THE PROSPERITY BIBLE

THE PROSPERITY BIBLE

The Greatest Writings of All Time on the Secrets to Wealth and Prosperity

NAPOLEON HILL, BENJAMIN FRANKLIN, JAMES ALLEN,
WALLACE D. WATTLES, ERNEST HOLMES,
FLORENCE SCOVEL SHINN,
AND OTHERS

A TarcherPerigee Book

tarcherperigee
an imprint of Penguin Random House LLC
penguinrandomhouse.com

First trade paperback edition 2011

Published simultaneously in Canada

Library of Congress Cataloging-in-Publication Data

The prosperity bible : landmark writings on the incredible prospering powers of the human mind / Napoleon Hill . . . [et al.].
p. cm.
ISBN 978-1-58542-614-0
1. Success. 2. Wealth. 3. New Thought. 4. Conduct of life. I. Hill, Napoleon, 1883–1970.
BF637.S8P75 2008 2007036468
650.1—dc22

ISBN 978-1-58542-914-1 (paperback edition)

Printed in the United States of America

14th Printing

BOOK DESIGN BY TANYA MAIBORODA

Neither the publisher nor the author is engaged in rendering professional advice or services to the individual reader. The ideas, procedures, and suggestions contained in this book are not intended as a substitute for consulting with your physician. All matters regarding your health require medical supervision. Neither the author nor the publisher shall be liable or responsible for any loss or damage allegedly arising from any information or suggestion in this book.

Publisher's Note

The nineteen books that compose *The Prosperity Bible* appear largely as they did in their original editions. Other than minor adjustments made for clarity, the publisher has retained the original spelling, usage, and style of each author.

As most of these works were initially published in the late nineteenth century or the first half of the twentieth century, they occasionally feature an antiquated reference or word choice. For purposes of historical accuracy, the publisher has left these intact.

Further information about these books and their authors appears in the About the Authors section on pages 1269–1272.

Contents

1. *Think and Grow Rich* by Napoleon Hill (1937 original edition) 1
2. *Acres of Diamonds* by Russell H. Conwell 187
3. *A Message to Garcia* by Elbert Hubbard 207
4. *As a Man Thinketh* by James Allen 213
5. *The Game of Life and How to Play It* by Florence Scovel Shinn 239
6. *The Science of Getting Rich* by Wallace D. Wattles 289
7. *Creative Mind and Success* by Ernest Holmes 361
8. *Prosperity* by Charles Fillmore 407
9. *In Tune with the Infinite* by Ralph Waldo Trine 507
10. *The Master Key System* by Charles F. Haanel 595
11. *The Secret of Success* by William Walker Atkinson 731
12. *The Art of Money Getting* by P. T. Barnum 773
13. *The Way to Wealth* by Benjamin Franklin 815
14. *The Secret of the Ages* by Robert Collier (1926 original edition) 831
15. *The Conquest of Poverty* by Helen Wilmans 999
16. *How to Attract Success* by F. W. Sears 1057
17. *The Power of Concentration* by Theron Q. Dumont 1113
18. *How to Grow Success* by Elizabeth Towne 1203
19. *The Mental Equivalent* by Emmet Fox 1253

About the Authors 1269

1

THINK AND GROW RICH

NAPOLEON HILL

(1937)

Contents

Publisher's Preface 5

Author's Preface 7

1. Introduction 13
2. Desire *(The First Step Toward Riches)* 23
3. Faith *(The Second Step Toward Riches)* 36
4. Auto-Suggestion *(The Third Step Toward Riches)* 49
5. Specialized Knowledge *(The Fourth Step Toward Riches)* 54
6. Imagination *(The Fifth Step Toward Riches)* 64
7. Organized Planning *(The Sixth Step Toward Riches)* 74
8. Decision *(The Seventh Step Toward Riches)* 103
9. Persistence *(The Eighth Step Toward Riches)* 111
10. Power of the Master Mind *(The Ninth Step Toward Riches)* 123
11. The Mystery of Sex Transmutation *(The Tenth Step Toward Riches)* 128
12. The Subconscious Mind *(The Eleventh Step Toward Riches)* 143
13. The Brain *(The Twelfth Step Toward Riches)* 149
14. The Sixth Sense *(The Thirteenth Step Toward Riches)* 154
15. How to Outwit the Six Ghosts of Fear *(Clearing the Brain for Riches)* 162

Publisher's Preface

This book conveys the experience of more than 500 men of great wealth, who began at scratch, with nothing to give in return for riches except thoughts, ideas, and organized plans.

Here you have the entire philosophy of money-making, just as it was organized from the actual achievements of the most successful men known to the American people during the past fifty years. It describes what to do, also, how to do it!

It presents complete instructions on how to sell your personal services.

It provides you with a perfect system of self-analysis that will readily disclose what has been standing between you and "the big money" in the past.

It describes the famous Andrew Carnegie formula of personal achievement by which he accumulated hundreds of millions of dollars for himself and made no fewer than a score of millionaires of men to whom he taught his secret.

Perhaps you do not need all that is to be found in the book—no one of the 500 men from whose experiences it was written did—but you may need one idea, plan, or suggestion to start you toward your goal. Somewhere in the book you will find this needed stimulus.

The book was inspired by Andrew Carnegie, after he had made his millions and retired. It was written by the man to whom Carnegie disclosed the astounding secret of his riches—the same man to whom the 500 wealthy men revealed the source of their riches.

In this volume will be found the thirteen principles of money-making essential to every person who accumulates sufficient money to guarantee financial independence. It is estimated that the research which went into the preparation, before the book was written, or could be written—research covering more than twenty-five years of continuous effort—could not be duplicated at a cost of less than $100,000.00.

Moreover, the knowledge contained in the book never can be duplicated, at any cost, for the reason that more than half of the 500 men who supplied the information it brings have passed on.

Riches cannot always be measured in money!

Money and material things are essential for freedom of body and mind, but there are some who will feel that the greatest of all riches can be evaluated only in terms of lasting friendships, harmonious family relationships, sympathy and understanding between business associates, and introspective harmony which brings one peace of mind measurable only in spiritual values!

All who read, understand, and apply this philosophy will be better prepared to attract and enjoy these higher estates which always have been and always will be denied to all except *those who are ready for them.*

Be prepared, therefore, when you expose yourself to the influence of this philosophy, to experience a changed life which may help you not only to negotiate your way through life with harmony and understanding, but also to prepare you for the accumulation of material riches in abundance.

THE PUBLISHER

Author's Preface

In every chapter of this book, mention has been made of the money-making secret which has made fortunes for more than five hundred exceedingly wealthy men whom I have carefully analyzed over a long period of years.

The secret was brought to my attention by Andrew Carnegie, more than a quarter of a century ago. The canny, lovable old Scotsman carelessly tossed it into my mind, when I was but a boy. Then he sat back in his chair, with a merry twinkle in his eyes, and watched carefully to see if I had brains enough to understand the full significance of what he had said to me.

When he saw that I had grasped the idea, he asked if I would be willing to spend twenty years or more, preparing myself to take it to the world, to men and women who, without the secret, might go through life as failures. I said I would, and with Mr. Carnegie's co-operation, I have kept my promise.

This book contains the secret, after having been put to a practical test by thousands of people, in almost every walk of life. It was Mr. Carnegie's idea that the magic formula, which gave him a stupendous fortune, ought to be placed within reach of people who do not have time to investigate how men make money, and it was his hope that I might test and demonstrate the soundness of the formula through the experience of men and women in every calling. He believed the formula should be taught in all public schools and colleges, and expressed the opinion that if it were properly taught it would so revolutionize the entire educational system that the time spent in school could be reduced to less than half.

His experience with Charles M. Schwab, and other young men of Mr. Schwab's type, convinced Mr. Carnegie that much of that which is taught in the schools is of no value whatsoever in connection with the business of earning a living or accumulating riches. He had arrived at this decision, because he had taken into his business one young man after another, many of them with but little schooling, and by coaching them in the use of this formula, developed in them rare leadership. Moreover, *his coaching made fortunes for every one of them who followed his instructions.*

In the chapter on Faith, you will read the astounding story of the organization of the giant United States Steel Corporation, as it was conceived and carried out by one of the young men through whom Mr. Carnegie proved that his formula will work *for all who are ready for it.* This single application of the secret, by that young man—Charles M. Schwab—made him a huge fortune in both money and opportunity. Roughly speaking, this particular application of the formula was worth *six hundred million dollars.*

These facts—and they are facts well known to almost everyone who knew Mr. Carnegie—give you a fair idea of what the reading of this book may bring to you, provided you *know what it is that you want.*

Even before it had undergone twenty years of practical testing, the secret was passed on to more than one hundred thousand men and women who have used it for their personal benefit, as Mr. Carnegie planned that they should. Some have made fortunes with it. Others have used it successfully in creating harmony in their homes. A clergyman used it so effectively that it brought him an income of upwards of $75,000.00 a year.

Arthur Nash, a Cincinnati tailor, used his near-bankrupt business as a "guinea pig" on which to test the formula. The business came to life and made a fortune for its owners. It is still thriving, although Mr. Nash has gone. The experiment was so unique that newspapers and magazines gave it more than a million dollars' worth of laudatory publicity.

The secret was passed on to Stuart Austin Wier, of Dallas, Texas. He was ready for it—so ready that he gave up his profession and studied law. Did he succeed? That story is told too.

I gave the secret to Jennings Randolph, the day he graduated from College, and he has used it so successfully that he is now serving his third term as a Member of Congress, with an excellent opportunity to keep on using it until it carries him to the White House.

While serving as Advertising Manager of the LaSalle Extension University, when it was little more than a name, I had the privilege of seeing J. G. Chapline, President of the University, use the formula so effectively that he has since made the LaSalle one of the great extension schools of the country.

The secret to which I refer has been mentioned no fewer than a hundred times, throughout this book. It has not been directly named, for it seems to work more successfully when it is merely uncovered and left in sight, where those who are ready, and searching for it, may pick it up. That is why Mr. Carnegie tossed it to me so quietly, without giving me its specific name.

If you are ready to put it to use, you will recognize this secret at least once in every chapter. I wish I might feel privileged to tell you how you will know if you are ready, but that would deprive you of much of the benefit you will receive when you make the discovery in your own way.

While this book was being written, my own son, who was then finishing the last year of his college work, picked up the manuscript of chapter two, read it, and discovered the secret for himself. He used the information so effectively that he went directly into a responsible position at a beginning salary greater than the average man ever earns. His story has been briefly described in chapter two. When you read it, perhaps you will dismiss any feeling you may have had, at the beginning of the book, that it promised too much. And, too, if you have ever been discouraged, if you have had difficulties to surmount which took the very soul out of you, if you have tried and failed, if you were ever handicapped by illness or physical affliction, this story of my son's discovery and use of the

Carnegie formula may prove to be the oasis in the Desert of Lost Hope, for which you have been searching.

This secret was extensively used by President Woodrow Wilson, during the World War. It was passed on to every soldier who fought in the war, carefully wrapped in the training received before going to the front. President Wilson told me it was a strong factor in raising the funds needed for the war.

More than twenty years ago, Hon. Manuel L. Quezon (then Resident Commissioner of the Philippine Islands), was inspired by the secret to gain freedom for his people. He has gained freedom for the Philippines, and is the first President of the free state.

A peculiar thing about this secret is that those who once acquire it and use it find themselves literally swept on to success, with but little effort, and they never again submit to failure! If you doubt this, study the names of those who have used it, wherever they have been mentioned, check their records for yourself, and be convinced.

There is no such thing as something for nothing!

The secret to which I refer cannot be had without a price, although the price is far less than its value. It cannot be had at any price by those who are not intentionally searching for it. It cannot be given away, it cannot be purchased for money, for the reason that it comes in two parts. One part is already in possession of those who are ready for it.

The secret serves equally well, all who are ready for it. Education has nothing to do with it. Long before I was born, the secret had found its way into the possession of Thomas A. Edison, and he used it so intelligently that he became the world's leading inventor, although he had but three months of schooling.

The secret was passed on to a business associate of Mr. Edison. He used it so effectively that, although he was then making only $12,000 a year, he accumulated a great fortune, and retired from active business while still a young man. You will find his story at the beginning of the first chapter. It should convince you that riches are not beyond your reach, that you can still be what you wish to be, that money, fame, recognition and happiness can be had by all who are ready and determined to have these blessings.

How do I know these things? You should have the answer before you finish this book. You may find it in the very first chapter, or on the last page.

While I was performing the twenty-year task of research, which I had undertaken at Mr. Carnegie's request, I analyzed hundreds of well known men, many of whom admitted that they had accumulated their vast fortunes through the aid of the Carnegie secret; among these men were:—

Henry Ford	Theodore Roosevelt
William Wrigley Jr.	John W. Davis
John Wanamaker	Elbert Hubbard
James J. Hill	Wilbur Wright
George S. Parker	William Jennings Bryan
E. M. Statler	Dr. David Starr Jordan
Henry L. Doherty	J. Odgen Armour
Cyrus H. K. Curtis	Charles M. Schwab
George Eastman	Harris F. Williams

Dr. Frank Gunsaulus
King Gillette
Judge Daniel T. Wright
Thomas A. Edison
F. W. Woolworth
Edward A. Filene
Arthur Brisbane
Wm. Howard Taft
Edward W. Bok
Elbert H. Gary
John H. Patterson
Stuart Austin Wier
George M. Alexander
Hon. Jennings Randolph
Clarence Darrow
Daniel Willard
Ralph A. Weeks
John D. Rockefeller
Frank A. Vanderlip
Col. Robert A. Dollar
Edwin C. Barnes
Woodrow Wilson
Luther Burbank
Frank A. Munsey
Dr. Alexander Graham Bell
Julius Rosenwald
Dr. Frank Crane
J. G. Chapline
Arthur Nash

These names represent but a small fraction of the hundreds of well-known Americans whose achievements, financially and otherwise, prove that those who understand and apply the Carnegie secret reach high stations in life. I have never known anyone who was inspired to use the secret, who did not achieve noteworthy success in his chosen calling. I have never known any person to distinguish himself, or to accumulate riches of any consequence, without possession of the secret. From these two facts I draw the conclusion that the secret is more important, as a part of the knowledge essential for self-determination, than any which one receives through what is popularly known as "education."

What is education, anyway? This has been answered in full detail.

As far as schooling is concerned, many of these men had very little. John Wanamaker once told me that what little schooling he had, he acquired in very much the same manner as a modern locomotive takes on water, by "scooping it up as it runs." Henry Ford never reached high school, let alone college. I am not attempting to minimize the value of schooling, but I am trying to express my earnest belief that those who master and apply the secret will reach high stations, accumulate riches, and bargain with life on their own terms, even if their schooling has been meager.

Somewhere, as you read, the secret to which I refer will jump from the page and stand boldly before you, if you are ready for it! When it appears, you will recognize it. Whether you receive the sign in the first or the last chapter, stop for a moment when it presents itself, and turn down a glass, for that occasion will mark the most important turning-point of your life.

We pass now, to chapter one, and to the story of my very dear friend, who has generously acknowledged having seen the mystic sign, and whose business achievements are evidence enough that he turned down a glass. As you read his story, and the others, remember that they deal with the important problems of life, such as all men experience. The problems arising from one's endeavor to earn a living, to find hope, courage, contentment and peace of mind; to accumulate riches and to enjoy freedom of body and spirit.

Remember, too, as you go through the book, that it deals with facts and not with fiction, its purpose being to convey a great universal truth through which all who are ready may learn, not only *what* to do, but also *how* to do it! and receive, as well, the needed stimulus to make a start.

As a final word of preparation, before you begin the first chapter, may I offer one brief suggestion which may provide a clue by which the Carnegie secret may be recognized? It is this—*all achievement, all earned riches, have their beginning in an idea!* If you are ready for the secret, you already possess one half of it; therefore, you will readily recognize the other half the moment it reaches your mind.

THE AUTHOR

CHAPTER 1

Introduction

THE MAN WHO "THOUGHT" HIS WAY INTO PARTNERSHIP WITH THOMAS A. EDISON

Truly, "thoughts are things," and powerful things at that, when they are mixed with definiteness of purpose, persistence, and a burning desire for their translation into riches, or other material objects.

A little more than thirty years ago, Edwin C. Barnes discovered how true it is that men really do think and grow rich. His discovery did not come about at one sitting. It came little by little, beginning with a burning desire to become a business associate of the great Edison.

One of the chief characteristics of Barnes' desire was that it was *definite.* He wanted to work *with* Edison, not *for* him. Observe, carefully, the description of how he went about translating his desire into reality, and you will have a better understanding of the thirteen principles which lead to riches.

When this desire, or impulse of thought, first flashed into his mind he was in no position to act upon it. Two difficulties stood in his way. He did not know Mr. Edison, and he did not have enough money to pay his railroad fare to Orange, New Jersey.

These difficulties were sufficient to have discouraged the majority of men from making any attempt to carry out the desire. But his was no ordinary desire! He was so determined to find a way to carry out his desire that he finally decided to travel by "blind baggage," rather than be defeated. (To the uninitiated, this means that he went to East Orange on a freight train.)

He presented himself at Mr. Edison's laboratory, and announced he had come to go into business with the inventor. In speaking of the first meeting between Barnes and Edison, years later, Mr. Edison said, "He stood there before me, looking like an ordinary tramp, *but there was something in the expression of his face which conveyed the impression that he was determined to get what he had come after.* I had learned, from years of experience with men, that when a man really desires a thing so deeply that he is willing to stake his entire future on a single turn of the wheel in order to get it, he is sure to win. I gave him the opportunity he asked for, *because I saw he had made up his mind to stand by until he succeeded.* Subsequent events proved that no mistake was made."

Just what young Barnes said to Mr. Edison on that occasion was far less important than *that which he thought.* Edison, himself, said so! It could not have been the young man's appearance which got him his start in the Edison office, for that was definitely against him. It was what he thought that counted.

If the significance of this statement could be conveyed to every person who reads it, there would be no need for the remainder of this book.

Barnes did not get his partnership with Edison on his first interview. He did get a chance to work in the Edison offices, at a very nominal wage, doing work that was unimportant to Edison, but most important to Barnes, because it gave him an opportunity to display his "merchandise" where his intended "partner" could see it.

Months went by. Apparently nothing happened to bring the coveted goal which Barnes had set up in his mind as his definite major purpose. But something important was happening in Barnes' mind. He was constantly intensifying his desire to become the business associate of Edison.

Psychologists have correctly said that "when one is truly ready for a thing, it puts in its appearance." Barnes was ready for a business association with Edison; moreover, he was determined to remain ready until he got that which he was seeking.

He did not say to himself, "Ah well, what's the use? I guess I'll change my mind and try for a salesman's job." But, he did say, "I came here to go into business with Edison, and I'll accomplish this end if it takes the remainder of my life." *He meant it!* What a different story men would have to tell if only they would adopt a definite purpose, and stand by that purpose until it had time to become an all-consuming obsession!

Maybe young Barnes did not know it at the time, but his bulldog determination, his persistence in standing back of a single desire, was destined to mow down all opposition, and bring him the opportunity he was seeking.

When the opportunity came, it appeared in a different form, and from a different direction than Barnes had expected. That is one of the tricks of opportunity. It has a sly habit of slipping in by the back door, and often it comes disguised in the form of misfortune, or temporary defeat. Perhaps this is why so many fail to recognize opportunity.

Mr. Edison had just perfected a new office device, known at that time as the Edison Dictating Machine (now the Ediphone). His salesmen were not enthusiastic over the machine. They did not believe it could be sold without great effort. Barnes saw his opportunity. It had crawled in quietly, hidden in a queer-looking machine which interested no one but Barnes and the inventor.

Barnes knew he could sell the Edison Dictating Machine. He suggested this to Edison, and promptly got his chance. He did sell the machine. In fact, he sold it so successfully that Edison gave him a contract to distribute and market it all over the nation. Out of that business association grew the slogan "Made by Edison and installed by Barnes."

The business alliance has been in operation for more than thirty years. Out of it Barnes has made himself rich in money, but he has done something infinitely greater: he has proved that one really may "Think and Grow Rich."

How much actual cash that original desire of Barnes' has been worth to him, I have no way of knowing. Perhaps it has brought him two or three million dollars, but the amount, whatever it is, becomes insignificant when compared with the greater asset he acquired in the form of definite knowledge that *an intangible impulse of thought can be transmuted into its physical counterpart* by the application of known principles.

Barnes literally *thought* himself into a partnership with the great Edison! He thought himself into a fortune. He had nothing to start with, except the capacity to know what he wanted, and the determination to stand by that desire until he realized it.

He had no money to begin with. He had but little education. He had no influence. But he did have initiative, faith, and the will to win. With these intangible forces he *made himself* number one man with the greatest inventor who ever lived.

Now, let us look at a different situation, and study a man who had plenty of tangible evidence of riches, but lost it, *because he stopped* three feet short of the goal he was seeking.

THREE FEET FROM GOLD

One of the most common causes of failure is the habit of quitting when one is overtaken by *temporary defeat.* Every person is guilty of this mistake at one time or another.

An uncle of R. U. Darby was caught by the "gold fever" in the gold-rush days, and went west to dig and grow rich. He had never heard that *more gold has been mined from the brains of men than has ever been taken from the earth.* He staked a claim and went to work with pick and shovel. The going was hard, but his lust for gold was definite.

After weeks of labor, he was rewarded by the discovery of the shining ore. He needed machinery to bring the ore to the surface. Quietly, he covered up the mine, retraced his footsteps to his home in Williamsburg, Maryland, told his relatives and a few neighbors of the "strike." They got together money for the needed machinery, and had it shipped. The uncle and Darby went back to work the mine.

The first car of ore was mined, and shipped to a smelter. The returns proved they had one of the richest mines in Colorado! A few more cars of that ore would clear the debts. Then would come the big killing in profits.

Down went the drills! Up went the hopes of Darby and Uncle! Then something happened! The vein of gold ore disappeared! They had come to the end of the rainbow, and the pot of gold was no longer there! They drilled on, desperately trying to pick up the vein again—all to no avail.

Finally, they decided to quit.

They sold the machinery to a junk man for a few hundred dollars, and took the train back home. Some "junk" men are dumb, but not this one! He called in a mining engineer to look at the mine and do a little calculating. The engineer advised that the project had failed, because the owners were not familiar with "fault lines." His calculations showed that the vein would be found just three feet from where the Darbys had stopped drilling! That is exactly where it was found!

The "junk" man took millions of dollars in ore from the mine, because he knew enough to seek expert counsel before giving up.

Most of the money which went into the machinery was procured through the efforts of R. U. Darby, who was then a very young man. The money came from his relatives and neighbors, because of their faith in him. He paid back every dollar of it, although he was years in doing so.

Long afterward, Mr. Darby recouped his loss many times over, *when he made the discovery* that desire can be transmuted into gold. The discovery came after he went into the business of selling life insurance.

Remembering that he lost a huge fortune, because he stopped three feet from gold, Darby profited by the experience in his chosen work, by the simple method of saying to himself, "I stopped three feet from gold, but I will never stop *because men say 'no'* when I ask them to buy insurance."

Darby is one of a small group of fewer than fifty men who sell more than a million dollars in life insurance annually. He owes his "stickability" to the lesson he learned from his "quitability" in the gold mining business.

Before success comes in any man's life, he is sure to meet with much temporary defeat, and, perhaps, some failure. When defeat overtakes a man, the easiest and most logical thing to do is to quit. That is exactly what the majority of men do.

More than five hundred of the most successful men this country has ever known told the author their greatest success came just one step *beyond* the point at which defeat had overtaken them. Failure is a trickster with a keen sense of irony and cunning. It takes great delight in tripping one when success is almost within reach.

A FIFTY CENT LESSON IN PERSISTENCE

Shortly after Mr. Darby received his degree from the "University of Hard Knocks," and had decided to profit by his experience in the gold mining business, he had the good fortune to be present on an occasion that proved to him that "No" does not necessarily mean no.

One afternoon he was helping his uncle grind wheat in an old-fashioned mill. The uncle operated a large farm on which a number of colored sharecrop farmers lived. Quietly, the door was opened, and a small colored child, the daughter of a tenant, walked in and took her place near the door.

The uncle looked up, saw the child, and barked at her roughly, "What do you want?"

Meekly, the child replied, "My mammy say send her fifty cents."

"I'll not do it," the uncle retorted. "Now you run on home."

"Yas sah," the child replied. *But she did not move.*

The uncle went ahead with his work, so busily engaged that he did not pay enough attention to the child to observe that she did not leave. When he looked up and saw her still standing there, he yelled at her, "I told you to go on home! Now go, or I'll take a switch to you."

The little girl said, "Yas sah," *but she did not budge an inch.*

The uncle dropped a sack of grain he was about to pour into the mill hopper, picked up a barrel stave, and started toward the child with an expression on his face that indicated trouble.

Darby held his breath. He was certain he was about to witness a murder. He knew his uncle had a fierce temper. He knew that colored children were not supposed to defy white people in that part of the country.

When the uncle reached the spot where the child was standing, she quickly stepped forward one step, looked up into his eyes, and screamed at the top of her shrill voice, *"My mammy's gotta have that fifty cents!"*

The uncle stopped, looked at her for a minute, then slowly laid the barrel stave on the floor, put his hand in his pocket, took out half a dollar, and gave it to her.

The child took the money and slowly backed toward the door, never taking her eyes off the man *whom she had just conquered.* After she had gone, the uncle sat down on a box and looked out the window into space for more than ten minutes. He was pondering, with awe, over the whipping he had just taken.

Mr. Darby, too, was doing some thinking. That was the first time in all his experience that he had seen a colored child deliberately *master* an adult white person. How did she do it? What happened to his uncle that caused him to lose his fierceness and become as docile as a lamb? What strange power did this child use that made her master over her superior? These and other similar questions flashed into Darby's mind, but he did not find the answer until years later, when he told me the story.

Strangely, the story of this unusual experience was told to the author in the old mill, on the very spot where the uncle took his whipping. Strangely, too, I had devoted nearly a quarter of a century to the study of the power which enabled an ignorant, illiterate colored child to conquer an intelligent man.

As we stood there in that musty old mill, Mr. Darby repeated the story of the unusual conquest, and finished by asking, 'What can you make of it? What strange power did that child use, that so completely whipped my uncle?"

The answer to his question will be found in the principles described in this book. The answer is full and complete. It contains details and instructions sufficient to enable anyone to understand, and apply the same force which the little child accidentally stumbled upon.

Keep your mind alert, and you will observe exactly what strange power came to the rescue of the child; you will catch a glimpse of this power in the next chapter. Somewhere in the book you will find an idea that will quicken your receptive powers, and place at your command, for your own benefit, this same irresistible power. The awareness of this power may come to you in the first chapter, or it may flash into your mind in some subsequent chapter. It may come in the form of a single idea. Or, it may come in the nature of a plan, or a purpose. Again, it may cause you to go back into your past experiences of failure or defeat, and bring to the surface some lesson by which you can regain all that you lost through defeat.

After I had described to Mr. Darby the power unwittingly used by the little colored child, he quickly retraced his thirty years of experience as a life insurance salesman, and frankly acknowledged that his success in that field was due, in no small degree, to the lesson he had learned from the child.

Mr. Darby pointed out: "Every time a prospect tried to bow me out, without buying, I saw that child standing there in the old mill, her big eyes glaring in defiance, and I said to myself, 'I've gotta make this sale.' The better portion of all sales I have made were made after people had said 'no.'"

He recalled, too, his mistake in having stopped only three feet from gold. "But," he said, "that experience was a blessing in disguise. It taught me *to keep on keeping on,* no matter how hard the going may be, a lesson I needed to learn before I could succeed in anything."

This story of Mr. Darby and his uncle, the colored child and the gold mine, doubtless will be read by hundreds of men who make their living by selling life insurance, and to all of these, the author wishes to offer the suggestion that Darby owes to these two experiences his ability to sell more than a million dollars of life insurance every year.

Life is strange, and often imponderable! Both the successes and the failures have their roots in simple experiences. Mr. Darby's experiences were common-place and simple enough, yet they held the answer to his destiny in life, therefore they were as important (to him) as life itself. He profited by these two dramatic experiences, because *he analyzed them,* and found the lesson they taught. But what of the man who has neither the time nor the inclination to study failure in search of knowledge that may lead to success? Where, and how, is he to learn the art of converting defeat into stepping stones to opportunity?

In answer to these questions, this book was written.

The answer called for a description of thirteen principles, but remember, as you read, the answer *you* may be seeking, to the questions which have caused you to ponder over the strangeness of life, may be found *in your own mind,* through some idea, plan, or purpose which may spring into your mind as you read.

One sound idea is all that one needs to achieve success. The principles described in this book contain the best, and the most practical of all that is known, concerning ways and means of creating useful ideas.

Before we go any further in our approach to the description of these principles, we believe you are entitled to receive this important suggestion. . . . When riches begin to come, they come so quickly, in such great abundance, that one wonders where they have been hiding during all those lean years. This is an astounding statement, and all the more so when we take into consideration the popular belief that riches come only to those who work hard and long.

When you begin to think and grow rich, you will observe that riches begin with a state of mind, with definiteness of purpose, with little or no hard work. You, and every other person, ought to be interested in knowing how to acquire that state of mind which will attract riches. I spent twenty-five years in research, analyzing more than 25,000 people, because I, too, wanted to know "how wealthy men become that way."

Without that research, this book could not have been written.

Here take notice of a very significant truth, viz: The business depression started in 1929, and continued on to an all-time record of destruction, until sometime after President Roosevelt entered office. Then the depression began to fade into nothingness. Just as an electrician in a theatre raises the lights so gradually that darkness is transmuted into light before you realize it, so did the spell of fear in the minds of the people gradually fade away and become faith.

Observe very closely: As soon as you master the principles of this philosophy, and begin to follow the instructions for applying those principles, your financial status will begin to improve, and everything you touch will begin to transmute itself into an asset for your benefit. Impossible? Not at all!

One of the main weaknesses of mankind is the average man's familiarity with the word "impossible." He knows all the rules which will not work. He knows all the things which cannot be done. This book was written for those who seek the rules which have made others successful, and are willing to *stake everything* on those rules.

A great many years ago I purchased a fine dictionary. The first thing I did with it was to turn to the word "impossible," and neatly clip it out of the book. That would not be an unwise thing for you to do.

Success comes to those who become success conscious.

Failure comes to those who indifferently allow themselves to become failure conscious.

The object of this book is to help all who seek it, to learn the art of changing their minds from failure consciousness to success consciousness.

Another weakness found in altogether too many people is the habit of measuring everything, and everyone, by *their own* impressions and beliefs. Some who will read this will believe that no one can think and grow rich. They cannot think in terms of riches, because their thought habits have been steeped in poverty, want, misery, failure, and defeat.

These unfortunate people remind me of a prominent Chinese, who came to America to be educated in American ways. He attended the University of Chicago. One day President Harper met this young Oriental on the campus, stopped to chat with him for a few minutes, and asked what had impressed him as being the most noticeable characteristic of the American people.

"Why," the Chinaman exclaimed, "the queer slant of your eyes. Your eyes are off slant!"

What do we say about the Chinese?

We refuse to believe that which we do not understand. We foolishly believe that our own limitations are the proper measure of limitations. Sure, the other fellow's eyes are "off slant," because they are not the same as our own.

Millions of people look at the achievements of Henry Ford, after he has arrived, and envy him, because of his good fortune, or luck, or genius, or whatever it is that they credit for Ford's fortune. Perhaps one person in every hundred thousand knows the secret of Ford's success, and those who do know are too modest, or too reluctant, to speak of it, *because of its simplicity.* A single transaction will illustrate the "secret" perfectly.

A few years back, Ford decided to produce his now famous V-8 motor. He chose to build an engine with the entire eight cylinders cast in one block, and instructed his engineers to produce a design for the engine. The design was placed on paper, but the engineers agreed, to a man, that it was simply *impossible* to cast an eight cylinder gas engine block in one piece.

Ford said, "Produce it anyway."

"But," they replied, "it's impossible!"

"Go ahead," Ford commanded, "and stay on the job until you succeed no matter how much time is required."

The engineers went ahead. There was nothing else for them to do, if they were to remain on the Ford staff. Six months went by, nothing happened. Another six months passed, and still nothing happened. The engineers tried every conceivable plan to carry out the orders, but the thing seemed out of the question: "*Impossible!*"

At the end of the year Ford checked with his engineers, and again they informed him they had found no way to carry out his orders.

"Go right ahead," said Ford, "I want it, and I'll have it."

They went ahead, and then, as if by a stroke of magic, the secret was discovered.

The Ford determination had won once more!

This story may not be described with minute accuracy, but the sum and substance of it is correct. Deduce from it, you who wish to think and grow rich, the secret of the Ford millions, if you can. You'll not have to look very far.

Henry Ford is a success, because he understands, and *applies* the principles of success. One of these is desire: knowing what one wants. Remember this Ford story as you read, and pick out the lines in which the secret of his stupendous achievement have been described. If you can do this, if you can lay your finger on the particular group of principles which made Henry Ford rich, you can equal his achievements in almost any calling for which you are suited.

YOU ARE "THE MASTER OF YOUR FATE, THE CAPTAIN OF YOUR SOUL," BECAUSE . . .

When Henley wrote the prophetic lines "I am the Master of my Fate, I am the Captain of my Soul," he should have informed us that we are the Masters of our Fate, the Captains of our Souls, *because* we have the power to control our thoughts.

He should have told us that the ether in which this little earth floats, in which we move and have our being, is a form of energy moving at an inconceivably high rate of vibration, and that the ether is filled with a form of universal power which adapts itself to the nature of the thoughts we hold in our minds; and influences us, in natural ways, to transmute our thoughts into their physical equivalent.

If the poet had told us of this great truth, we would know why it is that we are the Masters of our Fate, the Captains of our Souls. He should have told us, with great emphasis, that this power makes no attempt to discriminate between destructive thoughts and constructive thoughts, that it will urge us to translate into physical reality thoughts of poverty just as quickly as it will influence us to act upon thoughts of riches.

He should have told us, too, that our brains become magnetized with the dominating thoughts which we hold in our minds, and, by means with which no man is familiar, these "magnets" attract to us the forces, the people, the circumstances of life which harmonize with the nature of our *dominating* thoughts.

He should have told us that before we can accumulate riches in great abundance, we must magnetize our minds with intense desire for riches, that we must become "money conscious" until the desire for money drives us to create definite plans for acquiring it.

But, being a poet, and not a philosopher, Henley contented himself by stating a great truth in poetic form, leaving those who followed him to interpret the philosophical meaning of his lines.

Little by little, the truth has unfolded itself, until it now appears certain that the principles described in this book hold the secret of mastery over our economic fate.

We are now ready to examine the first of these principles. Maintain a spirit of open-mindedness, and remember as you read, they are the invention of no one man. The principles were gathered from the life experiences of more than 500 men who actually accumulated riches in huge amounts; men who began in poverty, with but little education, without influence. The principles worked for these men. You can put them to work for your own enduring benefit.

You will find it easy, not hard, to do.

Before you read the next chapter, I want you to know that it conveys factual information which might easily change your entire financial destiny, as it has so definitely brought changes of stupendous proportions to two people described.

I want you to know, also, that the relationship between these two men and myself is such that I could have taken no liberties with the facts, even if I had wished to do so. One of them has been my closest personal friend for almost twenty-five years, the other is my own son. The unusual success of these two men, success which they generously accredit to the principle described in the next chapter, more than justifies this personal reference as a means of emphasizing the far-flung power of this principle.

Almost fifteen years ago, I delivered the Commencement Address at Salem College, Salem, West Virginia. I emphasized the principle described in the next chapter, with so much intensity that one of the members of the graduating class definitely appropriated it, and made it a part of his own philosophy. The young man is now a Member of Congress, and an important factor in the present administration. Just before this book went to the publisher, he wrote me a letter in which he so clearly stated his opinion of the principle outlined in the next chapter that I have chosen to publish his letter as an introduction to that chapter.

It gives you an idea of the rewards to come.

My dear Napoleon:

My service as a Member of Congress having given me an insight into the problems of men and women, I am writing to offer a suggestion which may become helpful to thousands of worthy people.

With apologies, I must state that the suggestion, if acted upon, will mean several years of labor and responsibility for you, but I am enheartened to make the suggestion, because I know your great love for rendering useful service.

In 1922, you delivered the Commencement Address at Salem College, when I was a member of the graduating class. In that address, you planted in my mind an idea which has been responsible for the opportunity I now have to serve the people of my State, and will be responsible, in a very large measure, for whatever success I may have in the future.

The suggestion I have in mind is that you put into a book the sum and substance of the address you delivered at Salem College, and in that way give the people of America an opportunity to profit by your many years of experience and association with the men who, by their greatness, have made America the richest nation on earth.

I recall, as though it were yesterday, the marvelous description you gave of the method by which Henry Ford, with but little schooling, without a dollar, with no influential friends, rose to great heights. I made up my mind then, even before you had finished your speech, that I would make a place for myself, no matter how many difficulties I had to surmount.

Thousands of young people will finish their schooling this year, and within the next few years. Every one of them will be seeking just such a message of practical encouragement as the one I received from you. They will want to know where to turn, what to do, to get started in life. You can tell them, because you have helped to solve the problems of so many, many people.

If there is any possible way that you can afford to render so great a service, may I offer the suggestion that you include with every book one of your Personal Analysis Charts, in order that the purchaser of the book may have the benefit of a complete self-inventory, indicating, as you indicated to me years ago, exactly what is standing in the way of success.

Such a service as this, providing the readers of your book with a complete, unbiased picture of their faults and their virtues, would mean to them the difference between success and failure. The service would be priceless.

Millions of people are now facing the problem of staging a come-back, because of the depression, and I speak from personal experience when I say, I know these earnest people would welcome the opportunity to tell you their problems, and to receive your suggestions for the solution.

You know the problems of those who face the necessity of beginning all over again. There are thousands of people in America today who would like to know how they can convert ideas into money, people who must start at scratch, without finances, and recoup their losses. If anyone can help them, you can.

If you publish the book, I would like to own the first copy that comes from the press, personally autographed by you.

With best wishes, believe me,
Cordially yours,
Jennings Randolph

CHAPTER 2

Desire

THE STARTING POINT OF ALL ACHIEVEMENT

The First Step Toward Riches

When Edwin C. Barnes climbed down from the freight train in Orange, New Jersey, more than thirty years ago, he may have resembled a tramp, but his *thoughts* were those of a king!

As he made his way from the railroad tracks to Thomas A. Edison's office, his mind was at work. He saw himself *standing in Edison's presence.* He heard himself asking Mr. Edison for an opportunity to carry out the one consuming obsession of his life, a burning desire to become the business associate of the great inventor.

Barnes' desire was not a *hope!* It was not a *wish!* It was a keen, pulsating desire, which transcended everything else. It was definite.

The desire was not new when he approached Edison. It had been Barnes' *dominating desire* for a long time. In the beginning, when the desire first appeared in his mind, it may have been, probably was, only a wish, but it was no mere wish when he appeared before Edison with it.

A few years later, Edwin C. Barnes again stood before Edison, in the same office where he first met the inventor. This time his desire had been translated into reality. *He was in business with Edison.* The dominating dream of his life had become a reality. Today, people who know Barnes envy him, because of the "break" life yielded him. They see him in the days of his triumph, without taking the trouble to investigate the *cause* of his success.

Barnes succeeded because he chose a definite goal, placed all his energy, all his will power, all his effort, everything back of that goal. He did not become the partner of Edison the day he arrived. He was content to start in the most menial work, as long as it provided an opportunity to take even one step toward his cherished goal.

Five years passed before the chance he had been seeking made its appearance. During all those years not one ray of hope, not one promise of attainment of his desire had been held out to him. To everyone, except himself, he appeared only another cog in the Edison business wheel, but in his own mind, he was the partner of Edison every minute of the time, from the very day that he first went to work there.

It is a remarkable illustration of the power of a definite desire. Barnes won his goal, because he wanted to be a business associate of Mr. Edison, more than he wanted anything else. He created a plan by which to attain that purpose. But he burned all bridges behind him. He stood by his desire until it became the dominating obsession of his life—and—finally, a fact.

When he went to Orange, he did not say to himself, "I will try to induce Edison to give me a job of some sort." He said, "I will see Edison, and put him on notice that I have come to go into business with him."

He did not say, "I will work there for a few months, and if I get no encouragement, I will quit and get a job somewhere else." He did say, "I will start anywhere. I will do anything Edison tells me to do, but *before I am through,* I will be his associate."

He did not say, "I will keep my eyes open for another opportunity, in case I fail to get what I want in the Edison organization." He said, "There is but one thing in this world that I am determined to have, and that is a business association with Thomas A. Edison. I will burn all bridges behind me, and stake my entire future on my ability to get what I want."

He left himself no possible way of retreat. He had to win or perish!

That is all there is to the Barnes story of success!

A long while ago, a great warrior faced a situation which made it necessary for him to make a decision which insured his success on the battlefield. He was about to send his armies against a powerful foe, whose men outnumbered his own. He loaded his soldiers into boats, sailed to the enemy's country, unloaded soldiers and equipment, then gave the order to burn the ships that had carried them. Addressing his men before the first battle, he said, "You see the boats going up in smoke. That means that we cannot leave these shores alive unless we win! We now have no choice—*we win—or we perish!*" They won.

Every person who wins in any undertaking must be willing to burn his ships and cut all sources of retreat. Only by so doing can one be sure of maintaining that state of mind known as a burning desire to win, essential to success.

The morning after the great Chicago fire, a group of merchants stood on State Street, looking at the smoking remains of what had been their stores. They went into a conference to decide if they would try to rebuild, or leave Chicago and start over in a more promising section of the country. They reached a decision—all except one—to leave Chicago.

The merchant who decided to stay and rebuild pointed a finger at the remains of his store, and said, "Gentlemen, on that very spot I will build the world's greatest store, no matter how many times it may burn down."

That was more than fifty years ago. The store was built. It stands there today, a towering monument to the power of that state of mind known as a burning desire. The easy thing for Marshall Field to have done, would have been exactly what his fellow merchants did. When the going was hard, and the future looked dismal, they pulled up and went where the going seemed easier.

Mark well this difference between Marshall Field and the other merchants, because it is the same difference which distinguishes Edwin C. Barnes from thousands of other young men who have worked in the Edison organization. It is the same difference which distinguishes practically all who succeed from those who fail.

Every human being who reaches the age of understanding of the purpose of money wishes for it. *Wishing* will not bring riches. But *desiring* riches with a state of mind that becomes an obsession, then planning definite ways and means to acquire riches, and backing those plans with persistence which *does not recognize failure,* will bring riches.

The method by which desire for riches can be transmuted into its financial equivalent consists of six definite, practical steps, viz:

FIRST. Fix in your mind the *exact* amount of money you desire. It is not sufficient merely to say, "I want plenty of money." Be definite as to the amount. (There is a psychological reason for definiteness which will be described in a subsequent chapter.)

SECOND. Determine exactly what you intend to give in return for the money you desire. (There is no such reality as "something for nothing.")

THIRD. Establish a definite date when you intend to *possess* the money you desire.

FOURTH. Create a definite plan for carrying out your desire, and begin *at once,* whether you are ready or not, to put this plan into *action.*

FIFTH. Write out a clear, concise statement of the amount of money you intend to acquire, name the time limit for its acquisition, state what you intend to give in return for the money, and describe clearly the plan through which you intend to accumulate it.

SIXTH. Read your written statement aloud, twice daily, once just before retiring at night, and once after arising in the morning. As you read—see and feel and believe yourself already in possession of the money.

It is important that you follow the instructions described in these six steps. It is especially important that you observe and follow the instructions in the sixth paragraph. You may complain that it is impossible for you to "see yourself in possession of money" before you actually have it. Here is where a burning desire will come to your aid. If you truly desire money so keenly that your desire is an obsession, you will have no difficulty in convincing yourself that you will acquire it. The object is to want money, and to become so determined to have it that you convince yourself you will have it.

Only those who become "money conscious" ever accumulate great riches. "Money consciousness" means that the mind has become so thoroughly saturated with the desire for money, that one can see one's self already in possession of it.

To the uninitiated, who has not been schooled in the working principles of the human mind, these instructions may appear impractical. It may be helpful, to all who fail to recognize the soundness of the six steps, to know that the information they convey was received from Andrew Carnegie, who began as an ordinary laborer in the steel mills, but managed, despite his humble beginning, to make these principles yield him a fortune of considerably more than one hundred million dollars.

It may be of further help to know that the six steps here recommended were carefully scrutinized by the late Thomas A. Edison, who placed his stamp of approval upon them as being not only the steps essential for the accumulation of money, but necessary for the attainment of *any definite goal.*

The steps call for no "hard labor." They call for no sacrifice. They do not require one to become ridiculous, or credulous. To apply them calls for no great amount of education. But the successful application of these six steps does call for sufficient *imagination* to enable one to see, and to understand, that accumulation of money cannot be left to chance, good fortune, and luck. One must realize that all who have accumulated great fortunes first did a certain amount of dreaming, hoping, wishing, desiring, and planning *before* they acquired money.

You may as well know, right here, that you can never have riches in great quantities, unless you can work yourself into a white heat of desire for money, and actually believe you will possess it.

You may as well know, also, that every great leader, from the dawn of civilization down to the present, was a dreamer. Christianity is the greatest potential power in the world today, because its founder was an intense dreamer who had the vision and the imagination to see realities in their mental and spiritual form before they had been transmuted into physical form.

If you do not see great riches in your imagination, you will never see them in your bank balance.

Never in the history of America has there been so great an opportunity for practical dreamers as now exists. The six-year economic collapse has reduced all men, substantially, to the same level. A new race is about to be run. The stakes represent huge fortunes which will be accumulated within the next ten years. The rules of the race have changed, because we now live in a changed world that definitely favors the masses, those who had but little or no opportunity to win under the conditions existing during the depression, when fear paralyzed growth and development.

We who are in this race for riches should be encouraged to know that this changed world in which we live is demanding new ideas, new ways of doing things, new leaders, new inventions, new methods of teaching, new methods of marketing, new books, new literature, new features for the radio, new ideas for moving pictures. Back of all this demand for new and better things, there is one quality which one must possess to win, and that is definiteness of purpose, the knowledge of what one wants, and a burning desire to possess it.

The business depression marked the death of one age, and the birth of another. This changed world requires practical dreamers who can *and will* put their dreams into action. The practical dreamers have always been and always will be the pattern-makers of civilization.

We who desire to accumulate riches should remember the real leaders of the world always have been men who harnessed, and put into practical use, the intangible, unseen forces of unborn opportunity, and have converted those forces (or impulses of thought), into sky-scrapers, cities, factories, airplanes, automobiles, and every form of convenience that makes life more pleasant.

Tolerance and an open mind are practical necessities of the dreamer of today. Those who are afraid of new ideas are doomed before they start. Never has there been a time more favorable to pioneers than the present. True, there is no wild and woolly west to be conquered, as in the days of the Covered Wagon; but there is a vast business, financial, and industrial world to be remoulded and redirected along new and better lines.

In planning to acquire your share of the riches, let no one influence you to scorn the dreamer. To win the big stakes in this changed world, you must catch the spirit of the great pioneers of the past, whose dreams have given to civilization all that it has of value, the spirit which serves as the life-blood of our own country—your opportunity, and mine, to develop and market our talents.

Let us not forget, Columbus dreamed of an Unknown world, staked his life on the existence of such a world, and discovered it!

Copernicus, the great astronomer, dreamed of a multiplicity of worlds, and revealed them! No one denounced him as "impractical" *after* he had triumphed. Instead, the world worshipped at his shrine, thus proving once more that "success requires no apologies, failure permits no alibis."

If the thing you wish to do is right, and *you believe in it,* go ahead and do it! Put your dream across, and never mind what "they" say if you meet with temporary defeat, for "they," perhaps, do not know that every failure brings with it the seed of an equivalent success.

Henry Ford, poor and uneducated, dreamed of a horseless carriage, went to work with what tools he possessed, without waiting for opportunity to favor him, and now evidence of his dream belts the entire earth. He has put more wheels into operation than any man who ever lived, because he was not afraid to back his dreams.

Thomas Edison dreamed of a lamp that could be operated by electricity, began where he stood to put his dream into action, and despite more than *ten thousand failures,* he stood by that dream until he made it a physical reality. Practical dreamers do not quit!

Whelan dreamed of a chain of cigar stores, transformed his dream into action, and now the United Cigar Stores occupy the best corners in America.

Lincoln dreamed of freedom for the black slaves, put his dream into action, and barely missed living to see a united North and South translate his dream into reality.

The Wright brothers dreamed of a machine that would fly through the air. Now one may see evidence all over the world that they dreamed soundly.

Marconi dreamed of a system for harnessing the intangible forces of the ether. Evidence that he did not dream in vain may be found in every wireless and radio in the world. Moreover, Marconi's dream brought the humblest cabin, and the most stately manor house side by side. It made the people of every nation on earth back-door neighbors. It gave the President of the United States a medium by which he may talk to all the people of America at one time, and on short notice. It may interest you to know that Marconi's "friends" had him taken into custody, and examined in a psychopathic hospital, when he announced he had discovered a principle through which he could send messages through the air, without the aid of wires, or other direct physical means of communication. The dreamers of today fare better.

The world has become accustomed to new discoveries. Nay, it has shown a willingness to reward the dreamer who gives the world a new idea.

"The greatest achievement was, at first, and for a time, but a dream."

"The oak sleeps in the acorn. The bird waits in the egg, and in the highest vision of the soul, a waking angel stirs. Dreams are the seedlings of reality."

Awake, arise, and assert yourself, you dreamers of the world. Your star is now in the ascendency. The world depression brought the opportunity you have been waiting for. It taught people humility, tolerance, and open-mindedness.

The world is filled with an abundance of opportunity which the dreamers of the past never knew.

A burning desire to be and to do is the starting point from which the dreamer must take off. Dreams are not born of indifference, laziness, or lack of ambition.

The world no longer scoffs at the dreamer, nor calls him impractical. If you think it does, take a trip to Tennessee, and witness what a dreamer President has done in the way of harnessing and using the great water power of America. A score of years ago, such a dream would have seemed like madness.

You have been disappointed, you have undergone defeat during the depression, you have felt the great heart within you crushed until it bled. Take courage, for these experiences have tempered the spiritual metal of which you are made—they are assets of incomparable value.

Remember, too, that all who succeed in life get off to a bad start, and pass through many heartbreaking struggles before they "arrive." The turning point in the lives of those who succeed usually comes at the moment of some crisis, through which they are introduced to their "other selves."

John Bunyan wrote the *Pilgrim's Progress*, which is among the finest of all English literature, after he had been confined in prison and sorely punished, because of his views on the subject of religion.

O. Henry discovered the genius which slept within his brain after he had met with great misfortune, and was confined in a prison cell, in Columbus, Ohio. Being forced, through misfortune, to become acquainted with his "other self," and to use his imagination, he discovered himself to be a great author instead of a miserable criminal and outcast. Strange and varied are the ways of life, and stranger still are the ways of Infinite Intelligence, through which men are sometimes forced to undergo all sorts of punishment before discovering their own brains, and their own capacity to create useful ideas through imagination.

Edison, the world's greatest inventor and scientist, was a "tramp" telegraph operator; he failed innumerable times before he was driven, finally, to the discovery of the genius which slept within his brain.

Charles Dickens began by pasting labels on blacking pots. The tragedy of his first love penetrated the depths of his soul, and converted him into one of the world's truly great authors. That tragedy produced, first, *David Copperfield*, then a succession of other works that made this a richer and better world for all who read his books. Disappointment over love affairs generally has the effect of driving men to drink, and women to ruin; and this, because most people never learn the art of transmuting their strongest emotions into dreams of a constructive nature.

Helen Keller became deaf, dumb, and blind shortly after birth. Despite her greatest misfortune, she has written her name indelibly in the pages of the history of the great. Her entire life has served as evidence that *no one ever is defeated until defeat has been accepted as a reality.*

Robert Burns was an illiterate country lad; he was cursed by poverty, and grew up to be a drunkard in the bargain. The world was made better for his having lived, because he clothed beautiful thoughts in poetry, and thereby plucked a thorn and planted a rose in its place.

Booker T. Washington was born in slavery, handicapped by race and color. Because he was tolerant, had an open mind at all times, on all subjects, and was a dreamer, he left his impress for good on an entire race.

Beethoven was deaf, Milton was blind, but their names will last as long as time endures, because they dreamed and translated their dreams into organized thought.

Before passing to the next chapter, kindle anew in your mind the fire of hope, faith, courage, and tolerance. If you have these states of mind, and a working knowledge of the principles described, all else that you need will come to you, when you are ready for it. Let Emerson state the thought in these words: "Every proverb, every book, every byword that belongs to thee for aid and comfort shall surely come home through open or winding passages. Every friend whom not thy fantastic will, but the great and tender soul in thee craveth, shall lock thee in his embrace."

There is a difference between wishing for a thing and being ready to receive it. No one is *ready* for a thing until he *believes* he can acquire it. The state of mind must be belief, not mere hope or wish. Open-mindedness is essential for belief. Closed minds do not inspire faith, courage, and belief.

Remember, no more effort is required to aim high in life, to demand abundance and prosperity, than is required to accept misery and poverty. A great poet has correctly stated this universal truth through these lines:

I bargained with Life for a penny,
And Life would pay no more,
However I begged at evening
When I counted my scanty store.

For Life is a just employer,
He gives you what you ask,
But once you have set the wages,
Why, you must bear the task.

I worked for a menial's hire,
Only to learn, dismayed,
That any wage I had asked of Life,
Life would have willingly paid.

DESIRE OUTWITS MOTHER NATURE

As a fitting climax to this chapter, I wish to introduce one of the most unusual persons I have ever known. I first saw him twenty-four years ago, a few minutes after he was born. He came into the world without any physical sign of ears, and the doctor admitted, when pressed for an opinion, that the child might be deaf, and mute for life.

I challenged the doctor's opinion. I had the right to do so; I was the child's father. I, too, reached a decision, and rendered an opinion, but I expressed the opinion silently, in the secrecy of my own heart. I decided that my son would hear and speak. Nature could send me a child without ears, but Nature *could not induce me to accept* the reality of the affliction.

In my own mind I knew that my son would hear and speak. How? I was sure there must be a way, and I knew I would find it. I thought of the words of the immortal Emerson: "The whole course of things goes to teach us faith. We need only obey. There is guidance for each of us, and by lowly listening, we shall hear *the right word*."

The right word? Desire! More than anything else, I desired that my son should not be a deaf mute. From that desire I never receded, not for a second.

Many years previously, I had written, "Our only limitations are those we set up in our own minds." For the first time, I wondered if that statement were true. Lying on the bed in front of me was a newly born child, without the natural equipment of hearing. Even though he might hear and speak, he was obviously disfigured for life. Surely, this was a limitation which that child had not set up in his own mind.

What could I do about it? Somehow I would find a way to transplant into that child's mind my own burning desire for ways and means of conveying sound to his brain without the aid of ears.

As soon as the child was old enough to cooperate, I would fill his mind so completely with a burning desire to hear, that Nature would, by methods of her own, translate it into physical reality.

All this thinking took place in my own mind, but I spoke of it to no one. Every day I renewed the pledge I had made to myself, not to accept a deaf mute for a son.

As he grew older, and began to take notice of things around him, we observed that he had a slight degree of hearing. When he reached the age when children usually begin talking, he made no attempt to speak, but we could tell by his actions that he could hear certain sounds slightly. That was all I wanted to know! I was convinced that if he could hear, even slightly, he might develop still greater hearing capacity. Then something happened which gave me hope. It came from an entirely unexpected source.

We bought a victrola. When the child heard the music for the first time, he went into ecstasies, and promptly appropriated the machine. He soon showed a preference for certain records, among them, "It's a Long Way to Tipperary." On one occasion, he played that piece over and over, for almost two hours, standing in front of the victrola, *with his teeth clamped on the edge of the case.* The significance of this self-formed habit of his did not become clear to us until years afterward, for we had never heard of the principle of "bone conduction" of sound at that time.

Shortly after he appropriated the victrola, I discovered that he could hear me quite clearly when I spoke with my lips touching his mastoid bone, or at the base of the brain. These discoveries placed in my possession the necessary media by which I began to translate into reality my *Burning Desire* to help my son develop hearing and speech. By that time he was making stabs at speaking certain words. The outlook was far from encouraging, but desire backed by faith knows no such word as impossible.

Having determined that he could hear the sound of my voice plainly, I began, immediately, to transfer to his mind the desire to hear and speak. I soon discovered that the child enjoyed bedtime stories, so I went to work, creating stories designed to develop in him self-reliance, imagination, and a *keen desire to hear and to be normal.*

There was one story in particular which I emphasized by giving it some new and dramatic coloring each time it was told. It was designed to plant in his mind the thought that his affliction was not a liability, but an asset of great value. Despite the fact that all the philosophy I had examined clearly indicated that every adversity brings with it the seed of an equivalent advantage, I must confess that I had not the slightest idea *how* this affliction could ever become an asset. However, I continued my practice of wrapping that philosophy in bedtime stories, hoping the time would come when he would find some plan by which his handicap could be made to serve some useful purpose.

Reason told me plainly that there was no adequate compensation for the lack of ears and natural hearing equipment. Desire backed by faith pushed reason aside, and inspired me to carry on.

As I analyze the experience in retrospect, I can see now that my *son's faith in me* had much to do with the astounding results. He did not question anything I told him. I sold him the idea that he had a distinct *advantage* over his older brother, and that this advantage would reflect itself in many ways. For example, the teachers in school would observe that he had no ears, and, because of this, they would show him special attention and treat him with extraordinary kindness. They always did. His mother saw to that, by visiting the teachers and arranging with them to give the child the extra attention necessary. I sold him the idea, too, that when he became old enough to sell newspapers (his older brother had already become a newspaper merchant), he would have a big advantage over his brother, for the reason that people would pay him extra money for his wares, because they could see that he was a bright, industrious boy, despite the fact he had no ears.

We could notice that, gradually, the child's hearing was improving. Moreover, he had not the slightest tendency to be self-conscious because of his affliction. When he was about seven, he showed the first evidence that our method of servicing his mind was bearing fruit. For several months he begged for the privilege of selling newspapers, but his mother would not give her consent. She was afraid that his deafness made it unsafe for him to go on the street alone.

Finally, he took matters in his own hands. One afternoon, when he was left at home with the servants, he climbed through the kitchen window, shinnied to the ground, and set out on his own. He borrowed six cents in capital from the neighborhood shoemaker, invested it in papers, sold out, reinvested, and kept repeating until late in the evening. After balancing his accounts, and paying back the six cents he had borrowed from his banker, he had a net profit of forty-two cents. When we got home that night, we found him in bed asleep, with the money tightly clenched in his hand.

His mother opened his hand, removed the coins, and cried. Of all things! Crying over her son's first victory seemed so inappropriate. My reaction was the reverse. I laughed heartily, for I knew that my endeavor to plant in the child's mind an attitude of faith in himself had been successful.

His mother saw, in his first business venture, a little deaf boy who had gone out in the streets and risked his life to earn money. I saw a brave, ambitious, self-reliant little business man whose stock in himself had been increased a hundred percent, because he had gone into business on his own initiative, and had won. The transaction pleased me, because I knew that he had given evidence of a trait of resourcefulness that would go with him all through life. Later events proved this to be true. When his older brother wanted something, he would lie down on the floor, kick his feet in the air, cry for it—and get it. When the "little deaf boy" wanted something, he would plan a way to earn the money, then buy it for himself. He still follows that plan!

Truly, my own son has taught me that handicaps can be converted into stepping stones on which one may climb toward some worthy goal, unless they are accepted as obstacles, and used as alibis.

The little deaf boy went through the grades, high school, and college without being able to hear his teachers, excepting when they shouted loudly, at close range. He did not go to a school for the deaf. We would not permit him to learn the sign language. We were determined that he should live a normal life, and associate with normal children, and we stood by that decision, although it cost us many heated debates with school officials.

While he was in high school, he tried an electrical hearing aid, but it was of no value to him; due, we believed, to a condition that was disclosed when the child was six, by Dr. J. Gordon Wilson, of Chicago, when he operated on one side of the boy's head, and discovered that there was no sign of natural hearing equipment.

During his last week in college (eighteen years after the operation), something happened which marked the most important turning-point of his life. Through what seemed to be mere chance, he came into possession of another electrical hearing device, which was sent to him on trial. He was slow about testing it, due to his disappointment with a similar device. Finally he picked the instrument up, and more or less carelessly, placed it on his head, hooked up the battery, and lo! as if by a stroke of magic, his lifelong desire for normal hearing became a reality! For the first time in his life he heard practically as well as any person with normal hearing. "God moves in mysterious ways, His wonders to perform."

Overjoyed because of the Changed World which had been brought to him through his hearing device, he rushed to the telephone, called his mother, and heard her voice perfectly. The next day he plainly heard the voices of his professors in class, for the first time in his life! Previously he could hear them only when they shouted, at short range. He heard the radio. He *heard* the talking pictures. For the first time in his life, he could converse freely with other people, without the necessity of their having to speak loudly. Truly, he had come into possession of a Changed World. We had refused to accept Nature's error, and, by persistent desire, we had induced Nature to correct that error, through the only practical means available.

Desire had commenced to pay dividends, but the victory was not yet complete. The boy still had to find a definite and practical way to convert his handicap into an *equivalent asset.*

Hardly realizing the significance of what had already been accomplished, but intoxicated with the joy of his newly discovered world of sound, he wrote a letter to the manufacturer of the hearing aid, enthusiastically describing his experience. Something in his letter; something, perhaps which was not written on the lines, but back of them; caused the company to invite him to New York. When he arrived, he was escorted through the factory, and while talking with the Chief Engineer, telling him about his Changed World, a hunch, an idea, or an inspiration—call it what you wish—flashed into his mind. It was *this impulse of thought* which converted his affliction into an asset, destined to pay dividends in both money and happiness to thousands for all time to come.

The sum and substance of that impulse of thought was this: It occurred to him that he might be of help to the millions of deafened people who go through life without the benefit of hearing devices, if he could find a way to tell them the story of his Changed World. Then and there, he reached a decision to devote the remainder of his life to rendering useful service to the hard of hearing.

For an entire month, he carried on an intensive research, during which he analyzed the entire marketing system of the manufacturer of the hearing device, and created ways and means of communicating with the hard of hearing all over the world for the purpose of sharing with them his newly discovered Changed World. When this was done, he put in writing a two-year plan, based upon his findings. When he presented the plan to the company, he was instantly given a position, for the purpose of carrying out his ambition.

Little did he dream, when he went to work, that he was destined to bring hope and practical relief to thousands of deafened people who, without his help, would have been doomed forever to deaf mutism.

Shortly after he became associated with the manufacturer of his hearing aid, he invited me to attend a class conducted by his company, for the purpose of teaching deaf mutes to hear, and to speak. I had never heard of such a form of education, therefore I visited the class, skeptical but hopeful that my time would not be entirely wasted. Here I saw a demonstration which gave me a greatly enlarged vision of what I had done to arouse and keep alive in my son's mind the desire for normal hearing. I saw deaf mutes actually being taught to hear and to speak, through application of the self-same principle I had used, more than twenty years previously, in saving my son from deaf mutism.

Thus, through some strange turn of the Wheel of Fate, my son, Blair, and I have been destined to aid in correcting deaf mutism for those as yet unborn, because we are the only living human beings, as far as I know, who have established definitely the fact that deaf mutism can be corrected to the extent of restoring to normal life those who suffer with this affliction. It has been done for one; it will be done for others.

There is no doubt in my mind that Blair would have been a deaf mute all his life, if his mother and I had not managed to shape his mind as we did. The doctor who attended at his birth told us, confidentially, the child might never hear or speak. A few weeks ago, Dr. Irving Voorhees, a noted specialist on such cases, examined Blair very thoroughly. He was astounded when he learned how well my son now hears, and speaks, and said his examination indicated that "theoretically, the boy should not be able to hear at all." But the lad does hear, despite the fact that X-ray pictures show there is no opening in the skull, whatsoever, from where his ears should be to the brain.

When I planted in his mind the desire to hear and talk, and live as a normal person, there went with that impulse some strange influence which caused Nature to become bridge-builder, and span the gulf of silence between his brain and the outer world, by some means which the keenest medical specialists have not been able to interpret. It would be sacrilege for me to even conjecture as to how Nature performed this miracle. It would be unforgivable if I neglected to tell the world as much as I know of the humble part I assumed in the strange experience. It is my duty, and a privilege to say I believe, and not without reason, that nothing is impossible to the person who backs desire with enduring faith.

Verily, a burning desire has devious ways of transmuting itself into its physical equivalent. Blair desired normal hearing; now he has it! He was born with a handicap which might easily have sent one with a less defined desire to the street with a bundle of pencils and a tin cup. That handicap now promises to serve as the medium by which he will render useful service to many millions of hard of hearing, also, to give him useful employment at adequate financial compensation the remainder of his life.

The little "white lies" I planted in his mind when he was a child, by leading him to believe his affliction would become a great asset, which he could capitalize, has justified itself. Verily, there is nothing, right or wrong, which belief, plus burning desire, cannot make real. These qualities are free to everyone.

In all my experience in dealing with men and women who had personal problems, I never handled a single case which more definitely demonstrates the power of desire. Authors sometimes make the mistake of writing of subjects of which they have but superficial, or very elementary, knowledge. It has been my good fortune to have had the privilege of testing the soundness of the power of desire, through the affliction of my own son. Perhaps it was providential that the experience came as it did, for surely no one is better prepared than he to serve as an example of what happens when desire is put to the test. *If Mother Nature bends to the will of desire, is it logical that mere men can defeat a burning desire?*

Strange and imponderable is the power of the human mind! We do not understand the method by which it uses every circumstance, every individual, every physical thing within its reach, as a means of transmuting desire into its physical counterpart. Perhaps science will uncover this secret.

I planted in my son's mind the desire to hear and to speak as any normal person hears and speaks. That desire has now become a reality. I planted in his mind the desire to convert his greatest handicap into his greatest asset. That desire has been realized. The modus operandi by which this astounding result was achieved is not hard to describe. It consisted of three very definite facts. First, I mixed faith with the desire for normal hearing, which I passed on to my son. Second, I communicated my desire to him in every conceivable way available, through persistent, continuous effort, over a period of years. Third, he believed me!

As this chapter was being completed, news came of the death of Mme. Schuman-Heink. One short paragraph in the news dispatch gives the clue to this unusual woman's stupendous success as a singer. I quote the paragraph, because the clue it contains is none other than desire.

Early in her career, Mme. Schuman-Heink visited the director of the Vienna Court Opera, to have him test her voice. But, he did not test it. After taking one look at the awkward and poorly dressed girl, he exclaimed, none too gently: "With such a face, and with no personality at all, how can you ever expect to succeed in opera? My good child, give up the idea. Buy a sewing machine, and go to work. You can never be a singer."

Never is a long time! The director of the Vienna Court Opera knew much about the technique of singing. He knew little about the power of desire, when it assumes the proportion of an obsession. If he had known more of that power, he would not have made the mistake of condemning genius without giving it an opportunity.

Several years ago, one of my business associates became ill. He became worse as time went on, and finally was taken to the hospital for an operation. Just before he was wheeled into the operating room, I took a look at him, and wondered how anyone as thin and emaciated as he could possibly go through a major operation successfully. The doctor warned me that there was little if any chance of my ever seeing him alive again. But that was the doctor's opinion. It was not the opinion of the patient. Just before he was wheeled away, he whispered feebly, "Do not be disturbed, Chief. I will be out of here in a few days." The attending nurse looked at me with pity. But the patient did come through safely. After it was all over, his physician said, "Nothing but his own desire to live saved him. He never would have pulled through if he had not refused to accept the possibility of death."

I believe in the power of desire backed by faith, because I have seen this power lift men from lowly beginnings to places of power and wealth; I have seen it rob the grave of its victims; I have seen it serve as the medium by which men staged a comeback after having been defeated in a hundred different ways; I have seen it provide my own son with a normal, happy, successful life, despite Nature's having sent him into the world without ears.

How can one harness and use the power of desire? This has been answered through this and the subsequent chapters of this book. This message is going out to the world at the end of the longest, and perhaps, the most devastating depression America has ever known. It is reasonable to presume that the message may come to the attention of many who have been wounded by the depression, those who have lost their fortunes, others who have lost their positions, and great numbers who must reorganize their plans and stage a comeback. To all these I wish to convey the thought that all achievement, no matter what may be its nature, or its purpose, must begin with an intense, burning desire for something definite.

Through some strange and powerful principle of "mental chemistry" which she has never divulged, Nature wraps up in the impulse of strong desire "that something" which recognizes no such word as impossible, and accepts no such reality as failure.

CHAPTER 3

Faith

VISUALIZATION OF AND BELIEF IN ATTAINMENT OF DESIRE

The Second Step Toward Riches

Faith is the head chemist of the mind. When faith is blended with the vibration of thought, the subconscious mind instantly picks up the vibration, translates it into its spiritual equivalent, and transmits it to Infinite Intelligence, as in the case of prayer.

The emotions of faith, love, and sex are the most powerful of all the major positive emotions. When the three are blended, they have the effect of "coloring" the vibration of thought in such a way that it instantly reaches the subconscious mind, where it is changed into its spiritual equivalent, the only form that induces a response from Infinite Intelligence.

Love and faith are psychic, related to the spiritual side of man. Sex is purely biological, and related only to the physical. The mixing, or blending, of these three emotions has the effect of opening a direct line of communication between the finite, thinking mind of man, and Infinite Intelligence.

HOW TO DEVELOP FAITH

There comes, now, a statement which will give a better understanding of the importance the principle of auto-suggestion assumes in the transmutation of desire into its physical, or monetary equivalent; namely, faith is a state of mind which may be induced, or created, by affirmation or repeated instructions to the subconscious mind, through the principle of auto-suggestion.

As an illustration, consider the purpose for which you are, presumably, reading this book. The object is, naturally, to acquire the ability to transmute the intangible thought impulse of desire into its physical counterpart, money. By following the instructions laid down in the chapters on auto-suggestion, and the subconscious mind, as summarized in the chapter on auto-suggestion, you may convince the subconscious mind that you *believe* you will receive that for which you ask, and it will act upon that belief, which your subconscious mind passes back to you in the form of "faith," followed by definite plans for procuring that which you desire.

The method by which one develops faith, where it does not already exist, is extremely difficult to describe, almost as difficult, in fact, as it would be to describe the color of red to a blind man who has never seen color, and has nothing with which to compare what you describe to him. Faith is a state of mind which you may develop at will, after you have mastered the thirteen principles, because it is a state of mind which develops voluntarily, through application and use of these principles.

Repetition of affirmation of orders to your subconscious mind is the only known method of voluntary development of the emotion of faith.

Perhaps the meaning may be made clearer through the following explanation as to the way men sometimes become criminals. Stated in the words of a famous criminologist, "When men first come into contact with crime, they abhor it. If they remain in contact with crime for a time, they become accustomed to it, and endure it. If they remain in contact with it long enough, they finally embrace it, and become influenced by it."

This is the equivalent of saying that any impulse of thought which is repeatedly passed on to the subconscious mind is, finally, accepted and acted upon by the subconscious mind, which proceeds to translate that impulse into its physical equivalent, by the most practical procedure available.

In connection with this, consider again the statement, all thoughts which have been emotionalized (given feeling) and mixed with faith begin immediately to translate themselves into their physical equivalent or counterpart.

The emotions, or the "feeling" portion of thoughts, are the factors which give thoughts vitality, life, and action. The emotions of faith, love, and sex, when mixed with any thought impulse, give it greater action than any of these emotions can do singly.

Not only thought impulses which have been mixed with faith, but those which have been mixed with any of the positive emotions, or any of the negative emotions, may reach and influence the subconscious mind.

From this statement, you will understand that the subconscious mind will translate into its physical equivalent a thought impulse of a negative or destructive nature, just as readily as it will act upon thought impulses of a positive or constructive nature. This accounts for the strange phenomenon which so many millions of people experience, referred to as "misfortune," or "bad luck."

There are millions of people who believe themselves "doomed" to poverty and failure, because of some strange force over which they believe they have no control. They are the creators of their own "misfortunes," because of this negative belief, which is picked up by the subconscious mind, and translated into its physical equivalent.

This is an appropriate place at which to suggest again that you may benefit by passing on to your subconscious mind any desire which you wish translated into its physical or monetary equivalent, in a state of expectancy or belief that the transmutation will actually take place. Your belief, or faith, is the element which determines the action of your subconscious mind. There is nothing to hinder you from "deceiving" your subconscious mind when giving it instructions through auto-suggestion, as I deceived my son's subconscious mind.

To make this "deceit" more realistic, conduct yourself just as you would if you were already in possession of the material thing which you are demanding when you call upon your subconscious mind.

The subconscious mind will transmute into its physical equivalent, by the most direct and practical media available, any order which is given to it in a state of belief, or faith that the order will be carried out.

Surely, enough has been stated to give a starting point from which one may, through experiment and practice, acquire the ability to mix faith with any order given to the subconscious mind. Perfection will come through practice. It *cannot* come by merely *reading* instructions.

If it be true that one may become a criminal by association with crime (and this is a known fact), it is equally true that one may develop faith by voluntarily suggesting to the subconscious mind that one has faith. The mind comes, finally, to take on the nature of the influences which dominate it. Understand this truth, and you will know why it is essential for you to encourage the *positive emotions* as dominating forces of your mind, and discourage—and *eliminate*—negative emotions.

A mind dominated by positive emotions becomes a favorable abode for the state of mind known as faith. A mind so dominated may, at will, give the subconscious mind instructions, which it will accept and act upon immediately.

FAITH IS A STATE OF MIND WHICH MAY BE INDUCED BY AUTO-SUGGESTION

All down the ages, the religionists have admonished struggling humanity to "have faith" in this, that, and the other dogma or creed, but they have failed to tell people how to have faith. They have not stated that "faith is a state of mind, and that it may be induced by self-suggestion."

In language which any normal human being can understand, we will describe all that is known about the principle through which faith may be developed, where it does not already exist.

Have faith in yourself; faith in the Infinite.

Before we begin, you should be reminded again that:

Faith is the "eternal elixir" which gives life, power, and action to the impulse of thought!

The foregoing sentence is worth reading a second time, and a third, and a fourth. It is worth reading aloud!

Faith is the starting point of all accumulation of riches!

Faith is the basis of all "miracles," and all mysteries which cannot be analyzed by the rules of science!

Faith is the only known antidote for failure!

Faith is the element, the "chemical" which, when mixed with prayer, gives one direct communication with Infinite Intelligence.

Faith is the element which transforms the ordinary vibration of thought, created by the finite mind of man, into the spiritual equivalent.

Faith is the only agency through which the cosmic force of Infinite Intelligence can be harnessed and used by man.

Every one of the foregoing statements is capable of proof!

The proof is simple and easily demonstrated. It is wrapped up in the principle of auto-suggestion. Let us center our attention, therefore, upon the subject of self-suggestion, and find out what it is, and what it is capable of achieving.

It is a well known fact that one comes, finally, to believe whatever one repeats to one's self, *whether the statement be true or false.* If a man repeats a lie over and over, he will eventually accept the lie as truth. Moreover, he will believe it to be the truth. Every man is what he is because of the dominating thoughts which he permits to occupy his mind. Thoughts which a man deliberately places in his own mind, and encourages with sympathy, and with which he mixes any one or more of the emotions, constitute the motivating forces which direct and control his every movement, act, and deed!

Comes, now, a very significant statement of truth:

Thoughts which are mixed with any of the feelings of emotions constitute a "magnetic" force which attracts, from the vibrations of the ether, other similar or related thoughts. A thought thus "magnetized" with emotion may be compared to a seed which, when planted in fertile soil, germinates, grows, and multiplies itself over and over again, until that which was originally one small seed becomes countless millions of seeds of the same brand!

The ether is a great cosmic mass of eternal forces of vibration. It is made up of both destructive vibrations and constructive vibrations. It carries, at all times, vibrations of fear, poverty, disease, failure, misery; and vibrations of prosperity, health, success, and happiness, just as surely as it carries the sound of hundreds of orchestrations of music, and hundreds of human voices, all of which maintain their own individuality, and means of identification, through the medium of radio.

From the great storehouse of the ether, the human mind is constantly attracting vibrations which harmonize with that which dominates the human mind. Any thought, idea, plan, or purpose which one *holds* in one's mind attracts, from the vibrations of the ether, a host of its relatives, adds these "relatives" to its own force, and grows until it becomes the dominating, motivating master of the individual in whose mind it has been housed.

Now, let us go back to the starting point, and become informed as to how the original seed of an idea, plan, or purpose may be planted in the mind. The information is easily conveyed: any idea, plan, or purpose may be placed in the mind *through repetition of thought.* This is why you are asked to write out a statement of your major purpose, or Definite Chief Aim, commit it to memory, and repeat it, in audible words, day after day, until these vibrations of sound have reached your subconscious mind.

We are what we are because of the vibrations of thought which we pick up and register, through the stimuli of our daily environment.

Resolve to throw off the influences of any unfortunate environment, and to build your own life to order. Taking inventory of mental assets and liabilities, you will discover that your greatest weakness is lack of self-confidence. This handicap can be surmounted, and timidity translated into courage, through the aid of the principle of auto-suggestion. The application of this principle may be made through a simple arrangement of positive thought impulses stated in writing, memorized, and repeated, until they become a part of the working equipment of the subconscious faculty of your mind.

SELF-CONFIDENCE FORMULA

FIRST. I know that I have the ability to achieve the object of my Definite Purpose in life, therefore, I demand of myself persistent, continuous action toward its attainment, and I here and now promise to render such action.

SECOND. I realize the dominating thoughts of my mind will eventually reproduce themselves in outward, physical action, and gradually transform themselves into physical reality, therefore, I will concentrate my thoughts for thirty minutes daily upon the task of thinking of the person I intend to become, thereby creating in my mind a clear mental picture of that person.

THIRD. I know through the principle of auto-suggestion any desire that I persistently hold in my mind will eventually seek expression through some practical means of attaining the object back of it, therefore, I will devote ten minutes daily to demanding of myself the development of self-confidence.

FOURTH. I have clearly written down a description of my definite chief aim in life, and I will never stop trying until I shall have developed sufficient self-confidence for its attainment.

FIFTH. I fully realize that no wealth or position can long endure unless built upon truth and justice, therefore, I will engage in no transaction which does not benefit all whom it affects. I will succeed by attracting to myself the forces I wish to use, and the cooperation of other people. I will induce others to serve me, because of my willingness to serve others. I will eliminate hatred, envy, jealousy, selfishness, and cynicism, by developing love for all humanity, because I know that a negative attitude toward others can never bring me success. I will cause others to believe in me, because I will believe in them, and in myself.

I will sign my name to this formula, commit it to memory, and repeat it aloud once a day, with full faith that it will gradually influence my thoughts and actions so that I will become a self-reliant and successful person.

Back of this formula is a law of Nature which no man has yet been able to explain. It has baffled the scientists of all ages. The psychologists have named this law "auto-suggestion," and let it go at that.

The name by which one calls this law is of little importance. The important fact about it is—it works for the glory and success of mankind, IF it is used constructively. On the other hand, if used destructively, it will destroy just as readily. In this statement may be found a very significant truth; namely, that those who go down in defeat, and end their lives in poverty, misery, and distress, do so because of negative application of the principle of auto-suggestion. The cause may be found in the fact that all impulses of thought have a tendency to clothe themselves in their physical equivalent.

The subconscious mind (the chemical laboratory in which all thought impulses are combined, and made ready for translation into physical reality) makes no distinction between constructive and destructive thought impulses. It works with the material we feed it, through our thought impulses. The subconscious mind will translate into reality a thought driven by fear just as readily as it will translate into reality a thought driven by courage, or faith.

The pages of medical history are rich with illustrations of cases of "suggestive suicide." A man may commit suicide through negative suggestion, just as effectively as by any other means. In a midwestern city, a man by the name of Joseph Grant, a bank official, "borrowed" a large sum of the bank's money, without the consent of the directors. He lost the money through gambling. One afternoon, the Bank Examiner came and began to check the accounts. Grant left the bank, took a room in a local hotel, and when they found him, three days later, he was lying in bed, wailing and moaning, repeating over and over these words, "My God, this will kill me! I cannot stand the disgrace." In a short time he was dead. The doctors pronounced the case one of "mental suicide."

Just as electricity will turn the wheels of industry, and render useful service if used constructively, or snuff out life if wrongly used, so will the law of auto-suggestion lead you to peace and prosperity, or down into the valley of misery, failure, and death, according to your degree of understanding and application of it.

If you fill your mind with fear, doubt, and unbelief in your ability to connect with and use the forces of Infinite Intelligence, the law of auto-suggestion will take this spirit of unbelief and use it as a pattern by which your subconscious mind will translate it into its physical equivalent.

This statement is as true as the statement that two and two are four!

Like the wind which carries one ship East, and another West, the law of auto-suggestion will lift you up or pull you down, according to the way you set your sails of thought.

The law of auto-suggestion, through which any person may rise to altitudes of achievement which stagger the imagination, is well described in the following verse:

If you think *you are beaten, you are,*
If you think *you dare not, you don't*
If you like to win, but you think *you can't,*
It is almost certain you won't.

If you think *you'll lose, you're lost*
For out of the world we find,
Success begins with a fellow's will—
It's all in the state of mind.

If you think *you are outclassed, you are,*
You've got to think *high to rise,*
You've got to be sure of yourself *before*
You can ever win a prize.

Life's battles don't always go
To the stronger or faster man,

But soon or late the man who wins
Is the man WHO THINKS HE CAN*!*

Observe the words which have been emphasized, and you will catch the deep meaning which the poet had in mind.

Somewhere in your make-up (perhaps in the cells of your brain) there lies *sleeping* the seed of achievement which, if aroused and put into action, would carry you to heights such as you may never have hoped to attain.

Just as a master musician may cause the most beautiful strains of music to pour forth from the strings of a violin, so may you arouse the genius which lies asleep in your brain, and cause it to drive you upward to whatever goal you may wish to achieve.

Abraham Lincoln was a failure at everything he tried, until he was well past the age of forty. He was a Mr. Nobody from Nowhere, until a great experience came into his life, aroused the sleeping genius within his heart and brain, and gave the world one of its really great men. That "experience" was mixed with the emotions of sorrow and love. It came to him through Anne Rutledge, the only woman whom he ever truly loved.

It is a known fact that the emotion of love is closely akin to the state of mind known as faith, and this for the reason that love comes very near to translating one's thought impulses into their spiritual equivalent. During his work of research, the author discovered, from the analysis of the lifework and achievements of hundreds of men of outstanding accomplishment, that there was the influence of a woman's love back of nearly every one of them. The emotion of love, in the human heart and brain, creates a favorable field of magnetic attraction, which causes an influx of the higher and finer vibrations which are afloat in the ether.

If you wish evidence of the power of faith, study the achievements of men and women who have employed it. At the head of the list comes the Nazarene. Christianity is the greatest single force which influences the minds of men. The basis of Christianity is faith, no matter how many people may have perverted or misinterpreted the meaning of this great force, and no matter how many dogmas and creeds have been created in its name, which do not reflect its tenets.

The sum and substance of the teachings and the achievements of Christ, which may have been interpreted as "miracles," were nothing more nor less than faith. If there are any such phenomena as "miracles" they are produced only through the state of mind known as faith! Some teachers of religion, and many who call themselves Christians, neither understand nor practice faith.

Let us consider the power of faith, as it is now being demonstrated, by a man who is well known to all of civilization, Mahatma Gandhi, of India. In this man the world has one of the most astounding examples known to civilization of the possibilities of faith. Gandhi wields more potential power than any man living at this time, and this, despite the fact that he has none of the orthodox tools of power, such as money, battle ships, soldiers, and materials of warfare. Gandhi has no money, he has no home, he does not own a suit of clothes, but he does have power. How does he come by that power?

He created it out of his understanding of the principle of faith, and through his ability to transplant that faith into the minds of two hundred million people.

Gandhi has accomplished, through the influence of faith, that which the strongest military power on earth could not, and never will accomplish through soldiers and military equipment. He has accomplished the astounding feat of influencing two hundred million minds to coalesce and move in unison, as a single mind.

What other force on earth, except faith, could do as much?

There will come a day when employees as well as employers will discover the possibilities of faith. That day is dawning. The whole world has had ample opportunity, during the recent business depression, to witness what the lack of faith will do to business.

Surely, civilization has produced a sufficient number of intelligent human beings to make use of this great lesson which the depression has taught the world. During this depression, the world had evidence in abundance that widespread fear will paralyze the wheels of industry and business. Out of this experience will arise leaders in business and industry who will profit by the example which Gandhi has set for the world, and they will apply to business the same tactics which he has used in building the greatest following known in the history of the world. These leaders will come from the rank and file of the unknown men, who now labor in the steel plants, the coal mines, the automobile factories, and in the small towns and cities of America.

Business is due for a reform, make no mistake about this! The methods of the past, based upon economic combinations of force and fear, will be supplanted by the better principles of faith and cooperation. Men who labor will receive more than daily wages; they will receive dividends from the business the same as those who supply the capital for business; but first they must give more to their employers, and stop this bickering and bargaining by force, at the expense of the public. *They must earn the right to dividends!*

Moreover, and this is the most important thing of all—they will be led by leaders who will understand and apply the principles employed by Mahatma Gandhi. Only in this way may leaders get from their followers the spirit of full cooperation which constitutes power in its highest and most enduring form.

This stupendous machine age in which we live, and from which we are just emerging, has taken the soul out of men. Its leaders have driven men as though they were pieces of cold machinery; they were forced to do so by the employees who have bargained, at the expense of all concerned, to *get* and not to *give.* The watchword of the future will be human happiness and contentment, and when this state of mind shall have been attained, the production will take care of itself, more effectively than anything that has ever been accomplished where men did not, and could not, mix faith and individual interest with their labor.

Because of the need for faith and cooperation in operating business and industry, it will be both interesting and profitable to analyze an event which provides an excellent understanding of the method by which industrialists and business men accumulate great fortunes, by *giving* before they try to *get.*

The event chosen for this illustration dates back to 1900, when the United States Steel Corporation was being formed. As you read the story, keep in mind these fundamental facts and you will understand how ideas have been converted into huge fortunes.

First, the huge United States Steel Corporation was born in the mind of Charles M. Schwab, in the form of an idea he created through his imagination! Second, he mixed faith with his idea. Third, he formulated a plan for the transformation of his idea into physical and financial reality. Fourth, he put his plan into action with his famous speech at the University Club. Fifth, he applied, and followed-through on his plan with persistence, and backed it with firm decision until it had been fully carried out. Sixth, he prepared the way for success by a burning desire for success.

If you are one of those who have often wondered how great fortunes are accumulated, this story of the creation of the United States Steel Corporation will be enlightening. If you have any doubt that men can think and grow rich, this story should dispel that doubt, because you can plainly see in the story of the United States Steel the application of a major portion of the thirteen principles described in this book.

This astounding description of the power of an idea was dramatically told by John Lowell, in the *New York World-Telegram*, with whose courtesy it is here reprinted.

A PRETTY AFTER-DINNER SPEECH FOR A BILLION DOLLARS

"When, on the evening of December 12, 1900, some eighty of the nation's financial nobility gathered in the banquet hall of the University Club on Fifth Avenue to do honor to a young man from out of the West, not half a dozen of the guests realized they were to witness the most significant episode in American industrial history.

"J. Edward Simmons and Charles Stewart Smith, their hearts full of gratitude for the lavish hospitality bestowed on them by Charles M. Schwab during a recent visit to Pittsburgh, had arranged the dinner to introduce the thirty-eight-year-old steel man to eastern banking society. But they didn't expect him to stampede the convention. They warned him, in fact, that the bosoms within New York's stuffed shirts would not be responsive to oratory, and that, if he didn't want to bore the Stillmans and Harrimans and Vanderbilts, he had better limit himself to fifteen or twenty minutes of polite vaporings and let it go at that.

"Even John Pierpont Morgan, sitting on the right hand of Schwab as became his imperial dignity, intended to grace the banquet table with his presence only briefly. And so far as the press and public were concerned, the whole affair was of so little moment that no mention of it found its way into print the next day.

"So the two hosts and their distinguished guests ate their way through the usual seven or eight courses. There was little conversation and what there was of it was restrained. Few of the bankers and brokers had met Schwab, whose career had flowered along the banks of the Monongahela, and none knew him well. But before the evening was over, they—and with them Money Master Morgan—were to be swept off their feet, and a billion-dollar baby, the United States Steel Corporation, was to be conceived.

"It is perhaps unfortunate, for the sake of history, that no record of Charlie Schwab's speech at the dinner ever was made. He repeated some parts of it at a later date during a similar meeting of Chicago bankers. And still later, when the Government brought suit to dissolve the Steel Trust, he gave his own version, from the witness stand, of the remarks that stimulated Morgan into a frenzy of financial activity.

"It is probable, however, that it was a 'homely' speech, somewhat ungrammatical (for the niceties of language never bothered Schwab), full of epigram and threaded with wit. But aside from that it had a galvanic force and effect upon the five billions of estimated capital that was represented by the diners. After it was over and the gathering was still under its spell, although Schwab had talked for ninety minutes, Morgan led the orator to a recessed window where, dangling their legs from the high, uncomfortable seat, they talked for an hour more.

"The magic of the Schwab personality had been turned on, full force, but what was more important and lasting was the full-fledged, clear-cut program he laid down for the aggrandizement of Steel. Many other men had tried to interest Morgan in slapping together a Steel Trust after the pattern of the biscuit, wire and hoop, sugar, rubber, whisky, oil or chewing gum combinations. John W. Gates, the gambler, had urged it, but Morgan distrusted him. The Moore boys, Bill and Jim, Chicago stock jobbers who had glued together a match trust and a cracker corporation, had urged it and failed. Elbert H. Gary, the sanctimonious country lawyer, wanted to foster it, but he wasn't big enough to be impressive. Until Schwab's eloquence took J. P. Morgan to the heights from which he could visualize the solid results of the most daring financial undertaking ever conceived, the project was regarded as a delirious dream of easy-money crackpots.

"The financial magnetism that began, a generation ago, to attract thousands of small and sometimes inefficiently managed companies into large and competition-crushing combinations, had become operative in the steel world through the devices of that jovial business pirate, John W. Gates. Gates already had formed the American Steel and Wire Company out of a chain of small concerns, and together with Morgan had created the Federal Steel Company. The National Tube and American Bridge companies were two more Morgan concerns, and the Moore Brothers had forsaken the match and cookie business to form the 'American' group—Tin Plate, Steel Hoop, Sheet Steel—and the National Steel Company.

"But by the side of Andrew Carnegie's gigantic vertical trust, a trust owned and operated by fifty-three partners, those other combinations were picayune. They might combine to their heart's content but the whole lot of them couldn't make a dent in the Carnegie organization, and Morgan knew it.

"The eccentric old Scot knew it, too. From the magnificent heights of Skibo Castle he had viewed, first with amusement and then with resentment, the attempts of Morgan's smaller companies to cut into his business. When the attempts became too bold, Carnegie's temper was translated into anger and retaliation. He decided to duplicate every mill owned by his rivals. Hitherto, he hadn't been interested in wire, pipe, hoops, or sheet. Instead, he was content to sell such companies the raw steel and let them work it into whatever shape they wanted. Now, with Schwab as his chief and able lieutenant, he planned to drive his enemies to the wall.

"So it was that in the speech of Charles M. Schwab, Morgan saw the answer to his problem of combination. A trust without Carnegie—giant of them all—would be no trust at all, a plum pudding, as one writer said, without the plums.

"Schwab's speech on the night of December 12, 1900, undoubtedly carried the inference, though not the pledge, that the vast Carnegie enterprise could be brought under the

Morgan tent. He talked of the world future for steel, of reorganization for efficiency, of specialization, of the scrapping of unsuccessful mills and concentration of effort on the flourishing properties, of economies in the ore traffic, of economies in overhead and administrative departments, of capturing foreign markets.

"More than that, he told the buccaneers among them wherein lay the errors of their customary piracy. Their purposes, he inferred, had been to create monopolies, raise prices, and pay themselves fat dividends out of privilege. Schwab condemned the system in his heartiest manner. The shortsightedness of such a policy, he told his hearers, lay in the fact that it restricted the market in an era when everything cried for expansion. By cheapening the cost of steel, he argued, an ever-expanding market would be created; more uses for steel would be devised, and a goodly portion of the world trade could be captured. Actually, though he did not know it, Schwab was an apostle of modern mass production.

"So, the dinner at the University Club came to an end. Morgan went home, to think about Schwab's rosy predictions. Schwab went back to Pittsburgh to run the steel business for 'Wee Andra Carnegie,' while Gary and the rest went back to their stock tickers, to fiddle around in anticipation of the next move.

"It was not long coming. It took Morgan about one week to digest the feast of reason Schwab had placed before him. When he had assured himself that no financial indigestion was to result, he sent for Schwab—and found that young man rather coy. Mr. Carnegie, Schwab indicated, might not like it if he found his trusted company president had been flirting with the Emperor of Wall Street, the Street upon which Carnegie was resolved never to tread. Then it was suggested by John W. Gates the go-between, that if Schwab 'happened' to be in the Bellevue Hotel in Philadelphia, J. P. Morgan might also 'happen' to be there. When Schwab arrived, however, Morgan was inconveniently ill at his New York home, and so, on the elder man's pressing invitation, Schwab went to New York and presented himself at the door of the financier's library.

"Now certain economic historians have professed the belief that from the beginning to the end of the drama, the stage was set by Andrew Carnegie—that the dinner to Schwab, the famous speech, the Sunday night conference between Schwab and the Money King, were events arranged by the canny Scot. The truth is exactly the opposite. When Schwab was called in to consummate the deal, he didn't even know whether 'the little boss,' as Andrew was called, would so much as listen to an offer to sell, particularly to a group of men whom Andrew regarded as being endowed with something less than holiness. But Schwab did take into the conference with him, in his own handwriting, six sheets of copper-plate figures, representing to his mind the physical worth and the potential earning capacity of every steel company he regarded as an essential star in the new metal firmament.

"Four men pondered over these figures all night. The chief, of course, was Morgan, steadfast in his belief in the Divine Right of Money. With him was his aristocratic partner, Robert Bacon, a scholar and a gentleman. The third was John W. Gates, whom Morgan scorned as a gambler and used as a tool. The fourth was Schwab, who knew more about the processes of making and selling steel than any whole group of men then living. Throughout that conference, the Pittsburgher's figures were never questioned. If he said a company was worth so much, then it was worth that much and no more. He was insistent, too, upon including in the combination only those concerns he nominated. He had conceived a corporation in which there would be no duplication, not even to satisfy the greed of friends who wanted to unload their companies upon the broad Morgan shoulders. Thus he left out, by design, a number of the larger concerns upon which the Walruses and Carpenters of Wall Street had cast hungry eyes.

"When dawn came, Morgan rose and straightened his back. Only one question remained.

"'Do you think you can persuade Andrew Carnegie to sell?' he asked.

"'I can try,' said Schwab.

"'If you can get him to sell, I will undertake the matter,' said Morgan.

"So far so good. But would Carnegie sell? How much would he demand? (Schwab thought about $320,000,000). What would he take payment in? Common or preferred stocks? Bonds? Cash? Nobody could raise a third of a billion dollars in cash.

"There was a golf game in January on the frost-cracking heath of the St. Andrews links in Westchester, with Andrew bundled up in sweaters against the cold, and Charlie talking volubly, as usual, to keep his spirits up. But no word of business was mentioned until the pair sat down in the cozy warmth of the Carnegie cottage hard by. Then, with the same persuasiveness that had hypnotized eighty millionaires at the University Club, Schwab poured out the glittering promises of retirement in comfort, of untold millions to satisfy the old man's social caprices. Carnegie capitulated, wrote a figure on a slip of paper, handed it to Schwab and said, 'All right, that's what we'll sell for.'

"The figure was approximately $400,000,000, and was reached by taking the $320,000,000 mentioned by Schwab as a basic figure, and adding to it $80,000,000 to represent the increased capital value over the previous two years.

"Later, on the deck of a trans-Atlantic liner, the Scotsman said ruefully to Morgan, 'I wish I had asked you for $100,000,000 more.'

"'If you had asked for it, you'd have gotten it,' Morgan told him cheerfully.

"There was an uproar, of course. A British correspondent cabled that the foreign steel world was 'appalled' by the gigantic combination. President Hadley, of Yale, declared that unless trusts were regulated the country might expect 'an emperor in Washington within the next twenty-five years.' But that able stock manipulator, Keene, went at his work of shoving the new stock at the public so vigorously that all the excess water—estimated by some at nearly $600,000,000—was absorbed in a twinkling. So Carnegie had his millions, and the Morgan syndicate had $62,000,000 for all its 'trouble,' and all the 'boys,' from Gates to Gary, had their millions.

"The thirty-eight-year-old Schwab had his reward. He was made president of the new corporation and remained in control until 1930."

The dramatic story of "Big Business" which you have just finished was included in this book because it is a perfect illustration of the method by which *desire can be transmuted into its physical equivalent!*

I imagine some readers will question the statement that a mere, intangible desire can be converted into its physical equivalent. Doubtless some will say, "You cannot convert nothing into something!" The answer is in the story of United States Steel.

That giant organization was created in the mind of one man. The plan by which the organization was provided with the steel mills that gave it financial stability was created in the mind of the same man. His faith, his desire, his imagination, his persistence were the real ingredients that went into United States Steel. The steel mills and mechanical equipment acquired by the corporation, after it had been brought into legal existence, were incidental, but careful analysis will disclose the fact that the appraised value of the properties acquired by the corporation increased in value by an estimated six hundred million dollars, by the mere transaction which consolidated them under one management.

In other words, Charles M. Schwab's idea, plus the faith with which he conveyed it to the minds of J. P. Morgan and the others, was marketed for a profit of approximately $600,000,000. Not an insignificant sum for a single idea!

What happened to some of the men who took their share of the millions of dollars of profit made by this transaction is a matter with which we are not now concerned. The important feature of the astounding achievement is that it serves as unquestionable evidence of the soundness of the philosophy described in this book, because this philosophy was the warp and the woof of the entire transaction. Moreover, the practicability of the philosophy has been established by the fact that the United States Steel Corporation prospered, and became one of the richest and most powerful corporations in America, employing thousands of people, developing new uses for steel, and opening new markets; thus proving that the $600,000,000 in profit which the Schwab idea produced was earned.

Riches begin in the form of thought!

The amount is limited only by the person in whose mind the thought is put into motion. Faith removes limitations! Remember this when you are ready to bargain with Life for whatever it is that you ask as your price for having passed this way.

Remember, also, that the man who created the United States Steel Corporation was practically unknown at the time. He was merely Andrew Carnegie's "Man Friday" until he gave birth to his famous IDEA. After that he quickly rose to a position of power, fame, and riches.

There are no limitations to the mind
except those we *acknowledge*

Both *poverty* and *riches* are
the offspring of thought

CHAPTER 4

Auto-Suggestion

THE MEDIUM FOR INFLUENCING THE SUBCONSCIOUS MIND

The Third Step Toward Riches

Auto-suggestion is a term which applies to all suggestions and all self-administered stimuli which reach one's mind through the five senses. Stated in another way, auto-suggestion is self-suggestion. It is the agency of communication between that part of the mind where conscious thought takes place, and that which serves as the seat of action for the subconscious mind.

Through the dominating thoughts which one *permits* to remain in the conscious mind, (whether these thoughts be negative or positive, is immaterial), the principle of auto-suggestion voluntarily reaches the subconscious mind and influences it with these thoughts.

No thought, whether it be negative or positive, can enter the subconscious mind without the aid of the principle of auto-suggestion, with the exception of thoughts picked up from the ether. Stated differently, all sense impressions which are perceived through the five senses are stopped by the conscious thinking mind, and may be either passed on to the subconscious mind, or rejected, at will. The conscious faculty serves, therefore, as an outer-guard to the approach of the subconscious.

Nature has so built man that he has absolute control over the material which reaches his subconscious mind, through his five senses, although this is not meant to be construed as a statement that man always exercises this control. In the great majority of instances, he does not exercise it, which explains why so many people go through life in poverty.

Recall what has been said about the subconscious mind resembling a fertile garden spot, in which weeds will grow in abundance if the seeds of more desirable crops are not sown therein. Auto-suggestion is the agency of control through which an individual may voluntarily feed his subconscious mind on thoughts of a creative nature, or, by neglect, permit thoughts of a destructive nature to find their way into this rich garden of the mind.

You were instructed, in the last of the six steps described in the chapter on Desire, to read aloud twice daily the written statement of your desire for money, and to see and feel yourself already in possession of the money! By following these instructions, you communicate the object of your desire directly to your subconscious mind in a spirit of absolute faith. Through repetition of this procedure, you voluntarily create thought habits which are favorable to your efforts to transmute desire into its monetary equivalent.

Go back to these six steps described in chapter two, and read them again, very carefully, before you proceed further. Then (when you come to it), read very carefully the four instructions for the organization of your "Master Mind" group, described in the chapter on Organized Planning. By comparing these two sets of instructions with that which has been stated on auto-suggestion, you, of course, will see that the instructions involve the application of the principle of auto-suggestion.

Remember, therefore, when reading aloud the statement of your desire (through which you are endeavoring to develop a "money consciousness"), that the mere reading of the words is of no consequence—unless you mix emotion, or feeling, with your words. If you repeat a million times the famous Emil Coué formula, "Day by day, in every way, I am getting better and better," without mixing emotion and faith with your words, you will experience no desirable results. Your subconscious mind recognizes and acts upon only thoughts which have been well-mixed with emotion or feeling.

This is a fact of such importance as to warrant repetition in practically every chapter, because the lack of understanding of this is the main reason the majority of people who try to apply the principle of auto-suggestion get no desirable results.

Plain, unemotional words do not influence the subconscious mind. You will get no appreciable results until you learn to reach your subconscious mind with thoughts, or spoken words which have been well emotionalized with belief.

Do not become discouraged if you cannot control and direct your emotions the first time you try to do so. Remember, there is no such possibility as something for nothing. Ability to reach and influence your subconscious mind has its price, and you must pay that price. You cannot cheat, even if you desire to do so. The price of ability to influence your subconscious mind is everlasting persistence in applying the principles described here. You cannot develop the desired ability for a lower price. You, and you alone, must decide whether or not the reward for which you are striving (the "money consciousness") is worth the price you must pay for it in effort.

Wisdom and "cleverness" alone will not attract and retain money except in a few very rare instances, where the law of averages favors the attraction of money through these sources. The method of attracting money described here does not depend upon the law of averages. Moreover, the method plays no favorites. It will work for one person as effectively as it will for another. Where failure is experienced, it is the individual, *not the method,* which has failed. If you try and fail, make another effort, and still another, until you succeed.

Your ability to use the principle of auto-suggestion will depend, very largely, upon your capacity to concentrate upon a given desire until that desire becomes a burning obsession.

When you begin to carry out the instructions in connection with the six steps described in the second chapter, it will be necessary for you to make use of the principle of concentration.

Let us here offer suggestions for the effective use of concentration. When you begin to carry out the first of the six steps, which instructs you to "fix in your own mind the exact amount of money you desire," hold your thoughts on that amount of money by concentration, or fixation of attention, with your eyes closed, until you can actually see the physical appearance of the money. Do this at least once each day. As you go through these exercises, follow the instructions given in the chapter on faith, and see yourself actually in possession of the money!

Here is a most significant fact—the subconscious mind takes any orders given it in a spirit of absolute faith, and acts upon those orders, although the orders often have to be presented *over and over again,* through repetition, before they are interpreted by the subconscious mind. Following the preceding statement, consider the possibility of playing a perfectly legitimate "trick" on your subconscious mind, by making it believe, *because you believe it,* that you must have the amount of money you are visualizing, that this money is already awaiting your claim, that the subconscious mind must hand over to you practical plans for acquiring the money which is yours.

Hand over the thought suggested in the preceding paragraph to your imagination, and see what your imagination can or will do to create practical plans for the accumulation of money through transmutation of your desire.

Do not wait for a definite plan, through which you intend to exchange services or merchandise in return for the money you are visualizing, but begin at once to see yourself in possession of the money, demanding and expecting meanwhile that your subconscious mind will hand over the plan, or plans, you need. Be on the alert for these plans, and when they appear, put them into action immediately. When the plans appear, they will probably "flash" into your mind through the sixth sense, in the form of an "inspiration." This inspiration may be considered a direct "telegram," or message from Infinite Intelligence. Treat it with respect, and act upon it as soon as you receive it. Failure to do this will be fatal to your success.

In the fourth of the six steps, you were instructed to "Create a definite plan for carrying out your desire, and begin at once to put this plan into action." You should follow this instruction in the manner described in the preceding paragraph. Do not trust to your "reason" when creating your plan for accumulating money through the transmutation of desire. Your reason is faulty. Moreover, your reasoning faculty may be lazy, and, if you depend entirely upon it to serve you, it may disappoint you.

When visualizing the money you intend to accumulate (with closed eyes), *see yourself rendering the service, or delivering the merchandise you intend to give in return for this money. This is important!*

SUMMARY OF INSTRUCTIONS

The fact that you are reading this book is an indication that you earnestly seek knowledge. It is also an indication that you are a student of this subject. If you are only a student, there is a chance that you may learn much that you did not know, but you will learn only by assuming an attitude of humility. If you choose to follow some of the instructions but neglect or refuse to follow others—*you will fail!* To get satisfactory results, you must follow all instructions in a spirit of faith.

The instructions given in connection with the six steps in the second chapter will now be summarized, and blended with the principles covered by this chapter, as follows:

FIRST. Go into some quiet spot (preferably in bed at night) where you will not be disturbed or interrupted, close your eyes, and repeat aloud (so you may hear your own words) the written statement of the amount of money you intend to accumulate, the time limit for its accumulation, and a description of the service or merchandise you intend to give in return for the money. As you carry out these instructions, see yourself already in possession of the money.

For example:—Suppose that you intend to accumulate $50,000 by the first of January, five years hence, that you intend to give personal services in return for the money, in the capacity of a salesman. Your written statement of your purpose should be similar to the following:

"By the first day of January, 19. . , I will have in my possession $50,000, which will come to me in various amounts from time to time during the interim.

"In return for this money I will give the most efficient service of which I am capable, rendering the fullest possible quantity, and the best possible quality of service in the capacity of salesman of . . . (describe the service or merchandise you intend to sell).

"I believe that I will have this money in my possession. My faith is so strong that I can now see this money before my eyes. I can touch it with my hands. It is now awaiting transfer to me at the time and in the proportion that I deliver the service I intend to render in return for it. I am awaiting a plan by which to accumulate this money, and I will follow that plan when it is received."

SECOND. Repeat this program night and morning until you can see (in your imagination) the money you intend to accumulate.

THIRD. Place a written copy of your statement where you can see it night and morning, and read it just before retiring and upon arising until it has been memorized.

Remember, as you carry out these instructions, that you are applying the principle of auto-suggestion, for the purpose of giving orders to your subconscious mind. Remember, also, that your subconscious mind will act only upon instructions which are emotionalized, and handed over to it with "feeling." Faith is the strongest and most productive of the emotions. Follow the instructions given in the chapter on faith.

These instructions may, at first, seem abstract. Do not let this disturb you. Follow the instructions, no matter how abstract or impractical they may, at first, appear to be. The time will soon come, if you do as you have been instructed, *in spirit as well as in act,* when a whole new universe of power will unfold to you.

Scepticism, in connection with all new ideas, is characteristic of all human beings. But if you follow the instructions outlined, your scepticism will soon be replaced by belief, and this, in turn, will soon become crystallized into absolute faith. Then you will have arrived at the point where you may truly say, "I am the master of my fate, I am the captain of my soul!"

Many philosophers have made the statement that man is the master of his own *earthly* destiny, but most of them have failed to say *why* he is the master. The reason that man may be the master of his own earthly status, and especially his financial status, is thoroughly explained in this chapter. Man may become the master of himself, and of his environment, because he has the power to influence his own subconscious mind, and through it, gain the cooperation of Infinite Intelligence.

You are now reading the chapter which represents the keystone to the arch of this philosophy. The instructions contained in this chapter must be understood and applied with persistence if you are to succeed in transmuting desire into money.

The actual performance of transmuting desire into money involves the use of auto-suggestion as an agency by which one may reach, and influence, the subconscious mind. The other principles are simply tools with which to apply auto-suggestion. Keep this thought in mind, and you will, at all times, be conscious of the important part the principle of auto-suggestion is to play in your efforts to accumulate money through the methods described in this book.

Carry out these instructions as though you were a small child. Inject into your efforts something of the faith of a child. The author has been most careful to see that no impractical instructions were included, because of his sincere desire to be helpful.

After you have read the entire book, come back to this chapter, and follow in spirit, and in action, this instruction:

Read the entire chapter aloud once every night, until you become thoroughly convinced that the principle of auto-suggestion is sound, that it will accomplish for you all that has been claimed for it. As you read, *underscore with a pencil* every sentence which impresses you favorably.

Follow the foregoing instruction to the letter and it will open the way for a complete understanding and mastery of the principles of success.

CHAPTER 5

Specialized Knowledge

PERSONAL EXPERIENCES OR OBSERVATIONS

The Fourth Step Toward Riches

There are two kinds of knowledge. One is general, the other is specialized. General knowledge, no matter how great in quantity or variety it may be, is of but little use in the accumulation of money. The faculties of the great universities possess, in the aggregate, practically every form of general knowledge known to civilization. *Most of the professors have but little or no money.* They specialize on *teaching* knowledge, but they do not specialize on the organization or the use of knowledge.

Knowledge will not attract money, unless it is organized, and intelligently directed, through practical plans of action, to the definite end of accumulation of money. Lack of understanding of this fact has been the source of confusion to millions of people who falsely believe that "knowledge is power." It is nothing of the sort! Knowledge is only *potential* power. It becomes power only when, and if, it is organized into definite plans of action, and directed to a definite end.

This "missing link" in all systems of education known to civilization today may be found in the failure of educational institutions to teach their students how to organize and use knowledge after they acquire it.

Many people make the mistake of assuming that, because Henry Ford had but little "schooling," he is not a man of "education." Those who make this mistake do not know Henry Ford, nor do they understand the real meaning of the word "educate." That word is derived from the Latin word "educo," meaning to educe, to draw out, to develop from within.

An educated man is not, necessarily, one who has an abundance of general or specialized knowledge. An educated man is one who has so developed the faculties of his mind that he may acquire anything he wants, or its equivalent, without violating the rights of others. Henry Ford comes well within the meaning of this definition.

During the world war, a Chicago newspaper published certain editorials in which, among other statements, Henry Ford was called "an ignorant pacifist." Mr. Ford objected to the statements, and brought suit against the paper for libeling him. When the suit was tried in the Courts, the attorneys for the paper pleaded justification, and placed Mr. Ford, himself, on the witness stand, for the purpose of proving to the jury that he was ignorant. The attorneys asked Mr. Ford a great variety of questions, all of them intended to prove, by his own evidence, that, while he might possess considerable specialized knowledge pertaining to the manufacture of automobiles, he was, in the main, ignorant.

Mr. Ford was plied with such questions as the following:

"Who was Benedict Arnold?" and "How many soldiers did the British send over to America to put down the Rebellion of 1776?" In answer to the last question, Mr. Ford replied, "I do not know the exact number of soldiers the British sent over, but I have heard that it was a considerably larger number than ever went back."

Finally, Mr. Ford became tired of this line of questioning, and in reply to a particularly offensive question, he leaned over, pointed his finger at the lawyer who had asked the question, and said, "If I should really want to answer the foolish question you have just asked, or any of the other questions you have been asking me, let me remind you that I have a row of electric pushbuttons on my desk, and by pushing the right button, I can summon to my aid men who can answer any question I desire to ask concerning the business to which I am devoting most of my efforts. Now, will you kindly tell me, why I should clutter up my mind with general knowledge, for the purpose of being able to answer questions, when I have men around me who can supply any knowledge I require?"

There certainly was good logic to that reply.

That answer floored the lawyer. Every person in the courtroom realized it was the answer not of an ignorant man but of a man of education. Any man is educated who knows where to get knowledge when he needs it, and how to organize that knowledge into definite plans of action. Through the assistance of his "Master Mind" group, Henry Ford had at his command all the specialized knowledge he needed to enable him to become one of the wealthiest men in America. *It was not essential that he have this knowledge in his own mind.* Surely no person who has sufficient inclination and intelligence to read a book of this nature can possibly miss the significance of this illustration.

Before you can be sure of your ability to transmute desire into its monetary equivalent, you will require specialized knowledge of the service, merchandise, or profession which you intend to offer in return for fortune. Perhaps you may need much more specialized knowledge than you have the ability or the inclination to acquire, and if this should be true, you may bridge your weakness through the aid of your "Master Mind" group.

Andrew Carnegie stated that he, personally, knew nothing about the technical end of the steel business; moreover, he did not particularly care to know anything about it. The specialized knowledge which he required for the manufacture and marketing of steel he found available through the individual units of his "Master Mind" group.

The accumulation of great fortunes calls for power, and power is acquired through highly organized and intelligently directed specialized knowledge, but that knowledge does not, necessarily, have to be in the possession of the man who accumulates the fortune.

The preceding paragraph should give hope and encouragement to the man with ambition to accumulate a fortune who has not possessed himself of the necessary "education" to supply such specialized knowledge as he may require. Men sometimes go through life suffering from "inferiority complexes" because they are not men of "education." The man who can organize and direct a "Master Mind" group of men who possess knowledge useful in the accumulation of money is just as much a man of education as any man in the group. Remember this if you suffer from a feeling of inferiority because your schooling has been limited.

Thomas A. Edison had only three months of "schooling" during his entire life. He did not lack education, neither did he die poor.

Henry Ford had less than a sixth grade "schooling" but he has managed to do pretty well by himself, financially.

Specialized knowledge is among the most plentiful, and the cheapest, forms of service which may be had! If you doubt this, consult the payroll of any university.

IT PAYS TO KNOW HOW TO PURCHASE KNOWLEDGE

First of all, decide the sort of specialized knowledge you require, and the purpose for which it is needed. To a large extent your major purpose in life, the goal toward which you are working, will help determine what knowledge you need. With this question settled, your next move requires that you have accurate information concerning dependable sources of knowledge. The more important of these are:

(a) One's own experience and education

(b) Experience and education available through cooperation of others (Master Mind Alliance)

(c) Colleges and universities

(d) Public libraries (through books and periodicals in which may be found all the knowledge organized by civilization)

(e) Special training courses (through night schools and home study schools in particular)

As knowledge is acquired it must be organized and put into use, for a definite purpose, through practical plans. Knowledge has no value except that which can be gained from its application toward some worthy end. This is one reason why college degrees are not valued more highly. They represent nothing but miscellaneous knowledge.

If you contemplate taking additional schooling, first determine the purpose for which you want the knowledge you are seeking, then learn where this particular sort of knowledge can be obtained, from reliable sources.

Successful men, in all callings, never stop acquiring specialized knowledge related to their major purpose, business, or profession. Those who are not successful usually make the mistake of believing that the knowledge acquiring period ends when one finishes school. The truth is that schooling does but little more than to put one in the way of learning how to acquire practical knowledge.

With this Changed World which began at the end of the economic collapse came also astounding changes in educational requirements. The order of the day is specialization!

This truth was emphasized by Robert P. Moore, secretary of appointments of Columbia University.

SPECIALISTS MOST SOUGHT

"Particularly sought after by employing companies are candidates who have specialized in some field—business-school graduates with training in accounting and statistics, engineers of all varieties, journalists, architects, chemists, and also outstanding leaders and activity men of the senior class.

"The man who has been active on the campus, whose personality is such that he gets along with all kinds of people and who has done an adequate job with his studies, has a most decided edge over the strictly academic student. Some of these, because of their all-around qualifications, have received several offers of positions, a few of them as many as six.

"In departing from the conception that the 'straight A' student was invariably the one to get the choice of the better jobs, Mr. Moore said that most companies look not only to academic records but to activity records and personalities of the students.

"One of the largest industrial companies, the leader in its field, in writing to Mr. Moore concerning prospective seniors at the college, said:

"'We are interested primarily in finding men who can make exceptional progress in management work. For this reason we emphasize qualities of character, intelligence and personality far more than specific educational background.'"

"APPRENTICESHIP" PROPOSED

"Proposing a system of 'apprenticing' students in offices, stores and industrial occupations during the summer vacation, Mr. Moore asserts that after the first two or three years of college, every student should be asked 'to choose a definite future course and to call a halt if he has been merely pleasantly drifting without purpose through an unspecialized academic curriculum.

"'Colleges and universities must face the practical consideration that all professions and occupations now demand specialists,' he said, urging that educational institutions accept more direct responsibility for vocational guidance."

One of the most reliable and practical sources of knowledge available to those who need specialized schooling is the night schools operated in most large cities. The correspondence schools give specialized training anywhere the U. S. mails go, on all subjects that can be taught by the extension method. One advantage of home study training is the flexibility of the study programme which permits one to study during spare time. Another stupendous advantage of home study training (if the school is carefully chosen) is the fact that most courses offered by home study schools carry with them generous privileges of consultation which can be of priceless value to those needing specialized knowledge. No matter where you live, you can share the benefits.

Anything acquired without effort and without cost is generally unappreciated, often discredited; perhaps this is why we get so little from our marvelous opportunity in public schools. The self-discipline one receives from a definite programme of specialized study makes up, to some extent, for the wasted opportunity when knowledge was available without cost. Correspondence schools are highly organized business institutions. Their tuition fees are so low that they are forced to insist upon prompt payments. Being asked to pay, whether the student makes good grades or poor, has the effect of causing one to follow through with the course when he would otherwise drop it. The correspondence schools have not stressed this point sufficiently, for the truth is that their collection departments constitute the very finest sort of training on decision, promptness, action, and the habit of finishing that which one begins.

I learned this from experience, more than twenty-five years ago. I enrolled for a home study course in advertising. After completing eight or ten lessons I stopped studying, but the school did not stop sending me bills. Moreover, it insisted upon payment, whether I kept up my studies or not. I decided that if I had to pay for the course (which I had legally obligated myself to do), I should complete the lessons and get my money's worth. I felt, at the time, that the collection system of the school was somewhat too well organized, but I learned later in life that it was a valuable part of my training for which no charge had been made. Being forced to pay, I went ahead and completed the course. Later in life I discovered that the efficient collection system of that school had been worth much in the form of money earned, because of the training in advertising I had so reluctantly taken.

We have in this country what is said to be the greatest public school system in the world. We have invested fabulous sums for fine buildings, we have provided convenient transportation for children living in the rural districts so they may attend the best schools, but there is one astounding weakness to this marvelous system—it is free! One of the strange things about human beings is that they value only that which has a price. The free schools of America, and the free public libraries, do not impress people *because they are free.* This is the major reason why so many people find it necessary to acquire additional training after they quit school and go to work. It is also one of the major reasons why employers give greater consideration to employees who take home study courses. They have learned, from experience, that any person who has the ambition to give up a part of his spare time to studying at home has in him those qualities which make for leadership. This recognition is not a charitable gesture—it is sound business judgment upon the part of the employers.

There is one weakness in people for which there is no remedy. It is the universal weakness of lack of ambition! Persons, especially salaried people, who schedule their spare time to provide for home study, seldom remain at the bottom very long. Their action opens the way for the upward climb, removes many obstacles from their path, and gains the friendly interest of those who have the power to put them in the way of opportunity.

The home study method of training is especially suited to the needs of employed people who find, after leaving school, that they must acquire additional specialized knowledge but cannot spare the time to go back to school.

The changed economic conditions prevailing since the depression have made it necessary for thousands of people to find additional or new sources of income. For the majority of these, the solution to their problem may be found only by acquiring specialized knowledge. Many will be forced to change their occupations entirely. When a merchant finds that a certain line of merchandise is not selling, he usually supplants it with another that is in demand. The person whose business is that of marketing personal services must also be an efficient merchant. If his services do not bring adequate returns in one occupation, he must change to another, where broader opportunities are available.

Stuart Austin Wier prepared himself as a Construction Engineer and followed this line of work until the depression limited his market to where it did not give him the income he required. He took inventory of himself, decided to change his profession to law, went back to school, and took special courses by which he prepared himself as a corporation lawyer. Despite the fact the depression had not ended, he completed his training, passed the Bar Examination, and quickly built a lucrative law practice, in Dallas, Texas; in fact, he is turning away clients.

Just to keep the record straight, and to anticipate the alibis of those who will say, "I couldn't go to school because I have a family to support," or "I'm too old," I will add the information that Mr. Wier was past forty and married when he went back to school. Moreover, by carefully selecting highly specialized courses in colleges best prepared to teach the subjects chosen, Mr. Wier completed in two years the work for which the majority of law students require four years. It pays to know how to purchase knowledge!

The person who stops studying merely because he has finished school is forever hopelessly doomed to mediocrity, no matter what may be his calling. The way of success is the way of continuous pursuit of knowledge.

Let us consider a specific instance.

During the depression a salesman in a grocery store found himself without a position. Having had some bookkeeping experience, he took a special course in accounting, familiarized himself with all the latest bookkeeping and office equipment, and went into business for himself. Starting with the grocer for whom he had formerly worked, he made contracts with more than 100 small merchants to keep their books, at a very nominal monthly fee. His idea was so practical that he soon found it necessary to set up a portable office in a light delivery truck, which he equipped with modern bookkeeping machinery. He now has a fleet of these bookkeeping offices "on wheels" and employs a large staff of assistants, thus providing small merchants with accounting service equal to the best that money can buy, at very nominal cost.

Specialized knowledge plus imagination were the ingredients that went into this unique and successful business. Last year the owner of that business paid an income tax of almost ten times as much as was paid by the merchant for whom he worked when the depression forced upon him a temporary adversity which proved to be a blessing in disguise.

The beginning of this successful business was an idea!

Inasmuch as I had the privilege of supplying the unemployed salesman with that idea, I now assume the further privilege of suggesting another idea which has within it the possibility of even greater income. Also the possibility of rendering useful service to thousands of people who badly need that service.

The idea was suggested by the salesman who gave up selling and went into the business of keeping books on a wholesale basis. When the plan was suggested as a solution of his unemployment problem, he quickly exclaimed, "I like the idea, but I would not know how to turn it into cash." In other words, he complained he would not know how to market his bookkeeping knowledge *after he acquired it.*

So, that brought up another problem which had to be solved. With the aid of a young woman typist, clever at hand lettering, and who could put the story together, a very attractive book was prepared, describing the advantages of the new system of bookkeeping. The pages were neatly typed and pasted in an ordinary scrapbook, which was used as a silent salesman with which the story of this new business was so effectively told that its owner soon had more accounts than he could handle.

There are thousands of people, all over the country, who need the services of a merchandising specialist capable of preparing an attractive brief for use in marketing personal services. The aggregate annual income from such a service might easily exceed that received by the largest employment agency, and the benefits of the service might be made far greater to the purchaser than any to be obtained from an employment agency.

The idea here described was born of necessity, to bridge an emergency which had to be covered, but it did not stop by merely serving one person. The woman who created the idea has a keen imagination. She saw in her newly born brain-child the making of a new profession, one that is destined to render valuable service to thousands of people who need practical guidance in marketing personal services.

Spurred to action by the instantaneous success of her first "prepared plan to market personal services," this energetic woman turned next to the solution of a similar problem for her son, who had just finished college but had been totally unable to find a market for his services. The plan she originated for his use was the finest specimen of merchandising of personal services I have ever seen.

When the plan book had been completed, it contained nearly fifty pages of beautifully typed, properly organized information, telling the story of her son's native ability, schooling, personal experiences, and a great variety of other information too extensive for description. The plan book also contained a complete description of the position her son desired, together with a marvelous word picture of the exact plan he would use in filling the position.

The preparation of the plan book required several week's labor, during which time its creator sent her son to the public library almost daily, to procure data needed in selling his services to best advantage. She sent him, also, to all the competitors of his prospective employer, and gathered from them vital information concerning their business methods which was of great value in the formation of the plan he intended to use in filling the position he sought. When the plan had been finished, it contained more than half a dozen very fine suggestions for the use and benefit of the prospective employer. (The suggestions were put into use by the company.)

One may be inclined to ask, "Why go to all this trouble to secure a job?" The answer is straight to the point, also it is dramatic, because it deals with a subject which assumes the proportion of a tragedy with millions of men and women whose sole source of income is personal services.

The answer is, "Doing a thing well never is trouble! The plan prepared by this woman for the benefit of her son helped him get the job for which he applied, at the first interview, at a salary fixed by himself."

Moreover—and this, too, is important—the position did not require the young man to start at the bottom. He began as a junior executive, at an executive's salary.

"Why go to all this trouble?" do you ask.

Well, for one thing, the planned presentation of this young man's application for a position clipped off no less than ten years of time he would have required to get to where he began, had he "started at the bottom and worked his way up."

This idea of starting at the bottom and working one's way up may appear to be sound, but the major objection to it is this—too many of those who begin at the bottom never manage to lift their heads high enough to be seen by opportunity, so they remain at the bottom. It should be remembered, also, that the outlook from the bottom is not so very bright or encouraging. It has a tendency to kill off ambition. We call it "getting into a rut," which means that we accept our fate because we form the habit of daily routine, a habit that finally becomes so strong we cease to try to throw it off. And that is another reason why it pays to start one or two steps above the bottom. By so doing one forms the habit of looking around, of observing how others get ahead, of seeing opportunity, and of embracing it without hesitation.

Dan Halpin is a splendid example of what I mean. During his college days, he was manager of the famous 1930 National Championship Notre Dame football team, when it was under the direction of the late Knute Rockne.

Perhaps he was inspired by the great football coach to aim high, and not mistake temporary defeat for failure, just as Andrew Carnegie, the great industrial leader, inspired his young business lieutenants to set high goals for themselves. At any rate, young Halpin finished college at a mighty unfavorable time, when the depression had made jobs scarce, so, after a fling at investment banking and motion pictures, he took the first opening with a potential future he could find—selling electrical hearing aids on a commission basis. Anyone could start in that sort of job, and Halpin knew it, but it was enough to open the door of opportunity to him.

For almost two years, he continued in a job not to his liking, and he would never have risen above that job if he had not done something about his dissatisfaction. He aimed, first, at the job of Assistant Sales Manager of his company, and got the job. That one step upward placed him high enough above the crowd to enable him to see still greater opportunity; also, it placed him where opportunity could see him.

He made such a fine record selling hearing aids that A. M. Andrews, Chairman of the Board of the Dictograph Products Company, a business competitor of the company for which Halpin worked, wanted to know something about that man Dan Halpin who was taking big sales away from the long established Dictograph Company. He sent for Halpin. When the interview was over, Halpin was the new Sales Manager, in charge of the Acousticon Division. Then, to test young Halpin's metal, Mr. Andrews went away to Florida for three months, leaving him to sink or swim in his new job. He did not sink! Knute Rockne's spirit of "All the world loves a winner, and has no time for a loser," inspired him to put so much into his job that he was recently elected Vice-President of the company, and General Manager of the Acousticon and Silent Radio Division, a job which most men would be proud to earn through ten years of loyal effort. Halpin turned the trick in little more than six months.

It is difficult to say whether Mr. Andrews or Mr. Halpin is more deserving of eulogy, for the reason that both showed evidence of having an abundance of that very rare quality known as imagination. Mr. Andrews deserves credit for seeing in young Halpin a "go-getter" of the highest order. Halpin deserves credit for refusing to compromise with life by accepting and keeping a job he did not want, and that is one of the major points I am trying to emphasize through this entire philosophy—that we rise to high positions or remain at the bottom because of conditions we can control if we desire to control them.

I am also trying to emphasize another point, namely, that both success and failure are largely the results of habit! I have not the slightest doubt that Dan Halpin's close association with the greatest football coach America ever knew planted in his mind the same brand of desire to excel which made the Notre Dame football team world-famous. Truly, there is something to the idea that hero-worship is helpful, provided one worships a winner. Halpin tells me that Rockne was one of the world's greatest leaders of men in all history.

My belief in the theory that business associations are vital factors, both in failure and in success, was recently demonstrated, when my son Blair was negotiating with Dan Halpin for a position. Mr. Halpin offered him a beginning salary of about one half what he could have gotten from a rival company. I brought parental pressure to bear, and induced him to accept the place with Mr. Halpin, because I believe that close association with one who refuses to compromise with circumstances he does not like is an asset that can never be measured in terms of money.

The bottom is a monotonous, dreary, unprofitable place for any person. That is why I have taken the time to describe how lowly beginnings may be circumvented by proper planning. Also, that is why so much space has been devoted to a description of this new profession, created by a woman who was inspired to do a fine job of planning because she wanted her son to have a favorable "break."

With the changed conditions ushered in by the world economic collapse came also the need for newer and better ways of marketing personal services. It is hard to determine why someone had not previously discovered this stupendous need, in view of the fact that more money changes hands in return for personal services than for any other purpose. The sum paid out monthly, to people who work for wages and salaries, is so huge that it runs into hundreds of millions, and the annual distribution amounts to billions.

Perhaps some will find, in the idea here briefly described, the nucleus of the riches they desire! Ideas with much less merit have been the seedlings from which great fortunes have grown. Woolworth's Five and Ten Cent Store idea, for example, had far less merit, but it piled up a fortune for its creator.

Those seeing opportunity lurking in this suggestion will find valuable aid in the chapter on Organized Planning. Incidentally, an efficient merchandiser of personal services would find a growing demand for his services wherever there are men and women who seek better markets for their services. By applying the Master Mind principle, a few people with suitable talent could form an alliance, and have a paying business very quickly. One would need to be a fair writer, with a flair for advertising and selling, one handy at typing and hand lettering, and one should be a first-class business getter who would let the world know about the service. If one person possessed all these abilities, he might carry on the business alone, until it outgrew him.

The woman who prepared the "Personal Service Sales Plan" for her son now receives requests from all parts of the country for her cooperation in preparing similar plans for others who desire to market their personal services for more money. She has a staff of expert typists, artists, and writers who have the ability to dramatize the case history so effectively that one's personal services can be marketed for much more money than the prevailing wages for similar services. She is so confident of her ability that she accepts, as the major portion of her fee, a percentage of the *increased* pay she helps her clients to earn.

It must not be supposed that her plan merely consists of clever salesmanship by which she helps men and women to demand and receive more money for the same services they formerly sold for less pay. She looks after the interests of the purchaser as well as the seller of personal services, and so prepares her plans that the employer receives full value for the additional money he pays. The method by which she accomplishes this astonishing result is a professional secret which she discloses to no one excepting her own clients.

If you have the imagination, and seek a more profitable outlet for your personal services, this suggestion may be the stimulus for which you have been searching. The idea is capable of yielding an income far greater than that of the "average" doctor, lawyer, or engineer whose education required several years in college. The idea is saleable to those seeking new positions, in practically all positions calling for managerial or executive ability, and those desiring re-arrangement of incomes in their present positions.

There is no fixed price for sound ideas!

Back of all ideas is specialized knowledge. Unfortunately, for those who do not find riches in abundance, specialized knowledge is more abundant and more easily acquired than ideas. Because of this very truth, there is a universal demand and an ever-increasing opportunity for the person capable of helping men and women to sell their personal services advantageously. Capability means imagination, the one quality needed to combine specialized knowledge with ideas, in the form of organized plans designed to yield riches.

If you have imagination this chapter may present you with an idea sufficient to serve as the beginning of the riches you desire. Remember, the idea is the main thing. Specialized knowledge may be found just around the corner—any corner!

CHAPTER 6

Imagination

THE WORKSHOP OF THE MIND

The Fifth Step Toward Riches

The imagination is literally the workshop wherein are fashioned all plans created by man. The impulse, the desire, is given shape, form, and action through the aid of the imaginative faculty of the mind.

It has been said that man can create anything which he can imagine.

Of all the ages of civilization, this is the most favorable for the development of the imagination, because it is an age of rapid change. On every hand one may contact stimuli which develop the imagination.

Through the aid of his imaginative faculty, man has discovered, and harnessed, more of Nature's forces during the past fifty years than during the entire history of the human race, previous to that time. He has conquered the air so completely that the birds are a poor match for him in flying. He has harnessed the ether, and made it serve as a means of instantaneous communication with any part of the world. He has analyzed and weighed the sun at a distance of millions of miles, and has determined, through the aid of imagination, the elements of which it consists. He has discovered that his own brain is both a broadcasting and a receiving station for the vibration of thought, and he is beginning now to learn how to make practical use of this discovery. He has increased the speed of locomotion, until he may now travel at a speed of more than three hundred miles an hour. The time will soon come when a man may breakfast in New York, and lunch in San Francisco.

Man's only limitation, within reason, lies in his development and use of his imagination. He has not yet reached the apex of development in the use of his imaginative faculty. He has merely discovered that he has an imagination, and has commenced to use it in a very elementary way.

TWO FORMS OF IMAGINATION

The imaginative faculty functions in two forms. One is known as "synthetic imagination," and the other as "creative imagination."

Synthetic Imagination:—Through this faculty, one may arrange old concepts, ideas, or plans into new combinations. This faculty *creates* nothing. It merely works with the material of experience, education, and observation with which it is fed. It is the faculty used most by the inventor, with the exception of the "genius" who draws upon the creative imagination when he cannot solve his problem through synthetic imagination.

Creative Imagination:—Through the faculty of creative imagination, the finite mind of man has direct communication with Infinite Intelligence. It is the faculty through which "hunches" and "inspirations" are received. It is by this faculty that all basic or new ideas are handed over to man. It is through this faculty that thought vibrations from the minds of others are received. It is through this faculty that one individual may "tune in," or communicate with the subconscious minds of other men.

The creative imagination works automatically, in the manner described in subsequent pages. This faculty functions only when the conscious mind is vibrating at an exceedingly rapid rate, as for example, when the conscious mind is stimulated through the emotion of a *strong desire.*

The creative faculty becomes more alert, more receptive to vibrations from the sources mentioned, in proportion to its development through use. This statement is significant! Ponder over it before passing on.

Keep in mind as you follow these principles that the entire story of how one may convert desire into money cannot be told in one statement. The story will be complete only when one has mastered, assimilated, and begun to make use of all the principles.

The great leaders of business, industry, and finance, and the great artists, musicians, poets, and writers, became great because they developed the faculty of creative imagination.

Both the synthetic and creative faculties of imagination become more alert with use, just as any muscle or organ of the body develops through use.

Desire is only a thought, an impulse. It is nebulous and ephemeral. It is abstract, and of no value, until it has been transformed into its physical counterpart. While the synthetic imagination is the one which will be used most frequently in the process of transforming the impulse of desire into money, you must keep in mind the fact that you may face circumstances and situations which demand use of the creative imagination as well.

Your imaginative faculty may have become weak through inaction. It can be revived and made alert through use. This faculty does not die, though it may become quiescent through lack of use.

Center your attention, for the time being, on the development of the synthetic imagination, because this is the faculty which you will use more often in the process of converting desire into money.

Transformation of the intangible impulse, of desire, into the tangible reality, of money, calls for the use of a plan, or plans. These plans must be formed with the aid of the imagination, and mainly, with the synthetic faculty.

Read the entire book through, then come back to this chapter, and begin at once to put your imagination to work on the building of a plan, or plans, for the transformation of your desire into money. Detailed instructions for the building of plans have been given in almost every chapter. Carry out the instructions best suited to your needs; reduce your plan to writing, if you have not already done so. The moment you complete this, you will have definitely given concrete form to the intangible desire. Read the preceding sentence once more. Read it aloud, very slowly, and as you do so, remember that the moment you reduce the statement of your desire, and a plan for its realization, to writing, you have actually taken the first of a series of steps, which will enable you to convert the thought into its physical counterpart.

The earth on which you live, you, yourself, and every other material thing are the result of evolutionary change, through which microscopic bits of matter have been organized and arranged in an orderly fashion.

Moreover—and this statement is of stupendous importance—this earth, every one of the billions of individual cells of your body, and every atom of matter, *began as an intangible form of energy.*

Desire is thought impulse! Thought impulses are forms of energy. When you begin with the thought impulse, desire, to accumulate money, you are drafting into your service the same "stuff" that Nature used in creating this earth, and every material form in the universe, including the body and brain in which the thought impulses function.

As far as science has been able to determine, the entire universe consists of but two elements—matter and energy.

Through the combination of energy and matter has been created everything perceptible to man, from the largest star which floats in the heavens down to, and including, man himself.

You are now engaged in the task of trying to profit by Nature's method. You are (sincerely and earnestly, we hope) trying to adapt yourself to Nature's laws, by endeavoring to convert desire into its physical or monetary equivalent. You can do it! It has been done before!

You can build a fortune through the aid of laws which are immutable. But, first, you must become familiar with these laws, and learn to use them. Through repetition, and by approaching the description of these principles from every conceivable angle, the author hopes to reveal to you the secret through which every great fortune has been accumulated. Strange and paradoxical as it may seem, the "secret" is not a secret. Nature, herself, advertises it in the earth on which we live, the stars, the planets suspended within our view, in the elements above and around us, in every blade of grass, and every form of life within our vision.

Nature advertises this "secret" in the terms of biology, in the conversion of a tiny cell, so small that it may be lost on the point of a pin, into the human being now reading this line. The conversion of desire into its physical equivalent is, certainly, no more miraculous!

Do not become discouraged if you do not fully comprehend all that has been stated. Unless you have long been a student of the mind, it is not to be expected that you will assimilate all that is in this chapter upon a first reading.

But you will, in time, make good progress.

The principles which follow will open the way for understanding of imagination. Assimilate that which you understand, as you read this philosophy for the first time, then, when you reread and study it, you will discover that something has happened to clarify it, and give you a broader understanding of the whole. Above all, do not stop, nor hesitate in your study of these principles until you have read the book at least three times, for then you will not want to stop.

HOW TO MAKE PRACTICAL USE OF IMAGINATION

Ideas are the beginning points of all fortunes. Ideas are products of the imagination. Let us examine a few well known ideas which have yielded huge fortunes, with the hope that these illustrations will convey definite information concerning the method by which imagination may be used in accumulating riches.

The Enchanted Kettle

Fifty years ago, an old country doctor drove to town, hitched his horse, quietly slipped into a drug store by the back door, and began "dickering" with the young drug clerk.

His mission was destined to yield great wealth to many people. It was destined to bring to the South the most far-flung benefit since the Civil War.

For more than an hour, behind the prescription counter, the old doctor and the clerk talked in low tones. Then the doctor left. He went out to the buggy and brought back a large, old fashioned kettle, a big wooden paddle (used for stirring the contents of the kettle), and deposited them in the back of the store.

The clerk inspected the kettle, reached into his inside pocket, took out a roll of bills, and handed it over to the doctor. The roll contained exactly $500.00—the clerk's entire savings!

The doctor handed over a small slip of paper on which was written a secret formula. The words on that small slip of paper were worth a King's ransom! *But not to the doctor!* Those magic words were needed to start the kettle to boiling, but neither the doctor nor the young clerk knew what fabulous fortunes were destined to flow from that kettle.

The old doctor was glad to sell the outfit for five hundred dollars. The money would pay off his debts, and give him freedom of mind. The clerk was taking a big chance by staking his entire life's savings on a mere scrap of paper and an old kettle! He never dreamed his investment would start a kettle to overflowing with gold that would surpass the miraculous performance of Aladdin's lamp.

What the clerk *really purchased* was an idea!

The old kettle and the wooden paddle and the secret message on a slip of paper were incidental. The strange performance of that kettle began to take place after the new owner mixed with the secret instructions an ingredient of which the doctor knew nothing.

Read this story carefully; give your imagination a test! See if you can discover what it was that the young man added to the secret message which caused the kettle to overflow with gold. Remember, as you read, that this is not a story from *Arabian Nights*. Here you have a story of facts, stranger than fiction, facts which began in the form of an idea.

Let us take a look at the vast fortunes of gold this idea has produced. It has paid, and still pays, huge fortunes to men and women all over the world who distribute the contents of the kettle to millions of people.

The Old Kettle is now one of the world's largest consumers of sugar, thus providing jobs of a permanent nature to thousands of men and women engaged in growing sugar cane, and in refining and marketing sugar.

The Old Kettle consumes, annually, millions of glass bottles, providing jobs to huge numbers of glass workers.

The Old Kettle gives employment to an army of clerks, stenographers, copy writers, and advertising experts throughout the nation. It has brought fame and fortune to scores of artists who have created magnificent pictures describing the product.

The Old Kettle has converted a small Southern city into the business capital of the South, where it now benefits, directly, or indirectly, every business and practically every resident of the city.

The influence of this idea now benefits every civilized country in the world, pouring out a continuous stream of gold to all who touch it.

Gold from the kettle built and maintains one of the most prominent colleges of the South, where thousands of young people receive the training essential for success.

The Old Kettle has done other marvelous things.

All through the world depression, when factories, banks, and business houses were folding up and quitting by the thousands, the owner of this Enchanted Kettle went marching on, *giving continuous employment* to an army of men and women all over the world, and paying out extra portions of gold to those who, long ago, *had faith in the idea.*

If the product of that old brass kettle could talk, it would tell thrilling tales of romance in every language. Romances of love, romances of business, romances of professional men and women who are daily being stimulated by it.

The author is sure of at least one such romance, for he was a part of it, and it all began not far from the very spot on which the drug clerk purchased the Old Kettle. It was here that the author met his wife, and it was she who first told him of the Enchanted Kettle. It was the product of that kettle they were drinking when he asked her to accept him "for better or worse."

Now that you know the content of the Enchanted Kettle is a world famous drink, it is fitting that the author confess that the home city of the drink supplied him with a wife, also that the drink itself provides him with *stimulation of thought without intoxication,* and thereby it serves to give the refreshment of mind which an author must have to do his best work.

Whoever you are, wherever you may live, whatever occupation you may be engaged in, just remember in the future, every time you see the words "Coca-Cola," that its vast empire of wealth and influence grew out of a single idea, and that the mysterious ingredient the drug clerk—Asa Candler—mixed with the secret formula was . . . imagination!

Stop and think of that for a moment.

Remember, also, that the thirteen steps to riches, described in this book, were the media through which the influence of Coca-Cola has been extended to every city, town, village, and cross-roads of the world, and that any idea you may create, as *sound and meritorious* as Coca-Cola, has the possibility of duplicating the stupendous record of this world-wide thirst-killer.

Truly, thoughts are things, and their scope of operation is the world, itself.

What I Would Do If I Had a Million Dollars

This story proves the truth of that old saying "Where there's a will, there's a way." It was told to me by that beloved educator and clergyman, the late Frank W. Gunsaulus, who began his preaching career in the stockyards region of South Chicago.

While Dr. Gunsaulus was going through college, he observed many defects in our educational system, defects which he believed he could correct, if he were the head of a college. His *deepest desire* was to become the directing head of an educational institution in which young men and women would be taught to "learn by doing."

He made up his mind to organize a new college in which he could carry out his ideas, without being handicapped by orthodox methods of education.

He needed a million dollars to put the project across! Where was he to lay his hands on so large a sum of money? That was the question that absorbed most of this ambitious young preacher's thought.

But he couldn't seem to make any progress.

Every night he took that thought to bed with him. He got up with it in the morning. He took it with him everywhere he went. He turned it over and over in his mind until it became a consuming *obsession* with him. A million dollars is a lot of money. He recognized that fact, but he also recognized the truth that *the only limitation is that which one sets up in one's own mind.*

Being a philosopher as well as a preacher, Dr. Gunsaulus recognized, as do all who succeed in life, that definiteness of purpose is the starting point from which one must begin. He recognized, too, that definiteness of purpose takes on animation, life, and power when backed by a burning desire to translate that purpose into its material equivalent.

He knew all these great truths, yet he did not know where, or how to lay his hands on a million dollars. The natural procedure would have been to give up and quit, by saying, "Ah well, my idea is a good one, but I cannot do anything with it, because I never can procure the necessary million dollars." That is exactly what the majority of people would have said, but it is not what Dr. Gunsaulus said. What he said, and what he did, are so important that I now introduce him, and let him speak for himself.

"One Saturday afternoon I sat in my room thinking of ways and means of raising the money to carry out my plans. For nearly two years, I had been thinking, but I *had done nothing but think!*

"The time had come for action!

"I made up my mind, then and there, that I would get the necessary million dollars within a week. How? I was not concerned about that. The main thing of importance was the *decision* to get the money within a specified time, and I want to tell you that the moment I reached a definite decision to get the money within a specified time, a strange feeling of assurance came over me, such as I had never before experienced. Something inside me seemed to say, 'Why didn't you reach that decision a long time ago? The money was waiting for you all the time!'

"Things began to happen in a hurry. I called the newspapers and announced I would preach a sermon the following morning, entitled 'What I would do if I had a Million Dollars.'

"I went to work on the sermon immediately, but I must tell you, frankly, the task was not difficult, because I had been preparing that sermon for almost two years. The spirit back of it was a part of me!

"Long before midnight I had finished writing the sermon. I went to bed and slept with a feeling of confidence, for *I could see myself already in possession of the million dollars.*

"Next morning I arose early, went into the bathroom, read the sermon, then knelt on my knees and asked that my sermon might come to the attention of someone who would supply the needed money.

"While I was praying I again had that feeling of assurance that the money would be forthcoming. In my excitement, I walked out without my sermon, and did not discover the oversight until I was in my pulpit and about ready to begin delivering it.

"It was too late to go back for my notes, and what a blessing that I couldn't go back! Instead, my own subconscious mind yielded the material I needed. When I arose to begin my sermon, I closed my eyes, and spoke with all my heart and soul of my dreams. I not only talked to my audience, but I fancy I talked also to God. I told what I would do with a million dollars if that amount were placed in my hands. I described the plan I had in mind for organizing a great educational institution, where young people would learn to do practical things, and at the same time develop their minds.

"When I had finished and sat down, a man slowly arose from his seat, about three rows from the rear, and made his way toward the pulpit. I wondered what he was going to do. He came into the pulpit, extended his hand, and said, 'Reverend, I liked your sermon. I believe you can do everything you said you would, if you had a million dollars. To prove that I believe in you and your sermon, if you will come to my office tomorrow morning, I will give you the million dollars. My name is Phillip D. Armour.'"

Young Gunsaulus went to Mr. Armour's office and the million dollars was presented to him. With the money, he founded the Armour Institute of Technology.

That is more money than the majority of preachers ever see in an entire lifetime, yet the thought impulse back of the money was created in the young preacher's mind in a fraction of a minute. The necessary million dollars came as a result of an idea. Back of the idea was a DESIRE which young Gunsaulus had been nursing in his mind for almost two years.

Observe this important fact . . . he got the money within thirty-six hours after he reached a definite decision in his own mind to get it, and decided upon a definite plan for getting it!

There was nothing new or unique about young Gunsaulus' vague thinking about a million dollars, and weakly hoping for it. Others before him, and many since his time, have had similar thoughts. But there was something very unique and different about the decision he reached on that memorable Saturday, when he put vagueness into the background, and definitely said, "I will get that money within a week!"

God seems to throw Himself on the side of the man who knows *exactly* what he wants, *if he is determined* to get just that!

Moreover, the principle through which Dr. Gunsaulus got his million dollars is still alive! It is available to you! This universal law is as workable today as it was when the young preacher made use of it so successfully. This book describes, step by step, the thirteen elements of this great law, and suggests how they may be put to use.

Observe that Asa Candler and Dr. Frank Gunsaulus had one characteristic in common. Both knew the astounding truth that ideas can be transmuted into cash through the power of definite purpose, plus definite plans.

If you are one of those who believe that hard work and honesty, alone, will bring riches, perish the thought! It is not true! Riches, when they come in huge quantities, are never the result of hard work! Riches come, if they come at all, in response to definite demands, based upon the application of definite principles, and not by chance or luck.

Generally speaking, an idea is an impulse of thought that impels action, by an appeal to the imagination. All master salesmen know that ideas can be sold where merchandise cannot. Ordinary salesmen do not know this—that is why they are "ordinary."

A publisher of books, which sell for a nickel, made a discovery that should be worth much to publishers generally. He learned that many people buy titles, and not contents of books. By merely changing the name of one book that was not moving, his sales on that book jumped upward more than a million copies. The inside of the book was not changed in any way. He merely ripped off the cover bearing the title that did not sell, and put on a new cover with a title that had "box-office" value.

That, as simple as it may seem, was an idea! It was imagination.

There is no standard price on ideas. The creator of ideas makes his own price, and, if he is smart, gets it.

The moving picture industry created a whole flock of millionaires. Most of them were men who couldn't create ideas—but—they had the imagination to recognize ideas when they saw them.

The next flock of millionaires will grow out of the radio business, which is new and not overburdened with men of keen imagination. The money will be made by those who discover or create new and more meritorious radio programmes and have the imagination to recognize merit, and to give the radio listeners a chance to profit by it.

The sponsor! That unfortunate victim who now pays the cost of all radio "entertainment" soon will become idea conscious, and demand something for his money. The man who beats the sponsor to the draw, and supplies programmes that render useful service, is the man who will become rich in this new industry.

Crooners and light chatter artists who now pollute the air with wisecracks and silly giggles will go the way of all light timbers, and their places will be taken by real artists who interpret carefully planned programmes which have been designed to service the minds of men, as well as provide entertainment.

Here is a wide-open field of opportunity screaming its protest at the way it is being butchered, because of lack of imagination, and begging for rescue at any price. Above all, the thing that radio needs is new ideas!

If this new field of opportunity intrigues you, perhaps you might profit by the suggestion that the successful radio programmes of the future will give more attention to creating "buyer" audiences, and less attention to "listener" audiences. Stated more plainly, the builder of radio programmes who succeeds in the future must find practical ways to convert "listeners" into "buyers." Moreover, the successful producer of radio programmes in the future must key his features so that he can definitely show its effect upon the audience.

Sponsors are becoming a bit weary of buying glib selling talks, based upon statements grabbed out of thin air. They want, and in the future will demand, indisputable proof that the Whoosit programme not only gives millions of people the silliest giggle ever, but that the silly giggler can sell merchandise!

Another thing that might as well be understood by those who contemplate entering this new field of opportunity, radio advertising is going to be handled by an entirely new group of advertising experts, separate and distinct from the old time newspaper and magazine advertising agency men. The old timers in the advertising game *cannot read* the modern radio scripts, because they have been schooled to see ideas. The new radio technique demands men who can interpret ideas from a *written* manuscript in terms of *sound!* It cost the author a year of hard labor, and many thousands of dollars to learn this.

Radio, right now, is about where the moving pictures were when Mary Pickford and her curls first appeared on the screen. There is plenty of room in radio for those who can *produce or recognize* ideas.

If the foregoing comment on the opportunities of radio has not started your idea factory to work, you had better forget it. Your opportunity is in some other field. If the comment intrigued you in the slightest degree, then go further into it, and you may find the one idea you need to round out your career.

Never let it discourage you if you have no experience in radio. Andrew Carnegie knew very little about making steel—I have Carnegie's own word for this—but he made practical use of two of the principles described in this book, and made the steel business yield him a fortune.

The story of practically every great fortune starts with the day when a creator of ideas and a seller of ideas got together and worked in harmony. Carnegie surrounded himself with men who could do all that he could not do—men who created ideas, and men who put ideas into operation—and made himself and the others fabulously rich.

Millions of people go through life hoping for favorable "breaks." Perhaps a favorable break can get one an opportunity, but the safest plan is not to depend upon luck. It was a favorable "break" that gave me the biggest opportunity of my life—*but*—twenty-five years *of determined effort* had to be devoted to that opportunity before it became an asset.

The "break" consisted of my good fortune in meeting and gaining the cooperation of Andrew Carnegie. On that occasion Carnegie planted in my mind the *idea* of organizing the principles of achievement into a philosophy of success. Thousands of people have profited by the discoveries made in the twenty-five years of research, and several fortunes have been accumulated through the application of the philosophy. The beginning was simple. It was an idea which anyone might have developed.

The favorable break came through Carnegie, but what about the determination, definiteness of purpose, and the desire to attain the goal, and the persistent effort of twenty-five years? It was no ordinary desire that survived disappointment, discouragement, temporary defeat, criticism, and the constant reminding of "waste of time." It was a burning desire! An obsession!

When the idea was first planted in my mind by Mr. Carnegie, it was coaxed, nursed, and enticed to *remain alive.* Gradually, the idea became a giant under its own power, and it coaxed, nursed, and drove me. Ideas are like that. First you give life and action and guidance to ideas, then they take on power of their own and sweep aside all opposition.

Ideas are intangible forces, but they have more power than the physical brains that give birth to them. They have the power to live on, after the brain that creates them has returned to dust. For example, take the power of Christianity. That began with a simple idea, born in the brain of Christ. Its chief tenet was "Do unto others as you would have others do unto you." Christ has gone back to the source from whence He came, but His idea goes marching on. Some day, it may grow up, and come into its own, then it will have fulfilled Christ's deepest desire. The idea has been developing for only two thousand years. Give it time!

Success Requires
No Explanations

Failure Permits No Alibis

CHAPTER 7

Organized Planning

THE CRYSTALLIZATION OF DESIRE INTO ACTION

The Sixth Step Toward Riches

You have learned that everything man creates or acquires begins in the form of desire, that desire is taken on the first lap of its journey, from the abstract to the concrete, into the workshop of the imagination, where plans for its transition are created and organized.

In chapter two, you were instructed to take six definite, practical steps as your first move in translating the desire for money into its monetary equivalent. One of these steps is the formation of a definite, practical plan, or plans, through which this transformation may be made.

You will now be instructed how to build plans which will be practical, viz:

(a) Ally yourself with a group of as many people as you may need for the creation and carrying out of your plan, or plans, for the accumulation of money—making use of the "Master Mind" principle described in a later chapter. (Compliance with this instruction is *absolutely essential.* Do not neglect it.)

(b) Before forming your "Master Mind" alliance, decide what advantages, and benefits, *you* may offer the individual members of your group, in return for their cooperation. No one will work indefinitely without some form of compensation. No intelligent person will either request or expect another to work without adequate compensation, although this may not always be in the form of money.

(c) Arrange to meet with the members of your "Master Mind" group at least twice a week, and more often if possible, until you have jointly perfected the necessary plan, or plans, for the accumulation of money.

(d) Maintain perfect harmony between yourself and every member of your "Master Mind" group. If you fail to carry out this instruction to the letter, you may expect to meet with failure. The "Master Mind" principle *cannot* obtain where perfect harmony does not prevail.

Keep in mind these facts:—

FIRST. You are engaged in an undertaking of major importance to you. To be sure of success, you must have plans which are faultless.

SECOND. You must have the advantage of the experience, education, native ability, and imagination of other minds. This is in harmony with the methods followed by every person who has accumulated a great fortune.

No individual has sufficient experience, education, native ability, and knowledge to insure the accumulation of a great fortune without the cooperation of other people. Every plan you adopt, in your endeavor to accumulate wealth, should be the joint creation of yourself and every other member of your "Master Mind" group. You may originate your own plans, either in whole or in part, but see that those plans are checked and approved by the members of your "Master Mind" alliance.

If the first plan which you adopt does not work successfully, replace it with a new plan; if this new plan fails to work, replace it, in turn with still another, and so on, until you find a plan which does work. Right here is the point at which the majority of men meet with failure, because of their lack of persistence in creating new plans to take the place of those which fail.

The most intelligent man living cannot succeed in accumulating money—nor in any other undertaking—without plans which are practical and workable. Just keep this fact in mind, and remember when your plans fail that temporary defeat is not permanent failure. It may only mean that your plans have not been sound. Build other plans. Start all over again.

Thomas A. Edison "failed" ten thousand times before he perfected the incandescent electric light bulb. That is—he met with *temporary defeat* ten thousand times, before his efforts were crowned with success.

Temporary defeat should mean only one thing—the certain knowledge that there is something wrong with your plan. Millions of men go through life in misery and poverty, because they lack a sound plan through which to accumulate a fortune.

Henry Ford accumulated a fortune, not because of his superior mind, but because he adopted and followed a plan which proved to be sound. A thousand men could be pointed out, each with a better education than Ford's, yet each of whom lives in poverty, because he does not possess the right plan for the accumulation of money.

Your achievement can be no greater than your plans are sound. That may seem to be an axiomatic statement, but it is true. Samuel Insull lost his fortune of over one hundred million dollars. The Insull fortune was built on plans which were sound. The business depression forced Mr. Insull to change his plans; and the change brought "temporary defeat," because his new plans were not sound. Mr. Insull is now an old man; he may, consequently, accept "failure" instead of "temporary defeat," but if his experience turns out to be failure, it will be for the reason that he lacks the fire of persistence to rebuild his plans.

No man is ever whipped, until he quits—*in his own mind.*

This fact will be repeated many times, because it is so easy to "take the count" at the first sign of defeat.

James J. Hill met with temporary defeat when he first endeavored to raise the necessary capital to build a railroad from the East to the West, but he, too turned defeat into victory *through new plans.*

Henry Ford met with temporary defeat, not only at the beginning of his automobile career, but after he had gone far toward the top. He created new plans, and went marching on to financial victory.

We see men who have accumulated great fortunes, but we often recognize only their triumph, overlooking the temporary defeats which they had to surmount before "arriving."

No follower of this philosophy can reasonably expect to accumulate a fortune without experiencing "temporary defeat." When defeat comes, accept it as a signal that your plans are not sound, rebuild those plans, and set sail once more toward your coveted goal. If you give up before your goal has been reached, you are a "quitter." A quitter never wins—and—a winner never quits. Lift this sentence out, write it on a piece of paper in letters an inch high, and place it where you will see it every night before you go to sleep, and every morning before you go to work.

When you begin to select members for your "Master Mind" group, endeavor to select those who do not take defeat seriously.

Some people foolishly believe that only money can make money. This is not true! Desire, transmuted into its monetary equivalent, through the principles laid down here, is the agency through which money is "made." Money, of itself, is nothing but inert matter. It cannot move, think, or talk, but it can "hear" when a man who desires it calls it to come!

PLANNING THE SALE OF SERVICES

The remainder of this chapter has been given over to a description of ways and means of marketing personal services. The information here conveyed will be of practical help to any person having any form of personal services to market, but it will be of priceless benefit to those who aspire to leadership in their chosen occupations.

Intelligent planning is essential for success in any undertaking designed to accumulate riches. Here will be found detailed instructions to those who must begin the accumulation of riches by selling personal services.

It should be encouraging to know that practically all the great fortunes began in the form of compensation for personal services, or from the sale of ideas. What else, except ideas and personal services, would one not possessed of property have to give in return for riches?

Broadly speaking, there are two types of people in the world. One type is known as leaders, and the other as followers. Decide at the outset whether you intend to become a leader in your chosen calling, or remain a follower. The difference in compensation is vast. The follower cannot reasonably expect the compensation to which a leader is entitled, although many followers make the mistake of expecting such pay.

It is no disgrace to be a follower. On the other hand, it is no credit to remain a follower. Most great leaders began in the capacity of followers. They became great leaders because they were intelligent followers. With few exceptions, the man who cannot follow a leader intelligently cannot become an efficient leader. The man who can follow a leader most efficiently is usually the man who develops into leadership most rapidly. An intelligent follower has many advantages, among them the opportunity to acquire knowledge from his leader.

THE MAJOR ATTRIBUTES OF LEADERSHIP

The following are important factors of leadership:—

1. Unwavering courage based upon knowledge of self, and of one's occupation. No follower wishes to be dominated by a leader who lacks self-confidence and courage. No intelligent follower will be dominated by such a leader very long.
2. Self-control. The man who cannot control himself can never control others. Self-control sets a mighty example for one's followers, which the more intelligent will emulate.
3. A keen sense of justice. Without a sense of fairness and justice, no leader can command and retain the respect of his followers.
4. Definiteness of decision. The man who wavers in his decisions shows that he is not sure of himself. He cannot lead others successfully.
5. Definiteness of plans. The successful leader must plan his work, and *work his plan.* A leader who moves by guesswork, without practical, definite plans, is comparable to a ship without a rudder. Sooner or later he will land on the rocks.
6. The habit of doing more than paid for. One of the penalties of leadership is the necessity of willingness, upon the part of the leader, to do more than he requires of his followers.
7. A pleasing personality. No slovenly, careless person can become a successful leader. Leadership calls for respect. Followers will not respect a leader who does not grade high on all of the factors of a Pleasing Personality.
8. Sympathy and understanding. The successful leader must be in sympathy with his followers. Moreover, he must understand them and their problems.
9. Mastery of detail. Successful leadership calls for mastery of details of the leader's position.
10. Willingness to assume full responsibility. The successful leader must be willing to assume responsibility for the mistakes and the shortcomings of his followers. If he tries to shift this responsibility, he will not remain the leader. If one of his followers makes a mistake, and shows himself incompetent, the leader must consider that it is *he* who failed.
11. Cooperation. The successful leader must understand and *apply* the principle of cooperative effort and be able to induce his followers to do the same. Leadership calls for power, and power calls for cooperation.

There are two forms of Leadership. The first, and by far the most effective, is leadership of consent of, and with the sympathy of, the followers. The second is leadership by force, without the consent and sympathy of the followers.

History is filled with evidences that Leadership by Force cannot endure. The downfall and disappearance of "Dictators" and kings is significant. It means that people will not follow forced leadership indefinitely.

The world has just entered a new era of relationship between leaders and followers, which very clearly calls for new leaders, and a new brand of leadership in business and industry. Those who belong to the old school of Leadership by Force, must acquire an understanding of the new brand of leadership (cooperation) or be relegated to the rank and file of the followers. There is no other way out for them.

The relationship of employer and employee, or of leader and follower, in the future, will be one of mutual cooperation, based upon an equitable division of the profits of business. In the future, the relationship of employer and employee will be more like a partnership than it has been in the past.

Napoleon, Kaiser Wilhelm of Germany, the Czar of Russia, and the King of Spain were examples of Leadership by Force. Their leadership passed. Without much difficulty, one might point to the prototypes of these ex-leaders among the business, financial, and labor leaders of America who have been dethroned or slated to go. *Leadership by Consent* of the followers is the only brand which can endure!

Men may follow the forced leadership temporarily, but they will not do so willingly.

The new brand of leadership will embrace the eleven factors of leadership, described in this chapter, as well as some other factors. The man who makes these the basis of his leadership will find abundant opportunity to lead in any walk of life. The depression was prolonged, largely, because the world lacked leadership of the new brand. At the end of the depression, the demand for leaders who are competent to apply the new methods of leadership has greatly exceeded the supply. Some of the old type of leaders will reform and adapt themselves to the new brand of leadership, but generally speaking, the world will have to look for new timber for its leadership.

This necessity may be your opportunity!

THE 10 MAJOR CAUSES OF FAILURE IN LEADERSHIP

We come now to the major faults of leaders who fail, because it is just as essential to know what not to do as it is to know what to do.

1. Inability to organize details. Efficient leadership calls for ability to organize and to master details. No genuine leader is ever "too busy" to do anything which may be required of him in his capacity as leader. When a man, whether he is a leader or follower, admits that he is "too busy" to change his plans, or to give attention to any emergency, he admits his inefficiency. The successful leader must be the master of all details connected with his position. That means, of course, that he must acquire the habit of relegating details to capable lieutenants.

2. Unwillingness to render humble service. Truly great leaders are willing, when occasion demands, to perform any sort of labor which they would ask another to perform.

"The greatest among ye shall be the servant of all" is a truth which all able leaders observe and respect.

3. Expectation of pay for what they "know" instead of what they *do* with that which they know. The world does not pay men for that which they "know." It pays them for what they DO, or induce others to do.

4. Fear of competition from followers. The leader who fears that one of his followers may take his position is practically sure to realize that fear sooner or later. The able leader trains understudies to whom he may delegate, at will, any of the details of his position. Only in this way may a leader multiply himself and prepare himself to be at many places, and give attention to many things at one time. It is an eternal truth that men receive more pay for their ability to get others to perform than they could possibly earn by their own efforts. An efficient leader may, through his knowledge of his job and the magnetism of his personality, greatly increase the efficiency of others, and induce them to render more service and better service than they could render without his aid.

5. Lack of imagination. Without imagination, the leader is incapable of meeting emergencies, and of creating plans by which to guide his followers efficiently.

6. Selfishness. The leader who claims all the honor for the work of his followers is sure to be met by resentment. The really great leader claims none of the honors. He is contented to see the honors, when there are any, go to his followers, because he knows that most men will work harder for commendation and recognition than they will for money alone.

7. Intemperance. Followers do not respect an intemperate leader. Moreover, intemperance in any of its various forms destroys the endurance and the vitality of all who indulge in it.

8. Disloyalty. Perhaps this should have come at the head of the list. The leader who is not loyal to his trust, and to his associates, those above him, and those below him, cannot long maintain his leadership. Disloyalty marks one as being less than the dust of the earth, and brings down on one's head the contempt he deserves. Lack of loyalty is one of the major causes of failure in every walk of life.

9. Emphasis of the "authority" of leadership. The efficient leader leads by encouraging, and not by trying to instil fear in the hearts of his followers. The leader who tries to impress his followers with his "authority" comes within the category of leadership through force. If a leader is a real leader, he will have no need to advertise that fact except by his conduct—his sympathy, understanding, fairness, and a demonstration that he knows his job.

10. Emphasis of title. The competent leader requires no "title" to give him the respect of his followers. The man who makes too much over his title generally has little else to emphasize. The doors to the office of the real leader are open to all who wish to enter, and his working quarters are free from formality or ostentation.

These are among the more common of the causes of failure in leadership. Any one of these faults is sufficient to induce failure. Study the list carefully if you aspire to leadership, and make sure that you are free of these faults.

SOME FERTILE FIELDS IN WHICH "NEW LEADERSHIP" WILL BE REQUIRED

Before leaving this chapter, your attention is called to a few of the fertile fields in which there has been a decline of leadership, and in which the new type of leader may find an abundance of opportunity.

FIRST. In the field of politics there is a most insistent demand for new leaders, a demand which indicates nothing less than an emergency. The majority of politicians have, seemingly, become high-grade, legalized racketeers. They have increased taxes and debauched the machinery of industry and business until the people can no longer stand the burden.

SECOND. The banking business is undergoing a reform. The leaders in this field have almost entirely lost the confidence of the public. Already the bankers have sensed the need of reform, and they have begun it.

THIRD. Industry calls for new leaders. The old type of leaders thought and moved in terms of dividends instead of thinking and moving in terms of human equations! The future leader in industry, to endure, must regard himself as a quasi-public official whose duty it is to manage his trust in such a way that it will work hardship on no individual, or group of individuals. Exploitation of working men is a thing of the past. Let the man who aspires to leadership in the field of business, industry, and labor remember this.

FOURTH. The religious leader of the future will be forced to give more attention to the temporal needs of his followers, in the solution of their economic and personal problems of the present, and less attention to the dead past, and the yet unborn future.

FIFTH. In the professions of law, medicine, and education, a new brand of leadership, and to some extent, new leaders will become a necessity. This is especially true in the field of education. The leader in that field must, in the future, find ways and means of teaching people how to apply the knowledge they receive in school. He must deal more with practice and less with theory.

SIXTH. New leaders will be required in the field of Journalism. Newspapers of the future, to be conducted successfully, must be divorced from "special privilege" and relieved from the subsidy of advertising. They must cease to be organs of propaganda for the interests which patronize their advertising columns. The type of newspaper which publishes scandal and lewd pictures will eventually go the way of all forces which debauch the human mind.

These are but a few of the fields in which opportunities for new leaders and a new brand of leadership are now available. The world is undergoing a rapid change. This means that the media through which the changes in human habits are promoted must be adapted to the changes. The media here described are the ones which, more than any others, determine the trend of civilization.

WHEN AND HOW TO APPLY FOR A POSITION

The information described here is the net result of many years of experience during which thousands of men and women were helped to market their services effectively. It can, therefore, be relied upon as sound and practical.

MEDIA THROUGH WHICH SERVICES MAY BE MARKETED

Experience has proved that the following media offer the most direct and effective methods of bringing the buyer and seller of personal services together.

1. Employment bureaus. Care must be taken to select only reputable bureaus, the management of which can show adequate records of achievement of satisfactory results. There are comparatively few such bureaus.
2. Advertising in newspapers, trade journals, magazines, and radio. Classified advertising may usually be relied upon to produce satisfactory results in the case of those who apply for clerical or ordinary salaried positions. Display advertising is more desirable in the case of those who seek executive connections, the copy to appear in the section of the paper which is most apt to come to the attention of the class of employer being sought. The copy should be prepared by an expert, who understands how to inject sufficient selling qualities to produce replies.
3. Personal letters of application, directed to particular firms or individuals most apt to need such services as are being offered. Letters should be *neatly typed,* always, and signed by hand. With the letter should be sent a complete "brief" or outline of the applicant's qualifications. Both the letter of application and the brief of experience or qualifications should be prepared by an expert. (See instructions as to information to be supplied.)
4. Application through personal acquaintances. When possible, the applicant should endeavor to approach prospective employers through some mutual acquaintance. This method of approach is particularly advantageous in the case of those who seek executive connections and do not wish to appear to be "peddling" themselves.
5. Application in person. In some instances, it may be more effective if the applicant offers personally his services to prospective employers, in which event a complete written statement of qualifications for the position should be presented, for the reason that prospective employers often wish to discuss with associates one's record.

INFORMATION TO BE SUPPLIED IN A WRITTEN "BRIEF"

This brief should be prepared as carefully as a lawyer would prepare the brief of a case to be tried in court. Unless the applicant is experienced in the preparation of such briefs, an expert should be consulted, and his services enlisted for this purpose. Successful merchants employ men and women who understand the art and the psychology of advertising to present the merits of their merchandise. One who has personal services for sale should do the same. The following information should appear in the brief:

1. *Education.* State briefly, but definitely, what schooling you have had, and in what subjects you specialized in school, giving the reasons for that specialization.
2. *Experience.* If you have had experience in connection with positions similar to the one you seek, describe it fully; state names and addresses of former employers. Be sure to bring out clearly any special experience you may have had which would equip you to fill the position you seek.
3. *References.* Practically every business firm desires to know all about the previous records, antecedents, etc., of prospective employees who seek positions of responsibility. Attach to your brief photostatic copies of letters from:
    a. Former employers
    b. Teachers under whom you studied
    c. Prominent people whose judgement may be relied upon
4. *Photograph of self.* Attach to your brief a recent, unmounted photograph of yourself.
5. *Apply for a specific position.* Avoid application for a position without describing exactly what particular position you seek. Never apply for "just a position." That indicates you lack specialized qualifications.
6. *State your qualifications* for the particular position for which you apply. Give full details as to the reason you believe you are qualified for the particular position you seek. This is the most important detail of your application. It will determine, more than anything else, what consideration you receive.
7. *Offer to go to work on probation.* In the majority of instances, if you are determined to have the position for which you apply, it will be most effective if you offer to work for a week, or a month, or for a sufficient length of time to enable your prospective employer to judge your value without pay. This may appear to be a radical suggestion, but experience has proved that it seldom fails to win at least a trial. If you are sure of your qualifications, a trial is all you need. Incidentally, such an offer indicates that you have confidence in your ability to fill the position you seek. It is most convincing. If your offer is accepted, and you make good, more than likely you will be paid for your "probation" period. Make clear the fact that your offer is based upon:
    a. Your confidence in your ability to fill the position

  b. Your confidence in your prospective employer's decision to employ you after trial
  c. Your determination to have the position you seek

8. *Knowledge of your prospective employer's business.* Before applying for a position, do sufficient research in connection with the business to familiarize yourself thoroughly with that business, and indicate in your brief the knowledge you have acquired in this field. This will be impressive, as it will indicate that you have imagination, and a real interest in the position you seek.

Remember that it is not the lawyer who knows the most law but the one who best prepares his case who wins. If your "case" is properly prepared and presented, your victory will have been more than half won at the outset.

Do not be afraid of making your brief too long. Employers are just as much interested in purchasing the services of well-qualified applicants as you are in securing employment. In fact, the success of most successful employers is due, in the main, to their ability to select well-qualified lieutenants. They want all the information available.

Remember another thing: neatness in the preparation of your brief will indicate that you are a painstaking person. I have helped to prepare briefs for clients which were so striking and out of the ordinary that they resulted in the employment of the applicant without a personal interview.

When your brief has been completed, have it neatly bound by an experienced binder, and lettered by an artist, or printer, similar to the following:

BRIEF OF THE QUALIFICATIONS OF
Robert K. Smith
APPLYING FOR THE POSITION OF
{ Private Secretary to
The President of
THE BLANK COMPANY, INC. }

Change names each time brief is shown.

This personal touch is sure to command attention. Have your brief neatly typed or mimeographed on the finest paper you can obtain, and bound with a heavy paper of the book-cover variety; the binder to be changed, and the proper firm name to be inserted, if it is to be shown to more than one company. Your photograph should be pasted on one of the pages of your brief. Follow these instructions to the letter, improving upon them wherever your imagination suggests.

Successful salesmen groom themselves with care. They understand that first impressions are lasting. Your brief is your salesman. Give it a good suit of clothes, so it will stand out in bold contrast to anything your prospective employer ever saw, in the way of an application for a position. If the position you seek is worth having, it is worth going after with care. Moreover, if you sell yourself to an employer in a manner that impresses him with your individuality, you probably will receive more money for your services from the very start than you would if you applied for employment in the usual conventional way.

If you seek employment through an advertising agency or an employment agency, have the agent use copies of your brief in marketing your services. This will help to gain preference for you, both with the agent and the prospective employers.

HOW TO GET THE EXACT POSITION YOU DESIRE

Everyone enjoys doing the kind of work for which he is best suited. An artist loves to work with paints, a craftsman with his hands, a writer loves to write. Those with less definite talents have their preferences for certain fields of business and industry. If America does anything well, it offers a full range of occupations: tilling the soil, manufacturing, marketing, and the professions.

FIRST. Decide exactly what kind of a job you want. If the job doesn't already exist, perhaps you can create it.

SECOND. Choose the company, or individual, for whom you wish to work.

THIRD. Study your prospective employer as to policies, personnel, and chances of advancement.

FOURTH. By analysis of yourself, your talents, and capabilities, figure what you can offer, and plan ways and means of giving advantages, services, developments, ideas that *you believe* you can successfully deliver.

FIFTH. Forget about "a job." Forget whether or not there is an opening. Forget the usual routine of "have you got a job for me?" Concentrate on what *you can give.*

SIXTH. Once you have your plan in mind, arrange with an experienced writer to put it on paper in neat form, and in full detail.

SEVENTH. Present it to the *proper person with authority* and he will do the rest. Every company is looking for men who can give something of value, whether it be ideas, services, or "connections." Every company has room for the man who has a definite plan of action which is to the advantage of that company.

This line of procedure may take a few days or weeks of extra time, but the difference in income, in advancement, and in gaining recognition will save years of hard work at small pay. It has many advantages, the main one being that it will often save from one to five years of time in reaching a chosen goal.

Every person who starts or "gets in" half way up the ladder does so by deliberate and careful planning (excepting, of course, the Boss' son).

THE NEW WAY OF MARKETING SERVICES

"Jobs" are now "Partnerships"

Men and women who market their services to best advantage in the future must recognize the stupendous change which has taken place in connection with the relationship between employer and employee.

In the future, the "Golden Rule," and not the "Rule of Gold," will be the dominating factor in the marketing of merchandise as well as personal services. The future relationship between employers and their employees will be more in the nature of a partnership consisting of:

a. The employer
b. The employee
c. The public they serve

This new way of marketing personal services is called new for many reasons; first, both the employer and the employee of the future will be considered as fellow-employees whose business it will be to serve the public efficiently. In times past, employers and employees have bartered among themselves, driving the best bargains they could with one another, not considering that in the final analysis they were, in reality, bargaining at the expense of the third party, the public they served.

The depression served as a mighty protest from an injured public, whose rights had been trampled upon in every direction by those who were clamoring for individual advantages and profits. When the debris of the depression shall have been cleared away, and business shall have been once again restored to balance, both employers and employees will recognize that they are no longer privileged to drive bargains at the expense of those whom they serve. The real employer of the future will be the public. This should be kept uppermost in mind by every person seeking to market personal services effectively.

Nearly every railroad in America is in financial difficulty. Who does not remember the day when, if a citizen enquired at the ticket office, the time of departure of a train, he was abruptly referred to the bulletin board instead of being politely given the information?

The street car companies have experienced a "change of times" also. There was a time not so very long ago when street car conductors took pride in giving argument to passengers. Many of the street car tracks have been removed and passengers ride on a bus, whose driver is "the last word in politeness."

All over the country street car tracks are rusting from abandonment, or have been taken up. Wherever street cars are still in operation, passengers may now ride without argument, and one may even hail the car in the middle of the block, and the motorman will obligingly pick him up.

How times have changed! That is just the point I am trying to emphasize. Times have changed! Moreover, the change is reflected not merely in railroad offices and on street cars, but in other walks of life as well. The "public-be-damned" policy is now passé. It has been supplanted by the "we-are-obligingly-at-your-service, sir" policy.

The bankers have learned a thing or two during this rapid change which has taken place during the past few years. Impoliteness on the part of a bank official or bank employee today is as rare as it was conspicuous a dozen years ago. In the years past, some bankers (not all of them, of course) carried an atmosphere of austerity which gave every would-be borrower a chill when he even thought of approaching his banker for a loan.

The thousands of bank failures during the depression had the effect of removing the mahogany doors behind which bankers formerly barricaded themselves. They now sit at desks in the open, where they may be seen and approached at will by any depositor, or by anyone who wishes to see them, and the whole atmosphere of the bank is one of courtesy and understanding.

It used to be customary for customers to have to stand and wait at the corner grocery until the clerks were through passing the time of day with friends, and the proprietor had finished making up his bank deposit, before being waited upon. Chain stores, managed by courteous men who do everything in the way of service, short of shining the customer's shoes, have pushed the old-time merchants into the background. Time marches on!

"Courtesy" and "Service" are the watch-words of merchandising today, and apply to the person who is marketing personal services even more directly than to the employer whom he serves, because, in the final analysis, both the employer and his employee are employed by the public they serve. If they fail to serve well, they pay by the loss of their privilege of serving,

We can all remember the time when the gas-meter reader pounded on the door hard enough to break the panels. When the door was opened, he pushed his way in, uninvited, with a scowl on his face which plainly said, "What the hell did you keep me waiting for?" All that has undergone a change. The meter-man now conducts himself as a gentleman who is "delighted-to-be-at-your-service-sir." Before the gas companies learned that their scowling meter-men were accumulating liabilities never to be cleared away, the polite salesmen of oil burners came along and did a land office business.

During the depression, I spent several months in the anthracite coal region of Pennsylvania, studying conditions which all but destroyed the coal industry. Among several very significant discoveries was the fact that greed on the part of operators and their employees was the chief cause of the loss of business for the operators, and loss of jobs for the miners.

Through the pressure of a group of overzealous labor leaders, representing the employees, and the greed for profits on the part of the operators, the anthracite business suddenly dwindled. The coal operators and their employees drove sharp bargains with one another, adding the cost of the "bargaining" to the price of the coal, until, finally, they discovered they had built up a wonderful business for the manufacturers of oil burning outfits and the producers of crude oil.

"The wages of sin is death!" Many have read this in the Bible, but few have discovered its meaning. Now, and for several years, the entire world has been listening by force to a sermon which might well be called "Whatsoever a man soweth, that shall he also reap."

Nothing as widespread and effective as the depression could possibly be "just a coincidence." Behind the depression was a cause. Nothing ever happens without a cause. In the main, the cause of the depression is traceable directly to the worldwide habit of trying to reap without sowing.

This should not be mistaken to mean that the depression represents a crop which the world is being forced to reap without having sown. The trouble is that the world *sowed the wrong sort of seed.* Any farmer knows he cannot sow the seed of thistles, and reap a harvest of grain. Beginning at the outbreak of the world war, the people of the world began to sow the seed of service inadequate in both quality and quantity. Nearly everyone was engaged in the pastime of trying to get without giving.

These illustrations are brought to the attention of those who have personal services to market, to show that we are where we are, and what we are, because of *our own conduct!* If there is a principle of cause and effect, which controls business, finance, and transportation, this same principle controls individuals and determines their economic status.

WHAT IS YOUR "QQS" RATING?

The causes of success in marketing services effectively and permanently have been clearly described. Unless those causes are studied, analyzed, understood, and applied, no man can market his services effectively and permanently. Every person must be his own salesman of personal services. The quality and the quantity of service rendered, and the spirit in which it is rendered, determine to a large extent the price and the duration of employment. To market personal services effectively (which means a permanent market, at a satisfactory price, under pleasant conditions), one must adopt and follow the "QQS" formula, which means that quality, plus quantity, plus the proper spirit of cooperation, equals perfect salesmanship of service. Remember the "QQS" formula, but do more—apply it as a habit!

Let us analyze the formula to make sure we understand exactly what it means.

1. *Quality* of service shall be construed to mean the performance of every detail, in connection with your position, in the most efficient manner possible, with the object of greater efficiency always in mind.
2. *Quantity* of service shall be understood to mean the habit of rendering all the service of which you are capable, at all times, with the purpose of increasing the amount of service rendered as greater skill is developed through practice and experience. Emphasis is again placed on the word "habit."
3. *Spirit* of service shall be construed to mean the habit of agreeable, harmonious conduct which will induce cooperation from associates and fellow employees.

Adequacy of quality and quantity of service is not sufficient to maintain a permanent market for your services. The conduct, or the spirit in which you deliver service, is a strong determining factor in connection with both the price you receive and the duration of employment.

Andrew Carnegie stressed this point more than others in connection with his description of the factors which lead to success in the marketing of personal services. He emphasized again, and again, the necessity for harmonious conduct. He stressed the fact that he would not retain any man, no matter how great a quantity, or how efficient the quality of his work, *unless* he worked in a spirit of harmony. Mr. Carnegie insisted upon men being agreeable. To prove that he placed a high value upon this quality, he permitted many men *who conformed to his standards* to become very wealthy. Those who did not conform had to make room for others.

The importance of a pleasing personality has been stressed because it is a factor which enables one to render service in the proper spirit. If one has a personality which pleases, and renders service in a spirit of harmony, these assets often make up for deficiencies in both the quality and the quantity of service one renders. Nothing, however, can be successfully substituted for pleasing conduct.

THE CAPITAL VALUE OF YOUR SERVICES

The person whose income is derived entirely from the sale of personal services is no less a merchant than the man who sells commodities, and it might well be added, such a person is subject to exactly the same rules of conduct as the merchant who sells merchandise.

This has been emphasized because the majority of people who live by the sale of personal services make the mistake of considering themselves free from the rules of conduct, and the responsibilities attached to those who are engaged in marketing commodities.

The new way of marketing services has practically forced both employer and employee into partnership alliances, through which both take into consideration the rights of the third party, the public they serve.

The day of the "go-getter" has passed. He has been supplanted by the "go-giver." High-pressure methods in business finally blew the lid off. There will never be the need to put the lid back on, because, in the future, business will be conducted by methods that will require no pressure.

The actual capital value of your brains may be determined by the amount of income you can produce (by marketing your services). A fair estimate of the capital value of your services may be made by multiplying your annual income by sixteen and two-thirds, as it is reasonable to estimate that your annual income represents six percent of your capital value. Money rents for 6% per annum. Money is worth no more than brains. It is often worth much less.

Competent "brains," if effectively marketed, represent a much more desirable form of capital than that which is required to conduct a business dealing in commodities, because "brains" are a form of capital which cannot be permanently depreciated through depressions, nor can this form of capital be stolen or spent. Moreover, the money which is essential for the conduct of business is as worthless as a sand dune, until it has been mixed with efficient "brains."

THE THIRTY MAJOR CAUSES OF FAILURE

How Many of These Are Holding You Back?

Life's greatest tragedy consists of men and women who earnestly try, and fail! The tragedy lies in the overwhelmingly large majority of people who fail, as compared to the few who succeed.

I have had the privilege of analyzing several thousand men and women, 98% of whom were classed as "failures." There is something radically wrong with a civilization, and a system of education, which permit 98% of the people to go through life as failures. But I did not write this book for the purpose of moralizing on the rights and wrongs of the world; that would require a book a hundred times the size of this one.

My analysis work proved that there are thirty major reasons for failure, and thirteen major principles through which people accumulate fortunes. In this chapter, a description of the thirty major causes of failure will be given. As you go over the list, check yourself by it, point by point, for the purpose of discovering how many of these causes-of-failure stand between you and success.

1. Unfavorable hereditary background. There is but little, if anything, which can be done for people who are born with a deficiency in brain power. This philosophy offers but one method of bridging this weakness—through the aid of the Master Mind. Observe with profit, however, that this is the only one of the thirty causes of failure which may not be *easily corrected* by any individual.

2. Lack of a well-defined purpose in life. There is no hope of success for the person who does not have a central purpose, or *definite goal*, at which to aim. Ninety-eight out of every hundred of those whom I have analyzed had no such aim. Perhaps this was the major cause of their failure.

3. Lack of ambition to aim above mediocrity. We offer no hope for the person who is so indifferent as not to want to get ahead in life, and who is not willing to pay the price.

4. Insufficient education. This is a handicap which may be overcome with comparative ease. Experience has proven that the best-educated people are often those who are known as "self-made," or self-educated. It takes more than a college degree to make one a person of education. Any person who is educated is one who has learned to get whatever he wants in life without violating the rights of others. Education consists not so much of knowledge, but of knowledge effectively and persistently applied. Men are paid not merely for what they know, but more particularly for what they do with that which they know.

5. Lack of self-discipline. Discipline comes through self-control. This means that one must control all negative qualities. Before you can control conditions, you must first control yourself. Self-mastery is the hardest job you will ever tackle. If you do not conquer self, you will be conquered by self. You may see at one and the same time both your best friend and your greatest enemy by stepping in front of a mirror.

6. Ill health. No person may enjoy outstanding success without good health. Many of the causes of ill health are subject to mastery and control. These, in the main are:

   a. Overeating of foods not conducive to health
   b. Wrong habits of thought; giving expression to negatives
   c. Wrong use of, and over indulgence in, sex
   d. Lack of proper physical exercise
   e. An inadequate supply of fresh air, due to improper breathing

7. Unfavorable environmental influences during childhood. "As the twig is bent, so shall the tree grow." Most people who have criminal tendencies acquire them as the result of bad environment, and improper associates during childhood.

8. Procrastination. This is one of the most common causes of failure. "Old Man

Procrastination" stands within the shadow of every human being, waiting his opportunity to spoil one's chances of success. Most of us go through life as failures, because we are waiting for the "time to be right" to start doing something worthwhile. Do not wait. The time will never be "just right." Start where you stand, and work with whatever tools you may have at your command, and better tools will be found as you go along.

9. Lack of persistence. Most of us are good "starters" but poor "finishers" of everything we begin. Moreover, people are prone to give up at the first signs of defeat. There is no substitute for persistence. The person who makes persistence his watch-word discovers that "Old Man Failure" finally becomes tired, and makes his departure. Failure cannot cope with persistence.

10. Negative personality. There is no hope of success for the person who repels people through a negative personality. Success comes through the application of power, and power is attained through the cooperative efforts of other people. A negative personality will not induce cooperation.

11. Lack of controlled sexual urge. Sex energy is the most powerful of all the stimuli which move people into action. Because it is the most powerful of the emotions, it must be controlled, through transmutation, and converted into other channels.

12. Uncontrolled desire for "something for nothing." The gambling instinct drives millions of people to failure. Evidence of this may be found in a study of the Wall Street crash of '29, during which millions of people tried to make money by gambling on stock margins.

13. Lack of a well-defined power of decision. Men who succeed reach decisions promptly, and change them, if at all, very slowly. Men who fail reach decisions, if at all, very slowly, and change them frequently, and quickly. Indecision and procrastination are twin brothers. Where one is found, the other may usually be found also. Kill off this pair before they completely "hog-tie" you to the treadmill of failure.

14. One or more of the six basic fears. These fears have been analyzed for you in a later chapter. They must be mastered before you can market your services effectively.

15. Wrong selection of a mate in marriage. This a most common cause of failure. The relationship of marriage brings people intimately into contact. Unless this relationship is harmonious, failure is likely to follow. Moreover, it will be a form of failure that is marked by misery and unhappiness, destroying all signs of ambition.

16. Over-caution. The person who takes no chances generally has to take whatever is left when others are through choosing. Over-caution is as bad as under-caution. Both are extremes to be guarded against. Life itself is filled with the element of chance.

17. Wrong selection of associates in business. This is one of the most common causes of failure in business. In marketing personal services, one should use great care to select an employer who will be an inspiration, and who is, himself, intelligent and successful. We emulate those with whom we associate most closely. Pick an employer who is worth emulating.

18. Superstition and prejudice. Superstition is a form of fear. It is also a sign of ignorance. Men who succeed keep open minds and are afraid of nothing.

19. Wrong selection of a vocation. No man can succeed in a line of endeavor which he does not like. The most essential step in the marketing of personal services is that of selecting an occupation into which you can throw yourself wholeheartedly.

20. Lack of concentration of effort. The "jack-of-all-trades" seldom is good at any. Concentrate all of your efforts on one definite chief aim.

21. The habit of indiscriminate spending. The spend-thrift cannot succeed, mainly because he stands eternally in fear of poverty. Form the habit of systematic saving by putting aside a definite percentage of your income. Money in the bank gives one a very safe foundation of courage when bargaining for the sale of personal services. Without money, one must take what one is offered, and be glad to get it.

22. Lack of enthusiasm. Without enthusiasm one cannot be convincing. Moreover, enthusiasm is contagious, and the person who has it, under control, is generally welcome in any group of people.

23. Intolerance. The person with a "closed" mind on any subject seldom gets ahead. Intolerance means that one has stopped acquiring knowledge. The most damaging forms of intolerance are those connected with religious, racial, and political differences of opinion.

24. Intemperance. The most damaging forms of intemperance are connected with eating, strong drink, and sexual activities. Overindulgence in any of these is fatal to success.

25. Inability to cooperate with others. More people lose their positions and their big opportunities in life because of this fault than for all other reasons combined. It is a fault which no well-informed business man or leader will tolerate.

26. Possession of power that was not acquired through self effort. (Sons and daughters of wealthy men, and others who inherit money which they did not earn.) Power in the hands of one who did not acquire it gradually is often fatal to success. Quick riches are more dangerous than poverty.

27. Intention dishonesty. There is no substitute for honesty. One may be temporarily dishonest by force of circumstances over which one has no control, without permanent damage. But, there is no hope for the person who is dishonest by choice. Sooner or later, his deeds will catch up with him, and he will pay by loss of reputation, and perhaps even loss of liberty.

28. Egotism and vanity. These qualities serve as red lights which warn others to keep away. They are fatal to success.

29. Guessing instead of thinking. Most people are too indifferent or lazy to acquire facts with which to think accurately. They prefer to act on "opinions" created by guesswork or snapjudgments.

30. Lack of capital. This is a common cause of failure among those who start out in business for the first time, without sufficient reserve of capital to absorb the shock of their mistakes, and to carry them over until they have established a reputation.

31. Under this, name any particular cause of failure from which you have suffered that has not been included in the foregoing list.

In these thirty major causes of failure is found a description of the tragedy of life, which obtains for practically every person who tries and fails. It will be helpful if you can induce someone who knows you well to go over this list with you, and help to analyze you by the thirty causes of failure. It may be beneficial if you try this alone. Most people cannot see themselves as others see them. You may be one who cannot.

The oldest of admonitions is "Man, know thyself!" If you market merchandise successfully, you must know the merchandise. The same is true in marketing personal services. You should know all of your weaknesses in order that you may either bridge them or eliminate them entirely. You should know your strength in order that you may call attention to it when selling your services. You can know yourself only through *accurate* analysis.

The folly of ignorance in connection with self was displayed by a young man who applied to the manager of a well known business for a position. He made a very good impression until the manager asked him what salary he expected. He replied that he had no fixed sum in mind *(lack of a definite aim)*. The manager then said, "We will pay you all you are worth, after we try you out for a week."

"I will not accept it," the applicant replied, "because I am getting more than that where I am now employed."

Before you even start to negotiate for a readjustment of your salary in your present position, or to seek employment elsewhere, be sure that you are worth more than you now receive.

It is one thing to want money—everyone wants more—but it is something entirely different to be worth more! Many people mistake their wants for their just dues. Your financial requirements or wants have nothing whatever to do with your worth. Your value is established entirely by your ability to render useful service or your capacity to induce others to render such service.

TAKE INVENTORY OF YOURSELF

28 Questions You Should Answer

Annual self-analysis is an essential in the effective marketing of personal services, as is annual inventory in merchandising. Moreover, the yearly analysis should disclose a decrease in faults, and an increase in virtues. One goes ahead, stands still, or goes backward in life. One's object should be, of course, to go ahead. Annual self-analysis will disclose whether advancement has been made, and if so, how much. It will also disclose any backward steps one may have made. The effective marketing of personal services requires one to move forward even if the progress is slow.

Your annual self-analysis should be made at the end of each year, so you can include in your New Year's Resolutions any improvements which the analysis indicates should be made. Take this inventory by asking yourself the following questions, and by checking your answers with the aid of someone who will not permit you to deceive yourself as to their accuracy.

Self-Analysis Questionnaire for Personal Inventory

1. Have I attained the goal which I established as my objective for this year? (You should work with a definite yearly objective to be attained as a part of your major life objective).

2. Have I delivered service of the best possible quality of which I was capable, or could I have improved any part of this service?
3. Have I delivered service in the greatest possible quantity of which I was capable?
4. Has the spirit of my conduct been harmonious, and cooperative at all times?
5. Have I permitted the habit of procrastination to decrease my efficiency and if so, to what extent?
6. Have I improved my personality, and if so, in what ways?
7. Have I been persistent in following my plans through to completion?
8. Have I reached decisions promptly and definitely on all occasions?
9. Have I permitted any one or more of the six basic fears to decrease my efficiency?
10. Have I been either "over-cautious," or "under-cautious"?
11. Has my relationship with my associates in work been pleasant, or unpleasant? If it has been unpleasant, has the fault been partly, or wholly mine?
12. Have I dissipated any of my energy through lack of concentration of effort?
13. Have I been open minded and tolerant in connection with all subjects?
14. In what way have I improved my ability to render service?
15. Have I been intemperate in any of my habits?
16. Have I expressed, either openly or secretly, any form of egotism?
17. Has my conduct toward my associates been such that it has induced them to respect me?
18. Have my opinions and decisions been based upon guesswork, or accuracy of analysis and thought?
19. Have I followed the habit of budgeting my time, my expenses, and my income, and have I been conservative in these budgets?
20. How much time have I devoted to unprofitable effort which I might have used to better advantage?
21. How may I re-budget my time, and change my habits so I will be more efficient during the coming year?
22. Have I been guilty of any conduct which was not approved by my conscience?
23. In what ways have I rendered more service and better service than I was paid to render?
24. Have I been unfair to anyone, and if so, in what way?
25. If I had been the purchaser of my own services for the year, would I be satisfied with my purchase?
26. Am I in the right vocation, and if not, why not?
27. Has the purchaser of my services been satisfied with the service I have rendered, and if not, why not?
28. What is my present rating on the fundamental principles of success? (Make this rating fairly, and frankly, and have it checked by someone who is courageous enough to do it accurately.)

Having read and assimilated the information conveyed through this chapter, you are now ready to create a practical plan for marketing your personal services. In this chapter will be found an adequate description of every principle essential in planning the sale of personal services, including the major attributes of leadership; the most common causes of failure in leadership; a description of the fields of opportunity for leadership; the main causes of failure in all walks of life, and the important questions which should be used in self-analysis.

This extensive and detailed presentation of accurate information has been included, because it will be needed by all who must begin the accumulation of riches by marketing personal services. Those who have lost their fortunes, and those who are just beginning to earn money, have nothing but personal services to offer in return for riches, therefore it is essential that they have available the practical information needed to market services to best advantage.

The information contained in this chapter will be of great value to all who aspire to attain leadership in any calling. It will be particularly helpful to those aiming to market their services as business or industrial executives.

Complete assimilation and understanding of the information here conveyed will be helpful in marketing one's own services, and it will also help one to become more analytical and capable of judging people. The information will be priceless to personnel directors, employment managers, and other executives charged with the selection of employees, and the maintenance of efficient organizations. If you doubt this statement, test its soundness by answering in writing the twenty-eight self-analysis questions. That might be both interesting and profitable, even though you do not doubt the soundness of the statement.

WHERE AND HOW ONE MAY FIND OPPORTUNITIES TO ACCUMULATE RICHES

Now that we have analyzed the principles by which riches may be accumulated, we naturally ask, "where may one find favorable opportunities to apply these principles?" Very well, let us take inventory and see what the United States of America offer the person seeking riches, great or small.

To begin with, let us remember, *all of us,* that we live in a country where *every law-abiding citizen enjoys freedom of thought and freedom of deed unequaled anywhere in the world.* Most of us have never taken inventory of the advantages of this freedom. We have never compared our unlimited freedom with the curtailed freedom in other countries.

Here we have freedom of thought, freedom in the choice and enjoyment of education, freedom in religion, freedom in politics, freedom in the choice of a business, profession or occupation, freedom to accumulate and own without molestation, *all the property we can accumulate,* freedom to choose our place of residence, freedom in marriage, freedom through equal opportunity to all races, freedom of travel from one state to another, freedom in our choice of foods, and freedom to *aim for any station in life for which we have prepared ourselves,* even for the presidency of the United States.

We have other forms of freedom, but this list will give a bird's eye view of the most important, which constitute opportunity of the highest order. This advantage of freedom is all the more conspicuous because the United States is the only country guaranteeing to every citizen, whether native born or naturalized, so broad and varied a list of freedoms.

Next, let us recount some of the blessings which our widespread freedom has placed within our hands. Take the average American family for example (meaning, the family of average income) and sum up the benefits available to every member of the family, in this land of opportunity and plenty!

a. Food. Next to freedom of thought and deed come food, clothing, and shelter, the three basic necessities of life.

Because of our universal freedom the average American family has available, at its very door, the choicest selection of food to be found anywhere in the world, and at prices within its financial range.

A family of two, living in the heart of Times Square district of New York City, far removed from the source of production of foods, took careful inventory of the cost of a simple breakfast, with this astonishing result:

ARTICLES OF FOOD;	COST AT THE BREAKFAST TABLE:
Grape Fruit Juice (From Florida)	02
Rippled Wheat Breakfast food (Kansas Farm)	02
Tea (From China)	02
Bananas (From South America)	02½
Toasted Bread (From Kansas Farm)	01
Fresh Country Eggs (From Utah)	07
Sugar (From Cuba, or Utah)	00½
Butter and Cream (From New England)	03
GRAND TOTAL	20

It is not very difficult to obtain food in a country where two people can have breakfast consisting of all they want or need for a dime apiece! Observe that this simple breakfast was gathered, by some strange form of magic (?) from China, South America, Utah, Kansas and the New England States, and delivered on the breakfast table, ready for consumption, in the very heart of the most crowded city in America, at a cost well within the means of the most humble laborer.

The cost included all federal, state and city taxes! (Here is a fact the politicians did not mention when they were crying out to the voters to throw their opponents out of office because the people were being taxed to death.)

b. Shelter. This family lives in a comfortable apartment, heated by steam, lighted with electricity, with gas for cooking, all for $65.00 a month. In a smaller city, or a more sparsely settled part of New York City, the same apartment could be had for as low as $20.00 a month.

The toast they had for breakfast in the food estimate was toasted on an electric toaster, which cost but a few dollars, the apartment is cleaned with a vacuum sweeper that is run by electricity. Hot and cold water is available, at all times, in the kitchen and the bathroom. The food is kept cool in a refrigerator that is run by electricity. The wife curls her hair, washes her clothes and irons them with easily operated electrical equipment, on power obtained by sticking a plug in the wall. The husband shaves with an electric shaver, and they receive entertainment from all over the world, twenty four hours a day, if they want it, without cost, by merely turning the dial of their radio.

There are other conveniences in this apartment, but the foregoing list will give a fair idea of some of the concrete evidences of the freedom we, of America, enjoy. *(And this is neither political nor economic propaganda.)*

c. Clothing. Anywhere in the United States, the woman of average clothing requirements can dress very comfortably and neatly for less than $200.00 a year, and the average man can dress for the same, or less.

Only the three basic necessities of food, clothing, and shelter have been mentioned. The average American citizen has other privileges and advantages available in return for modest effort, not exceeding eight hours per day of labor. Among these is the privilege of automobile transportation, with which one can go and come at will, at very small cost.

The average American has security of property rights not found in any other country in the world. He can place his surplus money in a bank with the assurance that his government will protect it, and make good to him if the bank fails. If an American citizen wants to travel from one state to another he needs no passport, no one's permission. He may go when he pleases, and return at will. Moreover, he may travel by train, private automobile, bus, airplane, or ship, as his pocketbook permits. In Germany, Russia, Italy, and most of the other European and Oriental countries, the people cannot travel with so much freedom, and at so little cost.

THE "MIRACLE" THAT HAS PROVIDED THESE BLESSINGS

We often hear politicians proclaiming the freedom of America, when they solicit votes, but seldom do they take the time or devote sufficient effort to the analysis of the source or nature of this "freedom." Having no axe to grind, no grudge to express, no ulterior motives to be carried out, I have the privilege of going into a frank analysis of that mysterious, abstract, greatly misunderstood "something" which gives to every citizen of America more blessings, more opportunities to accumulate wealth, more freedom of every nature, than may be found in any other country.

I have the right to analyze the source and nature of this unseen power, because I know, and have known for more than a quarter of a century, many of the men who organized that power, and many who are now responsible for its maintenance.

The name of this mysterious benefactor of mankind is capital!

Capital consists not alone of money, but more particularly of highly organized, intelligent groups of men who plan ways and means of using money efficiently for the good of the public, and profitably to themselves.

These groups consist of scientists, educators, chemists, inventors, business analysts, publicity men, transportation experts, accountants, lawyers, doctors, and both men and women who have highly specialized knowledge in all fields of industry and business. They pioneer, experiment, and blaze trails in new fields of endeavor. They support colleges, hospitals, public schools, build good roads, publish newspapers, pay most of the cost of government, and take care of the multitudinous detail essential to human progress. Stated briefly, the capitalists are the brains of civilization, because they supply the entire fabric of which all education, enlightenment and human progress consists.

Money, without brains, always is dangerous. Properly used, it is the most important essential of civilization. The simple breakfast here described could not have been delivered to the New York family at a dime each, *or at any other price,* if organized capital had not provided the machinery, the ships, the railroads, and the huge armies of trained men to operate them.

Some slight idea of the importance of organized capital may be had by trying to imagine yourself burdened with the responsibility of collecting, without the aid of capital, and delivering to the New York City family, the simple breakfast described.

To supply the tea, you would have to make a trip to China or India, both a very long way from America. Unless you are an excellent swimmer, you would become rather tired before making the round trip. Then, too, another problem would confront you. What would you use for money, even if you had the physical endurance to swim the ocean?

To supply the sugar, you would have to take another long swim to Cuba, or a long walk to the sugar beet section of Utah. But even then, you might come back without the sugar, because organized effort and money are necessary to produce sugar, to say nothing of what is required to refine, transport, and deliver it to the breakfast table anywhere in the United States.

The eggs, you could deliver easily enough from the barn yards near New York City, but you would have a very long walk to Florida and return, before you could serve the two glasses of grapefruit juice.

You would have another long walk, to Kansas, or one of the other wheat growing states, when you went after the four slices of wheat bread.

The Rippled Wheat Biscuits would have to be omitted from the menu, because they would not be available except through the labor of a trained organization of men and suitable machinery, all of which call for capital.

While resting, you could take off for another little swim down to South America, where you would pick up a couple of bananas, and on your return, you could take a short walk to the nearest farm having a dairy and pick up some butter and cream. Then your New York City family would be ready to sit down and enjoy breakfast, and *you could collect your two dimes for your labor!*

Seems absurd, doesn't it? Well, the procedure described would be the only possible way these simple items of food could be delivered to the heart of New York City, if we had no capitalistic system.

The sum of money required for the building and maintenance of the railroads and steam ships used in the delivery of that simple breakfast is so huge that it staggers one's imagination. It runs into hundreds of millions of dollars, not to mention the armies of trained employees required to man the ships and trains. But, transportation is only a part of the requirements of modern civilization in capitalistic America. Before there can be anything to haul, something must be grown from the ground, or manufactured and prepared for market. This calls for more millions of dollars for equipment, machinery, boxing, marketing, and for the wages of millions of men and women.

Steam ships and railroads do not spring up from the earth and function automatically. They come in response to the call of civilization, through the labor and ingenuity and organizing ability of men who have imagination, faith, enthusiasm, decision, persistence! These men are known as capitalists. They are motivated by the desire to build, construct, achieve, render useful service, earn profits and accumulate riches. And, because they render service without which there would be no civilization, they put themselves in the way of great riches.

Just to keep the record simple and understandable, I will add that these capitalists are the selfsame men of whom most of us have heard soap-box orators speak. They are the same men to whom radicals, racketeers, dishonest politicians and grafting labor leaders refer as "the predatory interests," or "Wall Street."

I am not attempting to present a brief for or against any group of men or any system of economics. I am not attempting to condemn collective bargaining when I refer to "grafting labor leaders," nor do I aim to give a clean bill of health to all individuals known as capitalists.

The purpose of this book—*a purpose to which I have faithfully devoted over a quarter of a century*—is to present to all who want the knowledge, the most dependable philosophy through which individuals may accumulate riches in whatever amounts they desire.

I have here analyzed the economic advantages of the capitalistic system for the two-fold purpose of showing:

1. that all who seek riches must recognize and adapt themselves to the system that controls all approaches to fortunes, large or small, and
2. to present the side of the picture opposite to that being shown by politicians and demagogues who deliberately becloud the issues they bring up, by referring to organized capital as if it were something poisonous.

This is a capitalistic country, it was developed through the use of capital, and we who claim the right to partake of the blessings of freedom and opportunity, we who seek to accumulate riches here, may as well know that neither riches nor opportunity would be available to us if organized capital had not provided these benefits.

For more than twenty years it has been a somewhat popular and growing pastime for radicals, self-seeking politicians, racketeers, crooked labor leaders, and on occasion religious leaders, to take pot-shots at "Wall Street, the money changers, and big business."

The practice became so general that we witnessed during the business depression, the unbelievable sight of high government officials lining up with the cheap politicians, and labor leaders, with the openly avowed purpose of throttling the system which has made Industrial America the richest country on earth. The line-up was so general and so well organized that it prolonged the worst depression America has ever known. It cost millions of men their jobs, because those jobs were inseparably a part of the industrial and capitalistic system which form the very backbone of the nation.

During this unusual alliance of government officials and self-seeking individuals who were endeavoring to profit by declaring "open season" on the American system of industry, a certain type of labor leader joined forces with the politicians and offered to deliver voters in return for legislation designed to permit men to take riches away from industry by organized force of numbers, instead of the better method of giving a fair day's work for a fair day's pay.

Millions of men and women throughout the nation are still engaged in this popular pastime of trying to get without giving. Some of them are lined up with labor unions, where they demand shorter hours and more pay! Others do not take the trouble to work at all. They demand government relief and are getting it. Their idea of their rights of freedom was demonstrated in New York City, where violent complaint was registered with the Postmaster, by a group of "relief beneficiaries," because the Postmen awakened them at 7:30 A.M. to deliver Government relief checks. They demanded that the time of delivery be set up to 10:00 o'clock.

If you are one of those who believe that riches can be accumulated by the mere act of men who organize themselves into groups and demand more pay for less service, if you are one of those who demand Government relief without early morning disturbance when the money is delivered to you, if you are one of those who believe in trading their votes to politicians in return for the passing of laws which permit the raiding of the public treasury, you may rest securely on your belief, with certain knowledge that no one will disturb you, because this is a free country where every man may think as he pleases, where nearly everybody can live with but little effort, where many may live well without doing any work whatsoever.

However, you should know the full truth concerning this freedom of which so many people boast, and so few understand. As great as it is, as far as it reaches, as many privileges as it provides, it does not, and cannot bring riches without effort.

There is but one dependable method of accumulating, and legally holding riches, and that is by rendering useful service. No system has ever been created by which men can legally acquire riches through mere force of numbers, or without giving in return an equivalent value of one form or another.

There is a principle known as the law of economics! This is more than a theory. It is a law no man can beat.

Mark well the name of the principle, and remember it, because it is far more powerful than all the politicians and political machines. It is above and beyond the control of all the labor unions. It cannot be swayed, nor influenced nor bribed by racketeers or self-appointed leaders in any calling. Moreover, it has an all-seeing eye, and a perfect system of bookkeeping, in which it keeps an accurate account of the transactions of every human being engaged in the business of trying to get without giving. Sooner or later its auditors come around, look over the records of individuals both great and small, and demand an accounting.

"Wall Street, Big Business, Capital Predatory Interests," or whatever name you choose to give the system which has given us American Freedom, represents a group of men who understand, respect, and adapt themselves to this powerful law of economics! Their financial continuation depends upon their respecting the law.

Most people living in America like this country, its capitalistic system and all. I must confess I know of no better country, where one may find greater opportunities to accumulate riches. Judging by their acts and deeds, there are some in this country who do not like it. That, of course is their privilege; if they do not like this country, its capitalistic system, its boundless opportunities, *they have the privilege of clearing out!* Always there are other countries, such as Germany, Russia, and Italy, where one may try one's hand at enjoying freedom, and accumulating riches providing one is not too particular.

America provides all the freedom and all the opportunity to accumulate riches that any honest person may require. When one goes hunting for game, one selects hunting grounds where game is plentiful. When seeking riches, the same rule would naturally obtain.

If it is riches you are seeking, do not overlook the possibilities of a country whose citizens are so rich that women, alone, spend over two hundred million dollars annually for lip-sticks, rouge and cosmetics. Think twice, you who are seeking riches, before trying to destroy the Capitalistic System of a country whose citizens spend over fifty million dollars a year for greeting cards, with which to express their appreciation of their freedom!

If it is money you are seeking, consider carefully a country that spends hundreds of millions of dollars annually for cigarettes, the bulk of the income from which goes to only four major companies engaged in supplying this national builder of "nonchalance" and "quiet nerves."

By all means give plenty of consideration to a country whose people spend annually more than fifteen million dollars for the privilege of seeing moving pictures, and toss in a few additional millions for liquor, narcotics, and other less potent soft drinks and giggle-waters.

Do not be in too big a hurry to get away from a country whose people willingly, even eagerly, hand over millions of dollars annually for football, baseball, and prize fights.

And, by all means, stick by a country whose inhabitants give up more than a million dollars a year for chewing gum, and another million for safety razor blades.

Remember, also, that this is but the beginning of the available sources for the accumulation of wealth. Only a few of the luxuries and non-essentials have been mentioned. But, remember that the business of producing, transporting, and marketing these few items of merchandise gives regular employment to many millions of men and women, who receive for their services many millions of dollars monthly, and spend it freely for both the luxuries and the necessities.

Especially remember, that back of all this exchange of merchandise and personal services may be found an abundance of opportunity to accumulate riches. Here our American

Freedom comes to one's aid. There is nothing to stop you, or anyone from engaging in any portion of the effort necessary to carry on these businesses. If one has superior talent, training, experience, one may accumulate riches in large amounts. Those not so fortunate may accumulate smaller amounts. Anyone may earn a living in return for a very nominal amount of labor.

So—there you are!

Opportunity has spread its wares before you. Step up to the front, select what you want, create your plan, put the plan into action, and follow through with persistence. "Capitalistic" America will do the rest. You can depend upon this much—capitalistic America insures every person the opportunity to render useful service, and to collect riches in proportion to the value of the service.

The "System" denies no one this right, but it does not, and cannot, promise something for nothing, because the system, itself, is irrevocably controlled by the law of economics which neither recognizes nor tolerates for long, getting without giving.

The law of economics was passed by Nature! There is no Supreme Court to which violators of this law may appeal. The law hands out both penalties for its violation, and appropriate rewards for its observance, *without interference or the possibility of interference by any human being.* The law cannot be repealed. It is as fixed as the stars in the heavens, and subject to, and a part of the same system that controls the stars.

May one refuse to adapt one's self to the law of economics?

Certainly! This is a free country, where all men are born with equal rights, including the privilege of ignoring the law of economics.

What happens then?

Well, nothing happens until large numbers of men join forces for the avowed purpose of ignoring the law, and taking what they want by force. *Then comes the dictator, with well-organized firing squads and machine guns!*

We have not yet reached that stage in America! But we have heard all we want to know about how the system works. Perhaps we shall be fortunate enough not to demand personal knowledge of so gruesome a reality. Doubtless we shall prefer to continue with our freedom of speech, freedom of deed and freedom to render useful service in return for riches.

The practice, by Government officials of extending to men and women the privilege of raiding the public treasury in return for votes, sometimes results in election, but as night follows day, the final payoff comes; when every penny wrongfully used must be repaid with compound interest on compound interest. If those who make the grab are not forced to repay, the burden falls on their children, and their children's children, "even unto the third and fourth generations." There is no way to avoid the debt.

Men can, and sometimes do, form themselves into groups for the purpose of crowding wages up, and working hours down. There is a point beyond which they cannot go. It is the point at which the law of economics steps in, and the sheriff gets both the employer and the employees.

For six years, from 1929 to 1935, the people of America, both rich and poor, barely missed seeing the Old Man Economics hand over to the sheriff all the businesses, and industries and banks. It was not a pretty sight! It did not increase our respect for mob psychology through which men cast reason to the winds and start trying to get without giving.

We who went through those six discouraging years, when fear was in the saddle, and faith was on the ground, cannot forget how ruthlessly the law of economics exacted its toll from both rich and poor, weak and strong, old and young. We shall not wish to go through another such experience.

These observations are not founded upon short-time experience. They are the result of twenty-five years of careful analysis of the methods of both the most successful and the most unsuccessful men America has known.

CHAPTER 8

Decision

THE MASTERY OF PROCRASTINATION

The Seventh Step Toward Riches

Accurate analysis of over 25,000 men and women who had experienced failure disclosed the fact that lack of decision was near the head of the list of the 30 major causes of failure. This is no mere statement of a theory—*it is a fact.*

Procrastination, the opposite of decision, is a common enemy which practically every man must conquer.

You will have an opportunity to test your capacity to reach *quick* and *definite* decisions when you finish reading this book, and are ready to begin putting into action the principles which it describes.

Analysis of several hundred people who had accumulated fortunes well beyond the million dollar mark disclosed the fact that *every one of them* had the habit of reaching decisions promptly, and of changing these decisions slowly, if, and when they were changed. People who fail to accumulate money, *without exception,* have the habit of reaching decisions, if at all, very *slowly,* and *of changing these decisions quickly and often.*

One of Henry Ford's most outstanding qualities is his *habit* of reaching decisions quickly and definitely, and changing them slowly. This quality is so pronounced in Mr. Ford, that it has given him the reputation of being obstinate. It was this quality which prompted Mr. Ford to continue to manufacture his famous Model "T" (the world's ugliest car), when all of his advisors, and many of the purchasers of the car, were urging him to change it.

Perhaps, Mr. Ford delayed too long in making the change, but the other side of the story is, that Mr. Ford's firmness of decision yielded a huge fortune, before the change in model became *necessary.* There is but little doubt that Mr. Ford's habit of definiteness of decision assumes the proportion of obstinacy, but this quality is preferable to slowness in reaching decisions and quickness in changing them.

The majority of people who fail to accumulate money sufficient for their needs, are, generally, easily influenced by the "opinions" of others. They permit the newspapers and the "gossiping" neighbors to do their "thinking" for them. "Opinions" are the cheapest commodities on earth. Everyone has a flock of opinions ready to be wished upon anyone who will accept them. If you are influenced by "opinions" when you reach decisions, you will not succeed in any undertaking, much less in that of transmuting your own desire into money.

If you are influenced by the opinions of others, you will have no desire of your own.

Keep your own counsel, when you begin to put into practice the principles described here, by *reaching your own decisions* and following them. Take no one into your confidence, except the members of your "Master Mind" group, and be very sure in your selection of this group, that you choose only those who will be in complete sympathy and harmony with your purpose.

Close friends and relatives, while not meaning to do so, often handicap one through "opinions" and sometimes through ridicule, which is meant to be humorous. Thousands of men and women carry inferiority complexes with them all through life, because some well-meaning, but ignorant person destroyed their confidence through "opinions" or ridicule.

You have a brain and mind of your own. Use it, and reach your own decisions. If you need facts or information from other people, to enable you to reach decisions, as you probably will in many instances; acquire these facts or secure the information you need quietly, without disclosing your purpose.

It is characteristic of people who have but a smattering or a veneer of knowledge to try to give the impression that they have much knowledge. Such people generally do too much talking, and too little listening. Keep your eyes and ears wide open—and your mouth closed, if you wish to acquire the habit of prompt decision. Those who talk too much do little else. If you talk more than you listen, you not only deprive yourself of many opportunities to accumulate useful knowledge, but you also disclose your plans and purposes to people who will take great delight in defeating you, because they envy you.

Remember, also, that every time you open your mouth in the presence of a person who has an abundance of knowledge, you display to that person, your exact stock of knowledge, or your lack of it! Genuine wisdom is usually conspicuous through *modesty and silence.*

Keep in mind the fact that every person with whom you associate is, like yourself, seeking the opportunity to accumulate money. If you talk about your plans too freely, you may be surprised when you learn that some other person has beaten you to your goal by putting into action ahead of you, the plans of which you talked unwisely.

Let one of your first decisions be to keep a closed mouth and open ears and eyes.

As a reminder to yourself to follow this advice, it will be helpful if you copy the following epigram in large letters and place it where you will see it daily.

"Tell the world what you intend to do, but first show it."

This is the equivalent of saying that "deeds, and not words, are what count most."

FREEDOM OR DEATH ON A DECISION

The value of decisions depends upon the courage required to render them. The great decisions, which served as the foundation of civilization, were reached by assuming great risks, which often meant the possibility of death.

Lincoln's decision to issue his famous Proclamation of Emancipation, which gave freedom to the colored people of America, was rendered with full understanding that his act would turn thousands of friends and political supporters against him. He knew, too, that the carrying out of that proclamation would mean death to thousands of men on the battlefield. In the end, it cost Lincoln his life. That required courage.

Socrates' decision to drink the cup of poison, rather than compromise in his personal belief, was a decision of courage. It turned Time ahead a thousand years, and gave to people then unborn, the right to freedom of thought and of speech.

The decision of Gen. Robert E. Lee, when he came to the parting of the way with the Union, and took up the cause of the South, was a decision of courage, for he well knew that it might cost him his own life, that it would surely cost the lives of others.

But, the greatest decision of all time, as far as any American citizen is concerned, was reached in Philadelphia, July 4, 1776, when fifty-six men signed their names to a document, which they well knew would bring freedom to all Americans, or *leave every one of the fifty-six hanging from a gallows!*

You have heard of this famous document, but you may not have drawn from it the great lesson in personal achievement it so plainly taught.

We all remember the date of this momentous decision, but few of us realize what courage that decision required. We remember our history, as it was taught; we remember dates, and the names of the men who fought; we remember Valley Forge, and Yorktown; we remember George Washington, and Lord Cornwallis. But we know little of the real forces back of these names, dates, and places. We know still less of that intangible power, which insured us freedom *long before Washington's armies reached Yorktown.*

We read the history of the Revolution, and falsely imagine that George Washington was the Father of our Country, that it was he who won our freedom, while the truth is—Washington was only an accessory after the fact, because victory for his armies had been insured long before Lord Cornwallis surrendered. This is not intended to rob Washington of any of the glory he so richly merited. Its purpose, rather, is to give greater attention to the astounding power that was the real cause of his victory.

It is nothing short of tragedy that the writers of history have missed, entirely, even the slightest reference to the irresistible power, which gave birth and freedom to the nation destined to set up new standards of independence for all the peoples of the earth. I say it is a tragedy, because it is the selfsame power which must be used by every individual who surmounts the difficulties of Life, and forces Life to pay the price asked.

Let us briefly review the events which gave birth to this power. The story begins with an incident in Boston, March 5, 1770. British soldiers were patroling the streets, by their presence, openly threatening the citizens. The colonists resented armed men marching in their midst. They began to express their resentment openly, hurling stones as well as epithets, at the marching soldiers, until the commanding officer gave orders, "Fix bayonets. . . . Charge!"

The battle was on. It resulted in the death and injury of many. The incident aroused such resentment that the Provincial Assembly (made up of prominent colonists) called a meeting for the purpose of taking definite action. Two of the members of that Assembly were John Hancock, and Samuel Adams—long live their names! They spoke up courageously, and declared that a move must be made to eject all British soldiers from Boston.

Remember this—a decision, in the minds of two men, might properly be called the beginning of the freedom which we, of the United States now enjoy. Remember, too, that the decision of these two men called for faith, and courage, because it was dangerous.

Before the Assembly adjourned, Samuel Adams was appointed to call on the Governor of the Province, Hutchinson, and demand the withdrawal of the British troops.

The request was granted, the troops were removed from Boston, but the incident was not closed. It had caused a situation destined to change the entire trend of civilization. Strange, is it not, how the great changes, such as the American Revolution, and the World War, often have their beginnings in circumstances which seem unimportant? It is interesting, also, to observe that these important changes usually begin in the form of a definite decision in the minds of a relatively small number of people. Few of us know the history of our country well enough to realize that John Hancock, Samuel Adams, and Richard Henry Lee (of the Province of Virginia) were the real Fathers of our Country.

Richard Henry Lee became an important factor in this story by reason of the fact that he and Samuel Adams communicated frequently (by correspondence), sharing freely their fears and their hopes concerning the welfare of the people of their Provinces. From this practice, Adams conceived the idea that a mutual exchange of letters between the thirteen Colonies might help to bring about the coordination of effort so badly needed in connection with the solution of their problems. Two years after the clash with the soldiers in Boston (March '72), Adams presented this idea to the Assembly, in the form of a motion that a Correspondence Committee be established among the Colonies, with definitely appointed correspondents in each Colony, "for the purpose of friendly cooperation for the betterment of the Colonies of British America."

Mark well this incident! It was the beginning of the organization of the far-flung power destined to give freedom to you, and to me. The Master Mind had already been organized. It consisted of Adams, Lee, and Hancock. "I tell you further, that if two of you agree upon the earth concerning anything for which you ask, it will come to you from My Father, who is in Heaven."

The Committee of Correspondence was organized. Observe that this move provided the way for increasing the power of the Master Mind by adding to it men from all the Colonies. Take notice that this procedure constituted the first organized planning of the disgruntled Colonists.

In union there is strength! The citizens of the Colonies had been waging disorganized warfare against the British soldiers, through incidents similar to the Boston riot, but nothing of benefit had been accomplished. Their individual grievances had not been consolidated under one Master Mind. No group of individuals had put their hearts, minds, souls, and bodies together in one definite decision to settle their difficulty with the British once and for all, until Adams, Hancock, and Lee got together.

Meanwhile, the British were not idle. They, too, were doing some planning and "Master-Minding" on their own account, with the advantage of having back of them money, and organized soldiery.

The Crown appointed Gage to supplant Hutchinson as the Governor of Massachusetts. One of the new Governor's first acts was to send a messenger to call on Samuel Adams, for the purpose of endeavoring to stop his opposition—by fear.

We can best understand the spirit of what happened by quoting the conversation between Col. Fenton (the messenger sent by Gage) and Adams.

Col. Fenton: "I have been authorized by Governor Gage, to assure you, Mr. Adams, that the Governor has been empowered to confer upon you such benefits as would be satisfactory [endeavor to win Adams by promise of bribes] upon the condition that you engage to cease in your opposition to the measures of the government. It is the Governor's advice to you, Sir, not to incur the further displeasure of his majesty. Your conduct has been such as makes you liable to penalties of an Act of Henry VIII, by which persons can be sent to England for trial for treason, or misprision of treason, at the discretion of a governor of a province. But, by changing your political course, you will not only receive great personal advantages, but you will make your peace with the King."

Samuel Adams had the choice of two decisions. He could cease his opposition, and receive personal bribes, or he could continue, and run the risk of being hanged!

Clearly, the time had come when Adams was *forced* to reach *instantly,* a decision which could have cost his life. The majority of men would have found it difficult to reach such a decision. The majority would have sent back an evasive reply, but not Adams! He insisted upon Col. Fenton's word of honor, that the Colonel would deliver to the Governor the answer exactly as Adams would give it to him.

Adams' answer, "Then you may tell Governor Gage that I trust I have long since made my peace with the King of Kings. No personal consideration shall induce me to abandon the righteous cause of my Country. And, tell Governor Gage it is the advice of Samuel Adams to him, no longer to insult the feelings of an exasperated people."

Comment as to the character of this man seems unnecessary. It must be obvious to all who read this astounding message that its sender possessed loyalty of the highest order. *This is important.* (Racketeers and dishonest politicians have prostituted the honor for which such men as Adams died.)

When Governor Gage received Adams' caustic reply, he flew into a rage, and issued a proclamation which read, "I do, hereby, in his majesty's name, offer and promise his most gracious pardon to all persons who shall forthwith lay down their arms, and return to the duties of peaceable subjects, excepting only from the benefit of such pardon, Samuel Adams and John Hancock, whose offences are of too flagitious a nature to admit of any other consideration but that of condign punishment."

As one might say, in modern slang, Adams and Hancock were "on the spot!" The threat of the irate Governor forced the two men to reach another decision, equally as dangerous. They hurriedly called a secret meeting of their staunchest followers. (Here the Master Mind began to take on momentum.) After the meeting had been called to order, Adams locked the door, placed the key in his pocket, and informed all present that it was imperative that a Congress of the Colonists be organized, and that no man should leave the room until the decision for such a congress had been reached.

Great excitement followed. Some weighed the possible consequences of such radicalism (Old Man Fear). Some expressed grave doubt as to the wisdom of so *definite a decision* in defiance of the Crown. Locked in that room were two men immune to Fear, blind to the possibility of Failure. Hancock and Adams. Through the influence of their minds, the others were induced to agree that, through the Correspondence Committee, arrangements should be made for a meeting of the First Continental Congress, to be held in Philadelphia, September 5, 1774.

Remember this date. It is more important than July 4, 1776. If there had been no DECISION to hold a Continental Congress, there could have been no signing of the Declaration of Independence.

Before the first meeting of the new Congress, another leader, in a different section of the country was deep in the throes of publishing a "Summary View of the Rights of British America." He was Thomas Jefferson, of the Province of Virginia, whose relationship to Lord Dunmore (representative of the Crown in Virginia) was as strained as that of Hancock and Adams with their Governor.

Shortly after his famous Summary of Rights was published, Jefferson was informed that he was subject to prosecution for high treason against his majesty's government. Inspired by the threat, one of Jefferson's colleagues, Patrick Henry, boldly spoke his mind, concluding his remarks with a sentence which shall remain forever a classic, *"If this be treason, then make the most of it."*

It was such men as these who, without power, without authority, without military strength, without money, sat in solemn consideration of the destiny of the colonies, beginning at the opening of the First Continental Congress, and continuing at intervals for two years—until on June 7, 1776, Richard Henry Lee arose, addressed the Chair, and to the startled Assembly made this motion:

"Gentlemen, I make the motion that these United Colonies are, and of right ought to be free and independent states, that they be absolved from all allegiance to the British Crown, and that all political connection between them and the state of Great Britain is, and ought to be totally dissolved."

Lee's astounding motion was discussed fervently, and at such length that he began to lose patience. Finally, after days of argument, he again took the floor, and declared, in a clear, firm voice, "Mr. President, we have discussed this issue for days. It is the only course for us to follow. Why, then Sir, do we longer delay? Why still deliberate? Let this happy day give birth to an American Republic. Let her arise, not to devastate and to conquer, but to reestablish the reign of peace, and of law. The eyes of Europe are fixed upon us. She demands of us a living example of freedom, that may exhibit a contrast, in the felicity of the citizen, to the ever increasing tyranny."

Before his motion was finally voted upon, Lee was called back to Virginia, because of serious family illness, but before leaving, he placed his cause in the hands of his friend, Thomas Jefferson, who promised to fight until favorable action was taken. Shortly thereafter the President of the Congress (Hancock) appointed Jefferson as Chairman of a Committee to draw up a Declaration of Independence.

Long and hard the Committee labored, on a document which would mean, when accepted by the Congress, that every man who signed it, would be signing his own death warrant, should the Colonies lose in the fight with Great Britain, which was sure to follow.

The document was drawn, and on June 28, the original draft was read before the Congress. For several days it was discussed, altered, and made ready. On July 4, 1776, Thomas Jefferson stood before the Assembly, and fearlessly read the most momentous decision ever placed upon paper.

"When in the course of human events it is necessary for one people to dissolve the political bands which have connected them with another, and to assume, among the powers of the earth, the separate and equal station to which the laws of Nature, and of Nature's God entitle them, a decent respect to the opinions of mankind requires that they should declare the causes which impel them to the separation. . . ."

When Jefferson finished, the document was voted upon, accepted, and signed by the fifty-six men, every one staking his own life upon his decision to write his name. By that decision came into existence a nation destined to bring to mankind forever, the privilege of making decisions.

By decisions made in a similar spirit of Faith, and only by such decisions, can men solve their personal problems, and win for themselves high estates of material and spiritual wealth. Let us not forget this!

Analyze the events which led to the Declaration of Independence, and be convinced that this nation, which now holds a position of commanding respect and power among all nations of the world, was born of a decision created by a Master Mind, consisting of fifty-six men. Note well, the fact that it was their decision which insured the success of Washington's armies, because the *spirit* of that decision was in the heart of every soldier who fought with him, and served as a spiritual power which recognizes no such thing as failure.

Note, also (with great personal benefit) that the power which gave this nation its freedom, is the self-same power that must be used by every individual who becomes self-determining. This power is made up of the principles described in this book. It will not be difficult to detect, in the story of the Declaration of Independence, at least six of these principles; desire, decision, faith, persistence, the master mind, and organized planning.

Throughout this philosophy will be found the suggestion that thought, backed by strong desire, has a tendency to transmute itself into its physical equivalent. Before passing on, I wish to leave with you the suggestion that one may find in this story, and in the story of the organization of the United States Steel Corporation, a perfect description of the method by which thought makes this astounding transformation.

In your search for the secret of the method, do not look for a miracle, because you will not find it. You will find only the eternal laws of Nature. These laws are available to every person who has the faith and the courage to use them. They may be used to bring freedom to a nation, or to accumulate riches. There is no charge save the time necessary to understand and appropriate them.

Those who reach decisions promptly and definitely know what they want, and generally get it. The leaders in every walk of life decide quickly, and firmly. That is the major reason why they are leaders. The world has the habit of making room for the man whose words and actions show that he knows where he is going.

Indecision is a habit which usually begins in youth. The habit takes on permanency as the youth goes through graded school, high school, and even through college, without definiteness of purpose. The major weakness of all educational systems is that they neither teach nor encourage the habit of definite decision.

It would be beneficial if no college would permit the enrollment of any student, unless and until the student declared his major purpose in matriculating. It would be of still greater benefit, if every student who enters the graded schools were compelled to accept training in the habit of decision, and forced to pass a satisfactory examination on this subject before being permitted to advance in the grades.

The habit of indecision acquired because of the deficiencies of our school systems, goes with the student into the occupation he chooses . . . if . . . in fact, he chooses his occupation. Generally, the youth just out of school seeks any job that can be found. He takes the first place he finds, because he has fallen into the habit of indecision. Ninety-eight out of every hundred people working for wages today are in the positions they hold, because they lacked the definiteness of decision to plan a definite position, and the knowledge of how to choose an employer.

Definiteness of decision always requires courage, sometimes very great courage. The fifty-six men who signed the Declaration of Independence staked their lives on the decision to affix their signatures to that document. The person who reaches a definite decision to procure the particular job, and make life pay the price he asks, does not stake his life on that decision; he stakes his economic freedom. Financial independence, riches, desirable business and professional positions are not within reach of the person who neglects or refuses to expect, plan, and demand these things. The person who desires riches in the same spirit that Samuel Adams desired freedom for the Colonies, is sure to accumulate wealth.

In the chapter on Organized Planning, you will find complete instructions for marketing every type of personal services. You will find also detailed information on how to choose the employer you prefer, and the particular job you desire. These instructions will be of no value to you unless you definitely decide to organize them into a plan of action.

CHAPTER 9

Persistence

THE SUSTAINED EFFORT NECESSARY TO INDUCE FAITH

The Eighth Step Toward Riches

Persistence is an essential factor in the procedure of transmuting desire into its monetary equivalent. The basis of persistence is the power of will.

Will-power and desire, when properly combined, make an irresistible pair. Men who accumulate great fortunes are generally known as cold-blooded, and sometimes ruthless. Often they are misunderstood. What they have is will-power, which they mix with persistence, and place back of their desires to *insure* the attainment of their objectives.

Henry Ford has been generally misunderstood to be ruthless and cold-blooded. This misconception grew out of Ford s habit of following through in all of his plans with persistence.

The majority of people are ready to throw their aims and purposes overboard, and give up at the first sign of opposition or misfortune. A few carry on despite all opposition, until they attain their goal. These few are the Fords, Carnegies, Rockefellers, and Edisons.

There may be no heroic connotation to the word "persistence," but the quality is to the character of man what carbon is to steel.

The building of a fortune, generally, involves the application of the entire thirteen factors of this philosophy. These principles must be understood, they must be applied with persistence by all who accumulate money.

If you are following this book with the intention of applying the knowledge it conveys, your first test as to your persistence will come when you begin to follow the six steps described in the second chapter. Unless you are one of the two out of every hundred who already have a definite goal at which you are aiming, and a definite plan for its attainment, you may read the instructions, and then pass on with your daily routine, and never comply with those instructions.

The author is checking you up at this point, because lack of persistence is one of the major causes of failure. Moreover, experience with thousands of people has proved that lack of persistence is a weakness common to the majority of men. It is a weakness which may be overcome by effort. The ease with which lack of persistence may be conquered will depend *entirely* upon the intensity of one's desire.

The starting point of all achievement is desire. Keep this constantly in mind. Weak desires bring weak results, just as a small amount of fire makes a small amount of heat. If you find yourself lacking in persistence, this weakness may be remedied by building a stronger fire under your desires.

Continue to read through to the end, then go back to Chapter two, and start *immediately* to carry out the instructions given in connection with the six steps. The eagerness with which you follow these instructions will indicate clearly, how much, or how little you really desire to accumulate money. If you find that you are indifferent, you may be sure that you have not yet acquired the "money consciousness" which you must possess, before you can be sure of accumulating a fortune.

Fortunes gravitate to men whose minds have been prepared to "attract" them, just as surely as water gravitates to the ocean. In this book may be found all the stimuli necessary to "attune" any normal mind to the vibrations which will attract the object of ones desires.

If you find you are weak in persistence, center your attention upon the instructions contained in the chapter on "Power"; surround yourself with a "master mind" group, and through the cooperative efforts of the members of this group, you can develop persistence. You will find additional instructions for the development of persistence in the chapters on auto-suggestion, and the subconscious mind. Follow the instructions outlined in these chapters until your habit nature hands over to your subconscious mind, a clear picture of the object of your desire. From that point on, you will not be handicapped by lack of persistence.

Your subconscious mind works continuously, while you are awake, and while you are asleep.

Spasmodic, or occasional effort to apply the rules will be of no value to you. To get results, you must apply all of the rules until their application becomes a fixed habit with you. In no other way can you develop the necessary "money consciousness."

Poverty is attracted to the one whose mind is favorable to it, as money is attracted to him whose mind has been deliberately prepared to attract it, and through the same laws. Poverty consciousness will voluntarily seize the mind which is not occupied with the money consciousness. A poverty consciousness develops without *conscious* application of habits favorable to it. The money consciousness must be created to order, unless one is born with such a consciousness.

Catch the full significance of the statements in the preceding paragraph, and you will understand the importance of persistence in the accumulation of a fortune. Without persistence, you will be defeated, even before you start. With persistence you will win.

If you have ever experienced a nightmare, you will realize the value of persistence. You are lying in bed, half awake, with a feeling that you are about to smother. You are unable to turn over, or to move a muscle. You realize that you must begin to regain control over your muscles. Through persistent effort of will-power, you finally manage to move the fingers of one hand. By continuing to move your fingers, you extend your control to the muscles of one arm, until you can lift it. Then you gain control of the other arm in the same manner. You finally gain control over the muscles of one leg, and then extend it to the other leg. Then—with one supreme effort of will—you regain complete control over your muscular system, and "snap" out of your nightmare. The trick has been turned step by step.

You may find it necessary to "snap" out of your mental inertia, through a similar procedure, moving slowly at first, then increasing your speed, until you gain complete control over your will. Be persistent no matter how slowly you may, at first, have to move. With persistence will come success.

If you select your "Master Mind" group with care, you will have in it, at least one person who will aid you in the development of persistence. Some men who have accumulated great fortunes, did so because of necessity. They developed the habit of persistence, because they were so closely driven by circumstances, that they *had to become persistent.*

There is no substitute for persistence! It cannot be supplanted by any other quality! Remember this, and it will hearten you, in the beginning, when the going may seem difficult and slow.

Those who have cultivated the habit of persistence seem to enjoy insurance against failure. No matter how many times they are defeated, they finally arrive up toward the top of the ladder. Sometimes it appears that there is a hidden Guide whose duty is to test men through all sorts of discouraging experiences. Those who pick themselves up after defeat and keep on trying, arrive; and the world cries, "Bravo! I knew you could do it!" The hidden Guide lets no one enjoy great achievement without passing the persistence test. Those who can't take it, simply do not make the grade.

Those who can "take it" are bountifully rewarded for their persistence. They receive, as their compensation, whatever goal they are pursuing. That is not all! They receive something infinitely more important than material compensation—the knowledge that "every failure brings with it the seed of an equivalent advantage."

There are exceptions to this rule; a few people know from experience the soundness of persistence. They are the ones who have not accepted defeat as being anything more than temporary. They are the ones whose desires are so persistently applied that defeat is finally changed into victory. We who stand on the side-lines of Life see the overwhelmingly large number who go down in defeat, never to rise again. We see the few who take the punishment of defeat *as an urge to greater effort.* These, fortunately, never learn to accept Life's reverse gear. But what we do not see, what most of us never suspect of existing, is the silent but irresistible power which comes to the rescue of those who fight on in the face of discouragement. If we speak of this power at all we call it persistence, and let it go at that. One thing we all know, if one does not possess persistence, one does not achieve noteworthy success in any calling.

As these lines are being written, I look up from my work, and see before me, less than a block away, the great mysterious "Broadway," the "Graveyard of Dead Hopes," and the "Front Porch of Opportunity." From all over the world people have come to Broadway, seeking fame, fortune, power, love, or whatever it is that human beings call success. Once in a great while someone steps out from the long procession of seekers, and the world hears that another person has mastered Broadway. But Broadway is not easily nor quickly conquered. She acknowledges talent, recognizes genius, pays off in money, only *after* one has refused to quit.

Then we know he has discovered the secret of how to conquer Broadway. The secret is always inseparably attached to one word, persistence!

The secret is told in the struggle of Fannie Hurst, whose persistence conquered the Great White Way. She came to New York in 1915, to convert writing into riches. The conversion did not come quickly, but it came. For four years Miss Hurst learned about "The Sidewalks of New York" from first hand experience. She spent her days laboring, and her nights hoping. When hope grew dim, she did not say, "Alright Broadway, you win!" She said, "Very well, Broadway, you may whip some, but not me. I'm going to force you to give up."

One publisher *(The Saturday Evening Post)* sent her *thirty-six* rejection slips, before she "broke the ice" and got a story across. The average writer, like the "average" in other walks of life, would have given up the job when the first rejection slip came. She pounded the pavements for four years to the tune of the publisher's "no," because she was determined to win.

Then came the "payoff." The spell had been broken, the unseen Guide had tested Fannie Hurst, and she could take it. From that time on publishers made a beaten path to her door. Money came so fast she hardly had time to count it. Then the moving picture men discovered her, and money came not in small change, but in floods. The moving picture rights to her latest novel, *Great Laughter,* brought $100,000.00, said to be the highest price ever paid for a story before publication. Her royalties from the sale of the book probably will run much more.

Briefly, you have a description of what persistence is capable of achieving. Fannie Hurst is no exception. Wherever men and women accumulate great riches, you may be sure they first acquired persistence. Broadway will give any beggar a cup of coffee and a sandwich, but it demands persistence of those who go after the big stakes.

Kate Smith will say "amen" when she reads this. For years she sang, without money, and without price, before any microphone she could reach. Broadway said to her, "Come and get it, if you can take it." She did take it until one happy day Broadway got tired and said, "Aw, what's the use? You don't know when you're whipped, so name your price, and go to work in earnest." Miss Smith named her price! It was plenty. Away up in figures so high that one week's salary is far more than most people make in a whole year.

Verily it pays to be persistent!

And here is an encouraging statement which carries with it a suggestion of great significance—thousands of singers who excel Kate Smith are walking up and down Broadway looking for a "break"—without success. Countless others have come and gone, many of them sang well enough, but they failed to make the grade because they lacked the courage to keep on keeping on, until Broadway became tired of turning them away.

Persistence is a state of mind, therefore it can be cultivated. Like all states of mind, persistence is based upon definite causes, among them these:—

a. Definiteness of purpose. Knowing what one wants is the first and, perhaps, the most important step toward the development of persistence. A strong motive forces one to surmount many difficulties.

b. Desire. It is comparatively easy to acquire and to maintain persistence in pursuing the object of intense desire.

c. Self-reliance. Belief in one's ability to carry out a plan encourages one to follow the plan through with persistence. (Self-reliance can be developed through the principle described in the chapter on auto-suggestion.)

d. Definiteness of plans. Organized plans, even though they may be weak and entirely impractical, encourage persistence.

e. Accurate knowledge. Knowing that one's plans are sound, based upon experience or observation, encourages persistence; "guessing" instead of "knowing" destroys persistence.

f. Co-operation. Sympathy, understanding, and harmonious cooperation with others tend to develop persistence.

g. Will-power. The habit of concentrating one's thoughts upon the building of plans for the attainment of a definite purpose, leads to persistence.

h. Habit. Persistence is the direct result of habit. The mind absorbs and becomes a part of the daily experiences upon which it feeds. Fear, the worst of all enemies, can be effectively cured *by forced repetition of acts of courage.* Everyone who has seen active service in war knows this.

Before leaving the subject of persistence, take inventory of yourself, and determine in what particular, if any, you are lacking in this essential quality. Measure yourself courageously, point by point, and see how many of the eight factors of persistence you lack. The analysis may lead to discoveries that will give you a new grip on yourself.

SYMPTOMS OF LACK OF PERSISTENCE

Here you will find the real enemies which stand between you and noteworthy achievement. Here you will find not only the "symptoms" indicating weakness of persistence, but also the deeply seated subconscious causes of this weakness. Study the list carefully, and face yourself squarely if you really wish to know who you are, and what you are capable of doing. These are the weaknesses which must be mastered by all who accumulate riches.

1. Failure to recognize and to clearly define exactly what one wants.
2. Procrastination, with or without cause. (Usually backed up with a formidable array of alibis and excuses.)
3. Lack of interest in acquiring specialized knowledge.
4. Indecision, the habit of "passing the buck" on all occasions, instead of facing issues squarely. (Also backed by alibis.)
5. The habit of relying upon alibis instead of creating definite plans for the solution of problems.
6. Self-satisfaction. There is but little remedy for this affliction, and no hope for those who suffer from it.

7. Indifference, usually reflected in one's readiness to compromise on all occasions, rather than meet opposition and fight it.

8. The habit of blaming others for one's mistakes, and accepting unfavorable circumstances as being unavoidable.

9. Weakness of desire, due to neglect in the choice of motives that impel action.

10. Willingness, even eagerness, to quit at the first sign of defeat. (Based upon one or more of the 6 basic fears.)

11. Lack of organized plans, placed in writing where they may be analyzed.

12. The habit of neglecting to move on ideas, or to grasp opportunity when it presents itself.

13. Wishing instead of willing.

14. The habit of compromising with poverty instead of aiming at riches. General absence of ambition to *be,* to *do,* and to *own.*

15. Searching for all the short-cuts to riches, trying to get without giving a fair equivalent, usually reflected in the habit of gambling, endeavoring to drive "sharp" bargains.

16. Fear of criticism, failure to create plans and to put them into action, because of what other people will think, do, or say. This enemy belongs at the head of the list, because it generally exists in one's subconscious mind, where its presence is not recognized. (See the Six Basic Fears in a later chapter.)

Let us examine some of the symptoms of the Fear of Criticism. The majority of people permit relatives, friends, and the public at large to so influence them that they cannot live their own lives, because they fear criticism.

Huge numbers of people make mistakes in marriage, stand by the bargain, and go through life miserable and unhappy, because they fear criticism which may follow if they correct the mistake. (Anyone who has submitted to this form of fear knows the irreparable damage it does, by destroying ambition, self-reliance, and the desire to achieve.)

Millions of people neglect to acquire belated educations, after having left school, because they fear criticism.

Countless numbers of men and women, both young and old, permit relatives to wreck their lives in the name of duty, because they fear criticism. (Duty does not require any person to submit to the destruction of his personal ambitions and the right to live his own life in his own way.)

People refuse to take chances in business, because they fear the criticism which may follow if they fail. *The fear of criticism in such cases is stronger than the desire for success.*

Too many people refuse to set high goals for themselves, or even neglect selecting a career, because they fear the criticism of relatives and "friends" who may say "Don't aim so high, people will think you are crazy."

When Andrew Carnegie suggested that I devote twenty years to the organization of a philosophy of individual achievement my first impulse of thought was fear of what people might say. The suggestion set up a goal for me, far out of proportion to any I had ever conceived. As quick as a flash, my mind began to create alibis and excuses, all of them traceable to the inherent fear of criticism. Something inside of me said, "You can't do it—the job is too big, and requires too much time—what will your relatives think of you?—

how will you earn a living?—no one has ever organized a philosophy of success, what right have you to believe you can do it?—who are you, anyway, to aim so high?— remember your humble birth—what do you know about philosophy—people will think you are crazy—(and they did)—why hasn't some other person done this before now?"

These, and many other questions flashed into my mind, and demanded attention. It seemed as if the whole world had suddenly turned its attention to me with the purpose of ridiculing me into giving up all desire to carry out Mr. Carnegie's suggestion.

I had a fine opportunity, then and there, to kill off ambition before it gained control of me. Later in life, after having analyzed thousands of people, I discovered that most ideas are stillborn, and need the breath of life injected into them through definite plans of immediate action. The time to nurse an idea is at the time of its birth. Every minute it lives gives it a better chance of surviving. The fear of criticism is at the bottom of the destruction of most ideas which never reach the planning and action stage.

Many people believe that material success is the result of favorable "breaks." There is an element of ground for the belief, but those depending entirely upon luck are nearly always disappointed, because they overlook another important factor which must be present before one can be sure of success. It is the knowledge with which favorable "breaks" can be made to order.

During the Depression, W. C. Fields, the comedian, lost all his money, and found himself without income, without a job, and his means of earning a living (vaudeville) no longer existed. Moreover, he was past sixty, when many men consider themselves "old." He was so eager to stage a comeback that he offered to work without pay, in a new field (movies). In addition to his other troubles, he fell and injured his neck. To many that would have been the place to give up and quit. But Fields was persistent. He knew that if he carried on he would get the "breaks" sooner or later, and he did get them, but not by chance.

Marie Dressler found herself down and out, with her money gone, with no job, when she was about sixty. She, too, went after the "breaks," and got them. Her persistence brought an astounding triumph late in life, long beyond the age when most men and women are done with ambition to achieve.

Eddie Cantor lost his money in the 1929 stock crash, but he still had his persistence and his courage. With these, plus two prominent eyes, he exploited himself back into an income of $10,000 a week! Verily, if one has persistence, one can get along very well without many other qualities.

The only "break" anyone can afford to rely upon is a self-made "break." These come through the application of persistence. The starting point is definiteness of purpose.

Examine the first hundred people you meet, ask them what they want most in life, and ninety eight of them will not be able to tell you. If you press them for an answer, some will say—security, many will say—money, a few will say—happiness, others will say—fame and power, and still others will say—social recognition, ease in living, ability to sing, dance, or write, but none of them will be able to define these terms, or give the slightest indication of a plan by which they hope to attain these vaguely expressed wishes. Riches do not respond to wishes. They respond only to definite plans, backed by definite desires, through constant persistence.

HOW TO DEVELOP PERSISTENCE

There are four simple steps which lead to the habit of persistence. They call for no great amount of intelligence, no particular amount of education, and but little time or effort. The necessary steps are:—

1. A definite purpose backed by burning desire for its fulfillment.
2. A definite plan, expressed in continuous action.
3. A mind closed tightly against all negative and discouraging influences, including negative suggestions of relatives, friends and acquaintances.
4. A friendly alliance with one or more persons who will encourage one to follow through with both plan and purpose.

These four steps are essential for success in all walks of life. The entire purpose of the thirteen principles of this philosophy is to enable one to take these four steps as a matter of *habit.*

These are the steps by which one may control one's economic destiny.
They are the steps that lead to freedom and independence of thought.
They are the steps that lead to riches, in small or great quantities.
They lead the way to power, fame, and worldly recognition.
They are the four steps which guarantee favorable "breaks."
They are the steps that convert dreams into physical realities.
They lead, also, to the mastery of fear, discouragement, indifference.

There is a magnificent reward for all who learn to take these four steps. It is the privilege of writing one's own ticket, and of making Life yield whatever price is asked.

I have no way of knowing the facts, but I venture to conjecture that Mrs. Wallis Simpson's great love for a man was not accidental, nor the result of favorable "breaks" alone. There was a burning desire, and careful searching at every step of the way. Her first duty was to love. What is the greatest thing on earth? The Master called it love—not man made rules, criticism, bitterness, slander, or political "marriages," but love.

She knew what she wanted, not after she met the Prince of Wales, but long before that. Twice when she had failed to find it, she had the courage to continue her search. "To thine own self be true, and it must follow, as the night the day, thou canst not then be false to any man."

Her rise from obscurity was of the slow, progressive, persistent order, but it was sure! She triumphed over unbelievably long odds; and, no matter who you are, or what you may think of Wallis Simpson, or the king who gave up his Crown for her love, she is an astounding example of applied persistence, an instructor on the rules of self-determination, from whom the entire world might profitably take lessons.

When you think of Wallis Simpson, think of one who knew what she wanted, and shook the greatest empire on earth to get it. Women who complain that this is a man's world, that women do not have an equal chance to win, owe it to themselves to study carefully the life of this unusual woman, who, at an age which most women consider "old," captured the affections of the most desirable bachelor in the entire world.

And what of King Edward? What lesson may we learn from his part in the world's greatest drama of recent times? Did he pay too high a price for the affections of the woman of his choice?

Surely no one but he can give the correct answer.

The rest of us can only conjecture. This much we know, the king came into the world without his own consent. He was born to great riches, without requesting them. He was persistently sought in marriage; politicians and statesmen throughout Europe tossed dowagers and princesses at his feet. Because he was the first born of his parents, he inherited a crown, which he did not seek, and perhaps did not desire. For more than forty years he was not a free agent, could not live his life in his own way, had but little privacy, and finally assumed duties inflicted upon him when he ascended the throne.

Some will say, "With all these blessings, King Edward should have found peace of mind, contentment, and joy of living."

The truth is that back of all the privileges of a crown, all the money, the fame, and the power inherited by King Edward, there was an emptiness which could be filled only by love.

His greatest desire was for love. Long before he met Wallis Simpson, he doubtless felt this great universal emotion tugging at the strings of his heart, beating upon the door of his soul, and crying out for expression.

And when he met a kindred spirit, crying out for this same Holy privilege of expression, he recognized it, and without fear or apology, opened his heart and bade it enter. All the scandalmongers in the world cannot destroy the beauty of this international drama, through which two people found love, and had the courage to face open criticism, renounce all else to give it *holy* expression.

King Edward's decision to give up the crown of the world's most powerful empire, for the privilege of going the remainder of the way through life with the woman of his choice, was a decision that required courage. The decision also had a price, but who has the right to say the price was too great? Surely not He who said, "He among you who is without sin, let him cast the first stone."

As a suggestion to any evil-minded person who chooses to find fault with the Duke of Windsor, because his desire was for love, and for openly declaring his love for Wallis Simpson, and giving up his throne for her, let it be remembered that the open declaration was not essential. He could have followed the custom of clandestine liaison which has prevailed in Europe for centuries, without giving up either his throne, or the woman of his choice, and there would have been no complaint from either church or laity. But this unusual man was built of sterner stuff. His love was clean. It was deep and sincere. It represented the one thing which, above all else he truly desired, therefore, he took what he wanted, and paid the price demanded.

If Europe had been blessed with more rulers with the human heart and the traits of honesty of ex-king Edward, for the past century, that unfortunate hemisphere now seething with greed, hate, lust, political connivance, and threats of war, would have a different and a better story to tell. A story in which Love and not Hate would rule.

In the words of Stuart Austin Wier we raise our cup and drink this toast to ex-king Edward and Wallis Simpson:

> "Blessed is the man who has come to know that our muted thoughts are our sweetest thoughts.
>
> "Blessed is the man who, from the blackest depths, can see the luminous figure of love, and seeing, sing; and singing, say: 'Sweeter far than uttered lays are the thoughts I have of you.'"

In these words would we pay tribute to the two people who, more than all others of modern times, have been the victims of criticism and the recipients of abuse, because they found Life's greatest treasure, and claimed it. *

Most of the world will applaud the Duke of Windsor and Wallis Simpson, because of their persistence in searching until they found life's greatest reward. All of us can profit by following their example in our own search for that which we demand of life.

What mystical power gives to men of persistence the capacity to master difficulties? Does the quality of persistence set up in one's mind some form of spiritual, mental or chemical activity which gives one access to supernatural forces? Does Infinite Intelligence throw *itself* on the side of the person who still fights on, after the battle has been lost, with the whole world on the opposing side?

These and many other similar questions have arisen in my mind as I have observed men like Henry Ford, who started at scratch, and built an Industrial Empire of huge proportions, with little else in the way of a beginning but persistence. Or, Thomas A. Edison, who, with less than three months of schooling, became the world's leading inventor and converted persistence into the talking machine, the moving picture machine, and the incandescent light, to say nothing of half a hundred other useful inventions.

I had the happy privilege of analyzing both Mr. Edison and Mr. Ford, year by year, over a long period of years, and therefore, the opportunity to study them at close range, so I speak from actual knowledge when I say that I found no quality save persistence, in either of them, that even remotely suggested the major source of their stupendous achievements.

As one makes an impartial study of the prophets, philosophers, "miracle" men, and religious leaders of the past, one is drawn to the inevitable conclusion that persistence, concentration of effort, and definiteness of purpose, were the major sources of their achievements.

Consider, for example, the strange and fascinating story of Mohammed; analyze his life, compare him with men of achievement in this modern age of industry and finance, and observe how they have one outstanding trait in common, persistence!

If you are keenly interested in studying the strange power which gives potency to persistence, read a biography of Mohammed, especially the one by Essad Bey. This

---

*Mrs. Simpson read and approved this analysis.

brief review of that book, by Thomas Sugrue, in the *Herald-Tribune,* will provide a preview of the rare treat in store for those who take the time to read the entire story of one of the most astounding examples of the power of persistence known to civilization.

THE LAST GREAT PROPHET

Reviewed by Thomas Sugrue

"Mohammed was a prophet, but he never performed a miracle. He was not a mystic; he had no formal schooling; he did not begin his mission until he was forty. When he announced that he was the Messenger of God, bringing word of the true religion, he was ridiculed and labeled a lunatic. Children tripped him and women threw filth upon him. He was banished from his native city, Mecca, and his followers were stripped of their worldly goods and sent into the desert after him. When he had been preaching ten years he had nothing to show for it but banishment, poverty and ridicule. Yet before another ten years had passed, he was dictator of all Arabia, ruler of Mecca, and the head of a New World religion which was to sweep to the Danube and the Pyrenees before exhausting the impetus he gave it. That impetus was three-fold: the power of words, the efficacy of prayer and man's kinship with God.

"His career never made sense. Mohammed was born to impoverished members of a leading family of Mecca. Because Mecca, the crossroads of the world, home of the magic stone called the Caaba, great city of trade and the center of trade routes, was unsanitary, its children were sent to be raised in the desert by Bedouins. Mohammed was thus nurtured, drawing strength and health from the milk of nomad, vicarious mothers. He tended sheep and soon hired out to a rich widow as leader of her caravans. He traveled to all parts of the Eastern World, talked with many men of diverse beliefs and observed the decline of Christianity into warring sects. When he was twenty-eight, Khadija, the widow, looked upon him with favor, and married him. Her father would have objected to such a marriage, so she got him drunk and held him up while he gave the paternal blessing. For the next twelve years Mohammed lived as a rich and respected and very shrewd trader. Then he took to wandering in the desert, and one day he returned with the first verse of the Koran and told Khadija that the archangel Gabriel had appeared to him and said that he was to be the Messenger of God.

"The Koran, the revealed word of God, was the closest thing to a miracle in Mohammed's life. He had not been a poet; he had no gift of words. Yet the verses of the Koran, as he received them and recited them to the faithful, were better than any verses which the professional poets of the tribes could produce. This, to the Arabs, was a miracle. To them the gift of words was the greatest gift, the poet was all-powerful. In addition the Koran said that all men were equal before God,, that the world should be a democratic state Islam. It was this political heresy, plus Mohammed's desire to destroy all the 360 idols in the courtyard of the Caaba, which brought about his banishment. The idols brought the desert tribes to Mecca, and that meant trade. So the business men of Mecca, the capitalists, of which he had been one, set upon Mohammed. Then he retreated to the desert and demanded sovereignty over the world.

"The rise of Islam began. Out of the desert came a flame which would not be extinguished—a democratic army fighting as a unit and prepared to die without wincing. Mohammed had invited the Jews and Christians to join him; for he was not building a new religion. He was calling all who believed in one God to join in a single faith. If the Jews and Christians had accepted his invitation Islam would have conquered the world. They didn't. They would not even accept Mohammed's innovation of humane warfare. When the armies of the prophet entered Jerusalem not a single person was killed because of his faith. When the crusaders entered the city, centuries later, not a Moslem man, woman, or child was spared. But the Christians did accept one Moslem idea—the place of learning, the university."

CHAPTER 10

Power of the Master Mind

THE DRIVING FORCE

The Ninth Step Toward Riches

Power is essential for success in the accumulation of money.

Plans are inert and useless, without sufficient power to translate them into action. This chapter will describe the method by which an individual may attain and apply power.

Power may be defined as "organized and intelligently directed knowledge." Power, as the term is here used, refers to organized effort, sufficient to enable an individual to transmute desire into its monetary equivalent. Organized effort is produced through the coordination of effort of two or more people, who work toward a definite end, in a spirit of harmony.

Power is required for the accumulation of money! Power is necessary for the retention of money after it has been accumulated!

Let us ascertain how power may be acquired. If power is "organized knowledge," let us examine the sources of knowledge:

a. Infinite intelligence. This source of knowledge may be contacted through the procedure described in another chapter, with the aid of Creative Imagination.

b. Accumulated experience. The accumulated experience of man (or that portion of it which has been organized and recorded) may be found in any well-equipped public library. An important part of this accumulated experience is taught in public schools and colleges, where it has been classified and organized.

c. Experiment and research. In the field of science, and in practically every other walk of life, men are gathering, classifying, and organizing new facts daily. This is the source to which one must turn when knowledge is not available through "accumulated experience." Here, too, the Creative Imagination must often be used.

Knowledge may be acquired from any of the foregoing sources. It may be converted into power by organizing it into definite plans and by expressing those plans in terms of action.

Examination of the three major sources of knowledge will readily disclose the difficulty an individual would have, if he depended upon his efforts alone, in assembling knowledge and expressing it through definite plans in terms of action. If his plans are comprehensive, and if they contemplate large proportions, he must, generally, induce others to cooperate with him, before he can inject into them the necessary element of power.

GAINING POWER THROUGH THE "MASTER MIND"

The "Master Mind" may be defined as: "Coordination of knowledge and effort, in a spirit of harmony, between two or more people, for the attainment of a definite purpose."

No individual may have great power without availing himself of the "Master Mind." In a preceding chapter, instructions were given for the creation of plans for the purpose of translating desire into its monetary equivalent. If you carry out these instructions with persistence and intelligence, and use discrimination in the selection of your "Master Mind" group, your objective will have been half-way reached, even before you begin to recognize it.

So you may better understand the "intangible" potentialities of power available to you, through a properly chosen "Master Mind" group, we will here explain the two characteristics of the Master Mind principle, one of which is economic in nature, and the other psychic. The economic feature is obvious. Economic advantages may be created by any person who surrounds himself with the advice, counsel, and personal cooperation of a group of men who are willing to lend him wholehearted aid, in a spirit of perfect harmony. This form of cooperative alliance has been the basis of nearly every great fortune. Your understanding of this great truth may definitely determine your financial status.

The psychic phase of the Master Mind principle is much more abstract, much more difficult to comprehend, because it has reference to the spiritual forces with which the human race, as a whole, is not well acquainted. You may catch a significant suggestion from this statement: "No two minds ever come together without, thereby, creating a third, invisible, intangible force which may be likened to a third mind."

Keep in mind the fact that there are only two known elements in the whole universe, energy and matter. It is a well known fact that matter may be broken down into units of molecules, atoms, and electrons. There are units of matter which may be isolated, separated, and analyzed.

Likewise, there are units of energy.

The human mind is a form of energy, a part of it being spiritual in nature. When the minds of two people are coordinated in a spirit of harmony, the spiritual units of energy of each mind form an affinity, which constitutes the "psychic" phase of the Master Mind.

The Master Mind principle, or rather the economic feature of it, was first called to my attention by Andrew Carnegie, over twenty-five years ago. Discovery of this principle was responsible for the choice of my life's work.

Mr. Carnegie's Master Mind group consisted of a staff of approximately fifty men, with whom he surrounded himself, for the definite purpose of manufacturing and marketing steel. He attributed his entire fortune to the power he accumulated through this "Master Mind."

Analyze the record of any man who has accumulated a great fortune, and many of those who have accumulated modest fortunes, and you will find that they have either consciously, or unconsciously employed the "Master Mind" principle.

Great power can be accumulated through no other principle!

Energy is Nature's universal set of building blocks, out of which she constructs every material thing in the universe, including man, and every form of animal and vegetable life. Through a process which only Nature completely understands, she translates energy into matter.

Nature's building blocks are available to man, in the energy involved in thinking! Man's brain may be compared to an electric battery. It absorbs energy from the ether, which permeates every atom of matter, and fills the entire universe.

It is a well known fact that a group of electric batteries will provide more energy than a single battery. It is also a well known fact that an individual battery will provide energy in proportion to the number and capacity of the cells it contains.

The brain functions in a similar fashion. This accounts for the fact that some brains are more efficient than others, and leads to this significant statement—a group of brains coordinated (or connected) in a spirit of harmony will provide more thought-energy than a single brain, just as a group of electric batteries will provide more energy than a single battery.

Through this metaphor it becomes immediately obvious that the Master Mind principle holds the secret of the power wielded by men who surround themselves with other men of brains.

There follows, now, another statement which will lead still nearer to an understanding of the psychic phase of the Master Mind principle: When a group of individual brains are coordinated and function in Harmony, the increased energy created through that alliance becomes available to every individual brain in the group.

It is a well known fact that Henry Ford began his business career under the handicap of poverty, illiteracy, and ignorance. It is an equally well known fact that, within the inconceivably short period of ten years, Mr. Ford mastered these three handicaps, and that within twenty-five years he made himself one of the richest men in America. Connect with this fact, the additional knowledge that Mr. Ford's most rapid strides became noticeable, from the time he became a personal friend of Thomas A. Edison, and you will begin to understand what the influence of one mind upon another can accomplish. Go a step farther, and consider the fact that Mr. Ford's most outstanding achievements began from the time that he formed the acquaintances of Harvey Firestone, John Burroughs, and Luther Burbank (each a man of great brain capacity) and you will have further evidence that power may be produced through friendly alliance of minds.

There is little if any doubt that Henry Ford is one of the best informed men in the business and industrial world. The question of his wealth needs no discussion. Analyze Mr. Ford's intimate personal friends, some of whom have already been mentioned, and you will be prepared to understand the following statement:—

"Men take on the nature and the habits and the power of thought of those with whom they associate in a spirit of sympathy and harmony."

Henry Ford whipped poverty, illiteracy, and ignorance by allying himself with great minds, whose vibrations of thought he absorbed into his own mind. Through his association with Edison, Burbank, Burroughs, and Firestone, Mr. Ford added to his own brain power, the sum and substance of the intelligence, experience, knowledge, and spiritual forces of these four men. Moreover, he appropriated, and made use of the Master Mind principle through the methods of procedure described in this book.

This principle is available to you!

We have already mentioned Mahatma Gandhi. Perhaps the majority of those who have heard of Gandhi look upon him as merely an eccentric little man, who goes around without formal wearing apparel, and makes trouble for the British Government.

In reality, Gandhi is not eccentric, but he is the most powerful man now living. (Estimated by the number of his followers and their faith in their leader.) Moreover, he is probably the most powerful man who has ever lived. His power is passive, but it is real.

Let us study the method by which he attained his stupendous power. It may be explained in a few words. He came by power through inducing over two hundred million people to coordinate, with mind and body, in a spirit of harmony, for a definite purpose.

In brief, Gandhi has accomplished a miracle, for it is a miracle when two hundred million people can be induced—not forced—to cooperate in a spirit of harmony, for a limitless time. If you doubt that this is a miracle, try to induce any two people to cooperate in a spirit of harmony for *any length of time.*

Every man who manages a business knows what a difficult matter it is to get employees to work together in a spirit even remotely resembling harmony.

The list of the chief sources from which power may be attained is, as you have seen, headed by infinite intelligence. When two or more people coordinate in a spirit of harmony, and work toward a definite objective, they place themselves in position, through that alliance, to absorb power directly from the great universal storehouse of Infinite Intelligence. This is the greatest of all sources of power. It is the source to which the genius turns. It is the source to which every great leader turns (whether he may be conscious of the fact or not).

The other two major sources from which the knowledge, necessary for the accumulation of power, may be obtained are no more reliable than the five senses of man. The senses are not always reliable. Infinite Intelligence does not err.

In subsequent chapters, the methods by which Infinite Intelligence may be most readily contacted will be adequately described.

This is not a course on religion. No fundamental principle described in this book should be interpreted as being intended to interfere either directly, or indirectly, with any man's religious habits. This book has been confined, exclusively, to instructing the reader how to transmute the definite purpose of desire for money, into its monetary equivalent.

Read, *think,* and meditate as you read. Soon, the entire subject will unfold, and you will see it in perspective. You are now seeing the detail of the individual chapters.

Money is as shy and elusive as the "old time" maiden. It must be wooed and won by methods not unlike those used by a determined lover, in pursuit of the girl of his choice. And, coincidental as it is, the power used in the "wooing" of money is not greatly different from that used in wooing a maiden. That power, when successfully used in the pursuit of money must be mixed with faith. It must be mixed with desire. It must be mixed with persistence. It must be applied through a plan, and that plan must be set into action.

When money comes in quantities known as "the big money," it flows to the one who accumulates it, as easily as water flows down hill. There exists a great unseen stream of power, which may be compared to a river; except that one side flows in one direction, carrying all who get into that side of the stream, onward and upward to wealth—and the other side flows in the opposite direction, carrying all who are unfortunate enough to get into it (and not able to extricate themselves from it), downward to misery and poverty.

Every man who has accumulated a great fortune has recognized the existence of this stream of life. It consists of one's thinking process. The positive emotions of thought form the side of the stream which carries one to fortune. The negative emotions form the side which carries one down to poverty.

This carries a thought of stupendous importance to the person who is following this book with the object of accumulating a fortune.

If you are in the side of the stream of power which leads to poverty, this may serve as an oar, by which you may propel yourself over into the other side of the stream. It can serve you only through application and use. Merely reading, and passing judgment on it, either one way or another, will in no way benefit you.

Some people undergo the experience of alternating between the positive and negative sides of the stream, being at times on the positive side, and at times on the negative side. The Wall Street crash of '29 swept millions of people from the positive to the negative side of the stream. These millions are struggling, some of them in desperation and fear, to get back to the positive side of the stream. This book was written especially for those millions.

Poverty and riches often change places. The Crash taught the world this truth, although the world will not long remember the lesson. Poverty may, and generally does, voluntarily take the place of riches. When riches take the place of poverty, the change is usually brought about through well-conceived and carefully executed PLANS. Poverty needs no plan. It needs no one to aid it, because it is bold and ruthless. Riches are shy and timid. They have to be "attracted."

Anybody can wish for riches, and most people do, but only a few know that a definite plan, plus a burning desire for wealth, are the only dependable means of accumulating wealth.

CHAPTER 11

The Mystery of Sex Transmutation

The Tenth Step Toward Riches

The meaning of the word "transmute" is, in simple language, "the changing, or transferring of one element, or form of energy, into another."

The emotion of sex brings into being a state of mind.

Because of ignorance on the subject, this state of mind is generally associated with the physical, and because of improper influences, to which most people have been subjected, in acquiring knowledge of sex, things essentially physical have highly biased the mind.

The emotion of sex has back of it the possibility of three constructive potentialities, they are:—

1. The perpetuation of mankind.
2. The maintenance of health (as a therapeutic agency, it has no equal).
3. The transformation of mediocrity into genius through transmutation.

Sex transmutation is simple and easily explained. It means the switching of the mind from thoughts of physical expression, to thoughts of some other nature.

Sex desire is the most powerful of human desires. When driven by this desire, men develop keenness of imagination, courage, will-power, persistence, and creative ability unknown to them at other times. So strong and impelling is the desire for sexual contact that men freely run the risk of life and reputation to indulge it. When harnessed, and redirected along other lines, this motivating force maintains all of its attributes of keenness of imagination, courage, etc., which may be used as powerful creative forces in literature, art, or in any other profession or calling, including, of course, the accumulation of riches.

The transmutation of sex energy calls for the exercise of will-power, to be sure, but the reward is worth the effort. The desire for sexual expression is inborn and natural. The desire cannot, and should not be submerged or eliminated. But it should be given an outlet through forms of expression which enrich the body, mind, and spirit of man. If not given this form of outlet, through transmutation, it will seek outlets through purely physical channels.

A river may be dammed, and its water controlled for a time, but eventually, it will force an outlet. The same is true of the emotion of sex. It may be submerged and controlled for a time, but its very nature causes it to be ever seeking means of expression. If it is not transmuted into some creative effort it will find a less worthy outlet.

Fortunate, indeed, is the person who has discovered how to give sex emotion an outlet through some form of creative effort, for he has, by that discovery, lifted himself to the status of a genius.

Scientific research has disclosed these significant facts:

1. The men of greatest achievement are men with highly developed sex natures; men who have learned the art of sex transmutation.
2. The men who have accumulated great fortunes and achieved outstanding recognition in literature, art, industry, architecture, and the professions, were motivated by the influence of a woman.

The research from which these astounding discoveries were made went back through the pages of biography and history for more than two thousand years. Wherever there was evidence available in connection with the lives of men and women of great achievement, it indicated most convincingly that they possessed highly developed sex natures.

The emotion of sex is an "irresistible force," against which there can be no such opposition as an "immovable body," When driven by this emotion, men become gifted with a super power for action. Understand this truth, and you will catch the significance of the statement that sex transmutation will lift one to the status of a genius.

The emotion of sex contains the secret of creative ability.

Destroy the sex glands, whether in man or beast, and you have removed the major source of action. For proof of this, observe what happens to any animal after it has been castrated. A bull becomes as docile as a cow after it has been altered sexually. Sex alteration takes out of the male, whether man or beast, all the fight that was in him. Sex alteration of the female has the same effect.

THE TEN MIND STIMULI

The human mind responds to stimuli, through which it may be "keyed up" to high rates of vibration, known as enthusiasm, creative imagination, intense desire, etc. The stimuli to which the mind responds most freely are:—

1. The desire for sex expression
2. Love
3. A burning desire for fame, power, or financial gain, money
4. Music
5. Friendship between either those of the same sex, or those of the opposite sex
6. A Master Mind alliance based upon the harmony of two or more people who ally themselves for spiritual or temporal advancement
7. Mutual suffering, such as that experienced by people who are persecuted
8. Auto-suggestion

9. Fear
10. Narcotics and alcohol

The desire for sex expression comes at the head of the list of stimuli, which most effectively "step-up" the vibrations of the mind and start the "wheels" of physical action. Eight of these stimuli are natural and constructive. Two are destructive. The list is here presented for the purpose of enabling you to make a comparative study of the major sources of mind stimulation. From this study, it will be readily seen that the emotion of sex is, by great odds, the most intense and powerful of all mind stimuli.

This comparison is necessary as a foundation for proof of the statement that transmutation of sex energy may lift one to the status of a genius. Let us find out what constitutes a genius.

Some wiseacre has said that a genius is a man who "wears long hair, eats queer food, lives alone, and serves as a target for the joke makers." A better definition of a genius is, "a man who has discovered how to increase the vibrations of thought to the point where he can freely communicate with sources of knowledge not available through the ordinary rate of vibration of thought."

The person who thinks will want to ask some questions concerning this definition of genius. The first question will be, "How may one communicate with sources of knowledge which are not available through the ordinary rate of vibration of thought?"

The next question will be, "Are there known sources of knowledge which are available only to genii, and if so, what are these sources, and exactly how may they be reached?"

We shall offer proof of the soundness of some of the more important statements made in this book—or at least we shall offer evidence through which you may secure your own proof through experimentation, and in doing so, we shall answer both of these questions.

"GENIUS" IS DEVELOPED THROUGH THE SIXTH SENSE

The reality of a "sixth sense" has been fairly well established. This sixth sense is "Creative Imagination." The faculty of creative imagination is one which the majority of people never use during an entire lifetime, and if used at all, it usually happens by mere accident. A relatively small number of people use, with deliberation and purpose aforethought, the faculty of creative imagination. Those who use this faculty voluntarily, and with understanding of its functions, are genii.

The faculty of creative imagination is the direct link between the finite mind of man and Infinite Intelligence. All so-called revelations, referred to in the realm of religion, and all discoveries of basic or new principles in the field of invention take place through the faculty of creative imagination.

When ideas or concepts flash into one's mind, through what is popularly called a "hunch," they come from one or more of the following sources:—

1. Infinite Intelligence
2. One's subconscious mind, wherein is stored every sense impression and thought impulse which ever reached the brain through any of the five senses
3. From the mind of some other person who has just released the thought, or picture of the idea or concept, through conscious thought, or
4. From the other person's subconscious storehouse.

There are no other known sources from which "inspired" ideas or "hunches" may be received.

The creative imagination functions best when the mind is vibrating (due to some form of mind stimulation) at an exceedingly high rate. That is, when the mind is functioning at a rate of vibration higher than that of ordinary, normal thought.

When brain action has been stimulated, through one or more of the ten mind stimulants, it has the effect of lifting the individual far above the horizon of ordinary thought, and permits him to envision distance, scope, and quality of thoughts not available on the lower plane, such as that occupied while one is engaged in the solution of the problems of business and professional routine.

When lifted to this higher level of thought, through any form of mind stimulation, an individual occupies, relatively, the same position as one who has ascended in an airplane to a height from which he may see over and beyond the horizon line which limits his vision, while on the ground. Moreover, while on this higher level of thought, the individual is not hampered or bound by any of the stimuli which circumscribe and limit his vision while wrestling with the problems of gaining the three basic necessities of food, clothing, and shelter. He is in a world of thought in which the ordinary, work-a-day thoughts have been as effectively removed as are the hills and valleys and other limitations of physical vision, when he rises in an airplane.

While on this exalted plane of thought, the creative faculty of the mind is given freedom for action. The way has been cleared for the sixth sense to function, it becomes receptive to ideas which could not reach the individual under any other circumstances. The "sixth sense" is the faculty which marks the difference between a genius and an ordinary individual.

The creative faculty becomes more alert and receptive to vibrations, originating outside the individual's subconscious mind, the more this faculty is used, and the more the individual relies upon it, and makes demands upon it for thought impulses. This faculty can be cultivated and developed only through use.

That which is known as one's "conscience" operates entirely through the faculty of the sixth sense.

The great artists, writers, musicians, and poets become great, because they acquire the habit of relying upon the "still small voice" which speaks from within, through the faculty of creative imagination. It is a fact well known to people who have "keen" imaginations that their best ideas come through so-called "hunches."

There is a great orator who does not attain to greatness, until he closes his eyes and begins to rely entirely upon the faculty of Creative Imagination. When asked why he closed his eyes just before the climaxes of his oratory, he replied, "I do it, because, then I speak through ideas which come to me from within."

One of America's most successful and best-known financiers followed the habit of closing his eyes for two or three minutes before making a decision. When asked why he did this, he replied, "With my eyes closed, I am able to draw upon a source of superior intelligence."

The late Dr. Elmer R. Gates, of Chevy Chase, Maryland, created more than 200 useful patents, many of them basic, through the process of cultivating and using the creative faculty. His method is both significant and interesting to one interested in attaining to the status of genius, in which category Dr. Gates, unquestionably belonged. Dr. Gates was one of the really great, though less publicized scientists of the world.

In his laboratory, he had what he called his "personal communication room." It was practically sound proof, and so arranged that all light could be shut out. It was equipped with a small table, on which he kept a pad of writing paper. In front of the table, on the wall, was an electric pushbutton, which controlled the lights. When Dr. Gates desired to draw upon the forces available to him through his Creative Imagination, he would go into this room, seat himself at the table, shut off the lights, and concentrate upon the known factors of the invention on which he was working, remaining in that position until ideas began to "flash" into his mind in connection with the unknown factors of the invention.

On one occasion, ideas came through so fast that he was forced to write for almost three hours. When the thoughts stopped flowing, and he examined his notes, he found they contained a minute description of principles which had not a parallel among the known data of the scientific world. Moreover, the answer to his problem was intelligently presented in those notes. In this manner Dr. Gates completed over 200 patents, which had been begun, but not completed, by "half-baked" brains. Evidence of the truth of this statement is in the United States Patent Office.

Dr. Gates earned his living by "sitting for ideas" for individuals and corporations. Some of the largest corporations in America paid him substantial fees, by the hour, for "sitting for ideas."

The reasoning faculty is often faulty, because it is largely guided by one's accumulated experience. Not all knowledge, which one accumulates through "experience," is accurate. Ideas received through the creative faculty are much more reliable, for the reason that they come from sources more reliable than any which are available to the reasoning faculty of the mind.

The major difference between the genius and the ordinary "crank" inventor may be found in the fact that the genius works through his faculty of creative imagination, while the "crank" knows nothing of this faculty. The scientific inventor (such as Mr. Edison, and Dr. Gates) makes use of both the synthetic and the creative faculties of imagination.

For example, the scientific inventor, or "genius," begins an invention by organizing and combining the known ideas, or principles accumulated through experience, through the synthetic faculty (the reasoning faculty). If he finds this accumulated knowledge to be insufficient for the completion of his invention, he then draws upon the sources of knowledge available to him through his *creative* faculty. The method by which he does this varies with the individual, but this is the sum and substance of his procedure:

1. He stimulates his mind so that it vibrates on a higher-than-average plane, using one or more of the ten mind stimulants or some other stimulant of his choice.
2. He concentrates upon the known factors (the finished part) of his invention, and creates in his mind a perfect picture of unknown factors (the unfinished part) of his invention. He holds this picture in mind until it has been taken over by the subconscious mind, then relaxes by clearing his mind of all thought, and waits for his answer to "flash" into his mind.

Sometimes the results are both definite and immediate. At other times, the results are negative, depending upon the state of development of the "sixth sense," or creative faculty.

Mr. Edison tried out more than 10,000 different combinations of ideas through the synthetic faculty of his imagination before he "tuned in" through the creative faculty, and got the answer which perfected the incandescent light. His experience was similar when he produced the talking machine.

There is plenty of reliable evidence that the faculty of creative imagination exists. This evidence is available through accurate analysis of men who have become leaders in their respective callings, without having had extensive educations. Lincoln was a notable example of a great leader who achieved greatness, through the discovery, and use of his faculty of creative imagination. He discovered, and began to use this faculty as the result of the stimulation of love which he experienced after he met Anne Rutledge, a statement of the highest significance, in connection with the study of the source of genius.

The pages of history are filled with the records of great leaders whose achievements may be traced directly to the influence of women who aroused the creative faculties of their minds, through the stimulation of sex desire. Napoleon Bonaparte was one of these. When inspired by his first wife, Josephine, he was irresistible and invincible. When his "better judgment" or reasoning faculty prompted him to put Josephine aside, he began to decline. His defeat and St. Helena were not far distant.

If good taste would permit, we might easily mention scores of men, well known to the American people, who climbed to great heights of achievement under the stimulating influence of their wives, only to drop back to destruction after money and power went to their heads, and they put aside the old wife for a new one. Napoleon was not the only man to discover that sex influence, *from the right source,* is more powerful than any substitute of expediency, which may be created by mere reason.

The human mind responds to stimulation!

Among the greatest, and most powerful of these stimuli is the urge of sex. When harnessed and transmuted, this driving force is capable of lifting men into that higher sphere of thought which enables them to master the sources of worry and petty annoyance which beset their pathway on the lower plane.

Unfortunately, only the genii have made the discovery. Others have accepted the experience of sex urge, without discovering one of its major potentialities—a fact which accounts for the great number of "others" as compared to the limited number of genii.

For the purpose of refreshing the memory, in connection with the facts available from the biographies of certain men, we here present the names of a few men of outstanding achievement, each of whom was known to have been of a highly sexed nature. The genius which was theirs, undoubtedly found its source of power in transmuted sex energy:

George Washington	Thomas Jefferson
Napoleon Bonaparte	Elbert Hubbard
William Shakespeare	Elbert H. Gary
Abraham Lincoln	Oscar Wilde
Ralph Waldo Emerson	Woodrow Wilson
Robert Burns	John H. Patterson
Andrew Jackson	Enrico Caruso

Your own knowledge of biography will enable you to add to this list. Find, if you can, a single man, in all history of civilization, who achieved outstanding success in any calling, who was not driven by a well developed sex nature.

If you do not wish to rely upon biographies of men not now living, take inventory of those whom you know to be men of great achievement, and see if you can find one among them who is not highly sexed.

Sex energy is the creative energy of all genii. *There never has been, and never will be a great leader, builder, or artist lacking in this driving force of sex.*

Surely no one will misunderstand these statements to mean that all who are highly sexed are genii! Man attains to the status of a genius only when, and if, he stimulates his mind so that it draws upon the forces available, through the creative faculty of the imagination. Chief among the stimuli with which this "stepping up" of the vibrations may be produced is sex energy. The mere *possession of* this energy is not sufficient to produce a genius. The energy must be *transmuted* from desire for physical contact, into some other form of desire and action, before it will lift one to the status of a genius.

Far from becoming genii, because of great sex desires, the majority of men *lower* themselves, through misunderstanding and misuse of this great force, to the status of the lower animals.

WHY MEN SELDOM SUCCEED BEFORE FORTY

I discovered, from the analysis of over 25,000 people, that men who succeed in an outstanding way, seldom do so before the age of forty, and more often they do not strike their real pace until they are well beyond the age of fifty. This fact was so astounding that it prompted me to go into the study of its cause most carefully, carrying the investigation over a period of more than twelve years.

This study disclosed the fact that the major reason why the majority of men who succeed do not begin to do so before the age of forty to fifty, is their tendency to dissipate their energies through over indulgence in physical expression of the emotion of sex. The majority of men *never* learn that the urge of sex has other possibilities, which far transcend in importance, that of mere physical expression. The majority of those who make this discovery, do so *after having wasted many years* at a period when the sex energy is at its height, prior to the age of forty-five to fifty. This usually is followed by noteworthy achievement.

The lives of many men up to, and sometimes well past the age of forty, reflect a continued dissipation of energies, which could have been more profitably turned into better channels. Their finer and more powerful emotions are sown wildly to the four winds. Out of this habit of the male, grew the term, "sowing his wild oats."

The desire for sexual expression is by far the strongest and most impelling of all the human emotions, and for this very reason this desire, when *harnessed and transmuted* into action, other than that of physical expression, may raise one to the status of a genius.

One of America's most able business men frankly admitted that his attractive secretary was responsible for most of the plans he created. He admitted that her presence lifted him to heights of creative imagination, such as he could experience under no other stimulus.

One of the most successful men in America owes most of his success to the influence of a very charming young woman, who has served as his source of inspiration for more than twelve years. Everyone knows the man to whom this reference is made, but not everyone knows the real source of his achievements.

History is not lacking in examples of men who attained to the status of genii, as the result of the use of artificial mind stimulants in the form of alcohol and narcotics. Edgar Allan Poe wrote the "Raven" while under the influence of liquor, "dreaming dreams that mortal never dared to dream before." James Whitcomb Riley did his best writing while under the influence of alcohol. Perhaps it was thus he saw "the ordered intermingling of the real and the dream, the mill above the river, and the mist above the stream." Robert Burns wrote best when intoxicated, "For Auld Lang Syne, my dear, we'll take a cup of kindness yet, for Auld Lang Syne."

But let it be remembered that many such men have destroyed themselves in the end. Nature has prepared her own potions with which men may safely stimulate their minds so they vibrate on a plane that enables them to tune in to fine and rare thoughts which come from—no man knows where! No satisfactory substitute for Nature's stimulants has ever been found.

It is a fact well known to psychologists that there is a very close relationship between sex desires and spiritual urges—a fact which accounts for the peculiar behavior of people who participate in the orgies known as religious "revivals," common among the primitive types.

The world is ruled, and the destiny of civilization is established, by the human emotions. People are influenced in their actions, not by reason so much as by "feelings." The creative faculty of the mind is set into action entirely by emotions, and *not by cold reason.* The most powerful of all human emotions is that of sex. There are other mind stimulants, some of which have been listed, but no one of them, nor all of them combined, can equal the driving power of sex.

A mind stimulant is any influence which will either temporarily, or permanently, increase the vibrations of thought. The ten major stimulants, described, are those most commonly resorted to. Through these sources one may commune with Infinite Intelligence, or enter, at will, the storehouse of the subconscious mind, either one's own, or that of another person, a procedure *which is all there is of genius.*

A teacher, who has trained and directed the efforts of more than 30,000 sales people, made the astounding discovery that highly sexed men are the most efficient salesmen. The explanation is, that the factor of personality known as "personal magnetism" is nothing more nor less than sex energy. Highly sexed people always have a plentiful supply of magnetism. Through cultivation and understanding, this vital force may be drawn upon and used to great advantage in the relationships between people. This energy may be communicated to others through the following media:

1. The hand-shake. The touch of the hand indicates, instantly, the presence of magnetism, or the lack of it.
2. The tone of voice. Magnetism, or sex energy, is the factor with which the voice may be colored, or made musical and charming.
3. Posture and carriage of the body. Highly sexed people move briskly, and with grace and ease.
4. The vibrations of thought. Highly sexed people mix the emotion of sex with their thoughts, or may do so at will, and in that way, may influence those around them.
5. Body adornment. People who are highly sexed are usually very careful about their personal appearance. They usually select clothing of a style becoming to their personality, physique, complexion, etc.

When employing salesmen, the more capable sales manager looks for the quality of personal magnetism as the *first requirement* of a salesman. People who lack sex energy will never become enthusiastic nor inspire others with enthusiasm, and enthusiasm is one of the most important requisites in salesmanship, no matter what one is selling.

The public speaker, orator, preacher, lawyer, or salesman who is lacking in sex energy is a "flop," as far as being able to influence others is concerned. Couple with this the fact, that most people can be influenced only through an appeal to their emotions, and you will understand the importance of sex energy as a part of the salesman's native ability. Master salesmen attain the status of mastery in selling, because they, either consciously, or unconsciously, *transmute* the energy of sex into sales enthusiasm! In this statement may be found a very practical suggestion as to the actual meaning of sex transmutation.

The salesman who knows how to take his mind off the subject of sex, and direct it in sales effort with as much enthusiasm and determination as he would apply to its original purpose, has acquired the art of sex transmutation, whether he knows it or not. The majority of salesmen who transmute their sex energy do so without being in the least aware of what they are doing, or how they are doing it.

Transmutation of sex energy calls for more will power than the average person cares to use for this purpose. Those who find it difficult to summon will-power sufficient for transmutation, may gradually acquire this ability. Though this requires will-power, the reward for the practice is more than worth the effort.

The entire subject of sex is one with which the majority of people appear to be unpardonably ignorant. The urge of sex has been grossly misunderstood, slandered, and burlesqued by the ignorant and the evil minded, for so long that the very word sex is seldom used in polite society. Men and women who are known to be blessed—yes, blessed—with highly sexed natures, are usually looked upon as being people who will bear watching. Instead of being called blessed, they are usually called cursed.

Millions of people, even in this age of enlightenment, have inferiority complexes which they developed because of this false belief that a highly sexed nature is a curse. These statements, of the virtue of sex energy, should not be construed as justification for the libertine. The emotion of sex is a virtue only when used intelligently, and with discrimination. It may be misused, and often is, to such an extent that it debases, instead of enriches, both body and mind. The better use of this power is the burden of this chapter.

It seemed quite significant to the author, when he made the discovery that practically every great leader, whom he had the privilege of analyzing, was a man whose achievements were largely inspired by a woman. In many instances, the "woman in the case" was a modest, self-denying wife, of whom the public had heard but little or nothing. In a few instances, the source of inspiration has been traced to the "other woman." Perhaps such cases may not be entirely unknown to you.

Intemperance in sex habits is just as detrimental as intemperance in habits of drinking and eating. In this age in which we live, an age which began with the world war, intemperance in habits of sex is common. This orgy of indulgence may account for the shortage of great leaders. No man can avail himself of the forces of his creative imagination, while dissipating them. Man is the only creature on earth which violates Nature's purpose in this connection. Every other animal indulges its sex nature in moderation, and with purpose which harmonizes with the laws of nature. Every other animal responds to the call of sex only in "season." Mans inclination is to declare "open season."

Every intelligent person knows that stimulation in excess, through alcoholic drink and narcotics, is a form of intemperance which destroys the vital organs of the body, including the brain. Not every person knows, however, that over indulgence in sex expression may become a habit as destructive and as detrimental to creative effort as narcotics or liquor.

A sex-mad man is not essentially different than a dope-mad man! Both have lost control over their faculties of reason and will-power. Sexual over-indulgence may not only destroy reason and will-power, but it may also lead to either temporary, or permanent insanity. Many cases of hypochondria (imaginary illness) grow out of habits developed in ignorance of the true function of sex.

From these brief references to the subject, it may be readily seen that ignorance on the subject of sex transmutation forces stupendous penalties upon the ignorant on the one hand, and withholds from them equally stupendous benefits, on the other.

Widespread ignorance on the subject of sex is due to the fact that the subject has been surrounded with mystery and beclouded by dark silence. The conspiracy of mystery and silence has had the same effect upon the minds of young people that the psychology of prohibition had. The result has been increased curiosity, and desire to acquire more knowledge on this "verboten" subject; and to the shame of all lawmakers, and most physicians—by training best qualified to educate youth on that subject—information has not been easily available.

Seldom does an individual enter upon highly creative effort in any field of endeavor before the age of forty. The average man reaches the period of his greatest capacity to create between forty and sixty. These statements are based upon analysis of thousands of men and women who have been carefully observed. They should be encouraging to those who fail to arrive before the age of forty, and to those who become frightened at the approach of "old age," around the forty-year mark. The years between forty and fifty are, as a rule, the most fruitful. Man should approach this age, not with fear and trembling, but with hope and eager anticipation.

If you want evidence that most men do not begin to do their best work before the age of forty, study the records of the most successful men known to the American people, and you will find it. Henry Ford had not "hit his pace" of achievement until he had passed the age of forty. Andrew Carnegie was well past forty before he began to reap the reward of his efforts. James J. Hill was still running a telegraph key at the age of forty. His stupendous achievements took place after that age. Biographies of American industrialists and financiers are filled with evidence that the period from forty to sixty is the most productive age of man.

Between the ages of thirty and forty, man begins to learn (if he ever learns) the art of sex transmutation. This discovery is generally accidental, and more often than otherwise, the man who makes it is totally unconscious of his discovery. He may observe that his powers of achievement have increased around the age of thirty-five to forty, but in most cases, he is not familiar with the cause of this change; that Nature begins to harmonize the emotions of love and sex in the individual, between the ages of thirty and forty, so that he may draw upon these great forces, and apply them jointly as stimuli to action.

Sex, alone, is a mighty urge to action, but its forces are like a cyclone—they are often uncontrollable. When the emotion of love begins to mix itself with the emotion of sex, the result is calmness of purpose, poise, accuracy of judgment, and balance. What person, who has attained to the age of forty, is so unfortunate as to be unable to analyze these statements, and to corroborate them by his own experience?

When driven by his desire to please a woman, based solely upon the emotion of sex, a man may be, and usually is, capable of great achievement, but his actions may be disorganized, distorted, and totally destructive. When driven by his desire to please a woman, based upon the motive of sex alone, a man may steal, cheat, and even commit murder. But when the emotion of love is mixed with the emotion of sex, that same man will guide his actions with more sanity, balance, and reason.

Criminologists have discovered that the most hardened criminals can be reformed through the influence of a woman's *love.* There is no record of a criminal having been reformed solely through the sex influence. These facts are well known, but their cause is not. Reformation comes, if at all, through the *heart,* or the emotional side of man, *not* through his head, or reasoning side. Reformation means, "a change of heart." It does not mean a "change of head." A man may, because of reason, make certain changes in his personal conduct to avoid the consequences of undesirable effects, but genuine reformation comes only through a change of heart—through a desire to change.

Love, romance, and sex are all emotions capable of driving men to heights of super achievement. Love is the emotion which serves as a safety valve, and insures balance, poise, and constructive effort. When combined, these three emotions may lift one to an altitude of a genius. There are genii, however, who know but little of the emotion of love. Most of them may be found engaged in some form of action which is destructive, or at least, not based upon justice and fairness toward others. If good taste would permit, a dozen genii could be named in the field of industry and finance, who ride ruthlessly over the rights of their fellow men. They seem totally lacking in conscience. The reader can easily supply his own list of such men.

The emotions are states of mind. Nature has provided man with a "chemistry of the mind" which operates in a manner similar to the principles of chemistry of matter. It is a well-known fact that, through the aid of chemistry of matter, a chemist may create a deadly poison by mixing certain elements, none of which are—in themselves—harmful in the right proportions. The emotions may, likewise, be combined so as to create a deadly poison. The emotions of sex and jealousy, when mixed, may turn a person into an insane beast.

The presence of any one or more of the destructive emotions in the human mind, through the chemistry of the mind, sets up a poison which may destroy one's sense of justice and fairness. In extreme cases, the presence of any combination of these emotions in the mind may destroy one's reason.

The road to genius consists of the development, control, and use of sex, love, and romance. Briefly, the process may be stated as follows:

Encourage the presence of these emotions as the dominating thoughts in one's mind, and discourage the presence of all the destructive emotions. The mind is a creature of habit. It thrives upon the *dominating* thoughts fed it. Through the faculty of will-power, one may discourage the presence of any emotion, and encourage the presence of any other. Control of the mind, through the power of will, is not difficult. Control comes from persistence, and habit. The secret of control lies in understanding the process of transmutation. When any negative emotion presents itself in one's mind, it can be transmuted into a positive, or constructive emotion, by the simple procedure of changing one's thoughts.

There is no other road to genius than through voluntary self effort! A man may attain to great heights of financial or business achievement, solely by the driving force of sex energy, but history is filled with evidence that he may, and usually does, carry with him certain traits of character which rob him of the ability to either hold, or enjoy his fortune. This is worthy of analysis, thought, and meditation, for it states a truth, the knowledge of which may be helpful to women as well as men. Ignorance of this has cost thousands of people their privilege of happiness, even though they possessed riches.

The emotions of love and sex leave their unmistakable marks upon the features. Moreover, these signs are so visible, that all who wish may read them. The man who is driven by the storm of passion, based upon sex desires alone, plainly advertises that fact to the entire world, by the expression of his eyes, and the lines of his face. The emotion of love, when mixed with the emotion of sex, softens, modifies, and beautifies the facial expression. No character analyst is needed to tell you this—you may observe it for yourself.

The emotion of love brings out, and develops, the artistic and the aesthetic nature of man. It leaves its impress upon one's very soul, even after the fire has been subdued by time and circumstance.

Memories of love never pass. They linger, guide, and influence long after the source of stimulation has faded. There is nothing new in this. Every person, who has been moved by genuine love, knows that it leaves enduring traces upon the human heart. The effect of love endures, because love is spiritual in nature. The man who cannot be stimulated to great heights of achievement by love, is hopeless—he is dead, though he may seem to live.

Even the memories of love are sufficient to lift one to a higher plane of creative effort. The major force of love may spend itself and pass away, like a fire which has burned itself out, but it leaves behind indelible marks as evidence that it passed that way. Its departure often prepares the human heart for a still greater love.

Go back into your yesterdays, at times, and bathe your mind in the beautiful memories of past love. It will soften the influence of the present worries and annoyances. It will give you a source of escape from the unpleasant realities of life, and maybe—who knows?—your mind will yield to you, during this temporary retreat into the world of fantasy, ideas, or plans which may change the entire financial or spiritual status of your life.

If you believe yourself unfortunate, because you have "loved and lost," perish the thought. One who has loved truly, can never lose entirely. Love is whimsical and temperamental. Its nature is ephemeral, and transitory. It comes when it pleases, and goes away without warning. Accept and enjoy it while it remains, but spend no time worrying about its departure. Worry will never bring it back.

Dismiss, also, the thought that love never comes but once. Love may come and go, times without number, but there are no two love experiences which affect one in just the same way. There may be, and there usually is, one love experience which leaves a deeper imprint on the heart than all the others, but all love experiences are beneficial, except to the person who becomes resentful and cynical when love makes its departure.

There should be no disappointment over love, and there would be none if people understood the difference between the emotions of love and sex. The major difference is that love is spiritual, while sex is biological. No experience, which touches the human heart with a spiritual force, can possibly be harmful, except through ignorance, or jealousy.

Love is, without question, life's greatest experience. It brings one into communion with Infinite Intelligence. When mixed with the emotions of romance and sex, it may lead one far up the ladder of creative effort. The emotions of love, sex, and romance are sides of the eternal triangle of achievement-building genius. Nature creates genii through no other force.

Love is an emotion with many sides, shades, and colors. The love which one feels for parents, or children is quite different from that which one feels for one's sweetheart. The one is mixed with the emotion of sex, while the other is not.

The love which one feels in true friendship is not the same as that felt for one's sweetheart, parents, or children, but it, too, is a form of love.

Then, there is the emotion of love for things inanimate, such as the love of Nature's handiwork. But the most intense and burning of all these various kinds of love is that experienced in the blending of the emotions of love and sex. Marriages, not blessed with the eternal affinity of love, properly balanced and proportioned, with sex, cannot be happy ones—and seldom endure. Love, alone, will not bring happiness in marriage, nor will sex alone. When these two beautiful emotions are blended, marriage may bring about a state of mind, closest to the spiritual that one may ever know on this earthly plane.

When the emotion of romance is added to those of love and sex, the obstructions between the finite mind of man and Infinite Intelligence are removed. Then a genius has been born!

What a different story is this, than those usually associated with the emotion of sex. Here is an interpretation of the emotion which lifts it out of the commonplace, and makes of it potter's clay in the hands of God, from which He fashions all that is beautiful and inspiring. It is an interpretation which would, when properly understood, bring harmony out of the chaos which exists in too many marriages. The disharmonies often expressed in the form of nagging may usually be traced to *lack of knowledge* on the subject of sex. Where love, romance and the proper understanding of the emotion and function of sex abide, there is no disharmony between married people.

Fortunate is the husband whose wife understands the true relationship between the emotions of love, sex, and romance. When motivated by this holy triumvirate, no form of labor is burdensome, because even the most lowly form of effort takes on the nature of a labor of love.

It is a very old saying that "a man's wife may either make him or break him," but the reason is not always understood. The "making" and "breaking" is the result of the wife's understanding, or lack of understanding of the emotions of love, sex, and romance.

Despite the fact that men are polygamous, by the very nature of their biological inheritance, it is true that no woman has as great an influence on a man as his wife, unless he is married to a woman totally unsuited to his nature. If a woman permits her husband to lose interest in her, and become more interested in other women, it is usually because of her ignorance, or indifference toward the subjects of sex, love, and romance. This statement presupposes, of course, that genuine love once existed between a man and his wife. The facts are equally applicable to a man who permits his wife's interest in him to die.

Married people often bicker over a multitude of trivialities. If these are analyzed accurately, the real cause of the trouble will often be found to be indifference, or ignorance on these subjects.

Man's greatest motivating force is his desire to please woman! The hunter who excelled during prehistoric days, before the dawn of civilization, did so, because of his desire to appear great in the eyes of woman. Man's nature has not changed in this respect. The "hunter" of today brings home no skins of wild animals, but he indicates his desire for her favor by supplying fine clothes, motor cars, and wealth. Man has the same desire to please woman that he had before the dawn of civilization. The only thing that has changed, is his method of pleasing. Men who accumulate large fortunes, and attain to great heights of power and fame, do so, mainly, to satisfy their *desire to please women.* Take women out of their lives, and great wealth would be useless to most men. *It is this inherent desire of man to please woman, which gives woman the power to make or break a man.*

The woman who understands man's nature and tactfully caters to it, need have no fear of competition from other women. Men may be "giants" with indomitable will-power when dealing with other men, but they are easily managed by the women of their choice.

Most men will not admit that they are easily influenced by the women they prefer, because it is in the nature of the male to want to be recognized as the stronger of the species. Moreover, the intelligent woman recognizes this "manly trait" and very wisely makes no issue of it.

Some men know that they are being influenced by the women of their choice—their wives, sweethearts, mothers or sisters—but they tactfully refrain from rebelling against the influence because they are intelligent enough to know that no man is happy or complete without the modifying influence of the right woman. The man who does not recognize this important truth deprives himself of the power which has done more to help men achieve success than all other forces combined.

CHAPTER 12

The Subconscious Mind

THE CONNECTING LINK

The Eleventh Step Toward Riches

The subconscious mind consists of a field of consciousness, in which every impulse of thought that reaches the objective mind through any of the five senses, is classified and recorded, and from which thoughts may be recalled or withdrawn as letters may be taken from a filing cabinet.

It receives, and files, sense impressions or thoughts, regardless of their nature. You may voluntarily plant in your subconscious mind any plan, thought, or purpose which you desire to, translate into its physical or monetary equivalent. The subconscious acts first on the dominating desires which have been mixed with emotional feeling, such as faith.

Consider this in connection with the instructions given in the chapter on desire, for taking the six steps there outlined, and the instructions given in the chapter on the building and execution of plans, and you will understand the importance of the thought conveyed.

The subconscious mind works day and night. Through a method of procedure, unknown to man, the subconscious mind draws upon the forces of Infinite Intelligence for the power with which it voluntarily transmutes one's desires into their physical equivalent, making use, always of the most practical media by which this end may be accomplished.

You cannot *entirely* control your subconscious mind, but you can voluntarily hand over to it any plan, desire, or purpose which you wish transformed into concrete form. Read, again, instructions for using the subconscious mind, in the chapter on autosuggestion.

There is plenty of evidence to support the belief that the subconscious mind is the connecting link between the finite mind of man and Infinite Intelligence. It is the intermediary through which one may draw upon the forces of Infinite Intelligence at will. It, alone, contains the secret process by which mental impulses are modified and changed into their spiritual equivalent. It, alone, is the medium through which prayer may be transmitted to the source capable of answering prayer.

The possibilities of creative effort connected with the subconscious mind are stupendous and imponderable. They inspire one with awe.

I never approach the discussion of the subconscious mind without a feeling of littleness and inferiority due, perhaps, to the fact that man's entire stock of knowledge on this subject is so pitifully limited. The very fact that the subconscious mind is the medium of communication between the thinking mind of man and Infinite Intelligence is, of itself, a thought which almost paralyzes one's reason.

After you have accepted, as a reality, the existence of the subconscious mind, and understand its possibilities, as a medium for transmuting your desires into their physical or monetary equivalent, you will comprehend the full significance of the instructions given in the chapter on desire. You will also understand why you have been repeatedly admonished to make your desires clear, and to reduce them to writing. You will also understand the necessity of persistence in carrying out instructions.

The thirteen principles are the stimuli with which you acquire the ability to reach, and to influence your subconscious mind. Do not become discouraged, if you cannot do this upon the first attempt. Remember that the subconscious mind may be voluntarily directed *only through habit,* under the directions given in the chapter on faith. You have not yet had time to master faith. Be patient. Be persistent.

A good many statements in the chapters on faith and auto-suggestion will be repeated here, for the benefit of your subconscious mind. Remember, your subconscious mind functions voluntarily, *whether you make any effort to influence it or not.* This, naturally, suggests to you that thoughts of fear and poverty, and all negative thoughts serve as stimuli to your subconscious mind, *unless,* you master these impulses and give it more desirable food upon which it may feed.

The subconscious mind will not remain idle! If you fail to plant desires in your subconscious mind, it will feed upon the thoughts which reach it as the *result of your neglect.* We have already explained that thought impulses, both negative and positive are reaching the subconscious mind continuously, from the four sources which were mentioned in the chapter on Sex Transmutation.

For the present, it is sufficient if you remember that you are living *daily,* in the midst of all manner of thought impulses which are reaching your subconscious mind, without your knowledge. Some of these impulses are negative, some are positive. You are now engaged in trying to help shut off the flow of negative impulses, and to aid in voluntarily influencing your subconscious mind, through positive impulses of desire.

When you achieve this, you will possess the key which unlocks the door to your subconscious mind. Moreover, you will control that door so completely, that no undesirable thought may influence your subconscious mind.

Everything which man creates begins in the form of a thought impulse. Man can create nothing which he does not first conceive in thought. Through the aid of the imagination, thought impulses may be assembled into plans. The imagination, when under control, may be used for the creation of plans or purposes that lead to success in one's chosen occupation.

All thought impulses, intended for transmutation into their physical equivalent, voluntarily planted in the subconscious mind, must pass through the imagination, and be mixed with faith. The "mixing" of faith with a plan, or purpose, intended for submission to the subconscious mind, may be done only through the imagination.

From these statements, you will readily observe that voluntary use of the subconscious mind calls for coordination and application of all the principles.

Ella Wheeler Wilcox gave evidence of her understanding of the power of the subconscious mind when she wrote:

You never can tell what a thought will do
In bringing you hate or love—
For thoughts are things, and their airy wings
Are swifter than carrier doves.
They follow the law of the universe—
Each thing creates its kind,
And they speed O'er the track to bring you back
Whatever went out from your mind.

Mrs. Wilcox understood the truth, that thoughts which go out from one's mind, also imbed themselves deeply in one's subconscious mind, where they serve as a magnet, pattern, or blueprint by which the subconscious mind is influenced while translating them into their physical equivalent. Thoughts are truly things, for the reason that every material thing begins in the form of thought-energy.

The subconscious mind is more susceptible to influence by impulses of thought mixed with "feeling" or emotion, than by those originating solely in the reasoning portion of the mind. In fact, there is much evidence to support the theory, that only emotionalized thoughts have any action influence upon the subconscious mind. It is a well known fact that emotion or feeling rules the majority of people. If it is true that the subconscious mind responds more quickly to, and is influenced more readily by thought impulses which are well mixed with emotion, it is essential to become familiar with the more important of the emotions. There are seven major positive emotions, and seven major negative emotions. The negatives *voluntarily* inject themselves into the thought impulses, which insure passage into the subconscious mind. The positives must be injected, through the principle of auto-suggestion, into the thought impulses which an individual wishes to pass on to his subconscious mind. (Instructions have been given in the chapter on auto-suggestion.)

These emotions, or feeling impulses, may be likened to yeast in a loaf of bread, because they constitute the action element, which transforms thought impulses from the passive to the active state. Thus may one understand why thought impulses, which have been well mixed with emotion, are acted upon more readily than thought impulses originating in "cold reason."

You are preparing yourself to influence and control the "inner audience" of your subconscious mind, in order to hand over to it the desire for money, which you wish transmuted into its monetary equivalent. It is essential, therefore, that you understand the method of approach to this "inner audience." You must speak its language, or it will not heed your call. It understands best the language of emotion or feeling. Let us, therefore describe here the seven major positive emotions, and the seven major negative emotions, so that you may draw upon the positives, and avoid the negatives, when giving instructions to your subconscious mind.

THE SEVEN MAJOR POSITIVE EMOTIONS

The emotion of DESIRE
The emotion of FAITH
The emotion of LOVE
The emotion of SEX
The emotion of ENTHUSIASM
The emotion of ROMANCE
The emotion of HOPE

There are other positive emotions, but these are the seven most powerful, and the one's most commonly used in creative effort. Master these seven emotions (they can be mastered only by use) and the other positive emotions will be at your command when you need them. Remember, in this connection, that you are studying a book which is intended to help you develop a "money consciousness" *by filling your mind with positive emotions.* One does not become money conscious by filling one's mind with negative emotions.

THE SEVEN MAJOR NEGATIVE EMOTIONS
(To be avoided)

The emotion of FEAR
The emotion of JEALOUSY
The emotion of HATRED
The emotion of REVENGE
The emotion of GREED
The emotion of SUPERSTITION
The emotion of ANGER

Positive and negative emotions cannot occupy the mind at the same time. One or the other must dominate. It is your responsibility to make sure that positive emotions constitute the dominating influence of your mind. Here the law of habit will come to your aid. *Form the habit* of applying and using the positive emotions! Eventually, they will dominate your mind so completely, that the negatives *cannot enter it.*

Only by following these instructions literally, and continuously, can you gain control over your subconscious mind. The presence of a single negative in your conscious mind is sufficient to *destroy* all chances of constructive aid from your subconscious mind.

If you are an observing person, you must have noticed that most people resort to prayer only after everything else has failed! Or else they pray by a ritual of meaningless words. And because it is a fact that most people who pray, do so only after everything else has failed, they go to prayer with their minds filled with fear and doubt, *which are the emotions the subconscious mind acts upon,* and passes on to Infinite Intelligence. Likewise, that is the emotion which Infinite Intelligence receives, and acts upon.

If you pray for a thing, but have fear as you pray, that you may not receive it, or that your prayer will not be acted upon by Infinite Intelligence, your prayer *will have been in vain.*

Prayer does, sometimes, result in the realization of that for which one prays. If you have ever had the experience of receiving that for which you prayed, go back in your memory, and recall your actual state of mind, while you were praying, and you will know, for sure, that the theory here described is more than a theory.

The time will come when the schools and educational institutions of the country will teach the "science of prayer." Moreover, then prayer may be, and will be reduced to a science. When that time comes (it will come as soon as mankind is ready for it, and demands it), no one will approach the Universal Mind in a state of fear, for the very good reason that there will be no such emotion as fear. Ignorance, superstition, and false teaching will have disappeared, and man will have attained his true status as a child of Infinite Intelligence. A few have already attained this blessing.

If you believe this prophesy is far-fetched, take a look at the human race in retrospect. Less than a hundred years ago, men believed the lightning to be evidence of the wrath of God, and feared it. Now, thanks to the power of faith, men have harnessed the lightning and made it turn the wheels of industry. Much less than a hundred years ago, men believed the space between the planets to be nothing but a great void, a stretch of dead nothingness. Now, thanks to this same power of faith, men know that far from being either dead or a void, the space between the planets is very much alive, that it is the highest form of vibration known, excepting, perhaps, the vibration of thought. Moreover, men know that this living, pulsating, vibratory energy which permeates every atom of matter, and fills every niche of space, connects every human brain with every other human brain.

What reason have men to believe that this same energy does not connect every human brain with Infinite Intelligence?

There are no toll-gates between the finite mind of man and Infinite Intelligence. The communication costs nothing except Patience, Faith, Persistence, Understanding, and a sincere desire to communicate. Moreover, the approach can be made only by the individual himself. Paid prayers are worthless. Infinite Intelligence does no business by proxy. You either go direct, or you do not communicate.

You may buy prayer books and repeat them until the day of your doom, without avail. Thoughts which you wish to communicate to Infinite Intelligence, must undergo transformation, such as can be given only through your own subconscious mind.

The method by which you may communicate with Infinite Intelligence is very similar to that through which the vibration of sound is communicated by radio. If you understand the working principle of radio, you of course, know that sound cannot be communicated through the ether until it has been "stepped up," or changed into a rate of vibration which the human ear cannot detect. The radio sending station picks up the sound of the human voice, and "scrambles," or modifies it by stepping up the vibration millions of times. Only in this way, can the vibration of sound be communicated through the ether. After this transformation has taken place, the ether "picks up" the energy (which originally was in the form of vibrations of sound) carries that energy to radio receiving stations, and these receiving sets "step" that energy back down to its original rate of vibration so it is recognized as sound.

The subconscious mind is the intermediary, which translates one's prayers into terms which Infinite Intelligence can recognize, presents the message, and brings back the answer in the form of a definite plan or idea for procuring the object of the prayer. Understand this principle, and you will know why mere words read from a prayer book cannot, and will never serve as an agency of communication between the mind of man and Infinite Intelligence.

Before your prayer will reach Infinite Intelligence (a statement of the author's theory only), it probably is transformed from its original thought vibration into terms of spiritual vibration. Faith is the only known agency which will give your thoughts a spiritual nature. Faith and fear make poor bedfellows. *Where one is found, the other cannot exist.*

CHAPTER 13

The Brain

A BROADCASTING AND RECEIVING STATION FOR THOUGHT

The Twelfth Step Toward Riches

More than twenty years ago, the author, working in conjunction with the late Dr. Alexander Graham Bell, and Dr. Elmer R. Gates, observed that every human brain is both a broadcasting and receiving station for the vibration of thought.

Through the medium of the ether, in a fashion similar to that employed by the radio broadcasting principle, every human brain is capable of picking up vibrations of thought which are being released by other brains.

In connection with the statement in the preceding paragraph, compare, and consider the description of the Creative Imagination, as outlined in the chapter on Imagination. The Creative Imagination is the "receiving set" of the brain, which receives thoughts, released by the brains of others. It is the agency of communication between one's conscious, or reasoning mind, and the four sources from which one may receive thought stimuli.

When stimulated, or "stepped up" to a high rate of vibration, the mind becomes more receptive to the vibration of thought which reaches it through the ether from outside sources. This "stepping up" process takes place through the positive emotions, or the negative emotions. Through the emotions, the vibrations of thought may be increased.

Vibrations of an exceedingly high rate are the only vibrations picked up and carried, by the ether, from one brain to another. Thought is energy travelling at an exceedingly high rate of vibration. Thought, which has been modified or "stepped up" by any of the major emotions, vibrates at a much higher rate than ordinary thought, and it is this type of thought which passes from one brain to another, through the broadcasting machinery of the human brain.

The emotion of sex stands at the head of the list of human emotions, as far as intensity and driving force are concerned. The brain which has been stimulated by the emotion of sex, vibrates at a much more rapid rate than it does when that emotion is quiescent or absent.

The result of sex transmutation is the increase of the rate of vibration of thoughts to such a pitch that the Creative Imagination becomes highly receptive to ideas, which it picks up from the ether. On the other hand, when the brain is vibrating at a rapid rate, it not only attracts thoughts and ideas released by other brains through the medium of the ether, but it gives to one's own thoughts that "feeling" which is essential before those thoughts will be picked up and acted upon by one's subconscious mind.

Thus, you will see that the broadcasting principle is the factor through which you mix feeling, or emotion with your thoughts and pass them on to your subconscious mind.

The subconscious mind is the "sending station" of the brain, through which vibrations of thought are broadcast. The Creative Imagination is the "receiving set," through which the vibrations of thought are picked up from the ether.

Along with the important factors of the subconscious mind, and the faculty of the Creative Imagination, which constitute the sending and receiving sets of your mental broadcasting machinery, consider now the principle of auto-suggestion, which is the medium by which you may put into operation your "broadcasting" station.

Through the instructions described in the chapter on autosuggestion, you were definitely informed of the method by which desire may be transmuted into its monetary equivalent.

Operation of your mental "broadcasting" station is a comparatively simple procedure. You have but three principles to bear in mind, and to apply, when you wish to use your broadcasting station—the subconscious mind, creative imagination, and autosuggestion. The stimuli through which you put these three principles into action have been described—the procedure begins with desire.

GREATEST FORCES ARE "INTANGIBLE"

The depression brought the world to the very border-line of understanding of the forces which are intangible and unseen. Through the ages which have passed, man has depended too much upon his physical senses, and has limited his knowledge to physical things, which he could see, touch, weigh, and measure.

We are now entering the most marvelous of all ages—an age which will teach us something of the intangible forces of the world about us. Perhaps we shall learn, as we pass through this age, that the "other self" is more powerful than the physical self we see when we look into a mirror.

Sometimes men speak lightly of the intangibles—the things which they cannot perceive through any of their five senses, and when we hear them, it should remind us that *all of us are controlled by forces which are unseen and intangible.*

The whole of mankind has not the power to cope with, nor to control the intangible force wrapped up in the rolling waves of the oceans. Man has hot the capacity to understand the intangible force of gravity, which keeps this little earth suspended in mid-air, and keeps man from falling from it, much less the power to control that force. Man is entirely subservient to the intangible force which comes with a thunder storm, and he is just as helpless in the presence of the intangible force of electricity—nay, he does not even know what electricity is, where it comes from, or what is its purpose!

Nor is this by any means the end of man's ignorance in connection with things unseen and intangible. He does not understand the intangible force (and intelligence) wrapped up in the soil of the earth—*the force which provides him with every morsel of food he eats, every article of clothing he wears, every dollar he carries in his pockets.*

THE DRAMATIC STORY OF THE BRAIN

Last, but not least, man, with all of his boasted culture and education, understands little or nothing of the intangible force (the greatest of all the intangibles) of *thought.* He knows but little concerning the physical brain, and its vast network of intricate machinery through which the power of thought is translated into its material equivalent, but he is now entering an age which shall yield enlightenment on the subject. Already men of science have begun to turn their attention to the study of this stupendous thing called a brain, and, while they are still in the kindergarten stage of their studies, they have uncovered enough knowledge to know that the central switchboard of the human brain, the number of lines which connect the brain cells one with another, equal the figure one, followed by fifteen million ciphers.

"The figure is so stupendous," said Dr. C. Judson Herrick, of the University of Chicago, "that astronomical figures dealing with hundreds of millions of light years, become insignificant by comparison. ... It has been determined that there are from 10,000,000,000 to 14,000,000,000 nerve cells in the human cerebral cortex, and we know that these are arranged in definite patterns. These arrangements are not haphazard. They are orderly. Recently developed methods of electro-physiology draw off action currents from very precisely located cells, or fibers with micro-electrodes, amplify them with radio tubes, and record potential differences to a millionth of a volt."

It is inconceivable that such a network of intricate machinery should be in existence for the sole purpose of carrying on the physical functions incidental to growth and maintenance of the physical body. Is it not likely that the same system, which gives billions of brain cells the media for communication one with another, provides, also the means of communication with other intangible forces?

After this book had been written, just before the manuscript went to the publisher, there appeared in the *New York Times* an editorial showing that at least one great University, and one intelligent investigator in the field of mental phenomena, are carrying on an organized research through which conclusions have been reached that parallel many of those described in this and the following chapter. The editorial briefly analyzed the work carried on by Dr. Rhine, and his associates at Duke University, viz:—

WHAT IS "TELEPATHY"?

"A month ago we cited on this page some of the remarkable results achieved by Professor Rhine and his associates in Duke University from more than a hundred thousand tests to determine the existence of 'telepathy' and 'clairvoyance.' These results were summarized in the first two articles in *Harpers Magazine.* In the second which has now appeared, the author, E. H. Wright, attempts to summarize what has been learned, or what it seems reasonable to infer, regarding the exact nature of these 'extrasensory' modes of perception.

"The actual existence of telepathy and clairvoyance now seems to some scientists enormously probable as the result of Rhine's experiments. Various percipients were asked to name as many cards in a special pack as they could without looking at them and without other sensory access to them. About a score of men and women were discovered who could regularly name so many of the cards correctly that 'there was not one chance in many a million million of their having done their feats by luck or accident.'

"But how did they do them? These powers, assuming that they exist, do not seem to be sensory. There is no known organ for them. The experiments worked just as well at distances of several hundred miles as they did in the same room. These facts also dispose, in Mr. Wright's opinion, of the attempt to explain telepathy or clairvoyance through any physical theory of radiation. All known forms of radiant energy decline inversely as the square of the distance traversed. Telepathy and clairvoyance do not. But they do vary through physical causes as our other mental powers do. Contrary to widespread opinion, they do not improve when the percipient is asleep or half-asleep, but, on the contrary, when he is most wide-awake and alert. Rhine discovered that a narcotic will invariably lower a percipient's score, while a stimulant will always send it higher. The most reliable performer apparently cannot make a good score unless he tries to do his best.

"One conclusion that Wright draws with some confidence is that telepathy and clairvoyance are really one and the same gift. That is, the faculty that 'sees' a card face down on a table seems to be exactly the same one that 'reads' a thought residing only in another mind. There are several grounds for believing this. So far, for example, the two gifts have been found in every person who enjoys either of them. In every one so far the two have been of equal vigor, almost exactly. Screens, walls, distances, have no effect at all on either. Wright advances from this conclusion to express what he puts forward as no more than the mere 'hunch' that other extra-sensory experiences, prophetic dreams, premonitions of disaster, and the like, may also prove to be part of the same faculty. The reader is not asked to accept any of these conclusions unless he finds it necessary, but the evidence that Rhine has piled up must remain impressive."

In view of Dr. Rhine's announcement in connection with the conditions under which the mind responds to what he terms "extra-sensory" modes of perception, I now feel privileged to add to his testimony by stating that my associates and I have discovered what we believe to be the ideal conditions under which the mind can be stimulated so that the sixth sense described in the next chapter can be made to function in a practical way.

The conditions to which I refer consist of a close working alliance between myself and two members of my staff. Through experimentation and practice, we have discovered how to stimulate our minds (by applying the principle used in connection with the "Invisible Counselors" described in the next chapter) so that we can, by a process of blending our three minds into one, find the solution to a great variety of personal problems which are submitted by my clients.

The procedure is very simple. We sit down at a conference table, clearly state the nature of the problem we have under consideration, then begin discussing it. Each contributes whatever thoughts that may occur. The strange thing about this method of mind stimulation is that it places each participant in communication with unknown sources of knowledge definitely outside his own experience.

If you understand the principle described in the chapter on the Master Mind, you of course recognize the round-table procedure here described as being a practical application of the Master Mind.

This method of mind stimulation, through harmonious discussion of definite subjects, between three people, illustrates the simplest and most practical use of the Master Mind.

By adopting and following a similar plan any student of this philosophy may come into possession of the famous Carnegie formula briefly described in the introduction. If it means nothing to you at this time, mark this page and read it again after you have finished the last chapter.

The "Depression" was a blessing in disguise. It reduced the whole world to a new starting point that gives every one a new opportunity.

CHAPTER 14

The Sixth Sense

THE DOOR TO THE TEMPLE OF WISDOM

The Thirteenth Step Toward Riches

The "thirteenth" principle is known as the sixth sense, through which Infinite Intelligence may, and will communicate voluntarily, without any effort from, or demands by, the individual.

This principle is the apex of the philosophy. It can be assimilated, understood, and applied only by first mastering the other twelve principles.

The sixth sense is that portion of the subconscious mind which has been referred to as the Creative Imagination. It has also been referred to as the "receiving set" through which ideas, plans, and thoughts flash into the mind. The "flashes" are sometimes called "hunches" or "inspirations."

The sixth sense defies description! It cannot be described to a person who has not mastered the other principles of this philosophy, because such a person has no knowledge, and no experience with which the sixth sense may be compared. Understanding of the sixth sense comes only by meditation through mind development *from within.* The sixth sense probably is the medium of contact between the finite mind of man and Infinite Intelligence, and for this reason, *it is a mixture of both the mental and the spiritual.* It is believed to be the point at which the mind of man contacts the Universal Mind.

After you have mastered the principles described in this book, you will be prepared to accept as truth a statement which may, otherwise, be incredible to you, namely:

Through the aid of the sixth sense, you will be warned of impending dangers in time to avoid them, and notified of opportunities in time to embrace them.

There comes to your aid, and to do your bidding, with the development of the sixth sense, a "guardian angel" who will open to you at all times the door to the Temple of Wisdom.

Whether or not this is a statement of truth, you will never know, except by following the instructions described in the pages of this book, or some similar method of procedure.

The author is not a believer in, nor an advocate of "miracles," for the reason that he has enough knowledge of Nature to understand that Nature *never deviates from her established laws.* Some of her laws are so incomprehensible that they produce what appear to be "miracles." The sixth sense comes as near to being a miracle as anything I have ever experienced, and it appears so, only because I do not understand the method by which this principle is operated.

This much the author does know—that there is a power, or a First Cause, or an Intelligence, which permeates every atom of matter, and embraces every unit of energy perceptible to man—that this Infinite Intelligence converts acorns into oak trees, causes water to flow down hill in response to the law of gravity, follows night with day, and winter with summer, each maintaining its proper place and relationship to the other. This Intelligence may, through the principles of this philosophy, be induced to aid in transmuting desires into concrete, or material form. The author has this knowledge, because he has experimented with it—and has experienced it.

Step by step, through the preceding chapters, you have been led to this, the last principle. If you have mastered each of the preceding principles, you are now prepared to accept, *without being skeptical,* the stupendous claims made here. If you have not mastered the other principles, you must do so before you may determine, definitely, whether or not the claims made in this chapter are fact or fiction.

While I was passing through the age of "hero-worship" I found myself trying to imitate those whom I most admired. Moreover, I discovered that the element of faith, with which I endeavored to imitate my idols, gave me great capacity to do so quite successfully.

I have never entirely divested myself of this habit of hero-worship, although I have passed the age commonly given over to such. My experience has taught me that the next best thing to being truly great, is to emulate the great, by feeling and action, as nearly as possible.

Long before I had ever written a line for publication, or endeavored to deliver a speech in public, I followed the habit of reshaping my own character, by trying to imitate the nine men whose lives and life-works had been most impressive to me. These nine men were Emerson, Paine, Edison, Darwin, Lincoln, Burbank, Napoleon, Ford, and Carnegie. Every night, over a long period of years, I held an imaginary Council meeting with this group whom I called my "Invisible Counselors."

The procedure was this. Just before going to sleep at night, I would shut my eyes, and see, in my imagination, this group of men seated with me around my Council Table. Here I had not only an opportunity to sit among those whom I considered to be great, but I actually dominated the group, by serving as the Chairman.

I had a very definite purpose in indulging my imagination through these nightly meetings. My purpose was to rebuild my own character so it would represent a composite of the characters of my imaginary counselors. Realizing, as I did, early in life, that I had to overcome the handicap of birth in an environment of ignorance and superstition, I deliberately assigned myself the task of voluntary rebirth through the method here described.

BUILDING CHARACTER THROUGH AUTO-SUGGESTION

Being an earnest student of psychology, I knew, of course, that all men have become what they are, because of their dominating thoughts and desires. I knew that every deeply seated desire has the effect of causing one to seek outward expression through which that desire may be transmuted into reality. I knew that self-suggestion is a powerful factor in building character, that it is, in fact, the sole principle through which character is built.

With this knowledge of the principles of mind operation, I was fairly well armed with the equipment needed in rebuilding my character. In these imaginary Council meetings I called on my Cabinet members for the knowledge I wished each to contribute, addressing myself to each member in audible words, as follows:—

"Mr. Emerson, I desire to acquire from you the marvelous understanding of Nature which distinguished your life. I ask that you make an impress upon my subconscious mind, of whatever qualities you possessed, which enabled you to understand and adapt yourself to the laws of Nature. I ask that you assist me in reaching and drawing upon whatever sources of knowledge are available to this end.

"Mr. Burbank, I request that you pass on to me the knowledge which enabled you to so harmonize the laws of Nature that you caused the cactus to shed its thorns, and become an edible food. Give me access to the knowledge which enabled you to make two blades of grass grow where but one grew before, and helped you to blend the coloring of the flowers with more splendor and harmony, for you, alone, have successfully gilded the lily.

"Napoleon, I desire to acquire from you, by emulation, the marvelous ability you possessed to inspire men, and to arouse them to greater and more determined spirit of action. Also to acquire the spirit of enduring faith, which enabled you to turn defeat into victory, and to surmount staggering obstacles. Emperor of Fate, King of Chance, Man of Destiny, I salute you!

"Mr. Paine, I desire to acquire from you the freedom of thought and the courage and clarity with which to express convictions, which so distinguished you!

"Mr. Darwin, I wish to acquire from you the marvelous patience, and ability to study cause and effect, without bias or prejudice, so exemplified by you in the field of natural science.

"Mr. Lincoln, I desire to build into my own character the keen sense of justice, the untiring spirit of patience, the sense of humor, the human understanding, and the tolerance, which were your distinguishing characteristics.

"Mr. Carnegie, I am already indebted to you for my choice of a life-work, which has brought me great happiness and peace of mind. I wish to acquire a thorough understanding of the principles of *organized effort*, which you used so effectively in the building of a great industrial enterprise.

"Mr. Ford, you have been among the most helpful of the men who have supplied much of the material essential to my work. I wish to acquire your spirit of persistence, the determination, poise, and self-confidence which have enabled you to master poverty, organize, unify, and simplify human effort, so I may help others to follow in your footsteps.

"Mr. Edison, I have seated you nearest to me, at my right, because of the personal cooperation you have given me, during my research into the causes of success and failure. I wish to acquire from you the marvelous spirit of faith, with which you have uncovered so many of Natures secrets, the spirit of unremitting toil with which you have so often wrested victory from defeat."

My method of addressing the members of the imaginary Cabinet would vary, according to the traits of character in which I was, for the moment, most interested in acquiring. I studied the records of their lives with painstaking care. After some months of this nightly procedure, I was astounded by the discovery that these imaginary figures became, apparently *real.*

Each of these nine men developed individual characteristics, which surprised me. For example, Lincoln developed the habit of always being late, then walking around in solemn parade. When he came, he walked very slowly, with his hands clasped behind him, and once in a while, he would stop as he passed, and rest his hand, momentarily, upon my shoulder. He always wore an expression of seriousness upon his face. Rarely did I see him smile. The cares of a sundered nation made him grave.

That was not true of the others. Burbank and Paine often indulged in witty repartee which seemed, at times, to shock the other members of the cabinet. One night Paine suggested that I prepare a lecture on "The Age of Reason," and deliver it from the pulpit of a church which I formerly attended. Many around the table laughed heartily at the suggestion. Not Napoleon! He drew his mouth down at the corners and groaned so loudly that all turned and looked at him with amazement. To him the church was but a pawn of the State, not to be reformed, but to be used, as a convenient inciter to mass activity by the people.

On one occasion Burbank was late. When he came, he was excited with enthusiasm, and explained that he had been late, because of an experiment he was making, through which he hoped to be able to grow apples on any sort of tree. Paine chided him by reminding him that it was an apple which started all the trouble between man and woman. Darwin chuckled heartily as he suggested that Paine should watch out for little serpents, when he went into the forest to gather apples, as they had the habit of growing into big snakes. Emerson observed—"No serpents, no apples," and Napoleon remarked, "No apples, no state!"

Lincoln developed the habit of always being the last one to leave the table after each meeting. On one occasion, he leaned across the end of the table, his arms folded, and remained in that position for many minutes. I made no attempt to disturb him. Finally, he lifted his head slowly, got up and walked to the door, then turned around, came back, and laid his hand on my shoulder and said, "My boy, you will need much courage if you remain steadfast in carrying out your purpose in life. But remember, when difficulties overtake you, the common people have common sense. Adversity will develop it."

One evening Edison arrived ahead of all the others. He walked over and seated himself at my left, where Emerson was accustomed to sit, and said, "You are destined to witness the discovery of the secret of life. When the time comes, you will observe that life consists of great swarms of energy, or entities, each as intelligent as human beings *think* themselves to be. These units of life group together like hives of bees, and remain together until they disintegrate, *through lack of harmony.* These units have differences of opinion, the same as human beings, and often fight among themselves. These meetings which you are conducting will be very helpful to you. They will bring to your rescue some of the same units of life which served the members of your Cabinet, during their lives. These units are eternal. They never die! Your own thoughts and desires serve as the magnet which attracts units of life, from the great ocean of life out there. Only the friendly units are attracted—the ones which harmonize with the nature of your desires."

The other members of the Cabinet began to enter the room. Edison got up, and slowly walked around to his own seat. Edison was still living when this happened. It impressed me so greatly that I went to see him, and told him about the experience. He smiled broadly, and said, "Your dream was more a reality than you may imagine it to have been." He added no further explanation to his statement.

These meetings became so realistic that I became fearful of their consequences, and discontinued them for several months. The experiences were so uncanny, I was afraid if I continued them I would lose sight of the fact that the meetings were purely *experiences of my imagination.*

Some six months after I had discontinued the practice I was awakened one night, or thought I was, when I saw Lincoln standing at my bedside. He said, "The world will soon need your services. It is about to undergo a period of chaos which will cause men and women to lose faith, and become panic stricken. Go ahead with your work and complete your philosophy. That is your mission in life. If you neglect it, for any cause whatsoever, you will be reduced to a primal state, and be compelled to retrace the cycles through which you have passed during thousands of years."

I was unable to tell, the following morning, whether I had dreamed this, or had actually been awake, and I have never since found out which it was, but I do know that the dream, if it were a dream, was so vivid in my mind the next day that I resumed my meetings the following night.

At our next meeting, the members of my Cabinet all filed into the room together, and stood at their accustomed places at the Council Table, while Lincoln raised a glass and said, "Gentlemen, let us drink a toast to a friend who has returned to the fold."

After that, I began to add new members to my Cabinet, until now it consists of more than fifty, among them Christ, St. Paul, Galileo, Copernicus, Aristotle, Plato, Socrates, Homer, Voltaire, Bruno, Spinoza, Drummond, Kant, Schopenhauer, Newton, Confucius, Elbert Hubbard, Brann, Ingersoll, Wilson, and William James.

This is the first time that I have had the courage to mention this. Heretofore, I have remained quiet on the subject, because I knew, from my own attitude in connection with such matters, that I would be misunderstood if I described my unusual experience. I have been emboldened now to reduce my experience to the printed page, because I am now less concerned about what "they say" than I was in the years that have passed. One of the blessings of maturity is that it sometimes brings one greater courage to be truthful, regardless of what those who do not understand may think or say.

Lest I be misunderstood, I wish here to state most emphatically, that I still regard my Cabinet meetings as being purely imaginary, but I feel entitled to suggest that, while the members of my Cabinet may be purely fictional, and the meetings existent only in my own imagination, they have led me into glorious paths of adventure, rekindled an appreciation of true greatness, encouraged creative endeavor, and emboldened the expression of honest thought.

Somewhere in the cell-structure of the brain, is located an organ which receives vibrations of thought ordinarily called "hunches." So far, science has not discovered where this organ of the sixth sense is located, but this is not important. The fact remains that human beings do receive accurate knowledge, through sources other than the physical senses. Such knowledge, generally, is received when the mind is under the influence of extraordinary stimulation. Any emergency which arouses the emotions, and causes the heart to beat more rapidly than normal may, and generally does, bring the sixth sense into action. Anyone who has experienced a near accident while driving, knows that on such occasions, the sixth sense often comes to one's rescue, and aids, by split seconds, in avoiding the accident.

These facts are mentioned preliminary to a statement of fact which I shall now make, namely, that during my meetings with the "Invisible Counselors" I find my mind most receptive to ideas, thoughts, and knowledge which reach me through the sixth sense. I can truthfully say that I owe entirely to my "Invisible Counselors" full credit for such ideas, facts, or knowledge as I received through "inspiration."

On scores of occasions, when I have faced emergencies, some of them so grave that my life was in jeopardy, I have been miraculously guided past these difficulties through the influence of my "Invisible Counselors."

My original purpose in conducting Council meetings with imaginary beings was solely that of impressing my own subconscious mind, through the principle of auto-suggestion, with certain characteristics which I desired to acquire. In more recent years, my experimentation has taken on an entirely different trend. I now go to my imaginary counselors with every difficult problem which confronts me and my clients. The results are often astonishing, although I do not depend entirely on this form of Counsel.

You, of course, have recognized that this chapter covers a subject with which a majority of people are not familiar. The Sixth Sense is a subject that will be of great interest and benefit to the person whose aim is to accumulate vast wealth, but it need not claim the attention of those whose desires are more modest.

Henry Ford undoubtedly understands and makes practical use of the sixth sense. His vast business and financial operations make it necessary for him to understand and use this principle. The late Thomas A. Edison understood and used the sixth sense in connection with the development of inventions, especially those involving basic patents, in connection with which he had no human experience and no accumulated knowledge to guide him, as was the case while he was working on the talking machine, and the moving picture machine.

Nearly all great leaders, such as Napoleon, Bismarck, Joan of Arc, Christ, Buddha, Confucius, and Mohammed, understood, and probably made use of the sixth sense almost continuously. The major portion of their greatness consisted of their knowledge of this principle.

The sixth sense is not something that one can take off and put on at will. Ability to use this great power comes slowly, through application of the other principles outlined in this book. Seldom does any individual come into workable knowledge of the sixth sense before the age of forty. More often the knowledge is not available until one is well past fifty, and this, for the reason that the spiritual forces, with which the sixth sense is so closely related, do not mature and become usable except through years of meditation, self-examination, and serious thought.

No matter who you are, or what may have been your purpose in reading this book, you can profit by it without understanding the principle described in this chapter. This is especially true if your major purpose is that of accumulation of money or other material things.

The chapter on the sixth sense was included, because the book is designed for the purpose of presenting a complete philosophy by which individuals may unerringly guide themselves in attaining whatever they ask of life. The starting point of all achievement is desire. The finishing point is that brand of knowledge which leads to understanding—understanding of self, understanding of others, understanding of the laws of Nature, recognition and understanding of happiness.

This sort of understanding comes in its fullness only through familiarity with, and use of the principle of the sixth sense, hence that principle had to be included as a part of this philosophy, for the benefit of those who demand more than money.

Having read the chapter, you must have observed that while reading it, you were lifted to a high level of mental stimulation. Splendid! Come back to this again a month from now, read it once more, and observe that your mind will soar to a still-higher level of stimulation. Repeat this experience from time to time, giving no concern as to how much or how little you learn at the time, and eventually you will find yourself in possession of a power that will enable you to throw off discouragement, master fear, overcome procrastination, and draw freely upon your imagination. Then you will have felt the touch of that unknown "something" which has been the moving spirit of every truly great thinker, leader, artist, musician, writer, statesman. Then you will be in position to transmute your desires into their physical or financial counterpart as easily as you may lie down and quit at the first sign of opposition.

FAITH VS. FEAR!

Previous chapters have described how to develop faith, through Auto-suggestion, Desire and the Subconscious. The next chapter presents detailed instructions for the mastery of fear.

Here will be found a full description of the six fears which are the cause of all discouragement, timidity, procrastination, indifference, indecision, and the lack of ambition, self-reliance, initiative, self-control, and enthusiasm.

Search yourself carefully as you study these six enemies, as they may exist only in your subconscious mind, where their presence will be hard to detect.

Remember, too, as you analyze the "Six Ghosts of Fear," that they are nothing but ghosts because they exist only in one's mind.

Remember, also, that ghosts—creations of uncontrolled imagination—have caused most of the damage people have done to their own minds, therefore, ghosts can be as dangerous as if they lived and walked on the earth in physical bodies.

The Ghost of the Fear of Poverty, which seized the minds of millions of people in 1929, was so real that it caused the worst business depression this country has ever known. Moreover, this particular ghost still frightens some of us out of our wits.

CHAPTER 15

How to Outwit the Six Ghosts of Fear

Take Inventory of Yourself, As You Read This Closing Chapter, and Find Out How Many of the "Ghosts" Are Standing in Your Way

Before you can put any portion of this philosophy into successful use, your mind must be prepared to receive it. The preparation is not difficult. It begins with study, analysis, and understanding of three enemies which you shall have to clear out. These are indecision, doubt, and fear!

The Sixth Sense will never function while these three negatives, or any of them remain in your mind. The members of this unholy trio are closely related; where one is found, the other two are close at hand.

Indecision is the seedling of fear! Remember this, as you read. Indecision crystalizes into doubt, the two blend and become fear! The "blending" process often is slow. This is one reason why these three enemies are so dangerous. They germinate and grow *without their presence being observed.*

The remainder of this chapter describes an end which must be attained before the philosophy, as a whole, can be put into practical use. It also analyzes a condition which has, but lately, reduced huge numbers of people to poverty, and it states a truth which must be understood by all who accumulate riches, whether measured in terms of money or a state of mind of far greater value than money.

The purpose of this chapter is to turn the spotlight of attention upon the cause and the cure of the six basic fears. Before we can master an enemy, we must know its name, its habits, and its place of abode. As you read, analyze yourself carefully, and determine which, if any, of the six common fears have attached themselves to you.

Do not be deceived by the habits of these subtle enemies. Sometimes they remain hidden in the subconscious mind, where they are difficult to locate, and still more difficult to eliminate.

THE SIX BASIC FEARS

There are six basic fears, with some combination of which every human suffers at one time or another. Most people are fortunate if they do not suffer from the entire six. Named in the order of their most common appearance, they are:—

The fear of POVERTY
The fear of CRITICISM
The fear of ILL HEALTH
} at the bottom of most of one's worries
The fear of LOSS OF LOVE OF SOMEONE
The fear of OLD AGE
The fear of DEATH

All other fears are of minor importance, they can be grouped under these six headings.

The prevalence of these fears, as a curse to the world, runs in cycles. For almost six years, while the depression was on, we floundered in the cycle of fear of poverty. During the world-war, we were in the cycle of fear of death. Just following the war, we were in the cycle of fear of ill health, as evidenced by the epidemic of disease which spread itself all over the world.

Fears are nothing more than states of mind. One s state of mind is subject to control and direction. Physicians, as everyone knows, are less subject to attack by disease than ordinary laymen, for the reason that physicians do not fear disease. Physicians, without fear or hesitation, have been known to physically contact hundreds of people, daily, who were suffering from such contagious diseases as small-pox, without becoming infected. Their immunity against the disease consisted, largely, if not solely, in their absolute lack of fear.

Man can create nothing which he does not first conceive in the form of an impulse of thought. Following this statement, comes another of still greater importance, namely man's thought impulses begin immediately to translate themselves into their physical equivalent, whether those thoughts are voluntary or involuntary. Thought impulses which are picked up through the ether, by mere chance (thoughts which have been released by other minds) may determine one's financial, business, professional, or social destiny just as surely as do the thought impulses which one creates by intent and design.

We are here laying the foundation for the presentation of a fact of great importance to the person who does not understand why some people appear to be "lucky" while others of equal or greater ability, training, experience, and brain capacity, seem destined to ride with misfortune. This fact may be explained by the statement that *every human being has the ability to completely control his own mind,* and with this control, obviously, every person may open his mind to the tramp thought impulses which are being released by other brains, or close the doors tightly and admit only thought impulses of his own choice.

Nature has endowed man with absolute control over but one thing, and that is thought. This fact, coupled with the additional fact that everything which man creates, begins in the form of a thought, leads one very near to the principle by which fear may be mastered.

If it is true that all thought has a tendency to clothe itself in its physical equivalent (and this is true, beyond any reasonable room for doubt), it is equally true that thought impulses of fear and poverty cannot be translated into terms of courage and financial gain.

The people of America began to think of poverty, following the Wall Street crash of 1929. Slowly, but surely that mass thought was crystalized into its physical equivalent, which was known as a "depression." This had to happen, it is in conformity with the laws of Nature.

THE FEAR OF POVERTY

There can be no compromise between poverty and riches! The two roads that lead to poverty and riches travel in opposite directions. If you want riches, you must refuse to accept any circumstance that leads toward poverty. (The word "riches" is here used in its broadest sense, meaning financial, spiritual, mental and material estates.) The starting point of the path that leads to riches is desire. In chapter one, you received full instructions for the proper use of desire. In this chapter, on fear, you have complete instructions for preparing your mind to make practical use of desire.

Here, then, is the place to give yourself a challenge which will definitely determine how much of this philosophy you have absorbed. Here is the point at which you can turn prophet and foretell, accurately, what the future holds in store for you. If, after reading this chapter, you are willing to accept poverty, you may as well make up your mind to receive poverty. This is one decision you cannot avoid.

If you demand riches, determine what form, and how much will be required to satisfy you. You know the road that leads to riches. You have been given a road map which, if followed, will keep you on that road. If you neglect to make the start, or stop before you arrive, no one will be to blame, but you. This responsibility is yours. No alibi will save you from accepting the responsibility if you now fail or refuse to demand riches of Life, because the acceptance calls for but one thing—incidentally, the only thing you can control—and that is a state of mind. A state of mind is something that one assumes. It cannot be purchased, it must be created.

Fear of poverty is a state of mind, nothing else! But it is sufficient to destroy one's chances of achievement in any undertaking, a truth which became painfully evident during the depression.

This fear paralyzes the faculty of reason, destroys the faculty of imagination, kills off self-reliance, undermines enthusiasm, discourages initiative, leads to uncertainty of purpose, encourages procrastination, wipes out enthusiasm and makes self control an impossibility. It takes the charm from one's personality, destroys the possibility of accurate thinking, diverts concentration of effort, it masters persistence, turns the will-power into nothingness, destroys ambition, beclouds the memory and invites failure in every conceivable form; it kills love and assassinates the finer emotions of the heart, discourages friendship and invites disaster in a hundred forms, leads to sleeplessness, misery and unhappiness—and all this despite the obvious truth that we live in a world of over-abundance of everything the heart could desire, with nothing standing between us and our desires, excepting lack of a definite purpose.

The Fear of Poverty is, without doubt, the most destructive of the six basic fears. It has been placed at the head of the list, because it is the most difficult to master. Considerable courage is required to state the truth about the origin of this fear, and still greater courage to accept the truth after it has been stated. The fear of poverty grew out of man's inherited tendency to prey upon his fellow-man economically. Nearly all animals lower than man are motivated by instinct, but their capacity to "think" is limited, therefore, they prey upon one another physically. Man, with his superior sense of intuition, with the capacity to think and to reason, does not eat his fellow man bodily, he gets more satisfaction out of "eating" him financially. Man is so avaricious that every conceivable law has been passed to safeguard him from his fellow man.

Of all the ages of the world, of which we know anything, the age in which we live seems to be one that is outstanding because of man's money-madness. A man is considered less than the dust of the earth, unless he can display a fat bank account; but if he has money—never mind how he acquired it—he is a "king" or a "big shot"; he is above the law, he rules in politics, he dominates in business, and the whole world about him bows in respect when he passes.

Nothing brings man so much suffering and humility as poverty! Only those who have experienced poverty understand the full meaning of this.

It is no wonder that man *fears* poverty. Through a long line of inherited experiences man has learned, for sure, that some men cannot be trusted, where matters of money and earthly possessions are concerned. This is a rather stinging indictment, the worst part of it being that it is true.

The majority of marriages are motivated by the wealth possessed by one, or both of the contracting parties. It is no wonder, therefore, that the divorce courts are busy.

So eager is man to possess wealth that he will acquire it in whatever manner he can—through legal methods if possible— through other methods if necessary or expedient.

Self-analysis may disclose weaknesses which one does not like to acknowledge. This form of examination is essential to all who demand of Life more than mediocrity and poverty. Remember, as you check yourself point by point, that you are both the court and the jury, the prosecuting attorney and the attorney for the defense, and that you are the plaintiff and the defendant, also, that you are on trial. Face the facts squarely. Ask yourself definite questions and demand direct replies. When the examination is over, you will know more about yourself. If you do not feel that you can be an impartial judge in this self-examination, call upon someone who knows you well to serve as judge while you cross-examine yourself. You are after the truth. *Get it, no matter at what cost, even though it may temporarily embarrass you!*

The majority of people, if asked what they fear most, would reply, "I fear nothing." The reply would be inaccurate, because few people realize that they are bound, handicapped, whipped spiritually and physically through some form of fear. So subtle and deeply seated is the emotion of fear that one may go through life burdened with it, never recognizing its presence. Only a courageous analysis will disclose the presence of this universal enemy. When you begin such an analysis, search deeply into your character. Here is a list of the symptoms for which you should look:

Symptoms of the Fear of Poverty

INDIFFERENCE. Commonly expressed through lack of ambition; willingness to tolerate poverty; acceptance of whatever compensation life may offer without protest;

mental and physical laziness; lack of initiative, imagination, enthusiasm and self-control

INDECISION. The habit of permitting others to do one's thinking. Staying "on the fence."

DOUBT. Generally expressed through alibis and excuses designed to cover up, explain away, or apologize for one's failures, sometimes expressed in the form of envy of those who are successful, or by criticising them.

WORRY. Usually expressed by finding fault with others, a tendency to spend beyond one's income, neglect of personal appearance, scowling and frowning; intemperance in the use of alcoholic drink, sometimes through the use of narcotics; nervousness, lack of poise, self-consciousness and lack of self-reliance.

OVER-CAUTION. The habit of looking for the negative side of every circumstance, thinking and talking of possible failure instead of concentrating upon the means of succeeding. Knowing all the roads to disaster, but never searching for the plans to avoid failure. Waiting for "the right time" to begin putting ideas and plans into action, until the waiting becomes a permanent habit. Remembering those who have failed, and forgetting those who have succeeded. Seeing the hole in the doughnut, but overlooking the doughnut. Pessimism, leading to indigestion, poor elimination, auto-intoxication, bad breath and bad disposition.

PROCRASTINATION. The habit of putting off until tomorrow that which should have been done last year. Spending enough time in creating alibis and excuses to have done the job. This symptom is closely related to over-caution, doubt and worry. Refusal to accept responsibility when it can be avoided. Willingness to 'compromise rather than put up a stiff fight. Compromising with difficulties instead of harnessing and using them as stepping stones to advancement. Bargaining with Life for a penny, instead of demanding prosperity, opulence, riches, contentment and happiness. Planning what to do if and when overtaken by failure, instead of burning all bridges and making retreat impossible. Weakness of, and often total lack of self-confidence, definiteness of purpose, self-control, initiative, enthusiasm, ambition, thrift and sound reasoning ability. Expecting poverty instead of demanding riches. Association with those who accept poverty instead of seeking the company of those who demand and receive riches.

MONEY TALKS!

Some will ask, "why did you write a book about money? Why measure riches in dollars, alone?" Some will believe, and rightly so, that there are other forms of riches more desirable than money. Yes, there are riches which cannot be measured in terms of dollars, but there are millions of people who will say, "Give me all the money I need, and I will find everything else I want."

The major reason why I wrote this book on how to get money is the fact that the world has but lately passed through an experience that left millions of men and women paralyzed with the fear of poverty. What this sort of fear does to one was well described by Westbrook Pegler, in the New York World-Telegram, viz:

"Money is only clam shells or metal discs or scraps of paper, and there are treasures of the heart and soul which money cannot buy, but most people, being broke, are unable to keep this in mind and sustain their spirits. When a man is down and out and on the street, unable to get any job at all, something happens to his spirit which can be observed in the droop of his shoulders, the set of his hat, his walk and his gaze. He cannot escape a feeling of inferiority among people with regular employment, even though he knows they are definitely not his equals in character, intelligence or ability.

"These people—even his friends—feel, on the other hand, a sense of superiority and regard him, perhaps unconsciously, as a casualty. He may borrow for a time, but not enough to carry on in his accustomed way, and he cannot continue to borrow very long. But borrowing in itself, when a man is borrowing merely to live, is a depressing experience, and the money lacks the power of earned money to revive his spirits. Of course, none of this applies to bums or habitual ne'er-do-wells, but only to men of normal ambitions and self-respect.

WOMEN CONCEAL DESPAIR

"Women in the same predicament must be different. We somehow do not think of women at all in considering the down-and-outers. They are scarce in the breadlines, they rarely are seen begging on the streets, and they are not recognizable in crowds by the same plain signs which identify busted men. Of course, I do not mean the shuffling hags of the city streets who are the opposite number of the confirmed male bums. I mean reasonably young, decent and intelligent women. There must be many of them, but their despair is not apparent. Maybe they kill themselves.

"When a man is down and out he has time on his hands for brooding. He may travel miles to see a man about a job and discover that the job is filled or that it is one of those jobs with no base pay but only a commission on the sale of some useless knickknack which nobody would buy except out of pity. Turning that down, he finds himself back on the street with nowhere to go but just anywhere. So he walks and walks. He gazes into store windows at luxuries which are not for him, and feels inferior and gives way to people who stop to look with an active interest. He wanders into the railroad station or puts himself down in the library to ease his legs and soak up a little heat, but that isn't looking for a job, so he gets going again. He may not know it, but his aimlessness would give him away even if the very lines of his figure did not. He may be well dressed in the clothes left over from the days when he had a steady job, but the clothes cannot disguise the droop.

MONEY MAKES DIFFERENCE

"He sees thousands of other people, bookkeepers or clerks or chemists or wagon hands, busy at their work and envies them from the bottom of his soul. They have their independence, their self-respect and manhood, and he simply cannot convince himself that he is a good man, too, though he argue it out and arrive at a favorable verdict hour after hour.

"It is just money which makes this difference in him. With a little money he would be himself again.

"Some employers take the most shocking advantage of people who are down and out. The agencies hang out little colored cards offering miserable wages to busted men—$12 a week, $15 a week. An $17 a week job is a plum, and anyone with $25 a week to offer does not hang the job in front of an agency on a colored card. I have a want ad clipped from a local paper demanding a clerk, a good, clean penman, to take telephone orders for a sandwich shop from 11 A.M. to 2 P.M. for $8 a month—not $8 a week but $8 a month. The ad says also, 'State religion.' Can you imagine the brutal effrontery of anyone who demands a good, clean penman for 11 cents an hour inquiring into the victim's religion? But that is what busted people are offered."

THE FEAR OF CRITICISM

Just how man originally came by this fear, no one can state definitely, but one thing is certain—he has it in a highly developed form. Some believe that this fear made its appearance about the time that politics became a "profession." Others believe it can be traced to the age when women first began to concern themselves with "styles" in wearing apparel.

This author, being neither a humorist nor a prophet, is inclined to attribute the basic fear of criticism to that part of man's inherited nature which prompts him not only to take away his fellowman's goods and wares, but to justify his action by criticism of his fellow man's character. It is a well known fact that a thief will criticise the man from whom he steals—that politicians seek office, not by displaying their own virtues and qualifications, but by attempting to besmirch their opponents.

The fear of criticism takes on many forms, the majority of which are petty and trivial. Baldheaded men, for example, are bald for no other reason than their fear of criticism. Heads become bald because of the tight fitting bands of hats which cut off the circulation from the roots of the hair. Men wear hats, not because they actually need them, but mainly because "everyone is doing it." The individual falls into line and does likewise, lest some other individual criticise him. Women seldom have bald heads, or even thin hair, because they wear hats which fit their heads loosely, the only purpose of the hats being adornment.

But, it must not be supposed that women are free from the fear of criticism. If any woman claims to be superior to man with reference to this fear, ask her to walk down the street wearing a hat of the vintage of 1890.

The astute manufacturers of clothing have not been slow to capitalize this basic fear of criticism, with which all mankind has been cursed. Every season the styles in many articles of wearing apparel change. Who establishes the styles? Certainly not the purchaser of clothing, but the manufacturer. Why does he change the styles so often? The answer is obvious. He changes the styles so he can sell more clothes.

For the same reason the manufacturers of automobiles (with a few rare and very sensible exceptions) change styles of models every season. No man wants to drive an automobile which is not of the latest style, although the older model may actually be the better car.

We have been describing the manner in which people behave under the influence of fear of criticism as applied to the small and petty things of life. Let us now examine human behavior when this fear affects people in connection with the more important events of human relationship. Take for example practically any person who has reached the age of "mental maturity" (from 35 to 40 years of age, as a general average), and if you could read the secret thoughts of his mind, you would find a very decided disbelief in most of the fables taught by the majority of the dogmatists and theologians a few decades back.

Not often, however, will you find a person who has the courage to openly state his belief on this subject. Most people will, if pressed far enough, tell a lie rather than admit that they do not believe the stories associated with that form of religion which held people in bondage prior to the age of scientific discovery and education.

Why does the average person, even in this day of enlightenment, shy away from denying his belief in the fables which were the basis of most of the religions a few decades ago? The answer is, "because of the fear of criticism." Men and women have been burned at the stake for daring to express disbelief in ghosts. It is no wonder we have inherited a consciousness which makes us fear criticism. The time was, and not so far in the past, when criticism carried severe punishments — it still does in some countries.

The fear of criticism robs man of his initiative, destroys his power of imagination, limits his individuality, takes away his self-reliance, and does him damage in a hundred other ways. Parents often do their children irreparable injury by criticising them. The mother of one of my boyhood chums used to punish him with a switch almost daily, always completing the job with the statement, "You'll land in the penitentiary before you are twenty." He was sent to a Reformatory at the age of seventeen.

Criticism is the one form of service, of which everyone has too much. Everyone has a stock of it which is handed out, gratis, whether called for or not. One's nearest relatives often are the worst offenders. It should be recognized as a crime (in reality it is a crime of the worst nature) for any parent to build inferiority complexes in the mind of a child, through unnecessary criticism. Employers who understand human nature, get the best there is in men, not by criticism, but by constructive suggestion. Parents may accomplish the same results with their children. Criticism will plant fear in the human heart, or resentment, but it will not build love or affection.

Symptoms of the Fear of Criticism

This fear is almost as universal as the fear of poverty, and its effects are just as fatal to personal achievement, mainly because this fear destroys initiative, and discourages the use of imagination. The major symptoms of the fear are:

SELF-CONSCIOUSNESS. Generally expressed through nervousness, timidity in conversation and in meeting strangers, awkward movement of the hands and limbs, shifting of the eyes.

LACK OF POISE. Expressed through lack of voice control, nervousness in the presence of others, poor posture of body, poor memory.

PERSONALITY. Lacking in firmness of decision, personal charm, and ability to express opinions definitely. The habit of sidestepping issues instead of meeting them squarely. Agreeing with others without careful examination of their opinions.

INFERIORITY COMPLEX. The habit of expressing self-approval by word of mouth and by actions, as a means of covering up a feeling of inferiority. Using "big words" to impress others (often without knowing the real meaning of the words). Imitating others in dress, speech and manners. Boasting of imaginary achievements. This sometimes gives a surface appearance of a feeling of superiority.

EXTRAVAGANCE. The habit of trying to "keep up with the Joneses," spending beyond one's income.

LACK OF INITIATIVE. Failure to embrace opportunities for self-advancement, fear to express opinions, lack of confidence in ones own ideas, giving evasive answers to questions asked by superiors, hesitancy of manner and speech, deceit in both words and deeds.

LACK OF AMBITION. Mental and physical laziness, lack of self-assertion, slowness in reaching decisions, easily influenced by others, the habit of criticising others behind their backs and flattering them to their faces, the habit of accepting defeat without protest, quitting an undertaking when opposed by others, suspicious of other people without cause, lacking in tactfulness of manner and speech, unwillingness to accept the blame for mistakes.

THE FEAR OF ILL HEALTH

This fear may be traced to both physical and social heredity. It is closely associated, as to its origin, with the causes of fear of Old Age and the fear of Death, because it leads one closely to the border of "terrible worlds" of which man knows not, but concerning which he has been taught some discomforting stories. The opinion is somewhat general, also, that certain unethical people engaged in the business of "selling health" have had not a little to do with keeping alive the fear of ill health.

In the main, man fears ill health because of the terrible pictures which have been planted in his mind of what may happen if death should overtake him. He also fears it because of the economic toll which it may claim.

A reputable physician estimated that 75% of all people who visit physicians for professional service are suffering with hypochondria (imaginary illness). It has been shown most convincingly that the fear of disease, even where there is not the slightest cause for fear, often produces the physical symptoms of the disease feared.

Powerful and mighty is the human mind! It builds or it destroys.

Playing upon this common weakness of fear of ill health, dispensers of patent medicines have reaped fortunes. This form of imposition upon credulous humanity became so prevalent some twenty years ago that *Colliers' Weekly Magazine* conducted a bitter campaign against some of the worst offenders in the patent medicine business.

During the "flu" epidemic which broke out during the world war, the mayor of New York City took drastic steps to check the damage which people were doing themselves through their inherent fear of ill health. He called in the newspaper men and said to them, "Gentlemen, I feel it necessary to ask you not to publish any *scare headlines* concerning the 'flu' epidemic. Unless you cooperate with me, we will have a situation which we cannot control." The newspapers quit publishing stories about the "flu," and within one month the epidemic had been successfully checked.

Through a series of experiments conducted some years ago, it was proved that people may be made ill by suggestion. We conducted this experiment by causing three acquaintances to visit the "victims," each of whom asked the question, "What ails you? You look terribly ill." The first questioner usually provoked a grin, and a nonchalant "Oh, nothing, I'm alright," from the victim. The second questioner usually was answered with the statement, "I don't know exactly, but I do feel badly." The third questioner was usually met with the frank admission that the victim was actually feeling ill.

Try this on an acquaintance if you doubt that it will make him uncomfortable, but do not carry the experiment too far. There is a certain religious sect whose members take vengeance upon their enemies by the "hexing" method. They call it "placing a spell" on the victim.

There is overwhelming evidence that disease sometimes begins in the form of negative thought impulse. Such an impulse may be passed from one mind to another, by suggestion, or created by an individual in his own mind.

A man who was blessed with more wisdom than this incident might indicate, once said, "When anyone asks me how I feel, I always want to answer by knocking him down."

Doctors send patients into new climates for their health, because a change of "mental attitude" is necessary. The seed of fear of ill health lives in every human mind. Worry, fear, discouragement, disappointment in love and business affairs, cause this seed to germinate and grow. The recent business depression kept the doctors on the run, because every form of negative thinking may cause ill health.

Disappointments in business and in love stand at the head of the list of causes of fear of ill health. A young man suffered a disappointment in love which sent him to a hospital. For months he hovered between life and death. A specialist in suggestive therapeutics was called in. The specialist changed nurses, placing him in charge of a very *charming young woman* who began (by pre-arrangement with the doctor) to make love to him the first day of her arrival on the job. Within three weeks the patient was discharged from the hospital, still suffering, but with an entirely different malady. He was in love again. The remedy was a hoax, but the patient and the nurse were later married. Both are in good health at the time of this writing.

Symptoms of the Fear of Ill Health

The symptoms of this almost universal fear are:

AUTO-SUGGESTION. The habit of negative use of self-suggestion by looking for, and expecting to find the symptoms of all kinds of disease. "Enjoying" imaginary illness and speaking of it as being real. The habit of trying all "fads" and "isms" recommended by others as having therapeutic value. Talking to others of operations, accidents and other forms of illness. Experimenting with diets, physical exercises, reducing systems, without professional guidance. Trying home remedies, patent medicines and "quack" remedies.

HYPOCHONDRIA. The habit of talking of illness, concentrating the mind upon disease, and expecting its appearance until a nervous break occurs. Nothing that comes in bottles can cure this condition. It is brought on by negative thinking and nothing but positive thought can affect a cure. Hypochondria (a medical term for imaginary disease) is said to do as much damage on occasion, as the disease one fears might do. Most so-called cases of "nerves" come from imaginary illness.

EXERCISE. Fear of ill health often interferes with proper physical exercise, and results in over-weight, by causing one to avoid outdoor life.

SUSCEPTIBILITY. Fear of ill health breaks down Nature's body resistance, and creates a favorable condition for any form of disease one may contact.

The fear of ill health often is related to the fear of Poverty, especially in the case of the hypochondriac, who constantly worries about the possibility of having to pay doctor's bills, hospital bills, etc. This type of person spends much time preparing for sickness, talking about death, saving money for cemetery lots, and burial expenses, etc.

SELF-CODDLING. The habit of making a bid for sympathy, using imaginary illness as the lure. (People often resort to this trick to avoid work.) The habit of feigning illness to cover plain laziness, or to serve as an alibi for lack of ambition.

INTEMPERANCE. The habit of using alcohol or narcotics to destroy pains such as headaches, neuralgia, etc., instead of eliminating the cause.

The habit of reading about illness and worrying over the possibility of being stricken by it. The habit of reading patent medicine advertisements.

THE FEAR OF LOSS OF LOVE

The original source of this inherent fear needs but little description, because it obviously grew out of man's polygamous habit of stealing his fellow man's mate, and his habit of taking liberties with her whenever he could.

Jealousy, and other similar forms of dementia praecox grow out of man's inherited fear of the loss of love of someone. This fear is the most painful of all the six basic fears. It probably plays more havoc with the body and mind than any of the other basic fears, as it often leads to permanent insanity.

The fear of the loss of love probably dates back to the stone age, when men stole women by brute force. They continue to steal females, but their technique has changed. Instead of force, they now use persuasion, the promise of pretty clothes, motor cars, and other "bait" much more effective than physical force. Man's habits are the same as they were at the dawn of civilization, but he expresses them differently.

Careful analysis has shown that women are more susceptible to this fear than men. This fact is easily explained. Women have learned, from experience, that men are polygamous by nature, that they are not to be trusted in the hands of rivals.

Symptoms of the Fear of Loss of Love

The distinguishing symptoms of this fear are:—

JEALOUSY. The habit of being suspicious of friends and loved ones without any reasonable evidence of sufficient grounds. (Jealousy is a form of dementia praecox which sometimes becomes violent without the slightest cause.) The habit of accusing wife or husband of infidelity without grounds. General suspicion of everyone, absolute faith in no one.

FAULT FINDING. The habit of finding fault with friends, relatives, business associates and loved ones upon the slightest provocation, or without any cause whatsoever.

GAMBLING. The habit of gambling, stealing, cheating, and otherwise taking hazardous chances to provide money for loved ones, with the belief that love can be bought. The habit of spending beyond one's means, or incurring debts, to provide gifts for loved ones, with the object of making a favorable showing. Insomnia, nervousness, lack of persistence, weakness of will, lack of self-control, lack of self-reliance, bad temper.

THE FEAR OF OLD AGE

In the main, this fear grows out of two sources. First, the thought that old age may bring with it poverty. Secondly, and by far the most common source of origin, from false and cruel teachings of the past which have been too well mixed with "fire and brimstone," and other bogies cunningly designed to enslave man through fear.

In the basic fear of old age, man has two very sound reasons for his apprehension—one growing out of his distrust of his fellowman, who may seize whatever worldly goods he may possess, and the other arising from the terrible pictures of the world beyond, which were planted in his mind, through social heredity before he came into full possession of his mind.

The possibility of ill health, which is more common as people grow older, is also a contributing cause of this common fear of old age. Eroticism also enters into the cause of the fear of old age, as no man cherishes the thought of diminishing sex attraction.

The most common cause of fear of old age is associated with the possibility of poverty. "Poorhouse" is not a pretty word. It throws a chill into the mind of every person who faces the possibility of having to spend his declining years on a poor farm.

Another contributing cause of the fear of old age is the possibility of loss of freedom and independence, as old age may bring with it the loss of both physical and economic freedom.

Symptoms of the Fear of Old Age

The commonest symptoms of this fear are:

The tendency to slow down and develop an inferiority complex at the age of mental maturity, around the age of forty, falsely believing oneself to be "slipping" because of age. (The truth is that man's most useful years, mentally and spiritually, are those between forty and sixty.)

The habit of speaking apologetically of one's self as "being old" merely because one has reached the age of forty, or fifty, instead of reversing the rule and expressing gratitude for having reached the age of wisdom and understanding.

The habit of killing off initiative, imagination, and self-reliance by falsely believing one's self too old to exercise these qualities. The habit of the man or woman of forty dressing with the aim of trying to appear much younger, and affecting mannerisms of youth; thereby inspiring ridicule by both friends and strangers.

THE FEAR OF DEATH

To some this is the cruelest of all the basic fears. The reason is obvious. The terrible pangs of fear associated with the thought of death, in the majority of cases, may be charged directly to religious fanaticism. So-called "heathen" are less afraid of death than the more "civilized." For hundreds of millions of years man has been asking the still-unanswered questions, "whence" and "whither." Where did I come from, and where am I going?

During the darker ages of the past, the more cunning and crafty were not slow to offer the answer to these questions, for a price. Witness, now, the major source of origin of the fear of death.

"Come into my tent, embrace my faith, accept my dogmas, and I will give you a ticket that will admit you straightaway into heaven when you die," cries a leader of sectarianism. "Remain out of my tent," says the same leader, "and may the devil take you and burn you throughout eternity."

Eternity is a long time. Fire is a terrible thing. The thought of eternal punishment, with fire, not only causes man to fear death, it often causes him to lose his reason. It destroys interest in life and makes happiness impossible.

During my research, I reviewed a book entitled A *Catalogue of the Gods,* in which were listed the *30,000 gods* which man has worshiped. Think of it! Thirty thousand of them, represented by everything from a crawfish to a man. It is little wonder that men have become frightened at the approach of death.

While the religious leader may not be able to provide safe conduct into heaven, nor, by lack of such provision, allow the unfortunate to descend into hell, the possibility of the latter seems so terrible that the very thought of it lays hold of the imagination in such a realistic way that it paralyzes reason, and sets up the fear of death.

In truth, no man knows, and no man has ever known, what heaven or hell is like, nor does any man know if either place actually exists. This very lack of positive knowledge opens the door of the human mind to the charlatan so he may enter and control that mind with his stock of legerdemain and various brands of pious fraud and trickery.

The fear of death is not as common now as it was during the age when there were no great colleges and universities. Men of science have turned the spotlight of truth upon the world, and this truth is rapidly freeing men and women from this terrible fear of death. The young men and young women who attend the colleges and universities are not easily impressed by "fire" and "brimstone." Through the aid of biology, astronomy, geology, and other related sciences, the fears of the dark ages which gripped the minds of men and destroyed their reason have been dispelled.

Insane asylums are filled with men and women who have gone mad, because of the fear of death.

This fear is useless. Death will come, no matter what anyone may think about it. Accept it as a necessity, and pass the thought out of your mind. It must be a necessity, or it would not come to all. Perhaps it is not as bad as it has been pictured.

The entire world is made up of only two things, energy and matter. In elementary physics we learn that neither matter nor energy (the only two realities known to man) can be created nor destroyed. Both matter and energy can be transformed, but neither can be destroyed.

Life is energy, if it is anything. If neither energy nor matter can be destroyed, of course life cannot be destroyed. Life, like other forms of energy, may be passed through various processes of transition, or change, but it cannot be destroyed. Death is mere transition.

If death is not mere change, or transition, then nothing comes after death except a long, eternal, peaceful sleep, and sleep is nothing to be feared. Thus you may wipe out, forever, the fear of Death.

Symptoms of the Fear of Death

The general symptoms of this fear are:—

The habit of thinking about dying instead of making the most of life, due, generally, to lack of purpose, or lack of a suitable occupation. This fear is more prevalent among the aged, but sometimes the more youthful are victims of it. The greatest of all remedies for the fear of death is a burning desire for achievement, backed by useful service to others. A busy person seldom has time to think about dying. He finds life too thrilling to worry about death. Sometimes the fear of death is closely associated with the Fear of Poverty, where one's death would leave loved ones poverty-stricken. In other cases, the fear of death is caused by illness and the consequent breaking down of physical body resistance. The commonest causes of the fear of death are: ill-health, poverty, lack of appropriate occupation, disappointment over love, insanity, religious fanaticism.

OLD MAN WORRY

Worry is a state of mind based upon fear. It works slowly, but persistently. It is insidious and subtle. Step by step it "digs itself in" until it paralyzes ones reasoning faculty, destroys self-confidence and initiative. Worry is a form of sustained fear caused by indecision therefore it is a state of mind which can be controlled.

An unsettled mind is helpless. Indecision makes an unsettled mind. Most individuals lack the willpower to reach decisions promptly, and to stand by them after they have been made, even during normal business conditions. During periods of economic unrest (such as the world recently experienced), the individual is handicapped, not alone by his inherent nature to be slow at reaching decisions, but he is influenced by the indecision of others around him who have created a state of "mass indecision."

During the depression the whole atmosphere, all over the world, was filled with "Fearenza" and "Worryitis," the two mental disease germs which began to spread themselves after the Wall Street frenzy in 1929. There is only one known antidote for these germs; it is the habit of prompt and firm decision. Moreover, it is an antidote which every individual must apply for himself.

We do not worry over conditions, once we have reached a decision to follow a definite line of action. I once interviewed a man who was to be electrocuted two hours later. The condemned man was the calmest of some eight men who were in the death-cell with him. His calmness prompted me to ask him how it felt to know that he was going into eternity in a short while. With a smile of confidence on his face, he said, "It feels fine. Just think, brother, my troubles will soon be over. I have had nothing but trouble all my life. It has been a hardship to get food and clothing. Soon I will not need these things. I have felt fine ever since I learned for certain that I must die. I made up my mind then, to accept my fate in good spirit."

As he spoke he devoured a dinner of proportions sufficient for three men, eating every mouthful of the food brought to him, and apparently enjoying it as much as if no disaster awaited him. Decision gave this man resignation to his fate! Decision can also prevent ones acceptance of undesired circumstances.

The six basic fears become translated into a state of worry, through indecision. Relieve yourself, forever of the fear of death, by reaching a decision to accept death as an inescapable event. Whip the fear of poverty by reaching a decision to get along with whatever wealth you can accumulate without worry. Put your foot upon the neck of the fear of criticism by reaching a decision not to worry about what other people think, do, or say. Eliminate the fear of old age by reaching a decision to accept it, not as a handicap, but as a great blessing which carries with it wisdom, self-control, and understanding not known to youth. Acquit yourself of the fear of ill health by the decision to forget symptoms.

Master the fear of loss of love by reaching a decision to get along without love, if that is necessary.

Kill the habit of worry, in all its forms, by reaching a general, blanket decision that nothing which life has to offer is worth the price of worry. With this decision will come poise, peace of mind, and calmness of thought which will bring happiness.

A man whose mind is filled with fear not only destroys his own chances of intelligent action, but, he transmits these destructive vibrations to the minds of all who come into contact with him, and destroys, also, their chances.

Even a dog or a horse knows when its master lacks courage; moreover, a dog or a horse will pick up the vibrations of fear thrown off by its master, and behave accordingly. Lower down the line of intelligence in the animal kingdom, one finds this same capacity to pick up the vibrations of fear. A honey-bee immediately senses fear in the mind of a person—for reasons unknown, a bee will sting the person whose mind is releasing vibrations of fear, much more readily than it will molest the person whose mind registers no fear.

The vibrations of fear pass from one mind to another just as quickly and as surely as the sound of the human voice passes from the broadcasting station to the receiving set of a radio—and by the self-same medium.

Mental telepathy is a reality. Thoughts pass from one mind to another, voluntarily, whether or not this fact is recognized by either the person releasing the thoughts, or the persons who pick up those thoughts.

The person who gives expression, by word of mouth, to negative or destructive thoughts is practically certain to experience the results of those words in the form of a destructive "kick-back." The release of destructive thought impulses, alone, without the aid of words, produces also a "kick-back" in more ways than one. First of all, and perhaps most important to be remembered, the person who releases thoughts of a destructive nature must suffer damage through the breaking down of the faculty of creative imagination. Secondly, the presence in the mind of any destructive emotion develops a negative personality which repels people, and often converts them into antagonists. The third source of damage to the person who entertains or releases negative thoughts, lies in this significant fact—these thought-impulses are not only damaging to others, but they imbed themselves in the subconscious mind of the person releasing them, and there become a part of his character.

One is never through with a thought, merely by releasing it. When a thought is released, it spreads in every direction, through the medium of the ether, but it also plants itself *permanently* in the subconscious mind of *the person releasing it.*

Your business in life is presumably to achieve success. To be successful, you must find peace of mind, acquire the material needs of life, and above all, attain happiness. All of these evidences of success begin in the form of thought impulses.

You may control your own mind, you have the power to feed it whatever thought impulses you choose. With this privilege goes also the responsibility of using it constructively. You are the master of your own earthly destiny just as surely as you have the power to control your own thoughts. You may influence, direct, and eventually control your own environment, making your life what you want it to be—or, you may neglect to exercise the privilege which is yours, to make your life to order, thus casting yourself upon the broad sea of "Circumstance" where you will be tossed hither and yon, like a chip on the waves of the ocean.

THE DEVIL'S WORKSHOP

The Seventh Basic Evil

In addition to the Six Basic Fears, there is another evil by which people suffer. It constitutes a rich soil in which the seeds of failure grow abundantly. It is so subtle that its presence often is not detected. This affliction cannot properly be classed as a fear. It is more deeply seated and more often fatal than all of the six fears. For want of a better name, let us call this evil susceptibility to negative influences.

Men who accumulate great riches always protect themselves against this evil! The poverty stricken never do! Those who succeed in any calling must prepare their minds to resist the evil. If you are reading this philosophy for the purpose of accumulating riches, you should examine yourself very carefully, to determine whether you are susceptible to negative influences. If you neglect this self-analysis, you will forfeit your right to attain the object of your desires.

Make the analysis searching. After you read the questions prepared for this self-analysis, hold yourself to a strict accounting in your answers. Go at the task as carefully as you would search for any other enemy you knew to be awaiting you in ambush and deal with your own faults as you would with a more tangible enemy.

You can easily protect yourself against highway robbers, because the law provides organized cooperation for your benefit, but the "seventh basic evil" is more difficult to master, because it strikes when you are not aware of its presence, when you are asleep, and while you are awake. Moreover, its weapon is intangible, because it consists of merely—a state of mind. This evil is also dangerous because it strikes in as many different forms as there are human experiences. Sometimes it enters the mind through the well-meant words of one's own relatives. At other times, it bores from within, through one's own mental attitude. Always it is as deadly as poison, even though it may not kill as quickly.

How to Protect Yourself Against Negative Influences

To protect yourself against negative influences, whether of your own making, or the result of the activities of negative people around you, recognize that you have a will-power, and put it into constant use, until it builds a wall of immunity against negative influences in your own mind.

Recognize the fact that you, and every other human being, are, by nature, lazy, indifferent, and susceptible to all suggestions which harmonize with your weaknesses.

Recognize that you are, by nature, susceptible to all the six basic fears, and set up habits for the purpose of counteracting all these fears.

Recognize that negative influences often work on you through your subconscious mind, therefore they are difficult to detect, and keep your mind closed against all people who depress or discourage you in any way.

Clean out your medicine chest, throw away all pill bottles, and stop pandering to colds, aches, pains and imaginary illness.

Deliberately seek the company of people who influence you to think and act for yourself.

Do not expect troubles as they have a tendency not to disappoint.

Without doubt, the most common weakness of all human beings is the habit of leaving their minds open to the negative influence of other people. This weakness is all the more damaging, because most people do not recognize that they are cursed by it, and many who acknowledge it, neglect or refuse to correct the evil until it becomes an uncontrollable part of their daily habits.

To aid those who wish to see themselves as they really are, the following list of questions has been prepared. Read the questions and state your answers aloud, so you can hear your own voice. This will make it easier for you to be truthful with yourself.

Self-Analysis Test Questions

Do you complain often of "feeling bad," and if so, what is the cause?

Do you find fault with other people at the slightest provocation?

Do you frequently make mistakes in your work, and if so, why?

Are you sarcastic and offensive in your conversation?

Do you deliberately avoid the association of anyone, and if so, why?

Do you suffer frequently with indigestion? If so, what is the cause?

Does life seem futile and the future hopeless to you? If so, why?

Do you like your occupation? If not, why?

Do you often feel self-pity, and if so why?

Are you envious of those who excel you?

To which do you devote most time, thinking of success, or of failure?

Are you gaining or losing self-confidence as you grow older?

Do you learn something of value from all mistakes? Are you permitting some relative or acquaintance to worry you? If so, why?

Are you sometimes "in the clouds" and at other times in the depths of despondency?

Who has the most inspiring influence upon you? What is the cause?

Do you tolerate negative or discouraging influences which you can avoid?

Are you careless of your personal appearance? If so, when and why?

Have you learned how to "drown your troubles" by being too busy to be annoyed by them?

Would you call yourself a "spineless weakling" if you permitted others to do your thinking for you?

Do you neglect internal bathing until auto-intoxication makes you ill-tempered and irritable?

How many preventable disturbances annoy you, and why do you tolerate them?

Do you resort to liquor, narcotics, or cigarettes to "quiet your nerves"? If so, why do you not try will-power instead?

Does anyone "nag" you, and if so, for what reason? Do you have a definite major purpose, and if so, what is it, and what plan have you for achieving it?

Do you suffer from any of the Six Basic Fears? If so, which ones?

Have you a method by which you can shield yourself against the negative influence of others?

Do you make deliberate use of auto-suggestion to make your mind positive?

Which do you value most, your material possessions, or your privilege of controlling your own thoughts?

Are you easily influenced by others, against your own judgment?

Has today added anything of value to your stock of knowledge or state of mind?

Do you face squarely the circumstances which make you unhappy, or sidestep the responsibility?

Do you analyze all mistakes and failures and try to profit by them or, do you take the attitude that this is not your duty?

Can you name three of your most damaging weaknesses? What are you doing to correct them?

Do you encourage other people to bring their worries to you for sympathy?

Do you choose, from your daily experiences, lessons or influences which aid in your personal advancement?

Does your presence have a negative influence on other people as a rule?

What habits of other people annoy you most?

Do you form your own opinions or permit yourself to be influenced by other people?

Have you learned how to create a mental state of mind with which you can shield yourself against all discouraging influences?

Does your occupation inspire you with faith and hope?

Are you conscious of possessing spiritual forces of sufficient power to enable you to keep your mind free from all forms of fear?

Does your religion help you to keep your own mind positive?

Do you feel it your duty to share other people's worries? If so, why?

If you believe that "birds of a feather flock together" what have you learned about yourself by studying the friends whom you attract?

What connection, if any, do you see between the people with whom you associate most closely, and any unhappiness you may experience?

Could it be possible that some person whom you consider to be a friend is, in reality, your worst enemy, because of his negative influence on your mind?

By what rules do you judge who is helpful and who is damaging to you?

Are your intimate associates mentally superior or inferior to you?

How much time out of every 24 hours do you devote to:

a. your occupation

b. sleep
c. play and relaxation
d. acquiring useful knowledge
e. plain waste

Who among your acquaintances,

a. encourages you most
b. cautions you most
c. discourages you most
d. helps you most in other ways

What is your greatest worry? Why do you tolerate it?

When others offer you free, unsolicited advice, do you accept it without question, or analyze their motive?

What, above all else, do you most desire? Do you intend to acquire it? Are you willing to subordinate all other desires for this one? How much time daily do you devote to acquiring it?

Do you change your mind often? If so, why?

Do you usually finish everything you begin?

Are you easily impressed by other people's business or professional titles, college degrees, or wealth? Are you easily influenced by what other people think or say of you?

Do you cater to people because of their social or financial status?

Whom do you believe to be the greatest person living? In what respect is this person superior to yourself?

How much time have you devoted to studying and answering these questions? (At least one day is necessary for the analysis and the answering of the entire list.)

If you have answered all these questions truthfully, you know more about yourself than the majority of people. Study the questions carefully, come back to them once each week for several months, and be astounded at the amount of additional knowledge of great value to yourself, you will have gained by the simple method of answering the questions truthfully. If you are not certain concerning the answers to some of the questions, seek the counsel of those who know you well, especially those who have no motive in flattering you, and see yourself through their eyes. The experience will be astonishing.

You have absolute control over but one thing, and that is your thoughts. This is the most significant and inspiring of all facts known to man! It reflects man's Divine nature. This Divine prerogative is the sole means by which you may control your own destiny. If you fail to control your own mind, you may be sure you will control nothing else.

If you must be careless with your possessions, let it be in connection with material things. *Your mind is your spiritual estate!* Protect and use it with the care to which Divine Royalty is entitled. You were given a will-power for this purpose.

Unfortunately, there is no legal protection against those who, either by design or ignorance, poison the minds of others by negative suggestion. This form of destruction should be punishable by heavy legal penalties, because it may and often does destroy one's chances of acquiring material things which are protected by law.

Men with negative minds tried to convince Thomas A. Edison that he could not build a machine that would record and reproduce the human voice, "because" they said, "no one else had ever produced such a machine." Edison did not believe them. He knew that the mind could produce anything the mind could conceive and believe, and that knowledge was the thing that lifted the great Edison above the common herd.

Men with negative minds told F. W. Woolworth he would go "broke" trying to run a store on five and ten cent sales. He did not believe them. He knew that he could do anything, within reason, if he backed his plans with faith. Exercising his right to keep other men's negative suggestions out of his mind, he piled up a fortune of more than a hundred million dollars.

Men with negative minds told George Washington he could not hope to win against the vastly superior forces of the British, but he exercised his Divine right to believe, therefore this book was published under the protection of the Stars and Stripes, while the name of Lord Cornwallis has been all but forgotten.

Doubting Thomases scoffed scornfully when Henry Ford tried out his first crudely built automobile on the streets of Detroit. Some said the thing never would become practical. Others said no one would pay money for such a contraption. Ford said, "I'll belt the earth with dependable motor cars," and he did! His decision to trust his own judgment has already piled up a fortune far greater than the next five generations of his descendents can squander. For the benefit of those seeking vast riches, let it be remembered that practically the sole difference between Henry Ford and a majority of the more than one hundred thousand men who work for him, is this—Ford has a mind and controls it, the others have minds which they do not try to control.

Henry Ford has been repeatedly mentioned, because he is an astounding example of what a man with a mind of his own, and a will to control it, can accomplish. His record knocks the foundation from under that time-worn alibi, "I never had a chance." Ford never had a chance, either, but he created an opportunity and backed it with persistence until it made him richer than Croesus.

Mind control is the result of self-discipline and habit. You either control your mind or it controls you. There is no half-way compromise. The most practical of all methods for controlling the mind is the habit of keeping it busy with a definite purpose, backed by a definite plan. Study the record of any man who achieves noteworthy success, and you will observe that he has control over his own mind, moreover, that he exercises that control and directs it toward the attainment of definite objectives. Without this control, success is not possible.

"FIFTY-SEVEN" FAMOUS ALIBIS

By Old Man IF

People who do not succeed have one distinguishing trait in common. They know *all the reasons for failure,* and have what they believe to be air-tight alibis to explain away their own lack of achievement.

Some of these alibis are clever, and a few of them are justifiable by the facts. But alibis cannot be used for money. The world wants to know only one thing—have you achieved success?

A character analyst compiled a list of the most commonly used alibis. As you read the list, examine yourself carefully, and determine how many of these alibis, if any, are your own property. Remember, too, the philosophy presented in this book makes every one of these alibis obsolete.

IF I didn't have a wife and family . . .
IF I had enough "pull" . . .
IF I had money . . .
IF I had a good education . . .
IF I could get a job . . .
IF I had good health . . .
IF I only had time . . .
IF times were better . . .
IF other people understood me . . .
IF conditions around me were only different . . .
IF I could live my life over again . . .
IF I did not fear what "they" would say. . .
IF I had been given a chance . . .
IF I now had a chance . . .
IF other people didn't "have it in for me" . . .
IF nothing happens to stop me . . .
IF I were only younger . . .
IF I could only do what I want. . .
IF I had been born rich . . .
IF I could meet "the right people" . . .
IF I had the talent that some people have . . .
IF I dared assert myself. . .
IF I only had embraced past opportunities . . .
IF people didn't get on my nerves . . .
IF I didn't have to keep house and look after the children . . .
IF I could save some money . . .
IF the boss only appreciated me . . .
IF I only had somebody to help me . . .
IF my family understood me . . .
IF I lived in a big city . . .
IF I could just get started . . .
IF I were only free . . .
IF I had the personality of some people . . .
IF I were not so fat . . .
IF my talents were known . . .
IF I could just get a "break" . . .
IF I could only get out of debt . . .

IF I hadn't failed . . .
IF I only knew how . . .
IF everybody didn't oppose me . . .
IF I didn't have so many worries . . .
IF I could marry the right person . . .
IF people weren't so dumb . . .
IF my family were not so extravagant . . .
IF I were sure of myself. . .
IF luck were not against me . . .
IF I had not been born under the wrong star . . .
IF it were not true that "what is to be will be" . . .
IF I did not have to work so hard . . .
IF I hadn't lost my money . . .
IF I lived in a different neighborhood . . .
IF I didn't have a "past" . . .
IF I only had a business of my own . . .
IF other people would only listen to me . . .
IF * * * and this is the greatest of them all * * *

> I had the courage to see myself as I really am, I would *find out what is wrong with me, and correct it,* then I might have a chance to profit by my mistakes and learn something from the experience of others, for I know that there is something wrong with me, or I would now be where *I would have been if* I had spent more time analyzing my weaknesses, and less time building alibis to cover them.

Building alibis with which to explain away failure is a national pastime. The habit is as old as the human race, and *is fatal to success!* Why do people cling to their pet alibis? The answer is obvious. They defend their alibis because they create them! A man's alibi is the child of his own imagination. It is human nature to defend one's own brain-child.

Building alibis is a deeply rooted habit. Habits are difficult to break, especially when they provide justification for something we do. Plato had this truth in mind when he said, "The first and best victory is to conquer self. To be conquered by self is, of all things, the most shameful and vile."

Another philosopher had the same thought in mind when he said, "It was a great surprise to me when I discovered that most of the ugliness I saw in others, was but a reflection of my own nature."

"It has always been a mystery to me," said Elbert Hubbard, "why people spend so much time deliberately fooling themselves by creating alibis to cover their weaknesses. If used differently, this same time would be sufficient to cure the weakness, then no alibis would be needed."

In parting, I would remind you that "Life is a checkerboard, and the player opposite you is time. If you hesitate before moving, or neglect to move promptly, your men will be wiped off the board by time. You are playing against a partner who will not tolerate indecision!"

Previously you may have had a logical excuse for not having forced Life to come through with whatever you asked, but that alibi is now obsolete, because you are in possession of the Master Key that unlocks the door to Life's bountiful riches.

The Master Key is intangible, but it is powerful! It is the privilege of creating, *in your own mind,* a burning desire for a definite form of riches. There is no penalty for the use of the Key, but there is a price you must pay if you do not use it. The price is failure. There is a reward of stupendous proportions if you put the Key to use. It is the satisfaction that comes to all who *conquer self and force Life to pay whatever is asked.*

The reward is worthy of your effort. Will you make the start and be convinced?

"If we are related," said the immortal Emerson, "we shall meet." In closing, may I borrow his thought, and say, "If we are related, we have, through these pages, met."

2

ACRES OF DIAMONDS

RUSSELL H. CONWELL

(1921)

I am astonished that so many people should care to hear this story over again. Indeed, this lecture has become a study in psychology; it often breaks all rules of oratory, departs from the precepts of rhetoric, and yet remains the most popular of any lecture I have delivered in the fifty-seven years of my public life. I have sometimes studied for a year upon a lecture and made careful research, and then presented the lecture just once—never delivered it again. I put too much work on it. But this had no work on it—thrown together perfectly at random, spoken offhand without any special preparation, and it succeeds when the thing we study, work over, adjust to a plan, is an entire failure.

The "Acres of Diamonds" which I have mentioned through so many years are to be found in this city, and you are to find them. Many have found them. And what man has done, man can do. I could not find anything better to illustrate my thought than a story I have told over and over again, and which is now found in books in nearly every library.

In 1870 we went down the Tigris River. We hired a guide at Bagdad to show us Persepolis, Nineveh and Babylon, and the ancient countries of Assyria as far as the Arabian Gulf. He was well acquainted with the land, but he was one of those guides who love to entertain their patrons; he was like a barber that tells you many stories in order to keep your mind off the scratching and the scraping. He told me so many stories that I grew tired of his telling them and I refused to listen—looked away whenever he commenced; that made the guide quite angry.

I remember that toward evening he took his Turkish cap off his head and swung it around in the air. The gesture I did not understand and I did not dare look at him for fear I should become the victim of another story. But, although I am not a woman, I did look, and the instant I turned my eyes upon that worthy guide he was off again. Said he, "I will tell you a story now which I reserve for my particular friends!" So then, counting myself a particular friend, I listened, and I have always been glad I did.

He said there once lived not far from the River Indus an ancient Persian by the name of Al Hafed. He said that Al Hafed owned a very large farm with orchards, grain fields and gardens. He was a contented and wealthy man—contented because he was wealthy, and wealthy because he was contented. One day there visited this old farmer one of those ancient Buddhist priests, and he sat down by Al Hafed's fire and told that old farmer how this world of ours was made.

He said that this world was once a mere bank of fog, which is scientifically true, and he said that the Almighty thrust his finger into the bank of fog and then began slowly to move his finger around and gradually to increase the speed of his finger until at last he whirled that bank of fog into a solid ball of fire, and it went rolling through the universe, burning its way through other cosmic banks of fog, until it condensed the moisture without, and fell in floods of rain upon the heated surface and cooled the outward crust. Then the internal flames burst through the cooling crust and threw up the mountains and made the hills and the valleys of this wonderful world of ours. If this internal melted mass burst out and cooled very quickly it became granite; that which cooled less quickly became silver; and less quickly, gold; and after gold diamonds were made. Said the old priest, "A diamond is a congealed drop of sunlight."

This is a scientific truth also. You all know that a diamond is pure carbon, actually deposited sunlight—and he said another thing I would not forget: he declared that a diamond is the last and highest of God's mineral creations, as a woman is the last and highest of God's animal creations. I suppose that is the reason why the two have such a liking for each other. And the old priest told Al Hafed that if he had a handful of diamonds he could purchase a whole country, and with a mine of diamonds he could place his children upon thrones through the influence of their great wealth.

Al Hafed heard all about diamonds and how much they were worth, and went to his bed that night a poor man—not that he had lost anything, but poor because he was discontented and discontented because he thought he was poor. He said: "I want a mine of diamonds!" So he lay awake all night, and early in the morning sought out the priest.

Now I know from experience that a priest when awakened early in the morning is cross. He awoke that priest out of his dreams and said to him, "Will you tell me where I can find diamonds?" The priest said, "Diamonds? What do you want with diamonds?" "I want to be immensely rich," said Al Hafed, "but I don't know where to go." "Well," said the priest, "if you will find a river that runs over white sand between high mountains, in those sands you will always see diamonds." "Do you really believe that there is such a river?" "Plenty of them, plenty of them; all you have to do is just go and find them, then you have them." Al Hafed said, "I will go." So he sold his farm, collected his money at interest, left his family in charge of a neighbor, and away he went in search of diamonds.

He began very properly, to my mind, at the Mountains of the Moon. Afterwards he went around into Palestine, then wandered on into Europe, and at last, when his money was all spent, and he was in rags, wretchedness and poverty, he stood on the shore of that bay in Barcelona, Spain, when a tidal wave came rolling in through the Pillars of Hercules and the poor, afflicted, suffering man could not resist the awful temptation to cast himself into that incoming tide, and he sank beneath its foaming crest, never to rise in this life again.

When that old guide had told me that very sad story, he stopped the camel I was riding and went back to fix the baggage on one of the other camels, and I remember thinking to myself, "Why did he reserve that for his particular friends?" There seemed to be no beginning, middle or end—nothing to it. That was the first story I ever heard told or read in which the hero was killed in the first chapter. I had but one chapter of that story and the hero was dead.

When the guide came back and took up the halter of my camel again, he went right on with the same story. He said that Al Hafed's successor led his camel out into the garden to drink, and as that camel put its nose down into the clear water of the garden brook Al Hafed's successor noticed a curious flash of light from the sands of the shallow stream, and reaching in he pulled out a black stone having an eye of light that reflected all the colors of the rainbow, and he took that curious pebble into the house and left it on the mantel, then went on his way and forgot all about it.

A few days after that, this same old priest who told Al Hafed how diamonds were made, came in to visit his successor, when he saw that flash of light from the mantel. He rushed up and said, "Here is a diamond—here is a diamond! Has Al Hafed returned?" "No, no; Al Hafed has not returned and that is not a diamond; that is nothing but a stone; we found it right out here in our garden." "But I know a diamond when I see it," said he; "that is a diamond!"

Then together they rushed to the garden and stirred up the white sands with their fingers and found others more beautiful, more valuable diamonds than the first, and thus, said the guide to me, were discovered the diamond mines of Golconda, the most magnificent diamond mines in all the history of mankind, exceeding the Kimberley in its value. The great Kohinoor diamond in England's crown jewels and the largest crown diamond on earth in Russia's crown jewels, which I had often hoped she would have to sell before they had peace with Japan, came from that mine, and when the old guide had called my attention to that wonderful discovery he took his Turkish cap off his head again and swung it around in the air to call my attention to the moral.

Those Arab guides have a moral to each story, though the stories are not always moral. He said had Al Hafed remained at home and dug in his own cellar or in his own garden, instead of wretchedness, starvation, poverty and death—a strange land, he would have had "acres of diamonds"—for every acre, yes, every shovelful of that old farm afterwards revealed the gems which since have decorated the crowns of monarchs. When he had given the moral to his story, I saw why he had reserved this story for his "particular friends." I didn't tell him I could see it; I was not going to tell that old Arab that I could see it. For it was that mean old Arab's way of going around such a thing, like a lawyer, and saying indirectly what he did not dare say directly, that there was a certain young man that day traveling down the Tigris River that might better be at home in America. I didn't tell him I could see it.

I told him his story reminded me of one, and I told it to him quick. I told him about that man out in California, who, in 1847, owned a ranch out there. He read that gold had been discovered in Southern California, and he sold his ranch to Colonel Sutter and started off to hunt for gold. Colonel Sutter put a mill on the little stream in that farm and one day his little girl brought some wet sand from the raceway of the mill into the house and placed it before the fire to dry, and as that sand was falling through the little girl's fingers a visitor saw the first shining scales of real gold that were ever discovered in California; and the man who wanted the gold had sold his ranch and gone away, never to return.

I delivered this lecture two years ago in California, in the city that stands near that farm, and they told me that the mine is not exhausted yet, and that a one-third owner of that farm has been getting during these recent years twenty dollars of gold every fifteen minutes of his life, sleeping or waking. Why, you and I would enjoy an income like that!

But the best illustration that I have now of this thought was found here in Pennsylvania. There was a man living in Pennsylvania who owned a farm here and he did what I should do if I had a farm in Pennsylvania—he sold it. But before he sold it he concluded to secure employment collecting coal oil for his cousin in Canada. They first discovered coal oil there. So this farmer in Pennsylvania decided that he would apply for a position with his cousin in Canada. Now, you see, the farmer was not altogether a foolish man. He did not leave his farm until he had something else to do.

Of all the simpletons the stars shine on there is none more foolish than a man who leaves one job before he has obtained another. And that has especial reference to gentlemen of my profession, and has no reference to a man seeking a divorce. So I say this old farmer did not leave one job until he had obtained another. He wrote to Canada, but his cousin replied that he could not engage him because he did not know anything about the oil business. "Well, then," said he, "I will understand it." So he set himself at the study of the whole subject. He began at the second day of the creation, he studied the subject from the primitive vegetation to the coal oil stage, until he knew all about it. Then he wrote to his cousin and said, "Now I understand the oil business." And his cousin replied to him, "All right, then, come on."

That man, by the record of the country, sold his farm for eight hundred and thirty-three dollars—even money, "no cents." He had scarcely gone from that farm before the man who purchased it went out to arrange for watering the cattle and he found that the previous owner had arranged the matter very nicely. There is a stream running down the hillside there, and the previous owner had gone out and put a plank across that stream at an angle, extending across the brook and down edgewise a few inches under the surface of the water. The purpose of the plank across that brook was to throw over to the other bank a dreadful-looking scum through which the cattle would not put their noses to drink above the plank, although they would drink the water on one side below it.

Thus that man who had gone to Canada had been himself damming back for twenty-three years a flow of coal oil which the State Geologist of Pennsylvania declared officially, as early as 1870, was then worth to our state a hundred millions of dollars. The city of Titusville now stands on that farm and those Pleasantville wells flow on, and that farmer who had studied all about the formation of oil since the second day of God's creation clear down to the present time, sold that farm for $833, no cents—again I say, "no sense."

But I need another illustration, and I found that in Massachusetts, and I am sorry I did, because that is my old state. This young man I mention went out of the state to study—went down to Yale College and studied mines and mining. They paid him fifteen dollars a week during his last year for training students who were behind their classes in mineralogy, out of hours, of course, while pursuing his own studies. But when he graduated they raised his pay from fifteen dollars to forty-five dollars and offered him a professorship. Then he went straight home to his mother and said, "Mother, I won't work for forty-five dollars a week. What is forty-five dollars a week for a man with a brain like mine! Mother, let's go out to California and stake out gold claims and be immensely rich." "Now," said his mother, "it is just as well to be happy as it is to be rich."

But as he was the only son he had his way—they always do; and they sold out in Massachusetts and went to Wisconsin, where he went into the employ of the Superior Copper Mining Company, and he was lost from sight in the employ of that company at fifteen dollars a week again. He was also to have an interest in any mines that he should discover for that company. But I do not believe that he has ever discovered a mine—I do not know anything about it, but I do not believe he has. I know he had scarcely gone from the old homestead before the farmer who had bought the homestead went out to dig potatoes, and he was bringing them in a large basket through the front gateway, the ends of the stone wall came so near together at the gate that the basket hugged very tight. So he set the basket on the ground and pulled, first on one side and then on the other side.

Our farms in Massachusetts are mostly stone walls, and the farmers have to be economical with their gateways in order to have some place to put the stones. That basket hugged so tight there that as he was hauling it through he noticed in the upper stone next the gate a block of native silver, eight inches square; and this professor of mines and mining and mineralogy, who would not work for forty-five dollars a week, when he sold that homestead in Massachusetts, sat right on that stone to make the bargain. He was brought up there; he had gone back and forth by that piece of silver, rubbed it with his sleeve, and it seemed to say, "Come now, now, now, here is a hundred thousand dollars. Why not take me? But he would not take it. There was no silver in Newburyport; it was all away off—well, I don't know where; he didn't, but somewhere else—and he was a professor of mineralogy.

I do not know of anything I would enjoy better than to take the whole time tonight telling of blunders like that I have heard professors make. Yet I wish I knew what that man is doing out there in Wisconsin. I can imagine him out there, as he sits by his fireside, and he is saying to his friends. "Do you know that man Conwell that lives in Philadelphia?" "Oh, yes, I have heard of him." "And do you know that man Jones that lives in that city?" "Yes, I have heard of him." And then he begins to laugh and laugh and says to his friends, "They have done the same thing I did, precisely." And that spoils the whole joke, because you and I have done it.

Ninety out of every hundred people here have made that mistake this very day. I say you ought to be rich; you have no right to be poor. To live in Philadelphia and not be rich is a misfortune, and it is doubly a misfortune, because you could have been rich just as well as be poor. Philadelphia furnishes so many opportunities. You ought to be rich. But persons with certain religious prejudice will ask, "How can you spend your time advising the rising generation to give their time to getting money—dollars and cents—the commercial spirit?"

Yet I must say that you ought to spend time getting rich. You and I know there are some things more valuable than money; of course, we do. Ah, yes! By a heart made unspeakably sad by a grave on which the autumn leaves now fall, I know there are some things higher and grander and sublimer than money. Well does the man know, who has suffered, that there are some things sweeter and holier and more sacred than gold. Nevertheless, the man of common sense also knows that there is not any one of those things that is not greatly enhanced by the use of money. Money is power.

Love is the grandest thing on God's earth, but fortunate the lover who has plenty of money. Money is power: money has powers; and for a man to say, "I do not want money," is to say, "I do not wish to do any good to my fellowmen." It is absurd thus to talk. It is absurd to disconnect them. This is a wonderfully great life, and you ought to spend your time getting money, because of the power there is in money. And yet this religious prejudice is so great that some people think it is a great honor to be one of God's poor. I am looking in the faces of people who think just that way.

I heard a man once say in a prayer-meeting that he was thankful that he was one of God's poor, and then I silently wondered what his wife would say to that speech, as she took in washing to support the man while he sat and smoked on the veranda. I don't want to see any more of that kind of God's poor. Now, when a man could have been rich just as well, and he is now weak because he is poor, he has done some great wrong; he has been untruthful to himself; he has been unkind to his fellowmen. We ought to get rich if we can by honorable and Christian methods, and these are the only methods that sweep us quickly toward the goal of riches.

I remember, not many years ago, a young theological student who came into my office and said to me that he thought it was his duty to come in and "labor with me." I asked him what had happened, and he said: "I feel it is my duty to come in and speak to you, sir, and say that the Holy Scriptures declare that money is the root of all evil." I asked him where he found that saying, and he said he found it in the Bible. I asked him whether he had made a new Bible, and he said, no, he had not gotten a new Bible, that it was in the old Bible. "Well," I said, "if it is in my Bible, I never saw it. Will you please get the textbook and let me see it?"

He left the room and soon came stalking in with his Bible open, with all the bigoted pride of the narrow sectarian, who founds his creed on some misinterpretation of Scripture, and he puts the Bible down on the table before me and fairly squealed into my ear, "There it is. You can read it for yourself." I said to him, "Young man, you will learn, when you get a little older, that you cannot trust another denomination to read the Bible for you." I said, "Now, you belong to another denomination. Please read it to me, and remember that you are taught in a school where emphasis is exegesis." So he took the Bible and read it: "The love of money is the root of all evil." Then he had it right.

The Great Book has come back into the esteem and love of the people, and into the respect of the greatest minds of earth, and now you can quote it and rest your life and your death on it without more fear. So, when he quoted right from the Scriptures he quoted the truth. "The love of money is the root of all evil." Oh, that is it. It is the worship of the means instead of the end. Though you cannot reach the end without the means. When a man makes an idol of the money instead of the purposes for which it may be used, when he squeezes the dollar until the eagle squeals, then it is made the root of all evil. Think, if you only had the money, what you could do for your wife, your child, and for your home and your city. Think how soon you could endow the Temple College yonder if you only had the money and the disposition to give it; and yet, my friend, people say you and I should not spend the time getting rich. How inconsistent the whole thing is. We ought to be rich, because money has power.

I think the best thing for me to do is to illustrate this, for if I say you ought to get rich, I ought, at least, to suggest how it is done. We get a prejudice against rich men because of the lies that are told about them. The lies that are told about Mr. Rockefeller because he has two hundred million dollars—so many believe them; yet how false is the representation of that man to the world. How little we can tell what is true nowadays when newspapers try to sell their papers entirely on some sensation! The way they lie about the rich men is something terrible, and I do not know that there is anything to illustrate this better than what the newspapers now say about the city of Philadelphia.

A young man came to me the other day and said, "If Mr. Rockefeller, as you think, is a good man, why is it that everybody says so much against him?" It is because he has gotten ahead of us; that is the whole of it—just gotten ahead of us. Why is it Mr. Carnegie is criticized so sharply by an envious world! Because he has gotten more than we have. If a man knows more than I know, don't I incline to criticize somewhat his learning? Let a man stand in a pulpit and preach to thousands, and if I have fifteen people in my church, and they're all asleep, don't I criticize him? We always do that to the man who gets ahead of us. Why, the man you are criticizing has one hundred millions, and you have fifty cents, and both of you have just what you are worth.

One of the richest men in this country came into my home and sat down in my parlor and said: "Did you see all those lies about my family in the papers?" "Certainly I did; I knew they were lies when I saw them." "Why do they lie about me the way they do?" "Well," I said to him, "if you will give me your check for one hundred millions, I will take all the lies along with it." "Well," said he, "I don't see any sense in their thus talking about my family and myself. Conwell, tell me frankly, what do you think the American people think of me?" "Well," said I, "they think you are the blackest hearted villain that ever trod the soil!" "But what can I do about it?" There is nothing he can do about it, and yet he is one of the sweetest Christian men I ever knew. If you get a hundred millions you will have the lies; you will be lied about, and you can judge your success in any line by the lies that are told about you. I say that you ought to be rich.

But there are ever coming to me young men who say, "I would like to go into business, but I cannot." "Why not?" "Because I have no capital to begin on." Capital, capital to begin on! What! young man! Living in Philadelphia and looking at this wealthy generation, all of whom began as poor boys, and you want capital to begin on? It is fortunate for you that you have no capital. I am glad you have no money. I pity a rich man's son. A rich man's son in these days of ours occupies a very difficult position. They are to be pitied. A rich man's son cannot know the very best things in human life. He cannot. The statistics of Massachusetts show us that not one out of seventeen rich men's sons ever die rich. They are raised in luxury, they die in poverty. Even if a rich man's son retains his father's money, even then he cannot know the best things of life.

A young man in our college yonder asked me to formulate for him what I thought was the happiest hour in a man's history, and I studied it long and came back convinced that the happiest hour that any man ever sees in any earthly matter is when a young man takes his bride over the threshold of the door, for the first time, of the house he himself has earned and built, when he turns to his bride and with an eloquence greater than any language of mine, he sayeth to his wife, "My loved one, I earned this home myself; I earned it all. It is all mine, and I divide it with thee." That is the grandest moment a human heart may ever see. But a rich man's son cannot know that. He goes into a finer mansion, it may be, but he is obliged to go through the house and say, "Mother gave me this, mother gave me that, my mother gave me that, my mother gave me that," until his wife wishes she had married his mother.

Oh, I pity a rich man's son. I do. Until he gets so far along in his dudeism that he gets his arms up like that and can't get them down. Didn't you ever see any of them astray at Atlantic City? I saw one of these scarecrows once and I never tire thinking about it. I was at Niagara Falls lecturing, and after the lecture I went to the hotel, and when I went up to the desk there stood there a millionaire's son from New York. He was an indescribable specimen of anthropologic potency. He carried a goldheaded cane under his arm—more in its head than he had in his. I do not believe I could describe the young man if I should try. But still I must say that he wore an eye-glass he could not see through; patent leather shoes he could not walk in, and pants he could not sit down in—dressed like a grasshopper!

Well, this human cricket came up to the clerk's desk just as I came in. He adjusted his unseeing eye-glass in this wise and lisped to the clerk, because it's "Hinglish, you know," to lisp: "Thir, thir, will you have the kindness to fuhnish me with thome papah and thome envelopehs!" The clerk measured that man quick, and he pulled out a drawer and took some envelopes and paper and cast them across the counter and turned away to his books.

You should have seen that specimen of humanity when the paper and envelopes came across the counter—he whose wants had always been anticipated by servants. He adjusted his unseeing eye-glass and he yelled after that clerk: "Come back here, thir, come right back here. Now, thir, will you order a thervant to take that papah and thothe envelopehs and carry them to yondah dethk." Oh, the poor, miserable, contemptible American monkey! He couldn't carry paper and envelopes twenty feet. I suppose he could not get his arms down. I have no pity for such travesties of human nature. If you have no capital, I am glad of it. You don't need capital; you need common sense, not copper cents.

A. T. Stewart, the great princely merchant of New York, the richest man in America in his time, was a poor boy; he had a dollar and a half and went into the mercantile business. But he lost eighty-seven and a half cents of his first dollar and a half because he bought some needles and thread and buttons to sell, which people didn't want.

Are you poor? It is because you are not wanted and are left on your own hands. There was the great lesson. Apply it whichever way you will it comes to every single person's life, young or old. He did not know what people needed, and consequently bought something they didn't want, and had the goods left on his hands a dead loss. A. T. Stewart learned there the great lesson of his mercantile life and said "I will never buy anything more until

I first learn what the people want; then I'll make the purchase." He went around to the doors and asked them what they did want, and when he found out what they wanted, he invested his sixty-two and a half cents and began to supply a "known demand." I care not what your profession or occupation in life may be; I care not whether you are a lawyer, a doctor, a housekeeper, teacher or whatever else, the principle is precisely the same. We must know what the world needs first and then invest ourselves to supply that need, and success is almost certain.

A. T. Stewart went on until he was worth forty millions. "Well," you will say, "a man can do that in New York, but cannot do it here in Philadelphia." The statistics very carefully gathered in New York in 1889 showed one hundred and seven millionaires in the city worth over ten millions apiece. It was remarkable and people think they must go there to get rich. Out of that one hundred and seven millionaires only seven of them made their money in New York, and the others moved to New York after their fortunes were made, and sixty-seven out of the remaining hundred made their fortunes in towns of less than six thousand people, and the richest man in the country at that time lived in a town of thirty-five hundred inhabitants, and always lived there and never moved away. It is not so much where you are as what you are. But at the same time if the largeness of the city comes into the problem, then remember it is the smaller city that furnishes the great opportunity to make the millions of money.

The best illustration that I can give is in reference to John Jacob Astor, who was a poor boy and who made all the money of the Astor family. He made more than his successors have ever earned, and yet he once held a mortgage on a millinery store in New York, and because the people could not make enough money to pay the interest and the rent, he foreclosed the mortgage and took possession of the store and went into partnership with the man who had failed. He kept the same stock, did not give them a dollar of capital, and he left them alone and he went out and sat down upon a bench in the park.

Out there on that bench in the park he had the most important, and, to my mind, the pleasantest part of that partnership business. He was watching the ladies as they went by; and where is the man that wouldn't get rich at that business? But when John Jacob Astor saw a lady pass, with her shoulders back and her head up, as if she did not care if the whole world looked on her, he studied her bonnet; and before that bonnet was out of sight he knew the shape of the frame and the color of the trimmings, the curl of the—something on a bonnet. Sometimes I try to describe a woman's bonnet, but it is of little use, for it would be out of style tomorrow night.

So John Jacob Astor went to the store and said: "Now, put in the show window just such a bonnet as I describe to you because," said he, "I have just seen a lady who likes just such a bonnet. Do not make up any more till I come back." And he went out again and sat on that bench in the park, and another lady of a different form and complexion passed him with a bonnet of different shape and color, of course. "Now," said he, "put such a bonnet as that in the show window."

He didn't fill his show window with hats and bonnets which drive people away and then sit in the back of the store and bawl because the people go somewhere else to trade. He didn't put a hat or bonnet in that show window the like of which he had not seen before it was made up.

In our city especially, there are great opportunities for manufacturing, and the time has come when the line is drawn very sharply between the stockholders of the factory and their employees. Now, friends, there has also come a discouraging gloom upon this country and the laboring men are beginning to feel that they are being held down by a crust over their heads through which they find it impossible to break, and the aristocratic moneyowner-himself is so far above that he will never descend to their assistance. That is the thought that is in the minds of our people. But, friends, never in the history of our country was there an opportunity so great for the poor man to get rich as there is now and in the city of Philadelphia. The very fact that they get discouraged is what prevents them from getting rich. That is all there is to it. The road is open, and let us keep it open between the poor and the rich.

I know that the labor unions have two great problems to contend with, and there is only one way to solve them. The labor unions are doing as much to prevent its solving as are capitalists today, and there are positively two sides to it. The labor union has two difficulties; the first one is that it began to make a labor scale for all classes on a par, and they scale down a man that can earn five dollars a day to two and a half a day, in order to level up to him an imbecile that cannot earn fifty cents a day. That is one of the most dangerous and discouraging things for the working man. He cannot get the results of his work if he do better work or higher work or work longer; that is a dangerous thing, and in order to get every laboring man free and every American equal to every other American, let the laboring man ask what he is worth and get it—not let any capitalist say to him: "You shall work for me for half of what you are worth"; nor let any labor organization say: "You shall work for the capitalist for half your worth."

Be a man, be independent, and then shall the laboring man find the road ever open from poverty to wealth.

The other difficulty that the labor union has to consider, and this problem they have to solve themselves, is the kind of orators who come and talk to them about the oppressive rich. I can in my dreams recite the oration I have heard again and again under such circumstances. My life has been with the laboring man. I am a laboring man myself. I have often, in their assemblies, heard the speech of the man who has been invited to address the labor union. The man gets up before the assembled company of honest laboring men and he begins by saying: "Oh, ye honest, industrious laboring men, who have furnished all the capital of the world, who have built all the palaces and constructed all the railroads and covered the ocean with her steamships. Oh, you laboring men! You are nothing but slaves; you are ground down in the dust by the capitalist who is gloating over you as he enjoys his beautiful estates and as he has his banks filled with gold, and every dollar he owns is coined out of the heart's blood of the honest laboring man." Now, that is a lie, and you know it is a lie; and yet that is the kind of speech that they are hearing all the time, representing the capitalists as wicked and the laboring man so enslaved.

Why, how wrong it is! Let the man who loves his flag and believes in American principles endeavor with all his soul to bring the capitalists and the laboring man together until they stand side by side, and arm in arm, and work for the common good of humanity.

He is an enemy to his country who sets capital against labor or labor against capital. Suppose I were to go down through this audience and ask you to introduce me to the great inventors who live here in Philadelphia. "The inventors of Philadelphia," you would say, "why, we don't have any in Philadelphia. It is too slow to invent anything." But you do have just as great inventors, and they are here in this audience, as ever invented a machine. But the probability is that the greatest inventor to benefit the world with his discovery is some person, perhaps some lady, who thinks she could not invent anything.

Did you ever study the history of invention and see how strange it was that the man who made the greatest discovery did it without any previous idea that he was an inventor? Who are the great inventors? They are persons with plain, straightforward common sense, who saw a need in the world and immediately applied themselves to supply that need. If you want to invent anything, don't try to find it in the wheels in your head nor the wheels in your machine, but first find out what the people need, and then apply yourself to that need, and this leads to invention on the part of people you would not dream of before. The great inventors are simply great men; the greater the man the more simple the man; and the more simple a machine, the more valuable it is.

Did you ever know a really great man? His ways are so simple, so common, so plain, that you think any one could do what he is doing. So it is with the great men the world over. If you know a really great man, a neighbor of yours, you can go right up to him and say, "How are you, Jim, good morning, Sam." Of course you can, for they are always so simple.

When I wrote the life of General Garfield, one of his neighbors took me to his back door, and shouted, "Jim, Jim, Jim!" and very soon "Jim" came to the door and General Garfield let me in—one of the grandest men of our century. The great men of the world are ever so. I was down in Virginia and went up to an educational institution and was directed to a man who was setting out a tree. I approached him and said, "Do you think it would be possible for me to see General Robert E. Lee, the President of the University?" He said. "Sir, I am General Lee." Of course, when you meet such a man, so noble a man as that, you will find him a simple, plain man. Greatness is always just so modest and great inventions are simple.

I asked a class in school once who were the great inventors, and a little girl popped up and said, "Columbus." Well, now, she was not so far wrong. Columbus bought a farm and he carried on that farm just as I carried on my father's farm. He took a hoe and went out and sat down on a rock. But Columbus, as he sat upon that shore and looked out upon the ocean, noticed that the ships, as they sailed away, sank deeper into the sea the farther they went. And since that time some other "Spanish ships" have sunk into the sea. But as Columbus noticed that the tops of the masts dropped down out of sight, he said: "That is the way it is with this hoe handle; if you go around this hoe handle, the farther off you go the farther down you go. I can sail around to the East Indies." How plain it all was. How simple the mind—majestic like the simplicity of a mountain in its greatness. Who are the great inventors? They are ever the simple, plain, everyday people who see the need and set about to supply it.

I was once lecturing in North Carolina, and the cashier of the bank sat directly behind a lady who wore a very large hat. I said to that audience, "Your wealth is too near to you; you are looking right over it." He whispered to his friend, "Well, then, my wealth is in that hat." A little later, as he wrote me, I said, "Wherever there is a human need there is a greater fortune than a mine can furnish." He caught my thought, and he drew up his plan for a better hat pin than was in the hat before him and the pin is now being manufactured. He was offered fifty-two thousand dollars for his patent. That man made his fortune before he got out of that hall. This is the whole question: Do you see a need?"

I remember well a man up in my native hills, a poor man, who for twenty years was helped by the town in his poverty, who owned a widespreading maple tree that covered the poor man's cottage like a benediction from on high. I remember that tree, for in the spring—there were some roguish boys around that neighborhood when I was young—in the spring of the year the man would put a bucket there and the spouts to catch the maple sap, and I remember where that bucket was; and when I was young the boys were, oh, so mean, that they went to that tree before that man had gotten out of bed in the morning, and after he had gone to bed at night, and drank up that sweet sap, I could swear they did it.

He didn't make a great deal of maple sugar from that tree. But one day he made the sugar so white and crystalline that the visitor did not believe it was maple sugar; thought maple sugar must be red or black. He said to the old man: "Why don't you make it that way and sell it for confectionery?" The old man caught his thought and invented the "rock maple crystal," and before that patent expired he had ninety thousand dollars and had built a beautiful palace on the site of that tree. After forty years owning that tree he awoke to find it had fortunes of money indeed in it. And many of us are right by the tree that has a fortune for us, and we own it, possess it, do what we will with it, but we do not learn its value because we do not see the human need, and in these discoveries and inventions that is one of the most romantic things of life. I have received letters from all over the country and from England, where I have lectured, saying that they have discovered this and that, and one man out in Ohio took me through his great factories last spring, and said that they cost him $680,000, and, said he, "I was not worth a cent in the world when I heard your lecture 'Acres of Diamonds'; but I made up my mind to stop right here and make my fortune here, and here it is." He showed me through his unmortgaged possessions. And this is a continual experience now as I travel through the country, after these many years. I mention this incident, not to boast, but to show you that you can do the same if you will.

Who are the great inventors? I remember a good illustration in a man who used to live in East Brookfield, Mass. He was a shoemaker, and he was out of work and he sat around the house until his wife told him "to go out doors." And he did what every husband is compelled by law to do—he obeyed his wife. And he went out and sat down on an ash barrel in his back yard. Think of it! Stranded on an ash barrel and the enemy in possession of the house! As he sat on that ash barrel, he looked down into that little brook which ran through that back yard into the meadows, and he saw a little trout go flashing up the stream and hiding under the bank. I do not suppose he thought of Tennyson's beautiful poem:

"Chatter, chatter as I flow,
To join the brimming river,

Men may come, and men
may go, But I go on forever."

But as this man looked into the brook, he leaped off that ash barrel and managed to catch the trout with his fingers, and sent it to Worcester. They wrote back that they would give a five-dollar bill for another such trout as that, not that it was worth that much, but they wished to help the poor man. So this shoemaker and his wife, now perfectly united, that five-dollar bill in prospect, went out to get another trout. They went up the stream to its source and down to the brimming river, but not another trout could they find in the whole stream; and so they came home disconsolate and went to the minister. The minister didn't know how trout grew, but he pointed the way. Said he, "Get Seth Green's book, and that will give you the information you want."

They did so, and found all about the culture of trout. They found that a trout lays thirty-six hundred eggs every year and every trout gains a quarter of a pound every year, so that in four years a little trout will furnish four tons per annum to sell to the market at fifty cents a pound. When they found that, they said they didn't believe any such story as that, but if they could get five dollars apiece they could make something. And right in that same back yard with the coal sifter up stream and window screen down the stream, they began the culture of trout. They afterwards moved to the Hudson, and since then he has become the authority in the United States upon the raising of fish, and he has been next to the highest on the United States Fish Commission in Washington. My lesson is that man's wealth was out here in his back yard for twenty years, but he didn't see it until his wife drove him out with a mop stick.

I remember meeting personally a poor carpenter of Hingham, Massachusetts, who was out of work and in poverty. His wife also drove him out of doors. He sat down on the shore and whittled a soaked shingle into a wooden chain. His children quarreled over it in the evening, and while he was whittling a second one, a neighbor came along and said, "Why don't you whittle toys if you can carve like that?" He said, "I don't know what to make!"

There is the whole thing. His neighbor said to him: "Why don't you ask your own children?" Said he, "What is the use of doing that? My children are different from other people's children." I used to see people like that when I taught school. The next morning when his boy came down the stairway, he said, "Sam, what do you want for a toy?" "I want a wheelbarrow." When his little girl came down, he asked her what she wanted, and she said, "I want a little doll's wash-stand, a little doll's carriage, a little doll's umbrella," and went on with a whole lot of things that would have taken his lifetime to supply. He consulted his own children right there in his own house and began to whittle out toys to please them.

He began with his jack-knife, and made those unpainted Hingham toys. He is the richest man in the entire New England States, if Mr. Lawson is to be trusted in his statement concerning such things, and yet that man's fortune was made by consulting his own children in his own house. You don't need to go out of your own house to find out what to invent or what to make. I always talk too long on this subject. I would like to meet the great men who are here tonight. The great men! We don't have any great men in Philadelphia. Great men! You say that they all come from London, or San Francisco, or Rome, or

Manayunk, or anywhere else but there—anywhere else but Philadelphia—and yet, in fact, there are just as great men in Philadelphia as in any city of its size. There are great men and women in this audience.

Great men, I have said, are very simple men. Just as many great men here as are to be found anywhere. The greatest error in judging great men is that we think that they always hold an office. The world knows nothing of its greatest men. Who are the great men of the world? The young man and young woman may well ask the question. It is not necessary that they should hold an office, and yet that is the popular idea. That is the idea we teach now in our high schools and common schools, that the great men of the world are those who hold some high office, and unless we change that very soon and do away with that prejudice, we are going to change to an empire. There is no question about it. We must teach that men are great only on their intrinsic value, and not on the position they may incidentally happen to occupy. And yet, don't blame the young men saying that they are going to be great when they get into some official position.

I ask this audience again who of you are going to be great? Says a young man: "I am going to be great." "When are you going to be great?" "When I am elected to some political office." Won't you learn the lesson, young man; that it is prima facie evidence of littleness to hold public office under our form of government? Think of it. This is a government of the people, and by the people, and for the people, and not for the officeholder, and if the people in this country rule as they always should rule, an officeholder is only the servant of the people, and the Bible says that "the servant cannot be greater than his master."

The Bible says that "he that is sent cannot be greater than he who sent him." In this country the people are the masters, and the officeholders can never be greater than the people; they should be honest servants of the people, but they are not our greatest men. Young man, remember that you never heard of a great man holding any political office in this country unless he took that office at an expense to himself. It is a loss to every great man to take a public office in our country. Bear this in mind, young man, that you cannot be made great by a political election.

Another young man says, "I am going to be a great man in Philadelphia some time." "Is that so? When are you going to be great?" "When there comes another war! When we get into difficulty with Mexico, or England, or Russia, or Japan, or with Spain again over Cuba, or with New Jersey, I will march up to the cannon's mouth, and amid the glistening bayonets I will tear down their flag from its staff, and I will come home with stars on my shoulders, and hold every office in the gift of the government, and I will be great." "No, you won't! No, you won't; that is no evidence of true greatness, young man." But don't blame that young man for thinking that way; that is the way he is taught in the high school. That is the way history is taught in college. He is taught that the men who held the office did all the fighting.

I remember we had a Peace Jubilee here in Philadelphia soon after the Spanish War. Perhaps some of these visitors think we should not have had it until now in Philadelphia, and as the great procession was going up Broad Street I was told that the tally-ho coach stopped right in front of my house, and on the coach was Hobson, and all the people threw up their hats and swung their handkerchiefs, and shouted "Hurrah for Hobson!" I would have yelled too, because he deserves much more of his country that he has ever received. But suppose I go into the high school tomorrow and ask, "Boys, who sunk the Merrimac?" If they answer me "Hobson," they tell me seven-eighths of a lie—seven-eighths of a lie, because there were eight men who sunk the Merrimac. The other seven men, by virtue of their position, were continually exposed to the Spanish fire while Hobson, as an officer, might reasonably be behind the smoke-stack.

Why, my friends, in this intelligent audience gathered here tonight I do not believe I could find a single person that can name the other seven men who were with Hobson. Why do we teach history in that way? We ought to teach that however humble the station a man may occupy, if he does his full duty in his place, he is just as much entitled to the American people's honor as is a king upon a throne. We do teach it as a mother did her little boy in New York when he said, "Mamma, what great building is that?" "That is General Grant's tomb." "Who was General Grant?" "He was the man who put down the rebellion." Is that the way to teach history?

Do you think we would have gained a victory if it had depended on General Grant alone. Oh, no. Then why is there a tomb on the Hudson at all? Why, not simply because General Grant was personally a great man himself, but that tomb is there because he was a representative man and represented two hundred thousand men who went down to death for this nation and many of them as great as General Grant. That is why that beautiful tomb stands on the heights over the Hudson.

I remember an incident that will illustrate this, the only one that I can give tonight. I am ashamed of it, but I don't dare leave it out. I close my eyes now; I look back through the years to 1863; I can see my native town in the Berkshire Hills, I can see that cattle-show ground filled with people; I can see the church there and the town hall crowded, and hear bands playing, and see flags flying and handkerchiefs streaming—well do I recall at this moment that day.

The people had turned out to receive a company of soldiers, and that company came marching up on the Common. They had served out one term in the Civil War and had reenlisted, and they were being received by their native townsmen. I was but a boy, but I was captain of that company, puffed out with pride on that day—why, a cambric needle would have burst me all to pieces.

As I marched on the Common at the head of my company, there was not a man more proud than I. We marched into the town hall and then they seated my soldiers down in the center of the house and I took my place down on the front seat, and then the town officers filed through the great throng of people, who stood close and packed in that little hall. They came up on the platform, formed a half circle around it, and the mayor of the town, the "chairman of the selectmen" in New England, took his seat in the middle of that half circle.

He was an old man, his hair was gray; he never held an office before in his life. He thought that an office was all he needed to be a truly great man, and when he came up he adjusted his powerful spectacles and glanced calmly around the audience with amazing dignity. Suddenly his eyes fell upon me, and then the good old man came right forward and invited me to come up on the stand with the town officers. Invited me up on the stand! No town officer ever took notice of me before I went to war. Now, I should not say that. One town officer was there who advised the teachers to "whale" me, but I mean no "honorable mention."

So I was invited up on the stand with the town officers. I took my seat and let my sword fall on the floor, and folded my arms across my breast and waited to be received. Napoleon the Fifth! Pride goeth before destruction and a fall. When I had gotten my seat and all became silent through the hall, the chairman of the selectmen arose and came forward with great dignity to the table, and we all supposed he would introduce the Congregational minister, who was the only orator in the town, and who would give the oration to the returning soldiers.

But, friends, you should have seen the surprise that ran over that audience when they discovered that this old farmer was going to deliver that oration himself. He had never made a speech in his life before, but he fell into the same error that others have fallen into, he seemed to think that the office would make him an orator. So he had written out a speech and walked up and down the pasture until he had learned it by heart and frightened the cattle, and he brought that manuscript with him, and, taking it from his pocket, he spread it carefully upon the table. Then he adjusted his spectacles to be sure that he might see it, and walked far back on the platform and then stepped forward like this. He must have studied the subject much, for he assumed an elocutionary attitude; he rested heavily upon his left heel, slightly advanced the right foot, threw back his shoulders, opened the organs of speech, and advanced his right hand at an angle of forty-five.

As he stood in this elocutionary attitude this is just the way that speech went, this is it precisely. Some of my friends have asked me if I do not exaggerate it, but I could not exaggerate it. Impossible! This is the way it went; although I am not here for the story but the lesson that is back of it:

"Fellow citizens." As soon as he heard his voice, his hand began to shake like that, his knees began to tremble, and then he shook all over. He coughed and choked and finally came around to look at his manuscript. Then he began again: "Fellow citizens: We—are—we are—we are—we are—We are very happy—we are very happy—we are very happy—to welcome back to their native town these soldiers who have fought and bled—and come back again to their native town. We are especially—we are especially—we are especially—we are especially pleased to see with us today this young hero (that meant me~this young hero who in imagination (friends, remember, he said 'imagination,' for if he had not said that, I would not be egotistical enough to refer to it) this young hero who, in imagination, we have seen leading his troops—leading—we have seen leading—we have seen leading his troops on to the deadly breach. We have seen his shining—his shining—we have seen his shining—we have seen his shining—his shining sword —flashing in the sunlight as he shouted to his troops, 'Come on!'"

Oh dear, dear, dear, dear! How little that good, old man knew about war. If he had known anything about war, he ought to have known what any soldier in this audience knows is true, that it is next to a crime for an officer of infantry ever in time of danger to go ahead of his men. I, with my shining sword flashing in the sunlight, shouting to my troops: "Come on." I never did it. Do you suppose I would go ahead of my men to be shot in the front by the enemy and in the back by my own men? That is no place for an officer. The place for the officer is behind the private soldier in actual fighting.

How often, as a staff officer, I rode down the line when the rebel cry and yell was coming out of the woods, sweeping along over the fields, and shouted, "Officers to the rear! Officers to the rear!" and then every officer goes behind the line of battle, and the higher the officer rank, the farther behind he goes. Not because he is any the less brave, but because the laws of war require that to be done. If the general came up on the front line and were killed you would lose your battle anyhow, because he has the plan of the battle in his brain, and must be kept in comparative safety.

I, with my "shining sword flashing in the sunlight." Ah! There sat in the hall that day men who had given that boy their last hardtack, who had carried him on their backs through deep rivers. But some were not there; they had gone down to death for their country. The speaker mentioned them, but they were but little noticed, and yet they had gone down to death for their country, gone down for a cause they believed was right and still believe was right, though I grant to the other side the same that I ask for myself. Yet these men who had actually died for their country were little noticed, and the hero of the hour was this boy.

Why was he the hero? Simply because that man fell into the same foolishness. This boy was an officer, and those were only private soldiers. I learned a lesson that I will never forget. Greatness consists not in holding some office; greatness really consists in doing some great deed with little means, in the accomplishment of vast purposes from the private ranks of life, that is true greatness.

He who can give to this people better streets, better homes, better schools, better churches, more religion, more of happiness, more of God, he that can be a blessing to the community in which he lives tonight will be great anywhere, but he who cannot be a blessing where he now lives will never be great anywhere on the face of God's earth. "We live in deeds, not years, in feeling, not in figures on a dial; in thoughts, not breaths; we should count time by heart throbs, in the cause of right." Bailey says: "He most lives who thinks most."

If you forget everything I have said to you, do not forget this, because it contains more in two lines than all I have said. Bailey says: "He most lives who thinks most, who feels the noblest, and who acts the best."

3

A MESSAGE TO GARCIA

ELBERT HUBBARD

(1899)

In all this Cuban business there is one man stands out on the horizon of my memory like Mars at perihelion. When war broke out between Spain & the United States, it was very necessary to communicate quickly with the leader of the Insurgents, Garcia was somewhere in the mountain vastness of Cuba—no one knew where. No mail nor telegraph message could reach him. The President must secure his cooperation, and quickly.

What to do!

Some one said to the President, "There's a fellow by the name of Rowan will find Garcia for you, if anybody can."

Rowan was sent for and given a letter to be delivered to Garcia. How "the fellow by the name of Rowan" took the letter, sealed it up in an oil-skin pouch, strapped it over his heart, in four days landed by night off the coast of Cuba from an open boat, disappeared into the jungle, & in three weeks came out on the other side of the Island, having traversed a hostile country on foot, and delivered his letter to Garcia, are things I have no special desire now to tell in detail.

The point I wish to make is this: McKinley gave Rowan a letter to be delivered to Garcia; Rowan took the letter and did not ask, "Where is he at?" By the Eternal! there is a man whose form should be cast in deathless bronze and the statue placed in every college of the land. It is not book-learning young men need, nor instruction about this and that, but a stiffening of the vertebrae which will cause them to be loyal to a trust, to act promptly, concentrate their energies: do the thing—"Carry a message to Garcia!"

General Garcia is dead now, but there are other Garcias.

No man, who has endeavored to carry out an enterprise where many hands were needed, but has been well nigh appalled at times by the imbecility of the average man—the inability or unwillingness to concentrate on a thing and do it. Slip-shod assistance, foolish inattention, dowdy indifference, & half-hearted work seem the rule; and no man succeeds, unless by hook or crook, or threat, he forces or bribes other men to assist him; or mayhap, God in His goodness performs a miracle, & sends him an Angel of Light for an assistant. You, reader, put this matter to a test: You are sitting now in your office—six clerks are within call.

Summon any one and make this request: "Please look in the encyclopedia and make a brief memorandum for me concerning the life of Correggio."

Will the clerk quietly say, "Yes, sir," and go do the task?

On your life, he will not. He will look at you out of a fishy eye and ask one or more of the following questions:

Who was he?

Which encyclopedia?

Where is the encyclopedia?

Was I hired for that?

Don't you mean Bismarck?

What's the matter with Charlie doing it?

Is he dead?

Is there any hurry?

Shan't I bring you the book and let you look it up yourself?

What do you want to know for?

And I will lay you ten to one that after you have answered the questions, and explained how to find the information, and why you want it, the clerk will go off and get one of the other clerks to help him try to find Garcia—and then come back and tell you there is no such man. Of course I may lose my bet, but according to the Law of Average, I will not.

Now if you are wise you will not bother to explain to your "assistant" that Correggio is indexed under the C's, not in the K's, but you will smile sweetly and say, "Never mind," and go look it up yourself.

And this incapacity for independent action, this moral stupidity, this infirmity of the will, this unwillingness to cheerfully catch hold and lift, are the things that put pure Socialism so far into the future. If men will not act for themselves, what will they do when the benefit of their effort is for all? A first-mate with knotted club seems necessary; and the dread of getting "the bounce" Saturday night, holds many a worker to his place.

Advertise for a stenographer, and nine out often who apply, can neither spell nor punctuate—and do not think it necessary to.

Can such a one write a letter to Garcia?

"You see that bookkeeper," said the foreman to me in a large factory.

"Yes, what about him?"

"Well he's a fine accountant, but if I'd send him up town on an errand, he might accomplish the errand all right, and on the other hand, might stop at four saloons on the way, and when he got to Main Street, would forget what he had been sent for."

Can such a man be entrusted to carry a message to Garcia?

We have recently been hearing much maudlin sympathy expressed for the "downtrodden denizen of the sweat-shop" and the "homeless wanderer searching for honest employment," & with it all often go many hard words for the men in power.

Nothing is said about the employer who grows old before his time in a vain attempt to get frowsy ne'er-do-wells to do intelligent work; and his long patient striving with "help" that does nothing but loaf when his back is turned. In every store and factory there is a constant weeding-out process going on. The employer is constantly sending away "help" that have shown their incapacity to further the interests of the business, and others are being taken on. No matter how good times are, this sorting continues, only if times are hard and work is scarce, the sorting is done finer—but out and forever out, the incompetent and unworthy go.

It is the survival of the fittest. Self-interest prompts every employer to keep the best—those who can carry a message to Garcia.

I know one man of really brilliant parts who has not the ability to manage a business of his own, and yet who is absolutely worthless to any one else, because he carries with him constantly the insane suspicion that his employer is oppressing, or intending to oppress him. He cannot give orders; and he will not receive them. Should a message be given him to take to Garcia, his answer would probably be, "Take it yourself."

Tonight this man walks the streets looking for work, the wind whistling through his threadbare coat. No one who knows him dare employ him, for he is a regular fire-brand of discontent. He is impervious to reason, and the only thing that can impress him is the toe of a thick-soled No. 9 boot.

Of course I know that one so morally deformed is no less to be pitied than a physical cripple; but in our pitying, let us drop a tear, too, for the men who are striving to carry on a great enterprise, whose working hours are not limited by the whistle, and whose hair is fast turning white through the struggle to hold in line dowdy indifference, slip-shod imbecility, and the heartless ingratitude, which, but for their enterprise, would be both hungry & homeless.

Have I put the matter too strongly? Possibly I have; but when all the world has gone a-slumming I wish to speak a word of sympathy for the man who succeeds—the man who, against great odds has directed the efforts of others, and having succeeded, finds there's nothing in it: nothing but bare board and clothes.

I have carried a dinner pail & worked for day's wages, and I have also been an employer of labor, and I know there is something to be said on both sides. There is no excellence, per se, in poverty; rags are no recommendation; & all employers are not rapacious and high-handed, any more than all poor men are virtuous.

My heart goes out to the man who does his work when the "boss" is away, as well as when he is at home. And the man who, when given a letter for Garcia, quietly take the missive, without asking any idiotic questions, and with no lurking intention of chucking it into the nearest sewer, or of doing aught else but deliver it, never gets "laid off," nor has to go on a strike for higher wages. Civilization is one long anxious search for just such individuals. Anything such a man asks shall be granted; his kind is so rare that no employer can afford to let him go. He is wanted in every city, town and village—in every office, shop, store and factory. The world cries out for such: he is needed, & needed badly—the man who can carry a message to Garcia.

4

AS A MAN THINKETH

JAMES ALLEN

(1902)

"Mind is the Master power that moulds and makes,
And Man is Mind, and evermore he takes
The tool of Thought, and, shaping what he wills,
Brings forth a thousand joys, a thousand ills:—
He thinks in secret, and it comes to pass:
Environment is but his looking-glass."

Foreword

This little volume (the result of meditation and experience) is not intended as an exhaustive treatise on the much-written-upon subject of the power of thought. It is suggestive rather than explanatory, its object being to stimulate men and women to the discovery and perception of the truth that—

"They themselves are makers of themselves"

by virtue of the thoughts which they choose and encourage; that mind is the master weaver, both of the inner garment of character and the outer garment of circumstance, and that, as they may have hitherto woven in ignorance and pain they may now weave in enlightenment and happiness.

JAMES ALLEN
Broad Park Avenue,
Ilfracombe,
England.

Contents

1. Thought and Character 221
2. Effect of Thought on Circumstances 223
3. Effect of Thought on Health and the Body 229
4. Thought and Purpose 230
5. The Thought-Factor in Achievement 232
6. Visions and Ideals 234
7. Serenity 237

Thought and Character

The aphorism, "As a man thinketh in his heart so is he," not only embraces the whole of a man's being, but is so comprehensive as to reach out to every condition and circumstance of his life. A man is literally *what he thinks,* his character being the complete sum of all his thoughts.

As the plant springs from, and could not be without, the seed, so every act of a man springs from the hidden seeds of thought, and could not have appeared without them. This applies equally to those acts called "spontaneous" and "unpremeditated" as to those which are deliberately executed.

Act is the blossom of thought, and joy and suffering are its fruits; thus does a man garner in the sweet and bitter fruitage of his own husbandry.

> "Thought in the mind hath made us. What we are
> By thought was wrought and built. If a man's mind
> Hath evil thoughts, pain comes on him as comes
> The wheel the ox behind. . . .
> If one endure
> In purity of thought, joy follows him
> As his own shadow—sure."

Man is a growth by law, and not a creation by artifice, and cause and effect is as absolute and undeviating in the hidden realm of thought as in the world of visible and material things. A noble and Godlike character is not a thing of favor or chance, but is the natural result of continued effort in right thinking, the effect of long-cherished association with Godlike thoughts. An ignoble and bestial character, by the same process, is the result of the continued harboring of groveling thoughts.

Man is made or unmade by himself; in the armory of thought he forges the weapons by which he destroys himself; he also fashions the tools with which he builds for himself heavenly mansions of joy and strength and peace. By the right choice and true application of thought, man ascends to the Divine Perfection; by the abuse and wrong application of thought, he descends below the level of the beast. Between these two extremes are all the grades of character, and man is their maker and master.

Of all the beautiful truths pertaining to the soul which have been restored and brought to light in this age, none is more gladdening or fruitful of divine promise and confidence than this—that man is the master of thought, the molder of character, and the maker and shaper of condition, environment, and destiny.

As a being of Power, Intelligence, and Love, and the lord of his own thoughts, man holds the key to every situation, and contains within himself that transforming and regenerative agency by which he may make himself what he wills.

Man is always the master, even in his weakest and most abandoned state; but in his weakness and degradation he is the foolish master who misgoverns his "household." When he begins to reflect upon his condition, and to search diligently for the Law upon which his being is established, he then becomes the wise master, directing his energies with intelligence, and fashioning his thoughts to fruitful issues. Such is the *conscious* master, and man can only thus become by discovering *within himself* the laws of thought; which discovery is totally a matter of application, self-analysis, and experience.

Only by much searching and mining are gold and diamonds obtained, and man can find every truth connected with his being if he will dig deep into the mine of his soul; and that he is the maker of his character, the molder of his life, and the builder of his destiny, he may unerringly prove, if he will watch, control, and alter his thoughts, tracing their effects upon himself, upon others, and upon his life and circumstances, linking cause and effect by patient practice and investigation, and utilizing his every experience, even to the most trivial, everyday occurrence, as a means of obtaining that knowledge of himself which is Understanding, Wisdom, Power. In this direction, as in no other, is the law absolute that "He that seeketh findeth; and to him that knocketh it shall be opened"; for only by patience, practice, and ceaseless importunity can a man enter the Door of the Temple of Knowledge.

Effect of Thought on Circumstances

A man's mind may be likened to a garden, which may be intelligently cultivated or allowed to run wild; but whether cultivated or neglected, it must, and will, *bring forth.* If no useful seeds are *put* into it, then an abundance of useless weed seeds will *fall* therein, and will continue to produce their kind.

Just as a gardener cultivates his plot, keeping it free from weeds, and growing the flowers and fruits which he requires, so may a man tend the garden of his mind, weeding out all the wrong, useless, and impure thoughts, and cultivating toward perfection the flowers and fruits of right, useful, and pure thoughts. By pursuing this process, a man sooner or later discovers that he is the master gardener of his soul, the director of his life. He also reveals, within himself, the laws of thought, and understands, with ever-increasing accuracy, how the thought forces and mind elements operate in the shaping of his character, circumstances, and destiny.

Thought and character are one, and as character can only manifest and discover itself through environment and circumstance, the outer conditions of a person's life will always be found to be harmoniously related to his inner state. This does not mean that a man's circumstances at any given time are an indication of his *entire* character, but that those circumstances are so intimately connected with some vital thought element within himself that, for the time being, they are indispensable to his development.

Every man is where he is by the law of his being; the thoughts which he has built into his character have brought him there, and in the arrangement of his life there is no element of chance, but all is the result of a law which cannot err. This is just as true of those who feel "out of harmony" with their surroundings as of those who are contented with them.

As a progressive and evolving being, man is where he is that he may learn that he may grow; and as he learns the spiritual lesson which any circumstance contains for him, it passes away and gives place to other circumstances.

Man is buffeted by circumstances so long as he believes himself to be the creature of outside conditions, but when he realizes that he is a creative power, and that he may command the hidden soil and seeds of his being out of which circumstances grow, he then becomes the rightful master of himself.

That circumstances *grow* out of thought every man knows who has for any length of time practiced self-control and self-purification, for he will have noticed that the alteration in his circumstances has been in exact ratio with his altered mental condition. So true is this that when a man earnestly applies himself to remedy the defects in his character, and makes swift and marked progress, he passes rapidly through a succession of vicissitudes.

The soul attracts that which it secretly harbors; that which it loves, and also that which it fears; it reaches the height of its cherished aspirations; it falls to the level of its unchastened desires—and circumstances are the means by which the soul receives its own.

Every thought seed sown or allowed to fall into the mind, and to take root there, produces its own, blossoming sooner or later into act, and bearing its own fruitage of opportunity and circumstance. Good thoughts bear good fruit, bad thoughts bad fruit.

The outer world of circumstance shapes itself to the inner world of thought, and both pleasant and unpleasant external conditions are factors which make for the ultimate good of the individual. As the reaper of his own harvest, man learns both by suffering and bliss.

Following the inmost desires, aspirations, thoughts, by which he allows himself to be dominated (pursuing the will-o'-the-wisps of impure imaginings or steadfastly walking the highway of strong and high endeavor), a man at last arrives at their fruition and fulfillment in the outer conditions of his life. The laws of growth and adjustment everywhere obtain.

A man does not come to the almshouse or the jail by the tyranny of fate or circumstance, but by the pathway of groveling thoughts and base desires. Nor does a pure-minded man fall suddenly into crime by stress of any mere external force; the criminal thought had long been secretly fostered in the heart, and the hour of opportunity revealed its gathered power. Circumstance does not make the man; it reveals him to himself. No such conditions can exist as descending into vice and its attendant sufferings apart from vicious inclinations, or ascending into virtue and its pure happiness without the continued cultivation of virtuous aspirations; and man, therefore, as the lord and master of thought, is the maker of himself, the shaper and author of environment. Even at birth the soul comes to its own, and through every step of its earthly pilgrimage it attracts those combinations of conditions which reveal itself, which are the reflections of its own purity and impurity, its strength and weakness.

Men do not attract that which they *want*, but that which they *are*. Their whims, fancies, and ambitions are thwarted at every step, but their inmost thoughts and desires are fed with their own food, be it foul or clean. The "divinity that shapes our ends" is in ourselves; it is our very self. Man is manacled only by himself: thought and action are the jailers of Fate—they imprison, being base; they are also the angels of Freedom—they liberate, being noble. Not what he wishes and prays for does a man get, but what he justly earns. His wishes and prayers are only gratified and answered when they harmonize with his thoughts and actions.

In the light of this truth, what, then, is the meaning of "fighting against circumstances"? It means that a man is continually revolting against an *effect* without, while all the time he is nourishing and preserving its *cause* in his heart. That cause may take the form of a conscious vice or an unconscious weakness; but whatever it is, it stubbornly retards the efforts of its possessor, and thus calls aloud for remedy.

Men are anxious to improve their circumstances, but are unwilling to improve themselves; they therefore remain bound. The man who does not shrink from self-crucifixion can never fail to accomplish the object upon which his heart is set. This is as true of earthly as of heavenly things. Even the man whose sole object is to acquire wealth must be prepared to make great personal sacrifices before he can accomplish his object; and how much more so he who would realize a strong and well-poised life?

Here is a man who is wretchedly poor. He is extremely anxious that his surroundings and home comforts should be improved, yet all the time he shirks his work, and considers he is justified in trying to deceive his employer on the ground of the insufficiency of his wages. Such a man does not understand the simplest rudiments of those principles which are the basis of true prosperity, and is not only totally unfitted to rise out of his wretchedness, but is actually attracting to himself a still deeper wretchedness by dwelling in, and acting out, indolent, deceptive, and unmanly thoughts.

Here is a rich man who is the victim of a painful and persistent disease as the result of gluttony. He is willing to give large sums of money to get rid of it, but he will not sacrifice his gluttonous desires. He wants to gratify his taste for rich and unnatural viands and have his health as well. Such a man is totally unfit to have health, because he has not yet learned the first principles of a healthy life.

Here is an employer of labor who adopts crooked measures to avoid paying the regulation wage, and, in the hope of making larger profits, reduces the wages of his workpeople. Such a man is altogether unfitted for prosperity, and when he finds himself bankrupt, both as regards reputation and riches, he blames circumstances, not knowing that he is the sole author of his condition.

I have introduced these three cases merely as illustrative of the truth that man is the causer (though nearly always unconsciously) of his circumstances, and that, while aiming at a good end, he is continually frustrating its accomplishment by encouraging thoughts and desires which cannot possibly harmonize with that end. Such cases could be multiplied and varied almost indefinitely, but this is not necessary, as the reader can, if he so resolves, trace the action of the laws of thought in his own mind and life, and until this is done, mere external facts cannot serve as a ground of reasoning.

Circumstances, however, are so complicated, thought is so deeply rooted, and the conditions of happiness vary so vastly with individuals, that a man's *entire* soul condition (although it may be known to himself) cannot be judged by another from the external aspect of his life alone. A man may be honest in certain directions, yet suffer privations; a man may be dishonest in certain directions, yet acquire wealth; but the conclusion usually formed that the one man fails *because of his particular honesty*, and that the other prospers *because of his particular dishonesty*, is the result of a superficial judgment, which assumes that the dishonest man is almost totally corrupt, and the honest man almost entirely virtuous. In the light of a deeper knowledge and wider experience, such judgment is found to be erroneous. The dishonest man may have some admirable virtues which the other does not possess; and the honest man obnoxious vices which are absent in the other. The honest man reaps the good results of his honest thoughts and acts; he also brings upon himself the sufferings which his vices produce. The dishonest man likewise garners his own suffering and happiness.

It is pleasing to human vanity to believe that one suffers because of one's virtue; but not until a man has extirpated every sickly, bitter, and impure thought from his mind, and washed every sinful stain from his soul, can he be in a position to know and declare that his sufferings are the result of his good, and not of his bad qualities; and on the way to, yet long before he has reached, that supreme perfection, he will have found, working in his mind and life, the Great Law which is absolutely just, and which cannot, therefore, give good for evil, evil for good. Possessed of such knowledge, he will then know, looking back upon his past ignorance and blindness, that his life is, and always was, justly ordered, and that all his past experiences, good and bad, were the equitable outworking of his evolving, yet unevolved self.

Good thoughts and actions can never produce bad results; bad thoughts and actions can never produce good results. This is but saying that nothing can come from corn but corn, nothing from nettles but nettles. Men understand this law in the natural world, and work with it; but few understand it in the mental and moral world (though its operation there is just as simple and undeviating), and they, therefore, do not coöperate with it.

Suffering is *always* the effect of wrong thought in some direction. It is an indication that the individual is out of harmony with himself, with the Law of his being. The sole and supreme use of suffering is to purify, to burn out all that is useless and impure. Suffering ceases for him who is pure. There could be no object in burning gold after the dross had been removed, and a perfectly pure and enlightened being could not suffer.

The circumstances which a man encounters with suffering are the result of his own mental inharmony. The circumstances which a man encounters with blessedness are the result of his own mental harmony. Blessedness, not material possessions, is the measure of right thought; wretchedness, not lack of material possessions, is the measure of wrong thought. A man may be cursed and rich; he may be blessed and poor. Blessedness and riches are only joined together when the riches are rightly and wisely used; and the poor man only descends into wretchedness when he regards his lot as a burden unjustly imposed.

Indigence and indulgence are the two extremes of wretchedness. They are both equally unnatural and the result of mental disorder. A man is not rightly conditioned until he is a happy, healthy, and prosperous being; and happiness, health, and prosperity are the result of a harmonious adjustment of the inner with the outer, of the man with his surroundings.

A man only begins to be a man when he ceases to whine and revile, and commences to search for the hidden justice which regulates his life. And as he adapts his mind to that regulating factor, he ceases to accuse others as the cause of his condition, and builds himself up in strong and noble thoughts; ceases to kick against circumstances, but begins to *use* them as aids to his more rapid progress, and as a means of discovering the hidden powers and possibilities within himself.

Law, not confusion, is the dominating principle in the universe; justice, not injustice, is the soul and substance of life; and righteousness, not corruption, is the molding and moving force in the spiritual government of the world. This being so, man has but to right himself to find that the universe is right; and during the process of putting himself right, he will find that as he alters his thoughts toward things, and other people, things and other people will alter toward him.

The proof of this truth is in every person, and it therefore admits of easy investigation by systematic introspection and self-analysis. Let a man radically alter his thoughts, and he will be astonished at the rapid transformation it will effect in the material conditions of his life. Men imagine that thought can be kept secret, but it cannot; it rapidly crystallizes into habit and habit solidifies into circumstance. Bestial thoughts crystallize into habits of drunkenness and sensuality, which solidify into circumstances of destitution and disease: impure thoughts of every kind crystallize into enervating and confusing habits, which solidify into distracting and adverse circumstances: thoughts of fear, doubt, and indecision crystallize into weak, unmanly, and irresolute habits, which solidify into circumstances of failure, indigence, and slavish dependence: lazy thoughts crystallize into habits of uncleanliness and dishonesty, which solidify into circumstances of foulness and beggary: hateful and condemnatory thoughts crystallize into habits of accusation and violence, which solidify into circumstances of injury and persecution: selfish thoughts of all kinds crystallize into habits of self-seeking, which solidify into circumstances more or less distressing. On the other hand, beautiful thoughts of all kinds crystallize into habits of grace and kindliness, which solidify into genial and sunny circumstances: pure thoughts crystallize into habits of temperance and self-control, which solidify into circumstances of repose and peace: thoughts of courage, self-reliance, and decision crystallize into manly habits, which solidify into circumstances of success, plenty, and freedom: energetic thoughts crystallize into habits of cleanliness and industry, which solidify into circumstances of pleasantness: gentle and forgiving thoughts crystallize into habits of gentleness, which solidify into protective and preservative circumstances: loving and unselfish thoughts crystallize into habits of self-forgetfulness for others, which solidify into circumstances of sure and a biding prosperity and true riches.

A particular train of thought persisted in, be it good or bad, cannot fail to produce its results on the character and circumstances. A man cannot *directly* choose his circumstances, but he can choose his thoughts, and so indirectly, yet surely, shape his circumstances.

Nature helps every man to the gratification of the thoughts which he most encourages, and opportunities are presented which will most speedily bring to the surface both the good and evil thoughts.

Let a man cease from his sinful thoughts, and all the world will soften toward him, and be ready to help him; let him put away his weakly and sickly thoughts, and lo! opportunities will spring up on every hand to aid his strong resolves; let him encourage good thoughts, and no hard fate shall bind him down to wretchedness and shame. The world is your kaleidoscope, and the varying combinations of colors which at every succeeding moment it presents to you are the exquisitely adjusted pictures of your evermoving thoughts.

"You will be what you will to be;
Let failure find its false content
In that poor word, 'environment,'
But spirit scorns it, and is free.

"It masters time, it conquers space;
It cows that boastful trickster, Chance,
And bids the tyrant Circumstance
Uncrown, and fill a servant's place.

"The human Will, that force unseen,
The offspring of a deathless Soul,
Can hew a way to any goal.
Though walls of granite intervene,

"Be not impatient in delay.
But wait as one who understands;
When spirit rises and commands,
The gods are ready to obey."

Effect of Thought on Health and the Body

The body is the servant of the mind. It obeys the operations of the mind, whether they be deliberately chosen or automatically expressed. At the bidding of unlawful thoughts the body sinks rapidly into disease and decay; at the command of glad and beautiful thoughts it becomes clothed with youthfulness and beauty.

Disease and health, like circumstances, are rooted in thought. Sickly thoughts will express themselves through a sickly body. Thoughts of fear have been known to kill a man as speedily as a bullet, and they are continually killing thousands of people just as surely though less rapidly. The people who live in fear of disease are the people who get it. Anxiety quickly demoralizes the whole body, and lays it open to the entrance of disease; while impure thoughts, even if not physically indulged, will soon shatter the nervous system.

Strong, pure, and happy thoughts build up the body in vigor and grace. The body is a delicate and plastic instrument, which responds readily to the thoughts by which it is impressed, and habits of thought will produce their own effects, good or bad, upon it.

Men will continue to have impure and poisoned blood so long as they propagate unclean thoughts. Out of a clean heart comes a clean life and a clean body. Out of a defiled mind proceeds a defiled life and a corrupt body. Thought is the font of action, life, and manifestation; make the fountain pure, and all will be pure.

Change of diet will not help a man who will not change his thoughts. When a man makes his thoughts pure, he no longer desires impure food.

Clean thoughts make clean habits. The so-called saint who does not wash his body is not a saint. He who has strengthened and purified his thoughts does not need to consider the malevolent microbe.

If you would perfect your body, guard your mind. If you would renew your body, beautify your mind. Thoughts of malice, envy, disappointment, despondency, rob the body of its health and grace. A sour face does not come by chance; it is made by sour thoughts. Wrinkles that mar are drawn by folly, passion, pride.

Thought and Purpose

Until thought is linked with purpose there is no intelligent accomplishment. With the majority the bark of thought is allowed to "drift" upon the ocean of life. Aimlessness is a vice, and such drifting must not continue for him who would steer clear of catastrophe and destruction.

They who have no central purpose in their life fall an easy prey to petty worries, fears, troubles, and self-pityings, all of which are indications of weakness, which lead, just as surely as deliberately planned sins (though by a different route), to failure, unhappiness, and loss, for weakness cannot persist in a power-evolving universe.

A man should conceive of a legitimate purpose in his heart, and set out to accomplish it. He should make this purpose the centralizing point of his thoughts. It may take the form of a spiritual ideal, or it may be a worldly object, according to his nature at the time being; but whichever it is, he should steadily focus his thought forces upon the object which he has set before him. He should make this purpose his supreme duty, and should devote himself to its attainment, not allowing his thoughts to wander away into ephemeral fancies, longings, and imaginings. This is the royal road to self-control and true concentration of thought. Even if he fails again and again to accomplish his purpose (as he necessarily must until weakness is overcome), the *strength of character gained* will be the measure of his *true* success, and this will form a new starting point for future power and triumph.

Those who are not prepared for the apprehension of a *great* purpose, should fix the thoughts upon the faultless performance of their duty, no matter how insignificant their task may appear. Only in this way can the thoughts be gathered and focused, and resolution and energy be developed, which being done, there is nothing which may not be accomplished.

The weakest soul, knowing its own weakness, and believing this truth—*that strength can only be developed by effort and practice,* will, thus believing, at once begin to exert itself, and, adding effort to effort, patience to patience, and strength to strength, will never cease to develop, and will at last grow divinely strong.

As the physically weak man can make himself strong by careful and patient training, so the man of weak thoughts can make them strong by exercising himself in right thinking.

To put away aimlessness and weakness, and to begin to think with purpose, is to enter the ranks of those strong ones who only recognize failure as one of the pathways to attainment; who make all conditions serve them, and who think strongly, attempt fearlessly, and accomplish masterfully.

Having conceived of his purpose, a man should mentally mark out a *straight* pathway to its achievement, looking neither to the right nor the left. Doubts and fears should be rigorously excluded; they are disintegrating elements which break up the straight line of effort, rendering it crooked, ineffectual, useless. Thoughts of doubt and fear never accomplish anything, and never can. They always lead to failure. Purpose, energy, power to do, and all strong thoughts cease when doubt and fear creep in.

The will to do springs from the knowledge that we *can* do. Doubt and fear are the great enemies of knowledge, and he who encourages them, who does not slay them, thwarts himself at every step.

He who has conquered doubt and fear has conquered failure. His every thought is allied with power, and all difficulties are bravely met and wisely overcome. His purposes are seasonably planted, and they bloom and bring forth fruit which does not fall prematurely to the ground.

Thought allied fearlessly to purpose becomes creative force: he who *knows* this is ready to become something higher and stronger than a mere bundle of wavering thoughts and fluctuating sensations; he who *does* this has become the conscious and intelligent wielder of his mental powers.

The Thought-Factor in Achievement

All that a man achieves and all that he fails to achieve is the direct result of his own thoughts. In a justly ordered universe, where loss of equipoise would mean total destruction, individual responsibility must be absolute. A man's weakness and strength, purity and impurity, are his own, and not another man's; they are brought about by himself, and not by another; and they can only be altered by himself, never by another. His condition is also his own, and not another man's. His suffering and his happiness are evolved from within. As he thinks, so he is; as he continues to think, so he remains.

A strong man cannot help a weaker unless that weaker is *willing* to be helped, and even then the weak man must become strong of himself; he must, by his own efforts, develop the strength which he admires in another. None but himself can alter his condition.

It has been usual for men to think and to say, "Many men are slaves because one is an oppressor; let us hate the oppressor." Now, however, there is among an increasing few a tendency to reverse this judgment, and to say, "One man is an oppressor because many are slaves; let us despise the slaves." The truth is that oppressor and slave are cooperators in ignorance, and, while seeming to afflict each other, are in reality afflicting themselves. A perfect Knowledge perceives the action of law in the weakness of the oppressed and the misapplied power of the oppressor; a perfect Love, seeing the suffering which both states entail, condemns neither; a perfect Compassion embraces both oppressor and oppressed.

He who has conquered weakness, and has put away all selfish thoughts, belongs neither to oppressor nor oppressed. He is free.

A man can only rise, conquer, and achieve by lifting up his thoughts. He can only remain weak, and abject, and miserable by refusing to lift up his thoughts.

Before a man can achieve anything, even in worldly things, he must lift his thoughts above slavish animal indulgence. He may not, in order to succeed, give up *all* animality and selfishness, by any means; but a portion of it must, at least, be sacrificed. A man whose first thought is bestial indulgence could neither think clearly nor plan methodically; he could not find and develop his latent resources, and would fail in any undertaking. Not having commenced manfully to control his thoughts, he is not in a position to control affairs and to adopt serious responsibilities. He is not fit to act independently and stand alone. But he is limited only by the thoughts which he chooses.

There can be no progress, no achievement without sacrifice, and a man's worldly success will be in the measure that he sacrifices his confused animal thoughts, and fixes his mind on the development of his plans, and the strengthening of his resolution and self-reliance. And the higher he lifts his thoughts, the more manly, upright, and righteous he becomes, the greater will be his success, the more blessed and enduring will be his achievements.

The universe does not favor the greedy, the dishonest, the vicious, although on the mere surface it may sometimes appear to do so; it helps the honest, the magnanimous, the virtuous. All the great Teachers of the ages have declared this in varying forms, and to prove and know it a man has but to persist in making himself more and more virtuous by lifting up his thoughts.

Intellectual achievements are the result of thought consecrated to the search for knowledge, or for the beautiful and true in life and nature. Such achievements may be sometimes connected with vanity and ambition, but they are not the outcome of those characteristics; they are the natural outgrowth of long and arduous effort, and of pure and unselfish thoughts.

Spiritual achievements are the consummation of holy aspirations. He who lives constantly in the conception of noble and lofty thoughts, who dwells upon all that is pure and unselfish, will, as surely as the sun reaches its zenith and the moon its full, become wise and noble in character, and rise into a position of influence and blessedness.

Achievement, of whatever kind, is the crown of effort, the diadem of thought. By the aid of self-control, resolution, purity, righteousness, and well-directed thought a man ascends; by the aid of animality, indolence, impurity, corruption, and confusion of thought a man descends.

A man may rise to high success in the world, and even to lofty altitudes in the spiritual realm, and again descend into weakness and wretchedness by allowing arrogant, selfish, and corrupt thoughts to take possession of him.

Victories attained by right thought can only be maintained by watchfulness. Many give way when success is assured, and rapidly fall back into failure.

All achievements, whether in the business, intellectual, or spiritual world, are the result of definitely directed thought, are governed by the same law and are of the same method; the only difference lies in *the object of attainment.*

He who would accomplish little must sacrifice little; he who would achieve much must sacrifice much; he who would attain highly must sacrifice greatly.

Visions and Ideals

The dreamers are the saviors of the world. As the visible world is sustained by the invisible, so men, through all their trials and sins and sordid vocations, are nourished by the beautiful visions of their solitary dreamers. Humanity cannot forget its dreamers; it cannot let their ideals fade and die; it lives in them; it knows them as the *realities* which it shall one day see and know.

Composer, sculptor, painter, poet, prophet, sage, these are the makers of the afterworld, the architects of heaven. The world is beautiful because they have lived; without them, laboring humanity would perish.

He who cherishes a beautiful vision, a lofty ideal in his heart, will one day realize it. Columbus cherished a vision of another world, and he discovered it; Copernicus fostered the vision of a multiplicity of worlds and a wider universe, and he revealed it; Buddha beheld the vision of a spiritual world of stainless beauty and perfect peace, and he entered into it.

Cherish your visions; cherish your, ideals; cherish the music that stirs in your heart, the beauty that forms in your mind, the loveliness that drapes your purest thoughts, for out of them will grow all delightful conditions, all heavenly environment; of these, if you but remain true to them, your world will at last be built.

To desire is to obtain; to aspire is to achieve. Shall man's basest desires receive the fullest measure of gratification, and his purest aspirations starve for lack of sustenance? Such is not the Law: such a condition of things can never obtain: "Ask and receive."

Dream lofty dreams, and as you dream, so shall you become. Your Vision is the promise of what you shall one day be; your Ideal is the prophecy of what you shall at last unveil.

The greatest achievement was at first and for a time a dream. The oak sleeps in the acorn; the bird waits in the egg; and in the highest vision of the soul a waking angel stirs. Dreams are the seedlings of realities.

Your circumstances may be uncongenial, but they shall not long remain so if you but perceive an Ideal and strive to reach it. You cannot travel *within* and stand still *without.* Here is a youth hard pressed by poverty and labor; confined hours in an unhealthy workshop; unschooled, and lacking all the arts of refinement. But he dreams of better things:

he thinks of intelligence, of refinement, of grace and beauty. He conceives of, mentally builds up, an ideal condition of life; the vision of a wider liberty and a larger scope takes possession of him; unrest urges him to action, and he utilizes all his spare time and means, small though they are, to the development of his latent powers and resources. Very soon so altered has his mind become that the workshop can no longer hold him. It has become so out of harmony with his mentality that it falls out of his life as a garment is cast aside, and, with the growth of opportunities which fit the scope of his expanding powers, he passes out of it forever. Years later we see this youth as a full-grown man. We find him a master of certain forces of the mind which he wields with world-wide influence and almost unequaled power. In his hands he holds the cords of gigantic responsibilities; he speaks, and lo! lives are changed; men and women hang upon his words and remold their characters, and, sunlike, he becomes the fixed and luminous center around which innumerable destinies revolve. He has realized the Vision of his youth. He has become one with his Ideal.

And you, too, youthful reader, will realize the Vision (not the idle wish) of your heart, be it base or beautiful, or a mixture of both, for you will always gravitate toward that which you, secretly, most love. Into your hands will be placed the exact results of your own thoughts; you will receive that which you earn; no more, no less. Whatever your present environment may be, you will fall, remain, or rise with your thoughts, your Vision, your Ideal.

You will become as small as your controlling desire; as great as your dominant aspiration: in the beautiful words of Stanton Kirkham Davis, "You may be keeping accounts, and presently you shall walk out of the door that for so long has seemed to you the barrier of your ideals, and shall find yourself before an audience—the pen still behind your ear, the ink stains on your fingers—and then and there shall pour out the torrent of your inspiration. You may be driving sheep, and you shall wander to the city—bucolic and open mouthed; shall wander under the intrepid guidance of the spirit into the studio of the master, and after a time he shall say, 'I have nothing more to teach you.' And now you have become the master who did so recently dream of great things while driving sheep. You shall lay down the saw and the plane to take upon yourself the regeneration of the world."

The thoughtless, the ignorant, and the indolent, seeing only the apparent effects of things and not the things themselves, talk of luck, of fortune, and chance. Seeing a man grow rich, they say, "How lucky he is!" Observing another become intellectual, they exclaim, "How highly favored he is!" And noting the saintly character and wide influence of another, they remark, "How chance aids him at every turn!" They do not see the trials and failures and struggles which these men have voluntarily encountered in order to gain their experience; have no knowledge of the sacrifices they have made, of the undaunted efforts they have put forth, of the faith they have exercised, that they might overcome the apparently insurmountable, and realize the Vision of their heart. They do not know the darkness and the heartaches; they only see the light and joy, and call it "luck"; do not see the long and arduous journey, but only behold the pleasant goal, and call it "good fortune"; do not understand the process, but only perceive the result, and call it "chance."

In all human affairs there are *efforts,* and there are *results,* and the strength of the effort is the measure of the result. Chance is not. "Gifts," powers, material, intellectual, and spiritual possessions are the fruits of effort; they are thoughts completed, objects accomplished, visions realized.

The Vision that you glorify in your mind, the Ideal that you enthrone in your heart—this you will build your life by, this you will become.

Serenity

Calmness of mind is one of the beautiful jewels of wisdom. It is the result of long and patient effort in self-control. Its presence is an indication of ripened experience, and of a more than ordinary knowledge of the laws and operations of thought.

A man becomes calm in the measure that he understands himself as a thought-evolved being, for such knowledge necessitates the understanding of others as the result of thought, and as he develops a right understanding, and sees more and more clearly the internal relations of things by the action of cause and effect, he ceases to fuss and fume and worry and grieve, and remains poised, steadfast, serene.

The calm man, having learned how to govern himself, knows how to adapt himself to others; and they, in turn, reverence his spiritual strength, and feel that they can learn of him and rely upon him. The more tranquil a man becomes, the greater is his success, his influence, his power for good. Even the ordinary trader will find his business prosperity increase as he develops a greater self-control and equanimity, for people will always prefer to deal with a man whose demeanor is strongly equable.

The strong, calm man is always loved and revered. He is like a shade-giving tree in a thirsty land, or a sheltering rock in a storm. "Who does not love a tranquil heart, a sweet-tempered, balanced life? It does not matter whether it rains or shines, or what changes come to those possessing these blessings, for they are always sweet, serene, and calm. That exquisite poise of character which we call serenity is the last lesson of culture; it is the flowering of life, the fruitage of the soul. It is precious as wisdom, more to be desired than gold—yea, than even fine gold. How insignificant mere money-seeking looks in comparison with a serene life—a life that dwells in the ocean of Truth, beneath the waves, beyond the reach of tempests, in the Eternal Calm!

"How many people we know who sour their lives, who ruin all that is sweet and beautiful by explosive tempers, who destroy their poise of character, and make bad blood! It is a question whether the great majority of people do not ruin their lives and mar their happiness by lack of self-control. How few people we meet in life who are well-balanced, who have that exquisite poise which is characteristic of the finished character!"

Yes, humanity surges with uncontrolled passion, is tumultuous with ungoverned grief, is blown about by anxiety and doubt. Only the wise man, only he whose thoughts are controlled and purified, makes the winds and the storms of the soul obey him.

Tempest-tossed souls, wherever ye may be, under whatsoever conditions ye may live, know this—in the ocean of life the isles of Blessedness are smiling, and the sunny shore of your ideal awaits your coming. Keep your hand firmly upon the helm of thought. In the bark of your soul reclines the commanding Master; He does but sleep; wake Him. Self-control is strength; Right Thought is mastery; Calmness is power. Say unto your heart, "Peace, be still!"

5

THE GAME OF LIFE AND HOW TO PLAY IT

FLORENCE SCOVEL SHINN

(1925)

Contents

1. The Game 243
2. The Law of Prosperity 247
3. The Power of the Word 251
4. The Law of Nonresistance 255
5. The Law of Karma and The Law of Forgiveness 260
6. Casting the Burden (Impressing the Subconscious) 264
7. Love 268
8. Intuition or Guidance 273
9. Perfect Self-Expression or The Divine Design 278
10. Denials and Affirmations 283

The Game

Most people consider life a battle, but it is not a battle, it is a game.

It is a game, however, which cannot be played successfully without the knowledge of spiritual law, and the Old and the New Testaments give the rules of the game with wonderful clearness. Jesus Christ taught that it was a great game of *Giving and Receiving.*

"Whatsoever a man soweth that shall he also reap." This means that whatever man sends out in word or deed, will return to him; what he gives, he will receive.

If he gives hate, he will receive hate; if he gives love, he will receive love; if he gives criticism, he will receive criticism; if he lies he will be lied to; if he cheats he will be cheated. We are taught also, that the imaging faculty plays a leading part in the game of life.

"Keep thy heart (or imagination) with all diligence, for out of it are the issues of life." (Prov. 4:23.)

This means that what man images, sooner or later externalizes in his affairs. I know of a man who feared a certain disease. It was a very rare disease and difficult to get, but he pictured it continually and read about it until it manifested in his body, and he died, the victim of distorted imagination.

So we see, to play successfully the game of life, we must train the imaging faculty. A person with an imaging faculty trained to image only good, brings into his life "every righteous desire of his heart"—health, wealth, love, friends, perfect self-expression, his highest ideals.

The imagination has been called, "*The Scissors of The Mind,*" and it is ever cutting, cutting, day by day, the pictures man sees there, and sooner or later he meets his own creations in his outer world. To train the imagination successfully, man must understand the workings of his mind. The Greeks said: "Know Thyself."

There are three departments of the mind, the *subconscious, conscious and superconscious.* The subconscious, is simply power, without direction. It is like steam or electricity, and it does what it is directed to do; it has no power of induction.

Whatever man feels deeply or images clearly, is impressed upon the subconscious mind, and carried out in minutest detail.

For example: a woman I know, when a child, always "made believe" she was a widow. She "dressed up" in black clothes and wore a long black veil, and people thought she was very clever and amusing. She grew up and married a man with whom she was deeply in love. In a short time he died and she wore black and a sweeping veil for many years. The picture of herself as a widow was impressed upon the subconscious mind, and in due time worked itself out, regardless of the havoc created.

The conscious mind has been called mortal or carnal mind.

It is the human mind and sees life as it *appears to be.* It sees death, disaster, sickness, poverty and limitation of every kind, and it impresses the subconscious.

The *superconscious* mind is the God Mind within each man, and is the realm of perfect ideas.

In it, is the "*perfect pattern*" spoken of by Plato, *The Divine Design;* for there is a *Divine Design* for each person.

"*There is a place that you are to fill and no one else can fill, something you are to do, which no one else can do.*"

There is a perfect picture of this in the *superconscious mind.* It usually flashes across the conscious as an unattainable ideal—"something too good to be true."

In reality it is man's true destiny (or destination) flashed to him from the Infinite Intelligence which is *within himself.*

Many people, however, are in ignorance of their true destinies and are striving for things and situations which do not belong to them, and would only bring failure and dissatisfaction if attained.

For example: A woman came to me and asked me to "speak the word" that she would marry a certain man with whom she was very much in love. (She called him A. B.)

I replied that this would be a violation of spiritual law, but that I would speak the word for the right man, the "divine selection," the man who belonged to her by divine right.

I added, "If A. B. is the right man you can't lose him, and if he isn't, you will receive his equivalent." She saw A. B. frequently but no headway was made in their friendship. One evening she called, and said, "Do you know, for the last week, A. B. hasn't seemed so wonderful to me." I replied, "Maybe he is not the divine selection—another man may be the right one." Soon after that, she met another man who fell in love with her at once, and who said she was his ideal. In fact, he said all the things that she had always wished A. B. would say to her.

She remarked, "It was quite uncanny."

She soon returned his love, and lost all interest in A. B.

This shows the law of substitution. A right idea was substituted for a wrong one, therefore there was no loss or sacrifice involved.

Jesus Christ said, "Seek ye first the Kingdom of God and his righteousness; and all these things shall be added unto you," and he said the Kingdom *was within man.*

The Kingdom is the realm of *right ideas,* or the divine pattern.

Jesus Christ taught that man's words played a leading part in the game of life. "By your words ye are justified and by your words ye are condemned."

Many people have brought disaster into their lives through idle words.

For example: A woman once asked me why her life was now one of poverty of limitation. Formerly she had a home, was surrounded by beautiful things and had plenty of money. We found she had often tired of the management of her home, and had said repeatedly, "I'm sick and tired of things—I wish I lived in a trunk," and she added: "Today I am living in that trunk." She had spoken herself into a trunk. The subconscious mind has no sense of humor and people often joke themselves into unhappy experiences.

For example: A woman who had a great deal of money, joked continually about "getting ready for the poorhouse."

In a few years she was almost destitute, having impressed the subconscious mind with a picture of lack and limitation.

Fortunately the law works both ways, and a situation of lack may be changed to one of plenty.

For example: A woman came to me one hot summer's day for a "treatment" for prosperity. She was worn out, dejected and discouraged. She said she possessed just eight dollars in the world. I said, "Good, we'll bless the eight dollars and multiply them as Jesus Christ multiplied the loaves and the fishes," for He taught that *every man* had the power to bless and to multiply, to heal and to prosper.

She said, "What shall I do next?"

I replied, "Follow intuition. Have you a 'hunch' to do anything, or to go anywhere?" Intuition means, intuition, or to be taught from within. It is man's unerring guide, and I will deal more fully with its laws in a following chapter.

The woman replied: "I don't know—I seem to have a 'hunch' to go home; I've just enough money for carfare." Her home was in a distant city and was one of lack and limitation, and the reasoning mind (or intellect) would have said: "Stay in New York and get work and make some money." I replied, "Then go home—never violate a hunch." I spoke the following words for her: *"Infinite Spirit open the way for great abundance for——. She is an irresistible magnet for all that belongs to her by divine right."* I told her to repeat it continually also. She left for home immediately. In calling on a woman one day, she linked up with an old friend of her family.

Through this friend, she received thousands of dollars in a most miraculous way. She has said to me often, "Tell people about the woman who came to you with eight dollars and a hunch."

There is always *plenty on man's pathway;* but it can only be *brought into manifestation* through desire, faith or the spoken word. Jesus Christ brought out clearly that man must make the *first move.*

"Ask, and it shall be given you, seek, and ye shall find, knock, and it shall be opened unto you." (Mat. 7:7.)

In the Scriptures we read:

"Concerning the works of my hands, command ye me."

Infinite Intelligence, God, is ever ready to carry out man's smallest or greatest demands.

Every desire, uttered or unexpressed, is a demand. We are often startled by having a wish suddenly fulfilled.

For example: One Easter, having seen many beautiful rose-trees in the florists' windows, I wished I would receive one, and for an instant saw it mentally being carried in the door.

Easter came, and with it a beautiful rose-tree. I thanked my friend the following day, and told her it was just what I had wanted.

She replied, "I didn't send you a rose-tree, I sent you lilies!"

The man had mixed the order, and sent me a rose-tree simply because I had started the law in action, and *I had to have a rose-tree.*

Nothing stands between man and his highest ideals and every desire of his heart, but doubt and fear. When man can "wish without worrying," every desire will be instantly fulfilled.

I will explain more fully in a following chapter the scientific reason for this and how fear must be erased from the consciousness. It is man's only enemy—fear of lack, fear of failure, fear of sickness, fear of loss and a feeling of *insecurity on some plane.* Jesus Christ said: "Why are ye fearful, oh ye of little faith?" (Mat. 8:26.) So we can see we must substitute faith for fear, for fear is only inverted faith; it is faith in evil instead of good.

The object of the game of life is to see clearly one's good and to obliterate all mental pictures of evil. This must be done by impressing the subconscious mind with a realization of good. A very brilliant man, who has attained great success, told me he had suddenly erased all fear from his consciousness by reading a sign which hung in a room. He saw printed, in large letters this statement—"*Why worry, it will probably never happen.*" These words were stamped indelibly upon his subconscious mind, and he has now a firm conviction that only good can come into his life, therefore only *good can manifest.*

In the following chapter I will deal with the different methods of impressing the subconscious mind. It is man's faithful servant but one must be careful to give it the right orders. Man has ever a silent listener at his side—his subconscious mind.

Every thought, every word is impressed upon it and carried out in amazing detail. It is like a singer making a record on the sensitive disc of the phonographic plate. Every note and tone of the singer's voice is registered. If he coughs or hesitates, it is registered also. So let us break all the old bad records in the subconscious mind, the records of our lives which we do not wish to keep, and make new and beautiful ones.

Speak these words aloud, with power and conviction: "I now smash and demolish (by my spoken word) every untrue record in my subconscious mind. They shall return to the dust-heap of their native nothingness, for they came from my own vain imaginings. I now make my perfect records through the Christ within—The records *of Health, Wealth, Love and perfect Self-Expression.*" This is the square of life, *The Game completed.*

In the following chapters, I will show how man can *change* his *conditions by changing his words.* Any man who does not know the power of the word, is behind the times.

"Death and Life are in the power of the tongue."

(PROV. 18:21.)

The Law of Prosperity

"Yea, the Almighty shall be thy defense
and thou shalt have plenty of silver."

One of the greatest messages given to the race through the scriptures is that God is man's supply and that man can release, *through his spoken word,* all that belongs to him by divine right. He must, however, have *perfect faith in his spoken word.*

Isaiah said, "My word shall not return unto me void, but shall accomplish that where unto it is sent." We know now, that words and thoughts are a tremendous vibratory force, ever moulding man's body and affairs.

A woman came to me in great distress and said she was to be sued on the fifteenth of the month for three thousand dollars. She knew no way of getting the money and was in despair.

I told her God was her supply, and *that there is a supply for every demand.*

So I spoke the word! I gave thanks that the woman would receive three thousand dollars at the right time in the right way. I told her she must have perfect faith, and act her *perfect faith.* The fifteenth came but no money had materialized.

She called me on the phone and asked what she was to do.

I replied, "It is Saturday, so they won't sue you today. Your part is to act rich, thereby showing perfect faith that you will receive it by Monday." She asked me to lunch with her to keep up her courage. When I joined her at a restaurant, I said, "This is no time to economize. Order an expensive luncheon, act as if you have already received the three thousand dollars."

"All things whatsoever ye ask in prayer, *believing,* ye shall receive." "You must act as if you *had already received.*" The next morning she called me on the phone and asked me to stay with her during the day. I said, "No, you are divinely protected and God is never too late."

In the evening she phoned again, greatly excited and said, "My dear, a miracle has happened! I was sitting in my room this morning, when the doorbell rang. I said to the maid: 'Don't let anyone in.' The maid however, looked out the window and said, 'It's your cousin with the long white beard.'

"So I said, 'Call him back. I would like to see him.' He was just turning the corner, when he heard the maid's voice, and *he came back.*

"He talked for about an hour, and just as he was leaving he said, 'Oh, by the way, how are finances?'

"I told him I needed the money, and he said, 'Why, my dear, I will give you three thousand dollars the first of the month.'

"I didn't like to tell him I was going to be sued. What shall I do? I won't *receive it till* the first of the month, and I must have it tomorrow." I said, "I'll keep on 'treating.' "

I said, "Spirit is never too late. I give thanks she has received the money on the invisible plane and that it manifests on time." The next morning her cousin called her up and said, "Come to my office this morning and I will give you the money." That afternoon, she had three thousand dollars to her credit in the bank, and wrote checks as rapidly as her excitement would permit.

If one asks for success and prepares for failure, he will get the situation he has prepared for. For example: A man came to me asking me to speak the word that a certain debt would be wiped out.

I found he spent his time planning what he would say to the man when he did not pay his bill, thereby neutralizing my words. He should have seen himself paying the debt.

We have a wonderful illustration of this in the Bible, relating to the three kings who were in the desert, without water for their men and horses. They consulted the prophet Elisha, who gave them this astonishing message:

"Thus saith the Lord—Ye shall not see wind, neither shall ye see rain, yet make this valley full of ditches."

Man must prepare for the thing he has asked for, *when there isn't the slightest sign of it in sight.*

For example: A woman found it necessary to look for an apartment during the year when there was a great shortage of apartments in New York. It was considered almost an impossibility, and her friends were sorry for her and said, "Isn't it too bad, you'll have to store your furniture and live in a hotel." She replied, "*You needn't feel sorry for me, I'm a superman, and I'll get an apartment.*"

She spoke the words: "*Infinite Spirit, open the way for the right apartment.*" She knew there was a supply for every demand, and that she was "unconditioned," working on the spiritual plane, and that "one with God is a majority."

She had contemplated buying new blankets, when "the tempter," the adverse thought or reasoning mind, suggested, "Don't buy the blankets, perhaps, after all, you won't get an apartment and you will have no use for them." She promptly replied (to herself): "I'll dig my ditches by buying the blankets!" So she prepared for the apartment—acted as though she already had it.

She found one in a miraculous way, and it was given to her although there were over *two hundred other applicants.*

The blankets showed active faith.

It is needless to say that the ditches dug by the three kings in the desert were filled to over-flowing. (Read II Kings.)

Getting into the spiritual swing of things is no easy matter for the average person. The adverse thoughts of doubt and fear surge from the subconscious. They are the "army of the aliens" which must be put to flight. This explains why it is so often, "darkest before the dawn."

A big demonstration is usually preceded by tormenting thoughts.

Having made a statement of high spiritual truth one challenges the old beliefs in the subconscious, and "error is exposed" to be put out.

This is the time when one must make his affirmations of truth repeatedly, and rejoice and give thanks that he has already received. "Before ye call I shall answer." This means that "every good and perfect gift" is already man's awaiting his recognition.

Man can only receive what he sees himself receiving.

The children of Israel were told that they could have all the land they could see. This is true of every man. He has only the land within his own mental vision. Every great work, every big accomplishment, has been brought into manifestation through holding to the vision, and often just before the big achievement, comes apparent failure and discouragement.

The children of Israel when they reached the "Promised Land," were afraid to go in, for they said it was filled with giants who made them feel like grasshoppers. "And there we saw the giants and we were in our own sight as grasshoppers." This is almost every man's experience.

However, the one who knows spiritual law, is undisturbed by appearance, and rejoices while he is "yet in captivity." That is, he holds to his vision and gives thanks that the end is accomplished, he has received.

Jesus Christ gave a wonderful example of this. He said to his disciples: "Say not ye, there are yet four months and then cometh the harvest? Behold, I say unto you, lift up your eyes and look on the fields; for they are ripe already to harvest." His clear vision pierced the "world of matter" and he saw clearly the fourth dimensional world, things as they really are, perfect and complete in Divine Mind. So man must ever hold the vision of his journey's end and demand the manifestation of that which he has already received. It may be his perfect health, love, supply, self-expression, home or friends.

They are all finished and perfect ideas registered in Divine Mind (man's own superconscious mind) and must come through him, not to him. For example: A man came to me asking for treatments for success. It was imperative that he raise, within a certain time, fifty-thousand dollars for his business. The time limit was almost up, when he came to me in despair. No one wanted to invest in his enterprise, and the bank had flatly refused a loan. I replied: "I suppose you lost your temper while at the bank, therefore your power. You can control any situation if you first control yourself." "Go back to the bank," I added, "and I will treat." My treatment was: "You are identified in love with the spirit of everyone connected with the bank. Let the Divine Idea come out of this situation." He replied, "Woman, you are talking about an impossibility. Tomorrow is Saturday; the bank closes at twelve, and my train won't get me there until ten, and the time limit is up tomorrow, and anyway they won't do it. It's too late." I replied, "God doesn't need any time and is never too late. With Him all things are possible." I added, "I don't know anything about business, but I know all about God." He replied: "It all sounds fine when I sit here listening to you, but when I go out it's terrible." He lived in a distant city, and I did not hear from him for a week, then came a letter. It read: "You were right. I raised the money, and will never again doubt the truth of all that you told me."

I saw him a few weeks later, and I said, "What happened? You evidently had plenty of time, after all." He replied, "My train was late, and I got there just fifteen minutes to twelve. I walked into the bank quietly and said, 'I have come for the loan,' and they gave it to me without a question."

It was the last fifteen minutes of the time allotted to him, and Infinite Spirit was not too late. In this instance the man could never have demonstrated alone. He needed someone to help him hold to the vision. This is what one man can do for another.

Jesus Christ knew the truth of this when he said: "If two of you shall agree on earth as touching anything that they shall ask, it shall be done for them of my Father which is in heaven." One gets too close to his own affairs and becomes doubtful and fearful.

The friend or "healer" sees clearly the success, health, or prosperity, and never wavers, because he is not close to the situation.

It is much easier to "demonstrate" for someone else than for one's self, so a person should not hesitate to ask for help, if he feels himself wavering.

A keen observer of life once said, "no man can fail, if some one person sees him successful." Such is the power of the vision, and many a great man has owed his success to a wife, or sister, or a friend who "believed in him" and held without wavering to the perfect pattern!

The Power of the Word

"By thy words thou shalt be justified,
and by thy words thou shalt be condemned."

A person knowing the power of the word, becomes very careful of his conversation. He has only to watch the reaction of his words to know that they do "not return void." Through his spoken word, man is continually making laws for himself.

I knew a man who said, "I always miss a car. It invariably pulls out just as I arrive."

His daughter said: "I always catch a car. It's sure to come just as I get there." This occurred for years. Each had made a separate law for himself, one of failure, one of success. This is the psychology of superstitions.

The horse-shoe or rabbit's foot contains no power, but man's spoken word and belief that it will bring him good luck creates expectancy in the subconscious mind, and attracts a "lucky situation." I find however, this will not "work" when man has advanced spiritually and knows a higher law. One cannot turn back, and must put away "graven images." For example: Two men in my class had had great success in business for several months, when suddenly everything "went to smash." We tried to analyze the situation, and I found, instead of making their affirmations and looking to God for success and prosperity, they had each bought a "lucky monkey." I said: "Oh I see, you have been trusting in the lucky monkeys instead of God." "Put away the lucky monkeys and call on the law of forgiveness," for man has power to forgive or neutralize his mistakes.

They decided to throw the lucky monkeys down a coalhole, and all went well again. This does not mean, however, that one should throw away every "lucky" ornament or horse-shoe about the house, but he must recognize that the power back of it is the one and only power, God, and that the object simply gives him a feeling of expectancy.

I was with a friend, one day, who was in deep despair. In crossing the street, she picked up a horse-shoe. Immediately, she was filled with joy and hope. She said God had sent her the horse-shoe in order to keep up her courage.

It was indeed, at that moment, about the only thing that could have registered in her consciousness. Her hope became faith, and she ultimately made a wonderful demonstration. I wish to make the point clear that the men previously mentioned were depending on the monkeys, alone, while this woman recognized the power back of the horse-shoe.

I know, in my own case, it took a long while to get out of a belief that a certain thing brought disappointment. If the thing happened, disappointment invariably followed. I found the only way I could make a change in the subconscious, was by asserting, "There are not two powers, there is only one power, God, therefore, there are no disappointments, and this thing means a happy surprise." I noticed a change at once, and happy surprises commenced coming my way.

I have a friend who said nothing could induce her to walk under a ladder, I said, "If you are afraid, you are giving in to a belief in two powers, Good and Evil, instead of one. As God is absolute, there can be no opposing power, unless man makes the false of evil for himself. To show you believe in only One Power, God, and that there is no power or reality in evil, walk under the next ladder you see." Soon after, she went to her bank. She wished to open her box in the safe-deposit vault, and there stood a ladder on her pathway. It was impossible to reach the box without passing under the ladder. She quailed with fear and turned back. She could not face the lion on her pathway. However, when she reached the street, my words rang in her ears and she decided to return and walk under it. It was a big moment in her life, for ladders had held her in bondage for years. She retraced her steps to the vault, and the ladder was no longer there! This so often happens! If one is willing to do a thing he is afraid to do, he does not have to.

It is the law of nonresistance, which is so little understood.

Someone has said that courage contains genius and magic. Face a situation fearlessly, and there is no situation to face; it falls away of its own weight.

The explanation is, that fear attracted the ladder on the woman's pathway, and fearlessness removed it.

Thus the invisible forces are ever working for man who is always "pulling the strings" himself though he does not know it. Owing to the vibratory power of words, whatever man voices, he begins to attract. People who continually speak of disease, invariably attract it.

After man knows the truth, he cannot be too careful of his words. For example: I have a friend who often says on the 'phone, "Do come to see me and have a fine old-fashioned chat." This "old-fashioned chat" means an hour of about five hundred to a thousand destructive words, the principal topics being loss, lack, failure and sickness.

I reply: "No, I thank you, I've had enough old-fashioned chats in my life, they are too expensive, but I will be glad to have a new-fashioned chat, and talk about what we want, not what we don't want." There is an old saying that man only dares use his words for three purposes, to "heal, bless or prosper." What man says of others will be said of him, and what he wishes for another, he is wishing for himself.

"Curses, like chickens, come home to roost."

If a man wishes someone "bad luck," he is sure to attract bad luck himself. If he wishes to aid someone to success, he is wishing and aiding himself to success.

The body may be renewed and transformed through the spoken word and clear vision, and disease be completely wiped out of the consciousness. The metaphysician knows that all disease has a mental correspondence, and in order to heal the body one must first "heal the soul."

The soul is the subconscious mind, and it must be "saved" from wrong thinking.

In the twenty-third psalm, we read: "He restoreth my soul." This means that the subconscious mind or soul, must be restored with the right ideas, and the "mystical marriage" is the marriage of the soul and the spirit, or the subconscious and superconscious mind. They must be one. When the subconscious is flooded with the perfect ideas of the superconscious, God and man are one. "I and the Father are one." That is, he is one with the realm of perfect ideas; he is the man made in God's likeness and image (imagination) and is given power and dominion over all created things, his mind, body and affairs.

It is safe to say that all sickness and unhappiness come from the violation of the law of love. A new commandment I give unto you, "Love one another," and in the Game of Life, love or goodwill takes every trick.

For example: A woman I know, had, for years an appearance of a terrible skin disease. The doctors told her it was incurable, and she was in despair. She was on the stage, and she feared she would soon have to give up her profession, and she had no other means of support. She, however, procured a good engagement, and on the opening night, made a great "hit." She received flattering notices from the critics, and was joyful and elated. The next day she received a notice of dismissal. A man in the cast had been jealous of her success and had caused her to be sent away. She felt hatred and resentment taking complete possession of her, and she cried out, "Oh God don't let me hate that man." That night she worked for hours "in the silence."

She said, "I soon came into a very deep silence. I seemed to be at peace with myself, with the man, and with the whole world. I continued this for two following nights, and on the third day I found I was healed completely of the skin disease!" In asking for love, or goodwill, she had fulfilled the law, ("for love is the fulfilling of the law") and the disease (which came from subconscious resentment) was wiped out.

Continual criticism produces rheumatism, as critical, inharmonious thoughts cause unnatural deposits in the blood, which settle in the joints.

False growths are caused by jealousy, hatred, unforgiveness, fear, etc. Every disease is caused by a mind not at ease. I said once, in my class, "There is no use asking anyone 'What's the matter with you?' we might just as well say, 'Who's the matter with you?'" Unforgiveness is the most prolific cause of disease. It will harden arteries or liver, and affect the eyesight. In its train are endless ills.

I called on a woman, one day, who said she was ill from having eaten a poisoned oyster. I replied, "Oh, no, the oyster was harmless, you poisoned the oyster. What's the matter with you?" She answered, "Oh about nineteen people." She had quarrelled with nineteen people and had become so inharmonious that she attracted the wrong oyster.

Any inharmony on the external, indicates there is mental inharmony. "As the within, so the without."

Man's only enemies are within himself. "And a man's foes shall be they of his own household." Personality is one of the last enemies to be overcome, as this planet is taking its initiation in love. It was Christ's message—"Peace on Earth, good will towards man." The enlightened man, therefore, endeavors to perfect himself upon his neighbor. His work is with himself, to send out goodwill and blessings to every man, and the marvelous thing is, that if one blesses a man he has no power to harm him.

For example: A man came to me asking to "treat" for success in business. He was selling machinery, and a rival appeared on the scene with what he proclaimed, was a better machine, and my friend feared defeat. I said, "First of all, we must wipe out all fear, and know that God protects your interests, and that the divine idea must come out of the situation. That is, the right machine will be sold, by the right man, to the right man." And I added, "Don't hold one critical thought towards that man. Bless him all day, and be willing not to sell your machine, if it isn't the Divine Idea." So he went to the meeting, fearless and nonresistant, and blessing the other man. He said the outcome was very remarkable. The other man's machine refused to work, and he sold his without the slightest difficulty. "But I say unto you, love your enemies, bless them that curse you, do good to them that hate you, and pray for them which spitefully use you and persecute you."

Goodwill produces a great aura of protection about the one who sends it, and "No weapon that is formed against him shall prosper." In other words, love and goodwill destroy the enemies within one's self, therefore, one has no enemies on the external!

"There is peace on earth for him who sends goodwill to man!"

The Law of Nonresistance

"Resist not evil. Be not overcome of evil,
but overcome evil with good."

Nothing on earth can resist an absolutely nonresistant person.

The Chinese say that water is the most powerful element, because it is perfectly nonresistant. It can wear away a rock, and sweep all before it.

Jesus Christ said, "Resist not evil," for He knew in reality, there is no evil, therefore nothing to resist. Evil has come of man's "vain imagination," or a belief in two powers, good and evil.

There is an old legend, that Adam and Eve ate of "Maya the Tree of Illusion," and saw two powers instead of one power, God.

Therefore, evil is a false law man has made for himself, through psychoma or soul sleep. Soul sleep means, that man's soul has been hypnotized by the race belief (of sin, sickness and death, etc.) which is carnal or mortal thought, and his affairs have outpictured his illusions.

We have read in a preceding chapter, that man's soul is his subconscious mind, and whatever he feels deeply, good or bad, is outpictured by that faithful servant. His body and affairs show forth what he has been picturing. The sick man has pictured sickness, the poor man, poverty, the rich man, wealth.

People often say, "why does a little child attract illness, when it is too young even to know what it means?"

I answer that children are sensitive and receptive to the thoughts of others about them, and often outpicture the fears of their parents.

I heard a metaphysician once say, "If you do not run your subconscious mind yourself, someone else will run it for you."

Mothers often, unconsciously, attract illness and disaster to their children, by continually holding them in thoughts of fear, and watching for symptoms.

For example: A friend asked a woman if her little girl had had the measles. She replied promptly, "not yet!" This implied that she was expecting the illness, and, therefore, preparing the way for what she did not want for herself and child.

However, the man who is centered and established in right thinking, the man who sends out only goodwill to his fellow-man, and who is without fear, cannot be *touched or influenced by the negative thoughts of others.* In fact, he could then receive only good thoughts, as he himself, sends forth only good thoughts.

Resistance is Hell, for it places man in a "state of torment."

A metaphysician once gave me a wonderful recipe for taking every trick in the game of life, it is the acme of nonresistance. He gave it in this way; "At one time in my life, I baptized children, and of course, they had many names. Now I no longer baptize children, but I baptize events, but *I give every event the same name.* If I have a failure I baptize it success, in the name of the Father, and of the Son, and of the Holy Ghost!"

In this, we see the great law of transmutation, founded on nonresistance. Through his spoken word, every failure was transmuted into success.

For example: A woman who required money, and who knew the spiritual law of opulence, was thrown continually in a business-way, with a man who made her feel very poor. He talked lack and limitation and she commenced to catch his poverty thoughts, so she disliked him, and blamed him for her failure. She knew in order to demonstrate her supply, she must first feel that she *had received—a feeling of opulence must precede its manifestation.*

It dawned upon her, one day, that she was resisting the situation, and seeing two powers instead of one. So she blessed the man and baptized the situation "Success"! She affirmed, "As there is only one power, God, this man is here for my good and my prosperity" (just what he did not seem to be there for). Soon after that she met, *through this man,* a woman who gave her for a service rendered, several thousand dollars, and the man moved to a distant city, and faded harmoniously from her life. Make the statement, "Every man is a golden link in the chain of my good," for all men are God in manifestation, *awaiting the opportunity given by man, himself, to serve the divine plan of his life.*

"Bless your enemy, and you rob him of his ammunition." His arrows will be transmuted into blessings.

This law is true of nations as well as individuals. Bless a nation, send love and goodwill to every inhabitant, and it is robbed of its power to harm.

Man can only get the right idea of nonresistance, through spiritual understanding. My students have often said: "I don't want to be a door-mat," I reply, "when you use nonresistance with wisdom, no one will ever be able to walk over you."

Another example: One day I was impatiently awaiting an important telephone call. I resisted every call that came in and made no out-going calls myself, reasoning that it might interfere with the one I was awaiting.

Instead of saying, "Divine Ideas never conflict, the call will come at the right time," leaving it to Infinite Intelligence to arrange, I commenced to manage things myself—I made the battle mine, not God's and remained tense and anxious. The bell did not ring for about an hour, and I glanced at the 'phone and found the receiver had been off that length of time, and the 'phone was disconnected. My anxiety, fear and belief in interference, had brought on a total eclipse of the telephone. Realizing what I had done, I commenced blessing the situation at once; I baptized it "success," and affirmed, "I cannot lose any call that belongs to me by divine right; I am under *grace, and not under law.*"

A friend rushed out to the nearest telephone, to notify the Company to reconnect. She entered a crowded grocery, but the proprietor left his customers and attended to the call himself. My 'phone was connected at once, and two minutes later, I received a very important call, and about an hour afterward, the one I had been awaiting.

One's ships come in over a calm sea.

So long as man resists a situation, he will have it with him. If he runs away from it, it will run after him.

For example: I repeated this to a woman one day, and she replied, "How true that is! I was unhappy at home, I disliked my mother, who was critical and domineering; so I ran away and was married—but I married my mother, for my husband was exactly like my mother, and I had the same situation to face again." "Agree with thine adversary quickly."

That means, agree that the adverse situation is good, be undisturbed by it, and it falls away of its own weight. "None of these things move me," is a wonderful affirmation.

The inharmonious situation comes from some inharmony within man himself.

When there is, in him, no emotional response to an inharmonious situation, it fades away forever, from his pathway.

So we see man's work is ever with himself.

People have said to me, "Give treatments to change my husband, or my brother." I reply, "No, I will give *treatments to change you;* when you change, your husband and your brother will change."

One of my students was in the habit of lying. I told her it was a failure method and if she lied, she would be lied to. She replied, "I don't care, I can't possibly get along without lying."

One day she was speaking on the 'phone to a man with whom she was very much in love. She turned to me and said, "I don't trust him, I know he's lying to me." I replied, "Well, you lie yourself, so someone has to lie to you, and you will be sure it will be just the person you want the truth from." Some time after that, I saw her, and she said, "I'm cured of lying."

I questioned: "What cured you?"

She replied: "I have been living with a woman who lied worse than I did!"

One is often cured of his faults by seeing them in others.

Life is a mirror, and we find only ourselves reflected in our associates.

Living in the past is a failure method and a violation of spiritual law.

Jesus Christ said, "Behold, now is the accepted time." "Now is the day of Salvation."

Lot's wife looked back and was turned into a pillar of salt.

The robbers of time are the past and the future. Man should bless the past, and forget it, if it keeps him in bondage, and bless the future, knowing it has in store for him endless joys, but live *fully in the now.*

For example: A woman came to me, complaining that she had no money with which to buy Christmas gifts. She said, "Last year was so different; I had plenty of money and gave lovely presents, and this year I have scarcely a cent."

I replied, "You will never demonstrate money while you are pathetic and live in the past. Live fully in the *now,* and *get ready to give Christmas presents.* Dig your ditches, and the money will come." She exclaimed, "I know what to do! I will buy some tinsel twine, Christmas seals and wrapping paper." I replied, "Do that, and the *presents will come and stick themselves to the Christmas seals.*"

This too, was showing financial fearlessness and faith in God, as the reasoning mind said, "Keep every cent you have, as you are not sure you will get any more."

She bought the seals, paper and twine, and a few days before Christmas, received a gift of several hundred dollars. Buying the seals and twine had impressed the subconscious with expectancy, and opened the way for the manifestation of the money. She purchased all the presents in plenty of time.

Man must live suspended in the moment.

"Look well, therefore, to this Day! Such is the salutation of the Dawn."

He must be spiritually alert, ever awaiting his leads, taking advantage of every opportunity.

One day, I said continually (silently), "Infinite Spirit, don't let me miss a trick," and something very important was told to me that evening. It is most necessary to begin the day with right words.

Make an affirmation immediately upon waking.

For example:

"*Thy will be done this day! Today is a day of completion; I give thanks for this perfect day, miracle shall follow miracle and wonders shall never cease.*"

Make this a habit, and one will see wonders and miracles come into his life.

One morning I picked up a book and read, "Look with wonder at that which is before you!" It seemed to be my message for the day, so I repeated again and again, "Look with wonder at that which is before you."

At about noon, a large sum of money, was given me, which I had been desiring for a certain purpose.

In a following chapter, I will give affirmations that I have found most effective. However, one should never use an affirmation unless it is absolutely satisfying and convincing to his own consciousness, and often an affirmative is changed to suit different people.

For example: The following has brought success to many:

"I have a wonderful work, in a wonderful way, I give wonderful service, for wonderful pay!"

I gave the first two lines to one of my students, and she added the last two.

It made a *most powerful statement,* as there should always be perfect payment for perfect service, and a rhyme sinks easily into the subconscious. She went about singing it aloud and soon did receive wonderful work in a wonderful way, and gave wonderful service for wonderful pay.

Another student, a business man, took it, and changed the word work to business.

He repeated, "I have a wonderful business, in a wonderful way, and I give wonderful service for wonderful pay." That afternoon he made a forty-one-thousand dollar deal, though there had been no activity in his affairs for months.

Every affirmation must be carefully worded and completely "cover the ground."

For example: I knew a woman, who was in great need, and made a demand for work. She received a great deal of work, but was never paid anything. She now knows to add, "wonderful service for wonderful pay."

It is man's divine right to have plenty! More than enough!

"His barns should be full, and his cup should flow over!" This is God's idea for man, and when man breaks down the barriers of lack in his own consciousness, the Golden Age will be his, and every righteous desire of his heart fulfilled!

The Law of Karma and The Law of Forgiveness

Man receives only that which he gives. The Game of Life is a game of boomerangs. Man's thoughts, deeds and words, return to him sooner or later, with astounding accuracy.

This is the law of Karma, which is Sanskrit for "Comeback." "Whatsoever a man soweth, that shall he also reap."

For example: A friend told me this story of herself, illustrating the law. She said, "I make all my Karma on my aunt, whatever I say to her, some one says to me. I am often irritable at home, and one day, said to my aunt, who was talking to me during dinner. *'No more talk, I wish to eat in peace.'*

"The following day, I was lunching with a woman with whom I wished to make a great impression. I was talking animatedly, when she said: '*No more talk, I wish to eat in peace!*'"

My friend is high in consciousness, so her Karma returns much more quickly than to one on the mental plane.

The more man knows, the more he is responsible for, and a person with a knowledge of Spiritual Law, which he does not practice, suffers greatly, in consequence. "The fear of the Lord (law) is the beginning of wisdom." If we read the word Lord, law, it will make many passages in the Bible much clearer.

"Vengeance is mine, I will repay, saith the Lord" (law). It is the law which takes vengeance, not God. God sees man perfect, "created in His own image" (imagination) and given "power and dominion."

This is the perfect idea of man, registered in Divine Mind, awaiting man's recognition; for man can only be what he sees himself to be, and only attain what he sees himself attaining.

"Nothing ever happens without an on-looker" is an ancient saying.

Man sees first his failure or success, his joy or sorrow, before it swings into visibility from the scenes set in his own imagination. We have observed this in the mother picturing disease for her child, or a woman seeing success for her husband.

Jesus Christ said, "And ye shall know the truth and the truth shall make you free."

So, we see freedom (from all unhappy conditions) comes through knowledge—a knowledge of Spiritual Law.

Obedience precedes authority, and the law obeys man when he obeys the law. The law of electricity must be obeyed before it becomes man's servant. When handled ignorantly, it becomes man's deadly foe. *So with the laws of Mind!*

For example: A woman with a strong personal will, wished she owned a house which belonged to an acquaintance, and she often made mental pictures of herself living in the house. In the course of time, the man died and she moved into the house. Several years afterwards, coming into the knowledge of Spiritual Law, she said to me: "Do you think I had anything to do with that man's death?" I replied: "Yes, your desire was so strong, everything made way for it, but you paid your Karmic debt. Your husband, whom you loved devotedly, died soon after, and the house was a white elephant on your hands for years."

The original owner, however, could not have been affected by her thoughts had he been positive in the truth, nor her husband, but they were both under Karmic law. The woman should have said (feeling the great desire for the house), "Infinite Intelligence, give me the right house, equally as charming as this, the house *which is mine by divine right.*"

The divine selection would have given perfect satisfaction and brought good to all. The divine pattern is the only safe pattern to work by.

Desire is a tremendous force, and must be directed in the right channels, or chaos ensues.

In demonstrating, the most important step is the *first step, to "ask aright."*

Man should always demand only that which is his by *divine right.*

To go back to the illustration: Had the woman taken this attitude: "If this house, I desire, is mine, I cannot lose it, if it is not, give me its equivalent," the man might have decided to move out, harmoniously (had it been the divine selection for her) or another house would have been substituted. Anything forced into manifestation through personal will, is always "ill-got," and has "ever bad success."

Man is admonished, "My will be done not thine," and the curious thing is, man always gets just what he desires when he does relinquish personal will, thereby enabling Infinite Intelligence to work through him.

"Stand ye still and see the salvation of the Lord" (law).

For example: A woman came to me in great distress. Her daughter had determined to take a very hazardous trip, and the mother was filled with fear.

She said she had used every argument, had pointed out the dangers to be encountered, and forbidden her to go, but the daughter became more and more rebellious and determined. I said to the mother, "You are forcing your personal will upon your daughter, which you have no right to do, and your fear of the trip is only attracting it, for man attracts what he fears." I added, "Let go, and take your mental hands off; *put it in God's hands, and use this statement:* 'I put this situation in the hands of Infinite Love and Wisdom; if this trip is the Divine plan, I bless it and no longer resist, but if it is not divinely planned, I give thanks that it is now dissolved and dissipated.'" A day or two after that, her daughter said to her, "Mother, I have given up the trip," and the situation returned to its "native nothingness."

It is learning to "stand still," which seems so difficult for man. I have dealt more fully with this law in the chapter on nonresistance.

I will give another example of sowing and reaping, which came in the most curious way.

A woman came to me saying she had received a counterfeit twenty-dollar bill, given to her at the bank. She was much disturbed, for, she said, "the people at the bank will never acknowledge their mistake."

I replied, "Let us analyze the situation and find out why you attracted it." She thought a few moments and exclaimed: "I know it, I sent a friend a lot of stagemoney, just for a joke." So the law had sent her some stagemoney, for it doesn't know anything about jokes.

I said, "Now we will call on the law of forgiveness, and neutralize the situation."

Christianity is founded upon the law of forgiveness—Christ has redeemed us from the curse of the Karmic law, and the Christ within each man is his Redeemer and Salvation from all inharmonious conditions.

So I said: "Infinite Spirit, we call on the law of forgiveness and give thanks that she is under grace and not under law, and cannot lose this twenty dollars which is hers by divine right."

"Now," I said, "go back to the bank and tell them, fearlessly, that it was given you there by mistake."

She obeyed, and to her surprise, they apologized and gave her another bill, treating her most courteously.

So knowledge of the Law gives man power to "rub out his mistakes." Man cannot force the external to be what he is not.

If he desires riches, he must be rich first in consciousness.

For example: A woman came to me asking treatment for prosperity. She did not take much interest in her household affairs, and her home was in great disorder.

I said to her, "If you wish to be rich, you must be orderly. All men with great wealth are orderly—and order is heaven's first law." I added, "You will never become rich with a burnt match in the pincushion."

She had a good sense of humor and commenced immediately, putting her house in order. She rearranged furniture, straightened out bureau drawers, cleaned rugs, and soon made a big financial demonstration—a gift from a relative. The woman, herself, became made over, and keeps herself keyed-up financially, by being ever watchful of the *external and expecting prosperity, knowing God is her supply.*

Many people are in ignorance of the fact that gifts and things are investments, and that hoarding and saving invariably lead to loss.

"There is that scattereth and yet increaseth; and there is that withholdeth more than is meet, but it tendeth to poverty."

For example: I knew a man who wanted to buy a fur-lined overcoat. He and his wife went to various shops, but there was none he wanted. He said they were all too cheap-looking. At last, he was shown one, the salesman said was valued at a thousand dollars, but which the manager would sell him for five-hundred dollars, as it was late in the season.

His financial possessions amounted to about seven hundred dollars. The reasoning mind would have said, "You can't afford to spend nearly all you have on a coat," but he was very intuitive and never reasoned.

He turned to his wife and said, "If I get this coat, I'll make a ton of money!" So his wife consented, weakly.

About a month later, he received a ten-thousand-dollar commission. The coat made him feel so rich, it linked him with success and prosperity; without the coat, he would not have received the commission. It was an investment paying large dividends!

If man ignores these leadings to spend or to give, the same amount of money will go in an uninteresting or unhappy way.

For example: A woman told me, on Thanksgiving Day, she informed her family that they could not afford a Thanksgiving dinner. She had the money, but decided to save it.

A few days later, someone entered her room and took from the bureau drawer the exact amount the dinner would have cost.

The law always stands back of the man who spends fearlessly, with wisdom.

For example: One of my students was shopping with her little nephew. The child clamored for a toy, which she told him she could not afford to buy.

She realized suddenly that she was seeking lack, and not recognizing God as her supply!

So she bought the toy, and on her way home, *picked up, in the street, the exact amount of money she had paid for it.*

Man's supply is inexhaustible and unfailing when fully trusted, but faith or trust must precede the demonstration. "According to your faith be it unto you." "Faith is the substance of things hoped for, the evidence of things not seen—" for faith holds the vision steady, and the adverse pictures are dissolved and dissipated, and "in due season we shall reap, if we faint not."

Jesus Christ brought the good news (the gospel) that there was a higher law than the law of Karma—and that that law transcends the law of Karma. It is the law of grace, or forgiveness. It is the law which *frees man from the law of cause and effect—the law of consequence. "Under grace, and not under law."*

We are told that on this plane, man reaps where he has not sown; the gifts of God are simply poured out upon him. "All that the Kingdom affords is his." This continued state of bliss awaits the man who has overcome the race (or world) thought.

In the world thought there is tribulation, but Jesus Christ said: "Be of good cheer; I have overcome the world."

The world thought is that of sin, sickness and death. He saw their absolute unreality and said sickness and sorrow shall pass away and death itself, the last enemy, be overcome.

We know now, from a scientific standpoint, that death could be overcome by stamping the subconscious mind with the conviction of eternal youth and eternal life.

The subconscious, being simply power without direction, *carries out orders without questioning.*

Working under the direction of the superconscious (the Christ or God within man) the "resurrection of the body" would be accomplished.

Man would no longer throw off his body in death, it would be transformed into the "body electric," sung by Walt Whitman, for Christianity is founded upon the forgiveness of sins and "an empty tomb."

Casting the Burden

Impressing the Subconscious

When man knows his own powers and the workings of his mind, his great desire is to find an easy and quick way to impress the subconscious with good, for simply an intellectual knowledge of the Truth will not bring results.

In my own case, I found the easiest way is in "casting the burden."

A metaphysician once explained it in this manner. He said, "The only thing which gives anything weight in nature, is the law of gravitation, and if a boulder could be taken high above the planet, there would be no weight in that boulder; and that is what Jesus Christ meant when he said: 'My yoke is easy and my burden is light.'"

He had overcome the world vibration, and functioned in the fourth dimensional realm, where there is only perfection, completion, life and joy.

He said: "Come to me all ye that labor and are heavy laden, and I will give you rest." "Take my yoke upon you, for my yoke is easy and my burden is light."

We are also told in the fifty-fifth Psalm, to "cast thy burden upon the Lord." Many passages in the Bible state that the *battle is God's* not man's and that man is always to *"stand still" and see the Salvation of the Lord.*

This indicates that the superconscious mind (or Christ within) is the department which fights man's battle and relieves him of burdens.

We see, therefore, that man violates law if he carries a burden, and a burden is an adverse thought or condition, and this thought or condition has its root in the subconscious.

It seems almost impossible to make any headway directing the subconscious from the conscious, or reasoning mind, as the reasoning mind (the intellect) is limited in its conceptions, and filled with doubts and fears.

How scientific it then is, to cast the burden upon the superconscious mind (or Christ within) where it is "made light," or dissolved into its "native nothingness."

For example: A woman in urgent need of money, "made light" upon the Christ within, the superconscious, with the statement, "I cast this burden of lack on the Christ (within) and I go free to have plenty!"

The belief in lack was her burden, and as she cast it upon the superconscious with its belief of plenty, an avalanche of supply was the result.

We read, "The Christ in you the hope of glory."

Another example: One of my students had been given a new piano, and there was no room in her studio for it until she had moved out the old one. She was in a state of perplexity. She wanted to keep the old piano, but knew of no place to send it. She became desperate, as the new piano was to be sent immediately; in fact, was on its way, with no place to put it. She said it came to her to repeat, "I cast this burden on the Christ within, and I go free."

A few moments later, her phone rang, and a woman friend asked if she might rent her old piano, and it was moved out, a few minutes before the new one arrived.

I knew a woman, whose burden was resentment. She said, "I cast this burden of resentment on the Christ within, and I go free, to be loving, harmonious and happy." The Almighty superconscious, flooded the subconscious with love, and her whole life was changed. For years, resentment had held her in a state of torment and imprisoned her soul (the subconscious mind).

The statement should be made over and over and over, sometimes for hours at a time, silently or audibly, with quietness but determination.

I have often compared it to winding-up a victrola. We must wind ourselves up with spoken words.

I have noticed, in "casting the burden," after a little while, one seems to see clearly. It is impossible to have clear vision, while in the throes of carnal mind. Doubts and fear poison the mind and body and imagination runs riot, attracting disaster and disease.

In steadily repeating the affirmation, "I cast this burden on the Christ within, and go free," the vision clears, and with it a feeling of relief, and sooner or later comes *the manifestation of good, be it health, happiness or supply.*

One of my students once asked me to explain the "darkness before the dawn." I referred in a preceding chapter to the fact that often, before the big demonstration "everything seems to go wrong," and deep depression clouds the consciousness. It means that out of the subconscious are rising the doubts and fears of the ages. These old derelicts of the subconscious rise to the surface, *to be put out.*

It is then, that man should clap his cymbals, like Jehoshaphat, and give thanks that he is saved, even though he seems surrounded by the enemy (the situation of lack or disease). The student continued, "How long must one remain in the dark" and I replied, "Until one *can see in the dark,*" and *"Casting the burden enables one to see in the dark."*

In order to impress the subconscious, active faith is always essential.

"Faith without works is dead." In these chapters I have endeavored to bring out this point.

Jesus Christ showed active faith when "He commanded the multitude to sit down on the ground," before he gave thanks for the loaves and the fishes.

I will give another example showing how necessary this step is. In fact, active faith is the bridge, over which man passes to his Promised Land.

Through misunderstanding, a woman had been separated from her husband, whom she loved deeply. He refused all offers of reconciliation and would not communicate with her in any way.

Coming into the knowledge of Spiritual law, she denied the appearance of separation. She made this statement: "There is no separation in Divine Mind, therefore, I cannot be separated from the love and companionship which are mine by divine right."

She showed active faith by arranging a place for him at the table every day; thereby impressing the subconscious with a picture of his *return.* Over a year passed, but she never wavered, and *one day he walked in.*

The subconscious is often impressed through music. Music has a fourth dimensional quality and releases the soul from imprisonment. It makes wonderful things seem *possible, and easy of accomplishment!*

I have a friend who uses her victrola, daily, for this purpose. It puts her in perfect harmony and releases the imagination.

Another woman often dances while making her affirmations. The rhythm and harmony of music and motion carry her words forth with tremendous power.

The student must remember also, not to despise the "day of small things."

Invariably, before a demonstration, come "signs of land."

Before Columbus reached America, he saw birds and twigs which showed him land was near. So it is with a demonstration; but often the student mistakes it for the demonstration itself, and is disappointed.

For example: A woman had "spoken the word" for a set of dishes. Not long afterwards a friend gave her a dish which was old and cracked.

She came to me and said, "Well, I asked for a set of dishes, and all I got was a cracked plate."

I replied, "The plate was only signs of land. It shows your dishes are coming—look upon it as birds and seaweed," and not long afterwards the dishes came.

Continually "making believe" impresses the subconscious. If one makes believe he is rich, and makes believe he is successful, in "due time he will reap."

Children are always "making believe," and "except ye be converted, and become as little children, ye shall not enter the Kingdom of Heaven."

For example: I know of a woman who was very poor, but no one could make her *feel poor.* She earned a small amount of money from rich friends, who constantly reminded her of her poverty, and to be careful and saving. Regardless of their admonitions, she would spend all her earnings on a hat, or make someone a gift, and be in a rapturous state of mind. Her thoughts were always centered on beautiful clothes and "rings and things," but without envying others.

She lived in the world of the wondrous, and only riches seemed real to her. Before long she married a rich man, and the rings and things became visible. I do not know whether the man was the "Divine Selection," but opulence had to manifest in her life, as she had imaged only opulence.

There is no peace or happiness for man, until he has erased all fear from the subconscious.

Fear is misdirected energy and must be redirected, or transmuted into Faith.

Jesus Christ said, "Why are ye fearful, O ye of little faith?" "All things are possible to him that believeth."

I am asked, so often by my students, *"How can I get rid of fear?"*

I reply, *"By walking up to the thing you are afraid of."*

"The lion takes its fierceness from your fear."

Walk up to the lion, and he will disappear; run away and he runs after you.

I have shown in previous chapters, how the lion of lack disappeared when the individual spent money fearlessly, showing faith that God was his supply and therefore, unfailing.

Many of my students have come out of the bondage of poverty, and are now bountifully supplied, through losing all fear of letting money go out. The subconscious is impressed with the truth that *God is the Giver and the Gift;* therefore as one is one with the Giver, he is one with the Gift. A splendid statement is, "I now thank God the Giver for God the Gift."

Man has so long separated himself from his good and his supply, through thoughts of separation and lack, that sometimes, it takes dynamite to dislodge these false ideas from the subconscious, and the dynamite is a big situation.

We see in the foregoing illustration, how the individual was freed from his bondage by *showing fearlessness.*

Man should watch himself hourly to detect if his motive for action is fear or faith.

"Choose ye this day whom we shall serve," fear or faith.

Perhaps one's fear is of personality. Then do not avoid the people feared; be willing to meet them cheerfully, and they will either prove "golden links in the chain of one's good," or disappear harmoniously from one's pathway.

Perhaps one's fear is of disease or germs. Then one should be fearless and undisturbed in a germ-laden situation, and he would be immune.

One can only contract germs while vibrating at the same rate as the germ, and fear drags men down to the level of the germ. Of course, the disease laden germ is the product of carnal mind, as all thought must objectify. Germs do not exist in the superconscious or Divine Mind, therefore are the product of man's "vain imagination."

"In the twinkling of an eye," man's release will come when he realizes *there is no power in evil.*

The material world will fade away, and the fourth dimensional world, the "World of the Wondrous," will swing into manifestation.

"And I saw a new heaven, and a new earth—and there shall be no more death, neither sorrow nor crying, neither shall there be any more pain; for the former things are passed away."

Love

Every man on this planet is taking his initiation in love. "A new commandment I give unto you, that ye love one another." Ouspensky states, in "Tertium Organum," that "love is a cosmic phenomenon," and opens to man the fourth dimensional world, "The World of the Wondrous."

Real love is selfless and free from fear. It pours itself out upon the object of its affection, without demanding any return. Its joy is in the joy of giving. Love is God in manifestation, and the strongest magnetic force in the universe. Pure, unselfish love *draws to itself its own;* it does not need to seek or demand. Scarcely anyone has the faintest conception of real love. Man is selfish, tyrannical or fearful in his affections, thereby losing the thing he loves. Jealousy is the worst enemy of love, for the imagination runs riot, seeing the loved one attracted to another, and invariably these fears objectify if they are not neutralized.

For example: A woman came to me in deep distress. The man she loved had left her for other women, and said he never intended to marry her. She was torn with jealousy and resentment and said she hoped he would suffer as he had made her suffer; and added, "How could he leave me when I loved him so much?"

I replied, "You are not loving that man, you are hating him," and added, "*You can never receive what you have never given. Give a perfect love and you will receive a perfect love.* Perfect yourself on this man. Give him a perfect, *unselfish* love, demanding nothing in return, do not criticise or condemn, and *bless him wherever he is.*"

She replied, "No, I won't bless him unless I know where he is!"

"Well," I said, "that is not real love."

"When you *send out real love,* real love will return to you, either from this man or his equivalent, for if this man is not the divine selection, you will not want him. As you are one with God, you are one with the love which belongs to you by divine right."

Several months passed, and matters remained about the same, but she was working conscientiously with herself. I said, "When you are no longer disturbed by his cruelty, he will cease to be cruel, as you are attracting it through your own emotions."

Then I told her of a brotherhood in India, who never said, "Good morning" to each other. They used these words: "*I salute the Divinity in you.*" They saluted the divinity in every man, and in the wild animals in the jungle, and they were never harmed, for they *saw only God in every living thing.* I said, "Salute the divinity in this man, and say, 'I see your divine self only. I see you as God sees you, perfect, made in His image and likeness.'"

She found she was becoming more poised, and gradually losing her resentment. He was a Captain, and she always called him "The Cap."

One day, she said, suddenly, *"God bless the Cap wherever he is."*

I replied: "Now, that is real love, and when you have become a 'complete circle,' and are no longer disturbed by the situation, you will have his love, or attract its equivalent."

I was moving at this time, and did not have a telephone, so was out of touch with her for a few weeks, when one morning I received a letter saying, "We are married."

At the earliest opportunity, I paid her a call. My first words were, "What happened?"

"Oh," she exclaimed, "a miracle! One day I woke up and all suffering had ceased. I saw him that evening and he asked me to marry him. We were married in about a week, and I have never seen a more devoted man."

There is an old saying: *"No man is your enemy, no man is your friend, every man is your teacher."*

So one should become impersonal and learn what each man has to teach him, and soon he would learn his lessons and be free.

The woman's lover was teaching her selfless love, which every man, sooner or later, must learn.

Suffering is not necessary for man's development; it is the result of violation of spiritual law, but few people seem able to rouse themselves from their "soul sleep" without it. When people are happy, they usually become selfish, and automatically the law of Karma is set in action. Man often suffers loss through lack of appreciation.

I knew a woman who had a very nice husband, but she said often, "I don't care anything about being married, but that is nothing against my husband. I'm simply not interested in married life."

She had other interests, and scarcely remembered she had a husband. She only thought of him when she saw him. One day her husband told her he was in love with another woman, and left. She came to me in distress and resentment.

I replied, "It is exactly what you spoke the word for. You said you didn't care anything about being married, so the subconscious worked to get you unmarried."

She said, "Oh yes, I see. People get what they want, and then feel very much hurt."

She soon became in perfect harmony with the situation, and knew they were both much happier apart.

When a woman becomes indifferent or critical, and ceases to be an inspiration to her husband, he misses the stimulus of their early relationship and is restless and unhappy.

A man came to me dejected, miserable and poor. His wife was interested in the "Science of Numbers," and had had him read. It seems the report was not very favorable, for he said, "My wife says I'll never amount to anything because I am a two."

I replied, "I don't care what your number is, you are a perfect idea in Divine Mind, and we will demand the success and prosperity which are *already planned* for you by that Infinite Intelligence."

Within a few weeks, he had a very fine position, and a year or two later, he achieved a brilliant success as a writer. No man is a success in business unless he loves his work. The picture the artist paints for love (of his art) is his greatest work. The pot-boiler is always something to live down.

No man can attract money if he despises it. Many people are kept in poverty by saying: "Money means nothing to me, and I have a contempt for people who have it."

This is the reason so many artists are poor. Their contempt for money separates them from it.

I remember hearing one artist say of another, "He's no good as an artist, he has money in the bank."

This attitude of mind, of course, separates man from his supply; he must be in harmony with a thing in order to attract it.

Money is God in manifestation, as freedom from want and limitation, but it must be always kept in circulation and put to right uses. Hoarding and saving react with grim vengeance.

This does not mean that man should not have houses and lots, stocks and bonds, for "the barns of the righteous man shall be full." It means man should not hoard even the principal, if an occasion arises, when money is necessary. In letting it go out fearlessly and cheerfully he opens the way for more to come in, for God is man's unfailing and inexhaustible supply.

This is the spiritual attitude towards money and the great Bank of the Universal never fails!

We see an example of hoarding in the film production of "Greed." The woman won five thousand dollars in a lottery, but would not spend it. She hoarded and saved, let her husband suffer and starve, and eventually she scrubbed floors for a living.

She loved the money itself and put it above everything, and one night she was murdered and the money taken from her.

This is an example of where "love of money is the root of all evil." Money in itself, is good and beneficial, but used for destructive purposes, hoarded and saved, or considered more important than love, brings disease and disaster, and the loss of the money itself.

Follow the path of love, and all things are added, *for God is love,* and *God is supply;* follow the path of selfishness and greed, and the supply vanishes, or man is separated from it.

For example; I knew the case of a very rich woman, who hoarded her income. She rarely gave anything away, but bought and bought and bought things for herself.

She was very fond of necklaces, and a friend once asked her how many she possessed. She replied, "Sixty-seven." She bought them and put them away, carefully wrapped in tissue paper. Had she used the necklaces it would have been quite legitimate, but she was violating "the law of use." Her closets were filled with clothes she never wore, and jewels which never saw the light.

The woman's arms were gradually becoming paralyzed from holding on to things, and eventually she was considered incapable of looking after her affairs and her wealth was handed over to others to manage.

So man, in ignorance of the law, brings about his own destruction.

All disease, all unhappiness, come from the violation of the law of love. Man's boomerangs of hate, resentment and criticism, come back laden with sickness and sorrow. Love seems almost a lost art, but the man with the knowledge of Spiritual Law knows it must be regained, for without it, he has "become as sounding brass and tinkling cymbals."

For example: I had a student who came to me, month after month, to clean her consciousness of resentment. After a while, she arrived at the point where she resented only one woman, but that one woman kept her busy. Little by little she became poised and harmonious, and one day, all resentment was wiped out.

She came in radiant, and exclaimed, "You can't understand how I feel! The woman said something to me and instead of being furious I was loving and kind, and she apologized and was perfectly lovely to me.

"No one can understand the marvelous lightness I feel within!"

Love and goodwill are invaluable in business.

For example: A woman came to me, complaining of her employer. She said she was cold and critical and knew she did not want her in the position.

"Well," I replied, "salute the Divinity in the woman and send her love."

She said, "I can't; she's a marble woman."

I answered, "You remember the story of the sculptor who asked for a certain piece of marble. He was asked why he wanted it, and he replied, 'because there is an angel in the marble,' and out of it he produced a wonderful work of art."

She said, "Very well, I'll try it." A week later she came back and said, "I did what you told me to, and now the woman is very kind, and took me out in her car."

People are sometimes filled with remorse for having done someone an unkindness, perhaps years ago.

If the wrong cannot be righted, its effect can be neutralized by doing some one a kindness *in the present.*

"This one thing I do, forgetting those things which are behind and reaching forth unto those things which are before."

Sorrow, regret and remorse tear down the cells of the body, and poison the atmosphere of the individual.

A woman said to me in deep sorrow, "Treat me to be happy and joyous, for my sorrow makes me so irritable with the members of my family that I keep making more Karma."

I was asked to treat a woman who was mourning for her daughter. I denied all belief in loss and separation, and affirmed that God was the woman's joy, love and peace.

The woman gained her poise at once, but sent word by her son, not to treat any longer, because she was "so happy, it wasn't respectable."

So "mortal mind" loves to hang on to its griefs and regrets.

I knew a woman who went about bragging of her troubles, so, of course, she always had something to brag about.

The old idea was if a woman did not worry about her children, she was not a good mother.

Now, we know that mother-fear is responsible for many of the diseases and accidents which come into the lives of children.

For fear pictures vividly the disease or situation feared, and these pictures objectify, if not neutralized.

Happy is the mother who can say sincerely, that she puts her child in God's hands, and *knows* therefore, that he is divinely protected.

For example: A woman awoke suddenly, in the night, feeling her brother was in great danger. Instead of giving in to her fears, she commenced making statements of Truth, saying, "Man is a perfect idea in Divine Mind, and is always in his right place, therefore, my brother is in his right place, and is divinely protected."

The next day she found that her brother had been in close proximity to an explosion in a mine, but had miraculously escaped.

So man is his brother's keeper (in thought) and every man should know that the thing he loves dwells in "the secret place of the most high, and abides under the shadow of the Almighty."

"There shall no evil befall thee, neither shall any plague come nigh thy dwelling."

"Perfect love casteth out fear. He that feareth is not made perfect in love," and "Love is the fulfilling of the Law."

Intuition or Guidance

"In all thy ways acknowledge Him,
and He shall direct thy paths."

There is nothing too great of accomplishment for the man who knows the power of his word, and who follows his intuitive leads. By the word he starts in action unseen forces and can rebuild his body or remold his affairs.

It is, therefore, of the utmost importance to choose the right words, and the student carefully selects the affirmation he wishes to catapult into the invisible.

He knows that God is his supply, that there is a supply for every demand, and that his spoken word releases this supply.

"Ask and ye shall receive."

Man must make the first move. "Draw nigh to God and He will draw nigh to you."

I have often been asked just how to make a demonstration.

I reply: "Speak the word and then do not do anything until you get a definite lead." Demand the lead, saying, "Infinite Spirit, reveal to me the way, let me know if there is anything for me to do."

The answer will come through intuition (or hunch); a chance remark from someone, or a passage in a book, etc., etc. The answers are sometimes quite startling in their exactness. For example: A woman desired a large sum of money. She spoke the words: "Infinite Spirit, open the way for my immediate supply, let all that is mine by divine right now reach me, in great avalanches of abundance." Then she added: "Give me a definite lead, let me know if there is anything for me to do."

The thought came quickly, "Give a certain friend" (who had helped her spiritually) "a hundred dollars." She told her friend, who said, "Wait and get another lead, before giving it." So she waited, and that day met a woman who said to her, "I gave someone a dollar today; it was just as much for me, as it would be for you to give someone a hundred."

This was indeed an unmistakable lead, so she knew she was right in giving the hundred dollars. It was a gift which proved a great investment, for shortly after that, a large sum of money came to her in a remarkable way.

Giving opens the way for receiving. In order to create activity in finances, one should give. Tithing or giving one-tenth of one's income, is an old Jewish custom, and is sure to bring increase. Many of the richest men in this country have been tithers, and I have never known it to fail as an investment.

The tenth-part goes forth and returns blessed and multiplied. But the gift or tithe must be given with love and cheerfulness, for "God loveth a cheerful giver." Bills should be paid cheerfully; all money should be sent forth fearlessly and with a blessing.

This attitude of mind makes man master of money. It is his to obey, and his spoken word then opens vast reservoirs of wealth.

Man, himself, limits his supply by his limited vision. Sometimes the student has a great realization of wealth, but is afraid to act.

The vision and action must go hand in hand, as in the case of the man who bought the fur-lined overcoat.

A woman came to me asking me to "speak the word" for a position. So I demanded: "Infinite Spirit, open the way for this woman's right position," Never ask for just "a position"; ask for the right position, the place already planned in Divine Mind, as it is the only one that will give satisfaction.

I then gave thanks that she had already received, and that it would manifest quickly. Very soon, she had three positions offered her, two in New York and one in Palm Beach, and she did not know which to choose. I said, "Ask for a definite lead."

The time was almost up and was still undecided, when one day, she telephoned, "When I woke up this morning, I could smell Palm Beach." She had been there before and knew its balmy fragrance.

I replied: "Well, if you can smell Palm Beach from here, it is certainly your lead." She accepted the position, and it proved a great success. Often one's lead comes at an unexpected time.

One day, I was walking down the street, when I suddenly felt a strong urge to go to a certain bakery, a block or two away.

The reasoning mind resisted, arguing, "There is nothing there that you want."

However, I had learned not to reason, so I went to the bakery, looked at everything, and there was certainly nothing there that I wanted, but coming out I encountered a woman I had thought of often, and who was in great need of the help which I could give her.

So often, one goes for one thing and finds another.

Intuition is a spiritual faculty and does not explain, but simply *points the way.*

A person often receives a lead during a "treatment." The idea that comes may seem quite irrelevant, but some of God's leadings are "mysterious."

In the class, one day, I was treating that each individual would receive a definite lead. A woman came to me afterwards, and said: "While you were treating, I got the hunch to take my furniture out of storage and get an apartment." The woman had come to be treated for health. I told her I knew in getting a home of her own, her health would improve, and I added, "I believe your trouble, which is a congestion, has come from having things stored away. Congestion of things causes congestion in the body. You have violated the law of use, and your body is paying the penalty."

So I gave thanks that *"Divine order was established in her mind, body and affairs."*

People little dream of how their affairs react on the body. There is a mental correspondence for every disease. A person might receive instantaneous healing through the realization of his body being a perfect idea in Divine Mind, and, therefore, whole and perfect, but if he continues his destructive thinking, hoarding, hating, fearing, condemning, the disease will return.

Jesus Christ knew that all sickness came from sin, but admonished the leper after the healing, to go and sin no more, lest a worse thing come upon him.

So man's soul (or subconscious mind) must be washed whiter than snow, for permanent healing; and the metaphysician is always delving deep for the "correspondence."

Jesus Christ said, "Condemn not lest ye also be condemned."

"Judge not, lest ye be judged."

Many people have attracted disease and unhappiness through condemnation of others.

What man condemns in others, he attracts to himself.

For example: A friend came to me in anger and distress, because her husband had deserted her for another woman. She condemned the other woman, and said continually, "She knew he was a married man, and had no right to accept his attentions."

I replied, "Stop condemning the woman, bless her, and be through with the situation, otherwise, you are attracting the same thing to yourself."

She was deaf to my words, and a year or two later, became deeply interested in a married man, herself.

Man picks up a live-wire whenever he criticises or condemns, and may expect a shock.

Indecision is a stumbling-block in many a pathway. In order to overcome it, make the statement, repeatedly, *"I am always under direct inspiration; I make right decisions, quickly."*

These words impress the subconscious, and soon one finds himself awake and alert, making his right moves without hesitation. I have found it destructive to look to the psychic plane for guidance, as it is the plane of many minds and not "The One Mind."

As man opens his mind to subjectivity, he becomes a target for destructive forces. The psychic plane is the result of man's mortal thought, and is on the "plane of opposites." He may receive either good or bad messages.

The science of numbers and the reading of horoscopes, keep man down on the mental (or mortal) plane, for they deal only with the Karmic path.

I know of a man who should have been dead, years ago, according to his horoscope, but he is alive and a leader of one of the biggest movements in this country for the uplift of humanity.

It takes a very strong mind to neutralize a prophecy of evil. The student should declare, "Every false prophecy shall come to naught; every plan my Father in heaven has not planned, shall be dissolved and dissipated, the divine idea now comes to pass."

However, if any good message has ever been given one, of coming happiness, or wealth, harbor and expect it, and it will manifest sooner or later, through the law of expectancy.

Man's will should be used to back the universal will. "I will that the will of God be done."

It is God's will to give every man, every righteous desire of his heart, and man's will should be used to hold the perfect vision, without wavering.

The prodigal son said: "I will arise and go to my Father."

It is, indeed, often an effort of the will to leave the husks and swine of mortal thinking. It is so much easier, for the average person, to have fear than faith; *so faith is an effort of the will.*

As man becomes spiritually awakened he recognizes that any external inharmony is the correspondence of mental inharmony. If he stumbles or falls, he may know he is stumbling or falling in consciousness.

One day, a student was walking along the street condemning someone in her thoughts. She was saying, mentally, "That woman is the most disagreeable woman on earth," when suddenly three boy scouts rushed around the corner and almost knocked her over. She did not condemn the boy scouts, but immediately called on the law of forgiveness, and "saluted the divinity" in the woman. Wisdom's way are ways of pleasantness and all her paths are peace.

When one has made his demands upon the Universal, he must be ready for surprises. Everything may seem to be going wrong, when in reality, it is going right.

For example: A woman was told that there was no loss in Divine Mind, therefore, she could not lose anything which belonged to her; anything lost, would be returned, or she would receive its equivalent.

Several years previously, she had lost two thousand dollars. She had loaned the money to a relative during her lifetime, but the relative had died, leaving no mention of it in her will. The woman was resentful and angry, and as she had no written statement of the transaction, she never received the money, so she determined to deny the loss, and collect the two thousand dollars from the Bank of the Universal. She had to begin by forgiving the woman, as resentment and unforgiveness close the doors of this wonderful bank.

She made this statement, "I deny loss, there is no loss in Divine Mind, therefore, I cannot lose the two thousand dollars, which belong to me by divine right. '*As one door shuts another door opens.*'"

She was living in an apartment house which was for sale; and in the lease was a clause, stating that if the house was sold, the tenants would be required to move out within ninety days.

Suddenly, the landlord broke the leases and raised the rent. Again, injustice was on her pathway, but this time she was undisturbed. She blessed the landlord, and said, "As the rent has been raised, it means that I'll be that much richer, for God is my supply."

New leases were made out for the advanced rent, but by some divine mistake, the ninety days clause had been forgotten. Soon after, the landlord had an opportunity to sell the house. On account of the mistake in the new leases, the tenants held possession for another year.

The agent offered each tenant two hundred dollars if he would vacate. Several families moved; three remained, including the woman. A month or two passed, and the agent again appeared. This time he said to the woman, "Will you break your lease for the sum of fifteen hundred dollars?" It flashed upon her, "Here comes the two thousand dollars." She remembered having said to friends in the house, "We will all act together if anything more is said about leaving." So her *lead* was to consult her friends.

These friends said: "Well, if they have offered you fifteen hundred they will certainly give two thousand." So she received a check for two thousand dollars for giving up the apartment. It was certainly a remarkable working of the law, and the apparent injustice was merely opening the way for her demonstration.

It proved that there is no loss, and when man takes his spiritual stand, he collects all that is his from this great Reservoir of Good.

"I will restore to you the years the locusts have eaten."

The locusts are the doubts, fears, resentments and regrets of mortal thinking.

These adverse thoughts, alone, rob man; for "No man gives to himself but himself, and no man takes away from himself, but himself."

Man is here to prove God and "to bear witness to the truth," and he can only prove God by bringing plenty out of lack, and justice out of injustice.

"Prove me now herewith, saith the Lord of hosts, if I will not open you the windows of heaven, and pour out a blessing, that there shall not be room enough to receive it."

Perfect Self-Expression or The Divine Design

"No wind can drive my bark astray
nor change the tide of destiny."

There is for each man, perfect self-expression. There is a place which he is to fill and no one else can fill, something which he is to do, which no one else can do; it is his destiny!

This achievement is held, a perfect idea in Divine Mind, awaiting man's recognition. As the imaging faculty is the creative faculty, it is necessary for man to see the idea, before it can manifest.

So man's highest demand is for the *Divine Design of his life.*

He may not have the faintest conception of what it is, for there is, possibly, some marvelous talent, hidden deep within him.

His demand should be: *"Infinite Spirit, open the way for the Divine Design of my life to manifest; let the genius within me now be released; let me see clearly the perfect plan."*

The perfect plan includes health, wealth, love and perfect self-expression. This is the *square of life,* which brings perfect happiness. When one has made this demand, he may find great changes taking place in his life, for nearly every man has wandered far from the Divine Design.

I know, in one woman's case, it was as though a cyclone had struck her affairs, but readjustments came quickly, and new and wonderful conditions took the place of old ones.

Perfect self-expression will never be labor; but of such absorbing interest that it will seem almost like play. The student knows, also, as man comes into the world financed by God, the *supply* needed for his perfect self-expression will be at hand.

Many a genius has struggled for years with the problem of supply, when his spoken word, and faith, would have released quickly, the necessary funds.

For example: After the class, one day, a man came to me and handed me a cent.

He said: "I have just seven cents in the world, and I'm going to give you one; for I have faith in the power of your spoken word, I want you to speak the word for my perfect self-expression and prosperity."

I "spoke the word," and did not see him again until a year later. He came in one day, successful and happy, with a roll of yellow bills in his pocket. He said, "Immediately after you spoke the word, I had a position offered me in a distant city, and am now demonstrating health, happiness and supply."

A woman's perfect self-expression may be in becoming a perfect wife, a perfect mother, a perfect home-maker and not necessarily in having a public career.

Demand definite leads, and the way will be made easy and successful.

One should not visualize or force a mental picture. When he demands the Divine Design to come into his conscious mind, he will receive flashes of inspiration, and begin to see himself making some great accomplishment. This is the picture, or idea, he must hold without wavering.

The thing man seeks is seeking him—*the telephone was seeking Bell!*

Parents should never force careers and professions upon their children. With a knowledge of spiritual Truth, the Divine Plan could be spoken for, early in childhood, or prenatally.

A prenatal treatment should be: "Let the God in this child have perfect expression; let the Divine Design of his mind, body and affairs be made manifest throughout his life, throughout eternity."

God's will be done, not man's; God's pattern, not man's pattern, is the command we find running through all the scriptures, and the Bible is a book dealing with the science of the mind. It is a book telling man how to release his soul (or subconscious mind) from bondage.

The battles described are pictures of man waging war against mortal thoughts. "A man's foes shall be they of his own household." Every man is Jehoshaphat, and every man is David, who slays Goliath (mortal thinking) with the little white stone (faith).

So man must be careful that he is not the "wicked and slothful servant" who buried his talent. There is a terrible penalty to be paid for not using one's ability.

Often fear stands between man and his perfect self-expression. Stage-fright has hampered many a genius. This may be overcome by the spoken word, or treatment. The individual then loses all self-consciousness, and feels simply that he is a channel for Infinite Intelligence to express Itself through.

He is under direct inspiration, fearless, and confident; for he feels that it is the "Father within" him who does the work.

A young boy came often to my class with his mother. He asked me to "speak the word" for his coming examinations at school.

I told him to make the statement: "I am one with Infinite Intelligence. I know everything I should know on this subject." He had an excellent knowledge of history, but was not sure of his arithmetic. I saw him afterwards, and he said: "I spoke the word for my arithmetic, and passed with the highest honors; but thought I could depend on myself for history, and got a very poor mark." Man often receives a set-back when he is "too sure of himself," which means he is trusting to his personality and not the "Father within."

Another one of my students gave me an example of this. She took an extended trip abroad one summer, visiting many countries, where she was ignorant of the languages. She was calling for guidance and protection every minute, and her affairs went smoothly and miraculously. Her luggage was never delayed nor lost! Accommodations were always ready for her at the best hotels; and she had perfect service wherever she went. She returned to New York. Knowing the language, she felt God was no longer necessary, so looked after her affairs in an ordinary manner.

Everything went wrong, her trunks delayed, amid inharmony and confusion. The student must form the habit of "practicing the Presence of God" every minute. *"In all thy ways acknowledge him";* nothing is too small or too great.

Sometimes an insignificant incident may be the turning point in a man's life.

Robert Fulton, watching some boiling water, simmering in a tea kettle, saw a steamboat!

I have seen a student, often, keep back his demonstration, through resistance, or pointing the way.

He pins his faith to one channel only, and dictates just the way he desires the manifestation to come, which brings things to a standstill.

"My way, not your way!" is the command of Infinite Intelligence. Like all Power, be it steam or electricity, it must have a nonresistant engine or instrument to work through, and man is that engine or instrument.

Over and over again, man is told to "stand still." "Oh Judah, fear not; but tomorrow go out against them, for the Lord will be with you. You shall not need to fight this battle; set yourselves, stand ye still, and see the salvation of the Lord with you."

We see this in the incidents of the two thousand dollars coming to the woman through the landlord when she became *nonresistant* and *undisturbed,* and the woman who won the man's love "after all suffering had ceased."

The student's goal is *Poise! Poise* is *Power,* for it gives God-Power a chance to rush through man, to "will and to do Its good pleasure."

Poised, he thinks clearly, and makes "right decisions quickly." "He never misses a trick."

Anger blurs the visions, poisons the blood, is the root of many diseases, and causes wrong decision leading to failure.

It has been named one of the worst "sins," as its reaction is so harmful. The student learns that in metaphysics sin has a much broader meaning than in the old teaching. "Whatsoever is not of faith is sin."

He finds that fear and worry are deadly sins. They are inverted faith, and through distorted mental pictures, bring to pass the thing he fears. His work is to drive out these enemies (from the subconscious mind). "When Man is *fearless he is finished!"* Maeterlinck says, that "Man is God afraid."

So, as we read in the previous chapters: Man can only vanquish fear by walking up to the thing he is afraid of. When Jehoshaphat and his army prepared to meet the enemy, singing "Praise the Lord, for his mercy endureth forever," they found their enemies had destroyed each other, and there was nothing to fight.

For example: A woman asked a friend to deliver a message to another friend. The woman feared to give the message, as the reasoning mind said, "Don't get mixed-up in this affair, don't give that message."

She was troubled in spirit, for she had given her promise. At last, she determined to "walk up to the lion," and call on the law of divine protection. She met the friend to whom she was to deliver the message. She opened her mouth to speak it, when her friend said, "So-and-So has left town." This made it unnecessary to give the message, as the situation depended upon the person being in town. As she was willing to do it, she was not obliged to; as she did not fear, the situation vanished.

The student often delays his demonstration through a belief in incompletion. He should make this statement:

"In Divine Mind there is only completion, therefore, my demonstration is completed. My perfect work, my perfect home, my perfect health." Whatever he demands are perfect ideas registered in Divine Mind, and must manifest, "under grace in a perfect way." He gives thanks he has already received on the invisible, and makes active preparation for receiving on the visible.

One of my students was in need of a financial demonstration. She came to me and asked why it was not completed.

I replied: "Perhaps, you are in the habit of leaving things unfinished, and the subconscious has gotten into the habit of not completing (as the without, so the within)."

She said, "You are right. I often *begin things* and never finish them.

"I'll go home and finish something I commenced weeks ago, and I know it will be symbolic of my demonstration."

So she sewed assiduously, and the article was soon completed. Shortly after, the money came in a most curious manner.

Her husband was paid his salary twice that month. He told the people of their mistake, and they sent word to keep it.

When man asks, *believing, he must receive, for God creates His own channels!*

I have been sometimes asked, "Suppose one has several talents, how is he to know which one to choose?" Demand to be shown definitely. Say: "Infinite Spirit, give me a definite lead, reveal to me my perfect self-expression, show me which talent I am to make use of now."

I have known people to suddenly enter a new line of work, and be fully equipped, with little or no training. So make the statement: "*I am fully equipped for the Divine Plan of my life,*" and be fearless in grasping opportunities.

Some people are cheerful givers, but bad receivers. They refuse gifts through pride, or some negative reason, thereby blocking their channels, and invariably find themselves eventually with little or nothing. For example: A woman who had given away a great deal of money, had a gift offered her of several thousand dollars. She refused to take it, saying she did not need it. Shortly after that, her finances were "tied up," and she found herself in debt for that amount. Man should receive gracefully the bread returning to him upon the water—freely ye have given, freely ye shall receive.

There is always the perfect balance of giving and receiving, and though man should give without thinking of returns, he violates law if he does not accept the returns which come to him; for all gifts are from God, man being merely the channel.

A thought of lack should never be held over the giver.

For example: When the man gave me the one cent, I did not say: "Poor man, he cannot afford to give me that." I saw him rich and prosperous, with his supply pouring in. It was this thought which brought it. If one has been a bad receiver, he must become a good one, and take even a postage stamp if it is given him, and open up his channels for receiving.

The Lord loveth a cheerful receiver, as well as a cheerful giver.

I have often been asked why one man is born rich and healthy, and another poor and sick.

Where there is an effect there is always a cause; there is no such thing as chance.

This question is answered through the law of reincarnation. Man goes through many births and deaths, until he knows the truth which sets him free.

He is drawn back to the earth plane through unsatisfied desire, to pay his Karmic debts, or to "fulfill his destiny."

The man born rich and healthy has had pictures in his subconscious mind, in his past life, of health and riches; and the poor and sick man, of disease and poverty. Man manifests, on any plane, the sum total of his subconscious beliefs.

However, birth and death are man-made laws, for the "wages of sin is death"; the Adamic fall in consciousness through the belief in *two powers.* The real man, spiritual man, is birthless and deathless! He never was born and has never died—"As he was in the beginning, he is now, and ever shall be!"

So through the truth, man is set free from the law of Karma, sin and death, and manifests the man made in "His image and likeness." Man's freedom comes through fulfilling his destiny, bringing into manifestation the Divine Design of his life.

His Lord will say unto him: "Well done thou good and faithful servant, thou hast been faithful over a few things, I will make thee ruler over many things (death itself); enter thou into the joy of thy Lord (eternal life)."

Denials and Affirmations

"Thou shalt also decree a thing, and it shall be established unto thee."

All the good that is to be made manifest in man's life is already an accomplished fact in Divine Mind, and is released through man's recognition, or spoken word, so he must be careful to decree that only the Divine Idea be made manifest, for often, he decrees, through his "idle words," failure or misfortune.

It is, therefore, of the utmost importance, to word one's demands correctly, as stated in a previous chapter.

If one desires a home, friend, position or any other good thing, make the demand for the "divine selection."

For example: "Infinite Spirit, open the way for my right home, my right friend, my right position. I give thanks *it now manifests under grace in a perfect way.*"

The latter part of the statement is most important. For example: I knew a woman who demanded a thousand dollars. Her daughter was injured and they received a thousand dollars indemnity, so it did not come in a "perfect way." The demand should have been worded in this way: "Infinite Spirit, I give thanks that the one thousand dollars, which is mine by divine right, is now released, and reaches me under grace, in a perfect way."

As one grows in a financial consciousness, he should demand that the enormous sums of money, which are his by divine right, reach him under grace, in perfect ways.

It is impossible for man to release more than he thinks is possible, for one is bound by the limited expectancies of the subconscious. He must enlarge his expectancies in order to receive in a larger way.

Man so often limits himself in his demands. For example: A student made the demand for six hundred dollars, by a certain date. He did receive it but heard afterwards, that he came very near receiving a thousand dollars, but he was given just six hundred, as the result of his spoken word.

"They limited the Holy One of Israel." Wealth is a matter of consciousness. The French have a legend giving an example of this. A poor man was walking along a road when he met a traveler, who stopped him and said: "My good friend, I see you are poor. Take this gold nugget, sell it, and you will be rich all your days."

The man was overjoyed at his good fortune, and took the nugget home. He immediately found work and became so prosperous that he did not sell the nugget. Years passed, and he became a very rich man. One day he met a poor man on the road. He stopped him and said: "My good friend, I will give you this gold nugget, which, if you sell, will make you rich for life." The mendicant took the nugget, had it valued, and found it was only brass. So we see, the first man became rich through feeling rich, thinking the nugget was gold.

Every man has within himself a gold nugget; *it is his consciousness of gold, of opulence, which brings riches into his life.* In making his demands, man begins at his *journey's end,* that is, he declares *he has already received. "Before* ye call I shall answer."

Continually affirming establishes the belief in the subconscious.

It would not be necessary to make an affirmation more than once if one had perfect faith! One should not plead or supplicate, but give thanks repeatedly, that he has received.

"The desert shall *rejoice* and blossom as the rose." This rejoicing which is yet in the desert (state of consciousness) opens the way for release. The Lord's Prayer is in the form of command and demand, "Give us this day our daily bread, and forgive us our debts as we forgive our debtors," and ends in praise, "For thine is the Kingdom and the Power and the Glory, forever. Amen." "Concerning the works of my hands, command ye me." So prayer is command and demand, praise and thanksgiving. The student's work is in making himself believe that "with God all things are possible."

This is easy enough to state in the abstract, but a little more difficult when confronted with a problem. For example: It was necessary for a woman to demonstrate a large sum of money within a stated time. She knew she must *do something* to get a realization (for realization is manifestation), and she demanded a "lead."

She was walking through a department store, when she saw a very beautiful pink enamel papercutter. She felt the "pull" towards it. The thought came. "I haven't a papercutter good enough to open letters containing large cheques."

So she bought the papercutter, which the reasoning mind would have called an extravagance. When she held it in her hand, she had a flash of a picture of herself opening an envelope containing a large cheque, and in a few weeks, she received the money. The pink papercutter was her bridge of active faith.

Many stories are told of the power of the subconscious when directed in faith.

For example: A man was spending the night in a farmhouse. The windows of the room had been nailed down, and in the middle of the night he felt suffocated and made his way in the dark to the window. He could not open it, so he smashed the pane with his fist, drew in draughts of fine fresh air, and had a wonderful night's sleep.

The next morning, he found he had smashed the glass of a bookcase and the window had remained closed during the whole night. He had *supplied himself with oxygen, simply by his thought of oxygen.*

When a student starts out to demonstrate, he should never turn back. "Let not that man who wavers think that he shall receive anything of the Lord."

A colored student once made this wonderful statement, "When I asks the Father for anything, I puts my foot down, and I says: Father, I'll take nothing less than I've asked for, but more!" So man should never compromise: "Having done all—Stand." This is sometimes the most difficult time of demonstrating. The temptation comes to give up, to turn back, to compromise.

"He also serves who only stands and waits."

Demonstrations often come at the eleventh hour because man then lets go, that is, stops reasoning, and Infinite Intelligence has a chance to work.

"Man's dreary desires are answered drearily, and his impatient desires, long delayed or violently fulfilled."

For example: A woman asked me why it was she was constantly losing or breaking her glasses.

We found she often said to herself and others with vexation, "I wish I could get rid of my glasses." So her impatient desire was violently fulfilled. What she should have demanded was perfect eyesight, but what she registered in the subconscious was simply the impatient desire to be rid of her glasses; so they were continually being broken or lost.

Two attitudes of mind cause loss: depreciation, as in the case of the woman who did not appreciate her husband, *or fear of loss,* which makes a picture of loss in the subconscious.

When a student is able to let go of his problem (cast his burden) he will have instantaneous manifestation.

For example: A woman was out during a very stormy day and her umbrella was blown inside-out. She was about to make a call on some people whom she had never met and she did not wish to make her first appearance with a dilapidated umbrella. She could not throw it away, as it did not belong to her. So in desperation, she exclaimed: "Oh, God, you take charge of this umbrella, I don't know what to do."

A moment later, a voice behind her said: "Lady, do you want your umbrella mended?" There stood an umbrella mender.

She replied, "Indeed, I do."

The man mended the umbrella, while she went into the house to pay her call, and when she returned, she had a good umbrella. So there is always an umbrella mender at hand, on man's pathway, when one puts the umbrella (or situation) in God's hands.

One should always follow a denial with an affirmation.

For example: I was called on the phone late one night to treat a man whom I had never seen. He was apparently very ill. I made the statement: "I deny this appearance of disease. It is unreal, therefore cannot register in his consciousness; this man is a perfect idea in Divine Mind, pure substance expressing perfection."

There is no time or space, in Divine Mind, therefore the word reaches instantly its destination and does not "return void." I have treated patients in Europe and have found that the result was instantaneous.

I am asked so often the difference between visualizing and visioning. Visualizing is a mental process governed by the reasoning or conscious mind; visioning is a spiritual process, governed by intuition, or the superconscious mind. The student should train his mind to receive these flashes of inspiration, and work out the "divine pictures," through definite leads. When a man can say, "I desire only that which God desires for me," his false desires fade from the consciousness, and a new set of blueprints is given him by the Master

Architect, the God within. God's plan for each man transcends the limitation of the reasoning mind, and is always the square of life, containing health, wealth, love and perfect self-expression. Many a man is building for himself in imagination a bungalow when he should be building a palace.

If a student tries to force a demonstration (through the reasoning mind) he brings it to a standstill. "I will hasten it," saith the Lord. He should act only through intuition, or definite leads. "Rest in the Lord and wait patiently. Trust also in him, and he will bring it to pass."

I have seen the law work in the most astonishing manner. For example: A student stated that it was necessary for her to have a hundred dollars by the following day. It was a debt of vital importance which had to be met. I "spoke the word," declaring Spirit was "never too late" and that the supply was at hand.

That evening she phoned me of the miracle. She said that the thought came to her to go to her safe-deposit box at the bank to examine some papers. She looked over the papers, and at the bottom of the box, was a new one-hundred-dollar bill. She was astounded, and said she knew she had never put it there, for she had gone through the papers many times. It may have been a materialization, as Jesus Christ materialized the loaves and fishes. Man will reach the stage where his "word is made flesh," or materialized, instantly. "The fields, ripe with the harvest," will manifest immediately, as in all of the miracles of Jesus Christ.

There is a tremendous power alone in the name Jesus Christ. It stands for *Truth Made Manifest.* He said, "Whatsoever ye ask the Father, in my name, He will give it to you."

The power of this name raises the student into the fourth dimension, where he is freed from all astral and psychic influences, and he becomes "unconditioned and absolute, as God Himself is unconditioned and absolute."

I have seen many healings accomplished by using the words, "In the name of Jesus Christ."

Christ was both person and principle; and the Christ within each man is his Redeemer and Salvation.

The Christ within, is his own fourth dimensional self, the man made in God's image and likeness. This is the self which has never failed, never known sickness or sorrow, was never born and has never died. It is the "resurrection and the life" of each man! "No man cometh to the Father save by the Son," means, that God, the Universal, working on the place of the particular, becomes the Christ in man; and the Holy Ghost, means God-in-action. So daily, man is manifesting the Trinity of Father, Son and Holy Ghost.

Man should make an art of thinking. The Master Thinker is an artist and is careful to paint only the Divine Designs upon the canvas of his mind; and he paints these pictures with masterly strokes of power and decision, having perfect faith that there is no power to mar their perfection and that they shall manifest in his life the ideal made real.

All power is given man (through right thinking) to bring *his heaven* upon *his earth,* and this is the *goal of the "Game of Life."*

The simple rules are fearless faith, nonresistance and love!

May each reader be now freed from that thing which has held him in bondage through the ages, standing between him and his own, and "know the Truth which makes him free"—free to fulfill his destiny, to bring into manifestation the "*Divine Design of his life,* Health, Wealth, Love and Perfect Self-Expression." "Be ye transformed by the renewing of your mind."

DENIALS AND AFFIRMATIONS

(FOR PROSPERITY)

God is my unfailing supply, and large sums of money come to me quickly, under grace, in perfect ways.

(FOR RIGHT CONDITIONS)

Every plan my Father in heaven has not planned, shall be dissolved and dissipated, and the Divine Idea now comes to pass.

(FOR RIGHT CONDITIONS)

Only that which is true of God is true of me, for I and the Father are ONE.

(FOR FAITH)

As I am one with God, I am one with my good, for God is both the *Giver* and the *Gift*. I cannot separate the *Giver* from the *Gift*.

(FOR RIGHT CONDITIONS)

Divine Love now dissolves and dissipates every wrong condition in my mind, body and affairs. Divine Love is the most powerful chemical in the universe, and *dissolves everything* which is not of itself!

(FOR HEALTH)

Divine Love floods my consciousness with health, and every cell in my body is filled with light.

(FOR THE EYESIGHT)

My eyes are God's eyes, I see with the eyes of spirit. I see clearly the open way; there are no obstacles on my pathway. I see clearly the perfect plan.

(FOR GUIDANCE)

I am divinely sensitive to my intuitive leads, and give instant obedience to Thy will.

(FOR THE HEARING)

My ears are God's ears, I hear with the ears of spirit. I am nonresistant and am willing to be led. I hear glad tidings of great joy.

(FOR RIGHT WORK)

I have a perfect work
In a perfect way;
I give a perfect service
For perfect pay.

(FOR FREEDOM FROM ALL BONDAGE)

I cast this burden on the Christ within, and I go free!

6

THE SCIENCE OF GETTING RICH

WALLACE D. WATTLES

(1911)

Contents

Preface 293
1. The Right to Be Rich 295
2. There Is a Science of Getting Rich 297
3. Is Opportunity Monopolized? 300
4. The First Principle in the Science of Getting Rich 303
5. Increasing Life 306
6. How Riches Come to You 310
7. Gratitude 313
8. Thinking in the Certain Way 316
9. How to Use the Will 319
10. Further Use of the Will 322
11. Acting in the Certain Way 325
12. Efficient Action 329
13. Getting into the Right Business 332
14. The Impression of Increase 335
15. The Advancing Man 338
16. Some Cautions, and Concluding Observations 341
17. Summary of the Science of Getting Rich 344

HOW TO GET WHAT YOU WANT

Chapter 1 349
Chapter 2 351
Chapter 3 353
Chapter 4 356
Chapter 5 359

Preface

This book is pragmatical, not philosophical; a practical manual, not a treatise upon theories. It is intended for the men and women whose most pressing need is for money; who wish to get rich first, and philosophize afterward. It is for those who have, so far, found neither the time, the means, nor the opportunity to go deeply into the study of metaphysics, but who want results and who are willing to take the conclusions of science as a basis for action, without going into all the processes by which those conclusions were reached.

It is expected that the reader will take the fundamental statements upon faith, just as he would take statements concerning a law of electrical action if they were promulgated by a Marconi or an Edison; and, taking the statements upon faith, that he will prove their truth by acting upon them without fear or hesitation. Every man or woman who does this will certainly get rich; for the science herein applied is an exact science, and failure is impossible. For the benefit, however, of those who wish to investigate philosophical theories and so secure a logical basis for faith, I will here cite certain authorities.

The monistic theory of the universe—the theory that One is All, and that All is One; that one Substance manifests itself as the seeming many elements of the material world—is of Hindu origin, and has been gradually winning its way into the thought of the western world for two hundred years. It is the foundation of all the Oriental philosophies, and of those of Descartes, Spinoza, Leibnitz, Schopenhauer, Hegel, and Emerson.

The reader who would dig to the philosophical foundations of this is advised to read Hegel and Emerson for himself.

In writing this book I have sacrificed all other considerations to plainness and simplicity of style, so that all might understand. The plan of action laid down herein was deduced from the conclusions of philosophy; it has been thoroughly tested, and bears the supreme test of practical experiment; it works. If you wish to know how the conclusions were arrived at, read the writings of the authors mentioned above; and if you wish to reap the fruits of their philosophies in actual practice, read this book and do exactly as it tells you to do.

CHAPTER 1

The Right to Be Rich

Whatever may be said in praise of poverty, the fact remains that it is not possible to live a really complete or successful life unless one is rich. No man can rise to his greatest possible height in talent or soul development unless he has plenty of money; for to unfold the soul and to develop talent he must have many things to use, and he cannot have these things unless he has money to buy them with.

A man develops in mind, soul, and body by making use of things, and society is so organized that man must have money in order to become the possessor of things; therefore, the basis of all advancement for man must be the science of getting rich.

The object of all life is development; and everything that lives has an inalienable right to all the development it is capable of attaining.

Man's right to life means his right to have the free and unrestricted use of all the things which may be necessary to his fullest mental, spiritual, and physical unfoldment; or, in other words, his right to be rich.

In this book, I shall not speak of riches in a figurative way; to be really rich does not mean to be satisfied or contented with a little. No man ought to be satisfied with a little if he is capable of using and enjoying more. The purpose of Nature is the advancement and unfoldment of life; and every man should have all that can contribute to the power; elegance, beauty, and richness of life; to be content with less is sinful.

The man who owns all he wants for the living of all the life he is capable of living is rich; and no man who has not plenty of money can have all he wants. Life has advanced so far, and become so complex, that even the most ordinary man or woman requires a great amount of wealth in order to live in a manner that even approaches completeness. Every person naturally wants to become all that they are capable of becoming; this desire to realize innate possibilities is inherent in human nature; we cannot help wanting to be all that we can be. Success in life is becoming what you want to be; you can become what you want to be only by making use of things, and you can have the free use of things only as you become rich enough to buy them. To understand the science of getting rich is therefore the most essential of all knowledge.

There is nothing wrong in wanting to get rich. The desire for riches is really the desire for a richer, fuller, and more abundant life; and that desire is praiseworthy. The man who does not desire to live more abundantly is abnormal, and so the man who does not desire to have money enough to buy all he wants is abnormal.

There are three motives for which we live; we live for the body, we live for the mind, we live for the soul. No one of these is better or holier than the other; all are alike desirable, and no one of the three—body, mind, or soul—can live fully if either of the others is cut short of full life and expression. It is not right or noble to live only for the soul and deny mind or body; and it is wrong to live for the intellect and deny body or soul.

We are all acquainted with the loathsome consequences of living for the body and denying both mind and soul; and we see that *real* life means the complete expression of all that man can give forth through body, mind, and soul. Whatever he can say, no man can be really happy or satisfied unless his body is living fully in every function, and unless the same is true of his mind and his soul. Wherever there is unexpressed possibility, or function not performed, there is unsatisfied desire. Desire is possibility seeking expression, or function seeking performance.

Man cannot live fully in body without good food, comfortable clothing, and warm shelter; and without freedom from excessive toil. Rest and recreation are also necessary to his physical life.

He cannot live fully in mind without books and time to study them, without opportunity for travel and observation, or without intellectual companionship.

To live fully in mind he must have intellectual recreations, and must surround himself with all the objects of art and beauty he is capable of using and appreciating.

To live fully in soul, man must have love; and love is denied expression by poverty.

A man's highest happiness is found in the bestowal of benefits on those he loves; love finds its most natural and spontaneous expression in giving. The man who has nothing to give cannot fill his place as a husband or father, as a citizen, or as a man. It is in the use of material things that a man finds full life for his body, develops his mind, and unfolds his soul. It is therefore of supreme importance to him that he should be rich.

It is perfectly right that you should desire to be rich; if you are a normal man or woman you cannot help doing so. It is perfectly right that you should give your best attention to the Science of Getting Rich, for it is the noblest and most necessary of all studies. If you neglect this study, you are derelict in your duty to yourself, to God and humanity; for you can render to God and humanity no greater service than to make the most of yourself.

CHAPTER 2

There Is a Science of Getting Rich

There is a Science of Getting Rich, and it is an exact science, like algebra or arithmetic. There are certain laws which govern the process of acquiring riches; once these laws are learned and obeyed by any man, he will get rich with mathematical certainty.

The ownership of money and property comes as a result of doing things in a certain way; those who do things in this Certain Way, whether on purpose or accidentally, get rich; while those who do not do things in this Certain Way, no matter how hard they work or how able they are, remain poor.

It is a natural law that like causes always produce like effects; and, therefore, any man or woman who learns to do things in this Certain Way will infallibly get rich.

That the above statement is true is shown by the following facts:

Getting rich is not a matter of environment, for, if it were, all the people in certain neighborhoods would become wealthy; the people of one city would all be rich, while those of other towns would all be poor; or the inhabitants of one state would roll in wealth, while those of an adjoining state would be in poverty.

But everywhere we see rich and poor living side by side, in the same environment, and often engaged in the same vocations. When two men are in the same locality, and in the same business, and one gets rich while the other remains poor, it shows that getting rich is not, primarily, a matter of environment. Some environments may be more favorable than others, but when two men in the same business are in the same neighborhood, and one gets rich while the other fails, it indicates that getting rich is the result of doing things in a Certain Way.

And further, the ability to do things in this Certain Way is not due solely to the possession of talent, for many people who have great talent remain poor, while other who have very little talent get rich.

Studying the people who have gotten rich, we find that they are an average lot in all respects, having no greater talents and abilities than other men. It is evident that they do not get rich because they possess talents and abilities that other men have not, but because they happen to do things in a Certain Way.

Getting rich is not the result of saving, or "thrift"; many very penurious people are poor, while free spenders often get rich.

Nor is getting rich due to doing things which others fail to do; for two men in the same business often do almost exactly the same things, and one gets rich while the other remains poor or becomes bankrupt.

From all these things, we must come to the conclusion that getting rich is the result of doing things in a Certain Way.

If getting rich is the result of doing things in a Certain Way, and if like causes always produce like effects, then any man or woman who can do things in that way can become rich, and the whole matter is brought within the domain of exact science.

The question arises here, whether this Certain Way may not be so difficult that only a few may follow it. This cannot be true, as we have seen, so far as natural ability is concerned. Talented people get rich, and blockheads get rich; intellectually brilliant people get rich, and very stupid people get rich; physically strong people get rich, and weak and sickly people get rich.

Some degree of ability to think and understand is, of course, essential; but in so far natural ability is concerned, any man or woman who has sense enough to read and understand these words can certainly get rich.

Also, we have seen that it is not a matter of environment. Location counts for something; one would not go to the heart of the Sahara and expect to do successful business.

Getting rich involves the necessity of dealing with men, and of being where there are people to deal with; and if these people are inclined to deal in the way you want to deal, so much the better. But that is about as far as environment goes.

If anybody else in your town can get rich, so can you; and if anybody else in your state can get rich, so can you.

Again, it is not a matter of choosing some particular business or profession. People get rich in every business, and in every profession; while their next-door neighbors in the same vocation remain in poverty.

It is true that you will do best in a business which you like, and which is congenial to you; and if you have certain talents which are well developed, you will do best in a business which calls for the exercise of those talents.

Also, you will do best in a business which is suited to your locality; an ice-cream parlor would do better in a warm climate than in Greenland, and a salmon fishery will succeed better in the Northwest than in Florida, where there are no salmon.

But, aside from these general limitations, getting rich is not dependent upon your engaging in some particular business, but upon your learning to do things in a Certain Way. If you are now in business, and anybody else in your locality is getting rich in the same business, while you are not getting rich, it is because you are not doing things in the same Way that the other person is doing them.

No one is prevented from getting rich by lack of capital. True, as you get capital the increase becomes more easy and rapid; but one who has capital is already rich, and does not need to consider how to become so. No matter how poor you may be, if you begin to do things in the Certain Way you will begin to get rich; and you will begin to have capital. The getting of capital is a part of the process of getting rich; and it is a part of the result which invariably follows the doing of things in the Certain Way. You may be the poorest man on the continent, and be deeply in debt; you may have neither friends, influence, nor resources; but if you begin to do things in this way, you must infallibly begin to get rich, for like causes must produce like effects. If you have no capital, you can get capital; if you are in the wrong business, you can get into the right business; if you are in the wrong location, you can go to the right location; and you can do so *by beginning in your present business and in your present location* to do things in the Certain Way which causes success.

CHAPTER 3

Is Opportunity Monopolized?

No man is kept poor because opportunity has been taken away from him; because other people have monopolized the wealth, and have put a fence around it. You may be shut off from engaging in business in certain lines, but there are other channels open to you. Probably it would be hard for you to get control of any of the great railroad systems; that field is pretty well monopolized. But the electric railway business is still in its infancy, and offers plenty of scope for enterprise; and it will be but a very few years until traffic and transportation through the air will become a great industry, and in all its branches will give employment to hundreds of thousands, and perhaps to millions, of people. Why not turn your attention to the development of aerial transportation, instead of competing with J. J. Hill and others for a chance in the steam railway world?

It is quite true that if you are a workman in the employ of the steel trust you have very little chance of becoming the owner of the plant in which you work; but it is also true that if you will commence to act in a Certain Way, you can soon leave the employ of the steel trust; you can buy a farm of from ten to forty acres, and engage in business as a producer of foodstuffs. There is great opportunity at this time for men who will live upon small tracts of land and cultivate the same intensively; such men will certainly get rich. You may say that it is impossible for you to get the land, but I am going to prove to you that it is not impossible, and that you can certainly get a farm if you will go to work in a Certain Way.

At different periods the tide of opportunity sets in different directions, according to the needs of the whole, and the particular stage of social evolution which has been reached. At present, in America, it is setting toward agriculture and the allied industries and professions. Today, opportunity is open before the factory worker in his line. It is open before the business man who supplies the farmer more than before the one who supplies the factory worker; and before the professional man who waits upon the farmer more than before the one who serves the working class.

There is abundance of opportunity for the man who will go with the tide, instead of trying to swim against it.

So the factory workers, either as individuals or as a class, are not deprived of opportunity. The workers are not being "kept down" by their masters; they are not being "ground" by the trusts and combinations of capital. As a class, they are where they are because they do not do things in a Certain Way. If the workers of America chose to do so, they could follow the example of their brothers in Belgium and other countries, and establish great department stores and cooperative industries; they could elect men of their own class to office, and pass laws favoring the development of such co-operative industries; and in a few years they could take peaceable possession of the industrial field.

The working class may become the master class whenever they will begin to do things in a Certain Way; the law of wealth is the same for them as it is for all others. This they must learn; and they will remain where they are as long as they continue to do as they do. The individual worker, however, is not held down by the ignorance or the mental slothfulness of his class; he can follow the tide of opportunity to riches, and this book will tell him how.

No one is kept in poverty by a shortness in the supply of riches; there is more than enough for all. A palace as large as the Capitol at Washington might be built for every family on earth from the building material in the United States alone; and under intensive cultivation, this country would produce wool, cotton, linen, and silk enough to clothe each person in the world finer than Solomon was arrayed in all his glory; together with food enough to feed them all luxuriously.

The visible supply is practically inexhaustible; and the invisible supply really IS inexhaustible.

Everything you see on earth is made from one original substance, out of which all things proceed.

New Forms are constantly being made, and older ones are dissolving; but all are shapes assumed by One Thing.

There is no limit to the supply of Formless Stuff, or Original Substance. The universe is made out of it; but it was not all used in making the universe. The spaces in, through, and between the forms of the visible universe are permeated and filled with the Original Substance; with the Formless Stuff; with the raw material of all things. Ten thousand times as much as has been made might still be made, and even then we should not have exhausted the supply of universal raw material.

No man, therefore, is poor because nature is poor, or because there is not enough to go around.

Nature is an inexhaustible storehouse of riches; the supply will never run short. Original Substance is alive with creative energy, and is constantly producing more forms. When the supply of building material is exhausted, more will be produced; when the soil is exhausted so that food stuffs and materials for clothing will no longer grow upon it, it will be renewed or more soil will be made. When all the gold and silver has been dug from the earth, if man is still in such a stage of social development that he needs gold and silver, more will be produced from the Formless. The Formless Stuff responds to the needs of man; it will not let him be without any good thing.

This is true of man collectively; the race as a whole is always abundantly rich, and if individuals are poor, it is because they do not follow the Certain Way of doing things which makes the individual man rich.

The Formless Stuff is intelligent; it is stuff which thinks. It is alive, and is always impelled toward more life.

It is the natural and inherent impulse of life to seek to live more; it is the nature of intelligence to enlarge itself, and of consciousness to seek to extend its boundaries and find fuller expression. The universe of forms has been made by Formless Living Substance, throwing itself into form in order to express itself more fully.

The universe is a great Living Presence, always moving inherently toward more life and fuller functioning.

Nature is formed for the advancement of life; its impelling motive is the increase of life. For this cause, everything which can possibly minister to life is bountifully provided; there can be no lack unless God is to contradict himself and nullify his own works.

You are not kept poor by lack in the supply of riches; it is a fact which I shall demonstrate a little farther on that even the resources of the Formless Supply are at the command of the man or woman will act and think in a Certain Way.

CHAPTER 4

The First Principle in the Science of Getting Rich

Thought is the only power which can produce tangible riches from the Formless Substance. The stuff from which all things are made is a substance which thinks, and a thought of form in this substance produces the form.

Original Substance moves according to its thoughts; every form and process you see in nature is the visible expression of a thought in Original Substance. As the Formless Stuff thinks of a form, it takes that form; as it thinks of a motion, it makes that motion. That is the way all things were created. We live in a thought world, which is part of a thought universe. The thought of a moving universe extended throughout Formless Substance, and the Thinking Stuff moving according to that thought, took the form of systems of planets, and maintains that form. Thinking Substance takes the form of its thought, and moves according to the thought. Holding the idea of a circling system of suns and worlds, it takes the form of these bodies, and moves them as it thinks. Thinking the form of a slow-growing oak tree, it moves accordingly, and produces the tree, though centuries may be required to do the work. In creating, the Formless seems to move according to the lines of motion it has established; the thought of an oak tree does not cause the instant formation of a full-grown tree, but it does start in motion the forces which will produce the tree, along established lines of growth.

Every thought of form, held in thinking Substance, causes the creation of the form, but always, or at least generally, along lines of growth and action already established.

The thought of a house of a certain construction, if it were impressed upon Formless Substance, might not cause the instant formation of the house; but it would cause the turning of creative energies already working in trade and commerce into such channels as to result in the speedy building of the house. And if there were no existing channels through which the creative energy could work, then the house would be formed directly from primal substance, without waiting for the slow processes of the organic and inorganic world.

No thought of form can be impressed upon Original Substance without causing the creation of the form.

Man is a thinking center, and can originate thought. All the forms that man fashions with his hands must first exist in his thought; he cannot shape a thing until he has thought that thing.

And so far man has confined his efforts wholly to the work of his hands; he has applied manual labor to the world of forms, seeking to change or modify those already existing. He has never thought of trying to cause the creation of new forms by impressing his thoughts upon Formless Substance.

When man has a thought-force, he takes material from the forms of nature, and makes an image of the form which is in his mind. He has, so far, made little or no effort to cooperate with Formless Intelligence; to work "with the Father." He has not dreamed that he can "do what he seeth the Father doing." Man reshapes and modifies existing forms by manual labor; he has given no attention to the question whether he may not produce things from Formless Substance by communicating his thoughts to it. We propose to prove that he may do so; to prove that any man or woman may do so, and to show how. As our first step, we must lay down three fundamental propositions.

First, we assert that there is one original Formless Stuff, or Substance, from which all things are made. All the seemingly many elements are but different presentations of one element; all the many forms found in organic and inorganic nature are but different shapes, made from the same Stuff. And this Stuff is thinking Stuff; a thought held in it produces the form of the thought. Thought, in thinking Substance, produces shapes. Man is a thinking center, capable of original thought; if man can communicate his thought to original thinking Substance, he can cause the creation, or formation, of the thing he thinks about. To summarize this:

There is a thinking Stuff from which all things are made, and which, in its original state, permeates, penetrates, and fills the interspaces of the universe.

A thought, in this Substance, produces the thing that is imaged by the thought.

Man can form things in his thought, and, by impressing his thought upon Formless Substance, can cause the thing he thinks about to be created.

It may be asked if I can prove these statements; and without going into details, I answer that I can do so, both by logic and experience.

Reasoning back from the phenomena of form and thought, I come to one original thinking Substance; and reasoning forward from this thinking Substance, I come to man's power to cause the formation of the thing he thinks about.

And by experiment, I find the reasoning true; and this is my strongest proof.

If one man who reads this book gets rich by doing what it tells him to do, that is evidence in support of my claim; but if every man who does what it tells him to do gets rich, that is positive proof until someone goes through the process and fails. The theory is true until the process fails; and this process will not fail, for every man who does exactly what this book tells him to do will get rich.

I have said that men get rich by doing things in a Certain Way; and in order to do so, men must become able to think in a Certain Way.

A man's way of doing things is the direct result of the way he thinks about things.

To do things in a way you want to do them, you will have to acquire the ability to think the way you want to think; this is the first step toward getting rich.

To think what you want to think is to think TRUTH, regardless of appearances.

Every man has the natural and inherent power to think what he wants to think, but it requires far more effort to do so than it does to think the thoughts which are suggested by appearances. To think according to appearance is easy; to think truth regardless of appearances is laborious, and requires the expenditure of more power than any other work man is called upon to perform.

There is no labor from which most people shrink as they do from that of sustained and consecutive thought; it is the hardest work in the world. This is especially true when truth is contrary to appearances. Every appearance in the visible world tends to produce a corresponding form in the mind which observes it; and this can only be prevented by holding the thought of the TRUTH.

To look upon the appearance of disease will produce the form of disease in your own mind, and ultimately in your body, unless you hold the thought of the truth, which is that there is no disease; it is only an appearance, and the reality is health.

To look upon the appearances of poverty will produce corresponding forms in your own mind, unless you hold to the truth that there is no poverty; there is only abundance.

To think health when surrounded by the appearances of disease, or to think riches when in the midst of appearances of poverty, requires power; but he who acquires this power becomes a MASTER MIND. He can conquer fate; he can have what he wants.

This power can only be acquired by getting hold of the basic fact which is behind all appearances; and that fact is that there is one Thinking Substance, from which and by which all things are made.

Then we must grasp the truth that every thought held in this Substance becomes a form, and that man can so impress his thoughts upon it as to cause them to take form and become visible things.

When we realize this, we lose all doubt and fear, for we know that we can create what we want to create; we can get what we want to have, and can become what we want to be. As a first step toward getting rich, you must believe the three fundamental statements given previously in this chapter; and in order to emphasize them. I repeat them here:

There is a thinking Stuff from which all things are made, and which, in its original state, permeates, penetrates, and fills the interspaces of the universe.

A thought, in this Substance, produces the thing that is imaged by the thought.

Man can form things in his thought, and, by impressing his thought upon formless substance, can cause the thing he thinks about to be created.

You must lay aside all other concepts of the universe than this monistic one; and you must dwell upon this until it is fixed in your mind, and has become your habitual thought. Read these creed statements over and over again; fix every word upon your memory, and meditate upon them until you firmly believe what they say. If a doubt comes to you, cast it aside as a sin. Do not listen to arguments against this idea; do not go to churches or lectures where a contrary concept of things is taught or preached. Do not read magazines or books which teach a different idea; if you get mixed up in your faith, all your efforts will be in vain.

Do not ask why these things are true, nor speculate as to how they can be true; simply take them on trust.

The Science of Getting Rich begins with the absolute acceptance of this faith.

CHAPTER 5

Increasing Life

You must get rid of the last vestige of the old idea that there is a Deity whose will it is that you should be poor, or whose purposes may be served by keeping you in poverty.

The Intelligent Substance which is All, and in All, and which lives in All and lives in you, is a consciously Living Substance. Being a consciously Living Substance, it must have the nature and inherent desire of every living intelligence for increase of life. Every living thing must continually seek for the enlargement of its life, because life, in the mere act of living, must increase itself.

A seed, dropped into the ground, springs into activity, and in the act of living produces a hundred more seeds; life, by living, multiplies itself. It is forever Becoming More; it must do so, if it continues to be at all.

Intelligence is under this same necessity for continuous increase. Every thought we think makes it necessary for us to think another thought; consciousness is continually expanding. Every fact we learn leads us to the learning of another fact; knowledge is continually increasing. Every talent we cultivate brings to the mind the desire to cultivate another talent; we are subject to the urge of life, seeking expression, which ever drives us on to know more, to do more, and to be more.

In order to know more, do more, and be more we must have more; we must have things to use, for we learn, and do, and become, only by using things. We must get rich, so that we can live more.

The desire for riches is simply the capacity for larger life seeking fulfillment; every desire is the effort of an unexpressed possibility to come into action. It is power seeking to manifest which causes desire. That which makes you want more money is the same as that which makes the plant grow; it is Life, seeking fuller expression.

The One Living Substance must be subject to this inherent law of all life; it is permeated with the desire to live more; that is why it is under the necessity of creating things.

The One Substance desires to live more in you; hence it wants you to have all the things you can use.

It is the desire of God that you should get rich. He wants you to get rich because he can express himself better through you if you have plenty of things to use in giving him expression. He can live more in you if you have unlimited command of the means of life.

The universe desires you to have everything you want to have.

Nature is friendly to your plans.

Everything is naturally for you.

Make up your mind that this is true.

It is essential, however that *your purpose should harmonize with the purpose that is in All.*

You must want real life, not mere pleasure of sensual gratification. Life is the performance of function; and the individual really lives only when he performs every function, physical, mental, and spiritual, of which he is capable, without excess in any.

You do not want to get rich in order to live swinishly, for the gratification of animal desires; that is not life. But the performance of every physical function is a part of life, and no one lives completely who denies the impulses of the body a normal and healthful expression.

You do not want to get rich solely to enjoy mental pleasures, to get knowledge, to gratify ambition, to outshine others, to be famous. All these are a legitimate part of life, but the man who lives for the pleasures of the intellect alone will only have a partial life, and he will never be satisfied with his lot.

You do not want to get rich solely for the good of others, to lose yourself for the salvation of mankind, to experience the joys of philanthropy and sacrifice. The joys of the soul are only a part of life; and they are no better or nobler than any other part.

You want to get rich in order that you may eat, drink, and be merry when it is time to do these things; in order that you may surround yourself with beautiful things, see distant lands, feed your mind, and develop your intellect; in order that you may love men and do kind things, and be able to play a good part in helping the world to find truth.

But remember that extreme altruism is no better and no nobler than extreme selfishness; both are mistakes.

Get rid of the idea that God wants you to sacrifice yourself for others, and that you can secure his favor by doing so; God requires nothing of the kind.

What he wants is that you should make the most of yourself, for yourself, and for others; and *you can help others more by making the most of yourself than in any other way.*

You can make the most of yourself only by getting rich; so it is right and praiseworthy that you should give your first and best thought to the work of acquiring wealth.

Remember, however, that the desire of Substance is for all, and its movements must be for more life to all; it cannot be made to work for less life to any, because it is equally in all, seeking riches and life.

Intelligent Substance will make things for you, but it will not take things away from someone else and give them to you.

You must get rid of the thought of competition. You are to create, not to compete for what is already created.

You do not have to take anything away from anyone.

You do not have to drive sharp bargains.

You do not have to cheat, or to take advantage. You do not need to let any man work for you for less than he earns.

You do not have to covet the property of others, or to look at it with wishful eyes; no man has anything of which you cannot have the like, and that without taking what he has away from him.

You are to become a creator, not a competitor; you are going to get what you want, but in such a way that when you get it every other man will have more than he has now.

I am aware that there are men who get a vast amount of money by proceeding in direct opposition to the statements in the paragraph above, and may I add a word of explanation here. Men of the plutocratic type, who become very rich, do so sometimes purely by their extraordinary ability on the plane of competition; and sometimes they unconsciously relate themselves to Substance in its great purposes and movements for the general racial upbuilding through industrial evolution. Rockefeller, Carnegie, Morgan, et al., have been the unconscious agents of the Supreme in the necessary work of systematizing and organizing productive industry; and in the end, their work will contribute immensely toward increased life for all. Their day is nearly over; they have organized production, and *will soon be succeeded by the agents of the multitude, who will organize the machinery of distribution.*

The multimillionaires are like the monster reptiles of the prehistoric eras; they play a necessary part in the evolutionary process, but the same Power which produced them will dispose of them. And it is well to bear in mind that they have never been really rich; a record of the private lives of most of this class will show that they have really been the most abject and wretched of the poor.

Riches secured on the competitive plane are never satisfactory and permanent; they are yours today, and another's tomorrow. Remember, if you are to become rich in a scientific and certain way, you must rise entirely out of the competitive thought. You must never think for a moment that the supply is limited. Just as soon as you begin to think that all the money is being "cornered" and controlled by bankers and others, and that you must exert yourself to get laws passed to stop this process, and so on; in that moment you drop into the competitive mind, and your power to cause creation is gone for the time being; and what is worse, you will probably arrest the creative movements you have already instituted.

KNOW that there are countless millions of dollars' worth of gold in the mountains of the earth, not yet brought to light; and know that if there were not, more would be created from Thinking Substance to supply your needs.

KNOW that the money you need will come, even if it is necessary for a thousand men to be led to the discovery of new gold mines tomorrow.

Never look at the visible supply; look always at the limitless riches in Formless Substance, and KNOW that they are coming to you as fast as you can receive and use them. Nobody, by cornering the visible supply, can prevent you from getting what is yours.

So never allow yourself to think for an instant that all the best building spots will be taken before you get ready to build your house, unless you hurry. Never worry about the trusts and combines, and get anxious for fear they will soon come to own the whole earth. Never get afraid that you will lose what you want because some other person "beats you to it." That cannot possibly happen; you are not seeking any thing that is possessed by anybody else; you are causing what you want to be created from Formless Substance, and the supply is without limits. Stick to the formulated statement:

There is a thinking Stuff from which all things are made, and which, in its original state, permeates, penetrates, and fills the interspaces of the universe.

A thought, in this Substance, produces the thing that is imaged by the thought.

Man can form things in his thought, and, by impressing his thought upon Formless Substance, can cause the thing he thinks about to be created.

CHAPTER 6

How Riches Come to You

When I say that you do not have to drive sharp bargains, I do not mean that you do not have to drive any bargains at all, or that you are above the necessity for having any dealings with your fellow men. I mean that you will not need to deal with them unfairly; you do not have to get something for nothing, *but can give to every man more than you take from him.*

You cannot give every man more in cash market value than you take from him, but you can give him more in use value than the cash value of the thing you take from him. The paper, ink, and other material in this book may not be worth the money you pay for it; but if the ideas suggested by it bring you thousands of dollars, you have not been wronged by those who sold it to you; they have given you a great use value for a small cash value.

Let us suppose that I own a picture by one of the great artists, which, in any civilized community, is worth thousands of dollars. I take it to Baffin Bay, and by "salesmanship" induce an Eskimo to give a bundle of furs worth $500 for it. I have really wronged him, for he has no use for the picture; it has no use value to him; it will not add to his life.

But suppose I give him a gun worth $50 for his furs; then he has made a good bargain. He has use for the gun; it will get him many more furs and much food; it will add to his life in every way; it will make him rich.

When you rise from the competitive to the creative plane, you can scan your business transactions very strictly, and if you are selling any man anything which does not add more to his life than the thing he gives you in exchange, you can afford to stop it. You do not have to beat anybody in business. And if you are in a business which does beat people, get out of it at once.

Give every man more in use value than you take from him in cash value; then you are adding to the life of the world by every business transaction.

If you have people working for you, you must take from them more in cash value than you pay them in wages; but you can so organize your business that it will be filled with the principle of advancement, and so that each employee who wishes to do so may advance a little every day.

You can make your business do for your employees what this book is doing for you.

You can so conduct your business that it will be a sort of ladder, by which every employee who will take the trouble may climb to riches himself; and given the opportunity, if he will not do so it is not your fault.

And finally, because you are to cause the creation of your riches from Formless Substance which permeates all your environment, it does not follow that they are to take shape from the atmosphere and come into being before your eyes.

If you want a sewing machine, for instance, I do not mean to tell you that you are to impress the thought of a sewing machine on Thinking Substance until the machine is formed without hands, in the room where you sit, or elsewhere. But if you want a sewing machine, hold the mental image of it with the most positive certainty that it is being made, or is on its way to you. After once forming the thought, have the most absolute and unquestioning faith that the sewing machine is coming; never think of it, or speak, of it, in any other way than as being sure to arrive. Claim it as already yours.

It will be brought to you by the power of the Supreme Intelligence, acting upon the minds of men. If you live in Maine, it may be that a man will be brought from Texas or Japan to engage in some transaction which will result in your getting what you want.

If so, the whole matter will be as much to that man's advantage as it is to yours.

Do not forget for a moment that the Thinking Substance is through all, in all, communicating with all, and can influence all. The desire of Thinking Substance for fuller life and better living has caused the creation of all the sewing machines already made; and it can cause the creation of millions more, and will, whenever men set it in motion by desire and faith, and by acting in a Certain Way.

You can certainly have a sewing machine in your house; and it is just as certain that you can have any other thing or things which you want, and which you will use for the advancement of your own life and the lives of others.

You need not hesitate about asking largely; "it is your Father's pleasure to give you the kingdom," said Jesus.

Original Substance wants to live all that is possible in you, and wants you to have all that you can or will use for the living of the most abundant life.

If you fix upon your consciousness the fact that the desire you feel for the possession of riches is one with the desire of Omnipotence for more complete expression, your faith becomes invincible.

Once I saw a little boy sitting at a piano, and vainly trying to bring harmony out of the keys; and I saw that he was grieved and provoked by his inability to play real music. I asked him the cause of his vexation, and he answered, "I can feel the music in me, but I can't make my hands go right." The music in him was the URGE of Original Substance, containing all the possibilities of all life; all that there is of music was seeking expression through the child.

God, the One Substance, is trying to live and do and enjoy things through humanity. He is saying "I want hands to build wonderful structures, to play divine harmonies, to paint glorious pictures; I want feet to run my errands, eyes to see my beauties, tongues to tell mighty truths and to sing marvelous songs," and so on.

All that there is of possibility is seeking expression through men. God wants those who can play music to have pianos and every other instrument, and to have the means to cultivate their talents to the fullest extent; He wants those who can appreciate beauty to be able to surround themselves with beautiful things; He wants those who can discern truth to have every opportunity to travel and observe; He wants those who can appreciate dress to be beautifully clothed, and those who can appreciate good food to be luxuriously fed.

He wants all these things because it is Himself that enjoys and appreciates them; it is God who wants to play, and sing, and enjoy beauty, and proclaim truth and wear fine clothes, and eat good foods. "it is God that worketh in you to will and to do," said Paul.

The desire you feel for riches is the infinite, seeking to express Himself in you as He sought to find expression in the little boy at the piano.

So you need not hesitate to ask largely.

Your part is to focalize and express the desire to God.

This is a difficult point with most people; they retain something of the old idea that poverty and self-sacrifice are pleasing to God. They look upon poverty as a part of the plan, a necessity of nature. They have the idea that God has finished His work, and made all that He can make, and that the majority of men must stay poor because there is not enough to go around. They hold to so much of this erroneous thought that they feel ashamed to ask for wealth; they try not to want more than a very modest competence, just enough to make them fairly comfortable.

I recall now the case of one student who was told that he must get in mind a clear picture of the things he desired, so that the creative thought of them might be impressed on Formless Substance. He was a very poor man, living in a rented house, and having only what he earned from day to day; and he could not grasp the fact that all wealth was his. So, after thinking the matter over, he decided that he might reasonably ask for a new rug for the floor of his best room, and an anthracite coal stove to heat the house during the cold weather. Following the instructions given in this book, he obtained these things in a few months; and then it dawned upon him that he had not asked enough. He went through the house in which he lived, and planned all the improvements he would like to make in it; he mentally added a bay window here and a room there, until it was complete in his mind as his ideal home; and then he planned its furnishings.

Holding the whole picture in his mind, he began living in the Certain Way, and moving toward what he wanted; and he owns the house now, and is rebuilding it after the form of his mental image. And now, with still larger faith, he is going on to get greater things. It has been unto him according to his faith, and it is so with you and with all of us.

CHAPTER 7

Gratitude

The illustrations given in the last chapter will have conveyed to the reader the fact that the first step toward getting rich is to convey the idea of your wants to the Formless Substance.

This is true, and you will see that in order to do so it becomes necessary to relate yourself to the Formless Intelligence in a harmonious way.

To secure this harmonious relation is a matter of such primary and vital importance that I shall give some space to its discussion here, and give you instructions which, if you will follow them, will be certain to bring you into perfect unity of mind with God.

The whole process of mental adjustment and atonement can be summed up in one word, gratitude.

First, you believe that there is one Intelligent Substance, from which all things proceed; second, you believe that this Substance gives you everything you desire; and third, you relate yourself to it by a feeling of deep and profound gratitude.

Many people who order their lives rightly in all other ways are kept in poverty by their lack of gratitude. Having received one gift from God, they cut the wires which connect them with Him by failing to make acknowledgment.

It is easy to understand that the nearer we live to the source of wealth, the more wealth we shall receive; and it is easy also to understand that the soul that is always grateful lives in closer touch with God than the one which never looks to Him in thankful acknowledgment.

The more gratefully we fix our minds on the Supreme when good things come to us, the more good things we will receive, and the more rapidly they will come; and the reason simply is that the mental attitude of gratitude draws the mind into closer touch with the source from which the blessings come.

If it is a new thought to you that gratitude brings your whole mind into closer harmony with the creative energies of the universe, consider it well, and you will see that it is true. The good things you already have have come to you along the line of obedience to certain laws. Gratitude will lead your mind out along the ways by which things come; and it will keep you in close harmony with creative thought and prevent you from falling into competitive thought.

Gratitude alone can keep you looking toward the All, and prevent you from falling into the error of thinking of the supply as limited; and to do that would be fatal to your hopes.

There is a Law of Gratitude, and it is absolutely necessary that you should observe the law, if you are to get the results you seek.

The law of gratitude is the natural principle that action and reaction are always equal, and in opposite directions.

The grateful outreaching of your mind in thankful praise to the Supreme *is a liberation or expenditure of force; it cannot fail to reach that to which it addressed, and the reaction is an instantaneous movement toward you.*

"Draw nigh unto God, and He will draw nigh unto you." That is a statement of psychological truth.

And if your gratitude is strong and constant, the reaction in Formless Substance will be strong and continuous; the movement of the things you want will be always toward you. Notice the grateful attitude that Jesus took; how He always seems to be saying, "I thank Thee, Father, that Thou hearest me." You cannot exercise much power without gratitude; for it is gratitude that keeps you connected with Power.

But the value of gratitude does not consist solely in getting you more blessings in the future. Without gratitude you cannot long keep from dissatisfied thought regarding things as they are.

The moment you permit your mind to dwell with dissatisfaction upon things as they are, you begin to lose ground. You fix attention upon the common, the ordinary, the poor, and the squalid and mean; and your mind takes the form of these things. Then you will transmit these forms or mental images to the Formless, and the common, the poor, the squalid, and mean will come to you.

To permit your mind to dwell upon the inferior is to become inferior and to surround yourself with inferior things.

On the other hand, to fix your attention on the best is to surround yourself with the best, and to become the best.

The Creative Power within us makes us into the image of that to which we give our attention.

We are Thinking Substance, and thinking substance always takes the form of that which it thinks about.

The grateful mind is constantly fixed upon the best; therefore it tends to become the best; it takes the form or character of the best, and will receive the best.

Also, faith is born of gratitude. The grateful mind continually expects good things, and expectation becomes faith. The reaction of gratitude upon one's own mind produces faith; and every outgoing wave of grateful thanksgiving increases faith. He who has no feeling of gratitude cannot long retain a living faith; and without a living faith you cannot get rich by the creative method, as we shall see in the following chapters.

It is necessary, then, to cultivate the habit of being grateful for every good thing that comes to you; and to give thanks continuously.

And because all things have contributed to your advancement, you should include all things in your gratitude.

Do not waste time thinking or talking about the shortcomings or wrong actions of plutocrats or trust magnates. Their organization of the world has made your opportunity; all you get really comes to you because of them.

Do not rage against corrupt politicians; if it were not for politicians we should fall into anarchy, and your opportunity would be greatly lessened.

God has worked a long time and very patiently to bring us up to where we are in industry and government, and He is going right on with His work. There is not the least doubt that He will do away with plutocrats, trust magnates, captains of industry, and politicians as soon as they can be spared; but in the meantime, behold they are all very good. Remember that they are all helping to arrange the lines of transmission along which your riches will come to you, and be grateful to them all. This will bring you into harmonious relations with the good in everything, and the good in everything will move toward you.

CHAPTER 8

Thinking in the Certain Way

Turn back to chapter 6 and read again the story of the man who formed a mental image of his house, and you will get a fair idea of the initial step toward getting rich. You must form a clear and definite mental picture of what you want; you cannot transmit an idea unless you have it yourself.

You must have it before you can give it; and many people fail to impress Thinking Substance because they have themselves only a vague and misty concept of the things they want to do, to have, or to become.

It is not enough that you should have a general desire for wealth "to do good with"; everybody has that desire.

It is not enough that you should have a wish to travel, see things, live more, etc. Everybody has those desires also. If you were going to send a wireless message to a friend, you would not send the letters of the alphabet in their order, and let him construct the message for himself; nor would you take words at random from the dictionary. You would send a coherent sentence; one which meant something. When you try to impress your wants upon Substance, remember that it must be done by a coherent statement; you must know what you want, and be definite. You can never get rich, or start the creative power into action, by sending out unformed longings and vague desires.

Go over your desires just as the man I have described went over his house; see just what you want, and get a clear mental picture of it as you wish it to look when you get it.

That clear mental picture you must have continually in mind, as the sailor has in mind the port toward which he is sailing the ship; you must keep your face toward it all the time. You must no more lose sight of it than the steersman loses sight of the compass.

It is not necessary to take exercises in concentration, nor to set apart special times for prayer and affirmation, nor to "go into the silence," nor to do occult stunts of any kind. There things are well enough, but all you need is to know what you want, and to want it badly enough so that it will stay in your thoughts.

Spend as much of your leisure time as you can in contemplating your picture, but no one needs to take exercises to concentrate his mind on a thing which he really wants; it is the things you do not really care about which require effort to fix your attention upon them.

And unless you really want to get rich, so that the desire is strong enough to hold your thoughts directed to the purpose as the magnetic pole holds the needle of the compass, it will hardly be worthwhile for you to try to carry out the instructions given in this book.

The methods herein set forth are for people whose desire for riches is strong enough to overcome mental laziness and the love of ease, and make them work.

The more clear and definite you make your picture then, and the more you dwell upon it, bringing out all its delightful details, the stronger your desire will be; and the stronger your desire, the easier it will be to hold your mind fixed upon the picture of what you want.

Something more is necessary, however, than merely to see the picture clearly. If that is all you do, you are only a dreamer, and will have little or no power for accomplishment.

Behind your clear vision must be the purpose to realize it; to bring it out in tangible expression.

And behind this purpose must be an invincible and unwavering FAITH that the thing is already yours; that it is "at hand" and you have only to take possession of it.

Live in the new house, mentally, until it takes form around you physically. In the mental realm, enter at once into full enjoyment of the things you want.

"Whatsoever things ye ask for when ye pray, believe that ye receive them, and ye shall have them," said Jesus.

See the things you want as if they were actually around you all the time; see yourself as owning and using them. Make use of them in imagination just as you will use them when they are your tangible possessions. Dwell upon your mental picture until it is clear and distinct, and then take the Mental Attitude of Ownership toward everything in that picture. Take possession of it, in mind, in the full faith that it is actually yours. Hold to this mental ownership; do not waiver for an instant in the faith that it is real.

And remember what was said in the preceding chapter about gratitude; be as thankful for it all the time as you expect to be when it has taken form. The man who can sincerely thank God for the things which as yet he owns only in imagination, has real faith. He will get rich; he will cause the creation of whatsoever he wants.

You do not need to pray repeatedly for things you want; it is not necessary to tell God about it every day.

"Use not vain repetitions as the heathen do," Jesus said to his pupils, "for your Father knoweth ye have need of these things before ye ask Him."

Your part is to intelligently formulate your desires for the things which make for a larger life, and to get these desires arranged into a coherent whole; and then to impress this Whole Desire upon the Formless Substance, which has the power and the will to bring you what you want.

You do not make this impression by repeating strings of words; you make it by holding the vision with unshakable PURPOSE to attain it, and with steadfast FAITH that you do attain it.

The answer to prayer is not according to your faith while you are talking, but according to your faith while you are working.

You cannot impress the mind of God by having a special Sabbath day set apart to tell Him what you want, and then forgetting Him during the rest of the week. You cannot impress Him by having special hours to go into your closet and pray, if you then dismiss the matter from your mind until the hour of prayer comes again.

Oral prayer is well enough, and has its effect, especially upon yourself, in clarifying your vision and strengthening your faith; but it is not your oral petitions which get you what you want. In order to get rich you do not need a "sweet hour of prayer"; you need to "pray without ceasing." And by prayer I mean holding steadily to your vision, with the purpose to cause its creation into solid form, and the faith that you are doing so.

"Believe that ye receive them."

The whole matter turns on receiving, once you have clearly formed your vision. When you have formed it, it is well to make an oral statement, addressing the Supreme in reverent prayer; and from that moment you must, in mind, receive what you ask for. Live in the new house; wear the fine clothes; ride in the automobile; go on the journey, and confidently plan for greater journeys. Think and speak of all the things you have asked for in terms of actual present ownership. Imagine an environment, and a financial condition exactly as you want them, and live all the time in that imaginary environment and financial condition. Mind, however, that you do not do this as a mere dreamer and castle builder; hold to the FAITH that the imaginary is being realized, and to the PURPOSE to realize it. Remember that it is faith and purpose in the use of the imagination which make the difference between the scientist and the dreamer. And having learned this fact, it is here that you must learn the proper use of the Will.

CHAPTER 9

How to Use the Will

To set about getting rich in a scientific way, you do not try to apply your willpower to anything outside of yourself.

You have no right to do so, anyway.

It is wrong to apply your will to other men and women, in order to get them to do what you wish done.

It is as flagrantly wrong to coerce people by mental power as it is to coerce them by physical power. If compelling people by physical force to do things for you reduces them to slavery, compelling them by mental means accomplishes exactly the same thing; the only difference is in methods. If taking things from people by physical force is robbery, then taking things by mental force is robbery also; there is no difference in principle.

You have no right to use your willpower upon another person, even "for his own good"; for you do not know what is for his good. The Science of Getting Rich does not require you to apply power or force to any other person, in any way whatsoever. There is not the slightest necessity for doing so; indeed, any attempt to use your will upon others will only tend to defeat your purpose.

You do not need to apply your will to things, in order to compel them to come to you.

That would simply be trying to coerce God, and would be foolish and useless, as well as irreverent.

You do not have to compel God to give you good things, any more than you have to use your willpower to make the sun rise.

You do not have to use your willpower to conquer an unfriendly deity, or to make stubborn and rebellious forces do your bidding.

Substance is friendly to you, and is more anxious to give you what you want than you are to get it.

To get rich, you need only to use your willpower upon yourself.

When you know what to think and do, then you must use your will to compel yourself to think and do the right things. That is the legitimate use of the will in getting what you want—to use it in holding yourself to the right course. Use your will to keep yourself thinking and acting in the Certain Way.

Do not try to project your will, or your thoughts, or your mind out into space, to "act" on things or people.

Keep your mind at home; it can accomplish more there than elsewhere.

Use your mind to form a mental image of what you want, and to hold that vision with faith and purpose; and use your will to keep your mind working in the Right Way.

The more steady and continuous your faith and purpose, the more rapidly you will get rich, because you will make only POSITIVE impressions upon Substance; and you will not neutralize or offset them by negative impressions.

The picture of your desires, held with faith and purpose, is taken up by the Formless, and permeates it to great distances—throughout the universe, for all I know.

As this impression spreads, all things are set moving toward its realization; every living thing, every inanimate thing, and the things yet uncreated, are stirred toward bringing into being that which you want. All force begins to be exerted in that direction; all things begin to move toward you. The minds of people, everywhere, are influenced toward doing the things necessary to the fulfilling of your desires; and they work for you, unconsciously.

But you can check all this by starting a negative impression in the Formless Substance. Doubt or unbelief is as certain to start a movement away from you as faith and purpose are to start one toward you. It is by not understanding this that most people who try to make use of "mental science" in getting rich make their failure. Every hour and moment you spend in giving heed to doubts and fears, every hour you spend in worry, every hour in which your soul is possessed by unbelief, sets a current away from you in the whole domain of intelligent Substance. All the promises are unto them that believe, and unto them only. Notice how insistent Jesus was upon this point of belief; and now you know the reason why.

Since belief is all important, it behooves you to guard your thoughts; and as your beliefs will be shaped to a very great extent by the things you observe and think about, it is important that you should command your attention.

And here the will comes into use; for it is by your will that you determine upon what things your attention shall be fixed.

If you want to become rich, you must not make a study of poverty.

Things are not brought into being by thinking about their opposites. Health is never to be attained by studying disease and thinking about disease; righteousness is not to be promoted by studying sin and thinking about sin; and no one ever got rich by studying poverty and thinking about poverty.

Medicine as a science of disease has increased disease; religion as a science of sin has promoted sin, and economics as a study of poverty will fill the world with wretchedness and want.

Do not talk about poverty; do not investigate it, or concern yourself with it. Never mind what its causes are; you have nothing to do with them.

What concerns you is the cure.

Do not spend your time in charitable work, or charity movements; all charity only tends to perpetuate the wretchedness it aims to eradicate.

I do not say that you should be hard-hearted or unkind, and refuse to hear the cry of need; but you must not try to eradicate poverty in any of the conventional ways. Put poverty behind you, and put all that pertains to it behind you, and "make good."

Get rich; that is the best way you can help the poor.

And you cannot hold the mental image which is to make you rich if you fill your mind with pictures of poverty. Do not read books or papers which give circumstantial accounts of the wretchedness of the tenement dwellers, of the horrors of child labor, and so on. Do not read anything which fills your mind with gloomy images of want and suffering.

You cannot help the poor in the least by knowing about these things; and the widespread knowledge of them does not tend at all to do away with poverty.

What tends to do away with poverty is not the getting of pictures of poverty into your mind, but getting pictures of wealth into the minds of the poor.

You are not deserting the poor in their misery when you refuse to allow your mind to be filled with pictures of that misery.

Poverty can be done away with, not by increasing the number of well-to-do people who think about poverty but by increasing the number of poor people who purpose with faith to get rich.

The poor do not need charity; they need inspiration. Charity only sends them a loaf of bread to keep them alive in their wretchedness, or gives them an entertainment to make them forget for an hour or two; but inspiration will cause them to rise out of their misery. If you want to help the poor, demonstrate to them that they can become rich; prove it by getting rich yourself.

The only way in which poverty will ever be banished from this world is by getting a large and constantly increasing number of people to practice the teachings of this book.

People must be taught to become rich by creation, not by competition.

Every man who becomes rich by competition throws down behind him the ladder by which he rises, and keeps others down; but every man who gets rich by creation opens a way for thousands to follow him, and inspires them to do so.

You are not showing hardness of heart or an unfeeling disposition when you refuse to pity poverty, see poverty, read about poverty, or think or talk about it, or to listen to those who do talk about it. Use your willpower to keep your mind OFF the subject of poverty, and to keep it fixed with faith and purpose ON the vision of what you want.

CHAPTER 10

Further Use of the Will

You cannot retain a true and clear vision of wealth if you are constantly turning your attention to opposing pictures, whether they be external or imaginary.

Do not tell of your past troubles of a financial nature, if you have had them, do not think of them at all. Do not tell of the poverty of your parents, or the hardships of your early life; to do any of these things is to mentally class yourself with the poor for the time being, and it will certainly check the movement of things in your direction.

"Let the dead bury their dead," as Jesus said.

Put poverty and all things that pertain to poverty completely behind you.

You have accepted a certain theory of the universe as being correct, and are resting all your hopes of happiness on its being correct; and what can you gain by giving heed to conflicting theories?

Do not read religious books which tell you that the world is soon coming to an end; and do not read the writing of muckrakers and pessimistic philosophers who tell you that it is going to the devil.

The world is not going to the devil; it is going to God.

It is wonderful Becoming.

True, there may be a good many things in existing conditions which are disagreeable; but what is the use of studying them when they are certainly passing away, and when the study of them only tends to check their passing and keep them with us? Why give time and attention to things which are being removed by evolutionary growth, when you can hasten their removal only by promoting the evolutionary growth as far as your part of it goes?

No matter how horrible in seeming may be the conditions in certain countries, sections, or places, you waste your time and destroy your own chances by considering them.

You should interest yourself in the world's becoming rich.

Think of the riches the world is coming into, instead of the poverty it is growing out of; and bear in mind that the only way in which you can assist the world in growing rich is by growing rich yourself through the creative method—not the competitive one.

Give your attention wholly to riches; ignore poverty.

Whenever you think or speak of those who are poor, think and speak of them as those who are becoming rich; as those who are to be congratulated rather than pitied. Then they and others will catch the inspiration, and begin to search for the way out.

Because I say that you are to give your whole time and mind and thought to riches, it does not follow that you are to be sordid or mean.

To become really rich is the noblest aim you can have in life, for it includes everything else.

On the competitive plane, the struggle to get rich is a Godless scramble for power over other men; but when we come into the creative mind, all this is changed.

All that is possible in the way of greatness and soul unfoldment, of service and lofty endeavor, comes by way of getting rich; all is made possible by the use of things.

If you lack for physical health, you will find that the attainment of it is conditional on your getting rich.

Only those who are emancipated from financial worry, and who have the means to live a carefree existence and follow hygienic practices, can have and retain health.

Moral and spiritual greatness is possible only to those who are above the competitive battle for existence; and only those who are becoming rich on the plane of creative thought are free from the degrading influences of competition. If your heart is set on domestic happiness, remember that love flourishes best where there is refinement, a high level of thought, and freedom from corrupting influences; and these are to be found only where riches are attained by the exercise of creative thought, without strife or rivalry.

You can aim at nothing so great or noble, I repeat, as to become rich; and you must fix your attention upon your mental picture of riches, to the exclusion of all that may tend to dim or obscure the vision.

You must learn to see the underlying TRUTH in all things; you must see beneath all seemingly wrong conditions the Great One Life ever moving forward toward fuller expression and more complete happiness.

It is the truth that there is no such thing as poverty; that there is only wealth.

Some people remain in poverty because they are ignorant of the fact that there is wealth for them; and these can best be taught by showing them the way to affluence in your own person and practice.

Others are poor because, while they feel that there is a way out, they are too intellectually indolent to put forth the mental effort necessary to find that way and by travel it; and for these the very best thing you can do is to arouse their desire by showing them the happiness that comes from being rightly rich.

Others still are poor because, while they have some notion of science, they have become so swamped and lost in the maze of metaphysical and occult theories that they do not know which road to take. They try a mixture of many systems and fail in all. For these, again, the very best thing to do is to show the right way in your own person and practice; an ounce of doing things is worth a pound of theorizing.

The very best thing you can do for the whole world is to make the most of yourself.

You can serve God and man in no more effective way than by getting rich; that is, if you get rich by the creative method and not by the competitive one.

Another thing. We assert that this book gives in detail the principles of the science of getting rich; and if that is true, you do not need to read any other book upon the subject.

This may sound narrow and egotistical, but consider: there is no more scientific method of computation in mathematics than by addition, subtraction, multiplication, and division; no other method is possible. There can be but one shortest distance between two points. There is only one way to think scientifically, and that is to think in the way that leads by the most direct and simple route to the goal. No man has yet formulated a briefer or less complex "system" than the one set forth herein; it has been stripped of all nonessentials. When you commence on this, lay all others aside; put them out of your mind altogether.

Read this book every day; keep it with you; commit it to memory, and do not think about other "systems" and theories. If you do, you will begin to have doubts, and to be uncertain and wavering in your thought; and then you will begin to make failures.

After you have made good and become rich, you may study other systems as much as you please; but until you are quite sure that you have gained what you want, do not read anything on this line but this book, unless it be the authors mentioned in the Preface.

And read only the most optimistic comments on the world's news; those in harmony with your picture.

Also, postpone your investigations into the occult. Do not dabble in theosophy, Spiritualism, or kindred studies. It is very likely that the dead still live, and are near; but if they are, let them alone; mind your own business.

Wherever the spirits of the dead may be, they have their own work to do, and their own problems to solve; and we have no right to interfere with them. We cannot help them, and it is very doubtful whether they can help us, or whether we have any right to trespass upon their time if they can. Let the dead and the hereafter alone, and solve your own problem; get rich. If you begin to mix with the occult, you will start mental cross-currents which will surely bring your hopes to shipwreck. Now, this and the preceding chapters have brought us to the following statement of basic facts:—

There is a thinking Stuff from which all things are made, and which, in its original state, permeates, penetrates, and fills the interspaces of the universe.

A thought, in this Substance, produces the thing that is imaged by the thought.

Man can form things in his thought, and, by impressing his thought upon Formless Substance, can cause the thing he thinks about to be created.

In order to do this, man must pass from the competitive to the creative mind; he must form a clear mental picture of the things he wants, and hold this picture in his thoughts with the fixed PURPOSE to get what he wants, and the unwavering FAITH that he does get what he wants, closing his mind against all that may tend to shake his purpose, dim his vision, or quench his faith.

And in addition to all this, we shall now see that he must live and act in a Certain Way.

CHAPTER 11

Acting in the Certain Way

Thought is the creative power, or the impelling force which causes the creative power to act; thinking in a Certain Way will bring riches to you, but you must not rely upon thought alone, paying no attention to personal action. That is the rock upon which many otherwise scientific metaphysical thinkers meet shipwreck—the failure to connect thought with personal action.

We have not yet reached the stage of development, even supposing such a stage to be possible, in which man can create directly from Formless Substance without nature's processes or the work of human hands; man must not only think, but his personal action must supplement his thought.

By thought you can cause the gold in the hearts of the mountains to be impelled toward you; but it will not mine itself, refine itself, coin itself into double eagles, and come rolling along the roads seeking its way into your pocket.

Under the impelling power of the Supreme Spirit, men's affairs will be so ordered that someone will be led to mine the gold for you; other men's business transactions will be so directed that the gold will be brought toward you, and you must so arrange your own business affairs that you may be able to receive it when it comes to you. Your thought makes all things, animate and inanimate, work to bring you what you want; but your personal activity must be such that you can rightly receive what you want when it reaches you. You are not to take it as charity, nor to steal it; you must give every man more in use value than he gives you in cash value.

The scientific use of thought consists in forming a clear and distinct mental image of what you want; in holding fast to the purpose to get what you want; and in realizing with grateful faith that you do get what you want.

Do not try to "project" your thought in any mysterious or occult way, with the idea of having it go out and do things for you; that is wasted effort, and will weaken your power to think with sanity.

The action of thought in getting rich is fully explained in the preceding chapters; your faith and purpose positively impress your vision upon Formless Substance, which has THE SAME DESIRE FOR MORE LIFE THAT YOU HAVE; and this vision, received from you, sets all the creative forces at work IN AND THROUGH THEIR REGULAR CHANNELS OF ACTION, but directed toward you.

It is not your part to guide or supervise the creative process; all you have to do with that is to retain your vision, stick to your purpose, and maintain your faith and gratitude.

But you must act in a Certain Way, so that you can appropriate what is yours when it comes to you; so that you can meet the things you have in your picture, and put them in their proper places as they arrive.

You can really see the truth of this. When things reach you, they will be in the hands of other men, who will ask an equivalent for them.

And you can only get what is yours by giving the other man what is his.

Your pocketbook is not going to be transformed into a Fortunata's purse, which shall be always full of money without effort on your part.

This is the crucial point in the science of getting rich; right here, where thought and personal action must be combined. There are very many people who, consciously or unconsciously, set the creative forces in action by the strength and persistence of their desires, but who remain poor because they do not provide for the reception of the thing they want when it comes.

By thought, the thing you want is brought to you; by action you receive it.

Whatever your action is to be, it is evident that you must act NOW. You cannot act in the past, and it is essential to the clearness of your mental vision that you dismiss the past from your mind. You cannot act in the future, for the future is not here yet. And you cannot tell how you will want to act in any future contingency until that contingency has arrived.

Because you are not in the right business, or the right environment now, do not think that you must postpone action until you get into the right business or environment. And do not spend time in the present taking thought as to the best course in possible future emergencies; have faith in your ability to meet any emergency when it arrives.

If you act in the present with your mind on the future, your present action will be with a divided mind, and will not be effective.

Put your whole mind into present action.

Do not give your creative impulse to Original Substance, and then sit down and wait for results; if you do, you will never get them. Act now. There is never any time but now, and there never will be any time but now. If you are ever to begin to make ready for the reception of what you want, you must begin now.

And your action, whatever it is, must most likely be in your present business or employment, and must be upon the persons and things in your present environment.

You cannot act where you are not; you cannot act where you have been, and you cannot act where you are going to be; you can act only where you are.

Do not bother as to whether yesterday's work was well done or ill done; do today's work well.

Do not try to do tomorrow's work now; there will be plenty of time to do that when you get to it.

Do not try, by occult or mystical means, to act on people or things that are out of your reach.

Do not wait for a change of environment, before you act; get a change of environment by action.

You can so act upon the environment in which you are now, as to cause yourself to be transferred to a better environment.

Hold with faith and purpose the vision of yourself in the better environment, but act upon your present environment with all your heart, and with all your strength, and with all your mind.

Do not spend any time in daydreaming or castle building; hold to the one vision of what you want, and act NOW.

Do not cast about seeking some new thing to do, or some strange, unusual, or remarkable action to perform as a first step toward getting rich. It is probable that your actions, at least for some time to come, will be those you have been performing for some time past; but you are to begin now to perform these actions in the Certain Way, which will surely make you rich.

If you are engaged in some business, and feel that it is not the right one for you, do not wait until you get into the right business before you begin to act.

Do not feel discouraged, or sit down and lament because you are misplaced. No man was ever so misplaced but that he could not find the right place, and no man ever became so involved in the wrong business but that he could get into the right business.

Hold the vision of yourself in the right business, with the purpose to get into it, and the faith that you will get into it, and are getting into it; but ACT in your present business. Use your present business as the means of getting a better one, and use your present environment as the means of getting into a better one. Your vision of the right business, if held with faith and purpose, will cause the Supreme to move the right business toward you; and your action, if performed in the Certain Way, will cause you to move toward the business.

If you are an employee, or wage earner, and feel that you must change places in order to get what you want, do not "project" your thought into space and rely upon it to get you another job. It will probably fail to do so.

Hold the vision of yourself in the job you want, while you ACT with faith and purpose on the job you have, and you will certainly get the job you want.

Your vision and faith will set the creative force in motion to bring it toward you, and your action will cause the forces in your own environment to move you toward the place you want. In closing this chapter, we will add another statement to our syllabus:—

There is a thinking Stuff from which all things are made, and which, in its original state, permeates, penetrates, and fills the interspaces of the universe.

A thought, in this Substance, produces the thing that is imaged by the thought.

Man can form things in his thought, and, by impressing his thought upon Formless Substance, can cause the thing he thinks about to be created.

In order to do this, man must pass from the competitive to the creative mind; he must form a clear mental picture of the things he wants, and hold this picture in his thoughts with the fixed PURPOSE to get what he wants, and the unwavering FAITH that he does get what he wants, closing his mind to all that may tend to shake his purpose, dim his vision, or quench his faith.

That he may receive what he wants when it comes, man must act NOW upon the people and things in his present environment.

CHAPTER 12

Efficient Action

You must use your thought as directed in previous chapters, and begin to do what you can do where you are; and you must do ALL that you can do where you are.

You can advance only be being larger than your present place; and no man is larger than his present place who leaves undone any of the work pertaining to that place.

The world is advanced only by those who more than fill their present places.

If no man quite filled his present place, you can see that there must be a going backward in everything. Those who do not quite fill their present places are dead weight upon society, government, commerce, and industry; they must be carried along by others at a great expense. The progress of the world is retarded only by those who do not fill the places they are holding; they belong to a former age and a lower stage or plane of life, and their tendency is toward degeneration. No society could advance if every man was smaller than his place; social evolution is guided by the law of physical and mental evolution. In the animal world, evolution is caused by excess of life.

When an organism has more life than can be expressed in the functions of its own plane, it develops the organs of a higher plane, and a new species is originated.

There never would have been new species had there not been organisms which more than filled their places. The law is exactly the same for you; your getting rich depends upon your applying this principle to your own affairs.

Every day is either a successful day or a day of failure; and it is the successful days which get you what you want. If everyday is a failure, you can never get rich; while if every day is a success, you cannot fail to get rich.

If there is something that may be done today, and you do not do it, you have failed in so far as that thing is concerned; and the consequences may be more disastrous than you imagine.

You cannot foresee the results of even the most trivial act; you do not know the workings of all the forces that have been set moving in your behalf. Much may be depending on your doing some simple act; it may be the very thing which is to open the door of opportunity to very great possibilities. You can never know all the combinations which Supreme Intelligence is making for you in the world of things and of human affairs; your neglect or failure to do some small thing may cause a long delay in getting what you want.

Do, every day, ALL that can be done that day.

There is, however, a limitation or qualification of the above that you must take into account.

You are not to overwork, nor to rush blindly into your business in the effort to do the greatest possible number of things in the shortest possible time.

You are not to try to do tomorrow's work today, nor to do a week's work in a day.

It is really not the number of things you do, but the EFFICIENCY of each separate action that counts.

Every act is, in itself, either a success or a failure.

Every act is, in itself, either effective or inefficient.

Every inefficient act is a failure, and if you spend your life in doing inefficient acts, your whole life will be a failure.

The more things you do, the worse for you, if all your acts are inefficient ones.

On the other hand, every efficient act is a success in itself, and if every act of your life is an efficient one, your whole life MUST be a success.

The cause of failure is doing too many things in an inefficient manner, and not doing enough things in an efficient manner.

You will see that it is a self-evident proposition that if you do not do any inefficient acts, and if you do a sufficient number of efficient acts, you will become rich. If, now, it is possible for you to make each act an efficient one, you see again that the getting of riches is reduced to an exact science, like mathematics.

The matter turns, then, on the questions whether you can make each separate act a success in itself. And this you can certainly do.

You can make each act a success, because ALL Power is working with you; and ALL Power cannot fail.

Power is at your service; and to make each act efficient you have only to put power into it.

Every action is either strong or weak; and when every one is strong, you are acting in the Certain Way which will make you rich.

Every act can be made strong and efficient by holding your vision while you are doing it, and putting the whole power of your FAITH and PURPOSE into it.

It is at this point that the people fail who separate mental power from personal action. They use the power of mind in one place and at one time, and they act in another place and at another time. So their acts are not successful in themselves; too many of them are inefficient. But if ALL Power goes into every act, no matter how commonplace, every act will be a success in itself; and as in the nature of things every success opens the way to other successes, your progress toward what you want, and the progress of what you want toward you, will become increasingly rapid.

Remember that successful action is cumulative in its results. Since the desire for more life is inherent in all things, when a man begins to move toward larger life more things attach themselves to him, and the influence of his desire is multiplied.

Do, every day, all that you can do that day, and do each act in an efficient manner.

In saying that you must hold your vision while you are doing each act, however trivial or commonplace, I do not mean to say that it is necessary at all times to see the vision distinctly to its smallest details. It should be the work of your leisure hours to use your imagination on the details of your vision, and to contemplate them until they are firmly fixed upon memory. If you wish speedy results, spend practically all your spare time in this practice.

By continuous contemplation you will get the picture of what you want, even to the smallest details, so firmly fixed upon your mind, and so completely transferred to the mind of Formless Substance, that in your working hours you need only to mentally refer to the picture to stimulate your faith and purpose, and cause your best effort to be put forth. Contemplate your picture in your leisure hours until your consciousness is so full of it that you can grasp it instantly. You will become so enthused with its bright promises that the mere thought of it will call forth the strongest energies of your whole being.

Let us again repeat our syllabus, and by slightly changing the closing statements bring it to the point we have now reached.

There is a thinking Stuff from which all things are made, and which, in its original state, permeates, penetrates, and fills the interspaces of the universe.

A thought, in this Substance, produces the thing that is imaged by the thought.

Man can form things in his thought, and, by impressing his thought upon Formless Substance, can cause the thing he thinks about to be created.

In order to do this, man must pass from the competitive to the creative mind; he must form a clear mental picture of the things he wants, and do, with faith and purpose, all that can be done each day, doing each separate thing in an efficient manner.

CHAPTER 13

Getting into the Right Business

Success, in any particular business, depends for one thing upon your possessing in a well-developed state the faculties required in that business.

Without good musical faculty no one can succeed as a teacher of music; without well-developed mechanical faculties no one can achieve great success in any of the mechanical trades; without tact and the commercial faculties no one can succeed in mercantile pursuits. But to possess in a well-developed state the faculties required in your particular vocation does not ensure getting rich. There are musicians who have remarkable talent, and who yet remain poor; there are blacksmiths, carpenters, and so on who have excellent mechanical ability, but who do not get rich; and there are merchants with good faculties for dealing with men who nevertheless fail.

The different faculties are tools; it is essential to have good tools, but it is also essential that the tools should be used in the Right Way. One man can take a sharp saw, a square, a good plane, and so on, and build a handsome article of furniture; another man can take the same tools and set to work to duplicate the article, but his production will be a botch. He does not know how to use good tools in a successful way.

The various faculties of your mind are the tools with which you must do the work which is to make you rich; it will be easier for you to succeed if you get into a business for which you are well equipped with mental tools.

Generally speaking, you will do best in that business which will use your strongest faculties; the one for which you are naturally "best fitted." But there are limitations to this statement, also. No man should regard his vocation as being irrevocably fixed by the tendencies with which he was born.

You can get rich in ANY business, for if you have not the right talent for you can develop that talent; it merely means that you will have to make your tools as you go along, instead of confining yourself to the use of those with which you were born. It will be EASIER for you to succeed in a vocation for which you already have the talents in a well-developed state; but you CAN succeed in any vocation, for you can develop any rudimentary talent, and there is no talent of which you have not at least the rudiment.

You will get rich most easily in point of effort, if you do that for which you are best fitted; but you will get rich most satisfactorily if you do that which you WANT to do.

Doing what you want to do is life; and there is no real satisfaction in living if we are compelled to be forever doing something which we do not like to do, and can never do what we want to do. And it is certain that you can do what you want to do; the *desire* to do it is proof that you have within you the power which *can* do it.

Desire is a manifestation of power.

The desire to play music is the power which can play music seeking expression and development; the desire to invent mechanical devices is the mechanical talent seeking expression and development.

Where there is no power, either developed or undeveloped, to do a thing, there is never any desire to do that thing; and where there is strong desire to do a thing, it is certain proof that the power to do it is strong, and only requires to be developed and applied in the Right Way.

All things else being equal, it is best to select the business for which you have the best developed talent; but if you have a strong desire to engage in any particular line of work, you should select that work as the ultimate end at which you aim.

You can do what you want to do, and it is your right and privilege to follow the business or avocation which will be most congenial and pleasant.

You are not obliged to do what you do not like to do, and should not do it except as a means to bring you to the doing of the thing you want to do.

If there are past mistakes whose consequences have placed you in an undesirable business or environment, you may be obliged for some time to do what you do not like to do; but you can make the doing of it pleasant by knowing that it is making it possible for you to come to the doing of what you want to do.

If you feel that you are not in the right vocation, do not act too hastily in trying to get into another one. The best way, generally, to change business or environment is by growth.

Do not be afraid to make a sudden and radical change if the opportunity is presented, and you feel after careful consideration that it is the right opportunity; but never take sudden or radical action when you are in doubt as to the wisdom of doing so.

There is never any hurry on the creative plane; and there is no lack of opportunity.

When you get out of the competitive mind you will understand that you never need to act hastily. No one else is going to beat you to the thing you want to do; there is enough for all. If one space is taken, another and a better one will be opened for you a little farther on; there is plenty of time. When you are in doubt, wait. Fall back on the contemplation of your vision, and increase your faith and purpose; and by all means, in times of doubt and indecision, cultivate gratitude.

A day or two spent in contemplating the vision of what you want, and in earnest thanksgiving that you are getting it, will bring your mind into such close relationship with the Supreme that you will make no mistake when you do act.

There is a mind which knows all there is to know; and you can come into close unity with this mind by faith and the purpose to advance in life, if you have deep gratitude.

Mistakes come from acting hastily, or from acting in fear or doubt, or in forgetfulness of the Right Motive, which is more life to all, and less to none.

As you go on in the Certain Way, opportunities will come to you in increasing number; and you will need to be very steady in your faith and purpose, and to keep in close touch with the All Mind by reverent gratitude.

Do all that you can do in a perfect manner every day, but do it without haste, worry, or fear. Go as fast as you can, but never hurry.

Remember that in the moment you begin to hurry you cease to be a creator and become a competitor; you drop back upon the old plane again.

Whenever you find yourself hurrying, call a halt; fix your attention on the mental image of the thing you want, and begin to give thanks that you are getting it. The exercise of GRATITUDE will never fail to strengthen your faith and renew your purpose.

CHAPTER 14

The Impression of Increase

Whether you change your vocation or not, your actions for the present must be those pertaining to the business in which you are now engaged.

You can get into the business you want by making constructive use of the business you are already established in; by doing your daily work in a Certain Way.

And insofar as your business consists in dealing with other men, whether personally or by letter, the key thought of all your efforts must be to convey to their minds the impression of increase.

Increase is what all men and all women are seeking; it is the urge of the Formless Intelligence within them, seeking fuller expression.

The desire for increase is inherent in all nature; it is the fundamental impulse of the universe. All human activities are based on the desire for increase; people are seeking more food, more clothes, better shelter, more luxury, more beauty, more knowledge, more pleasure— increase in something, more life.

Every living thing is under this necessity for continuous advancement; where increase of life ceases, dissolution and death set in at once.

Man instinctively knows this, and hence he is forever seeking more. This law of perpetual increase is set forth by Jesus in the parable of the talents; only those who gain more retain any; from him who hath not shall be taken away even that which he hath.

The normal desire for increased wealth is not an evil or a reprehensible thing; it is simply the desire for more abundant life; it is aspiration.

And because it is the deepest instinct of their natures, all men and women are attracted to him who can give them more of the means of life.

In following the Certain Way as described in the foregoing pages, you are getting continuous increase for yourself, and you are giving it to all with whom you deal.

You are a creative center, from which increase is given off to all.

Be sure of this, and convey assurance of the fact to every man, woman, and child with whom you come in contact. No matter how small the transaction, even if it be only the selling of a stick of candy to a little child, put into it the thought of increase, and make sure that the customer is impressed with the thought.

Convey the impression of advancement with everything you do, so that all people shall receive the impression that you are an Advancing Man, and that you advance all who deal with you. Even to the people whom you meet in a social way, without any thought of business, and to whom you do not try to sell anything, give the thought of increase.

You can convey this impression by holding the unshakable faith that you, yourself, are in the Way of Increase; and by letting this faith inspire, fill, and permeate every action.

Do everything that you do in the firm conviction that you are an advancing personality, and that you are giving advancement to everybody.

Feel that you are getting rich, and that in so doing you are making others rich, and conferring benefits on all.

Do not boast or brag of your success, or talk about it unnecessarily; true faith is never boastful.

Wherever you find a boastful person, you find one who is secretly doubtful and afraid. Simply feel the faith, and let it work out in every transaction; let every act and tone and look express the quiet assurance that you are getting rich; that you are already rich. Words will not be necessary to communicate this feeling to others; they will feel the sense of increase when in your presence, and will be attracted to you again.

You must so impress others that they will feel that in associating with you they will get increase for themselves. See that you give them a use value greater than the cash value you are taking from them.

Take an honest pride in doing this, and let everybody know it; and you will have no lack of customers. People will go where they are given increase; and the Supreme, which desires increase in all, and which knows all, will move toward you men and women who have never heard of you. Your business will increase rapidly, and you will be surprised at the unexpected benefits which will come to you. You will be able from day to day to make larger combinations, secure greater advantages, and to go on into a more congenial vocation if you desire to do so.

But doing all this, you must never lose sight of your vision of what you want, or your faith and purpose to get what you want.

Let me here give you another word of caution in regard to motives.

Beware of the insidious temptation to seek for power over other men.

Nothing is so pleasant to the unformed or partially developed mind as the exercise of power or dominion over others. *The desire to rule for selfish gratification has been the curse of the world.* For countless ages kings and lords have drenched the earth with blood in their battles to extend their dominions; this not to seek more life for all, but to get more power for themselves.

Today, the main motive in the business and industrial world is the same; men marshal their armies of dollars, and lay waste the lives and hearts of millions in the same mad scramble for power over others. Commercial kings, like political kings, are inspired by the lust for power.

Jesus saw in this desire for mastery the moving impulse of that evil world He sought to overthrow. Read the twenty-third chapter of Matthew, and see how He pictures the lust of the Pharisees to be called "Master," to sit in the high places, to domineer over others, and to lay burdens on the backs of the less fortunate; and note how He compares this lust for dominion with the brotherly seeking for the Common Good to which He calls His disciples.

Look out for the temptation to seek for authority, to become a "master," to be considered as one who is above the common herd, to impress others by lavish display, and so on.

The mind that seeks for mastery over others is the competitive mind; and the competitive mind is not the creative one. In order to master your environment and your destiny, it is not at all necessary that you should rule over your fellow men and indeed, when you fall into the world's struggle for the high places, you begin to be conquered by fate and environment, and your getting rich becomes a matter of chance and speculation.

Beware of the competitive mind!! No better statement of the principle of creative action can be formulated than the favorite declaration of the late "Golden Rule" Jones of Toledo: "What I want for myself, I want for everybody."

CHAPTER 15

The Advancing Man

What I have said in the last chapter applies as well to the professional man and the wage-earner as to the man who is engaged in mercantile business.

No matter whether you are a physician, a teacher, or a clergyman, if you can give increase of life to others and make them sensible of the fact, they will be attracted to you, and you will get rich. The physician who holds the vision of himself as a great and successful healer, and who works toward the complete realization of that vision with faith and purpose, as described in former chapters, will come into such close touch with the Source of Life that he will be phenomenally successful; patients will come to him in throngs.

No one has a greater opportunity to carry into effect the teaching of this book than the practitioner of medicine; it does not matter to which of the various schools he may belong, for the principle of healing is common to all of them, and may be reached by all alike. The Advancing Man in medicine, who holds to a clear mental image of himself as successful, and who obeys the laws of faith, purpose, and gratitude, will cure every curable case he undertakes, no matter what remedies he may use.

In the field of religion, the world cries out for the clergyman who can teach his hearers the true science of abundant life. He who masters the details of the science of getting rich, together with the allied sciences of being well, of being great, and of winning love, and who teaches these details from the pulpit, will never lack for a congregation. This is the gospel that the world needs; it will give increase of life, and men will hear it gladly, and will give liberal support to the man who brings it to them.

What is now needed is a demonstration of the science of life from the pulpit. We want preachers who can not only tell us how, but who in their own persons will show us how. We need the preacher who will himself be rich, healthy, great, and beloved, to teach us how to attain to these things; and when he comes he will find a numerous and loyal following.

The same is true of the teacher who can inspire the children with the faith and purpose of the advancing life. He will never be "out of a job." And any teacher who has this faith and purpose can give it to his pupils; he cannot help giving it to them if it is part of his own life and practice.

What is true of the teacher, preacher, and physician is true of the lawyer, dentist, real estate man, insurance agent—of everybody.

The combined mental and personal action I have described is infallible; it cannot fail. Every man and woman who follows these instructions steadily, perseveringly, and to the letter, will get rich. The law of the Increase of Life is as mathematically certain in its operation as the law of gravitation; getting rich is an exact science.

The wage-earner will find this as true of his case as of any of the others mentioned. Do not feel that you have no chance to get rich because you are working where there is no visible opportunity for advancement, where wages are small and the cost of living high. Form your clear mental vision of what you want, and begin to act with faith and purpose.

Do all the work you can do, every day, and do each piece of work in a perfectly successful manner; put the power of success, and the purpose to get rich, into everything that you do.

But do not do this merely with the idea of currying favor with your employer, in the hope that he, or those above you, will see your good work and advance you; it is not likely that they will do so.

The man who is merely a "good" workman, filling his place to the very best of his ability, and satisfied with that, is valuable to his employer; and it is not to the employer's interest to promote him; he is worth more where he is.

To secure advancement, something more is necessary than to be too large for your place.

The man who is certain to advance is the one who is too big for his place, and who has a clear concept of what he wants to be; who knows that he can become what he wants to be and who is determined to BE what he wants to be.

Do not try to more than fill your present place with a view to pleasing your employer; do it with the idea of advancing yourself. Hold the faith and purpose of increase during work hours, after work hours, and before work hours. Hold it in such a way that every person who comes in contact with you, whether foreman, fellow workman, or social acquaintance, will feel the power of purpose radiating from you; so that everyone will get the sense of advancement and increase from you. Men will be attracted to you, and if there is no possibility for advancement in your present job, you will very soon see an opportunity to take another job.

There is a Power which never fails to present opportunity to the Advancing Man who is moving in obedience to law.

God cannot help helping you, if you act in a Certain Way; He must do so in order to help Himself.

There is nothing in your circumstances or in the industrial situation that can keep you down. If you cannot get rich working for the steel trust, you can get rich on a ten-acre farm; and if you begin to move in the Certain Way, you will certainly escape from the "clutches" of the steel trust and get on to the farm or wherever else you wish to be.

If a few thousands of its employees would enter upon the Certain Way, the steel trust would soon be in a bad plight; it would have to give its workingmen more opportunity, or go out of business. Nobody has to work for a trust; the trusts can keep men in so called hopeless conditions only so long as there are men who are too ignorant to know of the science of getting rich, or too intellectually slothful to practice it.

Begin this way of thinking and acting, and your faith and purpose will make you quick to see any opportunity to better your condition.

Such opportunities will speedily come, for the Supreme, working in All, and working for you, will bring them before you.

Do not wait for an opportunity to be all that you want to be; when an opportunity to be more than you are now is presented and you feel impelled toward it, take it. It will be the first step toward a greater opportunity.

There is no such thing possible in this universe as a lack of opportunities for the man who is living the advancing life.

It is inherent in the constitution of the cosmos that all things shall be for him and work together for his good; and he must certainly get rich if he acts and thinks in the Certain Way. So let wage-earning men and women study this book with great care, and enter with confidence upon the course of action it prescribes; it will not fail.

CHAPTER 16

Some Cautions, and Concluding Observations

Many people will scoff at the idea that there is an exact science of getting rich; holding the impression that the supply of wealth is limited, they will insist that social and governmental institutions must be changed before even any considerable number of people can acquire a competence.

But this is not true.

It is true that existing governments keep the masses in poverty, but this is because the masses do not think and act in the Certain Way.

If the masses begin to move forward as suggested in this book, neither governments nor industrial systems can check them; all systems must be modified to accommodate the forward movement.

If the people have the Advancing Mind, have the Faith that they can become rich, and move forward with the fixed purpose to become rich, nothing can possibly keep them in poverty.

Individuals may enter upon the Certain Way at any time, and under any government, and make themselves rich; and when any considerable number of individuals do so under any government, they will cause the system to be so modified as to open the way for others.

The more men who get rich on the competitive plane, the worse for others; the more who get rich on the creative plane, the better for others.

The economic salvation of the masses can only be accomplished by getting a large number of people to practice the scientific method set down in this book, and become rich. These will show others the way, and inspire them with a desire for real life, with the faith that it can be attained, and with the purpose to attain it.

For the present, however, it is enough to know that neither the government under which you live nor the capitalistic or competitive system of industry can keep you from getting rich. When you enter upon the creative plane of thought you will rise above all these things and become a citizen of another kingdom.

But remember that your thought must be held upon the creative plane; you are never for an instant to be betrayed into regarding the supply as limited, or into acting on the moral level of competition.

Whenever you do fall into old ways of thought, correct yourself instantly; for when you are in the competitive mind, you have lost the cooperation of the Mind of the Whole.

Do not spend any time in planning as to how you will meet possible emergencies in the future, except as the necessary policies may affect your actions today. You are concerned with doing today's work in a perfectly successful manner, and not with emergencies which may arise tomorrow; you can attend to them as they come.

Do not concern yourself with questions as to how you shall surmount obstacles which may loom upon your business horizon, unless you can see plainly that your course must be altered today in order to avoid them.

No matter how tremendous an obstruction may appear at a distance, you will find that if you go on in the Certain Way it will disappear as you approach it, or that a way over, through, or around it will appear.

No possible combination of circumstances can defeat a man or woman who is proceeding to get rich along strictly scientific lines. No man or woman who obeys the law can fail to get rich, any more than one can multiply two by two and fail to get four.

Give no anxious thought to possible disasters, obstacles, panics, or unfavorable combinations of circumstances; it is time enough to meet such things when they present themselves before you in the immediate present, and you will find that every difficulty carries with it the wherewithal for its overcoming.

Guard your speech. Never speak of yourself, your affairs, or of anything else in a discouraged or discouraging way.

Never admit the possibility of failure, or speak in a way that infers failure as a possibility.

Never speak of the times as being hard, or of business conditions as being doubtful. Times may be hard and business doubtful for those who are on the competitive plane, but they can never be so for you; you can create what you want, and you are above fear.

When others are having hard times and poor business, you will find your greatest opportunities.

Train yourself to think of and to look upon the world as a something which is Becoming, which is growing; and to regard seeming evil as being only that which is undeveloped. Always speak in terms of advancement; to do otherwise is to deny your faith, and to deny your faith is to lose it.

Never allow yourself to feel disappointed. You may expect to have a certain thing at a certain time, and not get it at that time; and this will appear to you like failure.

But if you hold to your faith you will find that the failure is only apparent.

Go on in the Certain Way, and if you do not receive that thing, you will receive something so much better that you will see that the seeming failure was really a great success.

A student of this science had set his mind on making a certain business combination which seemed to him at the time to be very desirable, and he worked for some, weeks to bring it about. When the crucial time came, the thing failed in a perfectly inexplicable way; it was as if some unseen influence had been working secretly against him. He was not disappointed; on the contrary, he thanked God that his desire had been overruled, and went steadily on with a grateful mind. In a few weeks an opportunity so much better came his way that he would not have made the first deal on any account; and he saw that a Mind which knew more than he knew had prevented him from losing the greater good by entangling himself with the lesser.

That is the way every seeming failure will work out for you, if you keep your faith, hold to your purpose, have gratitude, and do, every day, all that can be done that day, doing each separate act in a successful manner.

When you make a failure, it is because you have not asked for enough; keep on, and a larger thing then you were seeking will certainly come to you. Remember this.

You will not fail because you lack the necessary talent to do what you wish to do. If you go on as I have directed, you will develop all the talent that is necessary to the doing of your work.

It is not within the scope of this book to deal with the science of cultivating talent; but it is as certain and simple as the process of getting rich.

However, do not hesitate or waver for fear that when you come to any certain place you will fail for lack of ability; keep right on, and when you come to that place, the ability will be furnished to you. The same source of Ability which enabled the untaught Lincoln to do the greatest work in government ever accomplished by a single man is open to you; you may draw upon all the mind there is for wisdom to use in meeting the responsibilities which are laid upon you. Go on in full faith.

Study this book. Make it your constant companion until you have mastered all the ideas contained in it. While you are getting firmly established in this faith, you will do well to give up most recreations and pleasure; and to stay away from places where ideas conflicting with these are advanced in lectures or sermons. Do not read pessimistic or conflicting literature, or get into arguments upon the matter. Do very little reading, outside of the writers mentioned in the Preface. Spend most of your leisure time in contemplating your vision, and in cultivating gratitude, and in reading this book. It contains all you need to know of the science of getting rich; and you will find all the essentials summed up in the following chapter.

CHAPTER 17

Summary of the Science of Getting Rich

There is a thinking stuff from which all things are made, and which, in its original state, permeates, penetrates, and fills the interspaces of the universe.

A thought in this substance produces the thing that is imaged by the thought.

Man can form things in his thought, and by impressing his thought upon formless substance can cause the thing he thinks about to be created.

In order to do this, man must pass from the competitive to the creative mind; else he cannot be in harmony with the Formless Intelligence, which is always creative and never competitive in spirit.

Man may come into full harmony with the Formless Substance by entertaining a lively and sincere gratitude for the blessings it bestows upon him. Gratitude unifies the mind of man with the intelligence of Substance, so that man's thoughts are received by the Formless. Man can remain upon the creative plane only by uniting himself with the Formless Intelligence through a deep and continuous feeling of gratitude.

Man must form a clear and definite mental image of the things he wishes to have, to do, or to become; and he must hold this mental image in his thoughts, while being deeply grateful to the Supreme that all his desires are granted to him. The man who wishes to get rich must spend his leisure hours in contemplating his Vision, and in earnest thanksgiving that the reality is being given to him. Too much stress cannot be laid on the importance of frequent contemplation of the mental image, coupled with unwavering faith and devout gratitude. This is the process by which the impression is given to the Formless, and the creative forces set in motion.

The creative energy works through the established channels of natural growth, and of the industrial and social order. All that is included in his mental image will surely be brought to the man who follows the instructions given above, and whose faith does not waver. What he wants will come to him through the ways of established trade and commerce.

In order to receive his own when it shall come to him, man must be active; and this activity can only consist in more than filling his present place. He must keep in mind the Purpose to get rich through the realization of his mental image. And he must do, every day, all that can be done that day, taking care to do each act in a successful manner. He must give to every man a use value in excess of the cash value he receives, so that each transaction makes for more life; and he must so hold the Advancing Thought that the impression of increase will be communicated to all with whom he comes in contact.

The men and women who practice the foregoing instructions will certainly get rich; and the riches they receive will be in exact proportion to the definiteness of their vision, the fixity of their purpose, the steadiness of their faith, and the depth of their gratitude.

How to Get What You Want

CHAPTER 1

Getting what you want is success; and success is an effect, coming from the application of a cause. Success is essentially the same in all cases; the difference is in the things the successful people want, but not in the success. Success is essentially the same, whether it results in the attainment of health, wealth, development or position; success is attainment, without regard to the things attained. And it is a law in nature that like causes always produce like effects; therefore, since success is the same in all cases, the cause of success must be the same in all cases.

The cause of success is always in the person who succeeds; you will see that this must be true, because if the cause of success were in nature, outside the person, then all persons similarly situated would succeed.

The cause of success is not in the environment of the individual, because if it were, all persons within a given radius would be successful, and success would be wholly a matter of neighborhood; and we see that people whose environments are practically the same, and who live in the same neighborhood show us all degrees of success and failure; therefore, we know that the cause of success must be in the individual, and nowhere else.

It is, therefore, mathematically certain that you can succeed if you will find out the cause of success, and develop it to sufficient strength, and apply it properly to your work; for the application of a sufficient cause can not fail to produce a given effect. If there is a failure anywhere, of any kind, it is because the cause was either not sufficient or was not properly applied.

The cause of success is some power within you; you have the power to develop any power to a limitless extent; for there is no end to mental growth; you can increase the strength of this power indefinitely, and so you can make it strong enough to do what you want to do, and to get what you want to get; when it is strong enough you can learn how to apply it to the work, and therefore, you can certainly succeed. All you have to learn is what is the cause of success, and how it must be applied.

The development of the special faculties to be used in your work is essential. We do not expect anyone to succeed as a musician without developing the musical faculty; and it would be absurd to expect a machinist to succeed without developing the mechanical faculty, a clergyman to succeed without developing spiritual understanding and the use of words, or a banker to succeed without developing the faculty of finance. And in choosing a business, you should choose the one which will call for the use of your strongest faculties.

If you have good mechanical ability, and are not spiritually minded and have no command of language, do not try to preach; and if you have the taste and talent to combine colors and fabrics into beautiful creation in millinery and dress, do not learn typewriting or stenography; get into a business which will use your strongest faculties, and develop these faculties all you can; and even this is not enough to ensure success.

There are people with fine musical talent who fail as musicians; with good mechanical ability who fail as carpenters, blacksmiths, and machinists; with deep spirituality and fluent use of language who fail as clergymen; with keen and logical minds who fail as lawyers, and so on; the special faculties used in your work are the tools you use, but success does not depend alone on having good tools; it depends more on the power which uses and applies the tools. Be sure that your tools are the best and kept in the best condition; you can cultivate any faculty to any desired extent.

The application of the musical faculty causes success in music; that of the mechanical faculty causes success in mechanical pursuits; that of the financial faculty causes success in banking, and so on; and the something which applies these faculties, or causes them to be applied is the cause of success. The faculties are tools; the user of the tools is you, yourself; that in you which can cause you to use the tools in the right way, at the right time and in the right place is the cause of success.

What is this something in the person which causes him to use his faculties successfully?

What it is and how to develop it will be fully explained in the next section; but before taking that up you should read this section over several times, so as to fix upon your mind the impregnable logic of the statement that you can succeed. You can; and if you study the foregoing argument well, you will be convinced that you can; and to become convinced that you can succeed is the first requisite to success.

CHAPTER 2

The faculties of the human mind are the tools with which success is attained, and the right application of these tools to your work or business will do it successfully and get what you want. A few people succeed because they use their faculties successfully, and the majority, who have equally good faculties, fail because they use them unsuccessfully. There is something in the man who succeeds which enables him to use his faculties successfully, and this something must be cultivated by all who succeed; the question is, What is it?

It is hard to find a word which shall express it, and not be misleading. This something is Poise; and poise is peace and power combined; but it is more than poise, for poise is a condition, and this something is an action as well as a condition. This Something is Faith; but it is more than faith, as faith is commonly understood: As commonly understood, faith consists in the action of believing things which cannot be proved; and the Something which causes success is more than that. It is Conscious Power in Action.

It is ACTIVE POWER-CONSCIOUSNESS.

Power-Consciousness is what you feel when you know that you can do a thing; and you know HOW to do the thing. If I can cause you to KNOW that you can succeed, and to know that you know HOW to succeed, I have placed success within your grasp; for if you know that you can do a thing and know that you know how to do it, it is impossible that you should fail to do it, if you really try. When you are in full Power-Consciousness, you will approach the task in an absolutely successful frame of mind. Every thought will be a successful thought, every action a successful action; and if every thought and action is successful, the sum-total of all your actions cannot be failure.

What I have to do in these lessons, then, is to teach you how to create Power-Consciousness in yourself, so that you will know that you can do what you want to do and then to teach you how to do what you want to do. Read again the preceding section; it proves by unanswerable logic that you CAN succeed. It shows that all that is in any mind is in your mind; the difference, if any, being in development. It is a fact in nature that the undeveloped is always capable of development; we see then that the cause of success is in you, and is capable of full development.

Having read this you must believe that it is possible for you to succeed; but it is not enough for you to believe that you can; you must know that you can; and the subconscious mind must know it as well as the objective mind. People have a way of saying, "he can who thinks he can"; but this is not true. It is not even true that he can who knows he can, if only the objective mind is spoken of; for the subconscious mind will often completely set aside and overcome what is positively known by the objective mind. It is a true statement, however, that he can whose subconscious mind knows that he can; and it is especially true if his objective mind has been trained to do the work.

People fail because they think, objectively, that they can do things, but do not know, subconsciously, that they can do them. It is more than likely that your subconscious mind is even now impressed with doubts of your ability to succeed; and these must be removed, or it will withhold its power when you need it most.

The subconscious mind is the source from which power comes in the action of any faculty; and a doubt will cause this power to be withheld, and the action will be weak; therefore, your first step must be to impress your subconscious mind with that fact that you CAN. This must be done by repeated suggestions.

Practice the following mental exercise several times a day, and especially just before going to sleep: Think quietly about the subconscious mentality, which permeates your whole body as water permeates a sponge; as you think of this mind, try to feel it; you will soon be able to become conscious of it. Hold this consciousness, and say with deep, earnest feeling: "I CAN succeed! All that is possible to anyone is possible to me. I AM successful. I do succeed, for I am full of the Power of Success."

This is the simple truth. Realize that it is true, and repeat it over and over until your mentality is saturated through and through with the knowledge that YOU CAN DO WHAT YOU WANT TO DO. You can; other people have, and you can do more than anyone has ever done, for no one has ever yet used all the power that is capable of being used. It is within your power to make a greater success in your business than anyone has ever made before you.

Practice the above autosuggestion for a month with persistence, and you will begin to KNOW that you have within you that which CAN do what you want to do; and then you will be ready for the next section which will tell you how to proceed in doing what you want to do. But remember that it is absolutely essential that you should first impress upon the subconscious mind the knowledge that you CAN.

CHAPTER 3

Having filled your mentality, conscious and subconscious, with the faith that you CAN get what you want, the next question is one of the methods. You know that you can do it if you proceed in the right way; but which is the right way?

This much is certain; to get more, you must make constructive use of what you have. You cannot use what you have not; therefore, your problem is how to make the most constructive use of what you already have. Do not waste any time considering how you would use certain things if you had them; consider, simply, how to use what you have. It is also certain that you will progress more rapidly if you make the most perfect use of what you have. In fact, the degree of rapidity with which you attain what you want will depend upon the perfection with which you use what you have. Many people are at a standstill, or find things coming their way very slowly because they are making only partial use of present means, power, and opportunities.

You may see this point more plainly by considering an analogy in nature. In the process of evolution, the squirrels developed their leaping power to its fullest extent; then a continuous effort to advance brought forth the flying squirrel, which has a membrane uniting the legs in such a way as to form a parachute and enable the animal to sail some distance beyond an ordinary leap. A little extension of the parachute jump of the flying squirrel produced the bat, which has membranous wings and can fly; and continuous flight produced the bird with feathered wings. The transition from one plane to another was accomplished simply by perfecting and extending functions. If the squirrels had not kept leaping further and further, there would have been no flying squirrel, and no power of flight. Making constructive use of the leaping power produced flight. If you are only jumping half as far as you can, you will never fly.

In nature, we see that life advances from one plane to another by perfecting function on the lower plane. Whenever an organism contains more life than it can express by functioning perfectly on its own plane, it begins to perform the functions of the next higher, or larger plane. The first squirrel which began to develop the parachute membrane must have been a very perfect leaper. This is the fundamental principle of evolution, and of all attainment.

In accordance with this principle, then, you can advance only by more than filling your present place. You must do, perfectly, all that you can do now; and it is the law that by doing perfectly all that you can do now you will become able to do later things which you cannot do now. The doing to perfection of one thing invariably provides us with the equipment for doing the next larger thing, because it is a principle inherent in nature that life continuously advances. Every person who does one thing perfect is instantly presented with an opportunity to begin doing the next larger thing. This is the universal law of all life, and is unfailing.

First, do perfectly all that you can do now; keep on doing it perfectly until the doing of it becomes so easy that you have surplus power left after doing it; then by this surplus power you will get a hold on the work of a higher plane, and begin to extend your correspondence with environment.

Get into a business which will use your strongest faculties, even if you must commence at the bottom; then develop those faculties to the utmost. Cultivate power-consciousness, so that you can apply your faculties successfully, and apply them in doing perfectly everything you can do now, where you are now. Do not wait for a change of environment; it may never come. Your only way of reaching a better environment is by making constructive use of your present environment. Only the most complete use of your present environment will place you in a more desirable one.

If you wish to extend your present business, remember that you can only do it by doing in the most perfect manner the business you already have. When you put life enough into your business to more than fill it, the surplus will get you more business. Do not reach out after more until you have life to spare after doing perfectly all that you have to do now. It is of no advantage to have more work or more business than you have life to do perfectly; if that is the case, increase your vital power first. And remember, it is the perfection with which you do what you have to do now that extends your field and brings you in touch with a larger environment.

Bear in mind that the motive force which gets you what you want is life; and that what you want, in the last analysis, is only an opportunity to live more; and that, therefore, you can get what you want only through the operation of that universal law by which all life advances continuously into fuller expression. That law is that whenever an organism has more life than can find expression by functioning perfectly on a given plane, its surplus life lifts it to the next higher plane. When you put enough of yourself into your present work to do it perfectly, your surplus power will extend your work into a larger field. It is also essential that you should have in mind what you want, so that your surplus power may be turned in the right direction.

Form a clear conception of what you seek to accomplish, but do not let what you seek to accomplish interfere with doing perfectly what you have to do now. Your concept of what you want is a guide to your energies, and an inspiration to cause you to apply them to the utmost to your present work. Live for the future now.

Suppose that your desire is to have a department store, and you have only capital enough to start a peanut stand. Do not try to start a department store today, on a peanut-stand capital; but start the peanut stand in the full faith and confidence that you will be able to develop it into a department store. Look upon the peanut stand merely as the beginning of the department store, and make it grow; you can.

Get more business by using constructively the business you have now; get more friends by using constructively the friends you already have; get a better position by using constructively the one you now have; get more domestic happiness by the constructive use of the love that already exists in your home.

CHAPTER 4

You can obtain what you want only by applying your faculties to your work and your environment; you become able to apply your faculties successfully by acquiring Power-Consciousness; and you go forward by a concentration on today's work, and by doing perfectly everything that can be done at the present time. You can get what you want in the future only by concentrating all your energies upon the constructive use of whatever you are in relation with today. An indifferent or half-hearted use of the elements in today's environment will be fatal to tomorrow's attainment.

Do not desire for today what is beyond your ability to get today; but be sure you get today the very best that can be had. Never take less than the very best that can be had at the present time; but do not waste energy by desiring what cannot be had at the present time. If you always have the best that can be had, you will continue to have better and better things, because it is a fundamental principle in the universe that life shall continually advance into more life, and into the use of more and better things; this is the principle which causes evolution. But if you are satisfied with less than the best that can be had, you will cease to move forward.

Every transaction and relation of today, whether it be business, domestic, or social, must be made a stepping-stone to what you want in the future; and to accomplish this you must put into each more than enough life to fill it. There must be surplus power in everything you do. It is this surplus power which causes advancement and gets you what you want; where there is no surplus power there is no advancement and no attainment. It is the surplus of life above and beyond the functions of present environment which causes evolution; and evolution is advancing into more life, or getting what you want.

Suppose, for instance, you are in trade or a profession, and wish to increase your business; it will not do, when you sell goods or service to make the matter a merely perfunctory transaction, taking the customer's money, giving him good value, and letting him go away feeling that you had no interest in the matter beyond giving him a fair deal and profiting thereby. Unless he feels that you have a personal interest in him and his needs, and that you are honestly desirous to increase his welfare, you have made a failure and are losing ground.

When you can make every customer feel that you are really trying to advance his interests as well as your own, your business will grow. It is not necessary to give premiums, or heavier weights or better values than others give to accomplish this; it is done by putting life and interest into every transaction, however small.

If you desire to change your avocation, make your present business a stepping-stone to the one you want. As long as you are in your present business, fill it with life; the surplus will tend toward what you want.

Take a live interest in every man, woman, and child you meet in either a business or social way, and sincerely desire the best for them; they will soon begin to feel that your advancement is a matter of interest to them and they will unite their thoughts for your good. This will form a battery of power in your favor and will open ways of advancement for you.

If you are an employee and desire promotion, put life into everything you do; put in more than enough life and interest to fill each piece of work. But do not be servile; never be a flunkey; and above all things avoid the intellectual prostitution which is the vice of our times in many trades and most professions. I mean by this the being a mere hired apologist for and defender of immorality, graft, dishonesty, or vice in any form. The intellectual prostitute may rise in the service, but he is a lost soul.

Respect yourself; be absolutely just to all; put LIFE into every act and thought and fix Power-Conscious thought upon the fact that you are entitled to promotion; it will come as soon as you can more than fill your present place in every day. If it does not come from your present employer it will come from another; it is the law that whosoever more than fills his present place must be advanced. But for this law there could be no evolution, and no progress; but mark well what follows.

It is not enough that you should merely put surplus life into your business relations. You will not advance far if you are a good business man or employee, but a bad husband, an unjust father, or, an untrustworthy friend. Your failure in these respects will make you incapable of using your success for the advancement of life, and so you will not come under the operation of the constructive law. Many a man who fulfills the law in business is prevented from progressing because he is unkind to his wife, or deficient in some other relation of life. To come under the operation of the evolutionary force you must more than fill EVERY present relation.

A telegraph operator desired to get away from the key, and get onto a small farm; and he began to move in that direction by being "good" to his wife. He "courted" her, without any reference to his desire; and from being half indifferent she became interested and eager to help; soon they had a little piece of ground in the edge of the town, and she raised poultry and superintended a garden while he "pounded the key"; now they have a farm and he has obtained his desire. You can secure the cooperation, not only of your wife but of all the people around you by putting life and interest into all your relations with them.

Put into every relation, business, domestic, or social, more than enough life to fill that relation; have faith, which is Power-Consciousness; know what you want in the future, but have today the very best that can be obtained today; never be satisfied at any time with

less than the best that can be had at that time, but never waste energy in desiring what is not to be had now; use all things for the advancement of life for yourself and for all with whom you are related in any way. Follow out these principles of action and you cannot fail to get what you want; for the universe is so constructed that all things must work together for your good.

CHAPTER 5

Wealth-culture consists in making constructive use of the people and things in your environment.

First, get a clear mental picture of what you want. If your present business or profession is not the one most suitable to your talents and tastes, decide upon the one which is most suitable; and determine to get into that business or profession, and to achieve the very greatest success in it. Get a clear idea of what you want to do, and get a mental concept of the utmost success in that business or profession; and determine that you will attain to that. Give a great deal of time to forming this concept or mental picture; the more clear and definite it is, the easier will be your work. The man who is not quite sure what he wants to build will put up a wobbling and shaky structure.

Know what you want, and keep the picture of it in the background of your mind night and day; let it be like a picture on the wall of your room, always in your consciousness, night and day. And then begin to move toward it. Remember that if you have not the fully developed talent now, you can develop it as you go along; you can surely do what you want to do.

It is quite likely that at present you cannot do the thing you want to do because you are not in the right environment, and have not the necessary capital; but this does not hinder you from the beginning to move toward the right environment, and from beginning to acquire capital. Remember that you move forward only by doing what you can in your present environment.

Suppose that you have only capital enough to operate a newsstand, and your great desire is to own a department store; do not get the idea that there is some magical method by which you can successfully operate a department store on a newsstand capital. There is, however, a mental science method by which you can so operate a newsstand as to certainly cause it to grow into a department store.

Consider that your newsstand is one department of the store you are going to have; fix your mind on the department store, and begin to assimilate the rest of it. You will get it, if you make every act and thought constructive.

To make every act and thought constructive, everyone must convey the idea of increase. Steadily hold in mind the thought of advancement for yourself; know that you are advancing toward what you want, and act and speak in this faith. Then every word and act will convey the idea of advancement and increase to others, and they will be drawn to you. Always remember that what all people are seeking is increase.

First, study over the facts in regard to the great abundance until you know that there is wealth for you, and that you do not have to take this wealth from anyone else. Avoid the competitive spirit. You can readily see that if there is limitless abundance there is enough for you, without robbing anyone else. Then, knowing what it is the purpose of nature that you should have what you want, reflect upon the fact that you can get it only by acting. Consider that you can act only upon your present environment; and do not try to act now upon environment of the future.

Then remember that in acting upon your present environment, you must make every act a success in itself; and that in doing this you must hold the purpose to get what you want. You can hold this purpose only as you get a clear mental picture of what you want; be sure that you have that.

Also, remember that your actions will not have dynamic moving power unless you have an unwavering faith that you get what you want.

Form a clear mental picture of what you want; hold the purpose to get it; do everything perfectly, not in a servile spirit, but because you are a master mind; keep unwavering faith in your ultimate attainment of your goal, and you cannot fail to move forward.

7

CREATIVE MIND AND SUCCESS

ERNEST HOLMES

(1919)

Contents

1. Instruction 365

An Inquiry into the Truth 365
What Life Is 366
Man's Place in Creation 366
The Beginning of Understanding 367
Our Conditions Governed by Our Thinking 368
Unconscious Creation 369
First Steps 370
How to Attain Strength 371
What We Will Attract 372
More About the Power of Attraction 373
How to Attract Friends 374
The Control of Thought 375
Creating Atmosphere 376
The Power of Words 377
Why Belief Is Necessary 378
Where So Many Fail 379
Using the Imagination 379
Man's Right of Choice 380
Old Age and Opportunity 380
Demonstrating Success in Business 381
Money a Spiritual Idea 383
Action 383
Ideas of the Infinite 385
Don't Be a Leaner 386
Causes and Conditions 387
Mental Equivalents 388
One Law and Many Manifestations 390
Transcending Previous Conditions 390
Understanding and Misunderstanding 391

No Unusual Experience 393
Visualizing 393
Where Demonstration Takes Place 394

2. Practice 395
Treatments 395
Understanding and Guidance 395
How to Know Just What to Do 396
Following Up a Thought 397
The Single Stream of Thought 397
Enlarging Our Thought 398
Always Be Gathering 400
Mental Likeness 400
Keeping the Thing in Mind 401
Destroy All Thoughts That We Do Not Wish to Experience 402
Direct Practice for Prosperity 402
Race Consciousness 403
Developing Intuition 403
Presence of Activity 404
Drawing Your Own to You 405
The Final Word 406

PART 1

Instruction

AN INQUIRY INTO THE TRUTH

An inquiry into Truth is an inquiry into the cause of things as the human race sees and experiences them. The starting point of our thought must always begin with our experiences. We all know that life *is,* else we could not even think that we are. Since we *can* think, say, and feel, we *must* be. We live, we are conscious of life; therefore we must be and life must be. If we are life and consciousness (self-knowing) then it follows that we must have come from life and consciousness. Let us start, then, with this simple fact: *Life is and life is conscious of itself.*

But what is the nature of this life; is it physical, mental, material, or spiritual? A little careful thinking based upon logic, more than any merely personal opinion, will do much in clearing up some of these questions that at first seem to stagger us with their bigness.

How much of that which *is* may we call life? The answer would have to be: Life is *all* that there is; it is the reason for all that we see, hear, feel—all that we experience in any way. Now nothing from nothing leaves nothing, and it is impossible for something to proceed from nothing. Since something is, that from which it came must be all that is. *Life, then, is all that there is.* Everything comes from it, ourselves included.

The next question is, how do things come from life? How do the things that we see come from the things that we do not see? The things that we see must be real because we see them. To say they are not real will never explain them nor answer any question about them. God's world is not a world of illusion but one of divine realities. The truth must not explain away things that we see. It must explain what they are. We are living and experiencing varying degrees of consciousness and conditions. Only when the why of this living and of our experiences is understood will we know the least thing about the truth. Jesus did not say that things are illusions. He said that we must not judge from the standpoint of the seen but must judge righteously or with right judgment; and He meant that we must get behind the appearance and find out what caused it. So let us not in any way fool ourselves nor allow ourselves to believe we have always been fooled. We are living in a world of realities. Whatever we have experienced is a reality insofar as that experience is concerned, although if we had had a higher understanding of life, the unpleasant experience might have been avoided.

WHAT LIFE IS

In the first place, what do we mean by life? We mean that which we see, feel, hear, touch or taste, and the reason for it. We must have come into contact with all we know of life. We have already found what life is or we could not have had any of these experiences. "In the beginning was God" or life. Out of this life which is, everything which is made. So life must flow through all things. There is no such thing as dead matter. Moreover, life is one, and it cannot be changed except into itself. All forms are forms of this unity and must come and go through some inner activity. This inner activity of life or nature must be some form of self-consciousness or self-knowing. In our human understanding we would call this inner knowing, or consciousness, "thought." The Spirit, or Life, or God, must make things out of Himself, through self-recognition, or self-knowing or, as we would call it—*thinking.* Since God is all, there is nothing to hinder Him from doing what He wishes, and the question, "How do things come into being?" is answered: God makes them out of Himself. God thinks, or knows, and that thing which He thinks or knows appears from Himself, and is made out of Himself. There is no other possible explanation for what we see. Unless people are willing to begin here, they will never understand how it is that things are not material but spiritual.

MAN'S PLACE IN CREATION

But where does man come in? He *is;* therefore it follows that he, too, is made out of God, since God, or Spirit, is all. Being made out of God, we must partake of His nature, for we are "made in His image."

Man is a center of God in God. Whatever God is in the Universal, man must be in the individual world. The difference between God and man is one of degree and not of quality. Man is not self-made; he is made out of God.

The question might arise, why did God do this? No living person can answer this question. This is something that is known only of the Father. We might suppose that God made man to live with Him and to enjoy with Him. to be one with the Father. It is true, indeed, that those who have felt this most deeply have had a corresponding spiritual power that leads us to suppose that God really did make man as a companion. Man is the individual and God is the Universal. "For as the Father has life in Himself, so has He given to the Son to have life in himself." Man's mind is made out of God's mind, and all that man is or ever will be, all that he has or ever will have, must partake of the Divine nature. Man did not make it so, but it is so, and he must accept the fact and see what he can do with it. If he has the same power in his individual life that God has in the Universal, then this discovery will mean freedom from all bondage when he learns how to use his power. As God governs His Universal world so will man govern his individual world, always subject to the greater law and life. This could not be otherwise if we realize what follows from it, for so realizing we find ourselves living in a very different world from the one in which we thought we were living. God governs not through physical law as result, but first by inner knowing—then the physical follows. In the same way, man governs his world by the process which we will call, for want of a better name, the power of his thought.

Man's inner life is one with the Father. There can be no separation, for the self-evident reason that there is nothing to separate him from God, because there is nothing but life. The separation of two things implies putting a different element between them; but as there is nothing different from God, the unity of God and man is firmly established forever. "My Father and I are One" is a simple statement of a great soul who perceived life as it really is and not from the mere standpoint of outer conditions.

Taking as the starting point that man has the same life as God, it follows that he uses the same creative process. Everything is one, comes from the same source and returns again to it. "The things which are seen are not made of the things which do appear' What we see comes from what we do not see. This is the explanation of the whole visible universe, and is the only possible explanation.

As God's thought makes worlds and peoples them with all living things, so does our thought make our world and peoples it with all the experiences we have had. By the activity of our thought things come into our life, and we are limited because we have not known the truth; we have thought that outside things controlled us, when all the time we have had that within which could have changed everything and given us freedom from bondage.

The question, then, naturally arises: Why did God create man and *make him a free agent?* If God had created us in such a way as to compel us to do or to be anything that was not of our choosing, we should not have been individuals at all, we should be automatons. Since we know that we are individuals, we know that God made us thus; and we are just discovering the reason why. Let any man wake up to this, the greatest truth in all ages, and he will find it will answer all questions. He will be satisfied that things are what they are. He will perceive that he may use his own God-given power so to work, to think and to live that he will in no way hinder the greater law from operating *through* him. According to the clearness of his perception and the greatness of his realization of this power will he provide within himself a starting point through which God may operate. There will no longer be a sense of separation, but in its place will come that divine assurance that he is one with God, and thus will he find his freedom from all suffering, whether it be of body, mind, or estate.

THE BEGINNING OF UNDERSTANDING

Man is beginning to realize that he has life within himself as the great gift of God to him. If he really has life, if it is the same nature as the life of God, if he is an individual and has the right of self-choice which constitutes individuality; then it follows that he can do with his life what he wants to do: he can make out of himself that which he wishes. Freedom is his, but this freedom is within law and never outside it. Man must obey law. If he disobeys it, it has to act as law, and so acting has to punish him. This he cannot change but must submit to. Freedom comes to the individual from understanding the laws of his own life, and conforming to them, thereby subjecting them to his use, to the end of health, happiness, and success.

Law obtains throughout all nature, governing all things, both the seen and the unseen. Law is not physical or material but mental and spiritual. Law is God's method of operation. We should think of God as the great Spirit whose sole impulse is love, freely giving of Himself to all who ask and refusing none. God is our Father in every sense of the term, watching over, caring for and loving all alike. While all is love, yet, in order that things may not be chaotic, all is governed by law. And as far as you and I are concerned, *this law is always mental.*

OUR CONDITIONS GOVERNED BY OUR THINKING

It is easy for the average person to see how it is that mind can control, and to a certain extent govern, the functions of the body. Some can go even further than this and see that the body is governed entirely by consciousness. This they can see without much difficulty, but it is not so easy for them to see how it is that thought governs their conditions and decides whether they are to be successes or failures.

Here we will stop to ask the question: If our conditions are not controlled by thought, by what, then, are they controlled? Some will say that conditions are controlled by circumstances. But what are circumstances? Are they cause or are they effect? Of course they are always effect; everything that we see is an effect. An effect is something that follows a cause, and we are dealing with causation only; effects do not make themselves, but they are held in place by mind, or causation.

If this does not answer your thought, begin over again and realize that behind everything that is seen is the silent cause. In your life *you are that cause.* There is nothing but Mind, and nothing moves except as Mind moves it. We have agreed that, while God is love, yet your life is governed absolutely by Mind, or Law. In our lives of conditions we are the cause, and nothing moves except as our mind moves it.

The activity of our mind is thought. We are always acting because we are always thinking. At all times we are either drawing things to us or we are pushing them away from us. In the ordinary individual this process goes on without his ever knowing it consciously, but ignorance of the law will excuse no one from its effects.

"What," someone will say, "do you think that I thought failure or wanted to fail?" Of course not. You would be foolish to think that; but according to the law which we cannot deny, you must have thought things that would produce failure. Perhaps you thought that failure *might* come, or in some other way you gave it entrance to your mind.

Thinking back over the reason for things, you will find that you are surrounded by a Mind, or Law, that casts back at the thinker, manifested, everything that he thinks. If this were not true, man would not be an individual. Individuality can mean only the ability to think what we *want* to think. If that thought is to have power in our lives then there has to be something that will manifest it. Some are limited and bound by Law through ignorance. This law is sometimes called "Karma," it is the law that binds the ignorant and gives freedom to the wise.

We live in mind; and it can return to us only what we think into it. No matter what we may do, Law will always obtain. If we are thinking of ourselves as poor and needy, then Mind has no choice but to return what we have thought into it. At first this may be hard to realize, but the Truth will reveal to the seeker that Law could act in no other way. Whatever we think is the pattern, and mind is the builder. Jesus, realizing this law, said, "It is done unto you even as you have believed." Shall we doubt but that this great Way Shower knew what He was talking about? Did He not say, "It is done unto you"? What a wonderful thought. "It is done unto you." Nothing to worry about. "It is done unto you." With a tremendous grasp of the power of true spiritual thought, Jesus even called forth bread from the ethers of life, and at no time did He ever fail to demonstrate that when one knows the truth he is freed by that knowledge.

UNCONSCIOUS CREATION

The author once attended a patient who was suffering from a large growth. She was operated on and about fifty pounds of water were removed. In a few days the growth had returned. Where did it come from? Not from eating or drinking. Neither did it move from one part of the body to another part, as that would not have increased her weight. It must have been created from elements which she took in from the air. It had to come from something not physically seen, something appearing from nothing that we see. What we call "creation" is the same thing—the visible appearing from the invisible. Was not this phenomenon a creation?

Cases as remarkable as this are occurring every day. We should not deny this fact but try to explain it. In the case of this woman there must have been an activity of thought molded forth into form, else how could this growth have appeared? There is nothing manifest but that there is a cause for the manifestation. Investigation proves that behind every condition, whether of body or environment, there has been some thought, conscious or unconscious, which produced that condition. In the case of this woman the thought was not conscious. But creation is going on all the time; we should realize this and learn how to control it so that there may be created for us the things that we desire and not those that we do not want. Is it any wonder that the Bible says, "With all thy getting get understanding"?

Jesus understood all this, and so it was no more effort for Him to do what He did than it is for us to breathe or to digest our food. He *understood,* that is all. Because Jesus did understand and did use these great laws with objective consciousness, people thought He must be God. And when today something unusual occurs, people think that a miracle has been performed. Jesus was not God. He was the manifestation of God; and so are all people. "I say that ye are gods, and every one of you sons of the Most High."

A thinking person will be compelled to admit, in view of all this, that creation is first spiritual, through mental law, and then physical in its manifestation.

Man does not really create. He uses creative power that already is. Relatively speaking, he is the creative power in his own life; and so far as his thought goes, there is something that goes with it that has the power to bring forth into manifestation the thing thought of. Hitherto men have used this creative power in ignorance and so have brought upon themselves all kinds of conditions, but today hundreds of thousands are beginning to use these great laws of their being in a conscious, constructive way. Herein lies the great secret of the New Thought movements under their various names and cults and orders. All are using the same law even though some deny to others the real revelation. We should get into an attitude of mind wherein we recognize the Truth wherever we find it. The trouble with most of us is that unless we see sugar in a sugar bowl we think it must be something else, and so we stick to our petty prejudices instead of looking after principles.

FIRST STEPS

The first thing to realize is that since any thought manifests it necessarily follows that all thought does the same, else how should we know that the particular thought we were thinking would be the one that would create? Mind must cast back all or none. Just as the creative power of the soil receives all seeds put into it, and at once begins to work upon them, so mind must receive all thought and at once begin to operate upon it. Thus we find that all thought has some power in our lives and over our conditions. We are making our environments by the creative power of our thought. God has created us thus and we cannot escape it. By conforming our lives and thought to a greater understanding of Law we shall be able to bring into our experience just what we wish, letting go of all that we do not want to experience and taking in the things we desire.

Every person is surrounded by a thought atmosphere. This mental atmosphere is the direct result of thought which in its turn becomes the direct reason for the cause of that which comes into our lives. Through this power we are either attracting or repelling. Like attracts like and we attract to us just what we are in mind. It is also true that we become attracted to something that is greater than our previous experience by first embodying the atmosphere of our desire.

Every business, every place, every person, everything has a certain mental atmosphere of its own. This atmosphere decides what is to be drawn to it. For instance, you never saw a successful man who went around with an atmosphere of failure. Successful people think about success. A successful man is filled with that subtle something which permeates everything that he does with an atmosphere of confidence and strength. In the presence of some people we feel as though nothing were too great to undertake; we are uplifted; we are inspired to do great things, to accomplish; we feel strong, steady, sure. What a power we feel in the presence of big souls, strong men, noble women!

Did you ever stop to inquire *why* it is that such persons have this kind of an effect over you while others seem to depress, to drag you down, and in their presence you feel as though life were a load to carry? One type is positive, the other negative. In every physical respect they are just alike, but one has a mental and spiritual power which the other does not have, and without that power the individual can hope to do but little.

Which of these two do we like the better? With which do we want to associate? Certainly not with the one that depresses us; we have enough of that already. But what about the man who inspires us with our own worth? Ah, he is the man to whom we will turn every time. Before ever we reach him, in our haste to be near, even to hear his voice, do we not feel a strength coming to meet us? Do you think that this man who has such a wonderful power of attraction will ever want for friends? Will he ever have to look up a position? Already so many positions are open to him that he is weighing in his mind which one to take. He does not have to become a success; he already *is* a success.

Thoughts of failure, limitation, or poverty are negative and must be counted out of our lives for all time. Somebody will say, "But what of the poor; what are you going to do with them; are they to be left without help?" No; a thousand times no. The same Power is in them that is in all men. They will always be poor until they awake and realize what life is. All the charity on earth has never done away with poverty, and never will; if it could have done so it would have done so; it could not, therefore it has not. It will do a man a thousand times more good to show him how to succeed than it will to tell him he needs charity. We need not listen to all the calamity howlers. Let them howl if it does them any good. God has given us a Power and we must use it. We can do more toward saving the world by proving this law than all that charity has ever given it.

Right here, in the manifold world today, there is more money and provision than the world can use. Not even a fraction of the wealth of the world is used. Inventors and discoverers are adding to this wealth every day; they are the real people. But in the midst of plenty, surrounded by all the gifts of heaven, man sits and begs for his daily bread. He should be taught to realize that he has brought these conditions upon himself; that instead of blaming God, man, or the devil for the circumstances by which he is surrounded, he should learn to seek the Truth, to let the dead bury their dead. We should tell every man who will believe what his real nature is; show him how to overcome all limitations; give him courage; show him the way. If he will not believe, if he will not walk in the way, it is not our fault, and having done all we can, we must go our way. We may sympathize with *people* but never with trouble, limitation, or misery. If people still insist upon hugging their troubles to themselves, all the charity in the world will not help them.

Remember that God is that silent Power behind all things, always ready to spring into expression when we have provided the proper channels, which are receptive and positive faith in the evidence of things not seen with the physical eye but eternal in the heavens.

All is mind, and we must provide a receptive avenue for it as it passes out through us into the outer expression of our affairs. If we allow the world's opinion to control our thinking, then that will be our demonstration. If, on the other hand, we rise superior to the world, we shall do a new thing.

Remember that all people are making demonstrations, only most of them are making the ones they do not desire, but the only ones they can make with their present powers of perception.

HOW TO ATTAIN STRENGTH

Let us see that we use the right attitude of mind in all that we do, filling ourselves with such courage and power of strength that all thought of weakness flees before us. If any thought of weakness should come, ask this question: Is life weak? If life is not weak and if God is not discouraged, then you are not, never were, and never will be. I should like to see the sickly, discouraged thought that could withstand this attitude of mind.

No! Life is strong, and you are strong with the strength of the Infinite; forget all else as you revel in this strength. You are strong and can say I AM. You have been laboring under an illusion; now you are disillusioned. Now you know, and knowing is using the law in a constructive way. "I and my Father are One"; this is strength for the weak, and life for all who believe.

We can so fill ourselves with the drawing power of attraction that it will become irresistible. Nothing can hinder things from coming to the man who knows that he is dealing with the same Power that creates all from itself, moves all within itself, and yet holds all things in their places. I am one with the Infinite Mind. Let this ring through you many times each day until you rise to that Height that, looking, sees.

In order to be sure that we are creating the right kind of a mental atmosphere and so attracting what we want, we must at first watch our thinking, lest we create that which we should not like to see manifest. In other words, *we must think only what we wish to experience.* All is mind, and mind casts back at the thinker that only which he thinks. Nothing ever happens by chance. Law governs all life, and all people come under that law. But that law, so far as we are concerned, we ourselves set in motion, and we do this through the power of our thought.

Each person is living in a world of his own making, and he should speak only such words and think only such thoughts as he wishes to see manifested in his life. We must not hear, think, speak, read or listen to limitation of any kind. There is no way under heaven whereby we can think two kinds of thought and get only one result; it is impossible, and the sooner we realize it the sooner we shall arrive. This does not mean that we must be afraid to think lest we create the wrong image, but it does mean that the way most people think can produce nothing but failure; that is why so few succeed.

The person who is to succeed will never let his mind dwell on past mistakes. He will forgive the past in his life and in the lives of other people. If he makes a mistake he will at once forgive it. He will know that so long as he desires any good, there is nowhere in the universe anything that opposes him. God does not damn anyone or anything; man damns everyone and everything.

God does not make things by comparing His power with some other power. God knows that when He speaks it is done; and if we partake of the divine nature we must know the same thing in our lives that God knows in His.

"I am the master of my fate,
I am the captain of my soul."

WHAT WE WILL ATTRACT

We will always attract to us, in our lives and conditions, according to our thought. Things are but outer manifestations of inner mental concepts. Thought is not only power; it is also the form of all things. The conditions that we attract will correspond exactly to our mental pictures. It is quite necessary, then, that the successful business man should keep his mind on thoughts of happiness, which produce cheerfulness instead of depression; he should radiate joy, and should be filled with faith, hope, and expectancy. These cheerful, hopeful attitudes of mind are indispensable to the one who really wants to do things in life.

Put every negative thought out of your mind once and for all. Declare your freedom. Know that no matter what others may say, think or do, *you are a success,* now, and nothing can hinder you from accomplishing your good.

All the Power of the Universe is with you; feel it, know it, and then act as though it were true. This mental attitude alone will draw people and things to you.

Begin to blot out, one by one, all false beliefs, all idea that man is limited or poor or miserable. Use that wonderful power of choice that God has given to you. Refuse to think of failure or to doubt your own power.

See only what you wish to experience, and look at nothing else. No matter how many times the old thought returns, destroy it by knowing that it has no power over you; look it squarely in the face and tell it to go; it does not belong to you, and you must know—and stick to it—that you are now free.

Rise up in all the faith of one who knows what he is dealing with, and declare that you are one with Infinite Mind. Know that you cannot get away from this One Mind; that wherever you may go, there, right beside you, waiting to be used, is all the power there is in the whole universe. When you realize this you will know that in union with this, the only power, *you* are more than all else, *you* are more than anything that can ever happen.

MORE ABOUT THE POWER OF ATTRACTION

Always remember that Spirit makes things out of itself; it manifests in the visible world by becoming the thing that it wills to become. In the world of the individual the same process takes place. It is given to man to use creative Power, but with the using of this Power comes the necessity of using it as it is made to be used. If God makes things out of His thought before they come into manifestation, then we must use the same method.

You can attract only that which you first mentally become and feel yourself to be in reality, without any doubting. A steady stream of consciousness going out into creative mind will attract a steady manifestation of conditions; a fluctuating stream of consciousness will attract the corresponding manifestation or condition in your life. We must be consistent in our attitude of mind, never wavering. James says, "Ask in faith, nothing doubting, for he that doubteth is like a surge of the sea driven by the wind and tossed. For let not that man think that he shall receive anything of the Lord."

We are all immersed in an aura of our own thinking. This aura is the direct result of all that we have ever said, thought, or done; it decides what is to take place in our life; it attracts what is like itself and repels what is unlike itself. We are drawn toward those things that we mentally embody. Most of the inner processes of thought have been unconscious; but when we understand the Law all that we have to do is to embody consciously what we wish, and think of that only, and then we shall be drawn silently toward it.

We have this Law in our hands to do with as we will. We can draw what we want only as we let go of the old order and take up the new; and this we must do to the exclusion of all else. This is no weak man's job but an undertaking for a strong, self-reliant soul; and the end is worth the effort. The person who can keep his thoughts one-pointed is the one who will obtain the best results.

But this does not imply the necessity of strain or anything of a strenuous nature; on the contrary, strain is just what we must avoid. When we know that there is but one Power we shall not struggle, we shall know, and in calmness we shall see only what we know must be the Truth. This means a persistent, firm determination to think what we want to think, regardless of all outer evidence to the contrary. We look not to the seen but to the unseen. The king of Israel understood this when, looking upon the advancing host of the enemy, he said, "We have no might against this great company, but our eyes are upon Thee"—upon the One Power.

HOW TO ATTRACT FRIENDS

The man who has learned to love all people, no matter who they may be, will find plenty of people who will return that love to him. This is not mere sentiment, and it is more than a religious attitude of mind; it is a deep scientific fact, and one to which we should pay attention. The reason is this: As all is Mind, and as we attract to us what we first become, until we learn to love we are not sending out love vibrations, and not until we send out love vibrations can we receive love in return.

One of the first things to do is to learn to love everybody. If you have not done this, begin to do so at once. There is always more good than bad in people, and seeing the good tends to bring it forth. Love is the greatest healing and drawing power on earth. It is the very reason for our being, and that explains why it is that people should have something or somebody to love.

The life that has not loved has not lived; it is still dead. Love is the sole impulse for creation; and the man who does not have it as the greatest incentive in his life has never developed the real creative instinct. No one can swing out into the Universal without love, for the whole universe is based upon it.

When we find that we are Without friends, the thing to do is at once to send our thought out to the whole world,—send it full of love and affection. Know that this thought will meet the desires of some other person who is wanting the same thing, and in some way the two will be drawn together. Get over thinking that people are queer, that kind of thought will only produce misunderstanding and cause us to lose the friends that we now have. Think of the whole world as your friend; but you must also be the friend of the whole world. In this way and with this simple practice you will draw to you so many friends that the time will be too short to enjoy them all. Refuse to see the negative side of anyone. Refuse to let yourself misunderstand or be misunderstood. Do not be morbid. Know that everyone wants you to have the best; affirm this wherever you go and then you will find things just as you wish them to be.

The atmosphere created by a real lover of the race is so powerful that although his other shortcomings may be many, still the world will love him in return. "To him who loveth much, much will be forgiven." People are dying for real human interest, for some-one to tell them that they are all right. Which person do we like the better: the one who is always full of trouble and faultfinding, or the one who looks at the world as his friend and loves it? The question does not need to be asked; we know that we want the company of the person who loves and loving, forgets all else.

The only reason we think other people are "queer" is because they do not happen to think as we do. We must get over this little, petty attitude and see things in the large. The person who sees what he wants to see, regardless of what appears, will some day experience in the outer what he has so faithfully seen within.

From selfish motives alone, if from no loftier reason, we cannot afford to find fault or to hate or even to hold in mind anything against any living soul. The God who is love cannot hear the prayer of the man who is not love. Love and co-operation will yet be found to be the greatest business principle on earth. "God is Love."

We will make our unity with all people, with all life. We will affirm that God in us is unified with God in all. This One is now drawing into our life all love and fellowship. I am one with all people, with all things, with all life. As I listen in the silence the voice of all humanity speaks to me and answers the love that I hold out to it.

This great love that I now feel for the world is the love of God, and it is felt by all and returned from all. Nothing comes in between because there is nothing but love to come in between. I understand all people and that understanding is reflected back to me from all people. I help, therefore I am helped. I uplift, therefore I am uplifted. Nothing can mar this perfect picture of myself and my relations with the world; it is the truth, the whole truth, and nothing but the truth. I am now surrounded by all love, all friendship, all companionship, all health, all happiness, all success. I am one with life. I wait in the silence while the Great Spirit bears this message to the whole world.

THE CONTROL OF THOUGHT

The man who can control his thought can have and do what he wishes to have and to do; everything is his for the asking. He must remember that whatever he gets is his to use but not his to hold. Creation is always flowing by and we have as much of it as we can take and use; more would cause stagnation.

We are relieved of all thought of clinging to anybody or anything. Cannot the Great Principle of Life create for us faster than we can spend or use? The universe is inexhaustible; it is limitless; it knows no bounds and has no confines. We are not depending on a reed shaken by the wind, but on the *principle of life itself,* for all that we want, have, or ever shall have. It is not *some* power, or *a great* power, we affirm again; it is ALL POWER. All that we have to do is to believe this and act as though it were so, never wavering, not even once, no matter what happens. As we do this we shall find that things are steadily coming our way, and that they are coming without that awful effort that destroys the peace of the majority of the race. We know that there can be no failure in the Divine Mind, and this Mind is the Power on which we are depending.

Now just because we are depending upon Divine Mind we must not think that we do not have to do our share. God will work through us if we will let Him, but we must act in the outer as though we were sure of ourselves. Our part is to believe, and then to act in faith.

Jesus went to the tomb of Lazarus believing and knowing that God was working through Him. Often we may have to go somewhere or do something and we must know with deep conviction that there will be a power going with us that none can gainsay. When we feel this secure place in our thought, all that we will have to do is to act. There is no doubt but that the *creative power of the universe will answer; it always does.* And so we need not take the worry upon ourselves, but rather we will "make known our requests with thanksgiving."

When Jesus said, "All things whatsoever ye pray and ask for, believe that ye receive them and ye shall have them," he was uttering one of those many deep truths that were so clear to Him and that we are just beginning to see. He knew that everything is made out of Mind and that without that positive acceptance on the part of the individual there is no mold into which Mind can pour itself forth into form. In the Mind of God there is the correct mold, the true knowing, but in the mind of man there is not always this true knowing. Since God can do *for* us only by doing *through* us, nothing can be done for us unless we are positively receptive, but when we realize the law and how it works, then we will provide that complete inner acceptance. By so doing we permit the Spirit to do the work, to make the gift.

The reason we can make our requests known with thanksgiving is because we know from the beginning that we are to receive and therefore we cannot help being thankful. This grateful attitude to the Spirit puts us in very close touch with power and adds much to the reality of the thing that we are dealing with. Without it we can do but little. So let us cultivate all the gratitude that we can. In gratitude we will send our thoughts out into the world, and as it comes back it will come laden with the fruits of the Spirit.

CREATING ATMOSPHERE

To the student who has realized that all is Mind and that everything is governed by Law, there comes another thought: it is that he can create, or have created for him, from his own thinking. He can create such a strong mental atmosphere of success that its power of attraction will be irresistible. He can send his thought throughout the world and have it bring back to him whatever he wants. He can so fill his place of business with the power of success that it will draw from far and near. Thought will always bring back to us what we send out. First we must clear our thought of all unbelief. This book is written for those who believe; and to those who do believe it will come true in their lives.

Without mental clearness on the part of the thinker there can be no real creative work done. As water will reach only its own level, so Mind will return to us only what we first believe. We are always getting what we believe but not always what we want. Our thought has the power to reach, in the outer form of conditions, an exact correspondence to our inner convictions.

By thinking, you set in motion a Power that creates. It will be exactly as you think. You throw out into Mind an idea and Mind creates It for you and sets It on the path of your life. Think of It, then, as your greatest friend. It is always with you wherever you may be. It never deserts you. You are never alone. There is no doubt, no fear, no wondering; you *know.* You are going to use the only Power that there is in the Universe. You are going to use it for a definite purpose. You have already fixed this purpose in your thought; now you are going to speak it forth.

You are speaking it for your own good. You desire only the good and you know that only the good can come to you. You have made your unity with life, and now life is going to help you in your affairs.

You are going to establish in your rooms such an atmosphere of success that it will become an irresistible power; it will sweep everything before it as it realizes the greatness and the All-Mightiness of the One. You are so sure, that you will not even look to see if it is going to happen; you KNOW.

And now your word, which is one with the Infinite Life, is to be spoken in calm, perfect trust. It is to be taken up, and at once it is to be operated on. Perfect is the pattern and perfect will be the result. You see yourself surrounded by the thing that you desire. More than this, you *are* the *thing* that you desire. Your word is now establishing it forever; see this, feel it, know it. You are now encompassed by perfect life, by infinite activity, by all power, by all guidance. The power of the Spirit is drawing to you all people; it is supplying you with all good; it is filling you with all life, truth, and love.

Wait in perfect silence while that inner power takes it up. And then you know that it is done unto you. There goes forth from this word the power of the Infinite. "The words which I speak, they are spirit and they are life."

THE POWER OF WORDS

Man's word, spoken forth into Creative Mind, is endowed with power of expression. "By our words we are justified and by our words we are condemned." Our word has the exact amount of power that we put into it. This does not mean power through effort or strain but power through absolute conviction, or faith. It is like a little messenger who knows what he is doing and knows just how to do it. We speak into our words the intelligence which we are, and backed by that greater intelligence of the Universal Mind our word becomes a law unto the thing for which it is spoken. Jesus understood this far better than we do. Indeed, He absolutely believed it, for He said, "Heaven and earth shall pass away but my words shall not pass away till all be fulfilled."

This makes our word inseparable from Absolute Intelligence and Power. Now if any word has power it must follow that all words have power. Some words may have a greater power than others, according to our conviction, but all words have some power. How careful, then, we should be what kind of words we are speaking.

All this goes to prove that we really are one with the Infinite Mind, and that our words have the power of life within them; that the word is always with us and never far off. The word is within our own mouth. Every time we speak we are using power.

We are one in Mind with the whole universe; we are all eternally united in this Mind with real power. It is our own fault if we do not use this truth after we see it.

We should feel ourselves surrounded by this Mind, this great pulsating life, this all-seeing and all-knowing reality. When we do feel this near presence, this great power and life, then all we have to do is to speak forth into it, speak with all the positive conviction of the soul that has found its source, and above all else never fear but that it will be done unto us even as we have believed.

What wonderful power, what a newness of life and of power of expression, is waiting for those who really believe. What may the race not attain to when men wake up to the real facts of being? As yet the race has not begun to live, but the time is drawing near. Already thousands are using this great Power, and thousands are eagerly watching and waiting for the new day.

WHY BELIEF IS NECESSARY

Always when we pray we must believe. Our idea of prayer is not so much asking God for things as it is believing that we already have the things that we need. As we have said before, this *already-believing* Is necessary because all is Mind, and until we have provided that full acceptance we have not made a mold into which mind could pour itself and through which it could manifest. This positive belief is absolutely essential to real creative work; and if we do not at present have it, then we must develop it.

All is law, and cause and effect obtain through all life. Mind is cause, and what we term matter, or the visible, is effect. As water will freeze into the form that it is poured, so mind will solidify only into the forms that our thought takes. Thought is form. The individual provides the form; he never creates or even manifests—that is, of himself; there is something that does all this for him. His sole activity is the use of this Power. This Power is always at hand ready to be spoken into and at once ready to form the words into visible expression. But the mold that most of us provide is a very poor one, and we change it so quickly that it is more like a motion picture than anything else.

Already we have the Power; it is the gift of the Most High in its Finite Expression. But our ignorance of its use has caused us to create the wrong form, which in its turn has caused Mind to produce the form which we have thought into it. From this Law of Cause and Effect we may never hope to escape; and while we may think of it as a hard thing, at first, yet, when we understand, we shall see it as absolute justice without which there could be no real self-acting, individual life at all. Because of our Divine individuality, even God may have to wait our recognition of Him and His laws.

People in business will do well to remember this and so to form their thought that they will be willing to receive what they send out. No thought of discouragement or disorder should ever be created, but only positive assurance, strong thoughts of success, of Divine activity, the feeling that with God all things are possible, the belief that we are One with that Great Mind. These are the thoughts that make for success.

The realization that we are dealing with one and not with two powers enables us to think with clearness. We are not troubled about competition or opposition or failure because there is nothing but life, and this life is continually giving to us all that we could ask for, wish, or think into it. We can now see how essential it is that thought should be held one-pointed; that we should think always and only upon what we want, never letting our mind dwell on anything else. In this way the Spirit works through us.

WHERE SO MANY FAIL

The ordinary individual, sitting down to give a treatment to his business, unconsciously does just the thing that he should have avoided; and then he wonders why he did not get the desired results. Most people simply sit and wish for, or long for, something. They may even have a great desire or hope. They may even go so far as to believe that their desire is going to happen. All this is good as far as it goes, but it does not go far enough. What we must do is to provide that already-having-received attitude. This may seem hard at first but we can easily see that it is necessary; and as it is the only way that mind works, this is what we must do.

Power is, and Mind is, and life is; but they have to flow through us in order to express in our lives. We are dealing with law; and nature must be obeyed before it will work for us. Just realize that this law is as natural a law as any other of God's laws, and use it with the same intelligence that you would use the law of electricity; then you will get the desired results. We provide the thought form around which the divine energies play and to which they attract the conditions necessary for the fulfillment of the thought.

When we give a treatment this is all that we have to do, but before we can do even this we have to clear our minds of all fear, of every sense of separation from the Divine Mind. Law is; but we must enforce it, or use it, in our own lives. Nothing can happen to us that is not first an accepted belief in our own consciousness. We may not always be aware of what is going on within, but practice will enable us to control our thought more and more so that we shall be able to think what we want to think, regardless of what may seem to be the case.

Each person has within himself the capacity of knowing and making use of the law but it must be consciously developed. This is done by practice, and by willingness to learn and to utilize whatever we know so far as we have gone.

The individual who has the most power is the one who has the greatest realization of the Divine Presence, and to whom this means the most as an active principle of his life.

We all need more backbone and less wishbone. There is something which awaits only our recognition to spring into being, bringing with it all the Power in the universe.

USING THE IMAGINATION

Just imagine yourself surrounded by Mind, so plastic, so receptive, that it receives the slightest impression of your thought. Whatever you think it takes up and executes for you.

Every thought is received and acted upon. Not some but all thoughts. Whatever the pattern we provide, that will be our demonstration. If we cannot *get* over thinking that we are poor then we will still remain poor. As soon as we become rich in our thought then we will be rich in our expression. These are not mere words, but the deepest truth that has ever come to the human race. Hundreds of thousands of the most intelligent thinkers and the most spiritual people of our day are proving this truth. We are not dealing with illusions but with realities; pay no more attention to the one who ridicules these ideas than you would to the blowing of the wind.

In the center of your own soul choose what you want to become, to accomplish; keep it to yourself. Every day in the silence of absolute conviction know that it is now done. It is just as much done, as far as *you* are concerned, as it will be when you experience it in the outer. Imagine yourself to be what you Want to be. See only that which you desire, refuse even to think of the other. Stick to it, never doubt. Say many times a day, "I am that thing," realize what this means. It means that the great Universal power of Mind *is* that, and it cannot fail.

MAN'S RIGHT OF CHOICE

Man is created an individual and as such he has the power of choice. Many people seem to think that man should not choose, that since he has asked the Spirit to lead him, he need no longer act, or choose. This is taught by many teachers but is not consistent with our individuality. Unless we had this privilege, this power of choice, we would not be individuals. What we *do* need to learn is that the Spirit can choose through us. But when this happens it is an act on our part. Even though we say, "I will not choose," we are still choosing; because we are choosing not to choose.

We cannot escape the fact that we are made in such a way that at every step life is a constant choice. What we do need to do is to select what we feel to be right and know that the universe will never deny us anything. We choose and Mind creates. We should endeavor to choose that which will express always a greater life and we must remember that the Spirit is always seeking to express love and beauty through us. If we are attuned to these, and are working in harmony with the great creative power, we need have no doubt about its willingness to work for us.

We must know exactly what it is that we wish and get the perfect mental picture of it. We must believe absolutely that we now have it and never do or say anything that denies it.

OLD AGE AND OPPORTUNITY

One of the besetting errors of people is a belief that they are too old to do things. This comes from a lack of understanding what life really is. Life is consciousness and not years. The man or woman who is seventy years old should be better able to demonstrate than the man who is only twenty. He should have evolved a higher thought, and it is thought and not conditions that we are dealing with.

Amelia Barr was fifty-three before she wrote a book. After that she wrote over eighty, each of which had a large circulation. Mary Baker Eddy was sixty before she began her work, and she attended to all of her great activities until she passed from this plane to a higher one. The author of this book once took a man who was over sixty, one who thought his chance for success had gone, and through teaching him these principles in a year's time made him a prosperous business man. He is now doing well and was never before in his life so happy. The last time he was interviewed he said that business was increasing every day and that he had not begun yet. Every day he stands in his store and claims more activity. He speaks the word and realizes increase all the time. If this were not true then life would not be worth the living. What is a few years in eternity? We must get over these false notions about age and competition. In the truth the word competition is never mentioned. The people who think about it have never known the truth,

Life is what we make it from within and never from without. We are just as old as we think we are, no matter what the number of years may have been that we have lived on this planet.

DEMONSTRATING SUCCESS IN BUSINESS

All demonstrations take place within ourselves. Creation is eternally flowing through all things. The law is always working from that inner pattern. We do not struggle with conditions, we use principles which create conditions. What we can mentally encompass we can accomplish, no matter how hard it may seem from the outside.

All external things are but the outer rim of inner thought activity. You can easily prove this for yourself. If you are in business, say, running an ice cream stand or counter, and are not doing good business, look carefully into your own thought and see what you will find. You will find that it is an established belief there that business is not good. You are not feeling a sense of activity. You will not find within your thought any feeling of success. You are not expecting many customers.

Now suppose someone comes along and says to you: "What is the matter? Why are you not doing more business?" This is about what the answer would be: "People don't seem to want what I have to sell." Or perhaps something like this: "I am too old to compete with modern methods." Or even: "Well, times are hard." All this is negative thought.

Now this man to whom you are talking does not believe a word you have said. He knows that causation is in mind and not in matter, and he says: "The whole thing is in your own mind; the trouble with you is that you don't feel that you are a success."

Perhaps you have heard something of this before; if so you will ask him what he means, or perhaps you think he is talking about something peculiar; but we are taking it for granted that you are so anxious to do something to make your business a success that you will be willing to try anything, so you ask him to explain. He begins by telling you all is Mind; nothing moves but Mind moves it and that you are a center in this Mind. You do not understand how this relates in any way to your business, but he goes on to say that your thought decides whether your business shall be a success or a failure. Here you become indignant, and ask if he means to tell you that you want to fail. Of course he knows you do not, and he explains that while you wish success, you are thinking failure, fearing it, and that there is a law that makes your thought, never asking questions but at once sets about its fulfillment. You become interested and ask how this can be; in return you are asked this question: "How did anything come into being?" This sets you to thinking and of course you realize that there was a time when nothing existed but life; so whatever has come into being must have come from that life, for what we see must come from that which we do not see. You have to admit that. Then what you do not see must be the Cause of everything; and you must also admit that; and that Cause works by Law; this you are compelled to admit. Then this Law, being everywhere, must be in you; this is harder for you to see; but after much thought you begin to realize that it is so. Then you, without knowing where your thought processes were leading you, have conceded that you, yourself, are the reason for what happens in your life, be it success or failure.

God couldn't make you any other way and at the same time make you a self-choosing individual. This is plain.

Now what are you going to do about it? This is what you must do. For every time that you have thought failure you are going to replace it with strong radiant thoughts of success. You are going to speak activity into your business. You are going daily to see nothing but activity and to know that it is Law that you are using, Universal Law, and as such your thought is as sure as the thought of God.

Daily you are going to give to the Great Creative Mind exactly what you want to happen. You will see only what you desire and in the silence of your soul you will speak and it will be done unto you. You will come to believe that a great Divine Love flows through you and your affairs. You will be grateful for this Love.

It fills your lie. It satisfies your soul. You are a different man. You are so filled with activity and courage that when you meet people they will wonder at your energy. They will begin to wish simply to come in contact with you. They will feel uplifted.

In the course of a few months you will be a success. People will come to you and say: "How do you do it?" The answer will be the same that was given to you a few months ago. Let the man who is speaking to the public do the samething. Let him daily see throngs of people coming to hear him. Let him see nothing else. He will experience what he feels, and sees.

Always remember this. *Life is from within outward, and never from without inward.* You are the center of power in your own life.

Be sure and not take on false suggestion. The world is full of calamity howlers; turn from them, every one, no matter how great you think they may be; you haven't the time to waste over anything that is negative. You *are* a success, and you are giving to the Law, every day, just what you want done. And the Law is always working for you. All fear has gone and you know that there is but One Power in all the Universe. Happy is the man who knows this, the greatest of all Truths.

The whole thing resolves itself into our mental ability to control our thought. The man who can do this, can *have* what he wants, can *do* what he wishes, and *becomes* what he wills. Life, God, the Universe, is his.

MONEY A SPIRITUAL IDEA

Many people seem to think that money must be evil, but actually it is only an inordinate love of money that is characterized as the "root of all evil."

If *all* is an expression of life, then *money* is an expression of life, and as such, must be good. Without a certain amount of it in this life, we would have a hard time. But how to get it; that is the race problem. How shall we acquire wealth? Money didn't make itself, and not being self-creative it must be an effect. Behind it must be the Cause that projects it. That cause is never seen; no cause is ever seen. Consciousness is cause and people who have a money consciousness have the outward expression of it. People who have it as a sure reality in their mind, have it as an expression in their pocket. People who don't have this mental likeness don't have money in their pockets.

What we need to do is to acquire a money consciousness. This may seem very material, but the true idea of money is not material—it is spiritual. We need to make our unity with it. We can never do this while we hold it away from us by thinking that we haven't it. Let us change the method and begin to make our unity with supply by daily declaring that all the Power in the Universe is daily bringing to us all that we can use. Feel the presence of supply. Know that it is yours now.

Make yourself feel that you now have, and to you shall be given. Work with yourself until there is nothing in you that doubts. Money can not be kept away from the man who understands that all is Mind, and that Divine Law governs his life.

Daily give thanks for perfect supply. Feel it to be yours, that you have entered into the full possession of it now.

Refuse to talk poverty or limitation. Stick to it that you are rich. Get the million-dollar consciousness. There is no other way, and this will react into everything that you do.

See money coming to you from every source and from every direction. Know that everything is working for your good. Realize in your life the presence of an Omnipotent Power. Speak forth into It, and feel that It responds to your approach.

Whenever you see anything or anybody whom you think has more than you, at once affirm that you have the same thing. This doesn't mean that you have what is his, but that you have as much. It means that all you need is yours.

Whenever you think about anything big, at once say, "That means me." In this way you learn to unify yourself, in the Law, with large concepts, and according to the way that Law works, it will tend to produce that thing for you.

Never let yourself doubt for even a minute. Always be positive about yourself. Keep watch over the inner workings of your thought, and the Law will do the rest.

ACTION

The Universe is teeming with activity. There is motion everywhere. Nothing ever stands still. All activity comes from Mind. If we want to be in line with things we must move.

This doesn't mean that we must strain or struggle, but we must be willing to do our part by letting the Law work through us.

God can do for us only as we will allow Him to do through us. Intelligence gives us ideas and in our turn we work on them. But our work is no longer done in any sense of doubt or fear, for we know that we are dealing with something that never makes a mistake. We proceed with a calm confidence born of the inner trust in a Power that is Infinite. Behind all of our movements, then, is a great purpose, to let the Law work through us.

We must comply with the Law of Activity. We must be willing to take the way of outer activity. Jesus went to the tomb of Lazarus. We may have to go but there will accompany us something that never fails.

This Law of Activity we must use in our business. So many business places that we go into have such an atmosphere of inactivity, produce such a drowsy feeling, that we at once lose all interest in what is going on. We don't feel like buying. We leave that place without any apparent reason and go into another. Here we feel that all is life, all is motion, all is activity. We feel confident that this is the place we are looking for. We will buy here; we find just what we want; we are satisfied with our purchase and go away cheerful.

Now to create this activity something more than thought is essential. Not that it does not come first, but the one who has this thought of activity will naturally manifest it in vigorous, energetic movement which helps to produce a spirit of activity in his business and in everything he undertakes. Wherever you see a man who does not move, then you will find one whose thought is inactive; the two always go together.

A man in a store or place of business should always be moving his goods. He should always be doing something, People will see this and getting the thought of activity behind it will want to trade there. We are not attracted to a store that always has the same things on the same shelf. The world likes action, change. Action is Life.

Let a clerk in a store think activity and begin to manifest it, even though he may not be waiting on customers, and in a short time he will be waiting on them. Alertness is the word. Always be alert. *There must be mental alertness before there can be physical activity.*

Act as though things were happening even though they may not appear to be. Keep things moving and soon you will have to avoid the rush. Activity is genius. Half the stores that you go into make you sleepy before you *get* out, and you feel as though you can't get out fast enough. The other half are alive and those are the ones who are doing the business of the world.

The man who is active in his thought doesn't have to sit by himself to think; he works while he thinks and so complies with the Law which has to work through him. The thought of activity makes him move, and the thought of confidence makes his movements sure, and the thought of Supreme Guidance makes his work intelligent

We must be careful and not get into ruts; always be doing something new and different, and you will find life becomes a great game in which you are taking the leading part.

Life will never become tiresome to the active mind and body. It is so interesting that we wonder if we will ever get enough of it. Some people get into such lazy mental habits that a new idea cannot find entrance. Great things are done by people who think great thoughts and then go out into the world to make their dreams come true.

If you can't find anything new to do, go home and change the bed around, or the piano; put the cook stove in the parlor and eat on the back step for a time. It will start something moving and changing in you that will never stop. The wide awake person can find so many things to do that he hasn't time even to begin in this life and he knows that Eternity is necessary to carry out the ideals that he already has evolved.

Everything comes from Mind, but Mind acts on itself and we must act on ourselves and on conditions; not as a slave but as a master. Be interested in life, if you want life to be interested in you. Act in Life and Life will act through you. So will you also become one of the great people on earth.

IDEAS OF THE INFINITE

Suppose that we wish to draw from the Universal Mind some definite idea, some guidance, some information, some leading. How are we going to do this? First we must become convinced that we can do it.

Where do all the inventions come from? Where did Edison get his information about electricity? Where, if not direct from the Mind of the Universe? Everything that has ever come into the race comes direct from Mind.

It could come from nothing else.

Every invention is but a discovery of something that already is, although we may not have seen it. Where does the harmony of music come from? Where could it originate except in Mind? Does not a great musician listen and hear something that we do not hear? His ear is attuned to Harmony and he catches it straight from Life itself and interprets it to the world. We are surrounded by the music of the spheres but few of us ever catch the sound.

We are so filled with trouble that the Divine Melody is never heard. If we could see, if we could hear, if we could understand, if we only realized the presence of the All, what could we not do?

When a great thought springs up in the mind of an individual, when a great poem is written, when a great work of art is wrought by some receptive artist, it is simply a sign that the veil is thin between; he has caught a glimpse of reality.

But for most of us Inspiration is not to be depended on, and we must take the slower but none the less sure method of receiving straight from the Infinite. The method is a simple one and very effective. When you want to know a certain thing, or how to begin a certain line of action:

First, you must be quiet within yourself. You must not be confused by any outward appearance. Never become disturbed by effects. They didn't make themselves and have no intelligence to contradict you.

Be quiet until you realize the presence of absolute Intelligence all around you, of the Mind that knows. Now get a perfect picture of just what you desire. You cannot get a picture unless you know what it is you want. Put your mind in touch with Universal Mind, saying just what you are waiting for. Ask for it, believe that you are receiving it, and wait. After a few minutes declare that you now know, even though you may not seem to know, yet in the depths of consciousness you have received the impression. Give thanks that you now receive. Do this every day until you get some direction. It is sometimes a good thing to do this just before going to sleep.

Never, after you have done this, deny the knowledge that has been given you. The time will come when some idea will begin to take form. Wait for it and, when it does appear, act upon it with all the conviction of one who is perfectly sure of himself.

You have gotten understanding straight from the source of all understanding, knowledge from the source of knowledge. All can do this if they will be persistent. It is a sure direction and guidance and will never fail us. But we must be sure that we are not denying in other moments what we affirm in the moments of Faith. In this way we will make fewer mistakes and in time our lives will be controlled by supreme wisdom and understanding.

DON'T BE A LEANER

Never lean on other people. You have strength of your own that is great enough to do all that is necessary. The Almighty has implanted genius within the soul of everyone and what we need to do is to unearth that inner genius and cause it to shine forth. We will never do this while we look to others for guidance. "To thine own self repair, wait thou within the silence dim, and thou shalt find Him there."

All the power and intelligence of the Universe is already within, waiting to be utilized. The Divine Spark must be fanned into a blaze of the living Fire of your own divinity.

Self-reliance is the word to dwell on. Listen to your own voice; it will speak in terms that are unmistakable. Trust in your own self more than in all else. All great men have learned to do this. Every person, within his own soul, is in direct communication with the Infinite Understanding. When we depend on other people we are simply taking their light and trying to light our path with it. When we depend on ourselves we are depending on that inner voice that is God, speaking in and through man. "Man is the inlet and the outlet to all there is in God." God has made us and brought us up to where we recognize our own individuality; from now on we will have to let Him express through us. If it were different we should not be individuals. "Behold I stand at the door and wait." This is a statement of the near presence of power; but we, the Individual, must open the door. This door is our thought and we are the guardian of it, and when we do open the door we will find that the Divine Presence is right at hand, waiting, ready and willing to do for us all that we can believe.

We are strong with the strength of the Infinite. We are not weak. We are great and not mean. We are One with the Infinite Mind.

When you have a real thing to do, keep it to yourself. Don't talk about it. Just know in your own mind what it is that you want and keep still about it. Often when we think that we will do some big thing we begin to talk about it and the first thing we know all the power seems to be gone.

This is what happens. We are all sending out into Mind a constant stream of thought; the clearer it is, the better will it manifest; if it becomes doubtful it will not have so clear a manifestation. If it is confused it will manifest only confusion. All this is according to the Law of Cause and Effect, and we cannot change that Law. Too often, when we tell our friends what we are going to do, they confuse our thought by laughing about it, or by doubting our capacity to do so large a thing. Of course this would not happen if we were always positive, but when we become the least bit negative it will react and we will lose that power of clearness which is absolutely necessary to good creative work.

When you want to do a big thing, get the mental pattern, make it perfect, know just what it means, enlarge your thought, keep it to yourself, pass it over to the creative power behind all things, wait and listen, and when the impression comes, follow it with assurance. *Don't talk to anyone about it.* Never listen to negative talk or pay any attention to it and you will succeed where all others fail.

CAUSES AND CONDITIONS

When we realize that life is not fundamentally physical, but mental and spiritual, it will not be hard for us to see that by a certain mental and spiritual process we can demonstrate what we want.

We are not dealing with conditions but with causes. Causes originate only from the unseen side of life. This is not strange as the same might be said of electricity, or even of life itself. We do not see life, we only see what it does. This we call a condition. Of itself it is simply an effect. We are living in the outer world of effects and in the inner world of causes. These causes we set in motion by our thought, and, through the power inherent within the cause, expresses the thought as a condition. It follows that the cause must be equal to the effect and that the effect always evaluates with the cause held in mind. Everything comes from One Substance, and our thought qualifies that Substance and determines what is to take place in our life.

The whole teaching of the *Bhagavad Gita* is that there is but One and that it becomes to us just what we first believe into it. In other words we manifest the unmanifested. This in no way takes away from the omnipotence of God, but adds to it, for He has created something that is able to do this. God still rules in the Universe, but we are given the power to rule in our lives.

We must realize, then, absolutely that we are dealing with a Substance with which we have a right to deal, and by learning its laws we will be able to subject them to our use, just as Edison did with electricity. Law *is* but we must use it.

The substance that we deal with, in itself, is never limited, but we often are, because we draw only what we believe.

Because we are limited is no reason why the Universe should have limitation. Our limitation is only our unbelief; life can give us a big thing or a little thing. When it gives us a little thing, it is not limited, any more than life is limited when it makes a grain of sand, because it could just as well have made a planet. But in the great scheme of things all kinds of forms, small and large, are necessary, which, combined, make a complete whole. The power and substance behind everything remain Infinite.

Now this life can become to us only through us, and that becoming is the passing of Spirit into expression in our lives through the form of the thought that we give to it. In itself life is never limited; an ant has just as much life as an elephant though smaller in size. The question is not one of size but one of consciousness.

We are not limited by actual boundaries, but by false ideas about life and by a failure to recognize that we are dealing with the Infinite.

Limitation is an experience of the race, but it is not the fault of God, it is the fault of man's perception. And to prove that this is so, let any man break the bonds of this false sense of life and he at once begins to express less and less limitation. It is a matter of the growth of the inner idea.

People often say when they are told this, "Do you think that I decided to be poor and miserable; do you take me for a fool?" No, you are not a fool, but it is quite possible that you have been fooled, and most of us have been. I know of no one who has escaped being fooled about life; you may not have had thoughts of poverty but at the same time you may have had thoughts that have produced it. Just watch the process of your thinking and see how many times a day you think something that you would not want to happen. This will satisfy you that you need to be watchful, that your thought needs to be controlled.

What we need to do is to reverse the process of our thinking and see to it that we think only positive, constructive thoughts. A calm determination to think just what we want to think regardless of conditions will do much to put us on the highway to a greater realization of life.

Of course we will fall, of course the road is not easy, but we will be growing. Daily we will be giving to the Creative Mind a newer and a greater concept to be worked out into the life around us. Daily we will be overcoming some negative tendency. We must stick to it until we gain the mastery of all our thought and in that day we will rise never to fall again.

We must be good-natured with ourselves, never becoming discouraged or giving up until we overcome. Feel that you are always backed by an Omnipotent power and a kind Father of Love and the way will become easier.

MENTAL EQUIVALENTS

One of the most important things to remember is that we cannot demonstrate life beyond our mental ability to embody. We give birth to an idea only from within ourselves. What we are, we put into our thinking. What we are not, we cannot put into it.

If we are to draw from Life what we want, we must first think it forth into Life. It always produces what we think. In order to have success, we must first conceive it in our own thought. This is not because we are creators, but because the flow of Life into manifestation, through us, must take the form we give to it, and if we want a thing we must have within ourselves the mental equivalent before we get it.

This is what Jesus meant when he said that we must believe when we pray. This belief is providing within us that something which knows before it sees what it asks for.

For instance, suppose a man is praying for activity (our idea of prayer is the accepting of a thing before we get it) in his affairs. First, before this activity can come, he must have it within himself; he must come to see activity in everything; there must be something that corresponds to the thing that he wants; he must have a mental equivalent.

We find that we attract to ourselves as much of anything as we embody within. As water will reach only its own level, so our outward conditions will re-produce only our inner realizations.

A man will always draw to him just what he is. But we can learn to provide within the image of what we desire and so in a definite way use the law to get just what we need. If at first we do not have a great realization of activity we will have to work on what we do have, and as our outer conditions come up to meet the inner cause, we will find that it will be much easier to enlarge the inner receptivity for something greater and more worth while. Of one thing we may be assured—we must all start somewhere, and that somewhere is within ourselves. In this *within* we must make the affirmation, and there, too, we must do the real work of realization. At the first the way may seem hard, for we are constantly confronted with that which seems to be, and we are not always sure of ourselves nor strong enough to overcome, but we may rest content in the assurance that we are growing. Every day we will be providing a bigger concept of life, and with the inner growth we will have an enlarged power to speak forth into the Creative Mind, with the result that we shall get a fresh impulse and be doing a bigger thing for ourselves. Growth and realization are always from within and never from without.

The old race suggestion of fear and poverty and limitation must be done away with and daily we must clear our thought from all that limits the One from showing forth in our life.

Remember that you are dealing with One power, and not with two. This will make it easier, for you do not have to overcome any condition, because conditions flow from within out, and not from without in.

A man going to a new town will at once begin to attract to him just what he brings in his thought. He should be very careful what he thinks. He should know just what he wants and daily give it over to the Supreme Mind, knowing that It will work for him. Old thoughts must be destroyed, and new must take their places. Every time the old thought comes look it squarely in the face and declare that it has no part in your mind. It has no power over you. You state the Law and rely on it to the exclusion of all else. Daily try to see more and to understand more, feel every day that you are being especially looked after. There is no special creation for any individual, but we all specialize the Law every time we think into it. For all our thought is taken up and something is always done with it.

A good practice is to sit and realize that you are a center of Divine attraction, that all things are coming to you, that the power within is going out and drawing back all that you will ever need. Don't argue about it, just do it, and when you have finished leave it all to the Law, knowing that it will be done. Declare that all life, all love and power are now in your life. Declare that you are now in the midst of plenty. Stick to it even though you may not as yet see the result. It will work and those who believe the most always get the most. Think of the Law as your friend, always looking out for your interest. Trust completely in it and it will bring your good to you.

ONE LAW AND MANY MANIFESTATIONS

People often ask if the Law will not bring harm as well as good. This question would never be asked if people understood what Universal Law really means. Of course it will bring us what we think. All law will do the same thing. The law of electricity will either light our house or burn it down. We decide what we are to do with the Law. Law is always impersonal. There is no likelihood of using the Law for harmful purposes if we always use it for the more complete expression of life. We must not use it for any purpose that we would not like to experience ourselves. This should answer all questions of that nature. Do I really want the thing I ask for? Am I willing to take for myself what I ask for other people? How can we use the Law for evil if we desire only the good? We cannot and we should not bother about it. We want only the good for ourselves and for the whole world; when we have started causation, at once the Law will set to work carrying out our plans. Never distrust the Law and become afraid lest you misuse it. That is a great mistake, all Law is impersonal and cares not who uses it. It will bring to all just what is already in their thought. No person can long use it in a destructive way, for it will destroy him if he persists in doing wrong. We have no responsibility for any one except ourselves. Get over all idea that you must save the world; we have all tried and have all failed. We may, by demonstrating in our own lives, prove that the Law really exists as the great power behind all things. This is all that we can do. Every one must do the same thing for himself. Let the dead bury their dead, and see that you live. In this you are not selfish but are simply proving that law governs your life. All can do the same when they come to believe, and none until they believe.

TRANSCENDING PREVIOUS CONDITIONS

What if at times we attract something that we do not want? What about all the things that we have already attracted into our lives? Must we still suffer until the last farthing be paid? Are we bound by Karma? Yes, in a certain degree we are bound by what we have done; it is impossible to set law in motion and not have it produce. What we sow we must also reap, of that there is no doubt; but here is something to think about; the Bible also says that if a man repents his "sins are blotted out, and remembered no more forever." Here we have two statements which at first seem not to agree. The first says that we must suffer from what we have done, and the second that under certain conditions we will not have to suffer. What are those conditions? A changed attitude toward the Law. It means that we must stop thinking and acting in the wrong way.

When we do this we are taken out of the old order and established in the new. Someone will say: If that is true what about the Law of Cause and Effect? Is that broken? No, it is this way: The Law is not broken, it would still work out if we continued to use it in the wrong way; but when we reverse the cause; that is, think and act in a different way, then we have changed the flow of the Law. It is still the same Law but we have changed its flow, so that, instead of limiting us and punishing us, it frees and blesses. It is still the Law but we have changed our attitude toward it. We might throw a ball at the window, and if nothing stopped it, it would break the glass. Here is Law in motion. But if someone catches the ball before it reaches the window, the glass will not be broken. Neither the glass nor the Law will be broken. The flow of Law will be changed, that is all. So can we, no matter what has happened in the past, so transcend the old experience, that it will no longer have any effect upon us. So if we have attracted something that is not best to keep, we will remember that we do not have to keep it. It was the best that we knew at the time, and so was good as far as it went, but now we know more and can do better.

As Law works without variation, so does the Law of attraction work the same way. All that we have to do is to drop the undesired thing from our thought, forgive ourselves and start anew. We must never even think of it again. Let go of it once and for ail. Our various experiences will teach us more and more to try to mold all of our thoughts and desires, so that they will be in line with the fundamental purpose of the Great Mind, the expression of that which is perfect. To fear to make conscious use of the Law would be to paralyze all efforts of progress.

More and more will we come to see that a great cosmic plan is being worked out, and that all we have to do is to lend ourselves to it, in order that we may attain unto a real degree of life. As we do subject our thought to the greater purposes we are correspondingly blest, because we are working more in line with the Father, who from the beginning knew the end. We should never lose sight of the fact that we are each given the individual right to use the law, and that we cannot escape from using it.

Let us, then, go forward with the belief that a greater power is working through us; that all law is a law of good ; that we have planted our seed of thought in the Mind of the Absolute; and that we can go our way rejoicing in the Divine privilege of working with the Infinite.

UNDERSTANDING AND MISUNDERSTANDING

There are many persons who are constantly unhappy because they seem always to be misunderstood. They find it hard to use the Law of Attraction in an affirmative way, and they keep on drawing to themselves experiences which they would rather have avoided. The trouble with them is that there is always an undercurrent of thought which either neutralizes or destroys whatever helpful thoughts they have set in motion in their moments of greater strength. Such persons are usually very sensitive, and while this is a quality which is most creative when under control, it is most destructive when uncontrolled, because it is most chaotic. They should first come to know the Law and see how it works, and then treat themselves to overcome all sensitiveness. They should realize that everyone in the world is a friend, and prove this by never saying anything unkind to any one or about any one. They must within themselves see all people as perfect beings made in the Divine Image; and, seeing nothing else, they will in time be able to say that this is also the way that all people see them. Holding this as the law of their lives they will destroy all negative thought; and then, with that power which is always in a sensitive person, but which is now under control, they will find that life is theirs to do with as they please, the only requirement being that as they sow so must they also reap. We all know that anything that is unlike good is of short duration, but anything that embodies the good is like God, ever present and Eternal. We free ourselves through the same law under which we first bound ourselves.

The ordinary individual unknowingly does something that destroys any possibility of getting good results in the demonstration of prosperity. He affirms his good and makes his unity with it, and this is right, but he does not stop looking at it in others, which is wrong and is the cause of confusion. We cannot affirm a principle and deny it in the same breath. We must become what we want and we will never be able to do that while we still persist in seeing what we do not want, no matter where we see it. We cannot believe that something is possible for us without also believing the same for every individual.

One of the ways of attainment is, of a necessity, the way of universal love: coming to see all as the true sons of God, one with the Infinite Mind. This is no mere sentiment but the clear statement of a fundamental law and that man who does not obey it, is opposing the very thing that brought him into expression. It is true that through mental means alone he may bring to himself things and he may hold them as long as the will lasts. This is the ordinary way but we want to do more than compel things to appear. What we want is that things should gravitate to us because we are employing the same law that God uses. When we so attain this attitude of mind, then that which is brought into manifestation will never be lost, for it will be as eternal as the law of God and can never be destroyed forever. It is a comfort to know that we do not have to *make* things happen, but that the law of Divine love is all that we will ever need; it will relieve the overworked brain and the fagged muscle just to be still and know that we are One with the ALL in ALL.

How can we enter in, if at one and the same time we are believing for ourselves and beholding the beam in our brother's eye? Does that not obstruct the view and pervert our own natures? We must see only the good and let nothing else enter into our minds. Universal Love of all people and of all things is but returning love to the source of all love, to Him who creates all in love and holds all in divine care. The sun shines on all alike. Shall we separate and divide where God has so carefully united? We are dividing our own things when we do this, and sooner or later the Law of Absolute Justice that weighs out to each one his just measure will balance the account, and then we shall be obliged to suffer for the mistakes we have made. God does not bring this agony on us but we have imposed it on ourselves. If from selfish motives alone, we must love all things and look upon all things as good, made from the substance of the Father.

We can only hope to bring to ourselves that which we draw through the avenue of love. We must watch our thinking and if we have aught against any soul, get rid of it as soon as possible. This is the only safe and sure way. Did not Jesus at the supreme moment of sacrifice ask that the Father forgive all the wrong that was being done to Him? Shall we suppose that we can do it in a better way? If we do not at the present time love all people, then we must learn how to do it, and the way will become easier, when all condemnation is gone forever and we behold only good. God is good and God is Love; more than this we cannot ask nor conceive.

Another thing that we must eliminate is talking about limitation; we must not even think of it or read about it, or have any connection with it in any of our thinking, for we get only that which we think, no more and no less. This will be a hard thing to do. But if we remember that we are working out the science of being, though it may seem long and hard at times we sooner or later do it, and once done it is done forever. Every step in advance is an Eternal step, and will never have to be taken again. We are not building for a day or a year, but we are building for all time and for Eternity. So we will build the more stately mansion under the Supreme wisdom and the unfailing guidance of the Spirit, and we will do unto all, even as we would have them do unto us; there is no other way. The wise will listen, look and learn, then follow what they know to be the only way that is in line with the Divine will and purposes. So shall all see that God is good and in Him is no evil.

NO UNUSUAL EXPERIENCE

In demonstrating the truth of supply we do not have to experience any peculiar emotion or psychic experience. We do not have to feel any thrills or anything of that sort. While it is true that some of these things may come, yet we should remember that what we are doing is dealing with law, and that as law it will obey us, when we comply with its nature and contact it in the right way. What we are doing is stating something into Mind, and if the impression is clear in our own minds *that it is* and *that it is done* we have put all the activity we can put into it, until such a time as something happens in the external for us to work upon. So many people say, "I do wish that I could feel something, when I give a treatment." All this is a mistake and is an attempt to give a physical reason for life. What we do need to feel is that, since God is all and is good, He wants us to have only the good; and feeling this we should take what is already made for us. Our attitude toward such a good Father should constantly be one of thanksgiving. When we begin to prove the power of the truth we will always maintain this attitude. *Know* that you are dealing with a sure thing and that all you have to do is to think positively into it and wait for the results to come in the outer. Then do what your own good sense tells you to do, for this is the thought of God through you. More and more you will find that you are being led out of difficulty into that freedom which is the Divine birthright of every living soul. Go ahead, then, looking only at the things desired and never at the things not wanted. Victory will always be on the side that the majority of your thoughts rest on in absolute acceptance.

VISUALIZING

Some people visualize everything that they think and many think that it is impossible to make a demonstration unless they possess the power to visualize. This is not the case. While a certain amount of vision is necessary, on the other hand it must be remembered that we are dealing with a power that is like the soil of the ground, which will produce the plant when we plant seed. It does not matter if we have never before seen a plant like the one that is to be made for us. Our thought is the seed and mind is the soil. We are always planting and harvesting. All that we need to do is to plant only that which we want to harvest. This is not difficult to understand. We cannot think poverty and at the same time demonstrate plenty. If a person wants to visualize let him do so, and if he sees himself in full possession of his desire and knows that he is receiving, he will make his demonstration. If, on the other hand, he does not visualize, then let him simply state what he wants and absolutely believe that he has it and the result will always be the same.

Remember that you are always dealing with law and that this is the only way that anything could come into existence. Don't argue over it. That means that you have not as yet become convinced of the truth or you would not argue. Be convinced and rest in peace.

WHERE DEMONSTRATION TAKES PLACE

Does demonstration take place in the patient, the practitioner or in the mind of God? Let us see; *We are* in the mind of God and so it must take place there. But the patient is also in the mind of God or there would be two minds, and so it must take place in the mind of the patient, also. But that is the mind of God, so what does it matter where it takes place? We do not have to project our thought, because Mind is right at hand and never leaves us at any time. All that we have to do is to know within ourselves, and, when we are absolutely convinced, we will have made the demonstration.

As far as the practitioner is concerned, all that he has to do is to convince himself. Here his work begins and ends. There is a power that will look after the rest. Is this not the supreme attitude of faith in higher power? Of course it is, and the more of that faith that we have, the easier it will be for us and the quicker we will receive an answer to our prayer. If you have a simple, childlike faith it will produce; but it should give us a greater faith when we know something of the way that the law operates. It follows, then, that we should, by understanding, have so great a faith that we shall never fail to get the affirmative answer to all of our thoughts. Each victory will strengthen us until the time will come when we will no longer have to say *I hope* or *believe,* but *I know.*

PART 2

Practice

TREATMENTS

The way to give a treatment is first of all to absolutely believe that you can; believe that your word goes forth into a real Creative Power, which at once takes it up, and begins to operate upon it; feel that to this Power all things are possible. It knows nothing but Its own power to do that which It wishes to do. It receives the impress of your thought and acts upon it.

It is never safe to treat for anything that you do not wish to happen. This means that what you would want for another, you must first be willing to receive for yourself.

Believe then that your word is to be acted upon by an Almighty Power; feel its great reality, in and through all things you speak into it; and declare just what you wish it to do for you, never doubting in your own mind but that it will do just as you have directed.

All that a practitioner has to do is to convince himself, to know, to believe, and that thing will happen to him which he states. One of the first things, then, is to be definite; to have a mental likeness of the thing that you desire; to know exactly what you want. This mental likeness, this absolute acceptance of the fact that it now is, must never be overlooked; without it you will not accomplish your desired objective.

We sit down with our own souls, at peace with the world, at peace with ourselves; we realize that we are dealing with something that is a reality, something that cannot fail. We try to get a clear concept of the thing; we rest in that realization, while the Universal Creative Power takes it up and acts upon it.

We have stated just what we wanted done unto us; we have believed; we have believed that we have received; never again will we contradict the fact that we have stated. The person who can do this is sure of getting results.

UNDERSTANDING AND GUIDANCE

The inner man is always in immediate connection with the Infinite of understanding. We are immersed in a living Intelligence; we are surrounded by a Power that knows, for "in Him we live and move and have our being."

If our outer thought were never confused, we should at all times draw from this Infinite source of knowledge; we should be guided by It and never make mistakes; our minds would be like the smooth surface of a lake, unruffled by wind and storm.

But with most of us this is not the case; we become confused in the outer so that the surface of the mind is in turmoil, no longer clear and transparent, and we cannot get the clear vision, the real guidance, and we get things wrong because we do not see clearly.

The development of the understanding is learning to draw from the Infinite understanding; we can never do this while we are confused in our thinking.

The first thing to do when we wish a greater understanding is to be still and listen to the inner voice, to withdraw for a few moments into the silence of the soul taking here what we already know, and realizing that a greater intelligence is enlarging it.

Here we indefinitely take the pattern of our thought, the thing that we are working on, and ask for, and receive, new light; we hold this up in Divine Light and try to believe that we are being guided; we state that Supreme Intelligence and Absolute Power are acting upon our thought and bringing it to pass; it is now guiding us and we shall make no mistake; we hold ourselves in the secret place of the Most High, and abide under the shadow of the Almighty.

HOW TO KNOW JUST WHAT TO DO

Often we find ourselves confronted by the problem of how to begin. We are not sure *what* we want to do; we see no *way* to begin anything; see nothing to begin on; when we find ourselves in this position, humanly speaking, not knowing where to turn, then of all times we must be quiet and listen; then of all times we must trust that the same power that *started all things* will also *start us* in the right road for without some superior power we shall surely fail.

How often do people in the business world find themselves in this position? They realize that something must be done, but what? How can they get the right idea?

Here we must wait and know that the same Power that first thought a universe into being can also think our world and work into being. It knows all things; It knows how to begin and It cannot fail; we wish in some way to connect with this Power that will never fail us, so We may draw from it some idea with which to begin.

We must realize that there is something that wants to respond, to make manifest and in this realization wait for the idea; it may not come at first, but we must be patient, never doubting, and waiting thus in faith, it *will* come.

I once knew a businessman who was connected with a firm that had always been very successful, but at that time something had occurred that was causing them to lose out. This had gone on for a year and things were going from bad to worse. Failure seemed inevitable. He became interested in New Thought. He was told he could draw an idea from the Infinite and work it out on the plane of the visible. He told his partners that he wished to go home for a few days and that when he came back he would have worked out an idea which would put the business on a successful basis. They laughed at him, as people generally laugh at something they do not understand, but having no other plan they gave their consent. He went home and for three days sat in deep thought, claiming Supreme guidance and absolute leading of the Spirit. During this time a complete plan formulated in his mind as to the exact method to pursue in the business. He returned and told his plan to his partners. Again they laughed, saying it could not be done in business; could not be done any way; it would not work. But again they consented, knowing it was this or failure.

He then went to work carrying out all the details of his thought, following each leading that had come to him during those three days, and within a year he brought the failing business to a standard that transcended anything they had ever before experienced, He proved the law and became such an expert, that he gave up his business and devoted his entire time to helping other people do the same for themselves as he had done.

What this man did anyone can do if he will follow the same course and refuse to become discouraged. There is a Power that simply awaits our recognition of It, to spring into our thought as an unfailing leading, an unerring guidance. To those who lean on the ever outstretched arm of the Infinite, life is big with limitless possibilities.

We must wait and listen, then go about our outer business with an inner conviction that we are being led into a more perfect expression of life. All can do this.

FOLLOWING UP A THOUGHT

When we feel that we do have the right leading; when that something inside us tells us that we are led; then, no matter what it appears like, we must follow it up. Something beyond our intelligence is doing the thing through us and we must do nothing to contradict it.

Perhaps it will cause us to do something that seems to *go* contrary to the experience of the race. This makes no difference. All advance in invention and all advance along any line has always gone ahead of what the experience of the race thinks is possible.

Great men are the ones who get a vision and then go to work to make it come true, never looking to one side but with one-pointedness and calm determination, stick to the thing until it is accomplished. It may take much patience and a great deal of faith, but the end is as sure as is the reality of a Supreme Being itself.

Never hesitate to trust in that inner leading, never fear but it will be right. We are all in the midst of Supreme Intelligence; It presses against the doors of our thought, waiting to be known. We must be open to It at all times, ready to receive direction and to be guided into greater truths.

THE SINGLE STREAM OF THOUGHT

We are all in Mind and what we think into it is taken up and done unto us. This means that *as* we think it will be done. We cannot think one way one day and change our thought the next and hope to get the desired results. We must be very clear in our thought, sending out only such thoughts as we wish to see manifested in our condition.

Here is something worth remembering. Unless we are working with people who think as we do, we had better be working alone. One stream of thought, even though it may not be very powerful, will do more for us than many powerful streams that are at variance with each other. This means that, unless we are sure that we are working with people who harmonize, we would better work alone. Of course we cannot retire from business simply because people do not agree with us, but what we can do is to keep our thoughts to ourselves. We do not have to leave the world in order to control our thought; but we do have to learn that we can stay right in the world and still think just what we want to think, regardless of what others are thinking.

One single stream of thought, daily sent out into Creative Mind, will do wonders. Within a year the person who will practice this will have completely changed his conditions of life.

The way to practice this is daily to spend some time in thinking and in mentally seeing just what is wanted; see the thing just as it is wished and then affirm that this is now done. Try to feel that what has been stated is the truth.

Words and affirmations simply give shape to thought; they are not creative. Feeling is creative and the more feeling that is put into the word the greater power it will have over conditions. In doing this we think of the condition only as an effect, something that follows what we think. It cannot help following our thought. This is the way that all creation comes into expression.

It is a great help to realize mentally that at all times a great stream of thought and power is operating through us; it is constantly going out into Mind, where it is taken up and acted upon. Our business is to keep that stream of thought just where we want it to be: to be ready at any time to act when the impulse comes for action. Our action must never be negative, it must always be affirmative, for we are dealing with something that cannot fail. We may fail to realize, but the Power in itself is Infinite and cannot fail.

We are setting in motion in the Absolute a stream of thought that will never cease until it accomplishes its purpose. Try to feel this, be filled with a great joy as you feel that it is given to you to use this great and only Power.

Keep the thought clear and never worry about the way that things seem to be going. Let go of all outer conditions when working in Mind, for there is where things are made; there creation is going on, and It is now making something for us. This must be believed as never believed before; It must be known as the great reality; It must be felt as the only Presence. There is no other way to obtain.

Though all the Infinite may want to give, yet we must take, and, as far as we are concerned, that taking is mental. Though people may laugh at this, even that does not matter. "He laughs best who laughs last." We know in "what we believe," and that will be sufficient.

ENLARGING OUR THOUGHT

We can never stand still in our thought. Either we will be growing or else we will be going back. As we can attract to ourselves only that of which we first have a mental likeness, it follows that if we wish to attract larger things we must provide larger thoughts. This enlarging of consciousness is so necessary that too much cannot be said about it.

Most people get only a short way and then stop: they cannot seem to get beyond a certain point; they can do so much and no more. Why is it that a person in business does just about so much each year? We see people in all walks of life, getting so far, never going beyond a certain point. There must be a reason for everything; nothing happens, if all is governed by law, and we can come to no other conclusion.

When we look into the mental reason for things we find out why things happen. The man who gets so far and never seems to go beyond that point is still governed by law; when he allows his thoughts to take him out into larger fields of action, his conditions come up to his thought; when he stops enlarging his thought he stops growing. If he would still keep on in thought, realizing more and still more, he would find that in the outer form of things he would be doing greater things.

There are many reasons why a man stops thinking larger things. One of them is a lack of imagination. He cannot conceive of anything more to follow than that which has already happened. Another thought works like this: "This is as far as anyone can go in my business." Right here he signs his own death warrant. Often a person will say, "I am too old to do bigger things." There he stops. Some one else will say, "Competition is too great"; and here is where this man stops; he can go no further than his thought will carry him.

All this is unnecessary when we realize that life is first of all Consciousness, and then conditions follow. We see no reason why a man should not go on and on, and never stop growing. No matter what age or what circumstance, if life is thought, we can keep on thinking bigger things. There is no reason why a man who is already doing well should not be able mentally to conceive of a still better condition. What if we are active? There is always a greater activity possible. We can still see a little beyond what has come before. This is just what we should do, see, even though it be but a little beyond our former thought. If we always practice this, we will find that every year we shall be growing, every month we shall be advancing; and as time goes on we shall become really great. As there is no stopping in that Power which Is Infinite, as the Limitless is without bounds, so should we keep on trying to see more and greater possibilities in life.

We should definitely work every day for the expansion of thought. If we have fifty customers a day we should endeavor to believe that we have sixty. When we have sixty we should mentally see seventy. This should never stop; there is no stopping place in Mind.

Let go of everything else, drop everything else from your thought, and mentally see more coming to you than has ever come before; believe that Mind is establishing this unto you, and then go about your business in the regular way. Never see the limitation; never dwell upon it, and above all things else never talk limitation to anyone; this is the only way, and there is no other way to grow a larger thought. The man with the big thought is always the man who does big things in life. Get hold of the biggest thing that you can think of and claim it for your own; mentally see it and hold it as a thing already done, and you will prove to yourself that life is without bounds.

ALWAYS BE GATHERING

There is no reason why a person should ever stop. This does not mean that we should be miserly, trying to accumulate more and more to hold, but that our thought should so enlarge that it can not help gathering more and more, even though, on the other hand, or with the other hand, we are ever distributing that which we gather. Indeed, the only reason for having is that we may give out of that which we have.

No matter what big thing happens to us we should still be expecting more and more. Even when we think that we have at last arrived; right at the moment when it seems as though life had given us all that we could stand; right here let it be but a beginning for still greater things.

No matter how large the picture that you hold in mind, make it larger. The reason why so many people come to the point where they stop is that they come to a point where they stop growing in their own minds. They come to a point where they can see no more, thinking that because they have really done a big thing they should stop there. We must watch our thought for signs of inactivity. Nothing in the universe ever stops. Everything is built on a boundless basis, drawn from a limitless source, come forth from an Infinite sea of unmanifest life. We speak forth into this life and draw back from it all that we first think into it. Life is always limitless, and the only thing that limits us is our inability to conceive mentally, and we should draw more and more from that limitless source.

MENTAL LIKENESS

We can draw from the Infinite only as much as we first think into it. It is at this point that so many fail, thinking that all they need to do is to affirm what they want arid it will follow. While it *is* true that affirmations have real power, it is also true that they have *only* that which we speak into them.

As we cannot speak a word that we do not know, so we cannot make an affirmation that we do not understand. We really affirm only that which we know to be true; we know that to be true which we have experienced within ourselves. Although we may have heard or read that this or that thing is true, it is only when there is something within our own souls that corresponds or recognizes its truth, that it is true to us. This ought never to be lost sight of: we can effectively affirm only that which we know, and we know only that which we are. It is herein that we see the necessity of providing within a greater concept of life; a bigger idea of ourselves and a more expanded concept of the Universe in which we live, move, and have our being. This is a matter of inner growth together with the enlarging of all lines of thought and activity.

If we want to do a thing that is really worth doing, we must mentally grow until we are that thing, which we want to see made flesh. This may take time, but we should be glad to use all the time necessary to our own development.

But few people in limitation have a mental likeness of plenty. This likeness must be provided. The thought must be large enough to cover the whole of the thing desired; a small thought will produce only a small thing. The very fact that all is Mind proves this to be true. All *is* Mind and, because it is, we can draw from that Mind only that which we first think into it as a reality. We must become the thing we want. We must see it, think it, realize it, before the creative power of Mind can work it out for us. This is an inner process of the expansion of consciousness. It is a thought growing and realizing within. All can do this who wish and who will take the time and trouble, but it will mean work. The majority of people are too lazy to make the effort.

Daily we must train our thought to see that only which we wish to experience, and since we are growing into what we are mentally dwelling upon, we should put all small and insignificant thoughts and ideals out of our thinking and see things in a larger way. We must cultivate the habit of an enlarged mental horizon, daily seeing farther and farther ahead, and so experiencing larger and greater things in our daily life.

A good practice for the enlargement of thought is daily to see ourselves in a little bigger place, filled with more of activity, surrounded with increased influence and power; feel more and more that things are coming to us; see that much more is just ahead, and so far as possible, know that we now have all that we see and all that we feel. Affirm that you are that larger thing; that you are now entered into that larger life; feel that something within is drawing more to you; live with the idea and let the concept grow, expecting only the biggest and the best to happen. Never let small thoughts come into your mind, and you will soon find that a larger and greater experience has come into your life.

KEEPING THE THING IN MIND

Never let go of the mental image until it becomes manifested. Daily bring up the clear picture of what is wanted and impress it on the mind as an accomplished fact. This impressing on our own minds the thought of what we wish to realize will cause our own minds to impress the same thought on Universal Mind. In this way we shall be praying without ceasing. We do not have to hold continually the thought of something we want in order to get it, but the thought that we may inwardly become the thing we want. Fifteen minutes, twice each day, is time enough to spend in order to demonstrate anything, but the rest of the time ought also to be spent constructively. That is, we must stop all negative thinking and give over all wrong thought, holding fast to the realization that it is now done unto us. We must know that we are dealing with the only power there is in the Universe; that there is none other beside it, and that we are in it partaking of its nature and its laws. Always, behind the word that we send forth, must be the calm confidence in our ability to speak into the power, and the willingness of Mind to execute for us. We must gradually grow in confidence and in trust in the unseen world of spiritual activity. This is not hard, if we but remember that the Spirit makes things out of Itself by simply becoming the thing that it makes, and since there is no other power to oppose it, it will always work. The Spirit will never fail us if we never fail to believe in its goodness and its responsiveness. Life will become one grand song, when we realize that since God is for us, none can be against us. We shall cease merely to exist; we shall *live.*

DESTROY ALL THOUGHTS THAT WE DO NOT WISH TO EXPERIENCE

We must resolutely set our faces to the rising consciousness of the Son of Truth; seeing only the One Power we must destroy the adversary and leave the field to God or Good. All that is in any way negative must be wiped off the slate and we must daily come into the higher thought, to be washed clean of the dust and chaos of the objective life. In the silence of the soul's communion with the Great Cause of All Being, into the stillness of the Absolute, into the secret place of the Most High, back of the din and the ceaseless roar of life, we shall find a resting place and a place of real spiritual power. Speak in this inner silence and say, "I am one with the Almighty; I am one with all life, with all power, with all presence. I Am, I Am, I Am." Listen to the silence. From out of the seeming void the voice of peace will answer the waiting soul, "All is well."

Here we make known all our needs and wants, and here we receive first hand from the Infinite all that we shall ever need to make life healthy, happy, and harmonious. Few enter here, because of the belief that conditions and circumstances control. Know that there is no law but God's law; that the soul sets its own law in the Infinite and that our slightest wish is honored by the Father Mind.

Daily practice the truth and daily die to all error-thought. Spend more time receiving and realizing the presence of the Most High and less time worrying. Wonderful power will come to the one who believes and trusts in that Power in which he has come to believe. Know that all good and all God is with you; All Life and All Power; and never again say, "I fear," but always, "I trust, because 'I know in whom I have believed.'"

DIRECT PRACTICE FOR PROSPERITY

Suppose that you are doing a mail order business and sending out cards to the whole country. Take the cards into your hands, or simply think of them and declare into the only Mind that they will accomplish that for which they are sent out; know that every word written on them is truth and carries its own conviction with it; see them each reaching that place where it will be received with gladness and read with interest; declare this to be so *now;* feel it to be the truth; mentally assert that each card will find its way to the exact place where it will be wanted and where it will benefit the receiver; feel that each card is cared for by the Spirit; that it is a messenger of truth and power and that it will carry conviction and realization with it. When the word is spoken always feel that Mind at once takes it up and never fails to act upon it. Our place in the creative order is to know this and to be willing to do all that we can without hurry or worry, and, above all else, to trust absolutely in the Spirit to do the rest. He who sees most clearly and believes most implicitly will make the greatest demonstration. This one should be *you,* and will be you as soon as the false thought is gone and the realization that there is but the one Power and the one Presence comes. We are wrapped in an Infinite Love and Intelligence and we should cover ourselves with it and claim its protection from all evil. Declare that your word is the presence and the activity of the Power of all that is and wait for the perfect concept to unfold.

RACE CONSCIOUSNESS

One of the things which greatly hinders us from demonstrating a greater degree of prosperity we may call race thought or race consciousness. This is the result of all that the race has thought or believed. We are immersed in it, and those who are receptive to it are controlled by it. All thought seeks expression along the lines of least resistance. When we become negative or fearful we attract that kind of thought and condition. We must be sure of ourselves; we must be positive; we must not be aggressive, but absolutely sure and poised within. Negative people are always picking up negative conditions; they get into trouble easily. Persons who are positive draw positive things; they are always successful. Few people realize that the law of thought is the great reality; that thoughts produce things. When we come to understand this power of thought, we will carefully watch our thinking to see that no thought enters that we do not want made into a *thing.*

We can guard our minds by knowing that no negative thought can enter; we can daily practice by saying that no race thought of limitation can enter the mind; that Spirit forms itself around us and protects us from all fear and from all limitation. Let us clothe ourselves in the great realization that all power is ours and that nothing else can enter; let us fill the atmosphere of our homes, and places of business with streams of positive thought. Other people will feel this and will like to be near us and enter into the things that we enter into. In this way we shall be continually drawing only the best,

DEVELOPING INTUITION

If a person always lived near to Mind he would never make any great mistakes. Some seem to have the faculty of always knowing just what is best to do; they always succeed because they avoid making errors. We can also train ourselves that we will be guided by the Supreme Mind of the Universe; but we can never do this until we believe that we can receive direct from the source of all knowledge. This is done by sitting in the silence and knowing that the Spirit is inwardly directing us. We should try to feel that our thought is being permeated by the thought of the Spirit. We should expect It to direct but should never become discouraged if at once a direct impression is not received. The work is going on even if it is not seen or even felt. Thought is forming in our mind and in time will come forth as an idea. When the idea does come always trust in it even though it may not seem to be quite as we had expected. The first impressions are usually the most direct and the clearest; they are generally direct from the Mind of the Universe and should be carefully worked out into expression.

We declare as we sit in the silence that the Spirit of all knowledge is making known within us just what we should do; that it is telling us just what to say or where to go. Have absolute reliance on this as it is one of the most important things to do. We should always get that inner assurance before undertaking any new enterprise; being sure that we have really put the whole thing into the hands of life and that all that we have to do is to work it out in the outer. We shall learn to avoid mistakes when we learn to be directed by that inner voice that never makes mistakes. We should declare in the silence that Intelligence is guiding us and it will do so.

PRESENCE OF ACTIVITY

Suppose that your place of business does not seem to manifest any activity; that is, suppose that customers do not come. To the person in the business world the presence of customers generally means activity. Suppose that you have come to believe that the principle will work in the smallest as well as in the greatest things. What you want now is a greater activity. How are you going to see activity when there is none?

Here is a great question in Truth. Must we overlook that which we see, and that which we have experienced? Yes, absolutely; there is no other way. If we keep on seeing the thing as it appears we will never be able to change its appearance. What we must do, then, in spite of the seeming inactivity, is still to know and mentally to see and declare that we are in the midst of activity. Feel this to be true; mentally see the place crowded; know that it is packed full of customers all the time; declare that your word draws them in; have no sense of strain about it whatever; simply know that you are dealing with the only Power that there is; it will work; it must work. Realize when you have spoken the word that a greater Power has taken it up and that it is being established unto you. Have no idea of limitation; speak forth into Mind with perfect trust. If you have the ability mentally to see the place full, combine this with the word, and daily visualize it as being filled. Always combine faith in the Higher Power with all that you do; feel that you are being especially looked after. This is true. When a soul turns to the Universe of unmanifest life, at the same time It turns toward him. Jesus told this in the story of the Prodigal Son; the Father saw him afar off. Always there is that inward turning to us of the Parent Mind when we turn to It and place ourselves in closer contact with Life.

We must keep our mind clear so that when the Spirit brings the gift we will be open to receive it. Even God cannot force things upon us. We must receive even before we see.

"For the feeble hands and helpless,
Groping blindly in the darkness
Touch God's right hand in that darkness
And are lifted up and strengthened."

Always, when we believe, we will have that belief honored to the Spirit of Life. Mentally seeing just what we want; still seeing even though the heavens fall, we shall succeed in proving that the law of life is a law of liberty. God made man to have all that the Universe contained and then left him alone to discover his own nature.

Stop all striving and all struggle and within your own soul know the Truth and trust absolutely in it. Daily declare that you are being guided and protected and that the power of the Spirit is bringing all to pass, and wait in perfect peace and confidence. Such an attitude of mind will overcome anything and will prove that spiritual thought force is the only real power in the Universe.

DRAWING YOUR OWN TO YOU

Suppose that you wish to draw friends and companions to you; that you wish to enlarge your circle of friendships. This, too, can all be worked out by law, for everything can be worked out by the same law, the reason being that all is One and that the One becomes the many in expression. There are too many people in the world who are lonesome because they have a sense of separation from people. The thing to do is not to try to unify *with* people, but *with the Principle of Life* behind all people and things. This is working from the center and not the circumference; in this One Mind are the minds of all people. When you unite your thought with the whole you will be united with the parts of the whole. The first thing to do, then, is to realize that Life is your friend and companion; feel the divine companionship; feel that you are one with all life; declare that, as this thought awakens within your mind, so does it awaken within the mind of the whole race; feel that the world is being drawn to you; love the world and everyone who is in it; include all, if you would be included in all. The world seeks strength; be strong. The world loves love; embody it; see the good in all people; let go of all else. People will feel your love and will be drawn into it. Love is the greatest power in the Universe; it is at the base of all else; it is the cause of all that is. Feel your love to be like a great light lighting the pathway of the whole world; it will come back to you bringing so many friends that there will riot be time enough to enjoy them all. Become a real friend and you will have many friends.

Be sufficient unto yourself and at the same time include all else, and people will feel your strength and will have a desire to come into the radiance of it. Never become unhappy or morbid; always be cheerful and radiate good nature and happiness; never look depressed or down in the mouth; the world is attracted to the strongest center of cheer and good fellowship. Never allow your feelings to be hurt. No one wants to hurt you, and none could, even though they did want to; you are above all that. Wherever you go know that the Spirit of Truth goes before and prepares the way, bringing to you every friend and influence that will be necessary to your comfort and well being. This is not selfishness but good sense and will surely bring to you a harvest of friends and companions.

Declare unto Mind that you are now linked with all people and that all people are linked with you: see yourself surrounded with hosts of friends; mentally feel their presence and rejoice that all good is yours now. Do this no matter what seems to happen, and it will not be long before you will meet wonderful friends and will be brought into touch with the great of the world.

THE FINAL WORD

In the last analysis, man is just what he thinks himself to be; he is big in capacity if he thinks big thoughts; he is small if he thinks small thoughts. He will attract to himself what he thinks most about. He can learn to govern his own destiny when he learns to control his thoughts. In order to do this he must first realize that everything in the manifest universe is the result of some inner activity of Mind. This Mind is God, producing a universe by the activity of His own divine thoughts; man is in this Mind as a thinking center, and what he thinks governs his life, even as God's thought governs the Universe, by setting in motion all the cosmic activities. This is so easy to understand, and so plain as to use that we often wonder why we have been so long finding out this, the greatest of all truths of all the ages. Believing; thinking what is believed to be true; thinking into Mind each day that which is wished to be returned; eliminating negative thoughts; thinking positive thoughts; giving thanks to the Spirit of Life that it is so trusting always in the higher Law; never arguing with one's self or with others; using; these are the steps which, when followed, will bring us to where we shall not have to ask if it be true, for, having demonstrated, *we shall know.* The seed that falls into the ground shall bear fruit of its own kind; and nothing shall hinder it.

"He that hath ears to hear, let him hear."

8

PROSPERITY

CHARLES FILLMORE

(1936)

Foreword

It is perfectly logical to assume that a wise and competent Creator would provide for the needs of His creatures in their various stages of growth. The supply would be given as required and as the necessary effort for its appropriation was made by the creature. Temporal needs would be met by temporal things, mental needs by things of like character, and spiritual needs by spiritual elements. For simplification of distribution all would be composed of one primal spiritual substance, which under proper direction could be transformed into all products at the will of the operator. This is a crude yet true illustration of the underlying principles on which the human family is supplied on this earth. The Father has provided a universal seed substance that responds with magical power to the active mind of man. Faith in the increasing capacity of this seed substance, whether wrapped in visible husks or latent in invisible electrical units, always rewards man with the fruits of his labor.

The farmer may seem to get his supply from the seeds he plants, but he would never plant a seed unless he had faith in its innate capacity to increase, and that seed would never multiply without the quickening life of Spirit. Thus we see that all increase of substance depends on the quickening life of Spirit, and this fact gives us the key to mental processes that when used spiritually will greatly increase and at the same time simplify our appropriation of that inexhaustible substance which creative Mind has so generously provided.

In the following lessons we have attempted to explain man's lawful appropriation of the supplies spiritually and electrically provided by God. When we understand and adjust our mind to the realm or kingdom where these rich ideas and their electrical thought forms exist we shall experience in our temporal affairs what is called "prosperity."

We said "their electrical thought forms." Let us explain that all creative processes involve a realm of ideas and a realm of patterns or expressions of those ideas. The patterns arrest or "bottle up" the free electric units that sustain the visible thing. Thus creation is in its processes a trinity, and back of the visible universe are both the original creative idea and the cosmic rays that crystallize into earthly things. When we understand this trinity in its various activities we shall be able to reconcile the discoveries of modern science with the fundamentals of religion.

Modern science teaches us that space is heavily charged with energies that would transform the earth if they could be controlled. Sir Oliver Lodge says that a single cubic inch of the ether contains energy enough to run a forty-horse-power engine forty million years. The divergence of opinion among physicists as to the reality of the ether does not nullify the existence in space of tremendous potentialities. Sir Arthur Eddington says that about half the leading physicists assert that the ether exists and the other half deny its existence, but, in his words, "both parties mean exactly the same thing, and are divided only by words."

Spiritual understanding says that the ether exists as an emanation of mind and should not be confused in its limitations with matter. Mathematical measurements applied to the ether work it out of existence because its reality is in the Mind that conceived it and its being is governed and sustained by ideas, and ideas have no physical dimensions. So the ether will have existence and deposit matter only so long as Mind has use for it. When infinite Mind has completed the cycles of creation, both the invisible and the visible universes will be rolled up as a scroll and disappear and only Mind remain. "And all the host of heaven shall be dissolved, and the heavens shall be rolled together as a scroll; and all their host shall fade away."

It adds greatly to the stability of a Christian's faith to know that Jesus anticipated the discoveries of modern science of the existence of that kingdom called "the ether." He named it the kingdom of the heavens, and His illustrations of its possibilities are unsurpassed. He did not say it was a place the good would inherit after death but an estate we could have here and now. "It is your Father's good pleasure to give you the kingdom."

Jesus taught that we can incorporate life-giving rays into our mind, body, and affairs through faith. Where physicists merely describe the mechanical presence of life as energy, Jesus taught man how by the exercise of his mind he can make that life obey him. Instead of a universe of blind mechanical forces Jesus showed the universe to be persuaded and directed by intelligence.

What we need to realize above all else is that God has provided for the most minute needs of our daily life and that if we lack anything it is because we have not used our mind in making the right contact with the supermind and the cosmic ray that automatically flows from it.

Contents

1. Spiritual Substance, the Fundamental Basis of the Universe 413
2. Spiritual Mind, the Omnipresent Directive Principle of Prosperity 420
3. Faith in the Invisible Substance, the Key to Demonstration 427
4. Man, the Inlet and Outlet of Divine Mind 433
5. The Law That Governs the Manifestation of Supply 440
6. Wealth of Mind Expresses Itself in Riches 448
7. God Has Provided Prosperity for Every Home 455
8. God Will Pay Your Debts 462
9. Tithing, the Road to Prosperity 469
10. Right Giving, the Key to Abundant Receiving 476
11. Laying Up Treasures 483
12. Overcoming the Thought of Lack 489

Question Helps 497

LESSON 1

Spiritual Substance, the Fundamental Basis of the Universe

Divine mind is the one and only reality. When we incorporate the ideas that form this Mind into our mind and persevere in those ideas, a mighty strength wells up within us. Then we have a foundation for the spiritual body, the body not made with hands, eternal in the heavens. When the spiritual body is transmitted to the visible body and to all the things that we touch in the world about us.

Spiritual discernment reveals that we are now in the dawn of a new era, that the old methods of supply and support are fast passing away, and that new methods are waiting to be brought forth. In the coming commerce man will not be a slave to money. Humanity's daily needs will be met in ways that are not now thought practical. We shall serve for the joy of serving, and prosperity will flow to us and through us in streams of plenty. The supply and support that love and zeal will set in motion are not as yet largely used by man, but those who have tested their providing power are loud in their praise.

The dynamic power of the supermind in man has been sporadically displayed by men and women of every nation. It is usually connected with some religious rite in which mystery and priestly authority prevail. The so-called "'common herd" are kept in darkness with respect to the source of the superhuman power of occult adepts and holy men. But we have seen a "great light" in the discovery by physical scientists that the atom conceals electronic energies whose mathematical arrangement determines the character of all the fundamental elements of nature. This discovery has disrupted the science based on the old mechanical atomic theory, but has also given Christian metaphysicians a new understanding of the dynamics back of Spirit.

Science now postulates space rather than matter as the source of life. It says that the very air is alive with dynamic forces that await man's grasp and utilization and that these invisible, omnipresent energies possess potentialities far beyond our most exalted conception. What we have been taught about the glories of heaven pales into insignificance compared with the glories of the radiant rays—popularly referred to as the "ether." We are told by science that we have utilized very meagerly this mighty ocean of ether in producing from it the light and power of electricity. The seemingly tremendous force generated by the whirl of our dynamos is but a weak dribble from a universe of energy. The invisible waves that carry radio programs everywhere are but a mere hint of an intelligent power that penetrates and permeates every germ of life, visible and invisible. Scientific minds the world over have been tremendously moved by these revolutionary discoveries, and they have not found language adequate to explain their magnitude. Although a number of books have been written by scientists, setting forth guardedly the far-reaching effects that will inevitably follow man's appropriation of the easily accessible ether, none has dared to tell the whole story. The fact is that the greatest discovery of all ages is that of physical science that all things apparently have their source in the invisible, intangible ether. What Jesus taught so profoundly in symbols about the riches of the kingdom of the heavens has now been proved true.

According to the Greek, the language in which the New Testament has come down to us, Jesus did not use the word *heaven* but the word *heavens* in His teaching. He was not telling us of the glories of some faraway place called "heaven" but was revealing the properties of the "heavens" all around us, called both "space" and "ether" by physicists. He taught not only its dynamic but also its intelligent character, and said that the entity that rules it is within man: "The kingdom of God is within you." He not only described this kingdom of the heavens in numerous parables but made its attainment by man the greatest object of human existence. He not only set this as man's goal but attained it Himself, thereby demonstrating that His teaching is practical as well as true.

The scientists tell us that the ether is charged with electricity, magnetism, light rays, X rays, cosmic rays, and other dynamic radiations; that it is the source of all life, light, heat, energy, gravitation, attraction, repulsion; in short, that it is the interpenetrating essence of everything that exists on the earth. In other words, science gives to the ether all the attractions of heaven without directly saying so. Jesus epitomized the subject when He told His followers that it was the kingdom from which God clothed and fed all His children. "Seek ye first his kingdom, and his righteousness; and all these things shall be added unto you." Science says that the electrical particles that break into light in our earth's atmosphere are also a source of all substance and matter. Jesus said that He was the substance and bread that came from the heavens. When will our civilization begin really to appropriate and use this mighty ocean of substance and life spiritually as well as physically?

This inexhaustible mind substance is available at all times and in all places to those who have learned to lay hold of it in consciousness. The simplest, shortest, and most direct way of doing this was explained when Jesus said, "Whosoever . . . shall not doubt in his heart, but shall believe that what he said cometh to pass, he shall have it." When we know that certain potent ideas exist in the invisible mind expressions, named by science both "ether" and "space" and that we have been provided with the mind to lay hold of them, it is easy to put the law into action through thought and word and deed.

"There is a tide in the affairs of men,

Which, taken at the flood, leads on to fortune," said Shakespeare. That flood tide awaits us in the cosmic spaces, the paradise of God.

The spiritual substance from which comes all visible wealth is never depleted. It is right with you all the time and responds to your faith in it and your demands on it. It is not affected by our ignorant talk of hard times, though we are affected because our thoughts and words govern our demonstration. The unfailing resource is always ready to give. It has no choice in the matter; it must give, for that is its nature. Pour your living words of faith into the omnipresent substance, and you will be prospered though all the banks in the world close their doors. Turn the great energy of your thinking toward "plenty" ideas, and you will have plenty regardless of what men about you are saying or doing.

God is substance, but if by this statement we mean that God is matter, a thing of time or condition, then we should say that God is substanceless. God is not confined to that form of substance which we term matter. God is the intangible essence of that which man has formed into and named matter. Matter is a mental limitation of that divine substance whose vital and inherent character is manifest in all life expression.

God substance may be conceived as God energy, or Spirit light, and "God said, let there be light, and there was light." This is in harmony with the conclusions of some of the most advanced physicists. Sir James Jeans says, in "The Mysterious Universe," "The tendency of modern physics is to resolve the whole material universe into waves, and nothing but waves. These waves are of two kinds: bottled-up waves, which we call matter, and unbottled waves, which we call radiation, or light. The process of annihilation of matter is merely unbottling imprisoned wave energy, and setting it free to travel through space."

Spirit is not matter. Spirit is not person. In order to perceive the essence of Being we must drop from our mind all thought that God is in any way circumscribed or has any of the limitations that we associate with things or persons having form or shape. "Thou shalt not make unto thee a graven image, nor any likeness of *any thing* that is in heaven above, or that is in the earth beneath."

God is substance, not matter, because matter is formed, while God is the formless. God substance lies back of matter and form. It is the basis of all form yet does not enter into any form as a finality. Substance cannot be seen, touched, tasted, or smelled, yet it is more substantial than matter, for it is the only substantiality in the universe. Its nature is to "*sub*-stand" or "stand under" or behind matter as its support and only reality.

Job says, "The Almighty shall be thy defence, and thou shalt have plenty of silver." This refers to universal substance, for silver and gold are manifestations of an everywhere present substance and are used as symbols for it. Lew Wallace, in "Ben-Hur," refers to the kingdom as "beaten gold." You have doubtless in your own experience caught sight of this everywhere present substance in your silence, when it seemed like golden snowflakes falling all about you. This was the first manifestation from the overflow of the universal substance in your consciousness.

Substance is first given form in the mind, and as it becomes manifest it goes through a threefold activity. In laying hold of substance in the mind and bringing it into manifestation, we play a most important part. We do it according to our decree. "Thou shalt decree a thing, and it shall be established unto thee." We are always decreeing, sometimes consciously, often unconsciously, and with every thought and word we are increasing or diminishing the threefold activity of substance. The resulting manifestation conforms to our thought, "As he thinketh within himself, so is he."

There is no scarcity of the air you breathe. There is plenty of air, all you will ever need, but if you close your lungs and refuse to breathe, you will not get it and may suffocate for lack of air. When you recognize the presence of abundance of air and open your lungs to breathe it deeply, you get a larger inspiration. This is exactly what you should do with your mind in regard to substance. There is an all-sufficiency of all things, just as there is an all-sufficiency of air. The only lack *is* our own lack of appropriation. We must seek the kingdom of God and appropriate it aright before things will be added to us in fullness.

There is a kingdom of abundance of all things, and it may be found by those who seek it and are willing to comply with its laws. Jesus said that it is hard for a rich man to enter into the kingdom of heaven. This does not mean that it is hard because of his wealth, for the poor man gets in no faster and no easier. It is not money but the thoughts men hold about money, its source, its ownership, and its use, that keep them out of the kingdom. Men's thoughts about money are like their thoughts about all possessions; they believe that things coming out of the earth are theirs to claim and control as individual property, and may be hoarded away and depended on, regardless of how much other men may be in need of them. The same belief is prevalent among both rich and poor, and even if the two classes were suddenly to change places, the inequalities of wealth would not be remedied. Only a fundamental change in the thoughts of wealth could do that.

Before there is any fundamental social or economic change men must begin to understand their relationship to God and to one another as common heirs to the universal resource that is sufficient for all. They must give up some of their erroneous ideas about their "rights." They must learn that they cannot possess and lock up that which belongs to God without themselves suffering the effects of that sequestration. The poor man is not the greatest sufferer in this concentration of wealth, for he has not concentrated his faith in material things and chained his soul to them. Those who are rich in the things of this world are by their dependence on those things binding themselves to material things and are in material darkness.

Every thought of personal possession must be dropped out of mind before men can come into the realization of the invisible supply. They cannot possess money, houses, or land selfishly, because they cannot possess the universal ideas for which these symbols stand. No man can possess any idea as his own permanently. He may possess its material symbol for a little time on the plane of phenomena, but it is such riches that "moth and rust consume, and where thieves break through and steal."

Men possess as valuables their education, trade, ability, or intellectual talent. Ministers of the gospel possess scholarship or eloquence, and take pride in these spiritual possessions. Yet even these are burdens that must be unloaded before they may enter the kingdom of the heavens. The saint who is puffed up with his saintly goodness must unload his vanity before he gets in. Whoever is ambitious to do good, to excel his fellow men in righteousness, must lose his ambition and desire before he beholds the face of the all-providing Father.

The realm of causes may be compared to steam in a glass boiler. If the glass is clear one may look right at it and see nothing at all. Yet when an escape valve is touched the steam rushes out, condenses and becomes visible. But in this process it has also lost its power. Substance exists in a realm of ideas and is powerful when handled by one who is familiar with its characteristics. The ignorant open the valves of the mind and let ideas flow out into a realm with which they have nothing in common. The powerful ideas of substance are condensed into thoughts of time and space, which ignorance conceives as being necessary to their fruition. Thus their power is lost, and a weary round of seedtime and harvest is inaugurated to fulfill the demands of the world.

It is the mind that believes in personal possessions that limits the full idea. God's world is a world of results that sequentially follow demands. It is in this kingdom that man finds his true home. Labor has ceased for him who has found this inner kingdom. Divine supply is brought forth without laborious struggle: to desire is to have fulfillment.

This is the second step in demonstration for the one who has fully dedicated himself to the divine guidance. He immediately enters into easier experiences and more happiness than the world affords, when he covenants to follow only the good. There is an advanced degree along the same line of initiation into the mysteries of the divine. Before this step may be taken, a deeper and more thorough mental cleansing must be undergone. A higher set of faculties is then awakened within the body, and new avenues of expression are opened for the powers of the Spirit, not only in the body but also in the affairs of the individual. As he proceeds to exercise these faculties he may find some of them clogged by the crystals of dead thought that some selfish ideas have deposited, which makes him go through a fresh cleansing. If he is obedient to the Spirit and willing to follow without cavil or protest, the way is easy for him. If however he questions and argues, as did Job, he will meet many obstructions and his journey will be long and tedious.

Again, he who seeks the kingdom of substance for the sake of the loaves and fishes he may get out of it will surely be disappointed in the end. He may get the loaves and fishes, that is quite possible; but if there remains in his soul any desire to use them for selfish ends, the ultimate result will be disastrous.

Many people are seeking the aid of Spirit to heal them of their physical ills. They have no desire for the higher life, but having found their lusts and passions curtailed by physical infirmities, they want these erased in order that they may continue in their fleshly way. It is the experience of all who have dealt with Spirit that it is a vigorous bodily stimulant. It restores the vitality of the body until it is even more sensitive to pleasure or pain than it was before the spiritual quickening. This supersensitiveness makes it more susceptible and liable to more rapid waste if further indulgence is gratified. That is why those who receive spiritual treatment should be fully instructed in the Truth of Being. They should be shown that the indulgence of bodily passions is a sin against their success in every walk of life and especially in the way of finances and prosperity. If substance is dissipated, every kind of lack begins to be felt. Retribution always follows the indulgence of appetite and passion for mere sensation. Both sinners and saints suffer in this valley of folly. The alternative is to dedicate yourself to the Father's business. Make a definite and detailed covenant with the Father, lay your desires, appetites, and passions at His feet and agree to use all your substance in the most exalted way. Then you are seeking the kingdom, and all things else shall be added unto you.

We want to make this substance that faith has brought to our mind enduring and abiding, so that we do not lose it when banks fail or men talk of "hard times." We must have in our finances a consciousness of the permanency of the omnipresent substance as it abides in us. Some wealthy families succeed in holding their wealth while others dissipate it in one generation because they do not have the consciousness of abiding substance. For many of us there is either a feast or a famine in the matter of money and we need the abiding consciousness. There is no reason why we should not have a continuous even flow of substance both in income and outgo. If we have freely received we must also freely give and keep substance going, confident in our understanding that our supply is unlimited and that it is always right at hand in the omnipresent Mind of God.

In this understanding we can stand "the slings and arrows of outrageous fortune," depressions, losses, and financial failures and still see God as abundant substance waiting to come into manifestation. That is what Paul meant by taking up "the whole armor of God that ye may be able to withstand in the evil day," The substance that has in the past been manifest in our affairs is still here. It is the same substance and it cannot be taken away. Even though there seems to be material lack, there is plenty of substance for all. We are standing in the very midst of it. Like the fish we might ask, "Where is the water," when we live and move and have our being in it. It is in the water, in the air everywhere, abounding, glorious spiritual substance. Take that thought and hold it. Refuse to be shaken from your spiritual stand in the very midst of God's prosperity and plenty, and supply will begin to come forth from the ether and plenty will become more and more manifest in your affairs.

Jesus was so charged with spiritual substance that when the woman touched His garment the healing virtue went out from it and she was healed. There were thousands of people in the crowd, but only the woman who had faith in that substance got it. It was already established in her consciousness, and she knew that her needs would be met if she could make the contact. In this there is a lesson for us. We know that strength is manifest everywhere, for we see it in the mechanical world. A great locomotive starts from the depot, moving slowly at first, but when it gains momentum it speeds down the track like a streak. Thus it is with spiritual strength. Beginning sometimes with a very small thought, it takes on momentum and eventually becomes a powerful idea. Every one of us can strengthen his hold on the thought of divine substance until it becomes a powerful idea, filling the consciousness and manifesting itself as plenty in all our affairs.

As you lay hold of substance with your mind, make it permanent and enduring. Realize your oneness with it. You are unified with the one living substance, which is God, your all-sufficiency. From this substance you were created; in it you live and move and have your being; by it you are fed and prospered.

The spiritual substance is steadfast and immovable, enduring. It does not fluctuate with market reports. It does not decrease in "hard times" nor increase in "good times." It cannot be hoarded away to cause a deficiency in supply and a higher price. It cannot be exhausted in doles to meet the needs of privation. It is ever the same, constant, abundant, freely circulating and available.

The spiritual substance is a living thing, not an inanimate accumulation of bread that does not satisfy hunger nor water that fails to quench thirst. It is living bread and living water, and he that feeds on God's substance shall never hunger and never thirst. The substance is an abiding thing, not a bank deposit that can be withdrawn nor a fortune that can be lost. It is an unfailing principle that is as sure in its workings as the laws of mathematics. Man can no more be separated from his supply of substance than life can be separated from its source. As God permeates the universe and life permeates every cell of the body, so does substance flow freely through man, free from all limit or qualification.

In the new era that is even now at its dawn we shall have a spirit of prosperity. This principle of the universal substance will be known and acted on, and there will be no place for lack. Supply will be more equalized. There will not be millions of bushels of wheat stored in musty warehouses while people go hungry. There will be no overproduction or underconsumption or other inequalities of supply, for God's substance will be recognized and used by all people. Men will not pile up fortunes one day and lose them the next, for they will no longer fear the integrity of their neighbors nor try to keep their neighbor's share from him.

Is this an impractical Utopia? The answer depends on you. Just as soon as you individually recognize the omnipresent substance and put your faith in it, you can look for others around you to do the same. "A little leaven leaveneth the whole lump," and even one life that bears witness to the truth of the prosperity law will quicken the consciousness of the whole community.

Whoever you are and whatever your immediate need, you can demonstrate the law. If your thoughts are confused, become still and know. Be still and know that you are one with the substance and with the law of its manifestation. Say with conviction:

I am strong, immovable Spirit substance.

This will open the door of your mind to an inflow of substance-filled ideas. As they come, use them freely. Do not hesitate or doubt that they will bring results. They are God's ideas given to you in answer to your prayer and in order to supply your needs. They are substance, intelligent, loving, eager to manifest themselves to meet your need.

God is the source of a mighty stream of substance, and you are a tributary of that stream, a channel of expression. Blessing the substance increases its flow. If your money supply is low or your purse seems empty, take it in your hands and bless it. See it filled with the living substance ready to become manifest. As you prepare your meals bless the food with the thought of spiritual substance. When you dress, bless your garments and realize that you are being constantly clothed with God's substance. Do not center your thought on yourself, your interests, your gains or losses, but realize the universal nature of substance. The more conscious you become of the presence of the living substance the more it will manifest itself for you and the richer will be the common good of all.

Do not take anyone's word for it, but try the law for yourself. The other fellow's realization of substance will not guarantee your supply. You must become conscious of it for yourself. Identify yourself with substance until you make it yours; it will change your finances, destroy your fears, stop your worries, and you will soon begin to rejoice in the ever-present bounty of God.

Be still and turn within to the great source. See with the eye of faith that the whole world is filled with substance. See it falling all about you as snow-flakes of gold and silver and affirm with assurance:

Jesus Christ is now here raising me to His consciousness of the omnipresent, all-providing God substance, and my prosperity is assured.

I have unbounded faith in the all-present spiritual substance increasing and multiplying at my word.

LESSON 2

Spiritual Mind, the Omnipresent Directive Principle of Prosperity

Everything that appears in the universe had its origin in mind. Mind evolves ideas, and ideas express themselves through thoughts and words. Understanding that ideas have a permanent existence and that they evolve thoughts and words, we see how futile is any attempted reform that does not take them into consideration. This is why legislation and external rules of action are so weak and transient as reforms. Ideas generate thought currents, as a fire under a boiler generates steam. The idea is the most important factor in every act and must be given first place in our attention if we would bring about any results of a permanent character. Men formulate thoughts and thoughts move the world.

Ideas are centers of consciousness. They have a positive and a negative pole and generate thoughts of every conceivable kind. Hence a man's body, health, intelligence, finances, in fact everything about him, are derived from the ideas to which he gives his attention.

Man has never had a desire that could not somewhere, in the providence of God, be fulfilled. If this were not true, the universe would be weak at its most vital point. Desire is the onward impulse of the ever-evolving soul. It builds from within outward and carries its fulfillment with it as a necessary corollary.

All is mind. Then the things that appear must be expressions of mind. Thus mind is reality, and it also appears as phenomena. The is-ness of mind is but one side of it. Being is not limited to the level of is-ness; it has all possibilities, including that of breaking forth from its inherencies into the realm of appearances. Mind has these two sides, being and appearance, the visible and the invisible. To say that mind is all and yet deny that things do appear to have any place in the allness is to state but half the truth.

An idea is capable of statement as a proposition. The statement is made in response to a desire to know experimentally whether the proposition is capable of proof. A number of elements are involved in the statement of a proposition that are not integral parts of the proposition itself but necessary to its working out. In the simplest mathematical problem processes are used that are not preserved after the problem is solved yet that are necessary to its solution. The figures by the use of which we arrived at the solution are immediately forgotten, but they could not be dispensed with and it is to them we owe the outcome. The exact outcome of each step in the solution is a matter of experiment. The intermediate steps may be changed or retracted many times, but ultimately the problem is solved and the fulfillment of the desired result attained. If this is true of the simplest problem in arithmetic it is equally true of the creation of the universe. "As above, so below." Here is where many who have caught sight of the perfection and wholeness of the ideal fail to demonstrate. They deny the appearance because it does not express perfection in its wholeness.

The student in the depths of a mathematical problem who should judge thus would erase all his figures because the answer was not at once apparent, though he may have already completed a good part of the process leading up to the desired answer. We would not say that a farmer is wise who cuts down his corn in the tassel because it does not show the ripened ears. Do not jump to conclusions. Study a situation carefully in its various aspects before you decide. Consider both sides, the visible and the invisible, the within and the without.

The very fact that you have an ideal condition or world in your mind carries with it the possibility of its fulfillment in expression. Being cannot shirk expression. To think is to express yourself, and you are constantly thinking. You may deny that the things of the outer world have existence, yet as long as you live in contact with them you are recognizing them. When you affirm being and deny the expression of being, you are a "house divided against itself."

We have all wondered why we do not understand more truth than we do or why it is necessary to understand at all, since God is all-wise and all-present. Understanding is one of the essential parts of your I AM identity. Man is a focal point in God consciousness and expresses God. Therefore he must understand the processes that bring about that expression. Infinite Mind is here with all its ideas as a resource for man, and what we are or become is the result of our efforts to accumulate in our own consciousness all the attributes of infinite Mind. We have learned that we can accumulate ideas of power, strength, life, love, and plenty. How should we use these ideas or bring them into outer expression without understanding? Where shall we get this understanding save from the source of all ideas, the one Mind? "But if any of you lacketh wisdom, let him ask of God, who giveth to all liberally and upbraideth not; and it shall be given him."

In following the principles of mathematics we use rules. There is a rule of addition that we must observe when we add; other rules that must be followed when we subtract or multiply. The ideas of Divine Mind can only be expressed when we follow the rules or laws of mind, and these rules require understanding if we would follow them intelligently and achieve results. Man is given all power and authority over all the ideas of infinite Mind, and the idea of wisdom is one of them.

Closely associated with the idea of wisdom in Divine Mind is the idea of love. These ideas are the positive and the negative pole of the creative Principle. "Male and female created he them." The ideas of God-Mind are expressed through the conjunction of wisdom and love. God commanded that these two ideas should be fruitful and multiply and replenish the whole earth with thoughts in expression.

We have access to the divine realm from which all thoughts are projected into the world. We are constantly taking ideas from the spiritual world and forming them into our own conception of the things we desire. Sometimes the finished product does not satisfy or please us. That is because we have taken the idea away from its true parents, wisdom and love, and let it grow to maturity in an atmosphere of error and ignorance.

In the matter of money or riches we have taken the idea of pure substance from the spiritual realm, then have forgotten the substance idea and tried to work it out in a material atmosphere of thought. It was a wonderful idea, but when we took it away from its spiritual parents, wisdom and love, it became an unruly and disappointing child. Even if without love and understanding of substance you accumulate gold and silver, your store will not be stable or permanent. It will fluctuate and cause you worry and grief. There are many people who "don't know the value of a dollar," with whom money comes and goes, who are rich today and poor tomorrow. They have no understanding of the substance that is the underlying reality of all wealth.

To have adequate supply at all times, an even flow that is never enough to become a burden yet always enough to meet every demand, we must make union with the Spirit that knows how to handle ideas as substance. Men have the idea that material substance is limited, and they engage in competition trying to grab one another's money. Divine Mind has ideas of substance as unlimited and everywhere present, equally available to all. Since man's work is to express substance ideas in material form, we must find a way to connect ideas of substance with ideas of material expression, to adjust the ideas of man's mind with the ideas of Divine Mind. This is accomplished by faith through prayer.

That part of the Lord's Prayer which reads, "Give us this day our daily bread," is more correctly translated, "Give us today the substance of tomorrow's bread." By prayer we accumulate in our mind ideas of God as the substance of our supply and support. There is no lack of this substance in infinite Mind. Regardless of how much God gives, there is always an abundance left. God does not give us material things, but Mind substance—not money but ideas—ideas that set spiritual forces in motion so that things begin to come to us by the application of the law.

It may be that you solve your financial problem in your dreams. Men often think over their problems just before going to sleep and get a solution in their dreams or immediately upon awakening. This is because their minds were so active on the intellectual plane that they could not make contact with the silent inner plane where ideas work. When the conscious mind is stilled and one makes contact with the superconsciousness, it begins to show us how our affairs will work out or how we can help to bring about the desired prosperity.

This is the law of mind. The principle is within each one of us, but we must be spiritually quickened in life and in understanding before we can successfully work in accord with it. However we must not discount the understanding of the natural man. The mind in us that reasons and looks to the physical side of things has also the ability to look within. It is the door through which divine ideas must come. Jesus, the Son of man, called Himself "the door" and "the way." It is the divine plan that all expression or demonstration shall come through this gateway of man's mind. But above all this are the ideas that exist in the primal state of Being, and this is the truth of which we must become conscious. We must become aware of the source of our substance. Then we can diminish or increase the appearance of our supply or our finances, for their appearance depends entirely on our understanding and handling of the ideas of substance.

The time is coming when we shall not have to work for things, for our physical needs in the way of food and clothing, because they will come to us through the accumulation of the right ideas in our mind. We will begin to understand that clothing represents one idea of substance, food another, and that every manifest thing is representative of an idea.

In the 2d chapter of Genesis this living substance is called "dust of the ground" in the Hebrew, and Adam was formed from it. We find that the elemental substance is in our body. The kingdom of the heavens or the kingdom of God is within man. It is a kingdom of substance and of Mind. This Mind interpenetrates our mind and our mind interpenetrates and pervades our body. Its substance pervades every atom of our body. Are you giving it your attention, or do you still look to outer sources for supply? Are you meditating and praying for an understanding of this omnipresent substance? If you are, it will come, and it will demonstrate prosperity for you. When it does, you are secure, for nothing can take that true prosperity from you. It is the law that does not and cannot fail to operate when once set in operation in the right way.

This law of prosperity has been proved time and time again. All men who have prospered have used the law, for there is no other way. Perhaps they were not conscious of following definite spiritual methods, yet they have in some way set the law in operation and reaped the benefit of its unfailing action. Others have had to struggle to accomplish the same things. Remember that Elijah had to keep praying and affirming for a long time before he demonstrated the rain. He sent his servant out the first time, and there was no sign of a cloud. He prayed and sent him out again and again with the same result, but at last, after repeated efforts, the servant said he saw a little cloud. Then Elijah told them to prepare for rain, and the rain came. This shows a continuity of effort that is sometimes necessary. If your prosperity does not become manifest as soon as you pray and affirm God as your substance, your supply, and your support, refuse to give up. Show your faith by keeping up the work. You have plenty of Scripture to back you up. Jesus taught it from the beginning to the end of His ministry and demonstrated it on many occasions. Many have done the same thing in His name.

Jesus called the attention of His followers to the inner realm of mind, the kingdom of God substance. He pointed out that the lilies of the field were gloriously clothed, even finer than Solomon in all his glory. We do not have to work laboriously in the outer to accomplish what the lily does so silently and beautifully. Most of us rush around trying to work out our problems for ourselves and in our own way, with one idea, one vision: the material thing we seek. We need to devote more time to silent meditation and like the lilies of the field simply be patient and grow into our demonstrations. We should remember always that these substance ideas with which we are working are eternal ideas that have always existed and will continue to exist, the same ideas that formed this planet in the first place and that sustain it now.

A great German astronomer had worked the greater part of his life with a desire to know more about the stars. One night, quite suddenly and strangely enough—for he had given but little thought to the spiritual side of things—he broke right out into a prayer of thanksgiving because of the perfect order and harmony of the heavens. His prayer was "O God, I am thinking Thy thoughts after Thee." The soul of this man had at that moment made the contact and union with infinite Mind. But though this contact seemed to be made suddenly, it was the result of long study and the preparation of his mind and thought. Jesus expressed the same atonement with God at the moment of His supreme miracle, the raising of Lazarus. His words were "Father, I thank thee that thou heardest me. And I knew that thou hearest me always."

This gives us another side of the prosperity law. We open the way for great demonstrations by recognizing the Presence and praising it, by thanking the Father for Spiritual quickening. We quicken our life by affirming that we are alive with the life of Spirit; our intelligence by affirming our oneness with divine intelligence; and we quicken the indwelling, interpenetrating substance by recognizing and claiming it as our own. We should meditate in this understanding and give sincere thanks to the God of this omnipresent realm of ideas because we can think His thoughts after Him. We can thank the Father that His thoughts are our thoughts and that our natural mind is illumined by Spirit. We can illumine our mind any time by affirming this thought.

I thank Thee, Father, that I think Thy thoughts after Thee and that my understanding is illumined by Spirit.

Spiritual thoughts are infinite in their potentiality, each one being measured by the life, intelligence, and substance with which it is expressed. The thought is brought into expression and activity by the word. Every word is a thought in activity, and when spoken it goes out as a vibratory force that is registered in the all-providing substance.

The mightiest vibration is set up by speaking the name *Jesus Christ.* This is the name that is named "far above all rule, and authority," the name above all names, holding in itself all power in heaven and in earth. It is the name that has power to mold the universal substance. It is at one with the Father-Mother substance, and when spoken it sets forces into activity that bring results. "Whatsoever ye shall ask of the Father in my name, he may give it to you." "If ye shall ask anything in my name, that will I do." There could be nothing simpler, easier, or freer from conditions in demonstrating supply. "Hitherto [before the name *Jesus Christ* was given to the world] have ye asked nothing in my name: ask, and ye shall receive, that your joy may be made full."

The sayings of Jesus were of tremendous power because of His consciousness of God. They raised the God ideal far above what had ever before been conceived. These ideas so far transcended the thought plane of the people that even some of the disciples of Jesus would not accept them, and they "walked no more with him." Until fairly recent times most men have failed to grasp the lesson of the power of the spoken word expressing spiritual ideas. Jesus has never been taken literally, else men would have sought to overcome death by keeping His sayings. Few have taken His words in full faith, not only believing them but so saturating their minds with them that they become flesh of their flesh and bone of their bone, being incarnated in their very bodies, as Jesus intended.

The secret of demonstration is to conceive what is true in Being and to carry out the concept in thought, word, and act. If I can conceive a truth, there must be a way by which I can make that truth apparent. If I can conceive of an inexhaustible supply existing in the omnipresent ethers, then there is a way by which I can make that supply manifest. Once your mind accepts this as an axiomatic truth it has arrived at the place where the question of processes begins to be considered.

No one ever fully sees the steps that he must take in reaching a certain end. He may see in a general way that he must proceed from one point to another, but all the details are not definite unless he has gone over the same ground before. So in the demonstration of spiritual powers as they are expressed through man, we must be willing to follow the directions of someone who has proved his understanding of the law by his demonstrations.

We all know intuitively that there is something wrong in a world where poverty prevails and we would not knowingly create a world in which a condition of poverty exists. Lack of any kind is not possible in all God's universe. So when there is an appearance of poverty anywhere, it is our duty to deny it. Sorrow and suffering accompany poverty, and we wish to see them all blotted out. This desire is an index pointing the way to their disappearance. As the consciousness of the kingdom of heaven with its abundant life and substance becomes more and more common among men, these negative conditions will fade out of seeming existence.

Jesus said that all things should be added to those who seek the kingdom of heaven. We do not have to wait until we have fully entered the kingdom or attained a complete understanding of Spirit before prosperity begins to be manifest, but we do have to seek, to turn the attention in that direction. Then things begin to be added unto us. Thousands of people are proving the law in this age. They accept the promise of the Scriptures and are looking to God to supply their every need. In the beginning of their seeking they may have little to encourage them to believe that they will be provided for or helped along any particular line. But they carry out the command to seek and in faith act just as though they were receiving, and gradually there opens up to them new ways of making a living. Sometimes avenues are opened to them to which they are strangers, but they find pleasant experience and are encouraged to continue seeking the kingdom of God and rejoicing in its ever-increasing bounty.

Many such people today are wisely using their one talent. They may not have seen the holy of holies in the inner sanctuary, but they are getting closer to it. This is the step we must all take: begin to seek this kingdom of God's substance. Trust in the promise and see the result in the mental currents that are set in motion all about us. You may not be able to see at just what point success began, or what separate word of allegiance to the Father first took effect, but as the weeks or months go by you will observe many changes taking place in your mind, your body, and your affairs. You will find that your ideas have broadened immensely, that your little limited world has been transformed into a big world. You will find your mind more alert and you will see clearly where you were in doubt before, because you have begun thinking about realities instead of appearances. The consciousness of an omnipotent hand guiding all your affairs will establish you in confidence and security, which will extend to the body welfare and surroundings. There will be a lessening or entire absence of prejudice and faultfinding in you. You will be more forgiving and more generous and will not judge harshly. Other people will feel that there has been a change in you and will appreciate you more, showing it in many ways. Things will be coming your way, being added unto you indeed according to the promise.

All this is true not only of your own affairs. The effects extend also to those with whom you come in contact. They will also become more prosperous and happy. They may not in any way connect their improvement with you or your thoughts, but that does not affect the truth about it. All causes are essentially mental, and whoever comes into daily contact with a high order of thinking must take on some of it. Ideas are catching, and no one can live in an atmosphere of true thinking, where high ideas are held, without becoming more or less inoculated with them.

Do not expect miracles to be performed for you, but do expect the law with which you have identified yourself to work out your problem by means of the latent possibilities in and around you. Above all, *be yourself.* Let the God within you express Himself through you in the world without.

"Ye are gods,
And all of you sons of the Most High."

The idea of God covers a multitude of creative forces. In this case you are working to bring prosperity into your affairs. Hence you should fill your mind with images and thoughts of an all-providing all-supplying Father. The ancient Hebrews understood this. They had seven sacred names for Jehovah, each one of which represented some specific idea of God. They used the name *Jehovah-jireh* when they wished to concentrate on the aspect of substance. It means "Jehovah will provide," the mighty One whose presence and power provides, regardless of any opposing circumstance. To quicken the consciousness of the presence of God the Hebrews used the name *Jehovah-shammah* which means "Jehovah is there," "the Lord is present." Realize the Lord present as creative mind, throbbing in the ether as living productiveness.

Charge your mind with statements that express plenty. No particular affirmation will raise anyone from poverty to affluence, yet all affirmations that carry ideas of abundance will lead one into the consciousness that fulfills the law. Deny that lack has any place or reality in your thought or your affairs and affirm plenty as the only appearance. Praise what you have, be it ever so little, and insist that it is constantly growing larger.

Daily concentration of mind on Spirit and its attributes will reveal that the elemental forces that make all material things are here in the ether awaiting our recognition and appropriation. It is not necessary to know all the details of the scientific law in order to demonstrate prosperity. Go into the silence daily at a stated time and concentrate on the substance of Spirit prepared for you from the foundation of the world. This opens up a current of thought that will bring prosperity into your affairs. A good thought to hold in this meditation is this:

The invisible substance is plastic to my abundant thought, and I am rich in mind and in manifestation.

LESSON 3

Faith in the Invisible Substance, the Key to Demonstration

In this lesson we are considering the subject of faith especially as it applies to the demonstration of prosperity. In this study, as in all others, we must start in the one Mind. God had faith when He imaged man and the universe and through His faith brought all things into being. Man, being like God, must also base his creations on faith as the only foundation. Here then is our starting point in building a prosperity consciousness and making our world as we would have it. We all have faith, for it is innate in every man. Our question is how we may put it to work in our affairs.

Jesus gave us our best understanding of faith when He described Peter as a "rock" and asserted that His church, the ecclesia or "called-out ones," was to be built up with this rock or faith as its sure foundation. In this sense faith represents substance, the underlying, basic principle of all manifestation. "Now faith is assurance of *things* hoped for, a conviction of things not seen."

It is quite possible to possess a reality that cannot be seen, touched, or comprehended by any of the outer senses. It is faith when we are fully conscious of "things not seen" and have the "assurance of *things*" not yet manifest. In other words, faith is that consciousness in us of the reality of the invisible substance and of the attributes of mind by which we lay hold of it. We must realize that the mind makes real things. "Just a thought" or "just a mere idea," we sometimes lightly say, little thinking that these thoughts and ideas are the eternal realities from which we build our life and our world.

Faith is the perceiving power of the mind linked with a power to shape substance. You hear of a certain proposition that appeals to you and you say, "I have faith in that proposition." Some man whose character seems right is described to you and you say, "I have faith in that man." What do you mean by having faith? You mean that certain characteristics of men or things appeal to you, and these immediately begin a constructive work in your mind. What is that work? It is the work of making the proposition or man real to your consciousness. The character and attributes of the things in your mind become substantial to you because of your faith. The office of faith is to take abstract ideas and give them definite form in substance. Ideas are abstract and formless to us until they become substance, the substance of faith.

A very important work in soul culture is the establishment of a faith substance. Once we discern this law of soul building by faith, we find the Hebrew Scriptures full of illustrations of it. The 1st chapter of Luke's Gospel tells us how Elisabeth and Zacharias were told by an angel that they would have a son and that his name would be John. Zacharias was burning incense at the altar in the exercise of his duties as a priest. This means that when the mind is looking toward Spirit, even if it be in a blind way, and is seeking spiritual things, it will become spiritualized. The burning of incense typifies spiritualization. Zacharias represents the perceptive and Elisabeth the receptive qualities of the soul. When these two work in conjunction in prayer, meditation, and aspiration, the soul is open to the higher thoughts or angels that bring the promise of a new and definite state of consciousness. Zacharias doubted the promise of a son because his wife was past the age of childbearing, and because of his doubts he was stricken dumb. This means that when we perceive spiritual Truth and doubt it, we retard its outer expression; it cannot be spoken into manifestation through us because of our doubt. All the growth is then thrown upon the soul. Elisabeth "hid herself five months," but when the soul begins to feel the presence of the new ego or new state of consciousness, then we again come into faith expression: the speech of Zacharias is restored.

It was the same way in the bringing forth of Jesus. A promise was first made to Mary, and Joseph was assured that the child was the offspring of the Holy Spirit. This represents a still higher step in the work of faith. The bringing forth of John the Baptist is the intellectual perception of Truth. The intellect grasps Truth first. The next step is the bringing forth of substance and life in the subconsciousness. When we have given ourselves entirely to Spirit, we may do things without knowing exactly why. That is because faith is at work in us, and even if we do not know the law and cannot explain faith to the outer consciousness, it continues to do its perfect work and eventually brings forth the demonstration.

Do not fear the power that works out things in the invisible. When you get a strong perception of something that your inner mind tells you is true and good, act on it and your demonstration will come. That is the way a living faith works, and it is the law of your creative word.

Faith can also have understanding added to it. We call our spiritual faculties out of our subconsciousness. When Jesus did some of His most remarkable works He had with Him Peter, James, and John; Peter represents faith, James wisdom or judgment, and John love. These three faculties when expressed together in mind accomplish apparent miracles. You have called out faith in things spiritual, you have faith in God, and you have cultivated your unity with the one Mind; if you then use spiritual judgment and do your work in love, you have become "a teacher in Israel."

In order to have understanding of the law through which we gain or lose in the use of the invisible substance, we must use discrimination or judgment. There is a guiding intelligence always present that we can lay hold of and make our own. It is ours. It belongs to us and it is our birthright both to know it and to use it. Some metaphysicians mistakenly think that they must have hard experiences in order to appreciate the better things of life. They think poverty is a blessing because it educates people to the appreciation of plenty when they get it. They say that it is God's will for us to have some hard times and some good times, feasts and famines. This is not logically true when you consider God as principle. If you think of God as a man who arbitrarily gives or withholds by the exercise of His personal will, you might reach such a conclusion. But God is changeless, and if He gives one moment He will continue to give eternally. It is His nature to give, and His nature is eternally the same. When you talk of hard times, famines, lack, you are talking of something that has no place in the Mind of God. You are not acknowledging God in all your ways but are acknowledging error and affirming that the world has its source in outer things. You must turn around and get into this consciousness, that in Mind, in Spirit, there is abundance.

We often wonder how Jesus could multiply the five loaves and two fishes to meet the hunger of five thousand persons. It was done through a thorough understanding of this law. The five loaves represent the five-sense application of divine substance. The two fishes represent the yeast or multiplying power put into the substance, the source of the increase. We are told that if the yeast of a single setting of bread were allowed to increase, it would fill a space larger than this planet. This shows that there is no limit to the increasing power of elemental substance. It is for us to use as Jesus used this power. It was not a miracle but something that we all have within us as an unawakened ability and that we can learn to develop and use as Jesus did.

Jesus entered into the silence; prayed and blessed the substance at hand. If we would multiply and increase the power, substance, and life in us and at our command, we must get very still and realize that our resource is Spirit, that it *is* God, and that it is here in all its fullness. We must make contact with it in faith. Then we shall find it welling up within us. Some of you have no doubt had that experience. But if you just let it ooze away without understanding it, you get no benefit. Here is the key to this life and substance you feel when you sit in the silence. You must begin to speak these words with power and authority.

When there is world-wide belief in financial depression, lack of circulation, stagnation, things do not go as we expect and we develop fear, a belief in lack of circulation of money. But if we know the law, we do not come under this fear thought. At any time many persons make money; they use this law and take advantage of opportunity. We should bless everything that we have, for we can increase and multiply what we have by speaking words. Jesus said that His words were spirit and life. Did you ever think that your word is charged with great spiritual life force? It is. Be careful of your words. Man shall be held accountable for his lightest word. If you talk about substance in a negative way, your finances will be decreased, but if you talk about it in an appreciative, large way, you will be prospered.

If we could release the energy in the atoms the scientists tell us about, we could supply the world. This power lies within every one of us. We can begin by freeing the little ideas we have and making them fill the world with thoughts of plenty. We must realize that all power is given to us in heaven and in earth, as Jesus said. He told His apostles that they should receive power when the Holy Spirit had come upon them. They were told to go up into that upper room, in the crown of the head, where spiritual forces begin the formation of new ideas. After you get into the spiritual consciousness and receive the quickening, speak the word with authority and power, concentrating the attention at the power center in the throat. We find it effective to speak the words aloud and then sink back to "the other side" (Galilee), as Jesus often did, to rest and speak them again silently. You can send forth this vibratory energy of Spirit and break down the inertia caused by thoughts of fear and lack, carve out ways, open new avenues to the demonstration of your good.

To bring forth these undeveloped spiritual qualities we must believe in them. "For he that cometh to God must believe that he is." Lord, keep us from unbelief, from leaning on the things we see, from judging according to appearances.

You can conjure up in your mind a thousand imaginary things that will seem real to you. This shows that the mind creates by forming things according to its ideas. The world is awakening in a wonderful way to the truth about the creative power of the mind. Everywhere people are studying psychology or soul culture. The imagination builds things out of the one substance. If you will associate faith with it in its creative work, the things you make will be just as real as those that God makes. Whatever you make in mind and really put faith in will become substantial. Then you must be constantly on your guard as to what you believe, in order that you may bring what is for your good into manifestation.

In what do you have faith? In outer things? If so, you are building shadows without substance, shadows that cease as soon as your supporting thought is withdrawn from them, forms that will pass away and leave you nothing. If you would demonstrate true prosperity, you must turn from things and, as Jesus told His disciples, "have faith in God." Do not have faith in anything less than God, in anything other than the one Mind, for when your faith is centered there, you are building for eternity. Mind and the ideas of Mind will never pass away. There will never be an end to God. There will never be an end to Truth, which God is. There will never be an end to substance, which God is. Build with the divine substance, cultivate faith in realities and "lay up for yourselves treasures in heaven."

The foundation of every work is an idea. Faith *is* that quality of mind which makes the idea stand out as real, not only to ourselves but to others. When others have faith in the thing you are doing, making, or selling, they see it as real and worth while. Then your success and your prosperity are assured. Only that exists in whose becoming really visible or valuable you have great faith. If you say and believe, *"I have faith in the substance of God working in and through me to increase and bring abundance into my world,"* your faith will start to work mightily in the mind substance and make you prosperous. Whatever you put into substance along with faith will work out in manifestation in your world. We have seen it done and we have proved the law too many times to have any doubt.

The Scriptures are filled with illustrations of this activity of bringing things to pass through faith in substance. The characters of whom we read in the Scriptures represent ideas carrying forward their work in human souls. If we think that they existed only as people of thousands of years ago, we put our faith back thousands of years, instead of letting it work for us this minute in our everyday affairs of life. To demonstrate as Jesus did we must put our faith in the one substance and say, "*I have faith in God.*"

You demonstrate prosperity by an understanding of the prosperity law and by having faith in it, not by appealing to the sympathy of others, trying to get them to do something for you or give you something. Faithfulness and earnestness in the application of the prosperity law will assure you of success.

"Every good gift and every perfect gift is from above, coming down from the Father of lights, with whom can be no variation, neither shadow that is cast by turning."

"In all thy ways acknowledge him,
And he will direct thy paths."

Let us all know that just now we are in the very presence of creative Mind, the Mind that made the universe and everything in it. This Mind is here and at work right now as much as it ever was or ever will be. When we fully realize this, we increase the activity of Mind in us immeasurably. You must realize that God is Spirit and that Spirit is very real and powerful, and by far the most substantial thing in all the world.

It may be hard for those who have become attached to material things to realize that there is an invisible real life and substance that is much more substantial and real than the material. The men of science tell us that the invisible forces have a power that *is* millions of times more real and substantial than all the material world. When we read statements about some of the recent discoveries of science, which everyone accepts and talks about, we are truly amazed. Such statements made by religionists would be called preposterous and unbelievable. Yet religion has been making the same statements in different ways for thousands of years. Now science is helping religion by proving them.

In comparing substance and matter as regards their relative reality one scientific writer says that matter is merely a crack in the universal substance. It is universal substance that man is handling all the time with his spiritual mind. Through your thoughts you deal with the wonderful spiritual substance, and it takes form in your consciousness according to your thought about it. That is why we must hold the thought of divine wisdom and understanding: so that we may use these creative mind powers righteously. We use them all the time either consciously or unconsciously and we should use them to our advantage and blessing.

Every time you say, "I am a little short of funds," "I haven't as much money as I need," you are putting a limit on the substance in your own consciousness. Is that wisdom? You want a larger supply, not a limited supply, of substance. Therefore it is important to watch your thoughts so that the larger supply may come through your mind and into your affairs. Say to yourself, "*I am God's offspring, and I must think as God thinks. Therefore I cannot think of any lack or limitation.*" It is impossible that in this universal Mind that fills everything there can be any such thing as absence. There is no lack of anything anywhere in reality. The only lack *is* the fear of lack in the mind of man. We do not need to overcome any lack, but we must overcome the fear of lack.

This fear of lack led men to speculate in order to accumulate substance and have a lot of it stored up. This caused a still greater fear of lack in other men, and the situation grew worse and worse until it became generally believed that we must pile up the material symbols of substance for a possible lack in the future. We have tried that system and found that it fails us every time. We must learn to understand the divine law of supply and the original plan, which is that we have each day our daily bread. That is all we really want, just the amount of things we need for today's use, plus the absolute assurance that the supply for tomorrow's needs will be there when tomorrow comes. This assurance cannot be found in hoarding or piling up, as we have learned by experience. It can be had if we have faith and understand the truth about omnipresent, always available substance. Anything less than today's needs is not enough. Anything more than we need for today is a burden. Let us start with the fundamental proposition that there is plenty for you and for me and that the substance is here all the time, supplying us with every needful thing, according to our thought and word.

In the morning, immediately upon awakening, take a quiet meditative thought. A good foundation statement to hold in the silence is:

> *"Let the words of my mouth and the meditation of my heart*
> *Be acceptable in Thy sight,*
> *O Jehovah, my rock, and my redeemer."*

Think of the meaning of these words as you meditate on them. The words of your mouth and the thoughts of your heart are now and always molding the spiritual substance and bringing it into manifestation. They will not be acceptable to the Lord unless they bring into manifestation things that are true, lovely, and altogether good. After your morning meditation, when you have declared the omnipresence and the allness of the good, receive it as true and go forth to the day's activities with faith that all things needful are provided and your good must come. The soil and substance omnipresent has many names.

Jesus called it the kingdom of the heavens. Moses in Genesis named it the Garden of Eden. Science says it is the ether. We live in it as fishes live in the sea, and it lives in us and supplies us with all things according to our thoughts. When you start to your work, pause a moment and declare: *"I set God before me this day, to guide and guard, to protect and prosper me."* Or: *"The Spirit of the Lord goes before me this day and makes my way successful and prosperous."* Make this your proclamation for the day. Decree it to be so, and the Lord will bring it to pass. During the day, if a thought of lack or limitation should for a moment disturb you, banish it at once with the statement: "Jehovah is my shepherd; I shall not want."

When your mind comes around again to the subject of prosperity, realize most strongly that your prosperity comes from God. It came with you from God, from your contact with God-Mind in your silence, and your prosperity is right with you wherever you are. Supply may seem to come through outer channels, but your real success depends on your inner hold on the prosperity realization. Be thankful for supply that comes through outer channels, but do not limit God's giving to any one channel. Look unto Him and be prospered.

SOME PROSPERITY PRAYERS

I am always provided for because I have faith in Thee as my omnipresent abundance.

I have faith in Thee as my almighty resource and I trust Thee to preserve me in my prosperity.

I trust the universal Spirit of prosperity in all my affairs. I come to God because I believe that He is a rewarder of them that seek after Him.

LESSON 4

Man, the Inlet and Outlet of Divine Mind

The possessions of the Father are not in stocks and bonds but in the divine possibilities implanted in the mind and soul of every man. Through the mind of man ideas are brought into being. Through the soul of man God's wealth of love finds its expression.

It is well said that the mind is the crucible in which the ideal is transmuted into the real. This process of transformation is the spiritual chemistry we must learn before we are ready to work intelligently in the great laboratory of the Father's substance. There is no lack of material there to form what we will, and we can all draw on it as a resource according to our purpose. Wealth of consciousness will express itself in wealth of manifestation.

One who knows Principle has a certain inner security given him by the understanding of God-Mind. Our affirmations are for the purpose of establishing in our consciousness a broad understanding of the principles on which all life and existence depend. Our religion is based on a science in which ideas are related to Principle and to other ideas in a great universal Mind that works under mental laws. It is not a new religion nor a religious fad but points out the real and the true in any religion. If you know Principle, you are able to know at once whether a religion is founded on facts or has a basis of man-made ideas.

In order to demonstrate Principle we must keep establishing ourselves in certain statements of the law. The more often you present to your mind a proposition that is logical and true the stronger becomes that inner feeling of security to you. The mind of man is built on Truth and the clearer your understanding of Truth is the more substantial your mind becomes. There is a definite and intimate relation between what we call Truth and this universal substance of Being. When the one Mind is called into action in your mind by your thinking about it, it lays hold of the substance by the law of attraction or sympathy of thought. Thus the more you know about God the more successful you will be in handling your body and all your affairs. The more you know about God the healthier you will be, and of course the healthier you are the happier, more beautiful, and better you will be in every way. If you know how to take hold of the universal substance and mold it to your uses, you will be prosperous. Mind substance enters into every little detail of your daily life whether you realize the Truth or not. However, to establish yourself in a certain security in the possession and use of universal life, love, intelligence, and substance, you must get a consciousness of it by first mentally seeing the Truth.

All true action is governed by law. Nothing just happens. There are no miracles. There is no such thing as luck. Nothing comes by chance. All happenings are the result of cause and can be explained under the law of cause and effect. This is a teaching that appeals to the innate logic of our mind, yet we sometimes feel like doubting it when we see things happen that have no apparent cause. These happenings that seem miraculous are controlled by laws that we have not yet learned and result from causes that we have not been able to understand. Man does not demonstrate according to the law but according to his knowledge of the law, and that is why we must seek to learn more of it. God is law and God is changeless. If we would bring forth the perfect creation, we must conform to law and unfold in our mind, body, and affairs as a flower unfolds by the principle of innate life, intelligence, and substance.

The United States Congress establishes laws that rule the acts of all American citizens. Those who keep the laws are rewarded by the protection of the law. Congress does not see to it that men obey the laws. That is left to the executive department of the government. The same thing is true of the universal law. God has ordained the law but does not compel us to follow it. We have free will, and the manner of our doing is left entirely to us. When we know the law and work with it, we are rewarded by its protection and use it to our good. If we break the universal law, we suffer limitations, just as a convicted lawbreaker is limited to a cell or prison. The Holy Spirit is the executive official through whom Divine Mind enforces its laws.

You can see from this consideration that God has bestowed the power of Divine Mind on every man. You are using your organism, body, mind, and soul, to carry out a law that God established as a guide for all creation. If you righteously fulfill this mission, you cannot fail to get the righteous results. If you fail to live in accordance with the law—well, that is your affair. God cannot help it if you are not following the law and by it demonstrating health, happiness, prosperity, and all good. Blackstone said that law is a rule of action. So with God's law: if you follow the rules of action, you will demonstrate Truth. You will have all that God has prepared for you from the foundation of the world.

What are the rules of the law? First, God is good and all His creations are good. When you get that firmly fixed in your mind, you are bound to demonstrate good and nothing but good can come into your world. If you let in the thought that there is such a thing as evil and that you are as liable to evil as to good, then you may have conditions that conform to your idea of evil. But remember, evil and evil conditions are not recognized by Divine Mind. If you have thought of evil as a reality or as having any power over you, change your thought at once and begin to build up good brain cells that never heard about anything but good. Pray thus: *I am a child of the absolute good. God is good, and I am good. Everything that comes into my life is good, and I am going to have only the good.* Establish this consciousness and only the good will be attracted to you and your life will be a perpetual joy. I cannot tell you why this is true but I know that it is and that you can prove it for yourself to your satisfaction.

If you will start right now with the idea of universal and eternal goodness uppermost in your mind, talk only about the good, and see with the mind's eye everything and everybody as good, then you will soon be demonstrating all kinds of good. Good thoughts will become a habit, and good will manifest itself to you. You will see it everywhere. And people will be saying of you, "I know that that man is good and true. I have confidence in him. He makes me feel the innate goodness of all men." That is the way in which the one Mind expresses itself through man. It is the law. Those who live in accordance with the law will get the desired results. Those who fail to do so will get the opposite results.

The law also applies to our demonstrations of prosperity. We cannot be very happy if we are poor, and nobody needs to be poor. It is a sin to be poor. You may ask whether Jesus cited any example of poverty's being a sin? Yes. You will find it in the story of the prodigal son. That is often used as a text to preach to moral sinners, but a close study of it shows that Jesus was teaching the sin of lack and how to gain plenty. It is a wonderful prosperity lesson.

The prodigal son took his inheritance and went into a far country, where he spent it in riotous living and came to want. When he returned to his father's house he was not accused of moral shortcoming, as we should expect. Instead the father said, "Bring forth quickly the best robe and put it on him." That was a lesson in good apparel. It is a sin to wear poor clothes. This may seem to some to be rather a sordid way of looking at the teaching of Jesus, but we must be honest. We must interpret it as He gave it, not as we think it ought to be.

The next act of the father was to put a gold ring on the prodigal's finger, another evidence of prosperity. The Father's desire for us is unlimited good, not merely the means of a meager existence. The ring symbolizes the unlimited, that to which there is no end. It also represents omnipresence and omnipotence in the manifest world. When the father gave that ring to the son, he gave him the key to all life activity. It was the symbol of his being a son and heir to all that the father had. "All that is mine is thine." The Father gives us all that He has and is, omnipotence, omniscience, all love, and all substance when we return to the consciousness of His house of plenty.

"Put . . . shoes on his feet" was the father's next command to the servants. Feet represent that part of our understanding that comes into contact with earthly conditions. In the head or "upper room" we have the understanding that contacts spiritual conditions, but when we read in Scripture anything about the feet, we may know that it refers to our understanding of things of the material world.

The next thing the father did for his returned son was to proclaim a feast for him. That is not the way we treat moral sinners. We decree punishment for them; we send them to jail. But the Father gives a feast to those who come to Him for supply. He does not dole out only a necessary ration but serves the "fatted calf," universal substance and life in its fullness and richness.

The parable is a great lesson on prosperity, for it shows us that people who are dissipating their substance in sense ways are sinners and eventually fall into a consciousness of lack. It also proves that they may become lawful and prosperous again by returning to the Father-Mind. When there are so many lessons in the Bible for moral delinquents, there is no need to twist the meaning of this parable to that purpose. It is so plainly a lesson on the cause of lack and want. Jesus expressly states that the youth wasted his substance in a "far country," a place where the divine law of plenty was not realized. There is a very close relation between riotous living and want. Persons who waste their substance in sensation come to want in both physical and financial ways. If we would make the right use of the divine substance and the divine law, we must come back to the consciousness of the Father and conserve our body substance. Then health and prosperity will become naturally manifest. If we are not resourceful or secure in our use of the one divine substance, we are not secure in anything. Substance is a very important thing in our world, in fact the foundation of it. Therefore we should be secure in our understanding of it and use it according to God's law.

Then let us enter into the very Truth of Being and observe the divine law. Let us realize that our Father is always here and that we are in a "far country" only when we forget His presence. He is constantly giving us just what we will acknowledge and accept under His law. We can take our inheritance and divorce ourselves in consciousness from the Father, but we shall suffer the results, for then we shall not do things in divine wisdom and divine order, and there will be a "famine" in that land. Let us rather seek the divine wisdom to know how to handle our substance and the law of prosperity will be revealed to us. To come into this realization, declare with faith and all assurance: *The all-providing Mind is my resource, and I am secure in my prosperity.*

Primitive men did not contend for the products of nature so long as they could easily pick the fruits from the trees and sleep beneath the branches. When they began to live in caves contention arose over the best places, and the strongest were usually the victors. "Success leads to success." Those who were able to take the best did so and proved the law that "whosoever hath, to him shall be given, and he shall have abundance." This seems at first thought to be an unjust law, but it has always prevailed in the affairs of the world. Jesus, the greatest of metaphysicians, taught it as a divine law and gave it His commendation. He could not have done otherwise, for it is a righteous law that man shall have what he earns, that industry, effort, and ability be rewarded and laziness discouraged.

This law operates in every department of being. Those who seek the things that the material realm has to offer usually find them. Those who strive for moral excellence usually attain that goal. Those who aspire to spiritual rewards are also rewarded. The law is that we get what we want and work for, and all experience and history have proved it a good law. If this law were removed, world progress would cease and the race become extinct. Where there is no reward for effort, there will be no effort and society will degenerate. We may talk wisely about the inner urge, but when it has no outer field of action it eventually becomes discouraged and ceases to act.

When men evolve spiritually to a certain degree, they open up inner faculties that connect them with cosmic Mind, and attain results that are sometimes so startling that they seem to be miracle workers. What seems miraculous is the action of forces on planes of consciousness not previously understood. When a man releases the powers of his soul, he does marvels in the sight of the material-minded, but he has not departed from the law. He is merely functioning in a consciousness that has been sporadically manifested by great men in all ages. Man is greater than all the other creations of God-Mind because he has the ability to perceive and to lay hold of the ideas inherent in God-Mind and through faith bring them into manifestation. Thus evolution proceeds by man's laying hold of primal spiritual ideas and expressing them in and through his consciousness.

In the exercise of his I AM identity man needs to develop certain stabilizing ideas. One of them is continuity or loyalty to Truth. In the Scriptures and in life we have many examples of how love sticks to the thing on which it has set its mind. Nothing so tends to stabilize and unify all the other faculties of mind as love. That is why Jesus gave as the greatest commandment that we love God.

When you first begin to think of God as everywhere present substance, your mind will not adhere continuously to the idea. You will drop your attention after a while and think, "I haven't enough to meet all our bills." There you have made a break and have lost momentum in your ongoing, and you must patch it up quickly. Affirm, *"I am not going to be led astray. The old ideas are error and they are nothing. They have no power over me. I am going to stick to this proposition. God is love, the substance of my supply."*

Ruth, the Moabitish woman, became so attached to Naomi (spiritual thought) that she would not leave her but accompanied her back to Palestine. She was loyal and steadfast because of her love. What was the result of her stick-to-itiveness? She was at first a gleaner; then became the wife of a very rich man and was immortalized as one of the ancestresses of David. This lesson of abiding in our highest ideals is one that we must understand. Nothing is so important as sticking to the ideal and never giving up the work we have set out to accomplish. Affirm the law continuously and be loyal to it and you will become successful in its demonstration.

You have doubtless found that there is a spiritual law that brings into manifestation the thoughts we concentrate our attention on, a divine universal law of mind activity that is unfailing. Some adverse condition of your own thought has prevented a full demonstration. Do not let this swerve you from your loyalty to the law. You may seem to attain results very slowly, but that is the best reason for sticking closely to your ideal and not changing your mind. Be loyal to Principle and the adverse condition will break up. Then the true light will come and the invisible substance you have been faithfully affirming will begin to reveal itself to you in all its fullness of good.

Jesus stressed the idea that God has made abundant provision for all His children, even to the birds of the air and the lilies of the field. The Lord has clothed you with soul substance as gloriously as He did Solomon. But you must have faith in this all-providing substance of good and by your continuity of imagination set it to forming the things you desire. If you are persistent in working this idea in your conscious mind, it will eventually drop down into your subconscious mind and continue to work there where things take form and become manifest. Invisible substance, when your subconsciousness becomes filled with it to the overflowing point, will ooze out, as it were, into all your affairs. You will become more prosperous and successful so gradually, simply, and naturally that you will not realize that it derives from a divine source and in answer to your prayers. We must realize all the while however that whatever we put as seed into the subconscious soil will eventually bring forth after its kind and we must exercise the greatest caution so that we do not think or talk about insufficiency or allow others to talk to us about it. As we sow in mind so shall we reap in manifestation.

Some of our well-meaning friends have a way of loading us up with "hard-times" ideas that disperse this prosperity substance that we have accumulated. Sometimes even one adverse thought will cause it to escape; then we must go back and patch up the broken reservoir of substance thinking. We have to hold it in our mind in all its fullness and we should not let go of it for a minute lest the work of demonstration be delayed. When you retire at night, let your last thought be about the abundance of spiritual substance. See it filling all the house and the minds of all the people in the house. That potent thought will then sink into your subconsciousness and continue to work whether you are asleep or awake.

The law of supply is a divine law. This means that it is a law of mind and must work through mind. God will not go to the grocery and bring food to your table. But when you continue to think about God as your real supply, everything in your mind begins to awaken and to contact the divine substance, and as you mold it in your consciousness, ideas begin to come which will connect you with the visible manifestation. You first get the ideas in consciousness direct from their divine source, and then you begin to demonstrate in the outer. It is an exact law and it is scientific and unfailing. "First the blade, then the ear, then the full grain in the ear."

When you work in harmony with this universal law, every needed thing is abundantly supplied. Your part is simply to fulfill the law; that is, to keep your mind filled with mind substance, to store up spiritual substance until the mind is filled with it and it cannot help but manifest in your affairs in obedience to the law. "Whosoever hath, to him shall be given." But you are not fulfilling the law when you allow poverty-stricken thoughts to dwell in your mind. They draw other like thoughts, and your consciousness will have no room for the truth that prosperity is for you. Poverty or prosperity, it all depends on you. All that the Father has is yours, but you alone are responsible for the relationship of the Father's good to your life. Through conscious recognition of your oneness with the Father and His abundance you draw the living substance into visible supply.

Do not hesitate to think that prosperity is for you. Do not feel unworthy. Banish all thoughts of being a martyr to poverty. No one enjoys poverty, but some people seem to enjoy the sympathy and compassion they can excite because of it. Overcome any leaning in that direction and every belief that you were meant to be poor. No one is ever hopeless until he is resigned to his imagined fate. Think prosperity, talk prosperity, not in general but in specific terms, not as something for the other fellow but as your very own right. Deny every appearance of failure. Stand by your guns and affirm supply, support, and success in the very face of question and doubt, then give thanks for plenty in all your affairs, knowing for a certainty that your good is now being fulfilled in Spirit, in mind, and in manifestation.

A PROSPERITY TREATMENT

THE TWENTY-THIRD PSALM

(Revised)

The Lord is my banker; my credit is good.
He maketh me to lie down in the consciousness of omnipresent abundance;
He giveth me the key to His strongbox.
He restoreth my faith in His riches;
He guideth me in the paths of prosperity for His name's sake.

Yea, though I walk in the very shadow of debt,
I shall fear no evil, for Thou art with me;
Thy silver and Thy gold, they secure me.
Thou preparest a way for me in the presence of the collector;
Thou fillest my wallet with plenty; my measure runneth over.
Surely goodness and plenty will follow me all the days of my life,
And I shall do business in the name of the Lord forever.

LESSON 5

The Law That Governs the Manifestation of Supply

It is SAFE to say that all men are striving to fulfill the law of their being, but few have understood the law. The law is one of the most important things we can study, because only as we come to understand it and in proportion as we understand it can we comply with its requirements and demonstrate our divine possibilities through it.

In reading the Scriptures we gradually raise our consciousness of them as mere history and begin to apprehend them as setting forth the principle or law of life. We find the great Bible characters fitting into the pattern of our own consciousness, where they represent ideas. This makes the Bible a divine Book of Life rather than merely the history of a people. The idea of the law is symbolized by Moses. In our individual consciousness he is denial, the negative side of the law that precedes its affirmative expression. Moses gave the law as "Thou shalt not." Jesus represents the law in its affirmative expression "Thou shalt love the Lord thy God."

Moses could not go into the Promised Land, the four-dimensional state of consciousness, for there can be no negation there. Joshua, whose name has the same meaning as that of Jesus, entered the Promised Land and opened the way for the Children of Israel. He represents the first step in mind toward that full consciousness of the omnipresence and omnipotence of God that was attained in Jesus. Moses was the lawgiver, and Jesus was, in His own words, the fulfillment of the law.

We must begin to see this four-dimensional world within, with its innate capacity for all things. Everything is right here, all that ever was or ever could be, simply waiting to be brought forth into manifestation. The Lord has prepared a great feast and invited all of us to it, just as Jesus explained in parable. We have right here within and all around us this substance ready for our appropriation or eating. Eating is the outer symbol of mental appropriation. We begin to break bread by breaking the substance of mind, everywhere abundantly provided.

We have discovered that there is within us a life force that can be quickened into greater activity by thinking. Everyone has at some time demonstrated that he could overcome the negative condition of weakness by holding the thought of strength. Sometimes the strength follows the thought immediately, sometimes the thought must be persistently held for days or weeks. In demonstrating the law of ever-present abundance we should and do expect the same results. If the demonstration seems slow in coming, patience and persistence will win. That may be because the poverty consciousness has a tenacious hold and takes effort to be got rid of.

There is a law that governs the manifestation of supply, and we may learn that law and apply it by mental determination and faith in the logical sequences of spiritual realities. We have thought that the laws of God were mysterious and sacred, far removed from the ordinary individual, and that we had better try first to learn the laws of food, of medicine, of a thousand other secondary things. A strict metaphysician looks on all these temporal laws as secondary to the one law of God. That one law, we are told, *is* to be written in our heart, our inward parts. Then there is something within us that naturally responds to the law of God. If we accept this as true, that we know the one law by an inner intelligence and that all other laws are secondary to it, we are in a position to get results, to demonstrate prosperity.

In the natural world about us we see that everything is governed by law. We are told that the whole animal kingdom is guided by instinct. Many theories have been advanced to explain instinct in terms of material thought. Some philosophers have stated that it is something handed down from one generation to the next, incorporated in germ cells. Whether this is true or not, there is every evidence that there is a law either in or around the cells that controls their formation and duplicates the pattern laid down ages ago in Mother Eve and Father Adam. This is the law written in our inward parts, which is not a figure of speech but a recognized fact. We must look within for the law and not without. The laws we find in the outer are the secondary laws. The infinite, creative Mind has given to every one of us a key to the workings of this unfailing inner law. It is that everything we touch mentally or physically represents substance and that it is limited only by ourselves in our thought capacity. We cannot ask God for more substance, for the universe is full of it. We can and should ask for understanding to lay hold of it with our mind; that is, for an increase in our capacity. Back of the substance is the substance idea, and man is related to the cause side of this idea through his oneness with God.

You may think that you could live better and do more good if you had lots of money. Things would not be a bit better with you if you had a million dollars, unless you also had the understanding to use it for the good of yourself and others. Would you give a child a million dollars to go buy candy and ice cream for himself? We must evolve with our possessions until we get the ability to handle them. Then the law is fulfilled. The supply unfolds at the same rate as the need or ability to use substance is developed. Let us realize this law of unfolding substance and get busy to fulfill it in ourselves by developing our understanding and appreciation of it. We should pray for just as much each day as we need or can handle. "Give us this day our daily bread" is a prayer that conforms to the divine law and answers itself.

Infinite Mind has a lawful way for providing its children with supply for all their needs. Nothing is left to chance. God feeds the birds of the air and clothes the lilies of the field, and He will feed and clothe us unless we make it impossible by our refusal to accept His bounty. Paul said that the fulfilling of the law is love. That is exactly what we must do, love the Lord and love our neighbor as ourselves, and love our work. The law is there, in our inward parts, in our very heart. We know what to do. We don't have to pray or beg for God to give us anything. All we need do is to meditate quietly and affirm the presence and power of the great Giver of all, and then accept the gifts. To be true to the law is to stop looking to the without and to look within for supply. Looking to the within means fixing the mind on God as an ever-present Spirit that is also substance and power. Wrapped up within each of us is a great richness of thoughts. These thoughts are prisoners in the subconsciousness only waiting to be set free to go to work for us. They are waiting for the coming of the Son of God, who releases the prisoners and sets the captives free. This Son is now seeking expression in you; is you. Release your rich thoughts, set free your innate powers, and take from the rich substance of the Father what you will.

Through faith in the overcoming power of Jesus Christ, the sense mind will be overcome and the spiritual mind brought into control of your life and affairs. The sense mind is filled with lacks and limitations; the spiritual mind knows only limitless abundance. You are linked with the universal spiritual mind through the Christ Mind. It is through the Christ Mind that all things come to you; it is the channel to the all-mind of the Father. Make the unity of wholeness with the Christ Mind. Hold that you are master with the Master, one with the all-providing substance and that your prosperity runneth over. As you begin this process of unifying yourself consciously with the inner life and substance, it will begin to well up within you and to overflow into your affairs, so that you will be prosperous. Remain true to this inner life no matter what the outer appearance may be, and you cannot help but bring the good things of life into manifestation.

All manifest substance flows from a realm of light waves, according to the findings of modern physical science. James says, "Every good gift and every perfect gift is from above, coming down from the Father of lights." This is an exact statement of a scientific law, even to the use of the plural form of the word "lights," for as science states, one or more light particles, electrons, form the atom that is the basis of all material manifestation. God ideas then are the source of all that appears. Accept this as an absolute truth, an all-productive truth, and consciously connect your mind with the Father-Mind. Then you will begin to realize a never-failing prosperity that comes from Being itself.

The German philosopher and poet Goethe says, "The highest and most excellent thing in man is formless, and we should guard against giving it shape in anything less than noble dress." This is a recognition of the truth that man has the capacity within himself to give form to the formless substance. Jesus expressed the law by saying, "Whatsoever thou shalt bind on earth shall be bound in heaven; and whatsoever thou shalt loose on earth shall be loosed in heaven." This heaven is the realm of pure ideas in Mind. We are constantly incorporating these ideas into our mind and giving them form and shape according to our loyalty to Truth.

To every metaphysician this is a very important and very delicate process, because it is through this that we develop our soul. This soul development is often compared to the development of a photographic plate. The light puts the image on the sensitive plate in the first place, or as James says, it is a gift from "the Father of lights." There is then an image on the plate, but it is invisible and unmanifest until it goes through a developing process. Infinite Mind has imaged all its attributes in the soul of every man. But man must develop this image into the clear picture, and much of that work must be done in the dark with perfect faith in the law of manifestation. The photographer works in the darkroom, putting the plate through many processes. Sometimes the developer may make an error in some of the operations and the plate will come out with an imperfect image. So the human manifestation sometimes seems distorted, but the image of perfection imprinted by creative Mind is there. This perfect image is "Christ in you, the hope of glory."

Our body and affairs are first proofs of the development of the picture, but floating in our mind are the higher ideas, the real image to be developed. Our mind is engaged more or less in a chemical process. It is hard to find a line of demarcation between physical and mental chemistry, for they follow the same law. However what has been imaged can be brought out by the proper method of development. Whatever you image yourself as doing, you can do.

In our human understanding we have divorced this imaging power of the mind from the executive power. Now let us bring them together and unify them, for when imagination and will work together all things are possible to man. The will is symbolized in Scripture by the king. King Solomon was probably the world's richest man, and in so far as the world is concerned he was a great success. He demonstrated prosperity. He did not ask God for riches. Let us note that carefully. He asked God for wisdom, for ideas. God is mind and His gifts are not material but spiritual, not things but ideas. Solomon asked for and received the ideas and then developed them himself. Because he was wise all the world came to his court seeking wisdom and bringing riches in exchange for it. The King of Tyre brought the material he needed to build the Temple. The Queen of Sheba brought him great quantities of gold. From this we should get our cue: ask God for rich ideas (substance) and then put them to work in our affairs.

Do not hesitate to use the divine ideas that come to you, but do not forget their source or foundation. There are many people who are very active executives. The moment they get an idea they make use of it, but oftentimes they do not get far, because they forget the foundation on which such ideas rest and from which we must start to build. With a foundation of Truth, of spiritual ideas and substance we can build an enduring structure of prosperity. It will not be based on a false premise. It will stand when the rains descend and the floods come and the winds blow and beat upon it. We do not desire prosperity today and poverty tomorrow. We should seek for the steady, day-by-day realization of abundant supply.

Jesus understood and used this law of forming the formless substance by the power of imagination and will. When the woman touched the hem of His garment, some of this substance, of which He was vividly conscious, flowed from Him and healed her. He immediately remarked that someone had touched Him. Many had touched Him in the throng and no substance had left His body from those contacts, but the woman of faith was open to receive the healing substance and consciously appropriate it. This proved her faith, and Jesus told her to be of good cheer, for her faith had made her whole. The same substance was available to others who crowded against Him, but only the one who recognized it and laid hold of it received. Even so you and I shall receive no benefit, although substance is everywhere around us and in us, unless we recognize its presence by faith and lay hold of it by the hem of its garment (outer expression).

Jesus recognized the omnipresence of substance when He laid hold of it to multiply the loaves and the fishes. He dwelt in a consciousness of it at all times. Once He told the apostles when they asked Him to eat, "I have meat to eat that ye know not of." He built this divine substance into His body, cell by cell, replacing the mortal flesh with the spiritual substance, until His whole body was immortalized. He demonstrated it and told us how it was done. He said, "He that believeth on me, the works that I do shall he do also; and greater works than these shall he do." Then why are so many people poor, distressed, ill, or troubled? There is a way, a law, and a wisdom to apply the law, and there is an abundance of substance waiting to be formed by each of us into whatsoever we will, when we apply that law as a son of God.

There is an inherent faculty that instinctively lays hold of what it calls its own. Even little children like to have their own toys and to keep them separate from those of other children. There is nothing to be condemned in this, for it is the natural outworking of a divine law. It proves that we know, somewhere in our deepest being, that we have been provided for from the foundation of the world and are entitled to our own portion without question. The power of the mind to draw to us those things to which we are divinely entitled is a power that can be cultivated and should be.

We are now on the verge of a new state of mind in matters financial. Let us do away with the erroneous idea that men must be poor to be righteous. Money is man's instrument, not his master. Money was made for man, not man for money. Only those who put money above man and give it power in their minds by worshiping it, are the "rich" men to whom Jesus referred in His story about the camel and the needle's eye. It is not money that controls men, but the ideas they have about money. Ideas of poverty are just as powerful to enslave men as are ideas of wealth. Every man should be taught how to handle ideas, rather than money, so that they serve him rather than have dominion over him.

Some physical scientists are telling us that the time is near when men will manufacture from the ether, right at hand, everything that they need or desire. Man will not have to wait for seedtime and harvest when he learns to use the power of his mind. When we have that consciousness in which our ideas are tangible, all our demands will be quickly fulfilled by the higher law. Throw into your ideas all the life and power of your concentrated thought, and they will be clothed with reality.

When Jesus went into the wilderness of His (then) untried mental powers He was tempted to turn stones into bread. We all have had this temptation, and most of us have succumbed to it. We get our bread out of material things (stones) instead of out of the words that proceed from the mouth of God. It is the word, the idea, that feeds the soul of man. That is admitted. But we must realize that it is the word, the idea, that feeds the body and the affairs of man also, for unless the word is recognized and appropriated, there is a lack of the true substance and there is no satisfaction in the food. Fortunately the "Father knoweth that we have need of all these things," and in His compassion and mercy He feeds us with the substance even while we still try to assimilate the stones. If we would seek first the kingdom of God, the substance, the "things" would be added and we should consciously enjoy the fullness of living, the abundant life of Jesus Christ.

There is a universal law of increase. It is not confined to bank accounts but operates on every plane of manifestation. The conscious co-operation of man is necessary to the fullest results in the working of this law. You must use your talent, whatever it may be, in order to increase it. Have faith in the law. Do not reason too much but forge ahead in faith and boldness. If you let yourself think of any person or any outer condition as hindering your increase, this becomes a hindrance to you, for you have applied the law of increase to it. Fear of it may cause you to become timid and bury your talent, which defeats the law. Keep your eyes on the abundant inner reality and do not let the outer appearance cause you to falter.

Do not give too close study to yourself or your present condition. To dwell in mind upon your seeming limitations only prolongs their stay and makes your progress slow. A child loses sight of everything but his increase in size. The boy sees himself as a larger boy, even as a man. It is the childlike mind that finds the kingdom. Then look ahead to the perfect man you are to be in the Spirit and behold yourself as the beloved son in whom the Father is well pleased.

God gives the increase, we are told in the Scripture. This is to be remembered, for we so often think that increase is the result of our personal efforts. Increase comes by the operation of a universal law, and our part is to keep that law. Use the talent of life, and it will expand wonderfully. You do this by talking about life, praising it, and giving God thanks for it. Act as though you were alive and glad to be alive and you will gain a new realization of life, an increase in life itself.

Never allow yourself to come under the control of the "I can't" man. He believes in limitations, wraps his talent in them, and hides it away in the negative earth, and no increase is possible to him. Be positive in Spirit and you will succeed. All the negative talents that are buried away in the depths of material thought can be resurrected by Spirit and made positive, put to the right use, contributing to the increase of your good. Appetite and passion, which are decreasing and destructive in the material can be made increasing and constructive when directed to the things of Spirit. "Blessed are they that hunger and thirst after righteousness: for they shall be filled."

If there is any lack apparent in man's world it is because the requirements of the law of manifestation have not been met. This law is based on mind and its operation through thoughts and words. The key to the operation of mind is symbolically set forth in the Genesis account of the six days of creation. Man's mind goes through the identical steps in bringing an idea into manifestation. Between the perception of an idea and its manifestation there are six definite, positive movements, followed by a (seventh) "day" of rest, in which the mind relaxes and sees its work in process of fulfillment.

In bringing forth a manifestation of God's abundant supply, take the first step by saying, "Let there be light"; that is, let there be understanding. You must have a clear perception of the principle back of the proposition "God will provide." The one universal, eternal, substance of God, which is the source of all, must be discerned and relied on, while dependence on material things must be eliminated from thought. So long as you depend on money alone you are worshiping a false god and have not discerned the light. You must first enter into the understanding that God, omnipresent, omnipotent, and omniscient, is the source and that you can draw on this source without limit. If you have established that light, you have begun your demonstration and can go to the second step. A "firmament" must be established; that is, a firm place in the mind, a dividing of the true from the apparent. This is done through affirmation. As you affirm God as your supply and support, your words will in due season become substance to you, the substance of faith.

The third step is the forming of this substance into tangibility. "Let the dry land appear." Out of the omnipresent substance your mind forms whatever it wants by the power of imagination. If it is food you need, see yourself as bountifully supplied with food. If you have already taken the other steps, you can picture in mind the things you desire and bring them into your manifest world. If the other steps of understanding and faith have not been taken first, there will of course be no demonstration, for above all the creative law is orderly and works by progressive steps. Many people have tried to demonstrate by visualizing and concentrating and have failed because they have put the third step first. They have not developed understanding or faith. If you work according to the law, conforming to its orderly operation as revealed in the degrees of creation, you cannot fail, because when you have fulfilled the law you have found the kingdom.

Jesus recognized order as a fundamental factor in the law of increase. When He fed the multitude He made them sit down in companies. If you study the story carefully you will see that there was a great deal of preliminary preparation before the demonstration was made. There was a recognition of the seed ideas, the loaves and fishes carried by the small boy. There was a prayer of thanks for that supply and then it was blessed. All this preceded the actual appearing and appropriation of the supply. Every demonstration is based on the same law of increase and goes through the same orderly steps.

Pray, but let your prayer be affirmative, for that is the prayer of faith. A begging prayer filled with ifs is a prayer of doubt. Keep praying until affirmations become a habit of mind. The race thought of lack must be penetrated and so charged with the truth of God's omnipresent abundance that all consciousness of lack and poverty disappears from the face of the earth. The more we trust to the simplicity and infallibility of the law the better will be our individual demonstration and the more we shall contribute to the transformation of the race thought that causes lack and famine. Those who make the greatest spiritual demonstrations are not the wise of the world but the obedient children of the law on the bosom of infinite love.

See what you need as already manifest and as yours. Do not put it off to some uncertain future time. God wants you to have it now. Remember always God's omnipresence, and if doubts come in, do not entertain them. Say: *"I trust Omnipotence." "I refuse to be anxious about tomorrow or even the next minute. I know that God does provide for the fulfillment of His divine idea, and I am that divine idea."* This divine idea is the son, the perfect man, the Christ, brought forth on the sixth day. If you would have your inheritance, you must not omit this sixth-day realization. God expresses Himself as man and works through man to bring perfection into expression.

To give up all anxiety and trust in the Lord does not mean to sit down and do nothing. "My Father worketh even until now, and I work." We are to work as God works; to work with God, as a son follows the occupation of his father. We are to form what God has created. In the 1st chapter of Genesis we see how the Father works. The various steps in His method are clearly pointed out, and we shall have results only as we faithfully follow them. Some people think of prosperity as something separate from their spiritual experience, "outside the pale" of religion. They live in two worlds: in one for six days of the week when man runs things, and in the other on the seventh day when God is given a chance to show what He can do. It is personality's demonstration when people find themselves complaining of hard times and depression, but it is not the way to demonstrate God in the fullness of all things. Do all things to the glory of God seven days a week rather than one. Take God into all your affairs. Use this thought in the silence and bring God and His law of prosperity into your affairs: *I trust Thy universal law of prosperity in all my affairs.*

LESSON 6

Wealth of Mind Expresses Itself in Riches

Prosperity, according to Webster, is an advance or gain in anything good or desirable, successful progress toward, or attainment of a desired object. Prosperity does not mean the same thing to any two persons. To the wage earner an increase of a few dollars in the weekly income may seem like wonderful prosperity, for it means an increase in the comfort and welfare of his family. The man who engages in vast enterprises reckons prosperity in larger terms, and does not consider himself prosperous unless things are coming to him in a big way. Between these extremes are many ideas of prosperity, which shows quite plainly that prosperity is not in the possession of things but in the recognition of supply and in the knowledge of free and open access to an inexhaustible storehouse of all that is good or desirable.

In the great Mind of God there is no thought of lack, and such a thought has no rightful place in your mind. It is your birthright to be prosperous, regardless of who you are or where you may be. Jesus said to all men, "Seek ye first his kingdom, and his righteousness; and all these things shall be added unto you." This does not mean that if you belong to a certain church you will be prospered, for "righteousness" is not conforming to some particular religious belief but to the law of right thinking, regardless of creed, dogma, or religious form. Get into the prosperity thought and you will demonstrate prosperity. Cultivate the habit of thinking about abundance everywhere present, not only in the forms of imagination but in forms without. Jesus did not make a separation between the two as though they were at enmity. He said, "Render therefore unto Cæsar the things that are Cæsar's; and unto God the things that are God's." Put things in their right relation, the spiritual first and the material following, each where it belongs, and render to each its own.

Realize first of all that prosperity is not wholly a matter of capital or environment but a condition brought about by certain ideas that have been allowed to rule in the consciousness. When these ideas are changed the conditions are changed in spite of environment and all appearances, which must also change to conform to the new ideas. People who come into riches suddenly without building up a consciousness of prosperity soon part from their money. Those who are born and bred to riches usually have plenty all their life even though they never make the effort to earn a dollar for themselves. This is because the ideas of plenty are so interwoven into their thought atmosphere that they are a very part of themselves. They have the prosperity consciousness, in which there is no idea of any condition under which the necessities of life could be lacking.

We are sometimes asked whether we advocate the accumulation of riches. No. The accumulation of riches, as has been explained, is futile unless it is the outgrowth of a rich consciousness. We advocate the accumulation rather of rich ideas, ideas that are useful, constructive, and of service to the well-being of all mankind. The outer manifestation of riches may follow or it may not, but the supply for every need will be forthcoming because the man of rich ideas has confidence in an all-providing power that never fails. He may not have an extra dollar, but his ideas have merit and he has confidence, a combination that cannot fail to attract the money to carry him forward. This is true riches, not an accumulation of money, but access to an inexhaustible resource that can be drawn on at any time to meet any righteous demand. When a person has this rich consciousness there is no necessity for laying up gold or accumulating stocks and bonds or other property to ensure future supply. Such a one may be most generous with his wealth without fear of depletion, because his rich ideas will keep him in constant touch with abundance. Those who have the thought of accumulating material wealth, a thought that is dominant in the world today, are unbalanced. They have a fear of the loss of riches that makes their tenure insecure. Their prosperity is based on a wrong idea of the source of riches and eventually means disaster. The sin of riches is not in the possession but in the love of money, a material selfishness that leads to soul starvation.

It is not a crime to be rich nor a virtue to be poor, as certain reformers would have us think. The sin lies in hoarding wealth and keeping it from circulating freely to all who need it. Those who put wealth into useful work that contributes to the welfare of the masses are the salvation of the country. Fortunately, there are many in this country who have the prosperity consciousness. If we were all in a poverty consciousness, famines would be as common here as they are in India or China. Millions in those lands are held in the perpetual thought of poverty and they suffer want in all its forms from the cradle to the grave. The burden of the poverty thought reacts on the earth so that year after year it withholds its products and many people starve.

Universal Mind controls all nature and is in possession of all its products. "The earth is the Lord's, and the fulness thereof" is a great Truth. Puny, personal man uses all his craft to get control of the products of nature but is always defeated in the end. Only the universal man of Spirit is in indisputed possession, and to him the Father says, "All that is mine is thine." Jesus did not have title to a foot of land and evidently had no money, for the apostles carried whatever funds the company had.

He did not even burden Himself with a tub, as did Diogenes, and "had not where to lay his head." Yet He was always provided with entertainment of the best. He took it for granted that whatever He needed was His. The fish carried His pocketbook, and the invisible ethers furnished the sideboard from which He handed out food for thousands. He was rich in every way for He had the prosperity consciousness and proved that the earth with all its fullness does belong to the Lord, whose righteous sons are heirs to and in possession of all things.

The anxious thought must be eliminated and the perfect abandon of the child of nature assumed, and when to this attitude you add the realization of unlimited resources, you have fulfilled the divine law of prosperity.

The imagination is a wonderful creative power. It builds all things out of the one substance. When you associate it with faith, you make things just as real as those that God makes, for man is a co-creator with God. Whatever you form in the mind and have faith in will become substantial. Then you should be on guard as regards what you put your faith in. If it is material forms, shadows that cease to be as soon as your supporting thought is withdrawn from them, you are building temporary substance that will pass away and leave you nothing. Put your faith in the real or, as Jesus told His disciples, "have faith in God."

The real search of all people is for God. They may think they are looking for other things, but they must eventually admit that it is God they seek. Having once felt His presence within them, they are keenly conscious that only God can satisfy. The place where we meet God should be made so sure and so pure that we can never mistake His voice or be hidden from His face. This place we know as the mind, the inmost recess of the soul, the kingdom of the heavens within us.

It is not sufficient however to sit down and hold thoughts of abundance without further effort. That is limiting the law to thought alone, and we want it to be fulfilled in manifestation as well. Cultivating ideas of abundance is the first step in the process. The ideas that come must be used. Be alert in doing whatever comes to you to do, cheerful and competent in the doing, sure of the results, for it is the second step in the fulfilling of the law.

You can do anything with the thoughts of your mind. They are yours and under your control. You can direct them, coerce them, hush them, or crush them. You can dissolve one thought and put another in its stead. There is no other place in the universe where you are the absolute master. The dominion given you as your divine right is over your own thoughts only. When you fully apprehend this and begin to exercise your God-given dominion, you begin to find the way to God, the only door to God, the door of mind and thought.

If you are fearful that you will not be provided with the necessities of life for tomorrow, next week, or next year, or for your old age, or that your children will be left in want, deny the thought. Do not allow yourself for a moment to think of something that must be outside the realm of all careful, all-providing good. You know even from your outer experience that the universe is self-sustaining and that its equilibrium is established by law. The same law that sustains all sustains you as a part. Claim your identity under that law, your oneness with the all, and rest in the everlasting arms of Cause, which knows nothing of lack. If you are in a condition of poverty, this attitude of mind will attract to you opportunities to better your condition. Insulate your mind from the destructive thoughts of all those who labor under the belief in hard times. If your associates talk about the financial stringency, affirm all the more persistently your dependence on the abundance of God.

By doing this you place yourself under a divine law of demand and supply that is never influenced by the fluctuations of the market or the opinions of men. Every time you send out a thought of wholehearted faith in the I AM part of yourself, you set in motion a chain of causes that must bring the results you seek. Ask whatsoever you will in the name of the

Christ, the I AM, the divine within, and your demands will be fulfilled; both heaven and earth will hasten to do your bidding. But when you have asked for something, be on the alert to receive it when it comes. People complain that their prayers are not answered when, if we knew the truth, they are not awake to receive the answer when it comes. If you ask for money, do not look for an angel from the skies to bring it on a golden platter, but keep your eyes open for some fresh opportunity to make money, an opportunity that will come as sure as you live.

These are some tangible steps along the way to the larger manifestation you desire. No one is ever given the keys to the Father's storehouse of wealth until he has proved his faith and his reliability. Then he may go in and pass out the goods freely. If the men of the world, with their selfish ideas of "mine and thine," were given the power, without a thorough mental cleansing, of instantly producing whatever they desire, they would undoubtedly practice still greater oppressions on their fellows, and existing conditions would not be improved.

A stonecutter sees a block of marble as so many hours work, while Michelangelo sees it as an angel that it is his privilege to bring forth. This is the difference between those who see the material world as so much matter and those who look on it with the eyes of mind and the imagination that works toward perfection. One who paints a picture or makes a piece of sculpture first sees it in his mind. He first imagines or images it. If he wants a strong picture he makes force one of the elements of his image. If he wants beauty and character, he puts love into it. He may not see the perfect picture until all these elements are combined, then it requires but little effort to transfer it from his mind to the canvas or to the marble.

On the sixth day of creation, we are told, God "imaged" His man, made him in His image and likeness. This does not mean that God looks like man, a personal being with manlike form. We make a thing in our own image, the image we have in mind for the thing, and our creation does not resemble us in any way. God is without form, for He is Spirit. God is an idea that man has tried to objectify in various forms. He is the universal substance, the life that animates the substance, and the love that binds it together. Man just naturally gives some form to every idea he has, even the idea of God, for the formative faculty of the mind is always at work whether we are awake or asleep. We get material for forming mental pictures from without and from within.

This imaging or formative power of the mind could not make anything unless it had the substance out of which to form it. One could not make a loaf of bread without the flour and other ingredients. Yet with all the ingredients at hand one could not make a loaf unless one had the power of imaging the loaf in one's mind. This seems simple, but the fact is that the power to form the loaf is less common than the available material for the loaf. Flour and water are abundant, but only certain people can use them in the right way to form a palatable loaf of bread. So with this subject of prosperity. Substance is everywhere, filling all the universe. There is no lack. If we have not been successful in forming it into the things we have needed and wished for, it is not because of lack of substance but of lack of understanding how to use our imaging power.

The world goes through periods of seeming lack because the people have refused to build their prosperity on the inner, omnipresent, enduring substance, and on the contrary have tried to base it on the substance that they see in the outer. This outer substance, formed by the imaging power of men in past ages, seems to be limited, and men struggle for it, forgetting their own divine power to form their own substance from the limitless supply within. The lesson for all of us should be to build our prosperity on the inner substance.

Those who do demonstrate prosperity through the law of men have nothing permanent. All their possessions may be swept away in a moment. They have not built on the orderly law of God, and without the rich thoughts of God's bounteousness no one can have an enduring consciousness of supply.

No disease, poverty, or any other negative condition can enter into our domain unless we invite it. Nor can it remain with us unless we entertain it. Conscious power over all such conditions is one of our greatest delights and a part of our divine inheritance, but we must learn the law and apply the power in the right way.

Men have a consciousness of lack because they let Satan, the seroent of sense, tempt them. The Garden of Eden is within us here and now, and the subtle temptation to eat of the tree of sensation is also still with us. We have been given dominion over the animal forces of the body, the "beasts of the field," and must tame them, making them servants instead of masters of the body. Instead of feeding them we must make them feed us. When we overcome the animals within, it will be easy to train them in the without. This truth of overcoming is taught all through the Scriptures, and we can demonstrate it in our life, for God has endowed us with the power to overcome. We must lay hold of that inherent power and begin to use it constructively.

The whole human family seems to be sensation mad. All our economic and social troubles can be traced right back to the selfishness of the sense man. We can never overcome these conditions in the outer until we overcome their causes in the inner soul of ourselves. There is sure to be repetition of war and peace, plenty and famine, good times and depressions until we take the control of mind substance away from the sense man and give it to the spiritual man. We know that there is a spiritual man and we look forward in some ideal way to his coming, but he will never come until we bring him. We hope and pray for the coming of better things; but as Mark Twain said about the weather, "no one does anything about it." We can do something about the matter of self-control and each of us must if we are ever to improve our condition physically and financially as well as morally and spiritually. We must lift up this serpent of sense, as Moses lifted up the serpent in the wilderness, and control it in the name of Christ.

Eliminate all negative thoughts that come into your mind. Yet do not spend all your time in denials but give much of it to the clear realization of the everywhere present and waiting substance and life. Some of us have in a measure inherited "hard times" by entertaining the race thought so prevalent around us. Do not allow yourself to do this. Remember your identity, that you are a son of God and that your inheritance is from Him. You are the heir to all that the Father has. Let the I AM save you from every negative thought. The arrows that fly by day and the pestilence that threatens are these negative race thoughts in the mental atmosphere. The I AM consciousness, your Saviour, will lead you out of the desert of negation and into the Promised Land of plenty that flows with milk and honey.

Deny that you can lose anything. Let go of negative thoughts of financial loss or any other kind of loss and realize that nothing *is* ever lost in all the universe. There are opportunities everywhere, just as there have always been, to produce all that you need financially, or otherwise. God wants you to be a producer of new ideas. New ideas come to you from within. Do not think for a moment that you are limited to the ideas that come from without. Many of those ideas are outgrown anyway and have outlived their usefulness. That is why we go through periods of change; so that old outworn ideas can be discarded and replaced with new and better ones. There have been more inventions since the beginning of the so-called depression than in any previous similar period of American history. This shows that new ideas are within man, just waiting to be called out and put into expression. We can find new ways of living and new methods of work; we are not confined to the ways and methods of the past. When we commune with the Spirit within and ask for new ideas, they are always forthcoming. When these ideas from within us are recognized, they go to work and come to the surface. Then all the thoughts we have ever had, as well as the thoughts of other people, are added to them and new things are quickly produced. Let us quit slavishly depending on someone else for everything and become producers, for only in that direction lies happiness and success. Let us begin to concentrate on this inner man, this powerful man who produces things, who gets his ideas from a higher-dimensional realm, who brings ideas from a new territory, the land of Canaan.

What kind of character are you giving to this inner substance by your thoughts? Change your thought and increase your substance in the mind, as Elisha increased the oil for the widow. Get larger receptacles and plenty of them. Even a very small idea of substance may be added to and increased. The widow had a very small amount of oil, but as the prophet blessed it it increased until it filled every vessel she could borrow from the neighbors. We should form the habit of blessing everything that we have. It may seem foolish to some persons that we bless our nickels, dimes, and dollars, but we know that we are setting the law of increase into operation. All substance is one and connected, whether in the visible or the invisible. The mind likes something that *is* already formed and tangible for a suggestion to take hold of. With this image the mind sets to work to draw like substance from the invisible realm and thus increase what we have in hand. Jesus used the small quantity of loaves and fishes to produce a great quantity of—loaves and fishes. Elisha used a small amount of oil to produce a great amount of—oil. So when we bless our money or other goods, we are complying with a divine law of increase that has been demonstrated many times.

Another step in the demonstration of prosperity is the preparation of the consciousness to receive the increase. If we pray for rain, we should be sure that we have our umbrellas with us. You read in the 3d chapter of II Kings how Elisha caused the water to come from the invisible and fill trenches in the desert. But first the trenches had to be dug in the dry ground. That required faith, but the kings had it, and they dug trenches all over a large valley, just as Elisha had commanded. It was through the understanding of Elisha, who knew the truth about the invisible substance, that this seeming miracle was accomplished. Yet the trenches had to be prepared, and you must prepare your consciousness for the inflow of the universal substance. It obeys the law of nature, just as does water or any other visible thing, and flows into the place prepared for it. It fills everything you hold in your mind, whether vessels, trenches, or your purse.

It is not advisable to hold for too specific a demand. You might visualize a hundred dollars and get it when a thousand was coming your way. Do not limit the substance, to what you think you need or want; rather broaden your consciousness and give infinite Mind freedom to work, and every good and needful thing will be provided you. Make your statements broad and comprehensive so that your mind may expand to the Infinite rather than trying to cram the Infinite into your mind.

STATEMENTS TO BROADEN THE MIND AND FILL IT WITH THE RICHNESS OF SUBSTANCE

Infinite wisdom guides me, divine love prospers me, and I am successful in everything I undertake.

In quietness and confidence I affirm the drawing power of divine love as my magnet of constantly increasing supply.

I have unbounded faith in the omnipresent substance increasing and multiplying at my word of plenty, plenty, plenty.

Father, I thank Thee for unlimited increase in mind, money, and affairs.

LESSON 7

God Has Provided Prosperity for Every Home

The Home is the heart of the nation. The heart is the love center. Love is the world's greatest attractive power. The electromagnet that lifts the ingots of steel must first be charged with the electric current, for without the current it is powerless. So the heart of man, or the home that is the heart of the nation, must be aglow with God's love; then it becomes a magnet drawing all good from every direction. God has amply provided for every home, but the provision is in universal substance, which responds only to law. Through the application of the law the substance is drawn to us and begins to work for us.

It is the law of love that we have whatsoever we desire. As a father gives his children gifts so the Lord gives to us, because of love. When we desire aright, we put our thoughts into the supermind realm; we contact God-Mind and from it draw the invisible substance that is manifest in temporal things. The substance thus becomes a part of our mind and through it of our affairs. We draw spiritual substance to ourselves just as the magnet draws the iron. When we think about the love of God drawing to us the substance necessary for support and supply, that substance begins to accumulate all around us, and as we abide in the consciousness of it, it begins to manifest itself in all our affairs.

"Perfect love casteth out fear." Fear is a great breeder of poverty, for it breaks down positive thoughts. Negative thoughts bring negative conditions in their train. The first thing to do in making a demonstration of prosperity in the home is to discard all negative thoughts and words. Build up a positive thought atmosphere in the home, an atmosphere that is free from fear and filled with love. Do not allow any words of poverty or lack to limit the attractive power of love in the home. Select carefully only those words that charge the home atmosphere with the idea of plenty, for like attracts like in the unseen as well as the seen. Never make an assertion in the home, no matter how true it may look on the surface, that you would not want to see persist in the home. By talking poverty and lack you are making a comfortable place for these unwelcome guests by your fireside, and they will want to stay. Rather fill the home with thoughts and words of plenty, of love, and of God's substance; then the unwelcome guests will soon leave you.

Do not say that money is scarce; the very statement will scare money away from you.

Do not say that times are hard with you; the very words will tighten your purse strings until Omnipotence itself cannot slip a dime into it. Begin now to talk plenty, think plenty, and give thanks for plenty. Enlist all the members of the home in the same work. Make it a game. It's lots of fun, and, better than that, it actually works.

Every home can be prosperous, and there should be no poverty-stricken homes, for they are caused only by inharmony, fear, negative thinking and speaking. Every visible item of wealth can be traced to an invisible source. Food comes from grain, which was planted in the earth; but who sees or knows the quickening love that touches the seed and makes it bear a hundredfold? An unseen force from an invisible source acts on the tiny seeds, and supply for the multitude springs forth.

The physical substance that we name earth is the visible form of a superabundant mind substance, everywhere present, pervading all things, and inspiring all things to action. When the grain or seed is put into the earth, the quickening thought of the universe causes the little life germ to lay hold of the spiritual substance all about it and what we call matter proves to be a form of mind. "There is no matter; all is mind."

Words are also seeds, and when dropped into the invisible spiritual substance, they grow and bring forth after their kind. "Do *men* gather grapes of thorns, or figs of thistles?" Farmers and gardeners choose their seed with the greatest care. They reject every defective seed they find and in this way make sure of the coming crop. To have prosperity in your home you will have to exercise the same intelligent discrimination in the choice of your seed words.

You should expect prosperity when you keep the prosperity law. Therefore, be thankful for every blessing that you gain and as deeply grateful for every demonstration as for an unexpected treasure dropped into your lap. This will keep your heart fresh; for true thanksgiving may be likened to rain falling upon ready soil, refreshing it and increasing its productiveness. When Jesus had only a small supply He gave thanks for the little He had. This increased that little into such an abundance that a multitude was satisfied with food and much was left over. Blessing has not lost its power since the time Jesus used it. Try it and you will prove its efficacy. The same power of multiplication is in it today. Praise and thanksgiving impart the quickening spiritual power that produces growth and increase in all things.

You should never condemn anything in your home. If you want new articles of furniture or new clothes to take the place of those you now have, do not talk about your present things as old or shabby. Watch your words. See yourself clothed as befits a child of the King and see your house furnished just as pleases your ideal. Thus plant in the home atmosphere the seed of richness and abundance. It will all come to you. Use the patience, the wisdom, and the assiduity that the farmer employs in planting and cultivating, and your crop will be sure.

Your words of Truth are energized and vitalized by the living Spirit. Your mind is now open and receptive to an influx of divine ideas that will inspire you with the understanding of the potency of your own thoughts and words. You are prospered. Your home is a magnet of love, drawing to it all good from the unfailing and inexhaustible reservoir of supply. Your increase comes because of your righteous application of God's law in your home.

"The blessing of Jehovah, it maketh rich;
And he addeth no sorrow therewith."

Jesus showed men how to live in rest and peace, a simple life. Where the simplicity of His teaching is received and appreciated the people change their manner of living, doing away with ostentation and getting down to the simplicity and beauty of the things that are worth while. Every summer those who feel that they can, plan to go away for a vacation and many of them enjoy a small cabin in the woods where they can live a simple and natural life close to nature. This shows that they long to let go of the burdens of conventionality and rest in touch with the real of things. The soul wearies of the wear and tear of the artificial world, and now and then it must have a season of rest. Jesus invites, "Come unto me, all ye that labor and are heavy laden, and I will give you rest."

There is a great difference between the simple life and poverty. The two have been associated in the minds of some people, and this is the reason they shun the idea of the simple life. Even those who have come into some degree of spiritual understanding sometimes put out of mind all thought of a simple manner of living, because they fear that others will think they are failing to demonstrate prosperity. In such cases those who judge should remember to "judge not according to appearance," and those who are judged should be satisfied with the praise of God rather than with the praise of men. All those who base their prosperity on possessions alone have a purely material prosperity which, though it may seem great for a time, will vanish, because it is founded on the changing of the external and has no root within the consciousness.

There is a great similarity in the homes of nearly all people who have about the same-sized incomes. Each one unconsciously follows suggestion and furnishes his home with the same sort of things as his neighbors. Here and there are exceptions. Someone is expressing his or her individuality, overcoming mass suggestion and buying the kind of furniture he really wants or that is really comfortable and useful. This free, independent spirit has much in its favor in making a prosperity demonstration. The delusion that it is necessary to be just like other people or to have as much as other people have, causes a spirit of anxiety that hinders the exercise of faith in demonstration.

The simple life does not imply poverty and it is not ascetic. It is as different from the austere as it is from wanton luxury. It is the natural, free, childlike, mode of living, and one never really knows what true prosperity is until one comes into this simplicity and independence of spirit. The simple life is a state of consciousness. It is peace, contentment, and satisfaction in the joy of living and loving, and it is attained through thinking about God and worshiping Him in spirit and in truth.

You want to learn how to demonstrate prosperity in your home by the righteous exercise of powers and faculties that God has given you. Realize in the very beginning that you do have these powers and faculties. You are in possession of everything necessary for the demonstration of prosperity and can undertake it with the utmost confidence and faith. You can draw on the omnipresent substance throughout all eternity, yet it will never grow less, for it consists of ideas. Through thinking you take some of these ideas into your mind and they begin to become manifest in your affairs.

Love is one of the ideas that provide a key to the infinite storehouse of abundance. It opens up generosity in us. It opens up generosity in others when we begin to love and bless them. Will it also open up a spirit of generosity in God? It certainly will and does. If you consciously love and bless God, you will soon find that things are coming your way. It will surprise you that just thinking about God will draw to you the things you want and expect, and bring many other blessings that you had not even thought about. Thousands of persons have proved this law to their entire satisfaction, and we have many records that illustrate how people have demonstrated abundance in the very face of apparent lack, simply by thinking about the love of God and thanking Him for what they have. This law will demonstrate itself for you or for anyone who applies it faithfully, for "love never faileth."

Men in business and industry have demonstrated great amounts of money through love. They did not love God, but the love of money attracted the money to them. It drew the substance right to them and enabled them to accumulate money, but merely as material, without the divine idea that assures permanence. We hear about men in high finance going bankrupt quite as often as we hear about men making great fortunes. When we develop a spiritual consciousness, we transfer this personal love to a higher and more stable plane, from the love of money and material things to the love of God, and thus conceived it will attract to us all the resources of infinite Mind forever and ever. Once make a connection with the universal bank of God and you have a permanent source of wealth.

Jesus said that when we come to the altar to make an offering, we should have nothing in our heart against our brother. He said that before we can make contact with the love and power of God we must first make peace with our brother. This means that we must cultivate a love for our fellows in order to set the attractive force of love into operation. All we need do is quicken our love for others by thinking about love and casting out of our mind all hate and fear that would weaken the perfect working of that mighty magnet. As love attracts, hate dissipates. Before you approach God's altar of plenty, go and make friends with your brother men. Make friends even with the money powers. Do not envy the rich. Never condemn those who have money merely because they have it and you do not. Do not question how they got their money and wonder whether or not they are honest. All that is none of your business. Your business is to get what belongs to you, and you do that by thinking about the omnipresent substance of God and how you can lay hold of it through love. Get in touch with God riches in spirit, lay hold of them by love, and you will have sufficient for every day. "Love therefore is the fulfillment of the law."

The eternal law of Spirit goes right on operating regardless of what you may think, say, or do. It is ordained that love will bring you prosperity, and you need not wonder whether it will or how it will. "Be not therefore anxious, saying, What shall we eat? or, What shall we drink? or, Wherewithal shall we be clothed ?" Do not worry. Worry is a thief and a robber, for it keeps your good from you. It breaks the drawing law of love, the law that says, "Perfect love casteth out fear." Banish worry by quietly and confidently affirming the drawing power of divine love as the constantly active magnet that attracts your unfailing supply. A good affirmation to rout worry is one like this:

Divine love bountifully supplies and increases substance to meet my every need.

Nearly all books or articles that deal with success or prosperity stress the well-known virtues of honesty, industry, system and order, faithfulness, hard work. These make an excellent foundation and can be developed. Anyone with determination and will can overcome habits of laziness, carelessness, and weakness. The use of the will is very important in the demonstration of prosperity. If there is disorder or lack of system in your home, overcome it. Affirm: *I will to be orderly. I will be orderly. I will be systematic in all my work and affairs. I am systematic. I am orderly. I am efficient.*

It takes the use of the will to be persistent, and we must be persistent in making demonstrations. Spasmodic efforts count for little, and many people give up too easily. If things don't come out just right the first time they try, they say the law is wrong and make no further effort. Anything so much worth while as prosperity in the home, and especially a permanent and unfailing supply that continues to meet the daily needs year after year, is worth any effort that we can make. Then be patient but be persistent. Declare: *I am not discouraged. I am persistent. I go forward.*

When success fails to crown our very first efforts we become discouraged and quit. Then we try to console ourselves with the old thought that it is God's will for us to be poor. Poverty is not God's will, but man lays it to the charge of God to excuse his own feeling of inadequacy and defeat. God's will is health, happiness, and prosperity for every man; and to have all that is good and beautiful in the home is to express God's will for us. God's will is not expressed in a hovel, nor in any home where discord, lack, and unhappiness are entertained. Even a human guest would not stay long in such a home. To have a prosperous home prepare it as the abiding place of God, who gives prosperity to all His children and adds no sorrow therewith. Determine to know God's will and do it. Affirm: *I am determined to achieve success through doing God's will.* That sums up the whole law. God is more willing to give than we are to receive. What we need to do is to determine what is His will, what He is trying to give, and open ourselves to receive His bounty. We do that by willing to do His will. You can be and have anything that you will to be and to have. Will to be healthy. Will to be happy. Will to be prosperous.

There are many persons who will to be prosperous and who have made up their minds, as they think, very determinedly. But they have not overcome all doubts, and when their demonstration is delayed, as it is in such cases, the doubt increases until they lose faith altogether. What they need is more persistence and determination. The word *determined* is a good word, a strong, substantial word with power in it. Jesus said that His words were spirit and life and would never pass away. Emerson says that words are alive and if you cut one it will bleed. Use the word *determined* and emphasize it in your affirmations. If things do not seem to come fast enough, determine that you will be patient. If negative thoughts creep in, determine to be positive. If you feel worried about the results, determine to be optimistic. In response to every thought of lack or need determine to be prosperous. The Lord has prosperity to give, and those who are determined go after their share. Jesus was quite positive and very determined in all His affirmations. He made big claims for God, and demonstrated them. Without the slightest doubt that the money would be there, He told Peter to put his hand into the fish's mouth and take out the wanted money. His prayers were made of one strong affirmation after another. The Lord's Prayer is a series of determined affirmations. We claim the will of God *is* for us to be rich, prosperous, and successful. Make up your mind that such is God's will for you and your home and you will make your demonstration.

In the Old Testament, in the 4th chapter of II Kings, there is a fine prosperity lesson for any home. The widow represents one who has lost his consciousness of God's supply and support. That divine idea of God as all-abundance is our true support. The two children of this home represent the thoughts of debt, what the family owes, and what someone owes the family. The prophet is divine understanding. The house is the body consciousness. The pot of oil is faith in spiritual substance. The neighbors are outside thoughts, and their "empty vessels" are thoughts of lack. To go in "and shut the door," as the widow was told to do, is to enter the inner consciousness and shut out the thoughts of lack. This is followed by strong words of affirmation: "pouring" the substance into all the places that seem to be empty or to lack, until all are full. In conclusion it is affirmed that every obligation is met, every debt paid, and there is so much left over that there are no vessels left to hold it.

This compares with the promise of God "I will . . . open you the windows of heaven, and pour you out a blessing, that there shall not be room enough *to receive it.*" "Heaven" represents the mind. All this is done in the mind, and you can do it. Carry each step forward in your imagination exactly as if it were occurring in the without. Form your prosperity demonstration in your mind, then hold to the divine law of fulfillment. "And, having done all . . . stand." You may not be able to fill all the vessels with oil on your first attempt, but as you practice the method day by day your faith will increase and your results will be in proportion to your increasing faith.

Work at the problem until you prove it. Apply the principle and the solution is sure. If it does not come at once, check over your methods carefully and see wherein your work has not been true. Do not allow one empty thought to exist in your mind but fill every nook and corner of it with the word *plenty, plenty, plenty.*

If your purse seems empty, deny the lack and say, "*You are filled even now with the bounty of God, my Father, who supplies all my wants.*" If your rooms are empty, deny the appearance and determine that prosperity is manifest in every part of every room. Never think of yourself as poor or needy. Do not talk about hard times or the necessity for strict economy. Even "the walls have ears" and, unfortunately, memories too. Do not think how little you have but how much you have. Turn the telescope of your imagination around and look through the other end. "Revile not the king, no, not in thy thought; and revile not the rich in thy bedchamber: for a bird of the heavens shall carry the voice, and that which hath wings shall tell the matter."

"Blessed is the man that walketh not in the counsel of the wicked,
Nor standeth in the way of sinners,
Nor sitteth in the seat of scoffers:
But his delight is in the law of Jehovah;
And on his law doth he meditate day and night.
And he shall be like a tree planted by the streams of water.
That bringeth forth its fruit in its season,
Whose leaf also doth not wither;
And whatsoever he doeth shall prosper."

"Through wisdom is a house builded;
And by understanding it is established;
And by knowledge are the chambers filled
With all precious and pleasant riches."

"Jehovah will open unto thee his good treasure."

"And the Almighty will be thy treasure,
And precious silver unto thee."

"Jehovah is my shepherd; I shall not want."

"Trust in Jehovah, and do good;
Dwell in the land, and feed on his faithfulness."

"Jehovah will give grace and glory;
No good thing will he withhold from them that walk uprightly."

"That I may cause those that love me to inherit substance,
And that I may fill their treasuries."

"If ye be willing and obedient, ye shall eat the good of the land."

LESSON 8

God Will Pay Your Debts

Forgive us our debts, as we also have forgiven our debtors." In these words Jesus expressed an infallible law of mind, the law that one idea must be dissolved before another can take its place. If you have in your mind any thought that someone has wronged you, you cannot let in the cleansing power of Spirit and the richness of spiritual substance until you have cast out the thought of the wrong, have forgiven it fully. You may be wondering why you have failed to get spiritual illumination or to find the consciousness of spiritual substance. Perhaps the reason is here: a lack of room for the true thoughts because other thoughts fill your mind. If you are not receiving the spiritual understanding you feel you should have, you should search your mind carefully for unforgiving thoughts. "Thoughts are things" and occupy space in the mind realm. They have substance and form and may easily be taken as permanent by one not endowed with spiritual discernment. They bring forth fruit according to the seed planted in the mind, but they are not enduring unless founded in Spirit. Thoughts are alive and are endowed by the thinker with a secondary thinking power; that is, the thought entity that the I AM forms assumes an ego and begins to think on its own account. Thoughts also think but only with the power you give to them.

Tell me what kind of thoughts you are holding about yourself and your neighbors, and I can tell you just what you may expect in the way of health, finances, and harmony in your home. Are you suspicious of your neighbors? You cannot love and trust in God if you hate and distrust men. The two ideas love and hate, or trust and mistrust, simply cannot both be present in your mind at one time, and when you are entertaining one, you may be sure the other is absent. Trust other people and use the power that you accumulate from that act to trust God. There is magic in it: it works wonders; love and trust are dynamic, vital powers. Are you accusing men of being thieves, and fear that they are going to take away from you something that is your own? With such a thought generating fear and even terror in your mind and filling your consciousness with darkness, where is there room for the Father's light of protection? Rather build walls of love and substance around yourself. Send out swift, invisible messengers of love and trust for your protection. They are better guards than policemen or detectives.

Do not judge others as regards their guilt or innocence. Consider yourself and how you stand in the sight of the Father for having thoughts about another's guilt. Begin your reform with yourself. That means much to one who enjoys an understanding of mind and its laws, though it may mean little to the ordinary individual. He who knows himself superficially, just his external personality, thinks he has reformed when he has conformed to the moral and governmental laws. He may even be filled with his own self-righteousness and daily lift up his voice to praise God that he is not as other men are, that he has forgiven men their transgressions. He looks on all men who do not conform to his ideas of morality and religion as being sinners and transgressors and thanks God for his own insight and keenness. But he is not at peace. Something seems lacking. God does not talk to him "face to face," because the mind, where God and man meet, is darkened by the murky thought that other men are sinners. Our first work in any demonstration is to contact God, therefore we must forgive all men their transgressions. Through this forgiveness we cleanse our mind so that the Father can forgive us our own transgressions.

Our forgiving "all men" includes ourselves. You must also forgive yourself. Let the finger of denial erase every sin or "falling short" that you have charged up against yourself. Pay your debt by saying to that part of yourself which you think has fallen short: "Thou art made whole: sin no more, lest a worse thing befall thee." Then "loose him, and let him go." Treat sin as a mental transgression, instead of considering it as a moral deflection. Deny in thought all tendency to the error way and hold yourself firmly to the Christ Spirit, which is your divine self. Part company forever with "accusing conscience." Those who have resolved to sin no more have nothing in common with guilt.

"Shall I be in debt as long as I hold debts against others?" We find this to be the law of mind: a thought of debt will produce debt. So long as you believe in debt you will go into debt and accumulate the burdens that follow that thought. Whoever has not forgiven all men their debts is likely to fall into debt himself. Does this mean that you should give receipted bills to all those who owe you? No. That would not be erasing the thought of debt from your mind. First deny in mind that any man or woman owes you anything. If necessary, go over your list of names separately and sincerely forgive the thought of debt which you have been attaching to each person named. More bills may be collected in this way than in any other, for many of these people will pay what they owe when you send them this forgiving thought.

Debt is a contradiction of the universal equilibrium, and there is no such thing as lack of equilibrium in all the universe. Therefore in Spirit and in Truth there is no debt. However, men hold on to a thought of debt, and this thought is responsible for a great deal of sorrow and hardship. The true disciple realizes his supply in the consciousness of omnipresent, universally possessed abundance. Spirit substance is impartial and owned in common, and no thought of debt can enter into it.

Debts exist in the mind, and in the mind is the proper place to begin liquidating them. These thought entities must be abolished in mind before their outer manifestations will pass away and stay away. The world can never be free from the bondage of financial obligations until men erase from their minds the thoughts of "mine and thine" that generates debts and interest. Analyze the thought of debt and you will see that it involves a thought of lack. Debt is a thought of lack with absence at both ends; the creditor thinks he lacks what is owed him and the debtor thinks he lacks what is necessary to pay it, else he would discharge the obligation rather than continue it. There is error at both ends of the proposition and nothing in the middle. This being true, it should be easy to dissolve the whole thought that anyone owes us or that we owe anyone anything. We should fill our mind with thoughts of all-sufficiency, and where there is no lack there can be no debts. Thus we find that the way to pay our debts is by filling our mind with the substance of ideas that are the direct opposite of the thoughts of lack that caused the debts.

Ideas of abundance will more quickly and surely bring what is yours to you than any thoughts you can hold about debtors discharging their obligations to you. See substance everywhere and affirm it, not only for yourself but for everyone else. Especially affirm abundance for those whom you have held in the thought of owing you. Thus you will help them pay their debts more easily than if you merely erased their names from your book of accounts receivable. Help pay the other fellow's debts by forgiving him his debts and declaring for him the abundance that is his already in Spirit. The idea of abundance will also bring its fruits into your own life. Let the law of plenty work itself out in you and in your affairs. This is the way the Father forgives your debts: not by canceling them on His books but by erasing them from His mind. He remembers them no more against you when you deny their reality. The Father is the everywhere present Spirit in which all that appears has its origin. God's love sees you always well, happy, and abundantly provided for; but God's wisdom demands that order and right relation exist in your mind before it may become manifest in your affairs as abundance. His love would give you your every desire, but His wisdom ordains that you forgive your debtors before your debts are forgiven.

To remedy any state of limited finances or ill-health that has been brought about by worry one must begin by eliminating the worry that is the original cause. One must free one's mind from the burden of debt before the debt can be paid. Many people have found that the statement "*I owe no man anything but love*" has helped them greatly to counteract this thought of debt. As they used the words their minds were opened to an inflow of divine love and they faithfully co-operated with the divine law of forgiveness in thought, word, and deed. They built up such a strong consciousness of the healing and enriching power of God's love that they could live and work peacefully and profitably with their associates. Thus renewed constantly in health, in faith, and in integrity, they were able to meet every obligation that came to them.

The statement "*I owe no man anything but love*" does not mean that we can disclaim owing our creditors money or try to evade the payment of obligations we have incurred. The thing denied is the burdensome thought of debt or of lack. The work of paying debts is an inner work having nothing to do with the debts already owed but with the wrong thoughts that produced them. When one holds to the right ideas, burdensome debts will not be contracted. Debts are produced by thoughts of lack, impatient desire, and covetousness. When these thoughts are overcome, debts are overcome, forgiven, and paid in full, and we are free from them for all time.

Your thoughts should at all times be worthy of your highest self, your fellow man, and God. The thoughts that most frequently work ill to you and your associates are thoughts of criticism and condemnation. Free your mind of them by holding the thought "*There is now no condemnation in Christ Jesus.*" Fill your mind with thoughts of divine love, justice, peace, and forgiveness. This will pay your debts of love, which are the only debts you really owe. Then see how quickly and easily and naturally all your outer debts will be paid and all inharmonies of mind, body, and affairs smoothed out at the same time. Nothing will so quickly enrich your mind and free it from every thought of lack as the realization of divine love. Divine love will quickly and perfectly free you from the burden of debt and heal you of your physical infirmities, often caused by depression, worry, and financial fear. Love will bring your own to you, adjust all misunderstandings, and make your life and affairs healthy, happy, harmonious, and free, as they should be. Love indeed is the "fulfillment of the law."

The way is now open for you to pay your debts. Surrender them to God along with all your doubts and fears. Follow the light that is flooding into your mind. God's power, love, and wisdom, are here, for His kingdom is within you. Give Him full dominion in your life and affairs. Give Him your business, your family affairs, your finances, and let Him pay your debts. He is even now doing it, for it is His righteous desire to free you from every burden, and He is leading you out of the burden of debt, whether of owing or being owed. Meet every insidious thought, such as "I can't," "I don't know how," "I can't see the way," with the declaration *"Jehovah is my shepherd; I shall not want."* You "shall not want" the wisdom, the courage to do, or the substance to do with when you have once fully realized the scope of the vast truth that Almightiness is leading you into "green pastures . . . beside still waters."

In the kingdom of Truth and reality ideas are the coin of the realm. You can use the new ideas that divine wisdom is now quickening in your mind and start this very moment to pay your debts. Begin by thanking God for your freedom from the debt-burden thought. This is an important step in breaking the shackles of debt. The funds to pay all your bills may not suddenly appear in a lump sum; but as you watch and work and pray, holding yourself in the consciousness of God's leadership and His abundance, you will notice your funds beginning to grow "here a little, there a little," and increasing more and more rapidly as your faith increases and your anxious thoughts are stilled. For with the increase will come added good judgment and wisdom in the management of your affairs. Debt is soon vanquished when wisdom and good judgment are in control.

Do not yield to the temptation of "easy-payment plans," Any payment that drains your pay envelope before you receive it is not an easy payment. Do not allow false pride to tempt you to put on a thousand-dollar front on a hundred-dollar salary. There may be times when you are tempted to miss paying a bill in order to indulge a desire for some thing. This easily leads one into the habit of putting off paying, which fastens the incubus of debt on people before they realize it. It is the innocent-appearing forerunner of the debt habit and debt thought that may rob you of peace, contentment, freedom, integrity, and prosperity for years to come. The Divine Mind within you is much stronger than this desire mind of the body. Turn to it in a time like this, and affirm: *"Jehovah is my shepherd; I shall not want" this thing until it comes to me in divine order.*

Bless your creditors with the thought of abundance as you begin to accumulate the wherewithal to pay off your obligations. Keep the faith they had in you by including them in your prayer for increase. Begin to free yourself at once by doing all that is possible with the means you have and as you proceed in this spirit the way will open for you to do more; for through the avenues of Spirit more means will come to you and every obligation will be met. If you are a creditor, be careful of the kind of thoughts you hold over your debtor. Avoid the thought that he is unwilling to pay you or that he is unable to pay you. One thought holds him in dishonesty, and the other holds him subject to lack, and either of them tends to close the door to the possibility of his paying you soon. Think well and speak well of all those who owe you. If you talk about them to others avoid calling them names that you would not apply to yourself. Cultivate a genuine feeling of love for them and respect their integrity in spite of all appearances. Declare abundant supply for them and thus help them to prosper. Pray and work for their good as well as for your own, for yours is inseparable from theirs. You owe your debtor quite as much as he owes you and yours is a debt of love. Pay your debt to him and he will pay his to you. This rule of action never fails.

Far-seeing Christians look forward to an early resumtion of the economic system inaugurated by the early followers of Jesus. They had all things in common, and no man lacked anything. But before we can have a truly Christian community founded on a spiritual basis we must be educated into a right way of thinking about finances. If we should all get together and divide all our possessions, it would be but a short time until those who have the prevailing financial ideas would manipulate our finances, and plethora on one hand and lack on the other would again be established.

The world cannot be free from the bondage of debt and interest until men start to work in their minds to erase those things from consciousness. If the United States forgave the nations of Europe all their debts and wiped the slate clean, the law would not necessarily be fulfilled; for there would probably remain a thought that they still owed us and that we had made a sacrifice in canceling the obligations. We should not feel very friendly about it and would not truly forgive them, and in that case the error thought would be carried on. We must first forgive the error thought that they owe us money and that we would be losing money by canceling the debts. The man who is forced to forgive a debt does not forgive it.

Above all we should fill our mind with the consciousness of that divine abundance which is so manifest everywhere in the world today. There is as much substance as there ever was, but its free flow has been interfered with through selfishness. We must rid our mind of the selfish acquisitiveness that is so dominant in the race thought, and in that way do our part in the great work of freeing the world from avarice. It is the duty of every Christian metaphysician to help in the solution of this problem by affirming that the universal Spirit of supply is now becoming manifest as a distributing energy the world over; that all stored-up, hoarded, vicious thoughts are being dissolved; that all people have things in common, that no one anywhere lacks anything; and that the divine law of distribution of infinite supply that Jesus demonstrated is now being made manifest throughout the world. "The earth is the Lord's, and the fulness thereof."

There is a legitimate commerce that is carried on by means of what is called credit. Credit is a convenience to be used by those who appreciate its value and are careful not to abuse it, for to do so would be to ruin it. However, many persons are not equipped to use the credit system to advantage and are likely to abuse it. In the first place, few individuals are familiar with the intricacies of sound credit systems and often assume obligations without being certain of their ability to meet them, especially should some unforeseen complication arise. Frequently an individual loses all that he invests and finds himself involved in a burden of debt in addition. Such things are not in divine order and are largely responsible for retarding prosperity.

No one should assume an obligation unless he is prepared to meet it promptly and willingly when it comes due. One who knows God as his unfailing resource can be assured of his supply when it is needed. Then why should he plunge into debt when he is confident of his daily supply without debt? There are no creditors or debtors in God's kingdom. If you are in that kingdom, you need no longer be burdened with the thought of debt either as debtor or creditor. Under divine law there is no reaching out for things that are beyond one's present means. There is an ever-increasing richness of consciousness coming from the certain knowledge that God is infinite and unfailing supply. Outer things conform to the inner pattern, and riches are attracted to the one who lives close to the unselfish heart of God. His environment is made beautiful by the glory of the Presence, and there is satisfying and lasting prosperity in his affairs.

There is but one way to be free from debt. That is the desire to be free, followed by the realization that debt has no legitimate place in God's kingdom and that you are determined to erase it entirely from your mind. As you work toward your freedom you will find it helpful to have daily periods for meditation and prayer. Do not concentrate on debts or spoil your prayers by constantly thinking of debts. Think of that which you want to demonstrate, not that from which you seek freedom. When you pray, thank the Father for His care and guidance, for His provision and plenty, for His love and wisdom, for His infinite abundance and your privilege to enjoy it.

Here are a few prosperity prayers that may help establish you in the truth of plenty and erase the error thought of debt. They are offered as suggestions for forming your own prayers but may be used as given with excellent results.

I am no longer anxious about finances; Thou art my all-sufficiency in all things.

The Spirit of honesty, promptness, efficiency, and order is now expressed in me and in all that I do.

I am free from all limitations of mortal thought about quantities and values. The superabundance of riches of the Christ Mind are now mine, and I am prospered in all my ways.

THE TWENTY-THIRD PSALM

A Treatment to Free the Mind of the Debt Idea

Jehovah is my shepherd; I shall not want
He maketh me to lie down in green pastures:
He leadeth me beside still waters.
He restoreth my soul:
He guideth me in the paths of righteousness for his name's sake.
Yea, though I walk through the valley of the shadow of death,
I will fear no evil; for thou art with me;
Thy rod and thy staff, they comfort me.

Thou preparest a table before me in the presence of mine enemies:
Thou hast anointed my head with oil;
My cup runneth over.
Surely goodness and lovingkindness shall follow me all the days of my life:
And I shall dwell in the house of Jehovah for ever.

LESSON 9

Tithing, the Road to Prosperity

As Ye abound in everything, *in* faith, and utterance, and knowledge, and *in* all earnestness, and *in* your love to us, *see* that ye abound in this grace also."

"Honor Jehovah with thy substance,
And with the first-fruits of all thine increase:
So shall thy barns be filled with plenty,
And thy vats shall overflow with new wine."

Under the Mosaic law a tithe (or tenth) was required as the Lord's portion. Throughout the Old Testament the tithe or tenth is mentioned as a reasonable and just return to the Lord by way of acknowledging Him as the source of supply. After Jacob had seen the vision of the ladder with angels ascending and descending on it he set up a pillar and made a vow to the Lord, saying, "Of all that thou shalt give me I will surely give the tenth unto thee." In the 3d chapter of Malachi we find God's blessing directly connected with faithfulness in giving to the Lord's treasury, but gifts should be made because it is right and because one loves to give, not from a sense of duty or for the sake of reward.

That there will be a reward following the giving we are also assured by Jesus in a direct promise "Give, and it shall be given unto you; good measure, pressed down, shaken together, running over, shall they give unto your bosom. For with what measure ye mete it shall be measured to you again."

Promises of spiritual benefits and increase of God's bounty through the keeping of this divine law of giving and receiving, abound in all the Scriptures.

"There is that scattereth, and increaseth yet more;
And there is that withholdeth more than is meet, but it tendeth *only to want.*
The liberal soul shall be made fat;
And he that watereth shall be watered also himself."
"He that hath a bountiful eye shall be blessed;
For he giveth of his bread to the poor."
"He that soweth bountifully shall reap also bountifully."
"Blessed are ye that sow beside all waters."

We are living now under larger and fuller blessings from God than man has ever known. It is meet therefore that we give accordingly and remember the law of the tithe, for if a tenth was required under the law in those olden times, it is certainly no less fitting that we should give it cheerfully now. One of the greatest incentives to generous giving is a keen appreciation of the blessings secured to us through the redemptive work of Jesus Christ. "He that spared not His own Son, but delivered Him up for us all, how shall He not also with Him freely give us all things?" "Freely ye received, freely give." True giving is the love and generosity of the Spirit-quickened heart responding to the love and generosity of the Father's heart.

In his second letter Paul made a stirring appeal to the Corinthians for a generous gift to their poorer brethren in Jerusalem. He suggests some principles of giving that are always applicable, for giving is a grace that adds to the spiritual growth of all men in all times. Without giving the soul shrivels, but when giving is practiced as a part of Christian living, the soul expands and becomes Godlike in the grace of liberality and generosity. No restoration to the likeness of God can be complete unless mind, heart, and soul are daily opening out into that large, free, bestowing spirit which so characterizes our God and Father. Therefore it is not surprising that Paul classes the grace of giving with faith, knowledge, and love.

A very simple yet practical plan for exercising this grace of giving had been suggested by Paul in his first letter to the Corinthian church. "Upon the first day of the week," he said, "let each one of you lay by him in store, as he may prosper"; that is, each member was asked to contribute to the establishing of a treasury. This was to be the Lord's storehouse, into which each one was to put his offerings regularly and in proportion to his means. In adopting this plan the offerer became a steward of the Lord's goods and entered upon a course of training and discipline needed to make a good steward, for it takes wisdom to know how rightly to dispense the bounty of God. Perhaps no simpler way to begin one's growth in the grace of giving can be suggested for our own day. Those who have followed this method have usually found that they had more money to give than they had thought possible.

In order that the plan of giving may be successful there are several things that must be observed. First there must be a willing mind. "If the readiness is there, *it is* acceptable according as a *man* hath, not according as *he* hath not." "God loveth a cheerful giver." Secondly, the giving must be done in faith, and there must be no withholding because the offering seems small. Many of the instances of giving that are recorded in the Bible as worthy of special mention, commendation, and blessing are instances where the gift itself was small. The widow who fed Elijah in his time of famine gave him a cake made with her last handful of meal. For her faith and her generous spirit she was rewarded with a plentiful daily supply of food for herself and her sons, as well as for Elijah. "The jar of meal shall not waste, neither shall the cruse of oil fail."

This same truth is set forth beautifully in the New Testament, where it *is* clearly shown that not the amount of the offering but the spirit in which it is given determines its value and power. "And he [Jesus] sat down over against the treasury, and beheld how the multitude cast money into the treasury: and many that were rich cast in much. And there came a poor widow, and she cast in two mites, which make a farthing. And he called unto him his disciples, and said unto them, Verily I say unto you, This poor widow cast in more than all they that are casting into the treasury: for they all did cast in of their superfluity; but she of her want did cast in all that she had, *even* all her living."

This poor widow exemplified what it *is* to give in faith; and were ever two mites so great a gift as when they brought forth such praise from the Master Himself! The results of giving in faith are just as sure in this age as in the time of Jesus, for the law is unfailing in all ages.

A third requisite for keeping the law of giving and receiving *is* that the offering shall be a just and fair proportion of all that one receives. The amount was settled by Paul and the measure he gave was: "as he may prosper." There is a certain definiteness about this, and yet it admits of freedom for the giver to exercise his individual faith, judgment, and will.

The question of wise distribution is closely related to the matter of filling God's treasury. To whom shall we give and when are questions quite important. There are several truths that may be considered in this connection, but then each individual finds it necessary to trust to the Spirit of wisdom manifest in his own heart, since there are no rules or precedents that one can follow in detail. This is as it should be, for it keeps the individual judgment, faith, love, sympathy, and will alive and active. Yet a careful study of the underlying laws of spiritual giving will help one to exercise these divine faculties as they should be exercised. If we follow the Spirit of wisdom we shall not give to anything that is contrary to the teaching of Jesus, but spend every penny in the furtherance of the good news of life that He proclaims and in the promotion of the brotherhood of man that it is His mission to establish on earth among all those who become sons through Him.

True spiritual giving rewards with a double joy: first that which comes with the laying of the gift upon the altar or in the Lord's treasury; then the joy of sharing our part of God's bounty with others. One of the blessings is the satisfying knowledge that we are meeting the law and paying our debt of love and justice to the Lord. The other is the joy of sharing the Lord's bounty. Justice comes first; then generosity.

Even the so-called heathen recognize giving as a part of worship, for we find them coming with offerings when they worship their idols. All ages and all religious dispensations have stressed giving as a vital part of their worship. In this age, when we have so much, more is required of us, even to the giving of ourselves with all that we are and have. This privilege carries immeasurable benefits with it, for it looses us from the personal life, unifies us with the universal, and so opens our inner and outer life to the inflow and the outflow of the life, love, bounty and grace of God. This is the blessed result of faithful obedience to the law and exercise of the grace of giving.

The people were amazed when the prophet Malachi told them that they had been robbing God and desired to know wherein they had failed when they thought they had been serving the Lord so faithfully. People are as much amazed today to learn that they have been untrue to God's law, for the message of Malachi is for us quite as much as for the ancients. The Spirit of God gave this message through the prophet: "Bring ye the whole tithe into the store-house, that there may be food in my house, and prove me now herewith, saith Jehovah of hosts, if I will not open you the windows of heaven, and pour you out a blessing, that there shall not be room enough *to receive it.* And I will rebuke the devourer for your sakes, and he shall not destroy the fruits of your ground; neither shall your vine cast its fruit before the time in the field, saith Jehovah of hosts. And all nations shall call you happy; for ye shall be a delightsome land, saith Jehovah of hosts."

Study this 3d chapter of Malachi carefully if you would know the happy solution of the problem of giving and receiving. See how practical it is for people in every walk of life and for nations as well. It offers the solution to the problems of the farmer. It sets forth clearly a law of prosperity for all classes of people; for those who need protection for their crops from frosts, droughts, floods; for those who would escape the plagues, pestilences, and manifold things that would destroy their supply and support. It is a simple law but so effective: simply give a tithe or tenth or the "first-fruits" or their equivalent to the Lord. God should not be expected to meet all man's requirements in the matter of giving this protection and increase unless man fulfills the requirements of God. The act of giving complies with the divine law, because it involves the recognition of God as the giver of all increase; and unless we have a recognition of the source of our supply we have no assurance of continuing in its use.

Many people have doubts as to whether it will really do any good to ask the Lord for protection and for plenty in regard to crops or other supply. Many who are employed in cities or who are in business think it strange that they should believe in omnipresent prosperity. Thus unbelief is present with them at the very time when an unwavering faith is most necessary. There is a psychological reason why people should obey spiritual law. When a person obeys the law of God along any line, his faith immediately becomes strengthened in proportion and his doubts disappear. When anyone puts God first in his finances, not only in thought but in every act, by releasing his first fruits (a tenth part of his increase or income) to the Lord, his faith in omnipresent supply becomes a hundredfold stronger and he prospers accordingly. Obeying this law gives him an inner knowing that he is building his finances on a sure foundation that will not fail him.

Everything in the universe belongs to God, and though all things are for the use and enjoyment of man, he can possess nothing selfishly. When man learns that a higher law than human custom and desire is working in the earth to bring about justice, righteousness, and equalization, he will begin to obey that law by tithing, loving his neighbor, and doing unto others as he would have them do unto him. Then man will reach the end of all the troubles brought upon himself by his selfishness and greed, and will become healthy, prosperous, and happy.

The pastor of a small church in Georgia suggested to his congregation, composed largely of cotton farmers, that they dedicate a tenth part of their land to the Lord and ask Him for protection against the ravages of the boll weevil, which had devastated the crops in that vicinity for several years. Seven farmers in the congregation decided to do this. They took no measures to protect their crop on these dedicated acres, yet the pest did not attack the cotton there. The quality of the fiber was better on those acres than on any that adjoined them. The experiment was so successful in fact that practically all the farmers in that community have decided to follow the plan in the future.

Many experiences such as this are awakening men to respect our relation to the infinite principle of life, everywhere present, that we know as God. This divine element of life that manifests itself as growth and substance resides within the factors that combine to produce cotton, wheat, and all other forms of vegetation. Then certainly if the farmer works in acknowledged sympathy with this life principle, it will work in sympathy with him and for his good. Each contributing in love and understanding to the other, a larger crop will be the result, and a larger measure of prosperity for the farmer. Not only the farmer but the banker, the tradesman, the professional man can work in sympathy and harmony with this principle of growth and increase. The infinite life principle is as responsive in one field as another, and it is everywhere present. Even so-called inanimate objects are filled to the full with this infinite life, and even coined gold is tense with the desire to expand and to grow. The materials handled by the tradesman are made of the same substance that makes the universe and contain within themselves the germ of growth and increase. All men are therefore daily associated with life, and through rendering it the reverent acknowledgment that is its due and through witnessing this acknowledgment by dedicating a part of their increase they are prospered.

The tithe is the equivalent of the increased fertility of the land. If by acknowledging God as the giver of all life the farmer raises two or six or twenty bushels more on his field, that extra portion, which he would not have had otherwise, is the Lord's portion. In trade the tithe is the equivalent of the increased quality of goods. In professional life the tithe is the increased ability or the increased appreciation. The tithing principle can be applied in all of our industrial and social relationships. In every case where it has been applied and followed for a time, the tither has been, remarkably blessed; quite as much so as in the case of the cotton farmers and their tithe acres.

There are many people who wish to give but seem at a loss as to how to go about it or where to begin. They do not know how much they should give, or when or how often to offer their gifts, and there are a host of related questions. To answer these questions there must be found a definite basis for their giving, a rule to which they can conform. This is where the law of tithing fits beautifully, for it is a basis and a sound one, tested and proved for thousands of years. The tithe may be a tenth part of one's salary, wage, or allowance, of the net profits of business, or of money received from the sale of goods. It is based on every form of supply, no matter through what channel it may come, for there are many channels through which man is prospered. The tenth should be set apart for the upkeep of some spiritual work or workers. It should be set apart first even before one's personal expenses are taken out, for in the right relation of things God comes first always. Then everything else follows in divine order and falls into its proper place.

The great promise of prosperity is that if men seek God and His righteousness first, then all shall be added unto them. One of the most practical and sensible ways of seeking God's kingdom first is to be a tither, to put God first in finances. It is the promise of God, the logical thing to do, and the experience of all who have tried it, that all things necessary to their comfort, welfare, and happiness have been added to them in an overflowing measure. Tithing establishes method in giving and brings into the consciousness a sense of order and fitness that will be manifested in one's outer life and affairs as increased efficiency and greater prosperity.

Another blessing that follows the practice of tithing is the continual "letting go" of what one receives, which keeps one's mind open to the good and free from covetousness. Making an occasional large gift and then permitting a lapse of time before another is made will not give this lasting benefit, for one's mind channel may in the meantime become clogged with material thoughts of fear, lack, or selfishness. When a person tithes he is giving continuously, so that no spirit of grasping, no fear, and no thought of limitations gets a hold on him. There is nothing that keeps a person's mind so fearless and so free to receive the good constantly coming to him as the practice of tithing. Each day, week, pay day, whenever it is, the tither gives one tenth. When an increase of prosperity comes to him, as come it will and does, his first thought is to give God the thanks and the tenth of the new amount. The free, open mind thus stayed on God is certain to bring forth joy, real satisfaction in living, and true prosperity. Tithing is based on a law that cannot fail, and it is the surest way ever found to demonstrate plenty, for it is God's own law and way of giving.

"And all the tithe of the land, whether of the seed of the land, or of the fruit of the tree, is Jehovah's: it is holy unto Jehovah."

Let us give as God gives, unreservedly, and with no thought of return, making no mental demands for recompense on those who have received from us. A gift with reservations is not a gift; it is a bribe. There is no promise of increase unless we give freely, let go of the gift entirely, and recognize the universal scope of the law. Then the gift has a chance to go out and to come back multiplied. There is no telling how far the blessing may travel before it comes back, but it is a beautiful and encouraging fact that the longer it is in returning, the more hands it is passing through and the more hearts it is blessing. All these hands and hearts add something to it in substance, and it is increased all the more when it does return.

We must not try to fix the avenues through which our good is to come. There is no reason for thinking that what you give will come back through the one to whom you gave it. All men are one in Christ and form a universal brotherhood. We must put away any personal claim, such as "I gave to you, now you give to me," and supplant it with "Inasmuch as ye did it unto one of these my brethren, *even* these least, ye did it unto me." The law will bring each of us just what is his own, the reaping of the seeds he has sown. The return will come, for it cannot escape the law, though it may quite possibly come through a very different channel from what we expect. Trying to fix the channel through which his good must come to him is one of the ways in which the personal man shuts off his own supply.

The spiritual-minded man does not make selfish use of the law but gives because he loves to give. Because he gives with no thought of reward and no other motive than love, he is thrown more completely into the inevitable operation of the law and his return is all the more certain. He is inevitably enriched and cannot escape it. Jesus said, "Give, and it shall be given unto you; good measure, pressed down, shaken together, running over." He was not merely making a promise but stating a law that never fails to function.

So inexhaustible is the bounty of the Giver of all good that to him who has eyes to see it and faith to receive it God is an unfailing source of supply. The munificent Giver withholds nothing from him who comes in the name of a son and heir and lays claim to his portion. It is the Father's good pleasure to give us the kingdom, and all that the Father has is ours. But we must have the faith and the courage to claim it.

Men who accomplish great things in the industrial world are the ones who have faith in the money-producing power of their ideas. Those who would accomplish great things in the demonstration of spiritual resources must have faith to lay hold of the divine ideas and the courage to speak them into expression. The conception must be followed by the affirmation that the law is instantly fulfilled. Then the supply will follow in manifestation.

LESSON 10

Right Giving, the Key to Abundant Receiving

There is a law of giving and receiving and it requires careful study if we would use it in our prosperity demonstrations. It is a law of mind action, and it can be learned and applied the same as any other law. The teaching of Jesus stands out prominently, because it can be practically applied to the affairs of everyday life. It is not alone a religion in the sense that word is usually taken but is a rule of thinking, doing, living, and being. It is not only ethical but practical, and men have never yet sounded the depths of the simple but all-inclusive words of Jesus. To some people it is unthinkable to connect the teaching of Jesus with the countinghouse and the market place, but a deeper insight into their meaning and purpose, which the Spirit of Truth is now revealing to the world, shows that these lofty teachings are the most practical rules for daily living in all departments of life. They are vital to modern civilization and the very foundation of business stability. The law of giving and receiving that Jesus taught, "Give, and it shall be given unto you," is found to be applicable to all our commercial as well as our social relationships.

We have not been more successful in making this doctrine of Jesus a practical standard for everyday guidance because we have not understood the law on which it is based. Jesus would not have put forth a doctrine that was not true and not based on unchanging law, and we can be sure that this doctrine of giving and receiving is powerful enough to support all the affairs of civilization. We have not gone deeply enough into the teaching but have thought we understood it from a mere surface study. "Ye look at the things that are before your face," says Paul, and Jesus also warned us to "judge not according to appearance." We should form no conclusions until we have gone thoroughly into the causes and the underlying laws. The things we see outwardly are the effects that have arisen from causes that are invisible to us. There is an inner and an outer to everything: both the mental and the material conditions pervade the universe. Man slides at will up and down the whole gamut of cause and effect. The whole race slides into an effect almost unconsciously and so identifies the senses with the effect that the causes are lost sight of for thousands of years.

An awakening comes in time and the cause side of existence is again brought to the attention of men, as set forth, for example, in the doctrine of Jesus Christ. But men cannot grasp the great truth in a moment and cling to what is plainly visible to them, the effect side. The truth that things have a spiritual as well as a material identity and that the spiritual is the cause side and of greatest value, is a revelation that may be slow in coming to most people. In this instance it is the material side that they cling to, thinking it to be all and refusing to let go. Men have taken the letter or appearance side of the Jesus Christ doctrine and materialized it to fit their beliefs and customs. That is the reason why the Christ message has not purified commerce, society, and government. But it should be made spiritually operative in those fields. It will easily do the work desired when its mental side is studied and when it is understood and applied from the spiritual viewpoint.

There is need for reform in economics more than in any other department of everyday life. Money has been manipulated by greed until greed itself is sick and secretly asks for a panacea. But it does not look to the religion of Jesus Christ for healing. In fact that is the very last place it would apply for aid, because many of the advocates of the Jesus Christ doctrine are themselves economic dependents and have no solution for the economic problem—not understanding the power of their own religion. Yet no permanent remedy will ever be found for the economic ills of the world outside a practical application of the laws on which the doctrine of Jesus Christ is based.

The correctness of the solution of any problem is assured by the right relation of its elements. All true reform begins with the individual. Jesus began there. He did not clamor for legislation to control men or their actions. He called His twelve apostles and through them individually instituted that reform which has as its basis an appeal to the innate intelligence, honesty, and goodness in every man. He told them, "Go ye into all the world, and preach the gospel to the whole creation."

As people learn more definitely about the dynamic effect of thought and how ideas pass from mind to mind, they see more and more the wisdom of the Christ teaching. They are beginning to understand that there is one undeviating law of mind action and that all thinking and all speaking is amenable to it. Thus when Jesus said, "By thy words thou shalt be justified, and by thy words thou shalt be condemned," He taught the power of thoughts and words to bring results in accordance with the ideas back of them.

Following the metaphysical side of the teaching of Jesus, we have found that certain thoughts held in the minds of the people are causing widespread misery, disease, and death. We have also found that these thoughts can be dissolved or transformed and the whole man made over through his conscious volition. Paul well understood this process. He said, "Be ye transformed by the renewing of your mind."

Among the destructive thoughts that men indulge in and exercise are those forms of selfishness which we know as avarice, covetousness, money getting, the desire for financial gain and for possessing the things of the world. These thoughts threaten seriously to disturb the civilization of the world and the stability of the whole race. The sole thought of money getting is being allowed by men and women to generate its cold vapor in their souls until it shuts out all the sunlight of love and even of life. The remedy for the misery caused by destructive thoughts is not far to seek. It lies in constructive thinking along the lines that Jesus laid down. Indeed the remedy for all the ills to which flesh is heir lies in conformity to the divine law that Jesus revealed to His true followers. It is said of these true followers (Acts 4:32) that they were "of one heart and soul: and not one *of them* said that aught of the things which he possessed was his own; but they had all things common."

Many true Christians have observed this righteous law and sought to conform to it in community life. Such efforts have not always been successful, because there was not the necessary recognition of the mental factor and the discipline of ideas. So long as the idea of covetousness is lodged in the human mind as its dominant generating factor, there can be no successful community life. That idea must be eliminated from the mental plane first; the next step, the outer practice, will then be safe and successful.

Everywhere true metaphysicians are preparing themselves to be members in the great colony that Jesus is to set up, by working to eliminate from their mind all selfish ideas, along with all other discordant vibrations that produce inharmony among members of the same group. A step in this direction is the gradual introduction of the "freewill offering" plan to replace the world's commercial standard of reward for services. We are striving to educate the people on this question of giving and receiving and to let their own experience prove to them that there is a divine law of equilibrium in financial matters that corresponds to the law of balance and poise that holds the suns and the planets in place. In order to make a success of this great effort we must have the loving co-operation of everyone to whom we minister. The law is based on love and justice, and it equitably and harmoniously adjusts all the affairs of men. It goes even further, for it restores a harmony and balance in both mind and body that results in happiness and health as well as prosperity. Love and justice are mighty powers, and all things must eventually come under their influence, because even a few men and women of right motive can, by right thinking and consequent just action, introduce these ideas into the race consciousness and pave the way for their universal adoption. The movement has already begun and is rapidly gaining headway. Every student and reader is asked to give it impetus by resolving to be unselfish and just without compulsion.

The race consciousness is formed of thought currents and the dominant beliefs of all the people. A few men and women rise above these currents of thought and become independent thinkers. The dominating race idea of money getting as the goal of success is now being replaced by the idea of usefulness and good works. This idea must be carried out by individuals who have resolved to think and to act in the Jesus Christ way. To be one of these individuals and to contribute to the change in the race consciousness, first dedicate yourself in Spirit to the ministry of Jesus and resolve to carry forward the great work He has commissioned you to do. This does not mean that you must preach like Paul or necessarily carry on any extensive work in the outer. In the silence of your "inner chamber" you can do a mighty work of power by daily denying the beliefs in avarice and covetousness and affirming the universal sway of divine love and justice. You can make the idea of exact equity and justice between man and man the central theme of all your saying and doing. When you see examples of greed and avarice or when thoughts of these seek a place in your mind, remember the words of the Master: "What *is that* to thee? follow thou me."

Never for a moment allow yourself to entertain any scheme for getting the better of your fellows in any trade or bargain. Hold steadily to the law of equity and justice that is working in and through you, knowing for a certainty that you are supplied with everything necessary to fulfill all your requirements. Give full value for everything you get. Demand the same for everything you give, but do not try to enforce that demand by human methods. There is a better way: think of yourself as Spirit working with powerful spiritual forces, and know that the demands of Spirit must and will be met.

Do not plan to lay up for the future; let the future take care of itself. To entertain any fears or doubts on that point saps your strength and depletes your spiritual power. Hold steadily to the thought of the omnipresence of universal supply, its perfect equilibrium and its swift action in filling every apparent vacuum or place of lack. If you have been in the habit of hoarding or of practicing stringent economy change your thought currents to generosity. Practice giving, even though it may be in a small way. Give in a spirit of love and give when you cannot see any possibility of return. Put real substance into your gift by giving the substance of the heart with the token of money or whatever it is. Through the power of your word you can bless and spiritually multiply everything that you give. See yourself as the steward of God handing out His inexhaustible supplies. In this manner you are setting into action mental and spiritual forces that eventually bring large results into visibility. Be happy in your giving. God loves a cheerful giver because his mind and heart are open to the flow of the pure substance of Being that balances all things.

Do not give with any idea that you are bestowing charity. The idea of charity has infested the race consciousness for thousands of years and is responsible for the great army of human dependents. Do all you can to annul this mental error. There is no such thing as charity as popularly understood. Everything belongs to God and all His children are equally entitled to it. The fact that one has a surplus and gives some of it to another does not make the one a benefactor and the other a dependent. The one with the surplus is simply a steward of God and is merely discharging the work of his stewardship. When one asks for divine wisdom and understanding about giving it becomes a joy both to the giver and the recipient.

Followers of Jesus who are doing His work of teaching and healing should, like Him, receive freewill offerings for their ministry to the people. The majority of those who apply to teachers and healers recognize this law of giving and receiving, but there are quite a number who do not understand it. First there are those who are in bondage to the idea of avarice, and secondly, there are those who still are in bondage to the idea of charity. Both these classes need education and treatment to release them from mental limitation and mental disease. The avaricious suffer most in body and are the most difficult to heal, because of the mental bias that prompts them to get everything as cheaply as possible, including the kingdom of heaven. They must be patiently educated to be just because it is right, and to learn to "let go" of the acquisitive spirit and replace it with the spirit of generosity. They will do this readily enough as a mental drill but are not so willing to let go of the money symbol. However, continued treatments in the silence, supplemented with oral and written instruction, will eventually prevail and heal them.

There are many examples that could be given to prove the outworking of the law. The covetous idea has a great power over the body. It would avail little to treat the outer manifestation before first removing the inner cause from the mind. The salvation of such people is to learn to give generously and freely, not from compulsion or for the sake of reward but from a love of the giving. Some metaphysicians think to cure their patients of the hold of avaricious thoughts by charging them a good round price for their treatments. By the same token the medical doctor who charges the most is surest to heal his patients, and any service for which an exhorbitant price is charged is the best! Surely this would be a foolish idea. Metaphysical healing has become so popular that hundreds have gone into it as a business and are making of it an industry founded on the old commercial idea, just as cold and calculating, as hard and unyielding as the idea is in the ranks of the money-changers of mammon.

Surely there is a "more excellent way," one more in harmony with divine law, a way that permits the heart as well as the head and hand to be used in the grace of giving and receiving. Those who are using the freewill offering method meet with some criticism and opposition from those who hold to the commercial method and say that charging a definite sum is the legitimate way. They accuse Unity of fostering charity and poverty and keeping alive the spirit of getting something for nothing that is manifested by so many people. Our reply is that we are pursuing the only course that could ever effectually eradicate these erroneous states of consciousness and bring people into an understanding of the spiritual law of prosperity through giving in love.

Everyone should give as he receives; in fact, it is only through giving that he can receive. Until the heart is quickened at the center and the mind is opened up to Truth there is no permanent healing. Everyone can make a fair return for everything he gets. We aim to show moneyless paupers that they can *give* something in return for the good that has been done them. It may be to pass the true word to some other needy one, or merely to lift up their voice in thanksgiving and praise where before they were dumb. We recognize the necessity of some action of the mammon-bound mind. It must be made to let go somewhere before it can receive the light and the power of Spirit.

Our work is to bring men and women to the place of true and lasting dominion where they are superior to both riches and poverty. We can do this by showing them that they are spiritual beings, that they live in a spiritual world here and now, and that through the apprehension of the Truth of their being and their relation to God this dominion is to be realized.

The central and most vital fact that they must come to realize is that an idea has the power of building thought structures, which in turn materialize in the outer environment and affairs and determine every detail of their existence. Every man is a king ruling his own subjects. These subjects are the ideas existing in his mind, the "subjects" of his thought. Each man's ideas are as varied and show as many traits of character as the inhabitants of any empire. But they can all be brought into subjection and made to obey through the I AM power that is the ruler of the kingdom. In your domain of mind there may be colonies of alien ideas—the Philistines, Canaanites, and other foreign tribes, that the Children of Israel found in their Promised Land when they attempted to take possession of it. The story of the Children of Israel and how they gained the possession of that land is a symbolical representation of the experience of everyone who seeks to reclaim his own consciousness in the name of the Lord. The meaning in Hebrew of the name *Canaanite* is "merchant" or "trader"; in other words, a set of ideas that has to do with the commercial phase of life. Study the Children of Israel (spiritual ideas) in their experiences with these Canaanites and you will get many valuable hints on subduing and handling your own money-getting ideas.

You may allow avariciousness and stinginess to develop in your mind domain until the very blood in your body starts to dry up and your nerves are shaken and palsied with the fear of future poverty. If so, it is time these ideas were driven out and a new set of ideas settled in your domain to become active in building up a new state of consciousness (nation). Begin at once to let go of your all-consuming thoughts of gain. Think about generosity and begin to be generous for your own sake. "It is more blessed to give than to receive" will prove itself to you as the law, for you will be blessed by a new influx of ideas of life, health, and prosperity when you start giving.

Instead of being grasping and avaricious, perhaps you have gone to the other extreme and have cultivated ideas of small things financially. You may have been fostering poverty by holding ideas of pennies instead of dollars or of hundreds instead of thousands. You may be thinking that you cannot give because your income is small or your supply is limited. Your remedy is to cultivate ideas of abundance. Claim God as your inexhaustible resource; that all things are yours. But in order to set in motion the accumulated energy of your thought you must also begin to give. You may be able to give only pennies at first, but give them in the name and the spirit of your opulent God. Send them forth with all the love of your heart and say to them as they go, *"Divine love through me blesses and multiplies you."*

Your consciousness is like a stream of water. If the stream is in any way dammed up, the water settles in all the low places and becomes stagnant. The quickest way to purify and reclaim the low, "swampy" places in your consciousness is to let in the flood from above by opening the dam. Many people try to demonstrate God as their supply by repeating affirmations of abundance now present, but fail to deny and thus to let go of the old condition and old belief in lack by beginning to give as generously as possible. It is not the amount you give measured by standards of the world, it is the good will you send forth with the gift; which can be measured only by spiritual standards.

"God loveth a cheerful giver." The Greek word here translated cheerful is *hilarion,* which means really "hilarious, joyful." The gift may be measured in dollars and cents but God looks not on such standards, He looks on and loves the "joyful" giver. We read in Deuteronomy 28:47, 48, "Because thou servedst not Jehovah thy God with joyfulness, and with gladness of heart, by reason of the abundance of all things; therefore shalt thou serve thine enemies . . . in hunger, and in thirst, and in nakedness, and in want of all things." This shows that there is a definite relation between the cheerfulness or joyfulness of our giving and our prosperity. Whether we make a large or a small gift, let us make it with largeness of cheer and joy, even of hilarity, remembering that God loveth a "hilarious" giver. "Keep therefore the words of this covenant, and do them, that ye may prosper in all that ye do."

BLESSINGS THAT MAY BE PLACED ON OUR GIFTS

Divine love, through me, blesses and multiplies this offering.

The Father gives abundantly; I receive thankfully, and give again generously.

This is the bounty of God, and I send it forth with wisdom and joy.

Divine love bountifully supplies and increases this offering.

I give freely and fearlessly, fulfilling the law of giving and reciving.

LESSON 11

Laying Up Treasures

After the multitude had been fed by the increase of the loaves and fishes, Jesus commanded that they gather up the fragments so that nothing might be lost. "And they all ate, and were filled: and they took up that which remained over of the broken pieces, twelve baskets full." Any form of waste is a violation of the divine law of conservation. Everywhere in nature there is evidence of stored-up energy substance, ready for use when needed.

This reserve force is not material but spiritual. It is ready to be called into expression to meet any need. But when it is not put to use or called into expression, there is a manifestation of inharmony or lack either in the body of man or in its outer supply. It is in his wrong conception of this spiritual force that man makes the mistake of falling into the habit of hoarding instead of conserving. He tries to gather things together in the external in a vain effort to avert an imagined shortage in the future and he counts himself rich by the amount of his material possessions.

Spiritually awakened people are coming to know that all riches are spiritual and within the reach of all as divine ideas. They study the law of conservation as it pertains to the spiritual and seek to build up a large reserve consciousness of substance, life, strength, and power, rather than laying up material treasures that "moth and rust consume" and "thieves break through and steal."

Men and women scatter their energies to the four winds in the effort to satisfy the desires of the flesh, and then wonder why they do not demonstrate prosperity. If they only realized the truth that this same thought force can be conserved and controlled to express itself in constructive channels, they would soon be prosperous. Spirit must have substance to work on and there must be substance in the ideas of your mind. If your substance is going here, there, and everywhere, being spent in riotous thinking, how can it accumulate to the point of demonstration? Such a waste of substance is a violation of the law of conservation, a law that all should know. When you overcome your desire for dissipation, not the overt acts only but the inner desire, then you will begin to accumulate substance that must manifest itself as prosperity according to the law.

One of the fundamental principles in the study of Christianity is that God's great objective is the making of a perfect man. Man is the apex of creation, made in God's image and likeness, and endowed with full authority and dominion over his elemental thoughts. We sometimes think that we must succeed in some business or occupation before we can become rich or famous. This is a missing of the mark of "the high calling of God in Christ Jesus," which is to demonstrate the divine idea of a perfect man. The real object of life is not making money or becoming famous but the building of character, the bringing forth of the potentialities that exist in every one of us. A part of the divine plan is substantial provision by the Creator for all the mental and physical needs of His creation. We are not studying prosperity to become rich but to bring out those characteristics that are fundamental to prosperity. We must learn to develop the faculty that will bring prosperity and the character that is not spoiled by prosperity.

Faith is the faculty of mind that deals with the universal-substance idea. Faith is the substance of things hoped for. Everything in God is ideal, without form or shape but with all possibilities. He is omnipresent in our mind and in our body. It is in our body that we bring God into visible manifestation. Faith is the faculty that does this. It lays hold of the substance idea and makes it visible.

The scramble for wealth seems to be the only object of existence for certain minds. Writers of Biblical times were incessantly preaching against the evils of money. Yet Jehovah was always promising riches and honor to all those who kept His commandments. The gold and silver that God promised were spiritual rather than material. God is mind, and mind can give only ideas. These ideas can be translated into terms of gold or of anything else we desire, according to our thought. The only treasures that are worth saving are those we lay up in the heavens of the mind. The only gold that can be trusted to bring happiness is the gold of Spirit. Jesus says, "I counsel thee to buy of me gold refined by fire, that thou mayest become rich; and white garments, that thou mayest clothe thyself, *that* the shame of thy nakedness be not made manifest."

Paul tells us that "the love of money is a root of all kinds of evil." That means of course that by loving money man has in some way limited it. He has not loved the true source of money but has loved the thing rather than the Spirit that it expresses. He has broken the law by trying to grasp the thing and failing to acknowledge the idea that lies back of it. We must know this law, observing it in the handling of money, and make love the magnet of supply instead of becoming entangled in that selfishness and greed which is causing so much inharmony and suffering in the world today. We should know that there is a universal money substance and that it belongs to all of us in all its fullness.

In the parable of the sower Jesus uses a most striking phrase. Part of the good seed was choked out by thorns and the thorns represent the "deceitfulness of riches." Money is indeed a cheat. It promises ease and brings cares; it promises pleasures and pays with pain; it promises influence and returns envy and jealousy; it promises happiness and gives sorrow; it promises permanence and then flies away.

Metaphysically, it is better or at least safer to be poor than to be rich. Jesus taught this in the parable of the rich man and Lazarus. The rich man is pictured in torment, crying for the poor man to give him a drink of water. But if the rich are miserable, the poor who greatly desire to be rich are equally so. Poverty and riches are the two poles of a magnet whose pivot is a belief that the possession of matter will bring joy to the possessor. This belief is a delusion, and those who are attracted by this belief and allow their minds to be hypnotized by the desire for material possessions are to be pitied whether their desire is realized or not.

The real possessor of wealth is the one who feels that all things are his to use and to enjoy yet does not burden himself with the personal possession of anything. Diogenes was a most happy man though he lived in a tub. His philosophy has outlived the influence of the rich and powerful people who were his contemporaries. He walked around with a lantern at midday looking for an honest man, so they seem to have been as rare in his day as in ours.

However, the widespread desire for material possessions indicates that there is somewhere some good in it. The natural man is from the soil, formed of the dust of the ground, and loves his native element. The spiritual man is from above, originating in the heavens of the mind. He is given first place and like Jacob supplants the natural man. Men should not condemn the earth because of this, yet they should not love it to the exclusion of the heavens. They should understand that substance is the clay from which the Father makes the body of His people. "Your heavenly Father knoweth that ye have need of all these things . . . . But seek ye first his kingdom, and his righteousness; and all these things shall be added unto you."

The divine law holds that the earth is the Lord's and the fullness thereof. If this truth were thoroughly understood, men would begin at once to make all property public, available for the use and enjoyment of all the people. The early disciples of Jesus understood this and their religion required them to bring all their possessions and lay them at the feet of their leaders, to be distributed and used according to the needs of all. Paul's companion Barnabas gave his field. Ananias and Sapphira sold their land and brought part of the price to Peter but held back part of it. They had not overcome the fear of future lack and had not put their faith fully in the teaching and promises of the Master.

When we have recognized the truth of the omnipresence of God as substance and supply for every need, there will be no occasion for holding back part as Ananias and Sapphira did. We cannot hoard money in its material phase without breaking the law, which is that we have all the substance necessary for our supply. We ask the Lord for our "daily" bread and expect to have it but we do not get an accumulation that will spoil on our hands or that will deny the proper supply to any other man. The metaphysical idea of this part of the Lord's Prayer is "Give us this day the substance of tomorrow's bread." We ask not for bread but for the substance that Spirit arranges to manifest as bread, clothing, shelter, or the supply for any need we may have.

Substance in the form of money is given to us for constructive uses. It is given for use and to meet an immediate need, not to be hoarded away or be foolishly wasted. When you have found freedom from the binding thought of hoarding money, do not go to the opposite extreme of extravagant spending. Money is to be used, not abused. It is good to keep one's obligations paid. It is good to have some money on hand for good uses, such as hospitality, education, for developing industries that will contribute to the good of numbers of people, for the furtherance of spiritual work, for helping others to build useful and constructive lives, and for many other purposes and activities. But in such conservation of money one should keep ever in mind the necessity of a constructive motive back of the action. Money accumulated for a definite and definitely constructive purpose is quite a different thing from money hoarded with the fearful thought of a "rainy day" or a prolonged season of lack and suffering. Money saved for "rainy days" is always used for just that, for fear attracts that which is feared unfailingly. "The thing which I fear cometh upon me."

Money saved as "an opportunity fund" brings an increase of good, but money hoarded from fear as a motive or with any miserly thought in mind cannot possibly bring any blessing. Those who hold the thought of accumulation so dominant in the world today are inviting trouble and even disaster, because right along with this thought goes a strong affirmation of the fear of loss of riches. Their actions bespeak fear, and the loss they dread is certain to be manifested sooner or later. The worldly idea of prosperity is based on the wrong idea of supply. One may have the right idea about the source of riches as spiritual and yet have the wrong idea about the constancy of supply as an ever-present, freely flowing spiritual substance. God does not clothe the lilies in a moment and then leave them to the mercy of lack; He gives them the continuous supply necessary to their growth. We can rest assured that He will much more clothe us and keep us clothed from day to day according to our need. When we doubt this and place our dependence on stored-up money instead, we shut off the stream of divine supply. Then when our little accumulation is spent, stolen, or lost, we are like the prodigal son and we begin to be in want.

Jesus did not own a foot of land. Yet never did He lack for anything needed. Without laying up treasures on earth He was rich in His consciousness of the treasures of heaven within Himself, treasures ready to be manifested in the outer whenever He needed them.

We know perfectly well that sooner or later we shall have to let go of our earthly possessions. Does this bring the thought of death and of leaving the world behind? Then it shows what a powerful hold this race belief of worldly wealth has taken in your mind. Men can think of letting go of their material possessions only in connection with death. They seem to prefer death to giving up their idea of wealth. When they make such a choice they decree what shall come to pass for them. That is why it is hard for a "rich man" to enter into the kingdom of heaven. He has laid up treasures on earth and not enough in heaven. He has not made it possible for his mind to lay hold of the positive pole of wealth, the true idea of wealth. He is holding to the negative side of the wealth idea, and that side is always changing. Material things pass away unless they are firmly connected with the unchanging, positive Source.

True riches and real prosperity are in the understanding that there is an omnipresent substance from which all things come and that by the action of our mind we can unify ourselves with that substance so that the manifestations that come from it will be in line with our desires and needs. Instead of realizing the inexhaustible, eternal, and omnipresent nature of that substance, we have limited it in our thought We have thought that there is only about so much of it and that we had better hurry to get our share. We have thought that we must be careful how we spend it and put some of it away for a time when there won't be any more. In building up this consciousness of a limited supply we have concluded that it is necessary to be economical and more and more saving. We begin to pinch in our mind, and then our money becomes pinched, for as we think in our mind, so we manifest in our affairs. This attitude pinches the channel through which our substance comes to manifestation and slows down the even flow of our supply. Then comes depression, hard times, shortage, and we wonder why, looking for some way to lay the blame on the government, or on war, or on industry, or even on the Lord, but never by any chance do we put the blame where it belongs: on ourselves.

The "pinching attitude" of mind does even worse than bring people into want. If people would relax in mind, they would loosen up the nerves and muscles of the body. They must learn the cause of their strained, pinching mental attitude and let go of that first. Then the relief of the outer condition will become manifest as the condition itself did.

Nearly all of us have been brought up in the belief that economy is an important thing, even a virtue. We should save our money and have a bank account. Saving money is the recipe for success given by many of our wealthy men. It is not a bad idea. There must be money available in banks to carry on business and industry. By having a bank account we contribute to the welfare of the community, if we have the right idea; which is that the Lord is our banker.

The word *miser* is from the Latin root from which also comes "miserable." It describes the condition of those who love and hoard money, lands, or other material things. The stories that are told about misers are almost beyond credence, but nearly every day the press recounts the story of the pitiable straits to which misers have reduced themselves in order to add to their riches. They sometimes starve themselves to add a few dollars or even a few pennies to their hoarded store. The papers recently carried an item about a miser in New York worth eleven million dollars. He goes from office to office in one of his great office buildings and picks up the waste paper from the baskets, which he sells for a few cents. Another almost as wealthy will not buy an overcoat but keeps his body warm by pinning newspapers under his house coat. Such men are not only themselves miserable but they make miserable all those around them. A New York paper tells of a miser worth millions when he died. Once burglars broke into his home, but they succeeded in getting out again without losing anything.

You do not need to lay up treasures for the future when you know that the law of omnipresent good is providing for you from within. As you evolve into this inner law of mind, you draw to yourself more and more of the good things of life.

In your mind see plenty everywhere. Yes, it is hard sometimes to overcome the thought that there is not enough, for it is an insidious thought that has been in consciousness for a long time. But it can be done. It has been done and is being done by others. The prosperity law is not a theory but a demonstrated fact, as thousands can testify. Now is the time to open your mind and to see plenty. As you do so you will find that there is an increase in your supply. Deny out of mind every thought of lack and affirm the abundance of all good. The infinite substance that infinite Mind has given to you is all about you now, but you must lay hold of it. It is like the air, but you must breathe the air to get it. It is yours for the taking, but you must take it. You should cultivate this wonderful power of the mind to know that everything is bountiful and this power to lay hold of invisible substance in the mind and by faith bring it forth into manifestation. Know with Job that we have as much now, in reality and in Truth, as we ever had. There is no shortage, lack, or depression with God.

Do not be fearful, regardless of how outer appearances may affect others. Keep your head when all about you are losing theirs. Refuse to load up your mind with the old material thoughts of economy to the point of denial of what you really need. Eliminate the old limiting ideas. Assert your freedom and your faith as a child of God. Do not spend foolishly or save foolishly. The farmer does not throw away his wheat when he sows a field. He knows how much he must sow per acre and does not stint, for he knows that a stinted sowing will bring a stinted harvest. He sows bountifully but not extravagantly and he reaps bountifully as he has sown. "Whatsoever a man soweth, that shall he also reap." "He that soweth sparingly shall reap also sparingly; and he that soweth bountifully shall reap also bountifully."

We cannot help but see that apparent lack and hard times are the result of states of mind. We have such things in the manifest world because men have not squared their action with divine Principle. They have not used spiritual judgment. When they invest in stocks and property, they get the opinions of other men, sometimes those who call themselves experts. Then comes the crash, and even the experts prove how little they understand the real laws of wealth. We can go to an expert who really knows the law because He ordained it in the first place. And He is not far away, but right within ourselves. We can go within and meditate on these things in the silence, and the Lord will direct our personal finances. He will show us just how to get the most and give the most with our money and He will see to it that we have the supply that we need so that we may not be in want of anything needful to our good. This may not mean riches piled up or "saved for a rainy day," but it will insure our supply for today, the only day there *is* in Truth.

As we continue to grow in the consciousness of God as omnipresent life and substance we no longer have to put our trust in accumulations of money or other goods. We are sure that each day's need will be met, and we do not deprive ourselves of today's enjoyment and peace in order to provide for some future and wholly imaginary need. In this consciousness our life becomes divinely ordered, and there is a balance in supply and finances as in everything else. We do not deprive ourselves of what we need today; neither do we waste our substance in foolish ways nor deplete it uselessly. We do not expect or prepare for adversity of any kind, for to do so is not only to invite it but to show a doubt of God and all His promises. Many people bear burdens and deny themselves sufficient for their present needs in order to prepare for dark days that never come. When we look back over the past we find that most of our fears were groundless, and most of the things we dreaded so much never happened. However the things we prepared for probably did happen and found us not fully prepared even after all our efforts in that direction. This should enable us to trust God now and rest in the positive assurance that He will supply every need as it arises.

Things are never so bad as you think. Never allow yourself to be burdened with the thought that you are having a hard time. You do not want a soul structure of that kind and should not build it with those thoughts. You are living in a new age. Yesterday is gone forever; today is here forever. Something grander for man is now unfolding. Put yourself in line with the progress of thought in the new age and go forward.

LESSON 12

Overcoming the Thought of Lack

The Kingdom of heaven is like unto a net, that was cast into the sea, and gathered of every kind; which, when it was filled, they drew up on the beach; and they sat down, and gathered the good into vessels, but the bad they cast away."

The mind of man is like the net catching every kind of idea, and it is man's privilege and duty under the divine law to separate those that are good from those which are not good. In this process the currents of unselfish, spiritual love flowing through the soul act as great eliminators, freeing the consciousness of thoughts of hate, lack, and poverty, and giving the substance of Spirit free access into the consciousness and affairs.

In another parable Jesus explained the same process as a separation of the sheep from the goats. When this divine current of love and spiritual understanding begins its work, we must make this separation. We put the sheep, the good and obedient and profitable thoughts, on the right, and we put the goats, the stubborn, selfish, useless thoughts, on the left. Each must handle his own thoughts and overcome them by aligning them with the harmony and order of the divine thought. There is an infinite, omnipresent wisdom within us that will deal with these thoughts and guide us in making the discrimination between the right and the wrong when we trust ourselves fully to its intelligence. We can establish a connection between the conscious mind and the superconscious mind within us by meditation, by silence, and by speaking the word.

The superconscious mind within you discriminates among the kinds of food you assimilate, controls your digestion, your breathing, and the beating of your heart. It "doeth all things well," and it will help you do this important work of directing you in the thoughts you should hold and the ones you should cast out. As you develop this mind within yourself you will find that you can gradually turn over more and more of your affairs to its perfect discrimination. Nothing is too great for it to accomplish, nor is anything too trivial for it to handle with perfection and dispatch. This mind of the Spirit will guide you in perfect ways, even in the minute details of your life, if you will let it do so. But you must will to do its will and trust it in all your ways. It will lead you unfailingly into health, happiness, and prosperity, as it has done and is doing for thousands, if and when you follow it.

It is just as necessary that one should let go of old thoughts and conditions after they have served their purpose as it is that one should lay hold of new ideas and create new conditions to meet one's requirements. In fact we cannot lay hold of the new ideas and make the new conditions until we have made room for them by eliminating the old. If we feel that we cannot part with the goats, we shall have to do with fewer sheep. If we insist on filling the vessels with the bad fish, we shall have to do without the good. We are learning that thoughts are things and occupy "space" in mind. We cannot have new or better ones in a place already crowded with old, weak, inefficient thoughts. A mental house cleaning is even more necessary than a material one, for the without is but a reflection of the within. Clean the inside of the platter, where the food is kept as well as the outside that people see, taught Jesus.

Old thoughts must be denied and the mind cleansed in preparation before the affirmative Christ consciousness can come in. Our mind and even our body is loaded with error thoughts. Every cell is clothed with thought: every cell has a mind of its own. By the use of denial we break through the outer crust, the material thought that has enveloped the cells, and get down into the substance and the life within them. Then we make contact with that substance and life which our denials have exposed, and by it express the positive, constructive side of the law. When we consistently deny the limitations of the material, we begin to reveal the spiritual law that waits within ourselves to be fulfilled. When this law is revealed to our consciousness, we begin to use it to demonstrate all things that are good. That is the state of consciousness that Jesus had, the Christ consciousness.

Every man has a definite work to do in the carrying forward of the divine law of spiritual evolution. The law is set into action by our thinking and is continually supported by our thought as it develops our soul. Within us are the great potentialities of Spirit that, put into action, enable us to be, do, or have anything we will. Science tells us that each of us has enough energy within himself to run a universe, if we knew how to release and control it. We do this releasing by a process of letting go and taking hold: letting go of the old or that which has done its part and is no longer useful, and taking hold of the new ideas and inspirations that come from the superconscious mind. Jesus told Peter that what he should bind in earth would be bound in heaven and what he should loose in earth would be loosed in heaven. He was not talking about a geographical earth or a definite place in the skies called heaven. He was explaining to Peter the law of mind. The conscious mind is but the negative pole of a very positive realm of thought. That positive realm of thought, Jesus called "the kingdom of the heavens." It is not a place at all but is the free activity of the superconscious mind of man. Whatever we bind or limit in earth, in the conscious mind, shall be bound or limited in the ideal or heavenly realm, and whatever we loose and set free in the conscious mind (earth) shall be loosed and set free in the ideal, the heavenly. In other words, whatever you affirm or deny in your conscious mind determines the character of the supermind activities. Ail power is given unto you both in heaven and in earth through your thought.

We must carefully choose what thoughts we are going to loose in the mind and what thoughts we are going to bind, for they will come into manifestation in our affairs. "As he [man] thinketh within himself, so is he" and "whatsoever a man soweth [in the mind], that shall he also reap [in the manifestation]." We must loose all thoughts of lack and insufficiency in the mind and let them go, just as Jesus commanded be done with the wrappings that held Lazarus: "Loose him, and let him go." Loose all thoughts of lack and lay hold of thoughts of plenty. See the abundance of all good things, prepared for you and for all of us from the foundation of the world. We live in a very sea of inexhaustible substance, ready to come into manifestation when molded by our thought.

Some persons are like fish in the sea, saying, "Where is the water?" in the presence of spiritual abundance they cry, "Where will I get the money? How will I pay my bills? Will we have food or clothes or the necessities?" Plenty is here, all around, and when you have opened the eyes of Spirit in yourself, you will see it and rejoice.

We mold omnipresent substance with our mind and make from it all the things that our mind conceives. If we conceive lack and poverty we mold that. If we visualize with a bountiful eye we mold plenty from the ever-present substance. There is perhaps no step in spiritual unfoldment more important than the one we are taking here. We must learn to let go, to give up, to make room for the things we have prayed for and desired. This is called renunciation or elimination, sacrifice it may even seem to some people. It is simply the giving up and casting away of old thoughts that have put us where we are, and putting in their place new ideas that promise to improve our condition. If the new ideas fail to keep this promise, we cast them away in their turn for others, confident that we shall eventually find the right ideas that will bring that which we desire. We always want something better than we have. It is the urge of progress, of development and growth. As children outgrow their clothes we outgrow our ideals and ambitions, broadening our horizon of life as we advance. There must be a constant elimination of the old to keep pace with this growth. When we cling to the old ideals we hinder our advance or stop it altogether.

Metaphysicians speak of this eliminative work as denial. Denial usually comes first. It sweeps out the debris and makes room for the new tenant that is brought into the mind by the affirmation. It would not be wise to eliminate the old thoughts unless you knew that there are higher and better ones to take their place. But we need not fear this, because we know the divine truth that God is the source of all good and that all good things can be ours through the love and grace of Jesus Christ.

None of us has attained that supreme place in consciousness where he wholly gives up the material man and lives in the Spirit, as Jesus did, but we have a concept of such a life and His example showing that it can be attained. We shall attain it when we escape the mortal. This does not mean that we must die to get free from mortality, for mortality is but a state of consciousness. We die daily and are reborn by the process of eliminating the thought that we are material and replacing it with the truth that we are spiritual. One of the great discoveries of modern science is that every atom in this so-called material universe has within it superabundant life elements. God is life and Spirit, and He is in every atom. We release this spiritual life quality by denying the crust of materiality that surrounds the cells and affirming that they are Spirit and life. This is the new birth, which takes place first as a conception in the mind, followed by an outworking in body and affairs. We all want better financial conditions. Here is the way to obtain them: Deny the old thoughts of lack of money and affirm the new thought of spiritual abundance everywhere manifest.

Every lesson of Scripture illustrates some phase of mental action and can be applied to each individual life according to the need that is most pressing at the time of its perception. If you do not look for the mental lesson when reading Scripture, you get but the mere outer shell of Truth. If however you have the proper understanding of the characters in the narrative, knowing that they represent ideas in your own mind, you can follow them in their various movements and find the way to solve all the problems of your life. This does not mean that a study of the written Scriptures will itself solve your problems unless you come into the apprehension of the real Scriptures, the Bible of the ages, the Book of Life within your own consciousness. But a study of the outer symbols as given in the written Scriptures can and should lead you into the understanding of the Truth of Being.

In every person we find the conflicting ideas represented by the Children of Israel and the Philistines. They are pitted against each other in a conflict that goes on night and day. We call these warring thoughts Truth and error. When we are awakened spiritually we stand on the side of Truth, knowing that Truth thoughts are the chosen of the Lord, the Children of Israel. But the error thoughts sometimes seem so real and so formidable that we quake and cringe with fear in their presence.

We know that Truth will eventually prevail, but we put the victory off somewhere in the future and say that the error is so large and strong that we cannot cope with it now—we will wait until we have gathered more strength. Then we need to stand still and affirm the salvation of the Lord.

Ideas are not all of the same importance. Some are large and strong; some are small and weak. There are aggressive, dominating ideas that parade themselves, and brag about their power, and with threats of disaster keep us frightened into submission to their wicked reign. These domineering ideas of error have one argument that they always use to impress us, that of the fear of results if we should dare to come out and meet them in open opposition. This fear of opposing ideas, even when we know them to be wrong, seems to be woven into our very mental fabric. This fear is symbolized by the spear of Goliath which, as the story relates, "was like a weaver's beam."

What is the most fearful thought in the minds of men today? Is it not the power of money? Is not mammon the greatest Philistine, the Goliath in your consciousness? It is the same whether you are siding with the Philistines and are successful in your finances from a material viewpoint, or whether you are with the Israelites and tremble in your poverty. The daily appearance of this giant Goliath, the power of money, is something greatly feared. Neither the Philistines nor the Israelites are in possession of the Promised Land, neither side at peace or happy in any security, so long as this domineering giant parades his strength and shouts his boasts. This error idea claims he is stronger than the Lord of Israel. He must be killed before all the other error thoughts will be driven out of your consciousness and you can come into the consciousness of plenty, the Promised Land of milk and honey.

The whole world today trembles before this giant error idea, the belief that money is the ruling power. The nations of the world are under this dominion because men think that money is power. The rich and the poor alike are slaves to the idea. Kings and great men of the earth bow and cringe before the money kings. This is because man has given this power to money by his erroneous thinking. He has made the golden calf and now he falls before it in worship. Instead of making it his servant he has called it master and become its slave. The rule of this mad giant has been disastrous, and the end of it is rapidly approaching.

The first step in getting your mind free from this giant bugaboo is to get a clear perception of your right as a child of God. You know that you should put no other gods or powers before the true God. You know also that you should not be under the dominion of anything in the heavens above or the earth beneath, for you have been given dominion over all. You will never find a better time to come into the realization of the truth of who and what you are and what your rights are. Never was a more propitious time to seek a new and better state of consciousness. If you are in fear of the boasting Philistine giant, as so many around you are, begin now to seek a way, as did David, to give his "flesh unto the birds of the heavens." There is a way, a righteous way, that cannot fail, and it is your duty to find it. Follow each step of the way that is symbolically and beautifully set forth in the 17th chapter of I Samuel.

The name *David* means "the Lord's beloved," and David represents your righteous perception of your privileges as the child of God. You are not a slave to anything or to anybody in the universe. The threat of this Goliath, the power of money, holds no terrors for you in this consciousness. You have a smooth perception of Truth and you sling it straight to the center of his carnal thinking, his forehead. The weight of his shield and his armor does not intimidate you, for you see them for what they are, empty and meaningless show, vulnerable in many places to the true ideas with which you are armed.

Even the most ardent defenders of the money power will admit that it is a tyrant and that they would not have it rule their world if they could help it. It nearly always destroys its friends in the end. Any man who becomes a slave to money is eventually crushed by it. On the other side are whole armies of righteous people, Christians, who like the army of Israel think that this giant cannot be overcome. They are waiting for reinforcements, something larger and stronger in a physical way, with which to overcome this enemy. They forget that "the battle is Jehovah's."

Do you cringe before this giant when he comes out daily to impress you with his boastings and threats? It does not have to be so. You need not continue to fear. There is a little idea in your mind that can slay him. You perhaps have not considered this little idea of much importance. Perhaps you have kept it off on a lonely mountainside of your spiritual consciousness, herding the sheep, which are your innocent thoughts. Now let this David come forth, this perception of your rightful place in Divine Mind. Get a clear idea of where you really belong in creation and what your privileges are. Do you think for a moment that God has so ordained that men cannot escape from the terrible servitude of hard conditions? Of course not. That would be injustice, and God is above all just.

It is your privilege to step out at any time and accept the challenge of this boaster. The Lord has been with you in the slaying of the fear of sin and sickness (the bear and the lion), and He will still be with you in slaying the fear of poverty, which Goliath symbolizes. "The battle is Jehovah's," and He is with us to deliver us "out of the hand of the Philistines."

The weapons of the Lord's man are not carnal. He does not wage war after the manner of the world. He does not use armor of steel or brass, the protection of selfishness and the weapons of oppression. He goes forth in the simplicity of justice, knowing that his innocence is his defense. He uses only his shepherd's sling and smooth stones, words of Truth. This is the will and the words of Truth that it sends forth. They are disdained by the Philistines and many people laugh at the idea of using words to overcome conditions. But words do their work, the work whereto they are sent, and the great mass of materiality goes down before their sure aim.

We know that money was made for man and not man for money. No man needs to be a slave to his brother man or cringe before him to obtain money, which is the servant of all alike. We are not bound to the wheel of work, of ceaseless toil day after day, in order to appease the god of mammon on his own terms. We are children of the living God, who as a loving Father is right here in our midst, where we may claim Him as our support and our resource on such conditions as He lovingly reveals when we have acknowledged Him and denied mammon. This day has Jehovah delivered this proud Philistine into our hands, and the victory is ours. Praise God.

The five smooth stones chosen by David from the brook represent five irrefutable statements of Truth. These statements sent forth from a mind confident of itself, its cause, and its spiritual strength will crush the forehead of Goliath, error's giant. The statements are the following:

I am the beloved of the Lord. He is with me in all my righteous words, and they do accomplish that whereto I send them forth.

My cause is just, for it is my divine right to be supplied with all things whatsoever that the Father has placed at the disposal of His children.

I dissolve in my own mind and the minds of all others any thought that my own can be withheld from me. What is mine comes to me by the sure law of God, and in my clear perception of Truth I welcome it.

I am not fearful of poverty, and I am under obligations to no one. My opulent Father has poured out to me all resources, and I am a mighty channel of abundance.

I selfishly own nothing, yet all things in existence are mine to use and in divine wisdom to bestow upon others.

Do not hold yourself in poverty by the fear of lack and by practicing a pinching economy. If you believe that all that the Father has is yours, then there is surely no reason for skimping. Nothing will so broaden your mind and your world as the realization that all is yours. When you realize the boundlessness of your spiritual inheritance, nothing shall be lacking in all your world. See with the bountiful eye; for "he that hath a bountiful eye shall be blessed." This passage states an exact law, the law of increase.

Religious leaders in the past have spread the belief that it is a Christian duty to be poor and that poverty is a virtue. This is by no means the doctrine of Jesus. He accepted the proposition fully, without reservation or qualification, that God is our resource and that the Father has provided all things for His children. He is often described as being poor, without a place to lay His head, yet He had a parental home at Nazareth and was welcomed gladly into the homes of both the rich and the poor all over Palestine. He dressed as a rabbi, and His clothing was so rich and valuable that the Roman soldiers coveted the seamless robe He wore and cast lots for it. He found abundance in the kingdom of God where everything needful becomes manifest not through hard labor but through the realization of Truth.

Jesus seldom had need for money, because He went back of money to the idea it represents and dealt with money in the idea realm. Our government is back of all our paper dollars, else they would have no value. God is back of every material symbol, and it is in God rather than in the symbol that we should put our faith. He is back of our call for food and raiment and everything that we could need or desire. Jesus says all we need do is ask in faith and in His name, believing that we receive, and we shall have. And we should not hesitate to ask largely, for God can give much as easily as He can give a little.

Question Helps

LESSON 1. SPIRITUAL SUBSTANCE, THE FUNDAMENTAL BASIS OF THE UNIVERSE

1. What is Divine Mind?
2. What is man, and how is he connected with divine ideas?
3. What great change in methods of production and distribution seems about to be made? How will it affect our prosperity?
4. What is the ether of science and metaphysics? To what extent has man drawn on it, and what are its possibilities?
5. What did Jesus demonstrate regarding the kingdom of the ether?
6. What is the source of all material, according to science? According to Jesus?
7. What is the simplest and surest way to lay hold of substance?
8. Explain from this viewpoint how substance can never be depleted.
9. Why does God give to just and unjust alike, to all equally?
10. How does this truth of the ether help us better to understand the nature of God as pure being or Spirit?
11. What is symbolized by gold and silver? Why are they precious?
12. What is the threefold activity through which substance must go on its way to becoming manifest as material?
13. If substance is omnipresent and man can control its manifestation, why does man suffer from lack and limitation?
14. Explain the teaching of Jesus that it is hard for a rich man to enter the kingdom of the heavens.
15. What is meant by "property rights" and the right to wealth? What error *is* implied in this doctrine? To whom do ideas belong?
16. What are some of the "great possessions" that must be unloaded before we can enter the kingdom of consciousness?
17. After recognizing the existence, potentiality, and availability of universal substance, what is the next step in demonstration?

18. Can the kingdom be found by one with selfish motives? Why should we desire healing and prosperity?

19. What is the prosperity consciousness? Give examples. How can it be cultivated wisely?

20. What will be the social and economic results of a widespread prosperity consciousness in the whole race?

LESSON 2. SPIRITUAL MIND, THE OMNIPRESENT DIRECTIVE PRINCIPLE OF PROSPERITY

1. Why are ideas the most important things in life?
2. What is desire in origin, purpose, and result?
3. What is the difference between "is-ness" and "existence"?
4. What is the difference between "being" and "appearance"?
5. What is the relation of figures to the problem they help solve? How does this illustrate spiritual reality and material phenomena?
6. What is implied in the fact that man can conceive of an ideal world?
7. Should we deny the existence of material things? Can we do so successfully? What should we deny about the things of the outer?
8. What is the "I AM identity"? How does it differ from Divine Mind?
9. Why is spiritual understanding important? How is it gained?
10. What connection exists between ideas in Divine Mind?
11. What divine idea is back of riches? What ideas are the "parents" of this idea? How can this knowledge help us in demonstrating?
12. Are all men equally entitled to wealth? What ideas should accompany the acquiring, using, and spending of wealth?
13. Do we expect God to give us actual loaves of bread when we pray the Lord's Prayer? What does He give instead of material things?
14. Why do people have dreams? Do dreams help men with their problems?
15. What is the value of relaxation and the silence when we seek God's gifts?
16. What relation has prosperity demonstration to the kingdom-of-the-heavens consciousness?
17. What is the physical, psychological, and spiritual reason for preparing the way for the prosperity demonstration?
18. What does the parable of the lilies teach us about substance?
19. What effect does the attitude of thanksgiving and praise have upon our prosperity?
20. Why is asking in the name of Jesus Christ more effective than any other prayer?

LESSON 3. FAITH IN THE INVISIBLE SUBSTANCE, THE KEY TO DEMONSTRATION

1. What is the starting point in building a prosperity consciousness?
2. What is the relation between faith and substance?
3. What does it mean to "have" faith?

4. What is a "seeking" faith? For what does it seek?
5. Explain how doubt retards manifestation.
6. What is the difference between the conception of John the Baptist and that of Jesus?
7. How do love and understanding assist faith in its accomplishments?
8. Are difficult experiences necessary in life? Why do we have them?
9. Show that it is sinful to think and talk hard times, lack, and other limitations.
10. Explain the symbology of the five loaves and two fishes.
11. How does fear produce a stagnation in financial circulation? How does confidence or faith restore normal conditions?
12. How can we go into "the upper room" to wait for the power from on high?
13. How does your mind create? Are its creations always real?
14. Why should our faith be in Spirit rather than in material things?
15. Show how faith is essential to success in the professions, in manufacturing, in sales, and in other lines of activity.
16. What do the Bible characters represent to us today? What Bible personage represents faith?
17. Is science antagonistic to religion or helpful to its cause?
18. What is the relation between material and substance?
19. Is there any lack of anything anywhere? What are we to overcome?
20. What affirmations help most to banish fear and abide in the consciousness of plenty?

LESSON 4. MAN, THE INLET AND OUTLET OF DIVINE MIND

1. What is meant by Principle as applied to prosperity?
2. How do we establish a consciousness of Principle as related to us?
3. How can the study of Truth make one happier, healthier, more beautiful, more prosperous?
4. What is a miracle? Is prosperity miraculous?
5. How are the keepers of divine law rewarded, and its breakers punished?
6. What are the legislative, judicial, and executive phases of the divine law?
7. What is the first rule of the divine law?
8. What is the effect of thinking and speaking of everything as good?
9. Is there any virtue in poverty?
10. What is meant by the "far country," and what is the homeland of the prodigal son?
11. What is the psychological and spiritual effect of old clothes?
12. What is symbolized by the putting on of new shoes.
13. How is true substance wasted, and what is the connection between waste and want?
14. What is our best insurance of financial security?
15. How does the law "Seek and ye shall find" apply to prosperity?
16. Should one who works harder or has more ability receive a greater reward than another?

17. What power has love in helping one to demonstrate prosperity?

18. How does the subconscious mind help or hinder in demonstration?

19. What form does God's answer to prayer take? How do we know when a prayer is answered?

20. Must one be morally worthy to become prosperous?

LESSON 5. THE LAW THAT GOVERNS THE MANIFESTATION OF SUPPLY

1. What in our consciousness is represented by Moses? By Joshua? By Jesus?

2. What is the metaphysical significance of eating? How do we break bread in the four-dimensional world?

3. What retards manifestation when we work to attain the consciousness of abundance?

4. What do we mean by the "one law"? How may we know it? How keep it?

5. Explain how our ability to use wealth wisely to a large degree determines our prosperity.

6. Is it necessary to beseech God for prosperity? To ask? To thank?

7. How do we look or go "within"?

8. Compare the sense mind with the spiritual mind and show how true prosperity depends on the latter.

9. What is the light theory of matter formation, and how does it agree with the teaching of the New Testament?

10. Where and what is heaven? How is the soul formed?

11. How did King Solomon demonstrate great prosperity?

12. What is meant by "laying hold of" the substance?

13. How did Jesus develop His consciousness of omnipresent substance and what did that consciousness ultimately do for Him?

14. What is the true interpretation of "rich man" in the famous parable of the camel and the needle's eye?

15. How do we constantly "turn stones into bread," and what results?

16. What does the parable of the talents teach us regarding prosperity?

17. What six steps necessary to manifestation may be discerned in the story of creation?

18. What do we contribute to the world by raising our own consciousness to the prosperity level?

19. Analyze and explain the statement "*I trust Thy universal law of prosperity in all my affairs.*"

LESSON 6. WEALTH OF MIND EXPRESSES ITSELF IN RICHES

1. What is prosperity?

2. Explain the prosperity law that Jesus gave.

3. What relation has a prosperity consciousness to wealth in the outer?
4. What is the "sin of riches"?
5. What causes crop failure and famine in some countries?
6. Why did Jesus carry no money and own no property?
7. What is the only thing that can satisfy human longing, and where *is* it found?
8. Is the law of prosperity limited to thought? What else is needful?
9. Over what is man given dominion by his Creator?
10. How can man master his fear of financial lack?
11. Why are prosperity prayers sometimes unanswered?
12. What is the true idea of God, and how does man give it form?
13. What causes "depressions" in the affairs of men and nations?
14. What part does self-control in the matter of sensation play in prosperity demonstration?
15. What is the relative importance of denial and affirmation in the demonstration of prosperity?
16. Who are the real producers of wealth in the nation?
17. What is the law of increase as applied to Mind substance?
18. How should we prepare for an increased prosperity?
19. Should we be specific and definite in our prayers for increase?
20. Write a prosperity affirmation of your own embodying the four essential steps of recognition, love, faith, and praise.

LESSON 7. GOD HAS PROVIDED PROSPERITY FOR EVERY HOME

1. Of what great spiritual power *is* the home the symbol?
2. What has the "atmosphere" of a home to do with its prosperity? How may an atmosphere of worry and fear be changed?
3. Explain the importance of speaking true words in the home.
4. Aside from the feeling of religious duty, why should we be thankful for what we have and express our thanks often?
5. Is it good policy to condemn the furnishings in the home or to be apologetic about them?
6. Should our homes be ostentatious and rich looking to attract prosperity?
7. Why should we be individual in furnishing the home rather than following the "accepted" or "in-the-mode" style only?
8. How will a deep and sincere love for God attract prosperity?
9. Why must there be love and understanding between members of the family to insure a prosperous home?
10. Explain the law of "Love thy neighbor" as applied to home prosperity.
11. What is God's will for the home, and how does the home express it?
12. Explain how trying to live and do as others live and do may hold back our prosperity demonstration.
13. How can we use our will to help the demonstration of home prosperity?

14. Why should the individual express his own ideas in order to demonstrate?
15. Where and how is the prosperity demonstration started?
16. Do we have any personal claim on God's substance?
17. How do we "pour" substance into the "empty" places of the home?
18. Why is it necessary to have determination in order to demonstrate?
19. Does the possession of material things *give* satisfaction?

LESSON 8. GOD WILL PAY YOUR DEBTS

1. What law of mind is observed in true forgiveness?
2. Why should we trust rather than distrust people?
3. Is there any such thing as debt in Truth? Why?
5. Where must we start in forgiving our debtors and creditors?
5. How can we forgive ourselves for holding others in our debt?
6. What is the only sure way of getting out and staying out of debt?
7. Explain forgiveness as a good method of bill collecting.
8. How does God forgive our debts? How does His love pay our debts?
9. How do debt and worry about debt affect health? What is the remedy?
10. Does God have a place in modern business?
11. What are the merits and the dangers of installment buying?
12. What is the importance of paying all obligations promptly?
13. What kind of thoughts should one hold toward creditors? Debtors?
14. What dominant belief has caused world depression, and how must it be overcome?
15. What is our part in its overcoming?
16. Is the credit system responsible for widespread debt?
17. Does our faith in supply justify us in assuming obligations and trusting that we shall be able to pay when the time comes?
18. What is the value of prayer in gaining freedom from debt?

LESSON 9. TITHING, THE ROAD TO PROSPERITY

1. What is a "tithe," and how was tithing started?
2. What benefits accrue to the tither, according to the promises of the Bible?
3. Should one regard one's tithe as an investment that pays rewards?
4. In what way is giving a divine grace?
5. What was the practical plan that Paul suggested to the Corinthians?
6. What effect does a willing and cheerful spirit have on the giver, the gift, and the receiver?
7. How can faith be exercised in giving?
8. How should wisdom be employed in giving?
9. How can one who is puzzled about giving—as regards how much, when, and where—be helped by the decision to tithe?
10. What should tithing mean to the farmer? Businessman? Professional man? Mechanic? Laborer?

11. How does tithing help fulfill "the first and greatest commandment" about loving God and the neighbor?

12. Aside from Bible promises, do we have direct evidence that tithing increases prosperity? Cite instances.

13. Should the tithe have a definite place in the personal or family budget? Should we keep a record of our giving, as we do of other disbursements?

14. Why is the regular tithe, though it may be small, better than the occasional giving of a larger gift in a lump sum?

15. What is the psychological basis and effect of tithing?

16. What attitude should one assume toward a seemingly delayed demonstration?

17. Should we look for our good to come through the channel of those to whom we give or serve?

18. Why is it better to give without thought or expectation of return?

19. What must we do about receiving what God has and desires for us?

20. Discuss giving as a form of affirmation.

LESSON 10. RIGHT GIVING, THE KEY TO ABUNDANT RECEIVING

1. In what ways is the religion of Jesus applicable to the problems of daily living?

2. State briefly the law of giving and receiving that Jesus taught.

3. Why has the teaching of Jesus not been more effective in changing conditions in the world and in individual life?

4. Why is economic reform so much needed at the present time?

5. Can any effective reform be based on the material phase of the economic problem? Why?

6. Why do men who direct finance and business fail to seek any advice or assistance from the church?

7. Why is individual reform necessary before national or world changes can be made?

8. What do metaphysical teaching and study contribute toward world betterment?

9. How does the desire for the accumulation of money and goods affect the finer nature and sensibilities of people?

10. Does avarice or greed have any effect on the health of men?

11. What is the chief cause of stagnation in money circulation and its attendant evils?

12. What rule did Jesus give us for freeing ourselves from financial lack?

13. Is the method practiced by the early Christians practicable in the world as it is today?

14. What substitute is now being advocated for the commercial standard of payments for goods and service?

15. What is the divine law of equilibrium? Why does it not seem to operate in financial matters?

16. Is there any direct connection between poverty and ill-health? How may this problem be approached? Is there a problem at the other extreme—great wealth? How may it be solved?

17. What is meant by the "race consciousness"? Can we escape its effects? How can we help to change it for the better?
18. What should we do about saving money for the future?
19. What attitude should we take toward charity?

LESSON 11. LAYING UP TREASURES

1. What is the law of conservation as applied to spiritual substance?
2. What is the difference between hoarding and conserving?
3. Is accumulation of substance necessary to demonstration?
4. How is spiritual substance accumulated? How dissipated?
5. What is the true objective of man's life?
6. Explain why character development must be a part of our study of the demonstration of prosperity.
7. Is the ambition for wealth commendable or reprehensible?
8. Of what is gold the symbol, metaphysically understood?
9. What is the deceitfulness of riches? What is money?
10. Does great wealth bring happiness? Does extreme poverty make one any better than the rich? What is the truth about riches?
11. What is the only true deed or title to possessions?
12. What do we want when we ask for "our daily bread"?
13. How does the hoarding of money injure society?
14. Should we prepare for that "rainy day" by saving part of our money?
15. Was Jesus poor? Was He ever in want? What does it mean to turn stones into bread?
16. Explain the meaning of the rich man and the eye of the needle.
17. What are some of the financial and bodily results of the pinching attitude toward money?
18. What attitude toward hard times and lack is most helpful to us?
19. How shall we learn to get the most and give the most with the means we have at our disposal?

LESSON 12. OVERCOMING THE THOUGHT OF LACK

1. Why must we constantly examine our thoughts and separate them?
2. By what standard do we judge our thoughts?
3. What is the work of the superconscious mind in the body?
4. How may we use this superconscious mind in our outer affairs?
5. What is the importance of thought elimination or mental clean-up?
6. How do we go about this work of eliminating error thoughts?
7. What further benefits accrue from the use of denial words?
8. Where or what is the "kingdom of the heavens," and what is it like?
9. What is meant by "loosing in heaven"? What should we loose and what should we guard against loosing?

10. Where and what is "substance"? How do we contact it?
11. What is the result of clinging to past ideas and methods?
12. What is mortality? Do we escape it by dying? How otherwise?
13. Explain the new birth and the relation of denial to it.
14. What do Bible characters mean to us? What can they do for us?
15. What do David and Goliath stand for in consciousness?
16. What is the modern "golden calf" that most men worship?
17. Name some of the evil results of the error of money worship.
18. Would the doing away with money entirely solve the problem? What is the solution?
19. What "little but mighty" idea in consciousness is symbolized by David?
20. What are the weapons of this David that slay the giant fear?

9

IN TUNE WITH THE INFINITE

RALPH WALDO TRINE

(1897)

Contents

Preface 511

1. Fullness of Peace, Power, and Plenty: Prelude 513
2. The Supreme Fact of the Universe 514
3. The Supreme Fact of Human Life 516
4. Fullness of Life—Bodily Health and Vigor 525
5. The Secret, Power, and Effects of Love 542
6. Wisdom and Interior Illumination 549
7. The Realization of Perfect Peace 560
8. Coming into Fullness of Power 566
9. Plenty of All Things—The Law of Prosperity 575
10. How Men Have Become Prophets, Seers, Sages, and Saviours 581
11. The Basic Principle of All Religions—The Universal Religion 584
12. Entering Now into the Realization of the Highest Riches 587
13. "The Way" 592

Preface

There is a golden thread that runs through every religion in the world. There is a golden thread that runs through the lives and the teachings of all the prophets, seers, sages, and saviours in the world's history, through the lives of all men and women of truly great and lasting power. All that they have ever done or attained to has been done in full accordance with law. What one has done, all may do.

This same golden thread must enter into the lives of all who today, in this busy work-a-day world of ours, would exchange impotence for power, weakness and suffering for abounding health and strength, pain and unrest for perfect peace, poverty of whatever nature for fullness and plenty.

Each is building his own world. We both build from within and attract from without. Thought is the force with which we build, for thoughts are forces. Like builds like and like attracts like. In the degree that thought is spiritualized does it become more subtle and powerful in its workings. This spiritualizing is in accordance with law and is within the power of all.

Everything is first worked out in the unseen before it is manifested in the seen, in the ideal before it is realized in the real, in the spiritual before it shows forth in the material. The realm of the unseen is the realm of cause. The realm of the seen is the realm of effect. The nature of effect is always determined and conditioned by the nature of its cause.

To point out the great facts in connection with, and the great laws underlying the workings of the interior, spiritual, thought forces, to point them out so simply and so clearly that even a child can understand, is the author's aim. To point them out so simply and so clearly that all can grasp them, that all can take them and infuse them into everyday life, so as to mould it in all its details in accordance with what they would have it, is his purpose. That life can be thus moulded by them is not a matter of mere speculation or theory with him, but a matter of positive knowledge.

There is a divine sequence running throughout the universe. Within and above and below the human will incessantly works the Divine will. To come into harmony with it and thereby with all the higher laws and forces, to come then into league and to work in conjunction with them, in order that they can work in league and in conjunction with us, is to come into the chain of this wonderful sequence. This is the secret of all success. This is to come into the possession of unknown riches, into the realization of undreamed-of powers.

R. W. T.

CHAPTER 1

Fullness of Peace, Power, and Plenty

PRELUDE

The optimist is right. The pessimist is right. The one differs from the other as the light from the dark. Yet both are right. Each is right from his own particular point of view, and this point of view is the determining factor in the life of each. It determines as to whether it is a life of power or of impotence, of peace or of pain, of success or of failure.

The optimist has the power of seeing things in their entirety and in their right relations. The pessimist looks from a limited and a one-sided point of view. The one has his understanding illumined by wisdom, the understanding of the other is darkened by ignorance. Each is building his world from within, and the result of the building is determined by the point of view of each. The optimist, by his superior wisdom and insight, is making his own heaven, and in the degree that he makes his own heaven is he helping to make one for all the world beside. The pessimist, by virtue of his limitations, is making his own hell, and in the degree that he makes his own hell is he helping to make one for all mankind.

You and I have the predominating characteristics of an optimist or the predominating characteristics of a pessimist. We then are making, hour by hour, our own heaven or our own hell; and in the degree that we are making the one or the other for ourselves are we helping make it for all the world beside.

The word heaven means harmony. The word hell is from the old English *hell,* meaning to build a wall around, to separate; to be *helled* was to be shut off from. Now if there is such a thing as harmony there must be that something one can be in right relations with; for to be in right relations with anything is to be in harmony with it. Again, if there is such a thing as being *helled,* shut off, separated from, there must be that something from which one is held, shut off, or separated.

CHAPTER 2

The Supreme Fact of the Universe

The great central fact of the universe is that Spirit of Infinite Life and Power that is back of all, that animates all, that manifests itself in and through all; that self-existent principle of life from which all has come, and not only from which all has come, but from which all is continually coming. If there is an individual life, there must of necessity be an infinite source of life from which it comes. If there is a quality or a force of love, there must of necessity be an infinite source of love whence it comes. If there is wisdom, there must be the all-wise source back of it from which it springs. The same is true in regard to peace, the same in regard to power, the same in regard to what we call material things.

There is, then, this Spirit of Infinite Life and Power back of all which is the source of all. This Infinite Power is creating, working, ruling through the agency of great immutable laws and forces that run through all the universe, that surround us on every side. Every act of our every-day lives is governed by these same great laws and forces. Every flower that blooms by the wayside, springs up, grows, blooms, fades, according to certain great immutable laws. Every snowflake that plays between earth and heaven, forms, falls, melts, according to certain great unchangeable laws.

In a sense there is nothing in all the great universe but law. If this is true there must of necessity be a force behind it all that is the maker of these laws and a force greater than the laws that are made. This Spirit of Infinite Life and Power that is back of all is what I call God. I care not what term you may use, be it Kindly Light, Providence, the Over Soul, Omnipotence, or whatever term may be most convenient. I care not what the term may be as long as we are agreed in regard to the great central fact itself.

God, then, is this Infinite Spirit which fills all the universe with Himself alone, so that all is from Him and in Him, and there is nothing that is outside. Indeed and in truth, then, in Him we live and move and have our being. He is the life of our life, our very life itself. We have received, we are continually receiving our life from Him. We are partakers of the life of God: and though we differ from Him in that we are individualized spirits, while He is the Infinite Spirit including us as well as all else beside, yet *in essence the life of God and the life of man are identically the same, and so are one.* They differ not in essence, in quality; they differ in degree.

There have been and are highly illumined souls who believe that we receive our life from God after the manner of a divine inflow. And again, there have been and are those who believe that our life is one with the life of God, and so that God and man are one. Which is right? Both are right; both right when rightly understood.

In regard to the first: if God is the Infinite Spirit of Life back of all, whence all comes, then clearly our life as individualized spirits is continually coming from this Infinite Source by means of this divine inflow. In the second place, if our lives as individualized spirits are directly from, are parts of this Infinite Spirit of Life, then the degree of the Infinite Spirit that is manifested in the life of each must be identical in quality with that Source, the same as a drop of water taken from the ocean is, in nature, in characteristics, identical with that ocean, its source. And how could it be otherwise? The liability to misunderstanding in this latter case, however, is this: in that although the life of God and the life of man in essence are identically the same, the life of God so far transcends the life of individual man that it includes all else beside. In other words, so far as the quality of life is concerned, in essence they are the same; so far as the degree of life is concerned, they are vastly different.

In this light is it not then evident that both conceptions are true? and more, that they are one and the same? Both conceptions may be typified by one and the same illustration.

There is a reservoir in a valley which receives its supply from an inexhaustible reservoir on the mountain side. It is then true that the reservoir in the valley receives its supply by virtue of the inflow of the water from the larger reservoir on the mountain side. It is also true that the water in this smaller reservoir is in nature, in quality, in characteristics identically the same as that in the larger reservoir which is its source. The difference, however, is this: the reservoir on the mountain side, in the *amount* of its water, so far transcends the reservoir in the valley that it can supply an innumerable number of like reservoirs and still be unexhausted.

And so in the life of man. If, as I think we have already agreed, however we may differ in regard to anything else, there is this Infinite Spirit of Life back of all, the life of all, and so, from which all comes, then the life of individual man, your life and mine, must come by a divine inflow from this Infinite Source. And if this is true, then the life that comes by this inflow to man is necessarily the same in essence as is this Infinite Spirit of Life. There is a difference. It is not a difference in essence. It is a difference in degree.

If this is true, does it not then follow that in the degree that man opens himself to this divine inflow does he approach to God? If so, it then necessarily follows that in the degree that he makes this approach does he take on the God-powers. And if the God-powers are without limit, does it not then follow that the only limitations man has are the limitations he sets to himself, by virtue of not knowing himself?

CHAPTER 3

The Supreme Fact of Human Life

From the great central fact of the universe in regard to which we have agreed, namely, this Spirit of Infinite Life that is back of all and from which all comes, we are led to inquire as to what is the great central fact in human life. From what has gone before, the question almost answers itself.

The great central fact in human life, in your life and in mine, is the coming into a conscious, vital realization of our oneness with this Infinite Life, and the opening of ourselves fully to this divine inflow. This is the great central fact in human life, for in this all else is included, all else follows in its train. In just the degree that we come into a conscious realization of our oneness with the Infinite Life, and open ourselves to this divine inflow, do we actualize in ourselves the qualities and powers of the Infinite Life.

And what does this mean? It means simply this: that we are recognizing our true identity, that we are bringing our lives into harmony with the same great laws and forces, and so opening ourselves to the same great inspirations, as have all the prophets, seers, sages, and saviours in the world's history, all men of truly great and mighty power. For in the degree that we come into this realization and connect ourselves with this Infinite Source, do we make it possible for the higher powers to play, to work, to manifest through us.

We can keep closed to this divine inflow, to these higher forces and powers, through ignorance, as most of us do, and thus hinder or even prevent their manifesting through us. Or we can intentionally close ourselves to their operations and thus deprive ourselves of the powers to which, by the very nature of our being, we are rightful heirs. On the other hand, we can come into so vital a realization of the oneness of our real selves with this Infinite Life, and can open ourselves so fully to the incoming of this divine inflow, and so to the operation of these higher forces, inspirations, and powers, that we can indeed and in truth become what we may well term, God-men.

And what is a God-man? One in whom the powers of God are manifesting, though yet a man. No one can set limitations to a man or a woman of this type; for the only limitations he or she can have are those set by the self. Ignorance is the most potent factor in setting limitations to the majority of mankind; and so the great majority of people continue to live their little, dwarfed, and stunted lives simply by virtue of the fact that they do not realize the larger life to which they are heirs. They have never as yet come into a knowledge of the real identity of their true selves.

Mankind has not yet realized that the real self is one with the life of God. Through its ignorance it has never yet opened itself to the divine inflow, and so has never made itself a channel through which the infinite powers and forces can manifest. When we know ourselves merely as men, we live accordingly, and have merely the powers of men. When we come into the realization of the fact that we are God-men, then again we live accordingly, and have the powers of God-men. *In the degree that we open ourselves to this divine inflow are we changed from mere men into God-men.*

A friend has a beautiful lotus pond. A natural basin on his estate—his farm as he always calls it—is supplied with water from a reservoir in the foothills some distance away. A gate regulates the flow of the water from the main that conducts it from the reservoir to the pond. It is a spot of transcendent beauty. There, through the days of the perfect summer weather, the lotus flowers lie full blown upon the surface of the clear, transparent water. The June roses and other wild flowers are continually blooming upon its banks. The birds come here to drink and to bathe, and from early until late one can hear the melody of their song. The bees are continually at work in this garden of wild flowers. A beautiful grove, in which many kinds of wild berries and many varieties of brakes and ferns grow, stretches back of the pond as far as the eye can reach.

Our friend is a man, nay more, a God-man, a lover of his kind, and as a consequence no notice bearing such words as "Private grounds, no trespassing allowed," or "Trespassers will be prosecuted," stands on his estate. But at the end of a beautiful by-way that leads through the wildwood up to this enchanting spot, stands a notice bearing the words "All are welcome to the Lotus Pond." All love our friend. Why? They can't help it. He so loves them, and what is his is theirs.

Here one may often find merry groups of children at play. Here many times tired and weary looking men and women come, and somehow, when they go their faces wear a different expression,—the burden seems to be lifted; and now and then I have heard them when leaving, sometimes in a faint murmur, as if uttering a benediction, say, "God bless our brother-friend." Many speak of this spot as the Garden of God. My friend calls it his Soul Garden, and he spends many hours in quiet here. Often have I seen him after the others have gone, walking to and fro, or sitting quietly in the clear moonlight on an old rustic bench, drinking in the perfume of the wild flowers. He is a man of a beautifully simple nature. He says that here the real things of life come to him, and that here his greatest and most successful plans, many times as by a flash of inspiration, suggest themselves to him.

Everything in the immediate vicinity seems to breathe a spirit of kindliness, comfort, good-will, and good cheer. The very cattle and sheep as they come to the old stone-fence at the edge of the grove and look across to this beautiful spot seem, indeed, to get the same enjoyment that the people are getting. They seem almost to smile in the realization of their contentment and enjoyment; or perhaps it seems so to the looker-on, because he can scarcely help smiling as he sees the manifested evidence of their contentment and pleasure.

The gate of the pond is always open wide enough to admit a supply of water so abundant that it continually overflows a quantity sufficient to feed a stream that runs through the fields below, giving the pure mountain water in drink to the cattle and flocks that are grazing there. The stream then flows on through the neighbors' fields.

Not long ago our friend was absent for a year. He rented his estate during his absence to a man who, as the world goes, was of a very "practical" turn of mind. He had no time for anything that did not bring him direct "practical" returns. The gate connecting the reservoir with the lotus pond was shut down, and no longer had the crystal mountain water the opportunity to feed and overflow it. The notice of our friend, "All are welcome to the Lotus Pond," was removed, and no longer were the gay companies of children and of men and women seen at the pond. A great change came over everything. On account of the lack of the life-giving water the flowers in the pond wilted, and their long stems lay stretched upon the mud in the bottom. The fish that formerly swam in its clear water soon died and gave an offensive odor to all who came near. The flowers no longer bloomed on its banks. The birds no longer came to drink and to bathe. No longer was heard the hum of the bees; and more, the stream that ran through the fields below dried up, so that the cattle and the flocks no longer got their supply of clear mountain water.

The difference between the spot now and the lotus pond when our friend gave it his careful attention was caused, as we readily see, by the shutting of the gate to the pond, thus preventing the water from the reservoir in the hills which was the source of its life, from entering it. And when this, the source of its life, was shut off, not only was the appearance of the lotus pond entirely changed, but the surrounding fields were deprived of the stream to whose banks the flocks and cattle came for drink.

In this do we not see a complete parallel so far as human life is concerned? In the degree that we recognize our oneness, our connection with the Infinite Spirit which is the life of all, and in the degree that we open ourselves to this divine inflow, do we come into harmony with the highest, the most powerful, and the most beautiful everywhere. And in the degree that we do this do we overflow, so that all who come in contact with us receive the effects of this realization on our part. This is the lotus pond of our friend, he who is in love with all that is truest and best in the universe. And in the degree that we fail to recognize our oneness with this Infinite Source, and so close, shut ourselves to this divine inflow, do we come into that state where there seems to be with us nothing of good, nothing of beauty, nothing of power; and when this is true, those who come in contact with us receive not good, but harm. This is the spot of the lotus pond while the farm was in the hands of a renter.

There is this difference between the lotus pond and your life and mine. It has no power in itself of opening the gate to the inflow of the water from the reservoir which is its source. In regard to this it is helpless and dependent upon an outside agency. You and I have the power, the power within us, to open or to close ourselves to this divine inflow exactly as we choose. This we have through the power of mind, through the operation of thought.

There is the soul life, direct from God. This it is that relates us to the Infinite. There is, then, the physical life. This it is that relates us to the material universe about us. The thought life connects the one with the other. It is this that plays between the two.

Before we proceed farther let us consider very briefly the nature of thought. Thought is not, as is many times supposed, a mere indefinite abstraction, or something of a like nature. It is, on the contrary, a vital, living force, the most vital, subtle, and irresistible force there is in the universe.

In our very laboratory experiments we are demonstrating the great fact that thoughts are forces. They have form, and quality, and substance, and power, and we are beginning to find that there is what we may term a *science of thought.* We are beginning also to find that through the instrumentality of our thought forces we have creative power, not merely in a figurative sense, but creative power in reality.

Everything in the material universe about us, everything the universe has ever known, had its origin first in thought. From this it took its form. Every castle, every statue, every painting, every piece of mechanism, everything had its birth, its origin, first in the mind of the one who formed it before it received its material expression or embodiment. The very universe in which we live is the result of the thought energies of God, the Infinite Spirit that is back of all. And if it is true, as we have found, that we in our true selves are in essence the same and in this sense are one with the life of this Infinite Spirit, do we not then see that in the degree that we come into a vital realization of this stupendous fact, *we, through the operation of our interior, spiritual, thought forces, have in like sense creative power?*

Everything exists in the unseen before it is manifested or realized in the seen, and in this sense it is true that the unseen things are the real, while the things that are seen are the unreal. The unseen things are *cause;* the seen things are *effect.* The unseen things are the eternal; the seen things are the changing, the transient.

The *"power of the word"* is a literal scientific fact. Through the operation of our thought forces we have creative power. The spoken word is nothing more nor less than the outward expression of the workings of these interior forces. The spoken word is then, in a sense, the means whereby the thought forces are focused and directed along any particular line; and this concentration, this giving them direction, is necessary before any outward or material manifestation of their power can become evident.

Much is said in regard to "building castles in the air," and one who is given to this building is not always looked upon with favor. But castles in the air are always necessary before we can have castles on the ground, before we can have castles in which to live. The trouble with the one who gives himself to building castles in the air is not that he builds them in the air, but that he does not go farther and actualize in life, in character, in material form, the castles he thus builds. He does a part of the work, a very necessary part; but another equally necessary part remains still undone.

There is in connection with the thought forces what we may term, the drawing power of mind, and the great law operating here is one with that great law of the universe, that like attracts like. We are continually attracting to us from both the seen and the unseen side of life, forces and conditions most akin to those of our own thoughts.

This law is continually operating whether we are conscious of it or not. We are all living, so to speak, in a vast ocean of thought, and the very atmosphere around us is continually filled with the thought forces that are being continually sent or that are continually going out in the form of thought waves. We are all affected, more or less, by these thought forces, either consciously or unconsciously; and in the degree that we are more or less sensitively organized, or in the degree that we are negative and so are open to outside influences, rather than positive, thus determining what influences shall enter into our realm of thought, and hence into our lives.

There are those among us who are much more sensitively organized than others. As an organism their bodies are more finely, more sensitively constructed. These, generally speaking, are people who are always more or less affected by the mentalities of those with whom they come in contact, or in whose company they are. A friend, the editor of one of our great journals, is so sensitively organized that it is impossible for him to attend a gathering, such as a reception, talk and shake hands with a number of people during the course of the evening, without taking on to a greater or lesser extent their various mental and physical conditions. These affect him to such an extent that he is scarcely himself and in his best condition for work until some two or three days afterward.

Some think it unfortunate for one to be sensitively organized. By no means. It is a good thing, for one may thus be more open and receptive to the higher impulses of the soul within, and to all higher forces and influences from without. It may, however, be unfortunate and extremely inconvenient to be so organized unless one recognize and gain the power of closing himself, of making himself positive to all detrimental or undesirable influences. This power every one, however sensitively organized he may be, can acquire.

This he can acquire through the mind's action. And, moreover, there is no habit of more value to anyone, be he sensitively or less sensitively organized, than that of occasionally taking and holding himself continually in the attitude of mind—I close myself, I make myself positive to all things below, and open and receptive to all higher influences, to all things above. By taking this attitude of mind consciously now and then, it soon becomes a habit, and if one is deeply in earnest in regard to it, it puts into operation silent but subtle and powerful influences in effecting the desired results. In this way all lower and undesirable influences from both the seen and the unseen side of life are closed out, while all higher influences are invited, and in the degree that they are invited will they enter.

And what do we mean by the unseen side of life? First, the thought forces, the mental and emotional conditions in the atmosphere about us that are generated by those manifesting on the physical plane through the agency of physical bodies. Second, the same forces generated by those who have dropped the physical body, or from whom it has been struck away, and who are now manifesting through the agency of bodies of a different nature.

"The individual existence of man *begins* on the sense plane of the physical world, but rises through successive gradations of ethereal and celestial spheres, corresponding with his ever unfolding deific life and powers, to a destiny of unspeakable grandeur and glory. Within and above every physical planet is a corresponding ethereal planet, or soul world, as within and above every physical organism is a corresponding ethereal organism, or soul body, of which the physical is but the external counterpart and materialized expression. From this etherealized or soul planet, which is the immediate home of our arisen humanity, there rises or deepens in infinite gradations spheres within and above spheres, to celestial heights of spiritualized existence utterly inconceivable to the sense man. Embodiment, accordingly, is two-fold,—the physical being but the temporary husk, so to speak, in and by which the real and permanent ethereal organism is individualized and perfected, somewhat as 'the full corn in the ear' is reached by means of its husk, for which there is no further use. By means of this indestructible ethereal body and the corresponding ethereal spheres of environment with the social life and relations in the spheres, the individuality and personal life is preserved forever."

The fact of life in whatever form means the continuance of life, even though the form be changed. Life is the one eternal principle of the universe and so always continues, even though the form of the agency through which it manifests be changed. "In my Father's house are many mansions." And surely, because the individual has dropped, has gone out of the physical body, there is no evidence at all that the life does not go right on the same as before, not commencing,—for there is no cessation,—but commencing in the other form, exactly where it has left off here; for all life is a continuous evolution, step by step; there one neither skips nor jumps.

There are in the other form, then, mentalities and hence lives of all grades and influences, the same as there are in the physical form. If, then, the great law that like attracts like is ever operating, we are continually attracting to us from this side of life influences and conditions most akin to those of our own thoughts and lives. A grewsome thought that we should be so influenced, says one. By no means, all life is one; we are all bound together in the one common and universal life, and especially not when we take into consideration the fact that we have it entirely in our own hands to determine the order of thought we entertain, and consequently the order of influences we attract, and are not mere willowy creatures of circumstance, unless indeed we choose to be.

In our mental lives we can either keep hold of the rudder and so determine exactly what course we take, what points we touch, or we can fail to do this, and failing, we drift, and are blown hither and thither by every passing breeze. And so, on the contrary, welcome should be the thought, for thus we may draw to us the influence and the aid of the greatest, the noblest, and the best who have lived on the earth, whatever the time, wherever the place.

We cannot rationally believe other than that those who have labored in love and with uplifting power here are still laboring in the same way, and in all probability with more earnest zeal, and with still greater power.

"And Elisha prayed, and said, Lord, I pray thee, open his eyes, that he may see. And the Lord opened the eyes of the young man; and he saw: and, behold, the mountain *was full of horses and chariots of fire* round about Elisha."

While riding with a friend a few days ago, we were speaking of the great interest people are everywhere taking in the more vital things of life, the eagerness with which they are reaching out for a knowledge of the interior forces, their ever increasing desire to know themselves and to know their true relations with the Infinite. And in speaking of the great spiritual awakening that is so rapidly coming all over the world, the beginnings of which we are so clearly seeing during the closing years of this, and whose ever increasing proportions we are to witness during the early years of the coming century, I said, "How beautiful if Emerson, the illumined one so far in advance of his time, who labored so faithfully and so fearlessly to bring about these very conditions, how beautiful if he were with us today to witness it all! how he would rejoice !" "How do we know," was the reply, "that he is not witnessing it all? and more, that he is not having a hand in it all,—a hand even greater, perhaps, than when we *saw* him here?" Thank you, my friend, for this reminder. And, truly, "are they not all ministering spirits sent forth to minister to those who shall be heirs of salvation?"

As science is so abundantly demonstrating today,—the things that we see are but a very small fraction of the things that are. The real vital forces at work in our own lives and in the world about us are not seen by the ordinary physical eye. Yet they are the causes of which all things we see are merely the effects. Thoughts are forces; like builds like, and like attracts like. For one to govern his thinking, then, is to determine his life.

Says one of deep insight into the nature of things: "The law of correspondences between spiritual and material things is wonderfully exact in its workings. People ruled by the mood of gloom attract to them gloomy things. People always discouraged and despondent do not succeed in anything, and live only by burdening some one else. The hopeful, confident, and cheerful attract the elements of success. A man's front or back yard will advertise that man's ruling mood in the way it is kept. A woman at home shows her state of mind in her dress. A slattern advertises the ruling mood of hopelessness, carelessness, and lack of system. Rags, tatters, and dirt are always in the mind before being on the body. The thought that is most put out brings its corresponding visible element to crystallize about you as surely and literally as the visible bit of copper in solution attracts to it the invisible copper in that solution. A mind always hopeful, confident, courageous, and determined on its set purpose, and keeping itself to that purpose, attracts to itself out of the elements things and powers favorable to that purpose.

"Every thought of yours has a literal value to you in every possible way. The strength of your body, the strength of your mind, your success in business, and the pleasure your company brings others, depends on the nature of your thoughts. . . . In whatever mood you set your mind does your spirit receive of unseen substance in correspondence with that mood. It is as much a chemical law as a spiritual law. Chemistry is not confined to the elements we see. The elements we do not see with the physical eye outnumber ten thousand times those we do see. The Christ injunction, 'Do good to those who hate you,' is based on a scientific fact and a natural law. So, to do good is to bring to yourself all the elements in nature of power and good. To do evil is to bring the contrary destructive elements. When our eyes are opened, self-preservation will make us stop all evil thought. Those who live by hate will die by hate: that is, 'those who live by the sword will die by the sword.' Every evil thought is as a sword drawn on the person to whom it is directed. If a sword is drawn in return, so much the worse for both."

And says another who knows full well whereof he speaks: "The law of attraction works universally on every plane of *action,* and we attract whatever we desire or expect. If we desire one thing and expect another, we become like houses divided against themselves, which are quickly brought to desolation. Determine resolutely to expect only what you desire, then you will attract only what you wish for. . . . Carry any kind of thought you please about with you, and so long as you retain it, no matter how you roam over land or sea, you will unceasingly attract to yourself, knowingly or inadvertently, exactly and only what corresponds to your own dominant quality of thought. Thoughts are our private property, and we can regulate them to suit our taste entirely by steadily recognizing our ability so to do."

We have just spoken of the drawing power of mind. Faith is nothing more nor less than the operation of the *thought forces* in the form of an earnest desire, coupled with expectation as to its fulfillment. And in the degree that faith, the earnest desire thus sent out, is continually held to and watered by firm expectation, in just that degree does it either draw to itself, or does it change from the unseen into the visible, from the spiritual into the material, that for which it is sent.

Let the element of doubt or fear enter in, and what would otherwise be a tremendous force will be so neutralized that it will fail of its realization. Continually held to and continually watered by firm expectation, it becomes a force, a drawing power, that is irresistible and absolute, and the results will be absolute in direct proportion as it is absolute.

We shall find, as we are so rapidly beginning to find today, that the great things said in regard to faith, the great promises made in connection with it, are not mere vague sentimentalities, but are all great scientific facts, and rest upon great immutable laws. Even in our very laboratory experiments we are beginning to discover the laws underlying and governing these forces. We are now beginning, some at least, to use them understandingly and not blindly, as has so often and so long been the case.

Much is said today in regard to the will. It is many times spoken of as if it were a force in itself. But will is a force, a power, only in so far as it is a particular form of the manifestation of the thought forces; for it is by what we call the "will" that thought is focused and given a particular direction, and in the degree that thought is thus focused and given direction, is it effective in the work it is sent out to accomplish.

In a sense there are two kinds of will,—the human and the divine. The human will is the will of what, for convenience' sake, we may term the lower self. It is the will that finds its life merely in the realm of the mental and the physical,—the sense will. It is the will of the one who is not yet awake to the fact that there is a life that far transcends the life of merely the intellect and the physical senses, and which when realized and lived, does not do away with or minify these, but which, on the contrary, brings them to their highest perfection and to their powers of keenest enjoyment. The divine will is the will of the higher self, the will of the one who recognizes his oneness with the Divine, and who consequently brings his will to work in harmony, in conjunction with the divine will. "The Lord thy God *in the midst of thee* is mighty."

The human will has its limitations. So far and no farther, says the law. The divine will has no limitations. It is supreme. All things are open and subject to you, says the law, and so, in the degree that the human will is transmuted into the divine, in the degree that it comes into harmony with and so acts in conjunction with the divine, does it become supreme. Then it is that "thou shalt decree a thing and it shall be established unto thee." The great secret of life and of power, then, is to make and to keep one's conscious connection with this Infinite Source.

The power of every life, the very life itself, is determined by what it relates itself to. God is immanent as well as transcendent. He is creating, working, ruling in the universe today, in your life and in mine, just as much as He ever has been. We are too apt to regard Him after the manner of an absentee landlord, one who has set into operation the forces of this great universe, and then taken Himself away.

In the degree, however, that we recognize Him as immanent as well as transcendent, are we able to partake of His life and power. For in the degree that we recognize Him as the Infinite Spirit of Life and Power that is today, at this very moment, working and manifesting in and through all, and then, in the degree that we come into the realization of our oneness with this life, do we become partakers of, and so do we actualize in ourselves the qualities of His life. *In the degree that we open ourselves to the inflowing tide of this immanent and transcendent life, do we make ourselves channels through which the Infinite Intelligence and Power can work.*

It is through the instrumentality of the mind that we are enabled to connect the real soul life with the physical life, and so enable the soul life to manifest and work through the physical. The thought life needs *continually* to be illumined from within. This illumination can come in just the degree that through the agency of the mind we recognize our oneness with the Divine, of which each soul is an individual form of expression.

This gives us the inner guiding which we call intuition. "Intuition is to the spiritual nature and understanding practically what sense perception is to the sensuous nature and understanding. It is an inner spiritual sense through which man is opened to the direct revelation and knowledge of God, the secrets of nature and life, and through which he is brought into conscious unity and fellowship with God, and made to realize his own deific nature and supremacy of being as the son of God. Spiritual supremacy and illumination thus realized through the development and perfection of intuition under divine inspiration, gives the perfect inner vision and direct insight into the character, properties, and purpose of all things to which the attention and interest are directed. . . . It is, we repeat, a spiritual sense opening inwardly, as the physical senses open outwardly; and because it has the capacity to perceive, grasp, and know the truth at first hand, independent of all external sources of information, we call it intuition. All inspired teaching and spiritual revelations are based upon the recognition of this spiritual faculty of the soul, and its power to receive and appropriate them . . . Conscious unity of man in spirit and purpose with the Father, born out of his supreme desire and trust, opens his soul through this inner sense to immediate inspiration and enlightenment from the Divine Omniscience, and the co-operative energy of the Divine Omnipotence, under which he becomes a seer and a master.

"On this higher plane of realized spiritual life in the flesh the mind holds the impersonal attitude and acts with unfettered freedom and unbiased vision, grasping truth at first hand, independent of all external sources of information. Approaching all beings and things from the divine side, they are seen in the light of the Divine Omniscience. God's purpose in them, and so the truth concerning them, as it rests in the mind of God, are thus revealed by direct illumination from the Divine Mind, to which the soul is opened inwardly through this spiritual sense we call intuition." Some call it the voice of the soul; some call it the voice of God; some call it the sixth sense. It is our inner spiritual sense.

In the degree that we come into the recognition of our own *true* selves, into the realization of the oneness of our life with the Infinite Life, and in the degree that we open ourselves to this divine inflow, does this voice of intuition, this voice of the soul, this voice of God, speak clearly; and in the degree that we recognize, listen to, and obey it, does it speak ever more clearly, until by-and-by there comes the time when it is unerring, *absolutely unerring,* in its guidance.

CHAPTER 4

Fullness of Life—Bodily Health and Vigor

God is the Spirit of Infinite Life. If we are partakers of this life, and have the power of opening ourselves fully to its divine inflow, it means more, so far as even the physical life is concerned, than we may at first think. For very clearly, the life of this Infinite Spirit, from its very nature, can admit of no disease; and if this is true, no disease can exist in the body where it freely enters, through which it freely flows.

Let us recognize at the outset that, so far as the physical life is concerned, *all life is from within out.* There is an immutable law which says: "As within, so without; cause, effect." In other words, the thought forces, the various mental states and the emotions, all have in time their effects upon the physical body.

Some one says: "I hear a great deal said today in regard to the effects of the mind upon the body, but I don't know as I place very much confidence in this." Don't you? Some one brings you sudden news. You grow pale, you tremble, or perhaps you fall into a faint. It is, however, through the channel of your mind that the news is imparted to you. A friend says something to you, perhaps at the table, something that seems very unkind. You are hurt by it, as we say. You have been enjoying your dinner, but from this moment your appetite is gone. But what was said entered into and affected you through the channel of your mind.

Look! yonder goes a young man, dragging his feet, stumbling over the slightest obstruction in the path. Why is it? Simply that he is weak-minded, an idiot. In other words, *a falling state of mind is productive of a falling condition of the body.* To be sure minded is to be sure footed. To be uncertain in mind is to be uncertain in step.

Again, a sudden emergency arises. You stand trembling and weak with fear. Why are you powerless to move? Why do you tremble? And yet you believe that the mind has but little influence upon the body. You are for a moment dominated by a fit of anger. For a few hours afterwards you complain of a violent headache. And still you do not seem to realize that the thoughts and emotions have an effect upon the body.

A day or two ago, while conversing with a friend, we were speaking of worry. "My father is greatly given to worry," he said. "Your father is not a healthy man," I said. "He is not strong, vigorous, robust, and active." I then went on to describe to him more fully his father's condition and the troubles which afflicted him. He looked at me in surprise and said, "Why, you do not know my father?" "No," I replied. "How then can you describe so accurately the disease with which he is afflicted?" "You have just told me that your father is greatly given to worry. When you told me this you indicated to me cause. In describing your father's condition I simply connected with the cause its own peculiar effects."

Fear and worry have the effect of closing up the channels of the body, so that the life forces flow in a slow and sluggish manner. Hope and tranquillity open the channels of the body, so that the life forces go bounding through it is such a way that disease can rarely get a foothold.

Not long ago a lady was telling a friend of a serious physical trouble. My friend happened to know that between this lady and her sister the most kindly relations did not exist. He listened attentively to her delineation of her troubles, and then, looking her squarely in the face, in a firm but kindly tone said: "Forgive your sister." The woman looked at him in surprise and said: "I can't forgive my sister." "Very well, then," he replied, "keep the stiffness of your joints and your kindred rheumatic troubles."

A few weeks later he saw her again. With a light step she came toward him and said: "I took your advice. I saw my sister and forgave her. We have become good friends again, and I don't know how it is, but somehow or other from the very day, as I remember, that we became reconciled, my troubles seemed to grow less, and today there is not a trace of the old difficulties left; and really, my sister and I have become such good friends that now we can scarcely get along without one another." Again we have effect following cause.

We have several well-authenticated cases of the following nature: A mother has been dominated for a few moments by an intense passion of anger, and the child at her breast has died within an hour's time, so poisoned became the mother's milk by virtue of the poisonous secretions of the system while under the domination of this fit of anger. In other cases it has caused severe illness and convulsions.

The following experiment has been tried a number of times by a well-known scientist. Several men have been put into a heated room. Each man has been dominated for a moment by a particular passion of some kind; one by an intense passion of anger, and others by different other passions. The experimenter has taken a drop of perspiration from the body of each of these men, and by means of a careful chemical analysis he has been able to determine the particular passion by which each has been dominated. Practically the same results revealed themselves in the chemical analysis of the saliva of each of the men.

Says a noted American author, an able graduate of one of our greatest medical schools, and one who has studied deeply into the forces that build the body and the forces that tear it down: "The mind is the natural protector of the body. . . . Every thought tends to reproduce itself, and ghastly mental pictures of disease, sensuality, and vice of all sorts, produce scrofula and leprosy in the soul, which reproduces them in the body. Anger changes the chemical properties of the saliva to a poison dangerous to life. It is well known that sudden and violent emotions have not only weakened the heart in a few hours, but have caused death and insanity. It has been discovered by scientists that there is a chemical difference between that sudden cold exudation of a person under a deep sense of guilt and the ordinary perspiration; and the state of the mind can sometimes be determined by chemical analysis of the perspiration of a criminal, which, when brought into contact with selenic acid, produces a distinctive pink color. It is well known that fear has killed thousands of victims; while, on the other hand, *courage is a great invigorator.*

"Anger in the mother may poison a nursing child. Rarey, the celebrated horse-tamer, said that an angry word would sometimes raise the pulse of a horse ten beats in a minute. If this is true of a beast, what can we say of its power upon human beings, especially upon a child? Strong mental emotion often causes vomiting. Extreme anger or fright may produce jaundice. A violent paroxysm of rage has caused apoplexy and death. Indeed, in more than one instance, a single night of mental agony has wrecked a life. Grief, long-standing jealousy, constant care and corroding anxiety sometimes tend to develop insanity. Sick thoughts and discordant moods are the natural atmosphere of disease, and crime is engendered and thrives in the miasma of the mind."

From all this we get the great fact we are scientifically demonstrating today,—that the various mental states, emotions, and passions have their various peculiar effects upon the body, and each induces in turn, if indulged in to any great extent, its own peculiar forms of disease, and these in time become chronic.

Just a word or two in regard to their mode of operation. If a person is dominated for a moment by, say a passion of anger, there is set up in the physical organism what we might justly term a bodily thunder-storm, which has the effect of souring, or rather of corroding, the normal, healthy, and life-giving secretions of the body, so that instead of performing their natural functions they become poisonous and destructive. And if this goes on to any great extent, by virtue of their cumulative influences, they give rise to a particular form of disease, which in turn becomes chronic. So the emotion opposite to this, that of kindliness, love, benevolence, good-will, tends to stimulate a healthy, purifying, and life-giving flow of all the bodily secretions. All the channels of the body seem free and open; the life forces go bounding through them. And these very forces, set into a bounding activity, will in time counteract the poisonous and disease-giving effects of their opposites.

A physician goes to see a patient. He gives no medicine this morning. Yet the very fact of his going makes the patient better. He has carried with him the spirit of health; he has carried brightness of tone and disposition; he has carried hope into the sick chamber; he has left it there. In fact, the very hope and good cheer he has carried with him has taken hold of and has had a subtle but powerful influence upon the mind of the patient; and this mental condition imparted by the physician has in turn its effects upon the patient's body, and so through the instrumentality of this mental suggestion the healing goes on.

> *Know, then, whatever cheerful and serene*
> *Supports the mind, supports the body, too.*
> *Hence the most vital movement mortals feel*
> *Is* hope; *the balm and life-blood of the soul.*

We sometimes hear a person in weak health say to another, "I always feel better when you come." There is a deep scientific reason underlying the statement. "The tongue of the wise is health." The power of suggestion so far as the human mind is concerned is a most wonderful and interesting field of study. Most wonderful and powerful forces can be set into operation through this agency. One of the world's most noted scientists, recognized everywhere as one of the most eminent anatomists living, tells us that he has proven from laboratory experiments that the entire human structure can be completely changed, made over, within a period of less than one year, and that some portions can be entirely remade within a period of a very few weeks.

"Do you mean to say," I hear it asked, "that the body can be changed from a diseased to a healthy condition through the operation of the interior forces?" Most certainly; and more, this is the natural method of cure. The method that has as its work the application of drugs, medicines and external agencies is the artificial method. The only thing that any drug or any medicine can do is to remove obstructions, that the life forces may have simply a better chance to do their work. *The real healing process must be performed by the operation of the life forces within.* A surgeon and physician of world-wide fame recently made to his medical associates the following declaration: "For generations past the most important influence that plays upon nutrition, the *life principle* itself, has remained an unconsidered element in the medical profession, and the almost exclusive drift of its studies and remedial paraphernalia has been confined to the action of matter over mind. This has seriously interfered with the evolutionary tendencies of the doctors themselves, and consequently the psychic factor in professional life is still in a rudimentary or comparatively undeveloped state. But the light of the nineteenth century has dawned, and so the march of mankind in general is taken in the direction of the hidden forces of nature. Doctors are now compelled to join the ranks of students in psychology and follow their patrons into the broader field of mental therapeutics. There is no time for lingering, no time for skepticism or doubt or hesitation. *He who lingers is lost, for the entire race is enlisted in the movement.*"

I am aware of the fact that in connection with the matter we are now considering there has been a great deal of foolishness during the past few years. Many absurd and foolish things have been claimed and done; but this says nothing against, and it has absolutely nothing to do with the great underlying laws themselves. The same has been true of the early days of practically every system of ethics or philosophy or religion the world has ever known. But as time has passed, these foolish, absurd things have fallen away, and the great eternal principles have stood out ever more and more clearly defined.

I know *personally* of many cases where an entire and permanent cure has been affected, in some within a remarkably short period of time, through the operation of these forces. Some of them are cases that had been entirely given up by the regular practice, *materia medica.* We have numerous accounts of such cases in all times and in connection with all religions. And why should not the power of effecting such cures exist among us today? The *power does exist,* and it will be actualized in just the degree that we recognize the same great laws that were recognized in times past.

One person may do a very great deal in connection with the healing of another, but this almost invariably implies co-operation on the part of the one who is thus treated. In the cures that Christ performed he most always needed the co-operation of the one who appealed to him. His question almost invariably was, "Dost thou believe?" He thus stimulated into activity the life-giving forces within the one cured. If one is in a very weak condition, or if his nervous system is exhausted, or if his mind through the influence of the disease is not so strong in its workings, it may be well for him for a time to seek the aid and co-operation of another. But it would be far better for such a one could he bring himself to a vital realization of the omnipotence of his own interior powers.

One may cure another, but to be *permanently healed* one must do it himself. In this way another may be most valuable as a teacher by bringing one to a clear realization of the power of the forces within, but in every case, in order to have a permanent cure, the work of the self is necessary. Christ's words were almost invariably,—Go and sin no more, or, thy sins are forgiven thee, thus pointing out the one eternal and never-changing fact,—that all disease and its consequent suffering is the direct or the indirect result of the violation of law, either consciously or unconsciously, either intentionally or unintentionally.

Suffering is designed to continue only so long as sin continues, sin not necessarily in the theological, but always in the philosophical sense, though many times in the sense of both. The moment the violation ceases, the moment one comes into perfect harmony with the law, the cause of the suffering ceases; and though there may be residing within the cumulative effects of past violation, the cause is removed, and consequently there can be no more effects in the form of additions, and even the diseased condition that has been induced from past violation will begin to disappear as soon as the right forces are set into activity.

There is nothing that will more quickly and more completely bring one into harmony with the laws under which he lives than this vital realization of his oneness with the Infinite Spirit, which is the life of all life. In this there can be no disease, and nothing will more readily remove from the organism the obstructions that have accumulated there, or in other words, the disease that resides there, than this full realization and the complete opening of one's self to this divine inflow. "I shall put my spirit in you, and ye shall live."

The moment a person realizes his oneness with the Infinite Spirit he recognizes himself as a spiritual being, and no longer as a mere physical, material being. He then no longer makes the mistake of regarding himself as body, subject to ills and diseases, but he realizes the fact that he is spirit, spirit now as much as he ever will or can be, and that he is the builder and so the master of the body, the house in which he lives; and the moment he thus recognizes his power as master he ceases in any way to allow it the mastery over him. He no longer fears the elements or any of the forces that he now in his ignorance allows to take hold of and affect the body. The moment he realizes his own supremacy, instead of fearing them as he did when he was out of harmony with them, he learns to love them. He thus comes into harmony with them; or rather, he so orders them that they come into harmony with him. He who formerly was the slave has now become the master. The moment we come to love a thing it no longer carries harm for us.

There are almost countless numbers today, weak and suffering in body, who would become strong and healthy if they would only give God an opportunity to do His work. To such I would say, *Don't shut out the divine inflow.* Do anything else rather than this. Open yourselves to it. Invite it. In the degree that you open yourselves to it, its inflowing tide will course through your bodies a force so vital that the old obstructions that are dominating them today will be driven out before it. "My words are life to them that find them, and health to all their flesh."

There is a trough through which a stream of muddy water has been flowing for many days. The dirt has gradually collected on its sides and bottom, and it continues to collect as long as the muddy water flows through it. Change this. Open the trough to a swift-flowing stream of clear, crystal water, and in a very little while even the very dirt that has collected on its sides and bottom will be carried away. The trough will be entirely cleansed. It will present an aspect of beauty and no longer an aspect of ugliness. And more, the water that now courses through it will be of value; it will be an agent of refreshment, of health and of strength to those who use it.

Yes, in just the degree that you realize your oneness with this Infinite Spirit of Life, and thus actualize your latent possibilities and powers, you will exchange dis-ease for ease, inharmony for harmony, suffering and pain for abounding health and strength. And in the degree that you realize this wholeness, this abounding health and strength in yourself, will you carry it to all with whom you come in contact; for *we must remember that health is contagious as well as disease.*

I hear it asked, What can be said in a concrete way in regard to the practical application of these truths, so that one can hold himself in the enjoyment of perfect bodily health; and more, that one may heal himself of any existing disease? In reply, let it be said that the chief thing that can be done is to point out the great underlying principle, and that each individual must make his own application; one person cannot well make this for another.

First let it be said, that the very fact of one's holding the thought of perfect health sets into operation vital forces which will in time be more or less productive of the effect,—perfect health. Then speaking more directly in regard to the great principle itself, from its very nature, it is clear that more can be accomplished through the process of realization than through the process of affirmation, though for some affirmation may be a help, an aid to realization.

In the degree, however, that you come into a vital realization of your oneness with the Infinite Spirit of Life, whence all life in individual form has come and is continually coming, and in the degree that through this realization you open yourself to its divine inflow, do you set into operation forces that will sooner or later bring even the physical body into a state of abounding health and strength. For to realize that this Infinite Spirit of Life can from its very nature admit of no disease, and to realize that this, then, is the life in you, by realizing your oneness with it, you can so open yourself to its more abundant entrance that the diseased bodily conditions—effects—will respond to the influences of its all-perfect power, this either quickly or more tardily, depending entirely upon yourself.

There have been those who have been able to open themselves so fully to this realization that the healing has been instantaneous and permanent. The degree of intensity always eliminates in like degree the element of time. *It must, however, be a calm, quiet, and expectant intensity, rather than an intensity that is fearing, disturbed, and non-expectant.* Then there are others who have come to this realization by degrees.

Many will receive great help, and many will be entirely healed by a practice somewhat after the following nature: With a mind at peace, and with a heart going out in love to all, go into the quiet of your own interior self, holding the thought,—I am one with the Infinite Spirit of Life, the life of my life. I then as spirit, I a spiritual being, can in my own real nature admit of no disease. I now open my body, in which disease has gotten a foothold, I open it fully to the inflowing tide of this Infinite Life, and it now, even now, is pouring in and coursing through my body, and the healing process is going on. Realize this so fully that you begin to feel a quickening and a warming glow imparted by the life forces to the body. Believe the healing process is going on. Believe in and hold continually to it. Many people greatly desire a certain thing, but expect something else. They have greater faith in the power of evil than in the power of good, and hence remain ill.

If one will give himself to this meditation, realization, treatment, or whatever term it may seem best to use, at stated times, as often as he may choose, and then *continually hold himself in the same attitude of mind,* thus allowing the force to work continually, he will be surprised how rapidly the body will be exchanging conditions of disease and inharmony for health and harmony. There is no particular reason, however, for this surprise, for in this way he is simply allowing the Omnipotent Power to do the work, which will have to do it ultimately in any case.

If there is a local difficulty, and one wants to open this particular portion, in addition to the entire body, to this inflowing life, he can hold this particular portion in thought, for to fix the thought in this way upon any particular portion of the body stimulates or increases the flow of the life forces in that portion. It must always be borne in mind, however, that whatever healing may be thus accomplished, effects will not permanently cease until causes have been removed. In other words, *as long as there is the violation of law, so long disease and suffering will result.*

This realization that we are considering will have an influence not only where there is a diseased condition of the body, but even where there is not this condition it will give an increased bodily life, vigor, and power.

We have had many cases, in all times and in all countries, of healing through the operation of the interior forces, entirely independent of external agencies. Various have been the methods, or rather, various have been the names applied to them, but the great law underlying all is one and the same, and the same today. When the Master sent his followers forth, his injunction to them was to heal the sick and the afflicted, as well as to teach the people. The early church fathers had the power of healing, in short, it was a part of their work.

And why should we not have the power today, the same as they had it then? Are the laws at all different? Identically the same. Why, then? Simply because, with a few rare exceptions here and there, we are unable to get beyond the mere letter of the law into its real vital spirit and power. It is the letter that killeth, it is the spirit that giveth life and power. Every soul who becomes so individualized that he breaks through the mere letter and enters into the real vital spirit, *will have the power,* as have all who have gone before, and when he does, he will also be the means of imparting it to others, for he will be one who will move and who will speak with authority.

We are rapidly finding today, and we shall find even more and more, as time passes, that practically all disease, with its consequent suffering, has its origin in perverted mental and emotional states and conditions. *The mental attitude we take toward anything determines to a greater or lesser extent its effects upon us.* If we fear it, or if we antagonize it, the chances are that it will have detrimental or even disastrous effects upon us. If we come into harmony with it by quietly recognizing and inwardly asserting our superiority over it, in the degree that we are able successfully to do this, in that degree will it carry with it no injury for us.

No disease can enter into or take hold of our bodies unless it find therein something corresponding to itself which makes it possible. And in the same way, no evil or undesirable condition of any kind can come into our lives unless there is already in them that which invites it and so makes it possible for it to come. The sooner we begin to look within ourselves for the cause of whatever comes to us, the better it will be, for so much the sooner will we begin to make conditions within ourselves such that only *good* may enter.

We, who from our very natures should be masters of all conditions, by virtue of our ignorance are mastered by almost numberless conditions of every description.

Do I fear a draft? There is nothing in the draft—a little purifying current of God's pure air—to cause me trouble, to bring on a cold, perhaps an illness. The draft can affect me only in the degree that *I myself* make it possible, only in the degree that I allow it to affect me. We must distinguish between causes and mere occasions. The draft is not cause, nor does it carry cause with it.

Two persons are sitting in the same draft. The one is injuriously affected by it, the other experiences not even an inconvenience, but he rather enjoys it. The one is a creature of circumstances; he fears the draft, cringes before it, continually thinks of the harm it is doing him. In other words, he opens every avenue for it to enter and take hold of him, and so it—harmless and beneficent in itself—brings to him exactly what he has empowered it to bring. The other recognizes himself as the master over and not the creature of circumstances. He is not concerned about the draft. He puts himself into harmony with it, makes himself positive to it, and instead of experiencing any discomfort, he enjoys it, and in addition to its doing him a service by bringing the pure fresh air from without to him, it does him the additional service of hardening him even more to any future conditions of a like nature. But if the draft was cause, it would bring the same results to both. The fact that it does not, shows that it is not a cause, but a condition, and it brings to each, effects which correspond to the conditions it finds within each.

Poor draft! How many thousands, nay millions of times it is made the scapegoat by those who are too ignorant or too unfair to look their own weaknesses square in the face, and who instead of becoming imperial masters, remain cringing slaves. Think of it, what it means! A man created in the image of the eternal God, sharer of His life and power, born to have dominion, fearing, shaking, cringing before a little draft of pure life-giving air. But scapegoats are convenient things, even if the only thing they do for us is to aid us in our constant efforts at self-delusion.

The best way to disarm a draft of the bad effects it has been accustomed to bring one, is first to bring about a pure and healthy set of conditions within, then, to change one's mental attitude toward it. Recognize the fact that of itself it has no power, it has only the power you invest it with. Thus you will put yourself into harmony with it, and will no longer sit in fear of it. Then sit in a draft a few times and get hardened to it, as every one, by going at it judiciously, can readily do. "But suppose one is in delicate health, or especially subject to drafts?" Then be simply a little judicious at first; don't seek the strongest that can be found, especially if you do not as yet in your own mind feel equal to it, for if you do not, it signifies that you still fear it. That supreme regulator of all life, *good common sense,* must be used here, the same as elsewhere.

If we are born to have dominion, and that we are is demonstrated by the fact that some have attained to it,—and what one *has* done, soon or late all *can* do,—then it is not necessary that we live under the domination of any physical agent. In the degree that we recognize our own interior powers, then are we rulers and able to dictate; in the degree that we fail to recognize them, we are slaves, and are dictated to. We build whatever we find within us; we attract whatever comes to us, and all in accordance with spiritual law, for all natural law is spiritual law.

The whole of human life is cause and effect; there is no such thing in it as chance, nor is there even in all the wide universe. Are we not satisfied with whatever comes into our lives? The thing to do, then, is not to spend time in railing against the imaginary something we create and call fate, but to look to the within, and change the causes at work there, in order that things of a different nature may come, for there will come exactly what we cause to come. This is true not only of the physical body, but of all phases and conditions of life. We invite whatever comes, and did we not invite it, either consciously or unconsciously, it could not and it would not come. This may undoubtedly be hard for some to believe, or even to see, at first. But in the degree that one candidly and open-mindedly looks at it, and then studies into the silent, but subtle and, so to speak, omnipotent workings of the thought forces, and as he traces their effects within him and about him, it becomes clearly evident, and easy to understand.

And then whatever does come to one depends for its effects entirely upon his mental attitude toward it. Does this or that occurrence or condition cause you annoyance? Very well; it causes you annoyance, and so disturbs your peace merely because you allow it to. You are born to have absolute control over your own dominion, but if you voluntarily hand over this power, even if for a little while, to some one or to some thing else, then you of course become the creature, the one controlled.

To live undisturbed by passing occurrences you must first find your own centre. You must then be firm in your own centre, and so rule the world from within. He who does not himself condition circumstances allows the process to be reversed, and become a conditioned circumstance. Find your centre and live in it. Surrender it to no person, to no thing. In the degree that you do this will you find yourself growing stronger and stronger in it. And how can one find his centre? By realizing his oneness with the Infinite Power, and by living continually in this realization.

But if you do not rule from your own centre, if you invest this or that with the power of bringing you annoyance, or evil, or harm, then take what it brings, but cease your railing against the eternal goodness and beneficence of all things.

I swear the earth shall surely be complete
To him or her who shall be complete;
The earth remains jagged and broken
Only to him who remains jagged and broken.

If the windows of your soul are dirty and streaked, covered with matter foreign to them, then the world as you look out of them will be to you dirty and streaked and out of order. Cease your complainings, however; keep your pessimism, your "poor, unfortunate me" to yourself, lest you betray the fact that your windows are badly in need of something. But know that your friend, who keeps his windows clean, that the Eternal Sun may illumine all within and make visible all without,—know that he lives in a different world from yours.

Then, go wash your windows, and instead of longing for some other world, you will discover the wonderful beauties of this world; and if you don't find transcendent beauties on every hand here, the chances are that you will never find them anywhere.

The poem hangs on the berry-bush
When comes the poet's eye,
And the whole street is a masquerade
When Shakespeare passes by.

This same Shakespeare, whose mere passing causes all this commotion, is the one who put into the mouth of one of his creations the words: "The fault, dear Brutus, is not in our stars, but in ourselves, that we are underlings." And the great work of his own life is right good evidence that he realized full well the truth of the facts we are considering. And again he gave us a great truth in keeping with what we are considering when he said:

Our doubts are traitors,
And make us lose the good we oft might win
By fearing to attempt.

There is probably no agent that brings us more undesirable conditions than fear. We should live in fear of nothing, nor will we when we come fully to know ourselves. An old French proverb runs:

Some of your griefs you have cured,
And the sharpest you still have survived;
But what torments of pain *you endured*
From evils that never arrived.

Fear and lack of faith go hand in hand. The one is born of the other. Tell me how much one is given to fear, and I will tell you how much he lacks in faith. Fear is a most expensive guest to entertain, the same as worry is: so expensive are they that no one can afford to entertain them. *We invite what we fear, the same as, by a different attitude of mind, we invite and attract the influences and conditions we desire.* The mind dominated by fear opens the door for the entrance of the very things, for the actualization of the very conditions it fears.

"Where are you going?" asked an Eastern pilgrim on meeting the plague one day. "I am going to Bagdad to kill five thousand people," was the reply. A few days later the same pilgrim met the plague returning. "You told me you were going to Bagdad to kill five thousand people," said he, "but instead, you killed fifty thousand." "No," said the plague. "*I killed only five thousand,* as I told you I would: *the others died of fright.*"

Fear can paralyze every muscle in the body. Fear affects the flow of the blood, likewise the normal and healthy action of all the life forces. Fear can make the body rigid, motionless, and powerless to move.

Not only do we attract to ourselves the things we fear, but we also aid in attracting to others the conditions we in our own minds hold them in fear of. This we do in proportion to the strength of our own thought, and in the degree that they are sensitively organized and so influenced by our thought, and this, although it be unconscious both on their part and on ours.

Children, and especially when very young, are, generally speaking, more sensitive to their surrounding influences than grown people are. Some are veritable little sensitive plates, registering the influences about them, and embodying them as they grow. How careful in their prevailing mental states then should be those who have them in charge, and especially how careful should a mother be during the time she is carrying the child, and when every thought, every mental as well as emotional state has its direct influence upon the life of the unborn child. Let parents be careful how they hold a child, either younger or older, in the thought of fear. This is many times done, unwittingly on their part, through anxiety, and at times through what might well be termed over-care, which is fully as bad as under-care.

I know of a number of cases where a child has been so continually held in the thought of fear lest this or that condition come upon him, that the very things that were feared have been drawn to him, which probably otherwise never would have come at all. Many times there has been no adequate basis for the fear. In case there is a basis, then far wiser is it to take exactly the opposite attitude, so as to neutralize the force at work, and then to hold the child in the thought of wisdom and strength that it may be able to meet the condition and master it, instead of being mastered by it.

But a day or two ago a friend was telling me of an experience of his own life in this connection. At a period when he was having a terrific struggle with a certain habit, he was so continually held in the thought of fear by his mother and the young lady to whom he was engaged,—the engagement to be consummated at the end of a certain period, the time depending on his proving his mastery,—that he, very sensitively organized, *continually* felt the depressing and weakening effects of their negative thoughts. He could always tell exactly how they felt toward him; he was continually influenced and weakened by their fear, by their questionings, by their suspicions, all of which had the effect of lessening the sense of his own power, all of which had an endeavor-paralyzing influence upon him. And so instead of their begetting courage and strength in him, they brought him to a still greater realization of his own weakness and the almost worthless use of struggle.

Here were two who loved him dearly, and who would have done anything and everything to help him gain the mastery, but who, ignorant of the silent, subtle, ever-working and all-telling power of the thought forces, instead of imparting to him courage, instead of adding to his strength, disarmed him of this, and then added an additional weakness from without. In this way the battle for him was made harder in a three-fold degree.

Fear and worry and all kindred mental states are too expensive for any person, man, woman, or child, to entertain or indulge in. Fear paralyzes healthy action, worry corrodes and pulls down the organism, and will finally tear it to pieces. Nothing is to be gained by it, but everything to be lost. Long-continued grief at any loss will do the same. Each brings its own peculiar type of ailment. An inordinate love of gain, a close-fisted, hoarding disposition will have kindred effects. Anger, jealousy, malice, continual fault-finding, lust, has each its own peculiar corroding, weakening, tearing-down effects.

We shall find that not only are happiness and prosperity concomitants of righteousness,—living in harmony with the higher laws, but bodily health as well. The great Hebrew seer enunciated a wonderful chemistry of life when he said,—"As righteousness tendeth to life, so he that pursueth evil, pursueth it to his own death." On the other hand, "In the way of righteousness is life; and in the pathway thereof there is no death." The time will come when it will be seen that this means far more than most people dare *even to think as yet.* "It rests with man to say whether his soul shall be housed in a stately mansion of ever-growing splendor and beauty, or in a hovel of his own building,—a hovel at last ruined and abandoned to decay."

The bodies of almost untold numbers, living their one-sided, unbalanced lives, are every year, through these influences, weakening and falling by the wayside long before their time. Poor, poor houses! Intended to be beautiful temples, brought to desolation by their ignorant, reckless deluded tenants. Poor houses!

A close observer, a careful student of the power of the thought forces, will soon be able to read in the voice, in the movements, in the features, the effects registered by the prevailing mental states and conditions. Or, if he is told the prevailing mental states and conditions, he can describe the voice, the movements, the features, as well as describe, in a general way, the peculiar physical ailments their possessor is heir to.

We are told by good authority that a study of the human body, its structure, and the length of time it takes it to come to maturity, in comparison with the time it takes the bodies of various animals and their corresponding longevity, reveals the fact that its natural age should be nearer a hundred and twenty years than what we commonly find it today. But think of the multitudes all about us whose bodies are aging, weakening, breaking, so that they have to abandon them long before they reach what ought to be a long period of strong, vigorous middle life.

Then, the natural length of life being thus shortened, it comes to be what we might term a race belief that this shortened period is the natural period. And as a consequence many, when they approach a certain age, seeing that as a rule people at this period of life begin to show signs of age, to break and go down hill as we say, they, thinking it a matter of course and that it must be the same with them, by taking this attitude of mind, many times bring upon themselves these very conditions long before it is necessary. Subtle and powerful are the influences of the mind in the building and rebuilding of the body. As we understand them better it may become the custom for people to look forward with pleasure to the teens of their second century.

There comes to mind at this moment a friend, a lady well on to eighty years of age. An old lady, some, most people in fact, would call her, especially those who measure age by the number of the seasons that have come and gone since one's birth. But to call our friend old, would be to call black white. She is no older than a girl of twenty-five, and indeed younger, I am glad to say, or I am sorry to say, depending upon the point of view, than *many* a girl of this age. Seeking for the good in all people and in all things, she has found the good everywhere. The brightness of disposition and of voice that is hers today, that attracts all people to her and that makes her so beautifully attractive to all people, has characterized her all through life. It has in turn carried brightness and hope and courage and strength to hundreds and thousands of people through all these years, and will continue to do so, apparently, for many years yet to come.

No fears, no worryings, no hatreds, no jealousies, no sorrowings, no grievings, no sordid graspings after inordinant gain, have found entrance into her realm of thought. As a consequence her mind, free from these abnormal states and conditions, has not externalized in her body the various physical ailments that the great majority of people are lugging about with them, thinking in their ignorance, that they are natural, and that it is all in accordance with the "eternal order of things" that they should have them. Her life has been one of varied experiences, so that all these things would have found ready entrance into the realm of her mind and so into her life were she ignorant enough to allow them entrance. On the contrary she has been wise enough to recognize the fact that in one kingdom at least she is ruler,—the kingdom of her mind, and that it is hers to dictate as to what shall and what shall not enter there. She knows, moreover, that in determining this she is determining all the conditions of her life. It is indeed a pleasure as well as an inspiration to see her as she goes here and there, to see her sunny disposition, her youthful step, to hear her joyous laughter. Indeed and in truth, Shakespeare knew whereof he spoke when he said,—"It is the mind that makes the body rich."

With great pleasure I watched her but recently as she was walking along the street, stopping to have a word and so a part in the lives of a group of children at play by the wayside, hastening her step a little to have a word with a washerwoman toting her bundle of clothes, stopping for a word with a laboring man returning with dinner pail in hand from his work, returning the recognition from the lady in her carriage, and so imparting some of her own rich life to all with whom she came in contact.

And as good fortune would have it, while still watching her, an old lady passed her,—really old, this one, though at least ten or fifteen years younger, so far as the count by the seasons is concerned. Nevertheless she was bent in form and apparently stiff in joint and muscle. Silent in mood, she wore a countenance of long-faced sadness, which was intensified surely several fold by a black, sombre headgear with an immense heavy veil still more sombre looking if possible. Her entire dress was of this description. By this relic-of-barbarism garb, combined with her own mood and expression, she continually proclaimed to the world two things,—her own personal sorrows and woes, which by this very method she kept continually fresh in her mind, and also her lack of faith in the eternal goodness of things, her lack of faith in the love and eternal goodness of the Infinite Father.

Wrapped only in the thoughts of her own ailments, and sorrows, and woes, she received and she gave nothing of joy, nothing of hope, nothing of courage, nothing of value to those whom she passed or with whom she came in contact. But on the contrary she suggested to all and helped to intensify in many, those mental states all too prevalent in our common human life. And as she passed our friend one could notice a slight turn of the head which, coupled with the expression in her face, seemed to indicate this as her thought,—Your dress and your conduct are not wholly in keeping with a lady of your years. Thank God, then, thank God they are not. And may He in His great goodness and love send us an innumerable company of the same rare type; and may they live a thousand years to bless mankind, to impart the life-giving influences of their own royal lives to the numerous ones all about us who stand so much in need of them.

Would you remain always young, and would you carry all the joyousness and buoyancy of youth into your maturer years? Then have care concerning but one thing,—how you live in your thought world. This will determine all. It was the inspired one, Gautama, the Buddha, who said,—"The mind is everything; what you think you become." And the same thing had Ruskin in mind when he said,—"Make yourself nests of pleasant thoughts. None of us as yet know, for none of us have been taught in early youth, what fairy palaces we may build of beautiful thought,—*proof against all adversity.*" And would you have in your body all the elasticity, all the strength, all the beauty of your younger years? Then live these in your mind, making no room for unclean thought, and you will externalize them in your body. In the degree that you keep young in thought will you remain young in body. And you will find that your body will in turn aid your mind, for body helps mind the same as mind builds body.

You are continually building, and so externalizing in your body conditions most akin to the thoughts and emotions you entertain. And not only are you so building from within, but you are also continually drawing from without, forces of a kindred nature. Your particular kind of thought connects you with a similar order of thought from without. If it is bright, hopeful, cheerful, you connect yourself with a current of thought of this nature. If it is sad, fearing, despondent, then this is the order of thought you connect yourself with.

If the latter is the order of your thought, then perhaps unconsciously and by degrees you have been connecting yourself with it. You need to go back and pick up again a part of your child nature, with its careless and cheerful type of thought. "The minds of the group of children at play are unconsciously concentrated in drawing to their bodies a current of playful thought. Place a child by itself, deprive it of its companions, and soon it will mope and become slow of movement. It is cut off from that peculiar thought current and is literally 'out of its element.'

"You need to bring again this current of playful thought to you which has gradually been turned off. You are too serious or sad, or absorbed in the serious affairs of life. You can be playful and cheerful without being puerile or silly. You can carry on business all the better for being in the playful mood when your mind is off your business. There is nothing but ill resulting from the permanent mood of sadness and seriousness,—the mood which by many so long maintained makes it actually difficult for them to smile at all.

"At eighteen or twenty you commenced growing out of the more playful tendency of early youth. You took hold of the more serious side of life. You went into some business. You became more or less involved in its cares, perplexities and responsibilities. Or, as man or woman, you entered on some phase of life involving care or trouble. Or you became absorbed in some game of business which, as you followed it, left no time for play. Then as you associated with older people you absorbed their old ideas, their mechanical methods of thinking, their acceptance of errors without question or thought of question. In all this you opened your mind to a heavy, care-laden current of thought. Into this you glided unconsciously. That thought is materialized in your blood and flesh. The seen of your body is a deposit or crystallization of the unseen element ever flowing to your body from your mind. Years pass on and you find that your movements are stiff and cumbrous,—that you can with difficulty climb a tree as at fourteen. Your mind has all this time been sending to your body these heavy, inelastic elements, making your body what now it is. . . .

"Your change for the better must be gradual and can only be accomplished by bringing the thought current of an all-round symmetrical strength to bear on it,—by demanding of the Supreme Power to be led in the best way, by diverting your mind from the many unhealthy thoughts which habitually have been flowing into it without your knowing it, to healthier ones. . . .

"Like the beast, the bodies of those of our race have in the past weakened and decayed. This will not always be. Increase of spiritual knowledge will show the cause of such decay, and will show, also, how to take advantage of a Law or Force to build us up, renew ever the body and give it greater and greater strength, instead of blindly using that Law or Force, as has been done in the past, to weaken our bodies and finally destroy them."

Full, rich, and abounding health is the normal and the natural condition of life. Anything else is an abnormal condition, and abnormal conditions as a rule come through perversions. God never created sickness, suffering, and disease; they are man's own creations. They come through his violating the laws under which he lives. So used are we to seeing them that we come gradually, if not to think of them as natural, then to look upon them as a matter of course.

The time will come when the work of the physician will not be to treat and attempt to heal the body, but to heal the mind, which in turn will heal the body. In other words, the true physician will be a teacher; his work will be to keep people well, instead of attempting to make them well after sickness and disease comes on; and still beyond this there will come a time when each will be his own physician. In the degree that we live in harmony with the higher laws of our being, and so, in the degree that we become better acquainted with the powers of the mind and spirit, will we give less attention to the body,—no less *care,* but less *attention.*

The bodies of thousands today would be much better cared for if their owners gave them less thought and attention. As a rule, those who think least of their bodies enjoy the best health. Many are kept in continual ill health by the abnormal thought and attention they give them.

Give the body the nourishment, the exercise, the fresh air, the sunlight it requires, keep it clean, and then think of it as little as possible. In your thoughts, and in your conversation never dwell upon the negative side. Don't talk of sickness and disease. By talking of these you do yourself harm and you do harm to those who listen to you. Talk of those things that will make people the better for listening to you. Thus you will infect them with health and strength and not with weakness and disease.

To dwell upon the negative side is always destructive. This is true of the body the same as it is true of all other things. The following from one whose thorough training as a physician has been supplemented by extensive study and observations along the lines of the powers of the interior forces, are of special significance and value in this connection: "We can never gain health by contemplating disease, any more than we can reach perfection by dwelling upon imperfection, or harmony through discord. We should keep a high ideal of health and harmony constantly before the mind. . . .

"Never affirm or repeat about your health what you do not wish to be true. Do not dwell upon your ailments, nor study your symptoms. Never allow yourself to be convinced that you are not complete master of yourself. Stoutly affirm your superiority over bodily ills, and do not acknowledge yourself the slave of any inferior power. . . . I would teach children early to build a strong barrier between themselves and disease, by healthy habits of thought, high thinking, and purity of life. I would teach them to expel all thoughts of death, all images of disease, all discordant emotions, like hatred, malice, revenge, envy, and sensuality, as they would banish a temptation to do evil. I would teach them that bad food, bad drink, or bad air makes bad blood; that bad blood makes bad tissue, and bad flesh bad morals. I would teach them that healthy thoughts are as essential to healthy bodies as pure thoughts to a clean life. I would teach them to cultivate a strong will power, and to brace themselves against life's enemies in every possible way. I would teach the sick to have hope, confidence, cheer. Our thoughts and imaginations are the only real limits to our possibilities. No man's success or health will ever reach beyond his own confidence; as a rule, we erect our own barriers.

"Like produces like the universe through. Hatred, envy, malice, jealousy, and revenge all have children. Every bad thought breeds others, and each of these goes on and on, ever reproducing itself, until our world is peopled with their offspring. The true physician and parent of the future will not medicate the body with drugs so much as the mind with principles. The coming mother will teach her child to assuage the fever of anger, hatred, malice, with the great panacea of the world,—Love. The coming physician will teach the people to cultivate cheerfulness, good-will, and noble deeds for a health tonic as well as a heart tonic; and that a merry heart doeth good like a medicine."

The health of your body, the same as the health and strength of your mind, depends upon what you relate yourself with. This Infinite Spirit of Life, this Source of all Life, can from its very nature, we have found, admit of no weakness, no disease. Come then into the full, conscious, vital realization of your oneness with this Infinite Life, open yourself to its more abundant entrance, and full and ever-renewing bodily health and strength will be yours.

And good may ever conquer ill,
Health walk where pain has trod;
"As a man thinketh, so is he,"
Rise, then, and think with God.

The whole matter may then be summed up in the one sentence, "God is well and so are you." You must awaken to the knowledge of your *real being.* When this awakening comes, you will have, and you will see that you have, the power to determine what conditions are externalized in your body. You must recognize, you must realize yourself, as one with Infinite Spirit. God's will is then your will; your will is God's will, and "with God all things are possible." When we are able to do away with all sense of separateness by living continually in the realization of this oneness, not only will our bodily ills and weaknesses vanish, but all limitations along all lines.

Then "delight thyself in the Lord, and He shall give thee the desires of thine heart." Then will you feel like crying all the day long, "The lines are fallen unto me in pleasant places; yea, I have a goodly heritage." Drop out of mind your belief in good things and good events coming to you in the future. Come *now* into the real life, and coming, appropriate and actualize them *now*. Remember that only the best is good enough for one with a heritage so royal as yours.

We buy ashes for bread;
We buy diluted wine;
Give me the true,—
Whose ample leaves and tendrils curled
Among the silver hills of heaven,
Draw everlasting dew.

CHAPTER 5

The Secret, Power, and Effects of Love

This is the Spirit of Infinite Love. The moment we recognize ourselves as one with it we become so filled with love that we see only the good in all. And when we realize that we are all one with this Infinite Spirit, then we realize that in a sense we are all one with each other. When we come into a recognition of this fact, we can then do no harm to any one, to any thing. We find that we are all members of the one great body, and that no portion of the body can be harmed without all the other portions suffering thereby.

When we fully realize the great fact of the oneness of all life,—that all are partakers from this one Infinite Source, and so that the same life is the life in each individual,—then prejudices go and hatreds cease. Love grows and reigns supreme. Then, wherever we go, whenever we come in contact with the fellow-man, we are able to recognize the God within. We thus look only for the good, and we find it. It always pays.

There is a deep scientific fact underlying the great truth, "He that takes the sword shall perish by the sword." The moment we come into a realization of the subtle powers of the thought forces, we can quickly see that the moment we entertain any thoughts of hatred toward another, he gets the effects of these diabolical forces that go out from us, and has the same thoughts of hatred aroused in him, which in turn return to the sender. Then when we understand the effects of the passion, hatred or anger, even upon the physical body, we can see how detrimental, how expensive this is. The same is true in regard to all kindred thoughts or passions, envy, criticism, jealousy, scorn. In the ultimate we shall find that in entertaining feelings of this nature toward another, we always suffer far more than the one toward whom we entertain them.

And then when we fully realize the fact that selfishness is at the root of all error, sin, and crime, and that ignorance is the basis of all selfishness, with what charity we come to look upon the acts of all. It is the ignorant man who seeks his own ends at the expense of the greater whole. It is the ignorant man, therefore, who is the selfish man. The truly wise man is never selfish. He is a seer, and recognizes the fact that he, a single member of the one great body, is benefited in just the degree that the entire body is benefited, and so he seeks nothing for himself that he would not equally seek for all mankind.

If selfishness is at the bottom of all error, sin, and crime, and ignorance is the basis of all selfishness, then when we see a manifestation of either of these qualities, if we are true to the highest within us, we will look for and will see to call forth the good in each individual with whom we come in contact. When God speaks to God, then God responds, and shows forth as God. But when devil speaks to devil, then devil responds, and the devil is always to pay.

I sometimes hear a person say, "I don't see any good in him." No? Then you are no seer. Look deeper and you will find the very God in every human soul. But remember it takes a God to recognize a God. Christ always spoke to the highest, the truest, and the best in men. He knew and he recognized the God in each because he had first realized it in himself. He ate with publicans and sinners. Abominable, the Scribes and Pharisees said. They were so wrapped up in their own conceits, their own self-centredness, hence their own ignorance, that they had never found the God in themselves, and so they never dreamed that it was the real life of even publicans and sinners.

In the degree that we hold a person in the thought of evil or of error, do we suggest evil and error to him. In the degree that he is sensitively organized, or not well individualized, and so, subject to the suggestions of the thought forces from others, will he be influenced; and so in this way we may be sharers in the very evil-doing in which we hold another in thought. In the same way when we hold a person in the thought of the right, the good, and the true, righteousness, goodness, and truth are suggested to him, and thus we have a most beneficent influence on his life and conduct. If our hearts go out in love to all with whom we come in contact, we inspire love, and the same ennobling and warming influences of love always return to us from those in whom we inspire them. There is a deep scientific principle underlying the precept—If you would have all the world love you, you must first love all the world.

In the degree that we love will we be loved. Thoughts are forces. Each creates of its kind. Each comes back laden with the effect that corresponds to itself and of which it is the cause.

Then let your secret thoughts be fair—
They have a vital part, and share
In shaping words and moulding fate;
God's system is so intricate.

I know of no better practice than that of a friend who continually holds himself in an attitude of mind that he continually sends out his love in the form of the thought,—Dear everybody, I love you." And when we realize the fact that a thought invariably produces its effect before it returns, or before it ceases, we can see how he is continually breathing out a blessing not only upon all with whom he comes in contact, but upon all the world. These same thoughts of love, moreover, tokened in various ways, are continually coming to him from all quarters.

Even animals feel the effects of these forces. Some animals are much more sensitively organized than many people are, and consequently they get the effects of our thoughts, our mental states, and emotions much more readily than many people do. Therefore whenever we meet an animal we can do it good by sending out to it these thoughts of love. It will feel the effects whether we simply entertain or whether we voice them. And it is often interesting to note how quickly it responds, and how readily it gives evidence of its appreciation of this love and consideration on our part.

What a privilege and how enjoyable it would be to live and walk in a world where we meet only Gods. In such a world you can live. In such a world I can live. For in the degree that we come into this higher realization do we see only the God in each human soul; and when we are thus able to see Him in every one we meet, we then live in such a world.

And when we thus recognize the God in every one, we by this recognition help to call it forth ever more and more. What a privilege,—this privilege of yours, this privilege of mine! That hypocritical judging of another is something then with which we can have nothing to do; for we have the power of looking beyond the evolving, changing, error-making self, and seeing the real, the changeless, the eternal self which by and by will show forth in the full beauty of holiness. We are then large enough also to realize the fact that when we condemn another, by that very act we condemn ourselves.

This realization so fills us with love that we continually overflow it, and all with whom we come in contact feel its warming and life-giving power. These in turn send back the same feeling of love to us, and so we continually attract love from all quarters. Tell me how much one loves and I will tell you how much he has seen of God. Tell me how much he loves and I will tell you how much he lives with God. Tell me how much he loves and I will tell you how far into the Kingdom of Heaven,—the kingdom of harmony, he has entered, for "love is the fulfilling of the law."

And in a sense love is everything. It is the key to life, and its influences are those that move the world. Live only in the thought of love for all and you will draw love to you from all. Live in the thought of malice or hatred, and malice and hatred will come back to you.

For evil poisons; malice shafts
Like boomerangs return,
Inflicting wounds that will not heal
While rage and anger burn.

Every thought you entertain is a force that goes out, and every thought comes back laden with its kind. This is an immutable law. Every thought you entertain has moreover a direct effect upon your body. Love and its kindred emotions are the normal and the natural, those in accordance with the eternal order of the universe, for "God is love." These have a life-giving, health-engendering influence upon your body, besides beautifying your countenance, enriching your voice, and making you ever more attractive in every way. And as it is true that in the degree that you hold thoughts of love for all, you call the same from them in return, and as these have a direct effect upon your mind, and through your mind upon your body, it is as so much life force added to your own from without. You are then continually building this into both your mental and your physical life, and so your life is enriched by its influence.

Hatred and all its kindred emotions are the unnatural, the abnormal, the perversions, and so, out of harmony with the eternal order of the universe. For if love is the fulfilling of the law, then these, its opposites, are direct violations of law, and there can never be a violation of law without its attendant pain and suffering in one form or another. There is no escape from this. And what is the result of this particular form of violation? When you allow thoughts of anger, hatred, malice, jealousy, envy, criticism, or scorn to exercise sway, they have a corroding and poisoning effect upon the organism; they pull it down, and if allowed to continue will eventually tear it to pieces by externalizing themselves in the particular forms of disease they give rise to. And then in addition to the destructive influences from your own mind you are continually calling the same influences from other minds, and these come as destructive forces augmenting your own, thus aiding in the tearing down process.

And so love inspires love; hatred breeds hatred. Love and good-will stimulate and build up the body; hatred and malice corrode and tear it down. Love is a savor of life unto life; hatred is a savor of death unto death.

There are loyal hearts, there are spirits brave,
There are souls that are pure and true;
Then give to the world the best you have,
And the best will come back to you,

Give love, and love to your *heart will flow,*
A strength in your utmost need;
Have faith, and a score of hearts will show
Their faith in your *word and deed.*

I hear it said,—How in regard to one who bears me hatred, towards whom I have entertained no such thoughts and feelings, and so have not been the cause of his becoming my enemy? This may be true, but the chances are that you will have but few enemies if there is nothing of an antagonistic nature in your own mind and heart. Be sure there is nothing of this nature. But if hatred should come from another without apparent cause on your part, then meet it from first to last with thoughts of love and good-will. In this way you can, so to speak, so neutralize its effects that it cannot reach you and so cannot harm you. Love is positive, and stronger than hatred. Hatred can always be conquered by love.

On the other hand, if you meet hatred with hatred, you simply intensify it. You add fuel to the flame already kindled, upon which it will feed and grow, and so you increase and intensify the evil conditions. Nothing is to be gained by it, everything is to be lost. By sending love for hatred you will be able so to neutralize it that it will not only have no effect upon you, but will not be able even to reach you. But more than this, you will by this course sooner or later be able literally to transmute the enemy into the friend. Meet hatred with hatred and you degrade yourself. Meet hatred with love and you elevate not only yourself but also the one who bears you hatred.

The Persian sage has said, "Always meet petulance with gentleness, and perverseness with kindness. A gentle hand can lead even an elephant by a hair. Reply to thine enemy with gentleness. Opposition to peace is sin." The Buddhist says, "If a man foolishly does me wrong I will return him the protection of my ungrudging love. The more evil comes from him, the more good shall go from me." "The wise man avenges injuries by benefits," says the Chinese. "Return good for evil, overcome anger by love; hatred never ceases by hatred, but by love," says the Hindu.

The truly wise man or woman will recognize no one as an enemy. Occasionally we hear the expression, "Never mind; I'll get even with him." Will you? And how will you do it? You can do it in one of two ways. You can, as you have in mind, deal with him as he deals, or apparently deals, with you,—pay him, as we say, in his own coin. If you do this you will get even with him by sinking yourself to his level, and both of you will suffer by it. Or, you can show yourself the larger, you can send him love for hatred, kindness for ill-treatment, and so get even with him by raising him to the higher level. But remember that you can never help another without by that very act helping yourself; and if forgetful of self, then in most all cases the value to you is greater than the service you render another. If you are ready to treat him as he treats you, then you show clearly that there is in you that which draws the hatred and ill-treatment to you; you deserve what you are getting and should not complain, nor would you complain if you were wise. By following the other course you most effectually accomplish your purpose,—you gain a victory for yourself, and at the same time you do a great service for him; for which it is evident he stands greatly in need.

Thus you may become his saviour. He in turn may become the saviour of other error-making, and consequently care-encumbered men and women. Many times the struggles are greater than we can ever know. We need more gentleness and sympathy and compassion in our common human life. Then we will neither blame nor condemn. Instead of blaming or condemning we will sympathize, and all the more we will

Comfort one another,
For the way is often dreary,
And the feet are often weary,
And the heart is very sad.
There is a heavy burden bearing,
When it seems that none are caring,
And we half forget that ever we were glad.

Comfort one another
With the hand-clasp close and tender,
With the sweetness love can render,
And the looks of friendly eyes.
Do not wait with grace unspoken,
While life's daily bread is broken—
Gentle speech is oft like manna from the skies.

When we come fully to realize the great fact that all evil and error and sin with all their consequent sufferings come through ignorance, then wherever we see a manifestation of these in whatever form, if our hearts are right, we will have compassion, sympathy and compassion for the one in whom we see them. Compassion will then change itself into love, and love will manifest itself in kindly service. Such is the divine method. And so instead of aiding in trampling and keeping a weaker one down, we will hold him up until he can stand alone and become the master. But all life-growth is from within out, and one becomes a true master in the degree that the knowledge of the divinity of his own nature dawns upon his inner consciousness and so brings him to a knowledge of the higher laws; and in no way can we so effectually hasten this dawning in the inner consciousness of another, as by showing forth the divinity within ourselves simply by the way we live.

By example and not by precept. By living, not by preaching. By doing, not by professing. By living the life, not by dogmatizing as to how it should be lived. There is no contagion equal to the contagion of life. Whatever we sow, that shall we also reap, and each thing sown produces of its kind. We can kill not only by doing another bodily injury directly, but we can and we do kill by every antagonistic thought.

Not only do we thus kill, but while we kill we suicide. Many a man has been made sick by having the ill thoughts of a number of people centred upon him; some have been actually killed. Put hatred into the world and we make it a literal hell. Put love into the world and heaven with all its beauties and glories becomes a reality.

Not to love is not to live, or it is to live a living death. The life that goes out in love to all is the life that is full, and rich, and continually expanding in beauty and in power. Such is the life that becomes ever more inclusive, and hence larger in its scope and influence. The larger the man and the woman, the more inclusive they are in their love and their friendships. The smaller the man and the woman, the more dwarfed and dwindling their natures, the more they pride themselves upon their "exclusiveness." Any one—a fool or an idiot—can be exclusive. It comes easy. It takes and it signifies a large nature to be universal, to be inclusive. Only the man or the woman of a small, personal, self-centred, self-seeking nature is exclusive. The man or the woman of a large, royal, unself-centred nature never is. The small nature is the one that continually strives for effect. The larger nature never does. The one goes here and there in order to gain recognition, in order to attach himself to the world. The other stays at home and draws the world *to him.* The one loves merely himself. The other loves all the world; but in his larger love for all the world he finds himself included.

Verily, then, the more one loves the nearer he approaches to God, for God is the spirit of infinite love. And when we come into the realization of our oneness with this Infinite Spirit, then divine love so fills us that, enriching and enrapturing our own lives, from them it flows out to enrich the life of all the world.

In coming into the realization of our oneness with the Infinite Life, we are brought at once into right relations with our fellow-men. We are brought into harmony with the great law, that we find our own lives in losing them in the service of others. We are brought to a knowledge of the fact that all life is one, and so that we are all parts of the one great whole. We then realize that we can't do for another without at the same time doing for ourselves. We also realize that we cannot do harm to another without by that very act doing harm to ourselves. We realize that the man who lives to himself alone lives a little, dwarfed, and stunted life, because he has no part in this larger life of humanity. But the one who in service loses his own life in this larger life, has his own life increased and enriched a thousand or a million fold, and every joy, every happiness, everything of value coming to each member of this greater whole comes as such to him, for he has a part in the life of each and all.

And here let a word be said in regard to true service. Peter and John were one day going up to the temple, and as they were entering the gate they were met by a poor cripple who asked them for alms. Instead of giving him something to supply the day's needs and then leaving him in the same dependent condition for the morrow and the morrow, Peter did him a real service, and a real service for all mankind by saying, Silver and gold have I none, but such as I have I give unto thee. *And then he made him whole.* He thus brought him into the condition where he could help himself. In other words, the greatest service we can do for another is to help him to help himself. To help him directly might be weakening, though not necessarily. It depends entirely upon circumstances. But to help one to help himself is never weakening, but always encouraging and strengthening, because it leads him to a larger and stronger life.

There is no better way to help one to help himself than to bring him to a knowledge of himself. There is no better way to bring one to a knowledge of himself than to lead him to a knowledge of the powers that are lying dormant within his own soul. There is nothing that will enable him to come more readily or more completely into an awakened knowledge of the powers that are lying dormant within his own soul, than to bring him into the conscious, vital realization of his oneness with the Infinite Life and Power, so that he may open himself to it in order that it may work and manifest through him.

We will find that these same great truths lie at the very bottom of the solution of our social situation; and we will also find that we will never have a full and permanent solution of it until they are fully recognized and built upon.

CHAPTER 6

Wisdom and Interior Illumination

This is the Spirit of Infinite Wisdom, and in the degree that we open ourselves to it does the highest wisdom manifest itself to and through us. We can in this way go to the very heart of the universe itself and find the mysteries hidden to the majority of mankind,—hidden to them, though not hidden of themselves.

In order for the highest wisdom and insight we must have absolute confidence in the Divine guiding us, but not through the channel of some one else. And why should we go to another for knowledge and wisdom? With God is no respect of persons. Why should we seek these things second hand? Why should we thus stultify our own innate powers? Why should we not go direct to the Infinite Source itself? "If any man lack wisdom let him ask of God." "Before they call I will answer, and while they are yet speaking, I will hear."

When we thus go directly to the Infinite Source itself we are no longer slaves to personalities, institutions, or books. We should always keep ourselves open to suggestions of truth from these agencies. We should always regard them as agencies, however, and *never as sources.* We should never recognize them as masters, but simply as teachers. With Browning, we must recognize the great fact that—

Truth is within ourselves; it takes no rise
From outward things, whate'er you may believe.
There is an inmost centre in us all,
Where truth abides in fullness.

There is no more important injunction in all the world, nor one with a deeper interior meaning, than "To thine own self be true." In other words, be true to your own soul, for it is through your own soul that the voice of God speaks to you. This is the interior guide. This is the light that lighteth every man that cometh into the world. This is conscience. This is intuition. This is the voice of the higher self, the voice of the soul, the voice of God. "Thou shalt hear a voice behind thee, saying: This is the way, walk ye in it."

When Elijah was on the mountain it was after the various physical commotions and manifestations that he heard the "still, small voice," the voice of his own soul, through which the Infinite God was speaking. If we will but follow this voice of intuition, it will speak ever more clearly and more plainly, until by and by it will be absolute and unerring in its guidance. The great trouble with us is that we do not listen to and do not follow this voice within our own souls, and so we become as a house divided against itself. We are pulled this way and that, and we are never *certain* of anything. I have a friend who listens so carefully to this inner voice, who, in other words, always acts so quickly and so fully in accordance with his intuitions, and whose life as a consequence is so absolutely guided by them, that he always does the right thing at the right time and in the right way. He always knows when to act and how to act, and he is never in the condition of a house divided against itself.

But some one says, "May it not be dangerous for us to act always upon our intuitions? Suppose we should have an intuition to do harm to some one?" We need not be afraid of this, however, for the voice of the soul, this voice of God speaking through the soul, will never direct one to do harm to another, nor to do anything that is not in accordance with the highest standards. of right, and truth, and justice. And if you at any time have a prompting of this kind, know that it is not the voice of intuition; it is some characteristic of your lower self that is prompting you.

Reason is not to be set aside, but it is to be continually illumined by this higher spiritual perception, and in the degree that it is thus illumined will it become an agent of light and power. When one becomes thoroughly individualized he enters into the realm of all knowledge and wisdom; and to be individualized is to recognize no power outside of the Infinite Power that is back of all. When one recognizes this great fact and opens himself to this Spirit of Infinite Wisdom, he then enters upon the road to the true education, and mysteries that before were closed now reveal themselves to him. This must indeed be the foundation of all true education, this evolving from within, this evolving of what has been involved by the Infinite Power.

All things that it is valuable for us to know will come to us if we will but open ourselves to the voice of this Infinite Spirit. It is thus that we become seers and have the power of seeing into the very heart of things. There are no new stars, there are no new laws or forces, but we can so open ourselves to this Spirit of Infinite Wisdom that we can discover and recognize those that have not been known before; and in this way they become new to us. When in this way we come into a knowledge of truth we no longer need facts that are continually changing. We can then enter into the quiet of our own interior selves. We can open the window and look out, and thus gather the facts as we choose. This is true wisdom. "Wisdom is the knowledge of God." Wisdom comes by intuition. It far transcends knowledge. Great knowledge, knowledge of many things, may be had by virtue simply of a very retentive memory. It comes by tuition. But wisdom far transcends knowledge, in that knowledge is a mere incident of this deeper wisdom.

He who would enter into the realm of wisdom must first divest himself of all intellectual pride. He must become as a little child. Prejudices, preconceived opinions and beliefs always stand in the way of true wisdom. Conceited opinions are always suicidal in their influences. They bar the door to the entrance of truth.

All about us we see men in the religious world, in the world of science, in the political, in the social world, who through intellectual pride are so wrapped in their own conceits and prejudices that larger and later revelations of truth can find no entrance to them; and instead of growing and expanding, they are becoming dwarfed and stunted and still more incapable of receiving truth. Instead of actively aiding in the progress of the world, they are as so many dead sticks in the way that would retard the wheels of progress. This, however, they can never do. Such always in time get bruised, broken, and left behind, while God's triumphal car of truth moves steadily onward.

When the steam engine was still being experimented with, and before it was perfected sufficiently to come into practical use, a well-known Englishman—well known then in scientific circles—wrote an extended pamphlet proving that it would be impossible for it *ever* to be used in ocean navigation, that is, in a trip involving the crossing of the ocean, because it would be utterly impossible for any vessel to carry with it sufficient coal for the use of its furnace. And the interesting feature of the whole matter was that the very first steam vessel that made the trip from England to America, had among its cargo a part of the first edition of this carefully prepared pamphlet. There was only the one edition. Many editions might be sold now.

This seems indeed an amusing fact; but far more amusing is the man who voluntarily closes himself to truth because, forsooth, it does not come through conventional, or orthodox, or heretofore accepted channels; or because it may not be in full accord with, or possibly may be opposed to, established usages or beliefs. On the contrary—

Let there be many windows in your soul,
That all the glory of the universe
May beautify it. Not the narrow pane
Of one poor creed can catch the radiant rays
That shine from countless sources. Tear away
The blinds of superstition: let the light
Pour through fair windows, broad as truth itself
And high as heaven. . . . Tune your ear
To all the worldless music of the stars
And to the voice of nature, and your heart
Shall turn to truth and goodness as the plant
Turns to the sun. A thousand unseen hands
Reach down to help you to their peace-crowned heights
And all the forces of the firmament
Shall fortify your strength. Be not afraid
To thrust aside half-truths and grasp the whole.

There is a great law in connection with the coming of truth. It is this: Whenever a man or a woman shuts himself or herself to the entrance of truth on account of intellectual pride, preconceived opinions, prejudices, or for whatever reason, there is a great law which says that truth *in its fullness* will come to that one from no source. And on the other hand, when a man or a woman opens himself or herself fully to the entrance of truth from *whatever* source it may come, there is an equally great law which says that truth will flow in to him or to her from all sources, from all quarters. Such becomes the free man, the free woman, for it is the truth that makes us free. The other remains in bondage, for truth has had no invitation and will not enter where it is not fully and freely welcomed.

And where truth is denied entrance the rich blessings it carries with it cannot take up their abode. On the contrary, when this is the case, it sends an envoy carrying with it atrophy, disease, death, physically and spiritually as well as intellectually. And the man who would rob another of his free and unfettered search for truth, who would stand as the interpreter of truth for another, with the intent of remaining in this position, rather than endeavoring to lead him to the place where he can be his own interpreter, is more to be shunned than a thief and a robber. The injury he works is far greater, for he is doing direct and positive injury to the very life of the one he thus holds.

Who has ever appointed any man, whoever he may be, as the keeper, the custodian, the dispenser of God's illimitable truth? Many indeed are moved and so are called to be teachers of truth; but the true teacher will never stand as the interpreter of truth for another. The *true teacher* is the one whose endeavor is to bring the one he teaches to a true knowledge of himself and hence of his own interior powers, that he may become his own interpreter. All others are, generally speaking, those animated by purely personal motives, self-aggrandizement, or personal gain. Moreover, he who would claim to have all truth and the only truth, is a bigot, a fool, or a knave.

In the Eastern literature is a fable of a frog. The frog lived in a well, and out of his little well he had never been. One day a frog whose home was in the sea came to his well. Interested in all things, he went in. "Who are you? Where do you live?" said the frog in the well. "I am so and so, and my home is in the sea." "The sea? What is that? Where is that?" " It is a very large body of water, and not far away." " How big is your sea?" "Oh, very big." "As big as this?" pointing to a little stone lying near. "Oh, much bigger." "As big as this?" pointing to the board upon which they were sitting. "Oh, much bigger." "How much bigger, then?" " Why, the sea in which I live is bigger than your entire well; it would make millions of wells such as yours." "Nonsense, nonsense; you are a deceiver and a falsifier. Get out of my well. Get out of my well. I want nothing to do with any such frogs as you."

"Ye shall know the truth and the truth shall make you free," is the promise. Ye shall close yourselves to truth, ye shall live in your own conceits, and your own conceits shall make fools and idiots of you, would be a statement applicable to not a few, and to not a few who pride themselves upon their superior intellectual attainments. Idiocy is arrested mental growth. Closing one's self for whatever reason to truth and hence to growth, brings a certain type of idiocy, though it may not be called by this name. And on the other hand, another type is that arrested growth caused by taking all things for granted, without proving them for one's self, merely because they come from a particular person, a particular book, a particular institution. This is caused by one's always looking without instead of being true to the light within, and carefully tending it that it may give an everclearer light.

With brave and intrepid Walt Whitman, we should all be able to say—

From this hour I ordain myself loos'd of limits and imaginary lines,
Going where I list, my own master total and absolute,
Listening to others, considering well what they say,
Pausing, searching, receiving, contemplating,
Gently, but with undeniable will divesting myself of the holds that would hold me.

Great should be the joy that God's boundless truth is open to all, open *equally* to all, and that it will make each one its dwelling place in proportion as he earnestly desires it and opens himself to it.

And in regard to the wisdom that guides us in our daily life, there is nothing that it is right and well for us to know that may not be known when we recognize the law of its coming, and are able wisely to use it. Let us know that all things are ours as soon as we know how to appropriate them.

I hold it as a changeless law,
From which no soul can sway or swerve,
We have that in us which will draw
Whate'er we need or most deserve.

If the times come when we know not what course to pursue, when we know not which way to turn, the fault lies in ourselves. If the fault lies in ourselves then the correction of this unnatural condition lies also in ourselves. It is never necessary to come into such a state if we are awake and remain awake to the light and the powers within us. The light is ever shining, and the only thing that it is necessary for us diligently to see to is that we permit neither this thing nor that to come between us and the light.

"With Thee is the fountain of life; in Thy light shall we see light."

Let us hear the words of one of the most highly illumined men I have ever known, and one who as a consequence is never in the dark, when the time comes, as to what to do and how to do it. "Whenever you are in doubt as to the course you should pursue, after you have turned to every outward means of guidance, *let the inward eye see, let the inward ear hear,* and allow this simple, natural, beautiful process to go on unimpeded by questionings or doubts. . . . In all dark hours and times of unwonted perplexity we need to follow one simple direction, found, as all needed directions can be found, in the dear old gospel, which so many read, but alas, *so few interpret.* 'Enter into thine inner chamber and shut the door.' Does this mean that we must literally betake ourselves to a private closet with a key in the door? If it did, then the command could never be obeyed in the open air, on land or sea, and the Christ loved the lakes and the forests far better than the cramping rooms of city dwelling houses; still his counsels are so wide-reaching that there is no spot on earth and no conceivable situation in which any of us may be placed where we cannot follow them.

"One of the most intuitive men we ever met had a desk in a city office where several other gentlemen were doing business constantly and often talking loudly. Entirely undisturbed by the many various sounds about him, this self-centred, faithful man would, in any moment of perplexity, draw the curtains of privacy so completely about him that he would be as fully enclosed in his own psychic aura, and thereby as effectually removed from all distractions as though he were alone in some primeval wood. Taking his difficulty with him into the mystic silence in the form of a direct question, to which he expected a certain answer, he would remain utterly passive until the reply came, and never once through many years' experience did he find himself disappointed or misled. Intuitive perceptions of truth are the daily bread to satisfy our daily hunger; they come like the manna in the desert day by day; each day brings adequate supply for that day's need only. They must be followed instantly, for dalliance with them means their obscuration, and the more we dally the more we invite erroneous impressions to cover intuition with a pall of conflicting moral phantasy born of illusions of the terrence will.

"One condition is imposed by *universal law,* and this we must obey. Put all wishes aside save the one desire to know *truth;* couple with this one demand the fully consecrated determination to follow what is distinctly perceived as truth immediately it is revealed. No other affection must be permitted to share the field with this all-absorbing love of *truth* for its own sake. Obey this one direction and never forget that expectation and desire are bride and bridegroom and forever inseparable, and you will soon find your hitherto darkened way grow luminous with celestial radiance, for with the heaven within, all heavens without incessantly co-operate." This may be termed going into the "silence." This it is to perceive and to be guided by the light that lighteth every man that cometh into the world. This it is to listen to and be guided by the voice of your own soul, the voice of your higher self.

The soul is divine and in allowing it to become translucent to the Infinite Spirit it reveals all things to us. As man turns away from the Divine Light do all things become hidden. There is nothing hidden of itself. When the spiritual sense is opened, then it transcends all the limitations of the physical senses and the intellect. And in the degree that we are able to get away from the limitations set by them, and realize that so far as the real life is concerned it is one with the Infinite Life, then we begin to reach the place where this voice will always speak, where it will never fail us, if we follow it, and as a consequence where we will always have the divine illumination and guidance. To know this and to live in this realization is not to live in heaven hereafter, but to live in heaven here and now, *today and every day.*

No human soul need be without it. When we turn our face in the right direction it comes as simply and as naturally as the flower blooms and with winds blow. It is not to be bought with money or with price. It is a condition waiting simply to be realized, by rich and by poor, by king and by peasant, by master and by servant the world over. All are equal heirs to it. And so the peasant, if he find it first, lives a life far transcending in beauty and in real power the life of his king. The servant, if he find it first, lives a life surpassing the life of his master.

If you would find the highest, the fullest, and the richest life that not only this world but that any world can know, then do away with the sense of the separateness of your life from the life of God. Hold to the thought of your oneness. In the degree that you do this you will find yourself realizing it more and more, and as this life of realization is lived, you will find that no good thing will be withheld, for all things are included in this. Then it will be yours, without fears or forebodings, simply to do today what your hands find to do, and so be ready for tomorrow, *when it comes,* knowing that tomorrow will bring tomorrow's supplies for the mental, the spiritual, and the physical life. Remember, however, that tomorrow's supplies are not needed until tomorrow comes.

If one is willing to trust himself *fully* to the Law, the Law will never fail him. It is the half-hearted trusting to it that brings uncertain, and so, unsatisfactory results. Nothing is firmer and surer than Deity. It will never fail the one who throws himself wholly upon it. The secret of life then, is to live continually in this realization, whatever one may be doing, wherever one may be, by day and by night, both waking and sleeping. It can be lived in while we are sleeping no less than when we are awake. And here shall we consider a few facts in connection with sleep, in connection with receiving instruction and illumination while asleep?

During the process of sleep it is merely the physical body that is at rest and in quiet;

the soul life with all its activities goes right on. Sleep is nature's provision for the recuperation of the body, for the rebuilding and hence the replacing of the waste that is continually going on during the waking hours. It is nature's great restorer. If sufficient sleep is not allowed the body, so that the rebuilding may equalize the wasting process, the body is gradually depleted and weakened, and any ailment or malady, when it is in this condition, is able to find a more ready entrance. It is for this reason that those who are subject to it will take a cold, as we term it, more readily when the body is tired or exhausted through loss of sleep than at most any other time. The body is in that condition where outside influences can have a more ready effect upon it, than when it is in its normal condition. And when they do have an effect they always go to the weaker portions first.

Our bodies are given us to serve far higher purposes than we ordinarily use them for. Especially is this true in the numerous cases where the body is master of its owner. In the degree that we come into the realization of the higher powers of the mind and spirit, in that degree does the body, through their influence upon it, become less gross and heavy, finer in its texture and form. And then, because the mind finds a kingdom of enjoyment in itself, and in all the higher things it becomes related to, *excesses* in eating and drinking, as well as all others, naturally and of their own accord fall away. Then also falls away the desire for the heavier, grosser, less valuable kinds of food and drink, such as the flesh of animals, alcoholic drinks, and all things of the class that stimulate the body and the passions rather than build the body and the brain into a strong, clean, well-nourished, enduring, and fibrous condition. In the degree that the body thus becomes less gross and heavy, finer in its texture and form, is there less waste, and what there is is more easily replaced, so that it keeps in a more regular and even condition. When this is true, less sleep is actually required. And even the amount that is taken does more for a body of this finer type than it can do for one of the other nature.

As the body in this way grows finer, in other words, as the process of its evolution is thus accelerated, it in turn helps the mind and the soul in the realization of ever higher perceptions, and thus body helps mind the same as mind builds body. It was undoubtedly this fact that Browning had in mind when he said:

Let us cry "All good things
Are ours, nor soul helps flesh, more now
Than flesh helps soul."

Sleep, then, is for the resting and the rebuilding of the body. The soul needs no rest, and while the body is at rest in sleep the soul life is active the same as when the body is in activity.

There are some, having a deep insight into the soul's activities, who say that we travel when we sleep. Some are able to recall and bring over into the conscious, waking life the scenes visited, the information gained, and the events that have transpired. Most people are not able to do this and so much that might otherwise be gained is lost. They say, however, that it is in our power, in proportion as we understand the laws, to go where we will, and to bring over into the conscious, waking life all the experiences thus gained. Be this, however, as it may, it certainly is true that while sleeping we have the power, in a perfectly normal and natural way, to get much of value by way of light, instruction, and growth that the majority of people now miss.

If the soul life, that which relates us to Infinite Spirit, is always active, even while the body is at rest, why may not the mind so direct conditions as one falls asleep, that while the body is at rest, it may continually receive illumination from the soul and bring what it thus receives over into the conscious, waking life? This, indeed, can be done, and is done by some to great advantage; and many times the highest inspirations from the soul come in this way, as would seem most natural, since at this time all communications from the outer, material world no longer enter. I know those who do much work during sleep, the same as they get much light along desired lines. By charging the mind on going to sleep as to a particular time for waking, it is possible, as many of us know, to wake on the very minute. Not infrequently we have examples of difficult problems, problems that defied solution during waking hours, being solved during sleep.

A friend, a well-known journalist, had an extended newspaper article clearly and completely worked out for her in this way. She frequently calls this agency to her aid. She was notified by the managing editor one evening to have the article ready in the morning,—an article requiring more than ordinary care, and one in which quite a knowledge of facts was required. It was a matter in connection with which she knew scarcely anything, and all her efforts at finding information regarding it seemed to be of no avail.

She set to work, but it seemed as if even her own powers defied her. Failure seemed imminent. Almost in desperation she decided to retire, and putting the matter into her mind in such a way that she would be able to receive the greatest amount of aid while asleep, she fell asleep and slept soundly until morning. When she awoke her work of the previous evening was the first thing that came into her mind. She lay quietly for a few minutes, and as she lay there, the article, completely written, seemed to stand before her mind. She ran through it, arose, and without dressing took her pen and transcribed it on to paper, literally acting simply as her own amanuensis.

The mind acting intently along a particular line will continue so to act until some other object of thought carries it along another line. And since in sleep only the body is in quiet while the mind and soul are active, then the mind on being given a certain direction when one drops off to sleep, will take up the line along which it is directed, and can be made, in time, to bring over into consciousness the results of its activities. Some will be able very soon to get results of this kind; for some it will take longer. Quiet and continued effort will increase the faculty.

Then by virtue of the law of the drawing power of mind, since the mind is always active, we are drawing to us even while sleeping, influences from the realms kindred to those in which we in our thoughts are living before we fall asleep. In this way we can put ourselves into relation with what ever kinds of influence we choose and accordingly gain much during the process of sleep. In many ways the interior faculties are more open and receptive while we are in sleep than while we are awake. Hence the necessity of exercising even greater care as to the nature of the thoughts that occupy the mind as we enter into sleep, for there can come to us only what we by our own order of thought attract. We have it entirely in our own hands.

And for the same reason,—this greater degree of receptivity during this period,—we are able by understanding and using the law, to gain much of value more readily in this way than when the physical senses are fully open to the material world about us. Many will find a practice somewhat after the following nature of value: When light or information is desired along any particular line, light or information you feel it is right and wise for you to have, as, for example, light in regard to an uncertain course of action, then as you retire, first bring your mind into the attitude of peace and good-will for all. You in this way bring yourself into an harmonious condition, and in turn attract to yourself these same peaceful conditions from without.

Then resting in this sense of peace, quietly and calmly send out your earnest desire for the needed light or information; cast out of your mind all fears or forebodings lest it come not, for "in quietness and in confidence shall be your strength." Take the expectant attitude of mind, firmly believing and expecting that when you awake the desired results will be with you. Then on awaking, before any thoughts or activities from the outside world come in to absorb the attention, remain for a little while receptive to the intuitions or the impressions that come. When they come, when they manifest themselves clearly, then act upon them without delay. In the degree that you do this, in that degree will the power of doing it ever more effectively grow.

Or, if for unselfish purposes you desire to grow and develop any of your faculties, or to increase the health and strength of your body, take a corresponding attitude of mind, the form of which will readily suggest itself in accordance with your particular needs or desires. In this way you will open yourself to, you will connect yourself with, and you will set into operation within yourself, the particular order of forces that will make for these results. Don't be afraid to voice your desires. In this way you set into operation vibratory forces which go out and which make their impress felt somewhere, and which, arousing into activity or uniting with other forces, set about to actualize your desires. No good thing shall be withheld from him who lives in harmony with the higher laws and forces. There are no desires that shall not be satisfied to the one who knows and who wisely uses the powers with which he or she is endowed.

Your sleep will be more quiet, and peaceful, and refreshing, and so your power increased mentally, physically, and spiritually, simply by sending out as you fall asleep, thoughts of love and good-will, thoughts of peace and harmony for all. In this way you are connecting yourself with all the forces in the universe that make for peace and harmony.

A friend who is known the world over through his work along humane lines, has told me that many times in the middle of the night he is awakened suddenly and there comes to his mind, as a flash of inspiration, a certain plan in connection with his work. And as he lies there quietly and opens himself to it, the methods for its successful carrying out all reveal themselves to him clearly. In this way many plans are entered upon and brought to a successful culmination that otherwise would never be thought of, plans that seem, indeed, marvelous to the world at large. He is a man with a sensitive organism, his life in thorough harmony with the higher laws, and given wholly and unreservedly to the work to which he has dedicated it. Just how and from what source these inspirations come he does not fully know. Possibly no one does, though each may have his theory. But this we do know, and it is all we need to know now, at least,—that to the one who lives in harmony with the higher laws of his being, and who opens himself to them, they come.

Visions and inspirations of the highest order will come in the degree that we make for them the right conditions. One who has studied deeply into the subject in hand has said: "To receive education spiritually while the body is resting in sleep is a perfectly normal and orderly experience, and would occur definitely and satisfactorily in the lives of all of us, if we paid more attention to internal and consequently less to external states with their supposed but unreal necessities. . . . Our thoughts make us what we are here and hereafter, and our thoughts are often busier by night than by day, for when we are asleep to the exterior we can be wide awake to the interior world; and the unseen world is a substantial place, the conditions of which are entirely regulated by mental and moral attainments. When we are not deriving information through outward avenues of sensation, we are receiving instruction through interior channels of perception, and when this fact is understood for what it is worth, it will become a universal custom for persons to take to sleep with them the special subject on which they most earnestly desire particular instruction. The Pharaoh type of person dreams, and so does his butler and baker; but the Joseph type, which is that of the truly gifted seer, both dreams and interprets."

But why had not Pharaoh the power of interpreting his dreams? Why was Joseph the type of the "truly gifted seer?" Why did he not only dream, but had also the power to interpret both his own dreams and the dreams of others? Simply read the lives of the two. He who runs may read. In all true power it is, after all, living the life that tells. And in proportion as one lives the life does he not only attain to the highest power and joy for himself, but he also becomes of ever greater service to all the world. One need remain in no hell longer than he himself chooses to; and the moment he chooses not to remain longer, not all the powers in the universe can prevent his leaving it. One can rise to any heaven he himself chooses; and when he chooses so to rise, all the higher powers of the universe combine to help him heavenward.

When one awakes from sleep and so returns to conscious life, he is in a peculiarly receptive and impressionable state. All relations with the material world have for a time been shut off, the mind is in a freer and more natural state, resembling somewhat a sensitive plate, where impressions can readily leave their traces. This is why many times the highest and truest impressions come to one in the early morning hours, before the activities of the day and their attendant distractions have exerted an influence. This is one reason why many people can do their best work in the early hours of the day.

But this fact is also a most valuable one in connection with the moulding of everyday life. The mind is at this time as a clean sheet of paper. We can most valuably use this quiet, receptive, impressionable period by wisely directing the activities of the mind along the highest and most desirable paths, and thus, so to speak, set the pace for the day.

Each morning is a fresh beginning. We are as it were, just beginning life. We have it *entirely* in our own hands. And when the morning with its fresh beginning comes, all yesterdays should be yesterdays, with which we have nothing to do. Sufficient is it to know that the way we lived our yesterday has determined for us our today. And, again, when the morning with its fresh beginning comes, all tomorrows should be tomorrows, with which we have nothing to do. Sufficient to know that the way we live our today determines our tomorrow.

Every day is a fresh beginning,
Every morn is the world made new;
You who are weary of sorrow and sinning,

Here is a beautiful hope for you,
A hope for me and a hope for you.

All the past things are past and over,
The tasks are done, and the tears are shed.
Yesterday's errors let yesterday cover;
Yesterday's wounds, which smarted and bled,
Are healed with the healing which night has shed

. . . . . .

Let them go, since we cannot relieve them,
Cannot undo and cannot atone.
God in His mercy receive, forgive them!
Only the new days are our own.
Today is ours, and today alone.

Here are the skies all burnished brightly;
Here is the spent earth all reborn;
Here are the tired limbs springing lightly
To face the sun and to share with the morn
In the chrism of dew and the cool of dawn.

Every day is a fresh beginning,
Listen, my soul, to the glad refrain,
And, spite of old sorrow and older sinning,
And puzzles forecasted, and possible pain,
Take heart with the day and begin again.

Simply the first hour of this new day, with all its richness and glory, with all its sublime and eternity-determining possibilities, and each succeeding hour as it comes, but *not before* it comes. This is the secret of character building. This simple method will bring any one to the realization of the highest life that can be even conceived of, and there is nothing in this connection that can be conceived of that cannot be realized somehow, somewhen, somewhere.

This brings such a life within the possibilities of *all,* for there is *no one,* if really in earnest and if he really desires it, who cannot live to his highest for a single hour. But even though there should be, if he is *only earnest in his endeavor,* then, through the law that like builds like, he will be able to come a little nearer to it the next hour, and still nearer the next, and the next, until sooner or later comes the time when it becomes the natural, and any other would require the effort.

In this way one becomes in love and in league with the highest and best in the universe, and as a consequence, the highest and best in the universe becomes in love and in league with him. They aid him at every turn; they seem literally to move all things his way, because forsooth, he has first moved their way.

CHAPTER 7

The Realization of Perfect Peace

This is the Spirit of Infinite Peace, and the moment we come into harmony with it there comes to us an inflowing tide of peace, for peace is harmony. A deep interior meaning underlies the great truth, "To be spiritually minded is life and peace." To recognize the fact that we are spirit, and to live in this thought, is to be spiritually minded, and so to be in harmony and peace. Oh, the thousands of men and women all about us weary with care, troubled and ill at ease, running hither and thither to find peace, weary in body, soul, and mind; going to other countries, traveling the world over, coming back, and still not finding it. Of course they have not found it and they never will find it in this way, because they are looking for it where it is not. They are looking for it without when they should look within. Peace is to be found only within, and unless one find it there he will never find it at all.

Peace lies not in the external world. It lies within one's own soul. We may travel over many different avenues in pursuit of it, we may seek it through the channels of the bodily appetites and passions, we may seek it through all the channels of the external, we may chase for it hither and thither, but it will always be just beyond our grasp, because we are searching for it where it is not. In the degree, however, that we order the bodily appetites and passions in accordance with the promptings of the soul within will the higher forms of happiness and peace enter our lives; but in the degree that we fail in doing this will disease, suffering, and discontent enter in.

To be at one with God is to be at peace. The child simplicity is the greatest agency in bringing this full and complete realization, the child simplicity that recognizes its true relations with the Father's life. There are people I know who have come into such a conscious realization of their oneness with this Infinite Life, this Spirit of Infinite Peace, that their lives are fairly bubbling over with joy. I have particularly in mind at this moment a comparatively young man who was an invalid for several years, his health completely broken with nervous exhaustion, who thought there was nothing in life worth living for, to whom everything and everybody presented a gloomy aspect, and he in turn presented a gloomy aspect to all with whom he came in contact. Not long ago he came into such a vital realization of his oneness with this Infinite Power, he opened himself so completely to its divine inflow, that today he is in perfect health, and frequently as I meet him now he cannot resist the impulse to cry out, "Oh, it is a joy to be alive."

I know an officer on our police force who has told me that many times when off duty and on his way home in the evening, there comes to him such a vivid and vital realization of his oneness with this Infinite Power, and this Spirit of Infinite Peace so takes hold of and so fills him, that it seems as if his feet could scarcely keep to the pavement, so buoyant and so exhilarated does he become by reason of this inflowing tide.

He who comes into this higher realization never has any fear, for he has always with him a sense of protection, and the very realization of this makes his protection complete. Of him it is true,—"No weapon that is formed against thee shall prosper"; "There shall no ill come nigh thy dwelling"; "Thou shalt be in league with the stones of the field, and the beasts of the field shall be at peace with thee."

These are the men and the women who seem to live charmed lives. The moment we fear anything we open the door for the entrance of the actualization of the very thing we fear. An animal will never harm a person who is absolutely fearless in regard to it. The instant he fears he opens himself to danger; and some animals, the dog for example, can instantly detect the element of fear, and this gives them the courage to do harm. In the degree that we come into a full realization of our oneness with this Infinite Power do we become calm and quiet, undisturbed by the little occurrences that before so vex and annoy us. We are no longer disappointed in people, for we always read them aright. We have the power of penetrating into their very souls and seeing the underlying motives that are at work there.

A gentleman approached a friend the other day, and with great show of cordiality grasped him by the hand and said, "Why, Mr.——, I am so glad to see you." Quick as a flash my friend read him, and looking him steadily in the eye, replied, "No, you are mistaken, you are not glad to see me; but you are very much disconcerted, so much so that you are now blushing in evidence of it." The gentleman replied, "Well, you know in this day and age of conventionality and form we have to put on the show and sometimes make believe what we do not really feel." My friend once more looked him in the face and said, "Again you are mistaken. Let me give you one little word of advice: You will always fare better and will think far more of yourself, always to recognize and to tell the truth rather than to give yourself to any semblance of it."

As soon as we are able to read people aright we will then cease to be disappointed in them, we will cease to place them on pedestals, for this can never be done without some attendant disappointment. The fall will necessarily come, sooner or later, and moreover, we are thus many times unfair to our friends. When we come into harmony with this Spirit of Peace, evil reports and apparent bad treatment, either at the hands of friends or of enemies, will no longer disturb us. When we are conscious of the fact that in our life and our work we are true to that eternal principle of right, of truth, of justice that runs through all the universe, that unites and governs all, that always eventually prevails, then nothing of this kind can come nigh us, and come what may we will always be tranquil and undisturbed.

The things that cause sorrow, and pain, and bereavement will not be able to take the hold of as they now take, for true wisdom will enable us to see the proper place and know the right relations of all things. The loss of friends by the transition we call death will not cause sorrow to the soul that has come into this higher realization, for he knows that there is no such thing as death, for each one is not only a partaker, but an eternal partaker, of this Infinite Life. He knows that the mere falling away of the physical body by no means affects the real soul life. With a tranquil spirit born of a higher faith he can realize for himself, and to those less strong he can say—

Loving friends! be wise and dry
Straightway every weeping eye;
What you left upon the bier
Is not worth a single tear;
'Tis a simple sea-shell, one
Out of which the pearl has gone.
The shell was nothing, leave it there;
The pearl—the soul—was all, is here.

And so far as the element of separation is concerned, he realizes that to spirit there are no bounds, and that spiritual communion, whether between two persons in the body, or two persons, one in the body and one out of the body, is within the reach of all. In the degree that the higher spiritual life is realized can there be this higher spiritual communion.

The things that we open ourselves to always come to us. People in the olden times expected to see angels and they saw them; but there is no more reason why they should have seen them than that we should see them now; no more reason why they should come and dwell with them than that they should come and dwell with us, for the great laws governing all things are the same today as they were then. If angels come not to minister unto us it is because we do not invite them, it is because we keep the door closed through which they otherwise might enter.

In the degree that we are filled with this Spirit of Peace by thus opening ourselves to its inflow does it pour through us, so that we carry it with us wherever we go. In the degree that we thus open ourselves do we become magnets to attract peace from all sources; and in the degree that we attract and embody it in ourselves are we able to give it forth to others. We can in this way become such perfect embodiments of peace that wherever we go we are continually shedding benedictions. But a day or two ago I saw a woman grasp the hand of a man (his face showed the indwelling God), saying, "Oh, it does me so much good to see you. I have been in anxiety and almost in despair during the past few hours, but the very sight of you has rolled the burden entirely away." There are people all around us who are continually giving out blessings and comfort, persons whose mere presence seems to change sorrow into joy, fear into courage, despair into hope, weakness into power.

It is the one who has come into the realization of his own true self who carries this power with him and who radiates it wherever he goes,—the one who, as we say, has found his centre. And in all the great universe there is but one centre,—the Infinite Power that is working in and through all. The one who then has found his centre is the one who has come into the realization of his oneness with this Infinite Power, the one who recognizes himself as a spiritual being, for God is spirit.

Such is the man of power. Centred in the Infinite, he has thereby, so to speak, connected himself with, he has attached his belts to, the great power-house of the universe. He is constantly drawing power to himself from all sources. For, thus centred, knowing himself, conscious of his own power, the thoughts that go from his mind are thoughts of strength; and by virtue of the law that like attracts like, he by his thoughts is continually attracting to himself from all quarters the aid of all whose thoughts are thoughts of strength, and in this way he is linking himself with this order of thought in the universe.

And so to him that hath, to him shall be given. This is simply the working of a natural law. His strong, positive, and hence constructive thought is continually working success for him along all lines, and continually bringing to him help from all directions. The things that he sees, that he creates in the ideal, are through the agency of this strong constructive thought continually clothing themselves, taking form, manifesting themselves in the material. Silent, unseen forces are at work which will sooner or later be made manifest in the visible.

Fear and all thoughts of failure never suggest themselves to such a man; or if they do, they are immediately sent out of his mind, and so he is not influenced by this order of thought from without. He does not attract it to him. He is in another current of thought. Consequently the weakening, failure-bringing thoughts of the fearing, the vascillating, the pessimistic about him, have no influence upon him. The one who is of the negative, fearing kind not only has his energies and his physical agents weakened, or even paralyzed through the influence of this kind of thought that is born within him, but he also in this way connects himself with this order of thought in the world about him. And in the degree that he does this does he become a victim to the weak, fearing, negative minds all around him. Instead of growing in power, he increases in weakness. He is in the same order of thought with those of whom it is true,—and even that which they have shall be taken away from them. This again is simply the working of a natural law, the same as is its opposite. Fearing lest I lose even what I have I hide it away in a napkin. Very well. I must then pay the price of my "fearing lest I lose."

Thoughts of strength both build strength from within and attract it from without. Thoughts of weakness actualize weakness from within and attract it from without. Courage begets strength, fear begets weakness. And so courage begets success, fear begets failure. It is the man or the woman of faith, and hence of courage, who is the master of circumstances, and who makes his or her power felt in the world. It is the man or the woman who lacks faith and who as a consequence is weakened and crippled by fears and forebodings, who is the creature of all passing occurrences.

Within each one lies the cause of whatever comes to him. Each has it in his own hands to determine what comes. Everything in the visible, material world has its origin in the unseen, the spiritual, the thought world. This is the world of cause, the former is the world of effect. The nature of the effect is always in accordance with the nature of the cause. What one lives in his invisible, thought world, he is continually actualizing in his visible, material world. If he would have any conditions different in the latter he must make the necessary change in the former. A clear realization of this great fact would bring success to thousands of men and women who all about us are now in the depths of despair. It would bring health, abounding health and strength to thousands now diseased and suffering. It would bring peace and joy to thousands now unhappy and ill at ease.

And oh, the thousands all about us who are continually living in the slavery of fear. The spirits within that should be strong and powerful, are rendered weak and impotent. Their energies are crippled, their efforts are paralyzed. "Fear is everywhere,—fear of want, fear of starvation, fear of public opinion, fear of private opinion, fear that what we own today may not be ours tomorrow, fear of sickness, fear of death. Fear has become with millions a fixed habit. The thought is everywhere. The thought is thrown upon us from every direction. . . . To live in continual dread, continual cringing, continual fear of anything, be it loss of love, loss of money, loss of position or situation, is to take the readiest means to lose what we fear we shall."

By fear nothing is to be gained, but on the contrary, everything is to be lost. "I know this is true," says one, "but I am given to fear; it's natural to me and I can't help it." Can't help it! In saying this you indicate one great reason of your fear by showing that you do not even know yourself as yet. You must know yourself in order to know your powers, and not until you know them can you use them wisely and fully. Don't say you can't help it. If you think you can't, the chances are that you can't. If you think you can, and act in accordance with this thought, then not only are the chances that you can, but if you act fully in accordance with it, that you can and that you will is an absolute certainty. It was Virgil who in describing the crew which in his mind would win the race, said of them,—They can because they think they can. In other words, this very attitude of mind on their part will infuse a spiritual power into their bodies that will give them the strength and endurance which will enable them to win.

Then take the thought that you *can;* take it merely as a seed-thought, if need be, plant it in your consciousness, tend it, cultivate it, and it will gradually reach out and gather strength from all quarters. It will focus and make positive and active the spiritual force within you that is now scattered and of little avail. It will draw to itself force from without. It will draw to your aid the influence of other minds of its own nature, minds that are fearless, strong, courageous. You will thus draw to yourself and connect yourself with this order of thought. If earnest and faithful, the time will soon come when all fear will loose its hold; and instead of being an embodiment of weakness and a creature of circumstances, you will find yourself a tower of strength and a master of circumstances.

We need more faith in every-day life,—faith in the power that works for good, faith in the Infinite God, and hence faith in ourselves created in His image. And however things at times may seem to go, however dark at times appearances may be, the knowledge of the fact that "the Supreme Power has us in its charge as it has the suns and endless systems of worlds in space," will give us the supreme faith that all is well with us, the same as all is well with the world. "Thou wilt keep him in perfect peace whose mind is stayed on Thee."

There is nothing firmer, and safer, and surer than Deity. Then, as we recognize the fact that we have it in our own hands to open ourselves ever more fully to this Infinite Power, and call upon it to manifest itself in and through us, we will find in ourselves an ever increasing sense of power. For in this way we are working in conjunction with it, and it in turn is working in conjunction with us. We are then led into the full realization of the fact that all things work together for good to those that love the good. Then the fears and forebodings that have dominated us in the past will be transmuted into faith, and faith when rightly understood and rightly used is a force before which nothing can stand.

Materialism leads naturally to pessimism. And how could it do otherwise? A knowledge of the Spiritual Power working in and through us as well as in and through all things, a power that works for righteousness, leads to optimism. Pessimism leads to weakness. Optimism leads to power. The one who is centred in Deity is the one who not only outrides every storm, but who through the faith, and so, the conscious power that is in him, faces storm with the same calmness and serenity that he faces fair weather; for he knows well beforehand what the outcome will be. He knows that underneath are the everlasting arms. He it is who realizes the truth of the injunction, "Rest in the Lord, wait patiently for Him and He shall give thee thy heart's desire." All shall be given, simply given, to him who is ready to accept it. Can anything be clearer than this?

In the degree, then, that we work in conjunction with the Supreme Power do we need the less to concern ourselves about results. To live in the full realization of this fact and all that attends it brings peace, a full, rich, abiding peace,—a peace that makes the present complete, and that, going on before, brings back the assurance that as our days, so shall our strength be. The one who is thus centred, even in the face of all the unrest and the turmoil about us, can realize and say—

I stay my haste, I make delays,
For what avails this eager pace?
I stand amid eternal ways,
And what is mine shall know my face.

Asleep, awake, by night or day,
The friends I seek are seeking me;
No wind can drive my bark astray,
Nor change the tide of destiny.

. . . . . .

The waters know their own, and draw
The brooks that spring in yonder height;
So flows the good with equal law
Unto the soul of pure delight.

The stars come nightly to the sky;
The tidal wave unto the sea;
Nor time, nor space, nor deep, nor high,
Can keep my own away from me.

CHAPTER 8

Coming into Fullness of Power

This is the Spirit of Infinite Power, and in the degree that we open ourselves to it does power become manifest in us. With God all things are possible,—that is, in conjunction with God all things are possible. The true secret of power lies in keeping one's connection with the God who worketh all things; and in the degree that we keep this connection are we able literally to rise above every conceivable limitation.

Why, then, waste time in running hither and thither to acquire power? Why waste time with this practice or that practice? Why not go directly to the mountain-top itself, instead of wandering through the by-ways, in the valleys, and on the mountain sides? That man has absolute dominion, as taught in all the scriptures of the world, is true not of physical man, but of *spiritual man.* There are many animals, for example, larger and stronger, over which from a physical standpoint he would not have dominion, but he can gain supremacy over even these by calling into activity the higher mental, psychic, and spiritual forces with which he is endowed.

Whatever can't be done in the physical can be done in the spiritual. And in direct proportion as a man recognizes himself as spirit, and lives accordingly, is he able to transcend in power the man who recognizes himself merely as material. All the sacred literature of the world is teeming with examples of what we call miracles. They are not confined to any particular times or places. There is no age of miracles in distinction from any other period that may be an age of miracles. Whatever has been done in the world's history can be done again through the operation of the same laws and forces. These miracles were performed not by those who were more than men, but by those who through the recognition of their oneness with God became God-men, so that the higher forces and powers worked through them.

For what, let us ask, is a miracle? Is it something supernatural? Supernatural only in the sense of being above the natural, or rather, above that which is natural to man in his ordinary state. A miracle is nothing more nor less than this. One who has come into a knowledge of his true identity, of his oneness with the all-pervading Wisdom and Power, thus makes it possible for laws higher than the ordinary mind knows of to be revealed to him. These laws he makes use of; the people see the results, and by virtue of their own limitations, call them miracles and speak of the person who performs these apparently supernatural works as a supernatural being. But they as supernatural beings could themselves perform these supernatural works if they would open themselves to the recognition of the same laws, and consequently to the realization of the same possibilities and powers. And let us also remember that the supernatural of yesterday becomes, as in the process of evolution we advance from the lower to the higher, from the more material to the more spiritual, the common and the natural of today, and what seems to be the supernatural of today becomes in the same way the natural of tomorrow, and so on through the ages. Yes, it is the God-man who does the things that appear supernatural, the man who by virtue of his realization of the higher powers transcends the majority and so stands out among them. But any power that is possible to one human soul is possible to another. The same laws operate in every life. We can be men and women of power or we can be men and women of impotence. The moment one vitally grasps the fact that he can rise he will rise, and he can have absolutely no limitations other than the limitations he sets to himself. Cream always rises to the top. It rises simply because *it is the nature of cream to rise.*

We hear much said of "environment." We need to realize that environment should never be allowed to make the man, but that man should always, *and always can,* condition the environment. When we realize this we will find that many times it is not necessary to take ourselves out of any particular environment, because we may yet have a work to do there; but by the very force we carry with us we can so affect and change matters that we will have an entirely new set of conditions in an old environment.

The same is true in regard to "hereditary" traits and influences. We sometimes hear the question asked, "Can they be overcome?" Only the one who doesn't yet know himself can ask a question such as this. If we entertain and live in the belief that they cannot be overcome, then the chances are that they will always remain. The moment, however, that we come into a realization of our true selves, and so of the tremendous powers and forces within,—the powers and forces of the mind and spirit,—hereditary traits and influences that are harmful in nature will begin to lessen, and will disappear with a rapidity directly in proportion to the completeness of this realization.

There is no thing we cannot overcome;
Say not thy evil instinct is inherited,
Or that some trait inborn makes thy whole life forlorn,
And calls down punishment that is not merited.

Back of thy parents and grandparents lies
The Great Eternal Will! That too is thine
Inheritance,—strong, beautiful, divine,
Sure lever of success for one who tries.

. . . . . .

There is no noble height thou canst not climb;
All triumphs may be thine in Time's futurity,
If, whatso'er thy fault, thou dost not faint or halt;
But lean upon the staff of God's security.

Earth has no claim the soul cannot contest;
Know thyself part of the Eternal Source;
Naught can stand before thy spirit's force:
The soul's Divine Inheritance is best.

Again there are many who are living far below their possibilities because they are continually handing over their individualities to others. Do you want to be a power in the world? Then be yourself. Don't class yourself, don't allow yourself to be classed among the *second-hand,* among the *they-say* people. Be true to the highest within your own soul, and then allow yourself to be governed by no customs or conventionalities or arbitrary man-made rules that are not founded upon *principle.* Those things that are founded upon principle will be observed by the right-minded, the right-hearted man or woman, in any case.

Don't surrender your individuality, which is your greatest agent of power, to the customs and conventionalities that have gotten their life from the great mass of those who haven't enough force to preserve their individualities,—those who in other words have given them over as ingredients to the "mush of concession" which one of our greatest writers has said characterizes our modern society. If you do surrender your individuality in this way, you simply aid in increasing the undesirable conditions; in payment for this you become a slave, and the chances are that in time you will be unable to hold even the respect of those whom you in this way try to please.

If you preserve your individuality then you become a master, and if wise and discreet, your influence and power will be an aid in bringing about a higher, a better, and a more healthy set of conditions in the world. All people, moreover, will think more of you, will honor you more highly for doing this than if you show your weakness by contributing yourself to the same "mush of concession" that so many of them are contributing themselves to. With all classes of people you will then have an influence. "A great style of hero draws equally all classes, all extremes of society to him, till we say the very dogs believe in him."

To be one's self is the only worthy, and by all means the only satisfactory, thing to be. "May it not be good policy," says one, "to be governed sometimes by one's surroundings?" What is good policy? To be yourself, first, last and always.

This above all,—to thine own self be true;
And it must follow, as the night the day,
Thou canst not then be false to any man.

"When we appeal to the Supreme and our life is governed by a principle, we are not governed either by fear of public opinion or loss of others' approbation, and we may be sure that the Supreme will sustain us. If in any way we try to live to suit others we never shall suit them, and the more we try the more unreasonable and exacting do they become. The government of your life is a matter that lies entirely between God and yourself, and when your life is swayed and influenced from any other source you are on the wrong path." When we find the kingdom within and become centred in the Infinite, then we become a law unto ourselves. When we become a law unto ourselves, then we are able to bring others to a knowledge of laws higher than they are governed or many times even enslaved by.

When we have found this centre, then that beautiful simplicity, at once the charm and the power of a truly great personality, enters into our lives. Then all striving for effect,—that sure indicator of weakness and a lack of genuine power,—is absent. This striving for effect that is so common is always an indicator of a lack of something. It brings to mind the man who rides behind a dock-tailed horse. Conscious of the fact that there is not enough in *himself* to attract attention, in common with a number of other weaklings, he adopts the brutal method of having his horse's tail sawed off, that its unnatural, odd appearance may attract from people the attention that he of himself is unable to secure.

But the one who strives for effect is always fooled more than he succeeds in fooling others. The man and the woman of true wisdom and insight can always see the causes that prompt, the motives that underlie the acts of all with whom he or she comes in contact. "He is great who is what he is from nature and who never reminds us of others."

The men and the women who are truly awake to the real powers within are the men and women who seem to be doing so little, yet who in reality are doing so much. They seem to be doing so little because they are working with higher agencies, and yet are doing so much because of this very fact. They do their work on the higher plane. They keep so completely their connection with the Infinite Power that *It* does the work for them and they are relieved of the responsibility. They are the care-less people. They are care-less because it is the Infinite Power that is working through them, and with this Infinite Power they are simply cooperating.

The secret of the highest power is simply the uniting of the outer agencies of expression with the Power that works from within. Are you a painter? Then in the degree that you open yourself to the power of the forces within will you become great instead of mediocre. You can never put into permanent form inspirations higher than those that come through your own soul. In order for the higher inspirations to come through it, you must open your soul, you must open it fully to the Supreme Source of all inspiration. Are you an orator? In the degree that you come into harmony and work in conjunction with the higher powers that will speak through you will you have the real power of moulding and of moving men. If you use merely your physical agents, you will be simply a demagogue. If you open yourself so that the voice of God can speak through and use your physical agents, you will become a great and true orator, great and true in just the degree that you so open yourself.

Are you a singer? Then open yourself and let the God within pour forth in the spirit of song. You will find it a thousand times easier than all your long and studied practice without this, and other things being equal, there will come to you a power of song so enchanting and so enrapturing that its influence upon all who hear will be irresistible.

When my cabin or tent has been pitched during the summer on the edge or in the midst of a forest, I have sometimes lain awake on my cot in the early morning, just as the day was beginning to break. Silence at first. Then an intermittent chirp here and there. And as the unfolding tints of the dawn became faintly perceptible, these grew more and more frequent, until by and by the whole forest seemed to burst forth in one grand chorus of song. Wonderful! wonderful! It seemed as if the very trees, as if every grass-blade, as if the bushes, the very sky above, and the earth beneath, had part in this wonderful symphony.

Then, as I have listened as it went on and on, I have thought, What a study in the matter of song! If we could but learn from the birds. If we could but open ourselves to the same powers and allow them to pour forth in us, what singers, what movers of men we might have! Nay, what singers and what movers of men *we would have!*

Do you know the circumstances under which Mr. Sankey sang for the first time "The Ninety and Nine?" Says one of our able journals: "At a great meeting recently in Denver, Mr. Ira W. Sankey, before singing 'The Ninety and Nine,' which, perhaps, of all his compositions is the one that has brought him the most fame, gave an account of its birth. Leaving Glasgow for Edinburg with Mr. Moody, he stopped at a news-stand and bought a penny religious paper. Glancing over it as they rode on the cars, his eye fell on a few little verses in the corner of the page. Turning to Mr. Moody he said, 'I've found my hymn.' But Mr. Moody was busily engaged and did not hear a word. Mr. Sankey did not find time to make a tune for the verses, so he pasted them in his music scrapbook.

"One day they had an unusually impressive meeting in Edinburg, in which Dr. Bonar had spoken with great effect on 'The Good Shepherd.' At the close of the address Mr. Moody beckoned to his partner to sing. He thought of nothing but the Twenty-third Psalm, but that he had sung so often. His second thought was to sing the verses he had found in the newspaper, but the third thought was, how could it be done when he had no tune. Then a fourth thought came, and that was to sing them *anyway.* He put the verses before him, touched the keys of the organ, opened his mouth and sang, not knowing where he was going to come out. He finished the first verse amid profound silence. He took a long breath and wondered if he could sing the second the same way. He tried and succeeded; after that it was easy to sing it. When he finished the hymn the meeting was all broken down and the throngs were crying. Mr. Sankey says it was the most intense moment of his life. Mr. Moody said he never heard a song like it. It was sung at every meeting, and was soon going over the world."

When we open ourselves to the highest inspirations they never fail us. When we fail to do this we fail in attaining the highest results, whatever the undertaking.

Are you a writer? Then remember that the one great precept underlying all successful literary work is, *Look into thine own heart and write. Be true. Be fearless. Be loyal to the promptings of your own soul.* Remember that an author can never write more than he himself is. If he would write more, then he must be more. He is simply his own amanuensis. He in a sense writes himself into his book. He can put no more into it than he himself is.

If he is one of a great personality, strong in purpose, deep in feeling, open always to the highest inspirations, a certain indefinable something gets into his pages that makes them breathe forth a vital, living power, a power so great that each reader gets the same inspirations as those that spoke through the author. That that's written between the lines is many times more than that that's written in the lines. It is the spirit of the author that engenders this power. It is this that gives that extra twenty-five or thirty per cent that takes a book out of the class called medium and lifts it into the class called superior,—that extra per cent that makes it the one of the hundred that is truly successful, while the ninety-nine never see more than their first edition.

It is this same spiritual power that the author of a great personality puts into his work, that causes it to go so rapidly from reader to reader, for the only way that any book circulates in the ultimate is from mouth to mouth, any book that reaches a large circulation. It is this that many times causes a single reader, in view of its value to himself, to purchase numbers of copies for others. "A good poem," says Emerson, "goes about the world offering itself to reasonable men, who read it with joy and carry it to their reasonable neighbors. Thus it draws to it the *wise and generous souls,* confirming their secret thoughts, and through their sympathy *really publishing itself.*"

This is the type of author who writes not with the thought of having what he writes become literature, but he writes with the sole thought of reaching the hearts of the people, giving them something of vital value, something that will broaden, sweeten, enrich, and beautify their lives; that will lead them to the finding of the higher life and with it the higher powers and the higher joys. It most always happens, however, that if he succeeds in thus reaching the people, the becoming literature part somehow takes care of itself, and far better than if he aimed for it directly.

The one, on the other hand, who fears to depart from beaten paths, who allows himself to be bound by arbitrary rules, limits his own creative powers in just the degree that he allows himself so to be bound. "My book," says one of the greatest of modern authors, "shall smell of the pines and resound with the hum of insects. The swallow over my window shall interweave that thread or straw he carries in his bill into my web also." Far better, gentle sage, to have it smell of the pines and resound with the hum of insects than to have it sound of the rules that a smaller type of man gets by studying the works of a few great, fearless writers like yourself, and formulating from what he thus gains a handbook of rhetoric. "Of no use are the men who study to do exactly as was done before, who can never understand that *today is a new day.*"

When Shakespeare is charged with debts to his authors, Landor replies: "Yet he was more original than his originals. He breathed upon dead bodies and brought them into life." This is the type of man who doesn't move the world's way, but who moves the world his way.

I had rather be an amanuensis of the Infinite God, as it is my privilege literally to be, than a slave to the formulated rules of any rhetorician, or to the opinions of any critic. Oh, the people, the people over and over! Let me give something to them that will lighten the every-day struggles of our common life, something that will add a little sweetness here, a little hope there, something that will make more thoughtful, kind, and gentle this thoughtless, animal-natured man, something that will awaken into activity the dormant powers of this timid, shrinking little woman, powers that when awakened will be irresistible in their influence and that will surprise even herself. Let me give something that will lead each one to the knowledge of the divinity of every human soul, something that will lead each one to the conscious realization of *his own divinity,* with all its attendant riches, and glories, and powers,—let me succeed in doing this, and I can then well afford to be careless as to whether the critics praise or whether they blame. If it is blame, then under these circumstances it is as the cracking of a few dead sticks on the ground below, compared to the matchless music that the soft spring gale is breathing through the great pine forest.

Are you a minister, or a religious teacher of any kind? Then in the degree that you free yourself from the man-made theological dogmas that have held and that are holding and limiting so many, and in the degree that you open yourself to the Divine Breath, will you be one who will speak with authority. In the degree that you do this will you study the prophets less and be in the way of becoming a prophet yourself. The way is open for you exactly the same as it has ever been open for anyone.

If when born into the world you came into a family of the English-speaking race, then in all probability you are a Christian. To be a Christian is to be a follower of the *teachings* of Jesus, the Christ; to live in harmony with the same laws he lived in harmony with: in brief, *to live his life.* The great central fact of his teaching was this conscious union of man with the Father. It was the complete realization of this oneness with the Father on his part that made Jesus the Christ. It was through this that he attained to the power he attained to, that he spake as never man spake.

He never claimed for himself anything that he did not claim equally for all mankind. "The mighty works performed by Jesus were not exceptional, they were the natural and necessary concomitants of his state; he declared them to be in accordance with unvarying order; he spoke of them as no unique performances, but as the outcome of a state to which all might attain if they chose. As a teacher and demonstrator of truth, according to his own confession, he did nothing for the purpose of proving his solitary divinity. . . . The life and triumph of Jesus formed an epoch in the history of the race. His coming and victory marked a new era in human affairs; he introduced a new because a more complete ideal to the earth, and when his three most intimate companions saw in some measure what the new life really signified, they fell to the earth, speechless with awe and admiration."

By coming into this complete realization of his oneness with the Father, by mastering, absolutely mastering every circumstance that crossed his path through life, even to the death of the body, and by pointing out to us the great laws which are the same for us as they were to him, he has given us an ideal of life, an ideal for us to attain to *here and now,* that we could not have without him. *One has conquered first; all may conquer afterward.* By completely realizing it first for himself, and then by pointing out to others this great law of the at-one-ment with the Father, he has become probably the world's greatest saviour.

Don't mistake his mere person for his life and his teachings, an error that has been made in connection with most all great teachers by their disciples over and over again. And if you have been among the number who have been preaching a dead Christ, then for humanity's sake, for Christ's sake, for God's sake, and I speak most reverently, don't steal the people's time any longer, don't waste your own time more, in giving them stones in place of bread, dead form for the spirit of living truth. In his own words, "let the dead bury their dead." Come out from among them. Teach as did Jesus, *the living Christ.* Teach as did Jesus, *the Christ within.* Find this in all its transcendent beauty and power,—find it as Jesus found it, then you also will be one who will speak with authority. Then you will be able to lead large numbers of others to its finding. This is the pearl of great price.

It is the type of preacher whose soul has never as yet even perceived the *vital spirit* of the teachings of Jesus, and who as a consequence instead of giving this to the people, is giving them old forms and dogmas and speculations, who is emptying our churches. This is the type whose chief efforts seem to be in getting men ready to die. The Germans have a saying, Never go to the second thing first. We need men who will teach us first how to live. Living quite invariably precedes dying. This also is true, that when we once know how to live, and live in accordance with what we know, then the dying, as we term it, will in a wonderfully beautiful manner take care of itself. It is in fact the only way in which it can be taken care of.

It is on account of this emptying of our churches, for the reason that the people are tiring of mere husks, that many short-sighted people are frequently heard to say that religion is dying out. Religion dying out? How can anything die before it is really born? And so far as the people are concerned, religion is just being born, or rather they are just awaking to a vital, every-day religion. We are just beginning to get beyond the mere letter into its real, vital spirit. Religion dying out? Impossible even to conceive of. Religion is as much a part of the human soul as the human soul is a part of God. And as long as God and the human soul exist, religion will never die.

Much of the dogma, the form, the ceremony, the mere letter that has stood as religion,—and honestly, many times, let us be fair enough to say,—this, thank God, is rapidly dying out, and never so rapidly as it is today. By two methods it is dying. There is, first, a large class of people tired of or even nauseated with it all, who conscientiously prefer to have nothing rather than this. They are simply abandoning it, the same as a tree abandons its leaves when the early winter comes. There is, second, a large class in whom the Divine Breath is stirring, who are finding the Christ within in all its matchless beauty and redeeming power. And this new life is pushing off the old, the same as in the spring the newly awakened life in the tree pushes off the old, lifeless leaves that have clung on during the winter, to make place for the new ones. And the way this old dead leaf religion is being pushed off on every hand is indeed most interesting and inspiring to witness.

Let the places of those who have been emptying our churches by reason of their attempts to give stones for bread, husks and chaff for the life-giving grain, let their places be taken even for but a few times by those who are open and alive to these higher inspirations, and then let us again question those who feel that religion is dying out. "It is the live coal that kindles others, not the dead." Let their places be taken by those who have caught the inspiration of the Divine Breath, who as a consequence have a message of mighty value and import for the people, who by virtue of this same fact are able to present it with a beauty and a power so enrapturing that it takes captive the soul. Then we will find that the churches that today are dotted here and there with a few dozen people will be filled to overflowing, and there will not be even room enough for all who would enter. "Let the shell perish that the pearl may appear." We need no new revelations as yet. We need simply to find the vital spirit of those we already have. Then in due time, when we are ready for them, new ones will come, but not before.

"What the human soul, all the world over, needs," says John Pulsford, "is not to be harangued, however eloquently, about the old, accepted religion, but to be permeated, charmed, and taken captive by *a warmer and more potent Breath of God than they ever felt before.* And I should not be true to my personal experience if I did not bear testimony that this Divine Breath is as exquisitely adapted to the requirements of the soul's nature as a June morning to the plant. Nor does the morning breath leave the trees freer to delight themselves and develop themselves under its influence than the Breath of God allows each human mind to unfold according to its genius. Nothing stirs the central wheel of the soul like the Breath of God. The whole man is quickened, his senses are new senses, his emotions new emotions; his reason, his affections, his imagination, are all new-born. The change is greater than he knows; he marvels at the powers in himself which the Breath is opening and calling forth. He finds his nature to be an unutterable thing; he is sure therefore that the future must have inconceivable surprises in store. And herein lies the evidence, which I commend to my readers, of the existence of God, and of the Eternal human Hope. Let God's Breath kindle new spring-time in the soul, start into life its deeply buried germs, lead in heaven's summer; you will then have as clear evidence of God from within as you have of the universe from without. Indeed, your internal experience of life, and illimitable Hope in God will be nearer to you, and more prevailing, than all your external and superficial experience of nature and the world."

There is but one source of power in the universe. Whatever then you are, painter, orator, musician, writer, religious teacher, or whatever it may be, know that to catch and take captive the secret of power is so to work in conjunction with the Infinite Power, in order that it may continually work and manifest through you. If you fail in doing this, you fail in everything. If you fail in doing this, your work, whatever it may be, will be third or fourth rate, possibly at times second rate, but it positively never can be first rate. Absolutely impossible will it be for you ever to become a master.

Whatever estimate you put upon yourself will determine the effectiveness of your work along any line. As long as you live merely in the physical and the intellectual, you set limitations to yourself that will hold you as long as you so live. When, however, you come into the realization of your oneness with the Infinite Life and Power, and open yourself that it may work through you, you will find that you have entered upon an entirely new phase of life, and that an ever increasing power will be yours. Then it will be true that your strength will be as the strength of ten because your heart is pure.

O God! I am one forever
With Thee by the glory of birth;
The celestial powers proclaim it
To the utmost bounds of the earth.

I think of this birthright immortal,
And my being expands like a rose,
As an odorous cloud of incense
Around and above me flows.

A glorious song of rejoicing
In an innermost spirit I hear,
And it sounds like heavenly voices,
In a chorus divine and clear.

And I feel a power uprising,
Like the power of an embryo god;
With a glorious wall it surrounds me,
And lifts me up from the sod.

CHAPTER 9

Plenty of All Things—The Law of Prosperity

This is the Spirit of Infinite Plenty, the Power that has brought, that is continually bringing, all things into expression in material form. He who lives in the realization of his oneness with this Infinite Power becomes a magnet to attract to himself a continual supply of whatsoever things he desires.

If one hold himself in the thought of poverty, he will be poor, and the chances are that he will remain in poverty. If he hold himself, whatever present conditions may be, continually in the thought of prosperity, he sets into operation forces that will sooner or later bring him into prosperous conditions. The law of attraction works unceasingly throughout the universe, and the one great and never changing fact in connection with it is, as we have found, that like attracts like. If we are one with this Infinite Power, this source of all things, then in the degree that we live in the realization of this oneness, in that degree do we actualize in ourselves a power that will bring to us an abundance of all things that it is desirable for us to have. In this way we come into possession of a power whereby we can actualize at all times those conditions that we desire.

As all truth exists *now*, and awaits simply our perception of it, so all things necessary for present needs exist *now*, and await simply the power in us to appropriate them. God holds all things in His hands. His constant word is, My child, acknowledge me in all your ways, and in the degree that you do this, in the degree that you live this, then what is mine is yours. Jehovah-jireh,—the Lord will provide. "He giveth to all men liberally and upbraideth not." He giveth liberally to all men who put themselves in the right attitude to receive from Him. He forces no good things upon any one.

The old and somewhat prevalent idea of godliness and poverty has absolutely no basis for its existence, and the sooner we get away from it the better. It had its birth in the same way that the idea of asceticism came into existence, when the idea prevailed that there was necessarily a warfare between the flesh and the spirit. It had its origin therefore in the minds of those who had a distorted, a one-sided view of life. True godliness is in a sense the same as true wisdom. The one who is truly wise, and who uses the forces and powers with which he is endowed, to him the great universe always opens her treasure house. The supply is always equal to the demand,—equal to the demand when the demand is rightly, wisely made. When one comes into the realization of these higher laws, then the fear of want ceases to tyrannize over him.

Are you out of a situation? Let the fear that you will not get another take hold of and *dominate* you, and the chances are that it may be a long time before you will get another, or the one that you do get may be a very poor one indeed. Whatever the circumstances, you must realize that you have within you forces and powers that you can set into operation that will triumph over any and all apparent or temporary losses. Set these forces into operation and you will then be placing a magnet that will draw to you a situation that may be far better than the one you have lost, and the time may soon come when you will be even thankful that you lost the old one.

Recognize, working in and through you, the same Infinite Power that creates and governs all things in the universe, the same Infinite Power that governs the endless systems of worlds in space. Send out your thought,—thought is a force, and it has occult power of unknown proportions when rightly used and wisely directed,—send out your thought that the right situation or the right work will come to you at the right time, in the right way, and that you will recognize it when it comes. Hold to this thought, never allow it to weaken, hold to it, and continually water it with firm expectation. You in this way put your advertisement into a psychical, a spiritual newspaper, a paper that has not a limited circulation, but one that will make its way not only to the utmost bounds of the earth, but of the very universe itself. It is an advertisement, moreover, which if rightly placed on your part, will be far more effective than any advertisement you could possibly put into any printed sheet, no matter what claims are made in regard to its being "the great advertising medium." In the degree that you come into this realization and live in harmony with the higher laws and forces, in that degree will you be able to do this effectively.

If you wish to look through the "want" columns of the newspapers, then do it not in the ordinary way. Put the higher forces into operation and thus place it on a higher basis. As you take up the paper, take this attitude of mind: If there is here an advertisement that it will be well for me to reply to, the moment I come to it I will recognize it. Affirm this, believe it, expect it. If you do this in full faith you will somehow feel the intuition the moment you come to the right one, and this intuition will be nothing more nor less than your own soul speaking to you. When it speaks then act at once.

If you get the situation and it does not prove to be exactly what you want, if you feel that you are capable of filling a better one, then the moment you enter upon it take the attitude of mind that this situation is the stepping-stone that will lead you to one that will be still better. Hold this thought steadily, affirm it, believe it, expect it, and all the time be faithful, *absolutely faithful* to the situation in which you are at present placed. If you are *not* faithful to it then the chances are that it will not be the stepping-stone to something better, but to something poorer. If you are faithful to it, the time may soon come when you will be glad and thankful, when you will rejoice, that you lost your old position.

This is the law of prosperity: When apparent adversity comes, be not cast down by it, but make the best of it, and always look forward for better things, for conditions more prosperous. To hold yourself in this attitude of mind is to set into operation subtle, silent, and irresistible forces that sooner or later will actualize in material form that which is today merely an idea. But ideas have occult power, and ideas, when rightly planted and rightly tended, are the seeds that actualize material conditions.

Never give a moment to complaint, but utilize the time that would otherwise be spent in this way in looking forward and actualizing the conditions you desire. Suggest prosperity to yourself. See yourself in a prosperous condition. Affirm that you will before long be in a prosperous condition. Affirm it calmly and quietly, but strongly and confidently. Believe it, believe it absolutely. Expect it,—keep it continually watered with expectation. You thus make yourself a magnet to attract the things that you desire. Don't be afraid to suggest, to affirm these things, for by so doing you put forth an ideal which will begin to clothe itself in material form. In this way you are utilizing agents among the most subtle and powerful in the universe. If you are particularly desirous for anything that you feel it is good and right for you to have, something that will broaden your life or that will increase your usefulness to others, simply hold the thought that at the right time, in the right way, and through the right instrumentality, there will come to you or there will open up for you the way whereby you can attain what you desire.

I know of a young lady who a short time ago wanted some money very badly. She wanted it for a good purpose; she saw no reason why she shouldn't have it. She is one who has come into an understanding of the power of the interior forces. She took and held herself in the attitude of mind we have just pointed out. In the morning she entered into the silence for a few moments. In this way she brought herself into a more complete harmony with the higher powers. Before the day closed a gentleman called, a member of a family with which she was acquainted. He asked her if she would do for the family some work that they wanted done. She was a little surprised that they should ask her to do this particular kind of work, but she said to herself, "Here is a call. I will respond and see what it will lead to." She undertook the work. *She did it well.* When she had completed it there was put into her hands an amount of money far beyond what she had expected. She felt that it was an amount too large for the work she had done. She protested. They replied, "No; you have done us a service that transcends in value the amount we offer to pay you." The sum thus received was more than sufficient for the work she wished to accomplish.

This is but one of many instances in connection with the wise and effective use of the higher powers. It also carries a lesson,—Don't fold your hands and expect to see things drop into your lap, but set into operation the higher forces and then take hold of the first thing that offers itself. Do what your hands find to do, *and do it well.* If this work is not thoroughly satisfactory to you, then affirm, believe, and expect that it is the agency that will lead you to something better. "The basis for attracting the best of all the world can give to you is to first surround, own, and live in these things in mind, or what is falsely called imagination. All so-called imaginings are realities and forces of unseen element. Live in mind in a palace and gradually palatial surroundings will gravitate to you. But so living is *not* pining, or longing, or complainingly wishing. It is when you are 'down in the world,' calmly and persistently seeing yourself as up. It is when you are now compelled to eat from a tin plate, regarding that tin plate as only the certain step to one of silver. It is *not* envying and growling at other people who have silver plate. That growling is just so much capital stock taken from the bank account of mental force."

A friend who knows the power of the interior forces, and whose life is guided in every detail by them, has given a suggestion in this form: When you are in the arms of the bear, even though he is hugging you, look him in the face and laugh, but all the time keep your eye on the bull. If you allow all of your attention to be given to the work of the bear, the bull may get entirely out of your sight. In other words, if you yield to adversity the chances are that it will master you, but if you recognize in yourself the power of mastery over conditions then adversity will yield to you, and will be changed into prosperity. If when it comes you calmly and quietly recognize it, and use the time that might otherwise be spent in regrets, and fears, and forebodings, in setting into operation the powerful forces within you, it will soon take its leave.

Faith, absolute dogmatic faith, is the only law of true success. When we recognize the fact that a man carries his success or his failure with him, and that it does not depend upon outside conditions, we will come into the possession of powers that will quickly change outside conditions into agencies that make for success. When we come into this higher realization and bring our lives into complete harmony with the higher laws, we will then be able so to focus and direct the awakened interior forces, that they will go out and return laden with that for which they are sent. We will then be great enough to attract success, and it will not always be apparently just a little ways ahead. We can then establish in ourselves a centre so strong that instead of running hither and thither for this or that, we can stay at home and draw to us the conditions we desire. If we firmly establish and hold to this centre, things will seem continually to come our way.

The majority of people of the modern world are looking for things that are practical and that can be utilized in every-day life. The more carefully we examine into the laws underlying the great truths we are considering, the more we will find that they are not only eminently practical, but in a sense, and in the deepest and truest sense, they are the only practical things there are.

There are people who continually pride themselves upon being exceedingly "practical"; but many times those who of themselves think nothing about this are the most practical people the world knows. And, on the other hand, those who take great pride in speaking of their own practicality are many times the least practical. Or again, in some ways they may be practical, but so far as life in its totality is concerned, they are absurdly impractical.

What profit, for example, can there be for the man who, materially speaking, though he has gained the whole world, has never yet become acquainted with his own soul? There are multitudes of men all about us who are entirely missing the real life, men who have not learned even the a, b, c of true living. Slaves they are, abject slaves to their temporary material accumulations. Men who thinking they possess their wealth are on the contrary completely possessed by it. Men whose lives are comparatively barren in service to those about them and to the world at large. Men who when they can no longer hold the body,—the agency by means of which they are related to the material world,—will go out poor indeed, pitiably poor. Unable to take even the smallest particle of their accumulations with them, they will enter upon the other form of life naked and destitute.

The kindly deeds, the developed traits of character, the realized powers of the soul, the real riches of the inner life and unfoldment, all those things that become our real and eternal possessions, have been given no place in their lives, and so of the real things of life they are destitute. Nay, many times worse than destitute. We must not suppose that habits once formed are any more easily broken off in the other form of life than they are in this. If one voluntarily grows a certain mania here, we must not suppose that the mere dropping of the body makes all conditions perfect. All is law, all is cause and effect. As we sow, so shall we also reap, not only in this life but in all lives.

He who is enslaved with the sole desire for material possessions here will continue to be enslaved even after he can no longer retain his body. Then, moreover, he will have not even the means of gratifying his desires. Dominated by this habit, he will be unable to set his affections, for a time at least, upon other things, and the desire, without the means of gratifying it will be doubly torturing to him. Perchance this torture may be increased by his seeing the accumulations he thought were his now being scattered and wasted by spendthrifts. He wills his property, as we say, to others, but he can have no word as to its use.

How foolish, then, for us to think that any material possessions *are ours*. How absurd, for example, for one to fence off a number of acres of God's earth and say they are *his*. Nothing is ours that we cannot retain. The things that come into our hands come not for the purpose of being possessed, as we say, much less for the purpose of being hoarded. They come into our hands to be used, to be wisely used. We are stewards merely, and as stewards we shall be held accountable for the way we use whatever is entrusted to us. That great law of compensation that runs through all life is wonderfully exact in its workings, although we may not always fully comprehend it, or even recognize it when it operates in connection with ourselves.

The one who has come into the realization of the higher life no longer has a desire for the accumulation of enormous wealth, any more than he has a desire for any other *excess*. In the degree that he comes into the recognition of the fact that he is wealthy within, external wealth becomes less important in his estimation. When he comes into the realization of the fact that there is a source within from which he can put forth a power to call to him and actualize in his hands at any time a sufficient supply for all his needs, he no longer burdens himself with vast material accumulations that require his constant care and attention, and thus take his time and his thought from the real things of life. In other words, he first finds the *kingdom*, and he realizes that when he has found this, all other things follow in full measure.

It is as hard for a rich man to enter into the kingdom of heaven, said the Master,—he who having nothing had everything,—as it is for a camel to pass through the eye of a needle. In other words, if a man give all his time to the accumulation, the hoarding of outward material possessions far beyond what he can possibly ever use, what time has he for the finding of that wonderful kingdom, which when found, brings all else with it. Which is better, to have millions of dollars, and to have the burden of taking care of it all,—for the one always involves the other,—or to come into the knowledge of such laws and forces that every need will be supplied in good time, to know that no good thing shall be withheld, to know that we have it in our power to make the supply always equal to the demand?

The one who enters into the realm of this higher knowledge, never cares to bring upon himself the species of insanity that has such a firm hold upon so many in the world today. He avoids it as he would avoid any loathsome disease of the body. When we come into the realization of the higher powers, we will then be able to give more attention to the real life, instead of giving so much to the piling up of vast possessions that hamper rather than help. It is the medium ground that brings the true solution here, the same as it is in all phases of life.

Wealth beyond a certain amount cannot be used, and when it cannot be used it then becomes a hindrance rather than an aid, a curse rather than a blessing. All about us are persons with lives now stunted and dwarfed who could make them rich and beautiful, filled with a perennial joy, if they would begin wisely to use that which they have spent the greater portion of their lives in accumulating.

The man who accumulates during his entire life, and who leaves even all when he goes out for "benevolent purposes," comes far short of the ideal life. It is but a poor excuse of a life. It is not especially commendable in me to give a pair of old, worn-out shoes that I shall never use again to another who is in need of shoes. But it is commendable, if indeed doing anything we ought to do can be spoken of as being commendable, it is commendable for me to give a good pair of strong shoes to the man who in the midst of a severe winter is practically shoeless, the man who is exerting every effort to earn an honest living and thereby take care of his family's needs. And if in giving the shoes I also give myself, he then has a double gift, and I a double blessing.

There is no wiser use that those who have great accumulations can make of them than wisely to put them into life, into character, *day by day while they live.* In this way their lives will be continually enriched and increased. The time will come when it will be regarded as a disgrace for a man to die and leave vast accumulations behind him.

Many a person is living in a palace today who in the real life is poorer than many a one who has not even a roof to cover him. A man may own and live in a palace, but the palace for him may be a poorhouse still.

Moth and rust are nature's wise provisions—God's methods—for disintegrating and scattering, in this way getting ready for use in new forms, that which is hoarded and consequently serving no use. There is also a great law continually operating whose effects are to dwarf and deaden the powers of true enjoyment, as well as all the higher faculties of the one who hoards.

Multitudes of people are continually keeping away from them higher and better things because they are forever clinging on to the old. If they would use and pass on the old, room would be made for new things to come. Hoarding always brings loss in one form or another. Using, wisely using, brings an ever renewing gain.

If the tree should as ignorantly and as greedily hold on to this year's leaves when they have served their purpose, where would be the full and beautiful new life that will be put forth in the spring? Gradual decay and finally death would be the result. If the tree is already dead, then it may perhaps be well enough for it to cling on to the old, for no new leaves will come. But as long as the life in the tree is active, it is *necessary* that it rid itself of the old ones, that room may be made for the new.

Opulence is the law of the universe, an abundant supply for every need if nothing is put in the way of its coming. The natural and the normal life for us is this,—To have such a fullness of life and power by living so continually in the realization of our oneness with the Infinite Life and Power that we find ourselves in the constant possession of an abundant supply of all things needed.

Then not by hoarding but by wisely using and ridding ourselves of things as they come, an ever renewing supply will be ours, a supply far better adapted to present needs than the old could possibly be. In this way we not only come into possession of the richest treasures of the Infinite Good ourselves, but we also become open channels through which they can flow to others.

CHAPTER 10

How Men Have Become Prophets, Seers, Sages, and Saviours

I have tried thus far to deal fairly with you in presenting these vital truths, and have spoken of everything on the basis of our own reason and insight. It has been my aim to base nothing on the teachings of others, though they may be the teachings of those inspired. Let us now look for a moment at these same great truths in the light of the thoughts and the teachings as put forth by some of the world's great thinkers and inspired teachers.

The sum and substance of the thought presented in these pages is, you will remember, that the great central fact in human life is the coming into a conscious, vital realization of our oneness with the Infinite Life, and the opening of ourselves fully to this divine inflow. I and the Father are one, said the Master. In this we see how he recognized his oneness with the Father's life. Again he said, The words that I speak unto you I speak not of myself: but the Father that dwelleth in me, He doeth the works. In this we see how clearly he recognized the fact that he of himself could do nothing, only as he worked in conjunction with the Father. Again, my Father works and I work. In other words, my Father sends the power, I open myself to it, and work in conjunction with it.

Again he said, Seek ye first the kingdom of God and His righteousness, and all these things shall be added unto you. And he left us not in the dark as to exactly what he meant by this, for again he said, Say not Lo here nor lo there, know ye not that the kingdom of heaven is within you? According to his teaching, the kingdom of God and the kingdom of heaven were one and the same. If, then, his teaching is that the kingdom of heaven is within us, do we not clearly see that, putting it in other words, his injunction is nothing more nor less than, Come ye into a conscious realization of your oneness with the Father's life. As you realize this oneness you find the kingdom, and when you find this, all things else shall follow.

The story of the prodigal son is another beautiful illustration of this same great teaching of the Master. After the prodigal had spent everything, after he had wandered in all the realms of the physical senses in the pursuit of happiness and pleasure, and found that this did not satisfy but only brought him to the level of the animal creation, he then came to his senses and said, I will arise and go to my Father. In other words, after all these wanderings, his own soul at length spoke to him and said, You are not a mere animal. You are your Father's child. Arise and go to your Father, who holds all things in His hands. Again, the Master said, Call no man your Father upon the earth: for one is your Father, which is in heaven. Here he recognized the fact that the real life is direct from the life of God. Our fathers and our mothers are the agents that give us the bodies, the houses in which we live, but the real life comes from the Infinite Source of Life, God, who is our Father.

One day word was brought to the Master that his mother and his brethren were without, wishing to speak with him. Who is my mother and who are my brethren? said he. Whosoever shall do the will of my Father which is in heaven, the same is my brother, and my sister, and mother.

Many people are greatly enslaved by what we term ties of relationship. It is well, however, for us to remember that our true relatives are not necessarily those who are connected with us by ties of blood. Our truest relatives are those who are nearest akin to us in mind, in soul, in spirit. Our nearest relatives may be those living on the opposite side of the globe,—people whom we may never have seen as yet, but to whom we will yet be drawn, either in this form of life or in another, through that ever working and never failing law of attraction.

When the Master gave the injunction, Call no man your father upon the earth: for one is your Father, which is in heaven, he here gave us the basis for that grand conception of the fatherhood of God. And if God is equally the Father of all, then we have here the basis for the brotherhood of man. But there is, in a sense, a conception still higher than this, namely, the oneness of man and God, and hence the oneness of the whole human race. When we realize this fact, then we clearly see how in the degree that we come into the realization of our oneness with the Infinite Life, and so, every step that we make God-ward, we aid in lifting all mankind up to this realization, and enable them, in turn, to make a step Godward.

The Master again pointed out our true relations with the Infinite Life when he said, Except ye become as little children ye shall not enter into the kingdom of heaven. When he said, Man shall not live by bread alone, but by every word that proceedeth out of the mouth of God, he gave utterance to a truth of far greater import than we have as yet commenced fully to grasp. Here he taught that even the physical life can not be maintained by material food alone, but that one's connection with this Infinite Source determines to a very great extent the condition of even the bodily structure and activities. Blessed are the pure in heart for they shall see God. In other words, blessed are they who in all the universe recognize only God, for by such God shall be seen.

Said the great Hindu sage, Manu, He who in his own soul perceives the Supreme Soul in all beings, and acquires equanimity toward them all, attains the highest bliss. It was Athanasius who said, Even we may become Gods walking about in the flesh. The same great truth we are considering is the one that runs through the life and the teachings of Gautama, he who became the Buddha. People are in bondage, said he, because they have not yet removed the idea of *I*. To do away with all sense of separateness, and to recognize the oneness of the self with the Infinite, is the spirit that breathes through all his teachings. Running through the lives of all the mediæval mystics was this same great truth,—union with God.

Then, coming nearer to our own time, we find the highly illumined seer, Emanuel Swedenborg, pointing out the great laws in connection with what he termed, the divine influx, and how we may open ourselves more fully to its operations. The great central fact in the religion and worship of the Friends is, the inner light,—God in the soul of man speaking directly in just the degree that the soul is opened to Him. The inspired one, the seer who when with us lived at Concord, recognized the same great truth when he said, We are all inlets to the great sea of life. And it was by opening himself so fully to its inflow that he became one inspired.

All through the world's history we find that the men and the women who have entered into the realm of true wisdom and power, and hence into the realm of true peace and joy, have lived in harmony with this Higher Power. David was strong and powerful and his soul burst forth in praise and adoration in just the degree that he listened to the voice of God and lived in accordance with his higher promptings. Whenever he failed to do this we hear his soul crying out in anguish and lamentation. The same is true of every nation or people. When the Israelites acknowledged God and followed according to His leadings they were prosperous, contented, and powerful, and nothing could prevail against them. When they depended upon their own strength alone and failed to recognize God as the source of their strength, we find them overcome, in bondage, or despair.

A great immutable law underlies the truth, Blessed are they that hear the word of God and do it. Then follows all. We are wise in the degree that we live according to the higher light.

All the prophets, seers, sages, and saviours in the world's history became what they became, and consequently had the powers they had, through an entirely natural process. They all recognized and came into the conscious realization of their oneness with the Infinite Life. God is no respecter of persons. He doesn't create prophets, seers, sages, and saviours as such. He creates men. But here and there one recognizes his true identity, recognizes the oneness of his life with the Source whence it came. He lives in the realization of this oneness, and in turn becomes a prophet, seer, sage, or saviour. Neither is God a respecter of races or of nations. He has no chosen people; but here and there a race or nation becomes a respecter of God and hence lives the life of a chosen people.

There has been no age or place of miracles in distinction from any other age or place. What we term miracles have abounded in all places and at all times where conditions have been made for them. They are being performed today just as much as they ever have been when the laws governing them are respected. Mighty men, we are told they were, mighty men who walked with God; and in the words "who walked with God" lies the secret of the words "mighty men." Cause, effect.

The Lord never prospers any man, but the man prospers because he acknowledges the Lord, and lives in accordance with the higher laws. Solomon was given the opportunity of choosing whatever he desired; his better judgment prevailed and he chose wisdom. But when he chose wisdom he found that it included all else beside. We are told that God hardened Pharaoh's heart. I don't believe it. God never hardens any one's heart. Pharaoh hardened his own heart and God was blamed for it. But when Pharaoh hardened his heart and disobeyed the voice of God, the plagues came. Again, cause, effect. Had he, on the contrary, listened,—in other words, had he opened himself to and obeyed the voice of God, the plagues would not have come.

We can be our own best friends or we can be our own worst enemies. In the degree that we become friends to the highest and best within us, we become friends to all; and in the degree that we become enemies to the highest and best within us, do we become enemies to all. In the degree that we open ourselves to the higher powers and let them manifest through us, then by the very inspirations we carry with us do we become in a sense the saviours of our fellow-men, and in this way we all are, or may become, the saviours one of another. In this way you may become, indeed, one of the world's redeemers.

CHAPTER 11

The Basic Principle of All Religions—The Universal Religion

The great truth we are considering is the fundamental principle running through all religions. We find it in every one. In regard to it all agree. It is, moreover, a great truth in regard to which all people can agree, whether they belong to the same or to different religions. People always quarrel about the trifles, about their personal views of minor insignificant points. They always come together in the presence of great fundamental truths, the threads of which run through all. The quarrels are in connection with the lower self, the agreements are in connection with the higher self.

A place may have its factions that quarrel and fight among themselves, but let a great calamity come upon the land, flood, famine, pestilence, and these little personal differences are entirely forgotten and all work shoulder to shoulder in the one great cause. The changing, the evolving self gives rise to quarrels; the permanent, the soul self unites all in the highest efforts of love and service.

Patriotism is a beautiful thing; it is well for me to love my country, but why should I love my own country more than I love all others? If I love my own and hate others, I then show my limitations, and my patriotism will stand the test not even for my own. If I love my own country and in the same way love all other countries, then I show the largeness of my nature, and a patriotism of this kind is noble and always to be relied upon.

The view of God in regard to which we are agreed, that He is the Infinite Spirit of Life and Power that is back of all, that is working in and through all, that is the life of all, is a matter in regard to which all men, all religions can agree. With this view there can be no infidels or atheists. There are atheists and infidels in connection with many views that are held concerning God, and thank God there are. Even devout and earnest people among us attribute things to God that no respectable men or women would permit to be attributed to themselves. This view is satisfying to those who cannot see how God can be angry with his children, jealous, vindictive. A display of these qualities always lessens our respect for men and women, and still we attribute them to God.

The earnest, sincere heretic is one of the greatest friends true religion can have. Heretics are among God's greatest servants. They are among the true servants of mankind. Christ was one of the greatest heretics the world has ever known. He allowed himself to be bound by no established or orthodox teachings or beliefs. Christ is preeminently a type of the universal. John the Baptist is a type of the personal. John dressed in a particular way, ate a particular kind of food, belonged to a particular order, lived and taught in a particular locality, and he himself recognized the fact that he must decrease while Christ must increase. Christ, on the other hand, gave himself absolutely no limitations. He allowed himself to be bound by nothing. He was absolutely universal and as a consequence taught not for his own particular day, but for all time.

This mighty truth which we have agreed upon as the great central fact of human life is the golden thread that runs through all religions. When we make it the paramount fact in our lives we will find that minor differences, narrow prejudices, and all these laughable absurdities will so fall away by virtue of their very insignificance, that a Jew can worship equally as well in a Catholic cathedral, a Catholic in a Jewish synagogue, a Buddhist in a Christian church, a Christian in a Buddhist temple. Or all can worship equally well about their own hearth-stones, or out on the hillside, or while pursuing the avocations of every-day life. For true worship, only God and the human soul are necessary. It does not depend upon times, or seasons, or occasions. Anywhere and at any time God and man in the bush may meet.

This is the great fundamental principle of the universal religion upon which all can agree. This is the great fact that is permanent. There are many things in regard to which all cannot agree. These are the things that are personal, non-essential, and so as time passes they gradually fall away. One who doesn't grasp this great truth, a Christian, for example, asks, "But was not Christ inspired?" Yes, but he was not the only one inspired. Another who is a Buddhist asks, "Was not Buddha inspired?" Yes, but he was not the only one inspired. A Christian asks, "But is not our Christian Bible inspired?" Yes, but there are other inspired scriptures. A Brahmin or a Buddhist asks, "Are not the Vedas inspired?" Yes, but there are other inspired sacred books. Your error is not in believing that your particular scriptures are inspired, but your error is—and you show your absurdly laughable limitations by it—your inability to see that other scriptures are also inspired.

The sacred books, the inspired writings, all come from the same source,—God, God speaking through the souls of those who open themselves that He may thus speak. Some may be more inspired than others. It depends entirely on the relative degree that this one or that one opens himself to the Divine voice. Says one of the inspired writers in the Hebrew scriptures, Wisdom is the breath of the power of God, and *in all ages* entering into holy souls she maketh them friends of God and prophets.

Let us not be among the number so dwarfed, so limited, so bigoted as to think that the Infinite God has revealed Himself to one little handful of His children, in one little quarter of the globe, and at one particular period of time. This isn't the pattern by which God works. Of a truth I perceive that God is no respecter of persons, but in every nation he that revereth God and worketh righteousness is accepted of Him, says the Christian Bible.

When we fully realize this truth we will then see that it makes but little difference what particular form of religion one holds to, but it does make a tremendous difference how true he is to the *vital* principles of this one. In the degree that we love self less and love truth more, in that degree will we care less about converting people to our particular way of thinking, but all the more will we care to aid them in coming into the full realization of truth through the channels best adapted to them. The doctrine of our master, says the Chinese, consisted solely in integrity of heart. We will find as we search that this is the doctrine of every one who is at all worthy of the name of master.

The great fundamental principles of all religions are the same. They differ only in their minor details according to the various degrees of unfoldment of different people. I am sometimes asked, "To what religion do you belong?" What religion? Why, bless you, there is only one religion,—the religion of the living God. There are, of course, the various creeds of the same religion arising from the various interpretations of different people, but they are all of minor importance. The more unfolded the soul the less important do these minor differences become. There are also, of course, the various so-called religions. There is in reality, however, but one religion.

The moment we lose sight of this great fact we depart from the real, vital spirit of true religion and allow ourselves to be limited and bound by form. In the degree that we do this we build fences around ourselves which keep others away from us, and which also prevent our coming into the realization of universal truth; there is nothing worthy the name of truth that is not universal.

There is only one religion. "Whatever road I take joins the highway that leads to Thee," says the inspired writer in the Persian scriptures. "Broad is the carpet God has spread, and beautiful the colors he has given it." "The pure man respects every form of faith," says the Buddhist. "My doctrine makes no difference between high and low, rich and poor; like the sky, it has room for all, and like the water, it washes all alike." "The broad minded see the truth in different religions; the narrow minded see only the differences," says the Chinese. The Hindu has said, "The narrow minded ask, 'Is this man a stranger, or is he of our tribe?' But to those in whom love dwells, the whole world is but one family." "Altar flowers are of many species, but all worship is one." "Heaven is a palace with many doors, and each may enter in his own way." "Are we not all children of one Father?" says the Christian. "God has made of one blood all nations, to dwell on the face of the earth." It was a latter-day seer who said, "That which was profitable to the soul of man the Father revealed to the ancients; that which is profitable to the soul of man today revealeth He this day."

It was Tennyson who said, "I dreamed that stone by stone I reared a sacred fane, a temple, neither pagoda, mosque, nor church, but loftier, simpler, always open-doored to every breath from heaven, and Truth and Peace and Love and Justice came and dwelt therein."

Religion in its true sense is the most joyous thing the human soul can know, and when the real religion is realized, we will find that it will be an agent of peace, of joy, and of happiness, and never an agent of gloomy, long-faced sadness. It will then be attractive to all and repulsive to none. Let our churches grasp these great truths, let them give their time and attention to bringing people into a knowledge of their true selves, into a knowledge of their relations, of their oneness, with the Infinite God, and such joy will be the result, and such crowds will flock to them, that their very walls will seem almost to burst, and such songs of joy will continually pour forth as will make all people in love with the religion that makes for every-day life, and hence the religion that is true and vital. Adequacy for life, adequacy for every-day life here and now, must be the test of all true religion. If it does not bear this test, then it simply is not religion. We need an every-day, a this-world religion. All time spent in connection with any other is worse than wasted. The eternal life that we are now living will be well lived if we take good care of each little period of time as it presents itself day after day. If we fail in doing this, we fail in everything.

CHAPTER 12

Entering Now into the Realization of the Highest Riches

I hear the question, What can be said in a concrete way in regard to the method of coming into this realization? The facts underlying it are, indeed, most beautiful and true, but how can we actualize in ourselves the realization that carries with it such wonderful results?

The method is not difficult if we do not of ourselves make it difficult. The principal word to be used is the word,—Open. Simply to open your mind and heart to this divine inflow which is waiting only for the opening of the gate, that it may enter. It is like opening the gate of the trough which conducts the water from the reservoir above into the field below. The water, by virtue of its very nature, will rush in and irrigate the field if the gate is but opened. As to the realization of our oneness with this Infinite Life and Power, after seeing, as I think we have clearly seen by this time, the relations it bears to us and we to it, the chief thing to be said is simply,—Realize your oneness with it. The open mind and heart whereby one is brought into the receptive attitude is the first thing necessary. Then the earnest, sincere desire.

It may be an aid at first to take yourself for a few moments each day into the quiet, into the silence, where you will not be agitated by the disturbances that enter in through the avenues of the physical senses. There in the quiet alone with God, put yourself into the receptive attitude. Calmly, quietly, and expectantly desire that this realization break in upon and take possession of your soul. As it breaks in upon and takes possession of the soul, it will manifest itself to your mind, and from this you will feel its manifestations in every part of your body. Then in the degree that you open yourself to it you will feel a quiet, peaceful, illuminating power that will harmonize body, soul, and mind, and that will then harmonize these with all the world. You are now on the mountain top and the voice of God is speaking to you. *Then, as you descend, carry this realization with you.* Live in it, waking, working, thinking, walking, sleeping. In this way, although you may not be continually on the mountain top, you will nevertheless be continually living in the realization of all the beauty, and inspiration, and power you have felt there.

Moreover, the time will come when in the busy office or on the noisy street you can enter into the silence by simply drawing the mantle of your own thoughts about you and realizing that there and everywhere the Spirit of Infinite Life, Love, Wisdom, Peace, Power, and Plenty is guiding, keeping, protecting, leading you. This is the spirit of continual prayer. This it is to pray without ceasing. This it is to know and to walk with God. *This it is to find the Christ within.* This is the new birth, the second birth. First that which is natural, then that which is spiritual. It is thus that the old man Adam is put off and the new man Christ is put on. This it is to be saved unto life eternal, whatever one's form of belief or faith may be; for it is life eternal to know God. "The Sweet By and By" will be a song of the past. We will create a new song — "The Beautiful Eternal Now."

This is the realization that you and I can come into this very day, this very hour, this very minute, if we desire and if we will it. And if now we merely set our faces in the right direction, it is then but a matter of time until we come into the full splendors of this complete realization. To set one's face in the direction of the mountain and then simply to journey on, whether rapidly or more slowly, will bring him to it. But unless one set his face in the right direction and make the start, he will not reach it. It was Goethe who said:

Are you in earnest? Seize this very minute:
What you can do, or dream you can, begin it;
Boldness has genius, power, and magic in it.
Only engage and then the mind grows heated;
Begin and then the work will be completed.

Said the young man, Gautama Siddhârtha, I have awakened to the truth and I am resolved to accomplish my purpose,—Verily I shall become a Buddha. It was this that brought him into the life of the Enlightened One, and so into the realization of Nirvana right here in this life. That this same realization and life is within the possibilities of all here and now was his teaching. It was this that has made him the Light Bearer to millions of people.

Said the young man, Jesus, Know ye not that I must be about my Father's business? Making this the one great purpose of his life he came into the full and complete realization,—I and the Father are one. He thus came into the full realization of the Kingdom of Heaven right here in this life. That all could come into this same realization and life here and now was his teaching. It was this that has made him the Light Bearer to millions of people.

And so far as practical things are concerned, we may hunt the wide universe through and we shall find that there is no injunction more practical than, Seek ye first the kingdom of God and His righteousness and all other things shall be added unto you. And in the light of what has gone before, I think there is no one who is open to truth and honest with himself who will fail to grasp the underlying reason and see the great laws upon which it is based.

Personally I know lives that have so fully entered into the kingdom through the realization of their oneness with the Infinite Life and through the opening of themselves so fully to its divine guidance, that they are most wonderful concrete examples of the reality of this great and all-important truth. They are people whose lives are in this way guided not only in a general way, but literally in every detail. They simply live in the realization of their oneness with this Infinite Power, continually in harmony with it, and so continually in the realization of the kingdom of heaven. An abundance of all things is theirs. They are never at a loss for anything. The supply seems always equal to the demand. They never seem at a loss in regard to what to do or how to do it. Their lives are care-less lives. They are lives free from care because they are continually conscious of the fact that the higher powers are doing the guiding, and they are relieved of the responsibility. To enter into detail in connection with some of these lives, and particularly with two or three that come to my mind at this moment, would reveal facts that no doubt to some would seem almost incredible if not miraculous. But let us remember that what is possible for one life to realize is possible for all. This is indeed the natural and the normal life, that which will be the every-day life of every one who comes into and who lives in this higher realization and so in harmony with the higher laws. This is simply getting into the current of that divine sequence running throughout the universe; and when once in it, life then ceases to be a plodding and moves along day after day much as the tides flow, much as the planets move in their courses, much as the seasons come and go.

All the frictions, all the uncertainties, all the ills, the sufferings, the fears, the forebodings, the perplexities of life come to us because we are out of harmony with the divine order of things. They will continue to come as long as we so live. Rowing against the tide is hard and uncertain. To go with the tide and thus to take advantage of the working of a great natural force is safe and easy. To come into the conscious, vital realization of our oneness with the Infinite Life and Power is to come into the current of this divine sequence. Coming thus into harmony with the Infinite, brings us in turn into harmony with all about us, into harmony with the life of the heavens, into harmony with all the universe. And above all, it brings us into harmony with ourselves, so that body, soul, and mind become perfectly harmonized, and when this is so, life becomes full and complete.

The sense life then no longer masters and enslaves us. The physical is subordinated to and ruled by the mental; this in turn is subordinated to and continually illumined by the spiritual. Life is then no longer the poor, one-sided thing it is in so many cases; but the threefold, the all-round life with all its beauties and ever increasing joys and powers is entered upon. Thus it is that we are brought to realize that the middle path is the great solution of life; neither asceticism on the one hand nor license and perverted use on the other. Everything is for use, but all must be wisely used in order to be fully enjoyed.

As we live in these higher realizations the senses are not ignored but are ever more fully perfected. As the body becomes less gross and heavy, finer in its texture and form, all the senses become finer, so that powers we do not now realize as belonging to us gradually develop. Thus we come, in a perfectly natural and normal way, into the super-conscious realms whereby we make it possible for the higher laws and truths to be revealed to us. As we enter into these realms we are then not among those who give their time in speculating as to whether this one or that one had the insight and the powers attributed to him, but we are able *to know* for ourselves. Neither are we among those who attempt to lead the people upon the hearsay of some one else, but we know whereof we speak, and only thus can we speak with authority. There are many things that we cannot know until by living the life we bring ourselves into that state where it is possible for them to be revealed to us. "If any man will do His will, he shall know of the doctrine." It was Plotinus who said, The mind that wishes to behold God must itself become God. As we thus make it possible for these higher laws and truths to be revealed to us, we will in turn become enlightened ones, channels through which they may be revealed to others.

When one is fully alive to the possibilities that come with this higher awakening, as he goes here and there, as he mingles with his fellow-men, he imparts to all an inspiration that kindles in them a feeling of power kindred to his own. We are all continually giving out influences similar to those that are playing in our own lives. We do this in the same way that each flower emits its own peculiar odor. The rose breathes out its fragrance upon the air and all who come near it are refreshed and inspired by this emanation from the soul of the rose. A poisonous weed sends out its obnoxious odor; it is neither refreshing nor inspiring in its effects, and if one remain near it long he may be so unpleasantly affected as to be made even ill by it.

The higher the life the more inspiring and helpful are the emanations that it is continually sending out. The lower the life the more harmful is the influence it continually sends out to all who come in contact with it. Each one is continually radiating an atmosphere of one kind or the other.

We are told by the mariners who sail on the Indian Seas, that many times they are able to tell their approach to certain islands long before they can see them by the sweet fragrance of the sandalwood that is wafted far out upon the deep. Do you not see how it would serve to have such a soul playing through such a body that as you go here and there a subtle, silent force goes out from you that all feel and are influenced by; so that you carry with you an inspiration and continually shed a benediction wherever you go; so that your friends and all people will say,—His coming brings peace and joy into our homes, welcome his coming; so that as you pass along the street, tired, and weary, and even sin-sick men and women will feel a certain divine touch that will awaken new desires and a new life in them; that will make the very horse as you pass him turn his head with a strange, half-human, longing look? Such are the subtle powers of the human soul when it makes itself translucent to the Divine. To know that such a life is within our living here and now is enough to make one burst forth with songs of joy. And when the life itself is entered upon, the sentiment of at least one song will be:

Oh! I stand in the Great Forever,
All things to me are divine;
I eat of the heavenly manna,
I drink of the heavenly wine.

In the gleam of the shining rainbow
The Father's Love I behold,
As I gaze on its radiant blending
Of crimson and blue and gold.

In all the bright birds that are singing,
In all the fair flowers that bloom,
Whose welcome aromas are bringing
Their blessings of sweet perfume;

In the glorious tint of the morning,
In the gorgeous sheen of the night,
Oh! my soul is lost in rapture,
My senses are lost in sight.

As one comes into and lives continually in the full, conscious realization of his oneness with the Infinite Life and Power, then all else follows. This it is that brings the realization of such splendors, and beauties, and joys as a life that is thus related with the Infinite Power alone can know. This it is to come into the realization of heaven's richest treasures while walking the earth. This it is to bring heaven down to earth, or rather to bring earth up to heaven. This it is to exchange weakness and impotence for strength; sorrows and sighings for joy; fears and forebodings for faith; longings for realizations. This it is to come into fullness of peace, power, and plenty. This it is to be in tune with the Infinite.

CHAPTER 13

"The Way"

Life is not so complex if we do not so persistently make it so. We accept the results or the effects; but we concern ourselves all too little with the realm of cause. The springs of life are all from within. Invariably it is true—as is the inner so always and inevitably will be the outer.

There is a Divine current that will bear us with peace and safety on its bosom if we are sufficiently alert and determined to find it—and go with it. The natural, normal life is by a law divine under the guidance of the Spirit.

There is a mystic force that transcends the powers of the intellect and likewise of the body. There are certain faculties that we have that are not a part of the active, thinking mind; they transcend any possible activities of the active thinking mind. Through them we have intuitions, impulses, leadings, that instead of being merely the occasional, *should be the normal and habitual.*

They would be if we understood better the laws that pertain to them and observe them; for here, as in connection with everything in the universe and everything in human life, all is governed by law—the Elemental law of cause and effect. Supreme Intelligence, Creative Power, works only through law. There is an inner spirit or guide that rules and regulates the life when the life is brought into that state or condition whereby it can make itself known, and in turn, dominate the life.

Jesus, Master of the laws of life, and supreme revealer of them to men, had a full and practical knowledge of it. He not only abundantly demonstrated it in his own life, but he made clear the way whereby it may become the common possession of other lives; for—do not worry about your life—was his clear-cut and repeated command. He not only gave the injunction or command, but he demonstrated the method whereby the fears and forebodings and uncertainties of life, can be displaced by a force or a power that will bring them to an end.

It was embodied in his other injunction or command that he gave utterance to so repeatedly: "Seek ye first the Kingdom of God and His righteousness and all these things shall be added to you." And by all these things, he meant, all of the common needs and necessities of the daily life.

The finding of the Kingdom of God is the recognition of the indwelling Divine Life as the source and therefore as the Essence of our own lives. It is the bringing of men's minds and therefore acts into harmony with the Divine will and purpose. It is the saving of men from their lower conceptions and selves, and a lifting them up to a realization of their higher selves, which as he taught, is eternally one with God, the Father; and which, when realized, lifts a man's thoughts, acts, purposes and conduct—his entire life—up to that pattern or standard.

It was not merely a poetic fancy, but the recognition of a fundamental law, as well-known laws of modern psychology, mental and spiritual science, are now clearly demonstrating, that induced the Prophet to say: "And thine ears shall hear a word behind thee, saying, This is the way, walk ye in it, when ye turn to the right-hand and when ye turn to the left." And again: "The Lord in the midst of thee is mighty." And still again: "He that dwelleth in the secret place of the Most High shall abide under the shadow of the Almighty."

How often do the meagre accounts of the Master's life tell us of his going up to the mountain to pray—*for communion with the Father.* And then we find him invariably down among men, always where the need for help and for human service was the greatest.

This habit of taking a little time daily, alone in the quiet, in communion with one's Source, that the illumination and guidance of the Holy Spirit may become alive and active in the life, and going then about one's daily work ever open to and conscious of this Divine guidance, trusting and resting it in, strengthened and sustained always by this Divine power, will bring definiteness and direction, will bring hope and courage, will bring peace and power to every one who will heed the Master's injunction and will follow his example. These it has brought to great numbers to whom before, life was an enigma; and this because the life had been lived entirely from the outside.

The higher forces and powers of the inner life, those of the mind and spirit, always potential within, become of actual value only as they are recognized, realized, and used.

The Master's *Way of the Spirit,* the finding of the Kingdom within, leads into no blind alley. It leads out and triumphantly out onto the great plain of clear vision, of unselfcentred activity, of heroic endeavor and accomplishment.

If we would spend a fraction of the time that we spend in needless anxiety, in definite constructive thought, in "silent demand," visualizing the conditions that we would have, with faith in their fulfillment, we would soon know that the Master's illustration of the care-free bird is fact and not fancy—It is, he said, what life should be.

The little time spent in the quiet each day—alone with one's God—that we may make and keep our connection with the Infinite Source—our source and our life—will be a boon to any life. It will prove, if we are faithful, to be the most priceless possession that we have.

While it is impossible for one to make a formula for another that one should follow, the following may perchance contain some little suggestions—each must follow his or her own leading and therefore method:

My Father in Heaven, Infinite Spirit of life and love and wisdom and power, in whom I live and move and have my being, whence cometh my help, manifest Thyself in me.

Help me to open myself to the highest wisdom and insight and love and power, that

I may serve Thee and my fellow-men, and all my fellow-creatures faithfully, and that I may have the Divine guidance and care, and that all my needs be supplied.

Oh *Christ within,* enfold and lead me and reign supreme, that the One Life that is my life, I may realize and manifest ever more fully.

I am strong in the Infinite Spirit of life and love and wisdom and power. I have and shall have the Divine guidance and care; for it is the Father that worketh in me—My Father works and I work.

The following little motto—A resolve for today—may contain a little aid for the following of the *Way:*

I AM RESOLVED

I believe that my Brother intended that I take his teachings in the simple, frank, and open manner in which he gave them, out on the hill-side, by the calm blue waters of the Galilean sea, and out under the stars of heaven.

I believe that he knew what he meant, and that he meant what he said, when he gave the substance of all religion and the duty of man, as love to God, and love and service for his fellow-men.

I am therefore resolved at this, the beginning of another day, this fresh beginning of life, to go forth eager and happy and unafraid, in that I can come into the same filial relations of love and guidance and care with my Father in Heaven, that my Elder Brother realized and lived, and going before revealed to me.

I shall listen intently to know, and shall run with eager feet to do my Father's will, calm and quiet within, knowing that I shall have the Divine guidance and care, and that no harm therefore shall befall me; for I am now living in God's life and there I shall live forever.

I am resolved in all human contact to meet petulance with patience, questionings with kindness, hatred with love, eager always to do the kindly deed that brings the joy of service—and that alone makes human life truly human.

I shall seek no advantage for myself to the detriment or the harm of my neighbor, knowing that it is only through the law of mutuality that I can fully enjoy what I gain—or can even be a man.

I am resolved therefore so to live this day, that when the twilight comes and the night falls, I shall be not only another day's journey nearer home; but I shall have lived a man's part and done a man's work in the world—and shall indeed deserve my Father's love and care.

10

THE MASTER KEY SYSTEM

CHARLES F. HAANEL

(1917)

Contents

Foreword	599
Part One	605
Part Two	610
Part Three	616
Part Four	621
Part Five	626
Part Six	631
Part Seven	636
Part Eight	641
Part Nine	647
Part Ten	653
Part Eleven	658
Part Twelve	663
Part Thirteen	668
Part Fourteen	673
Part Fifteen	678
Part Sixteen	683
Part Seventeen	688
Part Eighteen	693
Part Nineteen	698

Part Twenty 703
Part Twenty-one 708
Part Twenty-two 713
Part Twenty-three 718
Part Twenty-four 723
About the Author 729

Foreword

Some men seem to attract success, power, wealth, attainment, with very little conscious effort; others conquer with great difficulty; still others fail altogether to reach their ambitions, desires and ideals. Why is this so? Why should some men realize their ambitions easily, others with difficulty, and still others not at all? The cause cannot be physical, else the most perfect men, physically, would be the most successful. The difference, therefore, must be mental—must be in the mind; hence mind must be the creative force, must constitute the sole difference between men. It is mind, therefore, which overcomes environment and every other obstacle in the path of men.

When the creative power of thought is fully understood, its effect will be seen to be marvelous. But such results cannot be secured without proper application, diligence, and concentration. The student will find that the laws governing in the mental and spiritual world are as fixed and infallible as in the material world. To secure the desired results, then, it is necessary to know the law and to comply with it. A proper compliance with the law will be found to produce the desired result with invariable exactitude. The student who learns that power comes from within, that he is weak only because he has depended on help from outside, and who unhesitatingly throws himself on his own thought, instantly rights himself, stands erect, assumes a dominant attitude, and works miracles.

It is evident, therefore, that he who fails to fully investigate and take advantage of the wonderful progress which is being made in this last and greatest science will soon be as far behind as the man who would refuse to acknowledge and accept the benefits which have accrued to mankind through an understanding of the laws of electricity.

Of course, mind creates negative conditions just as readily as favorable conditions, and when we consciously or unconsciously visualize every kind of lack, limitation and discord, we create these conditions; this is what many are unconsciously doing all the time.

This law as well as every other law is no respecter of persons, but is in constant operation and is relentlessly bringing to each individual exactly what he has created; in other words, "Whatsoever a man soweth that shall he also reap."

Abundance, therefore, depends upon a recognition of the laws of Abundance, and the fact that Mind is not only the creator, but the only creator of all there is. Certainly nothing can be created, before we know that it can be created and then make the proper effort. There is no more Electricity in the world today than there was fifty years ago, but until someone recognized the law by which it could be made of service, we received no benefit; now that the law is understood, practically the whole world is lit by it. So with the Law of Abundance; it is only those who recognize the law and place themselves in harmony with it who share in its benefits.

The scientific spirit now dominates every field of effort, relations of cause and effect are no longer ignored.

The discovery of a region of law marked an epoch in human progress. It eliminated the element of uncertainty and caprice in men's lives, and substituted law, reason and certitude.

Men now understand that for every result there is an adequate and definite cause, so that when a given result is desired, they seek the condition by which alone this result may be attained.

The basis upon which all law rests was discovered by inductive reasoning which consists of comparing a number of separate instances with one another until the common factor which gives rise to them all is seen.

It is this method of study to which the civilized nations owe the greater part of their prosperity and the more valuable part of their knowledge; it has lengthened life, it has mitigated pain, it has spanned rivers, it has brightened the night with the splendor of day, extended the range of vision, accelerated motion, annihilated distance, facilitated intercourse, and enabled men to descend into the sea, and into the air. What wonder then that men soon endeavored to extend the blessings of this system of study to their method of thinking, so that when it became plainly evident that certain results followed a particular method of thinking it only remained to classify these results.

This method is scientific, and it is the only method by which we shall be permitted retain that degree of liberty and freedom which we have been accustomed to look upon as an inalienable right, because a people is safe at home and in the world only if national preparedness means such things as growing surplus of health, accumulated efficiency in public and private business of whatever sort, continuous advance in the science and art of acting together, and the increasingly dominant endeavor to make all of these and all other aspects of national development center and revolve about ascending life, single and collective, for which science, art and ethics furnish guidance and controlling motives.

The Master Key is based on absolute scientific truth and will unfold the possibilities that lie dormant in the individual, and teach how they may be brought into powerful action, to increase the person's effective capacity, bringing added energy, discernment, vigor and mental elasticity. The student who gains an understanding of the mental laws which are unfolded will come into the possession of an ability to secure results hitherto undreamed of, and which has rewards hardly to be expressed in words.

It explains the correct use of both the receptive and active elements of the mental nature, and instructs the student in the recognition of opportunity; it strengthens the will and reasoning powers, and teaches the cultivation and best uses of imagination, desire, the emotions and the intuitional faculty. It gives initiative, tenacity of purpose, wisdom of choice, intelligent sympathy and a thorough enjoyment of life on its higher planes.

The Master Key teaches the use of Mind Power, true Mind Power, not any of the substitutes and perversions; it has nothing to do with Hypnotism, Magic or any of the more or less fascinating deceptions by which many are led to think that something can be had for nothing.

The Master Key cultivates and develops the understanding which will enable you to control the body and thereby the health. It improves and strengthens the Memory. It develops Insight, the kind of Insight which is so rare, the kind which is the distinguishing characteristic of every successful business man, the kind which enables men to see the possibilities as well as the difficulties in every situation, the kind which enables men to discern opportunity close at hand, for thousands fail to see opportunities almost within their grasp while they are industriously working with situations which under no possibility can be made to realize any substantial return.

The Master Key develops Mental Power, which means that others instinctively recognize that you are a person of force, of character—that they want to do what you want them to do; it means that you attract men and things to you; that you are what some people call "lucky," that "things" come your way, that you have come into an understanding of the fundamental laws of nature, and have put yourself in harmony with them; that you are in tune with Infinite; that you understand the Law of Attraction, the natural laws of growth, and the psychological laws on which all advantages in the social and business world rest.

Mental Power is creative power, it gives you the ability to create for yourself; it does not mean the ability to take something away from someone else. Nature never does things that way. Nature makes two blades of grass grow where one grew before, and Mind Power enables men to do the same thing.

The Master Key develops insight and sagacity, increased independence, the ability and disposition to be helpful. It destroys distrust, depression, fear, melancholia, and every form of lack, limitation and weakness, including pain and disease; it awakens buried talents, supplies initiative, force, energy, vitality—it awakens an appreciation of the beautiful in Art, Literature, and Science.

It has changed the lives of thousands of men and women, by substituting definite principles for uncertain and hazy methods—and principles for the foundation upon which every system of efficiency must rest.

Elbert Gary, the chairman of the United States Steel Corporation, said, "The services of advisors, instructors, efficiency experts in successful management are indispensable to most business enterprises of magnitude, but I deem the recognition and adoption of right principles to be of vastly more importance."

The Master Key teaches right principles, and suggests methods for making a practical application of the principles; in that it differs from every other course of study. It teaches that the only possible value which can attach to any principle is in its application. Many read books, take home study courses, attend lectures all their lives without ever making any progress in demonstrating the value of the principles involved. The Master Key suggests methods by which the value of the principles taught may be demonstrated and put in actual practice in the daily experience.

There is a change in the thought of the world. This change is silently transpiring in our midst, and is more important than any which the world has undergone since the downfall of Paganism.

The present revolution in the opinions of all classes of men, the highest and most cultured of men as well as those of the laboring class, stands unparalleled in the history of the world.

Science has of late made such vast discoveries, has revealed such an infinity of resources, has unveiled such enormous possibilities and such unsuspected forces, that scientific men more and more hesitate to affirm certain theories as established and indubitable or to deny certain other theories as absurd or impossible, and so a new civilization is being born; customs, creeds, and cruelty are passing; vision, faith and service are taking their place. The fetters of tradition are being melted off from humanity, and as the dross of materialism is being consumed, thought is being liberated and truth is rising full-orbed before an astonished multitude.

The whole world is on the eve of a new consciousness, a new power and a new consciousness, a new power and a new realization of the resources within the self. The last century saw the most magnificent material progress in history. The present century will produce the greatest progress in mental and spiritual power.

Physical science has resolved matter into molecules, molecules into atoms, atoms into energy, and it has remained for Sir Ambrose Fleming, in an address before the Royal Institution, to resolve this energy into mind. He says: "In its ultimate essence, energy may be incomprehensible by us except as an exhibition of the direct operation of that which we call Mind or Will."

Let us see what are the most powerful forces in nature. In the mineral world everything is solid and fixed. In the animal and vegetable kingdom it is in a state of flux, forever changing, always being created and re-created. In the atmosphere we find heat, light and energy. Each realm becomes finer and more spiritual as we pass from the visible to the invisible, from the coarse to the fine, from the low potentiality to high potentiality. When we reach the invisible we find energy in its purest and most volatile state.

And as the most powerful forces of nature are the invisible forces, so we find that the most powerful forces of man are his invisible forces, his spiritual force, and the only way in which the spiritual force can manifest itself is through the process of thinking. Thinking is the only activity which the spirit possesses, and thought is the only product of thinking.

Addition and subtraction are therefore spiritual transactions; reasoning is a spiritual process; ideas are spiritual conceptions; questions are spiritual searchlights and logic, argument and philosophy is spiritual machinery.

Every thought brings into action certain physical tissue, parts of the brain, nerve or muscle. This produces an actual physical change in the construction of the tissue. Therefore it is only necessary to have a certain number of thoughts on a given subject in order to bring about a complete change in the physical organization of a man.

This is the process by which failure is changed to success. Thoughts of courage, power, inspiration, harmony, are substituted for thoughts of failure, despair, lack, limitation and discord, and as these thoughts take root, the physical tissue is changed and the individual sees life in a new light, old things have actually passed away, all things have become new, he is born again, this time born of the spirit, life has a new meaning for him, he is reconstructed and is filled with joy, confidence, hope, energy. He sees opportunities for success to which he was heretofore blind. He recognizes possibilities which before had no meaning for him. The thoughts of success with which he has been impregnated are radiated to those around him, and they in turn help him onward and upward; he attracts to him new and successful associates, and this in turn changes his environment; so that by this simple exercise of thought, a man changes not only himself, but his environment, circumstances and conditions.

You will see, you must see, that we are at the dawn of a new day; that the possibilities are so wonderful, so fascinating, so limitless as to be almost bewildering. A century ago any man with a Gatling Gun could have annihilated a whole army equipped with the implements of warfare then in use. So it is at present. Any man with a knowledge of the possibilities contained in the Master Key has an inconceivable advantage over the multitude.

Part One

It is my privilege to enclose herewith Part One of the Master Key System. Would you bring into your life more power? Get the power consciousness. More health? Get the health consciousness. More happiness? Get the happiness consciousness. Live the spirit of these things until they become yours by right. It will then become impossible to keep them from you. The things of the world are fluid to a power within man by which he rules them.

You need not acquire this power. You already have it. But you want to understand it; you want to use it; you want to control it; you want to impregnate yourself with it, so that you can go forward and carry the world before you.

Day by day as you go on and on, as you gain momentum, as your inspiration deepens, as your plans crystallize, as you gain understanding, you will come to realize that this world is no dead pile of stones and timber, but that it is a living thing! It is made up of the beating hearts of humanity. It is a thing of life and beauty.

It is evident that it requires understanding to work with material of this description, but those who come into this understanding, are inspired by a new light, a new force, they gain confidence and greater power each day, they realize their hopes and their dreams come true, life has a deeper, fuller, clearer meaning than before.

And, now, Part One.

1. That much gathers more is true on every plane of existence and that loss leads to greater loss is equally true.

2. Mind is creative, and conditions, environment and all experiences in life are the result of our habitual or predominant mental attitude.

3. The attitude of mind necessarily depends upon what we think. Therefore, the secret of all power, all achievement and all possession depends upon our method of thinking.

4. This is true because we must "be" before we can "do," and we can "do" only to the extent which we "are," and what we "are" depends upon what we "think."

5. We cannot express powers that we do not possess. The only way by which we may secure possession of power is to become conscious of power, and we can never become conscious of power until we learn that all power is from within.

6. There is a world within—a world of thought and feeling and power; of light and life and beauty and, although invisible, its forces are mighty.

7. The world within is governed by mind. When we discover this world we shall find the solution for every problem, the cause for every effect; and since the world within is subject to our control, all laws of power and possession are also within our control.

8. The world without is a reflection of the world within. What appears without is what has been found within. In the world within may be found infinite Wisdom, infinite Power, infinite Supply of all that is necessary, waiting for unfoldment, development and expression. If we recognize these potentialities in the world within they will take form in the world without.

9. Harmony in the world within will be reflected in the world without by harmonious conditions, agreeable surroundings, the best of everything. It is the foundation of health and a necessary essential to all greatness, all power, all attainment, all achievement and all success.

10. Harmony in the world within means the ability to control our thoughts, and to determine for ourselves how any experience is to affect us.

11. Harmony in the world within results in optimism and affluence; affluence within results in affluence without.

12. The world without reflects the circumstances and the conditions of the consciousness within.

13. If we find wisdom in the world within, we shall have the understanding to discern the marvelous possibilities that are latent in this world within, and we shall be given the power to make these possibilities manifest in the world without.

14. As we become conscious of the wisdom in the world within, we mentally take possession of this wisdom, and by taking mental possession we come into actual possession of the power and wisdom necessary to bring into manifestation the essentials necessary for our most complete and harmonious development.

15. The world within is the practical world in which the men and women of power generate courage, hope, enthusiasm, confidence, trust and faith, by which they are given the fine intelligence to see the vision and the practical skill to make the vision real.

16. Life is an unfoldment, not accretion. What comes to us in the world without is what we already possess in the world within.

17. All possession is based on consciousness. All gain is the result of an accumulative consciousness. All loss is the result of a scattering consciousness.

18. Mental efficiency is contingent upon harmony; discord means confusion; therefore, he who would acquire power must be in harmony with natural law.

19. We are related to the world without by the objective mind. The brain is the organ of this mind and the cerebro-spinal system of nerves puts us in conscious communication with every part of the body. This system of nerves responds to every sensation of light, heat, odor, sound and taste.

20. When this mind thinks correctly, when it understands the truth, when the thoughts sent through the cerebro-spinal nervous system to the body are constructive, these sensations are pleasant, harmonious.

21. The result is that we build strength, vitality and all constructive forces into our

body, but it is through this same objective mind that all distress, sickness, lack, limitation and every form of discord and inharmony is admitted to our lives. It is therefore through the objective mind, by wrong thinking, that we are related to all destructive forces.

22. We are related to the world within by the subconscious mind. The solar plexus is the organ of this mind; the sympathetic system of nerves presides over all subjective sensations, such as joy, fear, love, emotion, respiration, imagination and all other subconscious phenomena. It is through the subconscious that we are connected with the Universal Mind and brought into relation with the infinite constructive forces of the Universe.

23. It is the coordination of these two centers of our being, and the understanding of their functions, which is the great secret of life. With this knowledge we can bring the objective and subjective minds into conscious cooperation and thus coordinate the finite and the Infinite. Our future is entirely within our own control. It is not at the mercy of any capricious or uncertain external power.

24. All agree that there is but one Principle or Consciousness pervading the entire Universe, occupying all space, and being essentially the same in kind at every point of its presence. It is all powerful, all wisdom and always present. All thoughts and things are within Itself. It is all in all.

25. There is but one consciousness in the universe able to think; and when it thinks, its thoughts become objective things to it. As this Consciousness is omnipresent, it must be present within every individual; each individual must be a manifestation of that Omnipotent, Omniscient and Omnipresent Consciousness.

26. As there is only one Consciousness in the Universe that is able to think it necessarily follows that your consciousness is identical with the Universal Consciousness, or, in other words, all mind is one mind. There is no dodging this conclusion.

27. The consciousness that focuses in your brain cells is the same consciousness which focuses in the brain cells of every other individual. Each individual is but the individualization of the Universal, the Cosmic Mind.

28. The Universal Mind is static or potential energy; it simply is; it can manifest itself only through the individual, and the individual can manifest himself only through the Universal. They are one.

29. The ability of the individual to think is his ability to act on the Universal and bring it into manifestation. Human consciousness consists only in the ability of man to think. Mind in itself is believed to be a subtle form of static energy, from which arises the activities called "thought," which is the dynamic phase of mind. Mind is static energy, thought is dynamic energy—the two phases of the same thing. Thought is therefore the vibratory force formed by converting static mind into dynamic mind.

30. As the sum of all attributes are contained in the Universal Mind, which is Omnipotent, Omniscient and Omnipresent, these attributes must be present at all times in their potential form in every individual. Therefore, when the individual thinks, the thought is compelled by its nature to embody itself in an objectivity or condition which will correspond with its origin.

31. Every thought therefore is a cause and every condition an effect; for this reason it is absolutely essential that you control your thoughts so as to bring forth only desirable conditions.

32. All power is from within, and is absolutely under your control; it comes through exact knowledge and by the voluntary exercises of exact principles.

33. It should be plain that when you acquire a thorough understanding of this law, and are able to control your thought processes, you can apply it to any condition; in other words, you will have come into conscious cooperation with Omnipotent law which is the fundamental basis of all things.

34. The Universal Mind is the life principle of every atom which is in existence; every atom is continually striving to manifest more life; all are intelligent, and all are seeking to carry out the purpose for which they were created.

35. A majority of mankind lives in the world without; few have found the world within, and yet it is the world within that makes the world without; it is therefore creative and everything which you find in your world without has been created by you in the world within.

36. This system will bring you into a realization of power which will be yours when you understand this relation between the world without and the world within. The world within is the cause, the world without the effect; to change the effect you must change the cause.

37. You will at once see that this is a radically new and different idea; most men try to change effects by working with effects. They fail to see that this is simply changing one form of distress for another. To remove discord, we must remove the cause, and this cause can be found only in the world within.

38. All growth is from within. This is evident in all nature. Every plant, every animal, every human is a living testimony to this great law, and the error of the ages is in looking for strength or power from without.

39. The world within is the Universal fountain of supply, and the world without is the outlet to the stream. Our ability to receive depends upon our recognition of this Universal Fountain, this Infinite Energy of which each individual is an outlet, and so is one with every other individual.

40. Recognition is a mental process, mental action is therefore the interaction of the individual upon the Universal Mind, and as the Universal Mind is the intelligence which pervades all space and animates all living things, this mental action and reaction is the law of causation, but the principle of causation does not obtain in the individual but in the Universal Mind. It is not an objective faculty but a subjective process, and the results are seen in an infinite variety of conditions and experiences.

41. In order to express life there must be mind; nothing can exist without mind. Everything which exists is some manifestation of this one basic substance from which and by which all things have been created and are continually being re-created.

42. We live in a fathomless sea of plastic mind substance. This substance is ever alive and active. It is sensitive to the highest degree. It takes form according to the mental demand. Thought forms the mold or matrix from which the substance expresses.

43. Remember that it is in the application alone that the value consists, and that a practical understanding of this law will substitute abundance for poverty, wisdom for ignorance, harmony for discord and freedom for tyranny, and certainly there can be no greater blessing than these from a material and social standpoint.

44. Now make the application: Select a room where you can be alone and undisturbed; sit erect, comfortably, but do not lounge; let your thoughts roam where they will but be perfectly still for from fifteen minutes to half an hour; continue this for three or four days or for a week until you secure full control of your physical being.

45. Many will find this extremely difficult; others will conquer with ease, but it is absolutely essential to secure complete control of the body before you are ready to progress. Next week you will receive instructions for the next step; in the meantime you must have mastered this one.

PART ONE. STUDY QUESTIONS WITH ANSWERS

1. What is the world without in its relation to the world within?
   The world without is a reflection of the world within.
2. Upon what does all possession depend?
   All possession is based on consciousness.
3. How is the individual related to the objective world?
   The individual is related to the objective world by the objective mind; the brain is the organ of this mind.
4. How is he related to the Universal Mind?
   He is related to the Universal Mind by the subconscious mind; the Solar Plexus is the organ of this mind.
5. What is the Universal Mind?
   Universal Mind is the life principle of every atom which is in existence.
6. How can the individual act on the Universal?
   The ability of the individual to think is his ability to act upon the Universal and bring it into manifestation.
7. What is the result of this action and interaction?
   The result of this action and interaction is cause and effect; every thought is a cause and every condition an effect.
8. How are harmonious and desirable conditions secured?
   Harmonious and desirable conditions are obtained by right thinking.
9. What is the cause of all discord, inharmony, lack and limitation?
   Discord, inharmony, lack and limitation are the result of wrong thinking.
10. What is the source of all power?
    The source of all power is the world within, the Universal Fountain of Supply, the Infinite Energy of which each individual is an outlet.

Part Two

Our difficulties are largely due to confused ideas and ignorance of our true interests. The great task is to discover the laws of nature to which we are to adjust ourselves. Clear thinking and moral insight are, therefore, of incalculable value. All processes, even those of thought, rest on solid foundations.

The keener the sensibilities, the more acute the judgment, the more delicate the taste, the more refined the moral feelings, the more subtle the intelligence, the loftier the aspiration—the purer and more intense are the gratifications which existence yields. Hence it is that the study of the best that has been thought in the world gives supreme pleasure.

The powers, uses and possibilities of the mind under the new interpretations are incomparably more wonderful than the most extravagant accomplishment, or even dreams of material progress.

Thought is energy. Active thought is active energy; concentrated thought is a concentrated energy. Thought concentrated on a definite purpose becomes power. This is the power which is being used by those who do not believe in the virtue of poverty, or the beauty of self-denial. They perceive that this is the talk of weaklings.

The ability to receive and manifest this power depends upon the ability to recognize the Infinite Energy ever dwelling in man, constantly creating and re-creating his body and mind, and ready at any moment to be made manifest through him in any needful manner. In exact proportion to the recognition of this truth will be the manifestation in the outer life of the individual.

Part Two explains the method by which this is accomplished.

1. The operations of the mind are produced by two parallel modes of activity, the one conscious, and the other subconscious. Professor Davidson says: "He who thinks to illuminate the whole range of mental action by the light of his own consciousness is not unlike the one who should go about to illuminate the universe with a rushlight."

2. The subconscious' logical processes are carried on with a certainty and regularity which would be impossible if there existed the possibility of error. Our mind is so designed that it prepares for us the most important foundations of cognition, whilst we have not the slightest apprehension of the modus operandi.

3. The subconscious soul, like a benevolent stranger, works and makes provision for our benefit, pouring only the mature fruit into our lap; thus ultimate analysis of thought processes shows that the subconscious is the theater of the most important mental phenomena.

4. It is through the subconscious that Shakespeare must have perceived, without effort, great truths which are hidden from the conscious mind of the student; that Phidias fashioned marble and bronze; that Raphael painted Madonnas and Beethoven composed symphonies.

5. Ease and perfection depend entirely upon the degree in which we cease to depend upon the consciousness; playing the piano, skating, operating the typewriter, the skilled trades, depend for their perfect execution on the process of the subconscious mind. The marvel of playing a brilliant piece on the piano, while at the same time conducting a vigorous conversation, shows the greatness of our subconscious powers.

6. We are all aware how dependent we are upon the subconscious, and the greater, the nobler, the more brilliant our thoughts are, the more it is obvious to ourselves that the origin lies beyond our ken. We find ourselves endowed with tact, instinct, sense of the beautiful in art, music, etc., of whose origin or dwelling place we are wholly unconscious.

7. The value of the subconscious is enormous; it inspires us; it warns us; it furnishes us with names, facts and scenes from the storehouse of memory. It directs our thoughts, tastes, and accomplishes tasks so intricate that no conscious mind, even if it had the power, has the capacity for.

8. We can walk at will; we can raise the arm whenever we choose to do so; we can give our attention through eye or ear to any subject at pleasure. On the other hand, we cannot stop our heartbeats nor the circulation of the blood, nor the growth of stature, nor the formation of nerve and muscle tissue, nor the building of the bones, nor many other important vital processes.

9. If we compare these two sets of action, the one decreed by the will of the moment, and the other proceeding in majestic, rhythmic course, subject to no vascillation, but constant at every moment, we stand in awe of the latter, and ask to have the mystery explained. We see at once that these are the vital processes of our physical life, and we cannot avoid the inference that these all-important functions are designedly withdrawn from the domain of our outward will with its variations and transitions, and placed under the direction of a permanent and dependable power within us.

10. Of these two powers, the outward and changeable has been termed the "Conscious Mind," or the "Objective Mind" (dealing with outward objects). The interior power is called the "Subconscious Mind," or the "Subjective Mind," and besides its work on the mental plane it controls the regular functions which make physical life possible.

11. It is necessary to have a clear understanding of their respective functions on the mental plane, as well as of certain other basic principles. Perceiving and operating through the five physical senses, the conscious mind deals with the impressions and objects of the outward life.

12. It has the faculty of discrimination, carrying with it the responsibility of choice. It has the power of reasoning—whether inductive, deductive, analytical or syllogistic—

and this power may be developed to a high degree. It is the seat of the will with all the energies that flow therefrom.

13. Not only can it impress other minds, but it can direct the subconscious mind. In this way the conscious mind becomes the responsible ruler and guardian of the subconscious mind. It is this high function which can completely reverse conditions in your life.

14. It is often true that conditions of fear, worry, poverty, disease, inharmony and evils of all kinds dominate us by reason of false suggestions accepted by the unguarded subconscious mind. All this the trained conscious mind can entirely prevent by its vigilant protective action. It may properly be called "the watchman at the gate" of the great subconscious domain.

15. One writer has expressed the chief distinction between the two phases of mind thus: "Conscious mind is reasoning will. Subconscious mind is instinctive desire, the result of past reasoning will."

16. The subconscious mind draws just and accurate inferences from premises furnished from outside sources. Where the premise is true, the subconscious mind reaches a faultless conclusion, but, where the premise or suggestion is an error, the whole structure falls. The subconscious mind does not engage in the process of proving. It relies upon the conscious mind, "the watchman at the gate," to guard it from mistaken impressions.

17. Receiving any suggestions as true, the subconscious mind at once proceeds to act thereon in the whole domain of its tremendous field of work. The conscious mind can suggest either truth or error. If the latter, it is at the cost of wide-reaching peril to the whole being.

18. The conscious mind ought to be on duty during every waking hour. When the "watchman" is "off guard," or when its calm judgment is suspended, under a variety of circumstances, then the subconscious mind is unguarded and left open to suggestion from all sources. During the wild excitement of panic, or during the height of anger, or the impulses of the irresponsible mob, or at any other time of unrestrained passion, the conditions are most dangerous. The subconscious mind is then open to the suggestion of fear, hatred, selfishness, greed, self-depreciation and other negative forces, derived from surrounding persons or circumstances. The result is usually unwholesome in the extreme, with effects that may endure to distress it for a long time. Hence, the great importance of guarding the subconscious mind from false impressions.

19. The subconscious mind perceives by intuition. Hence, its processes are rapid. It does not wait for the slow methods of conscious reasoning. In fact, it cannot employ them.

20. The subconscious mind never sleeps, never rests, any more than does your heart, or your blood. It has been found that by plainly stating to the subconscious mind certain specific things to be accomplished, forces are set in operation that lead to the result desired. Here, then, is a source of power which places us in touch with Omnipotence. Here in is a deep principle which is well worth our most earnest study.

21. The operation of this law is interesting. Those who put it into operation find that when they go out to meet the person with whom they anticipate a difficult interview,

something has been there before them and dissolved the supposed differences; everything is changed; all is harmonious; they find that when some difficult business problem presents itself they can afford to make delay and something suggests the proper solution; everything is properly arranged; in fact, those who have learned to trust the subconscious find that they have infinite resources at their command.

22. The subconscious mind is the seat of our principles and our aspirations. It is the fount of our artistic and altruistic ideals. These instincts can only be overthrown by an elaborate and gradual process of undermining the innate principles.

23. The subconscious mind cannot argue controversially. Hence, if it has accepted wrong suggestions, the sure method of overcoming them is by the use of a strong countersuggestion, frequently repeated, which the mind must accept, thus eventually forming new and healthy habits of thought and life, for the subconscious mind is the seat of Habit. That which we do over and over becomes mechanical; it is no longer an act of judgment, but has worn its deep grooves in the subconscious mind. This is favorable for us if the habit be wholesome and right. If it be harmful, and wrong, the remedy is to recognize the omnipotence of the subconscious mind and suggest present actual freedom. The subconscious being creative and one with our divine source will at once create the freedom suggested.

24. To sum up: The normal functions of the subconscious on the physical side have to do with the regular and vital processes, with the preservation of life and the restoration of health; with the care of offspring, which includes an instinctive desire to preserve all life and improve conditions generally.

25. On the mental side, it is the storehouse of memory; it harbors the wonderful thought messengers, who work, unhampered by time or space; it is the fountain of the practical initiative and constructive forces of life: It is the seat of habit.

26. On the spiritual side, it is the source of ideals, of aspiration, of the imagination, and is the channel through which we recognize our Divine Source, and in proportion as we recognize this divinity do we come into an understanding of the source of power.

27. Someone may ask: "How can the subconscious change conditions?" The reply is, because the subconscious is a part of the Universal Mind and a part must be the same in kind and quality as the whole; the only difference is one of degree. The whole, as we know, is creative, in fact, it is the only creator there is, consequently, we find that mind is creative, and as thought is the only activity which the mind possesses, thought must necessarily be creative also.

28. But we shall find that there is a vast difference between simply thinking, and directing our thought consciously, systematically and constructively; when we do this we place our mind in harmony with the Universal Mind, we come in tune with the Infinite, we set in operation the mightiest force in existence, the creative power of the Universal Mind. This, as everything else, is governed by natural law, and this law is the "Law of Attraction," which is that Mind is creative, and will automatically correlate with its object and bring it into manifestation.

29. Last week I gave you an exercise for the purpose of securing control of the phys-

ical body; if you have accomplished this you are ready to advance. This time you will begin to control your thought. Always take the same room, the same chair, and the same position, if possible. In some cases it is not convenient to take the same room, in this case simply make the best use of such conditions as may be available. Now be perfectly still as before, but inhibit all thought; this will give you control over all thoughts of care, worry and fear, and will enable you to entertain only the kind of thoughts you desire. Continue this exercise until you gain complete mastery.

30. You will not be able to do this for more than a few moments at a time, but the exercise is valuable, because it will be a very practical demonstration of the great number of thoughts which are constantly trying to gain access to your mental world.

31. Next week you will receive instructions for an exercise which may be a little more interesting, but it is necessary that you master this one first.

> Cause and effect is as absolute and undeviating in the hidden realm of thought as in the world of visible and material things. Mind is the master weaver, both of the interior garment of character and the outer garment of circumstance.
>
> —JAMES ALLEN

PART TWO.
STUDY QUESTIONS WITH ANSWERS

11. What are the two modes of mental activity?
Conscious and subconscious.
12. Upon what do ease and perfection depend?
Ease and perfection depend entirely upon the degree in which we cease to depend upon the conscious mind.
13. What is the value of the subconscious?
It is enormous; it guides us, warns us, it controls the vital processes and is the seat of memory.
14. What are some of the functions of the conscious mind?
It has the faculty of discrimination; it has the power of reasoning; it is the seat of the will and may impress the subconscious.
15. How has the distinction between the conscious and subconscious been expressed?
"Conscious mind is reasoning will. Subconscious mind is instinctive desire, the result of past reasoning will."
16. What method is necessary in order to impress the subconscious?
Mentally state what is wanted.
17. What will be the result?
If the desire is in harmony with the forward movement of the great Whole, forces will be set in motion which will bring about the result.
18. What is the result of the operation of this law?

Our environment reflects conditions corresponding to the predominant mental attitude which we entertain.

19. What name has been given to this law?
    The Law of Attraction.
20. How is the law stated?
    Thought is a creative energy, and will automatically correlate with its object and bring it into manifestation.

Part Three

You have found that the individual may act on the Universal, and that the result of this action and interaction is cause and effect. Thought, therefore, is the cause, and the experiences with which you meet in life are the effect.

Eliminate, therefore, any possible tendency to complain of conditions as they have been, or as they are, because it rests with you to change them and make them what you would like them to be.

Direct your effort to a realization of the mental resources, always at your command, from which all real and lasting power comes.

Persist in this practice until you come to a realization of the fact that there can be no failure in the accomplishment of any proper object in life if you but understand your power and persist in your object, because the mind-forces are ever ready to lend themselves to a purposeful will, in the effort to crystallize thought and desire into actions, events and conditions.

Whereas in the beginning each function of life and each action is the result of conscious thought, the habitual actions become automatic and the thought that controls them passes into the realm of the subconscious; yet it is just as intelligent as before. It is necessary that it become automatic, or subconscious, in order that the self-conscious mind may attend to other things. The new actions will, however, in their turn, become habitual, then automatic, then subconscious in order that the mind again may be freed from this detail and advanced to still other activities.

When you realize this, you will have found a source of power which will enable you to take care of any situation in life which may develop.

1. The necessary interaction of the conscious and subconscious mind requires a similar interaction between the corresponding systems of nerves. Judge Troward indicates the very beautiful method in which this interaction is effected. He says: The cerebro-spinal system is the organ of the conscious mind and the sympathetic is the organ of the subconscious. The cerebro-spinal is the channel through which we receive conscious perception from the physical senses and exercise control over the movements of the body. This system of nerves has its center in the brain.

2. The Sympathetic System has its center in a ganglionic mass at the back of the

stomach known as the Solar Plexus, and is the channel of that mental action which unconsciously supports the vital functions of the body.

3. The connection between the two systems is made by the vagus nerve which passes out of the cerebral region as a portion of the voluntary system to the thorax, sending out branches to the heart and lungs, and finally passing through the diaphragm, it loses its outer coating and becomes identified with the nerves of the Sympathetic System, so forming a connecting link between the two and making man physically a "single entity."

4. We have seen that every thought is received by the brain, which is the organ of the conscious; it is here subjected to our power of reasoning. When the objective mind has been satisfied that the thought is true it is sent to the Solar Plexus, or the brain of the subjective mind, to be made into our flesh, to be brought forth into the world as reality. It is then no longer susceptible to any argument whatever. The subconscious mind cannot argue; it only acts. It accepts the conclusions of the objective mind as final.

5. The Solar Plexus has been likened to the sum of the body, because it is a central point of distribution for the energy which the body is constantly generating. This energy is very real energy, and this sun is a very real sun, and the energy is being distributed by very real nerves to all parts of the body, and is thrown off in an atmosphere which envelops the body.

6. If this radiation is sufficiently strong the person is called magnetic; he is said to be filled with personal magnetism. Such a person may wield an immense power for good. His presence alone will often bring comfort to the troubled minds with which he comes in contact.

7. When the Solar Plexus is in active operation and is radiating life, energy and vitality to every part of the body, and to everyone whom he meets, the sensations are pleasant, the body is filled with health and all with whom he comes in contact experience a pleasant sensation.

8. If there is any interruption of this radiation the sensations are unpleasant, the flow of life and energy to some part of the body is stopped, and this is the cause of every ill to the human race, physical, mental or environmental.

9. Physical because the sun of the body is no longer generating sufficient energy to vitalize some part of the body; mental because the conscious mind is dependent upon the subconscious mind for the vitality necessary to support its thought, and environmental, because the connection between the subconscious mind and the Universal mind, is being interrupted.

10. The Solar Plexus is the point at which the part meets with the whole, where the finite becomes infinite, where the Uncreate becomes create, the Universal becomes individualized, the invisible becomes visible. It is the point at which life appears and there is no limit to the amount of life an individual may generate from this Solar center.

11. This center of energy is Omnipotent because it is the point of contact with all life and all intelligence. It can therefore accomplish whatever it is directed to accomplish, and herein lies the power of the conscious mind; the subconscious can and will carry out such plans and ideas as may be suggested to it by the conscious mind.

12. Conscious thought, then, is master of this sun center from which the life and energy of the entire body flows and the quality of the thought which we entertain determines

the quality of the thought which this sun will radiate, and the character of the thought which our conscious mind entertains will determine the character of the thought which this sun will radiate, and the nature of the thought which our conscious mind entertains will determine the nature of thought which this sun will radiate, and consequently will determine the nature of the experience which will result.

13. It is evident, therefore, that all we have to do is let our light shine; the more energy we can radiate, the more rapidly shall we be enabled to transmute undesirable conditions into sources of pleasure and profit. The important question, then, is how to let this light shine; how to generate this energy.

14. Non-resistant thought expands the Solar Plexus; resistant thought contracts it. Pleasant thought expands it; unpleasant thought contracts it. Thoughts of courage, power, confidence and hope all produce a corresponding state, but the one arch enemy of the Solar Plexus which must be absolutely destroyed before there is any possibility of letting any light shine is fear. This enemy must be completely destroyed; he must be eliminated; he must be expelled forever; he is the cloud which hides the sun; which causes a perpetual gloom.

15. It is this personal devil which makes men fear the past, the present and the future; fear themselves, their friends and their enemies; fear everything and everybody. When fear is effectually and completely destroyed, your light will shine, the clouds will disperse and you will have found the source of power, energy and life.

16. When you find that you are really one with the Infinite power, and when you can consciously realize this power by a practical demonstration of your ability to overcome any adverse condition by the power of your thought, you will have nothing to fear; fear will have been destroyed and you will have come into possession of your birthright.

17. It is our attitude of mind toward life which determines the experiences with which we are to meet; if we expect nothing, we shall have nothing; if we demand much, we shall receive the greater portion. The world is harsh only as we fail to assert ourselves. The criticism of the world is bitter only to those who cannot compel room for their ideas. It is fear of this criticism that causes many ideas to fail to see the light of day.

18. But the man who knows that he has a Solar Plexus will not fear criticism or anything else; he will be too busy radiating courage, confidence, and power; he will anticipate success by his mental attitude; he will pound barriers to pieces, and leap over the chasm of doubt and hesitation which fear places in his path.

19. A knowledge of our ability to consciously radiate health, strength and harmony will bring us into a realization that there is nothing to fear because we are in touch with Infinite Strength.

20. This knowledge can be gained only by making practical application of this information. We learn by doing; through practice the athlete becomes powerful.

21. As the following statement is of considerable importance, I will put it in several ways, so that you cannot fail to get the full significance of it. If you are religiously inclined, I would say, you can let your light shine. If your mind has a bias toward physical science, I would say you can wake the Solar Plexus; or, if you prefer the strictly scientific interpretation, I will say that you can impress your subconscious mind.

22. I have already told you what the result of this impression will be. It is the method

in which you are now interested. You have already learned that the subconscious is intelligent and that it is creative, and responsive to the will of the conscious mind. What, then, is the most natural way of making the desired impression? Mentally concentrate on the object of your desire; when you are concentrating you are impressing the subconscious.

23. This is not the only way, but it is a simple and effective way, and the most direct way, and consequently the way in which the best results are secured. It is the method which is producing such extraordinary results that many think that miracles are being accomplished.

24. It is the method by which every great inventor, every great financier, every great statesman has been enabled to convert the subtle and invisible force of desire, faith and confidence into actual, tangible, concrete facts in the objective world.

25. The subconscious mind is a part of the Universal mind. The Universal is the creative principle of the Universe, a part must be the same in kind and quality as the whole. This means that this creative power is absolutely unlimited; it is not bound by precedent of any kind, and consequently has no prior existing pattern by which to apply its constructive principle.

26. We have found that the subconscious mind is responsive to our conscious will, which means that the unlimited creative power of the Universal Mind is within control of the conscious mind of the individual.

27. When making a practical application of this principle, in accordance with the exercises given in the subsequent lessons, it is well to remember that it is not necessary to outline the method by which the subconscious will produce the results you desire. The finite cannot inform the Infinite. You are simply to say what you desire, not how you are to obtain it.

28. You are the channel by which the undifferentiated is being differentiated, and this differentiation is being accomplished by appropriation. It only requires recognition to set causes in motion which will bring about results in accordance with your desire, and this is accomplished because the Universal can act only through the individual, and the individual can act only through the Universal; they are one.

29. For your exercise this week, I will ask you to go one step further. I want you to not only be perfectly still, and inhibit all thought as far as possible, but relax, let go, let the muscles take their normal condition; this will remove all pressure from the nerves, and eliminate that tension which so frequently produces physical exhaustion.

30. Physical relaxation is a voluntary exercise of the will and the exercise will be found to be of great value, as it enables the blood to circulate freely to and from the brain and body.

31. Tension leads to mental unrest and abnormal mental activity of the mind; it produces worry, care, fear and anxiety. Relaxation is therefore an absolute necessity in order to allow the mental faculties to exercise the greatest freedom.

32. Make this exercise as thorough and complete as possible, mentally determine that you will relax every muscle and nerve, until you feel quiet and restful and at peace with yourself and the world.

33. The Solar Plexus will then be ready to function and you will be surprised at the result.

PART THREE.
STUDY QUESTIONS WITH ANSWERS

21. What system of nerves is the organ of the Conscious Mind?
The Cerebro-spinal.
22. What system of nerves is the organ of the subconscious mind?
The sympathetic.
23. What is the central point of distribution for energy which the body is constantly generating?
The solar plexus.
24. How may this distribution be interrupted?
By resistant, critical, discordant thoughts, but especially fear.
25. What is the result of such interruption?
Every ill with which the human race is afflicted.
26. How may this energy be controlled and directed?
By conscious thought.
27. How may fear be completely eliminated?
By an understanding and recognition of the true source of all power.
28. What determines the experiences with which we meet in life?
Our predominant mental attitude.
29. How may we awake the solar plexus?
Mentally concentrate upon the condition which we desire to see manifested in our lives.
30. What is the creative principle of the Universe?
The Universal Mind.

Part Four

Enclosed herewith I hand you Part Four. This part will show you why what you think, or do, or feel, is an indication of what you are.

Thought is energy and energy is power, and it is because all the religions, sciences and philosophies with which the world has heretofore been familiar have been based upon the manifestation of this energy instead of the energy itself, that the world has been limited to effects, while causes have been ignored or misunderstood.

For this reason we have God and the Devil in religion, positive and negative in science, and good and bad in philosophy.

The Master Key reverses the process; it is interested only in cause, and the letters received from students tell a marvelous story; they indicate conclusively that students are finding the cause whereby they may secure for themselves health, harmony, abundance, and whatever else may be necessary for their welfare and happiness.

Life is expressive and it is our business to express ourselves harmoniously and constructively. Sorrow, misery, unhappiness, disease and poverty are not necessities and we are constantly eliminating them.

But this process of eliminating consists in rising above and beyond limitation of any kind. He who has strengthened and purified his thought need not concern himself about microbes, and he who has come into an understanding of the Law of Abundance will go at once to the source of supply.

It is thus that fate, fortune, and destiny will be controlled as readily as a captain controls his ship, or an engineer, his train.

1. The "I" of you is not the physical body; that is simply an instrument which the "I" uses to carry out its purposes; the "I" cannot be the Mind, for the mind is simply another instrument which the "I" uses with which to think, reason, and plan.

2. The "I" must be something which controls and directs both the body and the mind; something which determines what they shall do and how they shall act. When you come into a realization of the true nature of this "I," you will enjoy a sense of power which you have never before known.

3. Your personality is made up of countless individual characteristics, peculiarities,

habits, and traits of character; these are the result of your former method of thinking, but they have nothing to do with the real "I."

4. When you say "I think" the "I" tells the mind what it shall think; when you say "I go" the "I" tells the physical body where it shall go; the real nature of this "I" is spiritual, and is the source of the real power which comes to men and women when they come into a realization of their true nature.

5. The greatest and most marvelous power which this "I" has been given is the power to think, but few people know how to think constructively, or correctly, consequently they achieve only indifferent results. Most people allow their thoughts to dwell on selfish purposes, the inevitable result of an infantile mind. When a mind becomes mature, it understands that the germ of defeat is in every selfish thought.

6. The trained mind knows that every transaction must benefit every person who is in any way connected with the transaction, and any attempt to profit by the weakness, ignorance or necessity of another will inevitably operate to his disadvantage.

7. This is because the individual is a part of the Universal. A part cannot antagonize any other part, but, on the contrary, the welfare of each part depends upon a recognition of the interest of the whole.

8. Those who recognize this principle have a great advantage in the affairs of life. They do not wear themselves out. They can eliminate vagrant thoughts with facility. They can readily concentrate to the highest possible degree on any subject. They do not waste time or money upon objects which can be of no possible benefit to them.

9. If you cannot do these things it is because you have thus far not made the necessary effort. Now is the time to make the effort. The result will be exactly in proportion to the effort expended. One of the strongest affirmations which you can use for the purpose of strengthening the will and realizing your power to accomplish, is, "I can be what I will to be."

10. Every time you repeat it realize who and what this "I" is; try to come into a thorough understanding of the true nature of the "I"; if you do, you will become invincible; that is, provided that your objects and purposes are constructive and are therefore in harmony with the creative principle of the Universe.

11. If you make use of this affirmation, use it continuously, night and morning, and as often during the day as you think of it, and continue to do so until it becomes a part of you; form the habit.

12. Unless you do this, you had better not start at all, because modern psychology tells us that when we start something and do not complete it, or make a resolution and do not keep it, we are forming the habit of failure; absolute, ignominious failure. If you do not intend to do a thing, do not start; if you do start, see it through even if the heavens fall; if you make up your mind to do something, do it; let nothing, no one, interfere; the "I" in you has determined, the thing is settled; the die is cast, there is no longer any argument.

13. If you carry out this idea, beginning with small things which you know you can control and gradually increase the effort, but never under any circumstances allowing your "I" to be overruled, you will find that you can eventually control yourself, and many men and women have found to their sorrow that it is easier to control a kingdom than to control themselves.

14. But when you have learned to control yourself you will have found the "World Within" which controls the world without; you will have become irresistible; men and things will respond to your every wish without any apparent effort on your part.

15. This is not so strange or impossible as it may appear when you remember that the "World Within" is controlled by the "I" and that this "I" is a part of or one with the Infinite "I" which is the Universal Energy or Spirit, usually called God.

16. This is not a mere statement or theory made for the purpose of confirming or establishing an idea, but it is a fact which has been accepted by the best religious thought as well as the best scientific thought.

17. Herbert Spender said: "Amid all the mysteries by which we are surrounded, nothing is more certain than that we are ever in the presence of an Infinite and Eternal Energy from which all things proceed."

18. Lyman Abbott, in an address delivered before the Alumni of Bangor Theological Seminary, said: "We are coming to think of God as dwelling in man rather than as operating on men from without."

19. Science goes a little way in its search and stops. Science finds the ever-present Eternal Energy, but Religion finds the Power behind this energy and locates it within man. But this is by no means a new discovery; the Bible says exactly the same thing, and the language is just as plain and convincing: "Know ye not that ye are the temple of the living God?" Here, then, is the secret of the wonderful creative power of the "World Within."

20. Here is the secret of power, of mastery. To overcome does not mean to go without things. Self-denial is not success. We cannot give unless we get; we cannot be helpful unless we are strong. The Infinite is not a bankrupt and we who are the representatives of Infinite power should not be bankrupts either, and if we wish to be of service to others we must have power and more power, but to get it we must give it; we must be of service.

21. The more we give the more we shall get; we must become a channel whereby the Universal can express activity. The Universal is constantly seeking to express itself, to be of service, and it seeks the channel whereby it can find the greatest activity, where it can do the most good, where it can be of greatest service to mankind.

22. The Universal cannot express through you as long as you are busy with your plans, your own purposes; quiet the senses, seek inspiration, focus the mental activity on the within, dwell in the consciousness of your unity with Omnipotence. "Still water runs deep"; contemplate the multitudinous opportunities to which you have spiritual access by the Omnipresence of power.

23. Visualize the events, circumstances and conditions which these spiritual connections may assist in manifesting. Realize the fact that the essence and soul of all things is spiritual and that the spiritual is the real, because it is the life of all there is; when the spirit is gone, the life is gone; it is dead; it has ceased to exist.

24. These mental activities pertain to the world within, to the world of cause; and conditions and circumstances which result are the effect. It is thus that you become a creator. This is important work, and the higher, loftier, grander and more noble ideals which you can conceive, the more important the work will become.

25. Over-work or over-play or over-bodily activity of any kind produces conditions of mental apathy and stagnation which make it impossible to do the more important work which results in a realization of conscious power. We should, therefore, seek the Silence frequently. Power comes through repose; it is in the Silence that we can be still, and when we are still, we can think, and thought is the secret of all attainment.

26. Thought is a mode of motion and is carried by the law of vibration the same as light or electricity. It is given vitality by the emotions through the law of love; it takes form and expression by the law of growth; it is a product of the spiritual "I," hence its Divine, spiritual, and creative nature.

27. From this it is evident that in order to express power, abundance or any other constructive purpose, the emotions must be called upon to give feeling to the thought so that it will take form. How may this purpose be accomplished? This is the vital point; how may we develop the faith, the courage, the feeling, which will result in accomplishment?

28. The reply is, by exercise; mental strength is secured in exactly the same way that physical strength is secured, by exercise. We think something, perhaps with difficulty the first time; we think the same thing again, and it becomes easier this time; we think it again and again; it then becomes a mental habit. We continue to think the same thing; finally it becomes automatic; we can no longer help thinking this thing; we are now positive of what we think; there is no longer any doubt about it. We are sure; we know.

29. Last week I asked you to relax, to let go physically. This week, I am going to ask you to let go mentally. If you practiced the exercise given you last week fifteen or twenty minutes a day in accordance with the instructions, you can no doubt relax physically; and anyone who cannot consciously do this quickly and completely is not a master of himself. He has not obtained freedom; he is still a slave to conditions. But I shall assume that you have mastered the exercise and are ready to take the next step, which is mental freedom.

30. This week, after taking your usual position, remove all tension by completely relaxing, then mentally let go of all adverse conditions, such as hatred, anger, worry, jealousy, envy, sorrow, trouble or disappointment of any kind.

31. You may say that you cannot "let go" of these things, but you can; you can do so by mentally determining to do so, by voluntary intention and persistence.

32. The reason that some cannot do this is because they allow themselves to be controlled by the emotions instead of by their intellect. But those who will be guided by the intellect will gain the victory. You will not succeed the first time you try, but practice makes perfect, in this as in everything else, and you must succeed in dismissing, eliminating and completely destroying these negative and destructive thoughts; because they are the seed which is constantly germinating into discordant conditions of every conceivable kind and description.

There is nothing truer than that the quality of thought which we entertain correlates certain externals in the outside world. This is the Law from which there is no escape. And it is this Law, this correlative of the thought with its object, that from time immemorial has led the people to believe in special providence.

—WILMANS

PART FOUR.
STUDY QUESTIONS WITH ANSWERS

31. What is thought?
Thought is spiritual energy.
32. How is it carried?
By the law of vibration.
33. How is it given vitality?
By the law of love.
34. How does it take form?
By the law of growth.
35. What is the secret of its creative power?
It is a spiritual activity.
36. How may we develop the faith, courage, and enthusiasm which will result in accomplishment?
By a recognition of our spiritual nature.
37. What is the secret of Power?
Service.
38. Why is this so?
Because we get what we give.
39. What is the Silence?
A physical stillness.
40. Of what value is it?
It is the first step to self-control, self-mastery.

Part Five

Enclosed herewith you will find Part Five. After studying this part carefully, you will see that every conceivable force or object or fact is the result of mind in action.

Mind in action is thought, and thought is creative. Men are thinking now as they never thought before.

Therefore, this is a creative age, and the world is awarding its richest prizes to the thinkers. Matter is powerless, passive, inert. Mind is force, energy, power. Mind shapes and controls matter. Every form which matter takes is but the expression of some pre-existing thought.

But thought works no magic transformations; it obeys natural laws; it sets in motion natural forces; it releases natural energies; it manifests itself in your conduct and actions, and these in turn react upon your friends and acquaintances, and eventually upon the whole of your environment. You can originate thought, and, since thoughts are creative, you can create for yourself the things you desire.

1. At least ninety per cent of our mental life is subconscious, so that those who fail to make use of this mental power live within very narrow limits.

2. The subconscious can and will solve any problem for us if we know how to direct it. The subconscious processes are always at work; the only question is, are we to be simply passive recipients of this activity, or are we to consciously direct the work? Shall we have a vision of the destination to be reached, the dangers to be avoided, or shall we simply drift?

3. We have found that mind pervades every part of the physical body and is always capable of being directed or impressed by authority coming from the objective or the more dominant portion of the mind.

4. The mind, which pervades the body, is largely the result of heredity, which, in turn, is simply the result of all the environments of all past generations on the responsive and ever-moving life forces. An understanding of this fact will enable us to use our authority when we find some undesirable trait of character manifesting itself.

5. We can consciously use all the desirable characteristics with which we have been provided and we can repress and refuse to allow the undesirable ones to be manifested.

6. Again, this mind which pervades our physical body is not only the result of hereditary tendencies, but is the result of home, business and social environment, where countless thousands of impressions, ideas, prejudices and similar thoughts have been received. Much of this has been received from others, the result of opinions, suggestions or statements; much of it is the result of our own thinking, but nearly all of it has been accepted with little or no examination or consideration.

7. The idea seemed plausible, the conscious received it, passed it on to the subconscious, where it was taken up by the Sympathetic System and passed on to be built into our physical body. "The word has become flesh."

8. This, then, is the way we are consistently creating and re-creating ourselves; we are today the result of our past thinking, and we shall be what we are thinking today, the Law of Attraction is bringing to us, not the things we should like, or the things we wish for, or the things someone else has, but it brings us "our own," the things which we have created by our thought processes, whether consciously or unconsciously. Unfortunately, many of us are creating these things unconsciously.

9. If either of us was building a home for ourself, how careful we would be in regard to the plans; how we should study every detail; how we should watch the material and select only the best of everything; and yet how careless we are when it comes to building our Mental Home, which is infinitely more important than any physical home, as everything which can possibly enter into our lives depends upon the character of the material which enters into the construction of our Mental Home.

10. What is the character of this material? We have seen that it is the result of the impressions which we have accumulated in the past and stored away in our subconscious Mentality. If these impressions have been of fear, of worry, of care, of anxiety; if they have been despondent, negative, doubtful, then the texture of the material which we are weaving today will be of the same negative material. Instead of being of any value, it will be mildewed and rotten and will bring us only more toil and care and anxiety. We shall be forever busy trying to patch it up and make it appear at least genteel.

11. But if we have stored away nothing but courageous thought, if we have been optimistic, positive, and have immediately thrown any kind of negative thought on the scrap pile, have refused to have anything to do with it, have refused to associate with it or become identified with it in any way, what then is the result? Our mental material is now of the best kind; we can weave any kind of material we want; we can use any color we wish; we know that the texture is firm, that the material is solid, that it will not fade, and we have no fear, no anxiety concerning the future; there is nothing to cover, there are no patches to hide.

12. These are psychological facts; there is no theory or guesswork about these thinking processes; there is nothing secret about them; in fact, they are so plain that every one can understand them. The thing to do is to have a mental housecleaning, and to have this housecleaning every day, and keep the house clean. Mental, moral and physical cleanliness are absolutely indispensable if we are to make progress of any kind.

13. When this mental housecleaning process has been completed, the material which is left will be suitable for the making of the kind of ideals or mental images which we desire to realize.

14. There is a fine estate awaiting a claimant. Its broad acres, with abundant crops, running water and fine timber, stretch away as far as the eye can see. There is a mansion, spacious and cheerful, with rare pictures, a well-stocked library, rich hangings, and every comfort and luxury. All the heir has to do is to assert his heirship, take possession, and use the property. He must use it; he must not let it decay; for use is the condition on which he holds it. To neglect it is to lose possession.

15. In the domain of mind and spirit, in the domain of practical power, such an estate is yours. You are the heir! You can assert your heirship and possess, and use this rich inheritance. Power over circumstances is one of its fruits, health, harmony and prosperity are assets upon its balance sheet. It offers you poise and peace. It costs you only the labor of studying and harvesting its great resources. It demands no sacrifice, except the loss of your limitations, your servitudes, your weakness. It clothes you with self-honor, and puts a scepter in your hands.

16. To gain this estate, three processes are necessary: You must earnestly desire it. You must assert your claim. You must take possession.

17. You admit that those are not burdensome conditions.

18. You are familiar with the subject of heredity. Darwin, Huxley, Haeckel, and other physical scientists have piled evidence mountain high that heredity is a law attending progressive creation. It is progressive heredity which gives man his erect attitude, his power of motion, the organs of digestion, blood circulation, nerve force, muscular force, bone structure and a host of other faculties on the physical side. There are even more impressive facts concerning heredity of mind force. All these constitute what may be called your human heredity.

19. But there is a heredity which the physical scientists have not compassed. It lies beneath and antecedent to all their researches. At a point where they throw up their hands in despair, saying they cannot account for what they see, this divine heredity is found in full sway.

20. It is the benignant force which decrees primal creation. It thrills down from the Divine, direct into every created being. It originates life, which the physical scientist has not done, nor ever can do. It stands out among all forces supreme, unapproachable. No human heredity can approach it. No human heredity measures up to it.

21. This Infinite Life flows through you; is you. Its doorways are but the faculties which comprise your consciousness. To keep open these doors is the Secret of Power. Is it not worthwhile to make the effort?

22. The great fact is, that the source of all life and all power is from within. Persons, circumstances and events may suggest need and opportunities, but the insight, strength and power to answer these needs will be found within.

23. Avoid counterfeits. Build firm foundations for your consciousness upon forces which flow direct from the Infinite source, the Universal Mind of which you are the image and likeness.

24. Those who have come into possession of this inheritance are never quite the same again. They have come into possession of a sense of power hitherto undreamed of. They can never again be timid, weak, vacillating, or fearful. They are indissolubly connected

with Omnipotence. Something in them has been aroused; they have suddenly discovered that they possess a tremendous latent ability of which they were heretofore entirely unconscious.

25. This power is from within, but we cannot receive it unless we give it. Use is the condition upon which we hold this inheritance. We are each of us but the channel through which the Omnipotent power is being differentiated into form; unless we give, the channel is obstructed and we can receive no more. This is true on every plane of existence and in every field of endeavor and all walks of life. The more we give, the more we get. The athlete who wishes to get strong must make use of the strength he has, and the more he gives the more he will get. The financier who wishes to make money must make use of the money he has, for only by using it can he get more.

26. The merchant who does not keep his goods going out will soon have none coming in; the corporation which fails to give efficient service will soon lack customers; the attorney who fails to get results will soon lack clients, and so it goes everywhere; power is contingent upon a proper use of the power already in our possession; what is true in every field of endeavor, every experience in life, is true of the power from which every other power known among men is begotten—spiritual power. Take away the spirit and what is left? Nothing.

27. If then the spirit is all there is, upon the recognition of this fact must depend the ability to demonstrate all power, whether physical, mental or spiritual.

28. All possession is the result of the accumulative attitude of mind, or the money consciousness; this is the magic wand which will enable you to receive the idea, and it will formulate plans for you to execute, and you will find as much pleasure in the execution as in the satisfaction of attainment and achievement.

29. Now, go to your room, take the same seat, the same position as heretofore, and mentally select a place which has pleasant associations. Make a complete mental picture of it, see the buildings, the grounds, the trees, friends, associations, everything complete. At first, you will find yourself thinking of everything under the sun, except the ideal upon which you desire to concentrate. But do not let that discourage you. Persistence will win, but persistence requires that you practice these exercises every day without fail.

PART FIVE.
STUDY QUESTIONS WITH ANSWERS

41. What proportion of our mental life is subconscious?
At least ninety per cent.
42. Is this vast mental storehouse generally utilized?
No.
43. Why not?
Few understand or appreciate the fact that it is an activity which they may consciously direct.
44. Where has the conscious mind received its governing tendencies?

From heredity—which means that it is the result of all the environments of all past generations.

45. What is the Law of Attraction bringing to us?
Our "Own."
46. What is our "Own"?
What we inherently are, and is the result of our past thinking, both conscious and subconscious.
47. Of what is the material with which we construct our mental home composed?
The thoughts which we entertain.
48. What is the Secret of Power?
A recognition of the omnipresence of omnipotence.
49. Where does it originate?
All life and all power is from within.
50. Upon what is the possession of power contingent?
Upon a proper use of the power already in our possession.

Part Six

It is my privilege to enclose Part Six. This part will give you an excellent understanding of the most wonderful piece of mechanism which has ever been created. A mechanism whereby you may create for yourself Health, Strength, Success, Prosperity or any other condition which you desire.

Necessities are demands, and demands create action, and actions bring about results. The process of evolution is constantly building our tomorrows out of our todays. Individual development, like Universal development, must be gradual with an ever-increasing capacity and volume.

The knowledge that if we infringe upon the rights of others, we become moral thorns and find ourselves entangled at every turn of the road, should be an indication that success is contingent upon the highest moral ideal, which is "The greatest good to the greatest number." Aspiration, desire and harmonious relations constantly and persistenly maintained will accomplish results. The greatest hindrance is erroneous and fixed ideas.

To be in tune with eternal truth we must possess poise and harmony within. In order to receive intelligence the receiver must be in tune with the transmitter.

Thought is a product of Mind and Mind is creative, but this does not mean that the Universal will change its modus operandi to suit us or our ideas, but it does mean that we can come into harmonious relationship with the Universal, and when we have accomplished this we may ask anything to which we are entitled, and the way will be made plain.

1. The Universal Mind is so wonderful that it is difficult to understand its utilitarian powers and possibilities and its unlimited producing effects.

2. We have found that this Mind is not only all intelligence but all substance. How, then, is it to be differentiated in form? How are we to secure the effect which we desire?

3. Ask any electrician what the effect of electricity will be and he will reply that "Electricity is a form of motion and its effect will depend upon the mechanism to which it is attached." Upon this mechanism will depend whether we shall have heat, light, power, music or any of the other marvelous demonstrations of power to which this vital energy has been harnessed.

4. What effect can be produced by thought? The reply is that thought is mind in mo-

tion (just as wind is air in motion), and its effect will depend entirely on the "mechanism to which it is attached."

5. Here, then, is the secret of all mental power; it depends entirely on the mechanism which we attach.

6. What is this mechanism? You know something of the mechanism which has been invented by Edison, Bell, Marconi and other electrical wizards, by which place and space and time have become only figures of speech, but did you ever stop to think that the mechanism which has been given you for transforming the Universal, Omnipresent Potential Power was invented by a greater inventor than Edison?

7. We are accustomed to examining the mechanism of the implements which we use for tilling the soil, and we try to get an understanding of the mechanism of the automobile which we drive, but most of us are content to remain in absolute ignorance of the greatest piece of mechanism which has ever come into existence, the brain of man.

8. Let us examine the wonders of this mechanism; perhaps we shall thereby get a better understanding of the various effects of which it is the cause.

9. In the first place, there is the great mental world in which we live and move and have our being; this world is omnipotent, omniscient and omnipresent; it will respond to our desire in direct ratio to our purpose and faith; the purpose must be in accordance with the law of our being, that is, it must be creative or constructive; our faith must be strong enough to generate a current of sufficient strength to bring our purpose into manifestation. "As thy faith is, so be it unto thee," bears the stamp of scientific test.

10. The effects which are produced in the world without are the result of the action and reaction of the individual upon the universal; that is the process which we call thinking; the brain is the organ through which this process is accomplished; think of the wonder of it all! Do you love music, flowers, literature, or are you inspired by the thought of ancient or modern genius? Remember, every beauty to which you respond must have its corresponding outline in your brain before you can appreciate it.

11. There is not a single virtue or principle in the storehouse of nature which the brain cannot express. The brain is an embryonic world, ready to develop at any time as necessity may arise. If you can comprehend that this is a scientific truth and one of the wonderful laws of nature, it will be easier for you to get an understanding of the mechanism by which these extraordinary results are being accomplished.

12. The nervous system has been compared to an electric circuit with its battery of cells in which force is originated, and its white matter to insulated wires by which the current is conveyed; it is through these channels that every impulse or desire is carried through the mechanism.

13. The spinal cord is the great motor and sensory pathway by which messages are conveyed to and from the brain; then, there is the blood supply plunging through the veins and arteries, renewing our energy and strength, the perfectly arranged structure upon which the entire physical body rests, and, finally, the delicate and beautiful skin, clothing the entire mechanism in a mantle of beauty.

14. This then is the "Temple of the living God" and the individual "I" is given control and upon his understanding of the mechanism which is within his control will the result depend.

15. Every thought sets the brain cells in action; at first the substance upon which the thought is directed fails to respond, but if the thought is sufficiently refined and concentrated, the substance finally yields and expresses perfectly.

16. This influence of the mind can be exerted upon any part of the body, causing the elimination of any undesirable effect.

17. A perfect conception and understanding of the laws governing in the mental world cannot fail to be of inestimable value in the transaction of business, as it develops the power of discernment and gives a clearer understanding and appreciation of facts.

18. The man who looks within instead of without cannot fail to make use of the mighty forces which will eventually determine his course in life and so bring him into vibration with all that is best, strongest and most desirable.

19. Attention or concentration is probably the most important essential in the development of mind culture. The possibilities of attention when properly directed are so startling that they would hardly appear credible to the uninitiated. The cultivation of attention is the distinguishing characteristic of every successful man or woman, and is the very highest personal accomplishment which can be acquired.

20. The power of attention can be more readily understood by comparing it with a magnifying glass in which the rays of sunlight are focused; they possess no particular strength as long as the glass is moved about and the rays directed from one place to another; but let the glass be held perfectly still and let the rays be focused on one spot for any length of time, and the effect will become immediately apparent.

21. So with the power of thought; let power be dissipated by scattering the thought from one object to another, and no result is apparent; but focus this power through attention or concentration on any single purpose for any length of time and nothing becomes impossible.

22. A very simple remedy for a very complex situation, some will say. All right, try it, you who have had no experience in concentrating the thought on a definite purpose or object. Choose any single object and concentrate your attention on it for a definite purpose for even ten minutes; you cannot do it; the mind will wander a dozen times and it will be necessary to bring it back to the original purpose, and each time the effect will have been lost and at the end of the ten minutes nothing will have been gained, because you have not been able to hold your thought steadily to the purpose.

23. It is, however, through attention that you will finally be able to overcome obstacles of any kind that appear in your path onward and upward, and the only way to acquire this wonderful power is by practice—practice makes perfect, in this as in anything else.

24. In order to cultivate the power of attention, bring a photograph with you to the same seat in the same room in the same position as heretofore. Examine it closely at least ten minutes, note the expression of the eyes, the form of the features, the clothing, the way the hair is arranged; in fact, note every detail shown on the photograph carefully. Now cover it and close your eyes and try to see it mentally; if you can see every detail perfectly and can form a good mental image of the photograph, you are to be congratulated; if not, repeat the process until you can.

25. This step is simply for the purpose of preparing the soil; next week we shall be ready to sow the seed.

26. It is by such exercises as these that you will finally be able to control your mental moods, your attitude, your consciousness.

27. Great financiers are learning to withdraw from the multitude more and more, that they may have more time for planning, thinking and generating the right mental moods.

28. Successful businessmen are constantly demonstrating the fact that it pays to keep in touch with the thought of other successful businessmen.

29. A single idea may be worth millions of dollars, and these ideas can only come to those who are receptive, who are prepared to receive them, who are in a successful frame of mind.

30. Men are learning to place themselves in harmony with the Universal Mind; they are learning the unity of all things; they are learning the basic methods and principles of thinking, and this is changing conditions and multiplying results.

31. They are finding that circumstances and environment follow the trend of mental and spiritual progress; they find that growth follows knowledge; action follows inspiration; opportunity follows perception; always the spiritual first, then the transformation into the infinite and illimitable possibilities of achievement.

32. As the individual is but the channel for the differentiation of the Universal, these possibilities are necessarily inexhaustible.

33. Thought is the process by which we may absorb the Spirit of Power, and hold the result in our inner consciousness until it becomes a part of our ordinary consciousness. The method of accomplishing this result by the persistent practice of a few fundamental principles, as explained in this System, is the Master Key which unlocks the storehouse of Universal Truth.

34. The two great sources of human suffering at present are bodily disease and mental anxiety. These may be readily traced to the infringement of some natural law. This is, no doubt, owing to the fact that so far knowledge has largely remained partial, but the clouds of darkness which have accumulated through long ages are beginning to roll away and with them many of the miseries that attend imperfect information.

> That a man can change himself, improve himself, re-create himself, control his environment, and master his own destiny is the conclusion of every mind who is wide-awake to the power of right thought in constructive action.
>
> —LARSEN

PART SIX.
STUDY QUESTIONS WITH ANSWERS

51. What are some of the effects which can be produced by electricity?
Heat, light, power, music.

52. Upon what do these various effects depend?
Upon the mechanism to which electricity is attached.

53. What is the result of the action and interaction of the individual mind upon the Universal?

    The conditions and experiences with which we meet.

54. How may these conditions be changed?

    By changing the mechanism by which the Universal is differentiated in form.

55. What is this mechanism?

    The brain.

56. How may it be changed?

    By the process we call thinking. Thoughts produce brain cells, and these cells respond to the corresponding thought in the Universal.

57. Of what value is the power of concentration?

    It is the very highest personal accomplishment which can be acquired, and the distinguishing characteristic of every successful man or woman.

58. How may it be acquired?

    By faithfully practicing the exercises in this System.

59. Why is this so important?

    Because it will enable us to control our thoughts, and since thoughts are causes conditions must be effects; if we can control the cause we can also control the effect.

60. What is changing conditions and multiplying results in the objective world?

    Men are learning the basic methods of constructive thinking.

Part Seven

Through all the ages man has believed in an invisible power, through which and by which all things have been created and are continually being re-created. We may personalize this power and call it God, or we may think of it as the essence or spirit, which permeates all things, but in either case the effect is the same.

So far as the individual is concerned, the objective, the physical, the visible, is the personal, that which can be cognized by the senses. It consists of body, brain and nerves. The subjective is the spiritual, the invisible, the impersonal.

The personal is conscious because it is a personal entity. The impersonal, being the same in kind and quality as all other Being, is not conscious of itself and has therefore been termed the subconscious.

The personal, or conscious, has the power of will and choice, and can therefore exercise discrimination in the selection of methods whereby to bring about the solution of difficulties.

The impersonal, or spiritual, being a part or one with the source, and origin of all power, can necessarily exercise no such choice, but, on the contrary, it has Infinite resources at its command. It can and does bring about results by methods concerning which the human or individual mind can have no possible conception.

You will therefore see that it is your privilege to depend upon the human will with all its limitations and misconceptions, or you may utilize the potentialities of Infinity by making use of the subconscious mind. Here, then, is the scientific explanation of the wonderful power which has been put within your control, if you but understand, appreciate and recognize it.

One method of consciously utilizing this omnipotent power is outlined in Part Seven.

1. Visualization is the process of making mental images, and the image is the mold or model which will serve as a pattern from which your future will emerge.

2. Make the pattern clear and make it beautiful; do not be afraid; make it grand; remember that no limitation can be placed upon you by anyone but yourself; you are not limited as to cost or material; draw on the Infinite for your supply, construct it in your imagination; it will have to be there before it will ever appear anywhere else.

3. Make the image clear and clean-cut, hold it firmly in the mind and you will gradually and constantly bring the thing nearer to you. You can be what "you will to be."

4. This is another psychological fact which is well known, but unfortunately, reading about it will not bring about any result which you may have in mind; it will not even help you to form the mental image, much less bring it into manifestation. Work is necessary—labor, hard mental labor, the kind of effort which so few are willing to put forth.

5. The first step is idealization. It is likewise the most important step, because it is the plan on which you are going to build. It must be solid; it must be permanent. The architect, when he plans a 30-storey building, has every line and detail pictured in advance. The engineer, when he spans a chasm, first ascertains the strength requirements of a million separate parts.

6. They see the end before a single step is taken; so you are to picture in your mind what you want; you are sowing the seed, but before sowing any seed you want to know what the harvest is to be. This is Idealization. If you are not sure, return to the chair daily until the picture becomes plain; it will gradually unfold; first the general plan will be dim, but it will take shape, the outline will take form, then the details, and you will gradually develop the power by which you will be enabled to formulate plans which will eventually materialize in the objective world. You will come to know what the future holds for you.

7. Then comes the process of visualization. You must see the picture more and more complete, see the detail, and, as the details begin to unfold the ways and means for bringing it into manifestation will develop. One thing will lead to another. Thought will lead to action, action will develop methods, methods will develop friends, and friends will bring about circumstances, and, finally, the third step, or Materialization, will have been accomplished.

8. We all recognize the Universe must have been thought into shape before it ever could have become a material fact. And if we are willing to follow along the lines of the Great Architect of the Universe, we shall find our thoughts taking form, just as the universe took concrete form. It is the same mind operating through the individual. There is no difference in kind or quality, the only difference is one of degree.

9. The architect visualizes his building, he sees it as he wishes it to be. His thought becomes a plastic mold from which the building will eventually emerge, a high one or a low one, a beautiful one or a plain one, his vision takes form on paper and eventually the necessary material is utilized and the building stands complete.

10. The inventor visualizes his idea in exactly the same manner. For instance, Nikola Tesla, he with the giant intellect, one of the greatest inventors of all ages, the man who has brought forth the most amazing realities, always visualizes his inventions before attempting to work them out. He did not rush to embody them in form and then spend his time in correcting defects. Having first built up the idea in his imagination, he held it there as a mental picture, to be reconstructed and improved by his thought. "In this way," he writes in the *Electrical Experimenter*, "I am enabled to rapidly develop and perfect a conception without touching anything. When I have gone so far as to embody in the invention every possible improvement I can think of, and see no fault anywhere, I put into concrete, the product of my brain. Invariably my devise works as I conceived it should; in twenty years there has not been a single exception."

11. If you can conscientiously follow these directions, you will develop Faith, the kind of Faith that is the "Substance of things hoped for, the evidence of things not seen"; you

will develop confidence, the kind of confidence that leads to endurance and courage; you will develop the power of concentration which will enable you to exclude all thoughts except the ones which are associated with your purpose.

12. The law is that thought will manifest itself in form, and only one who knows how to be the divine thinker of his own thoughts can ever take a Master's place and speak with authority.

13. Clearness and accuracy are obtained only by repeatedly having the image in mind. Each repeated action renders the image more clear and accurate than the preceding, and in proportion to the clearness and accuracy of the image will the outward manifestation be. You must build it firmly and securely in your mental world, the world within, before it can take form in the world without, and you can build nothing of value, even in the mental world unless you have the proper material. When you have the material you can build anything you wish, but make sure of your material. You cannot make broadcloth from shoddy.

14. This material will be brought out by millions of silent mental workers and fashioned into the form of the image which you have in mind.

15. Think of it! You have over five million of these mental workers, ready and in active use; brain cells they are called. Besides this, there is another reserve force of at least an equal number, ready to be called into action at the slightest need. Your power to think, then, is almost unlimited, and this means that your power to create the kind of material which is necessary to build for yourself any kind of environment which you desire is practically unlimited.

16. In addition to these millions of mental workers, you have billions of mental workers in the body, every one of which is endowed with sufficient intelligence to understand and act upon any message or suggestion given. These cells are all busy creating and re-creating the body, but, in addition to this, they are endowed with psychic activity whereby they can attract to themselves the substance necessary for perfect development.

17. They do this by the same law and in the same manner that every form of life attracts to itself the necessary material for growth. The oak, the rose, the lily, all require certain material for their most perfect expression and they secure it by silent demand, the Law of Attraction, the most certain way for you to secure what you require for your most complete development.

18. Make the Mental Image; make it clear, distinct, perfect; hold it firmly; the ways and means will develop; supply will follow the demand; you will be led to do the right thing at the right time and in the right way. Earnest Desire will bring about Confident Expectation, and this in turn must be reinforced by Firm Demand. These three cannot fail to bring about Attainment, because the Earnest Desire is the feeling, the Confident Expectation is the thought, and the Firm Demand is the will, and, as we have seen, feeling gives vitality to thought and the will holds it steadily until the law of growth brings it into manifestation.

19. Is it not wonderful that man has such tremendous power within himself, such transcendental faculties concerning which he had no conception? Is it not strange that we have always been taught to look for strength and power "without"? We have been taught to look everywhere but "within" and whenever this power manifested itself in our lives we were told that it was something supernatural.

20. There are many who have come to an understanding of this wonderful power, and who make serious and conscientious efforts to realize health, power, and other conditions, and seem to fail. They do not seem able to bring the law into operation. The difficulty in nearly every case is that they are dealing with externals. They want money, power, health and abundance, but they fail to realize that these are effects and can come only when the cause is found.

21. Those who will give no attention to the world without will seek only to ascertain the truth, will look only for wisdom, will find that this wisdom will unfold and disclose the source of all power, that it will manifest itself in thought and purpose which will create the external conditions desired. This truth will find expression in noble purpose and courageous action.

22. Create ideals only, give no thought to external conditions, make the world within beautiful and opulent and the world without will express and manifest the condition which you have within. You will come into a realization of your power to create ideals and these ideals will be projected into the world of effect.

23. For instance, a man is in debt. He will be continually thinking about the debt, concentrating on it, and as thoughts are causes the result is that he not only fastens the debt closer to him, but actually creates more debt. He is putting the great Law of Attraction into operation with the usual and inevitable result—Loss leads to greater "Loss."

24. What, then, is the correct principle? Concentrate on the things you want, not on the things you do not want. Think of abundance; idealize the methods and plans for putting the Law of Abundance into operation. Visualize the condition which the Law of Abundance creates; this will result in manifestation.

25. If the law operates perfectly to bring about poverty, lack and every form of limitation for those who are continually entertaining thoughts of lack and fear, it will operate with the same certainty to bring about conditions of abundance and opulence for those who entertain thoughts of courage and power.

26. This is a difficult problem for many; we are too anxious; we manifest anxiety, fear, distress; we want to do something; we want to help; we are like a child who has just planted a seed and every fifteen minutes goes and stirs up the earth to see if it is growing. Of course, under such circumstances, the seed will never germinate, and yet this is exactly what many of us do in the mental world.

27. We must plant the seed and leave it undisturbed. This does not mean that we are to sit down and do nothing, by no means; we will do more and better work than we have ever done before, new channels will constantly be provided, new doors will open; all that is necessary is to have an open mind, be ready to act when the time comes.

28. Thought force is the most powerful means of obtaining knowledge, and if concentrated on any subject will solve the problem. Nothing is beyond the power of human comprehension, but in order to harness thought force and make it do your bidding, work is required.

29. Remember that thought is the fire that creates the steam that turns the wheel of fortune, upon which your experiences depend.

30. Ask yourself a few questions and then reverently await the response; do you not now and then feel the self with you? Do you assert this self or do you follow the major-

ity? Remember that majorities are always led, they never lead. It was the majority that fought, tooth and nail, against the steam engine, the power loom and every other advance or improvement ever suggested.

31. For your exercise this week, visualize your friend, see him exactly as you last saw him, see the room, the furniture, recall the conversation, now see his face, see it distinctly, now talk to him about some subject of mutual interest; see his expression change, watch him smile. Can you do this? All right, you can; then arouse his interest, tell him a story of adventure, see his eyes light up with the spirit of fun or excitement. Can you do all of this? If so, your imagination is good, you are making excellent progress.

PART SEVEN.
STUDY QUESTIONS WITH ANSWERS

61. What is visualization?
The process of making mental pictures.

62. What is the result of this method of thought?
By holding the image or picture in mind, we can gradually but surely bring the thing nearer to us. We can be what we will to be.

63. What is Idealization?
It is a process of visualizing or idealizing the plans which will eventually materialize in our objective world.

64. Why are clearness and accuracy necessary?
Because "seeing" creates "feeling" and "feeling" creates "being." First the mental, then the emotional, then the illimitable possibilities of achievement.

65. How are they obtained?
Each repeated action renders the image more accurate than the former one.

66. How is the material for the construction of your mental image secured?
By millions of mental workers. Brain cells, they are called.

67. How are the necessary conditions for bringing about the materialization of your ideal in the objective world secured?
By the Law of Attraction. The natural law by which all conditions and experiences are brought about.

68. What three steps are necessary in order to bring this law into operation?
Earnest Desire, Confident Expectation, Firm Demand.

69. Why do many fail?
Because they concentrate on loss, disease and disaster. The law is operating perfectly; the things they fear are coming upon them.

70. What is the alternative?
Concentrate on the ideals which you desire to see manifested in your life.

Part Eight

In this Part you will find that you may freely choose what you think but the result of your thought is governed by an immutable law! Is not this a wonderful thought? Is it not wonderful to know that our lives are not subject to caprice or variability of any kind? That they are governed by law. This stability is our opportunity, because by complying with the law we can secure the desired effect with invariable precision.

It is the Law which makes the Universe one grand paean of Harmony. If it were not for law, the Universe would be a Chaos instead of a Cosmos.

Here, then, is the secret of the origin of both good and evil, this is all the good and evil there ever was or ever will be.

Let me illustrate. Thought results in action, if your thought is constructive and harmonious, the result will be good; if your thought is destructive or inharmonious, the result will be evil.

There is therefore but one law, one principle, on cause, one Source of Power, and good and evil are simply words which have been coined to indicate the result of our action, or our compliance or non-compliance with this law.

The importance of this is well illustrated in the lives of Emerson and Carlyle. Emerson loved the good and his life was a symphony of peace and harmony, Carlyle hated the bad, and his life was a record of perpetual discord and inharmony.

Here we have two grand men, each intent upon achieving the same ideal, but one makes use of constructive thought and is therefore in harmony with natural law, the other makes use of destructive thought and therefore brings upon himself discord of every kind and character.

It is evident therefore that we are to hate nothing, not even the "bad," because hatred is destructive, and we shall soon find that by entertaining destructive thought we are sowing the "wind" and in turn shall reap the "whirlwind."

1. Thought contains a vital principle, because it is the creative principle of the Universe and by its nature will combine with other similar thoughts.

2. As the one purpose of life is growth, all principles underlying existence must contribute to give it effect. Thought, therefore, takes form and the law of growth eventually brings it into manifestation.

3. You may freely choose what you think, but the result of your thought is governed by an immutable law. Any line of thought persisted in cannot fail to produce its result in the character, health and circumstances of the individual. Methods whereby we can substitute habits of constructive thinking for those which we have found produce only undesirable effects are therefore of primary importance.

4. We all know that this is by no means easy. Mental habits are difficult to control, but it can be done and the way to do it is to begin at once to substitute constructive thought for destructive thought. Form the habit of analyzing every thought. If it is necessary, if its manifestation in the objective will be a benefit, not only to yourself, but to all whom it may affect in any way, keep it; treasure it; it is of value; it is in tune with the Infinite; it will grow and develop and produce fruit a hundredfold. On the other hand, it will be well for you to keep this quotation from George Matthews Adams in mind, "Learn to keep the door shut, keep out of your mind, out of your office, and out of your world, every element that seeks admittance with no definite helpful end in view."

5. If your thought has been critical or destructive, and has resulted in any condition of discord or inharmony in your environment, it may be necessary for you to cultivate a mental attitude which will be conducive to constructive thought.

6. The imagination will be found to be a great assistance in this direction; the cultivation of the imagination leads to the development of the ideal out of which your future will emerge.

7. The imagination gathers up the material by which the Mind weaves the fabric in which your future is to be clothed.

8. Imagination is the light by which we can penetrate new worlds of thought and experience.

9. Imagination is the mighty instrument by which every discoverer, every inventor, opened the way from precedent to experience. Precedent said, "It cannot be done;" experience said, "It is done."

10. Imagination is a plastic power, molding the things of sense into new forms and ideals.

11. Imagination is the constructive form of thought which must precede every constructive form of action.

12. A builder cannot build a structure of any kind until he has first received the plans from the architect, and the architect must get them from his imagination.

13. The Captain of Industry cannot build a giant corporation which may coordinate hundreds of smaller corporations and thousands of employees, and utilize millions of dollars of capital until he has first created the entire work in his imagination. Objects in the material world are as clay in the potter's hand; it is in the Master Mind that the real things are created, and it is by the use of the imagination that the work is done. In order to cultivate the imagination it must be exercised. Exercise is necessary to cultivate mental muscle as well as physical muscle. It must be supplied with nourishment or it cannot grow.

14. Do not confuse Imagination with Fancy, or that form of daydreaming in which some people like to indulge. Daydreaming is a form of mental dissipation which may lead to mental disaster.

15. Constructive imagination means mental labor, by some considered to be the hard-

est kind of labor, but, if so, it yields the greatest returns, for all the great things in life have come to men and women who had the capacity to think, to imagine, and to make their dreams come true.

16. When you have become thoroughly conscious of the fact that Mind is the only creative principle, that it is Omnipotent, Omniscient and Omnipresent, and that you can consciously come into harmony with this Omnipotence through your power of thought, you will have taken a long step in the right direction.

17. The next step is to place yourself in position to receive this power. As it is Omnipresent, it must be within you. We know that this is so because we know that all power is from within, but it must be developed, unfolded, cultivated; in order to do this we must be receptive, and this receptivity is acquired just as physical strength is gained, by exercise.

18. The Law of Attraction will certainly and unerringly bring to you the conditions, environment, and experiences in life, corresponding with your habitual, characteristic, predominant mental attitude. Not what you think once in a while when you are in church, or have just read a good book, BUT your predominant mental attitude is what counts.

19. You cannot entertain weak, harmful, negative thoughts ten hours a day and expect to bring about beautiful, strong and harmonious conditions by ten minutes of strong, positive, creative thought.

20. Real power comes from within. All power that anybody can possibly use is within man, only waiting to be brought into visibility by his first recognizing it, and then affirming it as his, working it into his consciousness until he becomes one with it.

21. People say that they desire abundant life, and so they do, but so many interpret this to mean that if they will exercise their muscles or breathe scientifically, eat certain foods in certain ways, drink so many glasses of water every day of just a certain temperature, keep out of drafts, they will attain the abundant life they seek. The result of such methods is but indifferent. However, when man awakens to the truth, and affirms his oneness with all Life, he finds that he takes on the clear eye, the elastic step, the vigor of youth; he finds that he has discovered the source of all power.

22. All mistakes are but the mistakes of ignorance. Knowledge gaining and consequent power is what determines growth and evolution. The recognition and demonstration of knowledge is what constitutes power, and this power is spiritual power, and this spiritual power is the power which lies at the heart of all things; it is the soul of the universe.

23. This knowledge is the result of man's ability to think; thought is therefore the germ of man's conscious evolution. When man ceases to advance in his thoughts and ideals, his forces immediately begin to disintegrate and his countenance gradually registers these changing conditions.

24. Successful men make it their business to hold ideals of the conditions which they wish to realize. They constantly hold in mind the next step necessary to the ideal for which they are striving. Thoughts are the materials with which they build, and the imagination is their mental workshop. Mind is the ever-moving force with which they secure the persons and circumstance necessary to build their success structure, and imagination is the matrix in which all great things are fashioned.

25. If you have been faithful to your ideal, you will hear the call when circumstances are ready to materialize your plans and results will correspond in the exact ratio of your fidelity to your ideal. The ideal steadily held is what pre-determines and attracts the necessary conditions for its fulfillment.

26. It is thus that you may weave a garment of spirit and power into the web of your entire existence; it is thus that you may lead a charmed life and be forever protected from all harm; it is thus that you may become a positive force whereby conditions of opulence and harmony may be attracted to you.

27. This is the leaven which is gradually permeating the general consciousness and is largely responsible for the conditions of unrest which are everywhere evident.

28. In the last Part you created a mental image, you brought it from the invisible into the visible; this week I want you to take an object and follow it back to its origination, see of what it really consists. If you do this you will develop imagination, insight, perception, and sagacity. These come not by the superficial observation of the multitude, but by a keen analytical observation which sees below the surface.

29. It is the few who know that the things which they see are only effects, and understand the causes by which these effects were brought into existence.

30. Take the same position as heretofore and visualize a battleship; see the grim monster floating on the surface of the water; there appears to be no life anywhere about; all is silence; you know that by far the largest part of the vessel is under water; out of sight; you know that the ship is as large and as heavy as a twenty-story skyscraper; you know that there are hundreds of men ready to spring to their appointed task instantly; you know that every department is in charge of able, trained, skilled officials who have proven themselves competent to take charge of this marvelous piece of mechanism; you know that although it lies apparently oblivious to everything else, it has eyes which see everything for miles around, and nothing is permitted to escape its watchful vision; you know that while it appears quiet, submissive and innocent, it is prepared to hurl a steel projectile weighing thousands of pounds at an enemy many miles away; this and much more you can bring to mind with comparatively no effort whatever. But how did the battleship come to be where it is; how did it come into existence in the first place? All of this you want to know if you are a careful observer.

31. Follow the great steel plates through the foundries, see the thousands of men employed in their production; go still further back, and see the ore as it comes from the mine, see it loaded on barges or cars, see it melted and properly treated; go back still further and see the architect and engineers who planned the vessel; let the thought carry you back still further in order to determine why they planned the vessel; you will see that you are now so far back that the vessel is something intangible, it no longer exists, it is now only a thought existing in the brain of the architect; but from where did the order come to plan the vessel? Probably from the Secretary of Defense; but probably this vessel was planned long before the war was thought of, and that Congress had to pass a bill appropriating the money; possibly there was opposition, and speeches for or against the bill. Whom do these Congressmen represent? They represent you and me, so that our line of thought begins with the battleship and ends with ourselves, and we find in the last analysis that our own thought is responsible for this and many other things, of which we seldom think, and

a little further reflection will develop the most important fact of all and that is, if someone had not discovered the law by which this tremendous mass of steel and iron could be made to float upon the water, instead of immediately going to the bottom, the battleship could not have come into existence at all.

32. This law is that, "the specific gravity of any substance is the weight of any volume of it, compared with an equal volume of water." The discovery of this law revolutionized every kind of ocean travel, commerce and warfare, and made the existence of the battleship, aircraft carriers, and cruise ships possible.

33. You will find exercises of this kind invaluable. When the thought has been trained to look below the surface everything takes on a different appearance, the insignificant becomes significant, the uninteresting interesting; the things which we supposed to be of no importance are seen to be the only really vital things in existence.

Look to This Day for it is Life, the very Life of Life. In Its brief course lie all the Verities and Realities of your existence; The Bliss of Growth; The Glory of Action; The Splendor of Beauty; For Yesterday is but a Dream, And tomorrow is only a Vision: But Today well lived makes every Yesterday a Dream of Happiness, and Every Tomorrow a Vision of Hope. Look well, therefore, to This Day!

—FROM THE SANSKRIT

PART EIGHT. STUDY QUESTIONS WITH ANSWERS

71. What is the imagination?
    A form of constructive thought. The light by which we penetrate new worlds of thought and experience. The mighty instrument by which every inventor or discoverer opened the way from precedent to experience.
72. What is the result of imagination?
    The cultivation of the imagination leads to the development of the ideal out of which your future will emerge.
73. How may it be cultivated?
    By exercise; it must be supplied with nourishment or it cannot live.
74. How does imagination differ from daydreaming?
    Daydreaming is a form of mental dissipation, while imagination is a form of constructive thought which must precede every constructive action.
75. What are mistakes?
    The result of ignorance.
76. What is knowledge?
    The result of man's ability to think.
77. What is the power with which successful men build?
    Mind is the very moving force with which they secure the persons and circumstances necessary to complete their plans.

78. What pre-determines the result?
    The ideal held steadily in mind attracts the necessary conditions for its fulfillment.
79. What is the result of a keen analytical observation?
    The development of imagination, insight, perception and sagacity.
80. To what do these lead?
    Opulence and harmony.

Part Nine

In this Part you may learn to fashion the tools by which you may build for yourself any condition you desire. If you wish to change conditions you must change yourself. Your whims, your wishes, your fancies, your ambitions may be thwarted at every step, but your inmost thoughts will find expression just as certainly as the plant springs from the seed.

Suppose, then, we desire to change conditions, how are we to bring this about? The reply is simple: By the law of growth. Cause and effect are as absolute and undeviating in the hidden realm of thought as in the world of material things.

Hold in mind the condition desired; affirm it as an already existing fact. This indicates the value of a powerful affirmation. By constant repetition it becomes a part of ourselves. We are actually changing ourselves; are making ourselves what we want to be.

Character is not a thing of chance, but it is the result of continued effort. If you are timid, vacillating, self-conscious, or if you are over-anxious or harassed by thoughts of fear or impending danger, remember that it is axiomatic that "two things cannot exist in the same place at the same time."

Exactly the same thing is true in the mental and spiritual world; so that your remedy is plainly to substitute thoughts of courage, power, self-reliance and confidence for those of fear, lack and limitation.

The easiest and most natural way to do this is to select an affirmation which seems to fit your particular case.

The positive thought will destroy the negative as certainly as light destroys darkness, and the results will be just as effectual.

Act is the blossom of thought, and conditions are the result of action, so that you constantly have in your possession the tools by which you will certainly and inevitably make or unmake yourself, and joy or suffering will be the reward.

1. There are only three things which can possibly be desired in the "world without" and each of them can be found in the "world within." The secret of finding them is simply to apply the proper "mechanism" of attachment to the omnipotent power to which each individual has access.

2. The three things which all mankind desires and which are necessary for his highest expression and complete development are Health, Wealth and Love. All will admit that Health is absolutely essential; no one can be happy if the physical body is in pain. All will not so readily admit that Wealth is necessary, but all must admit that a sufficient supply at least is necessary, and what would be considered sufficient for one, would be considered absolute and painful lack for another; and as nature provides not only enough but abundantly, wastefully, lavishly, we realize that any lack or limitation is only the limitation which has been made by an artificial method of distribution.

3. All will probably admit that Love is the third, or maybe some will say the first essential necessary to the happiness of mankind; at any rate, those who possess all three, Health, Wealth, and Love, find nothing else which can be added to their cup of happiness.

4. We have found that the Universal substance is "All Health," "All Substance" and "All Love" and that the mechanism of attachment whereby we can consciously connect with this Infinite supply is in our method of thinking. To think correctly is therefore to enter into the "Secret Place of the Most High."

5. What shall we think? If we know this we shall have found the proper mechanism of attachment which will relate us to "Whatsoever things we desire." This mechanism may seem very simple when I give it to you, but read on; you will find that it is in reality the "Master Key," the "Aladdin's lamp," if you please; you will find that it is the foundation, the imperative condition, the absolute law of well-doing, which means, well-being.

6. To think correctly, accurately, we must know the "Truth." The truth then is the underlying principle in every business or social relation. It is a condition precedent to every right action. To know the truth, to be sure, to be confident, affords a satisfaction beside which no other is at all comparable; it is the only solid ground in a world of doubt, conflict and danger.

7. To know the Truth is to be in harmony with the Infinite and Omnipotent power. To know the truth is, therefore, to connect yourself with a power which is irresistible and which will sweep away every kind of discord, inharmony, doubt or error of any kind, because the "Truth is mighty and will prevail."

8. The humblest intellect can readily foretell the result of any action when he knows that it is based on truth, but the mightiest intellect, the most profound and penetrating mind loses its way hopelessly and can form no conception of the results which may ensue when his hopes are based on a premise which he knows to be false.

9. Every action which is not in harmony with Truth, whether through ignorance or design, will result in discord, and eventual loss in proportion to its extent and character.

10. How then are we to know the truth in order to attach this mechanism which will relate us to the Infinite?

11. We can make no mistake about this if we realize that truth is the vital principle of the Universal Mind and is Omnipresent. For instance, if you require health, a realization of the fact that the "I" in you is spiritual and that all spirit is one; that wherever a part is the whole must be, will bring about a condition of health, because every cell in the body must manifest the truth as you see it. If you see sickness; they will manifest sickness; if you see perfection they must manifest perfection. The affirmation, "I am whole, perfect, strong, powerful, loving, harmonious and happy" will bring about harmonious conditions. The

reason for this is that the affirmation is in strict accordance with the Truth, and when truth appears every form of error or discord must necessarily disappear.

12. You have found that the "I" is spiritual, it must necessarily then always be no less than perfect, the affirmation. "I am whole, perfect, strong, powerful, loving, harmonious and happy" is therefore an exact scientific statement.

13. Thought is a spiritual activity and spirit is creative, therefore the result of holding this thought in mind must necessarily bring about conditions in harmony with the thought.

14. If you require Wealth a realization of the fact that the "I" in you is one with the Universal mind which is all substance, and is Omnipotent, will assist you in bringing into operation the Law of Attraction which will bring you into vibration with those forces which make for success and bring about conditions of power and affluence in direct proportion with the character and purpose of your affirmation.

15. Visualization is the mechanism of the attachment which you require. Visualization is a very different process from seeing; seeing is physical, and is therefore related to the objective world, the "world without," but Visualization is a product of the imagination, and is therefore a product of the subjective mind, the "world within." It therefore possesses vitality; it will grow. The thing visualized will manifest itself in form. The mechanism is perfect; it was created by the Master Architect who "doeth all things well," but unfortunately sometimes the operator is inexperienced or inefficient, but practice and determination will overcome this defect.

16. If you require Love try to realize that the only way to get love is by giving it, that the more you give the more you will get, and the only way in which you can give it, is to fill yourself with it, until you become a magnet. The method was explained in another lesson.

17. He who has learned to bring the greatest spiritual truths into touch with the so-called lesser things of life has discovered the secret of the solution of his problem. One is always quickened, made more thoughtful, by his nearness of approach to great ideas, great events, great natural objects, and great men. Lincoln is said to have begotten in all who came near him the feeling awakened when one approaches a mountain, and this sense asserts itself most keenly when one comes to realize that he has laid hold upon things that are eternal, the power of Truth.

18. It is sometimes an inspiration to hear from someone who has actually put these principles to the test, someone who has demonstrated them in their own life. A letter from Frederick Andrews offers the following insight:

19. I was about thirteen years old when Dr. T. W. Marsee, since passed over, said to my mother: "There is no possible chance, Mrs. Andrews. I lost my little boy the same way, after doing everything for him that it was possible to do. I have made a special study of these cases, and I know there is no possible chance for him to get well."

20. She turned to him and said: "Doctor, what would you do if he were your boy?" and he answered, "I would fight, fight, as long as there is a breath of life to fight for."

21. That was the beginning of a long, drawn-out battle, with many ups and downs, the doctors all agreeing that there was no chance for a cure, though they encouraged and cheered us the best they could.

22. But at last the victory came, and I have grown from a little, crooked, twisted, cripple, going about on my hands and knees, to a strong, straight, well-formed man.

23. Now, I know you want the formula, and I will give it to you as briefly and quickly as I can.

24. I built up an affirmation for myself, taking the qualities I most needed, and affirming for myself over and over again, "I am whole, perfect, strong, powerful, loving, harmonious and happy." I kept up this affirmation, always the same, never varying, till I could wake up in the night and find myself repeating, "I am whole, perfect, strong, powerful, loving, harmonious and happy." It was the last thing on my lips at night and the first thing in the morning.

25. Not only did I affirm it for myself, but for others that I knew needed it. I want to emphasize this point. Whatever you desire for yourself, affirm it for others, and it will help you both. We reap what we sow. If we send out thoughts of love and health, they return to us like bread cast upon the waters; but if we send out thoughts of fear, worry, jealousy, anger, hate, etc., we will reap the results in our own lives.

26. It used to be said that man is completely built over every seven years, but some scientists now declare that we build ourselves over entirely every eleven months; so we are really only eleven months old. If we build the defects back into our bodies year after year, we have no one to blame but ourselves.

27. Man is the sum total of his own thoughts; so the question is, how are we going to entertain only the good thoughts and reject the evil ones? At first we can't keep the evil thoughts from coming, but we can keep from entertaining them. The only way to do this is to forget them—which means, get something for them. This is where the ready-made affirmation comes into play.

28. When a thought of anger, jealousy, fear or worry creeps in, just start your affirmation going. The way to fight darkness is with light—the way to fight cold is with heat—the way to overcome evils is with good. For myself, I never could find any help in denials. Affirm the good, and the bad will vanish.—Frederick Elias Andrews.

29. If there is anything you require, it will be well for you to make use of this affirmation; it cannot be improved upon. Use it just as it is; take it into the silence with you, until it sinks into your subconsciousness, so that you can use it anywhere, in your car, in the office, at home; this is the advantage of spiritual methods; they are always available. Spirit is omnipresent, ever ready; all that is required is a proper recognition of its omnipotence, and a willingness or desire to become the recipient of its beneficent effects.

30. If our predominant mental attitude is one of power, courage, kindliness and sympathy, we shall find that our environment will reject conditions in correspondence with these thoughts; if it is weak, critical, envious and destructive, we shall find our environment reflecting conditions corresponding to these thoughts.

31. Thoughts are causes and conditions are effects. Herein is the explanation of the origin of both good and evil. Thought is creative and will automatically correlate with its object. This is a cosmological law (a universal law), the Law of Attraction, the law of cause and effect; the recognition and application of this law will determine both beginning and end; it is the law by which in all ages and in all times the people were led to believe in the

power of prayer. "As thy faith is, so be it unto thee," is simply another, shorter and a better way of stating it.

32. This week visualize a plant; take a flower, the one you most admire, bring it from the unseen into the seen, plant the tiny seed, water it, care for it, place it where it will get the direct rays of the morning sun, see the seed burst; it is now a living thing, something which is alive and beginning to search for the means of subsistence. See the roots penetrating the earth, watch them shoot out in all directions and remember that they are living cells dividing and subdividing, and that they will soon number millions, that each cell is intelligent, that it knows what it wants and knows how to get it. See the stem shoot forward and upward, watch it burst through the surface of the earth, see it divide and form branches, see how perfect and symmetrical each branch is formed, see the leaves begin to form, and then the tiny stems, each one holding aloft a bud, and as you watch you see the bud begin to unfold and your favorite flower comes to view; and now if you will concentrate intently you will become conscious of a fragrance; it is the fragrance of the flower as the breeze gently sways the beautiful creation which you have visualized.

33. When you are enabled to make your vision clear and complete you will be enabled to enter into the spirit of a thing; it will become very real to you; you will be learning to concentrate and the process is the same, whether you are concentrating on health, a favorite flower, an ideal, a complicated business proposition or any other problem of life.

34. Every success has been accomplished by persistent concentration upon the object in view.

PART NINE.
STUDY QUESTIONS WITH ANSWERS

81. What is the imperative condition of all well-being?
Well doing.

82. What is the condition precedent to every right action?
Right thinking.

83. What is the underlying condition necessary in every business transaction or social relation?
To know the Truth.

84. What is the result of a knowledge of the Truth?
We can readily predict the result of any action that is based upon a true premise.

85. What is the result of any action based upon a false premise?
We can form no conception of the results which may ensue.

86. How may we know the Truth?
By a realization of the fact that Truth is the vital principle of the Universe and is therefore omnipresent.

87. What is the nature of Truth?
It is spiritual.

88. What is the secret of the solution to every problem?
To apply spiritual Truth.

89. What is the advantage of spiritual methods?
They are always available.
90. What are the necessary requirements?
A recognition of the omnipotence of spiritual power and a desire to become the recipient of its beneficent effects.

Thought means life, since those who do not think do not live in any high or real sense. Thinking makes the man.

—A. B. ALCOTT

Part Ten

If you get a thorough understanding of the thought contained in Part Ten, you will have learned that nothing happens without a definite cause. You will be enabled to formulate your plans in accordance with exact knowledge. You will know how to control any situation by bringing adequate causes into play. When you win, as you will, you will know exactly why.

The ordinary man, who has no definite knowledge of cause and effect, is governed by his feelings or emotions.

He thinks chiefly to justify his action. If he fails as a businessman, he says that luck is against him. If he dislikes music, he says that music is an expensive luxury. If he is a poor office man, he says that he could succeed better at some outdoor work. If he lacks friends, he says his individuality is too fine to be appreciated.

He never thinks his problem through to the end. In short, he does not know that every effect is the result of a certain definite cause, but he seeks to console himself with explanations and excuses. He thinks only in self-defense.

On the contrary, the man who understands that there is no effect without an adequate cause thinks impersonally. He gets down to bedrock facts regardless of consequences. He is free to follow the trail of truth wherever it may lead. He sees the issue clear to the end, and he meets the requirements fully and fairly, and the result is that the world gives him all that it has to give, in friendship, honor, love and approval.

1. Abundance is a natural law of the Universe. The evidence of this law is conclusive; we see it on every hand. Everywhere, nature is lavish, wasteful, extravagant. Nowhere is economy observed in any created thing. Profusion is manifested in everything. The millions and millions of trees and flowers and plants and animals and the vast scheme of reproduction where the process of creating and re-creating is forever going on, all indicate the lavishness with which nature has made provision for man. That there is an abundance for everyone is evident, but that many fail to participate in this abundance is also evident; they have not yet come into a realization of the Universality of all substance, and that mind is the active principle whereby we are related to the things we desire.

2. All wealth is the offspring of power; possessions are of value only as they confer

power. Events are significant only as they affect power; all things represent certain forms and degrees of power.

3. Knowledge of cause and effect as shown by the laws governing electricity, chemical affinity and gravitation enables man to plan courageously and execute fearlessly. These laws are called natural laws, because they govern in the physical world, but all power is not physical power; there is also mental power, and there is moral and spiritual power.

4. Spiritual power is superior because it exists on a higher plane. It has enabled man to discover the law by which these wonderful forces of Nature could be harnessed and made to do the work of hundreds and thousands of men. It has enabled man to discover laws whereby time and space have been annihilated and the law of gravitation to be overcome. The operation of this law is dependent upon spiritual contact, as Henry Drummond well says:

5. "In the physical world as we know it, there exists the organic and the inorganic. The inorganic of the mineral world is absolutely cut off from the plant or animal world; the passage is hermetically sealed. These barriers have never yet been crossed. No change of substance, no modification of environment, no chemistry, no electricity, no form of energy, no evolution of any kind can ever endow a single atom of the mineral world with the attribute of Life."

6. "Only by the bending down into this dead world of some living form can those dead atoms be gifted with the properties of vitality; without this contact with life they remain fixed in the inorganic sphere forever. Huxley says that the doctrine of Biogenesis (or life only from life) is victorious all along the line, and Tyndall is compelled to say: 'I affirm that no shred of trustworthy evidence exists to prove that life in our day has ever appeared independent of antecedent life.' "

7. "Physical laws may explain the inorganic, Biology explains and accounts for the development of the organic, but of the point of contact Science is silent. A similar passage exists between the natural world and the spiritual world; this passage is hermetically sealed on the natural side. The door is closed; no man can open it, no organic change, no mental energy, no moral effort, no progress of any kind can enable any human being to enter the spiritual world."

8. But as the plant reaches down into the mineral world and touches it with the mystery of Life, so the Universal Mind reaches down into the human mind and endows it with new, strange, wonderful and even marvelous qualities. All men or women who have ever accomplished anything in the world of industry, commerce or art have accomplished because of this process.

9. Thought is the connecting link between the Infinite and the finite, between the Universal and the individual. We have seen that there is an impassable barrier between the organic and the inorganic, and that the only way that matter can unfold is to be impregnated with life; as a seed reaches down into the mineral world and begins to unfold and reach out, the dead matter begins to live, a thousand invisible fingers begin to weave a suitable environment for the new arrival, and as the law of growth begins to take effect, we see the process continue until the Lily finally appears, and even "Solomon in all his glory was not arrayed like one of these."

10. Even so, a thought is dropped into the invisible substance of the Universal Mind, that substance from which all things are created, and as it takes root, the law of growth begins to take effect and we find that conditions and environment are but the objective form of our thought.

11. The law is that Thought is an active vital form of dynamic energy which has the power to correlate with its object and bring it out of the invisible substance from which all things are created into the visible or objective world. This is the law by which, and through which all things come into manifestation; it is the Master Key by which you are admitted into the Secret Place of the Most High and are "given dominion over all things." With an understanding of this law you may "decree a thing and it shall be established unto thee."

12. It could not be otherwise; if the soul of the Universe as we know it is the Universal Spirit, then the Universe is simply the condition which the Universal Spirit has made for itself. We are simply individualized spirit and are creating the conditions for our growth in exactly the same way.

13. This creative power depends upon our recognition of the potential power of spirit or mind and must not be confused with Evolution. Creation is the calling into existence of that which does not exist in the objective world. Evolution is simply the unfolding of potentialities involved in things which already exist.

14. In taking advantage of the wonderful possibilities opened up to us through the operation of this law, we must remember that we ourselves contribute nothing to its efficacy as the Great Teacher said: "It is not I that doeth the works, but the Father that dwelleth in me, He doeth the works." We must take exactly the same position; we can do nothing to assist in the manifestation, we simply comply with the law, and the All-originating Mind will bring about the result.

15. The great error of the present day is the idea that Man has to originate the intelligence whereby the Infinite can proceed to bring about a specific purpose or result. Nothing of this kind is necessary; the Universal Mind can be depended upon to find the ways and means for bringing about any necessary manifestation. We must, however, create the ideal, and this ideal should be perfect.

16. We know that the laws governing Electricity have been formulated in such a way that this invisible power can be controlled and used for our benefit and comfort in thousands of ways. We know that messages are carried around the world, that ponderous machinery does its bidding, that it now illuminates practically the whole world, but we know too that if we consciously or ignorantly violate its law by touching a live wire, when it is not properly insulated, the result will be unpleasant and possibly disastrous. A lack of understanding of the laws governing in the invisible world has the same result, and many are suffering the consequences all the time.

17. It has been explained that the law of causation depends upon polarity, a circuit must be formed; this circuit cannot be formed unless we operate in harmony with the law. How shall we operate in harmony with the law unless we know what the law is? How shall we know what the law is? By study, by observation.

18. We see the law in operation everywhere; all nature testifies to the operation of the

law by silently, constantly expressing itself in the law of growth. Where there is growth, there must be life; where there is life there must be harmony, so that everything that has life is constantly attracting to itself the conditions and the supply which is necessary for its most complete expression.

19. If your thought is in harmony with the creative principle of nature, it is in tune with the Infinite Mind, and it will form the circuit, it will not return to you void; but it is possible for you to think thoughts that are not in tune with the Infinite, and when there is no polarity, the circuit is not formed. What, then, is the result? What is the result when a dynamo is generating electricity, the circuit is cut off and there is no outlet? The dynamo stops.

20. It will be exactly the same with you, if you entertain thoughts which are not in accordance with the Infinite and cannot therefore be polarized; there is no circuit, you are isolated, the thoughts cling to you, harass you, worry you, and finally bring about disease and possibly death; the physician may not diagnose the case exactly in this way, he may give it some fancy name which has been manufactured for the various ills which are the result of wrong thinking, but the cause is the same nevertheless.

21. Constructive thought must necessarily be creative, but creative thought must be harmonious, and this eliminates all destructive or competitive thought.

22. Wisdom, strength, courage and all harmonious conditions are the result of power and we have seen that all power is from within; likewise, every lack, limitation or adverse circumstance is the result of weakness, and weakness is simply absence of power; it comes from nowhere, it is nothing—the remedy then is simply to develop power, and this is accomplished in exactly the same manner that all power is developed, by exercise.

23. This exercise consists in making an application of your knowledge. Knowledge will not apply itself. You must make the application. Abundance will not come to you out of the sky, neither will it drop into your lap, but a conscious realization of the law of attraction and the intention to bring it into operation for a certain, definite and specific purpose, and the will to carry out this purpose will bring about the materialization of your desire by a natural law of transference. If you are in business, it will increase and develop along regular channels, possibly new or unusual channels of distribution will be opened and when the law becomes fully operative, you will find that the things you seek are seeking you.

24. This week select a blank space on the wall, or any other convenient spot, from where you usually sit, mentally draw a black horizontal line about six inches long, try to see the line as plainly as though it were painted on the wall; now mentally draw two vertical lines connecting with this horizontal line at either end; now draw another horizontal line connecting with the two vertical lines; now you have a square. Try to see the square perfectly; when you can do so draw a circle within the square; now place a point in the center of the circle; now draw the point toward you about 10 inches; now you have a cone on a square base; you will remember that your work was all in black; change it to white, to red, to yellow.

25. If you can do this, you are making excellent progress and will soon be enabled to concentrate on any problem you may have in mind.

When any object or purpose is clearly held in thought, its precipitation, in tangible and visible form, is merely a question of time. The vision always precedes and itself determines the realization.

—LILLIAN WHITING

PART TEN.
STUDY QUESTIONS WITH ANSWERS

91. What is Wealth?
Wealth is the offspring of power.
92. Of what value are possessions?
Possessions are of value only as they confer power.
93. Of what value is a knowledge of cause and effect?
It enables men to plan courageously and execute fearlessly.
94. How does life originate in the inorganic world?
Only by the introduction of some living form. There is no other way.
95. What is the connecting link between the finite and the Infinite?
Thought is the connecting link.
96. Why is that so?
Because the Universal can manifest itself only through the individual.
97. Upon what does causation depend?
Upon polarity; a circuit must be formed; the Universal is the positive side of the battery of life, the individual is the negative, and thought forms the circuit.
98. Why do many fail to secure harmonious conditions?
They do not understand the law; there is no polarity; they have not formed the circuit.
99. What is the remedy?
A conscious recognition of the Law of Attraction with the intention of bring it into existence for a definite purpose.
100. What will be the result?
Thought will correlate with its object and bring it into manifestation, because thought is a product of the spiritual man, and spirit is the creative Principle of the Universe.

A vivid thought brings the power to paint it; and in proportion to the depth of its source is the force of its projection.

—EMERSON

Part Eleven

Your life is governed by law—by actual, immutable principles that never vary. Law is in operation at all times; in all places. Fixed laws underlie all human actions. For this reason, men who control giant industries are enabled to determine with absolute precision just what percentage of every hundred thousand people will respond to any given set of conditions.

It is well, however, to remember that while every effect is the result of a cause, the effect in turn becomes a cause, which creates other effects, which in turn create still other causes; so that when you put the Law of Attraction into operation you must remember that you are starting a train of causation for good or otherwise which may have endless possibilities.

We frequently hear it said, "A very distressing situation came into my life, which could not have been the result of my thought, as I certainly never entertained any thought which could have such a result." We fail to remember that like attracts like in the mental world, and that the thought which we entertain brings to us certain friendships, companionships of a particular kind, and these in turn bring about conditions and environment, which in turn are responsible for the conditions of which we complain.

1. Inductive reasoning is the process of the objective mind by which we compare a number of separate instances with one another until we see the common factor that gives rise to them all.

2. Induction proceeds by comparison of facts; it is this method of studying nature which has resulted in the discovery of a reign of law which has marked an epoch in human progress.

3. It is the dividing line between superstition and intelligence; it has eliminated the elements of uncertainty and caprice from men's lives and substituted law, reason, and certitude.

4. It is the "Watchman at the Gate" mentioned in a former lesson.

5. When, by virtue of this principle, the world to which the senses were accustomed had been revolutionized; when the sun had been arrested in his course, the apparently flat earth had been shaped into a ball and set whirling around him; when the inert matter had been resolved into active elements, and the universe presented itself wherever we directed

the telescope and microscope, full of force, motion and life; we are constrained to ask by what possible means the delicate forms of organization in the midst of it are kept in order and repair.

6. Like poles and like forces repel themselves or remain impenetrable to each other, and this cause seems in general sufficient to assign a proper place and distance to stars, men and forces. As men of different virtues enter into partnership, so do opposite poles attract each other, elements that have no property in common like acids and gases cling to each other in preference and a general exchange is kept up between the surplus and the demand.

7. As the eye seeks and receives satisfaction from colors complementary to those which are given, so do need, want and desire, in the largest sense, induce, guide and determine action.

8. It is our privilege to become conscious of the principle and act in accordance with it. Cuvier sees a tooth belonging to an extinct race of animals. This tooth wants a body for the performance of its function, and it defines the peculiar body it stands in need of with such precision that Cuvier is able to reconstruct the frame of this animal.

9. Perturbations are observed in the motion of Uranus. Leverrier needs another planet at a certain place to keep the solar system in order, and Neptune appears in the place and hour appointed.

10. The instinctive wants of the animal and the intellectual wants of Cuvier, the wants of nature and of the mind of Leverrier were alike, and thus the results; here the thoughts of an existence, there an existence. A well-defined lawful want, therefore, furnishes the reason for the more complex operations of nature.

11. Having recorded correctly the answers furnished by nature and stretched our senses with the growing science over her surface; having joined hands with the levers that move the earth; we become conscious of such a close, varied and deep contact with the world without, that our wants and purposes become no less identified with the harmonious operations of this vast organization, than the life, liberty, and happiness of the citizen is identified with the existence of his government.

12. As the interests of the individual are protected by the arms of the country, added to his own; and his needs may depend upon certain supply in the degree that they are felt more universally and steadily; in the same manner does conscious citizenship in the Republic of nature secure us from the annoyances of subordinate agents by alliance with superior powers; and by appeal to the fundamental laws of resistance or inducement offered to mechanical or chemical agents, distribute the labor to be performed between them and man to the best advantage of the inventor.

13. If Plato could have witnessed the pictures executed by the sun with the assistance of the photographer, or a hundred similar illustrations of what man does by induction, he would perhaps have been reminded of the intellectual midwifery of his master and, in his own mind might have arisen the vision of a land where all manual, mechanical labor and repetition is assigned to the power of nature, where our wants are satisfied by purely mental operations set in motion by the will, and where the supply is created by the demand.

14. However distant that land may appear, induction has taught men to make strides toward it and has surrounded him with benefits which are, at the same time, rewards for past fidelity and incentives for more assiduous devotion.

15. It is also an aid in concentrating and strengthening our faculties for the remaining part, giving unerring solution for individual as well as universal problems, by the mere operations of mind in the purest form.

16. Here we find a method, the spirit of which is, to believe that what is sought has been accomplished, in order to accomplish it: a method, bequeathed upon us by the same Plato who, outside of this sphere, could never find how the ideas became realities.

17. This conception is also elaborated by Swedenborg in his doctrine of correspondences; and a still greater teacher has said, "What things soever ye desire, when ye pray, believe that ye receive them, and ye shall have them." (Mark 11:24) The difference of the tenses in this passage is remarkable.

18. We are first to believe that our desire has already been fulfilled, its accomplishment will then follow. This is a concise direction for making use of the creative power of thought by impressing on the Universal subjective mind, the particular thing which we desire as an already existing fact.

19. We are thus thinking on the plane of the absolute and eliminating all consideration of conditions of limitation and are planting a seed which, if left undisturbed, will finally germinate into external fruition.

20. To review: Inductive reasoning is the process of the objective mind, by which we compare a number of separate instances with one another until we see the common factor that gives rise to them all. We see people in every civilized country on the globe, securing results by some process which they do not seem to understand themselves, and to which they usually attach more or less mystery. Our reason is given to us for the purpose of ascertaining the law by which these results are accomplished.

21. The operation of this thought process is seen in those fortunate natures that possess everything that others must acquire by toil, who never have a struggle with conscience because they always act correctly, and can never conduct themselves otherwise than with tact, learn everything easily, complete everything they begin with a happy knack, live in eternal harmony with themselves, without ever reflecting much what they do, or ever experiencing difficulty or toil.

22. The fruit of this thought is, as it were, a gift of the gods, but a gift which few as yet realize, appreciate, or understand. The recognition of the marvelous power which is possessed by the mind under proper conditions and the fact that this power can be utilized, directed, and made available for the solution of every human problem is of transcendental importance.

23. All truth is the same, whether stated in modern scientific terms or in the language of apostolic times. There are timid souls who fail to realize that the very completeness of truth requires various statements—that no one human formula will show every side of it.

24. Changing, emphasis, new language, novel interpretations, unfamiliar perspectives, are not, as some suppose, signs of departure from truth but on the contrary, they are evidence that the truth is being apprehended in new relations to human needs, and is becoming more generally understood.

25. The truth must be told to each generation and to every people in new and different terms, so that when the Great Teacher said—"Believe that ye receive and ye shall receive" or, when Paul said—"Faith is the substance of things hoped for, the evidence of things not seen" or, when modern science says—"The Law of Attraction is the law by which thought correlates with its object," each statement when subjected to analysis, is found to contain exactly the same truth. The only difference being in the form of presentation.

26. We are standing on the threshold of a new era. The time has arrived when man has learned the secrets of mastery and the way is being prepared for a new social order, more wonderful than anything ever heretofore dreamed of. The conflict of modern science with theology, the study of comparative religions, the tremendous power of new social movements, all of these are but clearing the way for the new order. They may have destroyed traditional forms which have become antiquated and impotent, but nothing of value has been lost.

27. A new faith has been born, a faith which demands a new form of expression, and this faith is taking form in a deep consciousness of power which is being manifested, in the present spiritual activity found on every hand.

28. The spirit which sleeps in the mineral, breathes in the vegetable, moves in the animal and reaches its highest development in man is the Universal Mind, and it behooves us to span the gulf between being and doing, theory and practice, by demonstrating our understanding of the dominion which we have been given.

29. By far the greatest discovery of all the centuries is the power of thought. The importance of this discovery has been a little slow in reaching the general consciousness, but it has arrived, and already in every field of research the importance of this greatest of all great discoveries is being demonstrated.

30. You ask in what does the creative power of thought consist? It consists in creating ideas, and these in turn objectify themselves by appropriating, inventing, observing, discerning, discovering, analyzing, ruling, governing, combining, and applying matter and force. It can do this because it is an intelligent creative power.

31. Thought reaches its loftiest activity when plunged into its own mysterious depth; when it breaks through the narrow compass of self and passes from truth to truth to the region of eternal light, where all which is, was or ever will be, melt into one grand harmony.

32. From this process of self-contemplation comes inspiration which is creative intelligence, and which is undeniably superior to every element, force or law of nature, because it can understand, modify, govern and apply them to its own ends and purposes and therefore possess them.

33. Wisdom begins with the dawn of reason, and reason is but an understanding of the knowledge and principles whereby we may know the true meaning of things. Wisdom, then, is illuminated reason, and this wisdom leads to humility, for humility is a large part of Wisdom.

34. We all know many who have achieved the seemingly impossible, who have realized lifelong dreams, who have changed everything including themselves. We have sometimes marveled at the demonstration of an apparently irresistible power, which seemed

to be ever available just when it was most needed, but it is all clear now. All that is required is an understanding of certain definite fundamental principles and their proper application.

35. For your exercise this week, concentrate on the quotation taken from the Bible, "Whatsoever things ye desire, when ye pray, believe that ye receive them and ye shall have them"; notice that there is no limitation, "Whatsoever things" is very definite and implies that the only limitation which is placed upon us in our ability to think, to be equal to the occasion, to rise to the emergency, to remember that Faith is not a shadow, but a substance, "the substance of things hoped for, the evidence of things not seen."

Death is but the natural process whereby all material forms are thrown into the crucible for reproduction in fresh diversity.

PART ELEVEN. STUDY QUESTIONS WITH ANSWERS

101. What is inductive reasoning?
The process of the objective mind by which we compare a number of separate instances with each other until we see the common factor which gives rise to them all.
102. What has this method of studying accomplished?
It has resulted in the discovery of a reign of law which has marked an epoch in human progress.
103. What is it that guides and determines action?
It is need, want and desire which in the largest sense induce, guide and determine action.
104. What is the formula for the unerring solution of every individual problem?
We are to believe that our desire has already been fulfilled; its accomplishment will then follow.
105. What great Teachers advocated it?
Jesus, Plato, Swedenborg.
106. What is the result of this thought process?
We are thinking on the plane of the absolute and planting a seed, which if left undisturbed will germinate into fruition.
107. Why is it scientifically exact?
Because it is natural law.
108. What is Faith?
"Faith is the substance of things hoped for, the evidence of things unseen."
109. What is the Law of Attraction?
The law by which Faith is brought into manifestation.
110. What importance do you attach to an understanding of this law?
It has eliminated the elements of uncertainty and caprice from men's lives and substituted law, reason, and certitude.

Part Twelve

Part Twelve is enclosed herewith. In the fourth paragraph you will find the following statement: "You must first have the knowledge of your power; second, the courage to dare; third, the faith to do." If you concentrate upon the thoughts given, if you give them your entire attention, you will find a world of meaning in each sentence, and will attract to yourself other thoughts in harmony with them, and you will soon grasp the full significance of the vital knowledge upon which you are concentrating.

Knowledge does not apply itself; we as individuals must make the application, and the application consists in fertilizing the thought with a living purpose.

The time and thought which most persons waste in aimless effort would accomplish wonders if properly directed with some special object in view. In order to do this, it is necessary to center your mental force upon a specific thought and hold it there, to the exclusion of all other thoughts. If you have ever looked through the viewfinder of a camera, you found that when the object was not in focus, the impression was indistinct and possibly blurred, but when the proper focus was obtained the picture was clear and distinct. This illustrates the power of concentration. Unless you can concentrate upon the object which you have in view, you will have but a hazy, indifferent, vague, indistinct and blurred outline of your ideal and the results will be in accordance with your mental picture.

1. There is no purpose in life that cannot be best accomplished through a scientific understanding of the creative power of thought.

2. This power to think is common to all. Man is, because he thinks. Man's power to think is infinite, consequently his creative power is unlimited.

3. We know that thought is building for us the thing we think of and actually bringing it nearer, yet we find it difficult to banish fear, anxiety or discouragement, all of which are powerful thought forces, and which continually send the things we desire further away, so that it is often one step forward and two steps backward.

4. The only way to keep from going backward is to keep going forward. Eternal vigilance is the price of success. There are three steps, and each one is absolutely essential. You must first have the knowledge of your power; second, the courage to dare; third, the faith to do.

5. With this as a basis you can construct an ideal business, an ideal home, ideal friends, and an ideal environment. You are not restricted as to material or cost. Thought is omnipotent and has the power to draw on the Infinite bank of primary substance for all that it requires. Infinite resources are therefore at your command.

6. But your ideal must be sharp, clear-cut, definite; to have one ideal today, another tomorrow, and a third next week, means to scatter your forces and accomplish nothing; your result will be a meaningless and chaotic combination of wasted material.

7. Unfortunately this is the result which many are securing, and the cause is self-evident. If a sculptor started out with a piece of marble and a chisel and changed his ideal every fifteen minutes, what result could he expect? And why should you expect any different result in molding the greatest and most plastic of all substances, the only real substance?

8. The result of this indecision and negative thought is often found in the loss of material wealth. Supposed independence which required many years of toil and effort suddenly disappears. It is often found then that money and property are not independence at all. On the contrary, the only independence is found to be a practical working knowledge of the creative power of thought.

9. This practical working method cannot come to you until you learn that the only real power which you can have is the power to adjust yourself to Divine and unchangeable principles. You cannot change the Infinite, but you can come into an understanding of natural laws. The reward of this understanding is a conscious realization of your ability to adjust your thought faculties with the Universal Thought which is Omnipresent. Your ability to cooperate with this Omnipotence will indicate the degree of success with which you meet.

10. The power of thought has many counterfeits which are more or less fascinating, but the results are harmful instead of helpful.

11. Of course, worry, fear, and all negative thoughts produce a crop after their kind; those who harbor thoughts of this kind must inevitably reap what they have sown.

12. Again, there are the Phenomena seekers who gormandize on the so-called proofs and demonstration obtained at materializing séances. They throw open their mental doors and soak themselves in the most poisonous currents which can be found in the psychic world. They do not seem to understand that it is the ability to become negative, receptive and passive, and thus drain themselves of all their vital force, which enables them to bring about these vibratory thought forms.

13. There are also the Hindu worshippers, who see in the materializing phenomena which are performed by the so-called adepts, a source of power, forgetting, or never seeming to realize that as soon as the will is withdrawn the forms wither, and the vibratory forces of which they are composed vanish.

14. Telepathy, or thought transference, has received considerable attention, but as it requires a negative mental state on the part of the receiver, the practice is harmful. A thought may be sent with the intention of hearing or seeing, but it will bring the penalty attached to the inversion of the principle involved.

15. In many instances, hypnotism is positively dangerous to the subject as well as the

operator. No one familiar with the laws governing in the mental world would think of attempting to dominate the will of another, for by so doing, he will gradually (but surely) divest himself of his own power.

16. All of these perversions have their temporary satisfaction and for some a keen fascination, but there is an infinitely greater fascination in a true understanding of the world of power within, a power which increases with use; is permanent instead of fleeting; which not only is potent as a remedial agency to bring about the remedy for past error or results of wrong thinking, but is a prophylactic agency protecting us from all manner and form of danger, and finally is an actual creative force with which we can build new conditions and new environment.

17. The law is that thought will correlate with its object and bring forth in the material world the correspondence of the thing thought or produced in the mental world. We then discern the absolute necessity of seeing that every thought has the inherent germ of truth in order that the law of growth will bring into manifestation good, for good alone can confer any permanent power.

18. The principle which gives the thought the dynamic power to correlate with its object, and therefore to master every adverse human experience, is the Law of Attraction, which is another name for love. This is an eternal and fundamental principle, inherent in all things, in every system of Philosophy, in every Religion, and in every Science. There is no getting away from the law of love. It is feeling that imparts vitality to thought. Feeling is desire, and desire is love. Thought impregnated with love becomes invincible.

19. We find this truth emphasized wherever the power of thought is understood, the Universal Mind is not only Intelligence, but it is substance, and this substance is the attractive force which brings electrons together by the Law of Attraction so that they form atoms; the atoms in turn are brought together by the same law and form molecules; molecules take objective forms; and so we find that the law of love is the creative force behind every manifestation, not only of atoms, but of worlds, of the Universe, of everything of which the imagination can form any conception.

20. It is the operation of this marvelous Law of Attraction which has caused men in all ages and all times to believe that there must be some personal being who responded to their petitions and desires, and manipulated events in order to comply with their requirements.

21. It is the combination of Thought and Love which forms the irresistible force called the Law of Attraction. All natural laws are irresistible, the law of gravitation, or electricity, or any other law operates with mathematical exactitude. There is no variation; it is only the channel of distribution which may be imperfect. If a bridge falls, we do not attribute the collapse to any variation of the law of gravitation. If a light fails us, we do not conclude that the laws governing electricity cannot be depended upon, and if the Law of Attraction seems to be imperfectly demonstrated by an inexperienced or uninformed person, we are not to conclude that the greatest and most infallible law upon which the entire system of creation depends has been suspended. We should rather conclude that a little more understanding of the law is required, for the same reason that a correct solution of a difficult problem in Mathematics is not always readily and easily obtained.

22. Things are created in the mental or spiritual world before they appear in the outward act or event; by the simple process of governing our thought forces today, we help create the events which will come into our lives in the future, perhaps even tomorrow. Educated desire is the most potent means of bringing into action the Law of Attraction.

23. Man is so constituted that he must first create the tools, or implements by which he gains the power to think. The mind cannot comprehend an entirely new idea until a corresponding vibratory brain cell has been prepared to receive it. This explains why it is so difficult for us to receive or appreciate an entirely new idea; we have no brain cell capable of receiving it; we are therefore incredulous; we do not believe it.

24. If, therefore, you have not been familiar with the omnipotence of the Law of Attraction, and the scientific method by which it can be put into operation, or if you have not been familiar with the unlimited possibilities which it opens to those who are enabled to take advantage of the resources it offers, begin now and create the necessary brain cells which will enable you to comprehend the unlimited powers which may be yours by cooperating with natural law. This is done by concentration or attention.

25. The intention governs the attention. Power comes through repose. It is by concentration that deep thoughts, wise speech, and all forces of high potentiality are accomplished.

26. It is in the Silence that you get into touch with the Omnipotent power of the subconscious mind from which all power is evolved.

27. He who desires wisdom, power, or permanent success of any kind will find it only within; it is an unfoldment. The unthinking may conclude that the silence is very simple and easily attained, but it should be remembered that only in absolute silence may one come into contact with Divinity itself; may learn of the unchangeable law and open for himself the channels by which persistent practice and concentration lead to perfection.

28. This week go to the same room, take the same chair, the same position as previously; be sure to relax, let go, both mentally and physically; always do this; never try to do any mental work under pressure; see that there are no tense muscles or nerves, that you are entirely comfortable. Now realize your unity with omnipotence; get into touch with this power, come into a deep and vital understanding, appreciation, and realization of the fact that your ability to think is your ability to act upon the Universal Mind, and bring it into manifestation, realize that it will meet any and every requirement; that you have exactly the same potential ability which any individual ever did have or ever will have, because each is but an expression or manifestation of the One, all are parts of the whole, there is no difference in kind or quality, the only difference being one of degree.

Thought cannot conceive of anything that may not be brought to expression.
He who first uttered it may be only the suggester, but the doer will appear.

—WILSON

PART TWELVE.
STUDY QUESTIONS WITH ANSWERS

111. How may any purpose in life be best accomplished?
Through a scientific understanding of the spiritual nature of thought.

112. What three steps are absolutely essential?
The knowledge of our power, the courage to dare, the faith to do.

113. How is the practical working knowledge secured?
By an understanding of natural laws.

114. What is the reward of an understanding of these laws?
A conscious realization of our ability to adjust ourselves to Divine and unchanging principle.

115. What will indicate the degree of success with which we meet?
The degree in which we realize that we cannot change the Infinite but must cooperate with it.

116. What is the principle which gives thought its dynamic power?
The Law of Attraction, which rests on vibration, which in turn rests upon the law of love. Thought impregnated with love becomes invincible.

117. Why is this law irresistible?
Because it is a natural law. All natural laws are irresistible and unchangeable and act with mathematical exactitude. There is no deviation or variation.

118. Why then does it sometimes seem to be difficult to find the solution to our problems in life?
For the same reason that it is sometimes difficult to find the correct solution to a difficult mathematical problem. The operator is uninformed or inexperienced.

119. Why is it impossible for the mind to grasp an entirely new idea?
We have no corresponding vibratory brain cell capable of receiving the idea.

120. How is wisdom secured?
By concentration; it is an unfoldment; it comes from within.

Part Thirteen

Physical science is responsible for the marvelous age of invention in which we are now living, but spiritual science is now setting out on a career whose possibilities no one can foretell.

Spiritual science has previously been the football of the uneducated, the superstitious, the mystical, but men are now interested in definite methods and demonstrated facts only.

We have come to know that thinking is a spiritual process, that vision and imagination preceded action and event, that the day of the dreamer has come.

The following lines by Mr. Herbert Kaufman are interesting in this connection.

"They are the architects of greatness, their vision lies within their souls, they peer beyond the veils and mists of doubt and pierce the walls of unborn Time. The belted wheel, the trail of steel, the churning screw, are shuttles in the loom on which they weave their magic tapestries. Makers of Empire, they have fought for bigger things than crowns and higher seats than thrones. Your homes are set upon the land a dreamer found. The pictures on its walls are visions from a dreamer's soul. They are the chosen few—the blazers of the way. Walls crumble and Empires fall, the tidal wave sweeps from the sea and tears a fortress from its rocks. The rotting nations drop off from Time's bough, and only things the dreamers make live on."

Part Thirteen, which follows, tells why the dreams of the dreamer come true. It explains the law of causation by which dreamers, inventors, authors, financiers, bring about the realization of their desires. It explains the law by which the thing pictured upon our mind eventually becomes our own.

1. It has been the tendency, and, as might be proved, a necessity for science to seek the explanation of everyday facts by a generalization of those others which are less frequent and form the exception. Thus does the eruption of the volcano manifest the heat which is continually at work in the interior of the earth and to which the latter owes much of her configuration.

2. Thus does the lightning reveal a subtle power constantly busy to produce changes in the inorganic world, and, as dead languages now seldom heard were once ruling among the nations, so does a giant tooth in Siberia, or a fossil in the depth of the earth not only

bear record of the evolution of past ages but thereby explain to us the origin of the hills and valleys which we inhabit today.

3. In this way a generalization of facts which are rare, strange, or form the exception, has been the magnetic needle guiding to all the discoveries of inductive science.

4. This method is founded upon reason and experience and thereby destroyed superstition, precedent and conventionality.

5. It is almost three hundred years since Lord Bacon recommended this method of study, to which the civilized nations owe the greater part of their prosperity and the more valuable part of their knowledge; purging the mind from narrow prejudices, denominated theories, more effectually than by the keenest irony; calling the attention of men from heaven to earth more successfully by surprising experiments than by the most forcible demonstration of their ignorance; educating the inventive faculties more powerfully by the near prospect of useful discoveries thrown open to all, than by talk of bringing to light the innate laws of our mind.

6. The method of Bacon has seized the spirit and aim of the great philosophers of Greece and carried them into effect by the new means of observation which another age offered; thus gradually revealing a wondrous field of knowledge in the infinite space of astronomy, in the microscopic egg of embryology, and the dim age of geology; disclosing an order of the pulse which the logic of Aristotle could never have unveiled, and analyzing into formerly unknown elements the material combinations which no dialectic of the scholastics could force apart.

7. It has lengthened life; it has mitigated pain; it has extinguished diseases; it has increased the fertility of the soil; it has given new securities to the mariner; it has spanned great rivers with bridges of form unknown to our fathers; it has guided the thunderbolt from heaven to earth; it has lighted up night with the splendor of day; it has extended the range of human vision; it has multiplied the power of the human muscles; it has accelerated motion; it has annihilated distance; it has facilitated intercourse, correspondence, all friendly offices, all dispatch of business; it has enabled men to descend into the depths of the sea, to soar into the air, to penetrate securely into the noxious recesses of the earth.

8. This then is the true nature and scope of induction. But the greater the success which men have achieved in the inductive science, the more does the whole tenor of their teachings and example impress us with the necessity of observing carefully, patiently, accurately, with all the instruments and resources at our command the individual facts before venturing upon a statement of general laws.

9. To ascertain the bearing of the spark drawn from the electric machine under every variety of circumstances, that we thus may be emboldened with Franklin to address, in the form of a kite, the question to the cloud about the nature of the lightning. To assure ourselves of the manner in which bodies fall with the exactness of a Galileo, that with Newton we may dare to ask the moon about the force that fastens it to the earth.

10. In short, by the value we set upon truth, by our hope in a steady and universal progress, not to permit a tyrannical prejudice to neglect or mutilate unwelcome facts, but to rear the superstructure of science upon the broad and unchangeable basis, of full attention paid to the most isolated as well as the most frequent phenomena.

11. An ever-increasing material may be collected by observation, but the accumulated facts are of very different value for the explanation of nature, and as we esteem most highly those useful qualities of men which are of the rarest occurrence, so does natural philosophy sift the facts and attach a pre-eminent importance to that striking class which cannot be accounted for by the usual and daily observation of life.

12. If then, we find that certain persons seem to possess unusual power, what are we to conclude? First, we may say, it is not so, which is simply an acknowledgment of our lack of information because every honest investigator admits that there are many strange and previously unaccountable phenomena constantly taking place. Those, however, who become acquainted with the creative power of thought, will no longer consider them unaccountable.

13. Second, we may say that they are the result of supernatural interference, but a scientific understanding of natural laws will convince us that there is nothing supernatural. Every phenomenon is the result of an accurate definite cause, and the cause is an immutable law or principle, which operates with invariable precision, whether the law is put into operation consciously or unconsciously.

14. Third, we may say that we are on "forbidden ground," that there are some things which we should not know. This objection was used against every advance in human knowledge. Every individual who ever advanced a new idea, whether a Columbus, a Darwin, a Galileo, a Fulton or an Emerson, was subjected to ridicule or persecution; so that this objection should receive no serious consideration; but, on the contrary, we should carefully consider every fact which is brought to our attention; by doing this we will more readily ascertain the law upon which it is based.

15. It will be found that the creative power of thought will explain every possible condition or experience, whether physical, mental or spiritual.

16. Thought will bring about conditions in correspondence with the predominant mental attitude. Therefore, if we fear disaster, as fear is a powerful form of thought, disaster will be the certain result of our thinking. It is this form of thought which frequently sweeps away the result of many years of toil and effort.

17. If we think of some form of material wealth we may secure it. By concentrated thought the required conditions will be brought about, and the proper effort put forth, which will result in bringing about the circumstances necessary to realize our desires; but we often find that when we secure the things we thought we wanted, they do not have the effect we expected. That is, the satisfaction is only temporary, or possibly is the reverse of what we expected.

18. What, then, is the proper method of procedure? What are we to think in order to secure what we really desire? What you and I desire, what we all desire, what every one is seeking, is Happiness and Harmony. If we can be truly happy we shall have everything the world can give. If we are happy ourselves we can make others happy.

19. But we cannot be happy unless we have health, strength, congenial friends, pleasant environment, sufficient supply, not only to take care of our necessities but to provide for those comforts and luxuries to which we are entitled.

20. The old orthodox way of thinking was to be "a worm," to be satisfied with our portion whatever it is; but the modern idea is to know that we are entitled to the best of every-

thing, that the "Father and I are one" and that the "Father" is the Universal Mind, the Creator, the Original Substance from which all things proceed.

21. Now admitting that this is all true in theory, and it has been taught for two thousand years, and is the essence of every system of Philosophy or Religion, how are we to make it practical in our lives? How are we to get the actual, tangible results here and now?

22. In the first place, we must put our knowledge into practice. Nothing can be accomplished in any other way. The athlete may read books and lessons on physical training all his life, but unless he begins to give out strength by actual work he will never receive any strength; he will eventually get exactly what he gives; but he will have to give it first. It is exactly the same with us; we will get exactly what we give, but we shall have to give it first. It will then return to us many fold, and the giving is simply a mental process, because thoughts are causes and conditions are effects; therefore in giving thoughts of courage, inspiration, health or help of any kind we are setting causes in motion which will bring about their effect.

23. Thought is a spiritual activity and is therefore creative, but make no mistake, thought will create nothing unless it is consciously, systematically, and constructively directed; and herein is the difference between idle thinking, which is simply a dissipation of effort, and constructive thinking, which means practically unlimited achievement.

24. We have found that everything we get comes to us by the Law of Attraction. A happy thought cannot exist in an unhappy consciousness; therefore the consciousness must change, and, as the consciousness changes, all conditions necessary to meet the changed consciousness must gradually change, in order to meet the requirements of the new situation.

25. In creating a Mental Image or an Ideal, we are projecting a thought into the Universal Substance from which all things are created. This Universal Substance is Omnipresent, Omnipotent and Omniscient. Are we to inform the Omniscient as to the proper channel to be used to materialize our demand? Can the finite advise the Infinite? This is the cause of failure; of every failure. We recognize the Omnipresence of the Universal Substance, but we fail to appreciate the fact that this substance is not only Omnipresent, but is Omnipotent and Omniscient, and consequently will set causes in motion concerning which we may be entirely ignorant.

26. We can best conserve our interests by recognizing the Infinite Power and Infinite Wisdom of the Universal Mind, and in this way become a channel whereby the Infinite can bring about the realization of our desire. This means that recognition brings about realization, therefore for your exercise this week make use of the principle, recognize the fact that you are a part of the whole, and that a part must be the same in kind and quality as the whole; the only difference there can possibly be, is in degree.

27. When this tremendous fact begins to permeate your consciousness, when you really come into a realization of the fact that you (not your body, but the Ego), the "I," the spirit which thinks is an integral part of the great whole, that it is the same in substance, in quality, in kind, that the Creator could create nothing different from Himself, you will also be able to say, "The Father and I are one" and you will come into an understanding of the beauty, the grandeur, the transcendental opportunities which have been placed at your disposal.

Increase in me that wisdom which discovers my truest interest,
strengthen my resolution to perform that which wisdom dictates.

—FRANKLIN

PART THIRTEEN.
STUDY QUESTIONS WITH ANSWERS

121. What is the method by which natural philosophers obtain and apply their knowledge?

To observe individual facts carefully, patiently, accurately, with all the instruments and resources at their command, before venturing upon a statement of general laws.

122. How may we be certain that this method is correct?

By not permitting a tyrannical prejudice to neglect or mutilate unwelcome facts.

123. What classes of facts are esteemed most highly?

Those which cannot be accounted for by the usual daily observation of life.

124. Upon what is this principle founded?

Upon reason and experience.

125. What does it destroy?

Superstition, precedent and conventionality.

126. How have these laws been discovered?

By a generalization of facts which are uncommon, rare, strange and form the exception.

127. How may we account for much of the strange and heretofore unexplainable phenomena which are constantly taking place?

By the creative power of thought.

128. Why is this so?

Because when we learn of a fact we can be sure that it is the result of a certain definite cause and that this cause will operate with invariable precision.

129. What is the result of this knowledge?

It will explain the cause of every possible condition, whether physical, mental or spiritual.

130. How will our best interest be conserved?

By a recognition of the fact that a knowledge of the creative nature of thought puts us in touch with Infinite power.

Part Fourteen

You have found from your study thus far that thought is a spiritual activity and is therefore endowed with creative power. This does not mean that some thought is creative, but that all thought is creative. This same principle can be brought into operation in a negative way, through the process of denial.

The conscious and subconscious are but two phases of action in connection with one mind. The relation of the subconscious to the conscious is quite analogous to that existing between a weather vane and the atmosphere.

Just as the least pressure of the atmosphere causes an action on the part of the weather vane, so does the least thought entertained by the conscious mind produce within your subconscious mind action in exact proportion to the depth of feeling characterizing the thought and the intensity with which the thought is indulged.

It follows that if you deny unsatisfactory conditions, you are withdrawing the creative power of your thought from these conditions. You are cutting them away at the root. You are sapping their vitality.

Remember that the law of growth necessarily governs every manifestation in the objective, so that a denial of unsatisfactory conditions will not bring about instant change. A plant will remain visible for some time after its roots have been cut, but it will gradually fade away and eventually disappear, so the withdrawal of your thought from the contemplation of unsatisfactory conditions will gradually, but surely, terminate these conditions.

You will see that this is an exactly opposite course from the one which we would naturally be inclined to adopt.

It will therefore have an exactly opposite effect to the one usually secured. Most persons concentrate intently upon unsatisfactory conditions, thereby giving the condition that measure of energy and vitality which is necessary in order to supply a vigorous growth.

1. The Universal Energy in which all motion, light, heat, and color have their origin, does not partake of the limitation of the many effects of which it is the cause, but it is supreme over them all. This Universal Substance is the source of all Power, Wisdom and Intelligence.

2. To recognize this Intelligence is to acquaint yourself with the knowing quality of

Mind and through it to move upon the Universal Substance, and bring it into harmonious relations in your affairs.

3. This is something that the most learned physical science teacher has not attempted—a field of discovery upon which he has not yet launched; in fact, but few of the materialistic schools have ever caught the first ray of this light. It does not seem to have dawned upon them that wisdom is just as much present everywhere as are force and substance.

4. Some will say, if these principles are true, why are we not demonstrating them? As the fundamental principle is obviously correct, why do we not get proper results? We do. We get results in exact accordance with our understanding of the law and our ability to make the proper application. We secured no results from the laws governing electricity until someone formulated the law and showed us how to apply it.

5. This puts us in an entirely new relation to our environment, opening up possibilities previously undreamed of, and this by an orderly sequence of law which is naturally involved in our new mental attitude.

6. Mind is creative and the principle upon which this law is based is sound and legitimate and is inherent in the nature of things; but this creative power does not originate in the individual, but in the Universal, which is the source and fountain of all energy and substance, the individual is simply the channel for the distribution of this energy. The individual is the means by which the Universal produces the various combinations which result in the formation of phenomena.

7. We know that scientists have resolved matter into an immense number of molecules; these molecules have been resolved into atoms, and the atoms into electrons. The discovery of electrons in high vacuum glass tubes containing fused terminals of hard metal indicates conclusively that these electrons fill all space; that they exist everywhere, that they are omnipresent. They fill all material bodies and occupy the whole of what we call empty space. This, then, is the Universal Substance from which all things proceed.

8. Electrons would forever remain electrons unless directed where to go to be assembled into atoms and molecules, and this director is Mind. A number of electrons revolving around a center of force constitutes an atom; atoms unite in absolutely regular mathematical ratios and form molecules, and these unite with each other to form a multitude of compounds which unite to build the Universe.

9. The lightest known atom is hydrogen and this is 1,700 times heavier than an electron. An atom of mercury is 300,000 times heavier than an electron. Electrons are pure negative electricity, and as they have the same potential velocity as all other cosmic energy, such as heat, light, electricity and thought, neither time nor space require consideration. The manner in which the velocity of light was ascertained is interesting.

10. The velocity of light was obtained by the Danish astronomer Roemer in 1676, by observing the eclipses of Jupiter's moons. When the earth was nearest to Jupiter, the eclipse appeared about eight and one-half minutes too soon for the calculations, and when the earth was most remote from Jupiter, they were about eight and one-half minutes too late. Roemer concluded the reason to be that it required 17 minutes for light

from the planet to traverse the diameter of the earth's orbit, which measured the difference of the distances of the earth from Jupiter. This calculation has since been verified, and proves that light travels about 186,000 miles a second.

11. Electrons manifest in the body as cells, and possess mind and intelligence sufficient for them to perform their functions in the human physical anatomy. Every part of the body is composed of cells, some of which operate independently; others in communities. Some are busy building tissue, while others are engaged in forming the various secretions necessary for the body. Some act as carriers of material; others are the surgeons whose work it is to repair damage; others are scavengers, carrying off waste; others are constantly ready to repel invaders or other undesirable intruders of the germ family.

12. All these cells are moving for a common purpose and each one is not only a living organism, but has sufficient intelligence to enable it to perform its necessary duties. It is also endowed with sufficient intelligence to conserve the energies and perpetuate its own life. It must, therefore, secure sufficient nourishment and it has been found that it exercises choice in the selection of such nourishment.

13. Each cell is born, reproduces itself, dies and is absorbed. The maintenance of health and life itself depends upon the constant regeneration of these cells.

14. It is therefore apparent that there is mind in every atom of the body; this mind is negative mind, and the power of the individual to think makes him positive, so that he can control this negative mind. This is the scientific explanation for metaphysical healing, and will enable anyone to understand the principle upon which this remarkable phenomenon rests.

15. This negative mind, which is contained in every cell of the body, has been called the subconscious mind, because it acts without our conscious knowledge. We have found that this subconscious mind is responsive to the will of the conscious mind.

16. All things have their origin in mind, and appearances are the result of thought. So that we see that things in themselves have no origin, permanency, or reality. Since they are produced by thought, they can be erased by thought.

17. In mental, as in natural science, experiments are being made and each discovery lifts man one step higher toward his possible goal. We find that every man is the reflection of the thought he has entertained during his lifetime. This is stamped on his face, his form, his character, his environment.

18. Back of every effect there is a cause, and if we follow the trail to its starting point, we shall find the creative principle out of which it grew. Proofs of this are now so complete that this truth is generally accepted.

19. The objective world is controlled by an unseen and, heretofore, unexplainable power. We have, heretofore, personalized this power and called it God. We have now, however, learned to look upon it as the permeating essence or Principle of all that exists—the Infinite or Universal Mind.

20. The Universal Mind, being infinite and omnipotent, has unlimited resources at its command, and when we remember that it is also omnipresent, we cannot escape the conclusion that we must be an expression or manifestation of that Mind.

21. A recognition and understanding of the resources of the subconscious mind will

indicate that the only difference between the subconscious and the Universal is one of degree. They differ only as a drop of water differs from the ocean. They are the same in kind and quality, the difference is one of degree only.

22. Do you, can you, appreciate the value of this all-important fact; do you realize that a recognition of this tremendous fact places you in touch with Omnipotence? The subconscious mind being the connecting link between the Universal Mind and the conscious mind, is it not evident that the conscious mind can consciously suggest thoughts which the subconscious mind will put into action, and as the subconscious is one with the Universal, is it not evident that no limit can be placed upon its activities?

23. A scientific understanding of this principle will explain the wonderful results which are secured through the power of prayer. The results which are secured in this way are not brought about by any special dispensations of providence, but on the contrary, they are the result of the operation of a perfectly natural law. There is, therefore, nothing either religious or mysterious about it.

24. Yet there are many who are not ready to enter into the discipline necessary to think correctly, even though it is evident that wrong thinking has brought failure.

25. Thought is the only reality; conditions are but the outward manifestations; as the thought changes, all outward or material conditions must change in order to be in harmony with their creator, which is thought.

26. But the thought must be clear-cut, steady, fixed, definite, unchangeable; you cannot take one step forward and two steps backward, neither can you spend twenty or thirty years of your life building up negative conditions as the result of negative thoughts, and then expect to see them all melt away as the result of fifteen or twenty minutes of right thinking.

27. If you enter into the discipline necessary to bring about a radical change in your life, you must do so deliberately, after giving the matter careful thought and full consideration, and then you must allow nothing to interfere with your decision.

28. This discipline, this change of thought, this mental attitude will not only bring you the material things which are necessary for your highest and best welfare, but will bring health and harmonious conditions generally.

29. If you wish harmonious conditions in your life, you must develop a harmonious mental attitude.

30. Your world without will be a reflection of your world within.

31. For your exercise this week, concentrate on Harmony, and when I say concentrate, I mean all that the word implies; concentrate so deeply, so earnestly, that you will be conscious of nothing but harmony. Remember, we learn by doing. Reading these lessons will get you nowhere. It is in the practical application that the value consists.

Learn to keep the door shut, keep out of your mind and out of your world, every element that seeks admittance with no definite helpful end in view.

—GEORGE MATHEW ADAMS

PART FOURTEEN.
STUDY QUESTIONS WITH ANSWERS

131. What is the source of all Wisdom, Power, and Intelligence?
The Universal Mind.

132. Where do all motion, light, heat, and color have their origin?
In the Universal Energy, which is one manifestation of the Universal Mind.

133. Where does the creative power of thought originate?
In the Universal Mind.

134. What is thought?
Mind in motion.

135. How is the Universal differentiated in form?
The individual is the means by which the Universal produces the various combinations which result in formation of phenomena.

136. How is this accomplished?
The power of the individual to think is his ability to act upon the Universal and bring it into manifestation.

137. What is the first form which the Universal takes so far as we know?
Electrons, which fill all space.

138. Where do all things have their origin?
In mind.

139. What is the result of a change of thought?
A change in conditions.

140. What is the result of a harmonious mental attitude?
Harmonious conditions in life.

Thought, immaterial though it may be, is the matrix that shapes the issues of life. The mind has been active in all fields during this fruitful century, but it is to science we must look for the thoughts that have shaped all thinking.

Part Fifteen

Experiments with parasites found on plants indicate that even the lowest order of life is enabled to take advantage of natural law. This experiment was made by Jacques Loch, M.D., Ph.D., a member of the Rockefeller Institute.

"In order to obtain the material, potted rose bushes are brought into a room and placed in front of a closed window. If the plants are allowed to dry out, the aphids (parasites), previously wingless, change to winged insects. After the metamorphosis, the animals leave the plants, fly to the window and then creep upward on the glass."

It is evident that these tiny insects found that the plants on which they had been thriving were dead, and that they could therefore secure nothing more to eat and drink from this source. The only method by which they could save themselves from starvation was to grow temporary wings and fly, which they did.

Experiments such as these indicate that Omniscience as well as Omnipotence is omnipresent and that the tiniest living thing can take advantage of it in an emergency.

Part Fifteen will tell you more about the law under which we live. It will explain that these laws operate to our advantage; that all conditions and experiences that come to us are for our benefit; that we gain strength in proportion to the effort expended, and that our happiness is best attained through a conscious cooperation with natural laws.

1. The laws under which we live are designed solely for our advantage. These laws are immutable and we cannot escape from their operation.

2. All the great eternal forces act in solemn silence, but it is in our power to place ourselves in harmony with them and thus express a life of comparative peace and happiness.

3. Difficulties, inharmonies, and obstacles indicate that we are either refusing to give out what we no longer need, or refusing to accept what we require.

4. Growth is attained through an exchange of the old for the new, of the good for the better; it is a conditional or reciprocal action, for each of us is a complete thought entity and this completeness makes it possible for us to receive only as we give.

5. We cannot obtain what we lack if we tenaciously cling to what we have. We are able to consciously control our conditions as we come to sense the purpose of what we attract, and are able to extract from each experience only what we require for our

further growth. Our ability to do this determines the degree of harmony or happiness we attain.

6. The ability to appropriate what we require for our growth continually increases as we reach higher planes and broader visions, and the greater our abilities to know what we require, the more certain we shall be to discern its presence, to attract it and to absorb it. Nothing may reach us except what is necessary for our growth.

7. All conditions and experiences that come to us do so for our benefit. Difficulties and obstacles will continue to come until we absorb their wisdom and gather from them the essentials of further growth.

8. That we reap what we sow is mathematically exact. We gain permanent strength exactly to the extent of the effort required to overcome difficulties.

9. The inexorable requirements of growth demand that we exert the greatest degree of attraction for what is perfectly in accord with us. Our highest happiness will be best attained through our understanding of, and conscious cooperation with natural laws.

10. In order to possess vitality thought must be impregnated with love. Love is a product of the emotions. It is therefore essential that the emotions be controlled and guided by the intellect and reason.

11. It is love which imparts vitality to thought and thus enables it to germinate. The Law of Attraction, or the law of love, for they are one and the same, will bring to it the necessary material for its growth and maturity.

12. The first form which thought will find is language, or words; this determines the importance of words; they are the first manifestation of thought—the vessels in which thought is carried. They take hold of the ether and by setting it in motion reproduce the thought to others in the form of sound.

13. Thought may lead to action of any kind, but whatever the action, it is simply the thought attempting to express itself in visible form. It is evident, therefore, that if we wish desirable conditions, we can afford to entertain only desirable thoughts.

14. This leads to the inevitable conclusion that if we wish to express abundance in our lives, we can afford to think abundance only, and as words are only thoughts taking form, we must be especially careful to use nothing but constructive and harmonious language, which when finally crystallized into objective forms, will prove to our advantage.

15. We cannot escape from the pictures we incessantly photograph on the mind, and this photography of erroneous conceptions is exactly what is being done by the use of words, when we use any form of language which is not identified with our welfare.

16. We manifest more and more life as our thought becomes clarified and takes higher planes. This is obtained with greater facility as we use word pictures that are clearly defined, and relieved of the conceptions attached to them on lower planes of thought.

17. It is with words that we must express our thoughts, and if we are to make use of higher forms of truth, we may use only such material as has been carefully and intelligently selected with this purpose in view.

18. This wonderful power of clothing thoughts in the form of words is what differentiates man from the rest of the animal kingdom; by the use of the written word he has been enabled to look back over the centuries and see the stirring scenes by which he has come into his present inheritance.

19. He has been enabled to come into communion with the greatest writers and thinkers of all time, and the combined record which we possess today is therefore the expression of Universal Thought as it has been seeking to take form in the mind of Man.

20. We know that the Universal Thought has for its goal the creation of form, and we know that the individual thought is likewise forever attempting to express itself in form, and we know that the word is a thought form, and a sentence is a combination of thought forms, therefore, if we wish our ideal to be beautiful or strong, we must see that the words out of which this temple will eventually be created are exact, that they are put together carefully, because accuracy in building words and sentences is the highest form of architecture in civilization and is a passport to success.

21. Words are thoughts and are therefore an invisible and invincible power which will finally objectify themselves in the form they are given.

22. Words may become mental places that will live forever, or they may become shacks which the first breeze will carry away. They may delight the eye as well as the ear; they may contain all knowledge; in them we find the history of the past as well as the hope of the future; they are living messengers from which every human and superhuman activity is born.

23. The beauty of the word consists in the beauty of the thought; the power of the word consists in the power of the thought, and the power of the thought consists in its vitality. How shall we identify a vital thought? What are its distinguishing characteristics? It must have principle. How shall we identify principle?

24. There is a principle of Mathematics, but none of error; there is a principle of health, but none of disease; there is a principle of truth, but none of dishonesty; there is a principle of light, but none of darkness, and there is a principle of abundance, but none of poverty.

25. How shall we know that this is true? Because if we apply the principle of Mathematics correctly we shall be certain of our results. Where there is health there will be no disease. If we know the Truth we cannot be deceived by error. If we let in light there can be no darkness, and where there is abundance there can be no poverty.

26. These are self-evident facts, but the all-important truth that a thought containing principle is vital and therefore contains life and consequently takes root, and eventually but surely and certainly displaces the negative thoughts, which by their very nature can contain no vitality, is one which seems to have been overlooked.

27. But this is a fact which will enable you to destroy every manner of discord, lack and limitation.

28. There can be no question but that he who "is wise enough to understand" will readily recognize that the creative power of thought places an invincible weapon in his hands and makes him a master of destiny.

29. In the physical world there is a law of compensation which is that "the appearance of a given amount of energy anywhere means the disappearance of the same amount somewhere else," and so we find that we can get only what we give; if we pledge ourselves to a certain action we must be prepared to assume the responsibility for the development of that action. The subconscious cannot reason. It takes us at our word; we have asked for

something; we are now to receive it; we have made our bed, we are now to lie in it; the die has been cast; the threads will carry out the pattern we have made.

30. For this reason Insight must be exercised so that the thought which we entertain contains no mental, moral or physical germ which we do not wish objectified in our lives.

31. Insight is a faculty of the mind whereby we are enabled to examine facts and conditions at long range, a kind of human telescope; it enables us to understand the difficulties, as well as the possibilities, in any undertaking.

32. Insight enables us to be prepared for the obstacles which we shall meet; we can therefore overcome them before they have any opportunity of causing difficulty.

33. Insight enables us to plan to advantage and turn our thought and attention in the right direction, instead of into channels which can yield no possible return.

34. Insight is therefore absolutely essential for the development of any great achievement, but with it we may enter, explore and possess any mental field.

35. Insight is a product of the world within and is developed in the Silence, by concentration.

36. For your exercise this week, concentrate on Insight; take your accustomed position and focus the thought on the fact that to have a knowledge of the creative power of thought does not mean to possess the art of thinking. Let the thought dwell on the fact that knowledge does not apply itself. That our actions are not governed by knowledge, but by custom, precedent and habit. That the only way we can get ourselves to apply knowledge is by a determined conscious effort. Call to mind the fact that knowledge unused passes from the mind, that the value of the information is in the application of the principle; continue this line of thought until you gain sufficient insight to formulate a definite program for applying this principle to your own particular problem.

Think truly, and thy thoughts shall the world's famine feed; Speak truly, and each word of thine shall be a fruitful seed; Live truly, and thy life shall be a great and noble creed.

—HORATIO BONAR

PART FIFTEEN.
STUDY QUESTIONS WITH ANSWERS

141. What determines the degree of harmony which we attain?

Our ability to appropriate what we require for our growth from each experience.

142. What do difficulties and obstacles indicate?

That they are necessary for our wisdom and spiritual growth.

143. How may these difficulties be avoided?

By a conscious understanding of and cooperation with natural laws.

144. What is the principle by which thought manifests itself in form?

The Law of Attraction.

145. How is the necessary material secured by which the growth, development and maturity of the idea take form?

The law of love, which is the creative principle of the Universe, imparts vitality to the thought, and the Law of Attraction brings the necessary substance by the law of growth.

146. How are desirable conditions secured?
By entertaining desirable thoughts only.
147. How are undesirable conditions brought about?
By thinking, discussing and visualizing conditions of lack, limitation, disease, inharmony and discord of every kind. This mental photography of erroneous conceptions is taken up by the subconscious and the law of attraction will inevitably crystallize it into objective form. That we reap what we sow is scientifically exact.
148. How can we overcome every kind of fear, lack, limitation, poverty, and discord?
By substituting principle for error.
149. How may we recognize principle?
By a conscious realization of the fact that Truth invariably destroys error. We do not have to laboriously shovel the darkness out; all that is necessary is to turn on the light. The same principle applies to every form of negative thought.
150. What is the value of Insight?
It enables us to understand the value of making application of the knowledge which we gain. Many seem to think that knowledge will automatically apply itself, which is by no means true.

To every man there openeth a way, And the high soul climbs the high way,
And the low soul gropes the low; And in between on the misty flats,
The rest drift to and fro. But to every man there openeth A high way
and a low And every man decideth The way his soul shall go.

Part Sixteen

The vibratory activities of the planetary Universe are governed by a law of periodicity. Everything that lives has periods of birth, growth, fruitage, and decline. These periods are governed by the Septimal Law.

The Law of Sevens governs the days of the week, the phases of the moon, the harmonies of sound, light, heat, electricity, magnetism, atomic structure. It governs the life of individuals and of nations, and it dominates the activities of the commercial world.

Life is growth, and growth is change; each seven-year period takes us into a new cycle. The first seven years is the period of infancy. The next seven the period of childhood, representing the beginning of individual responsibility. The next seven represents the period of adolescence. The fourth period marks the attainment of full growth. The fifth period is the constructive period, when men begin to acquire property, possessions, a home and family. The next from 35 to 42, is a period of reactions and changes, and this in turn is followed by a period of reconstruction, adjustment and recuperation, so as to be ready for a new cycle of sevens, beginning with the fiftieth year.

There are many who think that the world is just about to pass out of the sixth period; that it will soon enter into the seventh period, the period of readjustment, reconstruction and harmony; the period which is frequently referred to as the Millennium.

Those familiar with these cycles will not be disturbed when things seem to go wrong, but can apply the principle outlined in these lessons with the full assurance that a higher law will invariably control all other laws, and that through an understanding and conscious operation of spiritual laws, we can convert every seeming difficulty into a blessing.

1. Wealth is a product of labor. Capital is an effect, not a cause; a servant, not a master; a means, not an end.

2. The most commonly accepted definition of wealth is that it consists of all useful and agreeable things which possess exchange value. It is this exchange value which is the predominant characteristic of wealth.

3. When we consider the small addition made by wealth to the happiness of the possessor, we find that the true value consists not in its utility but in its exchange.

4. This exchange value makes it a medium for securing the things of real value whereby our ideals may be realized.

5. Wealth should then never be desired as an end, but simply as a means of accomplishing an end. Success is contingent upon a higher ideal than the mere accumulation of riches, and he who aspires to such success must formulate an ideal for which he is willing to strive.

6. With such an ideal in mind, the ways and means can and will be provided, but the mistake must not be made of substituting the means for the end. There must be a definite fixed purpose, an ideal.

7. Prentice Mulford said: "The man of success is the man possessed of the greatest spiritual understanding and every great fortune comes of superior and truly spiritual power." Unfortunately, there are those who fail to recognize this power; they forget that Andrew Carnegie's mother had to help support the family when they came to America, that Harriman's father was a poor clergyman with a salary of only $200 a year, that Sir Thomas Lipton started with only 25 cents. These men had no other power to depend upon, but it did not fail them.

8. The power to create depends entirely upon spiritual power; there are three steps, idealization, visualization and materialization. Every captain of industry depends upon this power exclusively. In an article in *Everybody's Magazine,* Henry M. Flagler, the Standard Oil multi-millionaire, admitted that the secret of his success was his power to see a thing in its completeness. The following conversation with the reporter shows his power of idealization, concentration and visualization, all spiritual powers:

9. "Did you actually vision to yourself the whole thing? I mean, did you, or could you, really close your eyes and see the tracks? And the trains running? And hear the whistles blowing? Did you go as far as that?" "Yes." "How clearly?" "Very clearly."

10. Here we have a vision of the law, we see "cause and effect," we see that thought necessarily precedes and determines action. If we are wise, we shall come into a realization of the tremendous fact that no arbitrary condition can exist for a moment, and that human experience is the result of an orderly and harmonious sequence.

11. The successful businessman is more often than not an idealist and is ever striving for higher and higher standards. The subtle forces of thought as they crystallize in our daily moods is what constitutes life.

12. Thought is the plastic material with which we build images of our growing conception of life. Use determines its existence. As in all other things our ability to recognize it and use it properly is the necessary condition for attainment.

13. Premature wealth is but the forerunner of humiliation and disaster, because we cannot permanently retain anything which we do not merit or which we have not earned.

14. The conditions with which we meet in the world without, correspond to the conditions which we find in the world within. This is brought about by the Law of Attraction. How then shall we determine what is to enter into the world within?

15. Whatever enters the mind through the senses or the objective mind will impress the mind and result in a mental image which will become a pattern for the creative energies. These experiences are largely the result of environment, chance, past thinking and other forms of negative thought, and must be subjected to careful analysis before being

entertained. On the other hand, we can form our own mental images, through our own interior processes of thought regardless of the thoughts of others, regardless of exterior conditions, regardless of environment of every kind, and it is by the exercise of this power that we can control our own destiny, body, mind and soul.

16. It is by the exercise of this power that we take our fate out of the hands of chance, and consciously make for ourselves the experiences which we desire, because when we consciously realize a condition, that condition will eventually manifest itself in our lives; it is therefore evident that in the last analysis thinking is the one great cause in life.

17. Therefore, to control thought is to control circumstances, conditions, environment, and destiny.

18. How then are we to control thought; what is the process? To think is to create a thought, but the result of the thought will depend upon its form, its quality and its vitality.

19. The form will depend upon the mental images from which it emanates; this will depend upon the depth of the impression, the predominance of the idea, the clarity of the vision, the boldness of the image.

20. The quality depends upon its substance, and this depends upon the material of which the mind is composed; if this material has been woven from thoughts of vigor, strength, courage, determination, the thought will possess these qualities.

21. And finally, the vitality depends upon the feeling with which the thought is impregnated. If the thought is constructive, it will possess vitality; it will have life, it will grow, develop, expand, it will be creative; it will attract to itself everything necessary for its complete development.

22. If the thought is destructive, it will have within itself the germ of its own dissolution; it will die, but in the process of dying, it will bring sickness, disease, and every other form of discord.

23. This we call evil, and when we bring it upon ourselves, some of us are disposed to attribute our difficulties to a Supreme Being, but this supreme being is simply Mind in equilibrium.

24. It is neither good nor bad, it simply is.

25. Our ability to differentiate it into form is our ability to manifest good or evil.

26. Good and evil therefore are not entities, they are simply words which we use to indicate the result of our actions, and these actions are in turn predetermined by the character of our thought.

27. If our thought is constructive and harmonious we manifest good; if it is destructive and discordant we manifest evil.

28. If you desire to visualize a different environment, the process is simply to hold the ideal in mind, until your vision has been made real; give no thought to persons, places or things; these have no place in the absolute; the environment you desire will contain everything necessary; the right persons, and the right things will come at the right time and in the right place.

29. It is sometimes not plain how character, ability, attainment, achievement, environment and destiny can be controlled through the power of visualization, but this is an exact scientific fact.

30. You will readily see that what we think determines the quality of mind, and that the quality of mind in turn determines our ability and mental capacity, and you can readily understand that the improvement in our ability will naturally be followed by increase in attainment and a greater control of circumstances.

31. It will thus be seen that natural laws work in a perfectly natural and harmonious manner; everything seems to "just happen." If you want any evidence of this fact simply compare results of your efforts in your own life, when your actions were prompted by high ideals and when you had selfish or ulterior motives in mind. You will need no further evidence.

32. If you wish to bring about the realization of any desire, form a mental picture of success in your mind, by consciously visualizing your desire; in this way you will be compelling success, you will be externalizing it in your life by scientific methods.

33. We can only see what already exists in the objective world, but what we visualize already exists in the spiritual world, and this visualization is a substantial token of what will one day appear in the objective world, if we are faithful to our ideal. The reason for this is not difficult; visualization is a form of imagination; this process of thinking forms impressions on the mind, and these impressions in turn form concepts and ideals, and they in turn are the plans from which the Master architect will weave the future.

34. The psychologists have come to the conclusion that there is but one sense, the sense of feeling, and that all other senses are but modifications of this one sense; this being true, we know why feeling is the very fountainhead of power, why the emotions so easily overcome the intellect, and why we must put feeling into our thought, if we wish results. Thought and feeling is the irresistible combination.

35. Visualization must, of course, be directed by the will; we are to visualize exactly what we want; we must be careful not to let the imagination run riot. Imagination is a good servant but a poor master, and unless it is controlled it may easily lead us into all kinds of speculations and conclusions which have no basis or foundation of fact whatever. Every kind of plausible opinion is liable to be accepted without any analytical examination and the inevitable result is mental chaos.

36. We must therefore construct only such mental images as are known to be scientifically true. Subject every idea to a searching analysis and accept nothing which is not scientifically exact. When you do this you will attempt nothing but what you know you can carry out and success will crown your efforts; this is what businessmen call far-sightedness; it is much the same as insight, and is one of the great secrets of success in all important undertakings.

37. For your exercise this week, try to bring yourself to a realization of the important fact that harmony and happiness are states of consciousness and do not depend upon the possession of things. That things are effects and come as a consequence of correct mental states. So that if we desire material possession of any kind our chief concern should be to acquire the mental attitude which will bring about the result desired. This mental attitude is brought about by a realization of our spiritual nature and our unity with the Universal Mind which is the substance of all things. This realization will bring about everything which is necessary for our complete enjoyment. This is scientific or correct thinking. When we succeed in bringing about this mental attitude it is comparatively easy

to realize our desire as an already accomplished fact; when we can do this we shall have found the "Truth" which makes us "free" from every lack or limitation of any kind.

A man might frame and let loose a star, to roll in its orbit, and yet not have done so memorable a thing before God as he who lets a golden-orbed thought to roll through the generations of time.

—H. W. BEECHER

PART SIXTEEN. STUDY QUESTIONS WITH ANSWERS

151. Upon what does wealth depend?
Upon an understanding of the creative nature of thought.
152. Upon what does its true value consist?
Upon its exchange value.
153. Upon what does success depend?
Upon spiritual power.
154. Upon what does this power depend?
Upon use; use determines its existence.
155. How may we take our fate out of the hands of chance?
By consciously realizing the conditions which we desire to see manifested in our lives.
156. What then is the great business of life?
Thinking.
157. Why is this so?
Because thought is spiritual and therefore creative. To consciously control thought is therefore to control circumstances, conditions, environment and destiny.
158. What is the source of all evil?
Destructive thinking.
159. What is the source of all good?
Scientific correct thinking.
160. What is scientific thinking?
A recognition of the creative nature of spiritual energy and our ability to control it.

The greatest events of an age are its best thoughts. It is the nature of thought to find its way into action.

—BOVEE

Part Seventeen

The kind of Deity which a man, consciously or unconsciously, worships, indicates the intellectual status of the worshipper.

Ask the Indian of God, and he will describe to you a powerful chieftain of a glorious tribe. Ask the Pagan of God, and he will tell you of a God of fire, a God of water, a God of this, that, and the other.

Ask the Israelite of God, and he will tell you of the God of Moses, who conceived it expedient to rule by coercive measures; hence, the Ten Commandments. Or of Joshua, who led the Israelites into battle, confiscated property, murdered the prisoners, and laid waste to cities.

The so-called heathen made "graven images" of their Gods, whom they were accustomed to worship, but among the most intelligent, at least, these images were but the visible fulcrums with which they were enabled to mentally concentrate on the qualities which they desired to externalize in their lives.

We of the twentieth century worship a God of Love in theory, but in practice we make for ourselves "graven images" of "Wealth," "Power," "Fashion," "Custom" and "Conventionality." We "fall down" before them and worship them. We concentrate on them and they are thereby externalized in our lives.

The student who masters the contents of Part Seventeen will not mistake the symbols for the reality; he will be interested in causes, rather than effects. He will concentrate on the realities of life, and will then not be disappointed in the results.

1. We are told that Man has "dominion over all things"; this dominion is established through Mind. Thought is the activity which controls every principle beneath it. The highest principle by reason of its superior essence and qualities necessarily determines the circumstances, aspects and relation of everything with which it comes in contact.

2. The vibrations of mental forces are the finest and consequently the most powerful in existence. To those who perceive the nature and transcendency of mental force, all physical power sinks into insignificance.

3. We are accustomed to look upon the Universe with a lens of five senses, and from these experiences our anthropomorphic conceptions originate, but true conceptions are only secured by spiritual insight. This insight requires a quickening of the vibrations of

the Mind, and is only secured when the mind is continuously concentrated in a given direction.

4. Continuous concentration means an even, unbroken flow of thought and is the result of patient, persistent, persevering and well-regulated system.

5. Great discoveries are the result of long-continued investigation. The science of mathematics requires years of concentrated effort to master it, and the greatest science—that of the Mind—is revealed only through concentrated effort.

6. Concentration is much misunderstood; there seems to be an idea of effort or activity associated with it, when just the contrary is necessary. The greatness of an actor lies in the fact that he forgets himself in the portrayal of his character, becoming so identified with it, that the audience is swayed by the realism of the performance. This will give you a good idea of true concentration; you should be so interested in your thought, so engrossed in your subject, as to be conscious of nothing else. Such concentration leads to intuitive perception and immediate insight into the nature of the object concentrated upon.

7. All knowledge is the result of concentration of this kind; it is thus that the secrets of Heaven and Earth have been wrested; it is thus that the mind becomes a magnet and the desire to know draws the knowledge, irresistibly attracts it, makes it your own.

8. Desire is largely subconscious; conscious desire rarely realizes its object when the latter is out of immediate reach. Subconscious desire arouses the latent faculties of the mind, and difficult problems seem to solve themselves.

9. The subconscious mind may be aroused and brought into action in any direction and made to serve us for any purpose, by concentration. The practice of concentration requires the control of the physical, mental, and physical being; all modes of consciousness whether physical, mental, or physical, must be under control.

10. Spiritual Truth is therefore the controlling factor; it is this which will enable you to grow out of limited attainment and reach a point where you will be able to translate modes of thought into character and consciousness.

11. Concentration does not mean mere thinking of thoughts, but the transmutation of these thoughts into practical values; the average person has no conception of the meaning of concentration. There is always the cry "to have" but never the cry "to be"; they fail to understand that they cannot have one without the other, that they must first find the "kingdom" before they can have the "things added." Momentary enthusiasm is of no value; it is only with unbounded self-confidence that the goal is reached.

12. The mind may place the ideal a little too high and fall short of the mark; it may attempt to soar on untrained wings and instead of flying, fall to earth; but that is no reason for not making another attempt.

13. Weakness is the only barrier to mental attainment; attribute your weakness to physical limitations or mental uncertainties and try again; ease and perfection are gained by repetition.

14. The astronomer centers his mind on the stars and they give forth their secrets; the geologist centers his mind on the construction of the earth and we have geology; so with all things. Men center their minds on the problems of life, and the result is apparent in the vast and complex social order of the day.

15. All mental discovery and attainment are the result of desire plus concentration; desire is the strongest mode of action; the more persistent the desire, the more authoritative the revelation. Desire added to concentration will wrench any secret from nature.

16. In realizing great thoughts, in experiencing great emotions that correspond with great thoughts, the mind is in a state where it appreciates the value of higher things.

17. The intensity of one moment's earnest concentration and the intense longing to become and to attain may take you further than years of slow normal and forced effort; it will unfasten the prison bars of unbelief, weakness, impotence and self-belittlement, and you will come into a realization of the joy of overcoming.

18. The spirit of initiative and originality is developed through persistence and continuity of mental effort. Business teaches the value of concentration and encourages decision of character; it develops practical insight and quickness of conclusion. The mental element in every commercial pursuit is dominant as the controlling factor, and desire is the predominating force; all commercial relations are the externalization of desire.

19. Many of the sturdy and substantial virtues are developed in commercial employment; the mind is steadied and directed; it becomes efficient. The principal necessity is the strengthening of the mind so that it rises superior to the distractions and wayward impulses of instinctive life and thus successfully overcomes in the conflict between the higher and lower self.

20. All of us are dynamos, but the dynamo of itself is nothing; the mind must work the dynamo; then it is useful and its energy can be definitely concentrated. The mind is an engine whose power is undreamed; thought is an omni-working power. It is the ruler and creator of all form and all events occurring in form. Physical energy is nothing in comparison with the omnipotence of thought, because thought enables man to harness all other natural power.

21. Vibration is the action of thought; it is vibration which reaches out and attracts the material necessary to construct and build. There is nothing mysterious concerning the power of thought; concentration simply implies that consciousness can be focalized to the point where it becomes identified with the object of its attention. As food absorbed is the essence of the body, so the mind absorbs the object of its attention, gives it life and being.

22. If you concentrate on some matter of importance, the intuitive power will be set in operation, and help will come in the nature of information which will lead to success.

23. Intuition arrives at conclusions without the aid of experience or memory. Intuition often solves problems that are beyond the grasp of the reasoning power. Intuition often comes with a suddenness that is startling; it reveals the truth for which we are searching, so directly that it seems to come from a higher power. Intuition can be cultivated and developed; in order to do this it must be recognized and appreciated; if the intuitive visitor is given a royal welcome when he comes, he will come again; the more cordial the welcome the more frequent his visits will become, but if he is ignored or neglected he will make his visits few and far apart.

24. Intuition usually comes in the Silence; great minds seek solitude frequently; it is here that all the larger problems of life are worked out. For this reason every businessman who can afford it has a private office, where he will not be disturbed; if you cannot afford

a private office you can at least find somewhere, where you can be alone a few minutes each day, to train the thought along lines which will enable you to develop that invincible power which is necessary to achieve.

25. Remember that fundamentally the subconscious is omnipotent; there is no limit to the things that can be done when it is given the power to act. Your degree of success is determined by the nature of your desire. If the nature of your desire is in harmony with natural law or the Universal Mind, it will gradually emancipate the mind and give you invincible courage.

26. Every obstacle conquered, every victory gained, will give you more faith in your power, and you will have greater ability to win. Your strength is determined by your mental attitude; if this attitude is one of success, and is permanently held with an unswerving purpose, you will attract to you from the invisible domain the things you silently demand.

27. By keeping the thought in mind, it will gradually take tangible form. A definite purpose sets causes in motion which go out in the invisible world and find the material necessary to serve your purpose.

28. You may be pursuing the symbols of power, instead of power itself. You may be pursuing fame instead of honor, riches instead of wealth, position instead of servitude; in either event you will find that they turn to ashes just as you overtake them.

29. Premature wealth or position cannot be retained because it has not been earned; we get only what we give, and those who try to get without giving always find that the law of compensation is relentlessly bringing about an exact equilibrium.

30. The race has usually been for money and other mere symbols of power, but with an understanding of the true source of power, we can afford to ignore the symbols. The man with a large bank account finds it unnecessary to load his pockets down with gold; so with the man who has found the true source of power; he is no longer interested in its shams or pretensions.

31. Thought ordinarily leads outwardly in evolutionary directions, but it can be turned within where it will take hold of the basic principles of things, the heart of things, the spirit of things. When you get to the heart of things it is comparatively easy to understand and command them.

32. This is because the Spirit of a thing is the thing itself, the vital part of it, the real substance. The form is simply the outward manifestation of the spiritual activity within.

33. For your exercise this week concentrate as nearly as possible in accordance with the method outlined in this lesson; let there be no conscious effort or activity associated with your purpose. Relax completely, avoid any thought of anxiety as to results. Remember that power comes through repose. Let the thought dwell upon your object, until it is completely identified with it, until you are conscious of nothing else.

34. If you wish to eliminate fear, concentrate on courage.

35. If you wish to eliminate lack, concentrate on abundance.

36. If you wish to eliminate disease, concentrate on health.

37. Always concentrate on the ideal as an already existing fact; this is the germ cell, the life principle which goes forth and sets in motion those causes which guide, direct and bring about the necessary relation, which eventually manifests itself in form.

Thought is the property of those only who can entertain it.
—EMERSON

PART SEVENTEEN.
STUDY QUESTIONS WITH ANSWERS

161. What is the true method of concentration?
To become so identified with the object of your thought that you are conscious of nothing else.
162. What is the result of this method of concentration?
Invisible forces are set in motion which irresistibly bring about conditions in correspondence with your thought.
163. What is the controlling factor in this method of thought?
Spiritual Truth.
164. Why is this so?
Because the nature of our desire must be in harmony with natural law.
165. What is the practical value of this method of concentration?
Thought is transmuted into character, and character is the magnet which creates the environment of the individual.
166. What is the controlling factor in every commercial pursuit?
The mental element.
167. Why is this so?
Because Mind is the ruler and creator of all form and all events occurring in form.
168. How does concentration operate?
By the development of the powers of perception, wisdom, intuition, and sagacity.
169. Why is intuition superior to reason?
Because it does not depend upon experience or memory and frequently brings about the solution to our problems by methods concerning which we are in entire ignorance.
170. What is the result of pursuing the symbol of the reality?
They frequently turn to ashes just as we overtake them, because the symbol is only the outward form of the spiritual activity within, therefore unless we can possess the spiritual reality, the form disappears.

Part Eighteen

In order to grow we must obtain what is necessary for our growth. This is brought about through the Law of Attraction. This principle is the sole means by which the individual is differentiated from the Universal.

Think for a moment, what would a man be if he were not a husband, father, or brother, if he were not interested in the social, economical, political or religious world. He would be nothing but an abstract theoretical ego. He exists, therefore, only in his relation to the whole, in his relation to other men, in his relation to society. This relation constitutes his environment and in no other way.

It is evident, therefore, that the individual is simply the differentiation of the one Universal Mind "which lighteth every man that cometh into the world," and his so-called individuality or personality consists of nothing but the manner in which he relates with the whole.

This we call his environment and is brought about by the Law of Attraction. Part Eighteen, which follows, has something more to say concerning this important law.

1. There is a change in the thought of the world. This change is silently transpiring in our midst, and is more important than any which the world has undergone since the downfall of Paganism.

2. The present revolution in the opinions of all classes of men, the highest and most cultured of men as well as those of the laboring class, stands unparalleled in the history of the world.

3. Science has of late made such vast discoveries, has revealed such an infinity of resources, has unveiled such enormous possibilities and such unsuspected forces, that scientific men more and more hesitate to affirm certain theories as established and beyond doubt or to deny other theories as absurd or impossible.

4. A new civilization is being born; customs, creeds, and precedent are passing; vision, faith and service are taking their place. The fetters of tradition are being melted off from humanity, and as the impurities of materialism are being consumed, thought is being liberated and truth is rising full robed before an astonished multitude.

5. The whole world is on the eve of a new consciousness, a new power, and a new realization within the self.

6. Physical Science has resolved matter into molecules, molecules into atoms, atoms into energy, and it has remained for Mr. J. A. Fleming, in an address before the Royal Institution, to resolve this energy into mind. He says, "In its ultimate essence, energy may be incomprehensible by us except as an exhibition of the direct operation of that which we call Mind or Will."

7. And this mind is the indwelling and ultimate. It is imminent in matter as in spirit. It is the sustaining, energizing, all-pervading Spirit of the universe.

8. Every living thing must be sustained by this omnipotent Intelligence, and we find the difference in individual lives to be largely measured by the degree of this intelligence, which they manifest. It is greater intelligence that places the animal in a higher scale of being than the plant, the man higher than the animal, and we find that this increased intelligence is again indicated by the power of the individual to control modes of action and thus to consciously adjust himself to his environment.

9. It is this adjustment that occupies the attention of the greatest minds, and this adjustment consists in nothing else than the recognition of an existing order in the Universal Mind, for it is well known that this mind will obey us precisely in proportion as we first obey it.

10. It is the recognition of natural laws that has enabled us to annihilate time and space, to soar in the air and to make iron float, and the greater the degree of intelligence the greater will be our recognition of these natural laws and the greater will be the power we can possess.

11. It is the recognition of the self as an individualization of this Universal Intelligence that enables the individual to control those forms of intelligence which have not yet reached this level of self-recognition; they do not know that this Universal Intelligence permeates all things ready to be called into action; they do not know that it is responsive to every demand, and they are therefore in bondage to the law of their own being.

12. Thought is creative and the principle on which the law is based is sound and legitimate and is inherent in the nature of things; but this creative power does not originate in the individual, but in the Universal, which is the source and foundation of all energy and substance; the individual is simply the channel for the distribution of this energy.

13. The individual is simply the means by which the Universal produces the various combinations which result in the formation of phenomena, which depends upon the law of vibration, whereby various rates of rapidity of motion in the primary substance form new substances only in certain exact numerical ratios.

14. Thought is the invisible link by which the individual comes into communication with the Universal, the finite with the Infinite, the seen with the Unseen. Thought is the magic by which the human is transformed into a being who thinks and knows and feels and acts.

15. As the proper apparatus has enabled the eye to discover worlds without number millions of miles away, so, with the proper understanding, man has been enabled to communicate with the Universal Mind, the source of all power.

16. The Understanding which is usually developed is about as valuable as a VCR

without a videotape; in fact, it is usually nothing more than a "belief," which means nothing at all. The savages of the Cannibal Islands believe something; but that proves nothing.

17. The only belief which is of any value to anyone is a belief that has been put to a test and demonstrated to be a fact; it is then no longer a belief, but has become a living Faith or Truth.

18. And this Truth has been put to the test by hundreds of thousands of people and has been found to be the Truth exactly in proportion to the usefulness of the apparatus which they used.

19. A man would not expect to locate stars hundreds of millions of miles away without a sufficiently strong telescope, and for this reason Science is continually engaged in building larger and more powerful telescopes and is continually rewarded by additional knowledge of the heavenly bodies.

20. So with understanding; men are continually making progress in the methods which they use to come into communication with the Universal Mind and its infinite possibilities.

21. The Universal Mind manifests itself in the objective, through the principle of attraction that each atom has for every other atom, in infinite degrees of intensity.

22. It is by this principle of combining and attracting that things are brought together. This principle is of universal application and is the sole means whereby the purpose of existence is carried into effect.

23. The expression of growth is met in a most beautiful manner through the instrumentality of this Universal Principle.

24. In order to grow we must obtain what is essential for our growth, but as we are at all times a complete thought entity, this completeness makes it possible for us to receive only as we give; growth is therefore conditioned on reciprocal action, and we find that on the mental plane like attracts like, that mental vibrations respond only to the extent of their vibratory harmony.

25. It is clear, therefore, that thoughts of abundance will respond only to similar thoughts; the wealth of the individual is seen to be what he inherently is. Affluence within is found to be the secret of attraction for affluence without. The ability to produce is found to be the real source of wealth of the individual. It is for this reason that he who has his heart in his work is certain to meet with unbounded success. He will give and continually give; and the more he gives, the more he will receive.

26. What do the great financiers of Wall Street, the captains of industry, the statesmen, the great corporation attorneys, the inventors, the physicians, the authors—what do each of these contribute to the sum of human happiness but the power of their thought?

27. Thought is the energy by which the Law of Attraction is brought into operation, which eventually manifests itself in abundance.

28. The Universal Mind is static Mind or Substance in equilibrium. It is differentiated into form by our power to think. Thought is the dynamic phase of mind.

29. Power depends upon consciousness of power; unless we use it, we shall lose it, and unless we are conscious of it, we cannot use it.

30. The use of this power depends upon attention; the degree of attention determines our capacity for the acquirement of knowledge which is another name for power.

31. Attention has been held to be the distinguishing mark of genius. The cultivation of attention depends upon practice.

32. The incentive of attention is interest; the greater the interest, the greater the attention; the greater the attention, the greater the interest, action and reaction; begin by paying attention; before long you will have aroused interest; this interest will attract more attention, and this attention will produce more interest, and so on. This practice will enable you to cultivate the power of attention.

33. This week concentrate upon your power to create; seek insight, perception; try to find a logical basis for the faith which is in you. Let the thought dwell on the fact that the physical man lives and moves and has his being in the sustainer of all organic life air, that he must breathe to live. Then let the thought rest on the fact that the spiritual man also lives and moves and has his being in a similar but subtler energy upon which he must depend for life, and that as in the physical world no life assumes form until after a seed is sown, and no higher fruit than that of the parent stock can be produced; so in the spiritual world no effect can be produced until the seed is sown and the fruit will depend upon the nature of the seed, so that the results which you secure depend upon your perception of law in the mighty domain of causation, the highest evolution of human consciousness.

> There is no thought in my mind but it quickly tends to convert itself
> into a power and organizes a huge instrumentality of means.
> —EMERSON

PART EIGHTEEN.
STUDY QUESTIONS WITH ANSWERS

171. How is the difference in individual lives measured?
By the degree of intelligence which they manifest.

172. What is the law by which the individual may control other forms of intelligence?
A recognition of the self as an individualization of the Universal Intelligence.

173. Where does the creative power originate?
In the Universal.

174. How does the Universal create form?
By means of the individual.

175. What is the connecting link between the individual and the Universal?
Thought.

176. What is the principle by which the means of existence is carried into effect?
The law of love.

177. How is this principle brought into expression?
By the law of growth.

178. Upon what condition does the law of growth depend?
Upon reciprocal action. The individual is complete at all times and this makes it possible to receive only as we give.
179. What is it that we give?
Thought.
180. What do we receive?
Thought, which is substance in equilibrium and which is constantly being differentiated in form by what we think.

Part Nineteen

Fear is a powerful form of thought. It paralyzes the nerve centers, thus affecting the circulation of the blood. This, in turn, paralyzes the muscular system, so that fear affects the entire being, body, brain and nerve, physical, mental, and muscular.

Of course the way to overcome fear is to become conscious of power. What is this mysterious vital force which we call power? We do not know, but then, neither do we know what electricity is.

But we do know that by conforming to the requirements of the law by which electricity is governed, it will be our obedient servant; that it will light our homes, our cities, run our machinery, and serve us in many useful capacities.

And so it is with vital force. Although we do not know what it is, and possibly may never know, we do know that it is a primary force which manifests itself through living bodies, and that by complying with the laws and principles by which it is governed, we can open ourselves to a more abundant inflow of this vital energy, and thus express the highest possible degree of mental, moral, and spiritual efficiency.

This part tells of a very simple way of developing this vital force. If you put into practice the information outlined in this lesson you will soon develop the sense of power which has ever been the distinguishing mark of genius.

1. The search for truth is no longer a haphazard adventure, but it is a systematic process, and is logical in its operation. Every kind of experience is given a voice in shaping its decision.

2. In seeking the truth we are seeking ultimate cause; we know that every human experience is an effect; then if we may ascertain the cause, and if we shall find that this cause is one which we can consciously control, the effect or the experience will be within our control also.

3. Human experience will then no longer be the football of fate; a man will not be the child of fortune, but destiny. Fate and fortune will be controlled as readily as a captain controls his ship, or an engineer his train.

4. All things are finally resolvable into the same element and as they are thus trans-

latable, one into the other, they must ever be in relation and may never be in opposition to one another.

5. In the physical world there are innumerable contrasts, and these may for convenience's sake, be designated by distinctive names. There are sizes, colors, shades or ends to all things. There is a North Pole, and a South Pole, an inside and an outside, a seen and an unseen, but these expressions merely serve to place extremes in contrast.

6. They are names given to two different parts of one quantity. The two extremes are relative; they are not separate entities, but are two parts or aspects of the whole.

7. In the mental world we find the same law; we speak of knowledge and ignorance, but ignorance is but a lack of knowledge and is therefore found to be simply a word to express the absence of knowledge; it has no principle in itself.

8. In the Moral World we again find the same law; we speak of good and evil, but Good is a reality, something tangible, while Evil is found to be simply a negative condition, the absence of Good. Evil is sometimes thought to be a very real condition, but it has no principle, no vitality, no life; we know this because it can always be destroyed by Good; just as Truth destroys Error and light destroys darkness, so Evil vanishes when Good appears; there is therefore but one principle in the Moral World.

9. We find exactly the same law obtaining in the spiritual world; we speak of Mind and Matter as two separate entities, but clearer insight makes it evident that there is but one operative principle and that is Mind.

10. Mind is the real and the eternal. Matter is forever changing; we know that in the eons of time a hundred years is but as a day. If we stand in any large city and let the eye rest on the innumerable large and magnificent buildings, the vast array of modern automobiles, cellular telephones, the electric lights, and all the other conveniences of modern civilization, we may remember that not one of them was there just over a century ago, and if we could stand on the same spot in a hundred years from now, in all probability we should find that but few of them remained.

11. In the animal kingdom we find the same law of change. The millions and millions of animals come and go, a few years constituting their span of life. In the plant world the change is still more rapid. Many plants and nearly all grasses come and go in a single year. When we pass to the inorganic, we expect to find something more substantial, but as we gaze on the apparently solid continent, we are told that it arose from the ocean; we see the giant mountain and are told that the place where it now stands was once a lake; and as we stand in awe before the great cliffs in the Yosemite Valley we can easily trace the path of the glaciers which carried all before them.

12. We are in the presence of continual change, and we know that this change is but the evolution of the Universal Mind, the grand process whereby all things are continually being created anew, and we come to know that matter is but a form which Mind takes and is therefore simply a condition. Matter has no principle; Mind is the only principle.

13. We have then come to know that Mind is the only principle which is operative in the physical, mental, moral and spiritual world.

14. We also know that this mind is static, mind at rest; we also know that the ability

of the individual to think is his ability to act upon the Universal Mind and convert it into dynamic mind, or mind in motion.

15. In order to do this fuel must be applied in the form of food, for man cannot think without eating, and so we find that even a spiritual activity such as thinking cannot be converted into sources of pleasure and profit except by making use of material means.

16. It requires energy of some kind to collect electricity and convert it into a dynamic power, it requires the rays of the sun to give the necessary energy to sustain plant life, so it also requires energy in the form of food to enable the individual to think and thereby act upon the Universal Mind.

17. You may know that thought constantly, eternally is taking form, is forever seeking expression, or you may not, but the fact remains that if your thought is powerful, constructive, and positive, this will be plainly evident in the state of your health, your business and your environment; if your thought is weak, critical, destructive and negative generally, it will manifest itself in your body as fear, worry and nervousness, in your finance as lack and limitation, and in discordant conditions in your environment.

18. All wealth is the offspring of power; possessions are of value only as they confer power. Events are significant only as they affect power; all things represent certain forms and degrees of power.

19. A knowledge of cause and effect as shown by the laws governing steam, electricity, chemical affinity and gravitation enables men to plan courageously and to execute fearlessly. These laws are called natural laws, because they govern the physical world, but all power is not physical power; there is also mental power, and there is moral and spiritual power.

20. What are our schools, our universities, but mental powerhouses, places where mental power is being developed?

21. As there are many mighty powerhouses for the application of power to ponderous machinery, whereby raw material is collected and converted into the necessities and comforts of life, so the mental powerhouses collect the raw material and cultivate and develop it into a power which is infinitely superior to all the forces of nature, marvelous though they may be.

22. What is this raw material which is being collected in these thousands of mental powerhouses all over the world and developed into a power which is evidently controlling every other power? In its static form it is Mind—in its dynamic form, it is Thought.

23. This power is superior because it exists on a higher plane, because it has enabled man to discover the law by which these wonderful forces of nature could be harnessed and made to do the work of hundreds and thousands of men. It has enabled man to discover laws whereby time and space have been annihilated, and the law of gravitation overcome.

24. Thought is the vital force or energy which is being developed and which has produced such startling results in the last half century as to bring about a world which would be absolutely inconceivable to a man existing only 50 or 25 years ago. If such results have been secured by organizing these mental powerhouses in 50 years, what may not be expected in another 50 years?

25. The substance from which all things are created is infinite in quantity; we know that light travels at the rate of 186,000 miles per second, and we know that there are stars so remote that it takes light 2,000 years to reach us, and we know that such stars exist in

all parts of the heaven; we know, too, that this light comes in waves, so that if the ether on which these waves travel was not continuous the light would fail to reach us; we can then only come to the conclusion that this substance, or ether, or raw material, is universally present.

26. How, then, does it manifest itself in form? In electrical science a battery is formed by connecting the opposite poles of zinc and copper, which causes a current to flow from one to the other and so provides energy. This same process is repeated in respect to every polarity, and as all form simply depends upon the rate of vibration and consequent relations of atoms to each other, if we wish to change the form of manifestation we must change the polarity. This is the principle of causation.

27. For your exercise this week, concentrate, and when I use the word concentrate, I mean all that the word implies; become so absorbed in the object of your thought that you are conscious of nothing else, and do this a few minutes every day. You take the necessary time to eat in order that the body may be nourished, why not take the time to assimilate your mental food?

28. Let the thought rest on the fact that appearances are deceptive. The earth is not flat, neither is it stationary; the sky is not a dome, the sun does not move, the stars are not small specks of light, and matter which was once supposed to be fixed has been found to be in a state of perpetual flux.

29. Try to realize that the day is fast approaching—its dawn is now at hand—when modes of thought and action must be adjusted to rapidly increasing knowledge of the operation of eternal principles.

Silent thought, is, after all, the mightiest agent in human affairs.

—CHANNING

PART NINETEEN.
STUDY QUESTIONS WITH ANSWERS

181. How are extremes placed in contrast?
They are designated by distinctive names, such as inside and outside, top and bottom, light and dark, good and bad.

182. Are these separate entities?
No, they are parts or aspects of one Whole.

183. What is the one creative Principle in the physical, mental and spiritual world?
The Universal Mind, or the Eternal Energy from which all things proceed.

184. How are we related to this creative Principle?
By our ability to think.

185. How does this creative Principle become operative?
Thought is the seed, which results in action and action results in form.

186. Upon what does form depend?
Upon the rate of vibration.

187. How may the rate of vibration be changed?
By mental action.

188. Upon what does mental action depend?
Upon polarity, action and reaction, between the individual and the Universal.

189. Does the creative energy originate in the individual or the Universal?
In the Universal, but the Universal can manifest itself only through the individual.

190. Why is the individual necessary?
Because the Universal is static, and requires energy to start it in motion. This is furnished by food which is converted into energy, which in turn enables the individual to think. When the individual stops eating he stops thinking; then he no longer acts upon the Universal; there is consequently no longer any action or reaction; the Universal is then only pure mind in static form—mind at rest.

Part Twenty

For many years there has been an endless discussion as to the origin of evil. Theologians have told us that God is Love, and that God is Omnipresent. If this be true, there is no place where God is not. Where, then, are Evil, Satan, and Hell?

Let us see:

God is Spirit.
Spirit is the Creative Principle of the Universe.
Man is made in the image and likeness of God.
Man is therefore a spiritual being.
The only activity which spirit possesses is the power to think.
Thinking is therefore a creative process.
All form is therefore the result of the thinking process.
The destruction of form must also be a result of the thinking process.
Fictitious representations of form are the result of the creative power of thought, as in Hypnotism.
Apparent representations of form are the result of the creative power of thought, as in Spiritualism.
Invention, organization and constructive work of all kinds are the result of the creative power of thought, as in concentration.
When the creative power of thought is manifested for the benefit of humanity, we call the result good.
When the creative power of thought is manifested in a destructive or evil manner, we call the result evil.

This indicates the origin of both good and evil; they are simply words which have been coined in order to indicate the nature of the result of the thinking or creative process. Thought necessarily precedes and predetermines action; action precedes and predetermines condition.

Part Twenty will throw more light upon this important subject.

1. The spirit of a thing is that thing; it is necessarily fixed, changeless and eternal. The spirit of you is—you; without the spirit you would be nothing. It becomes active through your recognition of it and its possibilities.

2. You may have all the wealth in Christendom, but unless you recognize it and make use of it, it will have no value; so with your spiritual wealth: unless you recognize it and use it, it will have no value. The one and only condition of spiritual power is use or recognition.

3. All great things come through recognition; the scepter of power is consciousness, and thought is its messenger, and this messenger is constantly molding the realities of the invisible world into the conditions and environments of your objective world.

4. Thinking is the true business of life, power is the result. You are at all times dealing with the magical power of thought and consciousness. What results can you expect so long as you remain oblivious to the power which has been placed within your control?

5. So long as you do this you limit yourself to superficial conditions, and make of yourself a beast of burden for those who think; those who recognize their power; those who know that unless we are willing to think we shall have to work, and the less we think the more we shall have to work, and the less we shall get for our work.

6. The secret of power is a perfect understanding of the principles, forces, methods and combinations of Mind, and a perfect understanding of our relationship to the Universal Mind. It is well to remember that this principle is unchangeable; if this were not so, it would not be reliable; all principles are changeless.

7. This stability is your opportunity; you are its active attribute, the channel for its activity; the Universal can act only through the individual.

8. When you begin to perceive that the essence of the Universal is within yourself—is you—you begin to do things; you begin to feel your power; it is the fuel which fires the imagination; which lights the torch of inspiration; which gives vitality to thought; which enables you to connect with all the invisible forces of the Universe. It is this power which will enable you to plan fearlessly, to execute masterfully.

9. But perception will come only in the Silence; this seems to be the condition required for all great purposes. You are a visualizing entity. Imagination is your workshop. It is here that your ideal is to be visualized.

10. As a perfect understanding of the nature of this power is a primary condition for its manifestation, visualize the entire method over and over again, so that you may use it whenever occasion requires. The infinity of wisdom is to follow the method whereby we may have the inspiration of the omnipotent Universal Mind on demand at any time.

11. We can fail to recognize this world within, and so exclude it from our consciousness, but it will still be the basic fact of all existence; and when we learn to recognize it, not only in ourselves, but in all persons, events, and things and circumstances we shall have found the "Kingdom of heaven" which we are told is "within" us.

12. Our failures are a result of the operation of exactly the same principle; the principle is unchangeable; its operation is exact, there is no deviation; if we think lack, limitation, discord, we shall find their fruits on every hand; if we think poverty, unhappiness or disease, the thought messengers will carry the summons as readily as any other kind of thought and the result will be just as certain. If we fear a coming calamity, we shall be

able to say with Job, "the thing I feared has come upon me"; if we think unkindly or ignorantly we shall thus attract to ourselves the results of our ignorance.

13. This power of thought, if understood and correctly used, is the greatest labor-saving device ever dreamed of, but if not understood or improperly used, the result will in all probability be disastrous, as we have already seen; by the help of this power you can confidently undertake things that are seemingly impossible, because this power is the secret of all inspiration, all genius.

14. To become inspired means to get out of the beaten path, out of the rut, because extraordinary results require extraordinary means. When we come into a recognition of the Unity of all things and that the source of all power is within, we tap the source of inspiration.

15. Inspiration is the art of imbibing, the art of self-realization; the art of adjusting the individual mind to that of the Universal Mind; the art of attaching the proper mechanism to the source of all power; the art of differentiating the formless into form; the art of becoming a channel for the flow of Infinite Wisdom; the art of visualizing perfection; the art of realizing the omnipresence of Omnipotence.

16. An understanding and appreciation of the fact that the infinite power is omnipresent and is therefore in the infinitely small as well as the infinitely large will enable us to absorb its essence; a further understanding of the fact that this power is spirit and therefore indivisible will enable us to appreciate its presence at all points at the same time.

17. An understanding of these facts, first intellectually and then emotionally, will enable us to drink deeply from this ocean of infinite power. An intellectual understanding will be of no assistance; the emotions must be brought into action; thought without feeling is cold. The required combination is thought and feeling.

18. Inspiration is from within. The Silence is necessary, the senses must be stilled, the muscles relaxed, repose cultivated. When you have thus come into possession of a sense of poise and power you will be ready to receive the information or inspiration or wisdom which may be necessary for the development of your purpose.

19. Do not confuse these methods with those of the clairvoyant; they have nothing in common. Inspiration is the art of receiving and makes for all that is best in life; your business in life is to understand and command these invisible forces instead of letting them command and rule you. Power implies service; inspiration implies power; to understand and apply the method of inspiration is to become a superman.

20. We can live more abundantly every time we breathe, if we consciously breathe with that intention. The IF is a very important condition in this case, as the intention governs the attention, and without the attention you can secure only the results which everyone else secures. That is, a supply equal to the demand.

21. In order to secure the larger supply your demand must be increased, and as you consciously increase the demand the supply will follow, you will find yourself coming into a larger and larger supply of life, energy and vitality.

22. The reason for this is not difficult to understand, but it is another of the vital mysteries of life which do not seem to be generally appreciated. If you make it your own, you will find it one of the great realities of life.

23. We are told that "In Him we live and move and have our being," and we are told

that "He" is a Spirit, and again that "He" is Love, so that every time we breathe, we breathe this life, love, and spirit. This is Pranic Energy, or Pranic Ether; we could not exist a moment without it. It is the Cosmic Energy; it is the Life of the Solar Plexus.

24. Every time we breathe we fill our lungs with air and at the same time vitalize our body with this Pranic Ether which is Life itself, so that we have the opportunity of making a conscious connection with All Life, All Intelligence and All Substance.

25. A knowledge of your relation and oneness with this Principle that governs the Universe and the simple method whereby you can consciously identify yourself with it gives you a scientific understanding of a law whereby you may free yourself from disease, from lack or limitation of any kind; in fact, it enables you to breathe the "breath of life" into your own nostrils.

26. This "breath of life" is a superconscious reality. It is the essence of the "I am." It is pure "Being" or Universal Substance, and our conscious unity with it enables us to localize it, and thus exercise the powers of this creative energy.

27. Thought is creative vibration and the quality of the conditions created will depend upon the quality of our thought, because we cannot express powers which we do not possess. We must "be" before we can "do" only to the extent to which we "are," and so what we do will necessarily coincide with what we "are" and what we are depends upon what we "think."

28. Every time you think you start a train of causation which will create a condition in strict accordance with the quality of the thought which originated it. Thought which is in harmony with the Universal Mind will result in corresponding conditions. Thought which is destructive or discordant will produce corresponding results. You may use thought constructively or destructively, but the immutable law will not allow you to plant a thought of one kind and reap the fruit of another. You are free to use this marvelous creative power as you will, but you must take the consequences.

29. This is the danger from what is called Will Power. There are those who seem to think that by force of will they can coerce this law; that they can sow seed of one kind and by "Will Power" make it bear fruit of another, but the fundamental principle of creative power is in the Universal, and therefore the idea of forcing a compliance with our wishes by the power of the individual will is an inverted conception which may appear to succeed for a while but is eventually doomed to failure—because it antagonizes the very power which it is seeking to use.

30. It is the individual attempting to coerce the Universal, the finite in conflict with the Infinite. Our permanent well-being will be best conserved by a conscious cooperation with the continuous forward movement of the Great Whole.

31. For your exercise this week, go into the Silence and concentrate on the fact that "In him we live and move and have our being" is literally and scientifically exact! That you ARE because He IS, that if He is Omnipresent He must be in you. That if He is all in all you must be in Him! That He is Spirit and you are made in "His image and likeness" and that the only difference between His spirit and your spirit is one of degree, that a part must be the same in kind and quality as the whole. When you can realize this clearly you will have found the secret of the creative power of thought, you will have found the origin of both good and evil, you will have found the secret of the wonderful power of concentra-

tion, you will have found the key to the solution of every problem whether physical, financial, or environmental.

The power to think consecutively and deeply and clearly, is an avowed and deadly enemy to mistakes and blunders, superstitions, unscientific theories, irrational beliefs, unbridled enthusiasm, fanaticism.

—HADDOCK

PART TWENTY. STUDY QUESTIONS WITH ANSWERS

191. Upon what condition does power depend?
Upon recognition and use.
192. What is recognition?
Consciousness.
193. How do we become conscious of power?
By thinking.
194. What then is the true business of life?
Correct scientific thinking.
195. What is correct scientific thinking?
The ability to adjust our thought processes to the will of the Universal. In other words, to cooperate with natural laws.
196. How is this accomplished?
By securing a perfect understanding of the principles, forces, methods and combinations of mind.
197. What is this Universal Mind?
The basic fact of all existence.
198. What is the cause of all lack, limitation, disease and discord?
It is due to the operation of exactly the same law; the law operates relentlessly and is continually bringing about conditions in correspondence with the thought which originated or created them.
199. What is inspiration?
The art of realizing the omnipresence of Omniscience.
200. Upon what do the conditions with which we meet depend?
Upon the quality of our thought. Because what we do depends upon what we are and what we are depends upon what we think.

Part Twenty-one

It is my privilege to enclose Part Twenty-one. In paragraph 7 you will find that one of the secrets of success, one of the methods of organizing victory, one of the accomplishments of the Master Mind is to think big thoughts.

In paragraph 8 you will find that everything which we hold in our consciousness for any length of time becomes impressed upon our subconsciousness and so becomes a pattern which the creative energy will wave into our life and environment. This is the secret of the wonderful power of prayer.

We know that the universe is governed by law; that for every effect there must be a cause, and that the same cause, under the same conditions, will invariably produce the same effect.

Consequently, if prayer has ever been answered, it will always be answered, if the proper conditions are complied with. This must necessarily be true; otherwise the universe would be a chaos instead of a cosmos. The answer to prayer is therefore subject to law, and this law is definite, exact and scientific, just as are the laws governing gravitation and electricity. An understanding of this law takes the foundation of Christianity out of the realm of superstition and credulity and places it upon the firm rock of scientific understanding.

But, unfortunately, there are comparatively few persons who know how to pray.

They understand that there are laws governing electricity, mathematics, and chemistry, but, for some inexplicable reason, it never seems to occur to them that there are also spiritual laws, and that these laws are also definite, scientific, exact, and operate with immutable precision.

1. The real secret of power is consciousness of power. The Universal Mind is unconditional; therefore, the more conscious we become of our unity with this mind, the less conscious we shall become of conditions and limitations, and as we become emancipated or freed from conditions we come into a realization of the unconditional. We have become free!

2. As soon as we become conscious of the inexhaustible power in the world within, we begin to draw on this power and apply and develop the greater possibilities which this discernment has realized, because whatever we become conscious of, is invariably manifested in the objective world, is brought forth into tangible expression.

3. This is because the Infinite Mind, which is the source from which all things proceed, is one and indivisible, and each individual is a channel whereby this Eternal Energy is being manifested. Our ability to think is our ability to act upon this Universal Substance, and what we think is what is created or produced in the objective world.

4. The result of this discovery is nothing less than marvelous, and means that mind is extraordinary in quality, limitless in quantity, and contains possibilities without number. To become conscious of this power is to become a "live wire"; it has the same effect as placing an ordinary wire in contact with a wire that is charged. The Universal is the live wire. It carries power sufficient to meet every situation which may arise in the life of every individual. When the individual mind touches the Universal Mind it receives all the power it requires. This is the world within. All science recognizes the reality of this world, and all power is contingent upon our recognition of this world.

5. The ability to eliminate imperfect conditions depends upon mental action, and mental action depends upon consciousness of power; therefore, the more conscious we become of our unity with the source of all power, the greater will be our power to control and master every condition.

6. Large ideas have a tendency to eliminate all smaller ideas so that it is well to hold ideas large enough to counteract and destroy all small or undesirable tendencies. This will remove innumerable petty and annoying obstacles from your path. You also become conscious of a larger world of thought, thereby increasing your mental capacity as well as placing yourself in position to accomplish something of value.

7. This is one of the secrets of success, one of the methods of organizing victory, one of the accomplishments of the Master-Mind. He thinks big thoughts. The creative energies of mind find no more difficulty in handling large situations, than small ones. Mind is just as much present in the Infinitely large as in the Infinitely small.

8. When we realize these facts concerning mind we understand how we may bring ourselves any condition by creating the corresponding conditions in our consciousness, because everything which is held for any length of time in the consciousness, eventually becomes impressed upon the subconscious and thus becomes a pattern which the creative energy will wave into the life and environment of the individual.

9. In this way conditions are produced and we find that our lives are simply the reflection of our predominant thoughts, our mental attitude; we see then that the science of correct thinking is the one science, that it includes all other sciences.

10. From this science we learn that every thought creates an impression on the brain, that these impressions create mental tendencies, and these tendencies create character, ability and purpose, and that the combined action of character, ability and purpose determines the experiences with which we shall meet in life.

11. These experiences come to us through the Law of Attraction; through the action of this law we meet in the world without the experiences which correspond to our world within.

12. The predominant thought or the mental attitude is the magnet, and the law is that "like attracts like"; consequently the mental attitude will invariably attract such conditions as correspond to its nature.

13. This mental attitude is our personality and is composed of the thoughts which we

have been creating in our own mind; therefore, if we wish a change in conditions all that is necessary is to change our thought; this will in turn change our mental attitude, which will in turn change our personality, which will in turn change the persons, things and conditions or the experiences with which we meet in life.

14. It is, however, no easy matter to change the mental attitude, but by persistent effort it may be accomplished; the mental attitude is patterned after the mental pictures which have been photographed on the brain; if you do not like the pictures, destroy the negatives and create new pictures; this is the art of visualization.

15. As soon as you have done this you will begin to attract new things, and the new things will correspond to the new pictures. To do this: impress on the mind a perfect picture of the desire which you wish to have objectified and continue to hold the picture in mind until results are obtained.

16. If the desire is one which requires determination, ability, talent, courage, power or any other spiritual power, these are necessary essentials for your picture; build them in; they are the vital part of the picture; they are the feeling which combines with thought and creates the irresistible magnetic power which draws the things you require to you. They give your picture life, and life means growth, and as soon as it begins to grow, the result is practically assured.

17. Do not hesitate to aspire to the highest possible attainments in anything you may undertake, for the mind forces are ever ready to lend themselves to a purposeful will in the effort to crystallize its highest aspirations into acts, accomplishments, and events.

18. An illustration of how these mind forces operate is suggested by the method in which all our habits are formed. We do a thing, then do it again, and again, and again, until it becomes easy and perhaps almost automatic; and the same rule applies in breaking any and all bad habits; we stop doing a thing, and then avoid it again, and again until we are entirely free from it; and if we do fail now and then, we should by no means lose hope, for the law is absolute and invincible and gives us credit for every effort and every success, even though our efforts and successes are perhaps intermittent.

19. There is no limit to what this law can do for you; dare to believe in your own idea; remember that nature is plastic to the ideal; think of the ideal as an already accomplished fact.

20. The real battle of life is one of ideas; it is being fought out by the few against the many; on the one side is the constructive and creative thought, on the other side the destructive and negative thought; the creative thought is dominated by an ideal, the passive thought is dominated by appearances. On both sides are men of science, men of letters, and men of affairs.

21. On the creative side are men who spend their time in laboratories, or over microscopes and telescopes, side by side with the men who dominate the commercial, political, and scientific world; on the negative side are men who spend their time investigating law and precedent, men who mistake theology for religion, statesmen who mistake might for right, and all the millions who seem to prefer precedent to progress, who are eternally looking backward instead of forward, who see only the world without, but know nothing of the world within.

22. In the last analysis there are but these two classes; all men will have to take their place on one side or the other; they will have to go forward, or go back; there is no standing still in a world where all is motion; it is this attempt to stand still that gives sanction and force to arbitrary and unequal codes of law.

23. That we are in a period of transition is evidenced by the unrest which is everywhere apparent. The complaint of humanity is as a roll of heaven's artillery, commencing with low and threatening notes and increasing until the sound is sent from cloud to cloud, and the lightning splits the air and earth.

24. The sentries who patrol the most advanced outposts of the Industrial, Political, and Religious world are calling anxiously to each other. What of the night? The danger and insecurity of the position they occupy and attempt to hold is becoming more apparent every hour. The dawn of a new era necessarily declares that the existing order of things cannot much longer be.

25. The issue between the old regime and the new, the crux of the social problem, is entirely a question of conviction in the minds of the people as to the nature of the Universe. When they realize that the transcendent force of spirit or mind of the Cosmos is within each individual, it will be possible to frame laws that shall consider the liberties and rights of the many instead of the privileges of the few.

26. As long as the people regard the Cosmic power as a power non-human and alien to humanity, so long will it be comparatively easy for a supposed privileged class to rule by Divine right in spite of every protest of social sentiment. The real interest of democracy is therefore to exalt, emancipate and recognize the divinity of the human spirit. To recognize that all power is from within. That no human being has any more power than any other human being, except such as may willingly be delegated to him. The old regime would have us believe that the law was superior to the law-makers; herein is the gist of the social crime of every form of privilege and personal inequality, the institutionalizing of the fatalistic doctrine of Divine election.

27. The Divine Mind is the Universal Mind; it makes no exceptions, it plays no favorites; it does not act through sheer caprice or from anger, jealousy or wrath; neither can it be flattered, cajoled or moved by sympathy or petition to supply man with some need which he thinks necessary for his happiness or even his existence. The Divine Mind makes no exceptions to favor any individual; but when the individual understands and realizes his Unity with the Universal principle he will appear to be favored because he will have found the source of all health, all wealth, and all power.

28. For your exercise this week, concentrate on the Truth. Try to realize that the Truth shall make you free, that is, nothing can permanently stand in the way of your perfect success when you learn to apply the scientifically correct thought methods and principles. Realize that you are externalizing in your environment your inherent soul potencies. Realize that the Silence offers an ever-available and almost unlimited opportunity for awakening the highest conception of Truth. Try to comprehend that Omnipotence itself is absolute silence, all else is change, activity, limitation. Silent thought concentration is therefore the true method of reaching, awakening, and then expressing the wonderful potential power of the world within.

The possibilities of thought training are infinite, its consequence eternal, and yet few take the pains to direct their thinking into channels that will do them good, but instead leave all to chance.

—MARDEN

PART TWENTY-ONE. STUDY QUESTIONS WITH ANSWERS

201. What is the real secret of power?
The consciousness of power, because whatever we become conscious of, is invariably manifested in the objective world, is brought forth into tangible expression.
202. What is the source of this power?
The Universal Mind, from which all things proceed, and which is one and indivisible.
203. How is this power being manifested?
Through the individual; each individual is a channel whereby this energy is being differentiated in form.
204. How may we connect with this Omnipotence?
Our ability to think is our ability to act on this Universal Energy, and what we think is what is produced or created in the objective world.
205. What is the result of this discovery?
The result is nothing less than marvelous, it opens unprecedented and limitless opportunity.
206. How, then, may we eliminate imperfect conditions?
By becoming conscious of our Unity with the source of all power.
207. What is one of the distinctive characteristics of the Master Mind?
He thinks big thoughts, he holds ideas large enough to counteract and destroy all petty and annoying obstacles.
208. How do experiences come to us?
Through the Law of Attraction.
209. How is this law brought into operation?
By our predominant mental attitude.
210. What is the issue between the old regime and the new?
A question of conviction as to the nature of the Universe. The old regime is trying to cling to the fatalistic doctrine of Divine election. The new regime recognizes the divinity of the individual, the democracy of humanity.

Part Twenty-two

In Part Twenty-two you will find that thoughts are spiritual seeds, which, when planted in the subconscious mind, have a tendency to sprout and grow, but unfortunately the fruit is frequently not to our liking.

The various forms of inflammation, paralysis, nervousness and diseased conditions generally, are the manifestation of fear, worry, care, anxiety, jealousy, hatred and similar thought.

The life processes are carried on by two distinct methods; first, the taking up and making use of nutritive material necessary for constructing cells; second, breaking down and excreting the waste material.

All life is based upon these constructive and destructive activities, and as food, water and air are the only requisites necessary for the construction of cells, it would seem that the problem of prolonging life indefinitely would not be a very difficult one.

However strange it may seem, it is the second or destructive activity that is, with rare exception, the cause of all disease. The waste material accumulates and saturates the tissues, which causes autointoxication. This may be partial or general. In the first case the disturbance will be local; in the second place it will affect the whole system.

The problem, then, before us in the healing of disease is to increase the inflow and distribution of vital energy throughout the system, and this can only be done by eliminating thoughts of fear, worry, care, anxiety, jealousy, hatred, and every other destructive thought, which tend to tear down and destroy the nerves and glands which control the excretion and elimination of poisonous and waste matter.

"Nourishing foods and strengthening tonics" cannot bestow life, because these are but secondary manifestations to life. The primary manifestation of life and how you may get in touch with it is explained in the Part which I have the privilege of enclosing herewith.

1. Knowledge is of priceless value, because by applying knowledge we can make our future what we wish it to be. When we realize that our present character, our present environment, our present ability, our present physical condition are all the result of past methods of thinking, we shall begin to have some conception of the value of knowledge.

2. If the state of our health is not all that could be desired, let us examine our method of thinking; let us remember that every thought produces an impression on the mind;

every impression is a seed which will sink into the subconscious and form a tendency; the tendency will be to attract other similar thoughts and before we know it we shall have a crop which must be harvested.

3. If these thoughts contain disease germs, the harvest will be sickness, decay, weakness, and failure; the question is, what are we thinking, what are we creating, what is the harvest to be?

4. If there is any physical condition which it is necessary to change, the law governing visualization will be found effective. Make a mental image of physical perfection, hold it in the mind until it is absorbed by the consciousness. Many have eliminated chronic ailments in a few weeks by this method, and thousands have overcome and destroyed all manner of ordinary physical disturbances by this method in a few days, sometimes in a few minutes.

5. It is through the law of vibration that the mind exercises this control over the body. We know that every mental action is a vibration, and we know that all form is simply a mode of motion, a rate of vibration. Therefore, any given vibration immediately modifies every atom in the body, every life cell is affected and an entire chemical change is made in every group of life cells.

6. Everything in the Universe is what it is by virtue of its rate of vibration. Change the rate of vibration and you change the nature, quality and form. The vast panorama of nature, both visible and invisible, is being constantly changed by simply changing the rate of vibration, and as thought is a vibration we can also exercise this power. We can change the vibration and thus produce any condition which we desire to manifest in our bodies.

7. We are all using this power every minute. The trouble is most of us are using it unconsciously and thus producing undesirable results. The problem is to use it intelligently and produce only desirable results. This should not be difficult, because we all have had sufficient experience to know what produces pleasant vibration in the body, and we also know the causes which produce the unpleasant and disagreeable sensations.

8. All that is necessary is to consult our own experience. When our thought has been uplifted, progressive, constructive, courageous, noble, kind or in any other way desirable, we have set in motion vibrations which brought about certain results. When our thought has been filled with envy, hatred, jealousy, criticism or any of the other thousand and one forms of discord, certain vibrations were set in motion which brought about certain other results of a different nature, and each of these rates of vibration, if kept up, crystallized in form. In the first case the result was mental, moral and physical health, and in the second case discord, inharmony and disease.

9. We can understand, then, something of the power which the mind possesses over the body.

10. The objective mind has certain effects on the body which are readily recognized. Someone says something to you which strikes you as ludicrous and you laugh, possibly until your whole body shakes, which shows that thought has control over the muscles of your body; or someone says something which excites your sympathy and your eyes fill with tears, which shows that thought controls the glands of your body; or someone says something which makes you angry and the blood mounts to your cheek, which shows that

thought controls the circulation of your blood. But as these experiences are all the results of the action of your objective mind over the body, the results are of a temporary nature; they soon pass away and leave the situation as it was before.

11. Let us see how the action of the subconscious mind over the body differs. You receive a wound; thousands of cells begin the work of healing at once; in a few days or a few weeks the work is complete. You may even break a bone. No surgeon on earth can weld the parts together (I am not referring to the insertion of rods or other devices to strengthen or replace bones). He may set the bone for you, and the subjective mind will immediately begin the process of welding the parts together, and in a short time the bone is as solid as it ever was. You may swallow poison; the subjective mind will immediately discover the danger and make violent efforts to eliminate it. You may become infected with a dangerous germ; the subjective will at once commence to build a wall around the infected area and destroy the infection by absorbing it in the white blood corpuscles which it supplies for the purpose.

12. These processes of the subconscious mind usually proceed without our personal knowledge or direction, and so long as we do not interfere the result is perfect, but, as these millions of repair cells are all intelligent and respond to our thought, they are often paralyzed and rendered impotent by our thoughts of fear, doubt, and anxiety. They are like an army of workmen, ready to start an important piece of work, but every time they get started on the undertaking a strike is called, or plans changed, until they finally get discouraged and give up.

13. The way to health is founded on the law of vibration, which is the basis of all science, and this law is brought into operation by the mind, the "world within." It is a matter of individual effort and practice. Our world of power is within; if we are wise we shall not waste time and effort in trying to deal with effects as we find them in the "world without," which is only an external, a reflection.

14. We shall always find the cause in the "world within"; by changing the cause, we change the effect.

15. Every cell in your body is intelligent and will respond to your direction. The cells are all creators and will create the exact pattern which you give them.

16. Therefore, when perfect images are placed before the subjective, the creative energies will build a perfect body.

17. Brain cells are constructed in the same way. The quality of the brain is governed by the state of mind, or mental attitude, so that if undesirable mental attitudes are conveyed to the subjective they will in turn be transferred to the body; we can therefore readily see that if we wish the body to manifest health, strength and vitality this must be the predominant thought.

18. We know then that every element of the human body is the result of a rate of vibration.

19. We know that mental action is a rate of vibration.

20. We know that a higher rate of vibration governs, modifies, controls, changes, or destroys a lower rate of vibration.

21. We know that the rate of vibration is governed by the character of brain cells, and finally,

22. We know how to create these brain cells; therefore,

23. We know how to make any physical change in the body we desire, and having secured a working knowledge of the power of mind to this extent, we have come to know that there is practically no limitation which can be placed upon our ability to place ourselves in harmony with natural law, which is omnipotent.

24. This influence or control over the body by mind is coming to be more and more generally understood, and many physicians are now giving the matter their earnest attention. Dr. Albert T. Shofield, who has written several important books on the subject, says, "The subject of mental therapeutics is still ignored in medical works generally. In our physiologies no references is made to the central controlling power that rules the body for its good, and the power of the mind over the body is seldom spoken of."

25. No doubt many physicians treat nervous diseases of functional origin wisely and well, but what we contend is that the knowledge they display was taught at no school, was learned from no book, but it is intuitive and empirical.

26. This is not as it should be. The power of mental therapeutics should be the subject of careful, special and scientific teaching in every medical school. We might pursue the subject of maltreatment, or want of treatment, further in detail and describe the disastrous results of neglected cases; but the task is an invidious one.

27. There can be no doubt that few patients are aware how much they can do for themselves. What the patient can do for himself, the forces he can set in motion are as yet unknown. We are inclined to believe that they are far greater than most imagine, and will undoubtedly be used more and more. Mental therapeutics may be directed by the patient himself to calming the mind in excitement, by arousing feelings of joy, hope, faith, and love; by suggesting motives for exertion, by regular mental work, by diverting the thoughts from the malady.

28. For your exercise this week concentrate on Tennyson's beautiful lines "Speak to Him, thou, for He hears, and spirit with spirit can meet, Closer is He than breathing, and nearer than hands and feet." Then try to realize that when you do "Speak to Him" you are in touch with Omnipotence.

29. This realization and recognition of this Omnipresent power will quickly destroy any and every form of sickness or suffering and substitute harmony and perfection. Then remember there are those who seem to think that sickness and suffering are sent by God; if so, every physician, every surgeon and every Red Cross nurse is defying the will of God and hospitals and sanitariums are places of rebellion instead of houses of mercy. Of course, this quickly reasons itself into an absurdity, but there are many who still cherish the idea.

30. Then let the thought rest on the fact that until recently theology has been trying to teach an impossible Creator, one who created beings capable of sinning and then allowed them to be eternally punished for such sins. Of course the necessary outcome of such extraordinary ignorance was to create fear instead of love, and so, after two thousand years of this kind of propaganda, Theology is now busily engaged in apologizing for Christendom.

31. You will then more readily appreciate the ideal man, the man made in the image

and likeness of God, and you will more readily appreciate the all-originating Mind that forms, upholds, sustains, originates, and creates all there is.

All are but parts of one stupendous whole, Whose body nature is, and God the soul.

Opportunity follows perception, action follows inspiration, growth follows knowledge, eminence follows progress. Always the spiritual first, then the transformation into the infinite and illimitable possibilities of achievement.

PART TWENTY-TWO. STUDY QUESTIONS WITH ANSWERS

211. How may sickness be eliminated?
By placing ourselves in harmony with natural law, which is Omnipotent.
212. What is the process?
A realization that man is a spiritual being and that this spirit must necessarily be perfect.
213. What is the result?
A conscious recognition of this perfection—first intellectually, then emotionally—brings about a manifestation of this perfection.
214. Why is this so?
Because thought is spiritual and therefore creative and correlates with its object and brings it into manifestation.
215. What natural law is brought into operation?
The law of vibration.
216. Why does this govern?
Because a higher rate of vibration governs, modifies, controls, changes, or destroys a lower rate of vibration.
217. Is this system of mental therapeutics generally recognized?
Yes, there are literally millions of people in this country who make use of it in one form or another (and obviously many more worldwide).
218. What is the result of this system of thought?
For the first time in the world's history every man's highest reasoning faculty can be satisfied by a demonstrable truth which is now fast flooding the world.
219. Is this system applicable to other forms of supply?
It will meet every human requirement or necessity.
220. Is this system scientific or religious?
Both. True science and true religion are twin sisters; where one goes, the other necessarily follows.

Part Twenty-three

In the Part which I have the honor to transmit herewith you will find that money weaves itself into the entire fabric of our very existence; that the law of success is service; that we get what we give, and for this reason we should consider it a great privilege to be able to give.

We have found that thought is the creative activity behind every constructive enterprise. We can therefore give nothing of more practical value than our thought.

Creative thought requires attention, and the power of attention is, as we have found, the weapon of the superman. Attention develops concentration, and concentration develops Spiritual Power, and Spiritual Power is the mightiest force in existence.

This is the science which embraces all sciences. It is the art which, above all arts, is relevant to human life. In the mastery of this science and this art there is opportunity for unending progression. Perfection in this is not acquired in six days, nor in six weeks, nor in six months. It is the labor of life. Not to go forward is to go backward.

It is inevitable that the entertainment of positive, constructive and unselfish thoughts should have a far-reaching effect for good. Compensation is the keynote of the universe. Nature is constantly seeking to strike an equilibrium. Where something is sent out something must be received; else there should be a vacuum formed.

By observance of this rule you cannot fail to profit in such measure as to amply justify your effort along this line.

1. The money consciousness is an attitude of mind; it is the open door to the arteries of commerce. It is the receptive attitude. Desire is the attractive force which sets the current in motion and fear is the great obstacle by which the current is stopped or completely reversed, turned away from us.

2. Fear is just the opposite from money consciousness; it is poverty consciousness, and as the law is unchangeable we get exactly what we give; if we fear we get what we feared. Money weaves itself into the entire fabric of our very existence; it engages the best thought of the best minds.

3. We make money by making friends, and we enlarge our circle of friends by making money for them, by helping them, by being of service to them. The first law of suc-

cess then is service, and this in turn is built on integrity and justice. The man who at least is not fair in his intention is simply ignorant; he has missed the fundamental law of all exchange; he is impossible; he will lose surely and certainly; he may not know it; he may think he is winning, but he is doomed to certain defeat. He cannot cheat the Infinite. The law of compensation will demand of him an eye for an eye and a tooth for a tooth.

4. The forces of life are volatile; they are composed of our thoughts and ideals and these in turn are molded into form; our problem is to keep an open mind, to constantly reach out for the new, to recognize opportunity, to be interested in the race rather than the goal, for the pleasure is in the pursuit rather than the possession.

5. You can make a money magnet of yourself, but to do so you must first consider how you can make money for other people. If you have the necessary insight to perceive and utilize opportunities and favorable conditions and recognize values, you can put yourself in position to take advantage of them, but your greatest success will come as you are enabled to assist others. What benefits one must benefit all.

6. A generous thought is filled with strength and vitality, a selfish thought contains the germs of dissolution; it will disintegrate and pass away. Great financiers are simply channels for the distribution of wealth; enormous amounts come and go, but it would be as dangerous to stop the outgo as the income; both ends must remain open; and so our greatest success will come as we recognize that it is just as essential to give as to get.

7. If we recognize the Omnipotent power that is the source of all supply we will adjust our consciousness to this supply in such a way that it will constantly attract all that is necessary to itself and we shall find that the more we give the more we get. Giving in this sense implies service. The banker gives his money, the merchant gives his goods, the author gives his thought, the workman gives his skill; all have something to give, but the more they can give, the more they get, and the more they get the more they are enabled to give.

8. The financier gets much because he gives much; he thinks; he is seldom a man that lets anyone else do his thinking for him; he wants to know how results are to be secured; you must show him; when you can do this he will furnish the means by which hundreds or thousands may profit, and in proportion as they are successful will he be successful. Morgan, Rockefeller, Carnegie and others did not get rich because they lost money for other people; on the contrary, it is because they made money for other people that they become the wealthiest men in the wealthiest country on the globe.

9. The average person is entirely innocent of any deep thinking; he accepts the ideas of others, and repeats them, in very much the same way as a parrot; this is readily seen when we understand the method which is used to form public opinion, and this docile attitude on the part of a large majority who seem perfectly willing to let a few persons do all their thinking for them is what enables a few men in a great many countries to usurp all the avenues of power and hold the millions in subjection. Creative thinking requires attention.

10. The power of attention is called concentration; this power is directed by the will; for this reason we must refuse to concentrate or think of anything except the things we desire. Many are constantly concentrating upon sorrow, loss and discord of every kind;

as thought is creative it necessarily follows that this concentration inevitably leads to more loss, more sorrow and more discord. How could it be otherwise? On the other hand, when we meet with success, gain, or any other desirable condition, we naturally concentrate upon the effects of these things and thereby create more, and so it follows that much leads to more.

11. How an understanding of this principle can be utilized in the business world is well told by an associate of mine:

12. "Spirit, whatever else it may or may not be, must be considered as the Essence of Consciousness, the Substance of Mind, the reality underlying Thought. And as all ideas are phases of the activity of Consciousness, Mind or Thought, it follows that in Spirit, and in it alone, is to be found the Ultimate Fact, the Real Thing, or Idea."

13. This being admitted, does it not seem reasonable to hold that a true understanding of Spirit, and its laws of manifestation, would be about the most "practical" thing that a "practical" person can hope to find? Does it not seem certain that if the "practical" men of the world could but realize this fact, they would "fall all over themselves" in getting to the place in which they might obtain such knowledge of spiritual things and laws? These men are not fools; they need only to grasp this fundamental fact in order to move in the direction of that which is the essence of all achievement.

14. Let me give you a concrete example. I know a man in Chicago whom I had always considered to be quite materialistic. He had made several successes in life; and also several failures. The last time I had a talk with him he was practically "down and out," as compared with his former business condition. It looked as if he had indeed reached "the end of his rope," for he was well advanced into the stage of middle-age, and new ideas came more slowly, and less frequently to him than in former years.

15. He said to me, in substance: "I know that all things that 'work out' in business are the result of Thought; any fool knows that. Just now, I seem to be short on thoughts and good ideas. But, if this 'All-Mind' teaching is correct, it should be possible for the individual to attain a 'direct connection' with Infinite Mind; and in Infinite Mind there must be the possibility of all kinds of good ideas which a man of my courage and experience could put to practical use in the business world, and make a big success thereof. It looks good to me; and I am going to look into it."

16. This was several years ago. The other day I heard of this man again. Talking to a friend, I said: "What has come of our old friend X? Has he ever gotten on his feet again?" The friend looked at me in amazement. "Why," said he, "don't you know about X's great success? He is the Big Man in the '______ Company' (naming a concern which has made a phenomenal success during the last eighteen months and is now well known, by reason of its advertisements, from one end of the country to another, and also abroad). He is the man who supplied the BIG IDEA for that concern. Why, he is about a half-million to the good and is moving rapidly toward the million mark; all in the space of eighteen months." I had not connected this man with the enterprise mentioned; although I knew of the wonderful success of the company in question. Investigation has shown that the story is true, and that the above stated facts are not exaggerated in the slightest.

17. Now, what do you think of that? To me, it means that this man actually made the "direct connection" with Infinite Mind—Spirit—and, having found it, he set it to work for him. He "used it in his business."

18. Does this sound sacrilegious or blasphemous? I hope not; I do not mean it to be so. Take away the implication of Personality, or Magnified Human Nature, from the conception of "The Infinite," and you have left the conception of an Infinite Presence-Power, the Quintessence of which is Consciousness—in fact, at the last, Spirit. As this man, also, at the last, must be considered as a manifestation of Spirit; there is nothing sacrilegious in the idea that he, being Spirit, should so harmonize himself with his Origin and Source that he would be able to manifest at least a minor degree of its Power. All of us do this, more or less, when we use our minds in the direction of Creative Thought. This man did more, he went about it in an intensely "practical" manner.

19. I have not consulted him about his method of procedure, though I intend doing so at the first opportunity, but he not only drew upon the Infinite Supply for the ideas which he needed (and which formed the seed of his success), but he also used the Creative Power of Thought in building up for himself an Idealistic Pattern of that which he hoped to manifest in material form, adding thereto, changing, improving its detail, from time to time—proceeding from the general outline to the finished detail. I judge this to be the facts of the case, not alone from my recollection of the conversation a few years ago, but also because I have found the same thing to be true in the cases of other prominent men who have made similar manifestation of Creative Thought.

20. Those who may shrink from this idea of employing the Infinite Power to aid one in his work in the material world, should remember that if the Infinite objected in the least to such a procedure the thing could never happen. The Infinite is quite able to take care of itself.

21. "Spirituality" is quite "practical," very "practical," intensely "practical." It teaches that Spirit is the Real Thing, the Whole Thing, and that Matter is but plastic stuff, which Spirit is able to create, mold, manipulate, and fashion to its will. Spirituality is the most "practical" thing in the world—the only really and absolutely "practical" thing that there is!

22. This week concentrate on the fact that man is not a body with a spirit, but a spirit with a body, and that it is for this reason that his desires are incapable of any permanent satisfaction in anything not spiritual. Money is therefore of no value except to bring about the conditions which we desire, and these conditions are necessarily harmonious. Harmonious conditions necessitate sufficient supply, so that if there appears to be any lack, we should realize that the idea or soul of money is service, and as this thought takes form, channels of supply will be opened, and you will have the satisfaction of knowing that spiritual methods are entirely practical.

We have discovered that premeditated, orderly thinking for a purpose matures that purpose into fixed form, so that we may be absolutely sure of the result of our dynamic experiment.

—FRANCIS LARIMER WARNER

PART TWENTY-THREE. STUDY QUESTIONS WITH ANSWERS

221. What is the first law of success?
Service.
222. How may we be of the most service?
Have an open mind; be interested in the race rather than the goal, in the pursuit rather than possession.
223. What is the result of a selfish thought?
It contains the germs of dissolution.
224. How will our greatest success be achieved?
By a recognition of the fact that it is just as essential to give as to receive.
225. Why do financiers frequently meet with great success?
Because they do their own thinking.
226. Why do the great majority in every country remain the docile and apparently willing tools of the few?
Because they let the few do all their thinking for them.
227. What is the effect of concentrating upon sorrow and loss?
More sorrow and more loss.
228. What is the effect of concentrating upon gain?
More gain.
229. Is this principle used in the business world?
It is the only principle which is ever used, or ever can be used; there is no other principle. The fact that it may be used unconsciously does not alter the situation.
230. What is the practical application of this principle?
The fact that success is an effect, not a cause, and if we wish to secure the effect we must ascertain the cause, or idea or thought by which the effect is created.

Nurture your mind with great thoughts; to believe in the heroic makes heroes.

—DISRAELI

Part Twenty-four

Enclosed you will find Part Twenty-four, your final lesson of this course. If you have practiced each of the exercises a few minutes every day, as suggested, you will have found that you can get out of life exactly what you wish by first putting into life that which you wish, and you will probably agree with the student who said: "The thought is almost overwhelming, so vast, so available, so definite, so reasonable and so usable."

The fruit of this knowledge is, as it were, a gift of the Gods; it is the "truth" that makes men free, not only free from every lack and limitation, but free from sorrow, worry and care, and, is it not wonderful to realize that this law is no respecter of persons, that it makes no difference what your habit of thought may be, the way has been prepared.

If you are inclined to be religious, the greatest religious teacher the world has ever known made the way so plain that all may follow. If your mental bias is toward physical science, the law will operate with mathematical certainty. If you are inclined to be philosophical, Plato or Emerson may be your teacher, but in either case, you may reach degrees of power to which it is impossible to assign any limit.

An understanding of this principle, I believe, is the secret for which the ancient Alchemists vainly sought, because it explains how gold in the mind may be transmuted into gold in the heart and in the hand.

1. When the scientists first put the Sun in the center of the Solar System and sent the earth spinning around it, there was immense surprise and consternation. The whole idea was self-evidently false; nothing was more certain than the movement of the Sun across the sky, and anyone could see it descend behind the western hills and sink into the sea; scholars raged and scientists rejected the idea as absurd, yet the evidence has finally carried conviction in the minds of all.

2. We speak of a bell as a "sounding body," yet we know that all the bell can do is to produce vibrations in the air. When these vibrations come at the rate of sixteen per second, they cause a sound to be heard in the mind. It is also possible for the mind to hear vibrations up to the rate of 38,000 vibrations per second. When the number increases beyond this, all is silence again; so that we know that the sound is not in the bell, it is in our own mind.

3. We speak and even think of the Sun as "giving light." Yet we know it is simply giving forth energy which produces vibrations in the ether at the rate of four hundred trillion a second, causing what are termed light waves, so that we know that what we call light is simply a form of energy and that the only light there is, is the sensation caused in the mind by the motion of the waves. When the number increases, the light changes in color, each change in color being caused by shorter and more rapid vibrations; so that although we speak of the rose as being red, the grass as being green, or the sky as being blue, we know that the colors exist only in our minds, and are the sensations experienced by us as the result of the vibrations of light waves. When the vibrations are reduced below four hundred trillion a second, they no longer affect us as light, but we experience the sensation of heat. It is evident, therefore, that we cannot depend upon the evidence of the senses for our information concerning the realities of things; if we did we should believe that the sun moved, that the world was flat instead of round, that the stars were bits of light instead of vast suns.

4. The whole range then of the theory and practice of any system of metaphysics consists in knowing the Truth concerning yourself and the world in which you live; in knowing that in order to express harmony, you must think harmony; in order to express health you must think health; and in order to express abundance you must think abundance; to do this you must reverse the evidence of the senses.

5. When you come to know that every form of disease, sickness, lack and limitation is simply the result of wrong thinking, you will have come to know "the Truth which shall make you free." You will see how mountains may be removed. If these mountains consist only of doubt, fear, distrust or other forms of discouragement, they are none the less real, and they need not only to be removed but to be "cast into the sea."

6. Your real work consists in convincing yourself of the truth of these statements. When you have succeeded in doing this you will have no difficulty in thinking the truth, and as has been shown, the Truth contains a vital principle and will manifest itself.

7. Those who heal diseases by mental methods have come to know this truth, they demonstrate it in their lives and the lives of others daily. They know that life, health and abundance are Omnipresent, filling all space, and they know that those who allow disease or lack of any kind to manifest themselves have as yet not come into an understanding of this great law.

8. As all conditions are thought creations and therefore entirely mental, disease and lack are simply mental conditions in which the person fails to perceive the truth; as soon as the error is removed, the condition is removed.

9. The method for removing this error is to go into the Silence and know the Truth; as all mind is one mind, you can do this for yourself or anyone else. If you have learned to form mental images of the conditions desired, this will be the easiest and quickest way to secure results; if not, results can be accomplished by argument, by the process of convincing yourself absolutely of the truth of your statement.

10. Remember, and this is one of the most difficult as well as most wonderful statements to grasp . . . remember that no matter what the difficulty is, no matter where it is, no matter who is affected, you have no patient but yourself; you have nothing to do but to convince yourself of the truth which you desire to see manifested.

11. This is an exact scientific statement in accordance with every system of Metaphysics in existence, and no permanent results are ever secured in any other way.

12. Every form of concentration, forming Mental Images, Argument, and Autosuggestion are all simply methods by which you are enabled to realize the Truth.

13. If you desire to help someone, to destroy some form of lack, limitation or error, the correct method is not to think of the person whom you wish to help; the intention to help them is entirely sufficient, as this puts you in mental touch with the person. Then drive out of your own mind any belief of lack, limitation, disease, danger, difficulty or whatever the trouble might be. As soon as you have succeeded in doing this the result will have been accomplished, and the person will be free.

14. But remember that thought is creative and consequently every time you allow your thought to rest on any inharmonious condition, you must realize that such conditions are apparent only, they have no reality, that spirit is the only reality and it can never be less than perfect.

15. All thought is a form of energy, a rate of vibration, but a thought of the Truth is the highest rate of vibration known and consequently destroys every form of error in exactly the same way that light destroys darkness; no form of error can exist when the "Truth" appears, so that your entire mental work consists in coming into an understanding of the Truth. This will enable you to overcome every form of lack, limitation or disease of any kind.

16. We can get no understanding of the truth from the world without; the world without is relative only; Truth is absolute. We must therefore find it in the "world within."

17. To train the mind to see Truth only is to express true conditions only, our ability to do this will be an indication as to the progress we are making.

18. The absolute truth is that the "I" is perfect and complete; the real "I" is spiritual and can therefore never be less than perfect; it can never have any lack, limitation, or disease. The flash of genius does not have origin in the molecular motion of the brain; it is inspired by the ego, the spiritual "I" which is one with the Universal Mind, and it is our ability to recognize this Unity which is the cause of all inspiration, all genius. These results are far reaching and have effect upon generations yet to come; they are the pillars of fire which mark the path that millions follow.

19. Truth is not the result of logical training or of experimentation, or even of observation; it is the product of a developed consciousness. Truth within a Caesar, manifests in a Caesar's deportment, in his life and his action; his influence upon social forms and progress. Your life and your actions and your influence in the world will depend upon the degree of truth which you are enabled to perceive, for truth will not manifest itself in creeds, but in conduct.

20. Truth manifests itself in character, and the character of a man should be the interpretation of his religion, or what to him is truth, and this will in turn be evidenced in the character of his possession. If a man complains of the drift of his fortune he is just as unjust to himself as if he should deny rational truth, though it stand patent and irrefutable.

21. Our environment and the innumerable circumstances and accidents of our lives already exist in the subconscious personality which attracts to itself the mental and phys-

ical material which is congenial to its nature. Thus our future being determined from our present, and if there should be apparent injustice in any feature or phase of our personal life, we must look within for the cause, try to discover the mental fact which is responsible for the outward manifestation.

22. It is this truth which makes you "free" and it is the conscious knowledge of this truth which will enable you to overcome every difficulty.

23. The conditions with which you meet in the world without are invariably the result of the conditions obtaining in the world within, therefore it follows with scientific accuracy that by holding the perfect ideal in mind you can bring about ideal conditions in your environment.

24. If you see only the incomplete, the imperfect, the relative, the limited, these conditions will manifest themselves in your life; but if you train your mind to see and realize the spiritual ego, the "I" which is forever perfect and complete, harmonious, wholesome, and healthful conditions only will be manifested.

25. As thought is creative, and the truth is the highest and most perfect thought which anyone can think, it is self-evident that to think the truth is to create that which is true and it is again evident that when truth comes into being that which is false must cease to be.

26. The Universal Mind is the totality of all mind which is in existence. Spirit is Mind, because spirit is intelligent. The words are, therefore, synonymous.

27. The difficulty with which you have to contend is to realize that mind is not individual. It is omnipresent. It exists everywhere. In other words, there is no place where it is not. It is, therefore, Universal.

28. Men have, heretofore, generally used the word "God" to indicate this Universal, creative principle; but the word "God" does not convey the right meaning. Most people understand this word to mean something outside of themselves; while exactly the contrary is the fact. It is our very life. Without it we would be dead. We would cease to exist. The minute the spirit leaves the body, we are as nothing. Therefore, spirit is really all there is of us.

29. Now, the only activity which the spirit possesses is the power to think. Therefore, thought must be creative, because spirit is creative. This creative power is impersonal and your ability to think is your ability to control it and make use of it for the benefit of yourself and others.

30. When the truth of this statement is realized, understood, and appreciated, you will have come into possession of the Master Key, but remember that only those who are wise enough to understand, broad enough to weigh the evidence, firm enough to follow their own judgment, and strong enough to make the sacrifice exacted, may enter and partake.

31. This week, try to realize that this is truly a wonderful world in which we live, that you are a wonderful being that many are awakening to a knowledge of the Truth, and as fast as they awake and come into a knowledge of the "things which have been prepared for them" they, too, realize that "Eye hath not seen, nor ear heard, neither hath it entered into the heart of man," the splendors which exist for those who find themselves in the Promised Land. They have crossed the river of judgment and have arrived at the point of

discrimination between the true and the false, and have found that all they ever willed or dreamed, was but a faint concept of the dazzling reality.

Though an inheritance of acres may be bequeathed, an inheritance of knowledge and wisdom cannot. The wealthy man may pay others for doing his work for him, but it is impossible to get his thinking done for him by another or to purchase any kind of self-culture.

—S. SMILES

PART TWENTY-FOUR.
STUDY QUESTIONS WITH ANSWERS

231. Upon what principle does the theory and practice of every system of Metaphysics in existence depend?

Upon a knowledge of the "Truth" concerning yourself and the world in which you live.

232. What is the "Truth" concerning yourself?

The real "I" or ego is spiritual and can therefore never be less than perfect.

233. What is the method of destroying any form of error?

To absolutely convince yourself of the "Truth" concerning the condition which you wish to see manifested.

234. Can we do this for others?

The Universal Mind in which "we live and move and have our being" is one and indivisible; it is therefore just as possible to help others as to help ourselves.

235. What is the Universal Mind?

The totality of all mind in existence.

236. Where is the Universal Mind?

The Universal Mind is omnipresent, it exists everywhere. There is no place where it is not. It is therefore within us. It is "The World within." It is our spirit, our life.

237. What is the nature of the Universal Mind?

It is spiritual and consequently creative. It seeks to express itself in form.

238. How may we act on the Universal Mind?

Our ability to think is our ability to act on the Universal Mind and bring it into manifestation for the benefit of ourselves or others.

239. What is meant by thinking?

Clear, decisive, calm, deliberate, sustained thought with a definite end in view.

240. What will be the result?

You will also be able to say, "It is not I that doeth the works, but the 'Father' that dwelleth within me, He doeth the works." You will come to know that the "Father" is the Universal Mind and that He does really and truly dwell within you, in other words, you will come to know that the wonderful promises made in the Bible are fact, not fiction, and can be demonstrated by anyone having sufficient understanding.

Temples have their sacred images, and we see what influence they have always had
over a great part of mankind; but, in truth, the ideas and images
in men's minds are the invisible powers that constantly govern them;
and to these they all pay universally a ready submission.

—JONATHAN EDWARDS

About the Author

Born in 1866, Charles F. Haanel achieved success as both a businessman and an author, rising to top positions at numerous corporations in his native St. Louis throughout his life. Often called the "Father of Personal Development," Haanel was among the earliest writers to popularize the "Law of Attraction." Haanel originally published *The Master Key System* as a correspondence course in 1912, before collecting the lessons and publishing them as a single volume in 1917. Haanel retained membership in many influential groups, such as the American Society for Psychical Research, and went on to write *Mental Chemistry* and *The New Psychology.* He died in 1949.

11

THE SECRET OF SUCCESS

WILLIAM WALKER ATKINSON

(1907)

Contents

1. The Secret of Success 735
The Fundamental Rules of Success. The Instinctive impulse how to Succeed. The Leaders among men. The Unfoldment of Individuality.

2. The Individual 738
Individuality and Personality. What the Self really is. What is the Individual which manifests the Power of the Self. The Master in the Brain.

3. Spiritedness 740
Spiritedness not a fanciful, vague quality, but a real, live, forceful Power in Man. The Assertion of Recognition of Mastery. A wonderful Soul-quality.

4. Latent Powers 744
The part played by Earnestness, Enthusiasm and Desire. The Manifestation of Will-Power. The Will, and what lies behind it.

5. Soul-Force 748
The Energy of Enthusiasm, and what it really means. What Enthusiasm accomplishes. How to communicate Enthusiasm.

6. The Power of Desire 752
The Motive Force that runs the world. A useful servant but a poor master. How to Create Desire. How to apply its wonderful Energy. How to extend the Mind Force by Desire.

7. The Law of Attraction 756
Nature's Great Law. From Atom to Man. How to draw to us the things we Desire or Fear. Desire Force. How to cultivate and master this great power of the Mind. Fearthought and how to overcome it.

8. Personal Magnetism 762
The Rationale of Personal Magnetism. What it is and what it does. How it affects others. The magnetic attraction manifested by certain people.

9. Attractive Personality 765

How to acquire an Attractive Personality. The Charm of Personality. The quality of Self Respect, Confidence and Mastery—What it does for one, and Develops its Personal qualities and traits that make for success, and how to acquire them.

An Afterword 771

LESSON 1

The Secret of Success

It is with some hesitation that we bring ourselves to write this little book, entitled "The Secret of Success." Not that we are not in sympathy with the subject—not that we do not believe that there is a "Secret of Success"—but because there has been so much written on the subject of "Success" that is the veriest twaddle—masses of platitudinous wordiness—that we hesitate to take the position of a teacher of Success. It is so easy to fill pages of paper with good advice—it is so much easier to say things than to do them—so much easier to formulate a code of precepts than to get out into the field of active endeavor and put into practice the same precepts. And you may imagine why we hesitate to assume a role which would lay us open to the suspicion of being one of the "do as I tell you, and not as I do" teachers of the Art of Success.

But there is another side of the question. There is besides the mere recital of a List of Good Qualities Leading to Success—a list with which every schoolboy and reader of the magazines is acquainted—a Something Else; and that Something Else is a suggestion that the Seeker for Success has a Something Within himself which if expressed into activity and action will prove of great value to him—a veritable Secret of Success, instead of a code of rules. And so we purpose to devote this little book to unfolding our idea of what this Something Within is, and what it will do for one who will unfold it and thus express it into action. So, therefore, do not expect to find this book a "Complete Compendium of Rules Conducive to Success, Approved of and Formulated by the Successful Men of the World who became acquainted with these Rules only after they had Attained Success, and consequently had Time and Inclination to Preach to Others." This is not a book of that sort. It is Quite Different. We hope you will like it—it will do you good in any event.

All people are striving and seeking for Success. Their ideas of Success may differ, but they are all agreed upon the desirability of Attainment. "Attainment"—that is the word which embodies the essence of that which we call Success. It is the "Getting-There" idea—the idea of Attainment—of Reaching the Goal for which we set out. That is the story—Attainment.

Many men and women have endeavored to point out the way to Success, and while some have rendered valuable service to those who were following them on the Path of Attainment, yet none have been able to tell the whole story of Success. And this is not to be wondered at, for the reason that on the road to Success each and every individual must be, in a measure, a law unto himself, or herself. No two temperaments are exactly alike—Nature delights in variety; no two sets of circumstances are precisely the same—infinite variety manifests here also. And so it would be folly to attempt to lay down rules of universal application which would surely lead all to the great goal of Success. One has but to look around him on all sides and see the different needs of the different individuals composing the crowd, in order to recognize the futility of any attempt to lay down lines of universal instruction on this subject. Each and every man who has succeeded has done so in a different way—generally along some original lines of action—in fact, the faculty or characteristic known as Individuality seems to have played an important part in the success of the majority of persons who have attained it. And Individuality renders those possessing it to a marked degree to be likely to depart from any set rules or laid-out courses of action. And so, it may be stated as a general principle that each must work out his own Success along the lines of his own Individuality, rather than by following any set rule or line of conduct.

In view of what we have just said, it may seem strange that feeling as we do we have ventured to write a little book entitled "The Secret of Success"—particularly as we have started the said book by declaring the impossibility of laying down any set rules on the subject. This may seem like a paradox, but a little examination will show you that it is not so. It is true that we believe that each and every person must work out his own Success, along the lines of his own Individuality, instead of along some cut-and-dried plan. And right here is where the "Secret of Success" comes in. "Along the lines of his own Individuality," we have just said—then it must follow that one must possess Individuality before he may work along its "lines." And in the measure that he possesses Individuality, so will he possess the first prerequisite to Success. And that is what we mean by "The Secret of Success"—INDIVIDUALITY.

Every person possesses dormant and latent Individuality—but only a few allow it to express itself. The majority of us are like human sheep trotting along complacently after some self-assertive bell-wether, whose tinkling bell serves to guide our footsteps. We have absorbed the notion somehow that these bell-wethers possess the sum and substance of human knowledge and power, and ability to think—-and instead of unfolding our own dormant powers, and latent possibilities, we allow them to remain in obscurity, and we trot along, jogitty-jogitty-jog after our pet bell-wether. People are very much like sheep in this way—they are obedient and imitative animals, and rather than assume the responsibility of directing their own footsteps, they wait until someone takes the lead, and then away they stampede after him. Is it any wonder that the leaders claim the choicest pickings for themselves, and allow the flock to get only the scrubby grass. Not a bit of it—they have earned the choice bits by reason of the lack of Individuality and Initiative on the part of those following them—in fact, they were chosen as leaders because of this self-assertive, and self-directive, quality. If they had stood back in a modest, mild manner, they would have been pushed aside by the flock who would disclaim them as leaders, in favor of others who knew how to push to the front.

Now, in this little book we shall not endeavor to awaken a spirit of "bell-wetherism" in you, nor to urge you to strive to lead the flock—there is nothing in the mere leading of people other than vainglory and petty self-satisfaction. The desirable thing is to possess sufficient Individuality and Initiate to be your own bell-wether—to be a law unto yourself, so far as other men are concerned. The great men—the strong men—care nothing for the flock which so obediently trots along after them. They derive no satisfaction from this thing which pleases only inferior minds, and gratifies only petty natures and ambitions. The big men—the great spirits of all ages—have derived more satisfaction from that inward conviction of strength and ability which they felt unfolding into activity within them, than in the plaudits of the mob, or in the servility of those imitative creatures who sought to follow in their footsteps.

And this thing called Individuality is a real thing, inherent in each of us, and which may be developed and brought into activity in each one of us if we go about it right. Individuality is the expression of our Self—that Self which is that which we mean when we say "I." Each of us is an Individual—an "I"— differing from every other "I" in the universe, so far as personal expression is concerned. And in the measure that we express and unfold the powers of that "I," so are we great, strong and successful. We all "have it in us"—it depends upon us to get it out into Expression. And this Individual Expression lies at the heart of the "Secret of Success." And that is why we use the term—and that is what we shall tell you about in this little book. It will pay you to learn this "Secret."

LESSON 2

The Individual

In our last lesson we stated that we considered the "Secret of Success" to consist principally of the Free Expression of the Individual—the "I." But before you will be able to apply this idea successfully, you must first awaken to a realization of what the Individual—the "I" within you—really is. This statement may appear ridiculous at first to many of you, but it will pay you to acquaint yourself fully with the idea behind it, for upon the true realization of the "I" comes Power.

If you will stop and take stock of yourself, you will find that you are a more complex being than you had at first considered yourself to be. In the first place there is the "I," which is the Real Self or the Individual, and there is the "Me," which is something attached to and belonging to the "I"—the Personality. For proof of this, let the "I" take stock of the "Me," and it will find that the latter consists of three phases or principles, i.e. (1) the Physical Body; (2) the Vital Energy; and (3) the Mind. Many persons are in the habit of regarding their bodies as the "I" part of them, but a little consideration will show them that the body is but a material covering, or machine through which and by means of which the "I" is able to manifest itself. A little thought will show that one may be vividly conscious of the "I Am" part of himself while totally oblivious of the presence of the physical body. This being so, it follows that the "I" is independent of the body, and that the latter falls into the "Me" classification. The physical body may exist after the "I" has left it—the dead body is not the "I." And the physical body is composed of countless particles which are changing places every moment of our lives—our body of today is entirely different from our body of a year ago.

Then comes the second principle of the "Me"—the Vital Energy, or what many call Life. This is seen to be independent of the body, which it energizes, but it, too, is transitory and changeable, and readily may be seen to be but a something used to animate and energize the body—an instrument of the "I," and therefore a principle of the "Me." What, then, is left to the "I" to examine and determine its nature? The answer that comes naturally to the lip is "The Mind, by which I know the truth of what you have just said." But stop a moment, you have said, speaking of the mind, "by which I know"—have you not, in saying this, acknowledged the mind to be a something through which the "I" acts? Think a moment—is the mind YOU? You are aware that your mental states change—your emotions vary—your feelings differ from time to time—your very ideas and thoughts are inconstant and are subject to outside influences, or else are moulded and governed by that which you call "I," or your Real Self. Then there must be something back of Mental States, Ideas, Feelings, Thoughts, etc., which is superior to them and which "knows" them just as one knows a thing apart from itself but which it uses. You say "I" feel; "I" think; "I" believe; "I" know; "I" will; etc., etc. Now which is the Real Self, the Mental States just mentioned or the "I" which is the subject or Real Cause of the mental phenomena? It is not the Mind that knows, but the "I" which uses the Mind in order to know. This may seem a little abstruse to you if you have never made a study of the subject, but think it over a little and the idea will clearly define itself in your mind.

We are not telling you these things merely to give you an idea of metaphysics, philosophy, or psychology—there are many books which go into these matters at length and in detail—so it is not for that reason. The real reason is that with a realization of the "I," or Real Self, comes a sense of Power that will manifest through you and make you strong. The awakening to a realization of the "I," in its clearness and vividness, will cause you to feel a sense of Being and Power that you have never before known. Before you can express Individuality, you must realize that you are an Individual. And you must be aware of this "I" within you before you can realize that you are an Individual.

The "Me" side of you is what is called Personality, or the outer appearance of yourself. Your personality is made up of countless characteristics, traits, habits of thought, expression, and motion—it is a bunch of peculiarities and personal traits that you have been thinking was the real "I" all this time. But it is not. Do you know what the idea of Personality arose from? Let us tell you. Turn to the pages of any good dictionary, and you will see that the word originated from the Latin word "Persona," meaning "a mask used by actors in ancient times," and which word in turn was derived from two other words, "sonare," meaning to "sound," and "per," meaning "through," the two words combined meaning "to sound through"—the idea being that the voice of the actor sounded through the mask of assumed personality or character. And Webster gives the following as one of the meanings of "Person," even to this day: "A character or part, as in a play; an assumed character." So that Personality means the part you are playing in the Great Play of Life, on the Stage of the Universe. The real Individual concealed behind the mask of Personality is YOU—the Real Self—the "I"—that part of you of which you are conscious when you say "I AM," which in your assertion of existence and latent power. "Individual" means something that cannot be divided or subtracted from—something that cannot be injured or hurt by outside forces—something REAL. And you are an Individual—a Real Self—an "I"— Something endowed with Life, Mind, and Power, to use as you will. A poet named Orr has said of it:

"Lord of a thousand worlds am I,
And I reign since time began;
And night and day, in cyclic sway,
Shall pass while their deeds I scan.
Yet time shall cease ere I find release,
For I AM the Soul of Man."

LESSON 3

Spiritedness

To many of you the tide of this lesson—Spiritedness—may seem to have some connection with "spirits," "disembodied entities," or else the "soul" or some higher part of it, to which the name Spirit is often applied. But, in this case, we use the word in a different sense, and yet in a sense approved by many advanced teachers and investigators of the occult and spiritual. One of the meanings of the word "spirit" as given by Webster is as follows: "Energy, vivacity, ardor, enthusiasm, courage," etc., while the same authority defines the word "spirited" as: "Animated; full of life and vigor, lively," etc. These definitions will give you a hint of the sense in which we are now using the term, but there is still more to it.

To us the word Spirit expresses the idea of the real essential nature of the Universal Power, and which is also manifested in man as the center of his being—his essential strength and power, from whence proceeds all that renders him an Individual. Spiritedness does not mean the quality of being ethereal, "goody-goody," spirituelle, other-worldly, or any thing of that sort. It means the state of being "animated," and "animated" means "possessed of life and vigor"—so that the state is really that of being filled with Power and Life. And that Power and Life comes from the very center of one's being—the "I AM" region or plane of mind and consciousness.

Spiritedness is manifested in different degrees among different men—and even among the animals. It is an elementary, fundamental, primitive quality and expression of Life, and does not depend upon culture, refinement or education—its development seems to depend upon such instinctive or intuitional recognition of the Something Within—the Power of the Individual which is derived from that Universal Power of which we are all expressions. And even some of the animals seem to possess it.

A recent writer on the "Taming of Animals" expresses this instinctive realization of Spiritedness among some of the higher animals as follows: "Put two male baboons in the same cage, and they will open their mouths, show all their teeth, and 'blow' at each other. But one of them, even though he may possess the uglier dentition, will blow with a difference, with an inward shakiness that marks him for the under dog at once. No test of battle is needed at all. It is the same with the big cats. Put two, or four, or a dozen lions in together, and they also, probably without a single contest, will soon discover which one of them possesses the mettle of the master. Thereafter he takes the choice of the meat; if he chooses, the rest shall not even begin to eat until he has finished; he goes first to the fresh pan of water. In short he is 'king of the cage.' Now, then, when a tamer goes into a den with a big cat that has taken a notion to act 'funny,' his attitude is almost exactly that of the 'king beast' above mentioned would be toward a subject rash and ill-advised enough to challenge his kingship."

You will notice in the above quotation, that the writer says clearly that it is not always the baboon with the fiercest tusks that is the master, neither does the "king lion" necessarily assert his dominion by winning physical fight—it is something far more subtle than the physical—it is the manifestation of some soul quality of the animal. And so it is with men, it is not always the biggest and strongest physically who rule—the ruler becomes so by reason of the mysterious soul quality which we call Spiritedness, and which men often call "nerve," or "mettle," or "sand." When two individuals come into contact with each other there is a mental struggle begun, from which one or the other emerges a victor, and one defeated. There is no physical struggle—there may not be even a word uttered—and yet soul grapples with soul as the two pairs of eyes gaze into each other, and a subtle something in each engages and grapples with a subtle something in the other. It may be all over in a moment, but the conflict is settled for the time, and each of the mental combatants knows that he is victor, or defeated, as the case may be. There may be no feeling of antagonism between the parties engaging, but nevertheless there seems to be an inward recognition on both sides that there is something between them that has to be settled at once. The parties may become the best of friends, and yet one of them always leads. And this leadership does not depend upon physical strength, intellectual attainment, or culture in the ordinary sense, but upon the manifestation and recognition of that subtle quality that we have called Spirit.

People unconsciously assert their recognition of this quality in themselves and others by their use of the term. We often hear of people "lacking spirit"; being "spiritless"; and of others having had "their spirit broken," etc. The term is used in the sense of "mettle." A "mettled" horse or man is "high-spirited," according to the dictionaries; and the same authorities define "mettlesome" as "full of spirit," so you see the term is used as we have employed it—but the explanation of the source of the "spiritedness" is not given. Breeders of thoroughbred racing horses will tell you that a horse having "spirit" will run a gamer race and will often outdistance and outwind a horse having higher physical characteristics, but less "spirit" or "class." Horsemen insist that the possession of "spirit" in a horse is recognized by the other horses, who are effected by it and become discouraged and allow themselves to be beaten, although often they may be better racing machines physically. This spirit is a fundamental vital strength possessed by all living things in degrees—and it may be developed and strengthened in one's self. In our next lesson we shall recite a few instances of its manifestation among men.

Oliver Wendell Holmes, in one of his books, gives the following vivid description of the conflict of spiritedness between two men: "The Koh-i-noor's face turned so white with rage that his blue-black mustache and beard looked fearful seen against it. He grinned with wrath, and caught at a tumbler, as if he would have thrown its contents at the speaker. The young Marylander fixed his clear, steady eye upon him, and laid his hand on his arm, carelessly almost, but the Jewel felt that he could not move it. It was no use. The youth was his master, and in that deadly Indian hug in which men wrestle with their eyes, over in five seconds, but which breaks one of their two backs, and is good for three score years and ten, one trial enough—settles the whole matter—just as when two feathered songsters of the barnyard, game and dunghill, come together. After a jump or two at each other, and a few sharp kicks, there is an end of it; and it is 'After you, monsieur,' with the beaten party in all the social relations for all the rest of his days."

Fothergill says: "Emily Brontë sketched out her ideal of a being possessed of immense will-power in a thorough ruffian—Heathcliff. A massive, muscular brute! Well, it was a girl's conception of a strong man; but I think I have seen some quiet, inoffensive-looking men in spectacles, who could very soon have shown the ruffian where the superiority lay."

A celebrated historical example of Spiritedness, under apparently overwhelming odds, is that of the interview between Hugo, Bishop of Lincoln, and Richard Coeur de Lion, in the church of Roche d'Andeli. In his desire to prosecute the war in Normandy, Richard demanded additional supplies and money from his barons and bishops, but Hugo refused to furnish men or money. He claimed that although the See of Lincoln was legally bound to supply men and money for military service within the four seas of Britain, the war in Normandy did not come under that head, and be defied the king. King Richard, called the Lion-Hearted, was a dangerous man to defy, and so when he summoned Bishop Hugo to Normandy, and the latter went forth to beard the lion in his den, few doubted the outcome, and the bishop's downfall was taken as a matter of course. When the bishop landed in Normandy he was met by two friendly barons who informed him that the king was in a terrible rage against him, and who advised him to send some humble, conciliatory message to him before entering the royal presence. But the bishop refused to do this, and proceeded boldly to meet his monarch. Richard was sitting at Mass when the bishop entered. Hugo walked up to him, and disregarding his frown, said "Kiss me, my lord King!" Richard turned wrathfully away, withholding his salute. But Hugo, gazing into his eyes, and shaking the royal shoulder vigorously, repeated his demand. "Thou hast not deserved it," roared the king, in anger and chagrin. "I have," retorted Hugo, shaking the royal shoulder the harder. The king gradually dropped his eyes from those of the bishop, and gave the kingly salute and kiss, and the bishop passed on calmly to take part in the service. Hugo afterward defied the king in his council chamber, and persisted in his refusal, and even ventured to rebuke his royal master for infidelity to the queen. The council was astounded, for knowing Richard's courage and fiery temper they expected to see Hugo crushed every moment—but instead he emerged the victor in the struggle of Spiritedness. The historian says: "The Lion was tamed for the moment. The king acknowledged nothing, but restrained his passion, remarking afterward, 'If all bishops were like my lord of Lincoln, not a prince among us could lift his head among them.'"

And this was not the first time that this doughty Bishop of Lincoln had vanquished a king. In his earlier days, shortly after King Henry Plantagenet had created him bishop, he became involved in a fierce dispute with that monarch. Henry was at Woodstock Park surrounded by his courtiers when Hugo approached. The king feigned not to see the bishop, taking no notice whatsoever of him. After a few moments of strained silence, the bishop, pushing aside a powerful earl who was seated by the king's side, took his place beside the king. The king pretended to be mending his leather glove. The bishop cheerfully and lightly said: "Your Majesty reminds me of your cousin at Falaise." Falaise was the place at which Henry's ancestor Duke Robert met Arlotta, the daughter of a tanner of leather, who bore him his illegitimate son who was afterward known as William the Conqueror. The Bishop's impudent allusion to the king's ancestry was too much for the latter, and he was badly worsted in the encounter and later acceded to the wishes of the bishop.

But as Fothergill truly says: "It is a great mistake to suppose that this Will is disposed to air itself on all occasions; far from it. It often has a tendency to conceal itself, and is not rarely found under an exterior of much pleasantness. There are men, and women, too, who prevent an appearance of such politeness that they seem to have no will of their own; they apparently exist merely to do what is agreeable to others; but just wait till the time comes, and then the latent will-power is revealed, and we find under this velvet glove the iron hand—and no mistake about it. It is the secret of the diplomatist. Talleyrand possessed it to a remarkable degree, and was a cool, bold, successful diplomat; Cavour also possessed this power and used it wisely. The blusterer and bragger are devoid of it." It is a subtle, tenuous Power, resting latent beneath the surface and out of evidence—but when needed it flashes forth like the dynamic electric spark, driving all before it. It is an elemental force of irresistible power.

LESSON 4

Latent Powers

The majority of you know by actual experience in everyday life that we have within our physical organism that which we call "second-wind." We have essayed some physical task, and after a bit found ourselves "winded," that is, short of breath, and we are tempted to stop and rest our panting bodies. But we have also found by experience that if we will stick to the task at hand the feeling of physical distress will usually pass away, and we will gain what is called our "second-wind." Now just what this "second-wind" is, is a matter that has long perplexed physiologists, and even to-day they have not been able to hand us down a very good guess at the underlying cause of the phenomenon. It seems to be a fresh start acquired by reason of the opening up of reserve stores of vital energy—latent physical power stored away for such emergencies. All persons who have engaged in athletic sports know very well the details of this peculiar physiological phenomenon—its actuality is too firmly established to admit of a doubt.

And, as is often the case, examination shows a curious parallel between the workings of Nature on the mental plane and on the physical. Just as there is a physical "second-wind," so is there a mental reserve force or latent energy upon which we can draw and thus get a fresh start. The phenomena attendant upon physical "second-wind," as noted above, is almost exactly duplicated by certain mental phenomena. We may be jaded while performing some tedious bit of mental work, and we begin to feel that we are "all in," when lo! some new interest arises—some new incentive presents itself—and away we are off with a full mental "second-wind" doing our work with a freshness, vigor and enthusiasm far surpassing the original effort. We have tapped on to a fresh source of supply of mental energy.

The majority of us have little or no conception of the reserve mental energies and forces contained within our being. We jog along at our customary gait, thinking that we are doing our best and getting all out of life that there is in it—think we are expressing ourselves to our utmost capacity. But we are living only in the first-wind mental state, and back of our working mentality are stores of wonderful mental energy and power—faculties lying dormant—powers lying latent—awaiting the magic command of the Will in order to awaken into activity and outward expression. We are far greater beings than we have realized—we are giants of power, if we did but know it. Many of us are like young elephants who allow themselves to be mastered by weak men, and put through their paces, little dreaming of the mighty strength and power concealed within their organisms.

Those of you who have read our little manual entitled "The Inner Consciousness" will recall what we said therein regarding the regions above and below the plane of the ordinary outer consciousness. And on those hidden planes of the mind are untold possibilities—the raw materials for mighty mental tasks and achievement—the storage batteries of wonderful accomplishment. The trouble with us is that we do not realize the existence of these faculties. We think that we are merely what we manifest in our ordinary dog-trot gait. Another trouble is that we have not had the incentive to action—we have lacked the interest to do great things—we haven't wanted to hard enough. This "want-to-hard-enough" is the great inciting power in life. Desire is the fire which rouses up the steam of Will. Without Incentive—and that means Desire—we accomplish nothing. Given the great, earnest, burning ardent Desire as an animating force—the great incentive to action, and we are able to get up this mental "second-wind"—yes, third, fourth, and fifth winds—tapping one plane of inward power after another, until we work mental miracles.

We wonder at the achievements of the great men in all walks of life, and we are apt to excuse ourselves by the sad remark that these people seem to "have it in them," while we have not. Nonsense, we all have it in us to do things a hundred times greater than we are doing. The trouble is not in the lack of power and mental material, but in the Desire and Interest, and Incentive to arouse into activity those wonderful storehouses of dynamic power within our mentality—we fail to call into operation the great mental "second-wind" that is at our disposal, and which is like all other natural powers and forces eager and anxious to be manifested and expressed. Yes, that's what we said, "anxious and eager," for all natural forces, penned up and in a static condition, seem to be bursting with desire to manifest and express into outer dynamic activity. This seems to be a law of life and nature. Nature and all in it seems to be eager for active expression. Have you not been surprised at yourselves at times, when under some slightly higher pressure and incentive. Something Within you seemed to break its bounds and fairly carry you off of your feet in its rush into active work. Have you not accomplished tasks under the stress of a sudden urgent need, that you would have deemed impossible in cold-blood. Have you not carried all before you when you "warmed-up" to the task, whereas your ordinary self would have stood around doing nothing under ordinary circumstances.

Earnestness and Enthusiasm are two great factors in bringing into operation these latent forces and dormant powers of the mentality. But one need not stand by and wait until you work yourself into a fit of fervor before the energies spring into action. You can by a careful training of the Will—or rather, by a careful training of yourself, use your Will—manage to get hold of the mental throttle, so that you may pull it down and turn on a full head of steam whenever necessary. And when you have once mastered this, you will find that you are not any more tired when running under full pressure than when you are crawling along. This is one of the Secrets of Success.

To many a person the term "The Will" means merely a firm steadfastness of mind, akin to Determination and Fixity of Purpose. To others it means something like Desire. To others it means "the power of choice," etc. But to occultists the Will is something far more than these things—it means a Vital Power—an Acting Force of the Mind—capable of dominating and ruling the other mental faculties as well as projecting itself beyond the mental organs of the individual and affecting others coming within its field of influence. And it is in this sense that we use the word "Will" in this lesson.

We have no desire to take the reader into the dim realms of metaphysics, or even into the lighter but still arduous paths of scientific psychology, but we must acquaint him with the fact of the existence of this thing that we call Will-Power, and its relation to the "I." Of all the mental faculties or powers, that of the Will is the closest to the "I" or Ego of the person. It is the Sword of Power clasped in the hand of the Ego. One may divorce himself in thought from the other mental faculties and states, but when he thinks of the "I" he is bound to think of it as possessing that power which we call Will. The Will is a primal, original power of the "I" which is always with it, from the beginning, and which will remain with it until the end. It is the force with which he rules (or should rule) his mental and physical kingdom—the power of which his Individuality manifests itself upon the outside world.

Desire is the great motive power inciting the Will to action in life. As we have shown you, the action of Will without the motive power of Desire is unthinkable, and therefore it follows that the culture and right direction of Desire carries with it the channel of expression and manifestation of the Will. You cultivate certain Desires, in order that the Will may flow out along these channels. By cultivating the Desire along certain lines, you are making channels along which the Will may flow in its rush toward expression and manifestation. So be sure to map out your Desire channels clearly by making the proper Mental Images of what you want—be sure and make the Desire channels deep and clear cut by the force of repeated attention and auto-suggestion.

History is filled with examples of men who had developed the use of the Will. We say "developed the use," rather than "developed the Will," for man does not develop his Will—his Will is always there ready for use—a man develops his ability to use the Will—perfects himself in its use. We have frequently used the following illustration, and have not been able to improve upon it: Man is like a trolley-car, with the upraised trolley-pole of his mind reaching out to the live wire of Will. Along that wire is flowing the current of Will-Power, which it "taps" and draws down into his mind, and by which he is able to move, and act and manifest power. But the power is always in the Wire, and his "developing" consists in the ability to raise the pole to the Wire, and thus "tap on" to its energy. If you will carry this idea in your mind, you will be able to apply this truth more easily in your everyday life.

A great promoter of the steel-pen, and electroplating industries, possesses this quality to a marked degree. It has been said of him that: "He had, to begin with, a strong, powerful, almost irresistible Will; and whoever and whatever he opposed, he surely conquered in the end." Buxton said: "The longer I live, the more certain I am that the great difference between men, between the feeble and the powerful, the great and the insignificant, is Energy—Invincible Determination—a purpose once fixed, and the Victory or Death. That quality will do anything that can be done in this world—and no talents, no circumstances, no opportunities, will make a two-legged creature a man without it." In this last quotation and the one preceding it, the idea of Persistence and Determination is identified closely with that of Will. And they are closely identified, the idea being that the Will should be held close, fast, and steadily against the task to be accomplished, just as the steel chisel is held firmly up against the object on the lathe, until its work is accomplished. It is not the mere Determination or Persistency that does the work—these would be of no avail unless the Will were there to do the cutting and shaping. But then again, there is a double-aspect of Will here—the Will in one phase does the work, while in another it forces the mind to hold it up against the task. So, in a sense the Will is the power back of Determination and Persistency, as well as the force doing the work—the cutting-edge of the chisel, as well as the firm hand that holds it to its work.

Simpson has said: "A passionate Desire and an unwearied Will can perform impossibilities, or what would seem to be such, to the cold and feeble." Disraeli said: "I have brought myself by long meditation to the conviction that a human being with a settled purpose must accomplish it, and that nothing can resist a Will which will stake even existence upon its fulfillment" Foster says: "It is wonderful how even the casualties of life seem to bow to a spirit that will not bow to them, and yield to subserve a design which they may, in their first apparent tendency, threaten to frustrate. When a firm, decisive spirit is recognized, it is curious to see how the space clears around a man and leaves him room and freedom." Mitchell has said: "Resolve is what makes a man manifest; not puny resolve; not crude determination; not errant purpose—but that strong and indefatigable Will which treads down difficulties and danger, as a boy treads down the heaving frost-lands of winter, which kindles his eye and brain with a proud pulse-beat toward the unattainable. Will makes men giants."

So, raise that mental trolley-pole, and touch the live-wire of Will.

LESSON 5

Soul-Force

You often have heard the word "Enthusiasm" used—have used it often yourself. But have you ever thought of what the word really means—from what source it originated—what is its essential spirit? Few have. The word "Enthusiasm" is derived from the Greek term meaning "to be inspired; to be possessed by the gods, etc.," the term having been originally used to designate the mental state of an inspired person who seems to be under the influence of a higher power. The term originally meant "inspired by a superhuman or divine power; ecstasy; etc." It is now used, according to Webster, in the sense of: "Enkindled and kindling fervor of soul; ardent and imaginative zeal or interest; lively manifestation of joy or zeal; etc." The word has acquired a secondary and unfavorable meaning in the sense of "visionary zeal; imaginative fervor; etc."; but its real and primary meaning is that ardent, lively zeal and interest in a thing, which seems to awaken into activity some inner forces of one's nature. Real enthusiasm means a powerful mental state exerted in favor of, or against, some idea.

A person filled with Enthusiasm seems indeed to be inspired by some power or being higher than himself—he taps on to a source of power of which he is not ordinarily conscious. And the result is that he becomes as a great magnet radiating attractive force in all directions and influencing those within his field of influence. For Enthusiasm is contagious and when really experienced by the individual renders him a source of inductive power, and a centre of mental influence. But the power with which he is filled does not come from an outside source—it comes from certain inner regions of his mind or soul—from his Inner Consciousness. Those who have read our little manual entitled "Inner Consciousness" will readily understand from what part of the mentality such power is derived. Enthusiasm is really "soul-power," and when genuine is so recognized and felt by those coming within its field of influence.

Without a certain amount of Enthusiasm no one ever has attained Success, and never will do so. There is no power in personal intercourse that can be compared to Enthusiasm of the right sort. It comprises Earnestness, Concentration, and Power, and there are a very few people that cannot be influenced in some degree by its manifestation by another. Few people realize the actual value of Enthusiasm. Many have succeeded by reason of its possession, and many have failed by reason of its lack. Enthusiasm is the steam that drives our mental machinery, and which indirectly thus accomplishes the great things in life. You cannot accomplish tasks properly yourself unless you manifest a degree of interest in them, and what is Enthusiasm but Interest plus Inspiration—Inspired Interest, that's what Enthusiasm is. By the power of Enthusiasm the great things of life are brought to expression and accomplishment.

Enthusiasm is not a thing which some possess and others lack. All persons have it potentially, but only a few are able to express it. The majority are afraid to let themselves "feel" a thing, and then to let the "feeling" express itself in powerful action, like the steam in an engine. The majority of persons do not know how to get up the steam of Enthusiasm. They fail to keep the fires of Interest and Desire kindled under their mental boiler, and the consequence is they fail to get up the steam of Enthusiasm. Enthusiasm may be developed, by cultivating interest and love of your task. Interest, confidence, and desire arouse Enthusiasm, and it remains for you to either concentrate it so that its effect will be directed straight toward the object, person or thing that you wish to move, or else allow it to dissipate itself in the air without result. Like steam, Enthusiasm may be dissipated or used—by concentrated direction it produces results; and by foolish waste and dissipation it fails to do so. The more interest you take in a thing, the greater does your confidence and desire grow—and from these arise the steam of Enthusiasm. So remember always that Interest is the mother of Enthusiasm.

The enthusiastic man naturally tends toward the optimistic frame of mind, and by doing so he diffuses an atmosphere of confident, cheerful expectation around him which tends to inspire confidence in others, and which aids him in his endeavors. He surrounds himself with a mental aura of Success—he vibrates Success—and those into whose presence he comes unconsciously take on his vibrations. Enthusiasm is very contagious, and one filled with the right quality, kind and degree of it unconsciously communicates his interest, earnestness and expectations to others. Enthusiasm plays an important part in that which is called Personal Magnetism. It is a live, warm, vital mental quality, and it quickens the pulse of the one using it, and those who are affected by it. It is different from the cold-blooded indifference that one meets with so often in business, and which causes many a sale to be lost, and many a good thing to be "turned down."

The man who lacks Enthusiasm is robbed of more than half his force of Personal Influence. No matter how good his arguments may be—no matter how meritorious his proposition may be—unless he possess the warm vital quality of Enthusiasm, his efforts are largely wasted, and his results impaired. Think over the salesmen who have approached you and remember how some of them produced the chilling effect of a damp cellar upon you, while others caused you to sit up and take notice in spite of yourself by reason of their earnest interest and enthusiasm. Analyze the impression produced upon you by the different people with whom you have come in contact, and then see how great an influence Enthusiasm exerts. And then remember the effect it produces upon yourself when you feel it. Enthusiasm is Mental Steam—remember that.

A few days ago there was erected a tablet, in one of the great colleges of the land, as a memorial to a former student in its halls. This young man saved the lives of seventeen people during a great storm on the lake. He swam out after them, one by one, and brought them all in alive. He fainted away from exhaustion, and when he recovered consciousness, his first words were "Boys, did I do my Best?"

The words of this young man express the great question that should urge every true seeker after Success to so live and act that he may be able to answer it in the affirmative. It is not so much a question of "did I do so much?" or "did I do as much as some one else?" as it is a matter of "DID I DO MY BEST?"

The man who does his best is never a failure. He is always a success, and if the best should be but a poor petty thing, still the world will place the laurel wreath of victory upon his brow when he accomplishes it. The one who does his best is never a "quitter," or a "shirker"—he stays right on his job until he has bestowed upon it the very best that there is in him to give at that particular time. Such a man can never be a failure.

The man who does his best is never heard asking the pessimistic question "What's the Use?" He doesn't care a whole lot about that part of it—his mind is fixed upon the idea that he is "on his job," and is not going to be satisfied with anything less than his Best. And when one really is able to answer the great question with an honest "Yes, I did my Best," then verily, he will be able to answer the "What's the Use?" question properly—it is "of use" to have brought out the Best work in oneself, if for no other reason than because it is a Man-Making process—a developer of the Self.

This infernal "What's the Use?" question seems to have been invented by some pessimistic imp of darkness to use in discouraging people making desperate struggles or leading forlorn hopes. It has brought down many a man into the Mire of Despondency and Failure. Chase it out of your mind whenever it appears, and replace it with the question "Am I doing my Best?" knowing that an affirmative answer settles the other question also. Anything is "Of Use" if done in the right spirit, in a worthy cause, and because one's own manhood demands it. Yea, even if one goes down to death in the doing of it—still it is a Success. Listen to this story, told in a recent magazine article:

It is a story of a sailor on the wreck of a German kerosene steamer, which was dashed against the rocks of the Newfoundland coast in the early part of 1901. She had taken fire, and had been run ashore on a submerged reef about an eighth of a mile from the coast. The coast-line itself was a wall some four hundred feet high. When morning dawned the fishermen on shore saw that her boats were all gone, and all the crew and officers had apparently been lost—all except three men. Two of these three men were seen standing on the bridge—the third was aloft, lashed to the rigging. Later, the watchers saw a tremendous wave strike the vessel, sweeping away the bridge and the two men who had been standing on it. Several hours later they saw the man in the rigging unlash himself and beat his arms against his body vigorously, evidently to restore the circulation, which had been almost stopped by the lashing and the extreme cold. The man then took off his coat, waved it to the fishermen on top of the cliff and then plunged into the sea. The first thought was that he bad given up the fight and committed suicide—but he was not that kind of a man. He struck out for shore, and reaching it made three separate attempts to secure a foothold on the rocks at the bottom of the cliff. But he failed—three times was he swept away by the surf, and finally, seeing the futility of his efforts, he swam away again, toward the ship. As the narrator well says: "At that crisis in the struggle ninety-nine men out of a hundred would have given up and allowed themselves to drown; but this man was not a quitter."

After a fierce battle with the waves the man regained the ship, and after a desperate struggle managed to board her. He climbed again into the rigging and waved his hand to the fishermen high up on the cliff, who were unable to help him. He lashed himself fast, and until dark could be seen signalling the fishermen above, to show them that he was still alive and game. When the following morning broke the fishermen saw that his head had fallen to his breast and he was motionless—frozen during the night. He was dead—his brave soul had gone forth to meet its Maker, and who can doubt that when that man confronted his Maker his eyes were looking firmly and bravely toward the Presence, and not bowed down in shame or fear. Such a man was indeed worthy to face his Maker, unabashed and unashamed. As the writer George Kennan has said in words that make one thrill: "That man died as a man in adverse circumstances ought to die, fighting to the last. You may call it foolish, and say that he might better have ended his sufferings by allowing himself to drown when he found that he could not make a landing at the base of the cliff; but deep down in your hearts you pay secret homage to his courage, his endurance, and his indomitable will. He was defeated at last, but so long as he had consciousness, neither fire nor cold nor tempest could break down his manhood."

The Caucasians have a favorite proverb which runs: "Heroism is endurance for one moment more." And that one moment more tells the difference between the "quitter" and the man who has "done his Best." No one is dead until his heart has ceased beating—and no one has failed so long as there is one more bit of fight in him. And that "one moment more" often is the moment in which the tide turns—the moment when the enemy relaxes his hold and drops back beaten.

LESSON 6

The Power of Desire

What is Desire? Let us see! Webster tells us that it is: "The natural longing to possess any seeming good; eager wish to obtain or enjoy," or in its abnormal and degenerate sense: "excessive or morbid longing; lust; appetite."

"Desire" is a much abused term—the public mind has largely identified it with its abnormal or degenerate phase, just mentioned, ignoring its original and true sense. Many use the word in the sense of an unworthy longing or craving, instead of in the true sense of "aspiration," "worthy craving and longing," etc. To call Desire "aspiration" renders it none the less Desire. To apply to it the term "laudable aim and ambition" does not take away from its character of Desire. There is no sense in endeavoring to escape the fact that Desire is the natural and universal impulse toward action, be the action good or bad. Without Desire the Will does not spring into action, and nothing is accomplished. Even the highest attainments and aims of the race are possible only when the steam of Will is aroused by the flame and heat of Desire.

Some of the occult teachings are filled with instructions to "kill out desire," and the student is warned to beware of it even in its most insidious and subtle forms, even to the extent of "avoiding even the desire to be desireless—even the desire not to desire. Now this is all nonsense, for if one "wishes," or "wants," or "is inclined," or "thinks best to," or "is pleased to" Kill Out Desire—in any of these cases he is but manifesting a Desire "not to desire," in spite of his use of other names. What is this "wishing to; wanting to; feeling like; inclination; being pleased to;" and all the rest, but just plain, clear, unadulterated Desire masquerading under some of these names. To proceed to "kill out desire" without "desiring" to do so is like trying to lift oneself by pulling on his own bootstraps. Folly. What is really meant is that the occultist should proceed to kill out the lower desires that he finds within his nature, and also to kill out the "attachment" for things. Regarding this last we would say that all true occultists know that even the best "things" are not good enough to rule and master one—nothing is good enough for the soul to allow itself to be unduly attached to it so that the thing rules the soul instead of the soul mastering the thing. That is what the teachings mean—avoidance of "attachment." And in this the occult teachers are clearly right. Desire is a frightful master—like fire it sweeps away the supports of the soul, leaving nothing but smouldering ashes. But, also like Fire, Desire is a splendid servant and by its harnessed power we are able to generate the steam of the Will and Activity, and to accomplish much in the world. Without proper Desire the world would be without activity. So do not make the mistake of using Desire any more than you would refuse to use fire—but in both cases keep the mastery in your own hands, and avoid allowing the control to pass from you to Desire.

Desire is the motive force that runs the world, as little as we care to admit it in many cases. Look around you and see the effects of Desire in every human act, good or bad. As a writer has said: "Every deed that we do, good or bad, is prompted by Desire. We are charitable because we Desire to relieve our inner distress at the sight of suffering; or from the Desire of sympathy; or from the Desire to be respected in this world; or to secure a comfortable place in the next. One man is kind because he Desires to be kind—because it gives him satisfaction to be kind; while another man is cruel from precisely the same kind of motive. One man does his duty because he Desires to do it—he obtains a higher satisfaction from duty well done than he would from the neglecting of it in accordance with some weaker desires. The religious man is religious because his religious desires are stronger than his irreligious ones—because he finds a higher satisfaction in religion than in the pursuits of the worldly-minded. The moral man is moral because his moral desires are stronger than his immoral ones—he obtains a greater satisfaction in being moral than in being the contrary. Everything we do is prompted by Desire in some shape or form—high or low. Man cannot be Desireless and act in any way. Desire is the motive power behind all action—it is a natural law of life. Everything from the atom to the monad; from the monad to the insect; from the insect to man; from man to Nature, acts and does things by reason of the power and force of Desire, the Animating Motive."

All the above at the first glance would seem to make of man a mere machine, subject to the power of any stray desire that might happen to come into his mind. But this is far from being so. Man acts not upon EVERY desire, but upon the STRONGEST Desire, or the Average of his Strongest Desires. This Average of Desires is that which constitutes his Nature or Character. And here is where the Mastery of the "I" comes in! Man need not be a slave or creature of his Desires if he will assert his Mastery. He may control, regulate, govern and guide his Desires in any direction that he pleases. Nay, more, he may even CREATE DESIRES by an action of his Will, as we shall see presently. By a knowledge of psychological laws he may neutralize unfavorable Desires, and grow and develop—yes, practically Create, new Desires in their place—all by the power of his Will, aided by the light of his Reason and Judgment. Man is the Master of his Mind.

"Yes," but some close reasoning critic may object; "yes, that is true enough, but even in that case is not Desire the ruling motive—must not one Desire create these new Desires before he can do so—is not Desire always precedent to action?" Very close reasoning this, good friends, but all advanced occultists know that there is a point in which the Principle of Desire shades and merges into its companion Principle, Will, and that a close reasoner and mental analyst may imagine a mental state in which one may be almost said to manifest a WILL to Will, rather than to merely Desire to Will. This state must be experienced before it can be understood—words cannot express it.

We have stated that it was in the power of man to Create Desire—not only to be its master when created, but to actually Create it by bringing it into being. And the statement is absolutely true, and is verified and proven by the most recent experiments and discoveries of modern psychology. Instead of man being a creature of Desire—and this indeed he is in many cases—he may become Master of Desire and even a Creator of it. By knowledge and Will he may reverse the ordinary order of things and, displacing the intruder from the throne, he may seat himself there in his rightful place, and then bid the late occupant do his will and obey his bidding. But the best way for the new occupant of the throne to bring about a reorganized court is to dismiss the old objectionable creatures of his mind and create new ones in their places. And here is how it may be done:

In the first place, one must think carefully over the tasks that he wishes to accomplish, then, using his judgment carefully, judicially and impartially—impersonally so far as is possible—he must take mental stock of himself and see in what points he is deficient, so far as the successful accomplishment of the task is concerned. Then let him analyze the task before him, in detail, separating the matter into as many clear defined divisions as possible, so that he may be able to see the Thing as It Is, in detail as well as in its entirety. Then let him take a similar inventory of the things which seem necessary for the accomplishment of the task—not the details that will arise only as the work progresses, day by day—but the general things which must be done in order that the task be brought to a successful conclusion. Then having taken stock of the task, the nature of the undertaking, and one's own qualifications and shortcomings—then Begin to Create Desire, according to the following plan:

The first step in the Creation of Desire is that of the forming of a clear, vital Mental Image of the qualities, things and details of the undertaking, as well as of the Completed Whole. By a Mental Image we mean a clear-cut, distinct mental picture in the Imagination of the things just named. Now, do not turn away with an impatient motion at the mention of the word Imagination. That is another word that you have only a mistaken idea of. Imagination means far more than the mere idle, fanciful use of that part of the mind that is believed by people to be "all there is to it." It isn't all, by a long way—in fact, the fanciful part may be said to be merely a shadow of the real Imaginative effort. Imagination is a real thing—it is a faculty of the mind by which it creates a matrix, mould, or pattern of things which the trained Will and Desire afterward materializes into objective reality. There has been nothing created by the hands and mind of man which did not have its first origin in the Imagination of some one. Imagination is the first step in Creation—whether of worlds or trifles. The mental pattern must always precede the material form. And so it is in the Creation of Desire. Before you can Create a Desire you must have a clear Mental Image of what you need to Desire.

You will find that this task of creating a Mental Image is a little harder than you had expected at the start. You will find it hard to form even a faint mental picture of that which you need. But be not discouraged, and persevere, for in this, as everything else, practice makes perfect. Each time you try to form the Mental Image it will appear a little clearer and more distinct, and the details will come into a little more prominence. Do not tire yourself at first, but lay aside the task until later in the day, or tomorrow. But practice and persevere and you will soon be able to SEE mentally the things you need, just as clearly as a memory picture of something you have already seen. We shall have more to say on this subject of Mental Imagery and Imagination in subsequent lessons.

Then, after having acquired the clear Mental Image of the things you wish to Desire, and thus attain, cultivate the focusing of the Attention upon these things. The word attention is derived from the Latin word "Attendere," meaning "to stretch forth," the original idea being that in Attention the mind was "stretched forth," or "extended" toward the object of attention, and this is the correct idea, for that is the way the mind operates in the matter. Keep the ideas before your attention as much as possible, so that the mind may take a firm grasp upon them, and make them a part of itself—by doing this you firmly impress the ideas upon the wax tablet of the mind.

Thus having fixed the idea clearly in your mind by means of the Imagination and Attention, until, as we have said, it becomes a fixture there, begin to cultivate an ardent DESIRE, LONGING, CRAVING DEMAND for the materialization of the things. Demand that you grow the qualities necessary for the task—Demand that your mental pictures materialize—Demand that the details be manifested as well as the Whole, making allowance for the "something better" which will surely arise to take the place of the original details, as you proceed—the Inner Consciousness will attend to these things for you.

Then Desire firmly, confident, and earnestly. Be not half-hearted in your demands and desires—claim and demand the WHOLE THING, and feel confident that it will work out into material objectivity and reality. Think of it, dream of it, and always LONG for it—you must learn to want it the worst way—learn to "want it hard enough." You can attain and obtain many things by "wanting them hard enough"—the trouble with most of us is that we do not want things hard enough—we mistake vague cravings and wishes for earnest, longing, demanding Desire and Want. Get to Desire and Demand the Thing just as you Demand and Desire your daily meals. That is "wanting it the worst way." This is merely a hint—surely you can supply the rest, if you are in earnest, and "want to hard enough."

LESSON 7

The Law of Attraction

There is in Nature a great Law—the Law of Attraction—by the operations of which all things—from atoms to men—are attracted toward each other in the degree of the common affinity of common use. The reverse of this law—which is merely another manifestation of its power—is what is called Repulsion, which is but the other pole of Attraction, and by the operations of which things tend to repel each other in the degree that they are unlike, opposing, and of no use to each other. The Law of Attraction is Universal, on all the planes of life, from the physical to the spiritual. Its operations are uniform and constant, and we may take the phenomena of one plane and thereby study the phenomena of another plane, for the same rule applies in each case—the same Law is in operation in the same way.

Beginning with the tiny corpuscles, electrons, or ions, of which the atoms are formed, we find manifested the Law of Attraction—certain electrons attract each other, and repel others still, thereby causing to spring into existing groups combinations and colonies of electrons which being in agreement and harmony manifest and constitute what are called atoms, which until recently were supposed to be the primal form of matter. Passing on the atoms themselves, we find many degrees of affinity and attraction existing between them which cause them to combine and form into molecules of which all masses of matter consist. For instance, every drop of water is composed of countless molecules of water. And each molecule of water is composed of two atoms of Hydrogen and one atom of Oxygen—the combination always being the same in every molecule of water. Now, why these atoms combine in just this way—the same invariable grouping and proportion? Not by chance, surely, for there is no such thing in Nature—there is a natural law back of every phenomenon. And in this case it is the Law of Attraction manifesting in the case of these atoms. And it is so in all chemical combinations—it is called Chemical Affinity. Sometimes an attached atom will come in contact with, or in proximity to, another atom, and then bang! goes the explosion of the molecule as the atom flies away from its partners and into the arms of the other atom for whom it has a greater affinity. There are marriages and divorces in the world of atoms, you will notice.

And in the cases of the molecules, it is found that certain molecules are attracted to others of the same kind, under what is called Cohesion, and thus masses of matter are composed. A piece of gold, silver, tin, glass, or other form of matter is composed of countless molecules held together tightly by Cohesion—and this Cohesion is merely another form of the Law of Attraction—the same that draws all things together. And underlying the Law of Attraction is to be found our old Principle of Desire and Will. You may shrug your shoulders at this mention of Desire and Will in connection with electrons, atoms, molecules—all forms of matter, but just wait a bit and see what the leading scientific authorities have to say on the subject.

Prof. Hakel, one of the world's greatest scientists—a materialist who would sneer at the teachings of Mental Science—even this man, naturally prejudiced against mentalistic theories, finds himself compelled to say: "The idea of chemical affinity consists in the fact that the various chemical elements perceive the qualitative differences in other elements—experience pleasure or revulsion at contact with them, and execute specific movements on this ground." He also positively and distinctly states that in the atoms there must be something corresponding to Desire for contact and association with other atoms, and Will to enable the atom to respond to the Desire. Law is constant throughout Nature, from atom to man—physical, mental and spiritual.

But what has all this to do with the Secret of Success? you may ask. Simply this, that the Law of Attraction is an important part in the Secret of Success, inasmuch as it tends to bring to us the things, persons and circumstances in accordance with our earnest Desire, Demand, and Will, just as it brings together the atoms and other particles of matter. Make yourself an atom of Living Desire and you will attract to yourself the person, things and circumstances fitting in with the accomplishment of your Desire. You will also get into rapport with those who are working along the same lines of thought, and will be attracted to them and they to you, and you will be brought into relations with persons, things and environments likely to work out the problem of your Desires—you will get "next to" the right persons and things. All by the operation of this great natural Law of Attraction. No Necromancy or Magic about it at all—nothing supernatural or mysterious—just the operations of a great Natural Law.

You can do little by yourself in Life, be you ever so strong and able. Life is a complex thing, and individuals are interdependent upon each other for the doings of things. One Individual, segregated from all the other Individuals, could accomplish little or nothing along the lines of outer activity. He must form combinations, arrangements, harmonies and agreements with others, and in accordance with environments and things, that is, he must create and use the proper environments and things, and draw to himself others with whom he must form combinations, in order to do things. And these persons, things and environments come to him—and be to them—by reason of this great Law of Attraction. And the way he sets into operation this great Law of Attraction is by the operation of his Desire, and along the lines of Mental Imagery. Do you see the connection now? So be careful to form, cultivate and manifest the right Desires—hold to them firmly, strongly and constantly, and you will set into operation this great Law, which forms an important part of the Secret of Success.

Desire-Force is the motive power leading the activities of Life. It is the basic vital power which animates the minds of living things and urges them forth to action. Without strong Desire no one accomplishes anything worthy of the name—and the greater the desire the greater will be the amount of energy generated and manifested, everything else being equal. That is to say, that given a dozen men of equal intellect, physical health and mental activity—equal in everything else except Desire, in short, the ones in whom the greatest Desire resides and is manifested will outstrip the others in attainment—and of these winners the one in who Desire burns like an unquenchable flame will be the one who will Master the others by the force of his primitive elementary power.

Not only does Desire give to the man that inward motive which leads to the unfoldment of the power within himself, but it does more than this; it causes to radiate from him the finer and more subtle mental and vital forces of his nature, which, flowing forth in all directions like the magnetic waves from the magnet, or the electric waves from the dynamo, influencing all who come within the field of force. Desire-Force is a real, active, effective force of Nature, and serves to attract, draw and bring to a center that which is in line with the nature of the Desire. The much-talked of Law of Attraction, of which so much is heard in Mental Science and the New Thought, depends largely upon the force and power of Desire. Desire-Force is at the center of the Law of Attraction. There is a tendency in Nature to attract and draw to the center of a Desire the things which are needed to fulfill that Desire. One's "own will come to him" by reason of this natural force, which lies behind and underneath the entire phenomena of Mental Influence. This being so, does it not become at once apparent why one who wishes to accomplish anything should be sure to create a strong Desire for it, and at the same time be sure to acquire the art of Visualization so as to form a dear Mental Picture of the thing Desired—a clear mould in which the materialized reality may manifest?

Have you ever come in contact with any of the great men of modern business life? If you have seen these people in action, you will have become conscious of a subtle, mysterious something about them—a something that you could actually feel—a something that seemed to draw you to fit into their schemes, planes and desires almost by an irresistible force. These people are all persons of the strongest kind of Desire—their Desire-Force manifests strongly and affects those with whom they come in contact. Not only this, but their Desire-Force flows from them in great waves, which occultists inform us soon manifest a circular or whirlpool-like motion, swing around and around the center of the Desire—these men become actual cyclones of Desire into which nearly everything that comes within its sweep is affected and swept into the vortex. Have we not evidences of this in the cases of all the great leaders of men—can we not see the operation of that mighty Law of Attraction which brings to them their own. We are apt to call this Will-Power, and so it is in a way, but back and under the Will in such cases is to be found the ardent, burning Desire which is the motive force of the attractive power.

This Desire-Force is a primitive, elemental thing. It is found in the animal kingdom, and among the lower races of men, perhaps more clearly than among the higher types of men, but only because in such instances it is seen stripped of the covering, sheaths, disguises and masks that surround the more civilized forms and planes of life. But remember this well, the same principle is manifest under and beneath the polished veneer of civilized life—the Desire-Force of the cultured leader of men is as elemental as that animating the fierce and shaggy cave-man or the wild Berserker who, naked and half-mad, rushed upon overwhelming hordes of his enemy, brushing them aside like flies—that is, if you will but look beneath the polished surface. In the old wild days Desire manifested its force on the physical plane—now it manifests on the Mental Plane—that is the only difference, the Force is the same in both cases.

While we write, there has just been produced on the stage a new play which illustrates this principle. The heroine, the daughter of an old New York family of high social standing and wealth, has a dream of her life in a former incarnation, in which she sees herself torn from the arms of her cave-dweller father by the mighty arms of a fierce savage chief, whose desire is manifested through the physical. She awakens from her dream, and to her horror soon discovers the face of her dream-captor on a man who comes into her father's life in New York. This man comes from the West, forceful, resourceful and desireful, beating down all before him in the game of finance. As of old, he places his foot on the neck of his enemies—but on the mental plane, this time, instead of the physical. The same old Desire for power is strong within him—the same old masterfulness manifests itself. This man says: "I have never quit; I have never been afraid." The same old Desire then flamed up in the savage now manifests in the Master of Wall Street, and between the force of its Attraction and the coupled and allied forces of his Will, he repeats the performances of his previous incarnation—but on the plane of mental forces and achievement this time—mind, not muscle, being the instrument through which the Desire manifests.

We give the above example merely as an illustration of the fact that Desire is the motive force that moves the Will into action, and which causes the varied activity of life, men and things. Desire-Force is a real power in life, and influences not only the powers and achievement of oneself, but also attracts, influences and compels other persons and things to swing in toward the center of the Desire sending forth the currents. In the Secret of Success, Desire plays a prominent part. Without a Desire for Success, there is no Success, can be none. The Law of Attraction is set into motion by Desire.

The majority of the principles advanced in this book have been in the nature of Positive injunctions—that is, you have been urged to do certain things rather than to not do the opposite or contrary. But here we come to a place in which the advice must be given along the negative lines—we must urge you not to do a certain thing. We allude to that great poisoner of the mind and Will known as Fear. We do not allude to physical fear—important though physical courage may be, and as regrettable as physical cowardice may be considered, still it is not a part of the purpose of this book to preach against the latter and advise a cultivation of the former quality—you will find much of that elsewhere. Our purpose here is to combat that subtle, insidious enemy of true Self-Expression which appears in the shape and guise of mental fear, forebodings which may be considered as Negative Thought just as the other principles mentioned in this work may be considered as Positive Thought.

Fear thought is that condition of the mind in which everything is seen through blue glasses—in which everything seems to bring a sense of the futility of endeavor—the "I Can't" principle of mentality, as contrasted with the "I Can and I Will" mental attitude. It is the noxious weed in the mental garden, which tends to kill the valuable plants to be found therein. It is the fly in the ointment—the spider in the cup of the Wine of Life. So far as we know the first person to use the word "Fear-thought"—which has now passed into common use—was Horace Fletcher, the well-known writer, who coined it to supplant the use of the word "Worry" in a certain sense. He had pointed out that Anger and Worry were the two great hindrances to a well-balanced, advanced and progressive mentality, but many misunderstood him and urged that to abolish Worry meant to cease taking any consideration of the morrow—a lack of common prudence and forethought. And so Fletcher coined the word "Fear-thought" to express a phase of his idea of "Forethought without Worry," and he entitled his second book on the subject, "Happiness, as found in Forethought minus Fearthought," a very happy expression of a very happy idea. Fletcher also was the first to advance the idea that Fear was not a thing-in-itself, but merely an expression of Fearthought—a manifestation of the state of mind known as Fear-thought. He and others who have written on the subject have taught that Fear might be abolished by the practice of abolishing Fearthought from the mind—by driving it out of the mental chamber—and the best teachers have taught that the best way to drive out Fear (or any other undesirable mental state) was by cultivating the thought of the opposite quality of mind by compelling the mind to dwell upon the mental picture of the desirable quality, and by the appropriate auto-suggestions. The illustration has often been stated that the way to drive darkness from a room is not to shovel it out, but to throw open the shutters and let the sunlight stream in, and that is the best way to neutralize Fearthought.

The mental processes have aptly been spoken of as "vibrations," a figure that has a full warrant in modern science. Then, by raising the vibration to the Positive pitch, the negative vibrations may be counteracted. By cultivating the qualities recommended in the other lessons of this book, Fearthought may be neutralized. The poison of Fearthought is insidious and subtle, but it slowly creeps through the veins until it paralyzes all useful efforts and action, until the heart and brain are affected and find it difficult to throw it off. Fearthought is at the bottom of the majority of failures and "going down" in life. As long as a man keeps his nerve and confidence in himself, he is able to rise to his feet after each stumble, and face the enemy resolutely—but let him feel the effects of Fearthought to such an extent that he cannot throw it off and he will fail to rise and will perish miserably. "There is nothing to fear except Fear," has well been said.

We have spoken elsewhere about the Law of Attraction which operates in the direction of attracting to us that which we Desire. But there is a reverse side to this—it is a poor rule that will not work both ways. Fear will set into motion the Law of Attraction just as well as Desire. Just as Desire draws to one the things he pictures in his mind as the Desired Thing, so will Fear draw to him the thing pictured in his mind as the Thing Feared. "The thing that I feared hath befallen me." And the reason is very simple, and the apparent contradiction vanishes when we examine the matter. What is the pattern upon which the Law of Attraction builds under the force of Desire? The Mental Image, of course. And so it is in the case of Fear—the person carries about the Mental Image or haunting picture of the Feared Thing, and the Law of Attraction brings it to him just as it brings the Desired Thing. Did you ever stop to think that Fear was the negative pole of Desire? The same laws work in both cases.

So avoid Fearthought as you would the poisonous draught that you know would cause your blood to become black and thick, and your breathing labored and difficult. It is a vile thing, and you should not rest content until you have expelled it from your mental system. You can get rid of it by Desire and Will, coupled with the holding of the Mental Image of Fearlessness. Drive it up by cultivating its opposite. Change your polarity. Raise your mental vibrations. Some one has said, "There is no Devil but Fear"—then send that Devil back to the place where he properly belongs, for if you entertain him hospitably he will make your heaven a hell in order that he may feel at home. Use the mental Big Stick on him.

LESSON 8

Personal Magnetism

We hear much about Personal Magnetism in these days. It is a peculiar quality of the mental being of the individual that serves to bring other persons into a mood or state of mind sympathetic with that of the magnetic person. Some men have this quality developed to a wonderful extent, and are able to bring about a harmonious agreement on the part of other persons in a short time, while others are almost entirely deficient in this respect and their very presence tends to arouse antagonism in the minds of others. The fact of Personal Magnetism is accepted without question by the majority of people, but few will agree upon any theory attempting to account for it.

Those who have studied the matter carefully know that the whole thing depends upon the mental states of the individual, and upon his ability to cause others to "catch" his mental vibrations. This "catching" is caused by what is known as Mental Induction. Induction, you know, is "that property or quality, or process by which one body having electrical or magnetic polarity produces it in another without direct contact." And Mental Induction is a manifestation of similar phenomena on the mental plane. Persons' mental states are "catching," or contagious, and if one infuses enough life and enthusiasm into his mental states they will affect the minds of persons with whom they come in contact. We have explained this matter in detail in the little book of this series entitled "Mental Influence."

It seems to us that the prime factor in successful Mental Induction, or manifestation of Personal Magnetism, is Enthusiasm. In another lesson in this book we have told you about Enthusiasm, and when you think of Personal Magnetism, it will be well for you to read what we have said about Enthusiasm also. Enthusiasm gives Earnestness to the person, and there is no mental state so effective as Earnestness. Earnestness makes itself felt strongly, and will often make a person give you attention in spite of himself. Walter D. Moody, a well-known writer on the subject of Salesmanship, says, truthfully, "It will be found that all men possessed of personal magnetism are very much in earnest. Their intense earnestness is magnetic." And this fact has been noted by nearly every student of the subject. But the earnestness must be more than a firm, confident, honest belief in the thing being presented to the attention of the other person. It must be a live, contagious earnestness, that can best be described as Enthusiasm—Enthusiastic Earnestness, that's the term.

This Enthusiastic Earnestness has much of the emotional in it—it appeals to the Emotional side of human nature, rather than to the Thinking-Reasoning side. And yet an argument based upon reason and conducted upon logical principles may be presented with Enthusiastic Earnestness with much greater effect than if the appeal to the reason is conducted in a cold, unemotional way. The average person is so constituted mentally that he thaws out under a manifestation of live, enthusiastic "feeling," and this impression includes much that is included under the term of Personal Magnetism. The "feeling" side of mentality is as important as the "thinking" side—and it is far more common and universal, for the majority of people really think very little, while everyone "feels."

A writer in the "early seventies" of the last century has said: "All of us emit a sphere, aura, or halo, impregnated with the very essence of ourselves; sensitives know it; so do our dogs and other pets; so does a hungry lion or tiger; aye, even flies, snakes and the insects, as we know to our cost. Some of us are magnetic—others not. Some of us are warm, attractive, love-inspiring and friendship-making, while others are cold, intellectual, thoughtful, reasoning, but not magnetic. Let a learned man of the latter type address an audience and it will soon tire of his intellectual discourse, and will manifest symptoms of drowsiness. He talks at them, but not into them—he makes them think, not feel, which is most tiresome to the majority of persons, and few speakers succeed who attempt to merely make people think—they want to be made to feel. People will pay liberally to be made to feel or laugh, while they will begrudge a dime for instruction or talk that will make them think. Pitted against a learned man of the type mentioned above, let there be a half-educated, but very loving, ripe and mellow man, with but nine-tenths of the logic and erudition of the first man, yet such a man carries along his crowd with perfect ease, and everybody is wide-awake, treasuring up every good thing that falls from his lips. The reasons are palpable and plain. It is heart against head; soul against logic; and soul is bound to win every time."

If you will notice the man and woman who are considered the most "magnetic," you will find that almost invariably they are people who have what is called "soul" about them—that is, they manifest and induce "feeling," or emotion. They manifest traits of character and nature similar to that manifested by actors and actresses. They throw out a part of themselves, which seems to affect those coming in contact with them. Notice a non-magnetic actor, and you will see that although he may be letter-perfect in his part, and may have acquired the proper mannerisms, gestures and other technical parts of his art, still he lacks a "something," and that something may be seen to be the ability to communicate "feeling." Now, those who are in the secret know full well that many of the successful actors, who seem to burn with passion, feeling and emotion on the stage, really feel but little of these qualities while acting—they are like phonographs, giving off sounds that have been registered in them. But if you will investigate still further, you will see that in studying their parts and practicing the same privately, these people induced a stimulated emotion, such as the part called for, and held it firmly in their minds, accompanying it with the appropriate gestures, etc., until it became firmly "set" there—impressed upon the tablets of the mentality as the record of a phonograph is likewise impressed upon the wax. Then, when afterward they played the part, the outward semblance of the feelings, with the motions, gestures, emphasis, etc., reproduced itself and impressed the audience. It is said that if an actor allows himself to be actually carried away with his part so that he feels the same keenly, the result will not be advantageous, for he is overcome with the feeling and its effect is upon himself rather than upon his audience. The best result is said to be obtained when one has first experienced and felt the emotion, and then afterward reproduces it in the manner above stated, without allowing it to control him.

We mention the above facts for the use of those who do not naturally possess the faculty or quality of Personal Magnetism to the required degree. Such people will find it to their advantage to endeavor to work up the desired feeling of Enthusiastic Earnestness in private, fixing the mental impression by frequent private rehearsals and practice, until it becomes registered in their "habit mind," to be reproduced upon occasions when needed. Be a good actor—that is the advice in such cases; and remember this, that frequent practice and private rehearsal makes the good actor. It is a far better thing to be able to induce feeling and enthusiasm in this way, rather to be lacking of it, on the one hand; or to be an "emotional inebriate" on the other hand. One may be rationally Enthusiastically Earnest, without being filled full of "slushy gush" or maudlin emotionalism. We think that the careful student will see just what is meant here, and will not misunderstand us. And remember, that through this repeated "acting" the desired quality will often become real and "natural."

LESSON 9

Attractive Personality

We have explained in our lesson on "Individuality," that what is known as the "Personality" was not the real "I" of the Individual, but that instead it formed the "Me" part of oneself—the outward appearance of the Individual. As we have told you, the word Personality really means the "mask" aspect of the Individual, the outward appearance of the part in the great drama of life that he is playing. And just as the actor may change his mask and costume, so may the Individual change, alter and replace his Personality by other features found desirable.

But nevertheless, while the Personality is not the real "I," it plays an important part in the drama of life, particularly as the audience pays more attention to the Personality, as a rule, than it does to the real Individual behind the mask. And so it is proper that every Individual should cultivate and acquire a Personality that will prove attractive to his audience, and render him acceptable to them. No, we are not preaching deception—we regard Individuality as the Real Self, and believe that one should build himself up to his highest and best according to the laws of Individual Unfoldment—but, nevertheless, so long as one must wear a Personality about him as he goes through life, we believe that it is not only to his advantage, but is also his duty, to make that Personality as pleasing and attractive as he is able to do so. You know that no matter how good, intelligent and high-minded a man may be, if he wears the mask of an unattractive and unpleasant Personality he is placed at a disadvantage, and drives away people whom he might benefit and who would be glad to love him if they could see behind his unattractive mask.

Nor are we speaking of one's personal physical appearance when we speak of unattractive and attractive masks. While one's physical appearance goes a good way in some cases, there is a charm of Personality that far transcends that fleeting appearance. There are many persons having beautiful faces and forms whose personality is far from charming, and who repel rather than attract. And there are others whose faces are homely and whose forms are far from shapely, who have, nevertheless, that "winning way about them" that attracts others to them. There are people whom we are always glad to see, and whose charm of manner makes us forget that they are not beautiful, in fact, even their homely faces seem to become transfigured when we are in their presence. That is what we mean by Personality, in the sense in which we are now using it. It bears a very close relationship to "Personal Magnetism," of which we spoke in our preceding lesson.

One of the first things that should be cultivated by those wishing to develop the Charm of Personality is a mental atmosphere of Cheerfulness. There is nothing so invigorating as the presence of a cheerful person—nothing so dispiriting as one of those Human Wet Blankets that cast a chill over everyone and everything with whom they come in contact. Think of your acquaintances and you will find that you will naturally place them in two classes—the Cheerful ones and the Gloomy ones. Sunny Jim is always preferred to Gloomy Gus—the one you will welcome, and the other you will fly from. The Japanese understand this law of Personality, and one of the first things that they teach their children is to preserve a cheerful, sunny exterior, no matter if their hearts are breaking. With them it is considered one of the most flagrant offenses against good form to carry their sorrows, griefs and pains into the presence of others. They reserve that side of their life for the privacy of their own chamber—to the outside world they present always a happy, sunny smile. And in this they are wise, for a number of reasons: (1) that they may induce a more buoyant and positive state of mind in themselves; (2) that they may attract cheerful persons and things to them by the Law of Attraction; and (3) that they may present an attractive Personality to others, and thereby be welcome and congenial associates and participants in the work of life. There is little welcome or help for the Gloomy Gus tribe in everyday business life—they are avoided as a pestilence—everyone has troubles enough of his own without those of other people added thereto. Remember the old lines:

"Laugh and the world laughs with you;
Weep and you weep alone.
For this sad old earth is in need of mirth,
And has troubles enough of its own."

So cultivate the Smile that Won't Come Off. It is a valuable asset of Personality. Not the silly, idiotic grin, but the Smile that means something—the Real Thing. And such a smile comes from within, and is more than skin-deep. If you want a Verbal Pattern upon which to model the mental state that will produce this outward appearance of Personality, here it is: "BRIGHT, CHEERFUL AND HAPPY." Frame it and hang it in a prominent place in your Mental Art Gallery. Commit it to memory and Visualize it, so that you may be able to see it before you like an illuminated electric sign—"BRIGHT, CHEERFUL AND HAPPY"—then endeavor to materialize the idea into reality within your mind. Think it out—act it out—and it will become real to you. Then will you have Something Worth While in the shape of Personality. This may seem simple and childish to you—but if you will work it out into actuality, it will be worth thousands of dollars to you, no matter in what walk of life you may be.

Another valuable bit of Personality is that of Self Respect. If you have real Self Respect it will manifest itself in your outward demeanor and appearance. If you haven't it, you had better start in and cultivate it—beginning from the outside. That is, cultivate the appearance of Self Respect, and then get busy building up a reality behind the "front." Remember that you are a MAN, or a WOMAN, as the case may be, and not a poor, crawling Worm of the Dust or Human Door Mat. Face the world firmly and fearlessly, keeping your eyes well to the front. HOLD UP YOUR HEAD! There is nothing like a stiff back-bone and a raised head for meeting the world. The man with bent head seems to apologize for living and being on the earth—and the world is apt to take such at their own valuation. An erect head enables one to walk past the dragons at the door of Success. A writer gives the following good advice on this subject: "Hold your ear lobes directly over your shoulders, so that a plumbline hung from the ears describes the line of your body. Be sure also not to carry the head either to the right or left, but vertical. Many men make the mistake, especially while waiting for a customer to finish some important piece of business, of leaning the head to the right or left. This indicates weakness. A study of men discloses the fact that the strong men never tilt the head. Their heads sit perfectly straight on strong necks. Their shoulders, held easily, yet firmly, in position, are inspiring in their strength-indicating poise. Every line of the body, in other words, denotes the thought of the bearer." The value of this advice lies not only in the fact that it gives to you the "appearance" of Self Respect (no trifling matter, by the way), but also that it tends to cultivate a corresponding mental state within you. For just as "Thought takes form in Action," so do Actions develop mental states—it is a rule that works both ways. So think Self Respect and act Self Respect. Let the "I AM" within you manifest itself. Don't crawl—don't cringe—don't grovel—but be a Real Human Being.

Another bit of Personality worth cultivating is the Art of Taking an Interest in Others. Many people go through the world so wrapped up in their own affairs that they convey the impression of being "apart" and aloof from others with whom they come in contact. This mental state manifests in a most unpleasant form of Personality. Such people are not only regarded as "cold" and lacking heart and soul, but they also give others the impression of selfishness and hardness, and the public is apt to let such a person alone—to leave him to his own selfish moods and mental states. Such a one never becomes popular—never becomes a good mixer among men. Taking an Interest in Others is an art that well repays the student of Success to cultivate. Of course one must always keep the main chance before him and not allow his own interests to suffer by reason of his interest in others—that goes without saying, for unreasonable altruism is just as one sided as undue selfishness. But there is a middle-course. You will find something of interest in every person with whom you come in contact, and if you will but turn your attention to that interest it will manifest itself in such a way that the person will be conscious of it, will appreciate it, and will be glad to respond by taking an interest in you. This is not deceit, or time-serving, or flattery—it is the Law of Compensation working on the mental plane—you get what you give. If you will stop and think a moment you will find that the people whose Personality seems the most attractive to you are the people who seem to Take an Interest in your own personality.

This Taking an Interest in Others manifests itself in many ways, one of which is in making you a Good Listener. Now, we do not mean that you should allow yourself to be made a dumping ground for all the talk of all the people with whom you come in contact—if you do this you will have time for nothing else. You must use ordinary judgment and tact in regulating the time you give to others, depending upon the person and the particular circumstances of the case. What we do mean is that while you are listening you should Listen Well. There is no more subtle compliment that one person can pay to another than Listening Well to him or her. To Listen Well is to Listen with Interest. And that is something that cannot be very well taught in a book. Perhaps the best way to express the idea is to say "Listen as you Would be Listened unto." The Golden Rule may be applied to many things and ideas, with benefit and good results. The man who listens well is well thought of by those to whom he listens. In this connection we are always reminded of the old story of Carlyle, who, as every one knows, was reputed to be a crusty, crabbed old chap, prone to sarcastic remarks and brusque treatment of those with whom he engaged in conversation. The tale goes that one day a man called upon Carlyle—and the man understood the Art of Listening Well. He so turned the conversation as to get Carlyle started on a subject dear to his heart—and then he kept quiet and Listened Well. Carlyle talked "a straight streak" for several hours, and grew quite enthusiastic over his topic. When at last the visitor arose to depart, he was forced to actually tear himself away from Carlyle, who, following him to the door, manifested unusual enthusiasm and good spirits, and bidding him good-bye, said warmly: "Come again, mon—come again and often—ye have a wonderfully bright mind, and I've enjoyed your conversation very much indeed—ye are a most delightful conversationalist."

Be careful not to bore people with your personal experiences—better forget your personal self in talking to others, except when it is right to the point to bring yourself in. People do not want to hear what a wonderful fellow you are—they want to tell you what wonderful people they are, which is very much more pleasant to them. Don't retail your woes, nor recite your many points of excellence. Don't tell what a wonderful baby you have—the other people have babies of their own to think about. You must endeavor to talk about things of interest to the other person, if he wants to do the talking himself. Forget yourself and Take an Interest in the Other Person.

Some of the best retail merchants impress upon their salespeople the advantage of cultivating the mental attitude and personality that will give the customer the impression that you are "on his side of the counter"—that is, that you are taking a personal interest in his being well-served, suited, well-treated and satisfied. The salesman who is able to create that impression is well advanced on the road to success in his particular line. This is a thing difficult to describe, but a little observation and thought and practice along the lines laid down in the preceding lessons will do much for you in this direction. A recent writer truthfully says on this subject: "Suppose, for instance, you are in trade or a profession, and wish to increase your business. It will not do, when you sell goods or services, to make the matter a merely perfunctory transaction, taking the customer's money, giving him good value and letting him go away feeling that you have no interest in the matter beyond giving him a fair deal and profiting thereby. Unless he feels that you have a personal interest in him and his needs, and that you are honestly desirous to increase his welfare, you have made a failure and are losing ground. When you can make every customer feel that you are really trying to advance his interests as well as your own, your business will grow. It is not necessary to give premiums, or heavier weights, or better values than others give to accomplish this; it is done by putting life and interest into every transaction, however small." This writer has stated the idea clearly, forcibly and truthfully, and you will do well to heed his advice and to put it into actual practice.

Another important point in Personality is Self Control, particularly in the matter of Keeping your Temper. Anger is a mark of weakness, not of strength. The man who loses his temper immediately places himself at a disadvantage. Remember the old saying: "Those whom the gods would destroy, they first make angry." Under the influence of anger a man does all sorts of foolish things that he afterwards regrets. He throws judgment, experience and caution to the winds, and acts like a crazy man. In fact, anger is a sort of madness—a phase of insanity—if you doubt this look carefully at the face of the first angry man you meet and see how irrational he looks and acts. It is a well-known fact that if one keeps cool while his opponent is angry, he has decidedly the best of the matter—for he is a sane man dealing with an irrational one. It is the better policy to allow the other fellow to "stew in his own fat" of anger, keeping cool yourself at the same time. It is a comparatively easy matter to cool down an angry man without becoming angry yourself—and as it takes two to make a quarrel, the matter is soon over. You will find that a control of the outward expression will give you control of your inner mental state. You will find that if you are able to control your voice, keeping it calm, steady and low-pitched, you will not fly into a passion, and more than this, you will find by so doing that the voice of the other fellow will gradually come down from its loud, boisterous tones, and in the end both of you will be pitching your voices in the same key—and you have set that key-note. This is worth remembering—this control of the voice—it is a secret well worth knowing and practicing.

While we are on the subject of voice, we would like to call your attention to a further control of voice, or rather a cultivation of voice. A man having a well-controlled, even, pleasant voice has an advantage over others having equal abilities in other directions, but lacking that one quality. The value of a vibrant, resonant, soft and flexible voice is great. If you have such a voice, you are blessed. If you lack it, why start to work and cultivate it? Oh, yes, you can! Did you ever hear of Nathan Sheppard, the well-known public speaker? Then listen to these words of his, telling of his natural disadvantages of voice, and how he overcame them and became a great speaker. He says: "When I made up my mind to devote my mind and body to public speaking, I was told by my teachers and governors that I would certainly fail; that my articulation was a failure, and it was; that my organs of speech were inadequate, and they were; and that if I would screw up my little mouth it could be put into my mother's thimble, and it could. Stinging words these certainly were, and cruel ones. I shall never forget them; possibly, however, they stung me into a persistency which I would never have known but for these words. At all events, that is the philosophy of the 'self-made' world of mankind. I may not have accomplished much, I do not claim to have accomplished much. It is something to have made a living out of my art for twenty years, and that I do claim to have done in spite of every obstacle and every discouragement, by turning my will upon my voice and vocal organs, by cultivating my elocutionary instincts and my ear for the cadences of rhetoric, by knowing what I and my voice and my feelings were about, by making the most of myself." After these words, anything that we might add regarding the possibility of acquiring a good voice by will, practice and desire would be superfluous. Pick out the kind of voice that you think best adapted to your work, and then cultivate it by practice, determination and desire. If Mr. Sheppard could become a famous public speaker with such obstacles as these, then for you to say "but I can't" is to stamp you as a weakling.

It has been suggested to us that we have a few words to say regarding the carriage or physical bearing of the person, as an important part of Personality—particularly in the phase of Walking. But we do not think that is necessary to add to what we have said in this lesson regarding the subject, in connection with what we have also said regarding the mental state of Self Respect. The main thing is to cultivate the Mental State of Self Respect, and the rest will follow as a natural consequence. Thought takes form in Action, and the man who has Self Respect imbedded in his mind will surely so carry and demean himself that he will give evidence of his mental state in his every physical action, gesture, carriage and motion. He must have it within, as well as without. One must pay attention to the exterior aspect of course, particularly in the matter of dress. One should cultivate Cleanliness and Neatness, of both body and clothing. To be well dressed does not mean to me showily clad—in fact, the person who is best dressed is inconspicuously dressed. Cultivate a quiet, refined taste, expressed in quality rather than in showiness. And above all—be Clean.

In conclusion, let us impress upon you again and again that that which we call Personality is but the outer mask of the Individual Within. The mask may be changed by an effort of the Will, aided by an intelligent discrimination. First find out what kind of Personality you should have, and then set to work to cultivate it—to grow it, in fact. Form the Mental Image of what you want to be—then think of it—desire it ardently—will that you shall have it—then Act It Out, over and over again; rehearsal after rehearsal, until you will actually materialize your ideal into objective reality. Make a good mental pattern or mould, and then pour in your mental material steadily, and lo! from the mould will come forth the Character and Personality that you desire and need. Then polish up this newborn Personality until it becomes radiant with the brightness of Culture.

You can be what you want to be—if you only want to hard enough. The Desire is the mother of the Actuality. Remember once more the old rule—EARNEST DESIRE—CONFIDENT EXPECTATION—FIRM RESOLVE—these are the three things that lead to ACCOMPLISHMENT.

And now that we have given you this little Secret of Success—USE IT. "It is Up to You" to "Make Good." We have "pressed the button—you must do the rest!"

An Afterword

On reading the foregoing pages after they have been set up in type, we are impressed with the idea that in spite of our determination, as expressed in the first few pages, not to attempt to lay down a code or rules or a course of conduct which should be considered as an infallible Guide to Success—in spite of our avowed determination not to pose as a teacher or preacher—we have nevertheless managed to do considerable in the direction of "laying down the law" so far as is concerned the naming of things to be done, or avoided.

However, we feel that the advice given is good, and that the various examples quoted are calculated to arouse within the mind of the reader the Spirit that leads to Success. And, with this thought, we send forth these pages to those who may attract them to themselves, or who may be attracted to them—under the Law of Attraction.

But we feel that we shall not have completed our task unless we, once more, remind the reader that Success is not to be gained by a blind and slavish following of anyone's rules or advice, our own any more than any other person's. There is no Royal Road to Success—no Patent Process by which the unsuccessful are to be magically transformed into Captains of Industry or Magnates of Wall Street. There is nothing more amusing, or pitiful, according to how one views it, than the bulk of Success Talk given to the public by self-appointed teachers and preachers. There is no one who can in a few pages point out to seekers after Success an infallible method whereby each and everyone may attain the Success and Attainment that their hearts crave. It is a cold, hard truth that each and every man must work out his own salvation in the matter of Success. Rules and advice may greatly assist—and they undoubtedly do this—but the real work must be accomplished by the individual. He must carve out his own Destiny, and there is no power above or below that will do the work for him if he refuses to perform it himself.

The old saying that "God helps him who helps himself" is true in more senses than one. It is true in the sense that the Higher Aid seems to refuse to come to the assistance of one who is not willing to strike out for himself and do his best. But it is true in another sense—this Aid does come to one who will throw heart and soul into the task set before him, and who will do each day's work the best he knows how, with hope in his soul, and a confident expectation of better things right ahead, around the turn of the road. The wise man is the one who takes courageously the step right ahead of him, planting his foot firmly and confidently upon it, although he is unable to see further ahead. To such a one, step after step is illuminated as he proceeds, and he reaches his goal, whereas the shrinking ones who have feared to take the obvious step because they could not see beyond it are still waiting for something to turn up. This waiting business is a poor policy—as Garfield said: "Don't wait for something to turn up—go out and turn something up." Take the step before you boldly and hopefully, and the next step will then appear. The thing to do is that which lies right before you to be done—do it the best you know how, feeling assured that in its doing you will be making progress toward the better things for which your heart has been longing. New ideas come while you are in action—in the doing of things comes the inspiration for the doing of greater things. You can always get a better "running start" when in action, which will give you an advantage over the best "standing start" imaginable. Get into action and motion.

In this little work we have endeavored to call your attention to something of far greater importance than a mere code of rules and general advice. We have pointed out to you the glorious fact that within each of you there is a Something Within which if once aroused would give you a greatly increased power and capacity. And so we have tried to tell you this story of the Something Within, from different view-points, so that you might catch the idea in several ways. We firmly believe that Success depends most materially upon a recognition and manifestation of this Something Within—we think that a study of the character and work of all successful men will show you that differ as they do in personal characteristics, they all manifest that consciousness of that Something Within them that gives them an assurance of Inward Power and Strength, from which proceeds Courage and Self-Confidence. You will find that the majority of successful men feel that there is a Something helping them—back of and behind their efforts. Some have called this Thing by the name of "Luck" or "Destiny," or some such term. But it is all a form of the same recognition of an Inward Power backing them up in their endeavors. They feel that they are "helped" in some way, although they are not quite sure of the nature of the helper—in fact, the majority of them do not stop to speculate upon its nature, they are too busy and are content with the knowledge that It is there. This Something Within is the Individual—the "I" in each of them—the source of the power which men manifest when they express it. And this little book is written in the hope that to many it may be the first step toward the recognition, unfoldment and manifestation of this Inward Power.

We earnestly urge upon you to cultivate this "I AM" consciousness—that you may realize the Power Within you. And then there will come naturally to you the correlated consciousness which expresses itself in the statement "I CAN and I WILL," one of the grandest affirmations of Power that man can make. This "I Can and I Will" consciousness is that expression of the Something Within which we trust that you will realize and manifest. We feel that back of all the advice that we can give you, this one thing is the PRIME FACTOR in the Secret of Success.

12

THE ART OF MONEY GETTING

P. T. BARNUM

(1880)

Contents

1. The Art of Money Getting 777
2. Don't Mistake Your Vocation 783
3. Select the Right Location 784
4. Avoid Debt 786
5. Persevere 788
6. Whatever You Do, Do It with All Your Might 790
7. Depend Upon Your Own Personal Exertions 791
8. Use the Best Tools 793
9. Don't Get Above Your Business 794
10. Learn Something Useful 797
11. Let Hope Predominate But Be Not Too Visionary 798
12. Do Not Scatter Your Powers 799
13. Be Systematic 800
14. Read the Newspapers 802
15. Beware of "Outside Operations" 803
16. Don't Endorse Without Security 804
17. Advertise Your Business 806
18. Be Polite and Kind to Your Customers 809
19. Be Charitable 810
20. Don't Blab 811
21. Preserve Your Integrity 812

CHAPTER 1

The Art of Money Getting

In the United States, where we have more land than people, it is not at all difficult for persons in good health to make money. In this comparatively new field there are so many avenues of success open, so many vocations which are not crowded, that any person of either sex who is willing, at least for the time being, to engage in any respectable occupation that offers, may find lucrative employment.

Those who really desire to attain an independence have only to set their minds upon it, and adopt the proper means, as they do in regard to any other object which they wish to accomplish, and the thing is easily done. But however easy it may be found to make money, I have no doubt many of my hearers will agree it is the most difficult thing in the world to keep it. The road to wealth is, as Dr. Franklin truly says, "as plain as the road to the mill." It consists simply in expending less than we earn; that seems to be a very simple problem. Mr. Micawber, one of those happy creations of the genial Dickens, puts the case in a strong light when he says that to have an income of twenty pounds per annum, and spend twenty pounds and sixpence, is to be the most miserable of men; whereas, to have an income of only twenty pounds, and spend but nineteen pounds and sixpence, is to be the happiest of mortals. Many of my readers may say, "We understand this; this is economy, and we know economy is wealth; we know we can't eat our cake and keep it also." Yet I beg to say that perhaps more cases of failure arise from mistakes on this point than almost any other. The fact is, many people think they understand economy when they really do not.

True economy is misapprehended, and people go through life without properly comprehending what that principle is. One says, "I have an income of so much and here is my neighbor who has the same; yet every year he gets something ahead and I fall short; why is it? I know all about economy." He thinks he does, but he does not. There are many who think that economy consists in saving cheese-parings and candle-ends, in cutting off two pence from the laundress' bill and doing all sorts of little, mean, dirty things. Economy is not meanness. The misfortune is, also, that this class of persons let their economy apply in only one direction. They fancy they are so wonderfully economical in saving a half-penny where they ought to spend two pence, that they think they can afford to squander in other directions. A few years ago, before kerosene oil was discovered or thought of, one might stop overnight at almost any farmer's house in the agricultural districts and get a very good supper, but after supper he might attempt to read in the sitting-room, and would find it impossible with the inefficient light of one candle. The hostess, seeing his dilemma, would say: "It is rather difficult to read here evenings; the proverb says you must have a ship at sea in order to be able to burn two candles at once; we never have an extra candle except on extra occasions."

These extra occasions occur, perhaps, twice a year. In this way the good woman saves five, six, or ten dollars in that time; but the information which might be derived from having the extra light would, of course, far outweigh a ton of candles.

But the trouble does not end here. Feeling that she is so economical in tallow candles, she thinks she can afford to go frequently to the village and spend twenty or thirty dollars for ribbons and furbelows, many of which are not necessary. This false economy may frequently be seen in men of business, and in those instances it often runs to writing-paper. You find good business men who save all the old envelopes, and scraps, and would not tear a new sheet of paper, if they could avoid it, for the world. This is all very well; they may in this way save five or ten dollars a year, but being so economical (only in note paper), they think they can afford to waste time; to have expensive parties, and to drive their carriages. This is an illustration of Dr. Franklin's "saving at the spigot and wasting at the bung-hole"; "penny wise and pound foolish." *Punch* in speaking of this "one idea" class of people says "they are like the man who bought a penny herring for his family's dinner and then hired a coach and four to take it home." I never knew a man to succeed by practising this kind of economy.

True economy consists in always making the income exceed the out-go. Wear the old clothes a little longer if necessary; dispense with the new pair of gloves; mend the old dress; live on plainer food if need be; so that, under all circumstances, unless some unforeseen accident occurs, there will be a margin in favor of the income. A penny here, and a dollar there, placed at interest, goes on accumulating, and in this way the desired result is attained. It requires some training, perhaps, to accomplish this economy, but when once used to it, you will find there is more satisfaction in rational saving, than in irrational spending. Here is a recipe which I recommend; I have found it to work an excellent cure for extravagance, and especially for mistaken economy: When you find that you have no surplus at the end of the year, and yet have a good income, I advise you to take a few sheets of paper and form them into a book and mark down every item of expenditure. Post it every day or week in two columns, one headed "necessaries" or even "comforts," and the other headed "luxuries," and you will find that the latter column will be double, treble, and frequently ten times greater than the former. The real comforts of life cost but a small portion of what most of us can earn. Dr. Franklin says, "It is the eyes of others and not our own eyes which ruin us. If all the world were blind except myself I should not care for fine clothes or furniture." It is the fear of what Mrs. Grundy may say that keeps the noses of many worthy families to the grindstone. In America many persons like to repeat "We are all free and equal," but it is a great mistake in more senses than one.

That we are born "free and equal" is a glorious truth in one sense, yet we are not all born equally rich, and we never shall be. One may say, "There is a man who has an income of fifty thousand dollars per annum, while I have but one thousand dollars; I knew that fellow when he was poor like myself, now he is rich and thinks he is better than I am; I will show him that I am as good as he is; I will go and buy a horse and buggy; no, I cannot do that, but I will go and hire one and ride this afternoon on the same road that he does, and thus prove to him that I am as good as he is."

My friend, you need not take that trouble; you can easily prove that you are "as good as he is", you have only to behave as well as he does; but you cannot make anybody believe that you are rich as he is. Besides, if you put on these "airs," and waste your time and spend your money, your poor wife will be obliged to scrub her fingers off at home, and buy her tea two ounces at a time, and everything else in proportion, in order that you may keep up "appearances," and, after all, deceive nobody. On the other hand, Mrs. Smith may say that her next-door neighbor married Johnson for his money, and "everybody says so." She has a nice one-thousand-dollar camel's-hair shawl, and she will make Smith get her an imitation one, and she will sit in a pew right next to her neighbor in church, in order to prove that she is her equal.

My good woman, you will not get ahead in the world, if your vanity and envy thus take the lead. In this country, where we believe the majority ought to rule, we ignore that principle in regard to fashion, and let a handful of people, calling themselves the aristocracy, run up a false standard of perfection, and in endeavoring to rise to that standard, we constantly keep ourselves poor; all the time digging away for the sake of outside appearances. How much wiser to be a "law unto ourselves" and say, "we will regulate our out-go by our income, and lay up something for a rainy day." People ought to be as sensible on the subject of money-getting as on any other subject. Like causes produce like effects. You cannot accumulate a fortune by taking the road that leads to poverty. It needs no prophet to tell us that those who live fully up to their means, without any thought of a reverse in this life, can never attain a pecuniary independence.

Men and women accustomed to gratify every whim and caprice will find it hard, at first, to cut down their various unnecessary expenses, and will feel it a great self-denial to live in a smaller house than they have been accustomed to, with less expensive furniture, less company, less costly clothing, fewer servants, a less number of balls, parties, theatergoings, carriage-ridings, pleasure excursions, cigar-smokings, liquor-drinkings, and other extravagances; but, after all, if they will try the plan of laying by a "nest-egg," or, in other words, a small sum of money, at interest or judiciously invested in land, they will be surprised at the pleasure to be derived from constantly adding to their little "pile," as well as from all the economical habits which are engendered by this course.

The old suit of clothes, and the old bonnet and dress, will answer for another season; the Croton or spring water will taste better than champagne; a cold bath and a brisk walk will prove more exhilarating than a ride in the finest coach; a social chat, an evening's reading in the family circle, or an hour's play of "hunt the slipper" and "blind man's buff," will be far more pleasant than a fifty or five hundred dollar party, when the reflection on the difference in cost is indulged in by those who begin to know the pleasures of saving. Thousands of men are kept poor, and tens of thousands are made so after they have acquired quite sufficiently to support them well through life, in consequence of laying their plans of living on too broad a platform. Some families expend twenty thousand dollars per annum, and some much more, and would scarcely know how to live on less, while others secure more solid enjoyment frequently on a twentieth part of that amount. Prosperity is a more severe ordeal than adversity, especially sudden prosperity. "Easy come, easy go" is an old and true proverb. A spirit of pride and vanity, when permitted to have full sway, is the undying canker-worm which gnaws the very vitals of a man's worldly possessions, let them be small or great, hundreds or millions. Many persons, as they begin to prosper, immediately expand their ideas and commence expending for luxuries, until in a short time their expenses swallow up their income, and they become ruined in their ridiculous attempts to keep up appearances, and make a "sensation."

I know a gentleman of fortune who says, that when he first began to prosper, his wife would have a new and elegant sofa. "That sofa," he says, "cost me thirty thousand dollars!" When the sofa reached the house, it was found necessary to get chairs to match; then sideboards, carpets, and tables "to correspond" with them, and so on through the entire stock of furniture; when at last it was found that the house itself was quite too small and old-fashioned for the furniture, and a new one was built to correspond with the new purchases; "thus," added my friend, "summing up an outlay of thirty thousand dollars, caused by that single sofa, and saddling on me, in the shape of servants, equipage, and the necessary expenses attendant upon keeping up a fine 'establishment,' a yearly outlay of eleven thousand dollars, and a tight pinch at that; whereas, ten years ago, we lived with much more real comfort, because with much less care, on as many hundreds. The truth is," he continued, "that sofa would have brought me to inevitable bankruptcy, had not a most unexampled tide of prosperity kept me above it, and had I not checked the natural desire to 'cut a dash.'"

The foundation of success in life is good health; that is the substratum of fortune; it is also the basis of happiness. A person cannot accumulate a fortune very well when he is sick. He has no ambition; no incentive; no force. Of course, there are those who have bad health and cannot help it; you cannot expect that such persons can accumulate wealth; but there are a great many in poor health who need not be so.

If, then, sound health is the foundation of success and happiness in life, how important it is that we should study the laws of health, which is but another expression for the laws of nature! The closer we keep to the laws of nature, the nearer we are to good health, and yet how many persons there are who pay no attention to natural laws, but absolutely transgress them, even against their own natural inclination. We ought to know that the "sin of ignorance" is never winked at in regard to the violation of nature's laws; their infraction always brings the penalty. A child may thrust its finger into the flames without knowing it will burn, and so suffers; repentance, even, will not stop the smart. Many of our ancestors knew very little about the principle of ventilation. They did now know much about oxygen, whatever other "gin" they might have been acquainted with; and consequently, they built their houses with little seven-by-nine-feet bedrooms, and these good old pious Puritans would lock themselves up in one of these cells, say their prayers, and go to bed. In the morning they would devoutly return thanks for the "preservation of their lives" during the night, and nobody had better reason to be thankful. Probably some big crack in the window, or in the door, let in a little fresh air, and thus saved them.

Many persons knowingly violate the laws of nature against their better impulses, for the sake of fashion. For instance, there is one thing that nothing living except a vile worm ever naturally loved, and that is tobacco; yet how many persons there are who deliberately train an unnatural appetite, and overcome this implanted aversion for tobacco, to such a degree that they get to love it. They have got hold of a poisonous, filthy weed, or rather that takes a firm hold of them. Here are married men who run about spitting tobacco juice on the carpet and floors, and sometimes even upon their wives besides. They do not kick their wives out of doors like drunken men, but their wives, I have no doubt, often wish they were outside of the house. Another perilous feature is that this artificial appetite, like jealousy, "grows by what it feeds on"; when you love that which is unnatural, a stronger appetite is created for the hurtful thing than the natural desire for what is harmless. There is an old proverb which says that "habit is second nature," but an artificial habit is stronger than nature. Take, for instance, an old tobacco-chewer; his love for the "quid" is stronger than his love for any particular kind of food. He can give up roast beef easier than give up the weed.

Young lads regret that they are not men; they would like to go to bed boys and wake up men; and to accomplish this they copy the bad habits of their seniors. Little Tommy and Johnny see their fathers or uncles smoke a pipe, and they say, "if I could only do that, I would be a man too; Uncle John has gone out and left his pipe of tobacco, let us try it." They take a match and light it, and then puff away. "We will learn to smoke; do you like it, Johnny?" That lad dolefully replies: "Not very much; it tastes bitter;" by and by he grows pale, but he persists and he soon offers up a sacrifice on the altar of fashion; but the boys stick to it and persevere until at last they conquer their natural appetites and become the victims of acquired tastes.

I speak "by the book," for I have noticed its effects on myself, having gone so far as to smoke ten or fifteen cigars a day, although I have not used the weed during the last fourteen years, and never shall again. The more a man smokes, the more he craves smoking; the last cigar smoked simply excites the desire for another, and so on incessantly.

Take the tobacco-chewer. In the morning, when he gets up, he puts a quid in his mouth and keeps it there all day, never taking it out except to exchange it for a fresh one, or when he is going to eat; oh! yes, at intervals during the day and evening, many a chewer takes out the quid and holds it in his hand long enough to take a drink, and then pop it goes back again. This simply proves that the appetite for rum is even stronger than that for tobacco. When the tobacco-chewer goes to your country seat and you show him your grapery and fruit house, and the beauties of your garden, when you offer him some fresh, ripe fruit, and say, "My friend, I have got here the most delicious apples, and pears, and peaches, and apricots; I have imported them from Spain, France, and Italy—just see those luscious grapes; there is nothing more delicious nor more healthy than ripe fruit, so help yourself; I want to see you delight yourself with these things;" he will roll the dear quid under his tongue and answer, "No, I thank you, I have got tobacco in my mouth." His palate has become narcotized by the noxious weed, and he has lost, in a great measure, the delicate and enviable taste for fruits. This shows what expensive, useless, and injurious habits men will get into. I speak from experience. I have smoked until I trembled like an aspen leaf, the blood rushed to my head, and I had a palpitation of the heart which I thought was heart disease, till I was almost killed with fright. When I consulted my physician, he said, "Break off tobacco using." I was not only injuring my health and spending a great deal of money, but I was setting a bad example. I obeyed his counsel. No young man in the world ever looked so beautiful, as he thought he did, behind a fifteen cent cigar or a meerschaum!

These remarks apply with tenfold force to the use of intoxicating drinks. To make money requires a clear brain. A man has got to see that two and two make four; he must lay all his plans with reflection and forethought, and closely examine all the details and the ins and outs of business. As no man can succeed in business unless he has a brain to enable him to lay his plans, and reason to guide him in their execution, so, no matter how bountifully a man may be blessed with intelligence, if the brain is muddled, and his judgment warped by intoxicating drinks, it is impossible for him to carry on business successfully. How many good opportunities have passed, never to return, while a man was sipping a "social glass" with his friend! How many foolish bargains have been made under the influence of the "nervine," which temporarily makes its victim think he is rich. How many important chances have been put off until to-morrow, and then forever, because the wine cup has thrown the system into a state of lassitude, neutralizing the energies so essential to success in business. Verily, "wine is a mocker." The use of intoxicating drinks as a beverage is as much an infatuation as is the smoking of opium by the Chinese, and the former is quite as destructive to the success of the business man as the latter. It is an unmitigated evil, utterly indefensible in the light of philosophy, religion, or good sense. It is the parent of nearly every other evil in our country.

CHAPTER 2

Don't Mistake Your Vocation

The safest plan, and the one most sure of success for the young man starting in life, is to select the vocation which is most congenial to his tastes. Parents and guardians are often quite too negligent in regard to this. It is very common for a father to say, for example: "I have five boys. I will make Billy a clergyman; John a lawyer; Tom a doctor, and Dick a farmer." He then goes into town and looks about to see what he will do with Sammy. He returns home and says, "Sammy, I see watch-making is a nice, genteel business; I think I will make you a goldsmith." He does this, regardless of Sam's natural inclinations, or genius.

We are all, no doubt, born for a wise purpose. There is as much diversity in our brains as in our countenances. Some are born natural mechanics, while some have great aversion to machinery.

Let a dozen boys of ten years get together, and you will soon observe two or three are "whittling" out some ingenious device; working with locks or complicated machinery. When they were but five years old, their father could find no toy to please them like a puzzle. They are natural mechanics; but the other eight or nine boys have different aptitudes. I belong to the latter class; I never had the slightest love for mechanism; on the contrary, I have a sort of abhorrence for complicated machinery. I never had ingenuity enough to whittle a cider tap so it would not leak. I never could make a pen that I could write with, or understand the principle of a steam engine. If a man was to take such a boy as I was, and attempt to make a watch-maker of him, the boy might, after an apprenticeship of five or seven years, be able to take apart and put together a watch; but all through life he would be working up hill and seizing every excuse for leaving his work and idling away his time. Watch-making is repulsive to him.

Unless a man enters upon the vocation intended for him by nature, and best suited to his peculiar genius, he cannot succeed. I am glad to believe that the majority of persons do find their right vocation. Yet we see many who have mistaken their calling, from the blacksmith up (or down) to the clergyman. You will see, for instance, that extraordinary linguist the "learned blacksmith," who ought to have been a teacher of languages; and you may have seen lawyers, doctors, and clergymen who were better fitted by nature for the anvil or the lapstone.

CHAPTER 3

Select the Right Location

After securing the right vocation, you must be careful to select the proper location. You may have been cut out for a hotel keeper, and they say it requires a genius to "know how to keep a hotel." You might conduct a hotel like clock-work, and provide satisfactorily for five hundred guests every day; yet, if you should locate your house in a small village where there is no railroad communication or public travel, the location would be your ruin. It is equally important that you do not commence business where there are already enough to meet all demands in the same occupation. I remember a case which illustrates this subject. When I was in London in 1858, I was passing down Holborn with an English friend and came to the "penny shows." They had immense cartoons outside, portraying the wonderful curiosities to be seen "all for a penny." Being a little in the "show line" myself, I said, "Let us go in here." We soon found ourselves in the presence of the illustrious showman, and he proved to be the sharpest man in that line I had ever met. He told us some extraordinary stories in reference to his bearded ladies, his albinos, and his armadillos, which we could hardly believe, but thought it "better to believe it than look after the proof." He finally begged to call our attention to some wax statuary, and showed us a lot of the dirtiest and filthiest wax figures imaginable. They looked as if they had not seen water since the Deluge.

"What is there so wonderful about your statuary?" I asked.

"I beg you not to speak so satirically," he replied. "Sir, these are not Madam Tussaud's wax figures, all covered with gilt and tinsel and imitation diamonds, and copied from engravings and photographs. Mine, sir, were taken from life. Whenever you look upon one of those figures, you may consider that you are looking upon the living individual."

Glancing casually at them, I saw one labelled "Henry VIII," and feeling a little curious upon seeing that it looked like Calvin Edson, the living skeleton, I said:

"Do you call that 'Henry the Eighth?'"

He replied, "Certainly, sir; it was taken from life at Hampton Court, by special order of his majesty, on such a day."

He would have given the hour of the day if I had insisted; I said, "Everybody knows that 'Henry VIII' was a great stout old king, and that figure is lean and lank; what do you say to that?"

"Why," he replied, "you would be lean and lank yourself, if you sat there as long as he has."

There was no resisting such arguments. I said to my English friend, "Let us go out; do not tell him who I am; I show the white feather; he beats me."

He followed us to the door, and seeing the rabble in the street, he called out, "ladies and gentlemen, I beg to draw your attention to the respectable character of my visitors," pointing to us as we walked away. I called upon him a couple of days afterwards; told him who I was, and said:

"My friend, you are an excellent showman, but you have selected a bad location."

He replied, "This is true, sir; I feel that all my talents are thrown away; but what can I do?"

"You can go to America," I replied. "You can give full play to your faculties over there; you will find plenty of elbow-room in America; I will engage you for two years; after that you will be able to go on your own account."

He accepted my offer and remained two years in my New York Museum. He then went to New Orleans and carried on a traveling show business during the summer. To-day he is worth sixty thousand dollars, simply because he selected the right vocation and also secured the proper location. The old proverb says, "Three removes are as bad as a fire," but when a man is in the fire, it matters but little how soon or how often he removes.

CHAPTER 4

Avoid Debt

Young men starting in life should avoid running into debt. There is scarcely anything that drags a person down like debt. It is a slavish position to get in, yet we find many a young man, hardly out of his "teens," running in debt. He meets a chum and says, "Look at this: I have got trusted for a new suit of clothes." He seems to look upon the clothes as so much given to him; well, it frequently is so, but, if he succeeds in paying and then gets trusted again, he is adopting a habit which will keep him in poverty through life. Debt robs a man of his self-respect, and makes him almost despise himself. Grunting and groaning and working for what he has eaten up or worn out, and now when he is called upon to pay up, he has nothing to show for his money; this is properly termed "working for a dead horse." I do not speak of merchants buying and selling on credit, or of those who buy on credit in order to turn the purchase to a profit. The old Quaker said to his farmer son, "John, never get trusted; but if thee gets trusted for anything, let it be for 'manure,' because that will help thee pay it back again."

Mr. Beecher advised young men to get in debt if they could to a small amount in the purchase of land, in the country districts. "If a young man," he says, "will only get in debt for some land and then get married, these two things will keep him straight, or nothing will." This may be safe to a limited extent, but getting in debt for what you eat and drink and wear is to be avoided. Some families have a foolish habit of getting credit at "the stores," and thus frequently purchase many things which might have been dispensed with.

It is all very well to say, "I have got trusted for sixty days, and if I don't have the money the creditor will think nothing about it." There is no class of people in the world who have such good memories as creditors. When the sixty days run out, you will have to pay. If you do not pay, you will break your promise, and probably resort to a falsehood. You may make some excuse or get in debt elsewhere to pay it, but that only involves you the deeper.

A good-looking, lazy young fellow was the apprentice boy, Horatio. His employer said, "Horatio, did you ever see a snail?" "I—think—I—have," he drawled out. "You must have met him then, for I am sure you never overtook one," said the "boss." Your creditor will meet you or overtake you and say, "Now, my young friend, you agreed to pay me; you have not done it, you must give me your note." You give the note on interest and it commences working against you; it is a "dead horse." The creditor goes to bed at night and wakes up in the morning better off than when he retired to bed, because his interest has increased during the night, but you grow poorer while you are sleeping, for the interest is accumulating against you.

Money is in some respects like fire; it is a very excellent servant but a terrible master. When you have it mastering you, when interest is constantly piling up against you, it will keep you down in the worst kind of slavery. But let money work for you, and you have the most devoted servant in the world. It is no "eye-servant." There is nothing animate or inanimate that will work so faithfully as money when placed at interest, well secured. It works night and day, and in wet or dry weather.

I was born in the blue-law State of Connecticut, where the old Puritans had laws so rigid that it was said, they fined a man for kissing his wife on Sunday. Yet these rich old Puritans would have thousands of dollars at interest, and on Saturday night would be worth a certain amount; on Sunday they would go to church and perform all the duties of a Christian. On waking up on Monday morning, they would find themselves considerably richer than the Saturday night previous, simply because their money placed at interest had worked faithfully for them all day Sunday, according to law!

Do not let it work against you; if you do there is no chance for success in life so far as money is concerned. John Randolph, the eccentric Virginian, once exclaimed in Congress, "Mr. Speaker, I have discovered the philosopher's stone: pay as you go." This is, indeed, nearer to the philosopher's stone than any alchemist has ever yet arrived.

CHAPTER 5

Persevere

When a man is in the right path, he must persevere. I speak of this because there are some persons who are "born tired"; naturally lazy and possessing no self-reliance and no perseverance. But they can cultivate these qualities, as Davy Crockett said:

"This thing remember, when I am dead,

"Be sure you are right, then go ahead."

It is this go-aheaditiveness, this determination not to let the "horrors" or the "blues" take possession of you, so as to make you relax your energies in the struggle for independence, which you must cultivate.

How many have almost reached the goal of their ambition, but, losing faith in themselves, have relaxed their energies, and the golden prize has been lost forever.

It is, no doubt, often true, as Shakespeare says:

"There is a tide in the affairs of men,

Which taken at the flood, leads on to fortune."

If you hesitate, some bolder hand will stretch out before you and get the prize. Remember the proverb of Solomon: "He becometh poor that dealeth with a slack hand; but the hand of the diligent maketh rich."

Perseverance is sometimes but another word for self-reliance. Many persons naturally look on the dark side of life, and borrow trouble. They are born so. Then they ask for advice, and they will be governed by one wind and blown by another, and cannot rely upon themselves. Until you can get so that you can rely upon yourself, you need not expect to succeed. I have known men, personally, who have met with pecuniary reverses, and absolutely committed suicide, because they thought they could never overcome their misfortune. But I have known others who have met more serious financial difficulties, and have bridged them over by simple perseverance, aided by a firm belief that they were doing justly, and that Providence would "overcome evil with good." You will see this illustrated in any sphere of life.

Take two generals; both understand military tactics, both educated at West Point, if you please, both equally gifted; yet one, having this principle of perseverance, and the other lacking it, the former will succeed in his profession, while the latter will fail. One may hear the cry, "The enemy are coming, and they have got cannon."

"Got cannon?" says the hesitating general.

"Yes."

"Then halt every man."

He wants time to reflect; his hesitation is his ruin; the enemy passes unmolested, or overwhelms him; while on the other hand, the general of pluck, perseverance, and self-reliance, goes into battle with a will, and, amid the clash of arms, the booming of cannon, the shrieks of the wounded, and the moans of the dying, you will see this man persevering, going on, cutting and slashing his way through with unwavering determination, inspiring his soldiers to deeds of fortitude, valor, and triumph.

CHAPTER 6

Whatever You Do, Do It with All Your Might

Work at it, if necessary, early and late, in season and out of season, not leaving a stone unturned, and never deferring for a single hour that which can be done just as well *now.* The old proverb is full of truth and meaning: "Whatever is worth doing at all, is worth doing well." Many a man acquires a fortune by doing his business thoroughly, while his neighbor remains poor for life, because he only half does it. Ambition, energy, industry, perseverance, are indispensable requisites for success in business.

Fortune always favors the brave, and never helps a man who does not help himself. It won't do to spend your time like Mr. Micawber, in waiting for something to "turn up." To such men one of two things usually "turns up": the poor-house or the jail; for idleness breeds bad habits, and clothes a man in rags. The poor spendthrift vagabond says to a rich man:

"I have discovered there is enough money in the world for all of us, if it was equally divided; this must be done, and we shall all be happy together."

"But," was the response, "if everybody was like you, it would be spent in two months, and what would you do then?"

"Oh! divide again; keep dividing, of course!"

I was recently reading in a London paper an account of a like philosophic pauper who was kicked out of a cheap boarding-house because he could not pay his bill, but he had a roll of papers sticking out of his coat pocket, which, upon examination, proved to be his plan for paying off the national debt of England without the aid of a penny. People have got to do as Cromwell said: "Not only trust in Providence, but keep the powder dry." Do your part of the work, or you cannot succeed. Mahomet, one night, while encamping in the desert, overheard one of his fatigued followers remark: "I will loose my camel, and trust it to God!" "No, no, not so," said the prophet, "tie thy camel, and trust it to God!" Do all you can for yourselves, and then trust to Providence, or luck, or whatever you please to call it, for the rest.

CHAPTER 7

Depend Upon Your Own Personal Exertions

The eye of the employer is often worth more than the hands of a dozen employees. In the nature of things, an agent cannot be so faithful to his employer as to himself. Many who are employers will call to mind instances where the best employees have overlooked important points which could not have escaped their own observation as a proprietor. No man has a right to expect to succeed in life unless he understands his business, and nobody can understand his business thoroughly unless he learns it by personal application and experience. A man may be a manufacturer; he has got to learn the many details of his business personally; he will learn something every day, and he will find he will make mistakes nearly every day. And these very mistakes are helps to him in the way of experiences if he but heeds them. He will be like the Yankee tin-peddler, who, having been cheated as to quality in the purchase of his merchandise, said: "All right, there's a little information to be gained every day; I will never be cheated in that way again." Thus a man buys his experience, and it is the best kind if not purchased at too dear a rate.

I hold that every man should, like Cuvier, the French naturalist, thoroughly know his business. So proficient was he in the study of natural history, that you might bring to him the bone, or even a section of a bone of an animal which he had never seen described, and, reasoning from analogy, he would be able to draw a picture of the object from which the bone had been taken. On one occasion his students attempted to deceive him. They rolled one of their number in a cow skin and put him under the professor's table as a new specimen. When the philosopher came into the room, some of the students asked him what animal it was. Suddenly the animal said, "I am the devil and I am going to eat you." It was but natural that Cuvier should desire to classify this creature, and examining it intently, he said:

"Divided hoof; graminivorous! it cannot be done."

He knew that an animal with a split hoof must live upon grass and grain, or other kind of vegetation, and would not be inclined to eat flesh, dead or alive, so he considered himself perfectly safe. The possession of a perfect knowledge of your business is an absolute necessity in order to ensure success.

Among the maxims of the elder Rothschild was one, an apparent paradox: "Be cautious and bold." This seems to he a contradiction in terms, but it is not, and there is great wisdom in the maxim. It is, in fact, a condensed statement of what I have already said. It is to say, "You must exercise your caution in laying your plans, but be bold in carrying them out." A man who is all caution, will never dare to take hold and be successful; and a man who is all boldness, is merely reckless, and must eventually fail. A man may go on "change" and make fifty or one hundred thousand dollars in speculating in stocks, at a single operation. But if he has simple boldness without caution, it is mere chance, and what he gains to-day he will lose to-morrow. You must have both the caution and the boldness, to ensure success.

The Rothschilds have another maxim: "Never have anything to do with an unlucky man or place." That is to say, never have anything to do with a man or place which never succeeds, because, although a man may appear to be honest and intelligent, yet if he tries this or that thing and always fails, it is on account of some fault or infirmity that you may not be able to discover but nevertheless which must exist.

There is no such thing in the world as luck. There never was a man who could go out in the morning and find a purse full of gold in the street to-day, and another to-morrow, and so on, day after day. He may do so once in his life; but so far as mere luck is concerned, he is as liable to lose it as to find it. "Like causes produce like effects." If a man adopts the proper methods to be successful, "luck" will not prevent him. If he does not succeed, there are reasons for it, although, perhaps, he may not be able to see them.

CHAPTER 8

Use the Best Tools

Men in engaging employees should be careful to get the best. Understand, you cannot have too good tools to work with, and there is no tool you should be so particular about as living tools. If you get a good one, it is better to keep him, than keep changing. He learns something every day, and you are benefited by the experience he acquires. He is worth more to you this year than last, and he is the last man to part with, provided his habits are good, and he continues faithful. If, as he gets more valuable, he demands an exorbitant increase of salary, on the supposition that you can't do without him, let him go. Whenever I have such an employee, I always discharge him; first, to convince him that his place may be supplied, and second, because he is good for nothing if he thinks he is invaluable and cannot be spared.

But I would keep him, if possible, in order to profit from the result of his experience. An important element in an employee is the brain. You can see bills up, "Hands Wanted," but "hands" are not worth a great deal without "heads." Mr. Beecher illustrates this, in this wise:

An employee offers his services by saying, "I have a pair of hands and one of my fingers thinks." "That is very good," says the employer. Another man comes along, and says "he has two fingers that think." "Ah! that is better." But a third calls in and says that "all his fingers and thumbs think." That is better still. Finally another steps in and says, "I have a brain that thinks; I think all over; I am a thinking as well as a working man!" "You are the man I want," says the delighted employer.

Those men who have brains and experience are therefore the most valuable and not to be readily parted with; it is better for them, as well as yourself, to keep them, at reasonable advances in their salaries from time to time.

CHAPTER 9

Don't Get Above Your Business

Young men after they get through their business training, or apprenticeship, instead of pursuing their avocation and rising in their business, will often lie about doing nothing. They say, "I have learned my business, but I am not going to be a hireling; what is the object of learning my trade or profession, unless I establish myself?"

"Have you capital to start with?"

"No, but I am going to have it."

"How are you going to get it?"

"I will tell you confidentially; I have a wealthy old aunt, and she will die pretty soon; but if she does not, I expect to find some rich old man who will lend me a few thousands to give me a start. If I only get the money to start with I will do well."

There is no greater mistake than when a young man believes he will succeed with borrowed money. Why? Because every man's experience coincides with that of Mr. Astor, who said, it was more difficult for him to accumulate his first thousand dollars, than all the succeeding millions that made up his colossal fortune. Money is good for nothing unless you know the value of it by experience. Give a boy twenty thousand dollars and put him in business, and the chances are that he will lose every dollar of it before he is a year older. Like buying a ticket in the lottery, and drawing a prize, it is "easy come, easy go." He does not know the value of it; nothing is worth anything, unless it costs effort. Without self-denial and economy, patience and perseverance, and commencing with capital which you have not earned, you are not sure to succeed in accumulating. Young men, instead of "waiting for dead men's shoes," should be up and doing, for there is no class of persons who are so unaccommodating in regard to dying as these rich old people, and it is fortunate for the expectant heirs that it is so. Nine out of ten of the rich men of our country to-day started out in life as poor boys, with determined wills, industry, perseverance, economy, and good habits. They went on gradually, made their own money, and saved it; and this is the best way to acquire a fortune. Stephen Girard started life as a poor cabin boy, and died worth nine million dollars. A. T. Stewart was a poor Irish boy; and he paid taxes on a million and a half dollars of income, per year. John Jacob Astor was a poor farmer boy, and died worth twenty millions. Cornelius Vanderbilt began life rowing a boat from Staten Island to New York; he presented our government with a steamship worth a million of dollars, and died worth fifty millions. "There is no royal road to learning," says the proverb, and I may say it is equally true, "There is no royal road to wealth." But I think there is a royal road to both. The road to learning is a royal one; the road that enables the student to expand his intellect and add every day to his stock of knowledge, until, in the pleasant process of intellectual growth, he is able to solve the most profound problems, to count the stars, to analyze every atom of the globe, and to measure the firmament—this is a regal highway, and it is the only road worth traveling.

So in regard to wealth. Go on in confidence, study the rules, and above all things, study human nature; for "the proper study of mankind is man," and you will find that while expanding the intellect and the muscles, your enlarged experience will enable you every day to accumulate more and more principal, which will increase itself by interest and otherwise, until you arrive at a state of independence. You will find, as a general thing, that the poor boys get rich and the rich boys get poor. For instance, a rich man at his decease leaves a large estate to his family. His eldest sons, who have helped him earn his fortune, know by experience the value of money, and they take their inheritance and add to it. The separate portions of the young children are placed at interest, and the little fellows are patted on the head, and told a dozen times a day, "You are rich; you will never have to work, you can always have whatever you wish, for you were born with a golden spoon in your mouth." The young heir soon finds out what that means; he has the finest dresses and playthings; he is crammed with sugar candies and almost "killed with kindness," and he passes from school to school, petted and flattered. He becomes arrogant and self-conceited, abuses his teachers, and carries everything with a high hand. He knows nothing of the real value of money, having never earned any; but he knows all about the "golden spoon" business. At college, he invites his poor fellow-students to his room, where he "wines and dines" them. He is cajoled and caressed, and called a glorious good fellow, because he is so lavish of his money. He gives his game suppers, drives his fast horses, invites his chums to fetes and parties, determined to have lots of "good times." He spends the night in frolics and debauchery, and leads off his companions with the familiar song, "we won't go home till morning." He gets them to join him in pulling down signs, taking gates from their hinges, and throwing them into back yards and horse-ponds. If the police arrest them, he knocks them down, is taken to the lock-up, and joyfully foots the bills.

"Ah! my boys," he cries, "what is the use of being rich, if you can't enjoy yourself?"

He might more truly say, "If you can't make a fool of yourself"; but he is "fast," hates slow things, and don't "see it." Young men loaded down with other people's money are almost sure to lose all they inherit, and they acquire all sorts of bad habits which, in the majority of cases, ruin them in health, purse, and character. In this country, one generation follows another, and the poor of to-day are rich in the next generation, or the third. Their experience leads them on, and they become rich, and they leave vast riches to their young children. These children, having been reared in luxury, are inexperienced and get poor; and after long experience another generation comes on and gathers up riches again in turn. And thus "history repeats itself," and happy is he who by listening to the experience of others avoids the rocks and shoals on which so many have been wrecked.

"In England, the business makes the man." If a man in that country is a mechanic or working-man, he is not recognized as a gentleman. On the occasion of my first appearance before Queen Victoria, the Duke of Wellington asked me what sphere in life General Tom Thumb's parents were in.

"His father is a carpenter," I replied.

"Oh! I had heard he was a gentleman," was the response of His Grace.

In this Republican country, the man makes the business. No matter whether he is a blacksmith, a shoemaker, a farmer, banker, or lawyer, so long as his business is legitimate, he may be a gentleman. So any "legitimate" business is a double blessing—it helps the man engaged in it, and also helps others. The farmer supports his own family, but he also benefits the merchant or mechanic who needs the products of his farm. The tailor not only makes a living by his trade, but he also benefits the farmer, the clergyman, and others who cannot make their own clothing. But all these classes of men may be gentlemen.

The great ambition should be to *excel* all others engaged in the same occupation.

The college-student who was about graduating, said to an old lawyer:

"I have not yet decided which profession I will follow. Is your profession full?"

"The basement is much crowded, but there is plenty of room *up-stairs*," was the witty and truthful reply.

No profession, trade, or calling, is overcrowded in the upper story. Wherever you find the most honest and intelligent merchant or banker, or the best lawyer, the best doctor, the best clergyman, the best shoemaker, carpenter, or anything else, that man is most sought for, and has always enough to do. As a nation Americans are too superficial—they are striving to get rich quickly, and do not generally do their business as substantially and thoroughly as they should, but whoever *excels* all others in his own line, if his habits are good and his integrity undoubted, cannot fail to secure abundant patronage, and the wealth that naturally follows. Let your motto then always be "Excelsior," for by living up to it there is no such word as fail.

CHAPTER 10

Learn Something Useful

Every man should make his son or daughter learn some trade or profession, so that in these days of changing fortunes—of being rich to-day and poor to-morrow—they may have something tangible to fall back upon. This provision might save many persons from misery, who by some unexpected turn of fortune have lost all their means.

CHAPTER 11

Let Hope Predominate but Be Not Too Visionary

Many persons are always kept poor, because they are too visionary. Every project looks to them like certain success, and therefore they keep changing from one business to another, always in hot water, always "under the harrow." The plan of "counting the chickens before they are hatched" is an error of ancient date, but it does not seem to improve by age.

CHAPTER 12

Do Not Scatter Your Powers

Engage in one kind of business only, and stick to it faithfully until you succeed, or until your experience shows that you should abandon it. A constant hammering on one nail will generally drive it home at last, so that it can be clinched. When a man's undivided attention is centered on one object, his mind will constantly be suggesting improvements of value, which would escape him if his brain was occupied by a dozen different subjects at once. Many a fortune has slipped through a man's fingers because he was engaged in too many occupations at a time. There is good sense in the old caution against having too many irons in the fire at once.

CHAPTER 13

Be Systematic

Men should be systematic in their business. A person who does business by rule, having a time and place for everything, doing his work promptly, will accomplish twice as much and with half the trouble of him who does it carelessly and slipshod. By introducing system into all your transactions, doing one thing at a time, always meeting appointments with punctuality, you find leisure for pastime and recreation; whereas the man who only half does one thing, and then turns to something else, and half does that, will have his business at loose ends, and will never know when his day's work is done, for it never will be done. Of course, there is a limit to all these rules. We must try to preserve the happy medium, for there is such a thing as being too systematic. There are men and women, for instance, who put away things so carefully that they can never find them again. It is too much like the "red tape" formality at Washington, and Mr. Dickens' "Circumlocution Office,"—all theory and no result.

When the "Astor House" was first started in New York City, it was undoubtedly the best hotel in the country. The proprietors had learned a good deal in Europe regarding hotels, and the landlords were proud of the rigid system which pervaded every department of their great establishment. When twelve o'clock at night had arrived, and there were a number of guests around, one of the proprietors would say, "Touch that bell, John"; and in two minutes sixty servants, with a water-bucket in each hand, would present themselves in the hall. "This," said the landlord, addressing his guests, "is our fire-bell; it will show you we are quite safe here; we do everything systematically." This was before the Croton water was introduced into the city. But they sometimes carried their system too far. On one occasion, when the hotel was thronged with guests, one of the waiters was suddenly indisposed, and although there were fifty waiters in the hotel, the landlord thought he must have his full complement, or his "system" would be interfered with. Just before dinner-time, he rushed down stairs and said, "There must be another waiter, I am one waiter short, what can I do?" He happened to see "Boots," the Irishman. "Pat," said he, "wash your hands and face; take that white apron and come into the dining-room in five minutes." Presently Pat appeared as required, and the proprietor said: "Now Pat, you must stand behind these two chairs, and wait on the gentlemen who will occupy them; did you ever act as a waiter?"

"I know all about it, sure, but I never did it."

Like the Irish pilot, on one occasion when the captain, thinking he was considerably out of his course, asked, "Are you certain you understand what you are doing?"

Pat replied, "Sure and I knows every rock in the channel."

That moment, "bang" thumped the vessel against a rock.

"Ah! be jabers, and that is one of 'em," continued the pilot. But to return to the dining-room. "Pat," said the landlord, "here we do everything systematically. You must first give the gentlemen each a plate of soup, and when they finish that, ask them what they will have next."

Pat replied, "Ah! an' I understand parfectly the vartues of shystem."

Very soon in came the guests. The plates of soup were placed before them. One of Pat's two gentlemen ate his soup; the other did not care for it. He said: "Waiter, take this plate away and bring me some fish." Pat looked at the untasted plate of soup, and remembering the injunctions of the landlord in regard to "system," replied:

"Not till ye have ate yer supe!"

Of course that was carrying "system" entirely too far.

CHAPTER 14

Read the Newspapers

Always take a trustworthy newspaper, and thus keep thoroughly posted in regard to the transactions of the world. He who is without a newspaper is cut off from his species. In these days of telegraphs and steam, many important inventions and improvements in every branch of trade are being made, and he who don't consult the newspapers will soon find himself and his business left out in the cold.

CHAPTER 15

Beware of "Outside Operations"

We sometimes see men who have obtained fortunes, suddenly become poor. In many cases, this arises from intemperance, and often from gaming, and other bad habits. Frequently it occurs because a man has been engaged in "outside operations," of some sort. When he gets rich in his legitimate business, he is told of a grand speculation where he can make a score of thousands. He is constantly flattered by his friends, who tell him that he is born lucky, that everything he touches turns into gold. Now if he forgets that his economical habits, his rectitude of conduct, and a personal attention to a business which he understood, caused his success in life, he will listen to the siren voices. He says:

"I will put in twenty thousand dollars. I have been lucky, and my good luck will soon bring me back sixty thousand dollars."

A few days elapse and it is discovered he must put in ten thousand dollars more; soon after, he is told, "It is all right," but certain matters not foreseen require an advance of twenty thousand dollars more, which will bring him a rich harvest; but before the time comes around to realize, the bubble bursts, he loses all he is possessed of, and then he learns what he ought to have known at the first, that however successful a man may be in his own business, if he turns from that and engages in a business which he don't understand, he is like Samson when shorn of his locks—his strength has departed, and he becomes like other men.

If a man has plenty of money, he ought to invest something in everything that appears to promise success, and that will probably benefit mankind; but let the sums thus invested be moderate in amount, and never let a man foolishly jeopardize a fortune that he has earned in a legitimate way, by investing it in things in which he has had no experience.

CHAPTER 16

Don't Endorse Without Security

I hold that no man ought ever to endorse a note or become security for any man, be it his father or brother, to a greater extent than he can afford to lose and care nothing about, without taking good security. Here is a man that is worth twenty thousand dollars; he is doing a thriving manufacturing or mercantile trade; you are retired and living on your money; he comes to you and says:

"You are aware that I am worth twenty thousand dollars, and don't owe a dollar; if I had five thousand dollars in cash, I could purchase a particular lot of goods and double my money in a couple of months; will you endorse my note for that amount?"

You reflect that he is worth twenty thousand dollars, and you incur no risk by endorsing his note; you like to accommodate him, and you lend your name without taking the precaution of getting security. Shortly after, he shows you the note with your endorsement canceled, and tells you, probably truly, that he made the profit that he expected by the operation; you reflect that you have done a good action, and the thought makes you feel happy. By and by, the same thing occurs again and you do it again; you have already fixed the impression in your mind that it is perfectly safe to endorse his notes without security.

But the trouble is, this man is getting money too easily. He has only to take your note to the bank, get it discounted, and take the cash. He gets money for the time being without effort; without inconvenience to himself. Now mark the result. He sees a chance for speculation outside of his business. A temporary investment of only $10,000 is required. It is sure to come back before a note at the bank would be due. He places a note for that amount before you. You sign it almost mechanically. Being firmly convinced that your friend is responsible and trustworthy, you endorse his notes as a "matter of course."

Unfortunately the speculation does not come to a head quite so soon as was expected, and another $10,000 note must be discounted to take up the last one when due. Before this note matures the speculation has proved an utter failure and all the money is lost. Does the loser tell his friend, the endorser, that he has lost half of his fortune? Not at all. He don't even mention that he has speculated at all. But he has got excited; the spirit of speculation has seized him; he sees others making large sums in this way (we seldom hear of the losers), and, like other speculators, he "looks for his money where he loses it." He tries again. Endorsing notes has become chronic with you, and at every loss he gets your signature for whatever amount he wants. Finally you discover your friend has lost all of his property and all of yours. You are overwhelmed with astonishment and grief, and you say, "It is a hard thing; my friend here has ruined me," but, you should add, "I have also ruined him." If you had said in the first place, "I will accommodate you, but I never endorse without taking ample security," he could not have gone beyond the length of his tether, and he would never have been tempted away from his legitimate business. It is a very dangerous thing, therefore, at any time, to let people get possession of money too easily; it tempts them to hazardous speculations, if nothing more. Solomon truly said, "He that hateth suretiship is sure."

So with the young man starting in business; let him understand the value of money by earning it. When he does understand its value, then grease the wheels a little in helping him to start business, but remember, men who get money with too great facility cannot usually succeed. You must get the first dollars by hard knocks, and at some sacrifice, in order to appreciate the value of those dollars.

CHAPTER 17

Advertise Your Business

We all depend, more or less, upon the public for our support. We all trade with the public—lawyers, doctors, shoemakers, artists, blacksmiths, showmen, opera singers, railroad presidents, and college professors. Those who deal with the public must be careful that their goods are valuable; that they are genuine, and will give satisfaction. When you get an article which you know is going to please your customers, and that when they have tried it, they will feel they have got their money's worth, then let the fact be known that you have got it. Be careful to advertise it in some shape or other, because it is evident that if a man has ever so good an article for sale, and nobody knows it, it will bring him no return. In a country like this, where nearly everybody reads, and where newspapers are issued and circulated in editions of five thousand to two hundred thousand, it would be very unwise if this channel was not taken advantage of to reach the public in advertising. A newspaper goes into the family, and is read by wife and children, as well as the head of the home; hence hundreds and thousands of people may read your advertisement, while you are attending to your routine business. Many, perhaps, read it while you are asleep. The whole philosophy of life is, first "sow," then "reap." That is the way the farmer does; he plants his potatoes and corn, and sows his grain, and then goes about something else, and the time comes when he reaps. But he never reaps first and sows afterwards. This principle applies to all kinds of business, and to nothing more eminently than to advertising. If a man has a genuine article, there is no way in which he can reap more advantageously than by "sowing" to the public in this way. He must, of course, have a really good article, and one which will please his customers; anything spurious will not succeed permanently because the public is wiser than many imagine. Men and women are selfish, and we all prefer purchasing where we can get the most for our money and we try to find out where we can most surely do so.

You may advertise a spurious article, and induce many people to call and buy it once, but they will denounce you as an imposter and swindler, and your business will gradually die out and leave you poor. This is right. Few people can safely depend upon chance custom. You all need to have your customers return and purchase again. A man said to me, "I have tried advertising and did not succeed; yet I have a good article."

I replied, "My friend, there may be exceptions to a general rule. But how do you advertise?"

"I put it in a weekly newspaper three times, and paid a dollar and a half for it."

I replied: "Sir, advertising is like learning—'a little is a dangerous thing'!"

A French writer says that "the reader of a newspaper does not see the first mention of an ordinary advertisement; the second insertion he sees, but does not read; the third insertion he reads; the fourth insertion, he looks at the price; the fifth insertion, he speaks of it to his wife; the sixth insertion, he is ready to purchase, and the seventh insertion, he purchases." Your object in advertising is to make the public understand what you have got to sell, and if you have not the pluck to keep advertising, until you have imparted that information, all the money you have spent is lost. You are like the fellow who told the gentleman if he would give him ten cents it would save him a dollar. "How can I help you so much with so small a sum?" asked the gentleman in surprise. "I started out this morning (hiccupped the fellow) with the full determination to get drunk, and I have spent my only dollar to accomplish the object, and it has not quite done it. Ten cents' worth more of whiskey would just do it, and in this manner I should save the dollar already expended."

So a man who advertises at all must keep it up until the public know who and what he is, and what his business is, or else the money invested in advertising is lost.

Some men have a peculiar genius for writing a striking advertisement, one that will arrest the attention of the reader at first sight. This fact, of course, gives the advertiser a great advantage. Sometimes a man makes himself popular by an unique sign or a curious display in his window. Recently I observed a swing sign extending over the sidewalk in front of a store, on which was the inscription in plain letters,

"Don't Read the Other Side."

Of course I did, and so did everybody else, and I learned that the man had made an independence by first attracting the public to his business in that way and then using his customers well afterwards.

Genin, the hatter, bought the first Jenny Lind ticket at auction for two hundred and twenty-five dollars, because he knew it would be a good advertisement for him. "Who is the bidder?" said the auctioneer, as he knocked down that ticket at Castle Garden. "Genin, the hatter," was the response. Here were thousands of people from the Fifth avenue, and from distant cities in the highest stations in life. "Who is 'Genin,' the hatter?" they exclaimed. They had never heard of him before. The next morning the newspapers and telegraph had circulated the facts from Maine to Texas, and from five to ten millions of people had read that the tickets sold at auction for Jenny Lind's first concert amounted to about twenty thousand dollars, and that a single ticket was sold at two hundred and twenty-five dollars, to "Genin, the hatter." Men throughout the country involuntarily took off their hats to see if they had a "Genin" hat on their heads. At a town in Iowa it was found that in the crowd around the post office, there was one man who had a "Genin" hat, and he showed it in triumph, although it was worn out and not worth two cents. "Why," one man exclaimed, "you have a real 'Genin' hat; what a lucky fellow you are." Another man said, "Hang on to that hat, it will be a valuable heir-loom in your family." Still another man in the crowd, who seemed to envy the possessor of this good fortune, said, "Come, give us all a chance; put it up at auction!" He did so, and it was sold as a keepsake for nine dollars and fifty cents! What was the consequence to Mr. Genin? He sold ten thousand extra hats per annum, the first six years. Nine-tenths of the purchasers bought of him, probably, out of curiosity, and many of them, finding that he gave them an equivalent for their money, became his regular customers. This novel advertisement first struck their attention, and then, as he made a good article, they came again.

Now I don't say that everybody should advertise as Mr. Genin did. But I say if a man has got goods for sale, and he don't advertise them in some way, the chances are that some day the sheriff will do it for him. Nor do I say that everybody must advertise in a newspaper, or indeed use "printers' ink" at all. On the contrary, although that article is indispensable in the majority of cases, yet doctors and clergymen, and sometimes lawyers and some others, can more effectually reach the public in some other manner. But it is obvious, they must be known in some way, else how could they be supported?

CHAPTER 18

Be Polite and Kind to Your Customers

Politeness and civility are the best capital ever invested in business. Large stores, gilt signs, flaming advertisements, will all prove unavailing if you or your employees treat your patrons abruptly. The truth is, the more kind and liberal a man is, the more generous will be the patronage bestowed upon him. "Like begets like." The man who gives the greatest amount of goods of a corresponding quality for the least sum (still reserving for himself a profit) will generally succeed best in the long run. This brings us to the golden rule, "As ye would that men should do to you, do ye also to them," and they will do better by you than if you always treated them as if you wanted to get the most you could out of them for the least return. Men who drive sharp bargains with their customers, acting as if they never expected to see them again, will not be mistaken. They will never see them again as customers. People don't like to pay and get kicked also.

One of the ushers in my Museum once told me he intended to whip a man who was in the lecture-room as soon as he came out.

"What for?" I inquired.

"Because he said I was no gentleman," replied the usher.

"Never mind," I replied. "He pays for that, and you will not convince him you are a gentleman by whipping him. I cannot afford to lose a customer. If you whip him, he will never visit the Museum again, and he will induce friends to go with him to other places of amusement instead of this, and thus you see, I should be a serious loser."

"But he insulted me," muttered the usher.

"Exactly," I replied, "and if he owned the Museum, and you had paid him for the privilege of visiting it, and he had then insulted you, there might be some reason in your resenting it, but in this instance he is the man who pays, while we receive, and you must, therefore, put up with his bad manners."

My usher laughingly remarked, that this was undoubtedly the true policy, but he added that he should not object to an increase of salary if he was expected to be abused in order to promote my interest.

CHAPTER 19

Be Charitable

Of course men should be charitable, because it is a duty and a pleasure. But even as a matter of policy, if you possess no higher incentive, you will find that the liberal man will command patronage, while the sordid, uncharitable miser will be avoided.

Solomon says: "There is that scattereth and yet increaseth; and there is that withholdeth more than meet, but it tendeth to poverty." Of course the only true charity is that which is from the heart.

The best kind of charity is to help those who are willing to help themselves. Promiscuous almsgiving, without inquiring into the worthiness of the applicant, is bad in every sense. But to search out and quietly assist those who are struggling for themselves is the kind that "scattereth and yet increaseth." But don't fall into the idea that some persons practice, of giving a prayer instead of a potato, and a benediction instead of bread, to the hungry. It is easier to make Christians with full stomachs than empty.

CHAPTER 20

Don't Blab

Some men have a foolish habit of telling their business secrets. If they make money they like to tell their neighbors how it was done. Nothing is gained by this, and ofttimes much is lost. Say nothing about your profits, your hopes, your expectations, your intentions. And this should apply to letters as well as to conversation. Goethe makes Mephistopheles say: "Never write a letter nor destroy one." Business men must write letters, but they should be careful what they put in them. If you are losing money, be specially cautious and not tell of it, or you will lose your reputation.

CHAPTER 21

Preserve Your Integrity

It is more precious than diamonds or rubies. The old miser said to his sons: "Get money; get it honestly, if you can, but get money." This advice was not only atrociously wicked, but it was the very essence of stupidity. It was as much as to say, "If you find it difficult to obtain money honestly, you can easily get it dishonestly. Get it in that way." Poor fool! Not to know that the most difficult thing in life is to make money dishonestly! Not to know that our prisons are full of men who attempted to follow this advice; not to understand that no man can be dishonest, without soon being found out, and that when his lack of principle is discovered, nearly every avenue to success is closed against him forever. The public very properly shun all whose integrity is doubted. No matter how polite and pleasant and accommodating a man may be, none of us dare to deal with him if we suspect "false weights and measures." Strict honesty not only lies at the foundation of all success in life (financially), but in every other respect. Uncompromising integrity of character is invaluable. It secures to its possessor a peace and joy which cannot be attained without it—which no amount of money, or houses and lands, can purchase. A man who is known to be strictly honest, may be ever so poor, but he has the purses of all the community at his disposal—for all know that if he promises to return what he borrows, he will never disappoint them. As a mere matter of selfishness, therefore, if a man had no higher motive for being honest, all will find that the maxim of Dr. Franklin can never fail to be true, that "honesty is the best policy."

To get rich is not always equivalent to being successful. "There are many rich poor men," while there are many others, honest and devout men and women, who have never possessed so much money as some rich persons squander in a week, but who are nevertheless really richer and happier than any man can ever be while he is a transgressor of the higher laws of his being.

The inordinate love of money, no doubt, may be and is "the root of all evil," but money itself, when properly used, is not only a "handy thing to have in the house," but affords the gratification of blessing our race by enabling its possessor to enlarge the scope of human happiness and human influence. The desire for wealth is nearly universal, and none can say it is not laudable, provided the possessor of it accepts its responsibilities, and uses it as a friend to humanity.

The history of money-getting, which is commerce, is a history of civilization, and wherever trade has flourished most, there, too, have art and science produced the noblest fruits. In fact, as a general thing, money-getters are the benefactors of our race. To them, in a great measure, are we indebted for our institutions of learning and of art, our academies, colleges, and churches. It is no argument against the desire for, or the possession of, wealth, to say that there are sometimes misers who hoard money only for the sake of hoarding and who have no higher aspiration than to grasp everything which comes within their reach. As we have sometimes hypocrites in religion, and demagogues in politics, so there are occasionally misers among money-getters. These, however, are only exceptions to the general rule. But when, in this country, we find such a nuisance and stumbling block as a miser, we remember with gratitude that in America we have no laws of primogeniture, and that in the due course of nature the time will come when the hoarded dust will be scattered for the benefit of mankind. To all men and women, therefore, do I conscientiously say, make money honestly, and not otherwise, for Shakespeare has truly said, "He that wants money, means, and content, is without three good friends."

13

THE WAY TO WEALTH

BENJAMIN FRANKLIN

(1758)

Introduction

This little treatise is much and justly admired, as well as its celebrated and ingenious author; in short, it is to be doubted whether any other work of the kind equal to it ever appeared. It has been repeatedly published, in different sizes; and made its appearance on both sides of the Atlantic. The London copy, from which this is printed, contains the following introduction:

"Dr. Franklin, wishing to collect into one piece all the sayings upon the following subjects, which he had dropped in the course of publishing the Almanac, called 'Poor Richard,' introduces Father Abraham for this purpose. Hence it is that Poor Richard is so often quoted, and that in the present title he is said to be improved. Notwithstanding the stroke of humor in the concluding paragraph of this address, Poor Richard Saunders and Father Abraham have proved, in America, that they are no common preachers; and shall we, brother Englishmen, refuse good sense and saving knowledge, because it comes from the other side of the water?"

Introduction

[illegible]

The Way to Wealth

Courteous Reader,—

I have heard that nothing gives an author so great pleasure, as to find his works respectfully quoted by others. Judge, then, how much I must have been gratified by an incident I am going to relate to you. I stopped my horse, lately, where a great number of people were collected at an auction of merchants' goods. The hour of the sale not being come, they were conversing on the badness of the times; and one of the company called to a plain, clean old man, with white locks, "Pray, Father Abraham, what think you of the times? Will not these heavy taxes quite ruin the country? How shall we ever be able to pay them? What would you advise us to?" Father Abraham stood up, and replied, "If you would have my advice, I will give it you in short, for 'a word to the wise is enough,' as Poor Richard says." They joined in desiring him to speak his mind, and, gathering around him, he proceeded as follows:—

"Friends," said he, "the taxes are indeed very heavy; and if those laid on by the government were the only ones we had to pay, we might more easily discharge them; but we have many others, and much more grievous to some of us. We are taxed twice as much by our idleness, three times as much by our pride, and four times as much by our folly; and from these taxes the commissioners cannot ease or deliver us, by allowing an abatement. However, let us hearken to good advice, and something may be done for us. 'God helps them that help themselves,' as Poor Richard says.

"I. It would be thought a hard government that should tax its people one-tenth part of their time to be employed in its service; but idleness taxes many of us much more. Sloth, by bringing on diseases, absolutely shortens life.

"'Sloth, like rust, consumes faster than labor wears; while the used key is always bright,' as Poor Richard says. 'But dost thou love life? Then do not squander time for that is the stuff life is made of,' as Poor Richard says. How much more than is necessary do we spend in sleep! forgetting that 'the sleeping fox catches no poultry, and that there will be sleeping enough in the grave,' as Poor Richard says.

"If time be of all things the most precious, 'wasting time must be,' as Poor Richard says, 'the greatest prodigality!' since, as he elsewhere tells us, 'Lost time is never found again; and what we call time enough, always proves little enough.' Let us, then, up and be doing, and doing to the purpose; so, by diligence, shall we do more with less perplexity. 'Sloth makes all things difficult, but industry all easy; and he that riseth late must trot all day, and shall scarce overtake his business at night; while laziness travels so slowly, that poverty soon overtakes him. Drive thy business, let not that drive thee; and early to bed, and early to rise, makes a man healthy, wealthy, and wise,' as Poor Richard says.

"So what signify wishing and hoping for better times? We may make these times better, if we bestir ourselves. 'Industry need not wish, and he that lives upon hope will die fasting. There are no gains without pains; then, help hands, for I have no lands;' or, if I have, they are smartly taxed. 'He that hath a trade, hath an estate; and he that hath a calling, hath an office of profit and honor,' as Poor Richard says. But then the trade must be worked at, and the calling well followed, or neither the estate nor the office will enable us to pay our taxes. If we are industrious, we shall never starve; for, 'at the working man's house hunger looks in, but dares not enter.' Nor will the bailiff or constable enter; for 'industry pays debts, while despair increaseth them.' What though you have found no treasure, nor has any rich relation left you a legacy; 'Diligence is the mother of good luck, and God gives all things to industry. Then plough deep, while sluggards sleep, and you shall have corn to sell and to keep.' Work while it is called to-day, for you know not how much you may be hindered tomorrow. 'One to-day is worth two to-morrows,' as Poor Richard says; and farther, 'Never leave that till to-morrow which you can do to-day.' If you were a servant, would you not be ashamed that a good master should catch you idle? Are you, then, your own master? Be ashamed to catch yourself idle, when there is so much to be done for yourself, your family, your country, and benevolent movements. Handle your tools without mittens; remember that 'the cat in gloves catches no mice,' as Poor Richard says. It is true, there is much to be done; and, perhaps, you are weak-handed: but stick to it steadily, and you will see great effects; for 'Constant dropping wears away stone; and by diligence and patience the mouse ate in two the cable; and little strokes fell great oaks.'

"Methinks I hear some of you say, 'Must a man afford himself no leisure?' I will tell thee, my friend, what Poor Richard says: 'Employ thy time well, if thou meanest to gain leisure; and since thou art not sure of a minute, throw not away an hour.' Leisure is time for doing something useful: this leisure the diligent man will obtain, but the lazy man never; for 'A life of leisure and a life of laziness are two things. Many, without labor, would live by their wits only; but they break for want of stock:' whereas, industry gives comfort, and plenty, and respect. 'Fly pleasures, and they will follow you. The diligent spinner has a large shift; and now I have a sheep and a cow, everybody bids me good morrow.'

"II. But with our industry we must likewise be steady, settled, and careful, and oversee our own affairs with our own eyes, and not trust too much to others; for, as Poor Richard says:—

'I never saw an oft-removed tree,
Nor yet an oft-removed family,
That throve so well as those that settled be.'

And again, 'Three removes are as bad as a fire:' and again, 'Keep thy shop, and thy shop will keep thee:' and again, 'If you would have your business done, go; if not, send:' And again,

> *'He that by the plough would thrive,*
> *Himself must either hold or drive.'*

And again, 'The eye of the master will do more work than both his hands:' and again, 'Want of care does us more damage than want of knowledge': and again, 'Not to oversee workmen, is to leave them your purse open.'

"Trusting too much to others' care is the ruin of many; for, 'In the affairs of this world, men are saved, not by faith, but by the want of it. But a man's own care is profitable; for if you would have a faithful servant, and one that you like, serve yourself. A little neglect may breed great mischief; for want of a nail, the shoe was lost; for want of a shoe, the horse was lost; and for want of a horse, the rider was lost;' being overtaken and slain by the enemy, all for want of a little care about a horse-shoe nail.

"III. So much for industry, my friends, and attention to one's own business; but to these we must add frugality, if we would make our industry more certainly successful. A man may, if he know not how to save as he gets, 'keep his nose all his life to the grindstone, and die not worth a groat at last. A fat kitchen makes a lean will': and

> *'Many estates are spent in getting,*
> *Since women for tea forsook spinning and knitting,*
> *And men for punch forsook hewing and splitting.'*

'If you would be wealthy, think of saving as well as of getting. The Indies have not made Spain rich, because her outgoes are greater than her incomes.'

"Away, then, with your expensive follies, and you will not then have so much cause to complain of hard times, heavy taxes, and chargeable families; for,

> *'Women and wine, game and deceit,*
> *Make the wealth small, and the want great.'*

And farther, 'What maintains one vice would bring up two children.' You may think, perhaps, that a little tea, or a little punch now and then, diet a little more costly, clothes a little finer, and a little entertainment now and then, can be no great matter; but remember, 'Many a little make a mickle.' Beware of little expenses; 'A small leak will sink a great ship,' as Poor Richard says: and again, 'Who dainties love, shall beggars prove;' and moreover, 'Fools make feasts, and wise men eat them.' Here you are all got together to this sale of fineries and nic-nacs. You call them goods; but, if you do not take care, they will prove evils to some of you. You expect they will be sold cheap, and, perhaps, they may for less than they cost: but if you have no occasion for them, they may be dear to you. Remember what Poor Richard says, 'Buy what thou hast no need of, and ere long thou shalt sell thy necessaries.' And again, 'At a great pennyworth pause awhile;' he means, that perhaps the cheapness is apparent only, and not real; or the bargain, by straitening thee in thy business, may do thee more harm than good: for in another place he says, 'Many have been ruined by buying good pennyworths.' Again, 'It is foolish to lay out money in a purchase of repentance;' and yet this folly is practised every day at auctions, for want of minding the Almanac. Many a one, for the sake of finery on the back, has gone with a hungry belly, and half starved his family. 'Silks and satins, scarlet and velvets, put out the kitchen fire,' as Poor Richard says. These are not the necessaries of life; they can scarcely be called the conveniences; and yet, only because they look pretty, how many want to have them! By these and other extravagances, the genteel are reduced to poverty, and forced to borrow of those whom they formerly despised, but who, through industry and frugality, have maintained their standing; in which case it appears plainly, that 'A ploughman on his legs is higher than a gentleman on his knees,' as Poor Richard says. Perhaps they have had a small estate left them, which they knew not the getting of; they think 'it is day, and will never be night;' that a little to be spent out of so much is not worth minding; but, 'Always taking out of the meal-tub, and never putting in, soon comes to the bottom,' as Poor Richard says: and then, 'when the well is dry, they know the worth of water.' But this they might have known before, if they had taken his advice. 'If you would know the value of money, go and try to borrow some; for he that goes a borrowing, goes a sorrowing,' as Poor Richard says; and, indeed, so does he that lends to such people, when he goes to get it in again. Poor Dick farther advises, and says,

'Fond pride of dress is sure a very curse:
Ere fancy you consult, consult your purse.'

And again, 'Pride is as loud a beggar as Want, and a great deal more saucy.' When you have bought one fine thing, you must buy ten more, that your appearance may be all of a piece; but Poor Dick says, 'It is easier to suppress the first desire, than to satisfy all that follow it. And it is as truly folly for the poor to ape the rich, as for the frog to swell, in order to equal the ox.'

'Vessels large may venture more,
But little boats should keep near shore.'

"It is, however, a folly soon punished; for, as Poor Richard says, 'Pride, that dines on vanity, sups on contempt. Pride breakfasted with Plenty, dined with Poverty, and supped with Infamy.' And, after all, of what use is this pride of appearance, for which so much is risked, so much is suffered? It cannot promote health, nor ease pain; it makes no increase of merit in the person, it creates envy, it hastens misfortune.

"But what madness it must be to run in debt for these superfluities! We are offered, by the terms of this sale, six months' credit; and that, perhaps, has induced some of us to attend it, because we cannot spare the ready money, and hope now to be fine without it. But, ah! think what you do when you run in debt: you give to another power over your liberty. If you cannot pay at the time, you will be ashamed to see your creditor; you will be in fear when you speak to him; you will make poor, pitiful, sneaking excuses; and, by degrees, come to lose your veracity, and sink into base downright lying; for, 'The second vice is lying, the first is running in debt,' as Poor Richard says; and again, to the same purpose, 'Lying rides upon Debt's back:' whereas a free-born man ought not to be ashamed or afraid to see or speak to any man living. But poverty often deprives a man of all spirit and virtue. 'It is hard for an empty bag to stand upright.' What would you think of that prince, or of that government, who should issue an edict forbidding you to dress like a gentleman or gentlewoman, on pain of imprisonment or servitude? Would not you say you are free, have a right to dress as you please, and that such an edict would be a breach of your privileges, and such a government tyrannical? And yet you are about to put yourself under that tyranny, when you run in debt for such dress! Your creditor has authority, at his pleasure, to deprive you of your liberty, by confining you in jail for life, or by selling you for a servant, if you should not be able to pay him. When you have got your bargain, you may, perhaps, think little of payment; but, as Poor Richard says, 'Creditors have better memories than debtors; creditors are a superstitious sect, great observers of set days and times.' The day comes round before you are aware, and the demand is made before you are prepared to satisfy it; or, if you bear your debt in mind, the term, which at first seemed so long, will, as it lessens, appear extremely short: Time will seem to have added wings to his heels as well as his shoulders. 'Those have a short Lent, who owe money to be paid at Easter.' At present, perhaps, you may think yourselves in thriving circumstances, and that you can bear a little extravagance without injury; but,

'For age and want save while you may:
No morning sun lasts a whole day.'

"Gain may be temporary and uncertain; but ever, while you live, expense is constant and certain; and 'It is easier to build two chimneys, than to keep one in fuel,' as Poor Richard says; so 'Rather go to bed supperless, than rise in debt.'

'Get what you can, and what you get hold;
'Tis the stone that will turn all your lead into gold.'

And when you have got the philosopher's stone, sure you will no longer complain of bad times, or of the difficulty of paying taxes.

"IV. This doctrine, my friends, is reason and wisdom; but, after all, do not depend too much upon your own industry, and frugality, and prudence, though excellent things; for they may all be blasted, without the blessing of Heaven; and, therefore, ask that blessing humbly, and be not uncharitable to those that at present seem to want it, but comfort and help them. Remember, Job suffered, and was afterwards prosperous.

"And now, to conclude: 'Experience keeps a dear school, but fools will learn in no other,' as Poor Richard says, and scarce in that; for it is true, 'We may give advice, but we cannot give conduct.' However, remember this, 'They that will not be counselled, cannot be helped;' and further, 'If you will not hear Reason, she will surely rap your knuckles,' as Poor Richard says."

Thus the old gentleman ended his harangue. The people heard it, and approved the doctrine, and immediately practised the contrary, just as if it had been a common sermon; for the auction opened, and they began to buy extravagantly. I found the good man had thoroughly studied my Almanacs, and digested all I had dropped on those topics during the course of twenty-five years. The frequent mention he made of me must have tired any one else; but my vanity was wonderfully delighted with it, though I was conscious that not a tenth part of the wisdom was my own, which he ascribed to me; but rather the gleanings that I had made of the sense of all ages and nations. However, I resolved to be the better for the echo of it; and though I had at first determined to buy stuff for a new coat, I went away, resolved to wear my old one a little longer. Reader, if thou wilt do the same, thy profit will be as great as mine. I am, as ever, thine to serve thee,

Richard Saunders.

Franklin's Advice to a Young Tradesman from an Old One

BY DR. BENJAMIN FRANKLIN

Remember that time is money. He that can earn 10*s.* a day by his labor, and goes abroad or sits idle one-half of that day, though he spend but 6*d.* during his diversion or idleness, ought not to reckon that the only expense; he has really spent, or rather thrown away, 5*s.* besides.

Remember that credit is money. If a man lets money lie in my hands after it is due, he gives me the interest, or so much as I can make of it during that time. This amounts to a considerable sum, if a man has a good and large credit, and makes good use of it.

Remember that money is of a prolific, generating nature. Money can beget money, and its offspring can beget more, and so on; 5*s.* turned, is 6*s.*; turned again, is 7*s.* 3*d.*; and so on till it becomes 100*l.* The more there is of it, the more it produces every turning; so that the profits rise quicker and quicker. He that kills a breeding sow, destroys all her offspring to the thousandth generation. He that murders a crown, destroys all that it might have produced, even scores of pounds.

Remember that six pounds a year is but a groat a day. For this little sum, which may daily be wasted in time or expense, unperceived, a man of credit may, on his own security, have the constant use and possession of 100*l.* So much in stock, briskly turned by an industrious man, produces great advantage.

Remember this saying: that *the good paymaster is lord of another man's purse.* He that is known to pay punctually and exactly at the time he promises, may at any time, and on any occasion, raise all the money his friends can spare. This is sometimes of great use; therefore, never keep borrowed money an hour beyond the time you promised, lest a disappointment shut up your friend's purse for ever.

The most trifling actions, that affect a man's credit, are to be regarded. The sound of your hammer at five in the morning, or nine at night, heard by a creditor, makes him easy six months longer. But if he sees you at a billiard table, or hears your voice at a tavern when you should be at work, he sends for his money the next day. Finer clothes than he or his wife wears, or greater expense in any particular than he affords himself, shocks his pride, and he duns you to humble you. Creditors are a kind of people that have the sharpest eyes and ears, as well as the best memories, of any in the world.

Good-natured creditors (and such one would always choose to deal with, if one could) feel pain when they are obliged to ask for money. Spare them that pain, and they will love you. When you receive a sum of money, divide it among them according to your debts. Do not be ashamed of paying a small sum, because you owe a greater. Money, more or less, is always welcome; and your creditor would sooner be at the trouble of receiving 10*l*. voluntarily brought him, though at ten different times or payments, than be obliged to go ten different times to demand it, before he can receive it in a lump. It shows that you are mindful of what you owe; it makes you appear a careful as well as an honest man, and that still increases your credit.

Beware of thinking all your own that you possess, and of living accordingly. It is a mistake that many people who have credit fall into. To prevent this, keep an exact account for some time of both your expenses and incomes. If you take the pains at first to mention particulars, it will have this good effect: you will discover how wonderfully small trifling expenses mount up to large sums, and will discern what might have been, and may for the future, be saved, without occasioning any great inconvenience.

In short, the way to wealth, if you desire it, is as plain as the way to market. It depends chiefly on two words—*industry* and *frugality;* that is, waste neither your time nor money, but make the best use of both. He that gets all he can, and saves all he gets (necessary expenses excepted), will certainly become rich; if that Being who governs the world, to whom all should look for a blessing on their honest endeavors, does not, in his wise providence, otherwise determine.

Franklin's Pro Bono Publico

A NEW WAY OF PAYING OLD DEBTS

The following letter was received by the editor of the *Leeds Mercury,* from a tradesman in Huddersfield.

"Why should excuse be born, or e'er begot?"
Shakespeare

Mr. Editor,—

A correspondent of yours, in the *Mercury* of last week, has taken some pains to instruct your readers in their *Christmas religious duties;* permit me to make the same experiment upon the *Christmas moral duties,* not of your readers only, for my philanthropy is more extensive; and, on the ground of *punctuality,* I wish to be the reformer of the world.

There is no talent, Sir, in the application of which some gentlemen more excel, than that of *excusing;* and when I tell you that I am a tradesman, obliged, from the nature of my business, to give credit, I hope you will not doubt that experience has qualified me to speak upon this subject, and to speak feelingly.

There are two kinds of *debtors*: those who *cannot* pay, and those who *will not* pay. The former have excuses *ready made;* the latter are *obliged* to *make* excuses. The former may be *sometimes* dishonest; the latter are never *very* honest. The former destroy hope at one blow; the latter protract its torments, till it expires from weakness. The former is an *acute distemper,* that kills in a few hours; the latter is a *chronic distemper,* worse than death. In a word, Sir, inability is tolerable, because *they* cannot cure it; *unwillingness* is painful, because I cannot shorten it.

In *forming excuses,* according to the common practice, the following rules are observed:—

1st. That the *same* excuse shall be as seldom repeated as possible.

2d. That the excuses be as various and *plausible* as possible.

3d. By way of maxim: every kind and degree of excuse deserves to be tried, because there is much less inconvenience in postponing a debt, than in paying it; and the advantages of *giving words* and *parting* with *money*, are on the side of the former.

To exemplify these rules, Mr. Editor, permit me to state the case of a bill which I sent to one of my customers last new-year (for, to be candid, the approach of that season has tempted me to trouble you on the present occasion). Now, mark the excuses in succession.

Jan. 1. "Oh! this is Mr. L—'s bill. Call again any day next week."

Jan. 9. "Not at home."—"When will he be at home?"—"Any time to-morrow."

Jan. 10. "Has a gentleman with him."—Waits an hour.—"Oh! ah! this is the bill—ay—hem!—look in on Tuesday."

Tuesday. "Not at home—gone to the Cloth-Hall."

Thursday. "Leave the bill, and I will look it over."

20. "There seems to be a mistake in the bill: I never had *this* article. Take it back to your master, and tell him to examine his books."

24. "Just gone out."

29. "I am busy now: tell your master I'll call on him as I go into the town."

Feb. 16. "Bless me! I quite forgot to call. This bill is not discharged! Bring me a receipt any time to-morrow or next day."

17. "Gone to London, and won't be at home till next month."

March 12. "What! did not I pay that bill before I went out of town?—Are you going farther?"

"Yes."—"Very well; call as you come back, and I'll settle."—Calls, and he is gone to dinner at Holmfirth.

16. "Plague on this bill! I don't believe I have so much cash in the house—can you give me change for a 100*l.* note?"—"No."—"Then call in as you pass to-morrow."

18. "Not at home."

25. *"Appoint a day!* Pray, what does your master mean? Tell him I'll call upon him, to know what he means by such a message."

April 14. "What! no discount?"—"Sir, it has been due these two years."—"There's your money, then."—"These notes won't pay."—"Then you must call again; I have no loose cash in the house."

And here ends the payment of 9*l.* 14s. 6*d.* with three doubtful notes.

But these are only a sample, after all, of the many excuses I must receive; and the most mortifying part of the business is, that such debtors are those who really can pay, but, by various delays, obtain the use of money, and, in some cases, tire out the patience of the creditor. I must say, indeed, that they are remarkably civil: they give me the prettiest words—they send their compliments and kind love "to Mrs. L—and the dear little ones"; but (plague on them!) they won't send the money.

As my fellow-tradesmen labor under the same hardships, in these respects, as myself, I hope you will not refuse this humble statement of our case; and, if it produces the payment of any one bill, which I should have to hunt after, you will merit the hearty thanks of Mr. Editor,

Your humble servant,
John L****.
Huddersfield, Christmas-day.

14

THE SECRET OF THE AGES

ROBERT COLLIER

(1926)

Contents

Foreword 837

1. The World's Greatest Discovery 839
In the Beginning— 840
The Purpose of Existence 841
The "Open, Sesame!" of Life 842

2. The Genie-of-Your-Mind 844
The Conscious Mind 846
The Subconscious Mind 846
The Universal Mind 852

3. The Primal Cause 855
Matter—Dream or Reality? 857
The Philosopher's Charm 859
The Kingdom of Heaven 860
"To Him That Hath"— 862
"To the Manner Born" 864

4. Desire—The First Law of Gain 867
The Magic Secret 869
"The Soul's Sincere Desire" 871

5. Aladdin & Company 875

6. See Yourself Doing It 882

7. "As a Man Thinketh" 887

8. The Law of Supply 892
The World Belongs to You 893
"Wanted" 897

9. The Formula of Success 900
The Talisman of Napoleon 901
"It Couldn't Be Done" 903

10. "This Freedom" 906
The Only Power 908

11. The Law of Attraction 911
A Blank Check 914

12. The Three Requisites 917

13. That Old Witch—Bad Luck 921
He Whom a Dream Hath Possessed 923
The Bars of Fate 924
Exercise 927

14. Your Needs Are Met 928
The Ark of the Covenant 930
The Science of Thought 932

15. The Master of Your Fate 935
The Acre of Diamonds 936

16. Unappropriated Millions 941

17. The Secret of Power 944

18. This One Thing I Do 946

19. The Master Mind 951

20. What Do You Lack? 955

21. The Sculptor and the Clay 960

22. Why Grow Old? 964
The Fountain of Youth 967

23. The Medicine Delusion 972

24. The Gift of the Magi 977
"Suffer Little Children to Come Unto Me" 991
L'Envoi 992

Index of Scriptural References and Quotations 995

"A fire-mist and a planet,
A crystal and a cell,
A jelly-fish and a saurian,
A cave where the cave-men dwell;
Then a sense of law and order,
A face upturned from the clod;
Some call it Evolution,
And others call it God."

REPRINTED FROM

THE NEW ENGLAND JOURNAL

Foreword

If you had more money than time, more millions than you knew how to spend, what would be your pet philanthropy? Libraries? Hospitals? Churches? Homes for the Blind, Crippled or Aged?

Mine would be "Homes"—but not for the aged or infirm. *For young married couples!*

I have often thought that, if ever I got into the "Philanthropic Billionaire" class, I'd like to start an Endowment Fund for helping young married couples over the rough spots in those first and second years of married life—especially the second year, when the real troubles come.

Take a boy and a girl and a cozy little nest—add a cunning, healthy baby—and there's nothing happier on God's green footstool.

But instead of a healthy babe, fill in a fretful, sickly baby—a wan, tired, worn-out little mother—a worried, dejected, heart-sick father—and there's nothing more pitiful.

A nurse for a month, a few weeks at the shore or mountains, a "lift" on that heavy Doctor's bill—any one of these things would spell H-E-A-V-E-N to that tiny family. But do they get it? Not often! And the reason? Because they are not poor enough for charity. They are not rich enough to afford it themselves. They belong to that great "Middle Class" which has to bear the burdens of both the poor and the rich—and take what is left for itself.

It is to them that I should like to dedicate this book. If I cannot endow Libraries or Colleges for them, perhaps I can point the way to get all good gifts for themselves.

For men and women like them do not need "charity"—nor even sympathy. What they do need is Inspiration—and Opportunity—the kind of Inspiration that makes a man go out and create his own Opportunity.

And that, after all, is the greatest good one can do anyone. Few people appreciate free gifts. They are like the man whom an admiring townsfolk presented with a watch. He looked it over critically for a minute. Then—"Where's the chain?" he asked.

But a way to win *for themselves* the full measure of success they've dreamed of but almost stopped hoping for—*that* is something every young couple would welcome with open arms. And it is something that, if I can do it justice, will make the "Eternal Triangle" as rare as it is today common, for it will enable husband and wife to work *together*—not merely for domestic happiness but for business success as well.

ROBERT COLLIER

CHAPTER 1

The World's Greatest Discovery

"You can do as much as you think you can,
But you'll never accomplish more;
If you're afraid of yourself, young man,
There's little for you in store.
For failure comes from the inside first,
It's there if we only knew it,
And you can win, though you face the worst,
*If you feel that you're going to do it."**

—EDGAR A. GUEST*

What, in your opinion, is the most significant discovery of this modern age?

The finding of Dinosaur eggs on the plains of Mongolia, laid—so scientists assert—some 10,000,000 years ago?

The unearthing of the Tomb of Tut-ankh-Amen, with its matchless specimens of a bygone civilization?

The radio-active time clock by which Professor Lane of Tufts College estimates the age of the earth at 1,250,000,000 years?

Wireless? The Aeroplane? Manmade thunderbolts?

No—not any of these. The really significant thing about them is that from all this vast research, from the study of all these bygone ages, men are for the first time beginning to get an understanding of that "Life Principle" which—somehow, some way—was brought to this earth thousands or millions of years ago. They are beginning to get an inkling of the infinite power it puts in their hands—to glimpse the untold possibilities it opens up.

This is the greatest discovery of modern times—that every man can call upon this "Life Principle" at will, that it is as much the servant of his mind as was ever Aladdin's fabled "Genie-of-the-lamp" of old; that he has but to understand it and work in harmony with it to get from it anything he may need—health or happiness, riches or success.

*From "A Heap o' Livin'." The Reilly & Lee Co.

To realize the truth of this, you have but to go back for a moment to the beginning of things.

IN THE BEGINNING—

It matters not whether you believe that mankind dates back to the primitive Ape-man of 500,000 years ago, or sprang full-grown from the mind of the Creator. In either event, there had to be a First Cause—a Creator. Some Power had to bring to this earth the first germ of Life, and the creation is no less wonderful if it started with the lowliest form of plant life and worked up through countless ages into the highest product of today's civilization, than if the whole were created in six days.

In the beginning, this earth was just a fire mist—six thousand or a billion years ago—what does it matter which?

The one thing that does matter is that some time, some way, there came to this planet the germ of Life—the Life Principle which animates all Nature—plant, animal, man. If we accept the scientists' version of it, the first form in which Life appeared upon earth was the humble Algae—a jelly-like mass which floated upon the waters. This, according to the scientists, was the beginning, the dawn of life upon the earth.

Next came the first bit of animal life—the lowly Amoeba, a sort of jelly fish, consisting of a single cell, without vertebrae, and with very little else to distinguish it from the water round about. But it had *life*—the first bit of *animal* life—and from that life, according to the scientists, we can trace everything we have and are today.

All the millions of forms and shapes and varieties of plants and animals that have since appeared are but different manifestations of *life*—formed to meet differing conditions. For millions of years this "Life Germ" was threatened by every kind of danger—from floods, from earthquakes, from droughts, from desert heat, from glacial cold, from volcanic eruptions—but to it each new danger was merely an incentive to finding a new resource, to putting forth Life in some new shape.

To meet one set of needs, it formed the Dinosaur—to meet another, the Butterfly. Long before it worked up to man, we see its unlimited resourcefulness shown in a thousand ways. To escape danger in the water, it sought land. Pursued on land, it took to the air. To breathe in the sea, it developed gills. Stranded on land, it perfected lungs. To meet one kind of danger, it grew a shell. For another, a sting. To protect itself from glacial cold, it grew fur. In temperate climes, hair. Subject to alternate heat and cold, it produced feathers. But ever, from the beginning, it showed its power to meet every changing condition, to answer every creature need.

Had it been possible to kill this "Life Idea," it would have perished ages ago, when fire and flood, drought and famine followed each other in quick succession. But obstacles, misfortunes, cataclysms were to it merely new opportunities to assert its power. In fact, it required obstacles to awaken it, to show its energy and resource.

The great reptiles, the monster beasts of antiquity, passed on. But the "Life Principle" stayed, changing as each age changed, always developing, always improving.

Whatever Power it was that brought this "Life Idea" to the earth, it came endowed with unlimited resource, unlimited energy, unlimited LIFE! No other force can defeat it. No obstacle can hold it back. All through the history of life and mankind you can see its directing intelligence—call it Nature, call it Providence, call it what you will—rising to meet every need of life.

THE PURPOSE OF EXISTENCE

No one can follow it down through the ages without realizing that the whole purpose of existence is GROWTH. Life is dynamic—not static. It is ever moving forward—not standing still. The one unpardonable sin of nature is to stand still, to stagnate. The Gigantosaurus, that was over a hundred feet long and as big as a house; the Tyrannosaurus, that had the strength of a locomotive and was the last word in frightfulness; the Pterodactyl or Flying Dragon—all the giant monsters of Prehistoric Ages—are gone. They ceased to serve a useful purpose. They did not know how to meet the changing conditions. They stood still—stagnated—while the life around them passed them by.

Egypt and Persia, Greece and Rome, all the great Empires of antiquity, perished when they ceased to grow. China built a wall about herself and stood still for a thousand years. Today she is the football of the Powers. In all Nature, to cease to grow is to perish.

It is for men and women who are not ready to stand still, who refuse to cease to grow, that this book is written. It will give you a clearer understanding of your own potentialities, show you how to work with and take advantage of the infinite energy all about you.

The terror of the man at the crossways, not knowing which road to take, will be no terror to you. Your future is of your own making. For the only law of Infinite Energy is the law of supply. The "Life Principle" is your principle. To survive, to win through, to triumphantly surmount all obstacles has been its everyday practice since the beginning of time. It is no less resourceful now than ever it was. You have but to supply the urge, to work in harmony with it, to get from it anything you may need.

For if this "Life Principle" is so strong in the lowest forms of animal life that it can develop a shell or a poison to meet a need; if it can teach the bird to circle and dart, to balance and fly; if it can grow a new limb on a spider to replace a lost one, how much more can it do for *you*—a reasoning, rational being, with a mind able to *work with* this "Life Principle," with an energy and an initiative to urge it on!

The evidence of this is all about you. Take up some violent form of exercise—rowing, tennis, swimming, riding. In the beginning your muscles are weak, easily tired. But keep on for a few days. The "Life Principle" promptly strengthens them, toughens them, to meet their new need. Do rough manual labor—and what happens? The skin of your hands becomes tender, blisters, hurts. Keep it up, and does the skin all wear off? On the contrary, the "Life Principle" provides extra thicknesses, extra toughness—calluses, we call them—to meet your need.

All through your daily life you will find this "Life Principle" steadily at work. Embrace it, work with it, take it to yourself, and there is nothing you cannot do. The mere fact that you have obstacles to overcome is in your favor, for when there is nothing to be done, when things run along too smoothly, this "Life Principle" seems to sleep. It is when you need it, when you call upon it urgently, that it is most on the job.

It differs from "Luck" in this, that fortune is a fickle jade who smiles most often on those who need her least. Stake your last penny on the turn of a card—have nothing between you and ruin but the spin of a wheel or the speed of a horse—and it's a thousand to one "Luck" will desert you! But it is just the opposite with the "Life Principle." As long as things run smoothly, as long as life flows along like a song, this "Life Principle" seems to slumber, secure in the knowledge that your affairs can take care of themselves.

But let things start going wrong, let ruin and disgrace stare you in the face—*then* is the time this "Life Principle" will assert itself if you but give it a chance.

THE "OPEN, SESAME!" OF LIFE

There is a Napoleonic feeling of power *that insures success* in the knowledge that this invincible "Life Principle" is behind your every act. Knowing that you have working with you a force which never yet has failed in anything it has undertaken, you can go ahead in the confident knowledge that it will not fail in your case, either. The ingenuity which overcame every obstacle in making you what you are is not likely to fall short when you have immediate need for it. It is the reserve strength of the athlete, the "second wind" of the runner, the power that, in moments of great stress or excitement, you unconsciously call upon to do the deeds which you ever after look upon as superhuman.

But they are in no wise superhuman. They are merely beyond the capacity of your conscious self. Ally your conscious self with that sleeping giant within you, rouse him daily to the task, and those "superhuman" deeds will become your ordinary, everyday accomplishments.

W. L. Cain, of Oakland, Oregon, writes: "I know that there is such a power, for I once saw two boys, 16 and 18 years of age, lift a great log off their brother, who had been caught under it. The next day, the same two boys, with another man and myself, tried to lift the end of the log, but could not even budge it."

How was it that the two boys could do at need what the four were unable to do later on, when the need had passed? Because they never stopped to question whether or not it *could* be done. They saw only the urgent need. They concentrated all their thought, all their energy on that one thing—never doubting, never fearing—and the Genie which is in all of us, waiting only for such a call, answered their summons and gave them the strength—not of two men, but of ten!

It matters not whether you are Banker or Lawyer, Business Man or Clerk. Whether you are the custodian of millions, or have to struggle for your daily bread. This "Life Principle" makes no distinction between rich and poor, high and low. The greater your need, the more readily will it respond to your call. Wherever there is an unusual task, wherever there is poverty or hardship or sickness or despair, *there* is this Servant of your Mind, ready and willing to help, asking only that you call upon him.

And not only is it ready and willing, but it is always ABLE to help. Its ingenuity and resource are without limit, It is Mind. It is Thought. It is the Telepathy that carries messages without the spoken or written word. It is the Sixth Sense that warns you of unseen dangers. No matter how stupendous and complicated, nor how simple your problem may be—the solution of it is somewhere in Mind, in Thought. And since the solution does exist, this Mental Giant can find it for you. It can KNOW, and it can DO, every right thing. Whatever it is necessary for you to know, whatever it is necessary for you to do, you can know and you can do if you will but seek the help of this Genie-of-your-Mind and work with it in the right way.

CHAPTER 2

The Genie-of-Your-Mind

"It matters not how strait the gate,
How charged with punishment the scroll,
I am the Master of my Fate;
I am the Captain of my Soul."

—HENLEY

First came the Stone Age, when life was for the strong of arm or the fleet of foot. Then there was the Iron Age—and while life was more precious, still the strong lorded it over the weak. Later came the Golden Age, and riches took the place of strength—but the poor found little choice between the slave drivers' whips of olden days and the grim weapons of poverty and starvation.

Now we are entering a new age—the Mental Age—when every man can be his own master, when poverty and circumstance no longer hold power and the lowliest creature in the land can win a place side by side with the highest.

To those who do not know the resources of mind these will sound like rash statements; but science proves beyond question that in the well springs of every man's mind are unplumbed depths—undiscovered deposits of energy, wisdom and ability. Sound these depths—bring these treasures to the surface—and you gain an astounding wealth of new power.

From the rude catamaran of the savages to the giant liners of today, carrying their thousands from continent to continent, is but a step in the development of Mind. From the lowly cave man, cowering in his burrow in fear of lightning or fire or water, to the engineer of today, making servants of all the forces of Nature, is but a measure of difference in mental development.

Man, without reasoning mind, would be as the monkeys are—prey of any creature fast enough and strong enough to pull him to pieces. At the mercy of wind and weather. A poor, timid creature, living for the moment only, fearful of every shadow.

Through his superior mind, he learned to make fire to keep himself warm; weapons with which to defend himself from the savage creatures round about; habitations to protect himself from the elements. Through mind he conquered the forces of Nature. Through mind he has made machinery do the work of millions of horses and billions of hands. What he will do next, no man knows, for man is just beginning to awaken to his own powers. He is just getting an inkling of the unfathomed riches buried deep in his own mind. Like the gold seekers of '49, he has panned the surface gravel for the gold swept down by the streams. Now he is starting to dig deeper to the pure vein beneath.

We bemoan the loss of our forests. We worry over our dwindling resources of coal and oil. We decry the waste in our factories. But the greatest waste of all, we pay no attention to—the waste of our own potential mind power. Professor Wm. James, the world-famous Harvard psychologist, estimated that the average man uses only 10% of his mental power. He has unlimited power—yet he uses but a tithe of it. Unlimited wealth all about him—and he doesn't know how to take hold of it. With God-like powers slumbering within him, he is content to continue in his daily grind—eating, sleeping, working—plodding through an existence little more eventful than the animals', while all of Nature, all of life, calls upon him to awaken, to bestir himself.

The power to be what you want to be, to get what you desire, to accomplish whatever you are striving for, abides within you. It rests with you only to bring it forth and put it to work. Of course you must know *how* to do that, but before you can learn how to use it, you must *realize* that you *possess* this power. So our first objective is to get acquainted with this power.

For Psychologists and Metaphysicians the world over are agreed in this—that Mind is all that counts. You can be whatever you make up your mind to be. You need not be sick. You need not be unhappy. You need not be poor. You need not be unsuccessful. You are not a mere clod. You are not a beast of burden, doomed to spend your days in unremitting labor in return for food and housing. You are one of the Lords of the Earth, with unlimited potentialities. Within you is a power which, properly grasped and directed, can lift you out of the rut of mediocrity and place you among the Elect of the earth—the lawyers, the writers, the statesmen, the big business men—the DOERS and the THINKERS. It rests with you only to learn to use this power which is yours—this Mind which can do all things.

Your body is for all practical purposes merely a machine which the mind uses. This mind is usually thought of as consciousness; but the *conscious part* of your mind is in fact the *very smallest part of it.* Ninety per cent of your mental life is subconscious, so when you make active use of only the conscious part of your mind you are using but a fraction of your real ability; you are running on low gear. And the reason why more people do not achieve success in life is because so many of them are content to run on low gear all their lives—on SURFACE ENERGY. If these same people would only throw into the fight the resistless force of their subconscious minds they would be amazed at their undreamed of capacity for winning success.

Conscious and subconscious are, of course, integral parts of the one mind. But for convenience sake let us divide your mind into three parts—the conscious mind, the subconscious mind and the Infinite, Subliminal or Universal Mind.

THE CONSCIOUS MIND

When you say "I see—I hear—I smell—I touch," it is your conscious mind that is saying this, for it is the force governing the five physical senses. It is the phase of mind with which you feel and reason—the phase of mind with which everyone is familiar. It is the mind with which you do business. It controls, to a great extent, all your voluntary muscles. It discriminates between right and wrong, wise and foolish. It is the generalissimo, in charge of all your mental forces. It can plan ahead—and get things done as it plans. Or it can drift along haphazardly, a creature of impulse, at the mercy of events—a mere bit of flotsam in the current of life.

For it is only through your conscious mind that you can reach the subconscious and the Universal Mind. Your conscious mind is the porter at the door, the watchman at the gate. It is to the conscious mind that the subconscious looks for all its impressions. It is on it that the subconscious mind must depend for the teamwork necessary to get successful results. You wouldn't expect much from an army, no matter how fine its soldiers, whose general never planned ahead, who distrusted his own ability and that of his men and who spent all his time worrying about the enemy instead of planning how he might conquer them. You wouldn't look for good scores from a ball team whose pitcher was at odds with the catcher. In the same way, you can't expect results from the subconscious when your conscious mind is full of fear or worry, or when it does not know what it wants.

The one most important province of your conscious mind is to center your thoughts on the thing you want, and to shut the door on every suggestion of fear or worry or disease.

If you once gain the ability to do that, nothing else is impossible to you.

For the subconscious mind does not reason inductively. It takes the thoughts you send in to it and works them out to their logical conclusion. Send to it thoughts of health and strength, and it will work out health and strength in your body. Let suggestions of disease, fear of sickness or accident, penetrate to it, either through your own thoughts or the talk of those around you, and you are very likely to see the manifestation of disease working out in yourself.

Your mind is master of your body. It directs and controls every function of your body. Your body is in effect a little universe in itself, and mind is its radiating center—the sun which gives light and life to all your system, and around which the whole revolves. And your *conscious thought* is master of this sun center. As Emile Coué puts it—"The conscious can put the subconscious mind over the hurdles."

THE SUBCONSCIOUS MIND

Can you tell me how much water, how much salt, how much of each different element there should be in your blood to maintain its proper specific gravity if you are leading an ordinary sedentary life? How much and how quickly these proportions must be changed if you play a fast game of tennis, or run for your car, or chop wood, or indulge in any other violent exercise?

Do you know how much water you should drink to neutralize the excess salt in salt fish? How much you lose through perspiration? Do you know how much water, how much salt, how much of each different element in your food should be absorbed into your blood each day to maintain perfect health?

No? Well, it need not worry you. Neither does anyone else. Not even the greatest physicists and chemists and mathematicians. But your subconscious mind knows.

And it doesn't have to stop to figure it out. It does it almost automatically. It is one of those "Lightning Calculators." And this is but one of thousands of such jobs it performs every hour of the day. The greatest mathematicians in the land, the most renowned chemists, could never do in a year's time the abstruse problems which your subconscious mind solves every minute.

And it doesn't matter whether you've ever studied mathematics or chemistry or any other of the sciences. From the moment of your birth your subconscious mind solves all these problems for you. While you are struggling along with the three R's, it is doing problems that would leave your teachers aghast. It supervises all the intricate processes of digestion, of assimilation, of elimination, and all the glandular secretions that would tax the knowledge of all the chemists and all the laboratories in the land. It planned and built your body from infancy on up. It repairs it. It operates it. It has almost unlimited power, not merely for putting you and keeping you in perfect health but for acquiring all the good things of life. Ignorance of this power is the sole reason for all the failures in this world. If you would intelligently turn over to this wonderful power all your business and personal affairs in the same way that you turn over to it the mechanism of your body, no goal would be too great for you to strive for.

Dr. Geo. C. Pitzer sums up the power of the subconscious mind very well in the following:

"The subconscious mind is a distinct entity. It occupies the whole human body, and, when not opposed in any way, it has absolute control over all the functions, conditions, and sensations of the body. While the objective (conscious) mind has control over all of our voluntary functions and motions, the subconscious mind controls all of the silent, involuntary, and vegetative functions. Nutrition, waste, all secretions and excretions, the action of the heart in the circulation of the blood, the lungs in respiration or breathing, and all cell life, cell changes and development are positively under the complete control of the subconscious mind. This was the only mind animals had before the evolution of the brain; and it could not, nor can it yet, reason inductively, but its power of deductive reasoning is perfect. And more, it can see without the use of physical eyes. It perceives by intuition. It has the power to communicate with others without the aid of ordinary physical means. It can read the thoughts of others. It receives intelligence and transmits it to people at a distance. Distance offers no resistance against the successful missions of the subconscious mind. It never dies. We call this the 'soul mind.' It is the living soul."

In "Practical Psychology and Sex Life" by David Bush, Dr. Winbigler is quoted as going even further. To quote him:

"It is this mind that carries on the work of assimilation and upbuilding whilst we sleep. . . .

"It reveals to us things that the conscious mind has no conception of until the consummations have occurred.

"It can communicate with other minds without the ordinary physical means.

"It gets glimpses of things that ordinary sight does not behold.

"It makes God's presence an actual, realizable fact, and keeps the personality in peace and quietness.

"It warns of approaching danger.

"It approves or disapproves of a course of conduct and conversation.

"It carries out all the best things which are given to it, providing the conscious mind does not intercept and change the course of its manifestation.

"It heals the body and keeps it in health, if it is at all encouraged."

It is, in short, the most powerful force in life, and when properly directed, the most beneficent. But, like a live electric wire, its destructive force is equally great. It can be either your servant or your master. It can bring to you evil or good.

The Rev. William T. Walsh, in a new book just published, explains the idea very clearly:

"The subconscious part in us is called the subjective mind, because it does not decide and command. It is a subject rather than a ruler. Its nature is to do what it is told, *or what really in your heart of hearts you desire.*

"The subconscious mind directs all the vital processes of your body. You do not think consciously about breathing. Every time you take a breath you do not have to reason, decide, command. The subconscious mind sees to that. You have not been at all conscious that you have been breathing while you have been reading this page. So it is with the mind and the circulation of blood. The heart is a muscle like the muscle of your arm. It has no power to move itself or to direct its action. Only mind, only something that can think, can direct our muscles, including the heart. You are not conscious that you are commanding your heart to beat. The subconscious mind attends to that. And so it is with the assimilation of food, the building and repairing of the body. In fact, all the vital processes are looked after by the subconscious mind."

"Man lives and moves and has his being" in this great subconscious mind. It supplies the "intuition" that so often carries a woman straight to a point that may require hours of cumbersome reasoning for a man to reach. Even in ordinary, everyday affairs, you often draw upon its wonderful wisdom.

But you do it in an accidental sort of way without realizing what you are doing.

Consider the case of "Blind Tom." Probably you've heard or read of him. You know that he could listen to a piece of music for the first time and go immediately to a piano and reproduce it. People call that abnormal. But as a matter of fact he was in this respect more normal than any of us. We are abnormal because we cannot do it.

Or consider the case of these "lightning calculators" of whom one reads now and then. It may be a boy seven or eight years old; but you can ask him to divide 7,649.437 by 326.2568 and he'll give you the result in less time than it would take you to put the numbers down on a piece of paper. You call him phenomenal. Yet you ought to be able to do the same yourself. Your subconscious mind can.

Dr. Hudson, in his book "The Law of Psychic Phenomena," tells of numerous such prodigies. Here are just a few instances:

"Of mathematical prodigies there have been upwards of a score whose calculations have surpassed, in rapidity and accuracy, those of the greatest educated mathematicians. These prodigies have done their greatest feats while but children from three to ten years old. In no case had these boys any idea how they performed their calculations, and some of them would converse upon other subjects while doing the sum. Two of these boys became men of eminence, while some of them showed but a low degree of objective intelligence.

"Whatcley spoke of his own gift in the following terms:

"'There was certainly something peculiar in my calculating faculty. It began to show itself at between five and six, and lasted about three years. I soon got to do the most difficult sums, always in my head, for I knew nothing of figures beyond numeration. I did these sums much quicker than anyone could upon paper, and I never remember committing the smallest error. When I went to school, at which time the passion wore off, I was a perfect dunce at cyphering, and have continued so ever since.'

"Professor Safford became an astronomer. At the age of ten he worked correctly a multiplication sum whose answer consisted of thirty-six figures. Later in life he could perform no such feats.

"Benjamin Hall Blyth, at the age of six, asked his father at what hour he was born. He was told that he was born at four o'clock. Looking at the clock to see the present time, he informed his father of the number of seconds he had lived. His father made the calculation and said to Benjamin, 'You are wrong 172,000 seconds.' The boy answered, 'Oh, papa, you have left out two days for the leap years 1820 and 1824,' which was the case.

"Then there is the celebrated case of Zerah Colburn, of whom Dr. Schofield writes:

"'Zerah Colburn could instantaneously tell the square root of 106,929 as 327, and the cube root of 268,336,125 as 645. Before the question of the number of minutes in forty-eight years could be written he said 25,228,810. He immediately gave the factors of 247,483 as 941 and 263, which are the only two; and being asked then for those of 36,083, answered none; it is a prime number. He could not tell how the answer came into his mind. He could not, on paper, do simple multiplication or division.'"

The time will come when, as H. G. Wells visioned in his "Men Like Gods," schools and teachers will no longer be necessary except to show us how to get in touch with the infinite knowledge our subconscious minds possess from infancy.

"The smartest man in the world," says Dr. Frank Crane in a recent article in *Liberty*, "is the Man Inside. By the Man Inside I mean that Other Man within each one of us that does most of the things we give ourselves credit for doing. You may refer to him as Nature or the Subconscious Self or think of him merely as a Force or a Natural Law, or, if you are religiously inclined, you may use the term God.

"I say he is the smartest man in the world. I know he is infinitely more clever and resourceful than I am or than any other man is that I ever heard of. When I cut my finger it is he that calls up the little phagocytes to come and kill the septic germs that might get into the wound and cause blood poisoning. It is he that coagulates the blood, stops the gash, and weaves the new skin.

"I could not do that. I do not even know how he does it. He even does it for babies that know nothing at all; in fact, does it better for them than for me.

"No living man knows enough to make toenails grow, but the Man Inside thinks nothing of growing nails and teeth and thousands of hairs all over my body; long hairs on my head and little fuzzy ones over the rest of the surface of the skin.

"When I practice on the piano I am simply getting the business of piano playing over from my conscious mind to my subconscious mind: in other words, I am handing the business over to the Man Inside.

"Most of our happiness, as well as our struggles and misery, comes from this Man Inside. If we train him in ways of contentment, adjustment, and decision he will go ahead of us like a well trained servant and do for us easily most of the difficult tasks we have to perform."

Dr. Jung, celebrated Viennese specialist, claims that the subconscious mind contains not only all the knowledge that it has gathered during the life of the individual, but that in addition it contains all the wisdom of past ages. That by drawing upon its wisdom and power the individual may possess any good thing of life, from health and happiness to riches and success.

You see, the subconscious mind is the connecting link between the Creator and ourselves, between Universal Mind and our conscious mind. It is the means by which we can appropriate to ourselves all the good gifts, all the riches and abundance which Universal Mind has created in such profusion.

Berthelot, the great French founder of modern synthetic chemistry, once stated in a letter to a close friend that the final experiments which led to his most wonderful discoveries had never been the result of carefully followed and reasoned trains of thought but that, on the contrary, "they came of themselves, so to speak, from the clear sky."

Charles M. Barrows, in "Suggestion Instead of Medicine," tells us that:

"If man requires another than his ordinary consciousness to take care of him while asleep, not less useful is this same psychical provision when he is awake. Many persons are able to obtain knowledge which does not come to them through their senses, in the usual way, but arrives in the mind by direct communication from another conscious intelligence, which apparently knows more of what concerns their welfare than their ordinary reason does. I have known a number of persons who, like myself, could tell the contents of letters in their mail before opening them. Several years ago a friend of mine came to Boston for the first time, arriving at what was then the Providence railroad station in Park Square. He wished to walk to the Lowell station on the opposite side of the city. Being utterly ignorant of the streets as well as the general direction to take he confidently set forth without asking the way, and reached his destination by the most direct path. In doing this he trusted solely to 'instinctive guidance,' as he called it, and not to any hints or clews obtained through the senses."

The geniuses of literature, of art, commerce, government, politics and invention are, according to the scientists, but ordinary men like you and me who have learned somehow, some way, to draw upon their subconscious minds.

Sir Isaac Newton is reported to have acquired his marvelous knowledge of mathematics and physics with no conscious effort. Mozart said of his beautiful symphonies that they just came to him. Descartes had no ordinary regular education. To quote Dr. Hudson:

"This is a power which transcends reason, and is independent of induction. Instances of its development might be multiplied indefinitely. Enough is known to warrant the conclusion that when the soul is released from its objective environment it will be enabled to perceive all the laws of its being, to 'see God as He is,' by the perception of the laws which He has instituted. It is the knowledge of this power which demonstrates our true relationship to God, which confers the warranty of our right to the title of 'sons of God,' and confirms our inheritance of our rightful share of his attributes and powers—our heirship of God, our joint heirship with Jesus Christ."

Our subconscious minds are vast magnets, with the power to draw from Universal Mind unlimited knowledge, unlimited power, unlimited riches.

"Considered from the standpoint of its activities," says Warren Hilton in "Applied Psychology," "the subconscious is that department of mind, which on the one hand directs the vital operations of the body, and on the other conserves, subject to the call of interest and attention, all ideas and complexes not at the moment active in consciousness.

"Observe, then, the possibility that lies before you. On the one hand, if you can control your mind in its subconscious activities, you can regulate the operation of your bodily functions, and can thus assure yourself of bodily efficiency and free yourself of functional disease. On the other hand, if you can determine just what ideas shall be brought forth from subconsciousness into consciousness, you can thus select the materials out of which will be woven your conscious judgments, your decisions and your emotional attitudes.

"To achieve control of your mind is, then, to attain (a) health, (b) success, and (c) happiness."

Few understand or appreciate, however, that the vast storehouse of knowledge and power of the subconscious mind can be drawn upon at will. Now and then through intense concentration or very active desire we do accidentally penetrate to the realm of the subconscious and register our thought upon it. Such thoughts are almost invariably realized. The trouble is that as often as not it is our negative thoughts—our fears—that penetrate. And these are realized just as surely as the positive thoughts. What you must manage to do is learn to communicate only such thoughts as you wish to see realized to your subconscious mind, for it is exceedingly amenable to suggestion. You have heard of the man who was always bragging of his fine health and upon whom some of his friends decided to play a trick. The first one he met one morning commented upon how badly he looked and asked if he weren't feeling well. Then all the others as they saw him made similar remarks. By noon time the man had come to believe them, and before the end of the day he was really ill.

That was a rather glaring example. But similar things are going on every day with all of us. We eat something that someone else tells us isn't good for us and in a little while we think we feel a pain. Before we know it we have indigestion, when the chances are that if we knew nothing about the supposed indigestible properties of the food we could eat it the rest of our days and never feel any ill effects.

Let some new disease be discovered and the symptoms described in the daily paper.

Hundreds will come down with it at once. They are like the man who read a medical encyclopedia and ended up by concluding he had everything but "housemaid's knee." Patent medicine advertisers realize this power of suggestion and cash in upon it. Read one of their ads. If you don't think you have everything the matter with you that their nostrums are supposed to cure, you are the exception and not the rule.

That is the negative side of it. Emile Coué based his system on the positive side—that you suggest to your subconscious mind that whatever ills it thinks you have are getting better. And it is good psychology at that. Properly carried out, it will work wonders. But there are better methods. And I hope to be able to show them to you before we reach the end of this book.

Suffice it now to say that your subconscious mind is exceedingly wise and powerful. That it knows many things that are not in books. That when properly used it has infallible judgment, unfailing power. That it never sleeps, never tires.

Your conscious mind may slumber. It may be rendered impotent by anaesthetics or a sudden blow. But your subconscious mind works on, keeping your heart and lungs, your arteries and glands ever on the job.

Under ordinary conditions, it attends faithfully to its duties, and leaves your conscious mind to direct the outer life of the body. But let the conscious mind meet some situation with which it is unable to cope, and, if it will only call upon the subconscious, that powerful Genie will respond immediately to its need.

You have heard of people who had been through great danger tell how, when death stared them in the face and there seemed nothing they could do, things went black before them and, when they came to, the danger was past. In the moment of need, their subconscious mind pushed the conscious out of the way, while it met and overcame the danger. Impelled by the subconscious mind, their bodies could do things absolutely impossible to their ordinary conscious selves.

For the power of the subconscious mind is unlimited. Whatever it is necessary for you to do in any right cause, it can give you the strength and the ability to do.

Whatever of good you may desire, it can bring to you. "The Kingdom of Heaven is within you."

THE UNIVERSAL MIND

Have you ever dug up a potato vine and seen the potatoes clustering underneath? How much of intelligence do you suppose one of these potatoes has? Do you think it knows anything about chemistry or geology? Can it figure out how to gather carbon gas from the atmosphere, water and all the necessary kinds of nutriment from the earth round about to manufacture into sugar and starch and alcohol? No chemist can do it. How do you suppose the potato knows? Of course it doesn't. It has no sense. Yet it does all these things. It builds the starch into cells, the cells into roots and vines and leaves—and into more potatoes.

"Just old Mother Nature," you'll say. But old Mother Nature must have a remarkable intelligence if she can figure out all these things that no human scientist has ever been able to figure. There must be an all-pervading Intelligence behind Mother Nature—the Intelligence that first brought life to this planet—the Intelligence that evolved every form of plant and animal—that holds the winds in its grasp—that is all-wise, all-powerful. The potato is but one small manifestation of this Intelligence. The various forms of plant life, of animals, of man—all are mere cogs in the great scheme of things.

But with this *difference*—that man is an active part of this Universal Mind. That he partakes of its creative wisdom and power and that by working in harmony with Universal Mind he can *do* anything, *have* anything, *be* anything.

There is within you—within everyone—this mighty resistless force with which you can perform undertakings that will dazzle your reason, stagger your imagination. There constantly resides within you a Mind that is all-wise, all-powerful, a Mind that is entirely apart from the mind which you consciously use in your everyday affairs yet which is one with it.

Your subconscious mind partakes of this wisdom and power, and it is through your subconscious mind that you can draw upon it in the attainment of anything you may desire. When you can intelligently reach your subconscious mind, you can be in communication with the Universal Mind.

Remember this: the Universal Mind is omnipotent. And since the subconscious mind is part of the Universal Mind, there is no limit to the things which it can do when it is given the power to act. Given any desire that is in harmony with the Universal Mind and you have but to hold that desire in your thought to attract from the invisible domain the things you need to satisfy it.

For mind does its building solely by the power of thought. Its creations take form according to its thought. Its first requisite is a mental image, and your desire held with unswerving purpose will form that mental image.

An understanding of this principle explains the power of prayer. The results of prayer are not brought about by some special dispensation of Providence. God is not a finite being to be cajoled or flattered into doing as you desire. But when you pray earnestly you form a mental image of the thing that you desire and you hold it strongly in your thought. Then the Universal Intelligence which is your intelligence—Omnipotent Mind—begins to work with and for you, and this is what brings about the manifestation that you desire.

The Universal Mind is all around you. It is as all-pervading as the air you breathe. It encompasses you with as little trouble as the water in the sea encompasses the fish. Yet it is just as thoroughly conscious of you as the water would be, were it intelligent, of every creature within it. "Are not two sparrows sold for a farthing? And one of them shall not fall on the ground without your Father. But the very hairs of your head are all numbered. Fear ye not, therefore, ye are of more value than many sparrows."

It seems hard to believe that a Mind busied with the immensities of the universe can consider such trivial affairs as our own when we are but one of the billions of forms of life which come into existence. Yet consider again the fish in the sea. It is no trouble for the sea to encompass them. It is no more trouble for the Universal Mind to encompass us. Its power, Its thought, are as much at our disposal as the sunshine and the wind and the rain. Few of us take advantage to the full of these great forces. Fewer still take advantage of the power of the Universal Mind. If you have any lack, if you are prey to poverty or disease, it is because you do not believe or do not understand the power that is yours. It is not a question of the Universal giving to you. It offers everything to everyone—there is no partiality. "Ho, everyone that thirsteth, come ye to the waters." You have only to take. "Whosoever will, let him take of the water of life freely."

"With all thy getting, get understanding," said Solomon. And if you will but get understanding, everything else will be added unto you.

To bring you to a realization of your indwelling and unused power, to teach you simple, direct methods of drawing upon it, is the beginning and the end of this course.

"And the earth was
Without form and void;
And darkness was upon
The face of the deep.
And the Spirit of God moved
Upon the face of the waters."

GENESIS 1:2

CHAPTER 3

The Primal Cause

This city, with all its houses, palaces, steam engines, cathedrals and huge, immeasurable traffic and tumult, what is it but a Thought, but millions of Thoughts made into one—a huge immeasurable Spirit of a Thought, embodied in brick, in iron, smoke, dust, Palaces, Parliaments, coaches, docks and the rest of it! Not a brick was made but some man had to *think* of the making of that brick.

—CARLYLE

For thousands of years the riddle of the universe has been the question of causation. Did the egg come first, or the chicken? "The globe," says an Eastern proverb, "rests upon the howdah of an elephant. The elephant stands upon a tortoise, swimming in a sea of milk." But then what? And what is life? As the Persian poet puts it—

"What without asking, hither hurried whence,
And without asking whither hurried hence?"

It has been said that every man, consciously or unconsciously, is either a materialist or an idealist. Certainly throughout the ages the schools of philosophy as well as individuals have argued and quarrelled, but always human thought through one or the other of these channels "has rolled down the hill of speculation into the ocean of doubt."

The materialist, roughly speaking, declares that nothing exists but matter and the forces inherent therein.

The idealist declares that all is mind or energy, and that matter is necessarily unreal.

The time has come when people have become dissatisfied with these unceasing theories which get them nowhere. And today, as the appreciation of a Primal Cause becomes more clearly defined, the spiritual instinct asserts itself determinedly.

"Give me a base of support," said Archimedes, "and with a lever I will move the world."

And the base of support is that all started with *mind*. In the beginning was nothing—a fire mist. Before anything could come of it there had to be an idea, a model on which to build. *Universal Mind* supplied that idea, that model. Therefore the primal cause is mind. Everything must start with an idea. Every event, every condition, every thing is first an idea in the mind of someone.

Before you start to build a house, you draw up a plan of it. You make an exact blueprint of that plan, and your house takes shape in accordance with your blueprint. Every material object takes form in the same way. Mind draws the plan. Thought forms the blueprint, well drawn or badly done as your thoughts are clear or vague. It all goes back to the one cause. The creative principle of the universe is mind, and thought is the eternal energy.

But just as the effect you get from electricity depends upon the mechanism to which the power is attached, so the effects you get from mind depend upon the way you use it. We are all of us dynamos. The power is there—unlimited power. But we've got to connect it up to something—set it some task—give it work to do—else are we no better off than the animals.

The "Seven Wonders of the World" were built by men with few of the opportunities or facilities that are available to you. They conceived these gigantic projects first in their own minds, pictured them so vividly that their subconscious minds came to their aid and enabled them to overcome obstacles that most of us would regard as insurmountable. Imagine building the Pyramids of Gizeh, enormous stone upon enormous stone, with nothing but bare hands. Imagine the labor, the sweat, the heartbreaking toil of erecting the Colossus of Rhodes, between whose legs a ship could pass! Yet men built these wonders, in a day when tools were of the crudest and machinery was undreamed of, by using the unlimited power of Mind.

Mind is creative, but it must have a model on which to work. It must have thoughts to supply the power.

There are in Universal Mind ideas for millions of wonders greater far than the "Seven Wonders of the World." And those ideas are just as available to you as they were to the artisans of old, as they were to Michael Angelo when he built St. Peter's in Rome, as they were to the architect who conceived the Woolworth Building, or the engineer who planned the Hell Gate Bridge.

Every condition, every experience of life is the result of our mental attitude. We can *do* only what we think we can do. We can *be* only what we think we can be. We can *have* only what we think we can have. What we do, what we are, what we have, all depend upon what we think. We can never express anything that we do not first have in mind. The secret of all power, all success, all riches, is in first thinking powerful thoughts, successful thoughts, thoughts of wealth, of supply. We must build them in our own mind first.

William James, the famous psychologist, said that the greatest discovery in a hundred years was the discovery of the power of the sub-conscious mind. It is the greatest discovery of all time. It is the discovery that man has within himself the power to control his surroundings, that he is not at the mercy of chance or luck, that he is the arbiter of his own fortunes, that he can carve out his own destiny. He is the master of all the forces round about him. As James Allen puts it:

"Dream lofty dreams, and as you dream, so shall you become. Your vision is the promise of what you shall one day be; your Ideal is the prophecy of what you shall at last unveil."

For matter is in the ultimate but a product of thought. Even the most material scientists admit that matter is not what it appears to be. According to physics, matter (be it the human body or a log of wood—it makes no difference which) is made up of an aggregation of distinct minute particles called atoms. Considered individually, these atoms are so small that they can be seen only with the aid of a powerful microscope, if at all.

MATTER—DREAM OR REALITY?

Until recently these atoms were supposed to be the ultimate theory regarding matter. We ourselves—and all the material world around us—were supposed to consist of these infinitesimal particles of matter, so small that they could not be seen or weighed or smelled or touched individually—but still particles of matter *and indestructible.*

Now, however, these atoms have been further analyzed, and physics tells us that they are not indestructible at all—that they are mere positive and negative buttons of force or energy called protons and electrons, without hardness, without density, without solidity, without even positive actuality. In short, they are vortices in the ether—whirling bits of energy—dynamic, never static, pulsating with life, but the life is *spiritual!* As one eminent British scientist put it—"Science now explains matter by *explaining it away!*"

And that, mind you, is what the solid table in front of you is made of, is what your house, your body, the whole world is made of—*whirling bits of energy!*

To quote the New York *Herald-Tribune* of March 11, 1926: "We used to believe that the universe was composed of an unknown number of different kinds of matter, one kind for each chemical element. The discovery of a new element had all the interest of the unexpected. It might turn out to be anything, to have any imaginable set of properties.

"That romantic prospect no longer exists. We know now that instead of many ultimate kinds of matter there are only two kinds. Both of these are really kinds of electricity. One is negative electricity, being, in fact, the tiny particle called the electron, familiar to radio fans as one of the particles vast swarms of which operate radio vacuum tubes. The other kind of electricity is positive electricity. Its ultimate particles are called protons. From these protons and electrons all of the chemical elements are built up. Iron and lead and oxygen and gold and all the others differ from one another merely in the number and arrangement of the electrons and protons which they contain. That is the modern idea of the nature of matter. *Matter is really nothing but electricity.*"

Can you wonder then that scientists believe the time will come when mankind *through mind* can control all this energy, can be absolute master of the winds and the waves, can literally follow the Master's precept—"If ye have faith as a grain of mustard seed, ye shall say unto this mountain, Remove hence to yonder place; and it shall remove; and nothing shall be impossible unto you."

For Modern Science is coming more and more to the belief that what we call *matter is a force subject wholly to the control of mind.*

How tenuous matter really is, is perhaps best illustrated by the fact that a single violin string, tuned to the proper pitch, could start a vibration that would shake down the Brooklyn Bridge! Oceans and mountains, rocks and iron, all can be reduced to a point little short of the purely spiritual. Your body is 85 per cent water, 15 per cent ash and phosphorus! And they in turn can be dissipated into gas and vapor. Where do we go from there?

Is not the answer that, to a great degree at least, and perhaps altogether, this world round about us is one of our mind's own creating? And that we can put into it, and get from it, pretty much what we wish? You see this illustrated every day. A panorama is spread before you. To you it is a beautiful picture; to another it appears a mere collection of rocks and trees. A girl comes out to meet you. To you she is the embodiment of loveliness; to another all that grace and beauty may look drab and homely. A moonlit garden, with its fragrant odors and dew-drenched grass, may mean all that is charming to you, while to another it brings only thoughts of asthma or fever or rheumatism. A color may be green to you that to another is red. A prospect may be inviting for you that to another is rugged and hard.

To quote "Applied Psychology," by Warren Hilton:

"The same stimulus acting on different organs of sense will produce different sensations. A blow upon the eye will cause you to 'see stars'; a similar blow upon the ear will cause you to hear an explosive sound. In other words, the vibratory effect of a touch on eye or ear is the same as that of light or sound vibrations.

"The notion you may form of any object in the outer world depends solely upon what part of your brain happens to be connected with that particular nerve-end that receives an impression from the object.

"You see the sun without being able to hear it because the only nerve-ends tuned to vibrate in harmony with the ether-waves set in action by the sun are nerve-ends that are connected with the brain center devoted to sight. 'If,' says Professor James, 'we could splice the outer extremities of our optic nerves to our ears, and those of our auditory nerves to our eyes, we should hear the lightning and see the thunder, see the symphony and hear the conductor's movements.'

"In other words, the kind of impressions we receive from the world about us, the sort of mental pictures we form concerning it, in fact, the character of the outer world, the nature of the environment in which our lives are cast—all these things depend for each one of us simply upon how he happens to be put together, upon his individual mental make-up."

In short, it all comes back to the old fable of the three blind men and the elephant. To the one who caught hold of his leg, the elephant was like a tree. To the one who felt of his side, the elephant was like a wall. To the one who seized his tail, the elephant was like a rope. The world is to each one of us the world of *his individual perceptions.*

You are like a radio receiving station. Every moment thousands of impressions are reaching you. You can tune in on whatever ones you like—on joy or sorrow, on success or failure, on optimism or fear. You can select the particular impressions that will best serve you, you can hear only what you want to hear, you can shut out all disagreeable thoughts and sounds and experiences, or you can tune in on discouragement and failure and despair.

Yours is the choice. You have within you a force against which the whole world is powerless. By using it, you can make what you will of life and of your surroundings.

"But," you will say, "objects themselves do not change. It is merely the difference in the way you look at them." Perhaps. But to a great extent, at least, we find what we look for, just as, when turn the dial on the radio, we tune in on whatever kind of entertainment or instruction we may wish to hear. And who can say that it is not our thoughts that put us here? Who, for the matter of that, can prove that our surroundings in waking hours are not as much the creature of our minds as are our dreams? You've had dreams many a time where every object seemed just as real as when you were awake. You've felt of the objects, you've pinched yourself, yet still you were convinced that you were actually *living* those dreams. May not your waking existence be largely the creation of your own mind, just as your dream pictures are?

Many scientists believe that it is, and that in proportion as you try to put into your surroundings the good things you desire, rather than the evil ones you fear, *you will find those good things.* Certain it is that you can do this with your own body. Just as certain that many people are doing it with the good things of life. They have risen above the conception of life in which matter is the master.

Just as the most powerful forces in nature are the invisible ones—heat, light, air, electricity—so the most powerful forces of man are his invisible forces, his thought forces. And just as electricity can fuse stone and iron, so can your thought forces control your body, so can they make or mar your destiny.

THE PHILOSOPHER'S CHARM

There was once a shrewd necromancer who told a king that he had discovered a way to make gold out of sand. Naturally the king was interested and offered him great rewards for his secret. The necromancer explained his process. It seemed quite easy, except for one thing. Not once during the operation must the king think of the word Abracadabra. If he did, the charm was broken and the gold would not come. The king tried and tried to follow the directions, but he could not keep that word Abracadabra out of his mind. And he never made the gold.

Dr. Winbigler puts the same idea in another way: "Inspiration, genius, power, are often interfered with by the conscious mind's interposing, by man's failing to recognize his power, afraid to assist himself, lacking the faith in himself necessary to stimulate the subconscious so as to arouse the genius asleep in each."

From childhood on we are assured on every hand—by scientists, by philosophers, by our religious teachers—that "ours is the earth and the fullness thereof." Beginning with the first chapter of Genesis, we are told that "God said, Let us make man in our image, after our likeness; and let them have dominion over the fish of the sea, and over the fowl of the air, and over the cattle, and over all the earth—and over every living thing that moveth upon the earth." All through the Old and the New Testament, we are repeatedly adjured to use these God-given powers. "He that believeth on me," said Jesus, "the works that I do shall he do also; and greater works than these shall he do." "If ye abide in me, and my words abide in you, ye shall ask what ye will, and it shall be done unto you." "For verily I say unto you, that whosoever shall say unto this mountain, Be thou removed, and be thou cast into the sea; and shall not doubt in his heart, but shall believe that those things which he saith shall come to pass; he shall have whatsoever he saith." "The kingdom of God is within you."

We hear all this, perhaps we even think we believe, but always, when the time comes to use these God-given talents, there is the "doubt in our heart."

Baudouin expressed it clearly: "To be ambitious for wealth and yet always expecting to be poor; to be always doubting your ability to get what you long for, is like trying to reach east by travelling west. There is no philosophy which will help a man to succeed when he is always doubting his ability to do so, and thus attracting failure.

"You will go in the direction in which you face. . . .

"There is a saying that every time the sheep bleats, it loses a mouthful of hay. Every time you allow yourself to complain of your lot, to say, 'I am poor; I can never do what others do; I shall never be rich; I have not the ability that others have; I am a failure; luck is against me,' you are laying up so much trouble for yourself.

"No matter how hard you may work for success, if your thought is saturated with the fear of failure, it will kill your efforts, neutralize your endeavors, and make success impossible."

And that is responsible for all our failures. We are like the old lady who decided she wanted the hill behind her house removed. So she got down on her knees and prayed the good Lord to remove it. The next morning she got up and hurried to the window. The hill was still in its same old place. "I knew it!" she snapped. "I gave Him his chance. But I knew all the time there was nothing to this prayer business."

Neither is there, as it is ordinarily done. Prayer is not a mere asking of favors. Prayer is not a paean of praise. Rather prayer is a realization of the God-power within you—of your right of dominion over your own body, your environment, your business, your health, your prosperity. It is an understanding that you are "heir of God and co-heir with Christ." And that as such, no evil has power over you, whereas you have all power for good. And "good" means not merely holiness. Good means happiness—the happiness of everyday people. Good means everything that is good in this world of ours—comforts and pleasures and prosperity for ourselves, health and happiness for those dependent upon us. There are no limits to "Good" except those we put upon it ourselves.

What was it made Napoleon the greatest conqueror of his day? Primarily his magnificent faith in Napoleon. He had a sublime belief in his destiny, an absolute confidence that the obstacle was not made which Napoleon could not find a way through, or over, or around. It was only when he lost that confidence, when he hesitated and vacillated for weeks between retreat and advance, that winter caught him in Moscow and ended his dreams of world empire. Fate gave him every chance first. The winter snows were a full month late in coming. But Napoleon hesitated—and was lost. It was not the snows that defeated him. It was not the Russians. It was his loss of faith in himself.

THE KINGDOM OF HEAVEN

"The Kingdom of Heaven is within you." Heaven is not some far-away state—the reward of years of tribulation here. Heaven is right here—here and now! When Christ said that

Heaven was within us, He meant just what He said—that the power for happiness, for good, for everything we need of life, is within each one of us.

That most of us fail to realize this Heaven—that many are sickly and suffering, that more are ground down by poverty and worry—is no fault of His. He gave us the power to overcome these evils; He stands ready and waiting to help us use it. If we fail to find the way, the fault is ours. To enjoy the Heaven that is within us, to begin here and now to live the life eternal, takes only a fuller understanding of the Power-that-is-within-us.

Even now, with the limited knowledge at our command, we can control circumstances to the point of making the world without an expression of our own world within, where the real thoughts, the real power, resides. Through this world within you can find the solution of every problem, the cause for every effect. Discover it—and all power, all possession is within your control.

For the world without is but a reflection of that world within. Your thought *creates* the conditions your mind images. Keep before your mind's eye the image of all you want to be and you will see it reflected in the world without. Think abundance, feel abundance, BELIEVE abundance, and you will find that as you think and feel and believe, abundance will manifest itself in your daily life. But let fear and worry be your mental companions, thoughts of poverty and limitation dwell in your mind, and worry and fear, limitation and poverty will be your constant companions day and night.

Your mental concept is all that matters. Its relation to matter is that of idea and form. There has got to be an idea before it can take form. As Dr. Terry Walter says:

"The impressions that enter the subconscious form indelible pictures, which are never forgotten, and whose power can change the body, mind, manner, and morals; can, in fact, revolutionize a personality.

"All during our waking hours the conscious mind, through the five senses, acts as constant feeder to the subconscious; the senses are the temporal source of supply for the content of the soul mind; therefore it is most important that we know and realize definitely and explicitly that every time we think a thought or feel an emotion, we are adding to the content of this powerful mind, good or bad, as the case may be. Life will be richer or poorer for the thoughts and deeds of today."

Your thoughts supply you with limitless energy which will take whatever form your mind demands. The thoughts are the mold which crystalizes this energy into good or ill according to the form you impress upon it. You are free to choose which. But whichever you choose, the result is sure. Thoughts of wealth, of power, of success, can bring only results commensurate with your idea of them. Thoughts of poverty and lack can bring only limitation and trouble.

"A radical doctrine," you'll say, and think me wildly optimistic. Because the world has been taught for so long to think that some must be rich and some poor, that trials and tribulations are our lot. That this is at best a vale of tears.

The history of the race shows that what is considered to be the learning of one age is ignorance to the next age.

Dr. Edwin E. Slosson, Editor of *Science Service,* speaking of the popular tendency to fight against new ideas merely because they were *new,* said: "All through the history of science, we find that new ideas have to force their way into the common mind in disguise, as though they were burglars instead of benefactors of the race."

And Emerson wrote: "The virtue in most request is conformity. Self-reliance is its aversion. It loves not realities and creators, but names and customs."

In the ages to come man will look back upon the poverty and wretchedness of so many millions today, and think how foolish we were not to take advantage of the abundance all about us. Look at Nature; how profuse she is in everything. Do you suppose the Mind that imaged that profuseness ever intended you to be limited, to have to scrimp and save in order to eke out a bare existence?

There are hundreds of millions of stars in the heavens. Do you suppose the Mind which could bring into being worlds without number in such prodigality intended to stint you of the few things necessary to your happiness?

What is money but a mere idea of mind, a token of exchange? The paper money you have in your pockets is supposed to represent so much gold or silver currency. There are billions upon billions of this paper money in circulation, yet all the gold in the world amounts to only about $8,000,000,000. Wealth is in ideas, not in money or property. You can control those ideas through mind.

Reduced to the ultimate—to the atom or to the electron—everything in this world is an idea of mind. All of it has been brought together through mind. If we can change the things we want back into mental images, we can multiply them as often as we like, possess all that we like.

"TO HIM THAT HATH"—

Take as an example the science of numbers. Suppose all numbers were of metal—that it was against the law to write figures for ourselves. Every time you wanted to do a sum in arithmetic you'd have to provide yourself with a supply of numbers, arrange them in their proper order, work out your problems with them. If your problems were too abstruse you might run out of numbers, have to borrow some from your neighbor or from the bank.

"How ridiculous," you say. "Figures are not things; they are mere ideas, and we can add them or divide them or multiply them or subtract them as often as we like. Anybody can have all the figures he wants."

To be sure he can. And when you get to look upon money in the same way, you will have all the money you want.

"To him that hath shall be given, and from him that hath not shall be taken away even that which he hath." To him that hath the right idea everything shall be given, and from him who hath not that right idea shall be taken away everything he hath.

Thought externalizes itself. What we are depends entirely upon the images we hold before our mind's eye. Every time we think, we start a chain of causes which will create conditions similar to the thoughts which originated it. Every thought we hold in our consciousness for any length of time becomes impressed upon our subconscious mind and creates a pattern which the mind weaves into our life or environment.

All power is from within and is therefore under our own control. When you can direct your thought processes, you can consciously apply them to any condition, for all that comes to us from the world without is what we've already imaged in the world within.

Do you want more money? Sit you down now quietly and realize that money is merely an idea. That your mind is possessed of unlimited ideas. That being part of Universal Mind, there is no such thing as limitation or lack. That somewhere, somehow, the ideas that shall bring you all the money you need for any right purpose are available for you. That you have but to put it up to your subconscious mind to find these ideas.

Realize that—*believe* it—and your need will be met. "What things soever ye desire, when ye pray, believe that ye receive it and ye shall have it." Don't forget that *"believe that ye receive it."* This it is that images the thing you want on your subconscious mind. And this it is that brings it to you. Once you can image the belief clearly on your subconscious mind, "whatsoever it is that ye ask for . . . ye shall have it."

For the source of all good, of everything you wish for, is the Universal Mind, and you can reach it only through the subconscious.

And Universal Mind will be to you whatever you believe it to be—the kind and loving Father whom Jesus pictured, always looking out for the well-being of his children—or the dread Judge that so many dogmatists would have us think.

When a man realizes that his mind is part of Universal Mind, when he realizes that he has only to take any right aspiration to this Universal Mind to see it realized, he loses all sense of worry and fear. He learns to dominate instead of to cringe. He rises to meet every situation, secure in the knowledge that everything necessary to the solution of any problem is in Mind, and that he has but to take his problem to Universal Mind to have it correctly answered.

For if you take a drop of water from the ocean, you know that it has the same properties as all the rest of the water in the ocean, the same percentage of sodium chloride. The only difference between it and the ocean is in volume. If you take a spark of electricity, you know that it has the same properties as the thunderbolt, the same power that moves trains or runs giant machines in factories. Again the only difference is in volume. It is the same with your mind and Universal Mind. The only difference between them is in volume. Your mind has the same properties as the Universal Mind, the same creative genius, the same power over all the earth, the same access to all knowledge. Know this, believe it, use it, and "yours is the earth and the fulness thereof." In the exact proportion that you believe yourself to be part of Universal Mind, sharing in Its all-power, in that proportion can you demonstrate the mastery over your own body and over the world about you.

All growth, all supply is from the world-within. If you would have power, if you would have wealth, you have but to image it on this world within, on your subconscious mind, through belief and understanding.

If you would remove discord, you have but to remove the wrong images—images of ill health, of worry and trouble from within. The trouble with most of us is that we live entirely in the world without. We have no knowledge of that inner world which is responsible for all the conditions we meet and all the experiences we have. We have no conception of "the Father that is within us."

The inner world promises us life and health, prosperity and happiness—dominion over all the earth. It promises peace and perfection for all its offspring. It gives you the right way and the adequate way to accomplish any normal purpose. Business, labor, professions, exist primarily in thought. And the outcome of your labors in them is regulated by thought. Consider the difference, then, in this outcome if you have at your command only the limited capacity of your conscious mind, compared with the boundless energy of the subconscious and the Universal Mind. "Thought, not money, is the real business capital," says Harvey S. Firestone, "and if you know absolutely that what you are doing is right, then you are bound to accomplish it in due season."

Thought is a dynamic energy with the power to bring its object out from the invisible substance all about us. Matter is inert, unintelligent. Thought can shape and control. Every form in which matter is today is but the expression of some thought, some desire, some idea.

You have a mind. You can originate thought. And thoughts are creative. Therefore you can create for yourself that which you desire. Once you realize this you are taking a long step toward success in whatever undertaking you have in mind.

More than half the prophecies in the Scriptures refer to the time when man shall possess the earth, when tears and sorrow shall be unknown, and peace and plenty shall be everywhere. That time will come. It is nearer than most people think possible. You are helping it along. Every man who is honestly trying to use the power of mind in the right way is doing his part in the great cause. For it is only through Mind that peace and plenty can be gained. The earth is laden with treasures as yet undiscovered. But they are every one of them known to Universal Mind, for it was Universal Mind that first imaged them there. And as part of Universal Mind, they can be known to you.

How else did the Prophets of old foretell, thousands of years ago, the aeroplane, the cannon, the radio? What was the genius that enabled Ezekiel to argue from his potter's wheel, his water wheel and the stroke of the lightning to an airplane, with its wheels within wheels, driven by electricity and guided by man? How are we to explain the descriptions of artillery in the Apocalypse and the astonishing declaration in the Gospels that the utterances of the chamber would be broadcast from the housetops?

"TO THE MANNER BORN"

Few of us have any idea of our mental powers. The old idea was that man must take this world as he found it. He'd been born into a certain position in life, and to try to rise above his fellows was not only the height of bad taste but sacrilegious as well. An All-wise Providence had decreed by birth the position a child should occupy in the web of organized society. For him to be discontented with his lot, for him to attempt to raise himself to a higher level, was tantamount to tempting Providence. The gates of Hell yawned wide for such scatterbrains, who were lucky if in this life they incurred nothing worse than the ribald scorn of their associates.

That is the system that produced aristocracy and feudalism. That is the system that feudalism and aristocracy strove to perpetuate.

The new idea—the basis of all democracies—is that man is not bound by any system, that he need not accept the world as he finds it. He can remake the world to his own ideas. It is merely the raw material. He can make what he wills of it.

It is this new idea that is responsible for all our inventions, all our progress. Man is satisfied with nothing. He is constantly remaking his world. And now more than ever will this be true, for psychology teaches us that each one has within himself the power to become what he wills.

Learn to control your thought. Learn to image upon your mind only the things you want to see reflected there.

You will never improve yourself by dwelling upon the drawbacks of your neighbors. You will never attain perfect health and strength by thinking of weakness or disease. No man ever made a perfect score by watching his rival's target. You have got to think strength, think health, think riches. To paraphrase Pascal—"Our achievements today are but the sum of our thoughts of yesterday."

For thought is energy. Mental images are concentrated energy. And energy concentrated on any definite purpose becomes power. To those who perceive the nature and transcendency of this force, all physical power sinks into insignificance.

What is imagination but a form of thought? Yet it is the instrument by which all the inventors and discoverers have opened the way to new worlds. Those who grasp this force, be their state ever so humble, their natural gifts ever so insignificant, become our leading men. They are our governors and supreme law-givers, the guides of the drifting host which follows them as by an irrevocable decree. To quote Glenn Clark in *The Atlantic Monthly,* "Whatever we have of civilization is their work, theirs alone. If progress was made they made it. If spiritual facts were discerned, they discerned them. If justice and order were put in place of insolence and chaos, they wrought the change. Never is progress achieved by the masses. Creation ever remains the task of the individual."

Our railroads, our telephones, our automobiles, our libraries, our newspapers, our thousands of other conveniences, comforts and necessities are due to the creative genius of but two per cent of our population.

And the same two per cent own a great percentage of the wealth of the country.

The question arises, Who are they? What are they? The sons of the rich? College men? No—few of them had any early advantages. Many of them have never seen the inside of a college. It was grim necessity that drove them, and somehow, some way, they found a method of drawing upon their Genie-of-the-Mind, and through that inner force they have reached success.

You don't need to stumble and grope. You can call upon your inner forces at will. There are three steps necessary:

First, to realize that you have the power.

Second, to know what you want.

Third, to center your thought upon it with singleness of purpose.

To accomplish these steps takes only a fuller understanding of the Power-that-is-within-you.

But what is this power? Where should you go to locate it? Is it a thing, a place, an object? Has it bounds, form or material shape? No! Then how shall you go about finding it?

If you have begun to *realize* that there is a power within you, if you have begun to arouse in your conscious mind the ambition and desire to use this power—you have started in the pathway of Wisdom. If you are willing to go forward, to endure the mental discipline of mastering this method, nothing in the world can hinder you or keep you from overcoming every obstacle.

Begin at once, today, to use what you have learned. All growth comes from practice. All the forces of life are active—peace—joy—power. The unused talent decays. Open the door—

"Behold I stand at the door and knock; if ANY MAN hear my voice and open the door, I will come in to him, and will sup with him and he with me."

So let us make use of this dynamo, which is *you.* What is going to start it working? Your *Faith,* the faith that is begotten of understanding. Faith is the impulsion, the propulsion of this power within. Faith is the confidence, the assurance, the enforcing truth, the knowing that the right idea of life will bring you into the reality of existence and the manifestation of the all-power.

All cause is in Mind—and Mind is everywhere. All the knowledge there is, all the wisdom there is, all the power there is, is all about you—no matter where you may be. Your Mind is part of it. You have access to it. If you fail to avail yourself of it, you have no one to blame but yourself. For as the drop of water in the ocean shares in all the properties of the rest of the ocean water so you share in that all-power, all-wisdom of Mind. If you have been sick and ailing, if poverty and hardship have been your lot, don't blame it on "fate." Blame yourself. "Yours is the earth and everything that's in it." But you've got to *take* it. The power is there—but *you* must *use* it. It is round about you like the air you breathe. You don't expect others to do your breathing for you. Neither can you expect them to use your Mind for you. Universal Intelligence is not only the mind of the Creator of the universe but it is also the mind of MAN, *your* intelligence, *your* mind. "Let this mind be in you, which was also in Christ Jesus!"

So start today by KNOWING that you can do anything you wish to do, have anything you wish to have, be anything you wish to be. The rest will follow.

"Ye shall ask what ye will and it shall be done unto you."

CHAPTER 4

Desire—The First Law of Gain

"Ah, Love! Could Thou and I with Fate conspire
To grasp this sorry Scheme of Things entire,
Would we not shatter it to bits—and then
Re-mold it nearer to the Heart's Desire!"
—"THE RUBAIYAT OF OMAR KHAYYAM"

If you had a fairy wishing ring, what one thing would you wish for? Wealth? Honor? Fame? Love? What one thing do you desire above everything else in life?

Whatever it is, you can have it. Whatever you desire wholeheartedly, with singleness of purpose—you can have. But the first and all-important essential is to know what this one thing is. Before you can win your heart's desire, you've got to get clearly fixed in your mind's eye what it is that you want.

It may sound paradoxical, but few people do know what they want. Most of them struggle along in a vague sort of way, hoping—like Micawber—for something to turn up. They are so taken up with the struggle that they have forgotten—if they ever knew—what it is they are struggling for. They are like a drowning man—they use up many times the energy it would take to get them somewhere, but they fritter it away in aimless struggles—without thought, without direction, exhausting themselves, while getting nowhere.

You've got to know what you want before you stand much chance of getting it. You have an unfailing "Messenger to Garcia" in that Genie-of-your-Mind—but YOU have got to formulate the message. Aladdin would have stood a poor chance of getting anything from his Genie if he had not had clearly in mind the things he wanted the Genie to get.

In the realm of mind, the realm in which is all practical power, you can possess what you want at once. You have but to claim it, to visualize it, to bring it into actuality—and it is yours for the taking. For the Genie-of-your-Mind can give you power over circumstances. Health, happiness and prosperity. And all you need to put it to work is an earnest, intense desire.

Sounds too good to be true? Well, let us go back for a moment to the start. You are infected with that "divine dissatisfaction with things as they are" which has been responsible for all the great accomplishments of this world—else you would not have gotten thus far in this book. Your heart is hungering for something better. "Blessed are they which do hunger and thirst after righteousness (right-wiseness) for they shall be filled." You are tired of the worry and grind, tired of the deadly dull routine and daily tasks that lead nowhere. Tired of all the petty little ills and ailments that have come to seem the lot of man here on earth.

Always there is something within you urging you on to bigger things, giving you no peace, no rest, no chance to be lazy. It is the same "something" that drove Columbus across the ocean; that drove Hannibal across the Alps; that drove Edison onward and upward from a train boy to the inventive wizard of the century; that drove Henry Ford from a poor mechanic at forty to probably the richest man in the world at sixty.

This "something" within you keeps telling you that you can do anything you want to do, be anything you want to be, have anything you want to have—and you have a sneaking suspicion that it may be right.

That "something" within you is your subconscious self, your part of Universal Mind, your Genie-of-the-brain. Men call it ambition, and "Lucky is the man," says Arthur Brisbane, "whom the Demon of Ambition harnesses and drives through life. This wonderful little coachman is the champion driver of all the world and of all history.

"Lucky you, if he is *your* driver.

"He will keep you going until you do something worth while—working, running and moving ahead.

"And that is how a real man ought to be driven.

"This is the little Demon that works in men's brains, that makes the blood tingle at the thought of achievement and that makes the face flush and grow white at the thought of failure.

"Every one of us has this Demon for a driver, IN YOUTH AT LEAST.

"Unfortunately the majority of us he gives up as very poor, hopeless things, not worth driving, by the time we reach twenty-five or thirty.

"How many men look back to their teens, when they were harnessed to the wagon of life with Ambition for a driver? When they could not wait for the years to pass and for opportunity to come?

"It is the duty of ambition to drive, and it is your duty to *keep Ambition alive and driving.*

"If you are doing nothing, if there is no driving, no hurrying, no working, *you may count upon it that there will be no results. Nothing much worth while in the years to come.*

"Those that are destined to be the big men twenty years from now, when the majority of us will be nobodies, *are those whom this demon is driving relentlessly, remorselessly, through the hot weather and the cold weather, through early hours and late hours.*

"Lucky YOU if you are in harness and driven by the Demon of Ambition."

Suppose you *have* had disappointments, disillusionments along the way. Suppose the fine point of your ambition has become blunted. Remember, there is no obstacle that there is not some way around, or over, or through—and if you will depend less upon the 10 per cent of your abilities that reside in your conscious mind, and leave more to the 90 per cent that constitute your subconscious, you can overcome all obstacles. Remember this—there is no condition so hopeless, no life so far gone, that mind cannot redeem it.

Every untoward condition is merely *a lack* of something. Darkness, you know, is not real. It is merely a lack of light. Turn on the light and the darkness will be seen to be nothing. It vanishes instantly. In the same way poverty is simply a lack of necessary supply. Find the avenue of supply and your poverty vanishes. Sickness is merely the absence of health. If you are in perfect health, sickness cannot hurt you. Doctors and nurses go about at will among the sick without fear—and suffer as a rule far less from sickness than does the average man or woman.

So there is nothing you have to *overcome. You* merely have to *acquire* something. And always Mind can show you the way. You can obtain from Mind anything you want, if you will learn how to do it. "I think we can rest assured that one can do and be practically what he desires to be," says Farnsworth in "Practical Psychology." And psychologists all over the world have put the same thought in a thousand different ways.

"It is not will, but desire," says Charles W. Mears, "that rules the world." "But," you will say, "I have had plenty of desires all my life. I've always wanted to be rich. How do you account for the difference between my wealth and position and power and that of the rich men all around me?"

THE MAGIC SECRET

The answer is simply that you have never focused your desires into one great dominating desire. You have a host of mild desires. You mildly wish you were rich, you wish you had a position of responsibility and influence, you wish you could travel at will. The wishes are so many and varied that they conflict with each other and you get nowhere in particular. You lack one *intense* desire, to the accomplishment of which you are willing to subordinate everything else.

Do you know how Napoleon so frequently won battles in the face of a numerically superior foe? By concentrating his men at the actual *point of contact!* His artillery was often greatly outnumbered, but it accomplished far more than the enemy's because instead of scattering his fire, he *concentrated it all on the point of attack!*

The time you put in aimlessly dreaming and wishing would accomplish marvels if it were concentrated on one definite object. If you have ever taken a magnifying glass and let the sun's rays play through it on some object, you know that as long as the rays were scattered they accomplished nothing. But focus them on one tiny spot and see how quickly they start something.

It is the same way with your mind. You've got to concentrate *on one idea at a time.*

"But how can I learn to concentrate?" many people write me. Concentration is not a thing to be learned. It is merely a thing to do. You concentrate whenever you become sufficiently interested in anything. Get so interested in a ball game that you jump up and down on your hat, slap a man you have never seen before on the back, embrace your nearest neighbor—*that* is concentration. Become so absorbed in a thrilling play or movie that you no longer realize the orchestra is playing or there are people around you—*that* is concentration.

And that is all concentration ever is—getting so interested in some one thing that you pay no attention to anything else that is going on around you.

If you want a thing badly enough, you need have no worry about your ability to concentrate on it. Your thoughts will just naturally center on it like bees on honey.

Hold in your mind the thing you most desire. Affirm it. Believe it to be an existing fact. Let me quote again the words of the Master, because there's nothing more important to remember in this whole book. "Therefore I say unto you, what things soever ye desire, when ye pray, *believe that ye receive them* and ye shall have them."

And again I say, the most important part is the *"believe that ye receive them."* Your subconscious mind is exceedingly amenable to suggestion. If you can truly believe that you have received something, can impress that belief upon your subconscious mind, depend upon it, it will see that you have it. For being a part of Universal Mind, it shares that Universal Mind's all-power. "The Father that is within me, He doeth the works." Your mind will respond to your desire in the exact proportion in which you believe. "As thy faith is, so be it unto thee."

The people who live in beautiful homes, who have plenty to spend, who travel about in yachts and fine cars, are for the most part people who started out to accomplish *some one definite thing.* They had one clear goal in mind, and everything they did centered on that goal.

Most men just jog along in a rut, going through the same old routine day after day, eking out a bare livelihood, with no definite desire other than the vague hope that fortune will some day drop in their lap. Fortune doesn't often play such pranks. And a rut, you know, differs from a grave only in depth. A life such as that is no better than the animals live. Work all day for money to buy bread, to give you strength to work all the next day to buy more bread. There is nothing to it but the daily search for food and sustenance. No time for aught but worry and struggle. No hope of anything but the surcease of sorrow in death.

You can have anything you want—if you want it badly enough. You can be anything you want to be, have anything you desire, accomplish anything you set out to accomplish—if you will hold to that desire with singleness of purpose; if you will understand and BELIEVE in your own powers to accomplish.

What is it that you wish in life? Is it health? In the chapter on health I will show you that you can be radiantly well—without drugs, without tedious exercises. It matters not if you are crippled or bedridden or infirm. Your body rebuilds itself entirely every eleven months. You can start now rebuilding along perfect lines.

Is it wealth you wish? In the chapter on success I will show you how you can increase your income, how you can forge rapidly ahead in your chosen business or profession.

Is it happiness you ask for? Follow the rules herein laid down and you will change your whole outlook on life. Doubts and uncertainty will vanish, to be followed by calm assurance and abiding peace. You will possess the things your heart desires. You will have love and companionship. You will win to contentment and happiness.

But desire must be impressed upon the subconscious before it can be accomplished.

Merely conscious desire seldom gets you anything. It is like the day-dreams that pass through your mind. Your desire must be visualized, must be persisted in, must be concentrated upon, must be impressed upon your subconscious mind. Don't bother about the means for accomplishing your desire—you can safely leave that to your subconscious mind. It knows how to do a great many things besides building and repairing your body. If you can visualize the thing you want, if you can impress upon your subconscious mind the *belief that you have it,* you can safely leave to it the finding of the means of getting it. Trust the Universal Mind to show the way. The mind that provided everything in such profusion must joy in seeing us take advantage of that profusion. "For herein is the Father glorified—that ye bear much fruit."

You do not have to wait until tomorrow, or next year, or the next world, for happiness. You do not have to die to be saved. "The Kingdom of Heaven is within you." That does not mean that it is up in the heavens or on some star or in the next world. It means *here* and *now!* All the possibilities of happiness are always here and always available. At the open door of every man's life there lies this pearl of great price—the understanding of man's dominion over the earth. With that understanding and conviction you can do everything which lies before you to do and you can do it to the satisfaction of everyone and the well-being of yourself. God and good are synonymous. And God—good—is absent only to those who believe He is absent.

Find your desire, impress it upon your thought, and you have opened the door for opportunity. And remember, in this new heaven and new earth which I am trying to show you, *the door of opportunity is never closed.* As a matter of fact, you constantly have *all that you will take.* So keep yourself in a state of receptivity. It is your business to receive abundantly and perpetually. The law of opportunity enforces its continuance and availability. "Every good gift and every perfect gift is from above and cometh down from the Father of light, with whom is *no variableness, neither shadow of turning.*"

Infinite Mind saith to every man, "Come ye to the open fountain." The understanding of the law of life will remedy every discord, giving "Beauty for ashes, the oil of joy for mourning, the garment of praise for the spirit of heaviness."

Believe that you share in that goodness and bounty. Act the part you wish to play in this life. Act healthy, act prosperous, act happy. Make such a showing with what you have that you will carry the conviction to your subconscious mind that all good and perfect gifts ARE yours. Register health, prosperity and happiness on your inner mind and some fine morning soon you will wake to find that *you are* healthy, prosperous and happy, that you *have* your dearest wish in life.

"THE SOUL'S SINCERE DESIRE"

Do you know what prayer is? Just an earnest desire that we take to God—to Universal Mind—for fulfillment. As Montgomery puts it—"Prayer is the soul's *sincere desire,* uttered or unexpressed." It is our Heart's Desire. At least, the only prayer that is worth anything is the prayer that asks for our real desires. That kind of prayer is heard. That kind of prayer is answered.

Mere lip prayers get you nowhere. It doesn't matter what your lips may say. The thing that counts is what your heart desires, what your mind images on your subconscious thought, and through it on Universal Mind. "Thou, when thou prayest, be not as the hypocrites are; for they love to pray standing in the synagogue and at the corners of the streets, that they may be seen of men. Verily I say unto you, they have their reward."

What was it these hypocrites that Jesus speaks of really wanted? "To be seen of men." And their prayers were answered. Their sincere desire was granted. They were seen of men. "They have their reward." But as for what their lips were saying, neither God nor they paid any attention to it.

"Thou, when thou prayest enter into thy closet, and when thou hast shut the door, pray to thy Father which is in secret, and thy Father which seeth in secret, shall reward thee openly." Go where you can be alone, where you can concentrate your thoughts on your one innermost sincere desire, where you can impress that desire upon your subconscious mind without distraction, and so reach the Universal Mind (the Father of all things).

But even sincere desire is not enough by itself. There must be BELIEF, too. "What things soever ye desire, when ye pray, believe that ye receive them and ye shall have them." You must realize God's ability to give you every good thing. You must believe in his readiness to do it. Model your thoughts after the Psalmists of old. They first asked for that which they wanted, then killed all doubts and fears by affirming God's power and His willingness to grant their prayers. Read any of the Psalms and you will see what I mean. So when you pray, ask for the things that you want. Then affirm God's readiness and His Power to grant your prayer.

Glenn Clark, in "The Soul's Sincere Desire," gives some wonderfully helpful suggestions along these lines. To quote him:

"For money troubles, realize: There is no want in Heaven, and affirm:

> "Our Heavenly Father, we know that thy Love is as infinite as the sky is infinite, and Thy Ways of manifesting that love are as unaccountable as the stars of the heavens.
>
> "Thy Power is greater than man's horizon, and Thy Ways of manifesting that Power are more numerous than the sands of the sea.
>
> "As Thou keepest the stars in their courses, so shalt Thou guide our steps in perfect harmony, without clash or discord of any kind, if we keep our trust in Thee. For we know Thou wilt keep him in perfect peace whose mind is stayed on Thee, because he trusteth in Thee. We know that, if we acknowledge Thee in all our ways, Thou wilt direct our paths. For Thou art the God of Love, Giver of every good and perfect gift, and there is none beside Thee. Thou art omnipotent, omniscient, and omnipresent, in all, through all, and over all, the only God. And Thine is the Kingdom, and the Power, and the Glory, forever, Amen.

"For aid in thinking or writing, realize: There is no lack of ideas, and affirm:

> "Thy wisdom is greater than all hidden treasures, and yet as instantly available for our needs as the very ground beneath our feet.

"For happiness: There is no unhappiness in Heaven, so affirm:

"Thy joy is brighter than the sun at noonday and Thy Ways of expressing that Joy as countless as the sunbeams that shine upon our path."

This is the kind of prayer the Psalmists of old had recourse to in their hours of trouble—this is the kind of prayer that will bring you every good and perfect gift.

Make no mistake about this—*prayer is effective.* It *can* do anything. It doesn't matter how trivial your desires may be—if it is RIGHT for you to have them, it is RIGHT for you to pray for them.

According to a United Press dispatch of May 3, 1926:

"Prayer belongs to the football field as much as to the pulpit, and a praying team stands a good chance of 'getting there,' Tim Lowry, Northwestern University football star, told a large church audience here.

"'Just before the Indiana–Northwestern game last year,' Tim said, 'we worried a great deal about the outcome. Then we saw that bunch of big husky Indiana players coming toward us and we knew something had to be done quick.

"'Fellows,' I said, 'I believe in prayer and we better pray.' We did and won a great victory.

"When the next game came, every fellow prayed again.

"You don't need to think that churches have a copyright on prayer."

In "Prayer as a Force," A. Maude Royden compares the man who trusts his desires to prayer with the swimmer who trusts himself to the water:

"Let me give you a very simple figure which I think may perhaps convey my meaning. If you are trying to swim you must believe that the sea is going to keep you afloat. You must give yourself to the sea. There is the ocean and there are you in it, and I say to you, 'According to your faith you will be able to swim!' I know perfectly well that it is literally according to your faith. A person who has just enough confidence in the sea and in himself to give one little hop from the ground will certainly find that the water will lift him but not very much; he will come down again. Persons who have enough confidence really to start swimming but no more, will not swim very far, because their confidence is so very small and they swim with such rapid strokes, and they hold their breath to such an extent, that by and by they collapse; they swim five or six, or twelve or fourteen strokes, but they do not get very far, through lack of confidence.

"Persons who know with assurance that the sea will carry them if they do certain things, will swim quite calmly, serenely, happily, and will not mind if the water goes right over them. 'Oh,' you say, 'that person is doing the whole thing!' *He can't do it without the sea!* You might hypnotize people into faith; you might say, 'You are now in the ocean; swim off the edge of this precipice' (which is really a cliff). You might make them do it, they might have implicit faith in you, you might hypnotize them into thinking they were swimming; but if they swam off the edge of the cliff they would fall. You can't swim without the sea! I might say to you, 'It lies with you whether you swim or not, according to your faith be it unto you'; but if the sea is not there you can't swim. That is exactly what I feel about God. 'According to your faith be it unto you.' Yes, certainly, if you try to swim in that ocean which is the love of God your faith will be rewarded, and according to your faith it will be to you. In exact proportion to your faith you will find the answer, like a scientific law. There is not one atom of faith you put in God that will not receive its answer."

But remember: you would not plant a valuable seed in your garden, and then, a day or a week later, go out and dig it up to see if it were sprouting. On the contrary, you would nourish it each morning with water. It is the same with your prayers. Don't plant the seed of your desire in your subconscious mind and then go out the next morning and tear it up with doubts and fears. Nourish it by holding in thought the thing you desire, by believing in it, visualizing it, SEEING it as an accomplished fact.

If you ask for my own formula for successful prayer, I would say—

1st. Center your thoughts on the thing that you want. Visualize it. Make a mental image of it. You are planting the seed of Desire. But don't be content with that. Planting alone will not make a seed of corn grow. It has to be warmed by sunshine, nurtured by rain. So with the seed of your Desire. It must be warmed by Faith, nurtured by constant Belief. So—

2nd. Read the 91st and the 23rd Psalms, just as a reminder of God's power and His readiness to help you in all your needs.

3rd. Don't forget to be thankful, not merely for past favors, *but for the granting of this favor you are now asking!*

To be able to thank God for it sincerely, in advance of its actual material manifestation, is the finest evidence of belief.

4th. BELIEVE! Picture the thing that you want so clearly, see it in your imagination so vividly, that for the moment, at least, you will actually BELIEVE THAT YOU HAVE IT!

It is this sincere conviction, registered upon your subconscious mind, and through it upon Universal Mind, that brings the answer to your prayers. Once convince your subconscious mind that you HAVE the thing you want, and you can forget it and go on to your next problem. Mind will attend to the bringing of it into being.

CHAPTER 5

Aladdin & Company

"But the feeble hands and helpless,
Groping blindly in the darkness,
Touch God's right hand in that darkness,
And are lifted up and strengthened."
—LONGFELLOW

It is not always the man who struggles hardest who gets on in the world. It is the direction as well as the energy of struggle that counts in making progress. To get ahead—you must swim with the tide. Men prosper and succeed who work in accord with natural forces. A given amount of effort with these forces carries a man faster and farther than much more effort used against the current. Those who work blindly, regardless of these forces, make life difficult for themselves and rarely prosper.

It has been estimated by wise observers that on the average something like 90 per cent of the factors producing success or failure lie outside a man's conscious efforts—separate from his daily round of details. To the extent that he cooperates with the wisdom and power of Universal Mind he is successful, well and happy. To the extent that he fails to cooperate, he is unsuccessful, sick and miserable.

All down the ages some have been enabled to "taste and see that the Lord is good." Prophets and Seers being blessed with the loving kindness of God have proclaimed a God of universal goodness, saying: "The earth is full of the goodness of the Lord"; "Thou wilt show me the path of life; in Thy presence is fullness of joy."

Now we know that this Infinite Good is not more available to one than it is to all. We know that the only limit to it is in our capacity to receive. If you had a problem in mathematics to work out, you would hardly gather together the necessary figures and leave them to arrange themselves in their proper sequence. You would know that while the method for solving every problem has been figured out, *you* have got to *work* it. The principles are there, but *you* have got to *apply* them.

The first essential is to understand the principle—to learn how it works—how to use it. The second—and even more important—part is to APPLY that understanding to the problem in hand.

In the same way, the Principle of Infinite Energy, Infinite Supply, is ever available. But that Energy, that Supply, is static. You've got to make it dynamic. You've got to understand the law. You've got to *apply* your understanding in order to solve your problems of poverty, discord, disease.

Science shows that it is possible to accomplish any good thing. But distrust of your ability to reach the goal desired often holds you back and failure is the inevitable result.

Only by understanding that there is but one power—and that this power is Mind, not circumstances or environment—is it possible to bring your real abilities to the surface and put them to work.

Few deny that intelligence governs the universe. It matters not whether you call this intelligence Universal Mind or Providence or God or merely Nature. All admit Its directing power. All admit that It is a force for good, for progress. But few realize that our own minds are a part of this Universal Mind in just the same way that the rays of the sun are part of the sun.

If we will work in harmony with It, we can draw upon Universal Mind for all power, all intelligence, in the same way that the sun's rays draw upon their source for the heat and light they bring the earth.

It is not enough to *know* that you have this power. You must put it into *practice*—not once, or twice, but *every hour and every day.* Don't be discouraged if at first it doesn't always work. When you first studied arithmetic, your problems did not always work out correctly, did they? Yet you did not on that account doubt the principle of mathematics. You knew that the fault was with your methods, not with the principle. It is the same in this. The power is there. Correctly used, it can do anything.

All will agree that the Mind which first brought the Life Principle to this earth—which imaged the earth itself and the trees and the plants and the animals—is all-powerful. All will agree that to solve any problem, to meet any need, Mind has but to *realize* the need and it will be met. What most of us do not understand or realize is that we ourselves, being part of Universal Mind, have this same power. Just as the drop of water from the ocean has all the properties of the great bulk of the water in the ocean. Just as the spark of electricity has all the properties of the thunderbolt. And having that power, we have only to realize it and use it to get from life any good we may desire.

In the beginning all was void—space—nothingness. How did Universal Mind construct the planets, the firmaments, the earth and all things on and in it from this formless void? *By first making a mental image on which to build.*

That is what you, too, must do. You control your destiny, your fortune, your happiness to the exact extent to which you can think them out, VIZUALIZE them, SEE them, and allow no vagrant thought of fear or worry to mar their completion and beauty. The quality of your thought is the measure of your power. Clear, forceful thought has the power of attracting to itself everything it may need for the fruition of those thoughts. As W. D. Wattles puts it in his "Science of Getting Rich":

"There is a thinking stuff from which all things are made and which, in its original state, permeates, penetrates, and fills the interspaces of the universe. A thought in this substance produces the thing that is imagined by the thought. Man can form things in his thought, and, by impressing his thought upon formless substance, can cause the thing he thinks about to be created."

The connecting link between your conscious mind and the Universal is thought, and every thought that is in harmony with progress and good, every thought that is freighted with the right idea, can penetrate to Universal Mind. And penetrating to it, it comes back with the power of Universal Mind to accomplish it. You don't need to originate the ways and means. The Universal Mind knows how to bring about any necessary results. There is but one right way to solve any given problem. When your human judgment is unable to decide what that one right way is, turn to Universal Mind for guidance. You need never fear the outcome, for if you heed its advice you cannot go wrong.

Always remember—your mind is but a conductor—good or poor as you make it—for the power of Universal Mind. And thought is the connecting energy. Use that conductor, and you will improve its conductivity. Demand much, and you will receive the more. The Universal is not a niggard in any of its gifts. "Ask and ye shall receive, seek and ye shall find, knock and it shall be opened unto you."

That is the law of life. And the destiny of man lies not in poverty and hardship, but in living up to his high estate in unity with Universal Mind, with the power that governs the universe.

To look upon poverty and sickness as sent by God and therefore inevitable is the way of the weakling. God never sent us anything but good. What is more, He has never yet failed to give to those who would use them the means to overcome any condition not of His making. Sickness and poverty are not of His making. They are not evidences of virtue, *but of weakness.* God gave us everything in abundance, and he expects us to manifest that abundance. If you had a son you loved very much, and you surrounded him with good things which he had only to exert himself in order to reach, you wouldn't like it if he showed himself to the world half-starved, ill-kempt and clothed in rags, merely because he was unwilling to exert himself enough to reach for the good things you had provided. No more, in my humble opinion, does God.

Man's principal business in life, as I see it, is to establish a contact with Universal Mind. It is to acquire an understanding of this power that is in him. "With all thy getting, get understanding," said Solomon.

> "*Happy is the man that findeth wisdom,*
> *And the man that getteth understanding.*
> *For the gaining of it is better than the gaining of silver.*
> *And the profit thereof than fine gold.*
> *She is more precious than rubies:*
> *And none of the things thou canst desire are to be compared unto her.*
> *Length of days is in her right hand:*
> *In her left hand are riches and honor.*
> *Her ways are ways of pleasantness,*

And all her paths are peace.
She is a tree of life to them that lay hold upon her.
And happy is every one that retaineth her."
—Proverbs

When you become conscious, even to a limited degree, of your one-ness with Universal Mind, your ability to call upon It at will for anything you may need, it makes a different man of you. Gone are the fears, gone are the worries. You know that your success, your health, your happiness will be measured only by the degree to which you can impress the fruition of your desires upon mind.

The toil and worry, the wearisome grind and the back-breaking work will go in the future as in the past to those who will not use their minds. The less they use them, the more they will sweat. And the more they work only from the neck down, the less they will be paid and the more hopeless their lot will become. *It is Mind that rules the world.*

But to use your mind to the best advantage doesn't mean to toil along with the mere conscious part of it. It means hitching up your conscious mind with the Man Inside You, with the little "Mental Brownies," as Robert Louis Stevenson called them, and then working together for a definite end.

"My Brownies! God bless them!" said Stevenson. "Who do one-half of my work for me when I am fast asleep, and in all human likelihood do the rest for me as well when I am wide awake and foolishly suppose that I do it myself. I had long been wanting to write a book on man's double being. For two days I went about racking my brains for a plot of any sort, and on the second night I dreamt the scene in 'Dr. Jekyll and Mr. Hyde' at the window; and a scene, afterward split in two, in which Hyde, pursued, took the powder and underwent the change in the presence of his pursuer."

Many another famous writer has spoken in similar strain, and every man who has problems to solve has had like experiences. You know how, after you have studied a problem from all angles, it sometimes seems worse jumbled than when you started on it. Leave it then for a while—forget it—and when you go back to it, you find your thoughts clarified, the line of reasoning worked out, your problem solved for you. It is your little "Mental Brownies" who have done the work for you!

The flash of genius does not originate in your own brain. Through intense concentration you've established a circuit through your subconscious mind with the Universal, and it is from It that the inspiration comes. All genius, all progress, is from the same source. It lies with you merely to learn how to establish this circuit at will so that you can call upon It at need. It can be done.

"In the Inner Consciousness of each of us," quotes Dumont in "The Master Mind," "there are forces which act much the same as would countless tiny mental brownies or helpers who are anxious and willing to assist us in our mental work, if we will but have confidence and trust in them. This is a psychological truth expressed in the terms of the old fairy tales. The process of calling into service these Inner Consciousness helpers is similar to that which we constantly employ to recall some forgotten fact or name. We find that we cannot recollect some desired fact, date, or name, and instead of racking our brains with an increased effort, we (if we have learned the secret) pass on the matter to the Inner

Consciousness with a silent command, 'Recollect this name for me,' and then go on with our ordinary work. After a few minutes—or it may be hours—all of a sudden, pop! will come the missing name or fact before us—flashed from the planes of the Inner Consciousness, by the help of the kindly workers or 'brownies' of those planes. The experience is so common that we have ceased to wonder at it, and yet it is a wonderful manifestation of the Inner Consciousness' workings of the mind. Stop and think a moment, and you will see that the missing word does not present itself accidentally, or 'just because.' There are mental processes at work for your benefit, and when they have worked out the problem for you they gleefully push it up from their plane on to the plane of the outer consciousness where you may use it.

"We know of no better way of illustrating the matter than by this fanciful figure of the 'mental brownies,' in connection with the illustration of the 'subconscious storehouse.' If you would learn to take advantage of the work of these Subconscious Brownies, we advise you to form a mental picture of the Subconscious Storehouse in which is stored all sorts of knowledge that you have placed there during your lifetime, as well as the impressions that you have acquired by race inheritance—racial memory, in fact. The information stored away has often been placed in the storage rooms without any regard for systematic storing, or arrangement, and when you wish to find something that has been stored away there a long time ago, the exact place being forgotten, you are compelled to call to your assistance the little brownies of the mind, which perform faithfully your mental command, 'Recollect this for me!' These brownies are the same little chaps that you charge with the task of waking you at four o'clock tomorrow morning when you wish to catch an early train—and they obey you well in this work of the mental alarm-clock. These same little chaps will also flash into your consciousness the report, 'I have an engagement at two o'clock with Jones'—when looking at your watch you will see that it is just a quarter before the hour of two, the time of your engagement.

"Well then, if you will examine carefully into a subject which you wish to master, and will pass along the results of your observations to these Subconscious Brownies, you will find that they will work the raw materials of thought into shape for you in a comparatively short time. They will analyze, systematize, collate, and arrange in consecutive order the various details of information which you have passed on to them, and will add thereto the articles of similar information that they will find stored away in the recesses of your memory. In this way they will group together various scattered bits of knowledge that you have forgotten. And, right here, let us say to you that you never absolutely forget anything that you have placed in your mind. You may be unable to recollect certain things, but they are not lost—sometime later some associative connection will be made with some other fact, and lo! the missing idea will be found fitted nicely into its place in the larger idea—the work of our little brownies. Remember Thompson's statement: 'In view of having to wait for the results of these unconscious processes, I have proved the habit of getting together material in advance, and then leaving the mass to digest itself until I am ready to write about it.' This subconscious 'digestion' is really the work of our little mental brownies.

"There are many ways of setting the brownies to work. Nearly everyone has had some experience, more or less, in the matter, although often it is produced almost unconsciously, and without purpose and intent. Perhaps the best way for the average person—or rather the majority of persons—to get the desired results is for one to get as clear an idea of what one really wants to know—as clear an idea or mental image of the question you wish answered. Then after rolling it around in your mind—mentally chewing it, as it were—giving it a high degree of voluntary attention, you can pass it on to your Subconscious Mentality with the mental command: '*Attend to this for me—work out the answer!*' or some similar order. This command may be given silently, or else spoken aloud—either will do. Speak to the Subconscious. Mentality—or its little workers—just as you would speak to persons in your employ, kindly but firmly. Talk to the little workers, and firmly command them to do your work. And then forget all about the matter—throw it off your conscious mind, and attend to your other tasks. Then in due time will come your answer—flashed into your consciousness—perhaps not until the very minute that you must decide upon the matter, or need the information. You may give your brownies orders to report at such and such a time—just as you do when you tell them to awaken you at a certain time in the morning so as to catch the early train, or just as they remind you of the hour of your appointment, if you have them all well trained."

Have you ever read the story by Richard Harding Davis of "The Man Who Could Not Lose"? In it the hero is intensely interested in racing. He has studied records and "dope" sheets until he knows the history of every horse backward and forward.

The day before the big race he is reclining in an easy chair, thinking of the morrow's race, and he drops off to sleep with that thought on his mind. Naturally, his subconscious mind takes it up, with the result that he dreams the exact outcome of the race.

That was mere fiction, of course, but if races were run solely on the speed and stamina of the horses, it would be entirely possible to work out the results in just that way. Unfortunately, other factors frequently enter into every betting game.

But the idea behind Davis' story is entirely right. The way to contact with your subconscious mind, the way to get the help of the "Man Inside You" in working out any problem is:

First, fill your mind with every bit of information regarding that problem that you can lay your hands on.

Second, pick out a chair or lounge or bed where you can recline in perfect comfort, where you can forget your body entirely.

Third, let your mind dwell upon the problem for a moment, not worrying, not fretting, but placidly, and then turn it over to the "Man Inside You." Say to him—"This is your problem. You can do anything. You know the answer to everything. Work this out for me!" And utterly relax. Drop off to sleep, if you can. At least, drop into one of those half-sleepy, half-wakeful reveries that keep other thoughts from obtruding upon your consciousness. Do as Aladdin did—summon your Genie, give him your orders, then forget the matter, secure in the knowledge that he will attend to it for you. When you waken, *you will have the answer!*

For whatever thought, whatever problem you can get across to your subconscious mind at the moment of dropping off to sleep, that "Man Inside You," that Genie-of-your-Mind will work out for you.

Of course, not everyone can succeed in getting the right thought across to the subconscious at the first or the second attempt. It requires understanding and faith, just as the working out of problems in mathematics requires an understanding of and faith in the principles of mathematics. But keep on trying, and you WILL do it. And when you do, *the results are sure.*

If it is something that you want, VISUALIZE it first in your mind's eye, see it in every possible detail, see yourself going through every move it will be necessary for you to go through when your wish comes into being. Build up a complete story, step by step, just as though you were acting it all out. Get from it every ounce of pleasure and satisfaction that you can. Be *thankful* for this gift that has come to you. Then relax; go on to sleep if you can; give the "Man Inside You" a chance to work out the consummation of your wish without interference.

When you waken, hold it all pleasurably in thought again for a few moments. Don't let doubts and fears creep in, but go ahead, confidently, knowing that your wish is working itself out. Know this, believe it—and if there is nothing harmful in it, IT WILL WORK OUT!

For somewhere in Universal Mind there exists the correct solution of every problem. It matters not how stupendous and complicated, nor how simple a problem may appear to be. There always exists the right solution in Universal Mind. And because this solution does exist, there also exists the ability to ascertain and to prove what that solution is. You can know, and you can do, every right thing. Whatever it is necessary for you to know, whatever it is necessary for you to do, you can know and you can do, if you will but seek the help of Universal Mind and be governed by its suggestions.

Try this method every night for a little while, and the problem does not exist that you cannot solve.

CHAPTER 6

See Yourself Doing It

You say big corporations scheme
To keep a fellow down;
They drive him, shame him, starve him, too,
If he so much as frown.
God knows I hold no brief for them;
Still, come with me to-day
And watch those fat directors meet,
For this is what they say:
"In all our force not one to take
The new work that we plan!
In all the thousand men we've hired
Where shall we find a man?"

—ST. CLAIR ADAMS*

You've often heard it said that a man is worth $2 a day from the neck down. How much he's worth from the neck up depends upon how much he is able to SEE.

"Without vision the people perish" did not refer to good eyesight. It was the eyes of the mind that counted in days of old just as they do today. Without them you are just so much power "on the hoof," to be driven as a horse or an ox is driven. And you are worth only a little more than they.

But given vision—imagination—the ability to visualize conditions and things a month or a year ahead; given the eyes of the mind—there's no limit to your value or to your capabilities.

The locomotive, the steamboat, the automobile, the aeroplane—all existed complete in the imagination of some man before ever they became facts. The wealthy men, the big men, the successful men, visioned their successes in their minds' eyes before ever they won them from the world.

*From "It Can Be Done." Copyright 1921, George Sully & Company.

From the beginning of time, nothing has ever taken on material shape without first being visualized in mind. The only difference between the sculptor and the mason is in the mental image behind their work. Rodin employed masons to hew his blocks of marble into the general shape of the figure he was about to form. *That was mere mechanical labor.* Then Rodin took it in hand and from that rough-hewn piece of stone there sprang the wondrous figure of "The Thinker." *That was art!*

"The difference was all in the imagination behind the hands that wielded mallet and chisel. After Rodin had formed his masterpiece, ordinary workmen copied it by the thousands. Rodin's work brought fabulous sums. The copies brought day wages. Conceiving ideas—*creating something*—is what pays, in sculpture as in all else. Mere hand-work is worth only hand wages.

"The imagination," says Glenn Clark in "The Soul's Sincere Desire," "is of all qualities in man the most God-like—that which associates him most closely with God. The first mention we read of man in the Bible is where he is spoken of as an 'image.' 'Let us make man in our image, after our likeness.' The only place where an image can be conceived is in the imagination. Thus man, the highest creation of God, was a creation of God's imagination.

"The source and center of all man's creative power—the power that above all others lifts him above the level of brute creation, and that gives him dominion, is his power of making images, or the power of the imagination. There are some who have always thought that the imagination was something which makes-believe that which is not. This is fancy—not imagination. Fancy would convert that which is real into pretense and sham; imagination enables one to see through the appearance of a thing to what it really *is*."

There is a very real law of cause and effect which makes the dream of the dreamer come true. It is the law of visualization—the law that calls into being in this outer material world everything that is real in the inner world. Imagination pictures the thing you desire. VISION idealizes it. It reaches beyond the thing that is, into the conception of what can be. Imagination gives you the picture. Vision gives you the impulse to make the picture your own.

Make your mental image clear enough, picture it vividly in every detail, and the Genie-of-your-Mind will speedily bring it into being as an everyday reality.

That law holds true of everything in life. There is nothing you can rightfully desire that cannot be brought into being through visualization.

Suppose there's a position you want—the general managership of your company. See yourself—just as you are now—sitting in the general manager's chair. See your name on his door. See yourself handling his affairs as you would handle them. Get that picture impressed upon your subconscious mind. See it! *Believe it!* The Genie-of-your-Mind will find the way to make it come true.

The keynote of successful visualization is this: See things as you would have them be instead of as they are. Close your eyes and make clear mental pictures. Make them look and act just as they would in real life. In short, day dream—but day dream with a purpose. Concentrate on the one idea to the exclusion of all others, and continue to concentrate on that one idea until it has been accomplished.

Do you want an automobile? A home? A factory? They can all be won in the same way.

They are in their essence all of them ideas of mind, and if you will but build them up in your own mind first, stone by stone, complete in every detail, you will find that the Genie-of-your-Mind can build them up similarly in the material world.

"The building of a trans-continental railroad from a mental picture," says C. W. Chamberlain in "The Uncommon Sense of Applied Psychology," "gives the average individual an idea that it is a big job. The fact of the matter is, the achievement, as well as the perfect mental picture, is made up of millions of little jobs, each fitting in its proper place and helping to make up the whole.

"A skyscraper is built from individual bricks, the laying of each brick being a single job which must be completed before the next brick can be laid."

It is the same with any work, any study. To quote Professor James:

"As we become permanent drunkards by so many separate drinks, so we become saints in the moral, and authorities and experts in the practical and scientific spheres, by so many separate acts and hours of working. Let no youth have any anxiety about the upshot of his education whatever the line of it may be. If he keep faithfully busy each hour of the working day he may safely leave the final result to itself. He can with perfect certainty count on waking some fine morning, to find himself one of the competent ones of his generation, in whatever pursuit he may have singled out. . . . Young people should know this truth in advance. The ignorance of it has probably engendered more discouragement and faint-heartedness in youths embarking on arduous careers than all other causes taken together."

Remember that the only limit to your capabilities is the one you place upon them. There is no law of limitation. The only law is of supply. Through your subconscious mind you can draw upon universal supply for anything you wish. The ideas of Universal Mind are as countless as the sands on the seashore. Use them. And use them lavishly, just as they are given. There is a little poem by Jessie B. Rittenhouse* that so well describes the limitations that most of us put upon ourselves that I quote it here:

"I bargained with Life for a penny,
And Life would pay no more,
However I begged at evening
When I counted my scanty store.

. . . . . .

"For Life is a just employer;
He gives you what you ask,
But once you have set the wages,
Why, you must bear the task.

"I worked for a menial's hire,
Only to learn, dismayed,
That any wage I had asked of Life,
Life would have paid."

*From "The Door of Dreams," Houghton, Mifflin & Co., Boston.

Aim high! If you miss the moon, you may hit a star. Everyone admits that this world and all the vast firmament must have been thought into shape from the formless void by some Universal Mind. That same Universal Mind rules today, and it has given to each form of life power to attract to itself whatever it needs for its perfect growth. The tree, the plant, the animal—each one finds its need.

You are an intelligent, reasoning creature. Your mind is part of Universal Mind. And you have power to *say* what you require for perfect growth. Don't be a niggard with yourself. Don't sell yourself for a penny. Whatever price you set upon yourself, life will give. So aim high. Demand much! Make a clear, distinct mental image of what it is you want. Hold it in your thought. Visualize it, see it, *believe it!* The ways and means of satisfying that desire will follow. For supply always comes on the heels of demand.

It is by doing this that you take your fate out of the hands of chance. It is in this way that you control the experiences you are to have in life. But be sure to visualize *only what you want.* The law works both ways. If you visualize your worries and your fears, you will make them real. Control your thought and you will control circumstances. Conditions will be what you make them.

Most of us are like factories where two-thirds of the machines are idle, where the workmen move around in a listless, dispirited sort of way, doing only the tenth part of what they could do if the head of the plant were watching and directing them. Instead of that, he is off idly dreaming or waiting for something to turn up. What he needs is someone to point out to him his listless workmen and idle machines, and show him how to put each one to working full time and overtime.

And that is what YOU need, too. You are working at only a tenth of *your* capacity. You are doing only a tenth of what *you* are capable of. The time you spend idly wishing or worrying can be used in so directing your subconscious mind that it will bring you anything of good you may desire.

Philip of Macedon, Alexander's father, perfected the "phalanx"—a triangular formation which enabled him to center the whole weight of his attack on one point in the opposing line. It drove through everything opposed to it. In that day and age it was invincible. And the idea is just as invincible today.

Keep the one thought in mind, SEE it being carried out step by step, and you can knit any group of workers into one homogeneous whole, all centered on the one idea. You can accomplish any one thing. You can put across any definite idea. Keep that mental picture ever in mind and you will make it as invincible as was Alexander's phalanx of old.

> *"It is not the guns or armament*
> *Or the money they can pay,*
> *It's the close cooperation*
> *That makes them win the day.*
> *It is not the individual*
> *Or the army as a whole*
> *But the everlasting team work*
> *of every bloomin' soul."*
>
> —J. MASON KNOX

The error of the ages is the tendency mankind has always shown to limit the power of Mind, or its willingness to help in time of need.

"Know ye not," said Paul, "that ye are the temples of the Living God?"

No—most of us do not know it. Or at least, if we do, we are like the Indian family out on the Cherokee reservation. Oil had been found on their land and money poured in upon them. More money than they had ever known was in the world. Someone persuaded them to build a great house, to have it beautifully furnished, richly decorated. The house when finished was one of the show places of that locality. But the Indians, while very proud of their showy house, continued to *live in their old sod shack!*

So it is with many of us. We may know that we are "temples of the Living God." We may even be proud of that fact. But we never take advantage of it to dwell in that temple, to proclaim our dominion over things and conditions. We never avail ourselves of the power that is ours.

The great Prophets of old had the forward look. Theirs was the era of hope and expectation. They looked for the time when the revelation should come that was to make men "sons of God." "They shall obtain joy and gladness, and sorrow and sighing shall flee away."

Jesus came to fulfill that revelation. "Ask and ye shall receive, that your joy may be full."

The world has turned in vain to matter and materialistic philosophy for deliverance from its woes. In the future the only march of actual progress will be in the mental realm, and this progress will not be in the way of human speculation and theorizing but in the *actual demonstration* of the Universal, Infinite Mind.

The world stands today within the Vestibule of the vast realm of divine intelligence, wherein is found the transcendent, practical power of Mind over all things.

"What eye never saw, nor ear ever heard,
What never entered the mind of man—
Even all that God has prepared for those who love Him."

CHAPTER 7

"As a Man Thinketh"

"Our remedies in ourselves do lie
Which we ascribe to heaven."
—SHAKESPEARE

In our great-grandfather's day, when witches flew around by night and cast their spell upon all unlucky enough to cross them, men thought that the power of sickness or health, of good fortune or ill, resided outside themselves.

We laugh today at such benighted superstition. But even in this day and age there are few who realize that the things they *see* are but *effects.* Fewer still who have any idea of the *causes* by which those effects are brought about.

Every human experience is an effect.

You laugh, you weep, you joy, you sorrow, you suffer or you are happy. Each of these is an effect, the cause of which can be easily traced.

But all the experiences of life are not so easily traceable to their primary causes. We save money for our old age. We put it into a bank or into safe bonds—and the bank breaks or the railroad or corporation goes into a receivership. We stay at home on a holiday to avoid risk of accident, and fall off a stepladder or down the stairs and break a limb. We drive slowly for fear of danger, and a speeding car comes from behind and knocks us into a ditch. A man goes over Niagara Falls in a barrel without harm, and then slips on a banana peel, breaks his leg, and dies of it.

What is the cause back of it all? If we can find it and control it, we can control the effect. We shall no longer then be the football of fate. We shall be able to rise above the conception of life in which matter is our master.

There is but one answer. The world without is a reflection of the world within. We image thoughts of disaster upon our subconscious minds and the Genie-of-our-Mind finds ways of bringing them into effect—even though we stay at home, even though we take every possible precaution. The mental image is what counts, be it for good or ill. It is a devastating or a beneficent force, just as we choose to make it. To paraphrase

Thackeray—"The world is a looking-glass, and gives back to every man the reflection of his own thought."

For matter is not *real* substance. Material science today shows that matter has no natural eternal existence. Dr. Willis R. Whitney, in an address before the American Chemical Society on August 8th, 1925, discussing "Matter—Is There Anything in It?" stated that "the most we know about matter is that it is almost entirely *space.* It is as empty as the sky. It is almost as empty as a perfect vacuum, although it usually contains a lot of energy." Thought is the only force. Just as polarity controls the electron, gravitation the planets, tropism the plants and lower animals—just so thought controls the action and the environment of man. And thought is subject wholly to the control of mind. Its direction rests with us.

Walt Whitman had the right of it when he said—"Nothing external to me has any power over me."

The happenings that occur in the material world are in themselves neither cheerful nor sorrowful, just as outside of the eye that observes them colors are neither green nor red. It is our thoughts that make them so. And we can color those thoughts according to our own fancy. We can make the world without but a reflection of the world within. We can make matter a force subject entirely to the control of our mind. For matter is merely our wrong view of what Universal Mind sees rightly.

We cannot change the past experience, but we can determine what the new ones shall be like. We can make the coming day just what we want it to be. We can *be* tomorrow what *we think* today. For the thoughts are causes and the conditions are the effects.

What is the reason for most failures in life? The fact that they first thought failure. They allowed competition, hard times, fear and worry to undermine their confidence. Instead of working aggressively ahead, spending money to make more money, they stopped every possible outlay, tried to "play safe," but expected others to continue spending with them. War is not the only place where "the best defensive is a strong offensive."

The law of compensation is always at work. Man is not at the caprice of fate. He is his own fate. "As a man thinketh in his heart, so is he." We are our own past thoughts, with the things that these thoughts have attracted to us added on.

The successful man has no time to think of failure. He is too busy thinking up new ways to succeed. You can't pour water into a vessel already full.

All about you is energy—electronic energy, exactly like that which makes up the solid objects you possess. The only difference is that the loose energy round about is unappropriated. It is still virgin gold—undiscovered, unclaimed. You can think it into anything you wish—into gold or dross, into health or sickness, into strength or weakness, into success or failure. Which shall it be? "There is nothing either good or bad," said Shakespeare, "but thinking makes it so." The understanding of that law will enable you to control every other law that exists. In it is to be found the panacea for all ills, the satisfaction of all want, all desire. It is Creative Mind's own provision for man's freedom.

Have you ever read Basil King's "Conquest of Fear"? If you haven't, do so by all means. Here is the way he visions the future:

"Taking Him (Jesus) as our standard we shall work out, I venture to think, to the following points of progress:

"*a.* The control of matter in furnishing ourselves with food and drink by means more direct than at present employed, as He turned water into wine and fed the multitudes with the loaves and fishes.

"*b.* The control of matter by putting away from ourselves, by methods more sure and less roundabout than those of today, sickness, blindness, infirmity, and deformity.

"*c.* The control of matter by regulating our atmospheric conditions as He stilled the tempest.

"*d.* The control of matter by restoring to this phase of existence those who have passed out of it before their time, or who can ill be spared from it, as He 'raised' three young people from 'the dead' and Peter and Paul followed His example.

"*e.* The control of matter in putting it off and on at will, as He in His death and resurrection.

"*f.* The control of matter in passing altogether out of it, as He in what we call His Ascension into Heaven."

Mortals are healthy or unhealthy, happy or unhappy, strong or weak, alive or dead, in the proportion that they think thoughts of health or illness, strength or weakness. Your body, like all other material things, manifests only what your mind entertains in belief. In a general way you have often noticed this yourself. A man with an ugly disposition (which is a mental state) will have harsh, unlovely features. One with a gentle disposition will have a smiling and serene countenance. All the other organs of the human body are equally responsive to thought. Who has not seen the face become red with rage or white with fear? Who has not known of people who became desperately ill following an outburst of temper? Physicians declare that just as fear, irritability and hate distort the features, they likewise distort the heart, stomach and liver.

Experiments conducted on a cat shortly after a meal showed that when it was purring contentedly, its digestive organs functioned perfectly. But when a dog was brought into the room and the cat drew back in fear and anger, the X-ray showed that its digestive organs were so contorted as to be almost tied up in a knot!

Each of us makes his own world—and he makes it through mind. It is a commonplace fact that no two people see the same thing alike. "A primrose by a river's brim, a yellow primrose was to him, and it was nothing more."

Thoughts are the causes. Conditions are merely effects. We can mould ourselves and our surroundings by resolutely directing our thoughts towards the goal we have in mind.

Ordinary animal life is very definitely controlled by temperature, by climate, by seasonal conditions. Man alone can adjust himself to any reasonable temperature or condition. Man alone has been able to free himself to a great extent from the control of natural forces through his understanding of the relation of cause and effect. And now man is beginning to get a glimpse of the final freedom that shall be his from all material causes when he shall acquire the complete understanding that mind is the only cause and that effects are what he sees.

"We moderns are unaccustomed," says one talented writer, "to the mastery over our own inner thoughts and feelings. That a man should be a prey to any thought that chances to take possession of his mind, is commonly among us assumed as unavoidable. It may be a matter of regret that he should be kept awake all night from anxiety as to the issue of a lawsuit on the morrow, but that he should have the power of determining whether he be kept awake or not seems an extravagant demand. The image of an impending calamity is no doubt odious, but its very odiousness (we say) makes it haunt the mind all the more pertinaciously, and it is useless to expel it. Yet this is an absurd position for man, the heir of all the ages, to be in: Hag-ridden by the flimsy creatures of his own brain. If a pebble in our boot torments us, we expel it. We take off the boot and shake it out. And once the matter is fairly understood, it is just as easy to expel an intruding and obnoxious thought from the mind. About this there ought to be no mistake, no two opinions. The thing is obvious, clear and unmistakable. It should be as easy to expel an obnoxious thought from the mind as to shake a stone out of your shoe; and until a man can do that, it is just nonsense to talk about his ascendency over nature, and all the rest of it. He is a mere slave, and a prey to the bat-winged phantoms that flit through the corridors of his own brain. Yet the weary and careworn faces that we meet by thousands, even among the affluent classes of civilization, testify only too clearly how seldom this mastery is obtained. How rare indeed to find a *man!* How common rather to discover a *creature* hounded on by tyrant thoughts (or cares, or desires), cowering, wincing under the lash.

"It is one of the prominent doctrines of some of the oriental schools of practical psychology that the power of expelling thoughts, or if need be, killing them dead on the spot, *must be* attained. Naturally the art requires practice, but like other arts, when once acquired there is no mystery or difficulty about it. It is worth practice. It may be fairly said that life only begins when this art has been acquired. For obviously when, instead of being ruled by individual thoughts, the whole flock of them in their immense multitude and variety and capacity is ours to direct and despatch and employ where we list, life becomes a thing so vast and grand, compared to what it was before, that its former condition may well appear almost ante-natal. If you can kill a thought dead, for the time being, you can do anything else with it that you please. And therefore it is that this power is so valuable. And it not only frees a man from mental torment (which is nine-tenths at least of the torment of life), but it gives him a concentrated power of handling mental work absolutely unknown to him before. The two are co-relative to each other."

There is no intelligence in matter—whether that matter be electronic energy made up in the form of stone, or iron, or wood, or flesh. It all consists of Energy, the universal substance from which Mind forms all material things. Mind is the only intelligence. It alone is eternal. It alone is supreme in the universe.

When we reach that understanding, we will no longer have cause for fear, because we will realize that Universal Mind is the creator of *life* only; that death is not an actuality—it is merely the *absence* of life—and life will be ever-present. Remember the old fairy story of how the Sun was listening to a lot of earthly creatures talking of a very dark place they had found? A place of Stygian blackness. Each told how terrifically dark it had seemed. The Sun went and looked for it. He went to the exact spot they had described. He searched everywhere. But he could find not even a tiny dark spot. And he came back and told the earth-creatures he did not believe there *was* any dark place.

When the sun of understanding shines on all the dark spots in our lives, we will realize that there is no cause, no creator, no power, except good; evil is not an entity—it is merely the *absence of good.* And there can be no ill effects without an evil cause. Since there is no evil cause, only good can have reality or power.

There is no beginning or end to good. From it there can be nothing but blessing for the whole race. In it is found no trouble. If God (or Good—the two are synonymous) is the only cause, then the only effect must be like the cause. "All things were made by Him; and without Him was not anything made that was made."

Don't be content with passively reading this. Use it! Practice it! Exercise is far more necessary to mental development that it is to physical. Practice the "daily dozen" of right thinking. Stretch your mind to realize how infinitely far it can reach out, what boundless vision it can have. Breathe out all the old thoughts of sickness, discouragement, failure, worry and fear. Breathe in deep, long breaths (thoughts) of unlimited health and strength, unlimited happiness and success. Practice looking forward—always looking forward to something better—better health, finer physique, greater happiness, bigger success. Take these mental breathing exercises every day. See how easily you will control your thoughts. How quickly you will see the good effects. You've got to think all the time. Your mind will do that anyway. And the thoughts are constantly building—for good or ill. So be sure to exhale all the thoughts of fear and worry and disease and lack that have been troubling you, and inhale only those you want to see realized.

CHAPTER 8

The Law of Supply

"They do me wrong who say I come no more
When once I knock and fail to find you in;
For every day I stand outside your door,
And bid you wake, and rise to fight and win.

"Wail not for precious chances passed away,
Weep not for golden ages on the wane!
Each night I burn the records of the day—
At sunrise every soul is born again!

—WALTER MALONE*

Have you ever run a race, or worked at utmost capacity for a protracted period, or swum a great distance? Remember how, soon after starting, you began to feel tired? Remember how, before you had gone any great distance, you thought you had reached your limit? But remember, too, how, when you kept on going, you got your second wind, your tiredness vanished, your muscles throbbed with energy, you felt literally charged with speed and endurance?

Stored in every human being are great reserves of energy of which the average individual knows nothing. Most people are like a man who drives a car in low gear, not knowing that by the simple shift of a lever he can set it in high and not merely speed up the car, but do it with far less expenditure of power.

The law of the universe is the law of supply. You see it on every hand. Nature is lavish in everything she does.

Look at the heavens at night. There are millions of stars there—millions of worlds—millions of suns among them. Surely there is no lack of wealth or profusion in the Mind that could image all of these; no place for limitation there! Look at the vegetation in the country round about you. Nature supplies all that the shrubs or trees may need for their

*Courtesy of Mrs. Ella Malone Watson.

growth and sustenance! Look at the lower forms of animal life—the birds and the wild animals, the reptiles and the insects, the fish in the sea. Nature supplies them bountifully with everything they need. They have but to help themselves to what she holds out to them with such lavish hand. Look at all the natural resources of the world—coal and iron and oil and all metals. There is plenty for everyone. We hear a lot about the exhaustion of our resources of coal and oil, but there is available coal enough to last mankind for thousands of years. There are vast oil fields practically untouched, probably others bigger still yet to be discovered, and when all these are exhausted, the extraction of oil from shales will keep the world supplied for countless more years.

There is abundance for everyone. But just as you must strain and labor to reach the resources of your "second wind," just so you must strive before you can make manifest the law of supply in nature.

THE WORLD BELONGS TO YOU

It is your estate. It owes you not merely a living but everything of good you may desire. You've got to *demand* these things of it, though. You've got to fear naught, dread naught, stop at naught. You've got to have the faith of a Columbus—crossing an unknown sea, holding a mutinous crew to the task long after they had ceased to believe in themselves or in him—*and giving to the world a new hemisphere.* You've got to have the faith of a Washington—defeated, discredited, almost wholly deserted by his followers, yet holding steadfast in spite of all—*and giving to America a new liberty.* You've got to *dominate*—not to cringe. *You've* got to make the application of the law of supply.

"Consider the lilies how they grow." The flowers, the birds, all of creation, are incessantly active. The trees and flowers in their growth, the birds and wild creatures in building their nests and finding sustenance, are always working—*but never worrying.* "Your Father knoweth that ye have need of these things." "And all these things shall be added unto you."

If all would agree to give up worrying—to be industrious but never anxious about the outcome—it would mean the beginning of a new era in human progress, an age of liberty, of freedom from bondage. Jesus set forth the universal law of supply when he said—"Therefore I say unto you, be not anxious for the morrow, what ye shall eat, or wherewithal ye shall be clothed—but seek first the kingdom of God, *and all those things shall be added unto you.*"

What is this "Kingdom of God"?

Jesus tells us—"The Kingdom of God is within you." It is the "Father within you" to which He so frequently referred. It is Mind—your part of Universal Mind. "Seek first the Kingdom of God." Seek first an understanding of this Power within you—learn to contact with it—to use it—"and all those things shall be added unto you."

All riches have their origin in Mind. Wealth is in ideas—not money. Money is merely the material medium of exchange for ideas. The paper money in your pockets is in itself worth no more than so many Russian rubles. It is the idea behind it that gives it value. Factory buildings, machinery, materials, are in themselves worthless without a manufacturing or a selling idea behind them. How often you see a factory fall to pieces, the machinery rust away, after the idea behind it gave out. Factories, machines, are simply the tools of trade. It is the idea behind them that makes them go.

So don't go out a-seeking of wealth. Look within you for ideas! "The Kingdom of God is within you." Use it—*purposefully!* Use it to THINK constructively. Don't say you are *thinking* when all you are doing is exercising your faculty of memory. As Dumont says in "The Master Mind"—"They are simply allowing the stream of memory to flow through their field of consciousness, while the Ego stands on the banks and idly watches the passing waters of memory flow by. They call this 'thinking,' while in reality there is no process of Thought under way."

They are like the old mountaineer sitting in the shade alongside his cabin. Asked what he did to pass the long hours away, he said—"Waal, sometimes I set and think; and sometimes I just set."

Dumont goes on to say, in quoting another writer: "When I use the word 'thinking,' I mean *thinking with a purpose, with an end in view, thinking to solve a problem.* I mean the kind of thinking that is forced on us when we are deciding on a course to pursue, on a life work to take up perhaps; the kind of thinking that was forced upon us in our younger days when we had to find a solution to a problem in mathematics; or when we tackled psychology in college. I do not mean 'thinking' in snatches, or holding petty opinions on this subject and on that. I mean thought on significant questions which lie outside the bounds of your narrow personal welfare. This is the kind of thinking which is now so rare—so sadly needed!"

The Kingdom of God is the Kingdom of Thought, of Achievement, of Health, of Happiness and Prosperity. "I came that ye might have life and have it more abundantly."

But you have got to *seek* it. You have got to do more than ponder. You have got to *think*—to think constructively—to seek how you may discover new worlds, new methods, new needs. The greatest discoveries, you know, have arisen out of things which everybody had *seen,* but only one man had NOTICED. The biggest fortunes have been made out of the opportunities which many men *had,* but only one man GRASPED.

Why is it that so many millions of men and women go through life in poverty and misery, in sickness and despair? Why? Primarily because they make a reality of poverty through their fear of it. They visualize poverty, misery and disease, and thus bring them into being. And secondly, they cannot demonstrate the law of supply for the same reason that so many millions cannot solve the first problem in algebra. The solution is simple—but they have never been shown the method. They do not understand the law.

The essence of this law is that you must *think* abundance, *see* abundance, *feel* abundance, *believe* abundance. Let no thought of limitation enter your mind. There is no lawful desire of yours for which, as far as mind is concerned, there is not abundant satisfaction. And if you can visualize it in mind, you can realize it in your daily world.

"Blessed is the man whose delight is in the *law* of the Lord: And he shall be like a tree planted by the rivers of water, that bringeth forth his fruit in his season: his leaf also shall not wither; and whatsoever he doeth shall prosper."

Don't worry. Don't doubt. Don't dig up the seeds of prosperity and success to see whether they have sprouted. Have faith! Nourish your seeds with renewed desire. Keep before your mind's eye the picture of the thing you want. BELIEVE IN IT! No matter if you seem to be in the clutch of misfortune, no matter if the future looks black and dreary—FORGET YOUR FEARS! Realize that the future is of your own making. There is no power that can keep you down but yourself. Set your goal. Forget the obstacles between. Forget the difficulties in the way. Keep only the goal before your mind's eye—*and you'll win it!*

Judge Troward, in his Edinburgh Lectures on Mental Science, shows the way:

"The initial step, then, consists in determining to picture the Universal Mind as the ideal of all we could wish it to be, both to ourselves and to others, together with the endeavor to reproduce this ideal, however imperfectly, in our own life; and this step having been taken, we can then cheerfully look upon it as our ever-present Friend, providing all good, guarding from all danger, and guiding us with all counsel. Similarly if we think of it as a great power devoted to supplying all our needs, we shall impress this character also upon it, and by the law of subjective mind, it will proceed to enact the part of that special providence which we have credited it with being; and if, beyond general care of our concerns, we would draw to ourselves some particular benefit, the same rule holds good of impressing our desire upon the universal subjective mind. And thus the deepest problems of philosophy bring us back to the old statement of the law: 'Ask and ye shall receive; seek and ye shall find; knock and it shall be opened unto you.' This is the summing-up of the natural law of the relation between us and the Divine Mind. It is thus no vain boast that mental science can enable us to make our lives what we will. And to this law there is no limit. What it can do for us today it can do tomorrow, and through all that procession of tomorrows that loses itself in the dim vistas of eternity. *Belief in limitation is the one and only thing that causes limitation,* because we thus impress limitation upon the creative principle; and in proportion as we lay that belief aside, our boundaries will expand, and increasing life and more abundant blessing will be ours."

You are not working for some firm merely for the pittance they pay you. You are part of the great scheme of things. And what you do has its bearing on the ultimate result. That being the case, you are working for Universal Mind, and Universal Mind is the most generous paymaster there is. Just remember that you can look to it for all good things. Supply is *where* you are and *what* you need.

Do you want a situation? Close your eyes and realize that somewhere is the position for which you of all people are best fitted, and which is best fitted to your ability. The position where you can do the utmost of good, and where life, in turn, offers the most to you. Realize that Universal Mind knows exactly where this position is, and that through your subconscious mind you, too, can know it. Realize that this is YOUR position, that it NEEDS you, that it belongs to you, that it is right for you to have it, that you are entitled to it. Hold this thought in mind every night for just a moment, then go to sleep knowing that your subconscious mind HAS the necessary information as to where this position is and how to get in touch with it. Mind you—not WILL have, but HAS. The earnest realization of this will bring that position to you, and you to it, as surely as the morrow will bring the sun. Make the law of supply operative and you find that the things you seek are seeking you.

Get firmly fixed in your own mind the definite conviction that you can do anything you greatly want to do. There is no such thing as lack of opportunity. There is no such thing as only one opportunity. You are subject to a law of boundless and perpetual opportunity, and you can enforce that law in your behalf just as widely as you need. Opportunity is infinite and ever present.

Berton Braley has it well expressed in his poem on "Opportunity":*

"For the best verse hasn't been rhymed yet,
The best house hasn't been planned,
The highest peak hasn't been climbed yet,
The mightiest rivers aren't spanned;
Don't worry and fret, faint hearted,
The chances have just begun,
For the Best jobs haven't been started,
The Best work hasn't been done."

Nothing stands in the way of a will which wants—an intelligence which knows. The great thing is to start. "Begin your work," says Ausonius. "To begin is to complete the first half. The second half remains. Begin again and the work is done." It matters not how small or unimportant your task may seem to be. It may loom bigger in Universal Mind than that of your neighbor, whose position is so much greater in the eyes of the world. Do it well—and Universal Mind will work with you.

But don't feel limited to any one job or any one line of work. Man was given dominion over all the earth. "And God said, Let us make man in our image, after our likeness: and let them have dominion over the fish of the sea, and over the fowl of the air, and over the cattle, and over all the earth, and over every creeping thing that creepeth upon the earth."

All of energy, all of power, all that can exercise any influence over your life, is in your hands through the power of thought. God—good—is the only power there is. Your mind is part of His mind. He is "the Father that is within you that doeth the works."

So don't put any limit upon His power by trying to limit your capabilities. You are not in bondage to anything. All your hopes and dreams can come true. Were you not given dominion over all the earth? And can anyone else take this dominion from you?

All the mysterious psychic powers about which you hear so much today are perfectly natural. I have them. You have them. They only await the time when they shall be allowed to assert their vigor and prove themselves your faithful servitors.

"Be not afraid!" Claim your inheritance. The Universal Mind that supplies all wisdom and power is *your* mind. And to the extent that you are governed by your understanding of its infinite law of supply you will be able to demonstrate plenty. "According to your faith, be it unto you."

"Analyze most of the great American fortunes of the past generation," says *Advertising and Selling Fortnightly,* "and you will find that they were founded on great faiths. One man's faith was in oil, another's in land, another's in minerals.

*From "A Banjo at Armageddon." Copyright 1917, George H. Doran Company.

"The fortunes that are being built today are just as surely being built on great faiths, but there is this difference: the emphasis of the faith has been shifted. Today it takes faith in a product or an opportunity, as it always did, but it takes faith in the public, in addition. Those who have the greatest faith in the public—the kind of faith possessed by Henry Ford and H. J. Heinz—*and make that faith articulate*—build the biggest fortunes."

"WANTED"

There is one question that bothers many a man. Should he stick to the job he has, or cast about at once for a better one? The answer depends entirely upon what you are striving for. The first thing is to set your goal. What is it you want? A profession? A political appointment? An important executive position? A business of your own?

Every position should yield you three things:

1. Reasonable pay for the present
2. Knowledge, training or experience that will be worth money to you in the future
3. Prestige or acquaintances that will be of assistance to you in attaining your goal

Judge every opening by those three standards. But don't overlook chances for valuable training, merely because the pay is small. Though it is a pretty safe rule that the concern with up-to-the-minute methods that it would profit you to learn also pays up-to-the-minute salaries.

Hold each job long enough to get from it every speck of information there is in it. Hold it long enough to learn the job ahead. Then if there seems no likelihood of a vacancy soon in that job ahead, find one that corresponds to it somewhere else.

Progress! Keep going ahead! Don't be satisfied merely because your salary is being boosted occasionally. Learn something every day. When you reach the point in your work that you are no longer adding to your store of knowledge or abilities, you are going backward, and it's time for you to move. Move upward in the organization you are with if you can—but MOVE!

Your actual salary is of slight importance compared with the knowledge and ability you add to your mind. Given a full storehouse there, the salary or the riches will speedily follow. But the biggest salary won't do you much good for long unless you've got the knowledge inside you to back it up.

It's like a girl picking her husband. She can pick one with a lot of money and no brains, or she can pick one with no money but a lot of ability. In the former case, she'll have a high time for a little while, ending in a divorce court or in her having a worthless young "rounder" on her hands and no money to pay the bills. In the other, the start will be hard, but she is likely to end up with a happy home she has helped to build, an earnest, hardworking husband who has "arrived"—*and happiness.*

Money ought to be a consideration in marriage—but never *the* consideration. Of course it's an easy matter to pick a man with neither money nor brains. But when it's a choice of money *or* brains—take the brains every time. Possessions are of slight importance compared to mind. Given the inquiring, alert type of mind—you can get any amount of possessions. But the possessions without the mind are nothing. Nine times out of ten the best thing that can happen to any young couple is to have to start out with little or nothing and work out their salvation together.

What is it *you* want most from life? Is it riches?

Picture yourself with all the riches you could use, with all the abundance that Nature holds out with such lavish hand everywhere. What would you do with it?

Day-dream for a while. Believe that you *have* that abundance *now.* Practice being rich in your own mind. See yourself driving that expensive car you have always longed for, living in the sort of house you have often pictured, well dressed, surrounded by everything to make life worth while. Picture yourself spending this money that is yours, lavishly, without a worry as to where more is coming from, knowing that there is no limit to the riches of Mind. Picture yourself doing all those things you would like to do, living the life you would like to live, providing for your loved ones as you would like to see them provided for. *See* all this in your mind's eye. *Believe* it to be true for the moment. *Know* that it will all be true in the not-very-distant future. Get from it all the pleasure and enjoyment you can.

It is the *first step* in making your dreams come true. You are creating the model in mind. And if you don't allow fear or worry to tear it down, Mind will re-create that model for you in your every-day life.

"All that the Father hath is yours," said Jesus. And a single glance at the heavens and the earth will show you that He has all riches in abundance. Reach out mentally and appropriate to yourself some of these good gifts. You've got to do it mentally before you can enjoy it physically. " 'Tis mind that makes the body rich," as Shakespeare tells us.

See the things that you want as *already yours.* Know that they will come to you at need. Then LET them come. Don't fret and worry about them. Don't think about your LACK of them. Think of them as YOURS, as *belonging* to you, as already in your possession.

Look upon money as water that runs the mill of your mind. You are constantly grinding out ideas that the world needs. Your thoughts, your plans, are necessary to the great scheme of things. Money provides the power. But it needs YOU, it needs your ideas, before it can be of any use to the world. The Falls of Niagara would be of no use without the power plants that line the banks. The Falls need these plants to turn their power to account. In the same way, money needs your ideas to become of use to the world.

So instead of thinking that you need money, realize that money needs YOU. Money is just so much wasted energy without work to do. Your ideas provide the outlet for it, the means by which money can do things. Develop your ideas, secure in the knowledge that money is always looking for such an outlet. When the ideas are perfected, money will gravitate your way without conscious effort on your part, if only you don't dam up the channels with doubts and fears.

"First have something good—then advertise!" said Horace Greeley. First have something that the world needs, even if it be only faithful, interested service—then open up your channels of desire, and dollars will flow to you.

And remember that the more you have to offer—the more of riches will flow to you. Dollars are of no value except as they are used.

You have seen the rich attacked time and again in newspapers and magazines. You have read numberless articles and editorials against them. You have heard agitators declaim against them by the hour. But have you ever heard one of them say a single word against the richest man of them all—Henry Ford? I haven't. And why? Because Henry Ford's idea of money is that it is something to be *used*—something to provide more jobs, something to bring more comfort, more enjoyment, into an increasingly greater number of lives.

That is why money flows to him so freely. That is why he gets so much out of life. And that is how you, too, can get in touch with Infinite Supply. Realize that it is not money you have to seek but a way to *use* money for the world's advantage. *Find the need!* Look at everything with the question—How could that be improved? To what new uses could this be put? Then set about supplying that need, in the absolute confidence that when you have found the way, money will flow freely to and through you. Do your part—and you can confidently look to Universal Mind to provide the means.

Get firmly in mind the definite conviction that YOU CAN DO ANYTHING RIGHT THAT YOU MAY WISH TO DO. Then set your goal and let everything you do, all your work, all your study, all your associations, be a step towards that goal. To quote Berton Braley again—

"If you want a thing bad enough
To go out and fight for it,
Work day and night for it,
Give up your time and your peace and your sleep for it,
If only desire of it
Makes you quite mad enough
Never to tire of it,
Makes you hold all other things tawdry and cheap for it,
If life seems all empty and useless without it
And all that you scheme and you dream is about it,
If gladly you'll sweat for it,
Fret for it,
Plan for it,
Lose all your terror of God or man for it,
If you'll simply go after that thing that you want,
With all your capacity,
Strength and sagacity,
Faith, hope and confidence, stern pertinacity,
If neither cold poverty, famished and gaunt,
Nor sickness nor pain
Of body or brain
Can turn you away from the thing that you want,
If dogged and grim you besiege and beset it,
*You'll get it!"**

*From "Things As They Are." Copyright 1916, George H. Doran Company, New York.

CHAPTER 9

The Formula of Success

"One ship drives east, and another drives west,
With the self-same winds that blow.
'Tis the set of the sails, and not the gales
Which tells us the way they go.

"Like the waves of the sea are the ways of fate
As we voyage along thru life.
'Tis the set of the soul which decides its goal
And not the calm or the strife."

—ELLA WHEELER WILCOX

What is the eternal question which stands up and looks you and every sincere man squarely in the eye every morning?

"How can I better my condition?" That is the real life question which confronts you, and will haunt you every day till you solve it.

Read this chapter carefully and I think you will find the answer to this important life question which you and every man must solve if he expects ever to have more each Monday morning, after pay day, than he had the week before.

To begin with, all wealth depends upon a clear understanding of the fact that mind—thought—is the only creator. The great business of life is thinking. Control your thoughts and you control circumstance.

Just as the first law of gain is desire, so the formula of success is BELIEF. Believe that you have it—see it as an existent fact—and anything you can rightly wish for is yours. Belief is "the substance of things hoped for, the evidence of things not seen."

You have seen men, inwardly no more capable than yourself, accomplish the seemingly impossible. You have seen others, after years of hopeless struggle, suddenly win their most cherished dreams. And you've often wondered, "What is the power that gives new life to their dying ambitions, that supplies new impetus to their jaded desires, that gives them a new start on the road to success?"

That power is belief—faith. Someone, something, gave them a new belief in themselves and a new faith in their power to win—and they leaped ahead and wrested success from seemingly certain defeat.

Do you remember the picture Harold Lloyd was in two or three years ago, showing a country boy who was afraid of his shadow? Every boy in the countryside bedeviled him. Until one day his grandmother gave him a talisman that she assured him his grandfather had carried through the Civil War and which, so she said, had the property of making its owner invincible. Nothing could hurt him, she told him, while he wore this talisman. Nothing could stand up against him. He believed her. And the next time the bully of the town started to cuff him around, he wiped up the earth with him. And that was only the start. Before the year was out he had made a reputation as the most daring soul in the community.

Then, when his grandmother felt that he was thoroughly cured, she told him the truth—that the "talisman" was merely a piece of old junk she'd picked up by the roadside—that she knew all he needed was *faith in himself,* belief that he could do these things.

THE TALISMAN OF NAPOLEON

Stories like that are common. It is such a well-established truth that you can do only what you think you can that the theme is a favorite one with authors. I remember reading a story years ago of an artist—a mediocre sort of artist—who was visiting the field of Waterloo and happened upon a curious lump of metal half buried in the dirt, which so attracted him that he picked it up and put it in his pocket. Soon thereafter he noticed a sudden increase in confidence, an absolute faith in himself, not only as to his own chosen line of work but in his ability to handle any situation that might present itself. He painted a great picture—just to show that he *could* do it. Not content with that, he visioned an empire with Mexico as its basis, actually led a revolt that carried all before it—until one day he lost his talisman. *And immediately his bubble burst.*

I instance this just to illustrate the point that it is *your own belief in yourself* that counts. It is the consciousness of dominant power within you that makes all things attainable. *You can do anything you think you can.* This knowledge is literally the gift of the gods, for through it you can solve every human problem. It should make of you an incurable optimist. It is the open door to welfare. *Keep it open*—by expecting to gain everything that is right.

You are entitled to every good thing. Therefore expect nothing but good. Defeat does not *need* to follow victory. You don't have to "knock wood" every time you congratulate yourself that things have been going well with you. Victory should follow victory—and it will if you "let this mind be in you which was also in Christ Jesus." It is the mind that means health and life and boundless opportunity and recompense. No limitation rests upon you. So don't let any enter your life. Remember that Mind will do every good thing for you. It will remove mountains for you.

"Bring ye all the tithes into the storehouse, and prove me now herewith, saith the Lord of hosts, if I will not open you the windows of heaven, and pour you out a blessing, that there shall not be room enough to receive it."

Bring all your thoughts, your desires, your aims, your talents, into the Storehouse—the Consciousness of Good, the law of infinite supply—and prove these blessings. There is every reason to know that you are entitled to adequate provision. Everything that is involved in supply is a thing of thought. Now reach out, stretch your mind, try to comprehend *unlimited thought, unlimited supply.*

Do not think that supply must come through one or two channels. It is not for you to dictate to Universal Mind the means through which It shall send Its gifts to you. There are millions of channels through which It can reach you. Your part is to impress upon Mind your need, your earnest desire, your boundless belief in the resources and the willingness of Universal Mind to help you. Plant the seed of desire. Nourish it with a clear visualization of the ripened fruit. Water it with sincere faith. But leave the means to Universal Mind.

Open up your mind. Clear out the channels of thought. Keep yourself in a state of receptivity. Gain a mental attitude in which you are constantly *expecting good.* You have the fundamental right to all good, you know. "According to your faith, be it unto you."

The trouble with most of us is that we are mentally lazy. It is so much easier to go along with the crowd than to break trail for ourselves. But the great discoverers, the great inventors, the great geniuses in all lines have been men who dared to break with tradition, who defied precedent, who believed that there is no limit to what Mind can do—and who stuck to that belief until their goal was won, in spite of all the sneers and ridicule of the wiseacres and the "It-can't-be-done'rs."

Not only that, but they were never satisfied with achieving just one success. They knew that the first success is like the first olive out of the bottle. All the others come out the more easily for it. They realized that they were a part of the Creative Intelligence of the Universe, and that the part shares all the properties of the whole. And that realization gave them the faith to strive for any right thing, the knowledge that the only limit upon their capabilities was the limit of their desires. Knowing that, they couldn't be satisfied with any ordinary success. They had to keep on and on and on.

Edison didn't sit down and fold his hands when he gave us the talking machine. Or the electric light. These great achievements merely opened the way to new fields of accomplishment.

Open up the channels between your mind and Universal Mind, and there is no limit to the riches that will come pouring in. Concentrate your thoughts on the particular thing you are most interested in, and ideas in abundance will come flooding down, opening up a dozen ways of winning the goal you are striving for.

But don't let one success—no matter how great—satisfy you. The Law of Creation, you know, is the Law of Growth. You can't stand still. You must go forward—or be passed by. Complacency—self-satisfaction—is the greatest enemy of achievement. You must keep looking forward. Like Alexander, you must be constantly seeking new worlds to conquer. Depend upon it, the power will come to meet the need. There is no such thing as failing powers, if we look to Mind for our source of supply. The only failure of mind comes from worry and fear—or from disuse.

William James, the famous psychologist, taught that "the more mind does, the more it can do." For ideas release energy. You can *do* more and better work than you have ever done. You can *know* more than you know now. You know from your own experience that under proper mental conditions of joy or enthusiasm, you can do three or four times the work without fatigue that you can ordinarily. Tiredness is more boredom than actual physical fatigue. You can work almost indefinitely when the work is a pleasure.

You've seen sickly persons, frail persons, who couldn't do an hour's light work without exhaustion, suddenly buckle down when heavy responsibilities were thrown upon them, and grow strong and rugged under the load. Crises not only draw upon the reserve power you have, but they help to create new power.

"IT COULDN'T BE DONE"

It may be that you have been deluded by the thought of incompetence. It may be that you have been told so often that you cannot do certain things that you've come to believe you can't. Remember that success or failure is merely a state of mind. Believe you cannot do a thing—and you can't. Know that you *can* do it—and you *will*. You must *see yourself doing it.*

"If you think you are beaten, you are;
If you think you dare not, you don't;
If you'd like to win, but you think you can't,
It's almost a cinch you won't;
If you think you'll lose, you've lost,
For out in the world you'll find
Success begins with a fellow's will—
It's all in the state of mind.

"Full many a race is lost
Ere even a race is run,
And many a coward fails
Ere even his work's begun.
Think big, and your deeds will grow,
Think small and you fall behind,
Think that you can, and you will;
It's all in the state of mind.

"If you think you are outclassed, you are;
You've got to think high to rise;
You've got to be sure of yourself before
You can ever win a prize.
Life's battle doesn't always go
To the stronger or faster man;
But sooner or later, the man who wins
Is the fellow who thinks he can."

There's a vast difference between a proper understanding of one's own ability and a determination to make the best of it—and offensive egotism. It is absolutely necessary for every man to believe in himself before he can make the most of himself. All of us have something to sell. It may be our goods, it may be our abilities, it may be our services. You've got to believe in yourself to make your buyer take stock in you at par and accrued interest. You've got to feel the same personal solicitude over a customer lost as a revivalist over a backslider, and hold special services to bring him back into the fold. You've got to get up every morning with determination if you're going to go to bed that night with satisfaction.

There's mighty sound sense in the saying that all the world loves a booster. The one and only thing you have to win success with is MIND. For your mind to function at its highest capacity, you've got to be charged with good cheer and optimism. No one ever did a good piece of work while in a negative frame of mind. Your best work is always done when you are feeling happy and optimistic.

And a happy disposition is the *result*—not the *cause*—of happy, cheery thinking. Health and prosperity are the *results* primarily of optimistic thoughts. *You* make the pattern. If the impress you have left on the world about you seems faint and weak, don't blame fate—blame your pattern! You will never cultivate a brave, courageous demeanor by thinking cowardly thoughts. You cannot gather figs from thistles. You will never make your dreams come true by choking them with doubts and fears. You've got to put foundations under your air castles, foundations of UNDERSTANDING and BELIEF. Your chances of success in any undertaking can always be measured by your BELIEF in yourself.

Are your surroundings discouraging? Do you feel that if you were in another's place success would be easier? Just bear in mind that your real environment is within you. All the factors of success or failure are in your inner world. *You* make that own inner world—and through it your outer world. You can choose the material from which to build it. If you've not chosen wisely in the past, you can choose again now the material you want to rebuild it with. The richness of life is within you. No one has failed so long as he can begin again.

Start right in and *do* all those things you feel you have it in you to do. Ask permission of no man. Concentrating your thought upon any proper undertaking will make its achievement possible. Your belief that you *can* do the thing gives your thought forces their power. Fortune waits upon you. Seize her boldly, hold her—and she is yours. She belongs rightfully to you. But if you cringe to her, if you go up to her doubtfully, timidly, she will pass you by in scorn. For she is a fickle jade who must be mastered, who loves boldness, who admires confidence.

A Roman boasted that it was sufficient for him to strike the ground with his foot and legions would spring up. And his very boldness cowed his opponents. It is the same with your mind. Take the first step, and your mind will mobilize all its forces to your aid. But the first essential is that you *begin.* Once the battle is started, all that is within and without you will come to your assistance, if you attack in earnest and meet each obstacle with resolution. But *you* have got to start things.

"The Lord helps them that help themselves" is a truth as old as man. It is, in fact, plain common sense. Your subconscious mind has all power, but your conscious mind is the watchman at the gate. *It* has got to open the door. It has got to press the spring that releases the infinite energy. No failure is possible in the accomplishment of any right object you may have in life, if you but understand your power and will perseveringly try to use it in the proper way.

The men who have made their mark in this world all had one trait in common—*they believed in themselves!* "But," you may say, "how can I believe in myself when I have never yet done anything worth while, when everything I put my hand to seems to fail?" You can't, of course. That is, you couldn't if you had to depend upon your conscious mind alone. But just remember what one far greater than you said—"I can of mine own self do nothing. The Father that is within me—He doeth the works."

That same "Father" is within you. And it is by knowing that He *is* in you, and that through Him you can do anything that is right, that you can acquire that belief in yourself which is so necessary. Certainly the Mind that imaged the heavens and the earth and all that they contain has all wisdom, all power, all abundance. With this Mind to call upon, you know there is no problem too difficult for you to undertake. The *knowing* of this is the first step. *Faith.* But St. James tells us—"Faith without works is dead." So go on to the next step. Decide on the one thing you want most from life. No matter what it may be. There is no limit, you know, to Mind. Visualize this thing that you want. See it, feel it, BELIEVE in it. Make your mental blue-print, and *begin to build!*

Suppose some people DO laugh at your idea. Suppose Reason does say— "It can't be done!" People laughed at Galileo. They laughed at Henry Ford. Reason contended for countless ages that the earth was flat. Reason said—or so numerous automotive engineers argued—that the Ford motor wouldn't run. But the earth *is* round—and the twelfth or fifteenth million Ford *is* on the road.

Let us start right now putting into practice some of these truths that you have learned. What do you want most of life right now? Take that one desire, concentrate on it, impress it upon your subconscious mind.

Psychologists have discovered that the best time to make suggestions to your subconscious mind is just before going to sleep, when the senses are quiet and the attention is lax. So let us take your desire and suggest it to your subconscious mind tonight. The two prerequisites are the earnest DESIRE and an intelligent, understanding BELIEF. Someone has said, you know, that education is three-fourths encouragement, and the encouragement is the suggestion that the thing can be done.

You know that you can have what you want, if you want it badly enough and can believe in it earnestly enough. So tonight, just before you drop off to sleep, concentrate your thought on this thing that you most desire from life. BELIEVE that you have it. SEE YOURSELF possessing it. FEEL yourself using it.

Do that every night until you ACTUALLY DO BELIEVE that you have the thing you want. When you reach that point, *YOU WILL HAVE IT!*

CHAPTER 10

"This Freedom"

"Ye shall know the truth
And the Truth shall make you free."

I have heard that quotation ever since I was a little child. Most of us have. But to me it was never anything much but a quotation—until a few years ago. It is only in the past several years that I have begun to get an inkling of the real meaning of it—an understanding of the comfort back of it. Perhaps to you, too, it has been no more than a sonorous phrase. If so, you will be interested in what I have since gotten from it.

To begin with, what is the "truth" that is so often referred to in all our religious teaching? The truth about what? And what is it going to free us from?

The truth as I see it now is the underlying reality in everything we meet in life. There is, for instance, one right way to solve any given problem in mathematics. That one right way is the truth as far as that problem is concerned. To know it is to free yourself from all doubt and vain imagining and error. It is to free yourself from any trouble that might arise through solving the problem incorrectly.

In the same way, there is but one BEST way of solving every situation that confronts you. That BEST way is the truth. To know it is to make you free from all worry or trouble in connection with that situation. For if it is met in the RIGHT way, only good can come of it.

Then there is your body. There is only one RIGHT idea of every organism in your body. One CORRECT method of functioning for each of them. And Universal Mind holds that RIGHT idea, that CORRECT method. The functioning of your body, the rebuilding of each cell and tissue, is the work of your subconscious mind. If you will constantly hold before it the thought that its model is perfection, that weakness or sickness or deformity is merely ABSENCE of perfection—not a reality in itself—in short, if you will realize the *Truth* concerning your body, your subconscious mind will speedily make you free and keep you free from every ill.

It matters not what is troubling you today. If you will KNOW that whatever it may seem to be is merely the absence of the true idea, if you will realize that the only thing that counts is the truth that Universal Mind knows about your body, you can make that truth manifest.

Affirm the good, the true—and the evil will vanish. It is like turning on the light—the darkness immediately disappears. For there is no actual substance in darkness—it is merely absence of light. Nor is there any substance in sickness or evil—it is merely the absence of health or good.

That is the truth that was the mentality of Jesus—what Paul describes as "the mind which was also in Christ Jesus."

Jesus declared that we should know the truth, and the truth would make us free. That truth was the power which He exercised. He had so perfect an understanding of truth that it gave Him absolute dominion over evil, enabled Him to heal diseases of every nature, even to raise the dead. The power that He exercised then was not confined to His time, nor limited to His own immediate followers. "Lo, I am with you always," He said, "even unto the end of the world." And He is just as available to us now as He was to His own disciples 1,900 years ago.

"I have given you power to tread serpents and scorpions under foot and to trample on all the power of the enemy; and in no case shall anything do you harm."

That gift was never meant to be confined to His own disciples or to any other one group. God has never dealt in special or temporary gifts. He gives to *all*—to all who will accept—to all who have an understanding heart.

All sickness, all poverty, all sorrow, is the result of the incorrect use of some gift of God, which in itself is inherently good. It is just as though we took the numbers that were given us to work out a problem and put them in the wrong places. The result would be incorrect, inharmonious. We would not be expressing the truth. The moment we rearrange those numbers properly, we get the correct answer—harmony—the *truth!* There was nothing wrong with the principle of mathematics before—the fault was all with us, with our incorrect arrangement of the figures.

What is true of the principle of mathematics is true of every principle. The principle is changeless, undying. It is only our expression of the principle that changes as our understanding of it becomes more thorough. Lightning held only terror for man until he made of electricity his servant. Steam was only so much waste until man learned to harness it. Fire and water are the most destructive forces known—until properly used, then they are man's greatest helpers. There is nothing wrong with any gift of God—once we find the way to use it. The truth is always there if we can find the principle behind it. The figures in mathematics are never bad. It is merely our incorrect arrangement of them.

The great need is an open mind and the desire for understanding. How far in the science of mathematics would you get if you approached the study of it with the preconceived notion that two plus two makes five, and nothing you heard to the contrary was going to change that belief? "Except ye turn, and become as little children, ye shall not enter into the kingdom of heaven." You must drop all your preconceived ideas, all your prejudices. You must never say—"Oh, that sounds like so-and-so. I don't want any of it." Just remember that any great movement must have at least a grain of truth back of it, else it could never grow to any size. Seek that grain of truth. Be open-minded. Keep your eyes and ears open for the truth. If you can do this, you will find that new wordings, different interpretations, are but the outer shell. You can still see the Truth beneath, the Christ that "before Abraham was, I am."

THE ONLY POWER

He who is looking for wisdom, power, or permanent success will find it only within. Mind is the only cause. Your body is healthy or sick according to the images of thought you impress upon your subconscious mind. If you will hold thoughts of health instead of sickness, if you will banish all thoughts of disease and decay, you can build up a perfect body. Dr. William S. Patten of New York says, "To know and to understand the organization of mind and to recognize the action of mind is the first and the only requisite of a sound body."

For all disease starts in mind. It may be in your own conscious mind, from reading of an epidemic or from meeting with circumstances which education has taught you will bring about disease. It may be suggested to your subconscious mind, as so frequently happens with young children, by the fears and worries and thoughts of contagion of those around you.

But whichever it is, it is FEAR that starts it. You visualize, consciously or unconsciously, the disease that you fear, and because that is the image held before your thought, your body proceeds to build in accordance with that model. You believe that disease is necessary, that you have got to expect a certain amount of it. You hear of it every day, and subconsciously at least you are constantly in fear of it. And through that very fear you create it, when if you would spend that same amount of time thinking and believing in the necessity of HEALTH, you would never need to know disease.

Disease is not sent by God. It is not a visitation of Providence. If it were, what would be the use of doctoring it? You couldn't fight against the power of God!

God never sent us anything but good. He never gave us disease. When we allow disease to take hold of us, it is because we have lost touch with God—lost the perfect model of us that He holds in mind. And what we have got to strive for is to get back the belief in that perfect model—to forget the diseased image we are holding in our thought.

Remember the story of Alexander and his famous horse, Bucephalus? No one could ride the horse because it was afraid of its shadow. But Alexander faced it towards the sun—and rode it without trouble. Face towards the sun and the shadows will fall behind you, too. Face towards the perfect image of every organ, and the shadows of disease will never touch you.

There is no germ in a draft capable of giving you a cold. There is no bacteria in exposure to the weather that can give you a fever or pneumonia. It is you that gives them to yourself. The draft doesn't reason this out. Neither does your body. They are both of them merely phases of matter. They are not intelligent. It is your conscious mind that has been educated to think that a cold must follow exposure to a draft. This it is that suggests it to your subconscious mind and brings the cold into being.

Before you decide again that you have a cold, ask yourself, Who is it that is taking this cold? It cannot be my nose, for it has no intelligence. It does only what my subconscious mind directs. And anyway, how could my nose know that a draft of air has been playing on the back of my neck? If it wasn't my nose that decided it, what was it? The only thing it can have been is my mind. Well, if mind can tell me to have a cold, surely it can stop that cold, too. So let's reverse the process, and instead of holding before the subconscious mind images of colds and fevers, think only of health and life and strength. Instead of trying to think back to discover how we "caught" cold, and thus strengthening the conviction that we have one, let us deny its existence and so knock the props out from under the creative faculties that are originating the cold. Let us hold before our subconscious mind only the perfect idea of nose and head and throat that is in Universal Mind. Let us make it use the Truth for its pattern, instead of the illusory ideas of conscious mind.

Every form of disease or sickness is solely the result of wrong thinking. The primary law of being is the law of health and life. When you recognize this, when you hold before your mind's eye only a perfect body, perfect organisms functioning perfectly, you will "realize the truth that makes you free."

Farnsworth in his "Practical Psychology" tells of a physician who has lived on a very restricted diet for years while at home. But about once a year he comes to New York for a week. While here, he eats anything and everything that his fancy dictates, and never suffers the least inconvenience. As soon as he gets home he has to return to his diet. Unless he sticks to his diet, he expects to be ill—*and he is ill.* "As a man thinketh, so is he." What one expects to get he is apt to get, especially where health is concerned. For matter has no sensation of its own. The conscious mind is what produces pain, is what feels, acts or impedes action.

Functional disorders are caused by certain suggestions getting into the subconsciousness and remaining there. They are not due to physical but to mental causes—due to wrong thinking. The basis of all functional disorders is in the mind, though the manifestation be dyspepsia, melancholia, palpitation of the heart, or any one of a hundred others. There is nothing organically wrong with the body. It is your mental image that is out of adjustment. Change the one and you cure the other.

In this day of the gymnasium and the daily dozen, it may sound impractical to suggest that it is the mind, not the body, which needs the care. But I am far from being the first to suggest it.

There is a very successful physician in London whose teaching is that gymnastic exercise does more harm than good. He contends that the only exercise necessary for the perfect development of the body is yawning and stretching.

I would go further than that. I would say that no physical exercise is *essential* to the perfect development of the body. That since the only cause is mind, the principal good of exercise is that when we go through the motions we are impressing upon our subconscious mind the picture of the perfect figure that we would have. And that mental visualization is what brings the results.

You can get the same results without the physical exercise by visualizing in your mind's eye the figure of the man you want to be, by intensely desiring it, by BELIEVING that you have it.

You can win to perfect health by knowing that there is but one right idea in Universal Mind for every organism in your body—that this right idea is perfect and undying—that you have only to hold it before you subconscious mind to see it realized in your body. *This is the truth that makes you free.*

CHAPTER 11

The Law of Attraction

For life is the mirror of king and slave.
'Tis just what you are and do;
Then give to the world the best you have,
And the best will come back to you.

—MADELINE BRIDGES

The old adage that "he profits most who serves best" is no mere altruism.

Look around you. What businesses are going ahead? What men are making the big successes? Are they the ones who grab the passing dollar, careless of what they offer in return? Or are they those who are striving always to give a little greater value, a little more work than they are paid for?

When scales are balanced evenly, a trifle of extra weight thrown into either side overbalances the other as effectively as a ton.

In the same way, a little better value, a little extra effort, makes the man or the business stand out from the great mass of mediocrity like a tall man among pigmies, and brings results out of all proportion to the additional effort involved.

It pays—not merely altruistically, but in good, hard, round dollars—to give a little more value than seems necessary, to work a bit harder than you are paid for. It's that extra ounce of value that counts.

For the law of attraction is service. We receive in proportion as we give out. In fact, we usually receive in far greater proportion. "Cast thy bread upon the waters and it will return to you an hundred-fold."

Back of everything is the immutable law of the Universe—that what you are is but the effect. Your thoughts are the causes. The only way you can change the effect is by first changing the cause.

People live in poverty and want because they are so wrapped up in their sufferings that they give out thoughts only of lack and sorrow. They expect want. They open the door of their mind only to hardship and sickness and poverty. True—they hope for something better—but their hopes are so drowned by their fears that they never have a chance.

You cannot receive good while expecting evil. You cannot demonstrate plenty while looking for poverty. "Blessed is he that expecteth much, for verily his soul shall be filled." Solomon outlined the law when he said:

> *"There is that scattereth, and increaseth yet more;*
> *And there is that withholdeth more than is meet, but it tendeth only to want.*
> *The liberal soul shall be made fat;*
> *And he that watereth shall be watered also himself."*

The Universal Mind expresses itself largely through the individual. It is continually seeking an outlet. It is like a vast reservoir of water, constantly replenished by mountain springs. Cut a channel to it and the water will flow in ever-increasing volume. In the same way, if you once open up a channel of service by which the Universal Mind can express itself through you, its gifts will flow in ever-increasing volume and YOU will be enriched in the process.

This is the idea through which great bankers are made. A foreign country needs millions for development. Its people are hard-working but lack the necessary implements to make their work productive. How are they to find the money?

They go to a banker—put their problem up to him. He has not the money himself, but he knows how and where to raise it. He sells the promise to pay of the foreign country (their bonds, in other words) to people who have money to invest. His is merely a service. But it is such an invaluable service that both sides are glad to pay him liberally for it.

In the same way, by opening up a channel between universal supply and human needs—by doing your neighbors or your friends or your customers service—you are bound to profit yourself. And the wider you open your channel—the greater service you give or the better values you offer—the more things are bound to flow through your channel, the more you are going to profit thereby.

But you've got to *use* your talent if you want to profit from it. It matters not how small your service—using it will make it greater. You don't have to retire to a cell and pray. That is a selfish method—selfish concern for your own soul to the exclusion of all others. Mere self-denial or asceticism as such does no one good. You've got to DO something, to USE the talents God has given you to make the world better for your having been in it.

Remember the parable of the talents. You know what happened to the man who went off and hid his talent, whereas those who made use of theirs were given charge over many things.

That parable, it has always seemed to me, expresses the whole law of life. The only right is to *use* all the forces of good. The only wrong is to *neglect* or to abuse them.

"Thou shalt love the Lord thy God. This is the first and the greatest Commandment." Thou shalt show thy love by using to the best possible advantage the good things (the "talents" of the parable) that He has placed in your hands. "And the second is like unto it. Thou shalt love thy neighbor as thyself." Thou shalt not abuse the good things that have been provided you in such prodigality, by using them against your neighbor. Instead, thou shalt treat him (love him) as you would be treated by him. Thou shalt use the good about you for the advantage of all.

If you are a banker, you've got to use the money you have in order to make more money. If you are a merchant, you've got to sell the goods you have in order to buy more goods. If you are a doctor, you must help the patient you have in order to get more practice. If you are a clerk, you must do your work a little better than those around you if you want to earn more money than they. And if you want more of the universal supply, you must use that which you have in such a way as to make yourself of greater service to those around you.

"Whosoever shall be great among you," said Jesus, "shall be your minister, and whosoever of you will be the chiefest, shall be servant of all." In other words, if you would be great, you must serve. And he who serves most shall be greatest of all.

If you want to make more money, instead of seeking it for yourself, see how you can make more for others. In the process you will inevitably make more for yourself, too. We get as we give—but we must give first.

It matters not where you start—you may be a day laborer. But still you can give—give a bit more of energy, of work, of thought, than you are paid for. "Whosoever shall compel thee to go a mile," said Jesus, "go with him twain." Try to put a little extra skill into your work. Use your mind to find some better way of doing whatever task may be set for you. It won't be long before you are out of the common labor class.

There is no kind of work that cannot be bettered by thought. There is no method that cannot be improved by thought. So give generously of your thought to your work. Think every minute you are at it—"Isn't there some way in which this could be done easier, quicker, better?" Read in your spare time everything that relates to your own work or to the job ahead of you. In these days of magazines and books and libraries, few are the occupations that are not thoroughly covered in some good work.

Remember in Lorimer's "Letters of a Self-Made Merchant to His Son," the young fellow that old Gorgan Graham hired against his better judgment and put in the "barrel gang" just to get rid of him quickly? Before the month was out the young fellow had thought himself out of that job by persuading the boss to get a machine that did the work at half the cost and with a third of the gang. Graham just had to raise his pay and put him higher up. But he wouldn't stay put. No matter what the job, he always found some way it could be done better and with fewer people. Until he reached the top of the ladder.

There are plenty of men like that in actual life. They won't stay down. They are as full of bounce as a cat with a small boy and a dog after it. Thrown to the dog from an upper window, it is using the time of falling to get set for the next jump. By the time the dog leaps for where it hit, the cat is up the tree across the street.

The true spirit of business is the spirit of that plucky old Danish sea captain, Peter Tordenskjold. Attacked by a Swedish frigate, after all his crew but one had been killed and his supply of cannon balls was exhausted, Peter boldly kept up the fight, firing pewter dinner plates and mugs from his one remaining gun.

One of the pewter mugs hit the Swedish captain and killed him, and Peter sailed off triumphant!

Look around YOU now. How can YOU give greater value for what you get? How can you SERVE better? How can you make more money for your employers or save more for your customers? Keep that thought ever in the forefront of your mind and *you'll never need to worry about making more for yourself!*

A BLANK CHECK

There was an article by Gardner Hunting in a recent issue of "Christian Business" that was so good that I reprint it here entire:

"All my life I have known in a vague way that getting money is the result of earning it; but I have never had a perfect vision of that truth till recently. Summed up now, the result of all my experience, pleasant and unpleasant, is that a man gets back exactly what he gives out, only multiplied.

"If I give to anybody service of a kind that he wants I shall get back the benefit myself. If I give more service I shall get more benefit. If I give a great deal more, I shall get a great deal more. But I shall get back more than I give. Exactly as when I plant a bushel of potatoes, I get back thirty or forty bushels, and more in proportion to the attention I give the growing crop. If I give more to my employer than he expects of me, he will give me a raise—and on no other condition. What is more, his giving me a raise does not depend on his fair-mindedness—he has to give it to me or lose me, because if he does not appreciate me somebody else will.

"But this is only part of it. If I give help to the man whose desk is next to mine, it will come back to me multiplied, even if he apparently is a rival. What I give to him, I give to the firm, and the firm will value it, because it is team-work in the organization that the firm primarily wants, not brilliant individual performance. If I have an enemy in the organization, the same rule holds; if I give him, with the purpose of helping him, something that will genuinely help him, I am giving service to the organization. Great corporations appreciate the peace-maker, for a prime requisite in their success is harmony among employees. If my boss is unappreciative, the same rule holds; if I give him more, in advance of appreciation, he cannot withhold his appreciation and keep his own job.

"The more you think about this law, the deeper you will see it goes. It literally hands you a blank check, signed by the Maker of Universal Law, and leaves you to fill in the amount—and the kind—of payment you want! Mediocre successes are those that obey this law a little way—that fill in the check with a small amount—but that stop short of big vision in it. If every employee would only get the idea of this law firmly fixed in him as a principle, not subject to wavering with fluctuating moods, the success of the organization would be miraculous. One of my fears is apt to be that, by promoting the other fellow's success, I am side-tracking my own; but the exact opposite is the truth.

"Suppose every employee would look at his own case as an exact parallel to that of his firm. What does his firm give for the money it gets from the public? Service! Service in advance! The better the service that is given out, the more money comes back. What does the firm do to bring public attention to its service? It advertises; that is part of the service. Now, suppose that I, as an employee, begin giving my service to the firm in advance of all hoped-for payment. Suppose I advertise my service. How do I do either? I cannot do anything constructive in that firm's office or store or plant or premises that is not service, from filing a letter correctly to mending the fence or pleasing a customer; from looking up a word for the stenographer, to encouraging her to look it up herself; demonstrating a machine to a customer or encouraging him to demonstrate it himself; from helping my immediate apparent rival to get a raise, to selling the whole season's output. As for advertising myself, I begin advertising myself the moment I walk into the office or the store or the shop in the morning; I cannot help it. Everybody who looks at me sees my advertisement. Everybody around me has my advertisement before his eyes all day long. So has the boss—my immediate chief and the head of the firm, no matter where they are. And if I live up to my advertising, nobody can stop me from selling my goods—my services! The more a man knocks me, the more he advertises me; because he calls attention to me; and if I am delivering something better than he says I am, the interested parties—my employers—will see it, and will not be otherwise influenced by what he says.

"More than that, I must give to every human being I come in contact with, from my wife to the bootblack who shines my shoes; from my brother to my sworn foe. Sometimes people will tell you to smile; but the smile I give has got to be a real smile that lives up to its advertising. If I go around grinning like a Cheshire cat, the Cheshire cat grin will be what I get back—multiplied! If I give the real thing, I'll get back the real thing—multiplied! If anybody objects that this is a selfish view to take, I answer him that any law of salvation from anything by anybody that has ever been offered for any purpose is a selfish view to take. The only unselfishness that has ever been truly taught is that of giving a lesser thing in hope of receiving a greater.

"Now, why am I so sure of this law? How can you be sure? I have watched it work; it works everywhere. You have only to try it, and keep on trying it and it will prove true for you. It is not true because I say so, nor because anybody else says so; it is just true. Theosophists call it the law of Karma; humanitarians call it the law of Service; business men call it the law of common sense; Jesus Christ called it the law of Love. It rules whether I know it or not, whether I believe it or not, whether I defy it or not. I *can't* break it! Jesus of Nazareth, without reference to any religious idea you may have about Him, without consideration as to whether He was or was not divine, was the greatest business Man that ever lived, and he said: 'Give and ye shall receive—good measure, pressed down, shaken together, running over!' And this happens to be so—not because He said it—but because it is the Truth, which we all, whether we admit it or not, worship *as* God. No man can honestly say that he does not put the truth supreme.

"It is the truth—the principle of giving and receiving—only there are few men who go the limit on it. But going the limit is the way to unlimited returns!

"What shall I give? What I have, of course. Suppose you believe in this idea—and suppose you should start giving it out, the idea itself, tactfully, wisely, and living it yourself in your organization. How long do you think it will be before you are a power in that organization, recognized as such and getting pay as such? It is more valuable than all the cleverness and special information you can possibly possess without it. What you have, give—to everybody. If you have an idea, do not save it for your own use only; give it. It is the best thing you have to give and therefore the thing best to give—and therefore the thing that will bring the best back to you. I believe that if a man would follow this principle, even to his trade-secrets, he would profit steadily more and more; and more certainly than he will by holding on to anything for himself. He would never have to worry about his own affairs—because he would be working on fundamental law. Law never fails—and it will be easy for you to discover what is or is not law. And if law is worth using part of the time, it is worth using all the time.

"Look around you first, with an eye to seeing the truth, and then put the thing to the test. Through both methods of investigation you will find a blank check waiting for you to fill in with 'whatsoever you desire,' and a new way to pray and to get what you pray for."

CHAPTER 12

The Three Requisites

"Waste no tears
Upon the blotted record of lost years,
But turn the leaf, and smile, oh smile, to see
The fair white pages that remain for thee.

"Prate not of thy repentance. But believe
The spark divine dwells in thee: let it grow.
That which the upreaching spirit can achieve
The grand and all creative forces know;
They will assist and strengthen as the light
Lifts up the acorn to the oak-tree's height.
Thou hast but to resolve, and lo! God's whole
Great universe shall fortify thy soul."

—ELLA WHEELER WILCOX

Sometime today or tomorrow or next month, in practically every commercial office and manufacturing plant in the United States, an important executive will sit back in his chair and study a list of names on a sheet of white paper before him.

Your name may be on it.

A position of responsibility is open and he is face-to-face with the old, old problem—"Where can I find the man?"

The faces, the words, the work, the impressions of various men will pass through his mind in quick review. What is the first question he will ask concerning each?

"Which man is strongest on initiative, which one can best assume responsibility?"

Other things being equal, THAT is the man who will get the job. For the first requisite in business as in social life is confidence in yourself—*knowledge of your power.* Given that, the second is easy—initiative or *the courage to start things.* Lots of men have ideas, but few have the confidence in themselves or the courage to start anything.

With belief and initiative, the third requisite follows almost as a matter of course—*the faith to go ahead* and do things in the face of all obstacles.

"Oh, God," said Leonardo da Vinci, "you sell us everything for the price of an effort."

Certainly no one had a better chance to know than he. An illegitimate son, brought up in the family of his father, the misfortune of his birth made him the source of constant derision. He had to do something to lift himself far above the crowd. And he did. "For the price of an effort" he became the greatest artist in Italy—probably the greatest in the world—in a day when Italy was famous for her artists. Kings and princes felt honored at being associated with this illegitimate boy. He made the name he had no right to famous for his work alone.

"Work out your own salvation," said Paul. And the first requisite in working it out is a knowledge of your power. "Every man of us has all the centuries in him."—Morley. All the ages behind you have bequeathed you stores of abilities which you are allowing to lie latent. Those abilities are stored up in your subconscious mind. Call upon them. Use them. As Whittier put it—

"All the good the past has had
Remains to make our own time glad."

Are you an artist? The cunning of a da Vinci, the skill of a Rembrandt, the vision of a Reynolds is behind those fingers of yours. Use the Genie-of-your-Mind to call upon them.

Are you a surgeon, a lawyer, a minister, an engineer, a business man? Keep before your mind's eye the biggest men who have ever done the things you now are doing. Use them as your model. And not as your model simply, but as your inspiration. Start in where they left off. Call upon the innermost recesses of your subconscious mind, for their skill, their judgment, their initiative. Realize that you have it in you to be as great as they. Realize that all that they did, all that they learned, all the skill they acquired is stored safely away in Universal Mind and that through your subconscious mind *you have ready access to it.*

The mind in you is the same mind that animated all the great conquerers of the past, all the great inventors, all the great artists, statesmen, leaders, business men. What they have done is but a tithe of what still remains to do—of what men in your day and your children's day will do. You can have a part in it. Stored away within you is every power that any man or woman ever possessed. It awaits only your call.

In "Thoughts on Business," we read: "It is a great day in a man's life when he truly begins to discover himself. The latent capacities of every man are greater than he realizes, and he may find them if he diligently seeks for them. A man may own a tract of land for many years without knowing its value. He may think of it as merely a pasture. But one day he discovers evidences of coal and finds a rich vein beneath his land. While mining and prospecting for coal he discovers deposits of granite. In boring for water he strikes oil. Later he discovers a vein of copper ore, and after that silver and gold. These things were there all the time—even when he thought of his land merely as a pasture. But they have a value only when they are discovered and utilized.

"Not every pasture contains deposits of silver and gold, neither oil nor granite, nor even coal. But beneath the surface of every man there must be, in the nature of things, a latent capacity greater than has yet been discovered. And one discovery must lead to another until the man finds the deep wealth of his own possibilities. History is full of the acts of men who discovered somewhat of their own capacity; but history has yet to record the man who fully discovered all that he might have been."

Everything that has been done, thought, gained, or been is in Universal Mind. And you are a part of Universal Mind. You have access to it. You can call upon it for all you need in the same way you can go to your files or to a library for information. If you can realize this fact, you will find in it the key to the control of every circumstance, the solution of every problem, the satisfaction of every right desire.

But to use that key, you've got to bear in mind the three requisites of faith in your powers, initiative, and courage to start. "Who would stand before a blackboard," says "Science and Health," "and pray the principle of mathematics to solve the problem? The rule is already established, and it is our task to work out the solution." In the same way, all knowledge you can need is in Universal Mind, but it is up to *you* to tap that mind.

And without the three requisites you will never do it.

Never let discouragement hold you back. Discouragement is the most dangerous feeling there is, because it is the most insidious. Generally it is looked upon as harmless, and for that very reason it is the more sinister. For failure and success are oftentimes separated by only the distance of that one word—Discouragement.

There is an old-time fable that the devil once held a sale and offered all the tools of his trade to anyone who would pay their price. They were spread out on the table, each one labeled—hatred, and malice, and envy, and despair, and sickness, and sensuality—all the weapons that everyone knows so well.

But off on one side, apart from the rest, lay a harmless-looking, wedge-shaped instrument marked "Discouragement." It was old and worn-looking, but it was priced far above all the rest. When asked the reason why, the devil replied:

"Because I can use this one so much more easily than the others. No one knows that it belongs to me, so with it I can open doors that are tight bolted against the others. Once I get inside I can use any tool that suits me best."

No one ever knows how small is the margin between failure and success. Frequently the two are separated only by the width of that one word—*discouragement.* Ask Ford, ask Edison, ask any successful man and he will tell you how narrow is the chasm that separates failure from success, how surely it can be bridged by perseverance and faith.

Cultivate confidence in yourself. Cultivate the feeling that you ARE succeeding. Know that you have unlimited power to do every right thing. Know that with Universal Mind to draw upon, no position is too difficult, and no problem too hard. "He that believeth on me, the works that I do shall he do also; and greater works than these shall he do." When you put limitations upon yourself, when you doubt your ability to meet any situation, you are placing a limit upon Universal Mind, for "The Father that is within me, He doeth the works."

With that knowledge of your power, with that confidence in the unlimited resources of Universal Mind, it is easy enough to show initiative, it is easy enough to find the courage to start things.

You have a right to dominion over all things—over your body, your environment, your business, your health. Develop these three requisites and you will gain that dominion.

Remember that you are a part of Universal Mind, and that the part shares every property of the whole. Remember that, as the spark of electricity is to the thunderbolt, so is your mind to Universal Mind. Whatever of good you may desire of life, whatever qualification, whatever position, you have only to work for it wholeheartedly, confidently, with singleness of purpose—*and you can get it.*

CHAPTER 13

That Old Witch—Bad Luck

"How do you tackle your work each day?
Are you scared of the job you find?
Do you grapple the task that comes your way
With a confident, easy mind?
Do you stand right up to the work ahead
Or fearfully pause to view it?
Do you start to toil with a sense of dread
Or feel that you're going to do it?

"What is the thought that is in your mind?
Is fear ever running through it?
If so, just tackle the next you find
By thinking you're going to do it."

—EDGAR A. GUEST*

Has that old witch—bad luck—ever camped on your doorstep? Have ill health, misfortune and worry ever seemed to dog your footsteps?

If so, you will be interested in knowing that YOU were the procuring cause of all that trouble. For fear is merely creative thought in negative form.

Remember back in 1920 how fine the business outlook seemed, how everything looked rosy and life flowed along like a song? We had crops worth ten billions of dollars. We had splendid utilities, great railways, almost unlimited factory capacity. Everyone was busy. The government had a billion dollars in actual money. The banks were sound. The people were well employed. Wages were good. Prosperity was general. *Then something happened.* A wave of fear swept over the country. The prosperity could not last. People wouldn't pay such high prices. There was too much inflation. What was the result?

As Job put it in the long ago, "The thing that I greatly feared has come upon me."

*From "A Heap o' Livin'." The Reilly & Lee Co.

The prosperity vanished almost overnight. Failures became general. Hundreds of thousands were thrown out of work. And all because of panic, fear.

'Tis true that readjustments were necessary. 'Tis true that prices were too high, that inventories were too big, that values generally were inflated. But it wasn't necessary to burst the balloon to let out the gas. There are orderly natural processes of readjustment that bring things to their proper level with the least harm to anyone.

But fear—panic—knows no reason. It brings into being overnight the things that it fears. It is the greatest torment of humanity. It is about all there is to Hell. *Fear is, in short, the devil.* It causes most of the sin, disaster, disease and misery of the world. It is the only thing you can put into business which won't draw dividends in either fun or dollars. If you guess right, you don't get any satisfaction out of it.

The real cause of all sickness is fear. You image some disease in your thought, and your body proceeds to build upon this model that you hold before it. You have seen how fear makes the face pallid, how it first stops the beating of the heart, then sets it going at trip-hammer pace. Fear changes the secretions. Fear halts the digestion. Fear puts lines and wrinkles into the face. Fear turns the hair gray.

Mind controls every function of the human body. If the thought you hold before your subconscious mind is the fear of disease, of colds or catarrh, of fever or indigestion, those are the images your subconscious mind will work out in your body. For your body itself is merely so much matter—an aggregation of protons and electrons, just as the table in front of you is an aggregation of these same buttons of force but with a different density. Take away your mind, and your body is just as inert, just as lifeless, just as senseless, as the table. Every function of your body, from the beating of your heart to the secretions in your glands, is controlled by mind. The digestion of your food is just as much a function of your mind as the moving of your finger. So the all-important thing is not what food you put into your stomach but what your mind decides shall be done with it. If your mind feels that certain food should make you sick, it *will* make you sick. If, on the other hand, your mind decides that though the food has no nutritive value, there is no reason why unintelligent matter should make you sick, mind will eliminate that food without harm or discomfort to you.

Your body is just like clay in the hands of a potter. Your mind can make of it what it will. The clay has nothing to say about what form it shall take. Neither have your head, your heart, your lungs, your digestive organs anything to say about how conditions shall affect them. They do not decide whether they shall be dizzy or diseased or lame. It is mind that makes this decision. They merely conform to it AFTER mind has decided it. Matter has undergone any and every condition without harm, when properly sustained by mind. And what it has done once, it can do again.

When you understand that your muscles, your nerves, your bones have *no* feeling or intelligence of their own, when you learn that they react to conditions only as mind directs that they shall react, you will never again think or speak of any organ as imperfect, as weak or ailing. You will never again complain of tired bodies, aching muscles or frayed nerves. On the contrary, you will hold steadfast to thoughts of exhaustless strength, of super-abundant vitality, knowing that, as Shakespeare said—"There is nothing, either good or bad, but thinking makes it so."

Never fear disaster, for the fear of it is an invitation to disaster to come upon you. Fear being vivid, easily impresses itself upon the sub-conscious mind. And by so impressing itself, it brings into being the thing that is feared. It is the Frankenstein monster that we all create at times, and which, created, turns to rend its creator. Fear that something you greatly prize will be lost and the fear you feel with create the very means whereby you will lose it. Fear is the Devil. It is the ravening lion roaming the earth seeking whom it may devour. The only safety from it is to deny it. The only refuge is in the knowledge that it has no power other than the power you give to it.

HE WHOM A DREAM HATH POSSESSED

You fear debt. So your mind concentrates upon it and brings about greater debts. You fear loss. And by visualizing that loss you bring it about.

The only remedy for fear is to know that evil has no power—that it is a nonentity—merely a lack of something. You fear ill health, when if you would concentrate that same amount of thought upon good health you would insure the very condition you fear to lose. Functional disturbances are caused solely by the mind through wrong thinking. The remedy for them is not drugs but right thinking, for the trouble is not in the organs but in the mind. Farnsworth in his "Practical Psychology" tells of a man who had conceived the idea when a boy that the eating of cherries and milk together had made him sick. He was very fond of both but always had to be careful not to eat them together, for whenever he did he had been ill. Mr. Farnsworth explained to him that there was no reason for such illness, because all milk sours anyway just as soon as it reaches the stomach. As a matter of fact it cannot be digested until it does sour. He then treated the man mentally for this wrong association of ideas, and after the one treatment the man was never troubled in this way again, though he had been suffering from it for forty-five years.

If you had delirium tremens, and thought you saw pink elephants and green alligators and yellow snakes all about you, it would be a foolish physician that would try to cure you of snakes. Or that would prescribe glasses to improve your eyesight, when he knew that the animals round about you were merely distorted visions of your mind.

The indigestion that you suffer from, the colds that bother you—in short, each and every one of your ailments—is just as much a distorted idea of your mind as would be the snakes of delirium tremens. Banish the idea and you banish the manifestation.

The Bible contains one continuous entreaty to cast out fear. From beginning to end, the admonition "Fear not" is insistent. Fear is the primary cause of all bodily impairment. Jesus understood this and He knew that it could be abolished. Hence His frequent entreaty, "Fear not, be not afraid."

Struggle there is. And struggle there will always be. But struggle is merely wrestling with trial. We need difficulties to overcome. But there is nothing to be afraid of. Everything is an effect of mind. Your thought forces, concentrated upon anything, will bring that thing into manifestation. Therefore concentrate them only upon good things, only upon those conditions you wish to see manifested. *Think* health, power, abundance, happiness. Drive all thoughts of poverty and disease, of fear and worry, as far from your mind as you drive filth from your homes. For fear and worry is the filth of the mind that causes all trouble, that brings about all disease. Banish it! Banish from among your associates any man with a negative outlook on life. Shun him as you would the plague. Can you imagine a knocker winning anything? He is doomed before he starts. Don't let him pull you down with him. "Fret not thyself," says the Psalmist, "else shalt thou be moved to do evil."

That wise old Psalmist might have been writing for us today. For there is no surer way of doing the wrong thing in business or in social life than to fret yourself, to worry, to fume, to want action of some kind, regardless of what it may be. Remember the Lord's admonition to the Israelites, "*Be still*—and know that I am God."

Have you ever stood on the shore of a calm, peaceful lake and watched the reflections in it? The trees, the mountains, the clouds, the sky, all were mirrored there—just as perfectly, as beautifully, as the objects themselves. But try to get such a reflection from the ocean! It cannot be done, because the ocean is always restless, always stirred up by winds or waves or tides.

So it is with your mind. You cannot reflect the richness and plenty of Universal Mind, you cannot mirror peace and health and happiness, if you are constantly worried, continually stirred by waves of fear, winds of anger, tides of toil and striving. You must relax at times. You must give mind a chance. You must realize that, when you have done your best, you can confidently lean back and leave the outcome to Universal Mind.

Just as wrong thinking produces discord in the body, so it also brings on a diseased condition in the realm of commerce. Experience teaches that we need to be protected more from our fears and wrong thoughts than from so-called evil influences external to ourselves. We need not suffer for another man's wrong, for another's greed, dishonesty, avarice or selfish ambition. But if we hug to ourselves the fear that we do have to so suffer, take it into our thought, allow it to disturb us, then we sentence ourselves. We are free to reject every suggestion of discord, and to be governed harmoniously, in spite of what anything or anybody may try to do to us.

Do you know why old army men would rather have soldiers of 18 or 20 than mature men of 30 or 40? Not because they can march farther. They can't! Not because they can carry more. They can't! But because when they go to sleep at night, they really sleep. *They wipe the slate clean!* When they awaken in the morning, they are ready for a new day and a new world.

But an older man carries the nervous strain of one day over to the next. He worries! With the result that at the end of a couple of months' hard campaigning, the older man is a nervous wreck.

And that is the trouble with most men in business. *They never wipe the slate clean! They worry!* And they carry each day's worries over to the next, with the result that some day the burden becomes more than they can carry.

THE BARS OF FATE

Fear results from a belief that there are really two powers in this world—Good and Evil. Like light and darkness. When the fact is that Evil is no more real than darkness. True, we lose contact with Good at times. We let the clouds of fear and worry come between us and the sunlight of Good and then all seems dark. But the sun is still shining on the other side of those clouds, and when we drive them away, we again see its light.

Realizing this, realizing that Good is ever available if we will but turn to it confidently in our need, what is there to fear? "Fear not, little flock," said Jesus, "for it is the Father's good pleasure to give you the kingdom." And again—"Son, thou art ever with me, and all that I have is thine."

If this means anything, it means that the Father is ever available to all of us, that we have but to call upon Him in the right way and our needs will be met. It doesn't matter what those needs may be.

If Universal Mind is the Creator of all, and if everything in the Universe belongs to It, then your business, your work, isn't really yours—but the "Father's." And He is just as much interested in its success, as long as you are working in accordance with His plan, as you can be.

Everyone will admit that Universal Mind can do anything good. Everyone will admit that It can bring to a successful conclusion any undertaking It may be interested in. If Mind created your business, if It inspired your work, then It is interested in its successful conclusion.

Why not, then, call upon Mind when you have done all you know how to do and yet success seems beyond your efforts? Why not put your problem up to Mind, secure in the belief that It CAN and WILL give you any right thing you may desire? I know that many people hesitate to pray for material things, but if Universal Mind made them, they must have been made for some good purpose, and as long as you intend to use them for good, by all means ask for them.

If you can feel that your business, your work, is a good work, if you can be sure that it is advancing the great Scheme of Things by ever so little, you will never again fear debt or lack or limitation. For "The earth is the Lord's and the fullness thereof." Universal Mind is never going to lack for means to carry on Its work. When Jesus needed fish and bread, fish and bread were provided in such abundance that a whole multitude was fed. When He needed gold, the gold coin appeared in the fish's mouth. Where you are, Mind is, and where Mind is, there is all the power, all the supply of the universe.

You are like the owner of a power house that supplies electricity for light and heat and power to the homes and the factories around you. There is unlimited electricity everywhere about you, but you have got to set your dynamo going to draw the electricity out of the air and into your power lines, before it can be put to practical account.

Just so, there are unlimited riches all about you, but you have got to set the dynamo of your mind to work to bring them into such form as will make them of use to yourself and the world.

So don't worry about any present lack of money or other material things. Don't try to win from others what they have. Go where the money is! The material wealth that is in evidence is so small compared with the possible wealth available through the right use of mind, that it is negligible by comparison. The great rewards are for the pioneers. Look at Carnegie, at Woolworth, at Ford! Every year some new field of development is opened, some new world discovered. Steam, gas, electricity, telegraphy, wireless, the automobile, the aeroplane—each opens up possibilities of new worlds yet to come.

A hundred years ago, people probably felt that everything had been discovered that could be discovered. That everything was already known that was likely ever to be known. Just as you may feel about things now. Yet look at the tremendous strides mankind has taken in the past hundred years. And they are as nothing to what the future holds for us, once man has learned to harness the truly unlimited powers of his subconscious mind.

There are billions of dollars' worth of treasure under every square mile of the earth's surface. There are millions of ways in which this old world of ours can be made a better place to live. Set your mind to work locating some of this treasure, finding some of those ways. Don't wait for someone else to blaze the trail.

No one remembers who else was on the *Santa Maria,* but Columbus' name will be known forever! Carnegie is said to have made a hundred millionaires, but he alone became almost a *billionaire!*

Have you ever read Kipling's "Explorer"?

" 'There's no sense in going further—it's the edge of cultivation,'
So they said, and I believed it—broke my land and sowed my crop—
Built my barns and strung my fences in the little border station
Tucked away below the foothills where the trails run out and stop.

"Till a voice, as bad as Conscience, rang interminable changes
On one everlasting Whisper day and night repeated—so:
'Something hidden. Go and find it. Go and look behind the Ranges—
Something lost behind the Ranges. Lost and waiting for you. Go!' "

Your mind is part and parcel of Universal Mind. You have the wisdom of all the ages to draw upon. Use it! Use it to do your work in a way it was never done before. Use it to find new outlets for your business, new methods of reaching people, new and better ways of serving them. Use it to uncover new riches, to learn ways to make the world a better place to live in.

Concentrate your thought upon these things, knowing that back of you is the vast reservoir of Universal Mind, that all these things are *already* known to It, and that you have but to make your contact for them to be known to you.

Optimism based on such a realization is never overconfidence. It is the joyous assurance of *absolute faith.* It is the assurance that made Wilson for a time the outstanding leader of the world. It is the assurance that heartened Lincoln during the black days of the Civil War. It is the assurance that carried Hannibal and Napoleon over the Alps, that left Alexander sighing for more worlds to conquer, that enabled Cortez and his little band to conquer a nation.

Grasp this idea of the availability of Universal Mind for your daily needs, and your vision will become enlarged, your capacity increased. You will realize that the only limits upon you are those you put upon yourself. There will be no such thing then as difficulties and opposition barring your way.

EXERCISE

You feed and nourish the body daily. But few people give any thought to nourishing that far more important part—the Mind. So let us try, each day, to set apart a few minutes' time to give the Mind a repast.

To begin with, *relax!* Stretch out comfortably on a lounge or in an easy chair and let go of every muscle, loosen every bit of tension, forget every thought of fear or worry. Relax mentally and physically.

Few people know how to relax entirely. Most of us are on a continual strain, and it is this strain that brings on physical disturbances—not any real work we may do. Here is a little exercise that will help you to thoroughly relax:

Recline comfortably on a lounge or bed. Stretch luxuriously first. Then when you are settled at your ease again, lift the right leg a foot or two. Let it drop limply. Repeat slowly twice. Do the same with the left leg. With the right arm. With the left arm. You will find then that all your muscles are relaxed. You can forget them and turn your thoughts to other things.

Try to realize the unlimited power that is yours. Think back to the dawn of time, when Mind first imaged from nothingness the heavens and the earth and all that in them is. Remember that, although your mind is to Universal Mind only as a drop of water to the ocean, this drop has all the properties of the great ocean; one in quality although not in quantity; your mind has all the creative power of Universal Mind.

"And God made man in His image, after His likeness." Certainly God never manifested anything but infinite abundance, infinite supply. If you are made in His image, there is no reason why you should ever lack for anything of good. You can manifest abundance, too.

Round about you is the same electronic energy from which Universal Mind formed the heavens and the earth. What do you wish to form from it? What do you want most from life? Hold it in your thought, visualize it, SEE it! Make your model clear-cut and distinct.

1. Remember, the first thing necessary is a sincere desire, concentrating your thought on one thing with singleness of purpose.
2. The second is visualization—SEEING YOURSELF DOING IT—imaging the object in the same way that Universal Mind imaged all of creation.
3. Next is faith—BELIEVING that you HAVE this thing that you want. Not that you are GOING to have it, mind you—but that you HAVE it.
4. And the last is gratitude—gratitude for this thing that you have received, gratitude for the power that enabled you to create it, gratitude for all the gifts that Mind has laid at your feet.

"Trust in the Lord . . . and verily thou shalt be fed.
"Delight thyself also in the Lord, and He shall give thee the desires of thy heart.
"Commit thy way unto the Lord, and He shall bring it to pass."

CHAPTER 14

Your Needs Are Met

"Arise, O Soul, and gird thee up anew,
Though the black camel Death kneel at this gate;
No beggar thou that thou for alms shouldst sue;
Be the proud captain still of thine own fate."

—KENYON

You've heard the story of the old man who called his children to his bedside to give them a few parting words of advice. And this was the burden of it.

"My children," he said, "I have had a great deal of trouble in my life—a great deal of trouble—*but most of it never happened.*"

We are all of us like that old man. Our troubles weigh us down—in prospect—but we usually find that when the actual need arrives, Providence has devised some way of meeting it.

Dr. Jacques Loeb, a member of the Rockefeller Institute, conducted a series of tests with parasites found on plants, which show that even the lowest order of creatures have the power to call upon Universal Supply for the resources to meet any unusual need.

"In order to obtain the material," reads the report of the tests, "potted rose bushes are brought into a room and placed in front of a closed window. If the plants are allowed to dry out, the aphides (parasites), previously wingless, change to winged insects. After the metamorphosis, the animals leave the plants, fly to the window and then creep upward on the glass.

"It is evident that these tiny insects found that the plants on which they had been thriving were dead, and that they could therefore secure nothing more to eat and drink from this source. The only method by which they could save themselves from starvation was to grow temporary wings and fly, which they did."

In short, when their source of sustenance was shut off and they had to find the means of migrating or perish, Universal Supply furnished the means for migration.

If Universal Mind can thus provide for the meanest of its creatures, is it not logical to suppose that It will do even more for us—the highest product of creation—if we will but call upon It, if we will but have a little faith? Viewed in the light of Mind's response to the need of those tiny parasites, does it seem so unbelievable that a sea should roll back while a people marched across it dry-shod? That a pillar of fire should lead them through the wilderness by night? That manna should fall from heaven, or water gush forth from a rock?

In moments of great peril, in times of extremity, when the brave soul has staked its all—those are the times when miracles are wrought, if we will but have faith.

That doesn't mean that you should rest supinely at your ease and let the Lord provide. When you have done all that is in you to do—when you have given of your best—don't worry or fret as to the outcome. Know that if more is needed, your need will be met. You can sit back with the confident assurance that having done your part, you can depend upon the Genie-of-your-Mind to do the rest.

When the little state of Palestine was in danger of being overrun by Egypt on the one hand, or gobbled up by Assyria on the other, its people were frantically trying to decide which horn of the dilemma to embrace, with which enemy they should ally themselves to stave off the other. "With neither," the Prophet Isaiah told them, "in calmly resting your safety lieth; in quiet trust shall be your strength."

So it is with most of the great calamities that afflict us. If we would only "calmly rest, quietly trust," how much better off we should be. But no—we must fret and worry, and nine times out of ten do the wrong thing. And the more we worry and fret, the more likely we are to go wrong.

All of Universal Mind that is necessary to solve any given problem, to meet any need, is wherever that need may be. Supply is always *where* you are and *what* you need. It matters not whether it be sickness or trouble, poverty or danger, the remedy is there, waiting for your call. Go at your difficulty boldly, knowing that you have infinite resources behind you, and you will find these forces closing around you and coming to your aid.

It's like an author writing a book. For a long time he works in a kind of mental fog, but let him persevere, and there flashes suddenly a light that clarifies his ideas and shows him the way to shape them logically. At the moment of despair, you feel a source of unknown energy arising in your soul.

That doesn't mean that you will never have difficulties. Difficulties are good for you. They are the exercise of your mind. You are the stronger for having overcome them. But look upon them as mere exercise. As "stunts" that are given you in order that you may the better learn how to use your mind, how to draw upon Universal Supply. Like Jacob wrestling with the Angel, don't let them go until they have blessed you—until, in other words, you have learned something from having encountered them.

Remember this: No matter how great a catastrophe may befall mankind, no matter how general the loss, you and yours can be free from it. There is always a way of safety. There is always an "ark" by which the understanding few can be saved from the flood. The name of that ark is Understanding—understanding of your inner powers.

When the children of Israel were being led into the promised land, and Joshua had given them their directions, they answered him: "All that thou commandest us we will do, and whithersoever thou sendest us, we will go. . . . Only the Lord thy God be with thee, as He was with Moses."

They came to the river Jordan, and it seemed an insurmountable barrier in their path, but Joshua commanded them to take the Ark of the Covenant, representing God's understanding with them, before them into the Jordan. They did it, and "the waters which came down from above stood and rose up upon an heap. . . . And the priests that bare the Ark of the Covenant of the Lord stood firm on dry ground in the midst of Jordan, and all the Israelites passed over on dry ground, until all the people were passed clean over Jordan."

THE ARK OF THE COVENANT

All through the Old Testament, when war and pestilence, fire and flood, were the common lot of mankind, there is constant assurance of safety for those who have this understanding, this "Covenant" with the Lord. "Because thou hast made the Lord which is my refuge—even the Most High—thy habitation, there shall no evil befall thee, neither shall any plague come nigh thy dwelling. For He shall give His angels charge over thee to keep thee in all thy ways."

That is His agreement with us—an agreement which gives us the superiority to circumstances which men have sought from time immemorial. All that is necessary on our side of the agreement is for us to remember the infinite powers that reside within us, to remember that our mind is part of Universal Mind and as such it can foresee, it can guard against and it can protect us from harm of any kind. We need not run away from trials or try to become stoical towards them. All we need is to bring our understanding to bear upon them—to know that no situation has ever yet arisen with which Universal Mind—and through it our own mind—was not fully competent to deal. To know that the right solution of every problem is in Universal Mind. That we have but to seek that solution and our trial is overcome.

"But where shall Wisdom be found? And where is the place of understanding? Acquaint now thyself with God, and be at peace."

If evil threatens us, if failure, sickness or accident seems imminent, we have only to decide that these evils do not come from Universal Mind, therefore they are unreal and have no power over us. They are simply the absence of the right condition which Universal Mind knows. Refuse, therefore, to see them, to acknowledge them—and seek through Mind for the right condition which shall nullify them.

If you will do this, you will find that you can appropriate from Mind whatever you require for your needs, *when* you require it. The greater your need, the more surely it will be met, if you can but realize this truth. "Fear not, little flock," said Jesus, "for it is your Father's good pleasure to give you the Kingdom."

Remember that your thought is all-powerful. That it is creative. That there is no limitation upon it of time or space. And that it is ever available.

Forget your worries. Forget your fears. In place of them, visualize the conditions you would like to see. Realize their availability. Declare to yourself that you already *have* all these things that you desire, that your needs *have* been met. Say to yourself: "How thankful I am that Mind has made all these good things available to me. I have everything that heart could desire to be grateful for."

Every time you do this, you are impressing the thought upon your sub-conscious mind. And the moment you can convince your subconscious mind of the truth of it—*that moment* your mind will proceed to *make* it true. This is the way to put into practice the Master's advice—"Believe that ye RECEIVE it, and ye SHALL HAVE it."

There is no condition so hopeless, no cause so far gone, that this truth will not save it. Time and again patients given over by their doctors as doomed have made miraculous recoveries through the faith of some loved one.

"I hope that everyone who reads this Book may gain as much from their first reading as I did," writes a happy subscriber from New York City. "I got such a clear understanding from that one reading that I was able to break the mental chain holding a friend to a hospital bed, and she left the hospital in three days, to the very great astonishment of the doctors handling the case."

In the same way, there are innumerable instances where threatened calamity has been warded off and good come instead. The great trouble with most of us is we do not *believe.* We insist upon looking for trouble. We feel that the "rainy day" is bound to come, and we do our utmost to make it a surety by keeping it in our thoughts, preparing for it, fearing it. "Cowards die many times before their deaths; the valiant never taste of death but once." We cross our bridges a dozen times before we come to them. We doubt ourselves, we doubt our ability, we doubt everyone and everything around us. And our doubts sap our energy, kill our enthusiasm, rob us of success. We are like the old lady who "enjoys poor health." We always place that little word "but" after our wishes and desires, feeling deep down that there are some things too good to be true. We think there is a power apart from Good which can withhold blessings that should be ours. We doubt, because we cannot see the way by which our desires can be fulfilled. We put a limit upon the good that can come to us.

"Prove me now herewith, saith the Lord of Hosts," cried the Prophet Malachi, "if I will not open you the windows of heaven and pour you out a blessing that there shall not be room enough to receive it . . . all nations shall call you blessed, for ye shall be a delightsome land."

Your mind is part of Universal Mind. And Universal Mind has all supply. You are entitled to, and you can have, just as much of that supply as you are able to appropriate. To expect less is to get less, for it dwarfs your power of receiving.

It doesn't matter what your longings may be, provided they are right longings. If your little son has his heart set on a train and you feel perfectly able to get him a train, you are not going to hand him a picture book instead. It may be that the picture book would have greater educational value, but the love you have for your son is going to make you try to satisfy his longings as long as those longings are not harmful ones.

In the same way, Universal Mind will satisfy *your* longings, no matter how trivial they may seem, as long as they are not harmful ones. "Delight thyself also in the Lord, and He shall give thee the desires of thine heart."

If we would only try to realize that God is not some far-off Deity, not some stern Judge but the beneficent force that we recognize as Nature—the life Principle that makes the flowers bud, and the plants grow, that spreads abundance about us with lavish hand. If we could realize that He is the Universal Mind that holds all supply, that will give us the toy of our childhood or the needs of maturity, that all we need to obtain from Him our Heart's Desire is a right understanding of His availability—then we would lose all our fears, all our worries, all our sense of limitation.

For Universal Mind is an infinite, unlimited source of good. Not only the source of general good but the specific good things you desire of life. To It there is no big or little problem. The removal of mountains is no more difficult than the feeding of a sparrow.

And to one—like the Master—with a perfect understanding, the "miracle" of raising Lazarus from the dead required no more effort than the turning of the water into wine. He knew that Universal Mind is all power—and there cannot be more than ALL. He knew that "to know God aright is life eternal." And Jesus knew God aright, so was able to demonstrate this knowledge of life eternal in overcoming sin, disease and death. For it is one and the same law that heals sin, sickness, poverty, heartaches or death itself. That law is the right understanding of Divine Principle.

But what does this ability to perform "miracles" consist of? What is the power or force by which we can prove this ability? Perhaps the simplest way is to begin with the realization that Universal Mind is man's working power.

THE SCIENCE OF THOUGHT

Can you stretch your mind a bit and try to comprehend this wonderful fact—that the ALL-POWERFUL, ALL-KNOWING, EVERLASTING CREATOR and Governor of the infinite universe, "who hath measured the waters in the hollow of his hand, and meted out heaven with the span, and comprehended the dust of the earth in a measure, and weighed the mountains in scales, and the hills in a balance," is your working power? In proportion as we understand this fact, and make use of it, in that same proportion are we able to perform our miracles.

Your work is inspired to the extent that you realize the presence of Universal Mind in your work. When you rely entirely on your own conscious mind, your work suffers accordingly. "I can of mine own self do nothing; for the Works which the Father hath given me to finish, the same works that I do bear witness of me." The miracles of Jesus bear witness of the complete recognition of God the Father as his working power.

And mind you, this inspiration, this working of Universal Mind with you, is available for all of your undertakings. Mind could not show Itself in one part of your life and withhold Itself from another, since It is all in all. Every rightly directed task, no matter how insignificant or menial it may appear to you, carries with it the inspiration of Universal Mind, since by the very nature of omnipotence, Its love and bestowals must be universal and impartial, "and whatsoever ye do, do it heartily as to the Lord."

Too many of us are like the maiden in the old Eastern legend. A Genie sent her into a field of grain, promising her a rare gift if she would pick for him the largest and ripest ear she could find. His gift to be in proportion to the size and perfection of the ear.

But he made this condition—she must pluck but one ear, and she must walk straight through the field without stopping, going back or wandering hither and thither.

Joyously she started. As she walked through the grain, she saw many large ears, many perfect ones. She passed them by in scorn, thinking to find an extra-large, super-perfect one farther along. Presently, however, the soil became less fertile, the ears small and sparse. She couldn't pick one of these! Would now that she had been content with an ordinary-sized ear farther back. But it was too late for that. Surely they would grow better again farther on!

She walked on—and on—and always they became worse—'till presently she found herself at the end of the field—*empty-handed as when she set out!*

So it is with life. Every day has its worthwhile rewards for work well done. Every day offers its chance for happiness. But those rewards seem so small, those chances so petty, compared with the big things we see ahead. So we pass them by, never recognizing that the great position we look forward to, the shining prize we see in the distance, is just the sum of all the little tasks, the heaped-up result of all the little prizes that we must win as we go along.

You are not commanded to pick out certain occupations as being more entitled to the Lord's consideration than others, but "whatsoever ye do." Whether it be in the exalted and idealistic realms of poetry, music and art; whether in the cause of religion or philanthropy; whether in government, in business, in science, or simply in household cares, "whatsoever ye do" you are entitled to, and *have* all of inspiration at your beck and call. If you seem to have less than all, it is because you do not utilize your gift.

"Now he that planteth and he that watereth are one; and every man shall receive his own reward according to his own labour. For we are labourers together with God." "All things are yours; and ye are Christ's and Christ's is God's."

How shall you take advantage of this Universal Supply? When next any need confronts you, when next you are in difficulties, close your eyes for a moment and realize that Universal Mind knows how that need can best be met, knows the solution of your difficulties. And that your sub-conscious mind, being part of the Universal Mind, can know this, too. So put your problem up to your sub-conscious mind with the sublime confidence that it will find the solution. Then forget it for a while. When the time comes, the need will be met.

Dr. Winbigler corroborates the working out of this idea in the following:

"Suggestions lodged in the mind can effect a complete change, morally and physically. If mankind would become in spirit 'as a little child,' trusting in God implicitly, the greatest power would be utilized in the establishment of health and equilibrium, and the results would be untold in comfort, sanity, and blessing, For instance, here is one who is suffering from worry, fear, and the vexations of life. How can he get rid of these things and relieve this suffering? Let him go to a quiet room or place, twice a day, lie down and relax every muscle, assume complete indifference to those things which worry him and the functions of the body, and quietly accept what God, through this law of demand and supply, can give. In a few days he will find a great change in his feelings, and the sufferings will pass away and life will look bright and promising. Infinite wisdom has established that law; and its utilization by those who are worried and fearful will secure amazing results in a short time.

"The real reason for the change is found in the possibility of recovery by using the laws that God has placed within our reach, and thus securing the coveted health and power for all that we want and ought to do. The subliminal life is the connecting link between man and God, and by obeying His laws, one's life is put in contact with infinite resources and all that God is able and willing to give. Here is the secret of all the cures of disease, and the foundation for the possibility of a joyful existence, happiness and eternal life. Suggestion is the method of securing what God gives, and the mind is the agent through which these gifts are received. This is not a matter of theory, but a fact. If any one who is sick or who desires to be kept well will have stated periods of relaxation, openmindedness, and faith, he can prove the beneficial and unvarying result of this method."

CHAPTER 15

The Master of Your Fate

"A craven hung along the battle's edge,
And thought, 'Had I a sword of keener steel—
That blue blade that the king's son bears,—but this blunt thing—!'
And lowering crept away and left the field.
Then came the king's son, wounded, sore bestead
And weaponless, and saw the broken sword,
And ran and snatched it, and with battle-shout
Lifted afresh he hewed his enemy down,
And saved a great cause that heroic day."

—EDWARD ROWLAND SILL*

Where will *you* be at 65? Five men in six at the age of 65 are living on charity. Just one in twenty is able to live without working at 65.

That is what the American Bankers Association found when it took one hundred healthy men at 25 and traced them to 65.

These hundred were healthy to start with. They all had the same chance for success. The difference lay in the way they used their MINDS. Ninety-five out of one hundred just do the tasks that are set them. They have no faith in themselves—no initiative—none of the courage that starts things. They are always directed or controlled by someone else.

At 65, where will *you* be? Dependent or independent? Struggling for a living—accepting charity from someone else—or at the top of the heap?

"I am the Master of my fate."

Until you have learned that, you will never attain life's full success. Your fate is in your own hands. *You* have the making of it. What you are going to be six months or a year from now depends upon what you think today.

So make your choice now:

Are you going to bow down to matter as the only power? Are you going to look upon

*From "Poems." Houghton, Mifflin Co.

your environment as something that has been wished upon you and for which you are in no way responsible?

Or are you going to try to realize in your daily life that matter is merely an aggregation of protons and electrons subject entirely to the control of Mind, that your environment, your success, your happiness are all of your own making, and that if you are not satisfied with conditions as they are, you have but to visualize them as you would have them be in order to change them?

The former is the easier way right now—the easy way that leads to the hell of poverty and fear and old age.

But the latter is the way that brings you to your Heart's Desire.

And merely because this Power of Universal Mind is invisible, is that any reason to doubt it? The greatest powers of Nature are invisible. Love is invisible, but what greater power is there in life? Joy is invisible, happiness, peace, contentment. The radio is invisible—yet you hear it. It is a product of the law governing sound waves. Law is invisible, yet you see the manifestation of different laws every day. To run a locomotive, you study the law of applying power, and you apply that law when you make the locomotive go.

These things are not the result of invention. The law has existed from the beginning. It merely waited for man to learn how to apply it. If man had known how to call upon Universal Mind to the right extent, he could have applied the law of sound waves, the law of steam, ages ago. Invention is merely a revelation and an unfoldment of Universal Wisdom.

That same Universal Wisdom knows millions of other laws of which man has not even a glimmering. You can call upon It. You can use that Wisdom as your own. By thinking of things as they might be instead of as they are, you will eventually find some great Need. And to find a need is the first step towards finding the supply to satisfy that need. You've got to know what you are after before you can send the Genie-of-your-Mind a-seeking of it in Universal Mind.

THE ACRE OF DIAMONDS

You remember the story of the poor Boer farmer who struggled for years to glean a livelihood out of his rocky soil, only to give it up in despair and go off to seek his fortune elsewhere. Years later, coming back to his old farm, he found it swarming with machinery and life—more wealth being dug out of it every day than he had ever dreamed existed. It was the great Kimberley Diamond Mine!

Most of us are like that poor Boer farmer. We struggle along under our surface power, never dreaming of the giant power that could be ours if we would but dig a little deeper—rouse that great Inner Self who can give us more even than any acre of diamonds.

As Orison Swett Marden put it:

"The majority of failures in life are simply the victims of their mental defeats. Their conviction that they cannot succeed as others do robs them of that vigor and determination which self-confidence imparts, and they don't even half try to succeed.

"There is no philosophy by which a man can do a thing when he thinks he can't. The reason why millions of men are plodding along in mediocrity today, many of them barely making a living, when they have the ability to do something infinitely bigger, is because they lack confidence in themselves. They don't believe they can do the bigger thing that would lift them out of their rut of mediocrity and poverty; they are not winners mentally.

"The way always opens for the determined soul, the man of faith and courage.

"It is the victorious mental attitude, the consciousness of power, the sense of mastership, that does the big things in this world. If you haven't this attitude, if you lack self-confidence, begin now to cultivate it.

"A highly magnetized piece of steel will attract and lift a piece of unmagnetized steel ten times its own weight. De-magnetize that same piece of steel and it will be powerless to attract or lift even a feather's weight.

"Now, my friends, there is the same difference between the man who is highly magnetized by a sublime faith in himself, and the man who is de-magnetized by his lack of faith, his doubts, his fears, that there is between the magnetized and the de-magnetized pieces of steel. If two men of equal ability, one *magnetized by a divine self-confidence,* the other de-magnetized by fear and doubt, are given similar tasks, one will succeed and the other will fail. The self-confidence of the one *multiplies his powers a hundredfold*; the lack of it subtracts a hundredfold from the power of the other."

Have you ever thought how much of your time is spent in choosing what you shall do, which task you will try, which way you shall go? Every day is a day of decision. We are constantly at crossroads, in our business dealings, our social relations, in our homes, there is always the necessity of a choice. How important then that we have faith in ourselves and in that Infinite intelligence within. "Commit thy works unto the Lord, and thy thoughts shall be established." "In all thy ways acknowledge him, and he shall direct thy paths."

In this ever-changing material age, with seemingly complex forces all about us, we sometimes cry out that we are driven by force of circumstances. Yet the fact remains that we do those things which we choose to do. For even though we may not wish to go a certain way, we allow ourselves to pursue it because it offers the least resistance.

"To every man there openeth
A way, and ways, and a way.
And the high soul climbs the high way,
And the low soul gropes the low:
And in between, on the misty flats,
The rest drift to and fro.
But to every man there openeth
A high way and a low,
And every man decideth
The way his soul shall go."

—JOHN OXENHAM

Now, how about you? Are you taking active control of your own thought? Are you imaging upon your subconcious mind only such things as you want to see realized? Are you thinking healthy thoughts, happy thoughts, successful thoughts?

The difference between the successful man and the unsuccessful one is not so much a matter of training or equipment. It is not a question of opportunity or luck. It is just in the way they each of them look at things.

The successful man sees an opportunity, seizes upon it, and moves upward another rung on the ladder of success. It never occurs to him that he may fail. He sees only the opportunity, he visions what he can do with it, and all the forces within and without him combine to help him win.

The unsuccessful man sees the same opportunity, he wishes that he could take advantage of it, but he is fearful that his ability or his money or his credit may not be equal to the task. He is like a timid bather, putting in one foot and then drawing it swiftly back again—and while he hesitates some bolder spirit dashes in and beats him to the goal.

Nearly every man can look back—and not so far back either with most of us—and say, "If I had taken that chance, I would be much better off now."

You will never need to say it again, once you realize that the future is entirely within your own control. It is not subject to the whims of fortune or the capriciousness of luck. There is but one Universal Mind and that mind contains naught but good. In it are no images of Evil. From it comes no lack of supply. Its ideas are as numberless as the grains of sand on the seashore. And those ideas comprise all wealth, all power, all happiness.

You have only to image vividly enough on your subconscious mind the thing you wish, to draw from Universal Mind the necessary ideas to bring it into being. You have only to keep in mind the experiences you wish to meet, in order to control your own future.

When Frank A. Vanderlip, former President of the National City Bank, was a struggling youngster, he asked a successful friend what one thing he would urge a young man to do who was anxious to make his way in the world. "Look as though you have already succeeded," his friend told him. Shakespeare expresses the same thought in another way—"Assume a virtue if you have it not." Look the part. Dress the part. Act the part. Be successful in your own thought first. It won't be long before you will be successful before the world as well.

David V. Bush, in his book "Applied Psychology and Scientific Living," says:

"Man is like the wireless operator. Man is subject to miscellaneous wrong thought currents if his mind is not in tune with the Infinite, or if he is not keyed up to higher vibrations than those of negation.

"A man who thinks courageous thoughts sends these courageous thought waves through the universal ether until they lodge in the consciousness of someone who is tuned to the same courageous key. Think a strong thought, a courageous thought, a prosperity thought, and these thoughts will be received by someone who is strong, courageous and prosperous.

"It is just as easy to think in terms of abundance as to think in terms of poverty. If we think poverty thoughts we become the sending and receiving stations for poverty thoughts. We send out a 'poverty' mental wireless and it reaches the consciousness of some poverty-stricken 'receiver.' We get what we think.

"It is just as easy to think in terms of abundance, opulence and prosperity as it is to think in terms of lack, limitation and poverty.

"If a man will raise his rate of vibration by faith currents or hope currents, these vibrations go through the Universal Mind and lodge in the consciousness of people who are keyed to the same tune. Whatever you think is sometime, somewhere, received by a person who is tuned to your thought key.

"If a man is out of work and he thinks thoughts of success, prosperity, harmony, position and growth, just as surely as his thoughts are things—as Shakespeare says—someone will receive his vibrations of success, prosperity, harmony, position and growth.

"If we are going to be timid, selfish, penurious and picayunish in our thinking, these thought waves which we have started in the universal ether will go forth until they come to a mental receiving station of the same caliber. 'Birds of a feather flock together,' and minds of like thinking are attracted one to the other.

"If you need money, all you have to do is to send up your vibrations to a strong, courageous receiving station, and someone who can meet your needs will be attracted to you or you to him."

When you learn that you are entitled to win—in any right undertaking in which you may be engaged—*you will win.* When you learn that you have a right to a legitimate dominion over your own affairs, *you will have dominion over them.* The promise is that we can do all things through the Mind that was in Christ.

Universal Mind plays no favorites. No one human being has any more power than any other. It is simply that few of us use the power that is in our hands. The great men of the world are in no wise SUPER Beings. They are ordinary creatures like you and me, who have stumbled upon the way of drawing upon their subconscious mind—and through it upon the Universal Mind. Speaking of Henry Ford's phenomenal success, his friend Thomas A. Edison said of him—"He draws upon his subconscious mind."

The secret of being what you have it in you to be is simply this: Decide now what it is you want of life, exactly what you wish your future to be. Plan it out in detail. Vision it from start to finish. See yourself as you are now, doing those things you have always wanted to do. Make them REAL in your mind's eye—feel them, live them, believe them, especially at the moment of going to sleep, when it is easiest to reach your subconscious mind—and you will soon be seeing them in real life.

It matters not whether you are young or old, rich or poor. The time to begin is NOW. It is never too late. Remember those lines of Appleton's:*

"I knew his face the moment that he passed
Triumphant in the thoughtless, cruel throng—
I gently touched his arm—he smiled at me—
He was the Man that Once I Meant to Be!

"Where I had failed, he'd won from life, Success;
Where I had stumbled, with sure feet he stood;
Alike—yet unalike—we faced the world,
And through the stress he found that life was good.
And I ? The bitter wormwood in the glass,

*From "The Quiet Courage." D. Appleton & Co., New York.

The shadowed way along which failures pass!
Yet as I saw him thus, joy came to me—
He was the Man that Once I Meant to Be!

"We did not speak. But in his sapient eyes
I saw the spirit that had urged him on,
The courage that had held him through the fight
Had once been mine. I thought, 'Can it be gone?'
He felt that unasked question—felt it so
His pale lips formed the one-word answer, 'No!'

. . . . . .

"Too late to win? No! Not too late for me—
He is the Man that Still I Mean to Be!"

CHAPTER 16

Unappropriated Millions

"Somebody said that it couldn't be done,
But he with a chuckle replied
That 'maybe it couldn't,' but he would be one
Who wouldn't say so till he'd tried.
So he buckled right in with the trace of a grin
On his face. If he worried he hid it.
He started to sing as he tackled the thing
That couldn't be done, and he did it."

—EDGAR A. GUEST*

The main difference between the mind of today and that of our great-great-grandfathers was that in their day conditions were comparatively static, whereas today they are dynamic. Civilization ran along for centuries with comparatively little change. Most people lived and died in the places where they were born. They followed their fathers' avocations. Seldom, indeed, did one of them break out of the class into which he had been born. Almost as seldom did they even *think* of trying to. No wonder, then, that civilization made little progress.

Today we are in the presence of continual change. Men are imbued with that divine unrest which is never satisfied with conditions as they are, which is always striving for improvement. And *thought* is the vital force behind all this change.

Your ability to think is your connecting link with Universal Mind, that enables you to draw upon It for inspiration, for energy, for power. Mind is the energy in *static* form. Thought is the energy in *dynamic* form.

And because life is dynamic—not static; because it is ever moving forward—not standing still; your success or failure depends entirely upon the *quality* of your thought.

For thought is creative energy. It brings into being the things that you think. Think

*From "The Path to Home." The Reilly & Lee Co.

the things you would see manifested, see them, *believe* them, and you can leave it to your subconscious mind to bring them into being.

Your mind is a marvelous storage battery of power on which you can draw for whatever things you need to make your life what you would have it be. It has within it all power, all resource, all energy—but YOU are the one that must use it. All that power is static unless you make it dynamic. In the moment of creative thinking your conscious mind becomes a Creator—it partakes of the power of Universal Mind. And there is nothing static about one who shares that All-power. The resistless Life Energy within him pushes him on to new growth, new aspirations. Just as the sap flowing through the branches of the trees pushes off the old dead leaves to make way for the new life, just so you must push away the old dead thoughts of poverty and lack and disease, before you can bring on the new life of health and happiness and unlimited supply.

This life is in all of us, constantly struggling for an outlet. Repress it—and you die. Doctors will tell you that the only reason people grow old is because their systems get clogged. The tiny pores in your arteries get stopped up. You don't throw off the old. You don't struggle hard enough, and the result is you fall an easy victim to failure and sickness and death.

Remember the story of Sinbad the Sailor, and the Old Man of the Sea? The Old Man's weight was as nothing when Sinbad first took him on his shoulders, but he clung there and clung there, slowly but surely sapping Sinbad's strength, and he would finally have killed him as he had killed so many others if Sinbad, by calling to his aid all his mental as well as his physical resources, had not succeeded in shaking him off.

Most of us have some Old Man of the Sea riding us, and because he clings tightly and refuses to be easily shaken off, we let him stay there, sapping our energies, using up our vitality, when to rid us of him it is only necessary to call to our aid ALL our resources, mental as well as physical, for one supreme effort.

When a storm arises, the hardy mariner doesn't turn off steam and drift helplessly before the wind. That might be the easy way, but that way danger lies. He turns on more steam and fights against the gale. And so should you. There is a something within you that thrives on difficulties. You prize that more which costs an effort to win. You need to blaze new trails, to encounter unusual hardships, in order to reach your hidden mental resources, just as the athlete needs to exert himself to the utmost to reach his "second wind."

Have you ever seen a turtle thrown on its back? For a while it threshes around wildly, reaching for something outside to take hold of that shall put it on its feet. Just as we humans always look for help outside ourselves first. But presently he draws all his forces within his shell, rests a bit to regain his strength, and then throws his whole force to one side—legs, head, tail, and all—*and over he goes!*

So it is with us. When we realize that the power to meet any emergency is within ourselves, when we stop looking outside for help and intelligently call upon Mind in our need, we shall find that we are tapping Infinite Resource. We shall find that we have but to center all those resources on the one thing we want most—to get anything from life that it has.

As Emerson put it, when we once find the way to get in touch with Universal Mind we are—

"... owner of the sphere,
Of the seven stars and the solar year,
Of Caesar's hand and Plato's brain,
Of the Lord Christ's heart and Shakespeare's strain."

CHAPTER 17

The Secret of Power

"The great were once as you.
They whom men magnify today
Once groped and blundered on life's way
Were fearful of themselves, and thought
By magic was men's greatness wrought.
They feared to try what they could do;
Yet Fame hath crowned with her success
The selfsame gifts that you possess."

—EDGAR A. GUEST*

There is a woman in one of the big eastern cities whose husband died a year or two ago and left her nearly $100,000,000. She has unlimited power in her hands—yet she uses none of it. She has unlimited wealth—yet she gets no more from it than if it were in the thousands instead of millions. She knows nothing of her power, of her wealth. She is insane.

You have just as great power in your hands—without this poor woman's excuse for not using it.

You have access to unlimited ideas, unlimited energy, unlimited wealth. The "Open, Sesame!" is through your subconscious mind.

So long as you limit yourself to superficial conditions, so long as you are a mere "hewer of wood or carrier of water" for those around you who *do* use their minds, you are in no better position than the beasts of burden.

The secret of power is in understanding the infinite resources of your own mind. When you begin to realize that the power to do anything, to be anything, to have anything, is within yourself, then *and then only* will you take your proper place in the world.

As Bruce Barton has it in "The Man Whom Nobody Knows"—

*Published by permission of the International Magazine Co. (*Cosmopolitan Magazine*). Copyright 1921.

"Somewhere, at some unforgettable hour, the daring filled His (Jesus) heart. He knew that He was bigger than Nazareth."

Again in speaking of Abraham Lincoln, Barton says—"Inside himself he felt his power, but where and when would opportunity come?" And later in the book—

"But to every man of vision the clear voice speaks. Nothing splendid has ever been achieved except by those who dared believe that *something inside them was superior to circumstance.*"

No doubt Jesus' friends and neighbors all ridiculed the idea of any such power within Him. Just as most people today laugh at the thought of a power such as that within themselves.

So they go on with their daily grind, with the gaunt spectres of sickness and need ever by their side, until death comes as a welcome relief. Are you going to be one of those? Or will you listen to that inner consciousness of power and find the "Kingdom of Heaven that is within you"? For whatever you become conscious of will be quickly brought forth into tangible form.

Don't judge your ability by what you have done in the past. Your work heretofore has been done with the help of your conscious mind alone. Add to that the infinite knowledge at the disposal of your subconscious mind, and what you have done is as nothing to what you will do in the future.

For knowledge does not apply itself. It is merely so much static energy. You must convert it into dynamic energy by the power of your thought. The difference between the $25-a-week clerk and the $25,000-a-year executive is solely one of thought. The clerk may have more brains than the executive—frequently *has* in actual weight of gray matter. He may even have a far better education. But he doesn't know how to apply his thought to get the greatest good from it.

If you have brains, *use* them. If you have skill, *apply* it. The world must profit by it, and therefore you.

We all have inspired moments when we see clearly how we may do great things, how we may accomplish wonderful undertakings. But we do not believe in them enough to make them come true. An imagination which begins and ends in day-dreaming is weakening to character.

Make the day-dreams come true. Make them so clear and distinct that they impress themselves upon your subconscious mind. There's nothing wrong with day-dreaming, except that most of us stop there. We don't try to make the dreams come true. The great inventor, Tesla, "dreams" every new machine complete and perfect in every particular before ever he begins his model for it. Mozart "dreamed" each of his wonderful symphonies complete before ever he put a note on paper. But they didn't stop with the dreaming. They visualized those dreams, *and then brought them into actuality.*

We lose our capacity to have visions if we do not take steps to realize them.

Power implies service, so concentrate all your thought on making your visions of great deeds come true. Thinking is the current that runs the dynamo of power. To connect up this current so that you can draw upon universal supply through your subconscious mind is to become a Super-man. Do this, and you will have found the key to the solution of every problem of life.

CHAPTER 18

This One Thing I Do

"How do you tackle your work each day?
Do you grapple the task that comes your way
With a confident, easy mind?
Do you start to toil with a sense of dread
Or feel that you're going to do it?

"You can do as much as you think you can,
But you'll never accomplish more;
If you're afraid of yourself, young man,
There's little for you in store.
For failure comes from the inside first,
It's there, if we only knew it,
And you can win, though you face the worst,
If you feel that you're going to do it."

—EDGAR A. GUEST*

How did the Salvation Army get so much favorable publicity out of the War? They were a comparatively small part of the "Services" that catered to the boys "over there," yet they carried off the lion's share of the glory. Do you know how they did it?

By concentrating on just one thing—DOUGHNUTS!

They served doughnuts to the boys—and they did it *well.* And that is the basis of all success in business—to focus on one thing and do that thing well. Better far to do one thing pre-eminently well than to dabble in forty.

Two thousand years ago, Porcius Marcus Cato became convinced, from a visit to the rich and flourishing city of Carthage, that Rome had in her a rival who must be destroyed. His countrymen laughed at him. He was practically alone in his belief. But he persisted. He concentrated all his thought, all his faculties, to that one end. At the end of every

*From "A Heap o' Livin'." The Reilly & Lee Co.

speech, at the end of every talk, he centered his hearers' thought on what he was trying to put over by epitomizing his whole idea in a single sentence—"Carthage must be destroyed!" And *Carthage was destroyed.*

If one man's concentration on a single idea could destroy a great nation, what can you not do when you apply that same principle to the *building* of a business?

I remember when I was first learning horsemanship, my instructor impressed this fact upon me: "Remember that a horse is an animal of one idea. You can teach him only one thing at a time."

Looking back, I'd say the only thing wrong with his instruction was that he took in too little territory. He need not have confined himself to the horse. Most humans are the same way.

In fact, you can put ALL humans into that class if you want a thing done well. For you cannot divide your thought and do justice to any one of the different subjects you are thinking of. You've got to do one thing at a time. The greatest success rule I know in business—the one that should be printed over every man's desk—is "This One Thing I Do." Take one piece of work at a time. Concentrate on it to the exclusion of all else. *Then finish it!* Don't half-do it, and leave it around to clutter up your desk and interfere with the next job. Dispose of it completely. Pass it along wherever it is to go. Be through with it *and forget it!* Then your mind will be clear to consider the next matter.

"The man who is perpetually hesitating which of two things he will do first," says William Wirt, "will do neither. The man who resolves, but suffers his resolution to be changed by the first counter-suggestion of a friend—who fluctuates from plan to plan and veers like a weather-cock to every point of the compass with every breath of caprice that blows—can never accomplish anything real or useful. It is only the man who first consults wisely, then resolves firmly, and then executes his purpose with inflexible perseverance, undismayed by those petty difficulties that daunt a weaker spirit, that can advance to eminence in any line."

Everything in the world, even a great business, can be resolved into atoms. And the basic principles behind the biggest business will be found to be the same as those behind the successful running of the corner newsstand. The whole practice of commerce is founded upon them. Any man can learn them, but only the alert and energetic can apply them. The trouble with most men is that they think they have done all that is required of them when they have earned their salary.

Why, that's only the beginning. Up to that point, you are working for someone else. From then on, you begin to work for yourself. Remember, you must *give* to *get.* And it is when you give that *extra* bit of time and attention and thought to your work that you begin to stand out above the crowd around you.

Norval Hawkins, for many years General Manager of Sales for the Ford Motor Company, wrote that "the greatest hunt in the Ford business right now is the MAN hunt." And big men in every industrial line echo his words. When it comes to a job that needs real ability, they are not looking for relatives or friends or men with "pull." They want a MAN—and they will pay any price for the right man.

Not only that but they always have a weather eye open for promising material. And the thing they value most of all is INITIATIVE.

But don't try to improve the whole works at once. Concentrate on one thing at a time. Pick some one department or some one process or some one thing and focus all your thought upon it. Bring to bear upon it the limitless resources of your subconscious mind. Then prepare a definite plan for the development of that department or the improvement of that process. Verify your facts carefully to make sure they are workable. *Then*—and not till then—present your plan.

In "Thoughts on Business," you read: "Men often think of a position as being just about so big and no bigger, when, as a matter of fact, a position is often what one makes it. A man was making about $1,500 a year out of a certain position and thought he was doing all that could be done to advance the business. The employer thought otherwise, and gave the place to another man who soon made the position worth $8,000 a year—at exactly the same commission.

"The difference was in the man—in other words, in what the two men thought about the work. One had a little conception of what the work should be, and the other had a big conception of it. One thought little thoughts, and the other thought big thoughts.

"The standards of two men may differ, not especially because one is naturally more capable than the other, but because one is familiar with big things and the other is not. The time was when the former worked in a smaller scope himself, but when he saw a wider view of what his work might be he rose to the occasion and became a bigger man. It is just as easy to think of a mountain as to think of a hill—when you turn your mind to contemplate it. The mind is like a rubber band—you can stretch it to fit almost anything, but it draws in to a smaller scope when you let go.

"Make it your business to know what is the best that might be in your line of work, and stretch your mind to conceive it, and then devise some way to attain it.

"Big things are only little things put together. I was greatly impressed with this fact one morning as I stood watching the workmen erecting the steel framework for a tall office building. A shrill whistle rang out as a signal, a man over at the engine pulled a lever, a chain from the derrick was lowered, and the whistle rang out again. A man stooped down and fastened the chain around the center of a steel beam, stepped back and blew the whistle once more. Again the lever was moved at the engine, and the steel beam soared into the air up to the sixteenth story, where it was made fast by little bolts.

"The entire structure, great as it was, towering far above all the neighboring buildings, was made up of pieces of steel and stone and wood, put together according to a plan. The plan was first imagined, then penciled, then carefully drawn, and then followed by the workmen. It was all a combination of little things.

"It is encouraging to think of this when you are confronted by a big task. *Remember that it is only a group of little tasks, any of which you can easily do.* It is ignorance of this fact that makes men afraid to try."

One of the most essential requisites in the accomplishment of any important work is patience. Not the patience that sits and folds its hands and waits—Micawber-like—for something to turn up. But the patience that never jeopardizes or upsets a plan by forcing it too soon. The man who possesses that kind of patience can always find plenty to do in the meantime.

Make your plan—then wait for the opportune moment to submit it. You'd be surprised to know how carefully big men go over suggestions from subordinates which show the least promise. One of the signs of a really big man, you know, is his eagerness to learn from everyone and anything. There is none of that "know it all" about him that characterized the German general who was given a book containing the strategy by which Napoleon had for fifteen years kept all the armies of Europe at bay. "I've no time to read about bygone battles," he growled, thrusting the book away, "I have my own campaign to plan."

There is priceless wisdom to be found in books. As Carlyle put it—"All that mankind has done, thought, gained or been—it is lying in matchless preservation in the pages of books."

The truths which mankind has been laboriously learning through countless ages, at who knows what price of sweat and toil and starvation and blood—all are yours for the effort of reading them.

And in business, knowledge was never so priceless or so easily acquired. Books and magazines are filled with the hows and whys, the rights and wrongs of buying and selling, of manufacturing and shipping, of finance and management. They are within the reach of anyone with the desire to KNOW.

Nothing pays better interest than judicious reading. The man who invests in more knowledge of his business than he needs to hold his job is acquiring capital with which to get a better job.

As old Gorgon Graham puts it in "The Letters of a Self-Made Merchant to His Son"—

> "I ain't one of those who believe that a half knowledge of a subject is useless, but it has been my experience that when a fellow has that half knowledge, he finds it's the other half which would really come in handy.
>
> "What you know is a club for yourself, and what you don't know is a meat-ax for the other fellow. That is why you want to be on the lookout all the time for information about the business and to nail a fact just as a sensible man nails a mosquito—the first time it settles near him."

The demands made upon men in business today are far greater than in any previous generation. To meet them, you've got to use your talents to the utmost. You've got to find in every situation that confronts you the best, the easiest and the quickest way of working it out. And the first essential in doing this is to plan your work ahead.

You'd be surprised at how much more work you can get through by carefully planning it, and then taking each bit in order and disposing of it before starting on the next.

Another thing—once started at work, don't let down. Keep on going until it is time to quit. You know how much power it takes to start an auto that is standing motionless. But when you get it going, you can run along in high at a fraction of the expenditure of gas. It is the same way with your mind. We are all mentally lazy. We hate to start using our minds. Once started, though, it is easy to keep along on high, if only we won't let down. For the moment we let down, we have that starting to do all over again. You can accomplish ten times as much, with far less effort or fatigue, if you will keep right on steadily instead of starting and stopping, and starting and stopping again.

Volumes have been written about personal efficiency, and general efficiency, and every other kind of efficiency in business. But boiled down, it all comes to this:

1. Know what you want
2. Analyze the thing you've got to do to get it.
3. Plan your work ahead.
4. Do one thing at a time.
5. Finish that one thing and send it on its way before starting the next.
6. Once started, KEEP GOING!

And when you come to some problem that "stumps" you, give your subconscious mind a chance.

Frederick Pierce, in "Our Unconscious Mind," gives an excellent method for solving business problems through the aid of the subconscious:

"Several years ago, I heard a successful executive tell a group of young men how he did his work, and included in the talk was the advice to prepare at the close of each day's business, a list of the ten most important things for the next day. To this I would add: Run them over in the mind just before going to sleep, not thoughtfully, or with elaboration of detail, but with the sure knowledge that the deeper centers of the mind are capable of viewing them constructively even though conscious attention is surrendered in sleep.

"Then, if there is a particular problem which seems difficult of solution, review its features lightly as a last game for the imaginative unconscious to play at during the night. Do not be discouraged if no immediate results are apparent. Remember that fiction, poetry, musical composition, inventions, innumerable ideas, spring from the unconscious, often in forms that give evidence of the highest constructive elaboration.

"Give your unconscious a chance. Give it the material, and stimulate it with keenly dwelt-on wishes along frank Ego Maximation lines. It is a habit which, if persisted in, will sooner or later present you with some very valuable ideas when you least expect them."

I remember reading of another man—a genius at certain kinds of work—who, whenever an especially difficult problem confronted him, "slept on it." He had learned the trick as a child. Unable to learn his lessons one evening, he had kept repeating the words to himself until he dozed in his chair, the book still in his hands. What was his surprise, on being awakened by his father a few minutes later to find that he knew them perfectly! He tried it again and again on succeeding evenings, and almost invariably it worked. Now, whenever a problem comes up that he cannot solve, he simply stretches out on a lounge in his office, thoroughly relaxes, *and lets his subconscious mind solve the problem!*

CHAPTER 19

The Master Mind

"One who never turned his back but marched breast forward,
Never doubted clouds would break,
Never dreamed though right were worsted
Wrong would triumph,
Held we fall to rise, are baffled to fight better,
Sleep to wake."
—BROWNING

Among your friends there is one of those men who doesn't have much use for the word "can't."

You marvel at his capacity for work.

You'll admire him the more the longer you know him.

You'll always respect him.

For he not only has made good, but he always will make good. He has found and appropriated to himself the "Talisman of Napoleon"—*absolute confidence in himself.*

The world loves a leader. All over the world, in every walk of life, people are eagerly seeking for someone to follow. They want someone else to do their thinking for them; they need someone to hearten them to action; they like to have someone else on whom to lay the blame when things go wrong; they want someone big enough to share the glory with them when success crowns his efforts.

But to instill confidence in them, that leader must have utter confidence in himself. A Roosevelt or a Mussolini who did not believe in himself would be inconceivable. It is that which makes men invincible—the Consciousness of their own Power. They put no limit upon their own capacities—therefore they have no limit. For Universal Mind sees all, knows all, and can do all, and we share in this absolute power to the exact extent to which we permit ourselves. Our mental attitude is the magnet that attracts from Universal Mind everything we may need to bring our desires into being. We make that magnet strong or weak as we have confidence in or doubt of our abilities. We draw to ourselves unlimited power or limit ourselves to humble positions according to our own beliefs.

A long time ago Emerson wrote: "There is one mind common to all individual men. Every man is an inlet to the same *and to all* of the same. He that is once admitted to the right of reason is made a freeman of the whole estate. What Plato has thought, he may think; what a saint has felt, he may feel; what at any time has befallen any man, he can understand. Who hath access to this Universal Mind, *is a party to all that is or can be done,* for this is the only and sovereign agent."

The great German physicist Nernst found that the longer an electric current was made to flow through a filament of oxide of magnesium, the greater became the conductivity of the filament.

In the same way, the more you call upon and use your subconscious mind, the greater becomes its conductivity in passing along to you the infinite resources of Universal Mind. The wisdom of a Solomon, the skill of a Michael Angelo, the genius of an Edison, the daring of a Napoleon, *all* may be yours. It rests with you only to form the contact with Universal Mind in order to draw from it what you will.

Think of this power as something that you can connect with any time. It has the answer to all of your problems. It offers you freedom from fear, from worry, from sickness, from accident. No man and no thing can interfere with your use of this power or diminish your share of it. No one, that is, but yourself.

Don Carlos Musser expresses it well in "You Are":

"Because of the law of gravitation the apple falls to the ground. Because of the law of growth the acorn becomes a mighty oak. Because of the law of causation, a man is 'as he thinketh in his heart.' Nothing can happen without its adequate cause."

Success does not come to you by accident. It comes as the logical result of the operation of law. Mind, working through your brain and your body, makes your world. That it is not a better world and a bigger one is due to your limited thoughts and beliefs. They dam back the flood of ideas that Mind is constantly striving to manifest through you. God never made a failure or a nobody. He offers to the highest and the lowest alike all that is necessary to happiness and success. The difference is entirely in the extent to which each of us AVAILS himself of that generosity.

There is no reason why you should hesitate to aspire to any position, any honor, any goal, for the Mind within you is fully able to meet any need. It is no more difficult for it to handle a great problem than a small one. Mind is just as much present in your little everyday affairs as in those of a big business or a great nation. Don't set it doing trifling sums in arithmetic when it might just as well be solving problems of moment to yourself and the world.

Start something! Use your initiative. Give your mind something to work upon. The greatest of all success secrets is initiative. It is the one quality which more than any other has put men in high places.

Conceive something. Conceive it first in your own mind. Make the pattern there and your subconscious mind will draw upon the plastic substance or energy all about you to make that model real.

Drive yourself. Force yourself. It is the dreamer, the man with imagination, who has made the world move. Without him, we would still be in the Stone Age.

Galileo looked at the moon and dreamed of how he might reach it. The telescope was the fruition of that dream. Watt dreamed of what might be done with steam—and our great locomotives and engines of today are the result. Franklin dreamed of harnessing the lightning—and today we have man-made thunderbolts.

Initiative, plus imagination, will take you anywhere. Imagination opens the eyes of the mind, and there is nothing good you can image there that is not possible of fulfillment in your daily life.

Imagination is the connecting link between the human and the Divine, between the formed universe and formless energy. It is, of all things human, the most God-like. It is our part of Divinity. Through it we share in the creative power of Universal Mind. Through it we can turn the most drab existence into a thing of life and beauty. It is the means by which we avail ourselves of all the good which Universal Mind is constantly offering to us in such profusion. It is the means by which we can reach any goal, win any prize.

What was it gave us the submarine, the aeroplane, wireless, electricity? Imagination. What was it that enabled man to build the Simplon Tunnel, the Panama Canal, the Hell Gate span? Imagination. What is it that makes us successful and happy, or poor and friendless? Imagination—or the lack of it.

It was imagination that sent Spanish and English and French adventurers to this new world. It was imagination that urged the early settlers westward—ever westward. It was imagination that built out railroads, our towns, our great cities.

Parents foolishly try to discourage imagination in their children, when all it needs is proper guidance. For imagination forms the world from which their future will take its shape. Restrain the one and you constrict the other. Develop the one in the right way, and there is no limit to the other. Uncontrolled, the imagination is like a rudderless ship. Or even, at times, like the lightning. But properly controlled, it is like the ship that carries riches from port to port. Or like the electric current, carrying unlimited power for industry and progress.

Do you want happiness? Do you want success? Do you want position, power, riches? *Image them!* How did God first make man? "In his image created He him." He "imaged" man in His Mind.

And that is the way everything has been made since time began. It was first imaged in Mind. That is the way everything you want must start—with a mental image.

So use your imagination! Picture in it your Heart's Desire. Imagine it—day-dream it so vividly, so clearly, that you will actually BELIEVE you HAVE it. In the moment that you carry this conviction to your subconscious mind—in that moment your dream will become a reality. It may be a while before you realize it, but the important part is done. You have created the model. You can safely leave it to your subconscious mind to do the rest.

When Jesus adjured His disciples—"Whatsoever ye desire, when ye pray, believe that ye RECEIVE it," He was not only telling them a great truth, but he was teaching what we moderns would call excellent psychology as well. For this "belief" is what acts upon the subconscious mind. It is through this "belief" that formless energy is compressed into material form.

Every man wants to get out of the rut, to grow, to develop into something better. Here is the open road—open to you whether you have schooling, training, position, wealth, or not. Remember this: Your subconscious mind knew more from the time you were a baby than is in all the books in all the colleges and libraries of the world.

So don't let lack of training, lack of education, hold you back. Your mind can meet every need—and will do so if you give it the chance. The Apostles were almost all poor men, uneducated men, yet they did a work that is unequalled in historical annals. Joan of Arc was a poor peasant girl, unable to read or write—*yet she saved France!* The pages of history are dotted with poor men, uneducated men, who thought great thoughts, who used their imaginations to master circumstances and became rulers of men. Most great dynasties started with some poor, obscure man. Napoleon came of a poor, humble family. He got his appointment to the Military Academy only through very hard work and the pulling of many political strings. Even as a Captain of Artillery he was so poverty-stricken that he was unable to buy his equipment when offered an appointment to India. Business today is full of successful men who have scarcely the rudiments of ordinary education. It was only after he had made his millions that Andrew Carnegie hired a tutor to give him the essentials of an education.

So it isn't training and it isn't education that make you successful. These help, but the thing that really counts is that gift of the Gods—*Creative Imagination!*

You have that gift. *Use it!* Make every thought, every fact, that comes into your mind *pay you a profit.* Make it work and produce for you. Think of things—not as they are but as they MIGHT be. Make them real, live and interesting. Don't merely dream—but *CREATE!* Then use your imagination to make that CREATION of advantage to mankind—and, incidentally, yourself.

CHAPTER 20

What Do You Lack?

"I read the papers every day, and oft encounter tales which show there's hope for every jay who in life's battle fails. I've just been reading of a gent who joined the has-been ranks, at fifty years without a cent, or credit at the banks. But undismayed he buckled down, refusing to be beat, and captured fortune and renown; he's now on Easy Street. Men say that fellows down and out ne'er leave the rockly track, but facts will show, beyond a doubt, that has-beens do come back. I know, for I who write this rhyme, when forty-odd years old, was down and out, without a dime, my whiskers full of mold. By black disaster I was trounced until it jarred my spine; I was a failure so pronounced I didn't need a sign. And after I had soaked my coat, I said (at forty-three), 'I'll see if I can catch the goat that has escaped from me.' I labored hard; I strained my dome, to do my daily grind, until in triumph I came home, my billy-goat behind. And any man who still has health may with the winners stack, and have a chance at fame and wealth—for has-beens do come back."

—WALT MASON*

Do you know why it is that the Bolsheviki are so opposed to religion?

Because religion, as it is commonly accepted, teaches man resignation to conditions as they are—teaches, in effect, that God created some men poor and some rich. That this unequal distribution is a perfectly natural thing. And that we must not rail against it because it will all be made right in the next world.

Napoleon, in his early Jacobin days, denounced religion for that very reason. But when he had won to power, when he planned to make himself Emperor, then he found he had need for that religion, and re-established the Church in France.

For, he reasoned, how can people be satisfied without religion? If one man is starv-

*From "Walt Mason—His Book." Barse & Hopkins, Newark, N.J.

ing, near another who is making himself sick by eating too much, how can you expect to keep the starving one resigned to his fate unless you teach him it will all be made right in some indefinite future state?

Organized society could not exist, as he planned it, without some being rich and some poor, and to keep the poor satisfied, there must be an authority to declare—"God wills it thus. But just be patient. In the hereafter all this will be different. YOU will be the ones then to occupy the places of honor."

Religion, in other words—as it is ordinarily taught—*is a fine thing to keep the common people satisfied!*

But Christianity was never meant for a weapon to keep the rich wealthy and secure, the poor satisfied and in their proper place. On the contrary, Christianity as taught by Jesus opened the way to all Good. And Christianity as it was practiced in its early years was an idealized form of Socialism that benefited each and all. No one was wealthier than his neighbors, it is true—but neither was any poverty-stricken. Theirs was the creed of the Three Musketeers—"All for one, and one for all!"

"Ask and ye shall receive," said Jesus. "Seek and ye shall find." That was not directed to the rich alone. That was to ALL men.

Providence has never made a practice of picking out certain families or certain individuals and favoring them to the detriment of other people—much as some of our "leading families" would have us believe it. It is only man that has arrogated to himself that privilege. We laugh now at the "divine right of Kings." It is just as ridiculous to think that a few have the right to all the good things of life, while the many have to toil and sweat to do them service.

To quote Rumbold's last words from the scaffold—"I never could believe that Providence had sent a few men into the world ready booted and spurred to ride, and millions ready saddled and bridled to be ridden."

There is nothing right in poverty. Not only that, but there is nothing meritorious in poverty. The mere fact that you are poor and ground down by fear and worry is not going to get you any forwarder in the hereafter. On the contrary, your soul is likely to be too pinched by want, too starved and shrivelled to be able to expand.

"The Kingdom of Heaven is within you." To me that means that Heaven is here and now. That if we want any happiness from it we've got to get it as we go along. I've never been much of a believer in accepting these promissory notes for happiness. Every time one of them falls due, you find you just have to renew it for another six months or a year, until one of these days you wake up and find that the bank has busted and all your notes are not worth the paper they are written on.

The Cumaean Sibyl is said to have offered Tarquin the Proud nine books for what he thought an exorbitant sum. So he refused. She burned three of the books, and placed the same price on the six as on the original nine. Again he refused. She burned three more books, and offered the remainder for the sum she had first asked. This time Tarquin accepted. The books were found to contain prophecies and invaluable directions regarding Roman policy, but alas, they were no longer complete.

So it is with happiness. If you take it as you go along, you get it in its entirety. But if you keep putting off the day when you shall enjoy it—if you keep taking promissory notes for happiness—every day will mean one day less of it that you will have. Yet the cost is just the same.

The purpose of existence is GROWTH. You can't grow spiritually or mentally without happiness. And by Happiness I don't mean a timid resignation to the "Will of God." That so-called "Will of God" is more often than not either pure laziness on the part of the resigned one or pure cussedness on the part of the one that is "putting something over" on him. It is the most sanctimonious expression yet devised to excuse some condition that no one has the energy or the ability to rectify.

No—by Happiness I mean the everyday enjoyment of everyday people. I mean love and laughter and honest amusement. Every one of us is entitled to it. Every one of us can have it—if he has the WILL and the ENERGY to get out and get it for himself.

Joyless work, small pay, no future, nothing to look forward to—God never planned such an existence. It is man-made—and you can be man enough to unmake it as far as you and yours are concerned.

God never made any man poor any more than He made any man sick. Look around you. All of Nature is bountiful. On every hand you see profusion—in the trees, in the flowers, in everything that He planned. The only Law of Nature is the law of Supply. Poverty is unnatural. It is man-made, through the limits man puts upon himself. God never put them there any more than He showed partiality by giving to some of His children gifts and blessings which He withheld from others. His gifts are just as available to you as to any man on earth. The difference is all in your understanding of how to avail yourself of the infinite supply all about you.

Take the worry clamps off your mentality and you will make the poverty clamps loosen up from your finances. Your affairs are so closely related to your consciousness that they too will relax into peace, order and plenty. Divine ideas in your spiritual consciousness will become active in your business, and will work out as your abundant prosperity.

As David V. Bush says in "Applied Psychology and Scientific Living"—"Thoughts are things; thoughts are energy; thoughts are magnets which attract to us the very things which we think. Therefore, if a man is in debt, he will, by continually thinking about debt, bring more debts to him. For thoughts are causes, and he fastens more debts on to himself and actually creates more obligations by thinking about debts.

"Concentrate and think upon things that you want; not on things which you ought not to have. Think of abundance, of opulence, of plenty, of position, harmony and growth, and if you do not see them manifested today, they will be realized to-morrow. If you must pass through straits of life where you do not outwardly see abundance, know that you have it within, and that in time it will manifest itself.

"I say, if you concentrate on debt, debt is what you will have; if you think about poverty, poverty is what you will receive. It is just as easy, when once the mind becomes trained, to think prosperity and abundance and plenty, as it is to think lack, limitation and poverty."

Prosperity is not limited to time or to place. It manifests when and where there is consciousness to establish it. It is attracted to the consciousness that is free from worry, strain and tension.

So never allow yourself to worry about poverty. Be careful, take ordinary business precautions—of course. But don't center your thought on your *troubles.* The more you think of them, the more tightly you fasten them upon yourself. Think of the *results* you are after—not of the difficulties in the way. Mind will find the way. It is merely up to you to choose the goal, then keep your thought steadfast until that goal is won.

The greatest short-cut to prosperity is to *LIVE IT!* Prosperity attracts. Poverty repels. To quote Orison Swett Marden—"To be ambitious for wealth and yet always expecting to be poor, to be always doubting your ability to get what you long for, is like trying to reach East by travelling West. There is no philosophy which will help a man to succeed when he is always doubting his ability to do so, and thus attracting failure."

Again: "No matter how hard you may work for success, if your thought is saturated with the fear of failure it will kill your efforts, neutralize your endeavors, and make success impossible."

The secret of prosperity lies in so vividly imaging it in your own mind that you literally exude prosperity. You feel prosperous, you look prosperous, and the result is that before long you ARE prosperous.

I remember seeing a play a number of years ago that was based on this thought. A young fellow—a chronic failure—was persuaded by a friend to carry a roll of $1,000 counterfeit bills in his pocket, and to show them, unostentatiously, when the occasion offered. Of course, everyone thought he had come into some legacy. The natural inference was that anyone who carried fifty or a hundred thousand-dollar bills in his pockets must have a lot more in the bank. Opportunities flocked to him. Opportunities to make good. Opportunities to make money. He made good! And that without having to spend any of this spurious money of his. For most business today is done on credit. I know many wealthy men who seldom carry anything but a little change in their pockets for tips. Everything they do, everything they buy, is "charged." And big deals are put through in the same way. If a man is believed to have plenty of money, if he has a reputation for honesty and fair-dealing, he may put through a transaction running into six or seven figures without paying one cent down. The thing that counts is not the amount of your balance at the Bank, but what others THINK of you, the IMAGE you have created in your own and in others' minds.

What do you lack? What thing do you want most? Realize that before it or any other thing can be, it must first be imaged in Mind. Realize, too, that when you can close your eyes and actually SEE that thing, *you have brought it into being*—you have drawn upon that invisible substance all about you—you have *created something.* Hold it in your thought, focus your mind upon it, "BELIEVE THAT YOU HAVE IT"—and you can safely leave its material manifestation to the Genie-of-your-Mind.

God is but another name for the invisible, everywhere-present, Source-of-things. Out of the air the seed gathers the essences which are necessary to its bountiful growth; out of the invisible ether our minds gather the rich ideas that stimulate us to undertake and to carry out enterprises that bring prosperity to us. Let us see with the eye of the mind a bountiful harvest; then our minds will be quickened with ideas of abundance, and plenty will appear, not only in our world but everywhere.

"As the rain cometh down and the snow from heaven, and returneth not thither, but watereth the earth, and maketh it bring forth and bud, and giveth seed to the sower and bread to the eater; so shall my word be that goeth forth out of my mouth: it shall not return unto me void, but it shall accomplish that which I please, and it shall prosper in the thing whereto I sent it."—Isaiah.

CHAPTER 21

The Sculptor and the Clay

"Eternal mind the Potter is,
And thought the eternal clay.
The hand that fashions is divine;
His works pass not away.
God could not make imperfect man
His model Infinite, Unhallowed thought
He could not plan—Love's work and Love must fit."

—ALICE DAYTON

When you step into your office on Monday morning, no doubt you have dreams of wonderful achievement. Your step is firm, your brain is clear and you have carefully thought out just WHAT you will do and HOW you will accomplish big things in your business. Perhaps the very plans you have in mind will influence your whole business career, and you have visions of the dollars that will be yours rolling into your bank account.

But do these dreams come true?

Are you always able to put through what you had planned to do—does your day's work have the snap and power you imagined it would have? Are you ever forced to admit that your dreams of big accomplishment are often shattered because of "fagged nerves" and lack of energy, because you have not the "pep"?

How easy it is to think back and see how success was in your grasp if only you had felt equal to that extra bit of effort, if only you had had the "pep," the energy to reach out and take it. The great men of the world have been well men, strong men. Sickness and hesitancy go hand in hand. Sickness means weakness, querulousness, lack of faith, lack of confidence in oneself and in others.

But there is no real reason for sickness or weakness, and there is no reason why you should remain weak or sick if you are so afflicted now.

Remember the story of the sculptor Pygmalion? How he made a statue of marble so beautiful that every woman who saw it envied it? So perfect was it that he fell in love with it himself, hung it with flowers and jewels, spent day after day in rapt admiration of it, until finally the gods took pity upon him and breathed into it the breath of life.

There is more than Pagan mythology to that story. There is this much truth in it—that any man can set before his mind's eye the image of the figure he himself would like to be, and then breathe the breath of life into it merely by keeping that image before his subconscious mind as the model on which to do its daily building.

For health and strength are natural. It is ill-health and weakness that are unnatural. Your body was meant to be lithe, supple, muscular, full of red-blooded energy and vitality. A clear brain, a powerful heart, a massive chest, wrists and arms of steel—all these were meant for you—all these you can have if you will but *know,* and *feel,* and *think aright.*

Just take stock of yourself for a moment. Are your muscles tough, springy and full of vim? Do they do all you ask of them—and then beg for more? Can you eat a good meal—and forget it?

If you can't, it's your own fault. You can have a body alive with vitality, a skin smooth and fine of texture, muscles supple and virile. You can be the man you have always dreamed of being, without arduous dieting, without tiresome series of exercises, merely by following the simple rules herein laid down.

For what is it that builds up the muscles, puts energy and vitality into your system, gives you the pep and vigor of youth? *Is it exercise?* Then why is it that so many day laborers are poor, weak, anaemic creatures, forced to lay off from one to three months every year on account of sickness? They get plenty of exercise and fresh air. Why is it that so many athletes die of tuberculosis or of weak hearts? They get the most scientific exercise year in and year out.

Just the other day I read of the sudden death of Martin A. Delaney, the famous trainer, known all over the country as a physical director. He taught thousands how to be strong, but "Athletic Heart" killed him at 55. Passersby saw him running for a car, then suddenly topple over dead.

"Exercise as a panacea for all human ills is dangerously overrated," Dr. Charles M. Wharton, in charge of health and physical education at the University of Pennsylvania, said today (March 20, 1926), according to an Associated Press despatch.

Dr. Wharton, who has been a trainer of men for thirty years and was an all-American guard on the Pennsylvania football team in 1895 and 1896, declared the search for the fountain of youth by exercise and diet has been commercialized to a point of hysteria.

"Some one should cry a halt against this wild scramble for health by unnatural means," said Dr. Wharton. "This indiscriminate adoption of severe physical training destroys the health of more people than it improves."

Dr. Wharton said he was appalled by the amount of physical defects and weaknesses developed by overindulgence in athletics by students in preparatory schools.

"I know I am presenting an unpopular viewpoint, and it may sound strange coming from a physical director.

"In gymnasium work at the University of Pennsylvania we try to place our young men in sports *which they will enjoy,* and thus get a physical stimulation from *relaxed play.*"

Is it diet? Then why is it that so many people you know, who have been dieting for years, are still such poor, flabby creatures? Doesn't it always work, or is it merely a matter of guess-work—and those were the cases where no one happened to guess right? Why is it that doctors disagree so on what is the correct diet? For years we have been taught to forswear too much meat. For years we have been told that it causes rheumatism and gout and hardening of the arteries—and a dozen or more other ailments.

Now comes Dr. Woods Hutchinson—a noted authority, quoted the world over—and says: "All the silly old prejudice against meat, that it heated the blood (whatever that means) and produced uric acid to excess, hardened the arteries, inflamed the kidneys, caused rheumatism, etc., has now been proved to be pure fairy tales, utterly without foundation in scientific fact.

"Red meats have nothing whatever to do with causing gout and rheumatism, because neither of these diseases is due to foods or drinks of any sort, but solely to what we call local infections. Little pockets of pus (matter) full of robber germs—mostly streptococci—around the roots of our teeth, in the pouches of our tonsils, in the nasal passages and sinuses of our foreheads and faces opening into them; . . . Our belief now is: 'No pockets of pus, no rheumatism or gout.' Food of any kind has absolutely nothing to do with the case.

"On the other hand, the very worst cases on record in all medical history of hardening and turning to lime (calcification) of the arteries all over the body, and in the kidneys and intestines particularly, have been found in Trappist and certain orders of Oriental monks who live almost exclusively upon starch and pulse—that is, peas, beans, and lentils, and abstain from meat entirely."

Then what is right? *Is it the combination of diet and exercise?* But surely the patients in sanitariums and similar institutions would have every chance to get just the right combination, yet how often you see them come out little, if any, better off than when they went in?

No. None of these is the answer. As a matter of fact, the principal good of either diet or exercise is that it keeps before the patient's mind the RESULT he is working for, and in that way tends to impress it upon his subconscious mind. That is why physical culturists always urge you to exercise in front of a mirror. If results are achieved, it is MIND that achieves them—not the movements you go through or the particular kind of food you eat.

Understand, I don't ask you to stop exercising. A reasonable amount of light, pleasant exercise is good for you mentally and physically. It develops your will power. It helps to impress upon your subconscious mind the image you want to see realized in your body. And it takes your mind off your troubles and worries, centering your thoughts instead upon your desires. Just where your thoughts should always be.

Outdoor exercise, tennis, horseback, swimming—any sort of active *game*—is the best rest there is for a tired mind. For mental tiredness comes from a too steady contemplation of one's problems. And anything that will take one's mind completely off them, and give the subconscious time to work out the solution, is good. That is why it so often happens that you go back to your work after a day of play—not merely refreshed but with so clear a mind that the problems which before seemed insurmountable are but as child's play to you.

You who envy the rosy cheek and sparkling eye of youth, who awake in the morning weary and unrefreshed, who go to your daily tasks with fagged brain and heavy tread—just remember that Perfect Youth or Perfect Health is merely a state of mind.

There is only one thing that puts muscles on your bones. There is only one thing that keeps your organs functioning with precision and regularity. There is only one thing that builds for you a perfect body. That one thing is your subconscious mind.

Every cell and tissue, every bone and sinew, every organ and muscle in your entire body is subject to the control of your subconscious mind. As it directs, so they build or function.

True, that subconscious mind accepts suggestions from your conscious mind. Hold before it the thought that the exercise you are taking is building muscle upon your arms or shoulders, and your subconscious mind will fall in readily with the suggestion and strengthen those muscles. Hold before it the thought that some particular food gives you unusual energy and "pep," and the subconscious mind will be entirely agreeable to producing the added vigor.

But have you ever noticed how some sudden joy (which is entirely a mental state) energizes and revitalizes you—*more than all the exercise or all the tonics you can take?* Have you ever noticed how martial music will relieve the fatigue of marching men? Have you ever noticed how sorrow (which is entirely a mental state) will depress and devitalize you, *regardless of any amount of exercise or health foods you may take?*

Each of us has within him all the essentials that go to the making of a Super-Man. But so has every acorn the essentials for making a great oak tree, yet the Japanese show us that even an oak may be stunted by continual pruning of its shoots. Negative and weak thoughts, thoughts of self-doubt, of mistrust, continually prune back the vigorous life ever seeking so valiantly to show forth the splendor and strength of the radiant inner self.

Choose what you will be! Your responsibility is to think, speak, act the true inner self. Your privilege is to show forth in this self the fullness of peace and plenty. Keep steadfastly in mind the idea of yourself that you want to see realized. Your daily, hourly and continual idea of yourself, your life, your affairs, your world, and your associates determines the harvest, the showing forth. Look steadfastly to your highest ideal of self, and your steadfast and lofty ideal will draw forth blessing and prosperity not only upon you but upon all who know you.

For mind is the only creator, and thought is the only energy. All that counts is the image of your body that you are holding in your thought. If heretofore that image has been one of weakness, of ill-health, change it *now*—TODAY. Repeat to yourself, the first thing upon awakening in the morning and the last thing before going to sleep at night—"My body was made in the image and likeness of God. God first imagined it in its entirety, therefore every cell and bone and tissue is perfect, every organ and muscle performing its proper function. That is the only model of me in Universal Mind. That is the only model of me that my Subconscious Mind knows. Therefore, since Mind—God—is the only creator, *that is the only model of me that I can have!*"

CHAPTER 22

Why Grow Old?

"And Moses was an hundred and twenty years old when he died:
his eye was not dim, nor his natural force abated."

Remember how you used to plough through great masses of work day after day and month after month, cheerily, enthusiastically, with never a sign of tiring or nervous strain? Remember how you used to enjoy those evenings, starting out as fresh from your office or shop as if you hadn't just put a hard day's work behind you?

No doubt you've often wondered why you can't work and enjoy yourself like that now, but solaced yourself with the moth-eaten fallacy that "as a man grows older he shouldn't expect to get the same fun out of life that he did in his earlier years."

Poor old exploded idea!

Youth is not a matter of time. It is a mental state. You can be just as brisk, just as active, just as light-hearted now as you were ten or twenty years ago. Genuine youth is just a perfect state of health. You can have that health, and the boundless energy and capacity for work or enjoyment that go with it. You can cheat time of ten, twenty or fifty years—not by taking thought of what you shall eat or what you shall drink, not by diet or exercise, but solely through a right understanding of what you should expect of your body.

"If only I had my life to live over again!" How often you have heard it said. How often you have thought it.

But the fact is that you CAN have it. You can start right now and live again as many years as you have already experienced. Health, physical freedom and full vigor need not end for you at 35 or 40—nor at 60 or 70. Age is not a matter of years. It is a state of mind.

In an address before the American Sociological Society a few months ago Dr. Hornell Hart of Bryn Mawr predicted, "Babies born in the year 2000 will have something like 200 years of life ahead of them, and men and women of 100 years will be quite the normal thing. But instead of being wrinkled and crippled, these centenarians will be in their vigorous prime."

Thomas Parr, an Englishman, lived to be 152 years old, and was sufficiently hale and hearty at the age of 120 to take unto himself a second wife. Even at 152, his death was not due to old age but to a sudden and drastic change in his manner of life. All his days he had lived upon simple fare, but his fame reaching the King, he was invited to London and there feasted so lavishly that he died of it.

In a despatch to *The New York Times* on February 14th last, I read of an Arab now in Palestine, one Salah Mustapha Salah Abu Musa, who at the age of 105 *is growing his third set of teeth!*

There is an ancient city in Italy which can be approached by sea only through a long stretch of shallow water full of rocks and cross currents. There is one safe channel, and it is marked by posts. In the days of the Sea Rovers the city used to protect itself by pulling up the posts whenever a rover hove in sight.

Mankind has taken to planting posts along its way to mark the flight of time. Every year we put in a new one, heedless of the fact that we are thus marking a clear channel for our Arch-Enemy, Age, to enter in from the sea of human belief.

But the fact is that there is no natural reason for man to grow old as soon as he does, *no biological reason for him to grow old at all!*

Why is it that the animals live eight to ten times their maturity, when man lives only about twice his? Why? Because man hastens decrepitude and decay by holding the thought of old age always before him.

Dr. Alexis Carrel, Noble Prize winner and member of the Rockefeller Institute, has demonstrated that living cells taken from a body, properly protected and fed, can be kept alive indefinitely. Not only that but they *grow!* In 1912 he took some tissue from the heart of an embryo chick and placed it in a culture medium. It is living and growing yet.

Recently Dr. Carrel showed a moving picture of these living cells before the American Institute of Electrical Engineers. They grow so fast that they double in size every twenty-four hours, and have to be trimmed daily!

The cells of your being can be made to live indefinitely when placed outside your body. Single-celled animals never die a natural death. They live on and on until something kills them. Now scientists are beginning to wonder if multi-cellular animals like man really need to die.

Under the title, "Immortality and Rejuvenation in Modern Biology," M. Metalnikov, of the Pasteur Institute, has just published a volume that should be read by all those who have decided that it is necessary to grow old and die.

Here is the first sentence of the concluding chapter of the book: "What we have just written forces us to maintain our conviction that immortality is the fundamental property of living organisms."

And further on:

"Old age and death are not a stage of earthly existence. . . ."

And that, mind you, is set forth under the aegis of a scientific establishment that has no equal in the world, and of a scholar universally respected.

As the *Journal of Paris* says in reviewing the article:

"Most religious and philosophic systems assert the immortality of the soul. But the positive sciences have shown themselves more skeptical on this point. This idea seems to them quite contradictory to all that we know, or think we know, of animal life. Animal life originates as a tiny germ, which becomes an embryo, developing into an adult organism, which grows old and finally dies. This means the disappearance of all the faculties of life that so clearly distinguish it from an inanimate object. There is no scientific evidence to show that at this moment the 'soul' does not disappear with the body, and that it continues its existence separately. Biologists cannot even conceive the possibility of separation of soul and body, so strong and indissoluble are the bonds that unite all our psychic manifestations with our bodily life. For them an immortal soul only can exist in an immortal body. What if it were so? What if our organism is really indestructible? It is this that M. Metalnikov attempts scientifically to prove.

"Death is a permanent and tangible phenomenon only in the case of man and the higher animals. It is not so for plants and for the simpler forms of animal life, the protozoans. These last, composed often of a single cell, just observable under the microscope, are however without the chief faculties that characterize the higher animals. They move about by means of vibratory hair-like processes, sustain themselves, seek their food, hunt animals still smaller than themselves, react to irritations of different kinds, and multiply. But this multiplication is not effected by means of special organs, as among the higher animals, but by the division of the whole organism into two equal parts. The common infusoria which abound in fresh water thus divide once or twice every twenty-four hours. Each daughter cell continues to live like the mother cell, of which it is the issue; it feeds, grows, and divides in its turn. And never, in this constantly renewed cycle in their lives, do we find the phenomenon of natural death, so characteristic and so universal in the higher animals. The infusorium is subject only to accidental death, such as we can cause by the addition of some poisonous element to the water in which it lives, or by heat.

"Experiments along this line were made long ago. The first were by de Saussure, in 1679. Having put an infusorium in a drop of water, he saw it divide under his eye. Four days later it was impossible to count the number of creatures. However, some authors thought that this reproductive facility was not unlimited. Maupas himself, who made a minute study of it forty years ago and succeeded in observing 700 successive generations of a single species, thought that it was finally subject to old age and to death.

"But the more recent works of Joukovsky at Heidelberg, of Koulaghine at Petrograd, of Calkins in England, of Weissmann, and still others, lead to an opposite opinion. The degeneration observed by these workers was due to autointoxication, caused by not renewing the culture-medium.

"Decisive experiments were made in Russia, dating from 1907, by Woodruff and by M. Metalnikov himself. Begun at Tsarskoe Selo, they continued until the tragic hours of the 1917 revolution, and were renewed at the University of Crimea. These investigators took an infusorium found in an aquarium, the Paramoecium caudatum, whose characteristics are well determined, and in thirteen years, in 1920, they had obtained 5,000 successive generations. . . .

"Thus we are bound to say that a unicellular body possesses within itself the power of immortality.

"And we ourselves are made up only by the juxtaposition of simple cells."

THE FOUNTAIN OF YOUTH

Four hundred years ago Ponce de León set sail into the mysteries of an unknown world in search of the Fountain of Youth, when all the time the secret of that fountain was right within himself.

For the fact is that no matter how many years have passed since you were born, *you are only eleven months old today!* Your body is constantly renewing itself. The one thing about it you can be surest of is CHANGE. Every one of the millions of cells of which it is composed is constantly being renewed. Even your bones are daily renewing themselves in this way.

These cells are building—building—building. Every day they tear down old tissue and rebuild it with new. There is not a cell in your body, not a muscle or tissue, not a bone, that is more than eleven months old! Why then should you feel age? Why should you be any less spry, any less cheerful, than these youngsters around you that you have been envying?

The answer is that you *need not*—if you will but realize your YOUTHFULNESS. Every organ, every muscle, tissue and cell of your body is subject to your subconscious mind. They rebuild exactly as that mind directs them. What is the model *you* are holding before your mind's eye? Is it one of age, of decrepitude? That is the model that most men use, because they know no better. That is the result that you see imaged upon their bodies.

But you need not follow their outworn models. You can hold before your mind's eye only the vision of youth, of manly vigor, of energy and strength and beauty—*and that is the model that your cells will use to build upon.*

Do you know what is responsible for the whole difference between Youth and Age? Just one thing. Youth looks *forward* always to something better. Age looks backward and sighs over its "lost" youth.

In youth we are constantly growing. We KNOW we have not yet reached our prime. We know we can expect to continually IMPROVE. We look forward to ever-increasing physical powers. We look forward to a finer, more perfect physique. We look forward to greater mental alertness. We have been educated to expect these things. Therefore we BELIEVE we shall get them—and we GET them!

But what happens after we get to be thirty or forty years of age? We think we have reached our prime. We have been taught that we can no longer look forward to greater growth—that all we can hope for is to "hold our own" for a little while, and then start swiftly downward to old age and decay. History shows that no nation, no institution and no individual can continue for any length of time to merely "hold his own." You must go forward—or back. You must move—or life will pass you by. Yours is the choice. If you will realize that there is never any end to GROWTH—that your body is constantly being rebuilt—that perfection is still so far ahead of you that you can continue GROWING towards it indefinitely—you need never know age. You can keep on growing more perfect, mentally and physically, every day. Every minute you live is a minute of conception and rebirth.

You may be weak and anaemic. You may be crippled or bent. No matter! You can start today to rebuild along new lines. In eleven months at the most, every one of those weak and devitalized cells, every one of those bent and crippled bones, will be replaced by new, strong, vigorous tissue.

Look at Annette Kellerman—crippled and deformed as a child—yet she grew up into the world's most perfectly formed woman. Look at Roosevelt—weak and anaemic as a young man—yet he made himself the envy of the world for boundless vigor and energy. And they are but two cases out of thousands I could quote. Many of the world's strongest men were weaklings in their childhood. It matters not what your age, what your condition—you can start now renewing your youth, growing daily nearer the model of YOU that is imaged in Universal Mind.

Arthur Brisbane says that at the age of 85 George F. Baker is doing the work of ten men.

That is what every man of 85 ought to be doing, for he should have not only the physical vigor and strength and enthusiasm of 21, but combined with them he should have the skill and experience, the ripened judgment of 85.

There is no more despairing pronouncement than the belief of the average man that he matures only to begin at once to deteriorate and decay. When the actual fact is, as stated in a recent utterance by the eminent Dr. Hammond, *there is no physiological reason* why a man should die. He asserted—and the statement is corroborated by scientists and physiologists—that the human body possesses inherent capacity to renew and continue itself and its functions indefinitely!

Your body wear out? Of course it does—just as all material things do. But with this difference—your body is being renewed just as fast as it wears out! Have you damaged some part of it? Don't worry. Down inside you is a chemical laboratory which can make new parts just as good or better than the old. Up in your subconscious mind is a Master Chemist with all the formulas of Universal Mind to draw upon, who can keep that chemical laboratory of yours making new parts just as fast as you can wear out the old.

But that Master Chemist is like all of us—like you. He is inclined to lazy a bit on the job—if you let him. Try to relieve him of some of his functions—and he won't bother about them further. Take to the regular use of drugs or other methods of eliminating the waste matter from the body, and your Master Chemist will figure that your conscious mind has taken over this duty from him—and he will leave it thereafter to your conscious mind. Lead him to believe that you no longer expect him to rebuild your body along such perfect lines as in youth—and he will slow down in his work of removing the old, worn-out tissues, and of replacing them with new, better material. The result? Arteries clogged with worn-out cells. Tissues dried and shrunken. Joints stiff and creaky. In short—Old Age.

The fault is not with the Master Chemist. It is with you. You didn't hold him to the job. When a business or an enterprise or an expedition fails, it is not the rank and file who are to blame—it is the directing head. He didn't give his men the right plans to work on. He didn't supply the proper leadership. He didn't keep them keyed up to their best work.

What would you think of an engineer who, with the best plans in the world, the best material with which to build, threw away his plans when he was half through with the job and let his men do as they pleased, ruining all his early work and all his fine material by putting the rest of it together any which way?

Yet that is what you do when you stop LOOKING FORWARD at 30 or 40, and decide thereafter to just grow old any which way. You throw away the wonderful model on which you have been building, you take the finest material in the world, and let your workmen put it together any way they like. In fact, you do worse than that. You tell them you don't expect much from them anymore. That any sort of a patched-up job they put together after that will be about as good as you can look for.

Man alive! What would you expect from ordinary workmen to whom you talked like that? Your inner workmen are no different. You will get from them just what you look for—no more, no less.

"Your time of life" should be the best time you have yet known. The engineer who has built forty bridges should be far more proficient than the one who has built only a few. The model you are passing on to your Master Chemist now ought to be a vastly more perfect model than the one you gave to him at twenty. Instead of feeling that your heart is giving out and your stomach weak, you ought to be boasting of how much better a heart you are now making than a few years ago, how much more perfectly your stomach is functioning than before you learned that you were its boss.

Of one thing you can be sure. God never decreed a law of decay and death. If there is any such law, it is man-made—and man can unmake it. The Life Principle that came to this planet thousands or millions of years ago brought no Death Principle with it. For death is like darkness—it is nothing in itself. Death is merely the absence of life, just as darkness is merely the absence of light. Keep that life surging—strongly.

In the Book of Wisdom, of the Apocryphal writings, you read:

"For God made not death; neither hath He pleasure in the destruction of the living.

"For He created all things that they might have being; and the generative powers of the world are healthsome, and there is no poison of destruction in them, nor hath death dominion upon the earth.

"For righteousness is immortal:

"But ungodly men with their works and words called death unto them.

"For God created man to be immortal, and made Him to be an image of His own proper being.

"But by the envy of the devil came death into the world."

"Whosoever liveth and believeth in me (understandeth me)," said Jesus, "shall never die."

And again—"If a man keep my saying, he shall never see death."

Universal Mind knows no imperfection—no decay—no death. It does not produce sickness and death. It is your *conscious* mind that has decreed these evils. Banish the thought—and you can banish the effect. Life was never meant to be measured by years.

I remember reading a story of a traveler who had journeyed to a land of perpetual sun. Since there was no sunrise and no sunset, no moons or changing seasons, there was no means of measuring time. Therefore to the inhabitants of that land, time did not exist. And having no time, they never thought to measure ages and consequently never grew old. Like organisms with a single cell, they did not die except by violence.

There is more truth than fiction to that idea. The measurement of life by the calendar robs youth of its vigor and hastens old age. It reminds me of the days of our grandparents, when a woman was supposed to doff her hat and don a bonnet at 40. And donning a bonnet was like taking the veil. She was supposed to retire to her chimney corner and make way for the younger generation.

Men and women ought to *grow* with years into greater health, broader judgment, maturer wisdom. Instead of becoming atrophied, and dead to all new ideas, their minds should through practice hold ever stronger images before them of youthful vigor and freshness. The Psalmist says—"But thou art the same, and thy years shall have no end."

No one need retire to the chimney corner, no matter how many years have passed over his head. Years should bring wisdom and greater health—not decrepitude. Many of the world's famous men did their greatest work long after the age when most men are in their graves. Tennyson composed the immortal lines of "Crossing the Bar" at the age of 80. Plato still had pen in hand at 81. Cato learned Greek at the same age. Humboldt completed his "Cosmos" in his ninetieth year, while John Wesley at 82 said—"It is twelve years now since I have felt any such sensation as fatigue."

You are only as old as your mind. Every function, every activity of your body, is controlled by your mind. Your vital organs, your blood that sends the material for rebuilding to every cell and tissue, the processes of elimination that remove all the broken down and waste material, all are dependent for their functioning upon the energy derived from your mind.

The human body can be compared to an electric transportation system. When the dynamo runs at full power every car speeds along, and everything is handled with precision. But let the dynamo slow down and the whole system lags.

That dynamo is your mind, and your thoughts provide the energy that runs it. Feed it thoughts of health and vigor and your whole system will reflect energy and vitality. Feed it thoughts of decrepitude and age, and you will find it slowing down to the halting pace you set for it.

You can grow old at 30. You can be young at 90. It is up to you. Which do you choose?

If you choose youth, then start this minute renewing your youth. Find a picture—or, better still, a statuette—of the man you would like to be, the form you would like to have. Keep it in your room. When you go to bed at night, *visualize* it in your mind's eye—hold it in your thought as *YOU*—as the man *YOU ARE GOING TO BE!*

The Journal of Education had the idea in their story of "The Prince and the Statue" in a recent issue:

"There was once a prince who had a crooked back. He could never stand straight up like even the lowest of his subjects. Because he was a very proud prince his crooked back caused him a great deal of mental suffering.

"One day he called before him the most skilful sculptor in his kingdom and said to him: 'Make me a noble statue of myself, true to my likeness in every detail with this exception—make this statue with a straight back. I wish to see myself as I might have been.'

"For long months the sculptor worked hewing the marble carefully into the likeness of the prince, and at last the work was done, and the sculptor went before the prince and said: 'The statue is finished; where shall I set it up?' One of the courtiers called out: 'Set it before the castle gate where all can see it,' but the prince smiled sadly, and shook his head. 'Rather,' said he, 'place it in a secret nook in the palace garden where only I shall see it.' The statue was placed as the prince ordered, and promptly forgotten by the world, but every morning, and every noon, and every evening the prince stole quietly away to where it stood and looked long upon it, noting the straight back and the unlifted head, and the noble brow. And each time he gazed, something seemed to go out of the statue and into him, tingling in his blood and throbbing in his heart.

"The days passed into months and the months into years; then strange rumors began to spread throughout the land. Said one: 'The prince's back is no longer crooked or my eyes deceive me.' Said another: 'The prince is more noble-looking or my eyes deceive me.' Said another: 'Our prince has the high look of a mighty man,' and these rumors came to the prince, and he listened with a queer smile. Then went he out into the garden to where the statue stood and, behold, it was just as the people said, his back had become as straight as the statue's, his head had the same noble bearing; he was, in fact, the noble man his statue proclaimed him to be."

A novel idea? Not at all! Two thousand five hundred years ago, in the Golden Age of Athens, when its culture led the world, Grecian mothers surrounded themselves with beautiful statues that they might bring forth perfect children and that the children in turn might develop into perfect men and women.

Eleven months from now *you* will have an entirely new body, inside and out. Not a single cell, not a single bit of tissue that is now in you will be there then. What changes do you want made in that new body? What improvements?

Get your new model clearly in your mind's eye. Picture it. VISUALIZE it! Look FORWARD daily to a better physique, to greater mental power.

Give that model to your Subconscious Mind to build upon—and before eleven months are out, that model *WILL BE YOU!*

CHAPTER 23

The Medicine Delusion

"I find the medicine worse than the malady."

—SHAKESPEARE

"We are getting rid of the drug illusion," declared Dr. Woods Hutchinson, the noted medical writer of America, at a luncheon given on June 6, 1925, by the English-Speaking Union to 700 American and Canadian doctors assembled in London, England.

"We are willing even to subscribe to the dictum of Oliver Wendell Holmes," the doctor added, "that if 99 per cent of all drugs we possess were thrown into the sea it would be a good thing for the human race, but rather hard on the fishes."

Sir Arbuthnot Lane, Surgeon to King George, seconded Dr. Hutchinson's remarks. "They might say," he went on, "that he was trying to establish a 'suicide club' for doctors. It practically came to that, because as the public became educated in matters of health the medical profession might disappear. It was in fact an anomaly that a medical profession should exist. If people were healthy, there was no reason to have doctors at all."

Twenty-five years ago, the charms of the Patent Medicine fakir and the incantations of the Indian Medicine Man were in the heyday of their popularity. So long as you talked about their aches and pains, their diseases and ailments, people would buy any kind of a nostrum that an unscrupulous fakir chose to palm off upon them. Patent medicine manufacturers made fabulous fortunes selling cheap whisky adulterated with burnt sugar and water, under a hundred different names for $1.00 the bottle. You could hardly pick up a magazine or newspaper without seeing a dozen of their lurid ads.

The day of the Indian Medicine Man and street-corner fakir has passed. And for a time, thanks to the crusade against them led by *Collier's*, and backed by a number of other reputable magazines, patent medicine manufacturers suffered an eclipse.

But they are back again today in a more respectable guise.

Pick up almost any small-town paper and you will find a dozen "sovereign remedies" for tired women or fretful children or run-down men. Concoctions, most of them, containing just enough alcohol to give you a pleasant sense of stimulation, enough burnt sugar to color them—and a whole lot of water.

But if that were all, no great harm would be done. If the peddling of drugs depended entirely—or even mostly—on Patent Medicine advertisers, the end of it would soon be in sight. But it doesn't. The worst offenders of all are the ones who, of all people, should know better—some of the doctors.

Understand, I don't mean all of them. And I don't mean the best of them. There are thousands of them like Dr. Woods Hutchinson who have the courage to get up and say that medicine itself cannot cure disease. That it never has cured disease. That Nature is the only Healer. Drugs can give you temporary relief from pain—yes. They can cleanse—yes. But as for *curing* anything, the drug is not made that can do it.

The principal good that the administering of a drug has is in its effect upon the mind of the patient. Men have been taught for so many years that drugging is the only way to cure disease, that when you give them something, they BELIEVE they are going to be cured, and to the extent that they believe, they ARE CURED.

The best proof of that is to let two patients suffering from the same complaint go to two different physicians—the one a doctor of the regular school, the other a homeopath. The regular doctor will administer a dose containing ten thousand times as much of the mother drug as the homeopath. In fact, there is so slight a trace of any drug in the homeopath's prescription that it might be called none at all. Yet it frequently happens that his patient will respond just as readily to his denatured dose as the other will to his drug.

Dr. Gour, in a recent issue of *Pearson's Magazine,* said: "A few years ago there appeared an article in the *Atlantic Monthly* written by a young woman physician who was with the Red Cross in Russia. Immediately following the Kerensky revolution, the Russian peasants who, for the first time in their lives, found that they could keep what they earned, began to think of going to doctors for ailments which had afflicted them for years, but which they could never before afford to have treated. Within two weeks' time this young physician exhausted her supply of medicine. But the rush of peasant patients continued and she was reduced to the placebo idea of administering colored waters with a slight amount of a single drug—quinine, if I recall correctly. For several weeks she obtained such wonderful results in every conceivable form of affliction that she said her faith in specific medication was completely lost."

In a despatch from Rome to the New York *Herald-Tribune,* under date of June 15, 1926, I read:

"Under the skeptical eyes of local doctors Don Luigi Garofalo, a priest in the Quarto sector of Naples, alleges that he is curing all the ills that flesh is heir to, from pneumonia to broken bones, by a practical application of the theory derived from the text, 'Man is of dust and to dust he shall return.' Don Luigi argues that from a homeopathic viewpoint dust should be a curative element. So from dust taken from the reddish earth near Pozznoli, which contains traces of sulphur and copper, he makes pills for the afflicted, but he contends that any other earth will do.

"The cures, most of which have been effected by means of the red earth, include the healing of broken limbs, tubercular cases, toothache, internal lesions, heart disease, mumps, paralysis and fevers."

Of course, it is not to be inferred from this that reliance can be placed upon red earth—or any other kind of earth—to cure you of any ill. But it shows that even so common, ordinary a thing as a bit of dirt can be used to arouse people from the lethargic condition in which sickness so frequently leaves them, and give them the power to help themselves.

Take another case. Your doctor prescribes regular doses of some drug. You take it once. It has the desired effect. You take it again. The effect is not quite so pronounced. You keep it up—and in a short time *the drug seems to have lost its efficacy.*

Why? The same chemical elements are there. And if you mix the same chemical elements in a retort, you will get the same results whether you do it once or a thousand times. Why doesn't it work the same way with drugs and your body?

Because the strongest factor in bringing about the desired effect in the beginning was your BELIEF—yours and that of your doctor. But as you kept on and on, your belief began to falter, until presently it died away altogether. You may have *hoped,* but the active belief suggestions to your subconscious mind had stopped carrying conviction.

Dr. Richard C. Cabot, Professor of Medicine at Harvard University, in a recent address, declared that "three-quarters of all illnesses are cured without the victims even knowing they have had them.

"Proof of this contention is to be found in post-mortem examinations, which time after time reveal indelible and unmistakable traces of disease which the subject has conquered all unknowingly. Ninety per cent of all typhoid cures itself, as does 75 per cent of all pneumonia. In fact, out of a total of 215 diseases known to medical science, there are only about eight or nine which doctors conquer—the rest conquer themselves."

He went on to say that "If nature, assisted by the proper mental and emotional moods, is capable of curing an ulcer in three or four weeks, why isn't it possible for the same force to heal a similar ulcer in a few minutes, when the curative processes have been speeded up abnormally?"

Great physicians have, on numerous occasions, maintained that there is no science in *medicating* people. In Preventive Medicine—yes. In Surgery. In Obstetrics. In a score of different lines that fall under the heading of the medical profession.

But the art of drugging is little ahead of where it was in the Middle Ages, when Egyptian mummies were in great demand among druggists and "powdered Pharaoh" was considered the greatest remedy for any ill that flesh was heir to.

Every day brings the discovery of some new drug, and the consequent dictum that the remedy previously prescribed was all a mistake—that it had little or no real value whatever.

One doctor says: "A medicine that will not kill you if you take an overdose is no good." Another: "The most prominent doctors now claim that there is not a single drug will do what it has been prescribed for in the past."

Dr. Douglas White, writing in *The Churchman,* sums it up thus:

"All cure of every disease is spiritual. Healing can never be imposed from without by either the surgeon or physician; it is the living organism which, helped by the skill of the one or the other, is enabled to work its way back to health. The whole principle of healing in all cases is the *vis medicatrix naturae.* And when we speak of nature, we are only personifying the principle of life which Christians call God."

In the *Medical Record* of September 25, 1920, Dr. Joseph Byrne, Professor of Neurology at Fordham University Medical School, said:

"At a conservative estimate it may be admitted that of all the ailments for which relief is sought, 90% or over are self limited and tend to get well. It may also be admitted that in over 90% of all human ailments, the *psychic* is the dominating factor."

In other words, Mind is the Healer. Drugs can sometimes make its work easier by removing obstructions, by killing off parasites. But the regular use of drugs is far more likely to harm than to heal. We might well quote to the druggists the old Hindoo proverb:

"God gives the mango;
The farmer plants the seed.
God cures the patient;
The doctor takes the fees."

In the Great War, the one drug that most proved its worth was Iodine. And what is Iodine? A *cleanser.* It killed germs. It cleansed wounds. But it has no healing power. And no healing was expected of it. It did all that was asked. It cauterized—cleansed—so that Nature (Mind) could do its own healing, unobstructed.

That would seem to be the most that should be expected of any drug—kill the germs of sickness or disease, cleanse so that Nature can the more easily do its rebuilding. And that is where the use of drugs should stop. Mind works best when it is interfered with least—when we throw ourselves entirely upon it for support, rather than share the responsibility with some outside agency.

Dr. Burnett Rae, a well-known English specialist, addressing a large audience on the subject of "Spiritual Healing and Medical Science," said the term "spiritual healing" was sometimes used in a manner which seemed to imply that there was a form of healing which was of a non-spiritual character, and that spiritual healing was incompatible with, or opposed to, medical practice. Healing could never be regarded as a purely physical process. He would go so far as to say that healing was always effected through the control of the mind, and medicinal remedies only set the machinery of the mind in motion. We are too apt to think of medical science as concerned with drugs or appliances and operations. *These might completely pass away during the next twenty or fifty years.*

It is not through drugs that the medical profession has done so much of good for the world. It is not through drugs that they have improved the general health, cleaned up plague spots, cut down infant mortality, lengthened the average life expectancy of mankind by fifteen years.

It is by scotching disease at its very source. It is by getting rid of artificially created *unwholesome* conditions, getting back to *natural wholesome* conditions.

What is it causes typhus? Filth—an entirely unwholesome condition, man-made. And how do doctors prevent the spread of typhus? By cleaning up—by getting back to *natural* wholesome conditions.

What is it causes typhoid? Impure water. And its prevention is simply the purifying of the water—getting back to Nature's perfect, wholesome supply.

Yellow fever has been practically stamped out of existence. Typhus is almost a forgotten plague, except in such backward places as parts of Russia and Asia.

Malaria has been conquered. And doctors predict that in another generation tuberculosis will be an almost forgotten malady.

How were these wonderful results brought about? Not through drugs—*but by cleaning up!* Cleaning out swamps and filth. Purifying water. Building drainage systems. Making everything round about as clean and wholesome as Nature herself.

Cleanliness—Purity—Sunshine!

God gave us in abundance all that is necessary for perfect health—clean air, pure water, clear sunshine. All we need to do is to keep these pure and clean, and to use all we possibly can of them. The greatest good the medical profession has done mankind is in discovering the value of these gifts of God and showing us how to use them.

The Chinese have long had the right idea—they pay their physicians to keep them well, not to cure them of sickness. And the thing that made the reputation of such men as Gorgas, Reed, Flexner, Carrel, was not their *cure* of disease—but their *prevention* of it.

That way lies the future of medicine—bringing our surroundings back to the *natural* wholesome conditions for which we were created. That way lies health and happiness for all—cleanliness inside and out, clean air, pure water, plenty of sunshine—*and right thinking!*

In the next chapter, I shall try to show you how you can apply the illimitable power of Mind hopefully towards the successful treatment of disease.

CHAPTER 24

The Gift of the Magi

"Sweep up the debris of decaying faiths;
Sweep down the cobwebs of worn-out beliefs,
And throw your soul wide open to the light
Of Reason and of Knowledge. Be not afraid
To thrust aside half-truths and grasp the whole."

—ELLA WHEELER WILCOX

All over the world, sick, weak and devitalized men and women are searching for health and strength. By the hundreds of thousands, they drag their weary and aching bones around, or languish on sick beds, waiting for someone to bring health to them corked up in a bottle.

But real, lasting health was never found in pill boxes or medicine bottles. There is one method—and only one—by which it can be gained and kept. That method is by using the power of the Subconscious Mind.

For a long time the doctors pooh-poohed any such idea. Then as the evidence piled up, they grudgingly admitted that nervous troubles and even functional disorders might be cured by mind.

Even now there are some who, as Bernard Shaw put it, "had rather bury a whole hillside ethically than see a single patient cured unethically. They will give credit to no method of healing outside the tenets of their own school."

Yet, as Warren Hilton has it in "Applied Psychology":

"All the literature of medicine, whether of ancient or modern times, abounds in illustrations of the power of the mind over the body in health and in disease. And medical science has always based much of its practice on this principle. No reputable school of medicine ever failed to instruct its students in practical applications of the principle of mental influence at the bedside of their patients. A brisk and cheery manner, a hopeful countenance, a supremely assured and confident demeanor—these things have always been regarded by the medical profession as but second in importance to sanitation and material remedies; *while the value of the sugar-coated bread pill when the diagnosis was uncertain, has long been recognized.*

"The properly trained nurse has always been expected to supplement the efforts of the attending physician by summoning the mental forces of the patient to his aid. She, therefore, surrounds the patient with an atmosphere of comfortable assurance. And by constantly advising him of his satisfactory progress toward speedy recovery she seeks to instil hope, confidence and mental effort.

"To quote Dr. Didama: 'The ideal physician irradiates the sick chamber with the light of his cheerful presence. He may not be hilarious—he is not indifferent—but he has an irrepressible good-nature which lifts the patient out of the slough of despond and places his feet on the firm land of health. In desperate cases, even a little harmless levity may be beneficial. A well-timed jest may break up a congestion; a pun may add pungency to the sharpest stimulant.' Dr. Oliver Wendell Holmes reduced this principle to its cash equivalent when he said that a cheerful smile might be worth five thousand dollars a year to a physician.

"Today, psychotherapy, or the healing of bodily disease by mental influence, has the unqualified endorsement of the American Therapeutic Society, the only national organization in America devoted exclusively to therapeutics. It has the enthusiastic support of men of such recognized international leadership in the scientific world and in the medical profession as Freud, Jung, Bleuler, Breuer, Prince, Janet, Babinski, Putnam, Gerrish, Sidis, Dubois, Munsterberg, Jones, Brill, Donley, Waterman and Taylor.

"The present attitude of reputable science toward the principle that the mind controls all bodily operations is, then, one of positive conviction. The world's foremost thinkers accept its truth. The interest of enlightened men and women everywhere is directed toward the mind as a powerful curative force and as a regenerative influence of hitherto undreamed-of resource."

The more progressive physicians everywhere now admit that there is practically no limit to how far mind can go in the cure of disease. As Dr. Walsh of Fordham University puts it: "Analysis of the statistics of diseases cured by mental influence shows that its results have been more strikingly manifest in organic than in the so-called nervous or functional diseases."

Everyone admits that the mind influences the body somewhat, for everyone has seen others grow pale with fear, or red with anger. Everyone has felt the stopping of the heartbeats at some sudden fright, the quickened breathing and the thumping of the heart caused by excitement. These and a hundred other evidences of the influence of mind over matter are common to all of us, and everyone will admit them.

But everyone does not know that our whole bodies seem to be nothing more or less than the outward expression of our thought. We sit in a draught, and education teaches us we should have a cold or fever. So we *have* a cold or fever. We eat something which we have been told is indigestible, and immediately we are assailed with pains. We see another yawn, and our impulse is to follow suit. In the same way, when we hear of sickness round about us, the fear of it visualizes it in our own minds and we, too, have it. The *fear* of these things seems to bring them about, the mental suggestion sent through to our subconscious minds. We have been educated in a medical age to think that most diseases are infectious or contagious. So the mere sight of a diseased person makes most of us withdraw into ourselves like a turtle within his shell. We fear we shall catch it—when one of the great dangers of disease is that very fear of it.

For years it has been accepted as an acknowledged fact that anyone trapped in a mine or other air-tight compartment would presently die of carbon dioxide poisoning—lack of oxygen. Now comes Houdini to prove that death for lack of oxygen is not necessary at all!

"Fear, and not poisoning by carbon dioxide, causes the death of miners and others trapped in air-tight compartments," in the opinion of Houdini, according to an Associated Press despatch of August 6, 1926.

Houdini had himself sunk in a sealed coffin in a swimming pool, without chance for a breath of outside air to reach him, and stayed there for an hour and a half, although, according to all previous scientific belief, he should have been dead at the end of four minutes. Yet Dr. W. J. McConnell of the United States Department of Mines, who examined Houdini before and after the experiment, reported no marked physical reactions from the test, and Houdini himself said he felt only a slight dizziness when he was released from the coffin!

"Anyone can do it," said Houdini. "The important thing is to *believe that you are safe.*"

The Chinese have a saying that when the plague comes, 5,000 people may die of the plague, but 50,000 will die of the fear of it.

Did you ever hurt a limb, or a finger, so that you thought you couldn't move it? And then, under the stress of some sudden emotion, forget all about the hurt and presently wake to find yourself using the finger or the limb just as readily and as painlessly as though there had never been anything wrong with it?

I have before me a clipping from *The New York Times* of March 29, 1925, telling of a cripple who had been paralyzed for six years, but under the spur of sudden fear, he ran up a stairway unaided, without crutch or cane. He had been treated in a number of hospitals but, because of an injury to his spine received in an auto accident, had been unable to walk without crutches or canes for six years. The patient in the bed next his own suddenly went crazy and attacked him, and in his fear this paralytic leaped from his bed and ran up a flight of stairs. According to the report, *the sudden fright cured him!*

Take the miracles of Lourdes, or of St. Anne of Beaupre, or of any of the dozens of shrines that dot the world. What is it that effects the cures? Two things—*Desire* and *Faith.* "What wouldst thou that I should do unto thee?" the Saviour asked the blind man who kept following and crying out to him. "Lord that I should receive my sight." And again of the cripple at the Pool of Bethesda Jesus asked—"Wouldst thou be made whole?"

Sounds like foolish questioning, doesn't it? But you remember the story of the famous Saint of Italy, who traveled from town to town healing the lame, the halt and the blind. A pilgrim hastening to a town where the Saint was expected met two lame beggars hurrying away. He asked them the reason for their haste, to be told, to his astonishment, it was because the Saint was coming to town. As they put it—"He will surely heal us, and where will our livelihood be then?"

So it is with many people today—not beggars, mind you—but people in every walk of life. They have become so wedded to their ailments, they "enjoy poor health" so thoroughly, that they are secretly a bit proud of it. Take away their complaints and they would be lost without them.

You must have the *sincere desire first.* That is prayer. Then the *faith*—the kind of faith that Jesus meant when he said—"Whatsoever ye ask for when ye pray, believe that ye *receive* it, and ye shall *have it.*" Mind you, not "believe ye are *going* to receive it." "Believe that ye *receive* it"—*now*—this very minute. Know that the REAL you, the image of you held in Universal Mind—in short, the *Truth* concerning every organ in your body—is perfect. "*Know the Truth.*" Believe that you HAVE this perfect image. On the day that you can truly believe this—carry this sincere conviction to your subconscious mind—on that day you WILL BE perfect.

This is the faith that Jesus meant when he said—"Thy faith hath made thee whole." This is the faith that is responsible for the miracles of Lourdes, for miraculous healings everywhere. It matters not whether you be Catholic or Protestant, Jew or Gentile. Desire and faith such as these will heal you.

A month or two ago I read in the newspapers of a farmer, blind for two years, who went out in the field and prayed "that he should receive his sight." At the end of the second day, his sight was completely restored. He was a Protestant. He went to no shrine—just out under the sky and prayed to God.

Today I have before me a clipping from the New York *Sun* of February 23, 1926, telling of Patrolman Dennis O'Brien of the Jersey City police force, who at the end of a Novena to Our Lady of Help at the Monastery of St. Michael's in Union City recovered the use of his legs, which had been paralyzed since the time, two years before, when a bullet had entered the base of his spine, severing the cord of motor and sensory nerves. He was a Catholic.

Then here is one from the New York *Sun* of June 26, 1926, telling how Miss Elsie Meyer of the Bronx, New York, was healed *overnight* of a tumorous growth that had troubled her for months:

"I realized last fall that there was an unusual growth on my body," she said. "It might have resulted from the strain of lifting a trunk. I wanted to know what it was, and I first went to a doctor, who informed me it was a tumorous growth and likely to become serious.

"But I would not be frightened and refused to receive any medical remedies in the way of cure. I have been a believer in faith healing and member of the Unity Society, a branch of the New Thought organization, for a number of years, so I went to a New Thought practioner. While this seemed to help me, the tumorous growth remained. I guess my faith wasn't strong enough at the time. That was last fall.

"I came to the congress with the same growth, apparently unaffected by any attempts to cure it. But after attending the healing meeting at the congress yesterday I left with firm faith that I would get the healing I had asked for. When I retired I noticed the tumor was still on my body, but when I awoke this morning it had disappeared."

The chronicles of every religion are full of just such miracles. And the reason for them is the same in every case—*prayer* and *faith.* Given these, no healing is impossible.

Suppose we go back for a moment to the lowly Amoeba, the first bit of animal life upon the earth. I know not whether you are Fundamentalist or Evolutionist. The facts are a bit harder to prove from the Evolution side of it, so let us argue from that angle.

The Amoeba, as you will recall from Chapter I, is the lowest form of animal life known to scientists, a sort of jelly-fish with but a single cell—without brains, without intelligence, possessing only LIFE. No one would ever contend that this jelly-fish could improve itself. No one would argue that it developed the next form of life out of its own mind or ideas.

Yet, according to science, the next form of life did develop from this jelly-like mass. The Amoeba certainly was not responsible for doing it. And it couldn't develop itself. So the conclusion is forced upon us that some outside Intelligence must have done it.

But there were no other living creatures. The Amoeba was alone of all animal life upon the planet. The condition of the water and atmosphere was such that few if any other forms of animals could have sustained life at that time. So the Intelligence which developed the next form of animal life must have been the same that created the Amoeba—that first brought LIFE to this Planet. That Intelligence is variously called God, Providence, Nature, the Life Principle, Mind, etc. For our purposes here let us call it Universal Mind.

Having formed life here on earth, Universal Mind proceeded to develop it. Starting with a single cell, It built cell upon cell, changing each form of life to meet the different conditions of atmosphere and environment that the cooling of the earth crust brought about. When the multi-cellular structure became complicated, It gave a brain to it to direct the different functions, just as you put a "governor" on a steam engine. When land appeared and the receding tides left certain animals high and dry for periods of hours, It gave these both lungs and gills—the one for the air, the other for the water.

When the creatures began to prey upon one another, It gave one speed, another a shell, a third an ink-like fluid, that each in its own way might escape and survive.

But always It progressed. Each new stage of life was an improvement over the previous one. And always It showed Its resourcefulness, Its ability to meet ANY need.

Finally, as the culmination of all Its efforts, It made MAN—a creature endowed not only with a brain like that of the lower animals but with the power of reason—"made in His image and likeness," sharing Infinite Intelligence—himself a Creator and a part of Universal Mind.

All through the creation—from the time of the one-celled Amoeba right up to Man—every scientist will admit that the directing intelligence of Universal Mind was on the job every minute, that It formed the models on which each new and different kind of animal was made, that each of these models was perfect—the one model best fitted to cope with the conditions it had to confront.

Certainly when It came to Man, It is not likely to have been any less successful in forming a perfect model than it was in making the tiger or the elephant. So we can take it, I assume, that all will admit that Man as formed by Universal Mind is perfect—that the idea of Man as it exists in Universal Mind is perfect in every particular.

And Universal Mind, from the very beginning, has never taken a step backward, has never stood still. Always it has PROGRESSED. So it would seem safe to assume that man is not going backward now—that he is a more perfect creature than he was 5,000, 10,000 or 100,000 years ago—that he is constantly drawing nearer and nearer the likeness of his Creator.

The next step seems just as logical. If there was inherent in even the earliest and lowest forms of life the power to develop whatever means was requisite to meet each new emergency, such as a shell or lungs or legs or wings—if this power is still inherent in the lower forms of life such as the Plant Parasites referred to in a previous chapter, does it not seem a certainty that *we* have the same power within ourselves, if only we knew how to call it forth?

Jesus proved that we have, and his disciples and followers added still further proof. After the third century of the Christian era, that power was allowed to lapse through disuse, but of late years thousands have been taking advantage of it for themselves and for others through psychology or religion. A new Church has been founded upon the words of James: "Faith without WORKS is dead." It differs from most Churches in that it teaches that Jesus meant ALL that he said when he commanded his disciples to "Go, preach, saying, The kingdom of heaven is at hand. *Heal the sick,* cleanse the lepers, raise the dead, cast out devils; freely ye have received, freely give." The sick, the lame, the halt and the blind have flocked to it literally by the hundred thousands. That thousands have been cured is beyond dispute. That many were cases which had been given up by the medical fraternity the doctors quite frankly admit.

And the basis of all these cures is that there is nothing miraculous about the cure of disease at all. That it is "Divinely Natural." That it requires merely understanding. That Mind is the only Creator. And that the only image Universal Mind holds of your body is a perfect image, neither young nor old but full of health, of vigor, of beauty and vitality. That all you have to do when assailed by disease is to go back to Universal Mind for a new conception of its perfect image—for the Truth concerning your body. Just as you would go back to the principle of mathematics for the Truth concerning any problem that worked out incorrectly. When you can make your subconscious mind copy after this Universal image—the *Truth*—instead of the diseased image you are holding in your thoughts, your sickness will vanish like the mere dream it is.

Does that sound too deep? Then look at it this way:

When you think an organ is diseased, it is your conscious mind that thinks this. Inevitably it sends this thought through to your subconscious mind, and the latter proceeds to build the cells of that organ along this imperfect, diseased model. Change the model—in other words, change your belief—and your subconscious mind will go back again to building along right lines.

Your body, you know, is simply an aggregation of millions upon millions of protons and electrons, held together by mind. They are the universal substance all about us, the plastic clay from which the sculptor Mind shapes the forms you see.

To quote the New York *Sun*: "Man's body is made up of trillions of miniature solar systems, each with whirling planets and a central sun. These tiny systems are the atoms of modern science. The atoms of all elements are made up of protons and electrons in varying quantities and arranged in various ways.

"But what are protons and electrons?

"The masters of physics have succeeded in weighing and measuring them. We know that they carry the smallest possible charges of electricity, and we are learning much about the way they behave; but students are beginning to doubt that they have real substance, that they are anything one could hit with a lilliputian hammer. Dr. H. G. Gale of the University of Chicago, addressing the Ohio Academy of Science the other day, said there was good reason to believe that electrons were composed entirely of electricity and that their mass or weight was only a manifestation of electrical force. According to this view, *nothing exists in the universe except electricity*—and perhaps ether."

Your subconscious mind partakes of the creative power of Mind and because of that, it is daily, hourly, changing the particles of electrical energy which constitute your body to conform to the image you hold before it.

The clay cannot reply to the sculptor. No more can these tiny particles of electricity. Your body has nothing to say as to whether it shall be diseased or crippled. It is MIND that decides this. Jesus understood this, and it was on the basis of this understanding that he was able to cure any and all manner of disease. He was not a magician or occult wonder-worker, aiming to set aside the laws of nature. He was a TEACHER, demonstrating those laws. He didn't pick the learned Scribes and Pharisees and let them in on the secret of his wonder working. On the contrary, the men he chose were simple fisher folk, and to them he gave the UNDERSTANDING that enabled them, too, to cure the sick, the halt and the blind.

For what is sickness? An illusion, a mortal dream—merely the *absence* of health. Bring back that health image, and the sickness immediately disappears. Universal Mind never created disease. The only image it knows of man is the *Truth*—the perfect image. The only idea it has of your body is a perfect, healthy idea. "For God is of purer eyes than to behold evil."

Then where does disease come from? Who created it? *No one did.* It is a mere illusion—just as, if you think a pin is sticking you, and you concentrate your thought on the pain, it becomes unbearable. Yet when you investigate, you find that no pin was sticking you at all—merely a hair, or bit of cinder lodged against the skin. How often have you had some fancied pain, only to have it promptly disappear when your physician assured you there was nothing wrong with you at all? It would be the same way with all sickness, all pain, if you would understand that it is merely fear or suggestion working on your conscious mind, and that if you will deny this belief of pain or sickness, your subconscious mind will speedily make that denial good. Don't render that mind impotent by thoughts of fear, doubt and anxiety. If you do, it is going to get like a working crew which is constantly being stopped by strikes or walk-outs or changes of plans. It will presently get discouraged and stop trying.

To quote Dr. Geo. E. Pitzer again—"In proper, healthy or normal conditions of life, the objective mind and the subjective mind act in perfect harmony with each other. When this is the case, healthy and happy conditions always prevail. But these two minds are not always permitted to act in perfect harmony with each other; this brings mental disturbances; excites physical wrongs, functional and organic diseases.

"Our unconscious is a tremendous storage plant full of potential energy which can be expended for beneficial or harmful ends. Like every apparatus for storing up power, it can be man's most precious ally, if man is familiar with it and, hence, not afraid of it. Ignorance and fear, on the other hand, can transform a live electric wire into an engine of destruction and death."

Even as long ago as Napoleon's day, men had begun to get an inkling of this. "Think that you are well," said the astute Tallyrand, "instead of thinking that you are sick." And the formula of the Quakers is that an energetic soul is "master of the body which it loves."

So keep in mind the one basic fact that covers the whole ground—that *Mind is all.* There is no other cause. When you drive the belief in disease from your subconscious mind, you will drive away the pain and all the other symptoms with it.

Few sick people have any idea how much they can do for themselves. There is an old saying that every man is "a fool or his own physician at 40." When the science of Mind is more generally understood, that saying will become literally true. Every man will find within himself the Mind which "healeth all thy diseases." For every function of your body is governed by your mind. When sickness or pain assails you, *deny it!* Cling steadfastly to the one idea that covers all—that Universal Mind made your every organ perfect; that the only image of each organ now in Universal Mind is this perfect image; and that this perfect idea is endowed with resources sufficient to meet any need.

Jesus' command—"Be ye therefore perfect, even as your father in Heaven is perfect"—was meant to be taken literally. And it can be followed literally if we will model our bodies upon the image He holds of us in Universal Mind. We are all sculptors, you know, but instead of marble or clay, our material is the plastic energy—protons and electrons—of which we and everything in this world about us are made. What are you making of it? What image are you holding in mind? Images of sickness? Of poverty? Of Limitation? Then you are reproducing these in your life.

Banish them! Forget them! Never let them enter your thought, and they will never again manifest themselves in your life.

You admit that mind influences your body to some extent, but you think your physical organs hold the preponderance of power. So you depend upon them, and make yourself their slave.

"Know ye not," says Paul, "that to whom ye yield yourselves servants to obey, his servants ye are to whom ye obey?"

By holding before yourself the thought that your organs are the master, you make them your master, and deprive yourself of the directing intelligence of your subconscious mind. When an organ ceases to function properly, you try to doctor it, when the part that needs attention is your mind. If you are running an electric machine, and the current becomes weak or is switched off, you don't take the machine part, or oil it or tamper with it to make it run better. You go to the source of the power to find what is wrong there.

In the same way, when anything seems wrong with the functioning of your body, the place to investigate is your subconscious mind. Your stomach has no intelligence, nor your heart, nor your liver, nor any other of your organs. Your liver, for instance, could never figure out how much sugar should be turned into your blood every minute to keep your bodily temperature at 98 degrees, when you are sitting in a room that is warmed to only 65 degrees. It doesn't know how much more sugar is required to keep that temperature normal when you go out into a driving gale 10 below zero. Yet it supplies the requisite amount—neither too much nor too little. And it does it instantaneously. Where does it get the information? *You* don't know it. No mortal man could figure it out in a year's time.

It gets it from your subconscious mind. It gets both the information and the directions to use it. And every other of your bodily organs gets its information in the same place. Your muscles are not self-acting. Take away mind and those muscles are just like any other bit of matter—lifeless, inert. They have nothing to say as to what they shall do. They merely obey the behests of mind.

Have you ever seen one of those great presses at work in a newspaper plant? They seem almost human in their intelligence. At one end, great rolls of paper feed in. At the other, out comes the finished newspaper, folded, ready for delivery. Everything is automatic. Everything as perfect as machinery can be made. The "fingers" that fold the papers seem almost lifelike in their deftness.

But shut off the life-giving electric current—and what happens? The machinery is powerless. Take away the directing human intelligence, and how long before that wonderful machine would be a mass of scrap—mere bits of steel and rubber? How long could it function of itself?

So it is with your body. A wonderful mechanism—the most complicated, yet the most perfect in the world. But switch off the current of your mental dynamo, take away the intelligence that directs the working of your every organ, and what is left? A bit of bone and flesh—inert and useless.

In the final analysis, your body is merely a piece of mechanism—dependent entirely upon mind. It has no power, no volition, of its own. It does as mind tells it to, insofar as mind believes itself to be the Master. Your eyes, for instance, are merely lenses which transmit light from the outer world to the brain within. They contract or elongate, they open or close, just as mind directs. And mind, in its turn, keeps them constantly nourished with new, life-giving blood, replacing old tissue, old cells, as fast as they wear out, rebuilding ever, so that your eyes may continue to function perfectly as long as your conscious mind is dependent upon them for its impressions of outer objects. It doesn't matter how old you may be or how much you use them. Your eyes are like any other muscles of your body—they improve in strength with use. Give them but enough rest intervals for mind to repair and rebuild the used tissue, keep before your subconscious mind the perfect image of eyes on which you expect it to rebuild, and you need never fear glasses, you need never worry about "your eyes going back on you."

What is it happens when your muscles refuse to work—fail to perform their functions properly? *You* are what has happened. You have switched off the current from some particular part. You have been holding the belief so long and so firmly that the muscles have the preponderance of power, that your subconscious mind has come to believe it, too. And when the nerve or muscle suffers an injury, the subconscious mind—at the suggestion of your conscious mind—gives up all dominion over it.

All disease, all sickness, all imperfections of the human body are due to this one cause—your belief that your body is the master, that it can act, that it can catch cold, or become diseased, without the consent of mind. This is the procuring cause of all suffering. One disease is no different from another in this. They are all due to that one erroneous belief.

If you will deny the power of your body over your mind, you can destroy all fear of disease. And when the fear goes, the foundation of the disease is gone.

The way to begin is to *refuse to believe* or to heed any complaint from your body. Have no fear of climate or atmosphere, of dampness or drafts. It is only when you believe them unhealthy that they are so to you. When your stomach sends a report of distress, when it tells you that something you have eaten is disagreeing with it, treat it as you would an unruly servant. Remind it that it is not the judge of what is or is not good for it. That it has no intelligence. That it is merely a channel through which the food you give it passes for certain treatment and selection. That if the food is not good it has but to pass it through to the eliminatory organs as speedily as may be.

Your stomach is entirely capable of doing this. Every organ you have is capable of withstanding any condition—given the right state of mind to direct it. The only reason that they succumb to sickness or disease or injury is because you tell them to. Men have fallen from great heights without injury. Men have taken the most deadly poison without harm. Men have gone through fire and flood and pestilence with not a scratch to show. And what men have done once they can do again. The fact that it *has* been done shows that your body does not *need* to suffer injury from these conditions. And if it does not need to, then it would seem that the only reason it ordinarily suffers is because your fear of injury is the thought you are holding before your subconscious mind and therefore that is the thought that it images on your body.

In a despatch from Stockholm to the New York *Herald-Tribune*, dated January 18, 1926, I read that Dr. Henry Markus and Dr. Ernest Sahlgren, Stockholm scientists, have been able, through hypnotic suggestion, to offset the effect of poisons on the human system to a marked degree.

The scientists put three subjects into hypnotic sleep and then administered drugs, carefully recording the effects on blood pressure and pulse, both with and without "suggestion." When a drug which acts to increase blood pressure was administered without "suggestion," the blood pressure readings ranged between 109 to 130 and pulse readings from 54 to 100. But when the drug was administered with the "suggestion" to the mind of the patient that it was merely so much harmless water, the blood pressures were from 107 to 116 and pulse readings all less than 67. From which one would judge that it was the patient's *belief* which affected him, far more than any power in the drug.

Bear this in mind when anyone tells you that certain foods are not good for you. You can eat what you like, if you do it in moderation. Just remember—no matter what you may eat—if you relish it, if you BELIEVE it to be good for you, *it will be good for you!*

But, you may say, is not this like the tenets of a well-known religion? What of that? If certain fundamental truths have been uncovered by another why not use them, regardless of whether or not we agree with the philosophy from which they are taken.

To quote again from Dr. Richard C. Cabot of the Harvard Medical School:

"There need be no conflict. There is opportunity for all sincere, humble-minded effort. Let us have no persecutions and no interference with the spread of truth and light from any source. Indictments against movements as powerful and sincere as Christian Science and Preventive Medicine are anachronistic. Let us all get busy along our own lines. 'With malice towards none, with charity for all, let us bind up the nation's wounds.'"

It has often seemed to me that if all the churches would take a leaf out of the book of ordinary Business Practice, forget their differences over dogma, and simply profit by the example that Mary Baker Eddy, Discoverer and Founder of Christian Science, has given them of building up an enormous following almost overnight, they would be much the better off thereby.

For what was it brought men and women into the Church in such vast numbers in the early day of Christianity? *Healing!* What was responsible for the phenomenal growth of the Christian Science Church? The *healing* of thousands of people of any and every kind of ill. What is it that people go to any Church for? To pray—*and to find how to get an answer to their prayers.* Show them the way to do this, show them the way to *heal* themselves of all their ills and lacks, and you will need to worry no more about the crowded theaters and the empty churches.

"If this be treason, make the most of it."

The moment any symptom of illness shows in your body, vigorously deny its existence. Say to yourself—"My body has no intelligence. Neither has any germ of disease. Therefore neither my body nor the disease can tell me I am sick. Mind is the only cause. And Mind has not directed them to make me sick. The only image of my body that Mind knows is a perfect, vigorous, healthy image. And that is the only image I am going to build on." Then forget the image of disease. It is only an illusion, and can be dispelled like any other illusion. Keep in your mind's eye the image of perfect health, of vigorous, boundless vitality.

Your body can not say it is sick. Therefore when the belief of sickness assails you, it must come either from your conscious mind or from outside suggestion. In either event, it is your job to see that no belief of sickness reaches your subconscious mind, that no fear of it, no thought of it, is imaged there.

To treat one who has already succumbed to the belief of sickness, explain to him, as I have explained to you here, that his body has no power for sickness or for health, any more than a log of wood has. That his body is merely an aggregation of millions of electrons—particles of electrical energy, really—subject wholly to his mind. That these particles of energy have neither substance nor intelligence; that they are constantly changing; and that the forms they take depend entirely upon the images he holds in his own mind.

His body is, in short, a mental concept. It is an exact reflection of the thought he is holding in mind of it. If he has been sick, it is because he has been holding sickly, weak and unhealthy thoughts in his mind. If he wishes to get well, it is first necessary for him to change his thought. Instead of doctoring the machine, he is to go direct to the power house and change the current. Let him repeat to himself, night and morning, this little formula:

"There is no permanence to matter. The one surest thing about it is *change.* Every cell, every tissue in my body is constantly being renewed. The old, worn-out tissues are being torn down and carried away. New, perfect ones are replacing them. And the model on which those new organisms are being re-built is the perfect model that is held in Divine Mind.

"For God made man in His image. That image was perfect then—*is* perfect now. It is the only image that Divine Mind knows of me. It is the only image on which my subconscious mind is ever again going to pattern its re-building. Every minute of every day I am growing more and more into the image of God—the *True Likeness* He holds of me in His thought."

If he will do that, if he will bear in mind that matter as such has no feeling, no intelligence; that it is the mind that feels, the mind that directs, and therefore he has nothing to fear from any external causes, his fear of the disease will vanish. And the patient does not exist who will not speedily recover when his fear of the disease is gone.

"Verily, verily, I say unto you," said Jesus, "if a man keep my saying, he shall never see death." And again—"This is the life eternal." "*Is*," you will notice, not "shall be."

"The subconscious mind is God's way of utilizing His energy," says the Rev. William T. Walsh, Rector of St. Luke's Church, New York City, in his book "Scientific Spiritual Healing." "God evolved the subconscious mind. It is His gift to us like all else that we possess, and because it is from Him we should give thanks and learn to use it intelligently.

"God has so fashioned us that we do not have to give conscious attention to the vital processes. He has given us what is called the subconscious mind which looks after all the vital functions. This mind can receive commands from us and has wonderful ability to carry them out, for it is a law that *every thought tends to realize itself* subconsciously in the body.

"If you allow evil thoughts to remain, they are received by the subconscious which tends to realize them in the body just as much as though they were good, wholesome, health-giving spiritual thoughts. For remember, the subconscious does not reason and judge. It only receives and obeys."

When you have an accident, don't immediately think that you must be hurt. On the contrary, deny at once that you can be hurt. The denial will take away the creative power of your thought from any damaging condition. More than that, if you will immediately call to mind the fact that the only image of your body that Universal Mind holds is a perfect image, and that this is the image on which your subconscious mind is building, you will find that this subconscious mind will speedily rebuild any damaged parts in accordance with that image.

As a matter of fact, if we could thoroughly realize that our bodies are made up merely of vortices of energy subject wholly to the control of mind, it should hurt us no more to run a knife through them than it does to run it through water. The water immediately resumes the shape of the vessel that holds it. Just so, our bodies should immediately resume the shape that mind holds them in.

But even with our present imperfect understanding, we can perform what the uninitiated would call miracles with our bodies. And each victory we win gives us a bit more of power over them. To conquer one diseased condition makes it easier to ward off or to conquer other diseased conditions. The body cannot oppose us. It is only the bias of education and the suggestions of those about us that we have to combat.

There is no necessity for disease. There is no necessity even for fatigue. "They that wait upon the Lord shall run and not be weary; and they shall walk and not faint." Those words from Holy Writ were meant literally—and they can be applied literally if you will govern your body by mind, and not let custom and popular belief make your body the master. Whatever it is right for you to do, you can do without fear, no matter if it entails long-continued toil, hardship or danger. Depend upon it, your mind can call to your aid all the forces of Nature if they are necessary to your emergency.

"Therefore I say unto you," quoth the Master, "take no thought for your life, what ye shall eat, or what ye shall drink; nor yet for your body, what ye shall put on. Is not the life more than meat and the body than raiment?"

Diet, exercise and rules of health never kept any one well of themselves. Often they attract the mind to the subject of sickness and thereby foster it.

Dieting is good insofar as it prevents gluttony. Temperance is just as important in eating as in the drinking of alcoholic liquor. But you can eat in moderation anything you like, anything that you relish and BELIEVE to be good for you, without fear of its disagreeing with you.

Reasonable exercise, too, is fine for both the body and the mind. Provided you do not make a fetich of it. It isn't the exercise that keeps you well—it is the mental image you hold in your thought.

The exercise merely helps to impress that mental image on your subconscious mind.

Electrical treatments, skin tonics, alcohol rubs, etc., all are useful only to the the extent that they center the attention of the subconscious mind upon the parts affected. Exactly the same results, even to that pleasant little tingling of the skin, can be effected by mind alone. I remember reading an article by Mrs. Vance Cheney, telling how she cured herself of paralysis of the legs in just that way. After lying for months under the care of doctors and masseurs, she tired of them and decided to depend entirely upon mind. So, several times a day, she would utterly relax in every nerve and muscle, then consciously send her thought down along the nerves of her legs to her feet. Presently there would be that little tingling sensation in her feet—evidence of increased circulation—followed after a time by a feeling of drowsiness. A few weeks of these treatments completely restored the use of her legs.

The same effort can be made to throw off any physical trouble. Put your hand upon the part affected. Try to visualize that organ as it should be. See it functioning perfectly. BELIEVE that it IS working normally again! Your thought brings the blood to the affected part, clears up the trouble, provides new cells, new tissue, while your belief that the organ IS functioning properly will bring about that normal condition.

This is a treatment, however, that must be used with discretion, for to consciously interfere in the regular functioning of the body without any real need for such interference results in confusion rather than help. It is like going down a flight of stairs rapidly. Pay no attention to the movement of your feet, and they flit over the steps with never a sign of hesitancy or faltering. But try to watch them step by step, and you will either have to slow up or you will presently miss a step, stumble or fall.

"The centipede was happy quite,
Until the toad, for fun,
Said, 'Pray, which leg goes after which?'
This stirred his mind to such a pitch,
He lay distracted in a ditch,
Considering how *to run."*

There is one rule that will help anyone keep healthy. That rule is to forget your nerves, throw away your pills and your medicine bottles, and hold before your mind's eye only the perfect image that Universal Mind has of your body. That is the surest way to keep free from sickness.

And if you are already sick, the same rule applies. Know that Universal Mind never created disease—that it is but an illusion of your conscious mind. Know that mind is the only creator, that as Shakespeare puts it, "There is nothing, either good or bad, but thinking makes it so." Know that you have the say as to what that thinking shall be. Know, therefore, that by holding a perfect image of your body in your thoughts you can make your body perfect.

Have you ever cut your finger? Who was it coagulated the blood, stopped the gash, wove new skin? Who was it called upon the little phagocytes to come and kill the septic germs?

Not your conscious mind, certainly. Most people don't even know there are "any such animals." Their conscious minds don't know the first thing about healing. Whence comes the information? Whence the directing genius? Where but from the same intelligence that keeps your heart and lungs on the job while you sleep, that regulates your liver and your kidneys, that attends to all the functions of your body?

That intelligence is your subconscious mind. With the proper co-operation on your part, your subconscious mind will attend to these duties indefinitely, keeping your every organ perfect, your every function regular as clockwork.

But it is exceedingly amenable to suggestion. Worry about sickness or contagion, hold before it the thought that you are getting old, or that some organ is becoming feeble, and it will be perfectly agreeable to bringing about the condition you suggest. Convince it that there is no danger from contagion, hold before it the thought of health and strength, and it will be just as prompt in manifesting them.

So what you must realize is this: Before anything can be made, there must be a model for it in mind. Before a house can be built, there must be a plan, a blueprint from which to build. Before you were created, Universal Mind held in thought the model on which you were made. That model was perfect then—is perfect now. The only idea of you that Universal Mind knows is a perfect model, where every cell and organism is formed along perfect lines.

True, many of us have built up imperfect models in our own thoughts, but we can get rid of them just as rapidly as we get rid of the fear of them.

Your body is changing every moment. Every cell, every organism, is constantly being rebuilt. Why rebuild along the old, imperfect lines? Why not build on the lines held in the thought of Universal Mind? You CAN do it! But the essence of it lies in the words of the Master: "Whatsoever things ye desire when ye pray, believe that ye RECEIVE them, and ye SHALL HAVE them."

It matters not what your ailment may be. It will respond to that treatment. Suppose, as an example, that your stomach has been troubling you, that you cannot eat what you would like, that you cannot assimilate your food, that you are weak and nervous is consequence. Every morning when you awake, and every night just before you drop off to sleep say to yourself—

"My stomach has neither intelligence nor feeling. It functions only as mind directs it.

Therefore I need have no worry about its being weak or diseased, for the only image that Mind knows of stomach is Its perfect image. And that perfect image can assimilate or remove anything I may put into it. It is perfect, as everything that Universal Mind makes is perfect. And being perfect, it can do anything right I may ask of it without fear or anxiety."

Concentrate on the one organ at a time, and repeat this formula to yourself night and morning. Say it, *feel* it, BELIEVE it—and you can do what you please with that organ. "As thy faith is, so be it done unto thee."

"SUFFER LITTLE CHILDREN TO COME UNTO ME"

"I can believe all you say about my fears and worries being responsible for my own illnesses," write many people, "but how about infants and little children? They have no fear. Why do they sicken and die?"

What many people do not understand is that the subconscious mind is just as amenable to suggestion from those round about you as it is from your own conscious mind. Otherwise you would be in no danger from anything you did not consciously know of. And the more ignorant you were, the safer you would be.

Suppose, for instance, you took a draught of what you believed to be pure "bootleg" whisky, but which in reality was no more than wood alcohol. Many others have done it. Your conscious mind would expect no harm from it—any more than did theirs. You would have no fear of the result. No more did they. So, you would say, you should experience no harm.

Yet you would probably die—or at least go blind—as have these others. Why? Because your subconscious mind would know the wood alcohol for what it is. Your own conscious belief, and the preponderance of opinion of those about you, have instilled the conviction in your subconscious mind that wood alcohol is dire poison. Therefore when you pour this poison into your system—even though you do not consciously recognize it as such—your subconscious mind proceeds to bring about the effects you would logically expect such a poison to produce.

It is the same with contagion, with the hundreds of diseases which most people scarcely know the names of but to which they are constantly falling victims. They don't know they have been exposed to contagion. They don't know that their systems are in such condition that certain diseases logically follow. But their subconscious minds do know it. And they have so thoroughly educated those minds to believe in the necessity for ill health, in the inevitability of sickness under certain conditions, that the subconscious proceeds to work out the contagion or the condition to its logical conclusion.

Grown people can change these subconscious convictions by the proper counter-suggestions, consciously given. But young children cannot reason. They accept the beliefs that are held by the generality of mankind, or that are strongly suggested to them by those nearest to them.

That is why babies and young children fall such easy victims to the fears of disease and contagion of their parents and those about them. That is why worry over a seeming epidemic so often results in the children catching it, even when they have apparently been in no way exposed to the contagion.

"Man," says a famous writer, "often has fear stamped upon him before his entrance into the outer world; he is reared in fear; all his life is passed in bondage of fear of disease and death and thus his whole mentality becomes cramped, limited, and depressed, and his body follows its shrunken pattern and specification. IS IT NOT SURPRISING THAT HEALTH EXISTS AT ALL? Nothing but the boundless Divine Love, exuberance, and vitality, constantly poured in, even though unconsciously to us, could in some degrees neutralize such an ocean of morbidity."

But the remedy is just as simple. Know that your children are primarily children of God. That the image He holds of them is perfect. And that His perfect image has within itself every power necessary to ward off disease of any kind.

Put your children actively under His care. Throw the responsibility upon Him. Depend upon it, when you do this in the right way, no harm can come near them. Whenever fear assails you, whenever your children are exposed to danger or contagion, realize that "He shall give His angels (his thoughts) charge over them, to lead them in all their ways."

If your children are sick or ailing, read these thoughts aloud to them just as though you were talking to a grown person. Only address yourself to their subconscious minds. Read over the past few pages. Repeat to them the little formula outlined above, adapting it to their own particular need. Above all, BELIEVE it! Your faith will work just as great wonders for your children as for yourself.

Never doubt. Never fear. Go at your problem just as you would approach a difficult problem in mathematics. In mathematics, you know that the problem does not exist for which you cannot find the solution, provided you follow the rules and work in the right way.

As long as you do your part, the principle of mathematics will do the rest. It is the same in all of life. Don't worry. Don't fret. Go at your problem in the right way, no matter how difficult it may seem; follow the rules herein laid down, and you can confidently look to the Principle of Being to bring you the answer.

L'ENVOI

"The Kingdom of Heaven is like unto a treasure hid in a field; the which when a man hath found, he hideth, and for joy thereof goeth and selleth all that he hath, and buyeth that field." This field is your own consciousness—a treasure you find within yourself—which others cannot see. But *you* know it for the in-dwelling Spirit—"the Father within you"—and are willing to sell all that you have because this treasure is worth more than all other possessions.

If you have begun to realize this treasure, and use it even in a small way, the most wonderful thing that can happen to anyone on this planet has happened to you. What does it mean? It means that an ordinary human being, afflicted with all the sufferings and fears and worries and superstitions of the average man, has learned the Law of Being. It means that he has acquired a power above all that of his would-be destroyers. It means that he has put his foot upon the Rock of Life, that the Doorway of Heaven is open before him, that all of Good is as free to him as the air he breathes.

"There hath not failed one word of all His good promises." "And we declare unto you glad tidings, how that the promise which was made unto the fathers, God hath fulfilled the same unto us."

Surely we have every reason to be grateful for all the good round about us. Surely we should be thankful for the infinite power that has been given to us.

And being truly grateful, by the way, is the surest evidence of real faith that there is. Faith, you know, is "the substance of things hoped for, the evidence of things not seen." Remember, when Jesus raised Lazarus from the dead, how He first prayed, *then thanked the Father for answering His prayer?* There was not yet any material evidence that the prayer had been answered. But Jesus had perfect faith in the Father. And it was justified. Immediately He had given thanks, Lazarus *came forth from the tomb!*

The world today is so much more wonderful than it was to former generations. Mankind has begun to glimpse its illimitable powers. The whole world is plastic and sensitive to new ideas. The soul of man is finding itself, and learning its relation to the Infinite. The veil between the visible and the invisible is being drawn aside. Through seeing the "Father do the works," we are becoming more assured of our own power, beginning to assert "the Father that is within us." We know that, given the right understanding, the works that Jesus did we can do also. We recognize his "miracles" as divinely natural laws, part of God's continuous plan.

So let us go with Him unto the Mount of Vision, taking as our motto His words—"See that thou make all things according to the pattern shewed thee in the Mount."

Index of Scriptural References and Quotations

These passages are quoted from the King James version of the Bible. Authorized, Revised, and from various modern translations.

According to your faith—Matthew 9:29
Acquaint now thyself with Him—Job 22:21
All things are yours—I Corinthians 3:22
All that thou commandest us—Joshua 1:16
All things were made by Him—John 1:3
And God said, Let us make man—Genesis 1:26
And Moses was an hundred and—Deuteronomy 34:7
And whatsoever ye do, do it heartily—Colossians 3:23
And the second is like unto it—Matthew 22:39
And we declare unto you glad—The Acts 13:32
And when thou prayest, be not—Matthew 6:5
Are not two sparrows sold—Matthew 10:29
Ask and it shall be given—Matthew 7:7
Ask and ye shall receive—John 16:24
As a man thinketh in his heart—Proverbs 23:7
As the rain cometh down and—Isaiah 55:10
Beauty for ashes, the oil of joy—Isaiah 61:3
Because thou hast made the Lord—Psalms 91:9, 10, 11
Before Abraham was, I am—John 8:58
Behold I stand at the door—Revelation 3:20
Behold, the kingdom of God—Luke 17:21
Believe that ye receive it—Mark 11:24
Beloved now are we the sons—I John 3:2
Be not afraid—Matthew 14:27
Be still, and know that I am God—Psalms 46:10
Be ye therefore perfect—Matthew 5:48
Blessed are they which do hunger—Matthew 5:6

Blessed is the man whose delight—Psalms 1:2, 3
But thou are the same—Psalms 102:27
But thou, when thou prayest—Matthew 6:6
But where shall wisdom be found?—Job 28:12
Cast thy bread upon the waters—Ecclesiastes 11:1
Come ye to the open fountain—Revelation 7:17
Commit thy works unto the Lord—Proverbs 16:3
Consider the lilies—Luke 12:27
Delight thyself also in the Lord—Psalms 37:4
Do men gather figs of thistles?—Matthew 7:16
Every good gift and every perfect—James 1:17
Except ye turn and become as—Matthew 18:3
Faith without works—James 2:17
Fear not little flock—Luke 12:32
For God made not death—Apocrypha, Book of Wisdom 1:13
For herein is the Father glorified—John 15:8
He shall give His angels charge—Psalms 91:11
He that believeth on me—John 14:12
Hewers of wood—Joshua 9:27
Ho, every one that thirsteth—Isaiah 55:1
I came that ye might have life—John 10:10
I can of mine own self—John 5:30, John 14:10
If ye have faith as a grain—Matthew 17:20
If ye abide in me and my words—John 15:7
If a man keep my saying, he shall—John 8:51
I have given you power—Luke 10:19
In all thy ways acknowledge—Proverbs 3:6
In returning and rest—Isaiah 30:15
Jacob wrestles with the angel—Genesis 34:24-26
Know ye not that ye are the temple—I Corinthians 3:16
Know ye not that to whom ye yield—Romans 6:16
Lazarus raised from the dead—John 11:1-44
Let this mind be in you—Philippians 2:5
Lo I am with you always—Matthew 28:20
Lord that I may receive—Luke 18:41
Ninety-first Psalm
Now he that planteth and he—I Corinthians, 3:8-9
O taste and see that the Lord—Psalms 34:8
Prophetic sons of God—Hosea 1:10
See that thou make all things—Hebrews 8:5
Seek ye first the kingdom—Matthew 7:33
Son thou art ever with me—Luke 15:31
Suffer the little children—Mark 10:4

The earth is full of the—Psalms 33:5
The earth is the Lord's—Psalms 24:1
The Father that dwelleth in me—John 14:10
The kingdom of heaven is like—Matthew 13:44
The loaves and fishes—Luke 9:12-17
The manna from heaven—Exodus 16:15
The mount of Vision—Exodus 24:13, 18
The pillar of fire—Exodus 13:21
The sea rolled back—Exodus 14:21-22
The substance of things—Hebrews 11:1
The thing that I greatly—Job 3:25
The tribute money—Matthew 17:27
The water from the rock—Exodus 17:6
The water turned into wine—John 2:1
The waters which came down—Joshua 3:16-17
Therefore I say unto you—Matthew 6:31-33
There hath not failed one—I Kings 8:56
There is that scattereth—Proverbs 11:24
They that wait upon the Lord, shall win—Isaiah 40:31
They shall obtain joy and—Isaiah 35:10
This is life eternal—John 17:3
This one thing I do—Philippians 3:13
Thou art of purer eyes than to behold—Habakkuk 1:13
Thou shall love the Lord—Matthew 22:37
Thou wilt show me the path—Psalms 16:11
Thy faith hath made thee whole—Luke 8:48
To him that hath—Matthew 25:29
To know aright is life—John 17:3
Trust in the Lord and—Psalms 37:3
Twenty-third Psalm
Verily, verily I say unto you—John 8:51
We shall see Him as he is—I John 3:2
What eye never saw—I Corinthians 2:9
What things soever ye—Mark 11:24
What wouldst thou that I—Mark 10:51
Where there is no vision—Proverbs 29:18
Who hath measured the waters—Isaiah 40:12
Who healeth all thy diseases—Psalms 103:3
Whosoever shall be great—Matthew 20:26, 27
Whosoever liveth and believeth—John 11:26
Whosoever shall compel thee—Matthew 5:41
Whosoever will let him take—Revelation 22:17
With all thy getting—Proverbs 4:7

Work out your own salvation—Philippians 2:12
Wouldst thou be made whole—John 5:16
Ye shall ask what ye will—John 15:7
Ye shall know the truth—John 8:32
Your Father knoweth that ye—Luke 12:30

15

THE CONQUEST OF POVERTY

HELEN WILMANS

(1899)

Dedication

To working men and women everywhere, the fruitage of whose toil is small; to those who would, but cannot toil because refused; to you now near the top of that great ladder climbed by brawn, who long to use your brain; to you now toiling in the mental world, who would build better than you have; to all, who long for greater wealth of purse and power and self, I dedicate this book.

Remember as you read it, that you, sir, are a man; you, madam, are a woman. Conditions cannot be your master when you know yourselves. The buds of wondrous promise are within us all.

Man! Woman! These are words of mighty power indeed when understood. Each human today is the temple of its god within. Turn on the light of selfhood as you read this book and let the light be strong. Discover self! If search be short or long, I say, discover self! Then, know thyself, and then record a solemn vow and let it be, I can—I will—I dare—I do

THE AUTHOR

Preface

Poverty is so widespread, its curses are so bitter and its effects so far reaching, that anything at all practical as a remedial agency can but be gladly welcomed.

The life story of successful people in the form of biography or autobiography always has an influence more or less healthful, but the real philosophy of success has been rarely if ever touched upon in any writings of this character. The laws which underlie and govern success have been unconsciously practiced by many, and those who have recorded the histories of such lives in the form of biographies or autobiographies nearly always relate the success without even an attempt at a discovery of the real secret of the success attained. Effect is treated rather than cause.

Another class of literature on success and how to attain it, how to get rich, etc., has been written by "literary" people who write for publishers at so much per page, and while theoretical essays of much seeming beauty have been written in this way, they cannot be said to possess the merit of truth born of experience. The lives of the authors are not, in such cases, in harmony with what is written. From the standpoint of success their lives are not demonstrations of what they seek to teach. While such authors often write much that sounds plausible, their writings nearly always contain much advice that is positively detrimental to the development of courageous selfhood, the real key to all power.

There are thousands to-day who know personally the author of this book. Those who do, know that words could hardly be found to over-estimate the grandeur of her womanhood. She stands a giant oak in the forest of the worlds great women. While master of many subjects, perhaps upon no other is she better capable of speaking than upon the subject of this work. From poverty she has evolved to a condition of opulence, commanding to-day an income aggregating tens of thousands of dollars annually. From a position of shrinking self-denial she has risen to a plane of powerful selfhood, and through its power has conquered all undesirable environments; not poverty alone, but disease. At a time of life counted by the world as old age, instead of getting ready to die she is preparing to live.

Her life story therefore is a significant lesson to all who are struggling with unfavorable conditions, even were it told alone and with no attempt to disclose the laws which governed her success.

This little book, while not purporting to be an autobiography, still marks the mile posts here and there, where courage guided her away from the paths of indecision out into the highway of self trust, as she gradually unfolded for herself and for the world the great principles of truth which she has so ably formulated into the school now known throughout the world as Mental Science, one of the greatest, indeed the greatest, of all contributions to truth in the nineteenth century.

Marking as it does a general outline of her experience thus far, and illuminated as it is by the light of her philosophy, its influence cannot fail to accomplish great good. The reader will find that cause as well as effect is treated, and he can read it with satisfaction born of the knowledge that each page was lighted by the lamp of experience as the author wrote. We feel, therefore, that in this book we are offering to the world a temple of truth. Its foundation is the bed-rock of experience. It is lighted by a life-giving philosophy, the practicability of the teachings of which is a matter of common demonstration, not alone by Mrs. Wilmans, but by many of her students.

Surely, then, this temple is not builded on the sands of theory, and though its spires reach into the clouds of the ideal, the highest points have habitable chambers. The ideal, to those who will read and heed, can be made the real, and though the storms of ignorant criticism should beat upon this house of the higher Law, it will not fall.

THE INTERNATIONAL SCIENTIFIC ASSOCIATION

Contents

Introduction 1007

1. In Bondage 1009
2. The First Step Toward Freedom 1011
3. The Dawn of Freedom 1019
4. Arrival at the Conscious Plane of Growth 1023
5. Practical Fruitage of the Conscious Plane 1026
6. The Potency of Desire 1028
7. Correlation of Thought to External Things 1031
8. Difficulties 1036
9. The Vitality of Proper Belief 1041
10. The Fear of Poverty 1046
11. Courage 1050
12. Conclusion 1053

Introduction

In writing this book, while I shall not make it an autobiography, I shall prove what I say as I go along by the test of personal experience, than which there is no better guide or teacher.

I shall expound as best I can the laws of individual financial success in the light of the philosophy of mind.

While reading it I request each reader to note:

First, the steady but slow unfoldment of selfhood, as I gradually recognized more and more of its powers after catching the first faint glimpses, and began unconsciously to hinder less and less the Law of Aspiration.

Second, I ask each to note how much more rapid has been my advancement since I arrived at the plane of conscious growth, where I came to an understanding of its laws.

Again, it will be of profit to observe that I am not indebted to environment or so-called "special gifts."

What I have accomplished thus far has been in obedience to the working of natural laws which can and will operate in any human organism that will tear down the embankments of fear which obstruct the river of growth, and open the flood gates of courage and self-trust, thus permitting natural law to take its course. What I am, natural law has made me, aided only by self recognition, and while I know the scope of my growth and power to be boundless, what I claim for myself I claim for each individual of the race. I do not forget that in their ignorance of, not the equality, but the unity of the race, selfish men have foolishly secured the enactment of statutory laws which help to effectually hold the masses of the people in chains; but I assert that any individual may, by himself, rise above his environments, and that as he rises by virtue of his knowledge of the higher Law he helps to make clearer the mental atmosphere, himself comes into a clear and yet clearer recognition of his true relations to society and his fellow men and thereby helps forward the coming of the time when all men shall know for a truth, that, while equality in all things is neither possible nor desirable, the unity of all is at all times absolute, and that to do to others as we would have them do to us is the practical, and the only practical road to such financial success as brings with it the happiness for which we are all seeking.

Introduction

CHAPTER 1

In Bondage

One of the darkest clouds that oppresses the divinely illuminated and universal hope of the race is poverty.

And poverty is born of two misconceptions: first, man does not know that opulence is universal, awaiting only the opening of his own mentality to give of itself freely in every manner of uses and luxuries; and second, that he has not the faintest conception of his own power to command it.

That poverty is innate in man I am convinced by my own experience. It manifests itself first in fear. Fear is at the bottom of all poverty; fear of others, and distrust of self which is another form of fear, and the most deadly form of all. I am convinced that every shade and degree of opulence depends upon a man's valuation of his own powers; opulence is not limited: it is we who are limited in our demand for it, and more especially in our expectation of it after we have sent out some feeble, half-fledged demand.

I have known poverty most thoroughly. I was held in a belief of its power all through the earlier part of my life; not during my childhood, however, but beginning when I was a very young woman and continuing until I found there was a Law that could command opulence, which by slow degrees I put in operation and became free.

In looking back upon my experience it does not seem that the hard work I had to do wore on my strength so bitterly as the feelings engendered by the situation. I was crushed. I looked up to others as my superiors, and was ready to take my place beneath them. This is always a pitiful thing, and a thing that leads constantly downward in the scale of being. Its effect upon one's womanhood or manhood is as demoralizing as the disintegrating effect of alcohol on the moral character of the inebriate.

Nor was this all. I was tortured day and night by fear of actual want. Where the next dollar was to come from was my continual thought. It was the last thing in my thought at night; it haunted my dreams, and in the morning—mornings made dark and dreadful by the same gaunt phantom—I would be awakened by becoming gradually conscious of a weight at my heart. Arising and sitting on the side of my bed the day would face me with threats that I had no courage to meet. A thousand times in my weakness and inability to resist the present, my tears would fall all the minutes I was hastening to clothe myself.

The weight at my heart was not imaginary; it was a palpable thing and did not entirely disappear for years after I began to conquer poverty and was on the upgrade to splendid success.

There was no valid reason for all this torture except that which existed in my mind. I had been so unappreciated that I had come to regard myself as an inferior creature, and to look upon all successful persons as being more happily endowed by nature than I. I accepted this as an actual fact and did not reason upon it. Indeed it was the unawakened condition of the power within me that was responsible for the whole situation.

Fear was at the bottom of it all. A natural timidity that my education increased instead of overcoming, and the constant distrust of myself, my own powers—these two conditions shut out the light of life for me and left me in the dark and the cold where the sunshine of truth was slow in reaching me.

But at last my reasoning powers showed signs of awakening; first on the subject of religion; then on other things, and my mind broke its fetters so that I began to see light. I threw off a hundred beliefs that were considered essential to man's salvation; and, as I kept on reasoning and my reason justified me in clinging fast to my own opinions, I slowly acquired a measure of individuality that enabled me to stand alone.

No, not alone; but to approach the place in the understanding of myself where I saw that it would be possible for me to stand alone, sometime.

My fears abated as I gradually perceived within myself a will that I argued would not be there unless it was meant for use. Previous to this I had supposed this will—when I caught sight of it at long intervals—was the Devil, and stood as the living opponent to God's will, which I tried, strenuously, to follow by crushing my own will.

But I shall not follow the course of reasoning I adopted at this period of my growth. It did pull me through every difficulty and changed me from the most despondent, hopeless, poverty-stricken person to the most hopeful and opulent one I know in all the world. I will give the course of reasoning I followed later on in this book; but now I will continue with my experiences, all of which constitute a perfect illustration of the ideas I mean to show forth as having the power in every instance, without fail, to cure poverty and establish wealth.

I consider that person wealthy who has enough and who spends fearlessly what he has. This is my condition, and while, since I came to the plane of conscious growth, I have expended money for anything I desired, it has come to me in greater abundance than the amount necessary to satisfy all immediate desires, the natural result being accumulation, which, to me, represents the over-plus of strength. I would not be afraid to spend the last dollar I possess in property or money, for I know that more would come to me. I know that a certain mental attitude, a certain quality of thought generated by the brain will put me in the way of getting what I want. Having mastered this quality of thought and come understandingly into the use of it, the supply is bound to be equal to my demand.

To describe the mental attitude or the quality of thought may prove rather difficult since it rests on a deep understanding of man and his powers. Perhaps I had better let my further experience demonstrate the idea, and after that give the necessary explanation. I may have to go into this experience at a tiresome length, but if the reader learns the secret from it he will be repaid for the reading.

CHAPTER 2

The First Step Toward Freedom

I was a farmer's wife and held up my end of the work without flinching; but we lost money each year, and the place was mortgaged and finally sold for debt. Perhaps there never was a more favorable situation for me than when I stood out on the roadside, after years of toil on that farm, with all my possessions in a valise, waiting for a wagon to come along that would carry me to town, five miles away. I did not suspect its being a favorable situation then. I had not a cent of money and no visible prospects ahead. It was strange that I had mustered sufficient courage to make the move I was then making. I was going to San Francisco, some ninety miles away (I lived in the mountainous region of Lake County, California). I was not only going there but I intended to find work more congenial than the work I had been doing so unceasingly for twenty years and more.

I cannot tell how I dared undertake such a trip, except that it was an unconscious obedience to the law of aspiration. I knew almost nothing about a city, and what little I did know made me still more timid concerning it. But I was so tired of life on the plane I had been living that I voluntarily closed the door on it forever, even if starvation were the result.

As I look back now I can see how for years I had been gradually coming out of the crushed feeling that rendered me so helpless, as far as facing the world was concerned. And yet the world was a great terror to me even then; my heart sank whenever I thought of being among the happy, busy, independent, prosperous people of the city; they seemed so fortunate and so easy in their minds; they had homes and plenty. Truly I was Hagar in the desert: an outcast.

And yet I would go on. I had not then become aware of the strength that now wells up every moment in my breast and makes me laugh at discouragements. It was no doubt there and held me to my purpose, in spite of my not seeing it. It was entirely undeveloped so far as my consciousness was concerned, but it had begun to grow within me, and even this small prophecy of its coming power held me to my purpose. It proved to be a great triumph to me that I dared to go, under the circumstances, and it marked a turning point in my life from the weakness that comes from self depreciation to the power that results from a high individual valuation.

When I reached the nearest village, which was Lower Lake, five miles from our mountain ranch, a place where every one knew me, I tried to borrow ten dollars to pay my traveling expenses to San Francisco. I asked one friend and another only to be refused; some of them did not have the money; others who could have obliged me were afraid to do so. The people were all poor except a few merchants, and, as we were in debt to them, I did not dare apply for a loan. I ran over the streets of that wretched little town until nine o'clock that night, then I bethought myself of the one hope left me. The village shoemaker had his shop and dwelling house under the same roof. From the street I saw a light in their rooms, and I rapped at the door. Both the man and his wife were startled; I presume that I was awfully pale, and I know that I was more resolute than I had ever been in my life before. I believe to this day that I frightened those people out of that ten dollars. I told them that I had asked dozens of people who professed friendship for me to let me have it and every one refused. "You," I said, "are the last hope I have, and it is a good hope, for I know you are going to lend it to me. I am leaving home for the city where I shall find something besides a slave's work and I shall pay you back very soon."

I did not say much more than this; the man shambled off to another room and came back with the money. He died of softening of the brain some two years later—I hope my night attack on his coffers was not the means of bringing it on. I would not like to be responsible for the death of one who did me a kindness.

But truly there was something strange about it. If I had thought of him at all in the morning, when I started in my quest for money, I should have put him down as the one most unlikely to let me have it. No, I am sure that he did not let me have it; I took it by mental force. Until I paid him, several weeks later, the circumstance scarcely left my mind an hour.

The next morning I was on the stage under full sail for the city. Oh, the glory of the thing! The exhilaration of that ride over the mountains; the splendor of the sunshine; the beauty of the trees and flowers; the gorges so far below the road, and the streams of crystal water cascading through them! I had been over the same road several times before, but never in the same frame of mind. There had been an awakening in my brain which brought out beauties in the air and sky and water never previously noted; it was evident that I was more alive than usual. It was the beginning of my becoming acquainted with myself.

I had never sought strength in myself; I had sought it in religion, in the advice of other persons, in books that were supposed to do good to those who read them; such means of grace profited me nothing. In fact, the more I depended on them the weaker and more irresolute I became.

But at last I was conscious of a small amount of resolution, even though the possession of it filled me with anxiety. I kept asking myself how I dared leave home, where I had food and clothes at least, to venture out into the wilderness of the world's ways without either money or friends. At first the answer seemed clear enough; it was to the effect that I had been measuring myself with other people and had reached the conclusion that I was as clear-headed as any body else and that, therefore, my chances of making a living outside of the drudgery of farm work were good.

As I neared the city, having spent seven out of my ten dollars, I began to sink in my own estimation, and as I did so my chances of success shrank too. Now note the correlation of thought and external things, as expressed in the situation just described. Thought, when positive, is all compelling; but, when negative, it has no power, either on the body or on external things. My thoughts weakened as the day waned; so when night came and I shudderingly walked the brilliant streets of the gay city, I was the most utterly hopeless creature that ever faced such a dismal situation.

I went to a lodging house where I paid one dollar for a room, and had less than two dollars left. The next morning I began to search for a room to live in. I found one in the cock-loft of a house kept by two old sisters, and a brother. It was a decent room and I became very happy in it later on. I paid one dollar and fifty-cents in advance for it and had almost nothing left. Up to this time I had bought nothing to eat. There were some crackers and remnants of a lunch in my satchel, put up in Lower Lake by a kind neighbor with whom I had spent the night, and these lasted a day or two. Then I went without anything for three full days.

All this time I was haunting the newspaper offices; I wanted some literary work to do. I had no special reason for believing myself fitted by nature or education for this kind of work, but all my aspirations had pointed toward literature from my babyhood, and now I could not consent to do any other kind of work. Matters really came to a life-and-death contest before I found a place where I could earn a living with my pen, but I clung to the hope and would be appeased by nothing else.

I had wealthy relatives in the city but I kept away from them. I read the "wants" in the papers when a paper chanced to fall in my way, and I knew that I could get a situation and large wages as either cook or housekeeper in some of the exceedingly wealthy families there. I knew the perplexities many of these families underwent because they could get no competent help. I knew of a woman who had taken a situation in one of these families and was paid two hundred dollars per month. I knew, also, that this woman was not my equal in such a capacity, and that I could easily obtain such work and such wages; but I would not have it.

I was certainly putting a very low valuation on my food in those days. I had never been hungry before, and really was not hungry then, or at least I was not conscious of being so. "I have had bread and butter all my life," I said to myself, "and bread and butter alone do not count for much just now. Unless my bread and butter can be made to feed a higher life than one occasioned by the drudgery I have done these twenty years, I do not want them. I cannot starve too soon."

I wanted what I wanted and I did not want anything else. I must have answered my own query as did the darkey, when asked where he was going: "Whar's I gwine? I's gwine whar I's gwine; dat's whar I's gwine." At last I found a little newspaper that was worrying out a precarious existence by carrying many patent medicine advertisements, and here the editor gave me work at six dollars a week. I asked him for a dollar in advance, and only obtained it when I told him I had been three days without food. I worked for him faithfully; wrote for the paper—a four-page weekly—and really secured a circulation of five or six hundred subscribers for it. It had no regular subscribers when I commenced work upon it; nothing but a home manufactured list, kept up for the purpose of deceiving the postal authorities.

When I had been working in the above capacity about six months, and was beginning to outgrow the anxieties that formerly made life a terror to me, the paper died suddenly and I was an orphan. The patent medicine men had withdrawn their patronage.

I was surprised to find that the catastrophe did not overwhelm me. I was not nearly so frightened as I had been when I made my first move toward freedom. "Something else will come," I said, and I said it because I was beginning to feel within myself the power to command that something.

And something else did come. It was a position on another paper at ten dollars a week. It did not last long, and again I was surprised to find myself quite indifferent and looking forward to something better yet.

My march was steadily upward, and, as I look back, I am aware that this was the case; because the external had to correspond with the internal me, and the internal me was constantly growing stronger.

I was constantly growing more confident in myself—not in my luck, not in special providence or the overruling power of God; but in my own individual self. I was daring to think better of myself. I had formerly considered myself weak and others strong. I now looked upon myself as being stronger than I had ever imagined before. And there was not one particle of increase in my belief in self that did not record itself in the external conditions of my life. The more I believed I could do, the more I accomplished.

I remember one morning, on wakening, it flashed through my brain that I was really a genius. The suggestion startled me. I was frightened for a moment. Then I sat up in bed and said to myself: I am not going to refuse the suggestion; it has come unbidden, but it is mine. As I continued to think I saw that everyone was a genius. That is, everybody had the power to develop out of himself, just as the leaves develop out of a tree, anything he wished to bring forth. The magnitude of the thought startled me; and yet I knew it was true then, quite as well as I know it now, after the confirmation of many years. That morning I had indeed taken a splendid step.

Let the reader ponder the last page of this chapter well, for it does, literally and in practical fact, furnish the key that unlocks the door of universal opulence to every soul that understands it.

Man is a miniature world. He is the world condensed into a working form, and he really has the privilege of being what he wishes to be, of doing what he wishes to do; the only trouble being that he does not know his own power—does not know himself.

"Man, know thyself" is the greatest injunction ever given. When a man knows himself he knows the God toward whom his aspirations have always ascended; for a man's own ideal—that supreme creature he has the power to become—is his God.

God's power is believed to be limitless; it is limitless; and the fact that it is embodied in the man and expressed through his uses, is no proof to the contrary.

But to return to my personal affairs. I really had less anxiety in my new life than ever before. I need not tell how, little by little, I saved the money to bring my children to me—it is told somewhere else in my printed works. But I must tell, even though I may have told it before, how the spirit of self confidence that had lain dormant in me so long, at last assumed proportions that made me question whether I wanted any position in any man's office any longer. Why could not I do something for myself? By this time two or three years had passed. I had learned to write a good article, and was making a reputation, which, though not extensive, was very valuable to me, since it procured for me a situation on a large Chicago paper where I had light work and excellent pay for a year or more.

But this spirit of independence, which is self growth, grew stronger in me all the time, as I trusted more and more the voice of the Law of Aspiration, or desire, and followed where it led. I was tired of being somebody's hired man, and longed to try my powers at work of my own. It used occasionally to happen that one of my editorials was condemned. This caused me to ask myself what right had the proprietor of the paper, or anybody else, to have my brain in his own power. He might well have in his own power the brains of those who do not object to such ownership, but with me it was different. My self-esteem had grown until I thought I could do as good work as the proprietor, or anybody else.

I am emphasizing the fact that with the growth of my self-esteem there was a corresponding improvement in my circumstances. This has been the case since the hour I stood in the road at the old farm gate waiting for a wagon to pass.

In other words, the thing you believe you can do, you can do; and if you will only be true to your belief, there is no power that can hinder you. The reason most men do not accomplish more is because they do not attempt more. But how are you to believe in your own power? You will have to affirm or declare a certain amount of faith in yourself, whether it is there or not; and then put that faith to the test by carrying it out in some external condition. Begin this way in small things and see them increase under your effort until you really do begin to feel the pride of self-conscious strength and individual mastery.

Oh, the glory of the thing and the opulence that waits on such a frame of mind! But I will go on with the illustration of this idea by still further recounting my personal experiences.

One dislikes to recount a circumstance that has already been written and published in some previous work, and I would not do what I am going to do were it not so necessary to the illustration of the subject in hand. The same thing has already appeared in one of my books called "A Search for Freedom."

The study of self develops the lifting power in a man; it shows him his own strength, and seeing his own strength he reaches out and takes without any fear of refusal, just what he wants. Excepting himself, there is no one to say "No" to him. But this reaching out to take possession of what he wants is no simple thought affair that loses itself in a succeeding troop of useless thoughts; it is thought armed with intelligent purpose and equipped for effort in the field of activities.

There are plenty of visionary guides to wealth nowadays, in which the writers tell you how, by holding certain thoughts, you can sit and do nothing while riches flow to you. There is nothing practical in this at this time, though the time may come when thought will have such power. But now the utmost that thought can do in this matter is to fill the person with vitality by showing him of what great things he is capable. It has been said, "Genius is only energy intensified, and energy is thought intensified and expressed in action." Thought shows a man that he does not have to be poor; that he does not have to ram stones in the street, or hammer iron, or dig ore, or drive horses for a living. It shows him, moreover, that there is no compulsion on him to work in grooves that are distasteful to him. Why? Because he sees that his own mind is fertile, and can hatch out ideas that will expand and grow, if he will only give them proper attention. He sees that he himself is as capable of arousing new hopes in the race and adding new uses to the operations of labor, as any other man.

But in order to accomplish anything he must think. Thought is the beginning of effort. The person who works for others, and plods steadily in a rut, has no need for thought. His boss thinks for him, and, if this goes on long enough, all the grand possibilities of his brain shrivel up and die because of non-use.

Capital needs and demands intelligent labor—men who think for themselves. Thought—original, creative thought—will bring its reward by increased remuneration as you work for others while growing to strength sufficient to enable you to work for yourself, thus making room for some one not yet quite so strong as yourself.

The slaves of capital are where they are, not because capital oppresses them, but because they will not use their brains. Employers everywhere honor the growing employee. No worthy man of money would hinder the growing mentality of the ambitious employee, but he could not if he would. Thought has power to redeem anyone by showing him a true estimate of his own worth. But so long as the so-called slaves of labor will not think, they can scarcely be called men. They are on a lower plane than that of men, and they are receiving treatment in conformity with the plane they are on. They have only their own ignorance to blame, and this is the thing they never think of blaming.

I repeat, knowledge of self is the lifting power; it individualizes. No man can seek a knowledge of himself introspectively without discovering the rudiments of mighty effort within himself, as I did. It is this discovery that lifts one in the scale of being, until he looks with level eyes into the eyes of all other men. When he is able to do this his fetters, no matter what they may have been, actually fall. Better positions in business open up to him; better surroundings come about him in answer to his increased consciousness of power. Let a man once proclaim himself a free man from his high point of intellectual seeing, and all the world hastens to respond.

In first looking abroad over the world, and seeing the inequality of position among the masses, we naturally resent it, and begin to search for some person or persons on whom we may lay the blame. In California where the capitalist fourished in extraordinary glory and where his tyranny was more felt than in any other state—owing to the fact that the mass of the laborers were the sons of the bravest men that the republic ever produced; namely, the pioneers who cut their way through such enormous obstacles to reach the land of gold in '49—there was the loudest possible call for sympathy and assistance from one so situated as I had been.

I wanted somebody to blame for the situation; somebody besides the laborers themselves, and I became an acceptable writer for the agnostic press.

I believed that certain social and political reforms were all that were necessary to enable men and women to rise in the scale of being, to much higher positions of thought and action than they had yet attained. And so I worked for the accomplishment of this end. That is, I did my little best for it. I was not widely known as a writer, and my influence was small; but I was in earnest and put my whole soul into the work, believing in it with great fervency.

But at every step I was disappointed. The people themselves, for whom I was laboring, were the greatest disappointment of all. They were dead to any sense of power within themselves, and were only alive to what they considered their wrongs. No thoughts of a higher intellectual growth stimulated them in their efforts to obtain greater financial independence. Their ideas of liberty, if gratified, would lead in the direction of unbridled license. They knew nothing of freedom in the true sense of the word. They had no idea that their fetters were of their own making no less than of their masters', and were all to be resolved into one short sentence—complete ignorance of their own undeveloped possibilities. They would not institute within themselves the search for what they needed in order to secure liberty. They did not know, and seemingly did not wish to know, that each man holds his own heaven in his personality, and that the careful unfolding of that personality will yield him all that he can ever desire. They preferred the clashing of opinions that were not based upon the foundation where individual growth begins; but, instead, were the mixed outcome of life's mistaken beliefs.

Instead of growing nearer to these people in sympathy I was growing away from them. At first I did not see the drift of the thing and made many futile attempts to regain my interest. I grew to hate the writing of a reform article. As to reading one from any of the numerous exchanges I simply could not do it. I was on the wrong track and intuition told me so, even in advance of reason.

It would be difficult for me to describe the confusion of mind I now fell into. My duties in the office of the paper on which I worked, though light, became a nightmare. The proprietor, the owner of the whole concern, was generosity itself. He was, and is, one of the noblest men I have ever met; my fast friend then and now; and if every soul on earth should prove a disappointment, the remembrance of him, his splendid manhood, his loyalty to his highest convictions of truth, and indeed his whole mentality, would always stand before me in justification of my unshaken faith in the godhood of man.

I am conscious now that this beloved friend was also losing faith in the reform for which he was laboring so faithfully; but at the time I left the paper I did not know it. He was still putting every effort of his strong, great life into his work, regardless of the fact that those for whom he thought and labored, and sacrificed, were so irresponsive and unthankful. He left the paper later, and has since applied his fine business ability to building up another enterprise, which has been wonderfully successful.

But when I left his paper he was displeased. He had a right to think me ungrateful. My action must have looked so to him. But I could not remain in the work. It is true that I was incapable of analyzing the impulse which prompted me to abandon it. I only recognized the impulse, and, because it was in the line of my growth, I was obedient to it.

I had made many a little conquest over my beliefs in my own weakness, and I was strong for a woman who had begun her career in such a state of morbid self-depreciation. I had developed rapidly from the condition of fear that had once been normal, and was standing at what seemed the open doorway of my own character; where, looking within, I saw many plants of great promise and vigor and wanted a chance to water them and dig about their roots, so that, in time, I should have much honest pride and comfort in them.

I had come to think my work degrading to the higher possibilities of my brain, and although those possibilities were too vague to be clearly defined, they were apparent enough to hold every secret thought of my mind true to them; so I was almost recklessly obedient to the ideal constantly beckoning me forward.

CHAPTER 3

The Dawn of Freedom

The morning came when, after dragging myself to the office, I sat at my desk, gloomy and despondent. I went presently to the proprietor's desk and told him that I wished to start a paper of my own. He told me the sea of journalism was very tempestuous and many ships were wrecked on it, that of the few which succeeded only a small number were real successes. He begged me for my own interest to remain where I was. When he saw that his argument failed to shake me, he turned back to his desk very gravely, and I felt that if I left his employment under these circumstances, I would lose the best friend I had in the world.

On the road to progress it often happens that the warmest friendship may become a tyranny that has to be broken. Nothing should hold the outward bound mind, and nothing could hold me. I would be free.

What a compelling force is an ideal! And yet, on that November morning, I had no glimpse of the ideal that usually presented so many allurements for attracting me from sober duty. It was simply the fact that I had reached another stage of growth, and must needs quit and look forward to the outlying filaments of the next experience that my developing life called for.

I sat at my desk, deliberately reasoning out the situation. My dear friend, the editor, had spoken of my bread and butter as being involved in the new effort. I thought about this and was filled with resentment at the idea. It had frightened me often enough in the earlier part of my career; but it could frighten me no longer. I would not show it the white feather. "Bread and butter are all right when they can be made to serve the purpose of building my ideal," I thought, "but not simply as a power with which to pump gas into another person's machine, I don't see what good this is doing me. This is one of the circumstances where my bread and butter instead of feeding me, are really starving me." So that point in the discussion between me and myself fell dead, never to be resurrected again.

As I write these words I go back to that time, and I know now (while I only believed then) that the logic I used at that time is one of the truest bits of wisdom that a growing soul can adopt. I did really lose all fear of want as completely as if liberated from earth-life and endued at that very moment with the highest angelic powers.

I arose, put on my cloak and hood, and went down into the street. The morning had been sunshiny, but cold, when I came. It was now gloomed over despairingly. I never saw a more dismal sky. The sleet, borne on a strong wind, struck me in the face; the sidewalks were coated with ice. As I stood at the foot of the stairs I opened my purse. I had only twenty-five cents. I had not a friend in the city but the one I had just left. I was my own sole dependence. There was no prop in the world on which I could lean, and I knew it with the most vivid sense of realization. More than this, I knew that there was no one I wanted to lean upon. I doubt whether in the history of the race there has been a soul who stood more erect in a position of such complete isolation. I was so far removed from fear and anxiety that I gloried in my aloneness. I walked those icy streets like a school boy just released from restraint. My years fell from me as completely as if death had turned my spirit loose in Paradise.

I returned to my boarding-house, to face the scowls of my landlord, whose prudent eye questioned my untimely return, and who shrewdly and rightly surmised that my next week's board bill would go unpaid. Then to my room and to pen and paper. I was fired by my sense of freedom, and what I wrote must have found an echo in hundreds of imprisoned spirits, for that article made my paper a success.

Late in the afternoon my landlord came in, embarrassed but resolute. He wanted to know how matters stood.

"Have you been discharged by the chief?"

"No, the chief has been discharged by me. I have refused to work for any person any longer."

"Is your bread insured?"

"I don't concede your right to question me, but I believe I am glad you take the liberty. My bread is insured."

"How?"

"I am going to start a paper of my own, and it is already a success even before it is born. Sit down while I read you the first article I have written for it."

He did so and I read the article. The subject was "I."

It was an article to stir the blood. It awakened interest wherever it was read, and brought me in frank, noble contact with many minds. It was a declaration of individuality; it would have been a protest against bonds, but for the fact that it sounded notes of freedom far above all thought of bonds. It had wings to it; those who read it were lifted into the air.

That it had this effect on me was not surprising; but when I saw its effect on my landlord, I was amazed. His face, which was naturally sodden, had become illuminated, and for the moment actually beautiful. (Oh there is a man, a woman, in every one of these shadows that walk the streets, if we could only reach them!)

After a pause my landlord said, "I have perfect confidence in your ability to succeed. In fact I am ready to gamble on you. I have twenty thousand dollars in bank and you can draw on me for all you need."

Then I confessed I was without means; but told him I confidently expected to "reach the persimmon" alone. I wouldn't take his money but I asked him to wait a few weeks for my board.

From that time on no queen could have been treated with more courtesy. One day, in my absence, the landlord moved my things down from my single room on the third floor, to a lovely suite of three rooms on the parlor floor. Again and again this generous man offered me money, which I steadily refused.

"Fate" was working rapidly in my favor at that time. Evidently the state of mental freedom I had achieved was putting a compulsion on externals in a very peremptory way. And oh, how happy I was! I drew the design for the heading of my paper and was so pleased with it that several times in the night I arose to look at it. I took it to the lithographer and had a plate made. It was sent to me by a boy several days after, without the bill.

When my writing was finished I went to the largest publishing house in the city and ordered twenty thousand copies of the paper, to be delivered at my room on a certain day.

In the meantime I was addressing wrappers as fast as I could, and making other preparations for mailing sample copies. At that time there was no trouble in getting thousands of sample copies into the mail; things have changed since then.

On the third day after my papers were mailed, I received eleven dollars on subscription. I told the landlord, and we danced around the table until we knocked off the ink bottle and so left a lasting impression of our joy. The next day brought more. Not long afterwards a rich man in Boston sent me two hundred and fifty dollars. Others sent considerable in smaller sums; altogether I felt that I could afford to pay my good friend, the landlord, but no! "Let me alone," he said, "I had need for you to owe me for your board, during the time of your trial. I am trying to get the Lord in debt to me; it is my only hope of salvation."

This was the beginning of my working for myself; it was the end of my working for wages. My freedom really dated from the day when, standing out in the snow, and counting the capital I had to begin life on, I found my inventory showed a total of twenty-five cents.

All along, as I advanced one step after another, I was inclined to examine the relations of my mind or state of thought, to matter, or external conditions. The result was I came to have a knowledge of the Law of Attraction, and how to use it in a way to benefit myself and others.

Experience has been the only teacher of any consequence I have ever had, and if I had not utilized the reasoning faculties that invited me to submit my experiences to the test of the most critical thought, I am sure I should never have found the right relation between the mind itself, as expressed in thought, and the same mind as carried out on the external plane and expressed in uses, in which case I should never have been able to tell my readers how they may command the wealth they need.

Some of our scientists who have at last found what they deserved to find earlier in their lives—that is, recognition of their own tremendous worth from the people—are now speaking boldly and understandingly of what they call "the correlation of forces." I was delighted when I first heard of this expression, "the correlation of forces." I had found that thought was a force, and bore a direct relation to the thing it was centered upon. I began to experiment with it. Before long I received the absolute assurance that a man is as he believes; that is, the thoughts in which he believes create his body and his external conditions also. No man not versed in Mental Science can conceive how much the above statement rests upon the Bible for proof. The characters in the Bible did what they believed they could do. Where doubt of their own ability to do the thing crept in, their faith was overshadowed and failure resulted.

After much thought I came to the conclusion that a man was worth his own valuation, provided that valuation was based on a dispassionate, logical examination of himself from the standpoint of pure reason—the reason that rests on a knowledge of man's place in the universe, and of how he came to be where he is.

Man must use his brain constantly. He needs to compare himself not only with other men but with other creatures and things, in order to recognize his advantage over all of them. He must know for a fact that nothing masters him; that he masters all things—not only of the present, but of the future as well. He must look forward to see the splendor of those intellectual gleams shooting beyond his experiences, and illuminating many an untried vista.

What! Does a sense of superiority actually lift a person in the scale of being? It surely does, for the reason that a man's body is his conscious intelligence, and it is because his body is his conscious intelligence that he is what he believes himself to be. In other words, a man is as he believes.

CHAPTER 4

Arrival at the Conscious Plane of Growth

I had now arrived at the conscious plane of growth, little dreaming, even after coming to an understanding of the Law, that it meant for me the immense fortifications of strength which it has proved. I did not dream that it meant the conquest of disease, not only for myself, but for others.

The name of C. C. Post has gone out to the world as an author and a clear and logical thinker in all the new lines of thought. When we were married, some sixteen years ago, we were both poor enough; but both of us had learned to think entirely beyond the present standard of thought. We took a complete course of lessons in Christian Science, and it did us immense good, by way of showing us the wrong end of the road to which the high ideal of our minds was constantly pointing. The wrong end of the road predicates the right end. They say, "All roads lead to Rome." This is true; in our case even the wrong road directed us aright. We were on that road and we had to think about it. This was the one thing necessary; anybody can unravel the mysteries of the whole span of life, can do anything on earth he wants to do, can learn anything he wants to learn, can command the power that created worlds if he will only think.

It was at this time that I begin to think more earnestly than ever before. I plunged into the remarkable assertion of Christian Science that there is nothing in all the universe but nothing, and that the one duty of the individual is to get rid of his individuality and lose himself in nothingness. I came out of my plunge with the knowledge that this idea was not only unsound, but that the direct reverse of it was true.

Individuality, then, became my great theme; the mighty and unfailing power vested in the individual; the creative power existing in the man. When I had come fully into this idea I could feel the chains break and fall from me. It even took a pressure off my lungs, so that my breathing was deeper from that hour. I also observed that every advancement I made in thinking showed forth in some new improvement in my body.

Thought is all powerful. Weak thought—by which I mean the thought you apply to yourself when discouraged—makes you weak, plants weakness in your body, renders you unfit for action and destroys your courage, even your ability, to advance along any line of intelligent development.

But you do not have to think weak thoughts of yourself, and you no sooner begin to affirm this fact than you observe a change. You want to hold long conversations with yourself, in which you affirm that you are capable of thinking well of yourself and have the right to do so. Say, "I can and I will," and let the meaning of these words permeate every particle of you. Very soon you will be stronger, and better calculated to undertake some good, paying enterprise.

Money comes through doing. But underneath the doing lies the mighty motor, thought—the finest, the most powerful, the most expansive, and the most creative substance there is. Thought is the world builder; but it has to build man first and then the man builds the world.

From that day in November, when I stood on the sleety pavement in Chicago with twenty-five cents in my purse, but with quite palpable wings in my brain, I have never really feared poverty. I did not make a fortune out of my paper; but I built it into a very fair business, which supplemented my husband's salary so that we lived comfortably, if not luxuriously. But Mr. Post was taken sick. He sank rapidly into consumption, and touched the verge of the grave before we had learned to use the power of thought with sufficient intelligence to bring him back to health. It was an awful thing to sit there helplessly and see that rare and beautiful life drift away. How hard I tried to put in practice the lessons I had learned in Christian Science. I could do nothing with them except to weaken him still more. At last I resolved that I would not let him die. I spoke the word of health for him, and spoke it so powerfully that it was like planting a monument in a substance so inflexible that nothing could shake it. I saw that monument constantly and it gave me strength, until I became as a god and knew that no power could come against me. It was at this time that the right road was pointed out to me by the discovery of the wrong road. It was here that the errors of Christian Science were made apparent. In that hour of rebellion against conditions which threatened to destroy a life that was dear to me, when intuition told me that by trusting my own thought I could save him; in that hour when I dared to think for myself thoughts which were in advance of the school whose disciple I had become, and from which I had hoped so much but was disappointed; in that hour of courage and self trust, was born the movement now known throughout the world as Mental Science. From an air-plant of Christian Science I had ripened into the fruitage of realistic idealism, and I dared to trust to that which told me another page of the infinite scroll of truth had been unfolded to me. Not alone for me, but through me for all mankind. I not only dared to trust these thoughts; but together we proceeded, a little later, to put them into practical execution, by formulating the truths made known to me.

Mr. Post began to get well, and he kept on getting well; but he had lost his editorial position—our principal means of support. I had sold my paper to get money to enable him to go South. So that we were faced by what to some would have seemed a very grim phantom indeed.

For a time I felt almost impatient. I had held the fort against death and had scored a splendid victory; but here we were without money, stung by small wants daily, and not knowing where to turn. It had been easier to fight the giant and gain the victory than to banish a horde of small annoyances like flies or mosquitoes. Necessity is often the mother of invention, and one day Mr. Post suggested that I write a set of lessons on Mental Science—the name we had decided to give this child of mental growth. We little dreamed then that this child would grow into a giant, with a world-wide influence; but we had faith and dared to do.

With my very soul on fire I began to write the lessons.

When they were completed there was no money to pay for printing them; so in the paper I had formerly owned, I advertised to the effect that the student could take one lesson at a time, copy and return it. My daughter, Mrs. Powers, helped me prepare six copies of each of the six lessons, and we really thought we were well equipped. There were only six lessons in the course, and I sold the entire set—to copy and return—for twenty-five dollars.

Some days later I received several letters asking questions about the lessons. One letter contained an order for twenty-five dollars. I had hard work to keep this money from looking large; but I managed it, and fixed up my expectations for more. And more came; a great deal more, and it continues to come. Of all the positive demands I have made, there has never been one on which I have insisted more unflinchingly than that one concerning money matters. Some annoyances about other things would and did come, for the fortification of self was not guarded in every direction; but there has been no weakening about money. It was essential to my freedom that I should have it; there was nothing in all the world to prevent me from having it, since I had so much to give in return. I had argued myself into a state of mental strength where I felt my mastery concerning it. So has every one plenty to give in return by simply unfolding his own self. His demand can be made just as emphatic.

I am sure that even now, after so many years of financial success, I could lose my power and drift back into poverty-stricken conditions, if I should permit my efforts to become clouded by fear. Fear is the only thing of which we should be afraid; it is the only real, live devil; all others are dead. So, now, the one great denial of my life is that of fear. "I am not afraid of poverty. I will not pinch down in my money spending. I will not economize as that word is commonly understood." This is my constant affirmation.

"It is not economy to acknowledge limitations to creative thought. I will live my life and not die all the way through it. I am greater than money and a thousand times more positive. In the nature of things it is for me to command and it to obey. This is the Law whose mandate is absolutely unchangeable. He who trusts the Law can come into the health of the Law and the opulence of the Law—an opulence which nothing but the man himself can stint."

CHAPTER 5

Practical Fruitage of the Conscious Plane

It was in consequence of Mr. Post's illness that we left Chicago and went to Georgia; he having gone in advance of myself and before I had come to a full understanding of my power to heal. While there we built a beautiful home, with large grounds and many trees and flowers. It was really a stately residence; but I never quite liked the location of it, and we sold it and came further south. The first winter we spent in Daytona, on the opposite side of the Halifax river from where we now live.

We bought land on the peninsula side and had the scrub palmetto roots grubbed out of the ground before we could do anything with it. The soil was absolutely virgin. The first house we put up was a beautiful little cottage of three rooms, under a group of stately palms by the river.

This was the first house we lived in after we came. Then, as others wished to come, we put up one wing of the Colonnades Hotel; then another wing, making quite a large house. Now another section of the building has been built with an additional fifty rooms.

Two beautiful boulevards, reaching across the peninsula from river to ocean, lined on both sides with stately palm trees and paved with shells, constitute handsome and attractive avenues for the comfort and convenience of pedestrians, carriages and bicycle riders. There are four other boulevards, with many intersecting avenues, laid out, some of them partly improved. We built a number of pretty cottages of different styles and sizes, and a large store building, the upper part of which is devoted to our publishing business, and the place is gradually assuming the appearance of a town. In short, from the small starting point of those first lessons a large business has grown—a business that never would have grown but for the fact that we coached our self-esteem along until we conquered fear and came out under the full sail of mastery.

You who read this will probably say, "Oh! yes, but C. C. Post and Helen Wilmans Post are not like the majority of people. They had capital in their brains, and some essential traits of character not possessed by everybody."

Now, I am going to deny my part of this charge completely. I have never met with a living soul whose nature it was to shrink from the world and be crushed by its opinions to the same degree that I have been. I have looked upon other people as gods, while at the same time I seemed to know that I was nobody. Yet I must say that deep down below all the crushed heart of me, I felt a confident sense of hope when I was alone and away from disturbing influences. I suppose I did actually, at such times, touch that principle of individualism that cannot do otherwise than speak for itself when uncovered. I could feel it. It was good company for me, and I was glad to be alone with it. I tried to cultivate it, and I know now that it was my savior.

There is not a person of ordinary intelligence alive who does not understand and thoroughly respond to the sentence just written. Every soul has found that he could strengthen himself by going down within himself and coming in contact with the strange bulwark of the true and undisturbed self that exists there. Every one, to a certain degree, has felt the shrinking of which I have spoken, though I hope no one has been made so wretched by it as I have been for hours and days at a time.

I wonder now at the persistence with which I endeavored to do something that would yield me the comfort of feeling myself a success, even in the smallest matters. Several years ago when I tried magazine writing, I do believe I wrote more than a hundred articles that were refused. How could I keep up the effort so constantly when I dreaded the results so greatly? I would actually tremble when those big brown envelopes were handed back to me, and a feeling of disgrace almost overpowered me.

I am telling this for the purpose of showing my reader how, with my growing determination, I made myself over as the years went on. I conquered slowly but surely. From the opinion of myself which constituted my weakness, I grew into another opinion which became my strength. Out of the limp rag of negation that I was, I literally made myself into a creature sufficiently positive to put a compulsion on the selfsame environment that had previously held me in compulsion. I know that if I could do this, with everything in the world against me, others can do it. It is no miraculous task to make ourselves over. Thought can do it, thought patiently held to and always true to the leading desire. And now as I look about me upon this little city by the sea, literally created by the power of our thought expressed in courageous action; as I stop to survey our splendid possessions and realize that all this change from poverty to opulence has taken place in the past few years, and only since I came to the conscious plane of growth; as I think of all this and then try to contemplate the boundless possibilities of the future, and then compare my present environment with that of millions who are toiling now as I toiled so long, in ignorance of their own powers, I wish—and I know that this desire is a prophecy of its fulfillment—that all men and all women may come to an understanding of themselves, and by reason of that knowledge break the chains which bind them in the slavery of poverty.

CHAPTER 6

The Potency of Desire

My own experience confirms the fact that the desires toward which I have been most unflinchingly persistent, have been the first to manifest objectively. Take, for instance, my desire for financial success. When I came into Mental Science I found that this was my leading desire. To be sure, I had many other desires that were very imperative; I desired youth and its symbols, health and its accompanying results; but I really desired money more than anything else. Why? Because I had been under the pressure of poverty so long that money represented a certain phase of freedom to me, without which no amount of health, strength or beauty could be enjoyed to any great extent. In other words, money did at that time promise a greater measure of freedom for my thoughts and for my body also, than any other thing. Therefore, the desire for money was my leading desire. I was a slave for the lack of it. Every thought of my life was chained to it, and could not escape. How could my spirit (thought-life) try its wings in the clearer atmosphere of the ideal under such circumstances?

I remember—as if it had been but yesterday—the very hour when I paused in my work and in my thinking, and made a compact with myself something like this: "I will have money, first of all; without money I can not move a step in the discovery of the mighty power latent in the human brain. This thing must go as I direct it, and I will submit to no dictation from any external source."

I spoke these words aloud and they have never wavered in their force. In speaking them I created a power in that line which went forth to its own accomplishment. Looking down within myself I came across the mental record of these words, and they seemed absolutely invulnerable—a sort of impregnable fortress that nothing could disrupt or weaken. The record of other resolutions faded or weakened at different times, but this never did. I had borne poverty until I simply would not bear it any longer. Disease, old age and death might come; but not poverty. It had been the monster which held the best part of my intellect in dreadful bondage, and I was done with it at all hazards.

This resolution received the emphasis of every atom of my body and mind, and no power on earth could break it down. No power on earth or in heaven ever does break down such a resolution. There was no wavering in it; there was no "God willing" in it; there was no "if it is for the best" in it. It was clear-cut positiveness, unblurred by a single flaw of irresolution. I had reached a point in mental suffering where life was not worth a straw to me unless I could have it on my own terms. So I stood up before "the powers that be," and made a statement of my terms. There was nothing to reject them (a thing I did not know at that time); so the statement stood for all there was in it, and it is standing yet.

As for my other desires, I have never come into so forceful a position with regard to them. I have been satisfied to see my health gradually improve and my mental powers gradually strengthen; and I have this same feeling yet about them. I can wait the slow development of time. With poverty, however, I could not wait. I would not. And I did not, for my resolution acted like the magician's wand, and efforts which I had put forth long before, rushed suddenly into success. Money enough came to release my thoughts from the eternal dollar, and to banish my fear of poverty. I did not want very much, because it easily becomes a burden, and enslaves the higher thought quite as much as its absence. What I wanted was freedom, and that was what I realized.

It is an inconsistent thing, while all growth is through accumulation, that society should place a ban upon the accumulation of wealth. Wealth is as necessary to our existence as the air we breathe. It is true that while we can manage to drag out meager, stinted lives without much wealth, still the lives we live are not in any way the lives we desire. We find ourselves in positions where our aspirations are shorn of their ascending power; our condition does indeed become sordid, simply because our faculties—so grand in their possibilities of expression—are tied down to a contemplation of the source from which our next meal is to come. There is nothing that can belittle a human brain so rapidly as this; nothing that can confine it to the contemplation of things unworthy of its scope; nothing that so soon will lead it into those mistakes which the world punishes as sins.

Why not abandon the effort on the brute plane—it is on the brute plane alone where the effort to accumulate seems sordid—and study the Law of Accumulation? There is a Law that governs it, and he who knows the Law well enough to practice it has put poverty under his feet forever. When I tell people this they say, "Oh, if I could only put poverty under my feet what would I not give?" They do not say, "Oh, if I could only understand the Law." Scarcely one of them cares for the Law; they want the results of understanding it while they remain indifferent to it. This is not a state of mind where anything valuable comes. The first thing to want is an understanding of the Law. "Give us wisdom" is the first demand, and in fact it is the only one. With wisdom, all other things flow in. Without wisdom, that is, without an understanding of the Law—there is no successful accumulation. There may be a spasmodic power to accumulate, but it is never to be relied upon. It may desert one at any hour, and it always deserts sometime. But the power to accumulate under a knowledge of the Law of Attraction never fails in even the smallest particular.

I am just as much assured of wealth to-day as if I had millions under lock and key. Why? Because I understand the Law by which our wants are supplied. What! Are you operating this mighty Law? you ask. Yes, I am operating it every day. I am building houses with it and operating it in improvements of use and beauty. I am accumulating wealth just as fast as I use it. If it seemed necessary to use it faster it would come to me faster. People have said to me, "Why don't you put your money out at interest?" My answer to this question is ready. To put money out on interest would clearly indicate that I have more confidence in money than in the power of the Law that brings it to me. It is a position that would wreck me. It is not my business to think of money except as one thinks of a tool with which to work. My business is to constantly seek a greater knowledge of my own power under the Law; for it is this knowledge alone that brings money. To put your trust in money is a sordid thing, and it brings its own reward in disappointed hopes. But to put your trust in yourself, knowing your relation to the Law, will actually put you in the way of accumulating everything that is necessary to make you a free man.

Let me not mislead any of my readers. The power of which I speak under the Law performs no miracles, but works itself out through the ordinary means lying thick about you. This power is simply a revelation to you of your own mastery. It gives you wisdom to carry your own faculties into external expression, and in doing this to obtain the reward that waits upon the doing. A knowledge of the Law of Attraction ingrained within you, will give you the power to carry any ideas of your own into practical success. Are you a drummer? Then you can sell twice as many goods as you could before you understood the Law. Are you a mechanic? It is in this department above all others that it reveals its might; it develops your constructiveness from one point to another until you see that there is no limit on this line. Are you a lawyer, a singer, an artist? It makes no difference what you are or what you desire to be. It is in this field of your operations that a knowledge of the Law of Attraction, as revealed by a study of Mental Science, will enable you to succeed.

This knowledge of the Law is something that can be learned easily and more inexpensively than the medical student learns his textbooks and masters the secrets of the human organism. Many persons have declared that it can be learned more easily than this; others have said that by "following the spirit" a man would come into a knowledge of it. But this is nonsense. The knowledge of this mighty thing requires intellectual application of the closest kind, and time for the mental ripening of the many facts it has to impart. Of course a slight knowledge of these facts will give the student some power in conquering the impediments that beset his path. Perfect conquest requires perfect knowledge, and there are no men—yea, and no gods—who can jump into this position at one bound. It requires work, study, and a testing of the knowledge as it slowly matures in the mind.

But suppose it does require a long time and unflagging effort; what is there in all the world so worthy of it? What else is there that bestows power to create in every direction and in every field of thought and action? I, who write these thoughts, am absolutely fearless. Neither time nor circumstance has any terrors for me. Poverty shakes his skeleton wand at me without producing a tremor. I am his master; not because I have houses and money in banks, but because I have the self-confidence—fully tested—that enables me to evolve the positive thought and to speak the positive word which externalizes my demand.

CHAPTER 7

Correlation of Thought to External Things

There is nothing truer than that the quality of thought which we entertain correlates certain externals in the outside world. This is the Law from which there is no escape. And it is this Law, this correlation of the thought with its object, that from time immemorial has led the people to believe in special providence. A man believes he is led by providence in a certain direction; the direction is not of his own choosing, so far as his consciousness is concerned. But providence had nothing to do with it; there was that in the man, unrecognized by himself, which related him to some thing or some condition on the external plane, and under the Law of Correlation he went in that direction. Every thought a man can have relates him to some external thing and draws him in the direction of it. This fact—on the plane where the thoughts of men are fleeting and of no comparative importance—has too frail an effect upon external life to be noticeable. But when much thought has been given to one subject, the result cannot be other than observable. Thus, continued thought upon disease allies us with the external conditions related to disease; or, more correctly speaking, it creates the disease. Thought on the subject of sin allies us with (so-called) sins, and renders us self-accusing, and accusers of others; while the belief that there is no sin, that the sins of the people are only the mistakes of an unripe and ignorant race, destroys the accusing spirit within us, so that we see ourselves and others in a nobler light and thus bring in a condition of peace and harmony.

A belief in poverty not only burdens and oppresses us until it makes us mentally poor, but it allies us with poverty-stricken conditions. Thought not only allies us with certain external things that represent its own character, but when we have ascended from physical to mental (which is a result of the study of Mental Science) it becomes creative. This is a marvelous thing; but if I know anything in the world, I know it is true.

What! Can a person by holding certain thoughts create wealth? Yes he can. A man by holding certain thoughts—if he knows the Law that relates effect and cause on the mental plane—can actually create wealth by the character of the thoughts he entertains. This creation must, at this time, be supplemented by courageous action, intensified by creative thought and knowledge of self; but such action is only a part of the thought. This Law is easy to understand, if one will only take the pains to investigate it.

Now, I want to write something practical on this subject, and it seems hard to do, because the very people I most desire to reach are those who have less faith in the power of mind to control matter than any other class. It seems that they will not believe; and until they do interest themselves in this wonderful subject enough to investigate its underlying principles, I do not know how I can persuade them to believe. While I cannot now enter extensively into the truths of Mental Science, except the phases especially bearing upon poverty, yet I believe that many who read this little book will thereby discover the road to the truth.

There is an almost universal reaching out for money. This reaching out is from the acquisitive faculties only, and its operations are confined to the competitive realm of the business world. It is a purely external proceeding; its mode of action is not rooted in the knowledge of the inner life, with its finer, more just, and spirtualized wants. It is but an extension of animality into the realm of the human, and no power can lift it to the divine plane the race is now approaching.

For all lifting on this plane is the result of spiritual growth. It is doing just what Christ said we must do in order to be rich. It is first seeking the kingdom of heaven within, where alone it exists. After this kingdom is discovered, then all these things (external wealth) shall be added.

What is there within a man that can be called the kingdom of heaven? When I answer this question not one reader out of ten will believe me—so utterly bankrupt of knowledge of their own internal wealth are the great majority of people. But I shall answer it, nevertheless, and it will be answered truly.

Heaven exists within us in the faculties latent in the human brain, the superabundance of which no man has ever dreamed. The weakest man living has the powers of a god folded within his organization; and they will remain folded until he learns to believe in their existence, and then tries to develop them. Men generally are not introspective, and this is why they are not rich. They are poverty-stricken in their own opinions of themselves and their powers, and they put the stamp of their own belief on everything they come in contact with. If a day laborer, let us say, does but look within himself long enough to perceive that he has an intellect that can be made as great and far reaching as that of the man he serves for a pittance that keeps body and soul together; if he sees this, and attaches due importance to it, the mere fact of his seeing it, has, to a degree, loosened his bonds and brought him face to face with better conditions.

But there is wanted something more than the fact of knowing that he is, or may become, by recognition of self, his employer's intellectual equal. There remains the fact that he needs also to know the Law and claim its provisions; namely, that his superior knowing relates him to a superior position. He must know this and trust it; for it is by holding this truth in faith and trust that he begins to ascend bodily. I would not be understood to advise blind bigotry. Far be it from my wish to incite unpleasant relations between employer and employee. Employers everywhere hail with delight the acquisition of employees who are not mere machines—they want brains in their business and are glad to pay for them. Cheap help is often the most expensive, in the sense of being the least profitable. As brain growth or development of thought power in the employee increases his value to the employer, and as the employee grows to the degree of strength where he is capable of doing for himself, there will be another not yet grown so strong to take his place.

The gradual recognition by a man of his own latent powers is the heaven within that is to be brought forward into the world and established in these conditions which correlate it. I have never taken a single step upward in the external world that was not the direct result of my recognition of some new power within my own brain. I have never sought wealth at all; I have simply sought to know myself. I have believed in my own greatness, and in your greatness equally. I have denied that man was a creeping worm of the dust. I have seen him as the seed germ of all attainment. I place no limitation upon his powers of progression. I scorn the word "impossible" as applied to what is in his power to be and to do. I think of his vast ability, and my own, with a jubilant feeling of surpassing triumph. I regard it as an assurance of present as well as prospective greatness, and a guarantee, eventually, of absolute mastery over all things and conditions which once mastered me. This frame of mind is well represented by the word "opulent." And in the direct measure of the power I have in holding it up before my perception, just in that measure is my business successful. Let me lose sight of this opulence of mental seeing, and my business declines. The most faithful and critical observation of this thing for several years has demonstrated its truth to a certainty. From this fact I deduce the following literal truths:

A mental poor-house projects from itself the spirit of a visible poor-house, and this spirit expresses itself in visible externals correlated to its character.

A mental palace sends forth the spirit of a visible palace with results that correlate it. And the same may be said of sickness and sin, of health and goodness.

But how is it possible for the man who is out of work, and who sees his children in rags and crying for bread, to conform to the conditions required? How can he perceive opulence when nothing but squalor meets his eyes? How can he calm his soul and enter into it by introspection, there to discover the mental wealth that the world has denied him a right to since birth? He does not dream that he is anything but one of the lowest and most unfortunate of beings. He sees nothing within himself that yields him a single hope. What can such a man do?

He can do nothing but conform to the Law, either on its negative or positive plane. He can recognize his manhood and his rights, the dignity of human nature and the godlike character of his own undying intellect, and be thereby raised in the scale of being; or he can fail to do this and be crushed out of life. More work and more money will relieve his present need and furnish him with implements for prolonging his existence; but no amount of money will give him that inner opulence which is the sure foundation for unchanging wealth; that opulence which is the purse of Fortunatus, and which can never be exhausted. Mental wealth, which is the recognition of innate ability, is the only true root of external wealth. External wealth that has not this root is but a floating air plant. There is no dependence to be placed in it.

A great many Christian and Mental Scientists say to me: "Why, I treat myself for success and for money nearly all the time. I resolutely refrain from holding thoughts of poverty, and I keep mental pictures of opulence before me with unvarying zeal, yet I am always poor. How is it the rule will not work with me?" I answer such a one in this way. I say to him or her: It is quite obvious from your statement that you are not seeking the kingdom of heaven within, but the externals of it without. Seek it first within; give no thought to the externals at all; they will group themselves around the internal kingdom when you have found it. Treat yourself for a knowledge of truth; treat yourself for the wisdom that will disclose and develop within your own brain the source of all power, giving no heed to the external, and the external will manifest itself in wealth. It will manifest itself in the production of creative thought—thought which will seek expression in noble, courageous action. You will begin to trust the voice of aspiration, and are to follow where it bids you.

Many people think that to seek religion as it is taught by the creeds is to seek the kingdom within. But this is not so. Do the creeds teach the opulence of man's innate capacity? Do they teach that the infinite spirit of strength and health and intelligence and beauty and power, which they call "God," is in man? No; they teach just the opposite. They teach man that he is nothing and that any good that he may perceive in himself, is not of himself, but of an outside God. They teach him that he is the most poverty-stricken wretch in life, that he is destitute of all merit, that he deserves nothing. Of all the poorhouses ever created in the mental realm there are none so utterly poverty-stricken as that which the creeds have erected. Did Jesus, their Master, teach this way? No, he did not. He knew that opulence existed in infinite diffusion. He knew the Law by which man's innate, mental opulence correlated him to the external opulence, and he taught it. Did He not say: "Consider the lilies of the field; they toil not, neither do they spin; yet Solomon in all his glory was not arrayed like one of these?"

What did this mean? It meant that the lily from its inner source of opulence simply expressed itself on the external plane. It is a tremendous lesson. The lily not doubting its own beauty, simply holding true to its sense of the beautiful, which was innate in it, expressed itself.

What men express themselves? Very few. And why? Because they do not know themselves. And not knowing themselves, how can they worthily express themselves in noble and courageous action, which is but thought in execution? They express the beggars they think they are; and their expression of themselves is correlated to the shreds and patches that form the beggar's surroundings.

For twenty years I have been telling men how rich they are. I have been looking at their undeveloped intellectual resources and searching them for new manifestations of genius ever since I can remember. I have seen them great and glorious, even when they looked upon themselves as pygmies. I have stood sponsor for the self-esteem of my friends and helped to develop that special bump, from a hole in the cranium to a decided protuberance. I was called "the liberator," because I could see so much more in other people than they could see in themselves; and this power of seeing does liberate the latent faculty in its structure and start it on its endless road to all growth. My husband used to say that my judgment of people was "goggle-eyed." I had a little daughter whose judgment was also "goggle-eyed." She, too, "saw men as trees walking." One day her father reprimanded her severely for her exaggerations—she had been playing with some urchins on the street, and had transformed them into angels. After her scolding she sat in her baby chair in a meditative mood, watching her father with an expression of motherly interest in her face, not unmixed with pity. She had been in a picture gallery a few days before, and had observed the unusual arrangement of the windows. Presently she lifted a dimpled cheek out of a dimpled hand, and said gently and encouragingly: "Papa, you're the doodest old fing wot ever lived, but your head ain't dot no sky-light in it."

It was a fact. His head had no window that opened upward. He lived in the city of Moan, in the state of Groan. There was enough of natural opulence in him to have turned the desert of his surroundings into paradise; but he could not see it, and we who—from the nature of the case—had to look through his eyes were awfully impoverished by his mental seeing.

CHAPTER 8

Difficulties

The difficulty that confronts me in making this book of great practical service to men and women in search for wealth is in the fact that they are expecting simply a set of business rules which, followed closely, will bring them what they desire. But there are no rules to formulate that can be operated successfully, and especially are there none for the man or woman who has no money to start business with. No amount of writing could make the thing practical in this direction. The only possible thing to do is to prove to the reader the great fact of the correlation of the forces within his own being as allied with the forces outside of himself; then he cannot fail to see that as he strengthens his own forces, he gains greater command over the external forces, until everything yields to him. A man could never lift so much as a chair if he believed he could not. We can believe with a belief that amounts to the knowing; and when we reach this point in belief we are there, body and intellect, every bit of us.

The brain can as easily speak a good word to the body as to speak an evil one, and the effect will follow. But men do not know this and so they are at the mercy of thousands of idle thoughts, generated by brains so low in the scale of development as to scarcely be capable of thought at all. It is this class of low irresponsible thoughts that forms the mental atmosphere we breathe and it keeps us weak in our own opinions until we learn how to combat and drive it away, and how to place our new thoughts, now being educated in strength, in the place of them.

The old thoughts have been saying all the past years: "You are a poor weakling; you are nothing of yourself; you were conceived in sin and born in iniquity; you are under the curse of your Creator and what you are to do about it no one knows. The odds are so greatly against you that effort is scarcely worth while. You have only a few years here at the best, and in the long run it is of very little consequence whether you obtain wealth and influence or not."

But let us suppose that your vitality is so great that even your desperate condition, ending so soon in the grave, does not daunt you, and you simply must make an effort.

Then the success of your effort (on the old plane of thought) will depend on what you think of yourself. If your fertile brain hatches business schemes by the dozen—all of them fine and grand and practical—and yet you fear to put them to the test, or if you put them to the test and do it with trembling indecision, then you fail. You might as well try to build a house out of loose sand and shape it in symmetry, as to build a splendid business scheme out of ideas that are shaken into incoherence by fears and anxieties.

What would you do in such a case? You would find out some plan by which you could harden your material; you would make your sand into brick, or, better still, into glass.

Just so with yourself when you see that you lack the firmness to carry out the enterprise you have conceived. You must harden and shape yourself. You do this by denials and affirmations. You summon your reasoning powers and examine your own capacity for the thing you are going to attempt; then hold this great Mental Science fact before you, that if you desire a certain faculty for creating wealth, or inventing machinery, or writing books, or doing any other noble, legitimate thing, you already have the capacity to do it. The desire is the first faint suggestion of the fact that the ability is also there. The desire could not be there without the ability to execute it.

You must know this, and you will know it if you reason on it. Let us suppose that God made you. If the gospel account of creation is correct then God is great above all His creatures; and He must be good and just. But suppose He made you so that there were hopes that took root in your brain all pointing to blissful realization, and yet there was no possibility of realization among them. What would this be but the promissory note of a ruined bank? What would it be but an outrageous swindle?

Or suppose that God did not make you; suppose that you are the result of evolution, the law of growth. Now the law of growth is simply the law of unfoldment; it is the unrolling of an individual life from some bud in the universal life, which, the farther it unrolls, the more of the universal life it shows forth. Already enough of the universal life has been brought forth or manifested on the external plane to prove to us that there can never be an end to it, either in quantity or variety, so long as there is no end to our demand. Every desire we have is a demand upon this universal life energy, and there is nothing in all the world to prevent it from responding to our demands unless we ourselves close the door between us and it by our doubts born of fear and anxiety.

Therefore, putting aside the questions of special creation and evolution, it remains that man is in his own hands and that he has the power to build himself; after which he is master of his surroundings.

One must think well of himself; he must love himself; he must take pride in every special faculty which he possesses. He need not make a fool of himself by trying to show off; but he must aggregate the strong points of his character and feel that he has the right to be proud of them. He must value his own opinion until he himself has dissected it and found it wanting. When he hears that another has formed a poor opinion of him, let him use his judgment in trying to discern whether that one's judgment is worth anything or not. If he concludes that it is, then he has a chance to make a correction in himself. This is character building, and it is one of the direct roads to wealth.

One of the great difficulties in the way of people becoming what they want to become and doing what they want to do is the fact that they accept opinions of others concerning themselves, and almost the entire world misjudges others by putting too small a valuation on them. All of us are under the wet blanket of an indiscriminating public, and it is smothering out our lives. We must kick this thing off. I recall how I felt when I first began to heal the sick; it really was not considered respectable to heal the sick by any but the long-established methods, and I could hardly endure it. I had belonged to a most respectable family, and really took sides with them against myself when they thought of me as doing something of which I should be ashamed. I became more strongly individualized in time, and I did it by taking sides with my own intelligent convictions and giving family prejudices the cold shoulder.

We are, all of us, apt to consider the opinions of other people when we are ready to do something different from what we have always been doing. This is a wrong thing, and is very injurious to character building. Perhaps it might be going too far to say that we would do well to shut our eyes and ears against the world's opinions and put our best thought into operation, supremely indifferent as to what the world thinks. It is better to go to this extreme than to let the opinions of others tie up our energies. Had I yielded to the opinions of others at the time I came to know that through the power of thought I could cure disease, my usefulness to the world would have been lessened, I would have been less successful financially and my self-hood would have been weakened rather than strengthened.

Sometimes a person will be strong in some certain directions and hold his own against the very Infernal Pit, if necessary, in order to accomplish what he has in his mind, and at the same time he may be very weak in another direction and permit the opinions of others to hold him as completely as if he were bound hand and foot. Here is a case in hand: Far out in one of the Western States a man lay dying of consumption. There was no question about his condition; he was actually dying. He came into possession of some of my Mental Science writings which banished his belief in the power of disease, and he declared that he would leave his bed and come to me. So he arose. But the question of money faced him. He could raise only five dollars, and with this he started on a journey of more than a thousand miles. How he managed I do not know. Of course he secured many a free ride on the cars; but he walked much of the way. When he reached here he refused all assistance, so far as charity was concerned, and asked for work. This was found for him and he recovered faster than ever. He was a young man of fair education and good natural ability. One year passed, then a second, then a third. His health had become perfect; he could work wherever other men worked, but always seemed unfitted for common occupations by reason of his own superiority. Why he did not start out as a teacher of the science that had saved his life, and concerning which he had such perfect confidence, was altogether unknown by even his most intimate friends. He has at times been almost as badly crippled financially as he used to be physically, and while he knows, from actual experience, that a knowledge of Mental Science can cure disease, he has never seemed able to apply it to the cure of poverty.

Sometimes I think that he has not really desired to be rid of poverty. He did desire to be rid of disease, and he desired it with an intensity of thought that resulted in his willingness to walk more than a thousand miles; but his desire for money, if he has it, has seemingly never been intense. This is one of the fundamental essentials to the acquisition of anything. An intense desire for any laudable acquisition is the prophecy of its sure fulfillment.

Coupled with this desire, let there be an implicit faith in self, and all will be well.

Many a good thought is born only to die because the brain that gave it birth was afraid to express the thought in action. The man of whom I have just been writing is capable of becoming very wealthy. He will be sometime. I think he is now rapidly coming to the period in conscious growth when he will see that his belief in poverty is just as false as was his former belief in disease. He actually believes that there is not enough money made now to go around and make everybody comfortable, let alone making each opulent. He forgets, as yet, that the laws of growth and change are steadily at work, and that the supply of the infinite is inexhaustible. The supply will always be equal to intelligent demand. The supply of money now in circulation and locked up in vaults is equal to the demand of all who come into an understanding of the laws of intelligent demand, and with the increase of those who understand these laws, the supply will increase. Conditions will always be met by the infinite. To say otherwise is an insult to the infinite spirit of Creativeness. This young man has recently nearly doubled his previous weekly income by accepting a position of some responsibility, which was really attracted to him by reason of his development. The position seemed to seek him rather than he the position. The only danger of his failing in that position is his belief in the poverty of the people. His correspondence to them betrays his belief in their poverty. But he is mastering it. When he comes into the same positive plane in regard to this false belief of the race that he reached some time since in regard to disease, opulence will be his.

He needs now to believe that he can become rich, and that no one is so poor now that he cannot become rich. He needs to think out business enterprises, then dare to put them into execution. In the words of a successful man of business, "Genius is only energy intensified, and energy is intensified thought expressed in action." The mistakes he has made thus far are, first, his lack of real desire to better his financial condition; second, his fear, lack of trust in self, and hesitancy in executing thought or "expressing if in action," when he has awakened to the necessity of money as a factor of complete freedom and happiness.

I have recounted this man's experience at much length, because his life is a good example, and fits many cases. Many, very many, master Mental Science to the extent of curing disease—and this is a great conquest—but fail for a time to apply it to poverty. I hope I have made plain the reasons for their failure. There is no need to postpone the working of the Law after it is understood. Each should learn the Law and then profit, through his understanding, by daring to put it into execution.

To prepare for a life of opulence absolutely full of the power that draws wealth, I must stand by the person I am. I must uphold my me, and never slacken one link of the good opinion I have formed of it. I must no more depreciate my ability than I would blaspheme God. Indeed, it is God I would be blaspheming, if I should weakly depreciate self.

There is no doubt but that I have had exceptional success so far as the making of money is concerned, and I know precisely how I came to have it. Up to the time when I had outgrown the belief that I was simply a crawling worm of the dust, I had no right to expect anything but the tramping-on such creatures receive. As I threw this feeling off I rose quite rapidly in my estimation of self. It was no fool's vanity that took possession of me, but a sense of justice and a feeling of strength. I not only rose in my own estimation, but I began to see all other people larger, and this added greatly to my happiness. As I grew happier I grew freer, and I found that my old laughing disposition had returned—none the worse for twenty years repose. But the great thing was that I had grown so bold that I did not hesitate to make a statement of my wants or to expect that they would be met and satisfied.

To be sure, if I made the statement that I wanted a certain amount of money, and the amount was larger than I could reasonably expect, I would distrust the result and receive nothing. Then I would have to wait for days, even weeks sometimes, before my mind ripened to a point where I felt that I could command a certain amount. I had to reach the point of feeling absolutely, or rather of knowing absolutely, that there was nothing to hinder me from receiving it. As soon as I touched this point, the thing was accomplished.

Now there was never anything mystical about the performance. I never proposed that a purse, having five thousand dollars in it, should fall into my lap, nor anything else remarkable. I simply started with the assertion that my business would net me a certain amount; perhaps double as much as it had ever done before in a similar length of time. I would then think out a plan of action by which my income would increase and diligently set to work to execute it.

My mind would then dwell upon it until I could see nothing preposterous or impossible in believing it would happen. And every hour, as I reverted to it and new thoughts were constantly born for prompt and courageous execution, it appeared more probable that I would get it, until at last I would know that I was going to get it, and I never failed. On the contrary I always received a few dollars more than I had ordered. It is true that the desire and demand is accompanied by action; but all the so-called industry, in the way of long hours of labor and great expenditure of effort that I could possibly have commanded, would never have yielded me one-half the returns that these positive thought currents, expressed in judicious and courageous action, have yielded me. Much so-called "energy" or "industry," is only a waste of force and is really nothing but slavery. Suppose I had been like Aladdin with his wonderful lamp, and that I had believed in its power to work wonders the same as he did, what would have been the result?

As truly as I am sitting here this beautiful night, I cannot find it in my brain to limit the creative power of thought, with or without expression in action, when it shall become possible for it to be accompanied with that quality of faith which has ripened into absolute knowing. I believe that if I had the same feeling of knowing, as regards the thing we call impossible, that I have concerning that which the brain accepts as possible, it would be done; in short, that the inception of all further progress begins in the brain and goes forth to try its strength on one thing and another, until at last it demonstrates some new fact. Thought is the beginning of all things. And thought is an actual substance generated by the brain. It goes forth as the pollen from the clover, and proves itself to be the seed of new forms of life and truth.

CHAPTER 9

The Vitality of Proper Belief

There is no denying the fact that next to disease poverty is the curse of the race. Indeed, you may cure a man of disease, and if, on being cured, he finds himself bound hand and foot by poverty, you might as well have left him to die, for life is no comfort to him. The eternal load of poverty that men and women carry is almost too much for the race to bear up under, and this poverty is increasing yearly, not only in our country, but in every country under the sun. What is it, and why does it increase?

I answer that it is an idea, a belief, founded in ignorance of the great fundamental truths of Mental Science. The first of these truths is that all substance is mind; that everything we see or feel, or of which the five senses can conceive, is a mental substance; in other words, that the entire universe is one mind, of which all objects, including man, are varied expressions. By saying that all is mind I do not wish to convey the idea that Mental Science denies the evidences of the senses. The things we see all about us are by no means a delusion. However, it is a scientific fact, now generally accepted by all who have investigated, that the basic factors of the universe may be variously termed ether and motion, substance and force, or mind and thought. There is one universal substance, and the highest form of this substance is thought. To one who understands this—who comprehends the laws of growth and change throughout all nature—the statement that all substance is, fundamentally, mental, is perfectly plain.

As an example, take a tree. You may cut it down and burn it, but it is not destroyed. Its form is changed; but every atom contained in it as a tree, still exists in smoke, gases, etc. The parts taken into the atmosphere may be breathed by man, and thus become a part of his tissue. The ashes nourish the soil; the soil nourishes vegetation; the vegetation is eaten by man. The very atoms which once composed the tree are now, in changed form, a part of man. That portion of the atoms of the vegetable which goes to nourish the body, becomes brain tissue and goes to produce thought—the highest, most positive and most powerful form of the universal substance. Any substance is capable of passing through this process and becoming thought. Therefore, everything is thought in an undeveloped state and capable of being evolved into thought.

The great truth that all is mind can only be thoroughly understood by a study of Mental Science. A knowledge of it transposes all things, all life, from the basis of the dead, immovableness of physical matter to the basis of living, thinking, active, ever changing, ever progressing mind, belief, thought, mental substance. It proves—actually proves—that all is mind, and therefore that man is just exactly what he thinks himself to be. Having proved this to the perfect satisfaction of every thinker who will take the time to investigate the subject, it will be seen that man is in his own hands, and the perfect master of his fate. If he is all mind, then he is what his beliefs are.

"Well," you say, "but this does not change him; his beliefs are fixed, and therefore his condition is fixed."

It is true that as we look at him to-day, all the great fundamental beliefs of his life are fixed; his belief in poverty is fixed; his belief in disease and death is fixed. But this is no reason why they should always remain fixed. He has other beliefs, outside of these great fixed beliefs, that are not in the same state of petrification. He changes his beliefs on many things, according to the fresh ideas which come into his life. At one time he believes himself fitted for a trade, and studies the trade with the intention of following it for life. Perhaps the trade is no sooner acquired than he changes his belief and thinks himself fitted for the study of law or medicine. Who will deny that this change in the man's belief will work out a very great change in his life? It will bring him into relation with entirely different people than his first belief would have done; it will give him environments of a different character, and will work changes in him and for him—in his surroundings and in his appearance—that will not end with him, but will show, in results, upon his children and grandchildren.

So much for the external changes resulting from changes in comparatively unimportant beliefs. But think how much greater will be the external changes that will result from a change in the great fixed beliefs in poverty, disease, old age and death. Remember that man is all mind; that as he thinks, or believes, so he is. This being the fact, he has the power to think or believe himself out of the old, fixed beliefs that now enslave him so completely.

But how? Can one believe anything he pleases? Can he believe a thing to be true simply because he wishes it to be true? Certainly not. His belief must depend upon his conviction. He must perceive, intellectually or mentally, that a thing is true before he can believe it. And I am not going to deny the fact that this means anything less than a new education for him—an education that lifts him out of his belief in physical matter to a belief in mind, and the constantly unfolding power of mind; an education that shows him how—being all mind—a knowledge of more truth is what he must have in order to gain the power which will show him his own mastery.

This knowledge will not come to men so long as they are satisfied with what they now know; and the majority of men care nothing about knowing more. They want more money and more strength, but they do not know that a knowledge of themselves and of their relation to the Law is the only thing that will give them permanent health, strength and riches, and that it will do this by simply showing them, in a clear, logical way, that their old, fossilized beliefs are errors; thereby converting them from error to truth, changing them all over, and proving to them their own power.

They do not know that mind alone is creative; and that—being all mind—it is in their power, through an increase in knowledge, to reach a point where they recognize themselves as creators of themselves and their conditions. And I make a plain, unvarnished statement of truth when I say that no man can know this except through the study of mind and the Law of Attraction that infuses it. He must understand Mental Science before he comes into the place of intellectual creativeness where he speaks the word that changes himself and his surroundings. He can only come into this high place of power by intelligent conviction. He cannot jump into it ignorantly; he reaches it by the knowing.

I came into this place by much thought and introspection; also by studying the Law of Growth as revealed to me in the habits of plants and trees and animals. I did not study books, for no book contained what I wanted. I wanted a knowledge of the Law of Attraction, which is the Law of Growth. Gradually, as I grew in the knowledge of the Law, I seemed to be able to co-operate with the Law, and to begin to share its life-giving power and its opulence. The Law is absolutely infinite in opulence; and this opulence becomes a personal endowment to the man who strives to understand it; who learns to perceive it, or to see it intellectually. In proportion as he learns to see the opulence of the Law his intellectual perception of poverty ceases. He wonders where the poverty is that formerly riveted all his beliefs to itself; and then he knows that poverty is seeing from a narrow and limited perception of the universal opulence, and that wealth is the result of a more enlarged intellectual perception.

This knowledge is a thing that cannot be picked up in a minute; it must be studied. As I said before, men do not want to study. "Give us the results of study," they cry, "but do the studying yourself if it suits your taste." But they will have to study for themselves. One person can no more study for another person than one tree can grow for another tree. Riches are waiting upon your mental awakening; they correlate a rich mentality. They are free as air; and yet you are like the travelers dying of thirst by the roadside when the spring that would save them is within a stone's throw.

As man is a purely mental creature, so are his surroundings all mental states; and as tone resounds to tone, so do your surroundings repeat your mental conditions from far and near. It is deep calling unto deep all through the shoreless ocean of mind. The sound you send forth comes back to you; and no sound can possibly reach your ears save the one you send out. Your poverty is the protracted echo of your own belief. Learn the science of mind that will change your belief, and, by changing it, change the whole world for you.

Labor unions and protective associations may combine to the end of time; but they cannot change this great, fundamental Law. The working people may inaugurate a war that will exterminate the nation; but they will not exterminate this truth. For though the last man of the race lay dead it will remain, eternal and unchangeable, waiting, in unshaken repose, the silent tread of a million ages, until in some new-fledged time some new-fledged soul shall open his eyes to a perception of it, and a world be saved and redeemed thereby.

As the race stands to-day there is nothing the matter with it but its ignorance; an ignorance that shows forth in poverty and disease and death. Congressmen cannot legislate its ignorance away; blood will not wipe it out; dynamite will not explode it; though the navies of the world be sunk, it will not be drowned. Only one thing will reach it; it has but one solvent on earth and that is intelligence—a knowledge of the law of omnipresent good; and this knowledge will only come through an earnest study of the mind and the Law that moves it.

At one period of my life I was interested in the labor movement. I often went to meetings of this class, and I kept the eyes and ears of my observation very widely open. The speakers were a complaining set, and they had a perfect right to complain; their situation warranted it; only they should have complained of themselves instead of their employers, for they were just precisely in the situation where the development of their manhood placed them. They had put their own valuation on themselves, and then wanted to kick the lid off of the universe because the men they acknowledged as bosses could not see them larger than they saw themselves. They were always talking about more wages, and the rights of labor. Why, labor has no rights until it is free! So long as labor is owned it is at the beck and call of its master, and its master can squeeze the life blood out of it if he so desires.

The man who mentally claims the most gets the most. Why? Because he is more unlimited in his power to recognize the universal opulence. Of course, in the present stage of the world's knowledge, this recognition is on the unconscious plane. Jay Gould knew no more of this Law than the man who worked for him on a salary of ten dollars per week. He was unconscious of the power by which he called to him the immense fortune he accumulated; but he had the power of seeing one of nature's grandest truths—namely, that there is no limit to the supply that answers demand. His brain was so constructed that he could see nothing but abundance. He could not see poverty; he did not believe in poverty; he believed in opulence. Moreover he had none of that sympathetic feeling by which he could enter into other people's beliefs in poverty, and therefore the appearance of poverty all about him did not shake his confidence. Opulence existed for him whether it existed for other men or not. This is what he recognized; and though his recognition was of the blind, unreasoning kind, like that of an animal, still it was recognition, and it brought him its own fruit.

To recognize this same fact—that opulence does exist everywhere—and to recognize it on the conscious or reasoning plane of life, will put a man in possession of wealth. To recognize that life is a grand, vital principle permeating all things from atoms to men, and that it manifests in each object just in proportion as the object recognizes it, will enable all persons to conquer death, and to cast their lives in such molds as their highest ideals may suggest.

Opulence of health and wealth and life are absolutely unlimited. Man can limit them in his perceptions, and take the consequences of doing so in a limited life, but the resources of the eternal fullness are not stinted thereby. Education is the only cure for poverty. The man may die before education comes to him, and he will die unless it does come, for he does not want education. He wants opulence without the education; he cares nothing for the heaven within, that a knowledge of these matters would yield. All he wants is the money and houses and land that he thinks would make him a heaven without. But the great bulk of men will never get it. Why? Because the spirit of a higher development is in the air; and this spirit has uttered its pronunciamento—namely, that seeing is being, and that he who will not see the truth cannot actualize it in his life and surroundings.

As yet there is no true understanding of the Law that renders opulence visible to the perceptions of the race. There is only an occasional perception of it in a few men, and this perception is not a thing they reason on or understand. It is an unconscious perception to which persons give no broad application, but limit it to themselves, and strengthen its effects in themselves by utterly ignoring all evidence of the poverty manifesting itself around them.

He who heals a patient of disease must recognize that nothing in the shape of disease exists; that life and health are omnipresent, filling all space, to the utter exclusion of disease. He must recognize that disease is simply a state of ignorance concerning the great truth that life and health are omnipresent. As all conditions are mental, disease is a mental condition, in which the diseased person fails to perceive the truth; he is in error concerning the truth.

A person can only recognize these great truths by an earnest study into the matter; but when he has once seen that they are true, and when he feels the force of their truth through his whole organism he cannot help healing. His very presence heals. He disperses a thought influence from himself every moment he lives that is positive to the thought influences of those who believe in disease, and consequently disperses their thought influences, leaving his own positive ones in their place.

This fact is no less true of that ignorant state of mind called "poverty," than of disease. There is no poverty. Men simply believe there is, and being mental creatures what they believe shows forth in their persons and surroundings. Oh, if I could only give the people the faintest idea of the opulence that abounds, what would I not give? But they will not listen. They pinch the dimes with straining fingers, fearing to let go lest no more will come. And indeed no more will come so long as they are ignorant of the fact that opulence is a part of the universal Law of Life.

What would I do with the poor man whose children are crying for bread?

I would educate him in the knowledge of Mental Science, or the power of mind, if I could; but he will not be educated. He prefers to grumble at "his boss," to call the advanced thinkers "cranks," and hatch plots against the government that may deluge a continent in blood, and will react with exterminating force upon himself. He is ready to do anything except think. Thought on the high plane—thought from the basis of that greatest of truths, all is good, and therefore all is health, opulence, life—would save him. Rejecting this, there is nothing before him but the clash of a warfare with those of his own kind—a contest that cannot give him what he truly wants, for only knowledge of the truth can do this.

Nevertheless every experience teaches; and when men have passed through the crisis that now threatens, only to find that they are still poor, that even the external symbols of wealth amount to nothing except as they are representatives of man's internal wealth, they will be ready for the education awaiting them in the great study of man's mentality and its relation to the Law of Life.

CHAPTER 10

The Fear of Poverty

I have something to say on the above subject which I hope may be of value to my readers by way of a practical illustration of the truths for which I stand sponsor. What I am going to say is the result of a correspondence with a dear friend whom I am treating for several diseases. She asked me to put my price down, and I did it; but I did it under great compunction.

Why did I have any compunction in giving her a reduction in my terms for treatment? You will say, it was because I wanted all the money I could obtain. But you would not touch the mark in this assertion; though it is a fact that I do want every cent for which I give a fair equivalent. It is a further fact that I love money; and the reason I love it is because money has another name and that other name is freedom.

In giving this friend a reduction in the price of treatments I compromised a very great principle; in fact I arrayed myself against it, and brought not only myself but her into negative relations with the Great Law of Opulence that runs absolutely unchecked—except by man's ignorance—through the universe.

I heal disease by refusing to recognize that disease is anything more than an ignorant belief, arising from non-recognition of the fact that all is Life, and that no individual opinion can possibly invalidate this fixed, unalterable and uncompromising truth. For me to admit that the belief in disease has any fixed foundation in absolute reality, would be to temporize with what I know to be false; and the result would be that every one of my patients who is strictly conjoined with me in thought, in accordance with my instructions, would become worse in less than an hour. My fear of disease (for any compromise with absolute truth, is caused by fear) would communicate itself to them, and show forth in a weakened condition of their bodies.

Now a part of this great Law that all is life is the further fact that all is opulence, and that there is not one particle of poverty in the universe. A belief in poverty, like a belief in disease, is ignorance of the Law of Opulence. Poverty is as much a disease as disease itself. Both are beliefs which are utterly false, but which take effect in individuals who believe in them, for the simple reason that every person and thing is all mind, and, as such, is representative of what it believes.

I heal because I do not believe in disease. I absolutely know that it is a false belief; and the patient, who, following my instructions, becomes conjoined with my thought, realizes the truth in this matter as I realize it, and he shows forth health. He cannot help but do so. He comes into my belief. I do not go into his belief, as would be the case if I sympathize with him and say, "Poor fellow, how he suffers." If I felt this I would take on his condition; and, instead of my curing him, he would make me sick. But I hold firmly for the ubiquity of the health or life principle; I deny that there is any power in disease; I hold in unshaken strength, to my highest convictions on this point; I will not compromise one inch by a recognition of his misconception of truth. And thus, holding in the might of a high understanding of absolute Law, I gradually lift him into its light, and his errors fall from him.

Now poverty is but one form of disease. It comes under the same head; it is ignorance of the Law of Opulence, which is a part of the Law of Life, just the same as disease is. So when my friend and patient asked me to put down the price for her, I did it; but I felt that I was wronging her, and myself too. I felt that I was recognizing poverty as a power that could possibly injure her and me also, because we were, for the time being, one in thought.

Having acceded to her request and reduced the price, I wrote a sort of protest, in which I tried to explain that it was the wrong thing to do. But she did not understand my explanation, and it seemed to hurt her. So I wrote her again as follows:

"I am sorry my letter hurt you. I only wished you to know the Law on the point, because it is generally unknown, and I have only learned something of it myself lately. My learning it has been the result of much thought on the subject, and of long experience in healing people. In treating for disease I do not recognize that there is any disease, and so that condition of thought called disease disappears from the patient. In treating for poverty, I do it by not recognizing that there is any poverty; and I notice that the least disposition on my part to recognize poverty; or even the desire to curtail expenses—which in reality is a recognition that poverty is stronger than opulence—always has a bad effect on the financial circumstances of the patient, and on my own financial circumstances as well. The fact is—believing as I do in absolute opulence—I have no excuse for not recognizing it. I do recognize it as an unfailing supply to every demand—opulence of health; opulence of youth; opulence of strength; opulence of money, and opulence of houses and lands, and all things desirable. And now, how can I hold true to my recognition of this supreme, never failing opulence, and yet keep trimming my sails to meet some possible contingency arising from fear that this opulence will fail? The position is absolutely contradictory, and it produces confusion, inharmony, and loss of mental power. With this loss of mental power, every patient I have relapses from the high position to which my previous fidelity to absolute truth has held him."

And now for a little illustration in proof of the facts I am trying to make plain here. Although I had known, in a small way, everything I have said about the mistake of recognizing poverty, yet I had gone steadily on recognizing it in my actions by giving such reductions as I have spoken of, even while denying it in my thought. But after writing to my friend as I did, the whole thing opened up to my view in a wonderful way. I saw that I had wronged her and jeopardized her financial condition. I had been weak in making any concession to her fear of caution. I should positively have held to my fixed charges. This firmness on my part based on a knowledge of the Law of Opulence—the Law that proclaims every moment that the supply is equal to the demand—would have put in operation the occult forces lying back of the scene, and she would far more readily have obtained the higher price I charged her, than the lower one to which I reduced it.

I am just as sure of this as that I live. But I disobeyed my higher convictions, and the occult power lying back of the scene was not set in action; but instead, it was rendered more obscure, and my friend's chances for wealth were positively injured. And now for the result as it affected me. My receipts vary only a trifle week by week. But the week after this letter was written they went down fully one-half. And I am sure it was because I compromised with the widespread fear of poverty that exists in the world.

"But," you say, "you have done the same thing before without taking the consequences in a falling off of your receipts, why did you happen to take the consequences of this one particular delinquency so suddenly?"

To which I reply; nothing happens. It all came by Law. I had not been fully conscious of the Law until the writing of that letter revealed it to me. The moment I was fully alive to a knowledge of the Law, its inexorable demand was upon me. I had to obey it or take the consequences of willful disobedience. I disobeyed, and took the consequences.

Again you say, "Why, here you have been for many years arguing for man's perfect mastery over all conditions, and now you virtually give the thing away by making him subject to a fixed Law. How is this?" I answer:

The Law exists; has always existed. Man cannot change it. It is absolutely perfect in its action. Man is a creator; but after he has learned the Law, he only creates in conformity with it. Previous to his understanding the Law, when he is on the unconscious plane of life, his creations are the most ephemeral beliefs; he creates disease and poverty, old age and death, and all manner of inharmony, the total result of which is chaos, or hell, such as finds representation in present race conditions.

But a knowledge of the Law of Life is absolutely essential to man's high and enduring creativeness. That which he creates after he comes into a knowledge of the Law alone endures. These creations alone are infused with the saving power of the Law. They alone are in consonance or harmony with it. That which is not in harmony with the Law passes away.

I do not deny man's power to create while he is in ignorance of the Law; but his creations are the representations of his ignorance. He is held by the Law unconsciously to himself, and he recognizes a power to create, without recognizing the perfection of that power. Therefore he creates by the best light his knowledge yields him. Disease, poverty, old age and death are creations in ignorance of the full power of the Law. Those who recognize a power in the Law that utterly ignores disease, poverty, old age and death, come into a state of unity or oneness with the Law, and they cease to be held by the race beliefs in disease, poverty, old age and death. They are virtually resurrected from the dead; they have become creators of new conditions, and are indeed the owners of the world.

They have ceased to fear the race beliefs in evil; and, because they are all mind, these race beliefs can never affect them again. But here is a continuation of my letter to this patient.

"If I reduce my price I shall be recognizing the possibility that you may become poor, and this will do you harm. If you go into a store with the intention of buying a dress for thirty dollars, and begin in your mind to say, 'I can't afford to spend this money, I do not dare spend it; money is scarce and I must economize,' you put yourself and your financial condition in the hands of that gaunt, bloodless and merciless skeleton, Poverty, and you will pay for it in loss."

This is the Law, and those who know it to be the Law will take the consequences of disobeying it. But those who do not understand it are literally beneath the reach of the Law, and its operation is not for them. They are in the bondage of fear; and until they learn positively that there is nothing on earth to fear, until they learn from irrefutable logic that they are masters of all conditions, the caution they exhibit is the proper thing. It belongs to the plane on which they live, and no amount of reckless daring will overcome the need of their conforming to it. Nothing but an understanding of the situation will overcome the necessity of their trimming their sails to meet the condition in which they live. They are living in the element of fear because they have not learned the great fact that they are masters and creators of conditions, and, therefore, do not have to fear; and so long as they are living in this element they are compelled to adapt their conduct to its requirements. It is only after they have ceased to live in this element, after they have risen above it by a course of reasoning proving them to be masters and creators, that they dare snap their fingers in the face of poverty, and act as if they possessed the whole world by spending money as lavishly as their desires prompt.

CHAPTER 11

Courage

I believe that, more than anything else, the race is lacking in courage. By courage I do not mean that element which enables men to march to battle in unbroken ranks or to face a bayonet charge without blanching. I mean that reliance on self which proves the absence of fear both of what others may think or say and of inability from any cause to accomplish what is desired.

Not one person in ten, no, not one in a hundred, either man or woman, does that which he likes to do, even if he has the courage to do it.

People are afraid of what their friends or the public or society will say, and most of all are afraid of failure if they attempt anything other than that which, in some accidental way, they find themselves to be already engaged in doing.

They lack faith in themselves, they have no true courage.

The truly courageous man is afraid of nothing, and least of all is he afraid of himself. He believes in himself and believing in himself believes in the perfection of the Law. He may not put this in words, may not say to himself, "I believe in the Law of Opulence," but he nevertheless acts upon such belief. He says, "I will succeed," he takes the Law into partnership, he plans, and he executes because he has courage.

It may not even have occurred to such a man to think of himself as being courageous. His courage is so much a part of him that he does not give it a name separate from himself. He says, "I," I will do so and so, and goes and does it without once thinking there is any reason why he should not succeed, whereas a man of less courage would approach the purpose of his desires haltingly, wondering if, possibly, he was wise in undertaking it, and how he ever had the courage to undertake it. And the difference in the way in which each approached the object of his desires is often the difference between success and failure.

The timid man is ever at a disadvantage both before his fellows and before the Law through which success is attained.

Confidence in self breeds confidence in others, and fear weakens both the brain that plans and the hand that executes.

It has been said that all the world loves a lover. It is also true that all the world falls into step with the man who walks, careless of who follows, with the air of one who knows that he is master. The mass of people have no opinions of their own, except such as they have inherited or received from others. To such as they have they cling tenaciously until some one arises whose strong individuality impresses them with a sense of his power, when lo! they drop their old beliefs to accept those of the one whose bearing proclaims him leader. Thus to his strength is added that of the masses by whom he is surrounded and a new set of ideas takes the place of the old.

The new may be little nearer the truth than were the old, but of this the Law of Opulence takes no account; it has served him who had the courage to command it and to make a co-partnership with it for the attainment of his ends.

Why should men be afraid of the opinions of other men; what harm can it do me that some, or that all men and women fail to see as I see? Am I not I? and am I not sufficient unto myself?

Why should the fact that others do not believe as I believe or think as I think distress me, or constrain me to believe with them?

A skilled performer upon the piano or other stringed instrument will receive applause from the audience, but who ever heard of an audience applauding a music box? It is genius that commands respect, not mechanical execution unaccompanied by a personality. But even genius without courage is valueless to its possessor, for distrusting itself it makes no use of itself, fails to accept the tender of co-partnership made to it by the Law, and so fails to accomplish its desires.

The world is full of geniuses; of men and women who would be really great if only they were not afraid to be themselves. Parrot-like they talk the language of their own babyhood and of that of the race, lacking the courage to speak the language of full grown men and women. Like sheep following each other where their leader jumped over a bar, they jump regardless of the fact that the bar had been removed before they reached the place where it had been. Lacking the courage which would enable them to apply their own knowledge or powers of observation and reason they make no demand upon the Law of Opulence, and for them, it has, therefore, no existence. Neither have they any personal existence before the Law, and of that which they create the Law's share goes not to them but to the few who, recognizing the Law are recognized by it.

If men dared to be their own selves, to think their own thoughts, and to accept the consequences of acting in accordance with their ambition, the world of society would scarce recognize itself in a week's time and the present unjust system for the distribution of wealth would pass in a day, giving place to one infinitely better for everybody. There are very few men or women to-day who are contented with things as they are, or who do not believe a better condition attainable if only everybody would consent to make the change. But each is afraid of suggesting such a thing lest others disapprove, and so the juggernaut rolls on, crushing the life out of new victims with every turn of its monster wheels. Courage to exercise their opinions wherever opportunity occurs is all that is lacking to remove half the obstacles that obstruct the road to happiness for the race, and if these were removed the other half would, as I verily believe, remove themselves.

Each soul must do its own thinking, and must be saved by its own power to (in consonance with the Law) think itself from its present negative condition in life to that high and positive condition where it perceives its own creativeness, and recognizes the fact that inherited beliefs do not save; but that the unrestrained power to create new thought, or new ideals, and to project them into the world of effects, alone can build each distinct individuality as it desires to be built.

Doubt is a giant, who with his club, pulverizes things, and dissolves them to their original elements. But in all his dissolving he has never dissolved Faith. Faith is the soul of all life; that mighty but intangible growth principle still stretching unseen tentacles upward, and taking hold of all that lies above the ordinary life plane. Not only taking hold of things above, but lifting up things below. It is the vine in human lives that climbs and climbs. Think how long Jack's wonderful bean stalk has been considered a fable. But it is the truth of all truths. It illustrates the faith of a world that grew and grew until some one brave enough to climb its dizzy heights went up and slew the giant Doubt, and redeemed the race forever from his paralyzing influence by making the impossible possible to every one of us.

There is nothing that ever says "no" to a man but himself. When he hears the word "no" spoken in opposition to his will, if he does but listen carefully he will find that it was but the non-recognition of the intellect that spoke it. In any and every enterprise the royal will asks for nothing but the brain's consent. To know this is to pass at once from the minor to the major chords of life. The gradually approaching knowledge of it is even now sending a stronger impulse through all the avenues of life. The people hear it and do not know what it is; but they are alert and listening. They are holding themselves in an attitude of intense expectancy. Something is coming; they are sure of it; they are ignorant of its character, and they will probably reject my suggestion that it is they themselves on the way from dead conditions to living ones, and that it is the rush of their own strong pinions that is filling the world with the strange, strong undercurrent of power whose swelling volume is momentarily increasing in strength.

CHAPTER 12

Conclusion

When I look back and see the worthlessness of my life and aims before I studied Mental Science, I am filled with a burning desire that all persons leave their present narrow, hampering walks, and come with me into the broad meadows and by the still waters of ever present blessedness, where happiness is the breath of life, and where all cares and anxieties are forgotten; where all belief of evil and forebodings of fear are left behind; where only faith and hope remain to project the new cellular tissue of our ever deepening and broadening personalities. For hope and faith do project the life cells into which flows the Vitalizing Principle—the god within; thus rendering us diseaseless incarnations of the great I Am.

By resolutely and sternly denying the doubt that would cloud my belief in man, by turning away from a view of him in his present embodiment, and holding trustingly and faithfully to my ideal picture of his glorious possibilities, and of the more than human power vested in him, I have come to that point where faith and hope are easy to me. I now see him a creature of infinite unfoldment, lacking nothing in all the world but the ability to appreciate himself.

Not knowing the law of his being, not knowing his oneness with the One Life, he depreciates himself. He takes the consequences of this depreciation in the bitter mistakes which he calls "sins," and in those ignorant denials or negations of his high privileges called "sickness" and poverty.

The truths I have offered to the public through my statements of the philosophy of mind, or Mental Science, are meant to teach man what a great creature he is. They are meant to remove at once and forever the crushing weight of a belief in his own helplessness and unworthiness—a belief that has been his bane and curse and defrauded him of his just dues in a universe that holds all for him; a belief that has shut off that infinite fountain of ever-flowing good which comes from an understanding of the fact that the supply is equal to the demand, and that a man may have what he wants if he will only learn how to take it; a belief that in limiting his own power he has limited the power of the Law in his thought; a belief that has damned, and is to-day damning, more souls than all the other infidelities ever foisted on an unreasoning and unresisting race. They are meant to teach man his own power by proving to him his own greatness; by showing him how divine are the faculties of his being; by proving to him that the best opinion he ever had of himself is not half so good as the truth will warrant. While it has been impossible in the treatise of this question of poverty, to any more than touch upon certain phases of Mental Science proper. I know that the right road is pointed out in this little book and my hope is that through it, many may find the way to liberty.

Personal vanity is that inflated belief one entertains concerning himself before a knowledge of his real worth comes to him, and of course we repudiate it. But self-esteem which rests on a basis of the knowledge of one's natural faculties, is another thing entirely. When a just appreciation of our own undying and ever unfolding faculties is presented for our consideration—yes, and for our love and veneration—it ceases to be a personal matter, and embraces every soul of the race in its broad and enthusiastic welcome of the potency which we see to be vested in all other men equally with ourselves. It is this broad and comprehensive understanding of the great natures we possess that shows us our power over error, poverty and sickness, and points out the way by which we can conquer all undesirable conditions.

Though I am even but a child in this wonderful knowledge of self, yet for some time past I have controlled circumstances to my liking, forbidden poverty admission to my doors, and refused to listen to the cry of disease; thereby banishing it far from my presence as a thing too weak and negative to keep step with my rapidly advancing pace in an understanding of the power of mind. The more I learn of man's inborn strength, of his own great power, the stronger and more irresistible I become, and the farther I am removed from the influences called "fate," "condition," "circumstances," "poverty" and "disease"—influences that were once my masters, but which will never be my masters again.

I have felt my way along the broadening process of life—from the not knowing my own worth and power, to the knowing it—by close and critical steps of thought, by challenging all ideas, and refusing to accept any that would not stand the test of practical experiment. I have forged my way through a hundred mistakes, and met many a bowlder that took all my strength to roll aside. And now it seems to me that no position is more thoroughly demonstrated by the works that result from it than mine. I do not intend to convey the idea that I have no more to learn, but only that I have at last found the principle that underlies all intelligent growth.

I thank myself—the power embodied in me—that I have been enabled to stand champion for the race through a recognition of the power embodied in every man and woman living. It is a position that has already lifted many souls from under the influence of self-depreciation to that high plane of thought where fear has fallen from them; where sin, sickness and poverty has ceased to be numbered among their belongings.

Do you know what this Mental Science movement means? It means the closing of the old dispensation, with its wretched beliefs in man's degeneracy and his inability to save himself, and the opening of the strong new era, wherein we see ourselves as our own saviors, through the power of that mighty influx of truth now pouring in upon us, the truth that comes from the inner, the unseen side of life, and that is verily and truly being materialized in our external selves this very hour; the truth that enables us to put the highest, noblest and grandest interpretation upon the writings of the spiritual leaders who have taught that "as thou, Father, art in me, and I in thee," they also may be one in us; the truth which teaches the unity of all and that each is indeed one with God, or good, the eternal principle of life.

Intelligent understanding of this great process, and how to co-operate with it so as to hasten its coming, is the work we are trying to do. The work was begun in a small way, modestly and quietly, and yet it carries the conviction of self-conscious worth, and could not consistently do otherwise. It teaches the student how to conquer disease in himself and others, and how to conquer all the hampering environments that cripple his life and make it so narrow and sordid and mean in his eyes. It gives him such an understanding of his own latent strength—intellectual and moral—that he feels the very foundations of his existence strengthen beneath him, while endless vistas of happy usefulness and noble prosperity open out before him.

Self-crushing has been the method of every previous system of training, and the result shows in a dwarfed, debased and diseased humanity. But now, at the beginning of the new era, there comes a change. Indeed the very words "new era," or "new order," mean nothing else and refer to nothing else but the reversal of public opinion on this very subject of self-esteem.

"Know thyself," is one of the great commandments. No matter by whom it was written, or whether it is found in the Bible or out of it, it is one of the greatest commandments. The more truly a man knows himself, the more he respects and reveres himself. The more he knows himself the more he knows the Law; the more he reveres himself the more he reveres the Law; for Law and man are one; they are the internal and external of the one omnipresent life. And to understand this fully is to make the atonement—the at-one-ment—between the life principle and man, by which man's life becomes identical with it, and he loses the very remembrance of sin, disease and poverty, and begins to step forth into a wonderful comprehension and fellowship with the divine life—that of unbroken progression in constantly increasing phases of happiness and power.

And this is what Mental Science is doing for the world. It is teaching man to know himself. In learning what he truly is, he cannot fail to learn that he has no fellowship with what we call "sin, sickness and poverty," and these negative conditions—which are but ignorant denials of absolute truth—fall from him like old and worn-out garments.

Everyone needs to learn all he possibly can on so great a subject. Never before has the truth risen in such a mighty tidal wave of power as it is now doing through the practical rendition of Christ's life and works in the magnificent system of new thought that is now not only proclaiming man's superiority to his environment, but demonstrating it to the easy comprehension of all. The numbers who are coming to a knowledge of Mental Science and its power to save are already great. The distant rumble of a mighty host advancing is already heard. Prejudice, fear, and false beliefs are being crushed under the feet of the advancing thousands. The darkness of ignorance is being dispelled by the light of reason, and the time will come when all mankind will rejoice in the knowledge of self, when each individual can step forth in his glorious self-hood and proclaim his own independence forever.

16

HOW TO ATTRACT SUCCESS

F. W. SEARS

(1914)

Contents

Publishers' Statement 1063

Author's Statement 1064

1. *What is Success?—The Laws that Make for Success.—"Declaring War on Poverty."—Must "Build Castles in the Air" Before Castles can be Built on the Ground.—Effect of Environment.—Fixed Habits.—What "Good Luck" and "Bad Luck" is.—Man is an Unconscious Creator but can become a Conscious One.—What Makes the Difference between Persons.—How to Create and Attract Success Permanently.* 1067

2. *How Man May be Classified.—Different Degrees of Unfoldment.—The Five General States of Consciousness.—What the "Sub-conscious Mind" Really Is.—The Mind of the Physical Body.—The Mind of the Ego or Astral Body.—The True Function of "Logic."—Mind of Physical Body Makes the Conditions by Which Mind of Astral Body May Manifest In and Through the Physical Body.—What the Imagination Is and its Proper Function.—"Impressions" and "Intuitions": Their Source, and How to Tell "Which is Which."* 1071

3. *Man Has the Power to Develop Every State of Consciousness.—How to Correct Too Emotional Natures; also Those That are Afraid.—The Faculties Used by the Successful Man.—What the Law of Force is and its Effects.—What the Law of Harmonious Attraction Is and its Effects.* 1075

4. *How Most Persons Have Gained Success.—Why It Has Not Been Permanent in Most Cases.—How Man in His Scramble for Money Resembles Chickens When They are Fed.—People and Things are Instruments in the Hands of God, the Great Universal Law.—Why Methods do not Affect One's Ability to Obtain Wealth But Do Affect the Ability to Retain It.—"Vacant Space" Filled with the One Universal Substance.—"A Million Dollars from Out a Blue Sky."—We Retain Things under Same Law We Obtain Them.—Wall Street Man's Experience.* 1077

5. *Most Rich Persons are Young Souls; have had but Few Incarnations.—Ignorant Use of Intellect Separates us from Abundance of Supply.—How Wealthy Persons Set Causes in Motion in One Incarnation which Relates Them with Poverty in the Next.—"Like Produces Like" on Every Plane of Consciousness.—Intellect the Governing Power in Material World.—Mental Imbeciles.—Soul and Spiritual Imbeciles.—The Two Brain Centers: Physical and Psychological.* 1080

6. *Intelligent Use of Intellect.—Physical and Intellectual Giants; Soul and Spiritual Pigmies.—God Gave Us All Power and the Faculties Through Which to Use It.—Man is Free to Use This Power in Any Way He Wishes.—No One Has Ever Enslaved Us But Ourselves.—Universal Energy is Neither "Good" nor "Bad."—Man can use it to Create Success or Failure, Abundance or Lack.—How Man Relates With the Law of Force.—How to Displace the Law of Force.—How to "Turn on the Light."—Down Broadway to the Battery.* 1082

7. *How to Obtain What We Want, When and Where We Want It.—What Having "The Faith of a Grain of Mustard Seed" Really Means.—What Makes a Thing "Natural" to Us.—Fixed Habits.* 1085

8. *Why Those Who Have "Faith" Do Not Succeed.—Why Only the Things We Do Not Want Materialize For Us.—How to Materialize the Things We Do Want.—Experience of Stenographer.—Experience of Business Man Who Attracted Nearly Ten Times as Much in Sixty Days Under the Law of Harmony as He Had in Six Months Previous Under Law of Force.* 1087

9. *The Relationship Between the Thing Created and the Energy Which Created it.—The Law of Cause and Effect.—How Each Life May Make the Affirmation "I Am Success NOW" Become a Scientific and Material Truth.—Why Continuously Thinking that "I Am a Failure" Makes Success Impossible.—Story of the "Lunkhead."* 1090

10. *Every Material Thing is the Objective Symbol of the Vibratory Rate of the Atoms which Compose it.—How to Demonstrate the Difference in the Vibration of Words.—How We Relate with Failure.—How to Turn Failure into Success.—Story of the Artist.—How Negative, Destructive Energy is Generated Unconsciously.—How to Displace it.—The Law of Life.* 1092

11. *How to Build a Success Consciousness.—A Personal Experience.—Each Life has an Inexhaustible Supply of Constructive Energy Upon which it May Draw.—How We May Relate with It.—Our Attitude Towards Things Governs their Effect on Us.—What our Attitude Should be Toward a Thief or Other Destructive Instrument.—"Children in Consciousness."—Defense is Neither Offense nor Attack.* 1095

12. *People are All in Different States of Unfoldment.—Recognition Determines what is Possible or Impossible for Each Life.—Story of the Street-Car Driver.—Man Becomes a Conscious Creator.—How.—People of the United States More Evenly Developed.—Unite the Imagination and Intellect more Harmoniously.—First "Build Castles in the Air" Before They Can Be Built on the Ground.* 1099

13. *The First Thing Necessary in Building a Consciousness of Money.—There is an Abundance of Money in the World.—"Chance," "Accident," or "Luck" does not Enter into Our Supply.—Why the "Other Fellow" has Money and We have None.—How We Can Relate With and Attract Money to Us—Our Part of the Work.—God's Part.—The True Law of Success.—Experience of Physician.* 1103

14. *"Vacant Space" Around Us is not Vacant.—Man is Like a Central Telephone Station.—What Connection do We Wish to Make?—"Am I to Buy Something I Want but for Which I Cannot Pay?"—Greatest Secret in Life.—Experience of a New York City Minister.—Who is the Successful Man?* 1106

15. *Summary of the Universal Laws which Make for Success.—Why We Refuse to Attack Any One.—This Attitude Does Not Take Away Our Initiative.—Personal Experience of the Author.—Why All Persons Living Will Not be Successful at the Same Time.—Who Will be Successful.—WILL YOU BE ONE OF THEM?* 1109

Publishers' Statement

To the Purchaser:

It is a self-evident fact that you wanted to get something out of this book or you would not have purchased it.

Therefore the first thing to do before you begin to read is to relax and become receptive to the lessons it teaches.

The second thing is to read slowly and try to *absorb* its lessons rather than learn them mentally.

The third thing is to remember that this book only *teaches* how to grow a constructive and harmonious consciousness; *you* will have to do the work of *applying* its lessons.

New habits are not formed in a day and the lessons which this book teaches will not be absorbed in one reading. The student who will devote not less than half an hour each day to their study and then *apply* them in living his daily life will receive untold benefit. It is dependent on *you alone* as to how valuable this book becomes to you.

The author has proven for himself everything he teaches. *He knows that everything he says is true,* and *you can know it* too but *you* will have to *apply* the lessons and prove them for yourself.

You will note that the author does not quote any "authorities" for any of his statements. The highest authority any soul can possibly have is its own God-self and it is this God-self in you which the proper and persistent study and application of these lessons will bring out into greater expression, and thus enable you to set the new causes in motion which will bring you success along any line you may desire.

THE PUBLISHERS

Author's Statement

Many books and treatises have been written on the subject of "Success" and the methods to be used in obtaining it. These works have been the honest statements of their authors who have used and found them successful. The student, in attempting to apply them, has usually been successful for a while but the day invariably came when he found that something was lacking, and the same methods which formerly brought success failed him in his need.

In the business world it has always been considered that the salesman who could sell a customer "something he did not want" was the best salesman. Men are taught "Business Psychology," which consists in controlling the "other fellow's" mind through the power of "Mental suggestion" and *making* him do what the salesman wants.

The world has not realized that the Law of Force was the controlling factor in these methods and that we can only retain a thing under the same Law by which it is obtained.

To be successful in anything one must be able to *retain* as well as *obtain* it; he must also be able to *obtain* it when he wants it, where he wants it, and be able to *retain* it as long as he wants it.

It is obvious then that when we *obtain* anything under the Law of Force we must be prepared to exert our Force all the time to a greater degree than can anyone else in order to be able to *obtain* what we want, when and where we want it, and to *retain* it as long as we want it.

Few men, that is few in comparison with the entire population of the world, are able to maintain this Law of Force against all comers for any great length of time, and so we have failure after failure. Some are able to maintain it for only a few months, others for several years, while those who are able to maintain it for a life-time against all-comers usually do so through making a sort of "truce" or combination—Trust—with others of their kind.

In this book is taught the true Law of Success, which is the "Law of Harmonious Attraction." Under this Law things come to us "because they *want* to come" and not because "we *make* them come;" they remain with us because they "*want* to do so." Instead of working to control the "other fellow" we learn to control ourselves and become so strong, powerful and harmonious in our attractive power that the things we want will "*want* us" so much that they cannot remain away.

The salesman who uses this Law finds that he is led to those who *want* to buy his goods, instead of to those whom he has to *force* into buying. The result is that he has a satisfied clientele instead of a dissatisfied one; that instead of having to dodge around the corner when he sees a former customer approaching, he goes up to meet him knowing that he will receive a hearty welcome and probably be given information which will help him make other sales.

The business man who uses this Law can go to bed at night with his mind free from the fear that he may wake up in the morning and find himself a pauper because his investments have proven to be bad or that some confidential clerk has absconded with his wealth.

The person who uses this Law to obtain Happiness or any other ideal will find that he has not been chasing an "ignus fatus" which disappears just as he thinks he has obtained it.

It is impossible for one working under any other Law to take away from us what we have gained under the Law of Harmonious Attraction, for this is the strongest and most powerful Law in the Universe; while those working under this Law will never *want* to take it away from us.

The Law of Harmonious Attraction, and the other Laws referred to in this book, are not new Laws, and the Author claims nothing for their discovery; they have existed throughout all time and have been used unconsciously to a greater or less extent throughout all the ages. The only claim the Author makes is for their revival and their conscious application by mankind along all lines, and the new application of them which he teaches.

The Author would teach the same common sense application of these Laws to the *energy which creates things* that the world uses in the handling of these things after they are created. Thus when one leaves his home he locks the doors and fastens the windows in order to prevent intruders from gaining entrance and stealing his valuables, but in his thought world he leaves the doors and windows open to all the thieves, tramps and vagabonds of the destructive thought currents. Man should learn to lock the "doors and windows" of his thought world against the "thieves and vagabonds"—vicious thoughts of all kinds—of that plane by forming the *fixed habit* of displacing them by constructive and harmonious thinking.

To the thousands of hungry souls that have battled long enough with the world under the Law of Force and who are ready to learn the larger Truth of the Law of Harmonious Attraction, is this book dedicated. All such will read and re-read it hundreds of times, get into the vibrations from which it was written and receive their own message of Harmony direct from the one great Source. Those who have not been beaten to earth again and again by the reaction of the Law of Force on their own lives and who are not ready for the great Truths contained herein will go on under their old Law, setting more and more destructive causes in motion until they too cry out for mercy and say, "Oh, God! Why hast thou forsaken me." Sometime they too will learn the lesson that "no one can save us from our own Laws but ourselves."

THE AUTHOR

CHAPTER 1

What is success? To be successful in anything is to have the ability and power to do the thing we want to do when and where we want to do it, or to have what we want, when we want it and as long as we want it.

Success is a thing which we can build for just as surely and as scientifically as the architect plans and builds the skyscraper or the engineer the wonderful tunnels and bridges of modern times.

The Laws which make for success are just as natural—although less generally understood—as are the laws which the architect and engineer use in their work.

A New York paper, in a recent editorial on "Declaring War on Poverty," among other things said, "Why then, does not the war begin? There is no reason—save the lack of organization for such a crusade. The men who want to abolish poverty, who know that it can be abolished and are able to abolish it, have not yet found a common standard around which to recruit their forces."

No, and they never will find a "common standard" until they learn the great truth that *everything begins and ends in consciousness—in the thought world,* the imagination, for that is where man does all his imaging—and that until the individual gets rid of a poverty consciousness, a poverty image, he will never be free permanently from a poverty environment.

Within each life lies the causes of whatever enters into it. Man is building his own world every moment of his life. He creates from with-in the energy which attracts from with-out. The thoughts he thinks are his own private property and they generate the power with which he builds from with-in and attracts from with-out. Like builds like and like attracts like. Man must first have "castles in the air" before he can have castles on the ground.

It is true that the man who is kept busy at good wages and given a pleasant and comfortable environment has the *external* things and conditions which will help him create a consciousness or image of abundance, but until he has *established* the *fixed habit* of *thinking constructively,* he will not continue to stay out of a poverty-stricken environment indefinitely.

Was the giving of a pleasant and comfortable environment to man and providing him with continuous employment an insurance against poverty the solution would be simple, easy and sure of quick accomplishment.

But we know that such a remedy has never effected a permanent cure; that *something more* than employment and environment is necessary. We know many men who have started out in life with everything their hearts could wish in both of these things, but the day came when their employment was gone and their environment poverty stricken.

What was it they lacked? What is that "something more" which is so necessary to the peace, happiness and success of man?

We have called it "bad luck," or rather the want of "good luck" heretofore, but it is neither. In the past we have been of the belief that success along any line was largely a matter of chance, or luck, but we know better to-day. We *know* that there is no such thing as either chance or luck, good or bad, in the universe.

"Good luck" is simply the effect of constructive and harmonious causes we have unconsciously set in motion sometime previous to its occurrence, while "bad luck" is the effect of destructive and inharmonious causes we have just as unconsciously set in motion and which we have not yet learned how to antidote or displace.

To-day we know that success is the consciousness of the abundance of supply and the recognition of our *oneness* with it. We may *believe* in the truth of this but until we *know* it beyond any question of a doubt it is impossible to materialize the belief at all times and under all circumstances.

We *know* that the things we have called luck, accident, chance, etc., simply *seem* so on the surface—on the external side of life—because we have only looked for their causes on the objective side; but when we look back of the external and go deeply into the energy which produced them we learn that all these so-called accidents, chance, luck, are the natural effects of natural Laws; that these Laws are as simple and easily understood as is the law that one and one makes two.

Before a spade is stuck into the ground in excavating for one of our immense skyscrapers the building has been entirely finished, even to the last coat of paint on the walls, in the consciousness—the thought world, the imagination—of the architect.

Before even one screw, nut, or bolt was made for the engines which generate the power on our ocean greyhounds the entire engine was completed in the consciousness—the thought world, the imagination—of the engineer who drafted the plans.

Both architect and engineer built "castles in the air" first, before their "air castles" could be materialized in objective form.

The engine which generates the steam does not know for what purpose the energy is to be used, and the masses have no greater knowledge of the use to which they will put the energy they create than does the engine; they work as unconsciously and as ignorantly of the effects of the energy they generate as does the engine.

Man, however, can become a conscious creator while the engine cannot, and in the consciousness or knowledge of this power does man have the advantage. When he neglects to develop or does not use his power, the effect is as disastrous to him as to the engine, for when the engine lies idle any length of time it rusts, becomes useless and fit only for the scrap pile. So with man, for when he fails to use his faculties and power they become atrophied from disuse and he too soon rusts out and becomes only fit for the scrap pile. On the other hand when man does develop and use his power the effect becomes more beneficial to him than to the engine.

Man is an individual creator; he not only creates his body but he also creates his environment.

MAN POSSESSES WITHIN HIMSELF ALL THE CREATIVE POWER OF THE UNIVERSE. This is a most stupendous statement, one which the masses cannot understand nor comprehend fully in their present state of consciousness, but each life may develop itself to where it not only understands but *knows* this truth. The only difference between persons is in the amount of this creative power each life expresses harmoniously.

There is absolutely nothing we have ever had in the past, have now, or ever will have, but what we have created for ourselves. Most of us have done the larger part of our work of creating unconsciously and ignorantly, and we have not stopped to see, study, and understand the relationship between the use we made of this energy and the things it has created for us. It has been so much easier to blame the disastrous effects to chance, accident, or luck.

On the objective plane we have learned that a sharp knife, drawn across the hand, cuts it; but what we have not yet learned is that when we *think* vicious thoughts of any kind—fear, worry, anger, hatred, resentment, resistance, impatience, intolerance, condemnation, criticism, envy, jealousy, etc.—such thoughts generate an energy which causes us to relate with the things on the objective plane, both in the physical body and its environment, that we do not want. It is this relationship of effect to cause which we must learn before we can begin to permanently abolish poverty or anything else we do not want.

Now do not understand that it is impossible to abolish poverty *temporarily,* or even for a lifetime in *some* lives, without either a knowledge or application of this truth, for such is not the case.

Some few lives—few as compared with the multitude of persons living at any time—may concentrate their entire creative power on the subject of money and amass great wealth and hold it too during their life in any incarnation and still *think* all these vicious thoughts and manifest them objectively, but "Be not deceived, for God—the great Universal Law—is not mocked, and whatsoever a man soweth that also shall he reap," and in the incarnations yet to come for such a life will it reap the effects of the energy it has created, either in poverty, sickness, or misery of some kind.

The object of these lessons is to teach how to create and attract success to us permanently—not temporarily; how to get what we want, get it when we want it, and keep it as long as we want it. When we know this Law, and it becomes such a *fixed habit* in our lives that we live it as unconsciously as we are now living, live it because we have developed such a consciousness that we do not know how to live any other way, there will be no need for "declaring war on poverty," disease, or misery, for we will then cease to generate the energy which relates us with these things.

Every moment of our lives, with every breath we draw, we are creating something. There has never been a second of time, all along down the ages past and gone, in which we have not created something for ourselves.

We are to-day, in body and environment, the effects of these creations of our past. We want to *know* this *now.* We also want to *know* that we will continue to create ourselves and our environment all down the future ages yet to come, not only here in this world but also in all the worlds through which we have yet to evolve in our return to our Source.

With this understanding thoroughly fixed in our consciousness let us learn how we may create consciously for success, and attract it to us under such Laws as will make it permanent in our lives.

CHAPTER 2

Man may be classified in a general way as being composed of five entirely different states of consciousness, degrees of unfoldment, or conditions of development, viz: Instinct, Intellect, Inspiration, Intuition, and Revelation. Bear in mind, however, that while the Instinct is a manifestation of the Physical plane, the Intellect of the Mental, the Inspirational of the Soul, the Intuitional and Revelational of the Spiritual, all these states of conciousness are just as much spiritual as is the latter, the difference being that they do not *express* as much. It is like ice, water, clouds and the invisible vapor, they are all one and the same but differ in their expression.

Most persons are over-developed in one of these states of consciousness and under-developed in the others, and that is why it is so hard for them to understand the other states. Few persons are so equally developed in all of them as to be able to impart their knowledge of the Inspirational, Intuitional and Revelational planes in such a way as may be understood by those manifesting only on the planes of Instinct and Intellect.

On the Physical plane of consciousness man expresses what is called "instinct." This is the "cell consciousness" referred to more at length in my lectures on "How We Create Ourselves," "How to Give Treatments," and others. This "cell consciousness"—which is really the intelligence in the cells of the physical body and in the atoms of the environment—is the only consciousness which is under the direction and control of the intellect and is therefore in reality the only "sub-conscious mind" there is, for the ego's mind is never subject to the conscious mind or intellect.

In the creating, destroying, re-creating and re-destroying of our bodies—which process is going on continuously every moment of our lives, awake or asleep—we attract to us atoms which will express the same degree of intelligence as those which harmonize with the energy we are momentarily creating by the thoughts we are thinking. As long as we remain wholly on the Physical plane of consciousness this process goes on under the Law of Instinct both as to our bodies and our environment.

The natural Law of this plane of Instinct is an unconscious recognition—an automatic manifestation—of our *oneness* with all life, and so we do not have "lack" or poverty in our bodies or environment. This is best illustrated in what we call the "uncivilized" tribes which used to predominate in the world, some of which are still in existence, although few remain in their former purely "Physical" or Instinctive state of consciousness. They did not work and did not need to for the Law of their lives led them to be born into an environment where Nature furnished them with sufficient to eat and wear without work.

Those who continued to live entirely in the physical side of their lives became overdeveloped in it, were unable to understand or appreciate any of the other states of consciousness and so continued to re-embody in a purely physical environment. We only need to study *all kinds* of people all over the world to be convinced of this truth.

As man went on in his evolutionary growth and unfoldment he began to use his physical brain—to think thoughts, to imagine or image things—and in this way he began to grow and develop his intellect. The more intellectual he grew, or as we call it the more "civilized" he became, the less instinctive he was, because, unconsciously to him, his intellect—his thoughts—dominated and controlled his "instinct"—the intelligence or mind of the cells of his body and environment—and they, obeying his "intellect," were deprived of their own initiative and the harmonious relationship which was *natural* to them, and he consequently attracted to his body and environment only such atoms as vibrated harmoniously with the thoughts he generated with the new faculty—his intellect.

To know the truth of this we only need to go back to the Indian of our own country and the frontiersman who, living largely in the instinctive side of their consciousness, could follow the trail of man or beast through pathless forests and could tell all about the person or animal they were following; when one who had developed his intellect and was living in that side of his life could not see anything to indicate the trail or that the forest had ever been penetrated before.

Some few men learned to combine their "instinct" and "intellect" and use the latter in further developing the former, and in all such cases they preserved their union—their *oneness*—with the Universal Life and knew no lack either in their body or environment.

The masses, however, unconsciously used their intellect to separate them from the One-Life, through the thoughts they generated and allowed to persist. They related in their thought world with the currents where lack, disease, fear, worry, anger, hatred, envy, jealousy, strife, resentment, resistance, impatience, intolerance, condemnation, criticism, and kindred thoughts found their home, and the more often they related with these currents the more did they attract to themselves, both in body and environment, the atoms which would make another inharmonious physical home where these conditions could manifest in material form.

As the result of the over-development of the "intellect" and the under-development of the other faculties we find men who are living in emaciated physical bodies, devoid of all sense of instinct, inspiration, intuition, and revelation, but with an intellect that in its "reason and logic" is tremendous, but entirely incapable of appreciating the instinct of the physical man, the inspiration of the dreamer, the intuition of the mystic, or the wonderful revelations which comes to one who harmoniously combines and develops all of these faculties. Such persons have not yet learned that the true function of "logic" is to teach us the constructive use of our reason or intellectual powers along harmonious lines.

These two states of consciousness, the Physical and Mental, deal solely with the states which have their initiative or origin in the physical body. When the physical body is destroyed by "death" these two states of consciousness cease to manifest; that is the Mental state ceases to manifest as soon as "death" ensues, and the Physical state—the intelligence in the cells of the body, the "sub-conscious mind"—at once goes to work to disintegrate the body and upon the completion of this it ceases to manifest in physical form. These two states of consciousness must have the objective body through which to manifest, otherwise their expression here on the material plane is impossible.

The other states of consciousness—the Soul or Inspirational, the Spiritual or Intuitional and Revelational—can manifest as well outside of the physical body as through it. It is true that in order for us to perceive the effects of their manifestations with our physical senses they must have a physical body of some kind through which to manifest, but they are separate and distinct from it and manifest through it rather than in it.

These states of consciousness are not under the dominion nor control of the Physical or Mental minds, neither do they in turn control the mentality in any way. The Physical mind—the cell consciousness or sub-conscious mind—is the only mind or intelligence which is under the control of the Mental mind or Intellect. The term "cell consciousness," as used here, includes not only the intelligence in the atoms or cells of the physical body but also that in the atoms of which the environment is composed. These are all under the control and domination of the Intellect or Mental mind.

While it is true that the Soul and Spiritual minds or states of consciousness are not in any way under the control of the Intellect, yet the latter can make conditions both in the physical body through which it is expressing and in the environment through which the Soul and Spiritual states of consciousness may express, and this is one of the true and constructive functions of the Intellect.

Through the Soul state of consciousness we derive all of our great wonderful inspirations which increase our vibrations and when this is accomplished under the intelligent direction of our intellect we attract to us the more harmonious and constructive material with which we rebuild our physical bodies and their environment.

Our Intellect should direct us to such places where we will get this inspiration. We may obtain it in many different ways; through association with those persons who have already developed it, through hearing lectures, reading books, visiting art galleries, going to theatres which produce plays that inspire, through viewing a beautiful sunset, through thinking of the wonderful power manifested by Nature in the raising of the lofty, snow clad peaks of the Rocky Mountains, or the never ending flow and ebb of the tides at the seashore, through the gigantic waves that the monster Ocean Liners ride so easily, and through the wonderful mechanism of the human body. All these inspire us with the wonder and greatness of existence, and when our Intellect permits us to revel in their inspiration it raises our vibrations and makes us just that much stronger and more powerful.

But when our Intellect refuses to allow us to revel in the inspiration which these and other wonderful things give us, when it belittles the creative power of the God-consciousness which manifests in all things, including man, when it places any kind of a limitation upon man's possibilities, then the vibrations of our atoms are slowed down and we draw from the formless energy everywhere around us only such atoms as vibrate at this slower rate, and it is in these currents where lack of all kinds is to be found.

The Spiritual state of consciousness is the vibration through which our intuition and revelation manifests. This is the vibration in which we get the real, the genuine, true-blue "hunches" of life. This is also the plane of consciousness from which our imagination obtains its most constructive and harmonious images.

The Imagination is a faculty which may be used by all of these different states of consciousness. Through its use we create everything we have both in body and environment, and the plane or state of consciousness from which we use it determines the kind and quality of the thing created. This most wonderful statement must be considered carefully in order to understand its stupendous import.

Many times people mistake an "impression" for an "intuition" and when the result proves different from what they expected they blame it on their "intuition," when, as a matter of fact, they themselves were to blame for not being able to differentiate between their "impression" and "intuition."

"Intuitions" never have their origin from anything on the objective plane, they always come from within, and are the result of our having, momentarily only perhaps, raised our physical vibrations to a point where this state of consciousness can manifest through the physical brain. Many persons do this frequently and unconsciously; they do not know how they do it and often do not know that they have done it, and then their Intellect steps in and tells them that such a thought was "all foolishness" and so they pay no attention to it. Afterward they frequently see their mistake and then they are wont to say "Had my foresight only been as good as my hindsight," etc. When we touch this state of consciousness and *know* it, and then follow the leading of our intuition we never go astray, for it is our highest state of consciousness trying to manifest through us and by continually listening to and following its instructions we develop it more and more.

Our Intellect was given us for the purpose of taking our intuitions and revelations and working them out intelligently in material form on the physical plane.

Can we imagine any more insane intuition, before it was materialized, than the reproduction of the human voice by machinery after the speaker is dead? Had not Edison by the intelligent use of his intellect worked out this dream into material form the phonograph would still be unknown. Without the Intellect to do this our intuitions and revelations would be as valueless to us on the physical plane as is an automobile without a chauffeur. The motor car, with an intelligent driver, can be made a most useful thing both for business and pleasure, and so with our inspirations, intuitions and revelations. That is why we should develop the Intellect, but it should be done intelligently and in a way that will enable us to use *all* of our faculties, Instinct, Inspiration, Intuition, and Revelation, as well as Mental, and not only some one or two of them.

"Impressions" have their origin solely in the objective side of life. They come as the result of the things we have learned on the objective plane through our physical senses. We may have learned them years ago, and perhaps forgotten, but they are stored up in the Intellect—the Mental mind—and come to us from that source. Having their origin in the objective world it depends on the basis or foundation on which they were originally built as to their value. "Impressions" are never safe to follow blindly because of the difficulty in determining their origin. It is interesting and instructive, sometimes, to follow them and see where they lead us. Many times this is the only way by which we learn to differentiate between them and our intuition.

CHAPTER 3

We all possess within us the power to unfold and develop, to the greatest perfection, every state of consciousness; in fact most of mankind manifest them all in some degree.

We have persons who are over-developed in some one of these different states and under-developed in the others; these find it difficult to express rationally, or understand anything which is not directly related to or connected with their own particular state of consciousness or unfoldment. Thus those who live continuously in the Inspirational, Intuitional or Revelational states—these are more generally known as the emotional states—to the exclusion of the Instinctive and Intellectual states, become so abnormal to the majority of mankind that they are called insane. They are the "Col. Mulberry Sellers" of the financial world, having great, wonderful inspiration and oft-times intuition and revelation as well, but lacking the intellectual development which would enable them to materialize their wonderful visions in a practical way on the objective plane.

On the other hand we have people who are over-developed intellectually; their Intellect has made them as hard as flint; they are what the world calls "practical" men; their Intellect is always in absolute control of every vibration; they would not permit of an increased heart beat nor allow themselves to be thrilled with an inspiration for anything; they pride themselves upon having absolute control of their "emotions" and would not allow any such a "weakness" to manifest in their lives; "An emotional nature is all right for women and children," they say, "but not for a man with red blood in his veins."

Such lives have yet to learn that it is not the emotional natures which are destructive any more than the mental, but it is the use to which we put such natures, such states of consciousness, which makes them constructive and successful or destructive and unsuccessful.

The successful business man is one who has some development of his inspirational and intuitional faculties but who guides and directs (instead of repressing) their manifestations with an intelligent application of his intellect.

When we live in any one of these states of consciousness to the exclusion of the others we can only relate with the things which are in its currents. We obtain such things under the Laws which prevail and control in that state of consciousness; and we can only retain them under the same Laws. But when we develop ourselves and learn to express in all of these states of consciousness, joining them all together in one harmonious expression, we learn to get what we want, get it when we want it, and keep it as long as we want it.

The Law under which we work in the Physical and Mental states of consciousness is the Law of Force. On the Physical plane this Law is expressed purely as brute force; whoever is the strongest, physically, is the most successful in this state of consciousness whether he be man or animal. On the Mental plane the expression of the Law of Force is more refined. In this state of consciousness men *make* others do their bidding through the developing and controlling of physical force by the intellect. The prize fighter or wrestler who has only physical strength stands no show whatever with the man who, even though of less physical strength, has developed his intellect and learned how to unite it harmoniously with his physical; while the machine—the product of man's intellect—can do the work of a hundred physical men and do it far better. In the world of business and finance the same truth prevails, and the man who has the sharpest and most developed intellect is the one man who has the greatest force in the purely Intellectual state of consciousness.

The Law which prevails in the Soul and Spiritual states of consciousness is the Law of Harmonious Attraction, the Law of Love.

This is a most wonderful Law although the words which symbolize it seem so simple. They are simple to us only because we have seldom or never seen beneath their purely intellectual interpretation. When we open ourselves to the inspiration of this Law of Harmonious Attraction and begin to study its operation by Nature we see that it is really the only Law which Nature, or God, uses throughout the universe.

The earth is held to its orbit in its journey around the sun through this wonderful Law of Harmonious Attraction. The sun throws out its great, beautiful love nature into space and entwines its arms around old Mother Earth, bringing life and vitality with every vibration, while the earth nestles and cuddles in the arms of the sun, evolving and developing the life within and upon it in this loving embrace.

The moon in its orbit around the earth is held under this same Law of Harmonious Attraction, and all mankind together with the things in all other kingdoms are held in the arms of old Mother Earth under this same Law of Love or Harmonious Attraction.

The seed when planted in the ground, under the same Law of Harmonious Attraction, sends its tiny rootlet down into the earth in order that it may be sure of a permanent supply of moisture, and its stem peeps out from under the clods, attracted there from the negative forces which surround it, in order to obtain the sunshine and rains and dews which are so necessary to its life and development.

Everywhere we look we can see some manifestation of this Law of Harmonious Attraction in Nature.

CHAPTER 4

The world has not had held before it many shining examples of success, financial or otherwise, by those who have obtained it under this Law of Harmonious Attraction. The success achieved by man has been largely the result of the use of the Law of Force, (and that is why it has not been permanent in most cases), through the intellectual and instinctive states of consciousness, and the world has therefore believed that the Law of Force was the real law of success.

The masses are like a lot of sheep and borrow their behavior from the few. In the matter of getting money they are like chickens about to be fed. A pan of food is placed in the center of the chicken-yard and the chickens come running toward it from all directions; the half dozen which reach it first grab something and start off on a run; the rest of the chickens, instead of going to the pan where the source of supply is and where there is an abundance of the food they want, run pell-mell, helter-skelter after the few chickens that have carried away with them only a small portion of the abundance of supply. The masses, like the chickens, instead of going to the source of the abundance of supply and creating something for themselves from out of the formless energy, spend their time running after the few who have related with abundance and who have money, and in devising schemes to relieve them of it, never once realizing that people and things are only instruments in the hands of God—the great Universal Law—to give to us just what we have created for ourselves and that it is impossible for them to give us anything else. We see the truth of this manifested many times when we try to help others but cannot do so. Something always intervenes and prevents it.

The *methods* we use do not affect our ability to obtain wealth or success temporarily but they do affect our ability to retain them permanently.

The world has not yet come into a realization that everywhere around us in this "vacant space," as we call it, there is a live, vital, seething mass of energy, far more vital and powerful than anything man has yet harnessed in material form, and to which he may go and draw from it an eternal abundance of everything he wants.

While it is true this vital substance is invisible to the physical sight yet it is none the less true that it exists, just as the electric fan revolving at a speed so rapid we cannot see it, yet when the current is shut off and the vibrations of the fan lowered it begins to materialize and we can see it then with our physical eyes.

So with this invisible substance, when we relate with it constantly and persistently in our consciousness in accordance with the image we have built and hold in our imagination we set up a strong, powerful vibration with our thoughts, and under the Law of Harmonious Attraction the atoms of this invisible substance with which we relate in our thought world begin to lower their vibrations and finally become materialized in form around us.

There is only one substance in the universe, and it is from this one substance that everything which we have ever materialized in form on the objective plane has been derived. This one substance may be differentiated into the myriads of material things we have had in the past, have now, or which we may create in the future, the differentiation being occasioned by the difference in the rate at which the atoms, composing the material form, vibrate.

When we understand this truth and use our Intuition to create as limitless a vision as we can of the thing we want, our Inspiration to increase our own bodily vibrations and relate us with the more rapid vibrating currents on the unseen side of life, and our Intellect to hold fast to this vision and inspiration, we have then effected a combination which, with these faculties working together in perfect harmony, will be able to reach out into the formless energy and attract the gold of the universe to us and differentiate it into form any time we may desire.

Now do not misunderstand me and get the idea that I either believe or teach that in our present state of consciousness it would be possible for any of us to sit with folded hands, with a blank, negative state of consciousness, and have a few million dollars drop into our laps from out the blue sky.

What I do mean is this: That through the operation of this Law of Harmonious Attraction we can make ourselves so full of the attractive power that over perfectly normal lines of transference on the objective plane, and in perfectly legitimate ways, old lines of transference will be increased, new ones opened up, and our earning capacity be increased way beyond what we have heretofore thought possible, and all this because people will *want* and love to do business with us rather than with those who try to *make* them through the use of the inharmonious Law of Force.

Under the Law of Force we are never sure of being able to retain what we do get. There is always the fear that we may make some unsafe investment, or that we will have something stolen from us, or that some one stronger and more powerful than we, or some one sharper, smarter, and less honest than we are will take it away from us, or that we will lose it in some way, or that whatever we do will be the "wrong" thing to do instead of the "right." This fear is well founded too, because we can only retain a thing under the same Law we obtained it. When we live under the Law of Force we always find some one, sometime and somewhere, who is able to use this Law more effectively than we can, and what we have obtained under it begins to leave us.

A Wall Street man once came to me with this story: He wanted to buy a property in New York. The price and terms had been satisfactorily agreed upon by both parties but the agent who was conducting the sale wanted the owner to pay him a larger commission than agreed. This the owner refused to do and the purchaser's contract expiring in the meantime the owner immediately sold the property to another party at a big advance in price.

This man did not learn, until it was too late, why his agent had not completed the sale. He had lived under the Law of Force all his life and so the Universal Law gave him what he had created for himself and took away, at the very last minute, this opportunity to make money, "through no fault of his" he and the world both said.

Later on this same man leased a property for hotel purposes and engaged another party to manage it. Through a combination of circumstances and conditions, made possible only through the inharmony he had created under the Law of Force, his Manager surreptitiously obtained a new lease in his own name and ousted the employer from possession.

This same man owned a property in process of development for which he was offered and refused $300,000 cash. Later on, through the men who managed the corporation but who only held enough stock by his permission to qualify as officers, he was sold out and only realized about $40,000 from the wreck.

"Luck" you say! Well, "luck" is only the *effect* of the energy we create in consciousness and it is for each and every one of us to say whether this *effect* shall be "good" or "bad luck."

Under the "Law of Harmonious Attraction" it is always "good luck" and remains so. Under the "Law of Force" as long as the *force* we use is stronger than that used by others we have "good luck" temporarily, but the fear that we will lose what we have is well grounded, for some day we run up against some one who uses the "Law of Force" better than we and our money melts away like dew before the morning sun.

These are only a few of the many negative registrations of the Law of Force in this man's life. For four years prior to coming to me this man had been having a "hand to mouth" existence and had about completely lost his courage.

He was under my care and instruction for nearly a year and in that time financed one big deal and got two other large ones under way, aggregating considerably more than the first one, and so far his profits have brought him a quarter of a million dollars.

All this came to him under the Law of Harmonious Attraction and through his consciously building for it under this Law. He ceased to fight for anything, knowing, as he looked back over his life, that resistance and resentment create an energy which is always destructive and that it is far better to let go of everything which can be held only under the "Law of Force" and use the energy toward creating something else under the "Law of Harmonious Attraction."

Under this Law of Harmonious Attraction all fear disappears, for we know that this Law is stronger and more powerful than is the Law of Force, and that it is impossible for any one working under the Law of Force to take anything away from us unless we first create the destructive energy in our own consciousness which permits the Universal Law to use them as such destructive instruments in our lives, and that those who are working under the Law of Harmonious Attraction will not *want* to take anything away from us. We know that what we have created for ourselves under the Law of Harmonious Attraction is our own, for it came to us harmoniously and constructively and because the "other fellow" *wanted* us to have it and so we can keep it as long as we want it.

CHAPTER 5

In analyzing these several states of consciousness it can readily be seen that one working on the Physical, or plane of Instinct, not yet having separated himself in his thought world from the abundance of supply is therefore still unconsciously related with it.

The majority of rich persons in the United States are still comparatively young souls, that is souls or egos who have not had many incarnations. They are living largely upon the plane of Instinct, and while they have Intellect and are usually very cultured, yet the fact that they have had but few incarnations in the physical body and have therefore not had the opportunity to create very much negative energy with their Intellect accounts for their not yet having set sufficient causes in motion to separate them from the abundance of supply.

There are some rich persons who are old souls and who are rich because they, either consciously or unconsciously, live under the Law of Harmonious Attraction most of the time; it is *natural* to them because they acquired the *habit* in former incarnations.

As we go on in our growth and unfoldment, incarnation after incarnation, the majority of us set negative, destructive causes in motion, through our Intellect, which separates us not only in consciousness but in the objective world from this abundance of supply.

Many of the very poor persons we have are those egos which, having lived through the plane of Instinct and developed a sense of the plane of Intellect, but not a sense of their responsibilities, have accumulated such a vast amount of destructive energy as to make it necessary for them to work it out through the poverty plane of consciousness.

It frequently occurs that lives which have had every whim, every wish, every desire satisfied in one incarnation become so satiated with money from the overabundance of supply which they have had, that through their very satiety they set causes in motion which in their next incarnation relates them with the direst kind of poverty.

A woman once had a beautiful wrap presented to her and was going into ecstasies in her delight with it when another woman said, "Oh! could I only find something which would give me the joy that wrap gives to that woman."

The latter woman had had an overabundance of supply all her life, having been born into an inheritance of wealth and never having expressed a desire, which money could purchase, without having it satisfied. She had become satiated with wealth and did not recognize that in the energy which she had put into her statement and in the consciousness back of her words she was setting causes in motion which, with that same state of consciousness continued and persisted in, could only have the effect some day, either in this or some future incarnation, of relating her with poverty.

Now what is the value of knowing and understanding these different planes of consciousness? Simply this: that "like produces like" and "like attracts like" on every plane of consciousness and in every rate of vibration throughout the entire universe, and that when we know the kind of causes we set in motion—the kind of energy we generate—we also know the kind of effects which will result.

The object of life is to join all of these states of consciousness together, make union with and live in them all harmoniously at one and the same time.

Our fixed point of contact with the world, that is the state of consciousness with which we contact it and the things on the objective plane, must necessarily be from only one of these planes of consciousness. One of them predominates until we reach a perfected state of development, an evolutionary unfoldment, which enables us to blend them all into one harmonious whole.

The state of consciousness which predominates in our lives determines our vibration, and the vibration in turn determines the currents in this formless energy everywhere around us with which we relate and the kind of atoms we draw from it to our bodies and environment.

The Mental plane, or the plane of Intellect, is the plane of consciousness which should predominate in the objective world, for it is only in this state of consciousness, acting through the physical body, that we are able to manifest on the objective plane. Should man's physical brain—the cerebro-spinal brain through which his Intellect operates—become atrophied from disuse or seriously impaired through injury, he becomes what we call an imbecile, his five physical senses are destroyed, his physical manifestations being only such as come from the instinct or intelligence in the physical cells of the body. On the other hand, when his solar-plexus—the psychological brain through which his inspirations, intuitions and revelations are conveyed to him—becomes atrophied from disuse or in any way seriously impaired through the improper use or the ignorant and destructive control of its functions by the Intellect, he becomes just as much of an imbecile on these higher planes of consciousness as he is on the Physical and Mental planes when his physical brain is impaired.

The world is full of soul imbeciles who cannot, in their present state of unfoldment, either understand or comprehend these larger truths. It is impossible to "prove" the existence of a tree or any other material object to one who is a mental imbecile, because the faculties by which such object can be discerned are undeveloped. And so with the "soul imbeciles;" their intellects may be gigantic but their faculties by which these larger truths may be perceived and understood are undeveloped. "Soul imbeciles" sometimes have great knowledge and wisdom but they always lack understanding. But no matter how atrophied their higher faculties may be they can be developed, and the human race as a whole is developing and unfolding them rapidly and therein lies our promise of the great future opening up before each one of us.

CHAPTER 6

Before we can manifest intelligently on the Physical plane we must develop the Intellect and through its intelligent use of all our faculties we are then fully equipped and able to master the external world and all its conditions. We can therefore readily see how very important the Mental or Intellectual state of consciousness is to us.

The masses have sensed this truth in a dim way, and so there has ever been the desire to cultivate the mind and improve the intellect.

In our hunger for intellectual development we have lost sight of the Soul or Inspirational, and Spiritual or Intuitional and Revelational unfoldment, and of the necessity for our growth along these lines keeping pace with our intellectual and physical attainments. The result could only be what it has been, viz.: a race of physical and intellectual giants, and soul and spiritual pigmies. Unintentionally and unconsciously we have used our Intellect to cover over and bury deeply the Soul and Spiritual states of consciousness. It is true we have tried to satisfy their incessant calls by devoting a small portion of one day out of seven to religious forms and ceremonies which in reality have only been an excuse for our neglecting their development the rest of the time and has better enabled us to bury them still more deeply rather than assist us in their unfoldment.

In the beginning God gave us all power and the faculties through which to use it; He also gave us the power to use these faculties in any way our desires might lead us. God never used the Law of Force in our lives; He never told us that we *must,* or *must not,* do anything. His hand has never been laid on our lives in any way; we have been free agents all down the ages past and gone and will continue to be free agents all along the ages yet to come to express ourselves in accordance with whatever causes we may set in motion. No one has ever enslaved us in any way but ourselves; no one ever set a cause in motion but ourselves for which we are in any way responsible; no one ever will set a cause in motion but ourselves for which we will ever be responsible.

In this material world our responsibility begins and ends in the Intellect, the Mental plane of consciousness. When we use our Intellect, consciously or unconsciously, to generate thoughts in the physical brain which in any way lower our vibrations or retard or repress our ability to express, we are using the Universal Energy destructively; on the other hand when we use our Intellect to generate thoughts in the physical brain which are harmonious and constructive, and so increase our vibrations and enable us to relate with more harmonious and constructive currents on the unseen side of life, we are using this Universal Energy constructively.

The Universal Energy—this one substance which pervades the universe, this One Life in all and through all—is neither "good" nor "bad" in itself; it simply IS. It is like fire which in itself is neither constructive nor destructive; it is the *use* of fire which determines its effect. When we use fire constructively it runs the commerce of the world both on land and sea; it heats our homes and our business places and keeps us from freezing in the winter time; it cooks our food, and in fact becomes one of the most beneficial agencies known to man. When we permit fire to get out from under our control and run riot it destroys our commerce both on land and sea; it destroys our homes and business places; it destroys our food, and it even destroys us, and so becomes one of the most devastating agencies known to man; but in itself it is neither "good" nor "bad."

And so with this Universal Energy. We can use it to materialize an abundance of supply for ourselves, or we can use it to create poverty and lack. God does not attempt to tell us *how we must use it* any more than He attempts to tell us how we must use the fire.

The question then is, "How shall we use our Intellect in order that we may build consciously for permanent success?"

One of the very first things to do is to displace in our consciousness every thought which will in any way relate us with this Law of Force; that is, all anger, hatred, worry, fear, envy, jealousy, impatience, intolerance, resentment, resistance, condemnation, criticism, etc., everything that creates the energy which relates us with this Law of Force. We should displace such thoughts with those of kindness, patience, tolerance, love (not simply the personal kind), peace, poise, harmony, etc., these generate a constructive energy and relate us with the currents wherein are contained the atoms which will produce in material form the harmonious and constructive things we want.

When we first attempt to train our minds to displace these old negative, destructive thoughts we find it necessary to continually and persistently affirm our *oneness* with the thing we want, no matter how far away from its materialization objectively we may seem to be. We must *fill* our thought world with the thought of the thing we want, displacing again and again the thoughts which come to us of the thing we do not want, and in accordance with our persistency in displacing them will we materialize the thing we do want soon or late.

Our work should be done without worry, fear, strain, effort, or tenseness of any kind. These old negative thoughts will come back again and again until we have formed the new habit of *filling* our thought world with the thoughts of the things that we want.

When night comes and everything turns from light to darkness, as it has done every night since the beginning of the world, we do not fret and fuss and fume and cry about it and say "Oh, what's the use of trying to get rid of this darkness? I have tried it again and again but I cannot get rid of it and there is no use of trying any more," but we just take the darkness as a matter of course and *turn on the light.*

We should use our Intellect to do this same thing in our thought world and no matter how often thoughts of poverty, lack and failure come to us, no matter how often we look into our pockets and find them empty, no matter how poor and poverty stricken our environment may tell us we are today, no matter how often we have failed to succeed in the past, no matter how dark the future may seem to us today, these are, one and all, like the "darkness" which comes to us every night and we should give them no more attention than we give to the night's darkness, but *"turn on the light"* by making strong powerful affirmations, such as "I have wealth *now,* I have an abundance of money *now,* I am wealth *now,* I am success *now.*"

Should we start to go down Broadway from 100th Street to the Battery and turn off Broadway at 99th Street, wander around for a while but finally return to Broadway, continuing on to 98th Street, turning off again and wandering around awhile on that street but finally returning to Broadway and continuing our journey, we could turn off Broadway at every cross-street we came to and it would not affect our ultimately reaching the end of our journey did we return to Broadway and continue our journey down town every time we recognized that we had gotten off Broadway. Our turning into the side streets would only delay our arrival at the Battery, *not prevent it.*

So with these negative, destructive thoughts of lack, poverty, anger, hatred, etc., which come to us from time to time; they will not prevent our ultimate success, but only delay it a little, when we learn to recognize that they create a destructive energy and we continuously and persistently displace them with constructive thoughts and affirmations every time we recognize that they have returned to us.

The length of time it will take us to arrive at our journey's end, that is form the *new fixed habit* in our lives of thinking constructively, will depend upon how often we "get off Broadway" and how long we stay off it on these side streets, that is how often we relate with the negative currents and remain in them—in their darkness—before we begin to displace them with the constructive thoughts.

CHAPTER 7

In order to obtain what we want, when and where we want it, we must continuously and persistently affirm our *oneness* with the thing we want. We must be like the "lily of the field which toils not, neither does it spin, but Solomon in all his glory was not arrayed like one of them." Side by side with the lily is the rose, the geranium, and other flowers, the weeds, the grass, perhaps many different kinds of vegetables are also growing in the garden near by; close at hand is the forest and the fruit orchard with their many different kinds of trees and varied fruits; all these are growing in the same ground, watered by the same rains and dews, kissed by the same sunshine, breathing the same air, and yet each draws to itself only the kind of material from earth and air, water, dew, and sunshine, which goes to make its particular kind. And side by side in this beautiful world of ours lives the man who has reached out into the formless energy and with his consciousness materialized the wealth of the universe, also the other man who has reached out into this same formless energy and materialized the lack and poverty. One has gathered the flowers, the other the weeds. Why?

We have always dismissed such questions with the answer—"Because it is *natural* to them." But what makes it *natural* to them? Jesus said that "When ye have the faith of a grain of mustard seed, ye shall remove mountains." We have never fully realized just what this word "faith" really meant in this connection. We have never looked upon the mustard seed, the lily, and the other things outside of the kingdom of man, as having intelligence or mind, or manifesting "faith," because the quality of their intelligence or mind and the action thereof was so different from the quality and action of what we called intelligence or mind in man. But now, understanding these different planes of consciousness in which man manifests, we can begin to see and understand how the things of the lesser kingdoms, the mineral, vegetable, and animal, may also manifest on and become common to at least one of these planes of consciousness, viz., the Physical or Instinctive plane.

The intelligence or consciousness in the atoms of the lily, mustard seed, etc., operating under the Law of Harmonious Attraction, vibrating at a rate peculiar to themselves, send out their conscious call into this one formless energy and everywhere, both on the seen and the unseen side of life, those atoms which are attuned to such call—like the wireless telegraph instruments receiving messages—hear, understand and obey and come rushing to answer it. There is no doubt, no fear, no worry, no anxiety in the consciousness of the lily, the mustard seed, etc., but what this result will occur, and the call is sent out with the utmost faith *knowing* that it will be answered.

It makes no difference how strong the call of the weed, the rose, the turnip, the cabbage, the apple, the corn, and everything else may be, it does not disturb the lily nor in anyway distract its attention from its own call. The lily never throws up its hands nor says "Oh, dear me! There's no use of me trying to get any life or sustenance where all these other things, bigger and stronger and more powerful than I, are calling for it;" it never says that "the big trees"—the trusts of the vegetable kingdom—"have gobbled up everything and we little fellows do not have any chance any more;" it never says, "I have done this all my life and still I am only a lily instead of a rose;" but holding continuously and persistently to the vision of the thing it wants to be, its call goes out morning, noon, and night, persistently and everlastingly for the thing it wants, and in response to its call the tiny rootlet creeps down into the earth and the stem peeps up into the sunshine from out the clods, and little by little, day by day, does the thing for which it continuously calls materialize in form.

When we learn to have the faith of the mustard seed, the lily, etc., that is when we have established in our lives the *fixed habit* of *filling* our thought world with the thought, the vision, the image of the thing we want, then that thing will begin to materialize in form around us like the lily and the mustard seed materialize their conscious call.

This faith—this consciousness—can be developed in every life, and somewhere down the line of our cosmic journey we one and all will develop it. Some will succeed in doing so in this incarnation, perhaps in a few days, a few weeks, or a few months, while others may take many incarnations in which to develop it. It is for each life to say how quickly the work will be accomplished for itself.

CHAPTER 8

Every day we meet persons who, upon being taught these things, will say that they have all this great faith; that they believe all these wonderful truths and practice them, yet they do not achieve success. Why? In all such cases I have found one of two things to be true, either their understanding of faith was like that of the old woman who prayed long and earnestly one night that God might remove the high hill at the back of her house in order that she might have a better view; upon arising the next morning she looked out of the window and finding the hill still there exclaimed, "Just as I expected!"

Occasionally, however, we do find those who undoubtedly have the faith and belief, and practice them with great understanding, and yet do not succeed. In such cases I have always found that an interior inharmony existed. Sometimes it had existed for so long and the persons had gotten so used to it that at first they honestly denied its existence, but a deeper study into their conciousness told the story of their interior inharmony, through which they generated the negative energy that prevented them from materializing the thing they wanted.

I have had many cases of patients and students who were strong, powerful creators, but who had reached a period in their existence where it seemed impossible for them to materialize any of their constructive creations; they materialized their destructive ones fast enough, but their constructive creations seemed impossible of actualization.

An examination into the conciousness and habits of such persons showed that their work was done under more or less of a strain; that they were invariably anxious or tense, rarely ever relaxing, with the result that they generated an inharmonious energy, constructed an inharmonious wall around them in which they were enclosed like a shell; this prevented the things that they had created, and which stood just outside of this wall or shell, from entering their atmosphere and materializing in form. Just as soon as this wall of inharmony could be dissipated and dissolved, through treatments for harmony, and the patients taught how to relate with the harmonious currents through deep breathing and proper affirmations, the things which had been created before in their thought world began to materialize in form around them.

A woman came to me once who said that for six months she had been answering an average of twenty advertisements a week for a position as stenographer but had failed to receive one reply to all her applications. Just think of the kind of a conciousness which could send out over 500 letters to people who wanted a stenographer (the kind of services she had to give) but yet could not relate with one reply, and was not even given an opportunity to demonstrate her ability. She said that when she "sent out her answers that she knew it would not do any good" and then she added most convincingly, "and it didn't."

Her trouble was that while she had built a position for herself in her consciousness she did not know it and was afraid to really believe in her own ability to create for herself the thing she wanted; there could only be one result from her holding the image that "it would not do any good" and she got that result.

I told her to continue doing exactly the same thing she had been doing, viz.: answer the advertisements for "stenographer wanted," and to send out each letter with the thought and affirmation that *it* was *the* one which would connect her with the position she had built for herself.

In less than one month she had six offers of a position and came to me to ask which one she should take. I told her to take which ever one appealed to her the most. She said the one she wanted did not pay as much as she desired. I told her to take it anyway as it was evident that was all the salary she had so far created for herself; that by taking it she was getting all she had attracted; that the position would give her work while she was creating a larger salary for herself in her consciousness. About three months afterwards she came to me and said that she was still at the same salary, and that she had been informed the position never had paid any more, so she would have to either *make* her employer pay her more or get another position. I told her that when she had created the increase in her own conciousness and then "let go" so the position could materialize that either her employer would voluntarily give her the increase or else some one would offer her another position at the increased salary she desired; that until she did create it for herself in her own consciousness she could not get *and hold* such increase. I told her that every time she thought of the question of salary she should *see* herself—that is imagine or image herself—drawing the salary she desired and that in accordance with the continuity and persistency with which she did this would she materialize it. In about a month she informed me that her employer had voluntarily raised her salary to the amount she desired.

A man came to me one day and said that his business had been "rotten" for several months and that he had to raise $2,000 with which to pay some bills and back salaries of employees or go to the wall; that he had about $2,500 owing him for which he was going to sue the parties unless they paid at once.

I told him that unless he had created the money for himself in his own thought world it would be useless for him to sue as he would not get it, and that when he had created it in his thought world it would not be necessary for him to sue. I also said to him that there was plenty of money in the world, also plenty right here in New York, and there was no reason, except his own ignorance, why he should not relate with and attract to himself all he wanted or needed; that he could have enough with which to pay all his bills and more with which to carry on his business, but that he would have to create it for himself before he could get it. I told him to FILL his imagination with the image, the thought, the idea, that he had several thousand dollars NOW; that he was free from all financial worry and had all the money NOW he needed or could use, and to hold persistently to that image, and every time the thought or image came into his field of consciousness which in any way dimmed or impaired that image to at once displace it with the new image I had given him. He had formed the habit of imaging lack and that he was now to change that habit and form the new one of imaging abundance of supply and his harmonious oneness with it; that as soon as this new image had displaced his old one he would materialize the abundance under the Law of Harmonious Attraction.

In less than one week he returned with this story: Upon leaving my office after the previous interview he had gone back to his place of business but had been there only a short time when an entire stranger came in and asked for an estimate on some work he wanted done. Upon returning for the estimate a few days afterwards my client was given the work which amounted to over $9,000 and also given an advance cash payment of $4,500 on account of the contract. In reporting the case my client said that in all his experience in the business covering some twenty years he never heard of anyone receiving a cash payment simply on an estimate and before any work had been done. This payment enabled my client to pay all his bills and left him with some ready cash as a working capital. As the result of following my instructions this man told me he took in over $20,000 in cash within sixty days from the time he first came to me although he had taken in less than $2,000 in the six months preceding that visit.

CHAPTER 9

The world has never understood the relationship between the energy we generate with our intellect through the thoughts which we permit to find lodgment in our physical brain, and the materialization of that energy in objective form. The relationship between the real cause and its materialized effect has been hidden too deeply to be discerned by those who lived only in their intellect to the exclusion of their other faculties.

The rich and purse-proud kings of finance seeing nothing but an abundance of supply in the world in which they live do not have a consciousness of poverty or lack but are like Marie Antoinette who when told that the people of France were starving because they had no bread asked, "Why don't they eat cake?" And they never do create such a consciousness until, through the accumulation of negative energy generated under the Law of Force through several incarnations of temporal power which their money gives to them, the time comes for them to reap the harvests of the causes they have set in motion, the seeds they have sown.

The masses, not knowing the Law of Cause and Effect—being ignorant of these truths and looking only on the objective side of life, seeing everywhere around them the physical expression of misery, poverty and lack—grow attached to the things of the senses and find it difficult to believe there is an abundance for them and that they can displace the image of lack and poverty—which they receive from this objective view—with one of opulence and abundance of supply such as the rich and wealthy have. Their intellect has been educated only to the point which will permit them to believe in what they call "facts," that is, the things which have been materialized and which can be determined by their five physical senses. Not knowing the relationship between the energy generated by the intellect in the thought world, and the things—the facts—which they find materialized in form around them it is natural to believe these material things are the real facts.

But when we learn this great truth—viz., that before anything can be materialized in form it must first be created in consciousness and then worked out into form through the intellect—and then apply this truth, not only to some things but to all things, we can then begin to see how when we say "I am success NOW," not only once but thousands of times a day, FILL our field of consciousness—our thought world, our imagination—with this inspired thought, this intuitive affirmation, this wonderful vibration, as continuously and persistently as do the mustard seed and the lily, that only one result can accrue and that is we become success.

Many who have used the intellect to bury the soul and spiritual states of consciousness will say that we cannot affirm "I am success NOW" when we "know we are flat failures," for that would be telling a lie. Of course we cannot under such circumstances, for as long as we have a consciousness that "we are failures," as long as we live in that thought and "know we are failures," God Himself cannot help us, and we continue to be failures. But the moment we get even a little glimmer of the light, the moment we begin to believe it is still possible that we might achieve success, and then begin to breathe deeply and affirm "I am success NOW," just that moment do we begin to relate with the success currents of the universe and in accordance with our persistency and continuity in the affirming of this new habit of thinking we are success NOW will we become successful.

One time a Vermont farmer was comparing himself to some of his old schoolmates; he said: "I am the biggest lunkhead that ever was and I know it. Now there is Joe Lake who didn't know half as much as I did; he was a regular lunkhead but didn't know it and now he is a Railroad President. Then there was Bill Johnson whom I always had to help with his lessons; he was another lunkhead but didn't know it and now he is President of a big Bank. Then there was Sam Williams who was always at the foot of the class; he was another lunkhead but didn't know it and now he is President of the biggest Trust Company in the country. Then there was John Wilson, the fool of the class; he was another lunkhead and didn't know it and now he is worth millions and at the head of some of the biggest corporations in the country. I was a lunkhead too, but the trouble with me was that I knew it and so I am still here on this rocky old farm."

The above homely story tells the law of success and of failure in a few words. We must never get the image that we are a "lunkhead" unless we want to be a failure. God—the great Universal Law—manipulates people and things in accordance with the image we hold continuously and persistently in our imagination.

CHAPTER 10

It is a well established scientific fact that every material thing is but the objective symbol of the vibratory rate of the atoms which compose it; that the reason there are no two persons just exactly alike, and no two things of any kind anywhere which are exactly alike, is because of the difference in the rate at which their atoms vibrate.

The reason "a" is "a" and not the letter "b" is because they are both objective symbols of different vibratory rates. Did they both symbolize exactly the same rates of vibration, motion or action, we would need but the one symbol. What is true of letters is also true of a combination of letters or words, and what is true of words is also true of a combination of words or sentences.

Suppose we take the words "I am success" and repeat them as fast as we can for five minutes, observing the vibrations which they set up within us and the thought currents with which they relate us. Then let us take the words " I am a failure," and repeat them as fast as we can for five minutes and observe the vibrations which are set up within us and the thought currents with which they relate us. We need only to make this one simple little experiment to convince ourselves of the difference in the vibratory rates which words symbolize and their effect upon us when we establish the habit of living in their currents.

The words "I am success NOW" repeated once or twice, or only a few times, do not affect us materially, but when they are repeated continuously and persistently and as rapidly as we can speak them, so that all other thoughts will be displaced completely, they will relate us with a strong, powerful vibration which will bring strength, courage, ambition, and a belief that success *is* possible for us.

On the other hand when we live in the thought of "I am a failure" and make such thoughts the law of our lives it can readily be seen that we relate with the currents in which failure, loss, lack and all the misery which these things bring are to be found.

This truth is so stupendous, yet so simple and so subtle, that it is hard for us to realize it; in fact many persons do not know that we are living in the failure thought currents most of the time but believe we are living in thoughts of success, so subtle is the action, and until we put our conscious mind on the thoughts we are thinking and learn through study the difference between constructive and destructive thoughts and their action it is hard for us to believe that we do have a failure consciousness. So strong is the habit of negative thinking in the mass mind that we have to watch persistently, continuously, intelligently and understandingly before we can displace it with the fixed habit of constructive thinking.

Should we go into the poor and poverty-stricken districts of any city in the world and interview the residents thereof we will occasionally find one who in the midst of his poverty-stricken environment says he knows he will be rich some day; not that he hopes he will but he *knows* he will. Should we follow up such lives we would find them gradually evolving out of the bondage of poverty into the freedom which comes with an abundance of supply.

When we are objectively poor but have a rich consciousness we can materialize wealth at once, but when we are poor both in our external expression and in our interior consciousness we must change the latter and develop a consciousness of the abundance of supply and our *oneness* with it before we can ever hope to materialize wealth and riches.

There was once an artist who was very poor. His studio was on the top floor of a tumbledown tenement and could only be reached by climbing half a dozen flights of ricketty stairs which endangered both life and limb every time they were scaled. When this man learned of the Law of Harmonious Attraction and the abundance of supply, and came into the conviction that it was possible for him to relate with it, he wrote the words *"I am wealth now,"* on large sheets of old wrapping paper and pinned them to the walls of his studio where they were constantly before him no matter which way he looked.

The few friends who visited him from time to time laughed at "his innocence, his foolishness," as they termed it, and in their "superior wisdom" they would exchange meaning glances, smile indulgently and tap their foreheads, saying, "Well I guess he is harmless anyway."

The artist let them have their fun while he went to work on what he determined would be his masterpiece, a picture which would bring him honor, fame, and wealth. Every time he mixed his paints he poured into their atoms the thought vibrations of *"I am wealth now."* With every touch of his brush upon the canvas he breathed this thought. Surrounded on all sides by poverty and lack he concentrated all the power of his inspiration and intuition, under the direction of his intellect, on wealth and success, never permitting a thought of fear, failure, or lack to find lodgment in his field of consciousness, his imagination. Every time such thought would try to gain entrance therein he closed his eyes and dreamed the dreams of wonderful wealth and success which his inspiration and intuition brought to him and then, living in that consciousness, in the wonderful, glorious, beautiful, harmonious vibrations which he touched, he resumed his work of painting.

Finally the picture was finished and placed on exhibition. It was a masterpiece in the world of art and brought fame and honor to the artist, and in a short time was sold at an almost fabulous price, thus materializing his conscious creation of wealth made in the midst of an environment of poverty.

Many persons say "Why I never had the slightest fear but what I would succeed and yet failure came to me. Why was it?" This is an experience which comes to some lives. The reason for it is simply this: Such persons generate the negative energy, which embodies in form as loss of money or lack of success, through thinking thoughts of anger, hatred, worry, fear, anxiety, impatience, intolerance, condemnation, criticism, envy, jealousy, strife, resentment, resistance, etc., and by being tense and repressing their energy. All these emotions generate a negative, destructive energy which must embody in form unless it is antidoted or displaced. The physical body and environment afford the only two places where this energy can so embody and when the time comes for its materialization it seeks out the lines of least resistance. Should this be the environment then we have loss of money, position, friends, family, etc., lack of success in whatever we may be doing, or some of the many irritations which come to us in our daily lives, the degree of registration depending on the amount of energy generated and materializing at that particular time. In this way do we have loss and lack of success without ever having either imaged or feared it.

When we find ourselves caught in any of these negative states of consciousness, instead of repressing the energy, we should displace the destructive thought or image with a constructive one and allow the energy to express along harmonious lines. Thus by displacing any of these thoughts or images, such as anger, etc., with the thought and image of "All is good," *filling* the imagination with this idea, saying it over as fast as we can and continuing to say it until we are carried by its vibrations out into the thought currents with which it relates us, we then express this energy constructively and are benefited by its expression instead of being torn to pieces by its expression as anger, or through its repression, both of which are highly destructive.

The Law of Life is Expression; the Law of Death is Repression; we should live to express but learn to express harmoniously and constructively.

CHAPTER 11

How may we build a consciousness by which we can materialize money and success? This is a question in which we are all interested and which we will all learn to solve somewhere down the line of our cosmic journey.

There is only one sure, certain and never-failing way and that is, first, last and all the time to *live in and affirm our oneness NOW with the currents which make for wealth, success and harmony.*

We do this by affirming "I am wealth NOW," "I am success NOW," "I am harmony NOW;" *filling* our thought world—our imagination, our field of consciousness—with these thoughts, displacing again and again all thoughts of failure, lack, inharmony, etc., until we have established the *fixed habit* of living in and breathing these constructive thoughts, until we do this unconsciously, do it because it has become *natural* to us.

Several years ago I began to establish the habit of concentrating upon the thought of health, wealth, and harmony as I walked to and from my office. I determined to build a consciousness of my *oneness* with these things and build it so strongly and powerfully that every atom of my body and environment would be so thoroughly impregnated with this thought and its image would be so deeply stamped thereon that the time would come when it would be impossible for me to attract even one atom to either my body or environment which did not vibrate in perfect harmony with these three conditions.

At first I had to put my conscious mind upon my thought world every time I started out to walk. Many times I would forget it entirely, again I would remember it only when I was near my journey's end, while frequently I remembered when I first started out.

No matter how often I forgot I kept persistently vowing that I never would forget it again with the result that today whenever I start to walk anywhere this habit has become so thoroughly *fixed* in my life that unconsciously and naturally, as the result of the habit, I begin to concentrate upon health, wealth, and harmony.

Slowly one by one the things which do not harmonize with these conditions are being sloughed off my life by the Universal Law and in their stead I am attracting the things which do harmonize with them.

All of us—young as well as old souls—have generated an inexhaustible supply of constructive energy in the past. It is stored up for us in the Universal Energy and we can relate with it at any time by continually and persistently realizing in our thought world that we have actually made the connection.

This accumulated energy may be likened unto an ocean of water on the physical plane the supply of which is limitless but which is all enclosed by dams or levees. Everywhere on all sides are little gates which, upon touching the proper button, may be opened and the water allowed to run along the channel into which it is directed. So this ocean of constructive energy which we have generated in the past may be drawn upon for anything we wish by touching, with our thought, the button which will raise the gate leading to the channel of wealth, of success, of harmony, or any other channel into which we may wish to direct this energy.

As long as we give power to the things of the objective plane we cannot say that the doing of certain things is "good" for every one, or that the doing of certain other things is "bad" for every one. There are some things that are more constructive in our lives than are others not because they are necessarily any better but because it is easier for us to take a more harmonious attitude toward them. It is therefore impossible for any teacher to lay down a law in the handling of *things* which is applicable to all persons under all conditions. This much we can say, however, that it is never the thing itself which is "good" or "bad," which brings joy or sorrow, success or failure, but it is the attitude we take toward the thing.

In order to gain success then we should take a harmonious and constructive attitude toward everything that comes and so keep ourselves perfectly harmonious, and in that way make of the thing simply a stepping-stone to our success.

What we permit ourselves to think about a thing is what controls our attitude toward it. Thus, for instance, when we permit ourselves to condemn a thing because we say it is "bad," or condemn some person for any cause whatever, that is taking a destructive attitude toward that thing or person and no matter how just we may think our position in the case may be we cannot relate with these negative, destructive currents in our thought world and expect constructive and harmonious effects, any more than we can expect to walk through a mud hole without getting mud on us.

A natural inquiry which would be made right here by the masses is this: "Supposing some one should steal our pocket-book, are we to say *that* is 'good' and not try to get it back or punish the thief should he be caught?"

Remember again that it is never the *thing* we do but it is the *way* we do it, *the consciousness back of the thing we do,* that makes it constructive or destructive. We always have a perfect right and it is always constructive to defend ourselves and our property but it is just as surely destructive for us to step over the line of defence and into the line of offence or attack. The line of demarcation between defence and offence is so slight and so subtle that it is difficult for the evolving soul to determine just where defence ends and offence begins. Like everything else, however, the beginning and ending are in the thought world, in our consciousness.

When we pursue a thief with the desire in our hearts to punish him, or when we attack some one in return in an attempt to "defend" ourselves from their attack, we are stepping over the boundary line of defence and are well into the vibrations of offence. When we condemn a thief, or anyone else, in our consciousness, no matter what they have done, we have again stepped over the line of defence and into that of offence. It is perfectly legitimate and constructive to analyze anything and everything as long as we do not criticize or condemn. Jesus said "I judge no man, neither doth my Father in Heaven (Father in Harmony) judge any man." He understood this Law of Harmony.

The man who sells "blue sky," knowing that it is only "blue sky," to an unsuspecting public in the belief on the part of the latter that they are buying well secured stocks or bonds, the man who sells cotton goods under the representation that it is all wool, the man who forecloses a mortgage because the owner of the property cannot pay it when due although he wants to pay it and would do so were it possible for him to earn the money, the man who breaks into our place of business or our home and takes away our valuables without our permission—are one and all in the same class in this respect, that is, they are all working under the Law of Force. It is the only law they have ever known and therefore the best thing they know how to do; they have not yet learned the Law of Harmonious Attraction, nor the destructive effects of the Law of Force.

It is true that the thief has learned that should he be caught he will undoubtedly be sent to prison. He does not fear to steal because it is wrong or destructive but only because he will be deprived of his liberty. The others, having nothing to fear in that respect—man-made laws being such as to protect them as far as prison sentences are concerned—go on under this Law of Force.

They are all simply children in consciousness—in their soul development and unfoldment. Were they two-year old children in physique and did these things we would not condemn them, so why, knowing that they are children in consciousness, no matter how old they may be in years as we measure time, should we condemn them? We should not. "Vengeance is mine, saith the Lord"—the Universal Law—"I will repay."

We know that under the Universal Law this is true. The Lord—the Universal Law—can only repay here on the objective plane through manipulating people and things, and so people and things become the instruments in the hands of the Lord—the Universal Law—which He uses to work out in us the effects of the causes we alone have created and set in motion.

When we allow our consciousness to be filled with the desire to punish the thief who steals our pocket-book we put ourselves in the negative destructive currents where the Lord—the Universal Law—can manipulate and use us as a destructive instrument to give to the thief the destructive effects of the destructive causes with which he related when he took the pocket-book under the Law of Force. In becoming such a destructive instrument we, in turn, set destructive causes in motion the effects of which we will have to reap later on, and some one else, through the manipulation of the Universal Law, will be used as the destructive instrument to work out in our lives the effects of such causes.

Again it would be impossible for any one to steal anything from us had we not some time before that created in our thought world, through destructive and inharmonious thinking, the energy which when embodied in form related us with such a loss. This being the case we can readily see that we must cease generating and relating with such negative energy should we desire to stop having such losses and discontinue registering the destructive effects of the negative energy we have created in the past.

In defending ourselves objectively against such a loss we have a perfect right to pursue the thief, capture him when we can, and obtain the return of our property. We also have a right to protect ourselves and society from the acts of such "children in consciousness" during the time they are being taught to displace the Law of Force with the Law of Harmonious Attraction, and for this purpose Schools of Detention—not prisons—should be established where those who commit such overt acts may be detained while taught more constructive methods.

In the meantime those on the outside of these Schools of Detention should also be taught this same truth to the end that mankind everywhere may cease to set these destructive causes in motion which relate us with the destructive effects.

CHAPTER 12

We are all souls unfolding from different planes of consciousness, we are in different states of development, and like the child whose intellect is being trained we must first learn the simple rules of arithmetic before we are prepared to solve the more difficult problems of geometry and higher mathematics.

We have recognized that in our present state of development and unfoldment it is impossible for us to get hold of and play with the moon and we therefore change our "want" rather than bewail the "fate" which keeps the moon away from us. Great wealth may be just as far away from us to-day, in our consciousness, as is the moon and so for the time being we change our "want" and use a lesser ideal towards which we find it less difficult to develop our consciousness.

We never lose sight of the greater ideal, but with the lesser one—the one which *seems possible* for us to accomplish *NOW*—we go steadily forward, developing our consciousness with the affirmation that we have this lesser thing *NOW* and we find that it does not take us long to materialize it objectively. This gives us greater faith and confidence in the power of our own creative ability and we increase our ideal and begin our work of mastering the new one; as fast as each new ideal is reached a still greater one comes into view, there being no limitation whatever to their greatness excepting such as we put on our inspiration, intuition and revelation with our intellect.

The following incident illustrates this truth.

Years ago, in one of our large and growing cities of the Middle West, a man was driving a street car at $1.10 a day.

In his dreams he saw himself in a policeman's uniform and, holding fast to that vision, in less than a year it was materialized.

He had no sooner donned the policeman's uniform than he dreamed another dream and saw himself passing step by step until he became a police captain and that dream was not long in materializing.

Still he was not satisfied but continued to build his "air-castles" and to live in his dreams; he saw himself in the position of Marshal of that county, a place which paid in fees over $50,000.00 a year, with a four-year term without re-election. By the intelligent use of his intellect it was not long before that dream in turn was materialized.

Having reached the pinnacle of success in official life, so far as money consideration for services was concerned, his dreams turned in another direction and he saw himself agent for a great public necessity having an exclusive control of its product, and this dream was materialized at the completion of his term as County Marshal.

Through the profits acquired by him in his progress in the development of his money consciousness he accumulated several million dollars, and to-day is the president and one of the principal owners of the street railway system in a city of nearly half a million population.

Had this man attempted to at once bridge the chasm between the street car driver at $1.10 a day and the millionaire owner of the street railway system he would have failed, but by putting aside his larger vision temporarily—although never losing sight of it—taking up and materializing these lesser visions, he was finally able to materialize the apparently impossible vision of his street car driver days.

During all his onward progress he used his intellect to hold fast to the dream vision which his inspiration, intuition and revelation brought him, doing that which he found nearest at hand to do with all his might and, as each new dream materialized, his inspirational, intuitional and revelational faculties unfolded to him the possibilities of still greater things to be accomplished, still larger things to be done, and God—the great Universal Law—manipulated people and things in the unfoldment of that life—as He does in every life—in accordance with the visions created and which are held continuously and persistently in the thought world by the intellect.

The lily of the field has limited itself to being a lily and as long as it remains in that state of consciousness it will continue to be a lily, reproducing itself again and again, but the day will come in its evolution and unfoldment when it will have a consciousness of something greater, something larger, something better, and it will then begin to evolve into this new and greater ideal.

So with man. In the physical state of consciousness we go on relating with and reproducing our kind until through our evolutionary growth we become intellectual. Before that time we are unconscious or instinctive creators, we are in our Garden of Eden, our Paradise, but *when we begin to use our intellectual faculty we become conscious creators and can create just what we may desire* and are held accountable under the Universal Law for the causes we set in motion—the energy we generate—by the use of this new faculty—the intellect. It is the inharmonious, ignorant and destructive use of the energy by our intellect that drives us out of our "Garden of Eden" and causes us to lose our "Paradise."

What we create and the extent and quality of our creations are determined by the faculties we use. When man lived wholly on the plane of instinct and only used that faculty he lived like the beasts of the field and roamed the country without home, clothing, or any of the things which civilized man calls the essentials of life.

As he commenced to use his intellect and develop the intellectual state of consciousness he began to use fires with which to warm his body and cook his food, clothing to cover his nakedness, and huts in which to sleep.

As his inspiration, intuition and revelation began to express he dreamed of more pretentious places of habitation, finer, better made and more comfortable garments to wear and, using his intellect intelligently, he realized and materialized these dreams.

Had he not been inspired with the idea of something better than the skin of animals for clothing, and tents, caves and huts for dwelling-places, and had not his intuitive and revelational faculties told him better things were possible, and had he not developed his intellect to where he could work out these dreams and visions in material form, he would still be in his instinctive state of consciousness and our civilization would not yet have dawned.

In studying and analyzing the history of the nations of the earth today it does not require a very deep thinking student to appreciate the fact that the people of the United States as a whole, have developed these five faculties more evenly and made their combination more harmonious than have the people of any other nation on the face of the globe.

It has required a most wonderful inspiration with great intuition and revelation, backed up by a powerful intellect, to work out into objective form the mighty buildings and the magnificent bridges, the great factories, the wonderful transportation facilities, the schools of learning, etc., which have been materialized here, and the colossal fortunes which have been accumulated in this country in the last half century.

The wonderful inventions of the past, such as the cotton gin, the sewing machine, the telegraph, the telephone, the phonograph, wireless telegraphy, the airships, the various kinds of farm machinery, machinery for making shoes, for making paper out of wood, for spinning cotton by which one man now does the work better and in less time than several dozen men used to do under the old methods, and those wonderful leviathans of the machinery world in use in digging the Panama Canal by which one machine in twelve minutes does the same amount of work which formerly took several hundred men several days to do, all these are the result of the great wonderful inspiration, the intuitive knowledge, and the master revelations their inventors had and which were worked out and materialized on the objective plane through the intelligent application of the intellect.

Some forty years ago Jules Verne, the noted French author, wrote three books entitled respectively "A Trip Around the World in Eighty Days," "Twenty Thousand Leagues under the Sea," and "A Journey to the Moon." The world laughed and pooh-poohed and made fun of the great "crazy" imagination, as they called it, of Jules Verne and said that it was impossible to accomplish any one of these three things; but a trip around the world may now be made in less than forty days, and submarine boats are an accomplished and materialized fact.

Neither one would ever have been materialized had they not been built first in the consciousness—the thought world, the imagination, for that is where we do our imaging—of some mind through the power of its inspirational, intuitional and revelational faculties and then through the intelligent application of the intellect worked out into material form.

Some day the world will learn the great lesson that we must first "build castles in the air"—in the thought world, the imagination—before we can build them on the ground.

The object of calling attention to these things is that the world may see plainly the power of the inspirational, intuitional and revelational faculties when intelligently used by the intellect and how necessary it is for us to develop these faculties and learn how to use them constructively by the intellect. Without the combination working together harmoniously it is impossible to achieve great success along any line.

While we are developing and equalizing the development of these faculties in our own lives we may through a combination of individuals, each of whom has developed a different one of these faculties but all working together harmoniously toward the one great end, achieve wonderful success, but it is necessary to have all of these faculties in expression, either in a single person or in a combination of persons, in order to produce great success.

CHAPTER 13

In the building of a consciousness for money, the first thing is to realize that there is an abundance of money in the world NOW.

When we stop and think for a moment we know that this statement is true. Should we have any doubt about it all we need to do is to visit the United States Treasury, or some great banking institution, and see the vast piles of money which they have in storage.

We can also take a stroll on Broadway and visit some of the "Lobster Palaces" along "The Great White Way," or some of the fashionable hotels and restaurants on Fifth Avenue, and we will have no difficulty whatever in coming away perfectly satisfied that there is an abundance of money in the world.

How can we help being satisfied of this truth when we see the men in such places pull out of their pockets rolls of money big as two fists, containing nothing less than $100 bills which they keep for small change, most of their roll being composed of $500 and $1000 bills, and then see them give the waiter a $500 bill with which to pay for a dinner costing perhaps $150, telling the waiter to keep the change.

While we realize that this method of reckless, extravagant, prodigal expenditure is destructive, yet we cannot help but admire the opulent consciousness of these spenders in New York's gay life.

I hear some one say "Yes, there is plenty of money in the world but the other fellows have it all while I do not have any."

Why do the "other fellows" have all the money, and why is our supply so limited? This is not the result of "chance," "accident," or "luck;" it is the normal effect of a perfectly natural law which every life uses, either intelligently or ignorantly, consciously or unconsciously, constructively or destructively; the method of using this law by each life determines its effect on the environment.

Those who are rich have *recognized* their *oneness with the abundance of supply.* They developed that recognition either in former incarnations and so were born into an environment of abundance in this one, or else they have developed it in this incarnation. When they developed it is immaterial in so far as the fact of their having developed it is concerned.

When we have lack it is because we have *recognized* our separation from this abundance of supply either in former incarnations and therefore were born into an environment of lack in this one, or else we have unconsciously and ignorantly developed that consciousness in this incarnation, for unless we had recognized in our consciousness our separation from the abundance of supply we never could have been separated from it on the material or objective plane.

The second step, therefore, is for us to begin to create a consciousness that it is possible for us here and now to relate with the abundance of supply just as well as anyone else.

The only way such a relationship can be established is through the people and things on the material plane, because the Universal Law can only manifest in objective form in the material world through them. Because of this fact many have obtained the idea that they must manipulate people and things in order to get the money but that is where we have made a big mistake.

While it is true that under the Law of Force we can and do manipulate people and things, just as the chickens run after and snatch the food from each other, and we can achieve temporary success and obtain large fortunes as long as we exert the stronger force, yet the time always comes somewhere down the line of our cosmic journey when some other life is able to manipulate the Law of Force in a stronger way than we and then our fortunes begin to crumble and melt away.

Under the Law of Harmonious Attraction the manipulation of people and things belongs to God—the great Universal Law—and is a part of the work with which we have absolutely nothing to do. This is a statement which will require careful study and consideration in order to begin to appreciate its great importance and wonderful action.

Our business is first, last, and all the time, through the power of our inspiration, intuition and revelation, to create and fill our imagination with this image and vision of the abundance of supply and our *oneness* with it, using our intellect with which to hold it so strongly and powerfully that all the poverty and lack of the objective plane cannot dim it, and then go on with the work in which we are now engaged on the objective plane, like the street car driver did, doing it with all the harmonious and attractive soul energy we are able to generate, and permit God—the Universal Law—to do the manipulating of people and things.

When we do this we will find that one by one new avenues, new and increased lines of transference, will open up to us and keep pace with our increasing development, just as they did in the street car driver's case and many other similar ones.

The principle—the law under which God works through man—is exactly the same as it is under which He works through the other kingdoms. The lily gets the vision and then God—the great Universal Law—has man plant the seed, then water, cultivate, and take care of it. God—the Universal Law—can only manifest on the material plane through the people and things of this plane because there is nothing else here.

When we understand this truth and attend to our part of the work and let God attend to His, working together in perfect harmony, He does for man what He does for the lily, and the money, as well as everything else, which comes to us under this Law of Harmonious Attraction, comes to us because *it wants to come* and not because we make it come against its desire.

The true Law of Success is the Law of Harmonious Attraction. Many lives are unconsciously working under this Law most of the time. Sometimes they ignorantly and unconsciously live in the currents of the Law of Force for a while and then they wonder why "bad luck" comes to them. When living under the Law of Harmonious Attraction they belong to the class of people to which the world refers as being so "lucky" that they "could fall into the water without getting wet."

When such people get caught in the negative currents of the Law of Force they frequently do not know how to get out of them and then their condition is pitiable.

I was teaching a class in "Abundance" once in which there were several physicians and other professional men. One of the physicians told me the following story: He was a specialist and used to treat fifty or more patients a day; he had so much work that it was necessary to employ assistants. When he was going to his office each day he always saw it filled, in his imagination, with patients, and he always found them there on his arrival. One day he was taken with a severe illness and was kept from his work for several months. During the time he was sick he saw his patients scattered and his practice dwindling to practically nothing. The result was that when he was able to take up his work again he had lost about all his practice and although it had been three years since that illness when he came to me he had not gotten back more than twenty-five per cent of his former business.

When I showed him how he had used the same law of unconscious imaging (but with pictures and ideas directly opposite to what he really wanted,) to destroy his practice that he originally used to build it he at once realized this and went to work to rebuild under the Law of Harmonious Attraction, and within the next forty-five days it increased to four-fifths of as much as it ever had been.

Under this law the money we accumulate comes to us on a plane of consciousness so high that we cannot lose it, because no force is strong enough to displace the power we have under the Law of Harmonious Attraction.

Under this law we have power without force, while under the Law of Force we have force without power, other than such as might or force gives us. But under that Law there is always some stronger force, some stronger might, which rises up at most inopportune times and displaces our force, our might.

CHAPTER 14

This vacant space everywhere around us is vacant only to our physical senses. It contains the material, in solution, for everything we have ever had materialized in objective form, or ever will have.

When we have obtained the vision of an abundance of supply and our *oneness* with it, and have formed the *fixed habit* of holding fast to it, we make of ourselves a magnet through which we relate with the harmonious and constructive currents and attract from this formless energy the atoms which make for abundance of supply in our lives.

We are all like a central telephone station. All around us is the switchboard with wires leading out to every part of the city, to the saloons, opium joints, brothels, and other places of degradation—these represent the destructive forces; other wires lead to the homes, churches, schools, and everything which symbolizes the constructive power. Each one of these wires has a socket while the operator has a plug which when inserted in any one of the sockets makes the connection complete. We can put the plug in a socket which will connect us with the poverty-stricken districts, the saloons, the opium joints, etc., or we can put the plug in a socket which will connect us with the homes, the churches, the institutions of learning and higher places of culture.

WHAT CONNECTION DO WE WISH TO MAKE? One with the constructive powers or one with the destructive forces? The operator—our will-power—will connect us with either.

When the plug is jammed away in the connection is strong and complete, but when it only touches the socket the connection is slight and weak.

So with each life. We have invisible rays—wires—running out in all directions from us which touch all the currents of the universe. We stand in the center with our intellect ready to execute the command of our will-power. Our will-power—the central operator—acts in accordance with the images or thoughts—subscribers' calls—which we allow to persist. When we live in or image—imagine—destructive thoughts we relate with the currents in which are located all the destructive things, the same as when we connect with any 'phone representing the destructive forces. It depends entirely upon where we put the plug of our thoughts as to what connection we make with these numerous currents, and that determines the relationship we establish.

When we put the plug in the thought current of lack and poverty, when we say or think or imagine, "I am poor," "I must economize," "I cannot afford to do it," "I am a lunkhead," or belittle ourselves in any way, we recognize in our consciousness, by such thought or action, our separation from the abundance of supply, and are creating a consciousness of poverty; we are holding up a vision or image of lack and through that very connection we attract from out this formless energy the material which goes to make for lack and poverty in our lives.

On the other hand when we put this thought plug into the socket which connects with the abundance of supply, when we recognize that it is impossible for us to have lack in our lives no matter how poverty-stricken our objective environment may be, when we *fill* our imagination with the image of our oneness with the abundance of supply and hold this image continuously and persistently, we are creating a consciousness of *wealth and success,* and we attract to us, by that very connection, the atoms from the formless energy which begin to materialize this abundance of supply in our environment.

One may ask, "Am I to go and buy something which I may want but for which I am not able to pay?" The proper attitude in such a case is this: Buy it in your thought world, *see* yourself owning it—that is imagine (image) your ownership of it—do this persistently and continuously in your thought world and in that way create a consciousness that it is yours NOW, recognize your *oneness* with it NOW and in accordance with your degree of *recognizing that oneness* will it materialize for you.

The greatest secret of life is RECOGNITION. From the moment we are born and instinctively turn to our mother's breast, recognizing that the life and sustenance for our physical body is to be found there, down to the period we call "death," we only get the things for our bodies and environment that we consciously or unconsciously recognize.

On the objective plane, when our income is limited, it is necessary to adjust our expenses to such limits as long as we retain the consciousness of limitation but there is no reason why we should retain that limitation in our consciousness. On the other hand there is every reason why we should at once go to work and develop a consciousnss which does not in any way recognize any limitations. That is one step towards removing the objective limitations.

When we have established the *fixed habit* in our lives of recognizing our oneness with everything we want, established it so firmly that it is just as *natural* as is the habit of breathing, then we will find that the way will be opened up on the objective plane for us to materialize whatever we may want just as rapidly as we determine that we really do want it and are willing to pay the price for obtaining it. The *price* to be paid under such conditions is to attract it to us under the Law of Harmony.

At a recent service in one of the New York churches the minister talked on "Faith." In order to illustrate his point he related the following incident. He was fond of playing golf; a small lake was one of the hazards on the links he used; he had made it many times and had never failed in the attempt. At the time of this incident and just as he was about to make the drive a friend said "Doctor, can you see the ball on the other side? Should you not be able to see it there it will fall in the lake." He made the drive and the ball fell into the lake. Why? Simply because he unconsciously allowed his friend's image of "seeing the ball fall into the lake" to displace his own image of "seeing the ball fall safely on the other shore." Had the friend given him the same image as his own, instead of giving him one of doubt, fear, anxiety or failure, the ball would have landed safely on the other shore as it always had done before.

Many times we have an image of success when some kind (?) friend, like that of the Doctor's, gives to us an image of doubt or failure and we unconsciously recognize it, instead of our own image of success, and failure is the inevitable result.

The man who is successful is the one who has *filled* his imagination with images, visions, and ideas of success, and who displaces as often as is necessary all thoughts and images of failure and lack which may come to him from every source.

There is never a moment of our lives but what we are imagining or imaging something, and when we image lack in our environment and our separation from the abundance of supply, that is what we will materialize; but when we learn to image consciously and persistently the thing we want, to *fill* our imagination with the abundance of supply, with the abundance of money, of food, of clothing, of joy, of happiness, of success, and our *oneness* with it, it is just as sure to materialize for us in form on the objective plane, in accordance with the degree and persistency with which we intelligently apply these laws, as it is for us to absorb the air into our lungs whenever we breathe.

CHAPTER 15

The universal laws which make for success are the Law of Harmonious Attraction, the Law of Non-Resistance in its positive application, the Law of Conscious Imaging or Ideation, and the Law of Persistent Application.

Under the Law of Harmonious Attraction we take an attitude which will make for harmony in our lives toward everything that comes to us. No matter how inharmonious has been our attitude in the past we now refuse to let any person or any thing disturb our harmony. The moment we recognize that we are becoming inharmonious we at once change our attitude and get back under the Law of Harmony.

Under the positive application of the Law of Non-Resistance we stand firm, but not resistant nor resentful, for the application of the principles and laws which are constructive and harmonious in our lives and we defend our position and our attitude against the fiercest onslaughts which the destructive forces of the universe may make upon us, through people and things, but in our defence we are exceedingly careful that we do not step over the boundary line which divides defence from offence. We refuse to attack anyone or any thing, because the moment we attack we cease to defend and begin to offend, thus getting into the destructive currents and becoming destructive in our creations and materializations. This attitude does not take away from us any of our initiative, but it does require that when we do take the initiative that our consciousness is free from all desire for revenge, free from all resentment, resistance, etc.; that our only desire is to uphold what we believe to be constructive and harmonious and not to convert the "other fellow" to our way of thinking. That the "other fellow" may take a destructive attitude towards us is not our concern; it is his business not to do so and when he is not *big* enough to be constructive and harmonious in his attitude that is his misfortune and he will have to take what goes with it until he learns his lesson of harmony.

Under the Law of Conscious Imaging or Ideation, through our inspirational, intuitional, and revelational faculties, we create the vision or image of the thing we want and by the intelligent use of our intellect we hold fast to this vision or image in our thought world and begin its creation in material form by doing the things which we find nearest at hand to do on the objective plane, doing them with all our might, doing them harmoniously, constructively, and without resentment or resistance, knowing that each thing we do under these laws brings us one step nearer to the materialization of our vision.

Under the Law of Persistent Application we go on day after day holding fast to our image of success, not resenting nor resisting any apparent failure of its immediate materialization, working harmoniously and constructively under these laws without looking for results. When we look for results we relate with the currents in which doubt, fear, worry, anxiety, lack, etc., are found and such relationship delays the materialization of results.

When we have built a consciousness which will enable us to live under these laws without looking for results, but because they are so deeply stamped upon our own consciousness and have become such a *fixed habit* in our lives that they are a part of our character and are *natural* to us, when we live under these laws because they are the highest and greatest and best thing we know how to live and because we cannot live under any others, then will we become the master of ourselves and our environment, and success will be ours along every line we may direct.

Let me tell you of a personal experience which I had a number of years ago in my business in the commercial world and which illustrates the unconscious use I made of these laws. At that time I was doing business largely on borrowed capital and the time came when it was necessary for me to raise $1,000 by a certain date or lose $10,000. I had reached the limit of my borrowing capacity at my bank and so went to friends in my efforts to raise the money. Every avenue on the objective plane seemed to be closed against me and nowhere did I receive any encouragement in the way of assistance.

I had made up my mind in the beginning, however, that I would raise the $1,000 and would not lose my $10,000 and no matter how often I met with a refusal I persisted in affirming that I had the money NOW.

As the days went by, and every avenue on the objective plane seemed closed to me, I made my affirmation that much stronger and more powerful, were it possible to do so, displacing instantly every thought of fear, anxiety, doubt, etc., refusing to allow them to find lodgment in my thought world.

The morning of the day upon which I had to pay the $1,000 arrived and without my having either the money or any idea from where it would come. As I walked down to my office that morning I said: "It has come to a showdown, for this is the day I must make the payment. I do not know from where the money is coming, but I do know that some way will be opened up to me and that is all I need know."

When I opened my mail I found a letter from one of my friends, to whom I had previously applied for the loan but who had not been able to let me have it at that time, enclosing his check for $1,000 and so I was saved.

This is what had occurred: A man who had owed him several thousand dollars paid the indebtedness before it was due, and my friend, knowing my need, at once sent me the $1,000.

"Pure luck and just a matter of chance" the unthinking world would say, but it was nothing of the kind. I had the inspiration that somewhere I would get that money. My intuition told me to hold fast to that belief and so I used my intellect to hold my conscious mind—the image in my imagination—in accordance with that inspiration and belief and to shut out from my thought world anything which would in any way impair that image.

The result was that the Universal Law, manipulating as it does people and things to accord with our vision—our image—caused this third party, who was entirely unknown to me, to pay his indebtedness before it was due and then have my friend send the amount I wished to borrow.

Had I allowed my intellect to dim the vision, the image, which my inspirational, intuitional, and revelational faculties gave me, had I allowed that vision, that image, to waver and permitted one instead which said it was impossible for me to get the money, I never would have gotten it, never could have gotten it, because the Universal Law manipulates people and things in accordance with the energy we generate in our thought world through the use we make by our intellect of our inspirational, intuitional and revelational faculties.

Were it possible to impart to the consciousness of all mankind this great truth, were it possible to stamp it upon the intelligence of each atom in the body and environment of every life, then teach each one how to apply it and develop in them the power or understanding of its application, poverty, lack, sorrow, misery, one and all, would be immediately banished from the face of the earth forever.

But this is not possible at the present time because we are all in such different states of unfoldment and we could just as well expect to teach every child how to solve problems in geometry and higher mathematics the moment it enters the kindergarten as we could expect to teach every life these greater truths and their power of application at once in their present state of unfoldment.

Some lives will immediately begin to absorb, digest, assimilate and make them their own, not because they are smarter or possess any greater power than do the lives which do not understand and therefore cannot at the present time assimilate these truths, but simply because the first class of lives have already developed these several faculties to a greater extent and the relationship between them is more harmonious in such lives.

The children in consciousness—those who have not yet developed these faculties—not only can do so but will do so somewhere down the line of their cosmic journey, and the sooner they begin to live in and practice these truths the sooner will such lives become the masters of themselves and their environment.

No matter how old we may be in years in this incarnation, no matter how wasted and spent and useless our lives seem to have been, it is never too late to begin. No matter how weak and puny and puerile our lives and our efforts may seem to us to have been, just know this, *know it beyond any question of a doubt, that we one and all possess within us all the great wonderful creative power of the universe and it is simply a matter of getting that power out into harmonious expression to enable us to become masters of ourselves and our environment under the Law of Harmonious Attraction, and attract success to us along any line we may wish.* WILL YOU BE ONE TO DO IT NOW?

17

THE POWER OF CONCENTRATION

THERON Q. DUMONT

(1915)

Contents

Introduction 1121

It is of the utmost value to learn how to concentrate. To make the greatest success of anything you must be able to concentrate your entire thought upon the idea you are working on. The person who is able to concentrate utilizes all constructive thoughts and shuts out all destructive ones. The greatest man would accomplish nothing if he lacked concentration.

1. Concentration Finds the Way 1123

Our two natures; one wants to advance; the other wants to pull us back. The one we concentrate on and develop determines what we will become. How you may change your whole career and accomplish miracles. We can be completely controlled by our concentrated thought. How can you make an "opportunity." One man's opportunity is usually another man's loss. A very beneficial practice. Why we get back what we give out. A wonderful encouraging tonic. Every man who is willing to put forth the necessary effort can be a success. The man who is best prepared to do things. How to make your services always in demand. How to reach the top. The man selected to manage is not usually a genius. He does not possess any more talent than others. What he does possess that others do not. Why a few succeed and so many fail.

2. The Self-Mastery: Self-Direction Power of Concentration 1127

Very few men possess the power to concentrate as they should. The cause of poor concentration. A very good practice. Concentration means strength of mind. The person unable to concentrate never accomplished a great deal. How many weaken their powers of concentration. How concentration can only be developed. How to control your every thought, wish and plan. What concentration is. The person who is able to concentrate gains the power to control others. Concentration makes the will and intellect act in unison. Why some people are not magnetic. When a powerful personal influence is generated. How to become influential. The cause of spasmodic, erratic concentration. How to centralize your attention. A quick way to develop concentration. The development of physical and mental concentration. How to learn a valuable lesson. One of the best ways to influence another. A good exercise. The real benefit of physical culture usually lost sight of. How to hold the faculties at work.

3. How to Gain What You Want Through Concentration 1134
The mistake made by those who do not understand the power of mental attraction. How to get what you want. We are not living in a "fairy age." Not the age for a "dreamer." The secret of getting what you concentrate on. How a messenger in a bank became its president. "Power to him whom power exerts."

4. Concentration, the Silent Force That Produces Results in All Business 1136
The power of thought. An experiment showing the power of thought. By concentrated thought you can make yourself what you please. How to greatly increase your efficiency. The face reflects how a person has spent his life. How to awaken possibilities within, that you never dreamed of. How to inspire confidence in those you deal with. The value of concentrating your thoughts in the proper channels. How to attract the good things without a great effort. By concentration you can revolutionize your life and gain happiness greater than you can imagine.

5. How Concentrated Thought Links All Humanity Together 1139
How you may become successful. The barriers to success can be controlled. How to realize your fondest ambitions. How to overcome destructive forces. How to become the master of circumstances. Through concentration you can mold your environment. You can get what you want. Sowing the thought seeds of success. Mind forces that are hardly dreamed of at present. A method for removing unfavorable conditions. Concentration makes you happy and gives you plenty to do.

6. The Training of the Will to Do 1142
The great secret of any accomplishment. Everything is possible today. The inner energy that controls all conscious acts. How you can become a genius. A mighty force at your disposal. Rules that will make you a "man" among men. The spirit that wins. Concentration develops determination and perseverance. Some special instructions. What will power is. You have as strong a will as anyone. You determine your own fate. The importance of learning to use your will.

7. The Concentrated Mental Demand 1146
The attitude of the mind affects the expression of the face. The wonderful power of the concentrated mental demand. How to desire something and exclude all distracting thoughts. The silent force of wonderful power within all of us. How to make plans work out. The mightiest power in the world is free for you to use. The motive power which supplies the energies necessary for achievement.

8. Concentration Gives Mental Poise 1149

The man who can concentrate is well poised. What you must do to be successful today. Concentration that is dangerous. How to make those you come in contact with feel as you do. The man who becomes a power in the world. You can control your life and actions. Successful lives are the concentrated lives. Why people do not get what they "concentrate" on.

9. Concentration Can Overcome Bad Habits 1153

Habit is but a powerful enemy and wonderful ally of concentration. Most people are controlled through the power of habit. Most people are imitators and copies of their past selves. All physical impressions are the carrying out of the actions of the will and intellect. How everyone could be made happier and successful. Some wonderful maxims. Habit the deepest law of human nature. How to overcome undesirable habits. Some special instructions by Dr. Oppenheim.

10. Business Results Gained Through Concentration 1157

A successful business not the result of chance. Failure not caused by luck. The intense desire that is necessary to make a business a success. Those who achieve permanent success deserve it. The man who is able to skillfully manage his business. How to realize your ambition. The successful business attitude. Your opinion should be as good as any one else. How many ruin their judgment. The man who gets the best results. A successful business not hard to build up; may be built up in a few years now whereas formerly it took a lifetime. How to do more and better work. How to attract the ideas thought out by others. Many attract forces and influences that they should not. Broaden the visions of those you come in contact with.

11. Concentrate on Courage 1161

Lack of courage creates financial, as well as mental and moral difficulties. The man without courage attracts all that is contemptible, weakening, demoralizing and destructive. It is just as easy to be courageous as cowardly. Courage concentrates the mental forces on the task at hand. Cowardice dissipates both mental and moral forces. How to banish doubts. No one knows what he can do until he tries. Once you understand the law everything is possible. How to build up courage to do as you wish. Difficulties soon melt away before the courageous.

12. Concentrate on Wealth 1164

No one was intended to be poor. Through wealth we can uplift ourselves and humanity. Uncongenial and unpleasant conditions are not conducive to proper thought. First step toward acquiring wealth. Most men of all ages have been comparatively rich. Wealth not altogether the result of being industrious. No one can become wealthy from his earnings. Why some have to be taught such painful lessons. How many attract poverty instead of riches. Why it is necessary to give a fair exchange for what we receive. How to make your society not only agreeable to others but sought after.

13. You Can Concentrate but Will You? 1167
All have the ability to concentrate. More ability not used than is used. Sometimes only a trifle keeps one from becoming a success. The fault is all your own. How to discover the cause if you are not making good. Make conditions favorable and do not expect them to shape themselves. Stumbling blocks but stepping stones. Hard passages can be bridged if you just concentrate on them. Why more people do not succeed. Don't be afraid of a rebuff. The man who knows no such thing as failure. Be ready for an opportunity when it comes. No circumstances can keep the determined man from succeeding.

14. The Art of Concentration by Means of Practical Exercises 1169
A daily habit will wonderfully increase your concentration. Seeing yourself as you would like to be. Instruction of the greatest importance. The great creative spirit of the universe. Why things manifest as they do. The cosmic intelligence. A most desired state. How to receive messages from the universal mind. How to develop power, unknown to you before. Make your mind a powerful transmitter of thought. The best time to practice concentration exercises. How to rejuvenate every cell of your brain and body. An exercise that will give you a self-poised manner, instead of a nervous strained appearance. Concentrating on the powers within. Concentration will save your energy. How to keep from getting irritable or nervous. The Eastern way of concentrating. Exercise in controlling desires.

15. Concentrate So You Will Not Forget 1181
Why people forget. An easy way to remember. How to deepen your impression. Exercise in Memory Concentration.

16. How Concentration Can Fulfill Your Desire 1183
The desire to do implies the ability to do. Man has within him the power to gratify his every wish. If you have been unable to satisfy your longings, it is time you learn how to use your God-given powers. Priceless knowledge and unlimited possibilities within you that is foreign to most people. How to concentrate on what you want and get it. The miraculous help we apparently receive at times. How one man started a business that pays him $6,000 a year. When you put forth the necessary concentrated effort you will receive great help from unknown sources.

17. Ideals Developed by Concentration 1186
Your happiness and success depends upon your ideals. A valuable lesson. Through concentration we can work out our ideals in physical life. What a different world this would be if we would build the right kind of ideals. Every time you change your ideal you think differently. Life is one continuous

unfoldment. You can be happy every step of its way or miserable as you please. How our grandest thoughts come to us.

18. Mental Control Through Creation 1188
An inventor's vision. Why it is easy to project your thoughts to another. How your mental powers can draw to you forces of a helpful nature. The big businessman must possess mental power of control. How to make a friend or relative succeed. How to generate enthusiasm and the spirit of success. Your environment is either helpful or harmful. Mental starvation. How to instill your thoughts and ideas into others. Influence that must be shaken off before you can advance. Our attitude has more to do with success than you realize.

19. A Concentrated Will Development 1192
A most effective and practical method of developing the Will. Practical exercises. Will training without exercises. Willpower can overcome big obstacles. The Will to win. Man an unknown quality until his powers are developed. Ability plentiful, but organizing, initiative and creative power not so plentiful. The driving force within.

20. Concentration Reviewed 1198
Those unable to concentrate will generally suffer from poverty and unhappiness. The best instructor will only help you to the extent you put it into practice. Gaining the mastery of your work, life powers and forces. Concentrate the dominant quality that makes men successful. Everyone can learn to concentrate better. An experiment to try. Final instructions.

Introduction

We all know that in order to accomplish a certain thing we must concentrate. It is of the utmost value to learn how to concentrate. To make a success of anything you must be able to concentrate your entire thought upon the idea you are working out.

Do not become discouraged, if you are unable to hold your thought on the subject very long at first. There are very few who can. It seems a peculiar fact that it is easier to concentrate on something that is not good for us, than on something that is beneficial. This tendency is overcome when we learn to concentrate consciously.

If you will just practice a few concentration exercises each day you will find you will soon develop this wonderful power.

Success is assured when you are able to concentrate for you are then able to utilize for your good all constructive thoughts and shut out all the destructive ones. It is of the greatest value to be able to think of only that which will be beneficial.

Did you ever stop to think what an important part your thoughts, concentrated thoughts, play in your life? This book shows their far-reaching and all-abiding effects.

These lessons you will find very practical. The exercises I have thoroughly tested. They are arranged so that you will notice an improvement from the very start, and this will give you encouragement. They point out ways in which you can help yourself.

Man is a wonderful creature, but he must be trained and developed to be useful. A great work can be accomplished by every man if he can be awakened to do his very best. But the greatest man would not accomplish much if he lacked concentration and effort. Dwarfs can often do the work of giants when they are transformed by the magic power of great mental concentration. But giants will only do the work of dwarfs when they lack this power.

We accomplish more by concentration than by fitness; the man that is apparently best suited for a place does not always fill it best. It is the man that concentrates on its every possibility that makes an art of both his work and his life.

All your real advancement must come from your individual effort.

This course of lessons will stimulate and inspire you to achieve success; it will bring you into perfect harmony with the laws of success. It will give you a firmer hold on your duties and responsibilities.

The methods of thought concentration given in this work if put into practice will open up interior avenues that will connect you with the everlasting laws of Being and their exhaustless foundation of unchangeable truth.

As most people are very different it is impossible to give instructions that will be of the same value to all. The author has endeavored in these lessons to awaken that within the soul which perhaps the book does not express. So study these lessons as a means of awakening and training that which is within yourself. Let all your acts and thoughts have the intensity and power of concentration.

To really get the full benefit of these lessons you should read a page, then close the book and thoughtfully recall its ideas. If you will do this you will soon cultivate a concentrated mental habit, which will enable you to read with ordinary rapidity and remember all that you read.

LESSON 1

Concentration Finds the Way

Everyone has two natures. One wants us to advance and the other wants to pull us back. The one that we cultivate and concentrate on decides what we are at the end. Both natures are trying to gain control. The will alone decides the issue. A man by one supreme effort of the will may change his whole career and almost accomplish miracles. You may be that man. You can be if you Will to be, for Will can find a way or make one.

I could easily fill a book, of cases where men plodding along in a matter-of-fact way, were all at once aroused and as if awakening from a slumber they developed the possibilities within them and from that time on were different persons. You alone can decide when the turning point will come. It is a matter of choice whether we allow our diviner self to control us or whether we will be controlled by the brute within us. No man has to do anything he does not want to do. He is therefore the director of his life if he wills to be. What we are to do, is the result of our training. We are like putty, and can be completely controlled by our will power.

Habit is a matter of acquirement. You hear people say: "He comes by this or that naturally, a chip off the old block," meaning that he is only doing what his parents did. This is quite often the case, but there is no reason for it, for a person can break a habit just the moment he masters the "I will." A man may have been a "good-for-nothing" all his life up to this very minute, but from this time on he begins to amount to something. Even old men have suddenly changed and accomplished wonders. "I lost my opportunity," says one. That may be true, but by sheer force of will, we can find a way to bring us another opportunity. There is no truth in the saying that opportunity knocks at our door but once in a lifetime. The fact is, opportunity never seeks us; we must seek it. What usually turns out to be one man's opportunity, was another man's loss. In this day one man's brain is matched against another's. It is often the quickness of brain action that determines the result. One man thinks "I will do it," but while he procrastinates the other goes ahead and does the work. They both have the same opportunity. The one will complain of his lost chance. But it should teach him a lesson, and it will, if he is seeking the path that leads to success.

Many persons read good books, but say they do not get much good out of them. They do not realize that all any book or any lesson course can do is to awaken them to their possibilities; to stimulate them to use their will power. You may teach a person from now until doom's day, but that person will only know what he learns himself. "You can lead him to the fountain, but you can't make him drink."

One of the most beneficial practices I know of is that of looking for the good in everyone and everything, for there is good in all things. We encourage a person by seeing his good qualities and we also help ourselves by looking for them. We gain their good wishes, a most valuable asset sometimes. We get back what we give out. The time comes when most all of us need encouragement; need buoying up. So form the habit of encouraging others, and you will find it a wonderful tonic for both those encouraged and yourself, for you will get back encouraging and uplifting thoughts.

Life furnishes us the opportunity to improve. But whether we do it or not depends upon how near we live up to what is expected of us. The first of each month, a person should sit down and examine the progress he has made. If he has not come up to "expectations" he should discover the reason, and by extra exertion measure up to what is demanded next time. Every time that we fall behind what we planned to do, we lose just so much, for that time is gone forever. We may find a reason for doing it, but most excuses are poor substitutes for action. Most things are possible. Ours may be a hard task, but the harder the task, the greater the reward. It is the difficult things that really develop us; anything that requires only a small effort, utilizes very few of our faculties, and yields a scanty harvest of achievement. So do not shrink from a hard task, for to accomplish one of these will often bring us more good than a dozen lesser triumphs.

I know that every man who is willing to pay the price can be a success. The price is not in money, but in effort. The first essential quality for success is the desire to do—to be something. The next thing is to learn how to do it; the next to carry it into execution. The man who is the best able to accomplish anything is the one with a broad mind; the man who has acquired knowledge, that may, it is true, be foreign to this particular case, but is, nevertheless, of some value in all cases. So the man who wants to be successful must be liberal; he must acquire all the knowledge that he can; he must be well posted not only in one branch of his business but in every part of it. Such a man achieves success.

The secret of success is to try always to improve yourself no matter where you are or what your position. Learn all you can. Don't see how little you can do, but how much you can do. Such a man will always be in demand, for he establishes the reputation of being a hustler. There is always room for him because progressive firms never let a hustler leave their employment if they can help it.

The man who reaches the top is the gritty, plucky, hard worker and never the timid, uncertain, slow worker. An untried man is seldom put in a position of responsibility and power. The man selected is one who has done something, achieved results in some line, or taken the lead in his department. He is placed there because of his reputation of putting vigor and virility into his efforts, and because he has previously shown that he has pluck and determination.

The man who is chosen at the crucial time is not usually a genius; he does not possess any more talent than others, but he has learned that results can only be produced by untiring concentrated effort. That "miracles" in business do not just "happen." He knows that the only way they will happen is by sticking to a proposition and seeing it through.

That is the only secret of why some succeed and others fail. The successful man gets used to seeing things accomplished and always feels sure of success. The man who is a failure gets used to seeing failure, expects it and attracts it to him.

It is my opinion that with the right kind of training every man could be a success. It is really a shame that so many men and women, rich in ability and talent, are allowed to go to waste, so to speak. Some day I hope to see a millionaire philanthropist start a school for the training of failures. I am sure he could not put his money to a better use. In a year's time the science of practical psychology could do wonders for him. He could have agencies on the lookout for men who had lost their grip on themselves; who had through indisposition weakened their will; who through some sorrow or misfortune had become discouraged. At first all they need is a little help to get them back on their feet, but usually they get a knock downwards instead. The result is that their latent powers never develop and both they and the world are the losers. I trust that in the near future, someone will heed the opportunity of using some of his millions in arousing men who have begun to falter. All they need to be shown is that there is within them an omnipotent source that is ready to aid them, providing they will make use of it. Their minds only have to be turned from despair to hope to make them regain their hold.

When a man loses his grip today, he must win his redemption by his own will. He will get little encouragement or advice of an inspiring nature. He must usually regain the right road alone. He must stop dissipating his energies and turn his attention to building a useful career. Today we must conquer our weakening tendencies alone. Don't expect anyone to help you. Just take one big brace, make firm resolutions, and resolve to conquer your weaknesses and vices. Really none can do this for you. They can encourage you; that is all.

I can think of nothing, but lack of health, that should interfere with one becoming successful. There is no other handicap that you should not be able to overcome. To overcome a handicap, all that is necessary to do is to use more determination and grit and will.

The man with grit and will may be poor today and wealthy in a few years; will power is a better asset than money; will can carry you over chasms of failure, if you but give it the chance.

The men who have risen to the highest positions have usually had to gain their victories against big odds. Think of the hardships many of our inventors have gone through before they became a success. Usually they have been very much misunderstood by relatives and friends. Very often they did not have the bare necessities of life, yet, by sheer determination and resolute courage, they managed to exist somehow until they perfected their inventions, which afterwards greatly helped in bettering the condition of others.

Everyone really wants to do something, but there are few who will put forward the needed effort to make the necessary sacrifice to secure it. There is only one way to accomplish anything and that is to go ahead and do it. A man may accomplish almost anything today, if he just sets his heart on doing it and lets nothing interfere with his progress. Obstacles are quickly overcome by the man who sets out to accomplish his heart's desire. The "bigger" the man, the smaller the obstacle appears. The "smaller" the man the greater the obstacle appears. Always look at the advantage you gain by overcoming obstacles, and it will give you the needed courage for their conquest.

Do not expect that you will always have easy sailing. Parts of your journey are likely to be rough. Don't let the rough places put you out of commission. Keep on with the journey. Just the way you weather the storm shows what material you are made of. Never sit down and complain of the rough places, but think how nice the pleasant stretches were. View with delight the smooth plains that are in front of you.

Do not let a setback stop you. Think of it as a mere incident that has to be overcome before you can reach your goal.

LESSON 2

The Self-Mastery: Self-Direction Power of Concentration

Man from a psychological standpoint of development is not what he should be. He does not possess the self-mastery, the self-directing power of concentration that is his by right.

He has not trained himself in a way to promote his self-mastery. Every balanced mind possesses the faculties whose chief duties are to engineer, direct and concentrate the operations of the mind, both in a mental and physical sense. Man must learn to control not only his mind but his bodily movements.

When the controlling faculties (autonomic) are in an untrained condition, the impulses, passions, emotions, thoughts, actions and habits of the person suffer from lack of regulation, and the procedure of mental concentration is not good, not because the mind is necessarily weak in the autonomic department of the faculties, but because the mind is not properly trained.

When the self-regulating faculties are not developed the impulses, appetites, emotions and passions have full swing to do as they please and the mind becomes impulsive, restless, emotional and irregular in its action.

This is what makes mental concentration poor.

When the self-guiding faculties are weak in development, the person always lacks the power of mental concentration. Therefore you cannot learn to concentrate until you develop these very powers that qualify you to be able to concentrate. So if you cannot concentrate one of the following is the cause:

1. Deficiency of the motor centers.
2. An impulsive and emotional mind.
3. An untrained mind.

The last fault can soon be removed by systematic practice. It is easiest to correct.

The impulsive and emotional state of mind can best be corrected by restraining anger, passion and excitement, hatred, strong impulses, intense emotions, fretfulness, etc. It is impossible to concentrate when you are in any of these excited states.

These can be naturally decreased by avoiding such food and drinks as have nerve weakening or stimulating influences, or a tendency to stir up the passions, the impulses and the emotions; it is a very good practice to watch and associate with those persons that are steady, calm, controlled and conservative.

Correcting the deficiency of the motor centers is harder because as the person's brain is undeveloped he lacks will power.

To cure this takes some time. Persons so afflicted may benefit by reading and studying my course, "The Master Mind."

Many have the idea that when they get into a negative state they are concentrating, but this is not so. They may be meditating, though not concentrating. Those who are in a negative state a good deal of the time cannot, as a rule, concentrate very well; they develop instead abstraction of the mind, or absence of mind. Their power of concentration becomes weaker and they find it difficult to concentrate on anything. They very often injure the brain, if they keep up this state. To be able to concentrate you must possess strength of mind. The person who is feeble-minded cannot concentrate his mind, because of lack of will. The mind that cannot center itself on a special subject, or thought, is weak; also the mind that cannot draw itself from a subject or thought is weak. But the person who can center his mind on any problem, no matter what it is, and remove any unharmonious impressions has strength of mind. Concentration, first, last and all the time, means strength of mind.

Through concentration a person is able to collect and hold his mental and physical energies at work. A concentrated mind pays attention to thoughts, words, acts and plans. The person who allows his mind to roam at will, will never accomplish a great deal in the world. He wastes his energies. If you work, think, talk and act aimlessly, and allow your brain to wander from your subject to foreign fields, you will not be able to concentrate. You concentrate at the moment when you say, "I want to, I can, I will."

SOME MISTAKES SOME PEOPLE MAKE

If you waste your time reading sensational stories or worthless newspaper items, you excite the impulsive and the emotional faculties, and this means you are weakening your power of concentration. You will not be a free engineer, able to pilot yourself to success.

Concentration of the mind can only be developed by watching yourself closely. All kinds of development commence with close attention. You should regulate your every thought and feeling. When you commence to watch yourself and your own acts and also the acts of other people, you use the faculties of autonomy, and, as you continue to do so, you improve your faculties, until in time you can engineer your every thought, wish and plan. To be able to focalize the mind on the object at hand in a conscious manner leads to concentration. Only the trained mind can focalize. To hold a thought before it until all the faculties shall have had time to consider that thought is concentration.

The person who cannot direct his thoughts, wishes, plans, resolutions and studies cannot possibly succeed to the fullest extent. The person who is impulsive one moment and calm the next has not the proper control over himself. He is not a master of his mind, nor of his thoughts, feelings and wishes. Such a person cannot be a success. When he becomes irritated, he irritates others and spoils all chances of any concerned doing their best. But the person who can direct his energies and hold them at work in a concentrated manner controls his every work and act, and thereby gains power to control others. He can make his every move serve a useful end and every thought a noble purpose.

In this day the man who gets excited and irritable should be looked upon as an undesirable person. The person of good breeding now speaks with slowness and deliberation. He is cultivating more and more of a reposeful attitude. He is consciously attentive and holds his mind to one thing at a time. He shuts out everything else. When you are talking to anyone give him your sole and undivided attention. Do not let your attention wander or be diverted. Give no heed to anything else, but make your will and intellect act in unison.

Start out in the morning and see how self-poised you can remain all day. At times take an inventory of your actions during the day and see if you have kept your determination. If not, see that you do tomorrow. The more self-poised you are the better will your concentration be. Never be in too much of a hurry; and, remember, the more you improve your concentration, the greater are your possibilities. Concentration means success, because you are better able to govern yourself and centralize your mind; you become more in earnest in what you do and this almost invariably improves your chances for success.

When you are talking to a person have your own plans in mind. Concentrate your strength upon the purpose you are talking about. Watch his every move, but keep your own plans before you. Unless you do, you will waste your energy and not accomplish as much as you should.

I want you to watch the next person you see who has the reputation of being a strong character, a man of force. Watch and see what a perfect control he has over his body. Then I want you to watch just an ordinary person. Notice how he moves his eyes, arms, fingers; notice the useless expenditure of energy. These movements all break down the vital cells and lessen the person's power in vital and nerve directions. It is just as important for you to conserve your nervous forces as it is the vital forces. As an example we see an engine going along the track very smoothly. Someone opens all the valves and the train stops. It is the same with you. If you want to use your full amount of steam, you must close your valves and direct your power of generating mental steam toward one end. Center your mind on one purpose, one plan, one transaction.

There is nothing that uses up nerve force so quickly as excitement. This is why an irritable person is never magnetic; he is never admired or loved; he does not develop those finer qualities that a real gentleman possesses. Anger, sarcasm and excitement weaken a person in this direction. The person who allows himself to get excited will become nervous in time, because he uses up his nerve forces and his vital energies. The person who cannot control himself and keep from becoming excited cannot concentrate.

When the mind can properly concentrate, all the energy of every microscopic cell is directed into one channel and then there is a powerful personal influence generated. Everyone possesses many millions of little trembling cells, and each one of these has a center where life and energy are stored up and generated. If this energy is not wasted but conserved and controlled, this person is influential or successful.

Just as it is impossible for a steam engine to run with all its valves open, so is it impossible for you to waste your energy and run at your top speed. Each neuron in the gray layers of the brain is a psychic center of thought and action, each one is pulsating an intelligent force of some kind, and when this force, your thoughts and motions, are kept in check by a conservative, systematic and concentrated mind, the result will be magnetism, vitality and health. The muscles, bones, ligaments, feet, hands and nerves, etc., are agents for carrying out the mandates of the mind. The sole purpose of the volitional faculties is to move the physical mechanism as the energy travels along the wires of nerves and muscles. Just for that reason, if you throw a voluntary control over these messages, impulses, thoughts, emotions, physical movements and over these physical instruments you develop your faculties of self-mastery and to the extent you succeed here, in proportion will you develop the power of concentration.

Any exercise or work that excites the mind, stimulates the senses, calls the emotions and appetites into action, confuses, terrifies or emotionalizes, weakens the power of concentration. This is why all kind of excitement is bad. This is the reason why persons who drink strong drinks, who allow themselves to get into fits of temper, who fight, who eat stimulating food, who sing and dance and thus develop their emotions, who are sudden, vehement and emotional, lack the power to concentrate. But those whose actions are slower and directed by their intelligence develop concentration. Sometimes dogmatic, wilful, excitable persons can concentrate, but it is spasmodic, erratic concentration instead of controlled and uniform concentration. Their energy works by spells; sometimes they have plenty, other times very little; it is easily excited; easily wasted. The best way to understand it is to compare it with the discharge of gun. If the gun goes off when you want it to, it accomplishes the purpose, but if it goes off before you are ready for it, you will not only waste ammunition, but it is also likely to do some damage. That is just what most persons do. They allow their energy to explode thus not only wasting it but endangering others. They waste their power, their magnetism and so injure their chance of success. Such persons are never well liked and never will be until they gain control over themselves.

It will be necessary for them to practice many different kinds of concentration exercises, and to keep them up for some time. They must completely overcome their sudden, erratic thoughts, and regulate their emotions and movements. They must from morning to night train the mind to be steady, and direct and keep the energies at work.

The lower area of the brain is the storehouse of the energy. Most all persons have all the dynamic energy they need if they would concentrate it. They have the machine, but they must also have the engineer, or they will not go very far. The engineer is the self-regulating, directing power. The person who does not develop his engineering qualities will not accomplish much in life. The good engineer controls his every act. All work assists in development. By what you do, you either advance or degenerate. This is a good idea to keep always in mind. When you are uncertain whether you should do something or not, just think whether by doing it you will grow or deteriorate, and act accordingly.

I am a firm believer in "work when you work, and play when you play." When you give yourself up to pleasure you can develop concentration by thinking of nothing else but pleasure; when your mind dwells on love, think of nothing but this and you will find you can develop a more intense love than you ever had before. When you concentrate your mind on the "you" or real self, and its wonderful possibilities, you develop concentration and a higher opinion of yourself. By doing this systematically, you develop much power, because you cannot be systematic without concentrating on what you are doing. When you walk out into the country and inhale the fresh air, studying vegetation, trees, etc., you are concentrating. When you see that you are at your place of business at a certain time each morning you are developing steadiness of habit and becoming systematic. If you form the habit of being on time one morning, a little late the next, and still later the following one, you are not developing concentration, but whenever you fix your mind on a certain thought and hold your mind on it at successive intervals, you develop concentration.

If you hold your mind on some chosen object, you centralize your attention, just like the lens of the camera centralizes on a certain landscape. Therefore always hold your mind on what you are doing, no matter what it is. Keep a careful watch over yourself, for unless you do your improvement will be very slow.

Practice inhaling long, deep breaths, not simply for the improvement of health, although that is no small matter, but also for the purpose of developing more power, more love, more life. All work assists in development.

You may think it foolish to try to develop concentration by taking muscular exercises, but you must not forget that the mind is associated with muscle and nerve. When you steady your nerves and muscles, you steady your mind. But let your nerves get out of order and your mind will become erratic and you will not possess the power of direction, which, in other words, is concentration. Therefore you understand how important exercises that steady the nerves and muscles are in developing concentration.

Everyone is continually receiving impulses that must be directed and controlled if one is to lead a successful life. That is the reason why a person must control the movements of his eyes, feet, fingers, etc.; this is another reason why it is important to control his breathing. The slow, deep, prolonged exhalations are of wonderful value. They steady the circulation, the heart action, muscles and nerves of the mind. If the heart flutters, the circulation is not regular, and when the lung action is uneven, the mind becomes unsteady and not fit for concentration. This is why controlled breathing is very important as a foundation for physical health.

You must not only concentrate your mind, but also the action of the eyes, ears and fingers. Each of these contain miniature minds that are controlled by the master engineer. You will develop much quicker if you thoroughly realize this.

If you have ever associated with big men, or read their biographies, you will find that they usually let the others do the talking. It is much easier to talk than it is to listen. There is no better exercise for concentration than to pay close attention when someone is talking. Besides learning from what they have to say, you may develop both mental and physical concentration.

When you shake hands with someone just think of your hand as containing hundreds of individual minds, each having an intelligence of its own. When you put this feeling into your handshake it shows personality. When you shake hands in a listless way, it demotes timidity, lack of force and power of personality. When the hand grip is very weak and stiff, the person has little love in his nature, no passion and no magnetism. When the hand shake is just the opposite, you will find that the nature is also. The loveless person is non-magnetic and he shows that he is by his non-magnetic handshake. When two developed souls shake hands, their clasps are never light. There is a thrill that goes through both when the two currents meet. Love arouses the opposite currents of the positive and negative natures. When there is no love, life loses its charm. The hand quickly shows when love is being aroused. This is why you should study the art of handshaking and develop your social affections. A person who loves his kind reflects love, but a person who hates reflects hate. The person with a bad nature, a hateful disposition, evil thoughts and feeling is erratic, freakish and fitful. When you allow yourself to become irritable, watch how you breathe and you will learn a valuable lesson. Watch how you breathe when you are happy. Watch your breathing when you harbor hate. Watch how you breathe when you feel in love with the whole world and noble emotions thrill you. When filled with good thoughts, you breathe a plentiful supply of oxygen into your lungs and love fills your soul. Love develops a person, physically, mentally and socially. Breathe deeply when you are happy and you will gain life and strength; you will steady your mind and you will develop your power of concentration and become magnetic and powerful.

If you want to get more out of life you must think more of love. Unless you have real affection for something, you have no sentiment, no sweetness, no magnetism. So arouse your love affections by your will and enter into a fuller life.

The hand of love always magnetizes, but it must be steady and controlled. Love can be concentrated in your handshake, and this is one of the best ways to influence another.

The next time you feel yourself becoming irritable, use your will and be patient. This is a very good exercise in self-control. It will help you to keep patient if you will breathe slowly and deeply. If you find you are commencing to speak fast, just control yourself and speak slowly and clearly. Keep from either raising or lowering your voice and concentrate on the fact that you are determined to keep your poise, and you will improve your power of concentration.

When you meet people of some consequence, assume a reposeful attitude before them. Do this at all times. Watch both them and yourself. Static exercises develop the motor faculties and increase the power of concentration. If you feel yourself getting irritable, nervous or weak, stand squarely on your feet with your chest up and inhale deeply and you will see that your irritability will disappear and a silent calm will pass over you.

If you are in the habit of associating with nervous, irritable people, quit it until you grow strong in the power of concentration, because irritable, angry, fretful, dogmatic and disagreeable people will weaken what powers of resistance you have.

Any exercises that give you better control of the ears, fingers, eyes, feet, help you to steady your mind; when your eye is steady, your mind is steady. One of the best ways to study a person is to watch his physical movements, for, when we study his actions, we are studying his mind. Because actions are the expressions of the mind. As the mind is, so is the action. If it is uneasy, restless, erratic, unsteady, its actions are the same. When it is composed, the mind is composed. Concentration means control of the mind and body. You cannot secure control over one without the other.

Many people who seem to lack ambition have sluggish minds. They are steady, patient and seemingly have good control, but this does not say they are able to concentrate. These people are indolent, inactive, slow and listless, because they lack energy; they do not lose control because they have little force to control. They have no temper and it therefore cannot disturb them. Their actions are steady because they possess little energy. The natural person is internally strong, energetic and forceful, but his energy, force and strength, thoughts and physical movements are well under his control.

If a person does not have energy, both mental and physical, he must develop it. If he has energy which he cannot direct and hold to a point he must learn to do so. A man may be very capable, but, unless he wills to control his abilities, they will not do him any good.

We hear so much talk about the benefit of physical culture, but the real benefit of this is really lost sight of. There is nothing that holds the faculties at work in a sustained and continuous manner as static exercises do. For, as stated before, when you learn to control the body, you are gaining control over the mind.

LESSON 3

How to Gain What You Want Through Concentration

The ignorant person may say, "How can you get anything by merely wanting it?" I say that through concentration you can get anything you want. Every desire can be gratified. But whether it is, will depend upon you concentrating to have that desire fulfilled. Merely wishing for something will not bring it. Wishing you had something shows a weakness and not a belief that you will really get it. So never merely wish, as we are not living in a "fairy age." You use up just as much brain force in "vain imaginings" as you do when you think of something worth while.

Be careful of your desires, make a mental picture of what you want and set your will to this until it materializes. Never allow yourself to drift without helm or rudder. Know what you want to do, and strive with all your might to do it, and you will succeed.

Feel that you can accomplish anything you undertake. Many undertake to do things, but feel when they start they are going to fail and usually they do. I will give an illustration. A man goes to a store for an article. The clerk says, "I am sorry, we have not it." But the man who is determined to get that thing inquires if he doesn't know where he can get it. Again receiving an unsatisfactory answer the determined buyer consults the manager and finally he finds where the article can be bought.

That is the whole secret of concentrating on getting what you want. And remember, your soul is a center of all-power, and you can accomplish what you will to. "I'll find a way or make one!" is the spirit that wins. I know a man who is now head of a large bank. He started there as a messenger boy. His father had a button made for him with a "P" on it and put it on his coat. He said, "Son, that 'P' is a reminder that some day you are to be the president of your bank. I want you to keep this thought in your mind. Every day do something that will put you nearer your goal." Each night after supper he would say, "Son, what did you do today?" In this way the thought was always kept in mind. He concentrated on becoming president of that bank, and he did. His father told him never to tell anyone what that "P" stood for. A good deal of fun was made of it by his associates. And they tried to find out what it stood for, but they never did until he was made president and then he told the secret.

Don't waste your mental powers in wishes. Don't dissipate your energies by trying to satisfy every whim. Concentrate on doing something really worth while. The man who sticks to something is not the man who fails.

"Power to him who power exerts."—Emerson.

Success today depends largely on concentrating on the interior law of force, for when you do this you awaken those thought powers or forces, which, when used in business, insures permanent results.

Until you are able to do this you have not reached your limit in the use of your forces. This great universe is interwoven with myriads of forces. You make your own place, and whether or not it is important depends upon you. Through the indestructible and Unconquerable Law you can in time accomplish all right things and therefore do not be afraid to undertake whatever you really desire to accomplish and are willing to pay for in effort. Anything that is right is possible. That which is necessary will inevitably take place. If something is right it is your duty to do it, though the whole world thinks it to be wrong. "God and one are always a majority," or in plain words, that omnipotent interior law which is God, and the organism that represents you is able to conquer the whole world if your cause is absolutely just. Don't say I wish I was a great man. You can do anything that is proper and you want to do. Just say: You can. You will. You must. Just realize this and the rest is easy. You have the latent faculties and forces to subdue anything that tries to interfere with your plans.

"Let-the-troubles-and-responsibilities-of-life-come-thick-and-fast. I-am-ready-for-them. My-soul-is-unconquerable. I-represent-the-Infinite-law-of-force,-or-of-all-power. This-God-within-is-my-all-sufficient-strength-and-ever-present-help-in-time-of-trouble. The-more-difficulties-the-greater-its-triumphs-through-me. The-harder-my-trials, the-faster-I-go-in-the-development-of-my-inherent-strength. Let-all-else-fail-me. This-interior-reliance-is-all-sufficient. The-right-must-prevail. I-demand-wisdom-and-power-to-know-and-follow-the-right. My-higher-self-is-all-wise. I-now-draw-nearer-to-it."

LESSON 4

Concentration, the Silent Force That Produces Results in All Business

I want you first to realize how powerful thought is. A thought of fear has turned a person's hair gray in a night. A prisoner condemned to die was told that if he would consent to an experiment and lived through it he would be freed. He consented. They wanted to see how much blood a person could lose and still live. They arranged that blood would apparently drop from a cut made in his leg. The cut made was very slight, from which practically no blood escaped. The room was darkened, and the prisoner thought the dropping he heard was really coming from his leg. The next morning he was dead through mental fear.

The two above illustrations will give you a little idea of the power of thought. To thoroughly realize the power of thought is worth a great deal to you.

Through concentrated thought power you can make yourself whatever you please. By thought you can greatly increase your efficiency and strength. You are surrounded by all kinds of thoughts, some good, others bad, and you are sure to absorb some of the latter if you do not build up a positive mental attitude.

If you will study the needless moods of anxiety, worry, despondency, discouragement and others that are the result of uncontrolled thoughts, you will realize how important the control of your thoughts are. Your thoughts make you what you are.

When I walk along the street and study the different people's faces I can tell how they spent their lives. It all shows in their faces, just like a mirror reflects their physical countenances. In looking in those faces I cannot help thinking how most of the people you see have wasted their lives.

The understanding of the power of thought will awaken possibilities within you that you never dreamed of. Never forget that your thoughts are making your environment, your friends, and as your thoughts change these will also. Is this not a practical lesson to learn? Good thoughts are constructive. Evil thoughts are destructive. The desire to do right carries with it a great power. I want you to thoroughly realize the importance of your thoughts, and how to make them valuable, to understand that your thoughts come to you over invisible wires and influence you.

If your thoughts are of a high nature, you become connected with people of the same mental caliber and you are able to help yourself. If your thoughts are tricky, you will bring tricky people to deal with you, who will try to cheat you.

If your thoughts are the right kind, you will inspire confidence in those with whom you are dealing.

As you gain the good will of others your confidence and strength will increase. You will soon learn the wonderful value of your thoughts and how serene you can become even when circumstances are the most trying.

Such thoughts of Right and Good Will bring you into harmony with people who amount to something in the world and who are able to give you help if you should need it, as nearly everyone does at times.

You can now see why it is so important to concentrate your thoughts in the proper channels. It is very necessary that people should have confidence in you. When two people meet they have not the time to look each other up. They accept each other according to instinct which can usually be relied on.

You meet a person and his attitude creates a suspicion in you. The chances are you cannot tell why, but something tells you, "Have no dealings with him, for if you do, you will be sorry." Thoughts produce actions. Therefore be careful of your thoughts. Your life will be molded by the thoughts you have. A spiritual power is always available to your thought, and when you are worthy you can attract all the good things without a great effort on your part.

The sun's rays shine down on our gardens, but we can plant trees that will interfere with the sun light. There are invisible forces ready to help you if you do not think and act to intercept these. These forces work silently. "You reap what you sow."

You have concentrated within powers that if developed will bring you happiness greater than you can even imagine. Most people go rushing through life, literally driving away the very things they seek. By concentration you can revolutionize your life, accomplish infinitely more and without a great effort.

Look within yourself and you will find the greatest machine ever made.

HOW TO SPEAK WISELY

In order to speak wisely you must secure at least a partial concentration of the faculties and forces upon the subject at hand. Speech interferes with the focusing powers of the mind, as it withdraws the attention to the external and therefore is hardly to be compared with that deep silence of the subconscious mind, where deep thoughts, and the silent forces of high potency are evolved. It is necessary to be silent before you can speak wisely. The person who is really alert and well poised and able to speak wisely under trying circumstances, is the person who has practiced in the silence. Most people do not know what the silence is and think it is easy to go into the silence, but this is not so. In the real silence we become attached to that interior law and the forces become silent, because they are in a state of high potency, or beyond the vibratory sounds to which our external ears are attuned. He who desires to become above the ordinary should open up for himself the interior channels which lead to the absolute law of the omnipotent. You can only do this by persistently and intelligently practicing thought concentration. Hold the thought: In-silence-I-will-allow-my-higher-self-to-have-complete-control. I-will-be-true-to-my-higher-self. I-realize-that-it-is-to-my-self-interest-to-live-up-to-my-best. I-demand-wisdom—so-that-I-may-act-wisely-for-myself-and-others.

In the next chapter I will tell you of the mysterious law, which links all humanity together, by the powers of co-operative thought, and chooses for us companionship and friends.

LESSON 5

How Concentrated Thought Links All Humanity Together

It is within your power to gratify your every wish. Success is the result of the way you think. I will show you how to think to be successful.

The power to rule and attract success is within yourself. The barriers that shut these off from you are subject to your control. You have unlimited power to think and this is the link that connects you with your omniscient source.

Success is the result of certain moods of mind or ways of thinking. These moods can be controlled by you and produced at will.

You have been evolved to what you are from a lowly atom because you possessed the power to think. This power will never leave you, but will keep urging you on until you reach perfection. As you evolve, you create new desires and these can be gratified. The power to rule lies within you. The barriers that keep you from ruling are also within you. These are the barriers of ignorance.

Concentrated thought will accomplish seemingly impossible results and make you realize your fondest ambitions. At the same time that you break down barriers of limitation new ambitions will be awakened. You begin to experience conscious thought constructions.

If you will just realize that through deep concentration you become linked with thoughts of omnipotence, you will kill out entirely your belief in your limitations and at the same time will drive away all fear and other negative and destructive thought forces which constantly work against you. In the place of these you will build up a strong assurance that your every venture will be successful. When you learn thus how to concentrate and reinforce your thought, you control your mental creations; they in turn help to mould your physical environment, and you become the master of circumstances and the ruler of your kingdom.

It is just as easy to surround your life with what you want as it is with what you don't want. It is a question to be decided by your will. There are no walls to prevent you from getting what you want, providing you want what is right. If you choose something that is not right, you are in opposition to the omnipotent plans of the universe and deserve to fail. But, if you will base your desires on justice and good will, you avail yourself of the helpful powers of universal currents, and instead of having a handicap to work against, can depend upon ultimate success, though the outward appearances may not at first be bright.

Never stop to think of temporary appearances, but maintain an unfaltering belief in your ultimate success. Make your plans carefully, and see that they are not contrary to the tides of universal justice. The main thing for you to remember is to keep at bay the destructive and opposing forces of fear and anger and their satellites.

There is no power so great as the belief which comes from the knowledge that your thought is in harmony with the divine laws of thought and the sincere conviction that your cause is right. You may be able seemingly to accomplish results for a time even if your cause is unjust, but the results will be temporary, and, in time, you will have to tear down your thought edifice and build on the true foundation of Right.

Plans that are not built on truth produce discordant vibrations and are therefore self-destructive. Never try to build until you can build right. It is a waste of time to do anything else. You may temorarily put aside your desire to do right, but its true vibrations will interfere with your unjust plans until you are forced back into righteous paths of power.

All just causes succeed in time, though temporarily they may fail. So if you should face the time when everything seems against you, quiet your fears, drive away all destructive thoughts and uphold the dignity of your moral and spiritual life.

"Where There Is A Will There Is A Way." The reason this is so is that the Will can make a way if given a chance to secure the assistance of aiding forces. The more it is developed the higher the way to which it will lead.

When everything looks gloomy and discouraging, then is the time to show what you are made of by rejoicing that you can control your moods by making them as calm, serene and bright as if prosperity were yours.

"Be faithful in sowing the thought seeds of success, in perfect trust that the sun will not cease to shine and bring a generous harvest in one season."

It is not always necessary to think of the success of a venture when you are actually engaged in it. For when the body is inactive the mind is most free to catch new ideas that will further the opportunity you are seeking. When you are actually engaged in doing something, you are thinking in the channels you have previously constructed and the work does not have to be done over again.

When you are in a negative mood the intuitions are more active, for you are not then controlling your thoughts by the will. Everything we do should have the approval of the intuition.

When you are in a negative mood you attract thoughts of similar nature through the law of affinity. That is why it is so important to form thoughts of a success nature to attract similar ones. If you have never made a study of this subject, you may think this is all foolishness, but it is a fact that there are thought currents that unerringly bring thoughts of a similar nature. Many persons who think of failure actually attract failure by their worries, their anxieties, their overactivity. These thoughts are bound to bring failure. When you once learn the laws of thought and think of nothing but Good, Truth, Success, you will make more progress with less efforts than you ever made before.

There are forces that can aid the mind that are hardly dreamed of by the average person. When you learn to believe more in the value of thought and its laws you will be led aright and your business gains will multiply.

The following method may assist you in gaining better thought control. If you are unable to control your fears, just say to your faulty determination, "Do not falter or be afraid, for I am not really alone. I am surrounded by invisible forces that will assist me to remove the unfavorable appearances." Soon you will have more courage. The only difference between the fearless man and the fearful one is in his will, his hope. So if you lack success, believe in it, hope for it, claim it. You can use the same method to brace up your thoughts of desire, aspiration, imagination, expectation, ambition, understanding, trust and assurance.

If you get anxious, angry, discouraged, undecided or worried, it is because you are not receiving the co-operation of the higher powers of your mind. By your Will you can so organize the powers of the mind that your moods change only as you want them to instead of as circumstances affect you.

I was recently asked if I advised concentrating on what you eat, or what you see while walking. My reply was that no matter what you may be doing, when in practice think of nothing else but that act at the time. The idea is to be able to control your unimportant acts, otherwise you set up a habit that it will be hard to overcome, because your faculties have not been in the habit of concentrating. Your faculties cannot be disorganized one minute and organized the next. If you allow the mind to wander while you are doing small things, it will be likely to get into mischief and make it hard to concentrate on the important act when it comes.

The man who is able to concentrate is the happy, busy man. Time does not drag with him. He always has plenty to do. He does not have time to think over past mistakes, which would make him unhappy.

If despite our discouragement and failures, we claim our great heritage, "life and truth and force, like an electric current," will permeate our lives until we enter into our "birthright in eternity."

The will does not act with clearness, decision and promptness unless it is trained to do so. There are comparatively few who really know what they are doing every minute of the day. This is because they do not observe with sufficient orderliness and accuracy to know what they are doing. It is not difficult to know what you are doing all the time, if you will just practice concentration and with a reposeful deliberation, and train yourself to think clearly, promptly, and decisively. If you allow yourself to worry or hurry in what you are doing, this will not be clearly photographed upon the sensitized plate of the subjective mind, and you therefore will not be really conscious of your actions. So practice accuracy and concentration of thought, and also absolute truthfulness and you will soon be able to concentrate.

LESSON 6

The Training of the Will to Do

The Will to Do is the greatest power in the world that is concerned with human accomplishment and no one can in advance determine its limits.

The things that we do now would have been a few ages ago impossibilities. Today the safe maxim is: "All things are possible."

The Will to Do is a force that is strictly practical, yet it is difficult to explain just what it is. It can be compared to electricity because we know it only through its cause and effects. It is a power we can direct and to just the extent we direct it do we determine our future. Every time you accomplish any definite act, consciously or unconsciously, you use the principle of the Will. You can Will to do anything whether it is right or wrong, and therefore the way you use your will makes a big difference in your life.

Every person possesses some "Will to Do." It is the inner energy which controls all conscious acts. What you will to do directs your life forces. All habits, good or bad, are the result of what you will to do. You improve or lower your condition in life by what you will to do. Your will has a connection with all avenues of knowledge, all activities, all accomplishment.

You probably know of cases where people have shown wonderful strength under some excitement, similar to the following. The house of a farmer's wife caught on fire. No one was around to help her move anything. She was a frail woman, and ordinarily was considered weak. On this occasion she removed things from the house that it later took three men to handle. It was the "Will to Do" that she used to accomplish her task.

Genius Is But A Will To Do Little Things With Infinite Pains. Little Things Well Done Open The Door Of Opportunity For Bigger Things.

The Will accomplishes its greater results through activities that grow out of great concentration in acquiring the power of voluntary attention to such an extent that we can direct it where we will and hold it steadily to its task until our aim is accomplished. When you learn so to use it, your Will Power becomes a mighty force. Almost everything can be accomplished through its proper use. It is greater than physical force because it can be used to control not only physical but mental and moral forces.

There are very few who possess perfectly developed and balanced Will Power, but those who do easily crush out their weak qualities. Study yourself carefully. Find out your greatest weakness and then use your will power to overcome it. In this way eradicate your faults, one by one, until you have built up a strong character and personality.

RULES FOR IMPROVEMENT

A desire arises. Now think whether this would be good for you. If it is not, use your Will Power to kill out the desire, but, on the other hand, if it is a righteous desire, summon all your Will Power to your aid, crush all obstacles that confront you and secure possession of the coveted Good.

SLOWNESS IN MAKING DECISIONS

This is a weakness of Will Power. You know you should do something, but you delay doing it through lack of decision. It is easier not to do a certain thing than to do it, but conscience says to do it. The vast majority of persons are failures because of the lack of deciding to do a thing when it should be done. Those who are successful have been quick to grasp opportunities by making a quick decision. This power of will can be used to bring culture, wealth and health.

SOME SPECIAL POINTERS

For the next week try to make quicker decisions in your little daily affairs. Set the hour you wish to get up and arise exactly at the fixed time. Anything that you should accomplish, do on or ahead of time. You want, of course, to give due deliberation to weighty matters, but by making quick decisions on little things you will acquire the ability to make quick decisions in bigger things. Never procrastinate. Decide quickly one way or the other even at the risk of deciding wrong. Practice this for a week or two and notice your improvement.

THE LACK OF INITIATIVE

This, too, keeps many men from succeeding. They have fallen into the way of imitating others in all that they do. Very often we hear the expression, "He seems clever enough, but he lacks initiative." Life for them is one continuous grind. Day after day they go through the same monotonous round of duties, while those who are "getting along" are using their initiative to get greater fullness of life. There is nothing so responsible for poverty as this lack of initiative, this power to think and do for ourselves.

YOU ARE AS GOOD AS ANYONE

You have will power, and if you use it, you will get your share of the luxuries of life. So use it to claim your own. Don't depend on anyone else to help you. We have to fight our own battles. All the world loves a fighter, while the coward is despised by all.

Every person's problems are different, so I can only say "analyze your opportunities and conditions and study your natural abilities." Form plans for improvement and then put them into operation. Now, as I said before, don't just say, "I am going to do so and so," but carry your plan into execution. Don't make an indefinite plan, but a definite one, and then don't give up until your object has been accomplished. Put these suggestions into practice with true earnestness, and you will soon note astonishing results, and your whole life will be completely changed. An excellent motto for one of pure motives is: Through my will power I dare do what I want to. You will find this affirmation has a very strengthening effect.

THE SPIRIT OF PERSEVERANCE

The spirit of "sticktoitiveness" is the one that wins. Many go just so far and then give up, whereas, if they had persevered a little longer, they would have won out. Many have much initiative, but instead of concentrating it into one channel, they diffuse it through several, thereby dissipating it to such an extent that its effect is lost.

Develop more determination, which is only the Will to Do, and when you start out to do something stick to it until you get results. Of course, before starting anything you must look ahead and see what the "finish leads to." You must select a road that will lead to "somewhere," rather than "nowhere." The journey must be productive of some kind of substantial results. The trouble with so many young men is that they launch enterprises without any end in sight. It is not so much the start as the finish of a journey that counts. Each little move should bring you nearer the goal which you planned to reach before the enterprise began.

Lack of perseverance is nothing but the lack of the Will to Do. It takes the same energy to say, "I will continue," as to say, "I give up." Just the moment you say the latter you shut off your dynamo, and your determination is gone. Every time you allow your determination to be broken you weaken it. Don't forget this. Just the instant you notice your determination beginning to weaken, concentrate on it and by sheer Will Power make it continue on the "job."

Never try to make a decision when you are not in a calm state of mind. If in a "quick temper," you are likely to say things you afterwards regret. In anger, you follow impulse rather than reason. No one can expect to achieve success if he makes decisions when not in full control of his mental forces.

Therefore make it a fixed rule to make decisions only when at your best. If you have a "quick temper," you can quickly gain control over it by simple rule of counting backwards. To count backwards requires concentration, and you thus quickly regain a calm state. In this way you can break the "temper habit."

It will do you a lot of good to think over what you said and thought the last time you were angry. Persevere until you see yourself as others see you. It would do no harm to write the scene out in story form and then sit in judgment of the character who played your part.

SPECIAL INSTRUCTIONS TO DEVELOP THE WILL TO DO

This is a form of mental energy, but requires the proper mental attitude to make it manifest. We hear of people having wonderful will power, which is really wrong. It should be said that they use their will power while with many it is a latent force. I want you to realize that no one has a monopoly on will power. There is plenty for all. What we speak of as will power is but the gathering together of mental energy, the concentration power at one point. So never think of that person as having a stronger will than yours. Each person will be supplied with just that amount of will power that he demands. You don't have to develop will power if you constantly make use of all you have, and remember the way in which you use it determines your fate, for your life is moulded to great extent by the use you make of your will. Unless you make proper use of it you have neither independence nor firmness. You are unable to control yourself and become a mere machine for others to use. It is more important to learn to use your will than to develop your intellect. The man who has not learned how to use his will rarely decides things for himself, but allows his resolutions to be changed by others. He fluctuates from one opinion to another, and of course does not accomplish anything out of the ordinary, while his brother with the trained will takes his place among the world's leaders.

LESSON 7

The Concentrated Mental Demand

The Mental Demand is the potent force in achievement. The attitude of the mind affects the expression of the face, determines action, changes our physical condition and regulates our lives.

I will not here attempt to explain the silent force that achieves results. You want to develop your mental powers so you can effect the thing sought, and that is what I want to teach you. There is wonderful power and possibility in the concentrated Mental Demand. This, like all other forces, is controlled by laws. It can, like all other forces, be wonderfully increased by consecutive, systematized effort.

The Mental Demand must be directed by every power of the mind and every possible element should be used to make the demand materialize. You can so intently desire a thing that you can exclude all distracting thoughts. When you practice this singleness of concentration until you attain the end sought, you have developed a Will capable of accomplishing whatever you wish.

As long as you can only do the ordinary things you will be counted in the mass of mediocrity. But just as quick as you surpass others by even comparatively small measure, you are classed as one of life's successes. So, if you wish to emerge into prominence, you must accomplish something more than the ordinary man or woman. It is easy to do this if you will but concentrate on what you desire, and put forth your best effort. It is not the runner with the longest legs or the strongest muscles who wins the race, but the one who can put forth the greatest desire force. You can best understand this by thinking of an engine. The engine starts up slowly, the engineer gradually extending the throttle to the top notch. It is then keyed up to its maximum speed. The same is true of two runners. They start off together and gradually they increase their desire to go faster. The one who has the greatest intensity of desire will win. He may outdistance the other by only a fraction of an inch, yet he gets the laurels.

The men who are looked upon as the world's successes have not always been men of great physical power, nor at the start did they seem very well adapted to the conditions which encompassed them. In the beginning they were not considered men of superior genius, but they won their success by their resolution to achieve results in their undertakings by permitting no set-back to dishearten them; no difficulties to daunt them. Nothing could turn them or influence them against their determination. They never lost sight of their goal. In all of us there is this silent force of wonderful power. If developed, it can overcome conditions that would seem insurmountable. It is constantly urging us on to great achievement. The more we become acquainted with it the better strategists we become, the more courage we develop and the greater the desire within us for self-expression in activity along many lines.

No one will ever be a failure if he becomes conscious of this silent force within that controls his destiny. But without the consciousness of this inner force, you will not have a clear vision, and external conditions will not yield to the power of your mind. It is the mental resolve that makes achievement possible. Once this has been formed it should never be allowed to cease to press its claim until its object is attained. To make plans work out it will, at times, be necessary to use every power of your mind. Patience, perseverance, and all the indomitable forces within one will have to be mustered and used with the greatest effectiveness.

Perseverance is the first element of success. In order to persevere you must be ceaseless in your application. It requires you to concentrate your thoughts upon your undertaking and bring every energy to bear upon keeping them focused upon it until you have accomplished your aim. To quit short of this is to weaken all future efforts.

The Mental Demand seems an unreal power because it is intangible; but it is the mightiest power in the world. It is a power that is free for you to use. No one can use it for you. The Mental Demand is not a visionary one. It is a potent force, which you can use freely without cost. When you are in doubt it will counsel you. It will guide you when you are uncertain. When you are in fear it will give you courage. It is the motive power which supplies the energies necessary to the achievement of the purpose. You have a large storehouse of possibilities. The Mental Demand makes possibilities realities. It supplies everything necessary for the accomplishment. It selects the tools and instructs how to use them. It makes you understand the situation. Every time you make a Mental Demand you strengthen the brain centers by drawing to you external forces.

Few realize the power of a Mental Demand. It is possible to make your demand so strong that you can impart what you have to say to another without speaking to him. Have you ever, after planning to discuss a certain matter with a friend, had the experience of having him broach the subject before you had a chance to speak of it? Have you ever, in a letter, made a suggestion to a friend that he carried out before your letter reached him? Have you ever wanted to speak to a person who, just then walked in or telephoned. I have had many such responses to thought and you and your friends have doubtless experienced them, too.

These two things are neither coincidences nor accidents, but are the results of Mental Demand launched by strong concentration.

The person who never wants anything gets little. To demand resolutely is the first step toward getting what you want.

The power of the Mental Demand seems absolute, the supply illimitable. The Mental Demand projects itself and causes to materialize the conditions and opportunities needed to accomplish the purpose. Do not think I over-estimate the value of the Mental Demand. It brings the fuller life if used for only righteous purposes. Once the Mental Demand is made, however, never let it falter. If you do the current that connects you with your desire is broken. Take all the necessary time to build a firm foundation, so that there need not be even an element of doubt to creep in. Just the moment you entertain "doubt" you lose some of the demand force, and force once lost is hard to regain. So whenever you make a mental demand hold steadfastly to it until your need is supplied.

I want to repeat again that Power of Mental Demand is not a visionary one. It is concentrated power only, and can be used by you. It is not supernatural power, but requires a development of the brain centers. The outcome is sure when it is given with a strong resolute determination.

No person will advance to any great extent, until he recognizes this force within him. If you have not become aware of it, you have not made very much of a success of your life. It is this "something" that distinguishes that "man" from other men. It is this subtle power that develops strong personality.

If you want a great deal you must demand a great deal. Once you make your demand, anticipate its fulfillment. It depends upon us. We are rewarded according to our efforts. The Power of Mental Demand can bring us what we want. We become what we determine to be. We control our own destiny.

Get the right mental attitude, then in accordance with your ability you can gain success.

And every man of AVERAGE ability, the ordinary man whom you see about you, can be really successful, independent, free of worry, HIS OWN MASTER, if he can manage to do just two things.

First, remain forever dissatisfied with what he IS doing and with what he HAS accomplished.

Second, develop in his mind a belief that the word "impossible" was not intended for him. Build up in his mind the confidence that enables the mind to use its power.

Many, especially the older men, will ask:

"How can I build up that self-confidence in my brain? How can I, after months and years of discouragement, of dull plodding, suddenly conceive and carry out a plan for doing something that will make life worthwhile and change the monotonous routine?"

"How can a man get out of a rut after he has been in it for years and has settled down to the slow jog-trot that leads to the grave?"

The answer is the thing can be done, and millions have done it.

One of the names most honored among the great men of France is that of Littre, who wrote and compiled the great French dictionary—a monument of learning. He is the man whose place among the forty immortals of France was taken by the great Pasteur, when the latter was elected to the Academy.

Littre BEGAN the work that makes him famous when he was more than sixty years old.

LESSON 8

Concentration Gives Mental Poise

You will find that the man who concentrates is well poised, whereas the man who allows his mind to wander is easily upset. When in this state wisdom does not pass from the subconscious storehouse into the consciousness. There must be mental quiet before the two consciousnesses can work in harmony. When you are able to concentrate you have peace of mind.

If you are in the habit of losing your poise, form the habit of reading literature that has a quieting power. Just the second you feel your poise slipping, say, "Peace," and then hold this thought in mind and you will never lose your self-control.

There cannot be perfect concentration until there is peace of mind. So keep thinking peace, acting peace, until you are at peace with all the world. For when once you have reached this state there will be no trouble to concentrate on anything you wish.

When you have peace of mind you are not timid or anxious, or fearful, or rigid and you will not allow any disturbing thought to influence you. You cast aside all fears, and think of yourself as a spark of the Divine Being, as a manifestation of the "One Universal Principle" that fills all space and time. Think of yourself thus as a child of the infinite, possessing infinite possibilities.

Write on a piece of paper, "I have the power to do and to be whatever I wish to do and be." Keep this mentally before you, and you will find the thought will be of great help to you.

THE MISTAKE OF CONCENTRATING ON YOUR BUSINESS WHILE AWAY

In order to be successful today, you must concentrate, but don't become a slave to concentration, and carry your business cares home. Just as sure as you do you will be burning the life forces at both ends and the fire will go out much sooner than was intended.

Many men become so absorbed in their business that when they go to church they do not hear the preacher because their minds are on their business. If they go to the theater they do not enjoy it because their business is on their minds. When they go to bed they think about business instead of sleep and wonder why they don't sleep. This is the wrong kind of concentration and is dangerous. It is involuntary. When you are unable to get anything out of your mind it becomes unwholesome as any thought held continuously causes weariness of the flesh. It is a big mistake to let a thought rule you, instead of ruling it. He who does not rule himself is not a success. If you cannot control your concentration, your health will suffer.

So never become so absorbed with anything that you cannot lay it aside and take up another. This is self-control.

CONCENTRATION IS PAYING ATTENTION TO A CHOSEN THOUGHT

Everything that passes before the eye makes an impression on the subconscious mind, but unless you pay attention to some certain thing you will not remember what you saw. For instance if you walked down a busy street without seeing anything that attracted your particular attention, you could not recall anything you saw. So you see only what attracts your attention. If you work you only see and remember what you think about. When you concentrate on something it absorbs your whole thought.

SELF-STUDY VALUABLE

Everyone has some habits that can be overcome by concentration. We will say for instance, you are in the habit of complaining, or finding fault with yourself or others; or imagining that you do not possess the ability of others; or feeling that you are not as good as someone else; or that you cannot rely on yourself; or harboring any similar thought or thoughts of weakness. These should be cast aside and instead thoughts of strength should be put in their place. Just remember every time you think of yourself as being weak, in some way you are making yourself so by thinking you are. Our mental conditions make us what we are. Just watch yourself and see how much time you waste in worrying, fretting and complaining. The more of it you do the worse off you are.

Just the minute you are aware of thinking a negative thought immediately change to a positive one. If you start to think of failure, change to thinking of success. You have the germ of success within you. Care for it the same as the setting hen broods over the eggs and you can make it a reality.

You can make those who you come in contact with feel as you do, because you radiate vibrations of the way you feel and your vibrations are felt by others. When you concentrate on a certain thing you turn all the rays of your vibrations on this. Thought is the directing power of all life's vibrations. If a person should enter a room with a lot of people and feel as if he were a person of no consequence no one would know he was there unless they saw him, and even if they did, they would not remember seeing him, because they were not attracted towards him. But let him enter the room feeling that he was magnetic and concentrating on this thought, others would feel his vibration. So remember the way you feel you can make others feel. This is the law. Make yourself a concentrated dynamo from which your thoughts vibrate to others. Then you are a power in the world. Cultivate the art of feeling, for as I said before you can only make others feel what you feel.

If you will study all of the great characters of history you will find that they were enthusiastic. First they were enthusiastic themselves, and then they could arouse others' enthusiasm. It is latent in everyone. It is a wonderful force when once aroused. All public men to be a success have to possess it. Cultivate it by concentration. Set aside some hour of the day, wherein to hold rapt converse with the soul. Meditate with sincere desire and contrite heart and you will be able to accomplish that which you have meditated on. This is the keynote of success.

"Think, speak and act just as you wish to be, And you will be that which you wish to be."

You are just what you think you are and not what you may appear to be. You may fool others but not yourself. You may control your life and actions just as you can control your hands. If you want to raise your hand you must first think of raising it. If you want to control your life you must first control your thinking. Easy to do, is it not? Yes it is, if you will but concentrate on what you think about.

For he only can
Who says he will.

"How can we secure concentration? To this question, the first and last answer must be: By interest and strong motive. The stronger the motive the greater the concentration."—Eustace Miller, M.D.

THE SUCCESSFUL LIVES ARE THE CONCENTRATED LIVES

The utterly helpless multitude who sooner or later have to be cared for by charity, are those who were never able to concentrate, and who have become the victims of negative ideas.

Train yourself so you will be able to centralize your thought and develop your brain power, and increase your mental energy, or you can be a slacker, a drifter, a quitter or a sleeper. It all depends on how you concentrate, or centralize your thoughts. Your thinking then becomes a fixed power and you do not waste time thinking about something that would not be good for you. You pick out the thoughts that will be the means of bringing you what you desire, and they become a material reality. Whatever we create in the thought world will some day materialize. That is the law. Don't forget this.

In the old days men drifted without concentration but this is a day of efficiency and therefore all of our efforts must be concentrated, if we are to win any success worth the name.

WHY PEOPLE OFTEN DO NOT GET WHAT THEY CONCENTRATE ON

Because they sit down in hopeless despair and expect it to come to them. But if they will just reach out for it with their biggest effort they will find it is within their reach. No one limits us but ourselves. We are what we are today as the result of internal conditions. We can control the external conditions. They are subject to our will.

Through our concentration we can attract what we want, because we became enrapport with the Universal forces, from which we can get what we want.

You have watched races no doubt. They all line up together. Each has his mind set on getting to the goal before the others. This is one kind of concentration. A man starts to think on a certain subject. He has all kinds of thoughts come to him, but by concentration he shuts out all these but the one he has chosen. Concentration is just a case of willing to do a certain thing and doing it.

If you want to accomplish anything first put yourself in a concentrating, reposeful, receptive, acquiring frame of mind. In tackling unfamiliar work make haste slowly and deliberately and then you will secure that interior activity, which is never possible when you are in a hurry or under a strain. When you "think hard" or try to hurry results too quickly, you generally shut off the interior flow of thoughts and ideas. You have often no doubt tried hard to think of something but could not, but just as soon as you stopped trying to think of it, it came to you.

LESSON 9

Concentration Can Overcome Bad Habits

Habits make or break us to a far greater extent than we like to admit. Habit is both a powerful enemy and wonderful ally of concentration. You must learn to overcome habits which are injurious to concentration and to cultivate those which increase it.

The large majority of people are controlled by their habits and are buffeted around by them like waves of the ocean tossing a piece of wood. They do things in a certain way because of the power of habit. They seldom ever think of concentrating on why they do them this or that way, or study to see if they could do them in a better way. Now my object in this chapter is to get you to concentrate on your habits so you can find out which are good and which are bad for you. You will find that by making a few needed changes you can make even those that are not good for you, of service; the good habits you can make much better.

The first thing I want you to realize is that all habits are governed consciously or unconsciously by the will. Most of us are forming new habits all the time. Very often, if you repeat something several times in the same way, you will have formed the habit of doing it that way. But the oftener you repeat it the stronger that habit grows and the more deeply it becomes embedded in your nature. After a habit has been in force for a long time, it becomes almost a part of you, and is therefore hard to overcome. But you can still break any habit by strong concentration on its opposite.

"All our life, so far as it has definite form, is but a mass of habits—practical, emotional, and intellectual — systematically organized, for our weal or woe, and bearing us irresistibly toward our destiny whatever the latter may be."

We are creatures of habits, "imitators and copiers of our past selves." We are liable to be "bent" or "curved" as we can bend a piece of paper, and each fold leaves a crease, which makes it easier to make the fold there the next time. "The intellect and will are spiritual functions; still they are immersed in matter, and to every movement of theirs corresponds a movement in the brain, that is, in their material correlative." This is why habits of thought and habits of willing can be formed. All physical impressions are the carrying out of the actions of the will and intellect. Our nervous systems are what they are today because of the way they have been exercised.

As we grow older most of us become more and more like automatic machines. The habits we have formed increase in strength. We work in our old characteristic way. Your associates learn to expect you to do things in a certain way. So you see that your habits make a great difference in your life, and as it is just about as easy to form good habits as it is bad, you should form only the former. No one but yourself is responsible for your habits. You are free to form the habits that you should and if everyone could realize the importance of forming the right kind of habits what a different world this would be. How much happier everyone would be. Then all instead of the few might win success.

Habits are formed more quickly when we are young, but if we have already passed the youthful plastic period the time to start to control our habits is right now, as we will never be any younger.

You will find the following maxims worth remembering.

FIRST MAXIM

"We must make our nervous system our ally instead of our enemy."

SECOND MAXIM

"In the acquisition of a new habit as in the leaving off of an old one, we must take care to launch ourselves with as strong and decided an initiative as possible."

The man who is in the habit of doing the right thing from boyhood, has only good motives, so it is very important for you that you concentrate assiduously on the habits that reinforce good motives. Surround yourself with every aid you can. Don't play with fire by forming bad habits. Make a new beginning today. Study why you have been doing certain things. If they are not for your good, shun them henceforth. Don't give in to a single temptation, for every time you do, you strengthen the chain of bad habits. Every time you keep a resolution you break the chain that enslaves you.

THIRD MAXIM

"Never allow an exception to occur till the new habit is securely rooted in your life."

Here is the idea, you never want to give in, until the new habit is fixed else you undo all that has been accomplished by previous efforts. There are two opposing inclinations. One wants to be firm, and the other wants to give in. By your will you can become firm, through repetition. Fortify your will to be able to cope with any and all opposition.

FOURTH MAXIM

"Seize the very first possible opportunity to act on every resolution you make, and on every emotional prompting you may experience in the direction of the habits you aspire to gain."

To make a resolution and not to keep it is of little value. So by all means keep every resolution you make, for you not only profit by the resolution, but if furnishes you with an exercise that causes the brain cells and physiological correlatives to form the habit of adjusting themselves to carry out resolutions. "A tendency to act, becomes effectively engrained in us in proportion to the uninterrupted frequency with which the actions actually occur, and the brain 'grows' to their use. When a resolve or a fine glow of feeling is allowed to evaporate without bearing fruit, it is worse than a chance lost."

If you keep your resolutions you form a most valuable habit. If you break them you form a most dangerous one. So concentrate on keeping them, whether important or unimportant, and remember it is just as important for this purpose to keep the unimportant, for by so doing you are forming the habit.

FIFTH MAXIM

"Keep the faculty of effort alive in you by a little gratuitous exercise every day."

The more we exercise the will, the better we can control our habits. "Every few days do something for no other reason than its difficulty, so that when the hour of dire need draws nigh, it may find you not unnerved or untrained to stand the test. Asceticism of this sort is like the insurance which a man pays on his house and goods. The tax does him no good at the time, and possibly may never bring him a return, but if the fire does come, his having paid it will be his salvation from ruin. So with the man who has daily insured himself to habits of concentrated attention, energetic volation, and self-denial in unnecessary things. "He will stand like a tower when everything rocks around him and his softer fellow-mortals are winnowed like chaff in the blast."

The young should be made to concentrate on their habits and be made to realize that if they don't they become walking bundles of injurious habits. Youth is the plastic state, and should be utilized in laying the foundations for a glorous future.

The great value of habit for good and evil cannot be over estimated. "Habit is the deepest law of human nature." No man is stronger than his habits, because his habits either build up his strength or decrease it.

WHY WE ARE CREATURES OF HABITS

Habits have often been called a labor-saving invention, because when they are formed they require less of both mental and material strength. The more deeply the habit becomes ingrained the more automatic it becomes. Therefore habit is an economizing tendency of our nature, for if it were not for habit we should have to be more watchful. We walk across a crowded street; the habit of stopping and looking prevents us from being hurt. The right kind of habits keeps us from making mistakes and mishaps. It is a well known fact that a chauffeur is not able to master his machine safely until he has trained his body in a habitual way. When an emergency comes he instantly knows what to do. Where safety depends on quickness the operator must work automatically. Habits means less risk, less fatigue, and greater accuracy.

"You do not want to become a slave to habits of a trivial nature. For instance, Wagner required a certain costume before he could compose corresponding parts of his operas. Schiller could never write with ease unless there were rotten apples in the drawer of his desk from which he could now and then obtain an odor which seemed to him sweet. Gladstone had different desks for his different activities, so that when he worked on Homer he never sat among habitual accompaniments of his legislative labors."

In order to over come undesirable habits, two things are necessary. You must have trained your will to do what you want it to do, and the stronger the will the easier it will be to break a habit. Then you must make a resolution to do just the opposite of what the habit is. Therefore one habit must replace another. If you have a strong will, you can tenaciously and persistently concentrate on removing the bad habit and in a very short time the good habit will gain the upper hand. I will bring this chapter to a close by giving Doctor Oppenheim's instructions for overcoming a habit:

"If you want to abolish a habit, and its accumulated circumstances as well, you must grapple with the matter as earnestly as you would with a physical enemy. You must go into the encounter with all tenacity of determination, with all fierceness of resolve—yea, even with a passion for success that may be called vindictive. No human enemy can be as insidious, so perservering, as unrelenting as an unfavorable habit. It never sleeps, it needs no rest.

"It is like a parasite that grows with the growth of the supporting body, and, like a parasite, it can best be killed by violent separation and crushing."

When life is stormy and all seems against us, that is when we often acquire wrong habits, and it is then that we have to make a gigantic effort to think and speak as we should; and even though we may feel the very reverse at that moment, the tiniest effort will be backed up by a tremendous Power and will lift us to a realization never felt before. It is not in the easy, contented moments of our life that we make our greatest progress, for then it requires no special effort to keep in tune. But it is when we are in the midst of trials and misfortunes, when we think we are sinking, being overwhelmed, then it is important for us to realize that we are linked to a great Power and if we live as we should, there is nothing that can occur in life, which could permanently injure us, nothing can happen that should disturb us. So always remember you have within you unlimited power, ready to manifest itself in the form which fills our need at the moment. If, when we have something difficult to solve, we would be silent like the child, we can get the inspiration when it comes; we will know how to act, we will find there is no need to hurry or disturb ourselves, that it is always wiser to wait for guidance from Within, than to act on impulses from Without.

LESSON 10

Business Results Through Concentration

A successful business is not usually the result of chance. Neither is a failure the result of luck. Most failures could be determined in advance if the founders had been studied. It is not always possible to start a money-making business at the start. Usually a number of changes have to be made. Plans do not work out as their creators thought they would. They may have to be changed a little, broadened it may be, here and there, and as you broaden your business you broaden your power to achieve. You gain an intense and sustained desire to make your business a success.

When you start a business you may have but a vague notion of the way you will conduct it. You must fill in the details as you go along. You must concentrate on these details. As you straighten out one after another, others will require attention. In this way you cover the field of "the first endeavor" and new opportunities open up for you.

When you realize one desire, another comes. But if you do not fulfill the first desire, you will not the second. The person who does not carry his desires into action is only a dreamer. Desire is a great creative force, if it is pure, intense and sustained. It is our desires that keep stirring us up to action and they will strengthen and broaden you if you make them materialize.

Every man who achieves success deserves it. When he first started out he did not understand how to solve the problems that afterwards presented themselves, but he did each thing as it came up in the very best way that he could, and this developed his power of doing bigger things. We become masters of business by learning to do well whatever we attempt. The man who has a thorough knowledge of his business can of course direct it much more easily and skillfully than the man who lacks that knowledge. The skilled business director can sit in his private office and still know acurately what is actually being done. He knows what should be done in any given time and if it is not accomplished he knows that his employees are not turning out the work that they should. It is then easy to apply the remedy.

Business success depends on well-concentrated efforts. You must use every mental force you can master. The more these are used the more they increase. Therefore the more you accomplish today the more force you will have at your disposal with which to solve your problems tomorrow.

If you are working for someone else today and wish to start in a business for yourself, think over carefully what you would like to do. Then when you have resolved what you want to do, you will be drawn towards it. There is a law that opens the way to the fulfillment of your desires. Of course back of your desire you must put forward the necessary effort to carry out your purpose; you must use your power to put your desires into force. Once they are created and you keep up your determination to have them fulfilled you both consciously and unconsciously work toward their materialization. Set your heart on your purpose; concentrate your thought upon it, direct your efforts with all your intelligence and in due time you will realize your ambition.

Feel yourself a success, believe you are a success and thus put yourself in the attitude that demands recognition and the thought current draws to you what you need to make you a success. Don't be afraid of big undertakings. Go at them with grit, and pursue methods that you think will accomplish your purpose. You may not at first meet with entire success, but aim so high that if you fall a little short you will still have accomplished much.

What others have done you can do. You may even do what others have been unable to do. Always keep a strong desire to succeed in your mind. Be in love with your aim and work, and make them, as far as possible, square with the rule of the greatest good to the greatest number and your life cannot be a failure.

The successful business attitude must be cultivated to make the most out of your life, the attitude of expecting great things from both yourself and others. It alone will often cause men to make good; to measure up to the best that is in them.

It is not the spasmodic spurts that count on a long journey, but the steady efforts. Spurts fatigue and make it hard for you to continue.

Rely on your own opinion. It should be as good as anyone else's. When once you reach a conclusion abide by it. Let there be no doubt, or wavering in your judgment. If you are uncertain about every decision you make, you will be subject to harassing doubts and fears which will render your judgment of little value. The man who decides according to what he thinks right and who learns from every mistake acquires a well balanced mind that gets the best results. He gains the confidence of others. He is known as the man who knows what he wants, and not as one who is as changeable as the weather. The man of today wants to do business with the man whom he can depend upon. Uncertainties in the business world are meeting with more disfavor. Reliable firms want to do business with men of known qualities, with men of firmness, judgment and reliability.

So if you wish to start in business for yourself, your greatest asset, with the single exception of a sound physique, is that of a good reputation.

A successful business is not hard to build if we can concentrate all our mental forces upon it. It is the man who is unsettled because he does not know what he wants who goes to the wall. We hear persons say that business is trying on the nerves, but it is the unsettling elements of fret and worry and suspense that are nerve-exhausting and not the business. Executing one's plans may cause fatigue, enjoyment comes with rest. If there has not been any unnatural strain, the recuperative powers replace what energy has been lost.

By attending to each day's work properly you develop the capacity to do a greater work tomorrow. It is this gradual development that makes possible the carrying out of big plans. The man who figures out doing something each hour of the day gets somewhere. At the end of each day you should be a step nearer your aim. Keep the idea in mind, that you mean to go forward, that each day must mark an advance and forward you will go. You do not even have to know the exact direction so long as you are determined to find the way. But you must not turn back once you have started.

Even brilliant men's conceptions of the possibilities of their mental forces are so limited and below their real worth that they are far more likely to belittle their possibilities than they are to exaggerate them. You don't want to think that an aim is impossible because it has never been realized in the past. Every day someone is doing something that was never done before. We are pushing ahead faster. Formerly it took decades to build up a big business, but today it is only but a matter of years, sometimes of months.

Plan each day's activities carefully and you can reach any height you aim at. If each thing you do is done with concise and concentrated thought you will be able to turn out an excellent quality and a large quantity of work. Plan to do so much work during the day and you will be astonished to see how much more you will do, than on other days, when you had not decided on any certain amount. I have demonstrated that the average business working force could do the same amount of work in six hours that they now do in eight, without using up any more energy. Never start to accomplish anything in an indecisive, indefinite, uncertain way. Tackle everything with a positiveness and an earnestness that will concentrate your mind and attract the very best associated thoughts. You will in a short time find that you will have extra time for planning bigger things.

The natural leader always draws to himself, by the law of mental attraction, ideas in his chosen subject that have ever been conceived by others. This is of the greatest importance and help. If you are properly trained you benefit much by others' thoughts, and providing you generate from within yourself something of value, they will benefit from yours. "We are heirs of all the ages," but we must know how to use our inheritance.

The confident, pushing, hopeful, determined man influences all with whom he associates, and inspires the same qualities in them. You feel that his is a safe example to follow and he arouses the same force within you that is pushing him onward and upward.

One seldom makes a success of anything that he goes at in a listless, spiritless way. To build up a business you must see it expanding in your mind before it actually takes tangible shape. Every great task that has ever been accomplished has first been merely a vision in the mind of its creator. Detail after detail has had to be worked out in his mind from his first faint idea of the enterprise. Finally a clear idea was formed and then the accomplishment, which was only the material result of the mental concept, followed.

The up-to-date businessman is not content to build only for the present, but is planning ahead. If he does not he will fall behind his competitor, who is. What we are actually doing today was carefully thought out and planned by others in the past. All progressive businesses are conducted this way. That is why the young businessman of today is likely to accomplish more in a few years than his father did in all his life. There is no reason why your work or business should fag you out. When it does there is something wrong. You are attracting forces and influence that you should not, because you are not in harmony with what you are doing. There is nothing so tiring as to try to do the work for which we are unfitted, both by temperament and training.

Each one should be engaged in a business that he loves; he should be furthering movements with which he is in sympathy. He will then only do his best work and take intense pleasure in his business. In this way, while constantly growing and developing his powers, he is at the same time rendering through his work, genuine and devoted service to humanity.

Business success is not the result of chance, but of scientific ideas and plans carried out by an aggressive and progressive management. Use your mental forces so that they will grow and develop. Remember that everything you do is the result of mental action, therefore you can completely control your every action. Nothing is impossible for you. Don't be afraid to tackle a difficult proposition. Your success will depend upon the use you make of your mind. That is capable of wonderful development. See that you make full use of it, and not only develop yourself but your associates. Try to broaden the visions of those with whom you come in contact and you will broaden your own outlook of life.

ARE YOU AFRAID OF RESPONSIBILITIES?

In order for the individual soul to develop, you must have responsibilities. You must manifest the omnipotence of the law of supply. The whole world is your legitimate sphere of activity. How much of a conqueror are you? What have you done? Are you afraid of responsibility, or are you ever dodging, flinching, or side-stepping it? If you are, you are not a Real Man. Your higher self never winces, so be a man and allow the powers of the higher self to manifest and you will find you have plenty of strength and you will feel better when you are tackling difficult propositions.

LESSON 11

Concentrate on Your Courage

Courage is the backbone of man. The man with courage has persistence. He states what he believes and puts it into execution. The courageous man has confidence. He draws to himself all the moral qualities and mental forces which go to make up a strong man. Whereas, the man without courage draws to himself all the qualities of a weak man, vacillation, doubt, hesitancy, and unsteadiness of purpose. You can therefore see the value of concentration on courage. It is a most vital element of success.

The lack of courage creates financial, as well as mental and moral difficulties. When a new problem comes, instead of looking upon it as something to be achieved, the man or woman without courage looks for reasons why it cannot be done and failure is naturally the almost inevitable result. This is a subject well worthy of your study. Look upon everything within your power as a possibility instead of as merely a probability and you will accomplish a great deal more, because by considering a thing as impossible, you immediately draw to yourself all the elements that contribute to failure. Lack of courage destroys your confidence in yourself. It destroys that forceful, resolute attitude so important to success.

The man without courage unconsciously draws to himself all that is contemptible, weakening, demoralizing and destructive. He then blames his luck when he does not secure the things he weakly desires. We must first have the courage to strongly desire something. A desire to be fulfilled must be backed by the strength of all our mental forces. Such a desire has enough commanding force to change all unfavorable conditions. The man with courage commands, whether he is on the battlefield or in business life.

What is courage? It is the Will to Do. It takes no more energy to be courageous than to be cowardly. It is a matter of the right training in the right way. Courage concentrates the mental forces on the task at hand. It then directs them thoughtfully, steadily, deliberately, while attracting all the forces of success, toward the desired end. Cowardice on the other hand, dissipates both our mental and moral forces, thereby inviting failure.

As we are creatures of habits, we should avoid persons who lack courage. They are easy to discover because of their habits of fear in attacking new problems. The man with courage is never afraid.

Start out today with the idea that there is no reason why you should not be courageous.

If any fear-thoughts come to you cast them off as you would the deadly viper. Form the habit of never thinking of anything unfavorable to yourself or anyone else. In dealing with difficulties, new or old, hold ever the thought, "I am courageous." Whenever a doubt crosses the threshold of your mind, banish it. Remember, you as master of your mind control its every thought, and here is a good one to often affirm, "I have courage because I desire it; because I need it; because I use it and because I refuse to become such a weakling as cowardice produces."

There is no justification for the loss of courage. The evils by which you will almost certainly be overwhelmed without it are far greater than those which courage will help you to meet and overcome. Right, then, must be the moralist who says that the only thing to fear is fear.

Never let another's opinion affect you; he cannot tell what you are able to do; he does not know what you can do with your forces. The truth is you do not know yourself until you put yourself to the test. Therefore, how can someone else know? Never let anyone else put a valuation on you.

Almost all wonderful achievements have been accomplished after it had been "thoroughly" demonstrated that they were impossibilities. Once we understand the law, things are possible. If they were impossibilities we could not conceive them.

Just the moment you allow someone to influence you against what you think is right, you lose that confidence in yourself that inspires courage and carries with it all the forces which courage creates. Just the moment you begin to swerve in your plan you begin to carry out another's thought and not your own. You become the directed and not the director. You forsake the courage and resolution of your own mind, and you therefore lack the very forces that you need to sustain and carry out your work. Instead of being self-reliant you become timid and this invites failure. When you permit yourself to be influenced from your plan by another, you are unable to judge as you should, because you have allowed another's influence to deprive you of your courage and determination without absorbing any of his in return so you are in much the same predicament, as you would be in if you turned over all your worldly possessions to another without getting "value received."

Concentrate on just the opposite of fear, want, poverty, sickness, etc. Never doubt your own ability. You have plenty, if you will just use it. A great many men are failures because they doubt their own capacity. Instead of building up strong mental forces which would be of the greatest use to them their fear-thoughts tear them down. Fear paralyzes energy. It keeps us from attracting the forces that go to make up success. Fear is the worst enemy we have.

There are few people who really know that they can accomplish much. They desire the full extent of their powers, but alas, it is only occasionally that you find a man who is aware of the great possibilities within him. When you believe with all your mind and heart and soul that you can do something, you thereby develop the courage to steadily and confidently live up to that belief. You have now gone a long way towards accomplishing it. The chances are that there will be obstacles, big and little, in your way, but resolute courage will overcome them and nothing else will. Strong courage eliminates the injurious and opposing forces by summoning their masters, the yet stronger forces that will serve you.

Courage is yours for the asking. All you have to do is to believe in it, claim it and use it. To succeed in business believe that it will be successful, assert that it is successful, and work like a beaver to make it so. Difficulties soon melt away before the courageous. One man of courage can fire with his spirit a whole army of men, whether it be military or industrial, because courage, like cowardice, is contagious.

The man of courage overcomes the trials and temptations of life; he commands success; he renders sound judgment; he develops personal influence and a forceful character and often becomes the mentor of the community which he serves.

HOW TO OVERCOME DEPRESSION AND MELANCHOLIA

Both of the former are harmful and make you unhappy. These are states that can be quickly overcome through concentrating more closely on the higher self, for when you do you cut off the connection with the harmful force currents. You can also drive away moods by simply choosing and fully concentrating on an agreeable subject. Through will power and thought control we can accomplish anything we want to do. There is wonderful inherent power within us all, and there is never any sufficient cause for fear, except ignorance.

Every evil is but the product of ignorance, and everyone who possesses the power to think has the power to overcome ignorance and evil. The pain that we suffer from doing evil are but the lessons of experience, and the object of the pain is to make us realize our ignorance. When we become depressed it is evidence that our thought faculties are combining improperly and thereby attracting the wrong force-currents.

All that it is necessary to do is to exercise the will and concentrate upon happy subjects. I will only think of objects worthy of my higher self and its powers.

LESSON 12

Concentrate on Wealth

It was never intended that man should be poor. When wealth is obtained under the proper conditions it broadens the life. Everything has its value. Everything has a good use and a bad use. The forces of mind, like wealth, can be directed either for good or evil. A little rest will re-create forces. Too much rest degenerates into laziness, and brainless, dreamy longings.

If you acquire wealth unjustly from others, you are misusing your forces; but if your wealth comes through the right sources you will be blessed. Through wealth we can do things to uplift ourselves and humanity.

Wealth is many persons' goal. It therefore stimulates their endeavor. They long for it in order to dress and live in such a way as to attract friends. Without friends they would not be so particular of their surroundings. The fact is the more attractive we make ourselves and our surroundings the more inspiring are their influences. It is not conducive to proper thought to be surrounded by conditions that are congenial and unpleasant.

So the first step toward acquiring wealth is to surround yourself with helpful influences; to claim for yourself an environment of culture, place yourself in it and be molded by its influences.

Most great men of all ages have been comparatively rich. They have made or inherited money. Without money they could not have accomplished what they did. The man engaged in physical drudgery is not likely to have the same high ideals as the man who can command comparative leisure.

Wealth is usually the fruit of achievement. It is not, however, altogether the result of being industrious. Thousands of persons work hard and never grow wealthy. Others with much less effort acquire wealth. Seeing possibilities is another step toward acquiring wealth. A man may be as industrious as he can possibly be, but if he does not use his mental forces he will be a laborer, to be directed by the man who uses to good advantage his mental forces.

No one can become wealthy in an ordinary lifetime, by mere savings from earnings. Many scrimp and economize all their lives; but by so doing waste all their vitality and energy. For example, I know a man who used to walk to work. It took him an hour to go and an hour to return. He could have taken a car and gone in twenty minutes. He saved ten cents a day but wasted an hour and a half. It was not a very profitable investment unless the time spent in physical exercise yielded him large returns in the way of health.

The same amount of time spent in concentrated effort to overcome his unfavorable business environment might have firmly planted his feet in the path of prosperity.

One of the big mistakes made by many persons of the present generation is that they associate with those who fail to call out or develop the best that is in them. When the social side of life is developed too exclusively, as it often is, and recreation or entertainment becomes the leading motive of a person's life, he acquires habits of extravagance instead of economy; habits of wasting his resources, physical, mental, moral and spiritual, instead of conserving them. He is, in consequence, lacking in proper motivation, his God-given powers and forces are undeveloped and he inevitably brings poor judgment to bear upon all the higher relationships of life, while, as to his financial fortunes, he is ever the leaner; often a parasite, and always, if opportunity affords, as heavy a consumer as he is a poor producer.

It seems a part of the tragedy of life that these persons have to be taught such painful lessons before they can understand the forces and laws that regulate life. Few profit by the mistakes of others. They must experience them for themselves and then apply the knowledge so gained in reconstructing their lives.

Any man who has ever amounted to anything has never done a great deal of detail work for long periods at any given time. He needs his time to reflect. He does not do his duties today in the same way as yesterday, but as the result of deliberate and concentrated effort, constantly tries to improve his methods.

The other day I attended a lecture on prosperity. I knew the lecturer had been practically broke for ten years. I wanted to hear what he had to say. He spoke very well. He no doubt benefited some of his hearers, but he had not profited by his own teachings. I introduced myself and asked him if he believed in his maxims. He said he did. I asked him if they had made him prosperous. He said not exactly. I asked him why. He answered that he thought he was fated not to experience prosperity.

In half an hour I showed that man why poverty had always been his companion. He had dressed poorly. He held his lectures in poor surroundings. By his actions and beliefs he attracted poverty. He did not realize that his thoughts and his surroundings exercised an unfavorable influence. I said: "Thoughts are moving forces; great powers. Thoughts of wealth attract wealth. Therefore, if you desire wealth you must attract the forces that will help you to secure it. Your thoughts attract a similar kind of thoughts. If you hold thoughts of poverty you attract poverty. If you make up your mind you are going to be wealthy, you will instill this thought into all your mental forces, and you will at the same time use every external condition to help you."

Many persons are of the opinion that if you have money it is easy to make more money. But this is not necessarily true. Ninety per cent of the men who start in business fail. Money will not enable one to accumulate much more, unless he is trained to seek and use good opportunities for its investment. If he inherits money the chances are that he will lose it. While, if he has made it, he not only knows its value, but has developed the power to use it as well as to make more if he loses it.

Business success today depends on foresight, good judgment, grit, firm resolution and settled purpose. But never forget that thought is as real a force as electricity. Let your thoughts be such, that you will send out as good as you receive; if you do not, you are not enriching others, and therefore deserve not to be enriched.

The man who tries to get all he can from others for nothing becomes so selfish and mean that he does not even enjoy his acquisitions. We see examples of this every day. What we take from others will in turn be taken from us. All obligations have to be met fairly and squarely. We cannot reach perfection until we discharge every obligation of our lives. We all realize this, so why not willingly give a fair exchange for all that we receive?

Again I repeat that the first as well as the last step in acquiring wealth is to surround yourself with good influence—good thought, good health, good home and business environment and successful business associates. Cultivate, by every legitimate means, the acquaintance of men of big caliber. Bring your thought vibrations in regard to business into harmony with theirs. This will make your society not only agreeable, but sought after, and, when you have formed intimate friendships with clean, reputable men of wealth, entrust to them, for investment, your surplus earnings, however small, until you have developed the initiative and business acumen to successfully manage your own investments. By this time you will, through such associations, have found your place in life which, if you have rightly concentrated upon and used your opportunities, will not be among men of small parts. With a competence secured, you will take pleasure in using a part of it in making the road you traveled in reaching your position easier for those who follow you,

There is somewhere in every brain the energy that will get you out of that rut and put you far up on the mountain of success if you can only use the energy.

You know that gasoline in the engine of an automobile doesn't move the car until the spark comes to explode the gasoline.

So it is with the mind of man. We are not speaking now of men of great genius, but of average, able citizens.

Each one of them has in his brain the capacity to climb over the word impossible and get into the successful country beyond.

And hope, self-confidence and the determination to do something supply the spark that makes the energy work.

LESSON 13

You Can Concentrate but Will You?

All have the ability to concentrate, but will you? You can, but whether you will or not depends on you. It is one thing to be able to do something, and another thing to do it. There is far more ability not used than is used. Why do not more men of ability make something of themselves? There are comparatively few successful men but many ambitious ones. Why do not more get along? Cases may differ, but the fault is usually their own. They have had chances, perhaps better ones than some others who have made good.

What would you like to do, that you are not doing? If you think you should be "getting on" better, why don't you? Study yourself carefully. Learn your shortcomings. Sometimes only a mere trifle keeps one from branching out and becoming a success. Discover why you have not been making good—the cause of your failure. Have you been expecting someone to lead you, or to make a way for you? If you have, concentrate on a new line of thought.

There are two things absolutely necessary for success—energy and the will to succeed. Nothing can take the place of either of these. Most of us will not have an easy path to follow so don't expect to find one. The hard knocks develop our courage and moral stamina. The persons who live in an indolent and slipshod way never have any. They have never faced conditions and therefore don't know how. The world is no better for their living.

We must make favorable conditions and not expect them to shape themselves. It is not the man who says, "It can't be done," but the man who goes ahead in spite of adverse advice, and shows that "it can be done" that "gets there" today. "The Lord helps those who help themselves," is a true saying. We climb the road to success by overcoming obstacles. Stumbling blocks are but stepping stones for the man who says, "I can and I will." When we see cripples, the deaf and dumb, the blind and those with other handicaps amounting to something in the world, the able-bodied man should feel ashamed of himself if he does not make good.

There is nothing that can resist the force of perseverance. The way ahead of all of us is not clear sailing, but all hard passages can be bridged, if you just think they can and concentrate on how to do it. But if you think the obstacles are unsurmountable, you will not of course try, and even if you do, it will be in only a half-hearted way—a way that accomplishes nothing.

Many men will not begin an undertaking unless they feel sure they will succeed in it. What a mistake! This would be right, if we were sure of what we could and could not do. But who knows? There may be an obstruction there now that might not be there next week. There may not be an obstruction there now that will be there next week. The trouble with most persons is that just as soon as they see their way blocked they lose courage. They forget that usually there is a way around the difficulty. It's up to you to find it. If you tackle something with little effort, when the conditions call for a big effort, you will of course not win. Tackle everything with a feeling that you will utilize all the power within you to make it a success. This is the kind of concentrated effort that succeeds.

Most people are beaten before they start. They think they are going to encounter obstacles, and they look for them instead of for means to overcome them. The result is that they increase their obstacles instead of diminishing them. Have you ever undertaken something that you thought would be hard, but afterwards found it to be easy? That is the way a great many times. The things that look difficult in advance turn out to be easy of conquest when once encountered. So start out on your journey with the idea that the road is going to be clear for you, and that if it is not you will clear the way. All men who have amounted to anything have cleared their way and they did not have the assistance that you will have today.

The one great keynote of success is to do whatever you have decided on. Don't be turned from your path, but resolve that you are going to accomplish what you set out to do. Don't be frightened at a few rebuffs for they cannot stop the man who is determined—the man who knows in his heart that success is only bought by tremendous resolution, by concentrated and whole-hearted effort.

"He who has a firm will," says Goethe, "molds the world to himself."

"People do not lack strength," says Victor Hugo; "they lack will."

It is not so much skill that wins victories as it is activity and great determination. There is no such thing as failure for the man who does his best. No matter what you may be working at, at the present time, don't let this make you lose courage. The tides are continually changing, and tomorrow or some other day they will turn to your advantage if you are a willing and are an ambitious worker. There is nothing that develops you and increases your courage like work. If it were not for work how monotonous life would at last become!

So I say to the man who wants to advance, "Don't look upon your present position as your permanent one. Keep your eyes open, and add those qualities to your makeup that will assist you when your opportunity comes. Be ever alert and on the watch for opportunities. Remember, we attract what we set our minds on. If we look for opportunities, we find them."

If you are the man you should be, someone is looking for you to fill a responsible position. So when he finds you, don't let your attention wander. Give it all to him. Show that you can concentrate your powers, that you have the makeup of a real man. Show no signs of fear, uncertainty or doubt. The man who is sure of himself is bound to get to the front. No circumstances can prevent him.

LESSON 14

The Art of Concentration by Means of Practical Exercises

Select some thought, and see how long you can hold your mind on it. It is well to have a clock at first and keep track of the time. If you decide to think about health, you can get a great deal of good from your thinking besides developing concentration. Think of health as being the greatest blessing there is in the world. Don't let any other thought drift in. Just the moment one starts to obtrude, make it get out.

Make it a daily habit of concentrating on this thought for, say, ten minutes. Practice until you can hold it to the exclusion of everything else. You will find it of the greatest value to centralize your thoughts on health. Regardless of your present condition, see yourself as you would like to be and blind to everything else. You will find it hard at first to forget your ailments, if you have any, but after a short while you can shut out these negative thoughts and see yourself as you want to be. Each time you concentrate you form a more perfect image of health, and, as you come into its realization, you become healthy, strong and wholesome.

I want to impress upon your mind that the habit of forming mental images is of the greatest value. It has always been used by successful men of all ages, but few realize its full importance.

Do you know that you are continually acting according to the images you form? If you allow yourself to mould negative images you unconsciously build a negative disposition. You will think of poverty, weakness, disease, fear, etc. Just as surely as you think of these will your objective life express itself in a like way. Just what we think, we will manifest in the external world.

In deep concentration you become linked with the great creative spirit of the universe, and the creative energy then flows through you, vitalizing your creations into form. In deep concentration your mind becomes attuned with the infinite and registers the cosmic energy that you are literally flooded with divine power. This is a most desired state. It is then we realize the advantages of being connected with the supra-consciousness. The supra-consciousness registers the higher cosmic vibrations. It is often referred to as the wireless station, the message recorded coming from the universal mind.

There are very few who reach this stage of concentration. Very few even know that it is possible. They think concentration means limitation to one subject, but this deeper concentration that brings us into harmony with the Infinite is that which produces and maintains health.

When you have once come in contact with your supra-consciousness you become the controller of your human thoughts. That which comes to you is higher than human thoughts. It is often spoken of as Cosmic Consciousness. Once it is experienced it is never forgotten. Naturally it requires a good deal of training to reach this state, but once you do, it becomes easier each time to do, and in the course of time you can become possessed of power which was unknown to you before. You are able to direct the expression of almost Infiinite Power while in this deeper state of concentration.

EXERCISES IN CONCENTRATION

The rays of the sun, when focused upon an object by means of a sun glass, produce a heat many times greater than the scattered rays of the same source of light and heat. This is true of attention. Scatter it and you get but ordinary results. But center it upon one thing and you secure much better results. When you focus your attention upon an object your every action, voluntary and involuntary, is in the direction of attaining that object. If you will focus your energies upon a thing to the exclusion of everything else, you generate the force that can bring you what you want.

When you focus your thought, you increase its strength. The exercises that follow are tedious and monotonous, but useful. If you will persist in them you will find they are very valuable, as they increase your powers of concentration.

Before proceeding with the exercises I will answer a question that just comes to me. This person says after he works all day he is too tired to practice any exercise. But this is not true. We will say he comes home all tired out, eats his supper and sits down to rest. If his work has been mental, the thought which has been occupying his mind returns to him and this prevents him from securing the rest he needs.

It is an admitted fact that certain thoughts call into operation a certain set of brain cells; the other cells, of course, are not busy at that time and are rested. Now if you take up something that is just different from what you have been doing during the day, you will use the cells that have not done anything and give those that have had work to do a rest. So you should regulate the evenings that you have and call forth an entirely different line of thought so as not to use the cells which you have tired out during the day. If you will center your attention on a new thought, you relieve the old cells from vibrating with excitement and they get their needed rest. The other cells that have been idle all day want to work, and you will find you can enjoy your evening while securing needed rest.

When once you have learned to master your thoughts, you will be able to change them just as easily as you change your clothes.

Remember, the real requisite of centering is to be able to shut out outside thoughts—anything foreign to the subject. Now, in order to control your intention first gain control over the body. This must be brought under direct control of the mind; the mind under the control of the will. Your will is strong enough to do anything you wish, but you must realize that it is. The mind can be greatly strengthened by being brought under the direct influence of the will. When the mind is properly strengthened by the impulse of the will it becomes a more powerful transmitter of thought, because it has more force.

THE BEST TIME TO CONCENTRATE IS

after reading something that is inspiring, as you are then mentally and spiritually exalted in the desired realm. Then is the time you are ready for deep concentration. If you are in your room first see that your windows are up and the air is good. Lie down flat on your bed without a pillow. See that every muscle is relaxed. Now breathe slowly, filling the lungs comfortably full of fresh air; hold this as long as you can without straining yourself; then exhale slowly. Exhale in an easy, rhythmic way. Breathe this way for five minutes, letting the Divine Breath flow through you, which will cleanse and rejuvenate every cell of brain and body.

You are then ready to proceed. Now think how quiet and relaxed you are. You can become enthusiastic over your condition. Just think of yourself as getting ready to receive knowledge that is far greater than you have ever received before. Now relax and let the spirit work in and through you and assist you to accomplish what you wish.

Don't let any doubts or fears enter. Just feel that what you wish is going to manifest. Just feel it already has, in reality it has, for just the minute you wish a thing to be done it manifests in the thought world. Whenever you concentrate just believe it is a success. Keep up this feeling and allow nothing to interfere and you will soon find you have become the master of concentration. You will find that this practice will be of wonderful value to you, and that rapidly you will be learning to accomplish anything that you undertake.

It will be necessary to first train the body to obey the commands of the mind. I want you to gain control of your muscular movements. The following exercise is especially good in assisting you to acquire perfect control of the muscles.

Exercise 1

Sit in a comfortable chair and see how still you can keep. This is not as easy as it seems. You will have to center your attention on sitting still. Watch and see that you are not making any involuntary muscular movements. By a little practice you will find you are able to sit still without a movement of the muscles for fifteen minutes. At first I advise sitting in a relaxed position for five minutes. After you are able to keep perfectly still, increase the time to ten minutes and then to fifteen. This is as long as it is necessary. But never strain yourself to keep still. You must be relaxed completely. You will find this habit of relaxing is very good.

Exercise 2

Sit in chair with your head up and your chin out, shoulders back. Raise your right arm until it is on the level with your shoulder, pointing to your right. Look around, with head only, and fix your gaze on your fingers, and keep the arm perfectly still for one minute. Do the same exercise with the left arm. When you are able to keep the arm perfectly steady, increase the time until you are able to do this five minutes with each arm. Turn the palm of the hand downward when it is outstretched, as this is the easiest position. If you will keep your eyes fixed on the tips of the fingers you will be able to tell if you are keeping your arm perfectly still.

Exercise 3

Fill a small glass full of water, and grasp it by the fingers; put the arm directly in front of you. Now fix the eyes upon the glass and try to keep the arm so steady that no movement will be noticeable. Do this first for one moment and then increase it to five. Do the exercise with first one arm and then the other.

Exercise 4

Watch yourself during the day and see that your muscles do not become tense or strained. See how easy and relaxed you can keep yourself. See how poised you can be at all times. Cultivate a self-poised manner, instead of a nervous, strained appearance. This mental feeling will improve your carriage and demeanor. Stop all useless gestures and movements of the body. These mean that you have not proper control over your body. After you have acquired this control, notice how "ill-at-ease" people are that have not gained this control. I have just been sizing up a salesman who has just left me. Part of his body kept moving all the time. I just felt like saying to him, "Do you know how much better appearance you would make if you would just learn to speak with your voice instead of trying to express what you say with your whole body?" Just watch those who interview you and see how they lack poise.

Get rid of any habit you have of twitching or jerking any part of your body. You will find you make many involuntary movements. You can quickly stop any of these by merely centering your attention on the thought, "I will not."

If you are in the habit of letting noises upset you, just exercise control; when the door slams, or something falls, etc., just think of these as exercises in self-control. You will find many exercises like this in your daily routine.

The purpose of the above exercises is to gain control over the involuntary muscular movement, making your actions entirely voluntary. The following exercises are arranged to bring your voluntary muscles under the control of the will, so that your mental forces may control your muscular movements.

Exercise 5

Move your chair up to a table, placing your hands upon it, clenching the fists, keeping the back of the hand on the table, the thumb doubled over the fingers. Now fix your gaze upon the fist for a while, then gradually extend the thumb, keeping your whole attention fixed upon the act, just as if it were a matter of greater importance. Then gradually extend your first finger, then your second and so on until you open the rest. Then reverse the process, closing first the last one opened and then the rest, and finally you will have the fist again in the original position with the thumb closed over the finger. Do this exercise with the left hand. Keep up this exercise first with one hand and then the other until you have done it five times with each hand. In a few days you can increase it to ten times.

The chances are that the above exercises will at first make you "tired," but it is important for you to practice these monotonous exercises so you can control your attention. It also gives you control over your muscular movement. The attention, of course, must be kept closely on each movement of the hand; if it is not, you of course lose the value of the exercise.

Exercise 6

Put the right hand on the knee, both fingers and thumb closed, except the first finger, which points out in front of you. Then move the finger slowly from side to side, keeping the attention fixed upon the end of the finger.

You can make up a variety of exercises like these. It is good training to plan out different ones. The main point you should keep in mind is that the exercise should be simple and that the attention should be firmly fixed upon the moving part of the body. You will find your attention will not want to be controlled and will try to drift to something more interesting. This is just where these exercises are of value, and you must control your attention and see it is held in the right place and does not wander away.

You may think these exercises very simple and of no value, but I promise you in a short time you will notice that you have a much better control over your muscular movements, carriage and demeanor, and you will find that you have greatly improved your power of attention, and can center your thoughts on what you do, which of course will be very valuable.

No matter what you may be doing, imagine that it is your chief object in life. Imagine you are not interested in anything else in the world but what you are doing. Do not let your attention get away from the work you are at. Your attention will no doubt be rebellious, but control it and do not let it control you. When once you conquer the rebellious attention you have achieved a greater victory that you can realize at the time. Many times afterwards you will be thankful you have learned to concentrate your closest attention upon the object at hand.

Let no day go by without practicing concentrating on some familiar object that is uninteresting. Never choose an interesting object, as it requires less attention. The less interesting it is the better exercise will it be. After a little practice you will find you can center your attention on uninteresting subjects at will.

The person who can concentrate can gain full control over his body and mind and be the master of his inclinations; not their slave. When you can control yourself you can control others. You can develop a Will that will make you a giant compared with the man who lacks Will Power. Try out your Will Power in different ways until you have it under such control that just as soon as you decide to do a thing you go ahead and do it. Never be satisfied with the "I did fairly well" spirit, but put forward your best efforts. Be satisfied with nothing else. When you have gained this you are the man you were intended to be.

Exercise 7. Concentration Increases the Sense of Smell

When you take a walk, or drive in the country, or pass a flower garden, concentrate on the odor of flowers and plants. See how many different kinds you can detect. Then choose one particular kind and try to sense only this. You will find that this strongly intensifies the sense of smell. This differentiation requires, however, a peculiarly attentive attitude. When sense of smell is being developed, you should not only shut out from the mind every thought but that of odor, but you should also shut out cognizance of every odor save that upon which your mind, for the time, is concentrated.

You can find plenty of opportunity for exercises for developing the sense of smell. When you are out in the air, be on the alert for the different odors. You will find the air laden with all kinds, but let your concentration upon the one selected be such that a scent of its fragrance in after years will vividly recall the circumstances of this exercise.

The object of these exercises is to develop concentrated attention, and you will find that you can, through their practice, control your mind and direct your thoughts just the same as you can your arm.

Exercise 8. Concentration on the Within

Lie down and thoroughly relax your muscles. Concentrate on the beating of your heart. Do not pay any attention to anything else. Think how this great organ is pumping the blood to every part of the body; try to actually picture the blood leaving the great reservoir and going in one stream right down to the toes. Picture another going down the arms to the tips of the fingers. After a little practice you can actually feel the blood passing through your system.

If, at any time, you feel weak in any part of the body, will that an extra supply of blood shall go there. For instance, if your eyes feel tired, picture the blood coming from the heart passing up through the head and out to the eyes. You can wonderfully increase your strength by this exercise. Men have been able to gain such control over the heart that they have actually stopped it from beating for five minutes. This, however, is not without danger, and is not to be practiced by the novice.

I have found the following a very, helpful exercise to take just before going to bed and on rising in the morning, say to yourself, "Every cell in my body thrills with life; every part of my body is strong and healthy." I have known a number of people to greatly improve their health in this way. You become what you picture yourself to be. If your mind thinks of sickness in connection with self you will be sick. If you imagine yourself in strong, vigorous health, the image will be realized. You will be healthy.

Exercise 9. Concentrating on Sleep

What is known as the water method is, although very simple, very effective in inducing sleep.

Put a full glass of clear water on a table in your sleeping room. Sit in a chair beside the table and gaze into the glass of water and think how calm it is. Then picture yourself getting into just as calm a state. In a short time you will find the nerves becoming quiet and you will be able to go to sleep. Sometimes it is good to picture yourself becoming drowsy to induce sleep, and, again, the most persistent insomnia has been overcome by one thinking of himself as some inanimate object—for instance, a hollow log in the depths of the cool quiet forest.

Those who are troubled with insomnia will find these sleep exercises that quiet the nerves very effective. Just keep the idea in your mind that there is no difficulty in going to sleep; banish all fear of insomnia. Practice these exercises and you will sleep.

By this time you should have awakened to the possibilities of concentration and have become aware of the important part it plays in your life.

Exercise 10. Concentration Will Save Energy and Appearance

Watch yourself and see if you are not in the habit of moving your hands, thumping something with your fingers or twirling your moustache. Some have the habit of keeping their feet going, as, for instance, tapping them on the floor. Practice standing before a mirror and see if you are in the habit of frowning or causing wrinkles to appear in the forehead. Watch others and see how they needlessly twist their faces in talking. Any movement of the face that causes the skin to wrinkle will eventually cause a permanent wrinkle. As the face is like a piece of silk, you can make a fold in it a number of times and it will straighten out of itself, but, if you continue to make a fold in it, it will in time be impossible to remove it.

By Concentration You Can Stop the Worry Habit

If you are in the habit of worrying over the merest trifles, just concentrate on this a few minutes and see how needless it is; if you are also in the habit of becoming irritable or nervous at the least little thing, check yourself instantly when you feel yourself becoming so; start to breathe deeply; say, "I will not be so weak; I am master of myself," and you will quickly overcome your condition.

Exercise 11. By Concentration You Can Control Your Temper

If you are one of those that flare up at the slightest "provocation" and never try to control yourself, just think this over a minute. Does it do you any good? Do you gain anything by it? Doesn't it put you out of poise for some time? Don't you know that this grows on you and will eventually make you despised by all who have any dealings with you? Everyone makes mistakes and, instead of becoming angry at their perpetrators, just say to them, "Be more careful next time." This thought will be impressed on them and they will be more careful. But, if you continually complain about their making a mistake, the thought of a mistake is impressed on them and they will be more likely to make mistakes in the future. All lack of self-control can be conquered if you will but learn to concentrate.

Many of you who read this may think you are not guilty of either of these faults, but if you will carefully watch yourself you will probably find that you are, if so, you will be greatly helped by repeating this affirmation each morning:

"I am going to try today not to make a useless gesture or to worry over trifles, or become nervous or irritable. I intend to be calm, and, no difference what may be the circumstances, I will control myself. Henceforth I resolve to be free from all signs that show lack of self-control."

At night quickly review your actions during the day and see how fully you realize your aim. At first you will, of course, have to plead guilty of violation a few times, but keep on, and you will soon find that you can live up to your ideal. After you have once gained self-control, however, don't relinquish it. For some time it will still be necessary to repeat the affirmation in the morning and square your conduct with it in the evening. Keep up the good work until, at last, the habit of self-control is so firmly fixed that you could not break it even though you tried.

I have had many persons tell me that this affirmation and daily review made a wonderful difference in their lives. You, too, will notice the difference if you live up to these instructions.

Exercise 12. Practice Talking Before a Glass

Make two marks on your mirror on a level with your eyes, and think of them as two human eyes looking into yours. Your eyes will probably blink a little at first. Do not move your head, but stand erect. Concentrate all your thoughts on keeping your head perfectly still. Do not let another thought come into your mind. Then, still keeping the head, eyes and body still, think that you look like a reliable man or woman should; like a person who anyone would have confidence in. Do not let your appearance be such as to justify the remark, "I don't like his appearance. I don't believe he can be trusted."

While standing before the mirror practice deep breathing. See that there is plenty of fresh air in the room, and that you are literally feasting on it. You will find that, as it permeates every cell, your timidity will disappear. It has been replaced by a sense of peace and power.

The one who stands up like a man and has control over the muscles of his face and eyes always commands attention. In his conversation, he can better impress those with whom he comes in contact. He acquires a feeling of calmness and strength that causes opposition to melt away before it.

Three minutes a day is long enough for the practice of this exercise.

Look at the clock before you commence the exercise, and if you find you can prolong the exercise for more than five minutes do so. The next day sit in a chair and, without looking at the picture, concentrate on it and see if you cannot think of additional details concerning it. The chances are you will be able to think of many more. It might be well for you to write down all you thought of the first day, and then add to the list each new discovery. You will find that this is a very excellent exercise in concentration.

Exercise 13. The Control of Sensations

Think how you would feel if you were cool; then how you would feel if you were cold; again, how you would feel if it were freezing. In this state you would be shivering all over. Now think of just the opposite conditions; construct such a vivid image of heat that you are able to experience the sensation of heat even in the coldest atmosphere. It is possible to train your imagination until you do this, and it can then be turned to practical account in making undesirable conditions bearable.

You can think of many very good exercises like this. For instance, if you feel yourself getting hungry or thirsty and for any reason you do not wish to eat, do not think of how hungry or thirsty you are, but just visualize yourself as finishing a hearty meal. Again, when you experience pain, do not increase it by thinking about it, but do something to divert your attention, and the pain will seem to decrease. If you will start practicing along this line systematically you will soon gain a wonderful control over the things that affect your physical comfort.

Exercise 14. The Eastern Way of Concentrating

Sit in a chair with a high back in upright position. Press one finger against the right nostril. Now take a long, deep breath, drawing the breath in gently as you count to ten; then expel the breath through the right nostril as you count to ten. Repeat this exercise with the opposite nostril. This exercise should be done at least twenty times at each sitting.

Exercise 15. Controlling Desires

Desires, which is one of the hardest forces to control, will furnish you with excellent exercises in concentration. It seems natural to want to tell others what you know; but, by learning to control these desires, you can wonderfully strengthen your powers of concentration. Remember, you have all you can do to attend to your own business. Do not waste your time in thinking of others or in gossiping about them.

If, from your own observation, you learn something about another person which is detrimental, keep it to yourself. Your opinion may afterwards turn out to be wrong anyway, but whether right or wrong, you have strengthened your will by controlling your desire to communicate your views.

If you hear good news resist the desire to tell it to the first person you meet and you will be benefited thereby. It will require the concentration of all your powers of resistance to prohibit the desire to tell. After you feel that you have complete control over your desires you can then tell your news. But you must be able to suppress the desire to communicate the news until you are fully ready to tell it. Persons who do not possess this power of control over desires are apt to tell things that they should not, thereby often involving both themselves and others in needless trouble.

If you are in the habit of getting excited when you hear unpleasant news, just control yourself and receive it without any exclamation of surprise. Say to yourself, "Nothing is going to cause me to lose my self-control." You will find from experience that this self-control will be worth much to you in business. You will be looked upon as a cool-headed business man, and this in time becomes a valuable business asset. Of course, circumstances alter cases. At times it is necessary to become enthused. But be ever on the lookout for opportunities for the practice of self-control. "He who ruleth his spirit is greater than he who ruleth a city."

Exercise 16. When You Read

No one can think without first concentrating his thoughts on the subject in hand. Every man and woman should train himself to think clearly. An excellent exercise is to read some short story and then write just an abridged statement. Read an article in a newspaper, and see in how few words you can express it. Reading an article to get only the essentials requires the closest concentration. If you are unable to write out what you read, you will know you are weak in concentration. Instead of writing it out you can express it orally if you wish. Go to your room and deliver it as if you were talking to some one. You will find exercises like this of the greatest value in developing concentration and learning to think.

After you have practiced a number of these simple exercises read a book for twenty minutes and then write down what you have read. The chances are that at first you will not remember very many details, but with a little practice you will be able to write a very good account of what you have read. The closer the concentration the more accurate the account will be.

It is a good idea when time is limited to read only a short sentence and then try to write it down word for word. When you are able to do this, read two or more sentences and treat similarly. The practice will produce very good results if you keep it up until the habit is fixed.

If you will just utilize your spare time in practicing exercises like those suggested you can gain wonderful powers of concentration. You will find that in order to remember every word in a sentence you must keep out every thought but that which you wish to remember, and this power of inhibition alone will more than compensate for the trouble of the exercise. Of course, success in all of the above depends largely upon cultivating, through the closest concentration, the power to image or picture what you read; upon the power, as one writer expresses it, of letting the mountains of which we hear loom before us and the rivers of which we read roll at our feet.

Exercise 17. Concentration Overcomes Bad Habits

If you have a habit that you want to get rid of, shut your eyes and imagine that your real self is standing before you. Now try the power of affirmation; say to yourself, "You are not a weakling; you can stop this habit if you want to. This habit is bad and you want to break it." Just imagine that you are someone else giving this advice. This is very valuable practice. You, in time, see yourself as others see you. The habit loses its power over you and you are free.

If you will just form the mental image of controlling yourself as another person might, you will take a delight in breaking bad habits. I have known a number of men to break themselves of drinking in this way.

Exercise 18. Watch Concentration

Sit in a chair and place a clock with a second hand on the table. Follow the second hand with your eyes as it goes around. Keep this up for five minutes, thinking of nothing else but the second hand. This is a very good exercise when you only have a few minutes to spare, if you are able to keep every other thought in the stream of consciousness subordinate to it. As there is little that is particularly interesting about the second hand, it is hard to do this, but in the extra effort of will power required to make it successful lies its value. Always try to keep as still as possible during these exercises.

In this way you can gain control over nerves and this quieting effect is very good for them.

Exercise 19. Faith Concentration

A belief in the power to concentrate is of course very important. I purposely did not put this exercise in the beginning where it naturally belongs because I wanted you to know that you could learn to concentrate. If you have practiced the above exercises you have now developed this concentration power to a considerable extent and therefore you have faith in the power of concentration, but you can still become a much stronger believer in it.

We will say that you have some desire or wish you want fulfilled, or that you need some special advice. You first clearly picture what is wanted and then you concentrate on getting it. Have absolute faith that your desires will be realized. Believe that it will according to your belief be fulfilled. Never, at this time, attempt to analyze the belief. You don't care anything about the whys and wherefores. You want to gain the thing you desire, and if you concentrate on it in the right way you will get it.

A CAUTION

Never think you will not succeed, but picture what is wanted as already yours, and yours it surely will be.

SELF-DISTRUST

Do you ever feel distrust in yourself? If you do, just ask yourself, which self do I mistrust? Then say: my higher self cannot be affected. Then think of the wonderful powers of the higher self. There is a way to overcome all difficulties, and it is a delight for the human soul to do so. Instead of wasting precious thought-force by dreading or fearing a disagreeable interview or event, instead devote the time and concentrated thought in how to make the best of the interview or event and you will find that it will not be as unpleasant as you thought it would be.

Most of our troubles are but imaginary, and it is the mental habit of so dreading them that really acts as a magnet in attracting those that really do come. Your evil circumstances are created or attracted by your own negative fears and wrong thoughts, and are a means of teaching you to triumph over all evils by discovering that which is inherent within yourself.

You will find it helpful in overcoming self-distrust to stop and think why you are concentrating your forces, and by so doing you become more closely attached to the higher self, which never distrusts.

LESSON 15

Concentrate So You Will Not Forget

A man forgets because he does not concentrate his mind on his purpose, especially at the moment he conceives it. We remember only that which makes a deep impression, hence we must first deepen our impressions by associating in our minds certain ideas that are related to them.

We will say a wife gives her husband a letter to mail. He does not think about it, but automatically puts it in his pocket and forgets all about it. When the letter was given to him had he said to himself, "I will mail this letter. The box is at the next corner and when I pass it I must drop this letter," it would have enabled him to recall the letter the instant he reached the mail box.

The same rule holds good in regard to more important things. For example, if you are instructed to drop in and see Mr. Smith while out to luncheon today, you will not forget it, if, at the moment the instruction is given, you say to yourself something similar to the following: "When I get too the corner of Blank Street, on my way to luncheon, I shall turn to the right and call on Mr. Smith." In this way the impression is made, the connection established and the sight of the associated object recalls the errand.

The important thing to do is to deepen the impression at the very moment it enters your mind. This is made possible, not only by concentrating the mind upon the idea itself, but by surrounding it with all possible association of ideas, so that each one will reinforce the others.

The mind is governed by laws of association, such as the law that ideas which enter the mind at the same time emerge at the same time, one assisting in recalling the others.

The reason why people cannot remember what they want to is that they have not concentrated their minds sufficiently on their purpose at the moment when it was formed.

You can train yourself to remember in this way by the concentration of the attention on your purpose, in accordance with the laws of association.

When once you form this habit, the attention is easily centered and the memory easily trained. Then your memory, instead of failing you at crucial moments, becomes a valuable asset in your every-day work.

EXERCISE IN MEMORY CONCENTRATION

Select some picture: put it on a table and then look at it for two minutes. Concentrate your attention on this picture, observe every detail; then shut your eyes and see how much you can recall about it. Think of what the picture represents; whether it is a good subject; whether it looks natural. Think of objects in foreground, middle ground, background; of details of color and form. Now open your eyes and hold yourself rigidly to the correction of each and every mistake. Close eyes again and notice how much more accurate your picture is. Practice until your mental image corresponds in every particular to the original.

Nature is a Wonderful Instructor. But there are very few who realize that when we get in touch with nature we discover ourselves. That by listening to her voice, with that curious, inner sense of ours, we learn the oneness of life and wake up to our own latent powers.

Few realize that the simple act of listening and concentrating is our best interior power, for it brings us into close contact with the highest, just as our other senses bring us into touch with the coarser side of human nature. The closer we live to nature the more developed is this sense. "So called" civilization has over developed our other senses at the expense of this one.

Children unconsciously realize the value of concentration—for instance: When a child has a difficult problem to solve, and gets some knotty point which he finds himself mentally unable to do—though he tries his hardest—he will pause and keep quite still, leaning on his elbow, apparently listening; then you will see, if you are watching, a sudden illumination come and he goes on happily and accomplishes his task. A child instinctively but unconsciously knows when he needs help, he must be quiet and concentrate.

All great people concentrate and owe their success to it. The doctor thinks over the symptoms of his patient, waits, listens for the inspiration, though quite unconscious, perhaps, of doing so. The one who diagnoses in this way seldom makes mistakes. An author thinks his plot, holds it in his mind, and then waits, and illumination conies. If you want to be able to solve difficult problems you must learn to do the same.

LESSON 16

How Concentration Can Fulfill Your Desire

"It is a spiritual law that the desire to do necessarily implies the ability to do."

You have all read of "Aladdin's Lamp," which accomplished such wonderful things. This, of course, is only a fairy story, but it illustrates the fact that man has within him the power, if he is able to use it, to gratify his every wish.

If you are unable to satisfy your deepest longings it is time you learned how to use your God-given powers. You will soon be conscious that you have latent powers within capable when once developed of revealing to you priceless knowledge and unlimited possibilities of success.

Man should have plenty of everything and not merely substance to live on as so many have. All natural desires can be realized. It would be wrong for the Infinite to create wants that could not be supplied. Man's very soul is in his power to think, and it, therefore, is the essence of all created things. Every instinct of man leads to thought, and in every thought there is great possibility because true thought development, when allied to those mysterious powers which perhaps transcend it, has been the cause of all the world's true progress.

In the silence we become conscious of "that something" which transcends thought and which uses thought as a medium for expression. Many have glimpses of "that something," but few ever reach the state where the mind is steady enough to fathom these depths. Silent, concentrated thought is more potent than spoken words, for speech distracts from the focusing power of the mind by drawing more and more attention to the without.

Man must learn more and more to depend on himself; to seek more for the Infinite within. It is from this source alone that he ever gains the power to solve his practical difficulties. No one should give up when there is always the resources of Infinity. The cause of failure is that men search in the wrong direction for success, because they are not conscious of their real powers that when used are capable of guiding them.

The Infinite within is foreign to those persons who go through life without developing their spiritual powers. But the Infinite helps only he who helps himself. There is no such thing as a special "providence." Man will not receive help from the Infinite except to the extent that he believes and hopes and prays for help from this great source.

CONCENTRATE ON WHAT YOU WANT, AND GET IT

The weakling is controlled by conditions. The strong man controls conditions. You can be either the conqueror or the conquered. By the law of concentration you can achieve your heart's desire. This law is so powerful that that which at first seems impossible becomes attainable.

By this law what you see first as a dream becomes a reality.

Remember that the first step in concentration is to form a mental image of what you wish to accomplish. This image becomes a thought-seed that attracts thoughts of a similar nature. Around this thought, when it is once planted in the imagination or creative region of the mind, you group or build associated thoughts which continue to grow as long as your desire is keen enough to compel close concentration.

Form the habit of thinking of something you wish to accomplish for five minutes each day. Shut every other thought out of consciousness. Be confident that you will succeed; make up your mind that all obstacles that are in your way will be overcome and you can rise above any environment.

You do this by utilizing the natural laws of the thought world which are all powerful.

A great aid in the development of concentration is to write out your thoughts on that which lies nearest your heart and to continue, little by little, to add to it until you have as nearly as possible exhausted the subject.

You will find that each day as you focus your forces on this thought at the center of the stream of consciousness, new plans, ideas and methods will flash into your mind. There is a law of attraction that will help you accomplish your purpose. An advertiser, for instance, gets to thinking along a certain line. He has formed his own ideas, but he wants to know what others think. He starts out to seek ideas and he soon finds plenty of books, plans, designs, etc., on the subject, although when he started he was not aware of their existence.

The same thing is true in all lines. We can attract those things that will help us. Very often we seem to receive help in a miraculous way. It may be slow in coming, but once the silent unseen forces are put into operation, they will bring results so long as we do our part. They are ever present and ready to aid those who care to use them. By forming a strong mental image of your desire, you plant the thought-seed which begins working in your interest and, in time, that desire, if in harmony with your higher nature, will materialize.

It may seem that it would be unnecessary to caution you to concentrate only upon achievement that will be good for you and work no harm to another, but there are many who forget others and their rights, in their anxiety to achieve success. All good things are possible for you to have, but only as you bring your forces into harmony with that law that requires that we mete out justice to fellow travelers as we journey along life's road. So first think over the thing wanted and if it would be good for you to have, say, "I want to do this; I am going to work to secure it. The way will be open for me."

If you fully grasp mentally the thought of success and hold it in mind each day, you gradually make a pattern or mold which in time will materialize. But by all means keep free from doubt and fear the destructive forces. Never allow these to become associated with your thoughts.

At last you will create the desired conditions and receive help in many unlooked-for ways that will lift you out of the undesired environment. Life will then seem very different to you, for you will have found happiness through awakening within yourself the power to become the master of circumstances instead of their slave.

To the beginner in this line of thought some of the things stated in this book may sound strange, even absurd, but, instead of condemning them, give them a trial. You will find they will work out.

The inventor has to work out his idea mentally before he produces it materially. The architect first sees the mental picture of the house he is to plan and from this works out the one we see. Every object, every enterprise, must first be mentally created.

I know a man who started in business with thirteen cents and not a dollar's worth of credit. In ten years he has built up a large and profitable business. He attributes his success to two things—belief that he would succeed and hard work. There were times when it did not look like he could weather the storm. He was being pressed by his creditors who considered him bankrupt. They would have taken fifty cents on the dollar for his notes and considered themselves lucky. But by keeping up a bold front he got an extension of time when needed. When absolutely necessary for him to raise a certain sum at a certain time he always did it. When he had heavy bills to meet he would make up his mind that certain people who owed him would pay by a certain date and they always did. Sometimes he would not receive their check until the last mail of the day of the extension, and I have known him to send out a check with the prospect of receiving a check from one of his customers the following day. He would have no reason other than his belief in the power of affecting the mind of another by concentration of thought for expecting that check, but rarely has he been disappointed.

Just put forth the necessary concentrated effort and you will be wonderfully helped from sources unknown to you.

Remember the mystical words of Jesus, the Master: "Whatsoever thing ye desire when ye pray; pray as if ye had already received and ye shall have."

LESSON 17

Ideals Developed by Concentration

Through our paltry stir and strife,
Glows the wished Ideal,
And longing molds in clay, what life
Carves in the marble real.

—LOWELL

We often hear people spoken of as idealists. The fact is we are all idealists to a certain extent, and upon the ideas we picture depends our ultimate success. You must have the mental image if you are to produce the material thing. Everything is first created in the mind. When you control your thoughts you become a creator. You receive divine ideas and shape them to your individual needs. All things of this world are to you just what you think they are. Your happiness and success depends upon your ideals.

You are responsible for every condition you go through, either consciously or unconsciously. The next step you take determines the succeeding step. Remember this; it is a valuable lesson. By concentrating on each step as you go along, you can save a lot of waste steps and will be able to choose a straight path instead of a roundabout road.

CONCENTRATE UPON YOUR IDEALS AND THEY WILL BECOME MATERIAL ACTUALITIES

Through concentration we work out our ideals in physical life. Your future depends upon the ideals you are forming now. Your past ideals are determining your present. Therefore, if you want a bright future, you must begin to prepare for it today.

If persons could only realize that they can only injure themselves, that when they are apparently injuring others they are really injuring themselves, what a different world this would be!

We say a man is as changeable as the weather. What is meant is his ideals change. Every time you change your ideal you think differently. You become like a rudderless boat on an ocean. Therefore realize the importance of holding to your ideal until it becomes a reality.

You get up in the morning determined that nothing will make you lose your temper. This is your ideal of a person of real strength and poise. Something takes place that upsets you completely and you lose your temper. If you had just thought a second of what a well-poised person implies you would not have become angry. You lose your poise when you forget your ideal. Each time we allow our ideals to be shattered we also weaken our will-power. Holding to your ideals develops will-power. Don't forget this.

Why do so many men fail? Because they don't hold to their ideal until it becomes a mental habit. When they concentrate on it to the exclusion of all other things it becomes a reality.

"I am that which I think myself to be."

Ideals are reflected to us from the unseen spirit. The laws of matter and spirit are not the same. One can be broken, but not the other. To the extent that ideals are kept is your future assured.

It was never intended that man should suffer. He has brought it upon himself by disobeying the laws of nature. He knows them so cannot plead ignorance. Why does he break them? Because he does not pay attention to those ideals flashed to him from the Infinite Spirit.

Life is but one continuous unfoldment, and you can be happy every step of the way or miserable, as you please; it all depends upon how we entertain those silent whisperings that come from we know not where. We cannot hear them with mortal ear, but from the silence they come as if they were dreams, not to you or me alone, but to everyone. In this way the grandest thoughts come to us, to use or abuse. So search not in treasured volumes for noble thoughts, but within, and bright and glowing vision will come to be realized now and hereafter.

You must give some hours to concentrated, consistent, persistent thought. You must study yourself and your weaknesses.

No man gets over a fence by wishing himself on the other side. He must climb.

No man gets out of the rut of dull, tiresome, monotonous life by merely wishing himself out of the rut. He must climb.

If you are standing still, or going backward, there is something wrong. You are the man to find out what is wrong.

Don't think that you are neglected, or not understood, or not appreciated.

Such thoughts are the thoughts of failure.

Think hard about the fact that men who have got what you envy got it by working for it.

Don't pity yourself, criticise yourself.

You know that the only thing in the world that you have got to count upon is yourself.

LESSON 18

Mental Control Through Creation

I attended a banquet of inventors recently. Each inventor gave a short talk on something he thought would be accomplished in the future. Many very much needed things were spoken of. One inventor spoke of the possibilities of wireless telephone. Distance, he said, would shortly be annihilated. He thought we would soon be able to talk to the man in the submarine forty fathoms below the surface and a thousand miles away. When he got through he asked if there were any who doubted what he said. No one spoke up. This was not a case of tactful politeness, as inventors like to argue, but a case where no one present really doubted that the inventor's vision would, in the future, materialize.

These shrewd men, some real geniuses, all thought we would in time be able to talk to those a thousand miles away without media. Now, if we can make an instrument so wonderful that we can send wireless messages a thousand miles, is there any reason why we should not through mental control transmit messages from one person to another? The wireless message should not be as easy to send as the projected thought.

The day will come when all business will employ highly developed persons to send out influences. These influences will be so dominating that employees will be partly controlled by them and so you will profit more and more by your mental powers and depend on them to draw to you all forces of a helpful nature. You will receive these unconsciously, but in case yours is the stronger personality they will carry them out the same as if you had spoken them.

This is being done even today. A finely organized company secures the combined effort of all its men. They may be each doing a different kind of work, but all work to bring about the very best results. The whole atmosphere is impregnated with a high standard of workmanship. Everyone feels he must do his best. He could not be in such surroundings and be satisfied to do anything but his best work.

A business will succeed only to the extent that the efforts of all are co-ordinated towards one result. At least one person is needed to direct all toward the desired end. The person at the head does not have to exactly outline to the others what steps to take, but he must possess the mental power of control over others.

An up-to-date business letter is not written in a casual, commonplace way today. The writer tries to convey something he thinks the receiver will be interested to know. In this way he awakens a responsive spirit. Sometimes just the addition of a word or two will change a letter of the matter-of-face style to one that compels a response. It is not always what is actually in a letter, but the spirit which it breathes that brings results. That intangible something that defies analysis is the projected thought of the master that brings back the harvest that it claims.

But we should not always claim success for ourselves only. If you are anxious that some friend or relative should succeed, think of this person as becoming successful. Picture him in the position you would like to see him in. If he has a weakness, desire and command that it be strengthened; think of his shortcomings which belong to his negative nature as being replaced by positive qualities. Take a certan part of the day to send him thoughts of an upbuilding nature. You can in this way arouse his mental powers into activity, and once aroused, they will assert themselves and claim their own.

We can accomplish a great deal more than many of us are ready to believe by sending to another our direct, positive and controlling suggestions of leadership, but whether a man is a success or not is greatly determined by the way he acts on the suggestions he receives.

We either advance or decline. We never stand still. Every time we accomplish something it gives us ability to do greater things. The bigger the attempt undertaken, the greater the things accomplished in the future. As a business grows, the head of the business also has to grow. He must advance and be ever the guiding influence. By his power to control, he inspires confidence in those associated with him. Often employees are superior to their employers in some qualities, and, if they had studied, instead of neglected their development, they could have been employers of more commanding influence than those whom they serve.

Through your mental power you can generate in another enthusiasm and the spirit of success, which somehow furnishes an impetus to do something worth while.

In concentrated mental control, there is a latent power more potent than physical force. The person becomes aware that the attitude of the mind has a power of controlling, directing and governing other forces. He has been placed in an attitude capable of acquiring that which he desires.

Any of us no matter how strong we are, are affected by the mental forces of our environment. There is no one who can remain neutral to influences. The mind cannot be freed from the forces of a place. If the environment of your place of business is not helpful, it will be harmful. That is why a change of position will often do a person a great deal of good.

No person was ever intended to live alone. If you are shut up with only your own thoughts you suffer from mental starvation. The mind becomes narrow; the mental powers weaken. Living alone often causes some of the milder forms of insanity. If children do not play with those their own age, but associate only with older people, they will take on the actions of the older people. The same is true of older persons if they associate with people younger than they are. They take on the spirit of youth. If you wish to retain your youth you need the influences of youth. Like attracts like all over the world.

The thought element plays a great part in our lives. Every business must not only command physical effort but it must also command thought effort. There must be coordination of thought. All employers should aim to secure employees who think along similar lines. They will work in fuller sympathy with each other. They will better understand each other. This enables them to help each other, which would be utterly impossible if they were not in sympathy with each other. It is this that goes to make up a perfect organization, which directs and influences them toward the one end. Instead of each person being a separate unit, each one is like a spoke in a big wheel. Each member carries his own load, and he would not think of shirking. Anyone working in such an atmosphere could not help turning out his best work.

All great leaders must be able to inspire this co-operative spirit. They first secure assistance through their mental control. They then make their assistants realize the value of mental control. Soon there is a close bond between them; they are working toward a single purpose. They profit by their combined effort. The result is that they accomplish much.

If your business is conducted in the right spirit, you can instill your thoughts and your ideas into your employees. Your methods and ideas become theirs. They don't know it, but your mental forces are shaping their work. They are just as certain to produce results as any physical force in nature.

The up-to-date businessman of the future is going to take pains to get his employees to think and reason better. He will not want them to become depressed or discouraged. There is time that instead of being wasted he will endeavor to have them use in concentrated effort that will be profitable to both employer and employed. There must be more of the spirit of justice entered into the business of the future.

There is a firm I know that will not hire an employee until he has filled out an application blank. No doubt those who fill it out think it is foolishness, but it is not. A capable manager can look over his application blank and pretty nearly tell if this person will fit into his management. The main thing he wants to know is the applicant's capacity for efficient co-operative effort. He wants persons who have faith in themselves. He wants them to realize that when they talk of misfortunes and become blue they are likely to communicate the same depressing influence to others. The up-to-date manager wants to guard against hiring employees who will obstruct his success.

You must realize that every moment spent in thinking of your difficulties of the past, every moment spent in bad company is attracting to you all that is bad; is attracting influences that must be shaken off before you can advance.

Many firms prefer to hire employees who never worked before so that they have nothing to unlearn. They are then not trained, but have no bad business habits to overcome. They are more easily guided and grasp the new methods more effectively because they are not contrary to what they have already learned. They are at once started on the right road, and as they co-operate readily they receive the mental support of the management in learning the methods that have been perfected. This inspires confidence in themselves and they soon become efficient and, finally, skilled workers.

Most big business firms today employ efficiency experts. Each day or week they are in a different department. They earn their money because they familiarize persons with very little business experience with plans that have taken the "expert" years of training and much money to perfect.

The attitude we take has a great deal more to do with our success than most of us realize. We must be able to generate those forces that are helpful. There is a wonderful power in the thought rightly controlled and projected and we must, through concentration, develop this power to the fullest possible extent.

We are surrounded by many forces of which we know but little at present. Our knowledge of these is to be wonderfully increased. Each year we learn more about these psychic forces which are full of possibilities of which we are not even dimly conscious. We must believe in mental control, learn more about it, and use it, if we want to command these higher powers and forces which will unquestionably direct the lives of countless future generations.

LESSON 19

A Concentrated Will Development

NEW METHOD

You will find in this chapter a most effective and most practical method of developing the will. You can develop a strong one if you want to. You can make your Will a dynamo to draw to you untold power. Exercises are given which will, if practiced, strengthen your will, just as you would strengthen your muscles by athletic exercises.

In starting to do anything, we must first commence with elementary principles. Simple exercises will be given. It is impossible to estimate the ultimate good to be derived from the mental cultivation that comes through these attempts at concentration. Even the simple exercises are not to be thought useless. "In no respect," writes Doctor Oppenheim, "can a man show a finer quality of will-power than in his own private, intimate life." We are all subjected to certain temptations. The Will decides whether we will be just, or unjust; pure of thought; charitable in opinion; forbearing in overlooking others' shortcomings; whether we live up to our highest standard. Since these are all controlled by the Will, we should find time for plenty of exercises for training of the will in our daily life.

You, of course, realize that your will should be trained. You must also realize that to do this requires effort that you alone can command. No one can call it forth for you.

To be successful in these exercises you must practice them in a spirit of seriousness and earnestness. I can show you how to train your will, but your success depends upon your mastery and application of these methods.

NEW METHODS OF WILL-TRAINING

Select a quiet room where you will not be interrupted; have a watch to determine the time, and a note-book in which to enter observations. Start each exercise with date and time of day.

Exercise 1

Time decided on. Select some time of the day when most convenient. Sit in a chair and look at the door-knob for ten minutes. Then write down what you experienced. At first it will seem strange and unnatural. You will find it hard to hold one position for ten minutes. But keep as still as you can. The time will seem long for it will probably be the first time you ever sat and did nothing for ten minutes. You will find your thoughts wandering from the door-knob, and you will wonder what there can be in this exercise. Repeat this exercise for six days.

10 P.M. 2ND DAY

NOTES. You should be able to sit quieter, and the time should pass more quickly. You will probably feel a little stronger because of gaining a better control of your will. It will brace you up, as you have kept your resolution.

10 P.M. 3RD DAY

NOTES. It may be a little harder for you to concentrate on the door-knob as perhaps you have a very busy day and your mind kept trying to revert to what you had been doing during the day. Keep on trying and you will finally succeed in banishing all foreign thoughts. Then you should feel a desire to gain still more control. There is a feeling of power that comes over you when you are able to carry out your will. This exercise will make you feel bigger and it awakens a sense of nobility and manliness. You will say, "I find that I can actually do what I want to and can drive foreign thoughts out. The exercise, I can now see, is valuable."

10 P.M. 4TH DAY

NOTES. "I found that I could look at the door-knob and concentrate my attention on it at once. Have overcome the tendency to move my legs. No other thoughts try to enter as I have established the fact that I can do what I want to do and not have to be directed. I feel that I am gaining in mental strength, I can now see the wonderful value of being the master of my own will-force. I know now if I make a resolution I will keep it. I have more self-confidence and I can feel my self-control increasing."

10 P.M. 5TH DAY

NOTES. "Each day I seem to increase the intensity of my concentration. I feel that I can center my attention on anything I wish."

10 P.M. 6TH DAY

NOTES. "I can instantly center my whole attention on the door-knob. Feel that I have thoroughly mastered this exercise and that I am ready for another."

You have practiced this exercise enough, but before you start another I want you to write a summary of just how successful you were in controlling the flitting impulses of the mind and will. You will find this an excellent practice. There is nothing more beneficial to the mind than to pay close attention to its own wonderful, subtle activities.

Exercise 2

Secure a package of playing cards. Select some time to do the exercise. Each day at the appointed time, take the pack in one hand and then start laying them down on top of each other just as slowly as you can, with an even motion. Try to get them as even as possible. Each card laid down should completely cover the under one. Do this exercise for six days.

1ST DAY

NOTES. Task will seem tedious and tiresome. Requires the closest concentration to make each card completely cover the preceding one. You will probably want to lay them down faster. It requires patience to lay them down so slowly, but benefit is lost if not so placed. You will find that at first your motions will be jerky and impetuous. It will require a little practice before you gain an easy control over your hands and arms. You probably have never tried to do anything in such a calm way. It will require the closest attention of your will. But you will find that you are acquiring a calmness you never had before. You are gradually acquiring new powers. You recognize how impulsive and impetuous you have been, and how, by using your will, you can control your temperament.

2ND DAY

NOTES. You start laying the cards down slowly. You will find that by practice you can lay them down much faster. But you want to lay them down slowly and therefore you have to watch yourself. The slow, steady movement is wearisome. You have to conquer the desire of wanting to hurry up. Soon you will find that you can go slowly or fast at will.

3RD DAY

NOTES. You still find it hard to go slowly. Your will urges you to go faster. This is especially true if you are impulsive, as the impulsive character finds it very difficult to do anything slowly and deliberately. It goes against the "grain." This exercise still is tiresome. But when you do it, it braces you up mentally. You are accomplishing something you do not like to do. It teaches you how to concentrate on disagreeable tasks. Writing these notes down you will find very helpful.

4TH DAY

NOTES. "I find that I am beginning to place the cards in a mathematical way. I find one card is not completely covering another. I am getting a little careless and must be more careful. I command my will to concentrate more. It does not seem so hard to bring it under control."

5TH DAY

NOTES. "I find that I am overcoming my jerky movements, that I can lay the cards down slowly and steadily. *I* feel that I am rapidly gaining more poise. I am getting better control over my will each day, and my will completely controls my movements. I begin to look on my will as a great governing power. I would not think of parting with the knowledge of will I have gained. I find it is a good exercise and know it will help me to accomplish my tasks."

6TH DAY

NOTES. "I begin to feel the wonderful possibilities of the will. It gives me strength to think of the power of will. I am able to do so much more and better work now, that I realize that I can control my will action. Whatever my task, my will is concentrated on it. I am to keep my will centered there until the task is finished. The more closely and, definitely I determine what I shall do, the more easily the will carries it out. Determination imparts compelling force to the will. It exerts itself more. The will and the end act and react on each other."

7TH DAY

NOTES. Now try to do everything you do today faster. Don't hurry or become nervous. Just try to do everything faster, but in a steady manner.

You will find that the exercises you have practiced in retardation have steadied your nerves, and thereby made it possible to increase your speed. The will is under your command. Make it carry out resolutions rapidly. This is how you build up your self-control and your self-command. It is then that the human machine acts as its author dictates.

You certainly should now be able to judge of the great benefit that comes from writing out your introspections each day. Of course you will not have the exact experiences given in these examples, but some of these will fit your case. Be careful to study your experiences carefully and make as true a report as you can. Describe your feelings just as they seem to you. Allow your fancies to color your report and it will be worthless. You have pictured conditions as you see them. In a few months, if you again try the same exercises, you will find your report very much better. By these introspections, we learn to know ourselves better and with this knowledge can wonderfully increase our efficiency. As you become used to writing out your report, it will be more accurate. You thus learn how to govern your impulses, activities and weaknesses.

Each person should try to plan exercises that will best fit his needs. If not convenient for you to practice exercises every day, take them twice or three times a week. But carry out any plan you decide to try. If you cannot devote ten minutes a day to the experiments start with five minutes and gradually increase the time. The exercises given are only intended for examples.

WILL TRAINING WITHOUT EXERCISE

There are many people who do not want to take the time to practice exercises, so the following instructions for training the will are given to them.

By willing and realizing, the will grows. Therefore the more you will, the more it grows, and builds up power. No matter whether your task is big or small, make it a rule to accomplish it in order to fortify your will. Form the habit of focusing your will in all its strength upon the subject to be achieved. You form in this way the habit of getting a thing done, of carrying out some plan. You acquire the feeling of being able to accomplish that which lies before you, no matter what it is. This gives you confidence and a sense of power that you get in no other way. You know when you make a resolution that you will keep it. You do not tackle new tasks in a half-hearted way, but with a bold, brave spirit. We know that the will is able to carry us over big obstacles. Knowing this despair never claims us for a victim. We have wills and are going to use them with more and more intensity, thus giving us the power to make our resolutions stronger, our actions freer and our lives finer and better.

The education of the will should not be left to chance. It is only definite tasks that will render it energetic, ready, persevering and consistent. The only way it can be done is by self-study and self-discipline. The cost is effort, time and patience, but the returns are valuable. There are no magical processes leading to will development, but the development of your will works wonders for you because it gives you self-mastery, personal power and energy of character.

CONCENTRATION OF THE WILL TO WIN

The adaptability of persons to their business environment is more a matter of determination than anything else. In this age we hear a good deal of talk about a man's aptitudes. Some of his aptitudes, some of his powers, may be developed to a wonderful extent, but he is really an unknown quality until all his latent powers are developed to their highest possible extent. He may be a failure in one line and a big success in another. There are many successful men who did not succeed well at what they first undertook, but they profited by their efforts in different directions, and this fitted them for higher things, whereas had they refused to adjust themselves to their environment, the tide of progress would have swept them into oblivion.

My one aim in all my works is to try and arouse in the individual the effort and determination to develop his full capacities, his highest possibilities. One thing I want you to realize at the start, that it is not so much ability, as it is the will to do that counts. Ability is very plentiful, but organizing initiative and creative power are not plentiful. It is easy to get employees, but to get someone to train them is harder. Their abilities must be directed to the work they can do. They must be shown how, while at this work, to conserve their energy and they must be taught to work in harmony with others, for most business concerns are dominated by a single personality.

CONCENTRATING ON DRIVING FORCE WITHIN

We are all conscious, at times, that we have somewhere within us an active driving force that is ever trying to push us onward to better deeds. It is that "force" that makes us feel determined at times to do something worth while. It is not thought, emotion or feeling. This driving force is something distinct from thought or emotion. It is a quality of the soul and therefore it has a consciousness all its own. It is the "I will do" of the will. It is the force that makes the will concentrate. Many have felt this force working within them, driving them on to accomplish their tasks. All great men and women become conscious that this supreme and powerful force is their ally in carrying out great resolutions.

This driving force is within all, but until you reach a certain stage you do not become aware of it. It is most useful to the worthy. It springs up naturally without any thought of training. It comes unprovoked and leaves unnoticed. Just what this force is we do not know, but we do know that it is what intensifies the will in demanding just and harmonious action.

The ordinary human being, merely as merchandise, if he could be sold as a slave, would be worth ten thousand dollars. If somebody gave you a five thousand dollar automobile you would take very good care of it. You wouldn't put sand in the carburetor, or mix water with the gasoline, or drive it furiously over rough roads, or leave it out to freeze at night.

Are you quite sure that you take care of your own body, your own health, your only real property, as well as you would take care of a five thousand dollar automobile if it were given to you?

The man who mixes whiskey with his blood is more foolish than a man would be if he mixed water with gasoline in his car.

You can get another car; you cannot get another body.

The man who misses sleep lives irregularly—bolts his food so that his blood supply is imperfect. That is a foolish man treating himself as he would not treat any other valuable piece of property.

Do you try to talk with men and women who know more than you do, and do you LISTEN rather than try to tell them what you know?

There are a hundred thousand men of fifty, and men of sixty, running along in the old rut, any one of whom could get out of it and be counted among the successful men if only the spark could be found to explode the energy within them now going to waste.

Each man must study and solve his own problem.

LESSON 20

Concentration Reviewed

In bringing this book to a close, I again want to impress you with the inestimable value of concentration, because those who lack this great power or, rather who fail to develop it, will generally suffer from poverty and unhappiness and their life's work will most often be a failure, while those who develop and use it will make the most of life's opportunities.

I have tried to make these lessons practical and I am sure that many will find them so. Of course the mere reading of them will not do you a great deal of good, but, if the exercises are practiced and worked out and applied to your own individual case, you should be able to acquire the habit of concentration in such measure as to greatly improve your work and increase your happiness.

But remember the best instruction can only help you to the extent to which you put it into practice. I have found it an excellent idea to read a book through first, and then reread it, and when you come to an idea that appeals to you, stop and think about it, then if applicable to you, repeat it over and over, that you will be impressed by it. In this way you can form the habit of picking out all the good things you read and these will have a wonderful influence on your character.

In this closing chapter, I want to impress you to concentrate on what you do, instead of performing most of your work unconsciously or automatically, until you have formed habits that give you the mastery of your work and your life powers and forces.

Very often the hardest part of work is thinking about it. When you get right into it, it does not seem so disagreeable. This is the experience of many when they first commence to learn how to concentrate. So never think it a difficult task, but undertake it with the "I Will Spirit" and you will find that its acquirement will be as easy as its application will be useful.

Read the life of any great man, and you will generally find that the dominant quality that made him successful was the ability to concentrate. Study those who have been failures and you will often find that lack of concentration was the cause.

"One thing at a time, and that done well, is a good rule as I can tell."

All men are not born with equal powers, but it is the way they are used that counts. "Opportunity knocks at every man's door." Those who are successful hear the knock and grasp the chance. The failures believe that luck and circumstances are against them. They always blame someone else instead of themselves for their lack of success. We get what is coming to us, nothing more or less. Anything within the universe is within your grasp. Just use your latent powers and it is yours. You are aided by both visible and invisible forces when you concentrate on either "to do" or "to be."

Everyone is capable of some concentration, for without it you would be unable to say or do anything. People differ in the power to concentrate because some are unable to Will to hold the thought in mind for the required time. The amount of determination used determines who has the strongest will. No one's is stronger than yours. Think of this whenever you go against a strong opponent.

Never say "I can't concentrate today." You can do it just the minute you say "I will." You can keep your thoughts from straying, just the same as you can control your arms. When once you realize this fact, you can train the will to concentrate on anything you wish. If it wanders, it is your fault. You are not utilizing your will. But, don't blame it on your will and say it is weak. The will is just the same whether you act as if it were weak or as if it were strong. When you act as if your will is strong you say, "I can." When you act as if it were weak you say, "I can't." It requires the same amount of effort in each case.

Some men get in the habit of thinking "I can't" and they fail. Others think "I can" and succeed. So remember, it is for you to decide whether you will join the army of "I can't" or "I can."

The big mistake with so many is that they don't realize that when they say "I can't," they really say, "I won't try." You cannot tell what you can do until you try. "Can't" means you will not try. Never say you cannot concentrate, for, when you do, you are really saying that you refuse to try.

Whenever you feel like saying, "I can't," say instead, "I possess all will and I can use as much as I wish." You only use as much as you have trained yourself to use.

AN EXPERIMENT TO TRY

Before going to bed tonight, repeat, "I am going to choose my own thoughts, and to hold them as long as I choose. I am going to shut out all thoughts that weaken or interfere; that make me timid. My Will is as strong as anyone else. While going to work the next morning, repeat this over. Keep this up for a month and you will find you will have a better opinion of yourself. These are the factors that make you a success. Hold fast to them always.

Concentration is nothing but willing to do a certain thing. All foreign thoughts can be kept out by willing that they stay out. You cannot realize your possibilities until you commence to direct your mind. You then do consciously what you have before done unconsciously. In this way you note mistakes, overcome bad habits and perfect your conduct.

You have at times been in a position that required courage and you were surprised at the amount you showed. Now, when once you arouse yourself, you have this courage all the time and it is not necessary to have a special occasion reveal it to you. My object in so strongly impressing this on your mind is to make you aware that the same courage, the same determination that you show at certain exceptionable times you have at your command at all times. It is a part of your vast resources. Use it often and well, in working out the highest destiny of which you are capable.

FINAL CONCENTRATION INSTRUCTION

You now realize that, in order to make your life worthy, useful and happy, you must concentrate. A number of exercises and all the needed instruction has been given. It now remains for you to form the highest ideal that you can in the present and live up to that ideal, and try to raise it. Don't waste your time in foolish reading. Select something that is inspiring, that you may become enrapport with those who think thoughts that are worth while. Their enthusiasm will inspire and enlighten you. Read slowly and concentrate on what you are reading. Let your spirit and the spirit of the author commune, and you will then sense what is between the lines—those great things which words cannot express.

Pay constant attention to one and one thing only for a given time and you will soon be able to concentrate. Hang on to that thought ceaselessly until you have attained your object. When you work, let your mind dwell steadily on your task. Think before you speak and direct your conversation to the subject under discussion. Do not ramble. Talk slowly, steadily and connectedly. Never form the hurry habit, but be deliberate in all you do. Assume static attitudes without moving a finger or an eyelid, or any part of your body. Read books that treat of but one continuous subject. Read long articles and recall the thread of the argument. Associate yourself with people who are steady, patient and tireless in their thought, action and work. See how long you can sit still and think on one subject without interruption.

CONCENTRATING ON THE HIGHER SELF

Father Time keeps going on and on. Every day he rolls around means one day less for you on this planet. Most of us only try to master the external conditions of this world. We think our success and happiness depends on us doing so. These are of course important and I don't want you to think they are not, but I want you to realize that when death comes, only those inherent and acquired qualities and conditions within the mentality—your character, conduct and soul growth—will go with you. If these are what they should be, you need not be afraid of not being successful and happy, for with these qualities you can mold external materials and conditions.

Study yourself. Find Your Strong Points and Make Them Stronger as Well as Your Weak Ones and Strengthen Them. Study yourself carefully and you will see yourself as you really are.

The secret of accomplishment is concentration, or the art of turning all your power upon just one point at a time.

If you have studied yourself carefully you should have a good line on yourself, and should be able to make the proper interior readjustments. Remember first, last and always, right thinking and right living necessarily results in happiness, and it is therefore within your power to obtain happiness. Anyone who is not happy does not claim his birthright.

Keep in mind that some day you are going to leave this world and think of what you will take with you. This will assist you to concentrate on the higher forces. Now start from this minute, to act according to the advice of the higher self in everything you do. If you do, its ever harmonious forces will necessarily insure to you a successful fulfillment of all your life purposes. Whenever you feel tempted to disobey your higher promptings, hold the thought.

"My-higher-self-insures-to-me-the-happiness-of-doing-that-which-best-answers my-true-relations-to-all-others."

You possess latent talents, that when developed and utilized are of assistance to you and others. But if you do not properly use them, you shirk your duty, and you will be the loser and suffer from the consequences. Others will also be worse off if you do not fulfill your obligations.

When you have aroused into activity your thought powers you will realize the wonderful value of these principles in helping you to carry out your plans. The right in the end must prevail. You can assist in the working out of the great plan of the universe and thereby gain the reward, or you can work against the great plan and suffer the consequences. The all consuming fires are gradually purifying all discordant elements. If you choose to work contrary to the law you will burn in its crucible, so I want you to learn to concentrate intelligently on becoming in harmony with your higher self. Hold the thought: "I will-live-for-my-best. I-seek-wisdom-self-knowledge, happiness-and-power-to-help-others. I-act-from-the-higher-self, therefore-only-the-best-can-come-to-me."

The more we become conscious of the presence of the higher self the more we should try to become a true representative of the human soul in all its wholeness and holiness, instead of wasting our time dwelling on some trifling external quality or defect. We should try to secure a true conception of what we really are so as not to over value the external furnishings. You will then not surrender your dignity or self-respect, when other ignorantly make a display of material things to show off. Only the person who realizes that he is a permanent Being knows what the true self is.

18

HOW TO GROW SUCCESS

ELIZABETH TOWNE

(1904)

DESTINY

Caught in the Gulf Stream of some great desire,
Know that thy life-trend rhythms to the mighty flow
And ebb of Life's full ocean. Also know
Each outreach of thy soul bears deep the seal
Of cosmic impulse, æons old That thing,
Heart-hungry, every fiber thrills to reach,
Hath sought thee down the ages, hungering, too;
In the birth-travail of this, thine ideal,
Dumb longing of the centuries finding speech.
Hunger is prophecy. Take heart; and fling
Doubt and despair forever from thy view.
Thy longing is the covenant cloud and fire
Forever faithful twixt thy goal and thee.
Kate follows faith. Desire is—Destiny.

—ESTHER HARLAN

How to Grow Success

SUCCESS. WHAT IT IS

Success is not money, nor is it fame. The King in the ancient fable turned to gold all that he touched, and starved to death. The "Sick Man of the East" has wealth galore and world-wide fame, but so abjectly afraid is he that he is never a moment alone; never tastes a dish that has not first been tried on a menial; and springs to his feet with pistol in hand if his best friend across the table happens to make a quick movement. Money and power he has, but not success.

SUCCESS *is liberty to command, coupled with a clear conscience and loving heart.* William Gladstone was a success Abraham Lincoln was another. Few men attain so complete a success as theirs. Jesus of Nazareth was a success, though most people imagine he was "poor." He was not. He wore seamless robes and fine linen and fared sumptuously in many elegant homes, *where he was more at liberty to command than were the masters themselves.* Nothing was too good for Jesus. To *own* all those homes would be a burden Jesus was too wise to assume. Liberty to command must not be overworked. lest it cease to be liberty and become the drudgery of *taking care* of things.

A successful man is not necessarily a rich man, but he *is* a man who can command *all he desires.* Among, money kings it is said J. Pierpont Morgan is not rated a very rich man. But he commands more money than any other man in the world. It is said men confide in him because of his fine business sense, gained by *using his own* judgment; and because "*he does exactly what he agrees to.*" He never asks advice and he keeps his mouth shut unless he has something special to say. Then he says it, in the simplest and fewest words possible. This is concentration, the mode of success.

Money is not success, but success *includes the power to command money.*

Success includes the liberty to command money enough to gratify all one's aspirations to better his own condition, and the condition of those dependent upon him. This does not mean that success includes money enough to enable one to outshine his neighbor. *No man with that aim in life was ever successful, or ever will be.*

Not to *out*-shine, but to *shine upon* his neighbors, is the successful man's mission.

SUCCESS IS ALIVE

It germinates, sprouts and grows. It grows first underground. In due time it appears and keeps on unfolding.

It is just as easy to grow success as to grow potatoes. Yes, it is easier; for success will grow *out* of potatoes, and *it will grow where potatoes won't.* There is not a spot on earth, or in heaven, or hell, that will not serve to sprout success in—not one. Success may outgrow a place and need transplanting; but it will *sprout anywhere.*

And at any time. Potatoes must be started at a certain time. The time to plant and tend success is NOW.

You plant potatoes and you *know* they will grow. You go off and do something else whilst they germinate and sprout. You can't *see* them grow but you KNOW they are growing, and whilst you are working away at other things you have a nice little warm glow in your heart, over the fine crop that is coming on out there in the tater patch. You *love* that patch. You planted it just as well as you could, with the best seed potatoes, and you are proud of it, even before there is the first peep of green. When that comes your love increases. You hoe every hill carefully and you take good care of the bugs. In due time you exhibit some of those spuds at the State Fair and you get a prize. And at last you *command more money* for your potatoes than others get for theirs.

Now do you imagine you had no success until you got the gold for those potatoes? Then you are greatly mistaken. You *planted success* with every blessed tater hill. You loved it and beamed on it, hoed the weeds away, picked the bugs off, and *reveled* in success all summer long. You *lived on success all summer.*

Perhaps you say, "Oh, that is a very pretty picture but *my* potato patch was a failure." Then you planted failure with your potatoes. When you were plowing and planting and hoeing you were telling yourself all the time that "there is no use—*nothing* ever did well for you—it seemed to be your lot to drudge and pinch and worry along and never have anything—there is John Smith over the way—*he can* take it easy and have fine stock and hire men to do the drudgery whilst he rides around and bosses—and here *you* are—everything is against you—damn the stones on this land anyhow—your spuds never do well—ground is no good—why can't you take it easy like other folks?" And so on, ad infinitum, *ad nauseam,* your mind meanders. Whilst you, with less than half a heart get through the "drudgery" any old way—just so you get through.

Potatoes are not the only thing you planted. You planted *thoughts* in every hill. You *cursed* every hill you planted—cursed it with mean thinking. You planted *failure* and you will reap ditto. Every idle thought will bring its meed of *failure* and subtract from the money that might have been yours.

It takes the finest seed potatoes, good land *and thinking to match,* to insure a good crop and good prices.

The successful man puts his thought *into* his work, The unsuccessful one turns his thought *away* from it: as if when be was supposed to be watering his garden he should turn the stream over the fence into the road, leaving his garden dry and gasping.

YOU MUST LOVE

And *think* about your work if you are to make a success of it and make it pay. "Blessed is that man who hath found his work." If you are doing work you dislike you will not succeed, and all the treatments in creation can't make you succeed.

Get into line with a work you do love—something in which you can express yourself.

If you think you must remain where you are then put your interest, your love, *yourself,* into that business. One touch of *yourself* will make business go. A young man laid in coal, opened shop, placed his card in the local paper and sat down to wait for custom that did not come. When he went home to dinner one day his wife remarked that she had a headache which had been aggravated by the noise of putting in coal at the next house. That young man went to the newspaper office and added a line to his ad—"Coal delivered without noise!" He delivered his coal in sacks. Yes, delivered it. One touch of *himself* did the business and he was custom-less no longer.

A man's success is measured on the unseen side by the amount of LOVE he feeds his work with; and on the seen side it is measured by money.

I do not mean that the amount of money a man manages to corner by fair means or foul, his own or his father's, is the measure of his success. Not at all. But the amount of real *love* a man puts INTO his work determines exactly the amount of money he or some other man can get *out* of it. If he respects himself *and the rest of mankind*—if he *knows that justice rules* NOW,—really *knows* it—he will himself get the money. If he "knows just what mean and grasping liars men are," he attracts men who will rob him of the money due his work. But in either event HE is at the bottom of the whole business.

The individual himself is Lord of his own circumstances; circumstances and other men are puppets in his hands. As a man realizes this he moves circumstances and people at will, *by pulling the right strings in himself.*

YOU MUST LOVE

People in order to be able to move them. You must be able to see them *as they see themselves,* and you must meet them *heart*-ily. Love is not sentimental gush; love is not a self announcer. Love is divine emotion—that which *moves outward* from the point where the Universal meets the personal. Love manifests in the person as pure GOOD WILL. It shines in his face, beams from his eyes and impels his every action. The successful man is a man of pure GOOD WILL.

Remember, Success is the liberty to command, *coupled with a clear conscience and loving heart.* In proportion as a man is possessed of *Good Will* his conscience is clear. Good Will is the outward-moving power of a loving heart.

Only such a heart ever has liberty to command.

In proportion as a man succeeds in *letting* Good Will flow outward to each person, thing or circumstance with which he comes in touch, in that proportion will he be able to *influence* persons, things and circumstances according to his will—his *Good Will*, which is just to all.

The art of succeeding is the art of *concentrating Good Will*, and *using it* for definite purposes. He that *doubteth* and yet doeth, directs *Evil Will*, not Good Will, and he is condemned in his own soul. Not only that, but he will reap outwardly what he has sown—*Evil Will.*

GOOD WILL

Must go out to all mankind, collectively and individually. A single grudge is a "worm i' the bud" of your success. Send out such positive, definite, *personal* Good Will that a grudge finds no room to grow by eating out *your* heart and success. It is *your* grudge that has the power to destroy your success—*your* grudge against person, place, work, or "fate." Spray your soul daily, hourly, with Good Will; and withhold not the spray from thy neighbor.

THE ESSENTIALS

Of success are these:

1. Good Will toward all. This includes justice, honesty, a clear conscience and loving heart.
2. An Aim; a stake to be reached.
2. Eternal stick-to-it-iveuess.
4. Concentration of thought and effort upon the *details* of reaching the stake set.

A man's aim in life is the *reflection* of his opinion of himself. A man with a pretty low opinion of himself has no aim at all. He feels himself merely a fallen twig borne helplessly on the bosom of life. Wake up, dearie, exalt yourself, and set your stake *just as high* us *you dare.* Then, as you find you can face your stake with a feeling that you are really going to make it after all, congratulate yourself upon your soul stature, *and move your stake higher.*

Listen to what somebody of the name of Buxton has said about the third essential to success.

"The longer I live, the more I am certain that the great difference between men, between the feeble and the powerful, the great and the insignificant, is *energy, invincible determination,*—a purpose once fixed, and then death or victory! That quality will do anything that can be done in this world; and no talents, no circumstances, no opportunities, will make a two-legged creature a man without it."

And Ella Wheeler Wilcox says:

"There is no chance, no destiny, no fate,
Can circumvent or hinder or control.
The firm resolve of a determined soul."

Another has said: "All things are possible to him that believeth." And I say unto you, "Go in to win and *stick to it.*"

Concentration of thought upon the details of getting there: You *can't afford* to waste thought upon grumblings and resentments, against individuals, circumstances or "fate." Yon may imagine you have brains enough to divide between your work and these petty fault findings and resentments; but you have not. Every idle thought subtracts a *definite* amount from your success *and your cash. Put* your thought into business.

This does not mean you are never to think of anything but business; but it *does* mean that you are never to separate thought *from Good Will.* Whatever you can think of with Good Will will aid you to self-expression; will increase your power.

Concentrate; on the *detail* of getting there. I was once lost above the snow line on a great mountain and had to retrace my steps upward to the point where I had taken the wrong trail. I was so anxious to get to that point that my whole soul seemed to leap up ward and away toward that place leaving me so utterly paralyzed that I was actually unable to take a step. In a few moments I collected myself and put my thought into the climbing, when I made the distance easily and quickly. Where the thought runs ahead like that the will, the real motive power of the body, actually goes out of the body, leaving it unable to accomplish what is expected of it. When you are *doing* something *put* your *thought* into it. Will follows thought and thus you work easily and effectively. When yon are relaxed and resting you may without injury let thought take any flight. "Whatsoever thy hand findeth to do, do it with thy might;" that is with *all* of thee—*thought* and will, as well as hands. Work done in this way actually *rejuvenates* the body; whilst a scattered mind scatters or disintegrates the body. You are a *unit—a* One. *Work* as a One.

NEVER FEAR FEAR

Fear is a great bugaboo and like moat bogies he is merely a shadow. No amount of fear will hinder your success if you will *keep your eye on the stake you have set,* and keep *sticking to it mentally,* fears or no fears. When I ride the wheel I see stones to be avoided. If I look at one and say to myself, "I am afraid—I'll probably run over it" —then I go over it every time. But I may have *more* fear—it may be a larger stone—but if I *say to myself, "I* shall go *around* that," I invariably *go* around it.

It is *the Word,* the mental statement, that determines whether I miss or hit those stones. I have proven by hundreds of careful observations that *fear* has absolutely *nothing* to do with it. I may be scared blue over something; I may not be able to keep my eyes off the obstacle; but if I *affirm* resolutely, "I shall *miss* that"—I miss it *every time.*

Our bodies are just bundles of mental statements, which are being hourly augmented and *revised* by more statements. It is these mental statements that *incite* motion. *Every thought* sends vibrations clear to the tips of the nerves and on out through the personal and universal auras. *Every thought incites corresponding muscular activity.* "Mind reading," is really "muscle reading," as Dr. Parkyn claims.

Fear literally has *no* power over your body except as you *state to yourself* that it has.

Deny it—*deny* that fear has power. Make persistent mental statements of what you desire; make them in the face of fear, until fear tucks his tail betwixt his legs and gets off the earth.

Kate Boehme gives this sentence to her students to "concentrate" upon: "I am open on my inner side to the inexhaustible ocean of Divine Love and Power. I flow forth from it and am one with it. All success is mine through the working of this power. I shall succeed in all my undertakings."

Be still and know.

Money Making

"Please treat me that I may be useful to the world. I will trust the money to follow."

All right; you will find the money following; but it will follow such a long way off that you will never see it except in some-other-body's possession.

"Make me useful to the world" is the cry of *self-depreciation;* it presupposes that you are *now* a weak, useless piece of furniture.

As you think of yourself so the world thinks. Just so long as you carry that prayer in your heart, just so long will you remain weak and useless *in your own esteem,* which the world will continue to reflect.

The world has an eye to the Main Chance. If you think you are worth little to the world the world will not fall over itself to lay its coin at your feet. It will take all you can give and when you've nothing more to give it will dump the remains in the potter's field. Possibly it may beautify its parks and soothe its conscience with a monument inscribed to you when you are well out of the way. And it may hold memorial services where it will congratulate itself on the bargain it got out of you.

But pay you?—never! Not a cent will you get beyond what you *really think in your heart* you are worth to the world.

Ungrateful? Hard? Wrong? Not at all. The world is governed by the immutable *Law* that "as a man thinketh so he is"; and the world is too wise to give gold for nothing.

Every man gets just as much gold out of the world as he *puts into it,* All things are thought made. Every man must *think his own gold into being.* Or, to turn it around that we may get a clearer view, there is money enough in existence but each individual must *stake his claim and then work it.*

The writer of those lines at the head of this article has never staked her claim. She "trusts" the world to *give* her money ready made in return for services which *she thinks* are of little or no value, but which she insists upon giving.

This is the beggar spirit pure and simple, and leads down to the depths of poverty. It is the same spirit that rules India—the spirit of self-depreciation, of self-effacement; the spirit which regards the individual as merely a microbe among teeming millions; the spirit of little i and big YOU.

"Big I and little you" is not a pretty spirit, but enshrined in the hearts of those starving millions he would have risen up and *demanded as his right* the sustenance which for centuries these poor "little i" people have been *denying themselves.* Not the British "big I" is to blame for these conditions, but the Indian *"little* i."

In our country it is not the "big I" corporations, trusts or individuals who are the cause of squalor and wretchedness. *It is the "little I" in the working man.* The only cure for poverty of mind or body is to *educate* the individual "little I" until he grows up.

These pinched conditions are necessary to wake up the individual to his own I AM—his "big I."

Every man gets the mental claim he stakes, works and *sticks* to.

Who ever heard of a rich man who never *aimed* to be rich? Many a man aims and fall short; stakes his claim and then gives it up because it is "too hard work," or "fate is against him;" but not one ever "makes his stake" without *first setting* his stake. This is all in his mind, but what is in his mind may, *by persevering effort,* come into visibility.

There are a few people in the world who seem to be exceptions to this rule. But you may depend upon it they only *seem.*

Every blessed accomplishment any human being evidences came in the same way—by *desiring* a definite thing and then putting forth intelligent, persistent effort in that direction. If you find a man to whom things "come easy" you may rest assured that in some prior state of existence he has staked his claim and put forth all the intelligent, repeated efforts necessary to work it. He has served his apprenticeship and mastered his art in some previous incarnation. In this incarnation he does it easily and the world wonders. This is just as true of a Carnegie or a Rockefeller or Elbert Hubbard as it is of a musical or an art genius. There is no royal road to anything.

Somewhere, somehow, sometime, every man must learn *all things* by his own persistent effort. And financiering is one of the all things.

Yes, he MUST learn to make money—literally to *make* money out of Himself.

Do you rebel at "must"? Well you might if another compelled you. But it is *the Law of your being* which says "I DESIRE it." And Desire is the Law.

You DESIRE wealth—money—the *ability to gratify your desires.*

But you want to cling to your old affectation that money is "filthy lucre" and not as "noble" an object of effort as "the good of mankind."

Oh, you dear dunce, *money* is the MEASURE of the "good" you can do mankind. Without money you can do nothing—but hire yourself out to some other man for bread and duds.

With money you can do *anything.* What your money cannot give to the world directly it will enable *you* to give to the world. It will give you Time in which to devote Ideas and Love to the world.

If Desire for money has been born in the midst of your poverty, bless it and cherish it and let it grow up. Don't starve it upon such watery sentimentality pap as "Oh, I *wish* we didn't have to have money. I'd so much rather be doing good to the world than working for money!"

If you were "doing good" that the world *wants* of you it would hasten to pay you money.

That's the trouble with folks who are always wailing to "do good"—they want to do good *their* way, never remembering that the World might object to their way. The World is perfectly willing you shall do good to *your* corner as much as you please but until you get your own corner ship shape the World objects to your meddling with it. If you do you'll find yourself on a rocky road.

When you get your own corner cosy and pretty, as an example of what you can do, then the world will come and gaze and ask you to tell how you did it. The World will even offer you $1,000 or so for a short magazine article on how you did it or how you'd advise other folks to do. The World wants the Ideas of a man who has demonstrated something for himself.

No, this is not because the World worships money at all. It don't. It worships Ideas and it will give all the gold it has for Ideas *externalized.*

As long as Ideas remain in Imagination they are not worth the second hand clothes and coarse grub of the Imaginer.

Let that Imaginer get a move on and externalize his thinks and the World shells out in a hurry.

The money you attract is the exact measure of value of the Ideas you have succeeded in externalizing.

If you have invented something or other and sold your Idea for a pittance to somebody else you needn't grumble because he is getting the money. He deserves it. It is as if you had given away or sold your baby at the hour of birth. He has *raised* your child. He has done more than ever you did toward making useful to the World your idea. So he gets a greater measure of money.

If you go about giving your Ideas—a literal piece of your mind—to the World at every turn you will never get beyond the second hand clothes stage. Other people may pick up your Ideas and make money on them. Well, you needn't feel robbed. You were too lazy to do anything but talk.

Some people—the "I want to do good to the World" kind—are prolific of Ideas perhaps, but they let somebody else incubate them and send 'em to market.

Learn to think for cash. Keep mum. Value your Ideas. Take good care of them. Keep your mouth shut so they don't catch cold. When you've borned a new Idea keep your eye on him. Don't let him get away until he is fit to be seen. Then present him to the World for Value Received.

This is a fine art and one that repays care and persistence and all the intelligence you can bring to bear.

To make money you must make Ideas practical to the World.

Making Ideas practical is *Self-expression.*

Self-expression is the mode of External life, growth, health, success, JOY.

Go in to win. There isn't a greater, grander, more God-like thing to do than to *make money.*

Now and Then

Discouragement is due to just one cause—letting the mind run on one thing whilst you are doing another. At such times you are a house divided against itself and you are falling. You are a stream of energy running in two channels instead of one, and you are therefore too weakened to accomplish anything in either channel. And you *feel* weak and discouraged. You are practicing mental scatteration, which is the way not to live. You are living in the death part of your consciousness and your body is *actually* disintegrating whilst you are doing it. You are letting go your life, your individuality. You are letting your desire and your will, which are all one force and the *only* one, spread out all over creation. You are allowing yourself to be pulled to pieces by conflicting centers of attraction outside you. You are become the puppet of environment for the time being.

Of course it don't feel good. It is an unnatural state, a painful state, to be in.

And you don't have to be there a single minute. Only your own ignorance can keep you there.

YOU are a center of attraction, with greater force than is in all your environment beside. You can literally *pull yourself together* and become master instead of puppet.

And it is the easiest thing in the world to do it, and the most natural. So natural that the tiniest infant can do it, and does it habitually.

LIVING is the art of adjusting one's self to the NOW. Whatever one is really adjusted to one enjoys. Whenever one is *not* enjoying, it is because he is hanging with one hand to the NOW and with the other to the fleeting past, or is straining out toward the future.

The NOW is the only point one can become thoroughly adjusted to, the only place one can really enjoy. And the only way one can enjoy the NOW is to put all of himself into it, so that there is no straining out in the different directions.

One no sooner becomes comfortably adjusted to the NOW than the NOW changes.

Well, LET it change and do thou likewise. Readjust as NOW readjusts. *Let go* what is fleeting away, accept what is arriving, and GET INTERESTED in cuddling comfortably down into it.

Dearie, this is something that *is all in your mind.* Keep adjusting your mind to things *as they come.*

Of course you will have a lot of Desires that certain particular things come. Well, every blessed one of those desired things *will* come. Desire is the Index to the Book of Life. Just read the index and smack your lips over the good things that are coming in that big book, and then settle down to *enjoy* every one of the chapters as it comes.

I know lots of folks think they must dip into the last chapter first, and then they lose interest in what comes before and skip slightingly over it all. They don't get half the pleasure of the book. But the Book of Life is a serial story and you can't get at the last chapter first, fortunately for you. So don't try. Just glance over the index, your desires, and then cuddle comfortably down with each chapter as it comes. ENJOY IT. And then enjoy the next and the next.

What is the use anyway in eternally hashing over the table of contents of our lives? Lots of us look backward continually and dwell upon the hard places. Why? Just because we want to be pitied and made much over—because we want somebody to get down with us and wail over the terrible things we have been through. Or if we have been through some nice things we want folks to weep with us because the particular chapter we are now giving the small part of our attention to isn't quite so nice.

It is astonishing how determined we are to weep and make other folks weep over our Book of Life. We are so set on "sympathy" that we don't even see one-tenth of the good cheer and fun and frolic and real wit that is so plentifully bespringling every Book of Life. We pass over the good things because we don't half read the NOW chapter.

Then if we have perchance grown tired of looking over the table of contents of our past lives we go stumbling over the future. We study our Desires assiduously but we *don't believe them.* We fret and strain after them, all the while fearing that the Book will not give us what the Index promises. See? So we fail to make the best of what goes before and we postpone the day of getting to the thing Desire promises, or when we get there we don't half enjoy it because we have failed to *pay attention* to what went before.

Now, dearie, this is no joke and no meaningless figure of speech. It is a literal FACT, as solid as any rock that ever grew. You never strive and strain over the table of contents of any printed book—you *never doubt* that it will all be in the book. So you get comfortably to work at the beginning and read one chapter at a time until you get to the Supreme Climax. Your desires are just as accurate and trustworthy an index to what is coming. Then LET it come and *enjoy the vicissitudes by which it comes.* Cuddle comfortably down with the NOW chapter and *pay attention* to each thing as it turns up. That is the way to GET THERE. See?

United We Achieve

Do I believe in turning *all* the attention upon each detail of every day work? Yes. Pour *all* your thought into *this* piece of work until you can do it to perfection and *with joy.* As long as you have irksome tasks or "drudgery" you may rest assured it is because you have not yet put in interested thought enough.

This is the finest "concentration" practice in the world—just to put your whole soul into the one thing you are doing! When you have used this practice long enough you will do the thing beautifully and with joy.

About this time you will find your thought force has flowed into this work and filled it *full* of energy *and is overflowing.* You will take happy little mental flights away from your work; little inspirations will come to you, and always your thought will come back to your work with joy.

Suppose your work just now is "five-finger exercises"—learning to use your fingers. If you put *all* your thought into each movement you will make each *accurately.* If you let your mind wander ever so little your fingers follow. Your exercises will be slovenly because your thought is divided and *you haven't enough to bear dividing.* If you practice with a divided mind it will take you five times as long to accomplish the art of using your fingers, and you will *never* use them to the best advantage. I hear daily some one across the street practicing scales. She runs one scale nicely because she *thinks* about it. After that I can read her wandering half-mind in those slovenly, uneven runs. I can tell when she is pleased or not, and I know the very instant she thinks of something nice she is going to do when she gets through that hour of "drudgery." You see her fingers are trying to express a divided mind, so their action is uncertain. And will always be so unless she mends her mind and turns it *all* into her fingers until her *fingers are full to overflowing.*

When this happens the thought flows, or overflows, in beautiful fancies which the fingers are ready to express. And *all* is pleasure.

Do you see now what "concentration" upon daily tasks is for? To *fill* your members, the different parts of your body, *with loving intelligence in expressing thought.* The everyday tasks set you in the school of life are the "scales" and "five finger exercises" that you *must* put your *soul* into mastering before that soul *can* express anything more beautiful in the way of life-symphonies.

There is a vast difference between putting *all* your thought into an action until you can do it sub-consciously, and your thought is freed on a higher plane, and the common way of putting half—or less—of your thought energy into "drudgery," done in a slipshod, ungraceful fashion, whilst the main body of your thought goes gallivanting around *where it has no business to be.*

Thought is *vitalizing,* energizing. When you try to work with half your thought switched *off* and *out* of your activities you rob and devitalize your body. To a fully vitalized body every act is *joy.* Whenever your work is "drudgery" stop short, call your thought home, take three or four very slow, full breaths of *fresh* air—straighten up to do it!—and then *quietly turn all* your thought into your actions. Every time you catch it wandering again bring it quietly, but firmly, back to business. This is the sort of "concentration" that gives self-command and fits you to think higher thoughts and *fill higher places.* And the moment you are *ready* the omnipresent Law of Attraction will whisk you into place.

I Want and I Am

I want so many things; or rather I want to be so many things—to be thoroughly healthy, beautiful, magnetic, cultured, a brilliant conversationalist, etc. I want lots of pretty clothes, beautiful things around me, money to gratify my ambitions. I am bewildered to know what to work at first. Am a clerk and have so little time to work at these things outside."

Don't you know the whole human race wants just those things, and don't you know that the whole human race is growing them? And all the unseen powers, the real powers, of the universe are working *with* the human race for the attainment of all that. And all the powers seen and unseen, are working for *your* attainment of them, and working just as whole-souledly, steadily and effectually as if *you* were the only creature in all creation. It is the working of these unseen powers in and through you that gives you the desire for such things. It is not *your* desire alone that is calling for these things—it is the whole universe calling *through* you. And all the powers of earth and heaven, yes, and hell too, will work through you to manifest them. All the powers *are* working through you NOW to manifest them.

You are not a separate and distinct creation rolling around loose in the world. You are a part of The Whole—a part that has its own peculiar position and uses in the economy of The Whole, and in all creation there is, never has been, and never will be, a duplicate of you. If you get misplaced in the world, or if you are not properly polished and beautified it is not you alone who suffer. The Whole travails in pain until *you* are satisfied and satisfying: until YOU *fit in* and glory in your fitness and beauty.

All the universe bestirs itself to help you fit in and be happy. All the beauty of the universe is pressing OUT through you into expression. All things that you desire are *welling up* within you, pressed upward by a ceaseless and almighty urge that CANNOT be gainsaid. Why, dearie, there is nothing you ever dreamed of, or hoped for, or longed for even in your moments of wildest imagining, that is not actually pressing, pressing, urging, to rise through you into visibility—that is not doing its best to well up and transform you and all your environment with its radiant, beautiful flow. Eye hath not seen nor ear heard, nor hath it yet entered into the heart of you to conceive the glories that are aching to flow through you and be free. There is more beauty, and art, and brilliance, wit and wisdom, fine raiment and *money* trying, trying to come upward and outward through YOU, dearie, than this blessed world has yet seen.

"Whether you believe it or not, *it is true.*

What is more, all these beautiful and desired things *are coming* through you. They are pressing out NOW, with fast increasing impetus.

IT IS TRUE, dearie, it is true.

Do you *want* to believe it? Do you want to help the universe into expression? Oh, you do.

But there are so many things, and you don't know where to begin. You don't have time for "these other things outside."

Well, *begin right where you are with the thing you are doing* NOW. You don't have to go outside to *let* the beautiful things of the universe come through you. You don't have to have special times for beauty culture, or health culture, or wisdom or money growing. Did you ever see a rose tree that had special hours for growing, or a rose that needed special times for improving its complexion or its perfume? No more do you need special times and places for such things. All desirable things well up within you and are radiated, just as the rose's beauty is radiated.

One of the greatest reasons why some people and corners of earth are not beautiful now is because they continually shut themselves up and try to get along any old way whilst they do up the so-called business of life. They promise themselves the ease and leisure to be beautiful and enjoy it away off some time in the future. Or, maybe, they just put it off until six o'clock, when the store closes. They try to live all day on business with a promise of what little beauty and leisure they can manage to crowd in after hours. The result is that when six o'clock comes they are literally starved—"too tired to move"—and must take that precious time that they meant to make beautiful, for resting. That is, they must needs lie down and *let the unseen beauties* rest them.

Beauty is harmony. Harmony may be seen, felt, tasted, smelt or heard. It may affect us through one or all the senses, either consciously or unconsciously. At night we sleep and the fine harmonies of the universe play through us and bring us into tune again. All unconsciously to us. Or, we may listen to exquisite music and so come consciously into harmony again. Or we see a beautiful, quiet place and *let* ourselves "catch" the harmony there expressed.

In either of these cases, or any other that we might think of, we simply *quit straining*—we quit *promising* ourselves beauty, harmony, at some other time. We LET GO and *enjoy* the harmony that IS NOW. We "vibrate with" the things that are and forget that tired feeling.

That tired feeling comes from *living on promises.* You see, promises point to something just out of reach and to save your life you can't help straining out after those promised good things. Your *energy* flows right out in the direction of the promised good things.

There *are* good things ahead—better things than any yet beheld. But, dearie, if you keep watching them they will ever *keep ahead. Your thought* FIXES *them in the future* and keeps them moving, just as every "tomorrow" is kept moving. I wish I could make you feel, as I feel, how *plastic* is the world and all that is therein, *including time and space.*

It is LITERALLY true that you are what you think, and WHEN you think it. There is really no future, *only as you think it.* Some people are literally almost *made up* of the future—they live so eternally on promises. Then there are so many poor, downhearted back-number folks who are in the same way nearly wholly composed of *the past.* Rarely do we meet one who is built of THE PRESENT. When we do meet such an one we see a radiant individual.

The knowledge that saves is the certainty that all that is, was, or ever will be, IS NOW.

When one knows *that,* he *lets go* and vibrates with the All-Love-Life NOW. He is an epitome of the universal harmonies. His life is not only a song but an exquisite blending of accompaniment beside. For him, and through him, the morning stars sing together NOW, heaven joys with him, and hell he has forgotten.

So it is not "time for these other things outside" that you need, dearie, but TIME NOW to *be* what you have been promising yourself. What you need is to haul taut on the life line and get those beautiful things right down into the NOW. Your visible self is a "statement of beliefs." Quit stating ANYTHING in the future tense. Say "I AM beauty, joy, everything I want—I AM! I AM!" Stick to it until you have made yourself *accept* the statement. That statement alone, lived on morning, noon and night, not to mention betweentimes, will work in you the mightiest revolution your world has ever seen. That statement LIVED ON will make a new creature of you—will move you to new ideas and activities—will open up the way for ALL those unseen beauties you so ardently desire to *literally come into the* NOW. This is no frill on the garment of Truth—it IS Truth itself. You prove Truth as you do the pudding. LIVE ON beauty NOW and yon will prove that all beauty IS now—that you ARE what you desire to be. You will find all you desire unfolding to your gaze, to ALL your senses.

Remember that what you desire is NOT *coming to* you, now or ever. It comes *through* you, from the unseen into the seen world. Whilst you are in the shop waiting upon a customer, the things you desire are *forming within you.* You cannot *see* the beauty you desire but you can *feel* it if you are mindful of it, if you look for it—you can feel it as a still, warm calmness at the center of you. *And your customer can see it shining in your face and feel its thrill in your quiet, whole-hearted attention.* It will mayhap quiet the turbulent waters of her soul. And it will surely help your soul into expression of the beauties you crave. Be still, dearie, and let the unseen harmonies be seen through you.

Every action that ever was made is really a vehicle for the letting of harmony from the unseen into the visible. The true art of living is only the art of *letting*—the art of being still.

Be still and know the I AM God within you.

Be still and *let* what you are into *this* act NOW.

Rejoice in what you ARE, as well as in what you have.

Dearie, this is an accurate description of each and every step of the way from behind that counter to *any place you may determine upon.*

Go in to WIN. Keep cool and sweet and BE NOW what you desire.

How to Be Wealthy

If you are afraid to use your money, if you are close, saving and skinflinty, in word, thought or deed, you are laying the foundation for unhappiness and poverty. The miser is not really rich, he is poor, *poor,* POOR." (W. E. T.) "I put it there because I want to be reminded of it all the time,—it has set me to thinking lots. I don't know where to draw the line between 'economy' and 'skinflinty,' and it gives me constant trouble to decide. It is awfully easy, I find, to follow out the economy bent till it becomes 'closeness,'—at the same time, it would be very easy to give myself the rein the other way, and 'just let her go' into extravagance. I suppose it might be said 'Draw the middle line,' but it is very hard to know where or what is the middle line,—and hence the question arises, on which side shall we err? My present opinion is that I had better err on the 'Let her go' side, as I am by nature strongly inclined to economy and self-denial. I am inclined to think that Economy with me would soon lead to penuriousness, and that therefore I should pursue the other tack. Besides what do these texts mean, if not that? 'Give and it shall be given unto you,—good measure, etc.,' and, 'If a man ask of you a coat, give him twain' (or something to that effect,)—give him twice what he asks for. As I look at the great God of Nature. He is extravagance itself,—the grain of wheat is multiplied many-fold,—the air we breathe, the water to drink are all in riotous profusion. And everything else till Man gets a hold of it, and surrounds it with his 'little fence,' and says, 'Thus far and no further.'"—Pigott.

It is not what you spend, nor what you spend it for, which makes the difference between wealth, opulence, and skinflintiness. Skinflintiness all lies in the attitude of mind which is constantly straining ahead to make a dollar buy *more* than a dollar's worth. The bargain counter conduces to skinflintiness, but it is a result and not a cause of it.

The man who, desiring a certain thing and having the dollar to pay for it, yet "hates to spend it," and thinks of a dozen other things he would like to have "thrown in" for the dollar,—such a man is a skinflint. He is not spending like a lord.

The man who, desiring a certain thing and having the dollar to pay, parts *willingly* with the dollar, even if it is a last one, and goes rejoicing on his way with the new purchase,—this man spends as he should. He is *willing* to pay *full* price, and he *enjoys* his purchase.

The skinflint's is spoiled with visions of a dozen other things he would *like* to have *squeezed out* of that dollar. He, of course, expresses it this way; "I've parted with that dollar for this thing, but there are a dozen other things I *'ought'* to have, too." You see, "ought" is a great word with a skinflint. I used to be one and I know the vernacular. He thinks he "ought" to be "saving" and "economical."

When he is a confirmed skinflint he always thinks the other fellow "ought" to come down on his price, and he parts with his dollar *only because he* MUST in *order to get that thing.* Sometimes he will wear out $2 worth of shoe leather travelling around town trying to find that article for ninety-nine cents. The skinflint is always nearsighted. He looks so closely at that dollar in his grasping fist that he fails to see his shoe leather and his *time and energy* expended in trying to *crawl out* of paying a full dollar. He "hates to do it." No matter how many other dollars he has he "hates" to pay out *this* one for this particular thing.

All this "tendeth to poverty" and it likewise generally attends poverty; though there are well-to-do folks who are skinflints—and on the road to penury.

We are most of us skinflinty in spots, especially when our income is shrinking and coal sky-rocketing. I used to be skinflinty in large spots, because I thought I had to to live at all And the closer I got the "tighter" money grew with me.

At last I "caught on" to the knack of spending like an opulent queen what I *did* have to spend, and from that day things began to get better. I do not mean that all at once I went to spending recklessly for all sorts of things I happened to fancy at the moment—a glass of ice-cream soda, or a new ribbon I saw in the window, a new shirtwaist I thought pretty—I still denied myself all "luxuries."

And right here I want to tell you that it is these little *wishes of the moment* which are the real leakages that keep our pocketbooks flat. Not only that, but the gratifying of every momentary whim *depletes your stock of Desire* just so much. The cutting off of these little leaks permits the tide of desire to rise higher within you, *for the accomplishment of things worth while.* In the same way it permits the rising of the money tide in your purse. Cogitate this well.

I not only did not fly into all sorts of momentary indulgences, but I began to put *more* thought than ever into *each* expenditure I made. I bought nothing that was not necessary, and I always "slept on it" before I decided that it *was* necessary. Then I consulted my cash and decided what was "the limit" I could use for this purpose. Then I went over in my mind all the things I *couldn't* have if I bought this. I let go *definitely* of *each one* of these. I said, "Get thee behind me—I *choose* this *one* thing and you may go away into forgetfulness—I *do not want you.*" Then I went down town and "looked around" until I found just the right thing to suit me. Sometimes it was on the bargain counter, sometimes among the new goods at highest price; but when I found it I was *pleased* with it, and I paid *gladly* for it, and took it home and *enjoyed it forever after.*

I used to be a great hand to be "sorry I hadn't got something else," but I never made a purchase in this new way which I did not enjoy fully until it was worn to shreds.

This was the beginning of opulence for me. After a time I found my desires growing *stronger and more definite* AND LESS NUMEROUS. And at the same time I began to discover *more money in my purse,* AND FEWER DRAINS UPON IT. I know by right of discovery and experience, that *this* is the road to wealth. And I know that what I have done in this line every one of you can do if you will. It will take you a longer or shorter time to accomplish just in proportion as you work faithfully at it *all* the time, or just spasmodically once in a while.

It is all a matter of establishing a right *habit* of thought. A few thoughts once in a while will not do it, but persistent effort *will.* Anybody with gumption enough to learn to read can learn to think opulently. And as soon as the *habit* is formed he will find that he *has* plenty for *all* his desires. More than this, spending will be a pleasure to him, and the thing bought a joy forever.

Factors of Success

Real and continued success is a mathematical result which any man or woman may obtain if he or she is willing to work carefully enough and long enough. When a man adds six and six together he is dead sure of twelve as the result—*if he makes no mistake.* He is sure of the same result if he multiplies four by three, or two by six. But if he gets careless and puts down any old figures he happens to think of he fails to get twelve as a result. If he puts down 5x4=12 he may fool himself for a moment or an hour, he may fool a few babies for an hour or a day, but he does not fool *the teacher,* who ruthlessly wipes his slate clean of both factors and result, and bids him try again.

There is another thing I want you to notice about the man who does not attain his result with the right factors—the man who puts down 5x4=12. "Why did he put down 5x4 instead of 3x4? He did it because he had not learned from experience that 5 "doesn't go in" 12 at all—because he did not know the factors of 12. He had to *guess* at them. Consequently he felt *doubt and uncertainty* all the time he was parading his little 5x4=12 for the benefit of the innocents. *He was not happy,* even though some of the innocents gushed admiringly over his smartness. Inside him there was the tension and trembling of fear that after all his problem was *not* correct and would not stand the test of time and the teacher. He had only *guessed* at it, instead of *proving* his problem until he understood just *how* each factor would affect the result.

Of course he would have had the same fear if he had *happened* to stumble on the correct factors. Only by *knowing* the factors and their relations to each other, by actual demonstration, could he have the sweet peace of certainty as to result.

I remember my first experience with the multiplication table—and a teacher who must have thought (if she thought at all) that she was training parrots. I had learned, of course, to add. Then suddenly I was to learn the 2x1=2 table by heart. I did, but I kept trembling inside for fear my memory would fail me and I'd state the wrong "answer." Then one day it dawned on me that the whole thing was simply *addition.* I set down 2 twice and, behold, 4. I set it down three times and added, and there was 6 just as the table gave it. I went through table after table in this way until I *understood* multiplication. Then it was all easy, and there was no more quivering and tension inside of me. And somehow I quit caring what the other children said about my written tables—I *knew* whether I was right or not, and their remarks failed to affect me either to depression or elation.

Life is a still-hunt for the factors of success. If we use the wrong factors the Great Teacher, Experience, wipes out our work and we have to do it all over again. This process is repeated until our wits are sharpened enough to find the right factors. Then success abides with us.

But what would you think of a man who went to a healer and asked her to "speak the Word" for 5x4 to equal 12? You would think him rather stupid, wouldn't you? And yet I receive just such requests as that, almost daily.

There are factors which simply won't "go in" success, any more than 5 will go in 12.

For instance, a man wrote me lately to "treat" him to hold his position and draw a higher salary. He is a man in government employ. He says a charge has been "trumped up" against him by "a woman of no character"—a false charge. But he says he has been taking advantage of the prestige given him by his government position to sell private goods, upon which he has made lots of money, and he fears this will tell against him. He says he did *not* neglect or injure his government work to do this, and he has been careful to attend faithfully to every detail; "but of course," he naively remarks, "it is really against the rules to sell goods as I have done." He wants me to "influence" the government to keep him and show up the falseness of the charges of the "woman of no character." In other words he wants government officials hypnotized into believing that 5x4=12—that he is all right, when he is not. Of course 4 will go in 12—the woman's charges may be utterly false; but there is the 5 that will *not* go—he has been breaking a rule and hoping to keep it quiet. The false charge only calls *attention* to his problem and then *all* the inaccuracies show up.

Now if this man has *learned* his lesson and this is really the *only* wrong factor he has been putting down he will *probably* be forgiven and get another chance—with mighty sharp eyes watching for his next slip. For this is really a splendidly kind and forgiving old world, and a man who has learned a lesson and really *means* to get his next problem *right* in *every* detail, can always find forgiveness and another opportunity.

But if this man's eyes waver when he talks—if he is only trying to avoid consequences without changing that 5-factor any more than he is obliged to—then the chances are he will get fired forthwith. After that he will go about explaining to folks how he has been "injured" by a "woman of no character," and dishonestly ousted from his position by cold-blooded men who think of nobody but themselves. Instead of correcting that 5 he will try adding an unlucky 13 to his little problem—he will tell folks it was the woman and the hard-hearted officials who lost him his position, when deep in *his heart* he *knows* it was the *broken rule* that played hob with him.

When you see people going around with a deprecatory air, telling how they have been injured and defrauded of their "rights" by somebody or other, you may set it right down in your little book that they are simply engaging the public's attention to keep it off their *real* shortcomings. Somewhere there is a figure 5 where a 3 should be, and they are making a big, black, unlucky 13 to keep your eyes off the 5. If you are a feel-er and not a thinker you will probably shed tears with him, and maybe loan him ten dollars or so. As time passes and you see nothing more of your ten dollars you may be able to open your eyes and see that false 5-factor in his statement.

There are a lot of things in this world that simply will not "go in" success. Disobedience to the letter *or spirit* of an employer's regulations is one of them. And every employer has a lot of *mental* regulations, besides the expressed ones, by which you must cheer-full abide if you are to *succeed* with him. He is not wholly conscious of all these little mental regulations himself, so how can he put them down in black and white! But if your *attentive desire* is turned toward pleasing him you will *feel* his desires as opportunity offers. You will please him and be successful.

Of course laziness, lack of promptitude, inattention to details, lack of order, slovenly dress, a glum or wooden expression, a slouchy, shuffling gait, a mind not on your work, an eye on the clock, a nose or tongue in other people's business, inaccuracy of statement, or "sticky fingers,"—all these are NOT factors which will go in success. Neither will the sort of ridicule and criticism some employes indulge in when the employer's back is turned.

And it makes no difference who your employer is. You may be *your own* employer, but still it remains true that none of these things will "go in" success. "When we get down to the foundations of things we find we are *all* employes of the One Spirit which is running this universe. There is no use trying to fool ourselves with the idea that we have nobody to please but our own small, personal selves.

In order to please ourselves, in order to realize the success we want we have got to *please the Spirit that's over us all.*

Consecration is the first requisite of success—consecration to the Spirit of Truth *as it speaks to the individual.*

It is not SAFE, *nor wise, to do or* THINK *that which you would blush to have proclaimed from the house-tops.*

That which is absolutely true to the Spirit of Truth neither shuns nor seeks exposure. When I say 3x4=12 there is nothing to blush for. If I say 5x4=12 I want either to hide it, for *fear* I am wrong; or else I want to parade it for the approbation of those too ignorant to detect my fallacy.

"*Blessed* is he that *doubteth* not in that which he alloweth"—or doeth. When in doubt *don't do it.*

Wait until you are *sure you will not regret;* then go ahead to victory. *Be still* and the Spirit of Truth will teach you.

Do not drive ahead on some doubtful line and try *to make* it come out right by "affirming" that it will.

Here is a wail from a woman. She says she went into the canvassing business expecting to succeed, and she has been treated to succeed, and she has continually affirmed that she would. But she failed. She "just hates" to ring door bells and she despises to meet strangers and she would never have gone into such work except for the money there was in it. Is it any wonder there was no money in it for her? Hating one's work is another factor which simply will not "go in" success.

There *must* be a degree of love for the work, outside the money there is in it.

And this love for your business must be cherished and coaxed to *grow*, or your business success will not grow.

Dearie, when you get right down to the foundation of things there is but *one* Law of Success, and that is the same Law which governs all creation—*the Law* of *Love.* The man who *loves* every bit of his work will coin his very highest *soul* into it. He will make it such a beautiful and glorified thing that the world will run to see, and will pay for his work almost any price he can ask.

Success is a certainly to him who *keeps in line* with his own ideals and aptitudes.

To Be Square

If you had a fine horse upon whose swiftness your fortunes depended, how would you treat it? Would you house it carelessly and make a pack-horse of it between races? Would you stuff it on all sorts of foods, keep it standing for weeks in the stable and then expect it to win the race for you? Would you keep it chasing over the country all night and then expect it to win next day? Of course you would not.

But you treat YOURSELF *that* way—and then go around clad in rags and a grieved expression because you have "failed" in the races for success.

In the races of life there are "classes" enough for all. *Every* man, woman and child may win his races and carry off his prizes—IF he takes proper care of himself and *observes carefully the rules of the race.*

With proper preparation and a good understanding any man can win his races.

By proper preparation I do not mean a college education. Nor do I mean even that a man's youth must be spent in any sort of school. There is Owen Kildare, for instance, whose story appears in February *Success.* He is now winning his races and wearing his laurels although his early life was spent as newsboy, prizefighter and all-around tough, and he never learned to read until he was thirty years old. Now, at thirty-eight, he is a successful story writer and a real helper in the world's work.

It is never too late *to catch on* to the principle of success. That is literally what one has to do in order to win the races.

Owen Kildare was a success even in the slums, and all his life was a schooling. *He was "square."* He lived up to his best understanding and his understanding grew.

Every man is *born into* just the school he needs to prepare him for success in life. If he is not "square" with himself and the class he is born into he stays perhaps a life-time in that class. Perhaps he drops down, down, down to the foot of the class. All because he is not "square" in his treatment of the lessons life presents to him. He shirks.

What does it mean to be "square"? It means a different thing to every man on earth, and yet it means always *one thing—to* do what *your own* spirit says is right, and to *keep your word,* actual or implied.

To be square requires a *steady purpose;* in other words, self-control.

To be square one must control it feelings instead of letting them run away with him. The boy who plays hookey when he feels like it is not square with himself nor the world. *There is an "ought" in his heart which he is not square with.*

Life is full of mournful fizzles who habitually play hookey when they *feel* like it. They *feel* like alighting this thing and that, and—they play hookey. They *feel* like lying abed late in the morning, though that little "ought" inside, and mayhap an employer outside, admonishes them to get up even if they don't happen to *feel* like it. Something is *expected* of them and they shirk. Tacitly their *word* is given to be on time, and they are not on time. They are not square.

The little "ought" inside is the well laid track upon which the individual's life may *safely* run. When he jumps that track and runs on *feeling alone* he is *not square* with the world and there is danger ahead. And he ploughs along in the wrong direction, injuring himself *and others.*

He follows feeling and lies abed. He is late at his work and dumpy when he gets there. His employer *feels* that he is not fairly treated. If he acts upon *his* feeling the sleepy-head will get his salary reduced.

Then he will tell folks what a stingy old curmudgeon his employer is. For he will never see that his own lack of square dealing has anything to do with his lack of funds or success. If there is anything the feeling-follower is really proficient in—anything where he shows himself a glorious genius—it is in *finding excuses* for himself and to himself. He never flies the smooth track of "ought" unless there was a great *big* bogie-man to throw him off. But his bogie-man somehow will never stand the camera test—they are big and valid excuses *only in his own mind.* The feeling-follower has an artistic imagination. He is ingenious.

If only he would exercise his ingenuity in keeping *on* the track he'd get his salary raised.

Of course the sense of oughtness is conscience, and conscience is a matter of education. The Hindoo mother thinks she ought to drown her baby girls in the Ganges. Owen Kildare used to think he ought to be a slugger. He religiously knocked down every fellow who failed to toe the scratch in slumdom. Roosevelt *et al* thinks he ought to knock down Spain for being mean to Cuba and the Filipinos. Tolstoi thinks he ought to resist nothing. All these people are winners in their own particular races because they square their acts with their "oughts."

And no two of them has just the same kind of an ought. Each has the conscience he is educated up to.

Conscience is a matter of education, but it has to be minded just the same. The Hindoo must mind *her* conscience and she will win her races. Tolstoi must mind his conscience if he would win his. *You* must mind *your* conscience if *you* would win.

And you must mind your conscience *at it* IS—not as you'd like to have it be. If your conscience tells you to hop out of bed *now* it will not do to lie still and philosophize about it, and explain away the "ought," and conjure up an excuse for flying its track.

You can silence the "ought" but you *can't convince it.* You can no more explain it away than you can explain away the shining steel rails between here and New York. You can ignore either—and get hurt. But they are *there.*

Until you can educate your conscience up to the point of letting you do what you want to do you would better do what it bids you even if you don't happen to *feel* like it.

The true preparation for success in life is to be had anywhere, in school or slum, in war or peace. All life's experiences are simply opportunities for you to *set the habit* of being square with the God in you *and the gods without.* This is character.

Did you ever watch a horse race? Perhaps there are half a dozen entries, every one of which has been fed, exercised and groomed to the highest state of perfection—each according to the best judgment of its own particular groom. Now they appear, ready, for the running. When the signal is given to start the horses are all wheeled around with the aim to keep them abreast as they pass under the wire ready for the signal, *"Go!"* But there are always some jockeys who are not *square.* They are so eager to *get ahead* of all the others that they swing too far ahead, and the whole lot have to be started over again. Time and again this false start is repeated, all because some of the jockeys are not *trying* to get a *fair* start—they are trying *to* get *the* start of the others; they want to take all the advantage they can get. They are not *square.* And did you ever see one of these unfair jockeys win the race? I never did.

The jockey who cannot control his feelings and start square gets rattled and urges his horse so excitedly that the horse "breaks" and "goes to pieces." Then when the jockey knows he has lost the race he takes it out on the poor horse, which finally comes in all panting and foam-covered at the tail of the race.

The same horse with a self-contained jockey would have won the race. The self-contained jockey rules his feelings and keeps to the track of "ought"—which is the track of wisdom and success.

It is easy for a man to do as he "ought" in little things. And if he takes pains to do it in little things he will find he has grown power to do as he "ought" when big things turn up. It is this doing as he ought—as *his own* soul says he ought, which enables a man to learn the lessons set for him in his particular class in life.

And it is the learning of the lessons in one class which fits him for those of a higher class.

This is why the shirk, who isn't square, has a hard row to hoe, and never gets promoted.

The "ought" in a man is the voice of the principle of his being.

Success is the result of obedience to this voice.

Your *feelings* are the race horse upon whose swiftness and right handling depend the races of your life.

You are not your feelings. *You* are the intelligence and will which govern and inform your feelings. You are the groom who cares for, and the jockey who directs the race horse of feeling.

Will you direct feeling, or will you let feeling run away with you?

Remember, feeling is your race horse. How will you treat it? Will you train it for the great events of life? Will you let it run loose without a purpose? Will you make a pack-mule of it, to carry petty and unnecessary burdens for Tom, Dick and Harry?

A good horse-trainer takes great care of the feelings of his horse. He never jerks the reins and yells at him. He never lets him stand uncurried and unfed in a dirty stable, with little yapping, snapping curs to torment him. He never loads him with unnecessary burdens and flogs him up hill and down.

But that is what men do with *themselves.* A man neglects his own brain and body and soul; he curses himself and his "luck"; he permits himself to be loaded with unnecessary annoyances; and then he jaws around about never being able to do as he wants to, and wonders what life is good for anyway.

A good horse trainer never pampers his horse either. He does not give him free access to the oat bin. Neither does he curry him daily to the last pitch of shininess, blanket him and keep him always under a roof.

A man stuffs himself at all hours, upon any sort of food which tempts his palate; he overdresses and underexercises himself; and cusses the world in general because his feelings are unruly.

A good horse trainer does not stuff his horse for supper and chase him around over the country until two o'clock in the morning as a preparation for next day's race. No. It takes a man or woman to do such things as that with *himself,* and then expect success.

If you want to be a real success in life you must have ONE purpose to which all other purposes an tributary. You must have ONE aim, and *all* the actions of your life must be so governed as to assist in the one direction.

This does not mean that a whole life-time must be devoted to a single pursuit; nor that you must have no other pursuits whilst you are following the one. But it *does* mean that no other pursuits shall come *before* the one—that you shall have no other gods before that.

If you neglect business for art, or art for business, *both* will fail. If you pursue art as a *recreation,* to better prepare you for business; if you pursue art when business does not call you; if at the *slightest* call of business you fly *instantly* with your *whole* soul, to that; you will make a success of business and the art will *help* you to do it. But if business is *the* present aim *everything* else must be dropped instantly and *willingly,* at its lightest call. Only so will business be a success. This is "concentration."

A race horse is not always racing; neither is the most successful man in any line, *always* thinking and working on that line. But he is always thinking and working on *tributaries* of his special line.

Clara Morris and Bernhardt find recreation in art, history, literature, outdoor life—things not necessarily connected at all with their stage life, but all of which tend to breadth and depth of character, and to splendid health, and thus add to the power of their work on the stage.

But Paderewski or Gabrilowitsch or Hoffmann would not turn to heavy manual labor for recreation, lest it stiffen their supple fingers.

Neither would any of these successful artists indulge in midnight carousals and unseasonable but highly seasoned feasts. With them, all things which will not assist them in their *main* purpose, are ruthlessly cut out entirely.

It is this self-command and *one-purpose-ness* which enables them to win their races. The *lack* of these is the ONE cause of *all* failures.

I find, upon looking however this article that, as a whole, it is quite a mixed metaphor. But never mind—it is like life itself, which is decidedly a mixed metaphor, and none the less interesting for the mixture.

One Thing at a Time

When I receive a letter which says the writer has "*so many* desires it is impossible to enumerate them," my heart shows a tendency to slip into my shoes. Such an one is really a hard case. *Desire* is the creator; but when desire is spread over a host of things it is no longer desire; it is mere shallow *wishing*, and accomplishes little. You can no more spread out your wishes and works over a multitude of things and bring success, than you can clean a dozen rooms all at once.

One thing at a time. Be definite. *What* do you want? Call them all up in a row for inspection. What will you have *first*? *Decide* upon one thing and then *banish* the other wishes until this one is realized. Make your mental demand for this ONE thing. Be still, and let the spirit tell you what to do, and how. Keep *affirming* it. *Be faith-full* to this one thing until you *realize* it.

"When it is well in sight call up your wishes again and make another selection. Then banish all others and WISH HARD, and AFFIRM harder, and work *faithfully* for that one.

One thing at a time and that *well* done, is the road to all accomplishment. And each thing well done increases your capacity. One thing properly "demonstrated" over makes way for better and *quicker* "demonstration" over the next thing.

When you are learning to do things it is wise to *begin* on the easy ones. So in choosing *which* of your desires shall engage *all* your attention NOW it is usually best to choose, not the hardest and biggest one, but the one nearest at hand and most reasonable and easy. Generally this is the *quickest* road to realizing the *big* desire, as well as the lesser ones.

Now ready, dearie. Look the desires over *judicially. Decide.* CHOOSE. Now go in to win and keep at it with *quiet confidence. Success is yours.*

I told you to get down to *one* desire at a time, and to work and treat for that alone. But sometimes it is hard to decide upon any one as the most important. Sift as you may, there will still seem to be several things equally urgent Now, dearie, you *can* work daily for several things provided you go rightly about it

When you go to school you work for success in geography, grammar, and arithmetic, and you succeed in all. Not only that, but you do *better* in each than you would probably do if you had one study alone. There is a lot in "getting your hand in" and *keeping* it in. "When one puts in so many hours every day, say four, in study, it soon becomes habit and you do it readily and easily; when perhaps one hour a day would scarcely enable you to get well interested before the hour would be over. But if you put the whole of four hours in on one study your mind would tire of the steady strain in one direction; whereas, if you divided the time among three studies your interest would be refreshed and your mind quickened by each change.

But what result would you expect if you sat down with all three text books before you, to put in four hours work at one stretch, dipping a moment into one book, then skipping to the others and back again innumerable times? How much interest could you take in such exercise of the mind? How much could you really take in? How many problems could you work out if you tried to carry the bounding of the Red Sea and the parsing of a sentence at the same time you worked at the problem? You would fail in *every* study for lack of *concentration.*

But that is what we are all prone to do with our life problems. We jumble them up together—and fizzle. Whilst we are doing our kitchen problem our minds are trying to practice on the piano, or make money, or "grow spiritual," or "treat" ourselves out of "conditions," or do *all* at once. Our thoughts fly hit and miss from one thing to another with "Oh, I wish this" and "I wish that"; and all the time our kitchen problem is slighted and we are acomplishing next to nothing if not *quite* nothing, with the other things.

Now if you have simmered your desires down to their last essence and there are still several, instead of one, just divide your time as wisely as possible between them. The better success you make on any *one* the greater will be your capacity for success in the others. Suppose you have a kitchen problem you can't *just now* get rid of. And you *want* musical opportunities, oh, so much. And you *must* have health and money. Now there are three things you want—opportunities to practice, health, and money; and there's that kitchen problem you *must* solve. And *the last shall be first.* Give the kitchen problem all the time and thought it needs. To slight that is to reduce the power for the others. Set your time for that. Now set another time for practice, another for health exercise and concentration, and another for concentration for money.

Take health, we'll say, *first* thing in the morning. Rise half an hour early, if need be, and make it from 6:30 to 7, perhaps, or earlier. Begin with breathing exercises and light gymnastics enough to *wake up* on. Follow with a cool shower or sponge bath and rubdown *if possible.* Then sit down or lie down for twenty minutes or more and "concentrate" on health and *nothing else.* Keep bringing your mind right down to the word "*Whole*"—"I AM WHOLE." Get *interested* in *imagining* how whole and strong and lovely you are. *Imagine* yourself as you *want* to be.

Now it will be time to change classes and take up your kitchen problem. So put your *whole* mind and body into that. Keep calling in your thought and interest and *putting* it *into* your work.

After a, few days of this you will find your kitchen problem solving beautifully. You will see new things to *omit,* and new ways of doing things, and you will find your kitchen problem becoming a real pleasure *and taking much less time.*

At another time take your hour, or half hour, for *money.* Sit straight and *alert,* take slow, full breaths, and *picture money pouring into your purse.* Get *enthused* over the picture and keep telling yourself it is *real* and the money is *yours.* But *never permit yourself to wonder* HOW *the money is to come, or through whom.* Simply picture it as coming to you from the "All-Encirling Good." Feel just as tickled over it as you can.

When this half hour money-study is over dismiss it entirely from mind, and keep dismiss it every time it happens to come in again.

When your practice hour has arrived put your whole mind and soul and *imagination* and *affirmation* into that. See yourself a Paderewski preparing for a unique career, and pour your *soul* into sounds for the joy of the whole world. Practice *exactly* the time you have allotted yourself, and use the *same* time *every* day.

Follow the same rule with all these other problems. Be prompt to the *second.* But if something unforeseen *does* happen to prevent, remember that the *most* important thing is to *keep sweet mentally;* and take the first minute you can for your exercises. All sorts of "upset" feelings put your mind out of tune so that you must use *more* time tuning up again before your mental exercises are at their best.

If you do *one* thing at a time as if that were the *only thing you'd ever have to do, with all eternity to do it in,* you can work for several things at once. Remember your school days and use the same principle these days. *Life* is *made up of school days.* And success is yours.

Last, but not least, remember to take *plenty of recesses* from your work and concentration and practices. If you filled your lungs full of air and then *kept* them full it would be only a matter of a little while until you'd die. It is by expanding and then relaxing, expanding and relaxing, that we keep the breath of life going. To try to keep the lungs full *all* the time would be death. The same law comes into all we do. To work steadily without playing and resting between times, would have the same effect as holding your breath. To work with, *all* your mind and soul and body, and then to *let go* with all your mind and soul and body is to complete a real breath of life. All work and no play, or all play and no work, makes us stupid and weak. But plenty of whole-souled work *alternated* with plenty of whole-souled rest, makes us strong and wise, and keeps us *growing.*

So take plenty of little recesses, dearie, every day. Go out and take a sun-bath and a soul-bath, and take slow, full, even breaths of the all-pervading love and wisdom and will of the universe. *Let* life live you. Fluff yourself all out loose and *let* the world-forces and the unseen forces play through you a while.

Then you will feel like being "strenuous" again when the time comes.

Joy Words

"All my life I have been searching for happiness in many different ways, but have never found the real thing."

You have been hunting happiness outside of you. You have expected happiness to flow from *things* into you. You have expected happiness as a result of making your environment fit you. All your efforts have been put forth in this direction, and you have constantly met with disappointment—and unhappiness. As everybody will whose happiness is pinned to his conditions.

Conditions, like people, are *growing* things; never two minutes in exactly the same state. If you pin your happiness to a thing, or a friend, you will probably have to unpin it before night.

Happiness, *real* happiness of the abiding, *growing* kind, *never* comes as a result of fitting circumstances to your notions. *It comes from fitting* YOURSELF *to* circumstances. In no other way can it be found.

After all this is much easier to do. There is but *One* of *you* to be adjusted; while all the rest of creation goes to make up your environment. And your power over yourself is practically unlimited; whilst your power over even your immediate environment is next to nothing. What power has a convict over his prison walls and keepers? But he has *all* power over his *mind;* and he has all power over his body *within the limits* set by his prison walls and his keeper's rules.

A convict can be a fool and fret away his life within those walls; he can sulk mentally, and refuse to use his physical powers as far as permitted. If he does this he falls sick and dies, an unhappy man; unhappy because he fretted over what he couldn't do, instead of doing what he could.

Or, the prisoner may use as he pleases that part of himself which cannot be walled in by any number of bolts and bars. He may think as high and as bravely and well as he *chooses:* and he may use his physical energies as bravely and well as he may. He may make the best of his opportunity to learn a trade, and to cheer and help others as he may, even in a prison. If he does this he will be in those grim environs a happier man than are three-quarters of the men who are outside prison walls. Not only this, but he will *win* from his keepers kindness and consideration not accorded the indifferent or defiant prisoner: and he will *shorten his term of sentence.* Still further than that, he will come forth from that prison a stronger, wiser, happier man than he has *ever* been before,—a man better equipped for success *for having been in that prison; a happier and more successful man than he would have been without that bit of education.* There are two of the world's greatest railroad magnates who are examples of this very thing; one of whom is making over London today.

Now, every human being is in a prison of circumstances. He is there because he deserves to be. He has "attracted" it to himself. It is the particular sort of prison he needs *just now.* It is stocked with just the sort of things he needs to exercise mind, will and muscles upon, to fit him for the next higher class *in the line of his desires.*

Will he *adjust himself* to it all and work happily, faithfully, willingly; and thus *shorten his sentence?* Or will he kick the walls and curse his work?—and *lengthen his sentence?* Will he *accept* things and work happily? Or will he grumble and kick, and be unhappy?

It all depends upon *himself.* His environment is his friend if he works *with* it; his foe if *he turns against it.* One is happy with his friends, no matter in what garb they come; one is unhappy with those he is *turned against,* no matter how richly they are dressed or how fair they may appear.

Do you really *want* to be happy? Do you want happiness enough to pay the price for it? Happiness is a jealous god. He simply will not live in the same heart with fault-finding, growls, dislikes. Do you want happiness badly enough to make you turn out all these things no matter *what* happens? Then happiness will come into you and *grow up* in you until it fills every crack and cranny of your being and makes you feel so good that you will entirely forget to growl and find fault and dislike things.

Happiness and Good Will are Siamese twins. You simply must have 'em both, or live without either. Growls and dislikes always send Good Will into the dark closet and then happiness flies away. You must CHOOSE Good Will, and keep on choosing, until it fills you and radiates such positive energy that growls and dislikes simply shrivel and cannot get into your mind or heart at all.

That reminds me of Kipling's "Just So Stories," but it isn't so imaginary as you might suppose. There are growls and dislikes flying through the air, seeking *dark auras* where they may abide. *You* have a Solar Center which is intended to do for your body and atmosphere what the sun does for its solar system. It is meant to radiate *Good Will,* or love, to fill you with light and real soul-warmth of the sort that is instant death to growls and dislikes—as light brings instant death to shadows.

But there is one little spot where a growl or grumble can always get in and *turn off* the Soul radiance and make your face and body and atmosphere all dark, so that all the other growls and dislikes will come in too, and hold high jinks where they ought not to be. Achilles had just one little spot on his heel (the feet represent the understanding, you know) where the enemy could hurt him. *You* have just one little spot where a growl can enter and shut off all your radiance of light and happiness,—the little spot of *Choice.*

If you *choose* a grumble as it presents its frowzy, bristly head, it hops over the sill and comes in. And the very first thing it does is to touch the button and shut off your *Good Will* radiations. Next it throws open the doors and windows of your mind and invites in all its relations.

To keep out growls just paste up a big notice:

NO GROWLS ADMITTED! NOT EVEN ON BUSINESS!

If a growl is impudent enough to come in when you are not looking just throw him down stairs, and all the king's horses and all the king's men can't put him together again.

Now growls are quite as intelligent as other folks. If they get an unvarying and decidedly warm brogan they give it up and go hunt for somebody who is in the *habit* of letting 'em in. All you have to do is to cultivate the habit of firing them. Then your Solar Center will shine brighter and brighter and Good Will and Happiness will hold open house to every little thought-body that's nice.

And your sentence will be commuted and you will go into a bigger, better place.

And happiness will keep right on growing.

Smile. Smile alike upon just or unjust.

Get interested in seeing how happy you *can* be.

Take a few minutes the first thing every morning to cultivate *real* happiness, which is joy. Sit down with a pencil and paper, in a good, comfortable, *straight-backed* chair. Place the paper on the table and hold the pencil ready for business. Now say to yourself, *"Joy"*; and as you say it make a firm, bold dot with your pencil. Repeat. Make the next dot firmly *right over* the first one—right *in* it, I mean—simply make the one mark blacker and firmer. And mentally *put* that single word *"Joy"* right *into* that firm pencil dot. Put the real JOY into it. See how perfectly *One* you can make the pencil mark and the mental word. Bring JOY *down to a fine point.* Do this twenty-five or thirty times at a sitting, saying *Joy* very positively with each dot of the pencil. Do it all very *deliberately,* calmly, positively, resolutely.

Then go quietly about your work. You will be surprised to see how smoothly and pleasantly your work goes.

Whenever things seem to get into a snarl, or you feel discouraged or burdened, drop everything like a hot potato, go into another room and use this little Joy-exercise a few minutes. It's magic. Just *do* it and see.

And you will be surprised to see how little time it takes: and you will be amazed at how *much* time it *saves:* time saved from wrangles and jangles, to be used in Joy.

This is what the Bible means when it says, *"Break off thy sins by tightness."* Break off jangles with Joy brought down to a fine point.

Success Letters

1

Attention, please! Attention is to you what the lens is to a camera—it *focusses power* for you. *Keep your attention upon* SUCCESS, upon opulence; until SUCCESS is imprinted upon every brain cell—I AM Success. *When* you take your Kodak for an outing you only turn it upon what you *want* to preserve. But you deliberately focus your *attention* upon what you *don't* want preserved. What nonsense! Turn to Success, to *all* you desire, as the needle to the pole. *Refuse* to see the opposite—deny it—smash the negatives. Keep on filling yourself with I AM SUCCESS pictures. Keep cool; keep *aiming.* The Word is with you daily and Success is sure as sunrise to every one of you who pays ATTENTION to what you *want,* instead of to what you *don't* want. *Think* success; *act* success; FEEL success.

2

Now look pleasant. How do you expect to attract customers, friends or money to a vinegar visage or a doleful wail? Nature abhors glumness and escheweth the glum, and every live thing flees at sight of the smileless and loiters not until he is out of ear-shot of the complainer.

Don't imagine you may be an exception to the rule. You are not. "Birds of a feather cleave together"—if you want pleasant people and things and plenty of gold and greenbacks you must make yourself akin to them. Nice people and gold and greenbacks look pleasant. Go thou and do likewise. Never mind how you feel inside. *Look Pleasant!* SMILE!

A smile not only attracts all the good things in the universe, but it is the most powerful of auto-suggestions for what you desire. A smile not only shines outward from your face, warming up and attracting friends and money, but it also shines *inward,* reaching at last the solar center, the sun of you. The smile born on the surface of you will vibrate inward; the solar sun will catch its rhythm and smile back. And the smile of the solar sun is to you what the smile of Old Sol is to the earth—*life* and JOY.

The shine of your solar center is what grows SUCCESS.

So look pleasant, please, whilst I speak the Word for you. Look pleasant; act pleasant; and *you are* pleasant.

Keep cool; keep sweet; keep aiming.

Success is growing!

3

How do you *think*, Sweetheart? How do you *do?* How do you *feel* is of no consequence so I'll not ask it.

Stop your efforts now for a few minutes and *get your bearings* again.

What are you *aiming* for? SUCCESS IN BUSINESS, which is simply the RESULT of self-expression.

Self-expression has a money value and he who most freely ex-presses (presses out) himself, his thought, into the visible, *practical* world receives most money from the world.

You have within you unlimited force which only needs expression to bring you unlimited, *visible* wealth. *How to get it out* has been the question.

I say unto you that the way to get it out is to *put it into each thing you find to do.*

WAKE UP!—and *see how much thought* you can put into the *one thing* in hand. The more thought force you *put in* to what you do the more Self you have ex-pressed—*pressed out* of yourself. See? *And the more money you will bring.*

And one thing done that way is always a stepping stone to something better *and each brings you nearer to the goal of your desire.*

That goal is *fixed* and *every* experience takes you nearer, *but every half-done thing is a loitering by the way.*

Not because the thing *must* be done (that is a matter of choice) *but because you have lost the opportunity to press out yourself* and there is really a *fixed quantity of Self* that must be expressed before you can attract money in great measure.

It is the *expressed* self which is the magnet.

Now let's see "where we are at." We DESIRE Success; Success is our objective point—real, *money* Success. We are getting there by *putting ourselves* into each thing that turns up—by GETTING INTERESTED in it and doing it with a WILL.

Now there is one thing right here to be guarded: When we are *putting ourselves* into anything we must be quiet and *take pains not to spill ourselves* and thus *waste* energy. We are to be quietly confident so that we put into each thing *just the right amount* of Self, of thought energy, and not let it *slop over.* I see you are catching on.

NOW we are ready for a new month and the best one yet. The Word is with you. Steady now. Keep cool. Keep sweet. Keep at it. SUCCESS IS OURS.

4

LET GO; be still; and *concentrate your efforts.* One day at a time is all you can live. LIVE it and LET the Law work out the future. The WORD is with you and *all you desire* IS MAN-

IFESTING. No matter how you *feel—it* IS manifesting. Keep cool, keep sweet, keep at it. Success is sure.

5

"I am so glad to have you say you would rather heal poverty than any other dis-ease, because it is the trunk of which ninety-nine other diseases are only branches. That appealed to me more than any I've read yet. I work from eight in the morning until six and after, striving to succeed, and sometimes it is very discouraging. If I could only put aside the annoying things, that worry the life out of one. Tell me how to stop it, or throw it off, please."

Quit fighting your best friends and you will more quickly realize the success you desire. Your best friends are the little things; the little things that annoy you now. Wake up and SEE that these little things bring only good to you. Each one of them is a little *opportunity.* Think of the opportunities you have wasted by impatience! Not to mention the time wasted afterward in fretting over what occurred! Think of the *thought force* wasted over all these little happenings! Yes, think about it. And turn over a new leaf. Every one of these little things is a *golden opportunity to practice concentration.* Put your mind to seeing how beautifully you can meet each little emergency and make the best of it. Take pride in seeing how cheerfully you can accept the consequences that *seem* to be against you. You will find out later that it was the best thing that could have happened. Soon you will cease to have such annoyances *because you will have loved them into pleasures.*

6

"June was a great deal the best month we have had since going into business here. But since then business has been dull and A hasn't the faith in it that he did have. Does his lack of faith have any effect on your treatments of him?"

I don't care how much or how little faith he has, or if he has none at all. There are ebbs and floods in the pocket book of every human being who isn't a "hired man." Any millionaire will tell you his floods were always succeeded by ebbs. But each new flood rose higher. "When the tide receded he hatched up new schemes to take advantage of the next rise. Faith or no faith, if you will keep cool; keep sweet; keep your wits awake and GET READY for the rise, it will come.

7

Fret not thy heart because of evil doers. Things are not always what they seem. Remember thy Creator—thy THINKER. *Think what thou* DESIREST. AFFIRM it. Stamp thy stout foot and affirm it again. Keep cool as a cucumber; keep sweet as a wild rose; keep steady as Old

Sol; keep at it. *You are succeeding.* The Word is with you and SUCCESS GROWS. Just AIM, Sweetheart, and grumble never—inside or out.

8

CONCENTRATE; CONCENTRATE; *concentrate.* Got things down to a fine point. Keep cool; keep sweet; keep *aiming. Let* your sun-center shine alike on just and unjust. Both are elements of SUCCESS. Steady, Sweetheart.

9

Now straighten up, dearie, and stand at ATTENTION. Close your eyes and look upward. Now *feel* all through you the invisible One Power that is too fine and mighty to feel with eyes open. *Take into your being* this subtle power in a full, slow, even breath. Hold your chest expanded whilst that power renews and fills you. Then *gently,* lovingly, steadily, breathe it *out* upon the *object you are aiming for.* Take three draughts of power, of God, before you stop, and do it whenever you think of it. Then turn your whole attention to the *next thing* there is to do, and see how much ingenuity and loving thought you can put into the doing. The WORD is in every breath you thus take and all you desire is growing.

10

You have been applying yourself closely to business. You have been breathing *out* more than you breathed in. So you have nearly drained yourself of vital force. That is what makes you see things through gray spectacles, if not blue. That is why you feel like saying, "What's the use?" Whenever you feel thus you may know right away that you are expending more force than you are taking in.

There is no need of this. The supply of vital energy is really and truly UNLIMITED for every one of you. All you have to do is to inhale it *with lungs and brain.* You can take in all the force you need for *anything* you want to do. But you can no more take in enough force in the morning to keep you running all day without that tired feeling, than you can take in BREATH enough to run you a day or a week. Your brains are a pair of lungs that you have to USE. You have to take IN statements of power, and then turn the power upon your work. And you have to do it many, many times a day until you learn to be literally conscious of your power all the time.

Whenever you get to seeing gray or blue just let go, straighten up, and use *both* pairs of your lungs. Face the SUN, with eyes turned *upward,* and take three of the deepest, slowest, fullest draughts of power that you can manage. Think "Power, *power,* POWER"—and think it emphatically and *slowly.* It is not necessary to face the visible sun always, but face the I AM SUN in *you.* And cast your eyes upward, because all power comes from above. See?

Now you feel like a new being and are ready to give out your power again—ready to put I AM into *I Do.*

In addition to this, if it is possible, change your kind of work for a time. When one keeps right at one thing he is very apt to keep on *breathing out.* His force gets to running out and it just keeps on running that way from habit. It takes THOUGHT to make any change. And with us highstrung people it takes a lot of very *deliberate* thought to get our nerves to keep open to *receive* as much vital energy as we give out. We keep on giving out until our nerves collapse, just as a rubber tube will from which all the water is sucked out. This is *literally* true. We start in to put our energy into some piece of work and the *attraction* of that work just sucks us dry and collapses our nerves.

It takes THOUGHT to keep ourselves from being ruled by our work. And ruined, too. But we CAN keep from it! Oh, yes! There is just nothing we can't do when once we see the point and go in to WIN.

And we not only can rule these things, but we *glory in doing it.* We GLORY in our power and in showing it! When once we get the notion of using our power on *ourselves* we are on the high road to greater achievements than the world has ever before dreamed of! And we are on that road NOW. And we are making rapid progress. We rejoice in our growth, and our appetite is whetted for more Self-command and more growth. Oh, we are The People and we are inheriting the earth! And the sun, too! Glory to the I AM in us!

11

Your realization of Success is growing. Oh, yes, IT IS. You have ups and downs and when you look down you *feel* down and it *seems* to you that success, is not growing. All because you look *down* instead of UP. Do you know that if you had $1,000,000 a year, like Mr. Schwab of the steel trust, if you kept looking at it and comparing it with what you *might* have had, or what somebody else has, you'd feel as poor and unsuccessful as you possibly could under *these* conditions? And if you owned the earth you'd compare it with Jupiter and grumble because you couldn't annex that. You see that is because you let yourself drop back into the old-fashioned habit of thinking success *consists in things.* Success consists in ability to ENJOY YOURSELF in the process of *evolving* things. Mr. Schwab enjoys his ability to *create* things, and the $1,000,000 is simply the *result,* the proof of his success. *The joy of doing* is the real success. Plenty of money flocks to the joyful doer who *believes* that justice rules—that his own comes to him. Mr. Schwab says he used to work over hours and out of shop, anywhere he saw something to be done whether there was to be extra pay or not. But he says that all *the time he* KNEW *that somehow, somewhere, from somebody, he would draw good pay for* EVERY MINUTE'S WORK PUT IN. Now, dearie, that is the secret of success in less than a nutshell. Put in your best licks with joy NOW and glory in *what is coming.* Set your stake as high as you dare and KNOW that it is yours. But remember this: Mr. Schwab *was success* from the first. He enjoyed every bit of the work it took to fit him for his present position. And it is *not* the $1,000,000 which is now his success, but *his joy in doing and in* KNOWING *that all he does will be well paid for.* Success is WITHIN and wells outward into *acts.* Remember, REMEMBER. And keep remembering. ACT as if it is true. Keep sweet and keep cheerily working *out* your ideals. I AM with you for success NOW. You ARE all you desire to be—*work it out.*

12

Success is the natural result of intelligent effort. Failure is the natural result of unintelligent effort. The *degree* of success in any man's life is determined by the exact amount of intelligence *he puts into* his efforts.

Take a careful inventory of *today's* efforts, dearie. How much of it is done perfunctorily, grumblingly, from *habit,* or "compulsion"; and *not* because you have *waked up,* surveyed conditions and *ideals,* and decided that under these circumstances, and JUST NOW, THIS is the highest, best thing you can do? Unless you have thus *decided,* this particular effort you are engaged in is *not* an intelligent effort and therefore is NOT adding to your success. It is a thoughttless effort, a drudgery, and is *wasting your energy and your success.*

Now quit, SHORT. If you cannot *put* intelligence, WILL, *interest,* into *this* effort and make it serve a purpose, then stop short and sit or lie perfectly relaxed until you *can* make your efforts tell. *Far* better do *nothing at all* than to waste energy in such wasteful effort. At least *be still* and *let energy accumulate.*

After a bit you will find yourself again able to put *intelligence* into your motions. When you do not know just what to do and how to do it, BE STILL. Be still all over—see how still you *can* be. Intelligence and power will well up inside and *fill* you again, to overflowing. *Then* you will know what to do and how, and it will be joy to do it. In the meantime, whether you are putting intelligence into effort *or into being still,* SUCCESS GROWS. I AM with you.

13

Wake up now, drop the burden of feelings, symptoms, and responsibilities and get interested heart and soul in the thing you decide is the work of now—the best thing to do under existing conditions. Do it as a child does things—with no thought beyond, or *before either.* See how much fun and freedom you can put into it! Then do the next thing you want to do, and do it with a will. Put your imagination into your work and play at it!

Ditto when you rest. Relax your body definitely and all over and rise into the realm of imagination. See what wild and happy flights you can take. Picture yourself as you *desire* to be—stretch your imagination in this direction! Then AFFIRM all those happy things for yourself, in the present tense—say, "I AM all those things!—and by thunder I'll prove it!!"

Then go in to win some more—to prove some more—to *work out* some more of the delightful things that are *within you.* Don't you know your imagination is within you? And whatever you see in imagination is within you. *And anything that is within you can be worked out.* And I'll whisper something else to you, dearie—*imagination is the only source of power or not-power.* An imagination filled with desirable things is inspiration—the real thing that enables you to do anything. And an imagination filled with undesirable things is a paralyzer. Think about it now and see if it is not so.

And imagination is the one place where you can do *anything.* Yon can imagine good things or bad things at will. So be sensible, dearie, and imagine good things and then *work them out.* It is fun to work out good things! If you find working is not fun, just stop short and see how far you can stretch your imagination again, in desirable directions. That's where the power comes from. Go often into your power house.

14

Be still and know.

Be still and know.

BE STILL AND KNOW.

Know what! Know that *you are what you will to be.* Be still and WILL success. Be still. Relax. *Let go* definitely of everything you don't want. Wave your hand and banish each one. Then *let go* each thing you *do* want. LET GO. You were tired and strained from hanging on. You were so strained that the life force could not flow through and fill you and *forward your work.* Now you are resting, all limp and loose, and life is pouring through your body and *re-charging* it with the magnetism that *attracts to you what you desire.* Now you are rested and filled with quiet, good feeling and WILL.

Rise now and see how well you can *use* your fresh energy. SUCCESS IS YOURS and I AM with you.

15

Good! Brace up again and go in to WIN. You ARE succeeding; better than you realize yet. My WORD is with you constantly. Walk straight up to the mark of your desires and you will find every lion is but a lamb. Keep at it. You will gain confidence with every attempt, and win beyond your expectations.

I AM with you and success is yours.

All things work together to bring about what *you* desire.

Desire for This, That and The Other

You will never reach the place where you have all you want to spend except by commanding yourself to spend, and to *want* to spend, less than your income, whatever that may happen to be; for having all you want to spend is a *state of mind,* not a matter of hundreds, thousands or millions of dollars income. With all Anna Gould's millions her French husband, de Castellane, has never had all he wanted to spend.

You will never have "enough for your needs" except by *ruling your needs;* for this too is a state of mind, not a matter of the size of your income. You " need" what you *think* you need; and in order to have "enough for your needs," you must *change your mind* as to your needs.

This is the only sure way to do it. To enlarge your income will never do it, because *your "needs" will grow with your income, as long as your state of mind remains unchanged, always outstripping your income.* Your "needs" will continue to suck the life out of your income and howl for more. Try it if you will, but you will only prove that what I tell you about is true. And I know from a full experience.

To seek to increase your income to cover your needs is to follow a will-o'-the-wisp which will lead you into quagmires of dissatisfaction if not debt. That way lies defeat.

Every human being is a little garden patch of desires, where one desire or set of desires must thrive at the expense of another desire or set of desires; just as your strawberry plants must thrive at the expense of the weeds which try so hard to grow along with your berry plants. As you nip those weeds in the bud in order to give the strawberry plants a chance to grow and bear fruit, so in the garden of your heart you must continually nip in the bud the undesirable desires in order to allow the desirable desires to gain in stature and bear fruit.

All our beautiful flowers had their beginnings in weeds. The gardener gave a tiny young weed its particular place in his garden; he gave it rich earth and plenty of moisture; he sheltered it from cold winds and allowed no other weeds, *nor even his choicest plants,* to grow near to it and sap its energy and he *clipped innumerable little* sprouts and buds from that weed and from the earth *near it,* as fast as they appeared, leaving only one bud to mature, and just leaves enough to give that one bud plenty of breathing capacity. So in time there were *roots* enough for a great sprawling weed with scores of little gnarly shoots and flowers; but there was only one slender stalk with a single bloom; and *such* a bloom!—no weed had ever before borne such a flower. Then the seeds of that one flower were planted, and the tiny plants tended as the first one had been; and behold, a still larger and more beautiful flower. Then after many generations of this careful tending and clipping process, a plant was allowed to bear several blooms, *all* of which were so large and beautiful that you'd never dream their great-grandmother was that gnarly little weed that tried to elbow everything else out of the garden.

The desire to live within your income is a homely and necessary plant which should be cultivated at all hazards. Where this desire is not thrifty and strong you will find it surrounded by weeds which are trying to grow at its expense—weeds of Desire for This, That and The Other (all good things in themselves but *not* good in their effects *unless procured without straining your income)* which if allowed foothold will eventually mature and bring forth the gnarled flowers and bitter fruits of theft, embezzlement and even murder.

Such men as the world and their old friends have learned to execrate as betrayers of public and private trust, such men as Butler and Blair of St. Louis and Holley of Holyoke and innumerable defaulting cashiers, etc., are men who have permitted the weeds of Desire for This, That and The Other to completely choke out the Desire to Keep Within Their Income. We know their fate and abhor it, even if we are charitable enough not to abhor them.

But many of us are on the same tack without realizing it. The man or woman who Has It Charged is growing a weed of Desire for This, That and The Other at the expense of the Desire to Keep Within Income; they are crowding out the homely plant of Honesty by letting the weeds choke it. If they keep at it long enough and have courage enough and opportunity enough they will be Blairs or Holleys. The weeds of Desire for This, That and The Other will possess them.

But the common run of us are too cowardly and our opportunities too limited (probably because we *are* cowardly) to enable us to shine so conspicuously as Getters of This, That and The Other for which we cannot pay. *We dosn't* go *too* far. Fear of punishment, either by the public authorities or an angry God, or by the hell fires inside of us, deters us from outright stealing of This, That and The Other. So we *cut off the tops of some of our* weeds—we run in debt *as far as we dare,* for This, That and The Other, *and promise* to pay, when we know perfectly well that unless a miracle occurs we can't do it; when we know that unless our *wildest* hopes are realized (which seldom are) we shall not be able to pay when the time comes; *when we know that emergencies are continually arising to prevent us from keeping promises.* We cut off the tops of our *tallest* weeds of Desire for This, That and The Other, but we *leave the roots* and the "most necessary" sprouts—we "only Have It Charged when it's absolutely necessary;" which is in 999 cases out of 1,000 a mere sophistry.

There *might* be in any life an occasional time when it is "absolutely necessary" to Have It Charged or to borrow—which is the same thing—just as there might come up a weed over night; *but there is* NEVER a *continued necessity for buying what one has not the money to pay for.*

Of course this does not refer to Having It Charged as a matter of convenience, when one *already has in bank* the money to pay for it. I refer to the habit of buying today that which one hopes to pay for out of tomorrow's work; the living this week on money one hopes to earn next week; the spending of money which is still On The Books; or *even living this week off money we expect to receive on Saturday night.* All living ahead of *the money in hand,* no matter when that money may be "due," is done at the expense of that homely plant, the Desire to Live Within Your Income, the essence of which is *Honesty.* And that plant, dearie, is the ONLY one from which we can distill the essence of Honesty. That is why I so strongly desire us to cultivate it.

The *habit* of Having It Charged is an ugly, gnarled and distorted weed whose root is the Desire for This, That and The Other; Desire which has been permitted to burrow and spread itself until it is in a fair way to completely starve that homely plant from which we distill Honesty.

The only thing to do is to *let die* that old root of Desire for This, That and The Other; to kill it by *refusing to feed it.*

They say love grows by what it feeds upon. That is the way all desire grows; *until is absorbs everything in sight and dies for the want of other worlds to conquer.*

Don't you know how, when you get the new chair you desired, the one like "Mrs. Smith's," immediately your room looks shabby and you find yourself desiring a new cushion or two to match—and new curtains—and then a new carpet to take the place of the old one which looks old fashioned now beside the new chair—*and* a dozen other things? And then when the door is open into the next room *that* looks shabby and you desire new things for that. And so your Desire for This, That and The Other goes running like a noxious weed in an untended garden, all over your house and premises, and yourself and children and husband, until it sucks the life all out of your income and the *peace out of your heart* and the hearts of those around you.

All these things are lovely in themselves, but *when purchased at the price of your conscience and the peace of mind of yourself and husband they are not expedient;* that is, *they do not speed your soul's expression;* they do not help you to express the *best* of yourself. In other words *they retard your development.*

It is by the best use of *what we have* that we learn our lessons and get ready for more things in a higher class. What would you think of a third reader pupil who insisted upon working in high school classes? And yet that is what every one of us does when he insists upon having that for which he cannot pay; and those of us who persist in that course come to a grand smash at last and are set back into their proper classes. Very often they find that class in the penitentiary; more often they find it in the lack of faith of their neighbors, who have learned by experience (their own and each others') *not to trust them.* So perforce they come down to their class and quit Having It Charged because nobody will charge it.

But he does not even yet live within his means because he wants to; and right action is incomplete unless rooted in strong *desire.* His heart-garden is overrun with those noxious weeds of Desire for This, That and The Other but he is now so placed that he must root out the majority of them, thus allowing the growth of Desire to Live Within His Income. When every attempt to Have It Charged meets with a cold rebuff one has an incentive to root out the desire to Have It Charged. So the Desire for This, That and The Other is not only lopped off at the top but it is starved at the bottom—paralyzed by fear of rebuffs.

I once read a remarkable story about two men who had let their heart-gardens overrun with Desire for This, That and The Other to such an extent that Honesty was a mere gasping rootlet without signs of life. One of these men was sentenced to five years in the penetentiary, which he served—after snugly caching his half of the stolen money. The other narrowly escaped.

The one who went to prison hatched while there a beautiful scheme for getting even with the world. He had been sent to prison for appropriating a paltry little $10,000 while such men as Rockefeller stole millions and were toadied; now he proposed to get even by stealng a cool half million from the world.

Upon his release he hunted up his old pal, who, after spending his $5,000, had been having a hard time because nobody would let him Have It Charged and everybody was afraid to trust him to do anything more responsible than janitor work, which he had never learned to do. Smith was his name. The other man's name after his release from prison was Johnson.

Johnson found Smith ripe for the new scheme, which was this: Smith was to go away to a new city where nobody knew him (Johnson could not trust himself because his gait reminded the observer of the prison lock-step); Smith was to change his name; to hire a modest office and pay for it out of Johnson's money of which a thousand or two were to be banked in Smith's new name, with more forthcoming from Johnson when needed; he was to buy good but plain furnishings and Have Them Charged; and promptly on presentation of the bill he was to pay with a check. This was done to impress people that Smith Bought Things and Paid Cash. If the things had not been Charged Smith would not have been so quickly brought to the town's notice as a Man of Means and Honesty. As soon as Smith's credit was established he was to begin to borrow money; first small sums and then larger as his credit grew; every time taking care to pay *ahead* of time, receiving the regular discount. In short, Smith was to live for five years as a strictly honest man who had everything Charged and Paid When He Said He Would, and who was Getting Rich Fast.

Johnson calculated that in five years of this sort of living Smith's credit would be good for a cool $500,000 in cash. At the expiration of the five years Smith was to borrow all he could lay his hands on and with Johnson skip for parts unknown.

The scheme worked like a charm. At the expiration of the five years Smith could command over $500,000 in cash, outside of his flourishing business, which, of course, could not be turned into cash without rousing suspicion of some sort and thus hurting his credit. And all these years Smith had lived *well,* though not extravagantly, as another aid in growing his credit.

Then, before the date for the final coup, he went to see Johnson, whom he had kept informed secretly of his progress. And what do you think Smith said? His first words were, "Johnny, I *can't do it;* five years of *living* like an honest man have made me prize honesty above everything else; I *can't* throw away the clean credit I have made, nor desert the fine business I have built up; my *heart and pride are in it* and to desert now would kill me."

And how do you suppose Johnson took it? He drew a long breath and—smiled. "Smithy," he said, "I'm with you; these five years of helping you to be square, of taking pride in your success, have made me see things I never dreamed of before; why, Smithy, it's *eas-*

ier to get an honest living than a dishonest one, ain't it?—and a feller *feels* a *heap* better while he's a-doin' it, don't he?" So Smith and Johnson shook hands solemnly and lived honest ever after. Johnson went home with Smith and they worked together to still further build the business and grow an Honest Credit, which they guarded as the apple of their eye.

Smith and Johnson were cultivating an ugly weed—the Desire to Get Even. In order to satisfy this weed they must have an enormous credit. *In order to grow an enormous credit they must live* STRICTLY WITHIN THEIR MEANS, seeing to it that their Means always kept *well* ahead of their Desire for This, That and The Other. By living this way five years they learned to want above ALL things to live within their means; *they found the noxious weed of Desire to Get Even had lived its short life* (all weeds are shortlived) *and died a natural death.*

Dearie, cultivate carefully that homely plant. Desire to Live Within Your Means. Let nothing hinder, for verily there is no limit to the income and the credit you can grow if only you keep the weeds of This, That and The Other well subdued.

And there are a thousand other virtues which will grow alongside the Desire to Live Within Your Income, which would shrivel and die among the weeds of Desire for This, That and The Other. But that's another story.

19

THE MENTAL EQUIVALENT

EMMET FOX

(1943)

This booklet is the substance of two lectures
delivered by Emmet Fox at Unity School of Christianity,
Kansas City, Mo.

WE ARE all supremely interested in one subject. There is one thing that means more to us than all the other things in the world put together, and that is our search for God and the understanding of His nature. The aim of the metaphysical movement is to teach the practice of the presence of God.

We practice the presence of God by seeing Him everywhere, in all things and in all people, despite any appearances to the contrary. As we look about the world with the eyes of the flesh, we see inharmony, fear, and all sorts of difficulties; but our leader Jesus Christ taught us, saying, "Judge not according to appearance, but judge righteous judgment." So when we see the appearance of evil we look through it to the truth that lies back of it. As soon as we see this truth, and see it spiritually, the appearance changes, because this is a mental world. Now most people do not know this: they think it is a material world, and that is why humanity has so many problems. After nineteen centuries of formal Christianity the world is passing through desperate difficulties. But we know the Truth; we do not judge by appearances. We know that we live in a mental world, and to know that is the key to life.

If a child could be taught only one thing, it should be taught that this is a mental world. I would let all the other things go and teach him that.

Whatever enters into your life is but the material expression of some belief in your own mind. The kind of body you have, the kind of home you have, the kind of work you do, the kind of people you meet, are all conditioned by and correspond to the mental concepts you are holding. The Bible teaches that from beginning to end. I am putting it in the language of metaphysics; the Bible gives it in the language of religion, but it is the same Truth.

About twenty years ago I coined the phrase "mental equivalent." And now I want to say that for anything that you want in your life—a healthy body, a satisfactory vocation, friends, opportunities, and above all the understanding of God—you must furnish a mental equivalent. Supply yourself with a mental equivalent, and the thing must come to you. Without a mental equivalent it cannot come. Now as to the things in your life that you would like to be rid of, (everyone has such things in his life). Perhaps bodily difficulties or faults of character are the most important. We all have habits of thought and action, and we all have business, family, and personal conditions we would like to be rid of. If we rid our mind of the mental equivalent of them, they must go.

Everything that you see or feel on the material plane, whether it is your body, your home, your business, or your city, is but the expression in the concrete of a mental equivalent held by you. Everything in your city is the embodiment of mental equivalents held by the citizens. Everything in your country is the embodiment of mental equivalents held by the people of the country; and the state of the world embodies the mental equivalent of the two thousand million people who make up the world.

What about war? That is the physical expression of a mental equivalent held by the human race. The human race has believed in the old bogey of fear. It has believed that you can enrich yourself by taking something belonging to someone else. It has believed in death. It has believed in lack. It has believed that aggression pays and that helping yourself to other people's things is a good policy. We have all believed this in some degree. The natural result of this has been to precipitate in the outer a picture of war, death, suffering, and so on. Because humanity had the mental equivalent of war the war came.

Today the world is beginning to get the mental equivalent of peace, and that is why peace will come. A new world will come. The new world will be worth living in. In the great new world that is going to come a little later on—and it will come sooner than some people think—there will be peace, harmony, and understanding between man and man and between nation and nation; but *always the thing you see in the outer is the precipitation on the physical plane of a mental equivalent held by one or more people.*

Now of course I borrowed this expression "mental equivalent" from physics and chemistry. We speak of the mechanical equivalent of heat, for example, and engineers constantly have to work out the equivalent of one kind of energy in another kind of energy. They have to discover how much electricity they will need to do certain mechanical work, such as driving a compressor. They have to find out how much coal will be needed to produce so much electricity, and so on. In like manner *there is a mental equivalent of every object or occurrence on the physical plane.*

The secret of successful living is to build up the mental equivalent that you want; and to get rid of, to expunge, the mental equivalent that you do not want.

Suppose you have rheumatism. I have friends in London who have it all the time; in fact, rheumatism used to be called the national British disease. Some people there have it beginning in October and lasting until March; others only have it until Christmas; others do not get it before Christmas and then have it until February. Of two men living in the same town, doing the same work, eating the same food, drinking the same water, why does one have to have rheumatism from October until February and the other does not have it at all or has it at a different time? Why? Because they have furnished the mental equivalent for what they get. Why is a quarrelsome person always in trouble? He makes New York too hot to hold him, so he goes to Chicago. He thinks he will like it in Chicago; but pretty soon he has enemies in Chicago, so he goes down to Kansas City. He has heard there are nice people there. But soon he is in trouble again. Why? He has what we call a quarrelsome disposition. He has the mental equivalent of strife.

There is another man, and wherever he goes there is peace. If there is a quarrelsome family and he visits them, there is peace while he is there. He has the mental equivalent of peace and true divine love.

So the key to life is to build in the mental equivalents of what you want and to expunge the equivalents of what you do not want. How do you do it? You build in the mental equivalents by thinking quietly, constantly, and persistently of the kind of thing you want, and by thinking that has two qualities: *clearness* or definiteness, and *interest.* If you want to build anything into your life—if you want to bring health, right activity, your true place, inspiration; if you want to bring right companionship, and above all if you want understanding of God—form a mental equivalent of the thing which you want by thinking about it a great deal, by thinking clearly and with interest. Remember *clarity* and *interest;* those are the two poles.

Universal Polarity

The law of polarity is of course a cosmic law. Everything is produced by two other things. Anything that is ever produced anywhere in the universe is produced by two other things. That is the law of polarity. In the organic world we see it as parenthood. In the inorganic world, the world of physics and chemistry, we see it as the protons and electrons. That is how the material universe is built up; it always takes two things to produce a third. And that is the real ultimate meaning back of the Trinity.

There were Trinitarian doctrines before the time of Christ. They had trinities in ancient Egypt and India and in Chaldea and Babylonia—always there is the trinity: father, mother, child: activity, material, production. Go where you like, seek where you will, you find the Trinity.

In the building up of thought the two poles are clarity of thought and warmth of feeling; the knowledge and the feeling. Ninety-nine times in a hundred the reason why metaphysical students do not demonstrate is that they lack the feeling in their treatments. They speak the Truth, oh, yes! "I am divine Spirit. I am one with God." But they do not feel it. The second pole is missing. When they talk about their troubles they are full of feeling, but when they speak of Truth they are about as cold as a dead fish; and I cannot think of anything chillier than a cold fish unless it is a metaphysician who has lost his contact with God. They say, "I am divine Spirit," and they say it with no feeling; but when they say, "I have a terrible pain!" it is loaded with feeling, and so the pain they get and the pain they keep.

A man is out of work and he says: "God is my infinite supply. Man is always in his true place." It is said perfunctorily, with no feeling. But if someone asks him whether he has found work, he says: "I have been out of work two years. I wrote letters. I went after that job, but they were prejudiced against me. They wouldn't give me a chance." As soon as he gets on the negative side, the feeling comes in, and he demonstrates that—he remains unemployed. To think clearly and with feeling leads to demonstration, because you have then built a *mental equivalent.*

Think of the conditions you want to produce. If you want to be healthy, happy, prosperous, doing a constructive work, having a continuous understanding of God, you do not picture it necessarily, but you think it, feel it, and get interested in it. What we call "feeling" in connection with thought is really interest. Feeling is not excitement. Did you ever hear of anything coming from excitement except apoplexy? True "feeling" in thought is *interest.*

You cannot show me any man or woman who is successful in his field, from president down to shoeblack, who is not interested in his work; nor can you show me any man who has his heart in his work who is not successful. The most successful shoeblack you have in town here is vitally interested in his work. He has his heart in it. He is a colored boy, and he loves his work. He did such good work that I gave him an extra tip when he finished polishing my shoes, but no money could really pay him for his work. He was so tickled as he did his work, he loved it so much, that I did not really pay him. He paid himself. He enjoyed it. And he had a line of people waiting for him.

You build a mental equivalent for what you want by getting interested in it. That is the way you create feeling. If you want health, get interested in health. If you want the right place, get interested in service, doing something that is really serving your fellow man.

The reason people do not get ahead in business is that they try to think up schemes to get their fellow men's money instead of thinking up opportunities for service. The successful man gets interested in what he wants to do, and gets rid of things he is not interested in.

How are you going to expunge the wrong mental equivalents? Suppose you have a mental equivalent of resentment, or unemployment, or criticism, or not understanding God. When somebody talks about God, it does not interest you much, you get sleepy or bored. Perhaps you do not get along with people—not that you quarrel with them, but they quarrel with you—the quarrel happens! What is to be done?

The only way to expunge a wrong mental equivalent is to supply the opposite. Think the right thing. The right thought automatically expunges the wrong thought. If you say: "I am not going to think resentment any more. I don't believe in it. There is nothing to it. I am not going to think of it any more," what are you thinking about except resentment? You are still thinking resentment all the time and strengthening the mental equivalent of resentment. Forget it! Think of health and bodily ease and peace and harmony and speak the word for it. Then you are building up a mental equivalent of health. If you want your true place—if your problem is unemployment, no job, the wrong job, or a job you do not like—if you say, "I am not going to think unemployment any more," you are wrong. That is thinking "unemployment," is it not? Think "true place."

If I say to you, "Don't think of the Statue of Liberty in New York," you know what you are thinking about. You are not thinking of anything except the Statue of Liberty. There she is, complete with torch in her hand! I said, "Don't think of her," but you do.

Now I am going to say that some time ago I visited, near Springfield, Illinois, a perfect reproduction of the village of New Salem as it was in the days of Abraham Lincoln. Even the log cabin is furnished as it was in his day. The National Park Commission has done it all.

Now you have forgotten the Statue of Liberty for a few seconds, haven't you? You have been thinking of New Salem. I gave you a different idea. That is the key to the management of your mind, the management of your thinking, and therefore the key to the management of your destiny.

Do not dwell on negative things but replace them, supplant them, with the right, constructive things. The law of mind is that you can only get rid of one thought by substituting another. If a carpenter drives a nail into a wooden wall or into a beam, there it is. Now if he takes a second nail and drives it against the first, the first is driven out and falls on the floor and the second one takes the place of the first one. That is what happens in the mind when you substitute one image for another. For everything in life there has to be a mental equivalent.

If you will start in this very day and refuse to think of your mistakes—and of course that includes the mistakes of other people—if you will cease to think of mistakes and hold the right concepts instead, cease to think fear and think of divine love instead, cease to think lack and think prosperity and the presence of God's abundance instead—and then if you will think as clearly as possible and get *interested;* you will be building a mental equivalent of happiness and prosperity.

If your thought is very vague, you do not build a mental equivalent. If your thought is lacking in interest, you do not build a mental equivalent. So make your thoughts as clear and definite as possible. Never strain. As soon as you start straining, taking the clenching-the-fist attitude, saying, "I am going to get what I want; I am going to get it if it kills me," all mental building stops.

We have all been told to relax. I have seen people tense up as soon as they were told to relax. They were going to relax if it killed them; and of course they missed the whole point.

Get the thought of what you want as clear as you can. Be definite but not too specific.

If you live in an apartment and say, "I want a house in the country or in the suburbs, and I want it to have a porch and a large yard with trees and flowers," that is all right. But do not say, "I must have a certain house—the one at 257 Ninth Street or 21 Fifth Avenue."

Suppose you go shopping. Well, you should know what you are shopping for. You should have some definite idea. If you say, "I want something, I don't know what—I will leave it to God"; if you say, "I want a business, it may be a farm or a shop I want—I will leave it to Divine Mind," you are foolish. What are you here for? You must have some desires and wishes, because you represent God here. So you must say, "Yes, I want a shop; and I know the kind of shop I want."

I know a woman who demonstrated a hat shop. She had no capital, but she wanted to go into business. She wanted a hat shop. She loves to make hats. She has a natural flair for it. She can make hats that look well on the homeliest people; and this is the art of millinery, isn't it? She was a good businesswoman, so she built the mental equivalent of a hat shop. She did not say, "I must be in a certain block on a certain street." She did not say, "I am going to get a hat shop if it kills me" or "I am going to get a hat shop, and I want Jane Smith's hat shop." She built a definite mental equivalent, and that is the right way. If you say, "I want a strong, healthy body," and build up a mental equivalent for it by constantly thinking of your body as perfect, that is fine. Do not think of details very much. Do not say, "First of all I'm going to get my teeth fixed up with right thought, and I'll let my bald head wait" or "Maybe I should get my bald head fixed up first, because my teeth can wait." It is the details that are wrong. The evil of outlining lies in going into small details and in saying, "I want it in my time, in my way, whether

God wants it or not." Apart from that (going too much into small details) you must have definite ideas.

Do not strain to get your ideas clear. They will be clearer the second day or the fifty-second day. If you have a pair of field glasses and you look at something and want the focus clearer, you slowly turn the wheel until the focus is clear.

Getting your mental equivalent may take you a week or a month or a year. *Charge it with interest,* like an electric charge, or it is dead. Love is the only way. You cannot be interested in a thing unless you love it. If you love it, it is filled with interest, it is filled with energy and life, and it comes true.

There is an interesting story about Napoleon. He thought a big nose was a sign of strong character. He said, "Give me a man with plenty of nose." If someone came to him and said that a certain officer ought to be promoted, he would say: "Has he got plenty of nose? Give me a man with a big nose." If an officer was killed, he replaced him with someone with a big nose. You know what happened. The law sent him Wellington, and Wellington destroyed him. Wellington had the largest nose in English history. He said himself it was more of a handle than a nose. Take that as a joke if you like, but it does carry an important lesson.

The doctrine of the mental equivalent is the essence of the metaphysical teaching; the doctrine that you will get whatever you provide the mental equivalent for.

I have known some very, very remarkable cases where people furnished the mental equivalent and out of the blue came things they never could have hoped for in the ordinary way. I know many men and women in London and New York and other places who seemingly had no human chance to attain success; but they got hold of this knowledge of mental equivalents, they quietly and faithfully applied this knowledge; and sometime sooner or later the thing they wanted came to them, without any help from anything outside; and it stayed with them and brought a blessing.

Building a New Mental Equivalent

It is your bounden duty to demonstrate, and in order to do so successfully you need to know why you should do so. Why should you demonstrate at all? Some people say, "Since God is all, and everything is perfect, why should I seek to demonstrate His law?" Because you have to prove the harmony of being in your own life. That is why. If there were no need to demonstrate, one might just as well go to bed and stay there or, more simply still, stroll around to the nearest undertaker.

Of course we are here on earth to express God, and true expression is what we call demonstration, because it demonstrates the law of Being. It is your duty to be healthy, prosperous, and free. It is your duty to express God to the utmost of your power; and you have no right to relinquish your efforts until you have accomplished this. Until you have excellent health and are visibly regenerating, until you have found your true place and right activity, until you are free from conscious fear, anxiety, and criticism, you are not demonstrating, and you must find out why and correct the error, whatever it is.

Jesus has told us that we always demonstrate our consciousness, and Unity is teaching the same truth today. You always demonstrate what you habitually have in your mind. What sort of mind have you? I am not going to tell you—and do not let anyone else tell you either, because they do not know. People who like you will think your mentality is better than it is; those who do not like you will think it is worse. So do not ask anybody about your mentality; but examine your conditions and see what you are demonstrating. This method is scientific and infallible.

If an automobile engineer is working out a new design for an engine, if he is going to do something different about the valves, for instance, he doesn't say: "I wonder what Smith thinks about this. I like Smith. If Smith is against this I won't try it." Nor does he say, "I won't try this idea because it comes from France, and I don't like those people." He is impersonal and perfectly unemotional about it. He says, "I will test it out, and decide by the results I obtain."

Then he tries it out, measuring the results carefully, and decides accordingly. He does not laugh, or cry, or get excited, or bang the table; but he tests out the idea scientifically and judges only by results.

That is how you should handle your mentality. That is how you should practice the metaphysical teaching. You demonstrate the state of your mind at any given time. You experience in the outer what you really think in the inner. This is the meaning of the old saying "As within so without." Note carefully that in the Bible the word "within" always means thought and the word "without" means manifestation or experience. That is why Jesus said that the kingdom of heaven (health, harmony, and freedom) is within. Harmonious thought means harmonious experience. Fear thought or anger thought means suffering or frustration.

This brings me to the most important thing I want to say, namely that if you want to change your life; if you want to be healthier, happier, younger, more prosperous; above all, if you want to get nearer to God—and I know that you do—*you must change your thought and keep it changed.* That is the secret of controlling your life, and there is no other way. Jesus Himself could not have done it in any other way, because this is a cosmic law. Change your thought and keep it changed. We have all been taught this very thing since the metaphysical movement began. I heard it stated in those very words many times nearly forty years ago in London; but most of us are slow to realize the importance of it. If you want to change some condition in your life, you must change your thought about it and keep it changed. Then the condition will change accordingly. All that anyone else can do for you is to help you change your thought. That is what a metaphysician can do for you, but you yourself must keep it changed. No one else can think for you. "No man can save his brother's soul or pay his brother's debt."

To change your thought and keep it changed is the way to build a new mental equivalent; it is the secret of accomplishment. You already have a mental equivalent for everything that is in your life today; and you must destroy the patterns for the things you do not want, and then they will disappear. You must build a new pattern or mental equivalent for the things you want, and then they will come into your life.

Of course changing your thought for a short time is the easiest thing in the world. Everyone does this when he goes to a metaphysical meeting. The beautiful atmosphere and the positive instruction make people feel optimistic. The teacher reminds the audience of the Truth of Being, and they think, "I believe that, and I am going to practice it." But five minutes after they have left the meeting they forget about it, perhaps for hours. The trouble with most students is not that they do not change their thought but that they do not keep it changed.

If you want health you must cease to think sickness and fear, and you must get the habit of thinking health and harmony. There can be no sickness without fear. You cannot be adversely affected by anything if you really have no fear concerning it. Everyone has many fears in the subconscious mind that he is not consciously aware of, but they are operating just the same.

A man said: "I entered a town in a foreign country in the east of Europe during a typhoid epidemic. I did not know there was any typhoid. I never thought about it. I didn't know the language and couldn't read the papers. They were printed in Greek. Yet I got typhoid and had quite a siege. How do you account for that?"

The explanation is that he believed in typhoid fever. He believed one can catch it from others, and that it makes one very ill, for so many days, and therefore he had a subconscious fear of it. He subconsciously knew there was typhoid around, and as it always does, the subconscious enacted or dramatized his real beliefs and fears, and presented him with a good hearty case of typhoid.

If he had really believed that he was a child of God who could not be hurt by anything, he would not have had typhoid.

Change your thought and keep it changed, not for ten seconds or even ten days but steadily and permanently. Then you will build a new mental equivalent, and *a mental equivalent is always demonstrated.*

The secret of harmony and success is to concentrate your thought upon harmony and success. That is why I teach that attention is the key to life. What you attend to or concentrate upon you bring into your life, because you are building a mental equivalent.

Many people fail to concentrate successfully because they think that concentration means will power. They actually try to concentrate with their muscles and blood vessels. They frown. They clench their hands. Unwittingly they are thinking of an engineer's drill or a carpenter's bit and brace. They suppose that the harder you press the faster you get through. But all this is quite wrong.

Forget the drill and think of a photographic camera. In a camera there is of course no question of pressure. There the secret lies in *focus.* If you want to photograph something you focus your camera lens quietly, steadily, and persistently on it for the necessary length of time. Suppose I want to photograph a vase of flowers. What do I do? Well, I do not press it violently against the lens of the camera. That would be silly. I place the vase in front of the camera and keep it there. But suppose that after a few moments I snatch away the vase and hold a book in front of the camera, and then snatch that away, and hold up a chair, and then put the flowers back for a few moments, and so forth. You know what will happen to my photograph. It will be a crazy blur. Is not that what people do to their minds when they cannot keep their thoughts concentrated for any length of time? They think health for a few minutes and then they think sickness or fear. They think prosperity and then they think depression. They think about bodily perfection and then they think about old age and their pains and aches. Is it any wonder that man is so apt to demonstrate the "marred image"?

Note carefully that I did not advocate taking one thought and trying to hold it by will power. That is bad. You must allow a train of *relevant* thoughts to have free play in your mind, one leading naturally to the next, but they must all be positive, constructive, and harmonious, and appertaining to your desire; and you must think quietly and without effort. Then you will get the mental equivalent of all-round success, and then success itself will follow; success in health, in social relationships, in your work, in your spiritual development.

Maintaining the New Equivalent

It is always good to make a practical experiment, so I advise you to take a single problem in your life—something you want to get rid of or something you want to obtain—and change your thought about this thing, and keep it changed. Do not be in a hurry to select your problem; take your time.

Do not tell anyone you are doing this. If you tell a friend about it you are thereby strongly affirming the existence of the problem, which is the very thing you are trying to get rid of. If you tell your friend that you are going to work on your rheumatism or on lack, you are making these things very real to your subconscious mind. Also your spiritual energy is leaking away, as electricity does in what we call a "ground."

Take your problem and change your mind concerning it, and keep it changed for a month, and you will be astonished at the results you will get. If you really do keep your thought changed you will not have to wait a month. If you really change your thought and keep it changed, the demonstration may come in a few hours. But to keep tensely looking for the demonstration is really affirming the existence of the problem, is it not? The secret is to keep your thought changed into the new condition. So keep your thought carefully, quietly expressive of the new condition that you want to produce. Believe what you are thinking, and to prove that you believe it you must act the part.

By changing your mind about your problem in this way and keeping it changed, you are building a new mental equivalent, a mental equivalent of harmony and success, and that mental equivalent, as we know, must be outpictured in your experience.

For a while you will find that your thought will keep slipping back into the old rut. Such is the force of habit. But if you are quietly persistent you will gain the victory. It is always a little difficult to change a habit, but it can be done, and then the new right habit becomes easier than the old wrong habit, and that is how a new mental equivalent is built.

Change your mind and keep it changed.

Do not talk about the negative thing or act as if it were there. Act your part as though the new condition were already in being in the outer. If you will do this, the new condition will presently appear in the outer, because the outer is always but the projection or outpicturing of the inner.

We project our own belief and call it experience, and this gives us the clue to the difference between a true action and a false or unreal action.

What is true action? A true action is one that really changes things, that gets you somewhere. A false action does not. For example, if your car has traction it is moving. That is a true action, and you will presently reach your destination; but if it does not have traction there will be movement, vibration, but you will not get anywhere. You are wearing out the engine and perhaps the tires, but you do not get anywhere. The same thing happens when a soldier is "marking time" as we say. He is tiring himself and wearing out his shoes but not getting anywhere. These are examples of false action.

Suppose you have a difficult letter to write or a sermon or a lecture to prepare. Suppose you sit in front of a sheet of paper and draw curlicues or cut the pencil to pieces or tear your hair. These would be false actions, and many people do just that. Such actions get you nowhere. To decide what you are going to say, to start a current of thought and then write it down, is true action. You will note that the difference is that in the false action you begin from the outside. You had not prepared your thoughts. You tried to begin by writing. With the true action you got your thoughts in order first and then the writing or outer activity followed. A false action means deadlock; a true action is always fruitful.

True activity is always from within outward. False activity tries to work from without inward. One is centrifugal and the other centripetal, if you want to be technical. If you are working from within out, your work is alive and will be productive. If you are working from outside inward, your work is dead, and it will have a bad effect on you.

Artists and literary people speak of "potboilers." You know what a potboiler is. It is a picture that you paint or a story that you write, not because you are interested but just to keep the monetary returns coming in. It is never good, because it is not the result of inspiration. It is done from the outside and is a false action. It is a common saying among writers that three potboilers will kill any talent; and that is true. The proper way to paint a picture is to see beauty somewhere, in a landscape or in a beautiful face, or wherever you please. You thrill to that beauty, and then you go to the canvas and express your inspiration there. That is art, and that is true action. It inspires other people and it helps and develops you yourself.

If you write a story or a novel because you have observed life, because you have seen certain things happen and studied certain people, and write it all down because you are alive with it, that is a true action and you write a great book. Dickens, George Eliot, Balzac, and all the great authors wrote in that way. But if you say, "I will do fifteen hundred words a day and give my publishers the 'mixture as before' and that will secure my income," your work will be dead. And this policy will kill any talent that you may have.

If you are in business and you are interested in your job and love it, your work is a positive action and must ultimately bring you success. Even if the work is uncongenial but nevertheless you say, "This is my job for the moment; I am going to do it as well as I can, and then something better will open up," you are working from within outward. Your work is a positive action, and before long something really congenial will come to you.

Most people know that these things are true. They know that they are true for pictures and stories and business life, but they do not realize that they are equally true for the things of the soul. Yet such is the case. If you pray and meditate from the outside just because you think it is a duty or because you will feel guilty if you do not, your prayers will be dead. You will get no demonstration and make no spiritual progress, and you will get no joy. But if you feel that when you are praying and meditating you are visiting with God, and that these moments are the happiest in the twenty-four hours, then you are working from within outward. Your spiritual growth will be fruitful, and you will grow very rapidly in spiritual understanding. When you pray in this way there is no strain and your soul is filled with peace.

The great enemy of prayer is a sense of tension. When you are tense you are always working from the outside inward. Tension in prayer is probably the greatest cause of failure to demonstrate. Remember that the mind always stops working when you are tense. When you think, "I must demonstrate this" or "I must get that in three days," you are tense; you are using your will power, and you will do more harm than good.

Remember this: The door of the soul opens inward. If you will remember this it will save you years and years of waiting for demonstrations. Write in your notebook, the one you carry in your pocket—not the notebook you keep locked in your desk, because that is a mausoleum—or better still, write it on a card, and place it on your dresser: "The door of the soul opens inward." And pray to God that you may remember that truth every time you turn to Him in prayer. You know what it means when a door opens inward: the harder you push against it the tighter you close it. When you press or force or hurl yourself against it you only close it on yourself. When you relax and draw back, you give it a chance to open. In all theaters and other public buildings the doors open outward. The law insists upon this because crowds are apt to become panic-stricken and then they push, and if the doors opened inward the people would imprison themselves and be killed. *The door of the soul opens inward!* That is the law. Relax mentally, draw away from your problem spiritually, and the action of God will open the door for you and you will be free.

There is an old legend of the Middle Ages that is very instructive. It seems that a citizen was arrested by one of the Barons and shut up in a dungeon in his castle. He was taken down dark stairs, down, down, down, by a ferocious-looking jailer who carried a great key a foot long. The door of a cell was opened, and he was thrust into a dark hole. The door shut with a bang, and there he was.

He lay in that dark dungeon for twenty years. Each day the jailer would come, the big door would be opened with a great creaking and groaning, a pitcher of water and a loaf of bread would be thrust in and the door closed again.

Well, after twenty years the prisoner decided that he could not stand it any longer. He wanted to die but he did not want to commit suicide, so he decided that the next day when the jailer came he would attack him. The jailer would then kill him in self-defense, and thus his misery would be at an end. He thought he would examine the door carefully so as to be ready for tomorrow and, going over, he caught the handle and turned it. To his amazement the door opened, and upon investigation he found that there was no lock upon it and never had been, and that for all those twenty years he had not been locked in, except in belief.

At any time in that period he could have opened the door if only he had known it. He thought it was locked, but it was not. He groped along the corridor and felt his way upstairs. At the top of the stairs two soldiers were chatting, and they made no attempt to stop him. He crossed the great yard without attracting attention. There was an armed guard on the drawbridge at the great gate, but they paid no attention to him, and he walked out a free man.

He went home unmolested and lived happily ever after. He could have done this any time through those long years since his arrest if he had known enough, but he did not. He was a captive, not of stone and iron but of false belief. He was not locked in; he only thought he was. Of course this is only a legend, but it is an extremely instructive one.

We are all living in some kind of prison, some of us in one kind, some in another; some in a prison of lack, some in a prison of remorse and resentment, some in a prison of blind, unintelligent fear, some in a prison of sickness. But always the prison is in our thought and not in the nature of things.

There is no truth in our seeming troubles. There is no reality in lack. There is no power in time or conditions to make us old or tired or sick.

The Jesus Christ teaching, and the Unity movement in particular, comes to us and says: "You are not locked in a prison of circumstances. You are not chained in any dungeon. In the name of God, turn the handle, walk out, and be free."

Build a mental equivalent of freedom, of vibrant physical health, of true prosperity, of increasing understanding and achievement for God. Build it by thinking of it, having faith in it and acting the part, and the old limitation equivalent will gradually fade out, for the door is unlocked and the voice of God in your heart says, "Be free."

About the Authors

JAMES ALLEN was born in Leicester, England, in 1864. He took his first job at fifteen to support his family, after his father was murdered while looking for work in America. Allen worked as a private secretary with various manufacturing companies until 1902, when he left to devote himself fully to writing. He soon finished his first book, *From Poverty to Power,* and then moved to Ilfracombe, England, where he went on to write eighteen more books before his death in 1912. Originally published in 1902, *As a Man Thinketh* is his second and most widely celebrated work, cited by generations of prosperity authors.

WILLIAM WALKER ATKINSON was born in Baltimore, Maryland, in 1862. Atkinson became an attorney in 1894, a career move that led to financial success but precipitated a complete mental and physical breakdown. He coped with his breakdown by reading New Thought literature, and became an important and influential figure within the early movement, publishing magazines such as *Suggestion, New Thought,* and *Advanced Thought,* as well as contributing to Elizabeth Towne's *The Nautilus.* Atkinson was the author of *The Secret of Success,* as well as many titles written under pseudonyms such as Yogi Ramacharka, The Three Initiates, and Theron Q. Dumont. An honorary president of the International New Thought Alliance, Atkinson died in California in 1932.

Best known as the most outrageous and controversial showman of the nineteenth century, P. T. BARNUM was born in Bethel, Connecticut, in 1810. After failing at an early career as a shopkeeper, Barnum founded the weekly paper *The Herald of Freedom* in 1829, and began his career as a showman in 1835. He spent the next several decades running Barnum's American Museum in New York City, where he maintained a collection of famous oddities. He toured with a notorious sideshow that included performers like "General" Tom Thumb and Jumbo the Elephant, and that eventually developed into the first modern three-ring circus. Barnum served two terms in the Connecticut state legislature, beginning in 1865, and was the mayor of Bridgeport, Connecticut, for a single year in 1875. Barnum was also a successful author. His autobiography, which came out in a variety of editions and titles, was second only to the New Testament in number of copies printed in the nineteenth century. His most enduring work is *The Art of Money Getting.* He died in 1891 in Bridgeport.

Born in St. Louis, Missouri, in 1885, ROBERT COLLIER trained to become a priest early in his life, before settling on a career in business, achieving success in the fields of advertising, publishing, and engineering. After recovering from a chronic illness with the help of mental healing, Collier began studying New Thought, metaphysical, and success principles. He distilled these principles into a popular and influential pamphlet series, collected into a single volume as *The Secret of the Ages* in 1926, and later revised by Collier in 1948. He died in 1950. Collier's original 1926 work is reproduced here.

Born in 1843, RUSSELL H. CONWELL was trained as a lawyer, served as a Union soldier, and worked as an international journalist. He was ordained and worked as a Baptist minister before founding Temple University in Philadelphia, in 1888, to meet the educational needs of the younger members of his congregation. Conwell served as Temple University's first president, and his Conwell School of Theology became the Gordon-Conwell Theological Seminary, one of the largest interdenominational seminaries in the United States. *Acres of Diamonds* began as an inspirational lecture he delivered more than six thousand times before his death in 1925.

THERON Q. DUMONT was a pseudonym used by WILLIAM WALKER ATKINSON in the early twentieth century.

Born in 1854, on an Indian reservation near St. Cloud, Minnesota, CHARLES FILLMORE spent much of his early life unsuccessfully speculating on real estate and traveling the country seeking a cure for his wife Myrtle's tuberculosis before co-founding the New Thought–based Unity movement with her. Their magazine, *Unity*, was first published in 1891, and in 1906, he and Myrtle were among the first to become ordained Unity ministers. The Unity movement eventually oversaw multiple magazines such as *Modern Thought*, *Daily Word*, and *Wee Wisdom*. It also maintained its own printing plant, and ran the town Unity Village in Lee's Summit, Missouri. Fillmore died in 1948.

Born in 1886 in Ireland, EMMET FOX was trained as an electrical engineer but instead pursued a life as a spiritual teacher and lecturer in the United States. In 1931, he became the minister of the Church of the Healing Christ in New York City. An acclaimed and influential philosopher, spiritual teacher, and writer whose works, such as *The Sermon on the Mount*, were an early inspiration for Alcoholics Anonymous, he died in France in 1951.

Patriot, politician, inventor, philosopher, author, and businessman BENJAMIN FRANKLIN was born in Boston, Massachusetts, in 1706. As a young man, Franklin moved to Philadelphia, where he became a printer and newspaper editor, publishing *Poor Richard's Almanac* and *The Pennsylvania Gazette*. Franklin became a hero to colonial America because of his work to repeal the Stamp Act and other unpopular British measures in the colonies, as well as his service as a diplomat during the Revolutionary War. Franklin helped negotiate and then write the Treaty of Paris, which ended the Revolutionary War. A signer of the Declaration of Independence and the U.S. Constitution, a Pennsylvania delegate to the Continental Congress, inventor of technology such as the lightning rod, bifocals, and the Franklin stove, and creator of the first public library and fire department, Franklin remains an inspirational figure to countless Americans. He died in 1790.

Born in 1866, CHARLES F. HAANEL achieved success as both a businessman and an author, rising to top positions at numerous corporations in his native St. Louis throughout his life. Often called the "Father of Personal Development," Haanel was among the earliest writers to popularize the "Law of Attraction." Haanel originally published *The Master Key System* as a correspondence course in 1912, before collecting the lessons and publishing them as a single volume in 1917. Haanel retained membership in many influential groups, such as the American Society for Psychical Research, and went on to write *Mental Chemistry* and *The New Psychology.* He died in 1949. His 1917 edition of *The Master Key System* is reproduced here.

NAPOLEON HILL was born in 1883, in Virginia, and died in 1970 after a long and successful career as a consultant to business leaders, a lecturer, and an author. *Think and Grow Rich* is the all-time bestseller in its field, having sold 15 million copies worldwide, and setting the standard for today's motivational thinking.

The founder of the worldwide Religious Science movement, ERNEST HOLMES was born on a small farm in Lincoln, Maine, in 1887. As a young man, he moved to California, where he spent most of his career writing, speaking, starting a seminary, and founding a successful network of metaphysical churches. Largely self-educated, Holmes was a uniquely gifted scholar with a vast command of the world's spiritual philosophies. His many inspirational books include the classic textbook of his ideas, *The Science of Mind,* and a wide range of shorter works such as *Creative Mind, This Thing Called You, The Art of Life, Creative Mind and Success,* and *The Hidden Power of the Bible.* He died in California in 1960.

Journalist ELBERT HUBBARD was born in Bloomington, Illinois, in 1856. A founder of the Arts and Crafts movement community Roycroft, in East Aurora, New York, Hubbard acted as publisher and editor of two popular magazines, *The Philistine* and *The Fra.* Hubbard died aboard the ship *Lusitania* in 1915, after it was torpedoed and sunk by a German submarine. He was en route to Europe, on a trip to encourage the end of World War I. His famous motivational essay *A Message to Garcia* was made into a silent film by Thomas Edison in 1916 and a "talkie" by George Marshall in 1936. Copies were provided for all U.S. Marines and U.S. Navy enlistees during both World Wars.

Born in Camden, New Jersey, in 1871, FLORENCE SCOVEL SHINN spent many years working as an artist and illustrator of children's literature in New York City before writing her New Thought classic *The Game of Life and How to Play It.* Unable to find a publisher, she published the book herself in 1925. Shinn went on to write *Your Word Is Your Wand* and *The Secret Door to Success,* and became widely regarded as an important American spiritual teacher. She died in 1940.

F. W. SEARS spent his early life studying medicine, and earned a master's degree in psychology before going on to pen the Books Without an If series. This series outlined his philosophy of the Law of Harmonious Convergence—that things come to us and stay with us because they want to, not because we desire them to. He lived and worked in the early twentieth century.

Born in 1860, ELIZABETH TOWNE founded the highly influential New Thought magazine *The Nautilus* by herself in 1898, as a single mother casting about for income. With second husband William E. Towne, Elizabeth established a business distributing New Thought literature in their town of Holyoke, Massachusetts. With more than fifty thousand readers at its peak, and featuring contributors such as Ella Wheeler Wilcox, William Walker Atkinson, and Orison Swett Marden, *The Nautilus* was one of the most successful and influential New Thought publications of its time. Towne was the author of thirteen books, including *Experiences in Self-Healing.* In 1924, she was elected head of the New Thought Alliance. *The Nautilus* ended its more than half-century print run in 1953.

An influential figure in the early New Thought movement, RALPH WALDO TRINE was born in 1866, in Mount Morris, Illinois. The author of more than a dozen books, he started off as a correspondent for the *Boston Daily Evening Transcript* before writing his widely popular *In Tune with the Infinite.* Informed by the ideas of thinkers as varied as Ralph Waldo Emerson, Johann Gottlieb Fichte, and Henry Drummond, *In Tune with the Infinite* went on to sell more than 2 million copies. Trine died in 1958, in Claremont, California.

A progressive social reformer and New Thought pioneer, WALLACE D. WATTLES was born in 1860 in the United States. He popularized creative-thought principles in his groundbreaking classics *The Science of Getting Rich, The Science of Being Great,* and *The Science of Being Well.* A great influence on future generations of success writers, he died in 1911.

Born in 1831, HELEN WILMANS left a life as a farmer's wife to move to San Francisco and begin a successful career in newspaper journalism. A one-time student of the respected New Thought teacher Emma Curtis Hopkins, Wilmans was a highly influential early practitioner and teacher of mental science, as well as a publisher of the periodicals *Freedom* and *The Woman's World.* She died in 1907.